WORD
BIBLICAL
COMMENTARY

WORD
BIBLICAL
COMMENTARY

Volume 34B

Mark 8:27–16:20

CRAIG A. EVANS

Publishers Since 1798

THOMAS NELSON PUBLISHERS
Nashville

Word Biblical Commentary
Mark 8:27–16:20
Copyright © 2001 by Thomas Nelson, Inc.

Library of Congress Cataloging-in-Publication Data
Main entry under title:

Word biblical commentary.

   Includes bibliographies.
   1. Bible—Commentaries—Collected works.
BS491.2.W67   22.7′7   81–71768
ISBN 0–8499–0253–3 (v. 34B) AACR2

Printed in Colombia

Scripture quotations in the body of the commentary, unless otherwise indicated, are generally from the Revised Standard Version of the Bible, Old Testament Section, Copyright 1952, New Testament Section, First Edition, Copyright 1946, Second Edition, © 1971 by the Division of Christian Education of the National Council of Churches of Christ in the USA and are used by permission. The author's own translation of the Scripture text appears in italic type under the heading *Translation*.

The Graeca, Hebraica, and Semitica fonts used to print this work are available from Linguist's Software, Inc., P.O. Box 580, Edmonds, WA 98020-0580 USA: tel. (206) 775-1130.

08 07 06 05 04 03 02   —   5 4 3 2

To
the memory of
Robert A. Guelich

Introduction

The following paragraphs are intended to augment and in some instances to update the *Introduction* found in the first volume of the Word Biblical Commentary on Mark (WBC 34A) by R. A. Guelich. Because Markan priority continues to be challenged and because the sequence of the composition of the Synoptic Gospels is vital for exegesis, it will be useful to review this question at some length. It will also be useful to say a few more things about the genre of the Gospel of Mark, for the genre itself may provide some insight into the evangelist's theology and purpose for writing. A few paragraphs will be devoted to the textual preservation of Mark and to recent claims of the great antiquity of Gospel fragments. Certain aspects of Mark's theology will also be taken up, in order primarily to orient the reader to issues and themes that will be treated in this, the second volume of the commentary. Finally, a few paragraphs are devoted to the specific question of why the Markan evangelist wrote his Gospel and what approach should be taken in its interpretation. Here I think some important points need to be made about the Roman world in which Mark was written, read, and heard.

Are the Synoptics the Oldest Gospels?

Bibliography

Bell, H. I., and **Skeat, T. C.** *Fragments of an Unknown Gospel and Other Early Christian Papyri.* London: British Museum, 1935. **Beyschlag, K.** "Das Petrusevangelium." In *Die verborgene Überlieferung von Christus.* Munich: Siebenstern Taschenbuch, 1969. 27–64. **Blomberg, C. L.** "Tradition and Redaction in the Parables of the Gospel of Thomas." In *The Jesus Tradition Outside the Gospels.* Ed. D. Wenham. Gospel Perspectives 5. Sheffield: JSOT, 1984. 177–205. **Brown, R. E.** "The *Gospel of Peter* and Canonical Gospel Priority." *NTS* 33 (1987) 321–43. ———. "The Gospel of Thomas and St John's Gospel." *NTS* 9 (1962–63) 155–77. ———. "The Relation of 'The Secret Gospel of Mark' to the Fourth Gospel." *CBQ* 36 (1974) 466–85. **Cameron, R. D.** *The Other Gospels: Non-Canonical Gospel Texts.* Philadelphia: Westminster, 1982. ———. *Parable and Interpretation in the Gospel of Thomas.* FFNT 2.2. Sonoma, CA: Polebridge, 1986. ——— and **Fallon, F. T.** "The Gospel of Thomas: A Forschungsbericht and Analysis." *ANRW* 2.25.6 (1988) 4195–4251. **Carrez, M.** "Quelques aspects christologiques de l'Évangile de Thomas." In *The Four Gospels 1992.* FS F. Neirynck, ed. F. Van Segbroeck et al. BETL 100. Leuven: Leuven UP, 1992. 2263–76. **Chilton, B. D.** "The Gospel according to Thomas as a Source of Jesus' Teaching." In *The Jesus Tradition Outside the Gospels.* Ed. D. Wenham. Gospel Perspectives 5. Sheffield: JSOT, 1984. 155–75. **Crossan, J. D.** *The Cross That Spoke: The Origins of the Passion Narrative.* San Francisco: Harper & Row, 1988. ———. *Four Other Gospels: Shadows on the Contours of Canon.* Minneapolis: Winston-Seabury, 1985. ———. *The Historical Jesus: The Life of a Mediterranean Jewish Peasant.* San Francisco: HarperCollins, 1991. ———. "The Parable of the Wicked Husbandmen." *JBL* 90 (1971) 451–65. **Davies, S. L.** "The Christology and Protology of the *Gospel of Thomas.*" *JBL* 111 (1992) 663–82. ———. *The Gospel of Thomas and Christian Wisdom.* New York: Seabury, 1983. **Dehandschutter, B.** "L'Évangile de Thomas comme collection de paroles de Jésus." In *Logia—Les Paroles de Jésus—The Sayings of Jesus.* Ed.

Contents

Editorial Preface

The launching of the Word Biblical Commentary brings to fulfillment an enterprise of several years' planning. The publishers and the members of the editorial board met in 1977 to explore the possibility of a new commentary on the books of the Bible that would incorporate several distinctive features. Prospective readers of these volumes are entitled to know what such features were intended to be; whether the aims of the commentary have been fully achieved time alone will tell.

First, we have tried to cast a wide net to include as contributors a number of scholars from around the world who not only share our aims but are in the main engaged in the ministry of teaching in university, college, and seminary. They represent a rich diversity of denominational allegiance. The broad stance of our contributors can rightly be called evangelical, and this term is to be understood in its positive, historic sense of a commitment to Scripture as divine revelation and the truth and power of the Christian gospel.

Then, the commentaries in our series are all commissioned and written for the purpose of inclusion in the Word Biblical Commentary. Unlike several of our distinguished counterparts in the field of commentary writing, there are no translated works, originally written in a non-English language. Also, our commentators were asked to prepare their own rendering of the biblical text from the original languages and to use those languages as the basis of their own comments and exegesis. What may be claimed as distinctive with this series is that it is based on the biblical languages, yet it seeks to make the technical and scholarly approach to the theological understanding of Scripture understandable by—and useful to—the fledgling student, the working minister, and colleagues in the guild of professional scholars and teachers as well.

Finally, a word must be said about the format of the series. The layout, in clearly defined sections, has been consciously devised to assist readers at different levels. Those wishing to learn about the textual witnesses on which the translation is offered are invited to consult the section headed *Notes*. If the readers' concern is with the state of modern scholarship on any given portion of Scripture, they should turn to the sections on *Bibliography* and *Form/Structure/Setting*. For a clear exposition of the passage's meaning and its relevance to the ongoing biblical revelation, the *Comment* and concluding *Explanation* are designed expressly to meet that need. There is therefore something for everyone who may pick up and use these volumes.If these aims come anywhere near realization, the intention of the editors will have been met, and the labor of our team of contributors rewarded.

General Editors: *Bruce M. Metzger*
David A. Hubbard†
Glenn W. Barker†
Old Testament: *John D. W. Watts*
New Testament: *Ralph P. Martin*

Author's Preface

More than a decade ago Martin Hengel remarked ruefully that "we are at the threshold of a new epoch of exegetical whim" in which "Mark simply becomes a cryptogram the key to which has to be guessed at" (M. Hengel, *Studies in the Gospel of Mark* [Philadelphia: Fortress, 1985] 140 n. 9). He was right, but I think American scholarship entered this epoch several years earlier. The fruit of it has been a seemingly unending harvest of subjective guesswork that has spawned a variety of speculative theories of what issues the evangelist faced and how he (or she) went about addressing them. What is impressive in all of this is the ingenuity of the individual interpreters and the even greater cleverness of the evangelist. We are told that Mark's narrative is a cipher that—for those sufficiently acquainted with the insiders' secret code—corrects Christology, ecclesiology, and/or eschatology. We are to believe, for example, that the narrative is ironic; what appears to be valued is in fact denigrated.

According to some interpreters the characters of the narrative symbolize certain persons or groups within the Markan church. Some are lionized; others are demonized. In step with this hermeneutic we are asked to believe that the disciples themselves represent members of the Markan community who hold to false theological views. To discredit the theology of his opponents, the evangelist must show how the apostles once held to this theology (!). This is surely one of the most incredible interpretations. Are we seriously to think that the earliest narrative of the ministry and death of Jesus would be composed in order to portray (falsely) the apostles as cowardly, stupid, disloyal, and unreliable? Would a frightened, persecuted Christian community find its much needed reassurance in such a portrait? How many first-century Christians would have been inspired to take up the cross and follow Jesus, when, as it turns out, his closest friends and followers, the first to proclaim the resurrection, had never been able to understand their Master and accept his teaching? Such lines of interpretation boggle the mind.

Gospel interpretation has passed through a strange season. Not long ago we were told that the *Gospel of Peter* provides us with the earliest account of the passion and resurrection (J. D. Crossan, *The Cross That Spoke: The Origins of the Passion Narrative* [San Francisco: Harper & Row, 1988]). This means that Mark drew not on early and reliable tradition but on a fantastic story of giant angels and a talking cross. Moreover, the Jesus Seminar would have us believe that the *Gospel of Thomas* yields more authentic material than does the Gospel of Mark. Indeed, we have been told that Mark's apologetic effort to present the Christian faith as innocent, from a Roman perspective, is responsible for two thousand years of social and political ills that have plagued the West, culminating in the horrors of the Holocaust (B. L. Mack, *A Myth of Innocence: Mark and Christian Origins* [Philadelphia: Fortress, 1988]). And, thanks to Morton Smith's discovery of an alleged long-lost letter of Clement, which refers to a "Secret Gospel of Mark" (M. Smith, *Clement of Alexandria and a Secret Gospel of Mark* [Cambridge: Harvard UP, 1973]; id., *The Secret Gospel: The Discovery and Interpretation of the Secret Gospel according to Mark* [New York: Harper & Row, 1973]), some scholars believe that we are now in a position to reconstruct the history of Gospel origins with greater precision (see, e.g., H. Koester, *Ancient Christian Gospels: Their History and*

Development [London: SCM Press; Philadelphia: Trinity Press International, 1990] 295–303). The fact that the seventeenth-century book that contains this Clementine letter has not been subjected to the usual scholarly and critical scrutiny given such discoveries and the fact that Clement of Alexandria naively passed on all sorts of apocryphal traditions about various writings supposedly authored by Peter or other apostles have not sufficiently troubled these scholars.

But signs of a springtime of sobriety can now be detected. With refreshing emphasis and clarity of thought, Robert Gundry's recent commentary challenges the regnant view that Mark's Gospel is a cipher of some sort. In Mark he finds no messianic secret, no Christology of irony, no ecclesiastical enemies lurking between the lines, no symbolism, and no apocalyptic agenda. "Mark's meaning," Gundry avers, "lies on the surface. He writes a straightforward apology for the Cross, for the shameful way in which the object of Christian faith and subject of Christian proclamation died, and hence for Jesus as the Crucified One" (R. H. Gundry, *Mark: A Commentary on His Apology for the Cross* [Grand Rapids, MI: Eerdmans, 1993] 1). This commentary is in essential agreement with Gundry's interpretation.

Alongside Gundry's useful commentary, we have Raymond Brown's magisterial two-volume work on the passion: R. E. Brown, *The Death of the Messiah: From Gethsemane to the Grave*, ABRL, 2 vols. (New York: Doubleday, 1993). Critical of Brown's preference for historical verisimilitude and his supposed failure to bring post-Holocaust sensitivities to bear on his interpretation of first-century documents, J. D. Crossan (*Who Killed Jesus? Exposing the Roots of Anti-Semitism in the Gospel Story of the Death of Jesus* [San Francisco: HarperCollins, 1995]) once again tries to explain what really happened by an appeal to the *Gospel of Peter*. This imaginative reconstruction of the origin and history of the passion story at times indulges in special pleading and improbable hypotheses and assumptions.

Perhaps we should keep in mind that the evangelist Mark did not hold a tenured post in a university in a liberal-minded society. I doubt much that he indulged in deconstruction theory. I doubt seriously that he thought of his Gospel as a play, whose characters represented various figures. I doubt too that he indulged in double-talk, intending his readers to take much of what he said in an opposite, ironic sense. Perhaps it would be wise to see if Mark makes sense, as it stands, in the context of the first-century Roman Empire.

Herein lies what I think is the real point behind Mark's Gospel. His work does indeed constitute an apology for the cross, as Gundry has argued. But it is an apologetic that boldly challenges the emperor's claim to divinity and his demand for the absolute loyalty of his subjects. There is nothing mysterious here that needs to be ferreted out of the text. The opening words, "The beginning of the good news of Jesus Christ, Son of God" (Mark 1:1), would have had an unmistakably imperial ring to them in the ears of the people of the Roman Empire. For from the time of Augustus on, the Roman caesars were called "son of God," and their accessions to the throne, their victories, and their achievements were hailed as "good news." They were called "savior" and "lord" and at death were thought to take their place in heaven. Their post-mortem deification was considered the greatest honor. Death by crucifixion, in sharp contrast, was considered the greatest dishonor. (There is no better treatment of this subject than what is offered in M. Hengel, *Crucifixion* [London: SCM Press; Philadelphia: Fortress, 1977].)

The problem that Mark and early Christians faced is thus plainly evident. How can the crucified Jesus be regarded "Son of God," "Lord," and "Savior" of humankind? For Mark it is all or nothing. If Jesus really is the fulfillment of OT prophecies and if his disciples' confession of his messianic status has any credibility, then he must be recognized and proclaimed as the *true* son of God. Jesus can have no rivals. Hence, Mark announces Jesus' identity at the outset, an identity that is subsequently recognized by divine authority above (Mark 1:11; 9:7) and Roman authority below (Mark 15:39). The Roman emperor might not like this "good news," but true followers of Jesus are ready and willing to follow their Master to the cross, if need be (Mark 8:27–38). I urge the reader to study the final part of the Introduction for further discussion and documentation of this line of interpretation.

The second volume of this commentary was thrust upon me following the sudden and unexpected death of Robert A. Guelich, Professor of New Testament at Fuller Theological Seminary, Pasadena, California. Dr. Guelich was much loved and appreciated by colleagues and students, as the memorial services for him in the summer and fall of 1991 amply attested. I very much sense that I am trying to walk in shoes that are too big for me to fill.

I was loathe not to make use of what Bob Guelich left behind by way of notes on Mark 8:27–16:20. He had written up a rough translation, along with several textual notes. Parts of some of these notes were included. I was also influenced by his translation in many places. He also wrote out rough drafts of commentary on three pericopes in chap. 11: (1) the cursing of the fig tree (vv 12–14, 20–21), (2) lessons of faith and prayer (vv 22–26), and (3) the questions about authority (vv 27–33). I incorporated as much of this material as possible, editing and supplementing it as I felt appropriate. For what readers find good and acceptable in these parts of the commentary, they should give the credit to Bob: for what is found wanting, they may assign the blame to me. All else that Bob left behind consisted of lists of bibliography (mostly concerned with chap. 13), abstracts, and notes extracted from various commentaries.

Finally, a word needs to be said about the translations. I have attempted to render the Greek as literally as possible, without making the text unduly awkward. Present-tense verbs are left in the present tense, instead of hiding them as aorists (which is what modern versions usually do). My purpose is to help the reader appreciate the Markan evangelist's style of writing, especially those readers who wish to study the Greek text itself but who are not advanced in their knowledge of the language. By rendering the historical present as the present (e.g., "he says" and "he goes," instead of "he said" and "he went"), I wish to allow the evangelist to signal "in vivid fashion the main action of the story or a new turn of events in a story already begun with" a historical present (see E. C. Maloney, "The Historical Present in the Gospel of Mark," in *To Touch the Text: Biblical and Related Studies,* FS J. A. Fitzmyer, ed. M. P. Horgan and P. J. Kobelski [New York: Crossroad, 1989] 67–78, with quotation from p. 78).

I close with an expression of thanks to Professor Ralph Martin, who invited me to take on this project and who patiently awaited its completion some years beyond what I had originally projected. I also appreciate the editorial work of Dr. Lynn Losie and Mrs. Melanie McQuere. Finally, my thanks to my wife, Ginny, for helping with the indexes.

CRAIG A. EVANS

May 2000
Trinity Western University

Abbreviations

A. General Abbreviations

abs.	absolute	MS(S)	manuscript(s)
adj.	adjective, adjectival	MT	Masoretic Text
adv.	adverb, adverbial	n.	note
aor.	aorist	n.d.	no date
Aram.	Aramaic	NHC	Nag Hammadi Codex
ca.	*circa,* about	no.	number
cf.	*confer,* compare	n.s.	new series
chap(s).	chapter(s)	NT	New Testament
Copt.	Coptic	obj.	object, objective
diss.	dissertation	OL	Old Latin
DSS	Dead Sea Scrolls	OT	Old Testament
ed(s).	editor(s), edited by	par.	parallel
e.g.	*exempli gratia,* for example	passim	here and there
esp.	especially	pf.	perfect
ET	English translation	prep.	preposition
et. al.	*et alii,* and others	pres.	present
frg.	fragment	ptc.	participle
FS	*Festschrift,* volume written in honor of	repr.	reprint
		rev.	revised, reviser, revision
fut.	future	sg.	singular
gen.	genitive	s.v.	*sub verbo,* under the word
Gk.	Greek	Syr.	Syriac
Heb.	Hebrew	Tg(s).	Targum(s); Targumic
id.	*idem,* the same	tr.	translator, translated by, translation
i.e.	*id est,* that is		
imper.	imperative	UP	University Press
impf.	imperfect	v, vv	verse, verses
indic.	indicative	Vg.	Vulgate
lit.	literally	voc.	vocative
LXX	Septuagint	vol(s).	volume(s)
masc.	masculine	x	times (2x = two times)

B. Abbreviations for Translations and Paraphrases

ASV	American Standard Version, American Revised Version (1901)	NEB	New English Bible
		NIV	New International Version
		NRSV	New Revised Standard Version
AV	Authorized Version	REB	Revised English Bible
KJV	King James Version (1611) = AV	RSV	Revised Standard Version
NASB	New American Standard Bible		

C. Abbreviations of Commonly Used Periodicals, Reference Works, and Serials

AASF	Annales Academiae scientiarum fennicae	ASTI	Annual of the Swedish Theological Institute
AASFDHL	AASF dissertationes humanarum litterarum	ATANT	Abhandlungen zur Theologie des Alten und Neuen Testaments
AB	Anchor Bible		
ABD	D. N. Freedman (ed.), Anchor Bible Dictionary	ATD	Das Alte Testament Deutsch
ABR	Australian Biblical Review	ATR	Anglican Theological Review
ABRL	Anchor Bible Reference Library	AUSS	Andrews University Seminary Studies
AER	American Ecclesiastical Review	AVTRW	Aufsätze und Vorträge zur Theologie und Religionswissenschaft
AGJU	Arbeiten zur Geschichte des antiken Judentums und des Urchristentums	AzTh	Arbeiten zur Theologie
AGSU	Arbeiten zur Geschichte des Spätjudentums und Urchristentums	BA	Biblical Archaeologist
		BAC	Biblioteca de autores cristianos
AJSL	American Journal of Semitic Languages and Literature	BAG	W. Bauer, W. F. Arndt, and F. W. Gingrich, Greek-English Lexicon of the NT (1957)
AJT	American Journal of Theology		
AnBib	Analecta biblica	BAR	Biblical Archaeology Review
AnPhil	J. Marouzeau (ed.), L'année philologique	BASOR	Bulletin of the American Schools of Oriental Research
ANRW	Aufstieg und Niedergang der römischen Welt		
		BBB	Bonner biblische Beiträge
ANTJ	Arbeiten zum Neuen Testament und Judentum	BBR	Bulletin for Biblical Research
		BBET	Beiträge zur biblischen Exegese und Theologie
APAMS	American Philosophical Association Monograph Series	BCPE	Bulletin de Centre protestant d'études
ARAB	D. D. Luckenbill (ed.), Ancient Records of Assyria and Babylonia, 2 vols.	BDF	F. Blass, A. Debrunner, and R. W. Funk, A Greek Grammar of the NT
		BeO	Bibbia e oriente
ArBib	The Aramaic Bible	BETL	Bibliotheca ephemeridum theologicarum lovaniensium
ARSP	Archiv für Rechts- und Sozialphilosophie		
ASB	Austin Seminary Bulletin		
ASNU	Acta seminarii neotestamentici upsaliensis	BEvT	Beiträge zur evangelischen Theologie
AsSeign	Assemblées du Seigneur	BGBE	Beiträge zur Geschichte der biblischen Exegese

BHT	Beiträge zur historischen Theologie	CBQMS	Catholic Biblical Quarterly Monograph Series
Bib	*Biblica*		
BibB	Biblische Beiträge	*CClCr*	*Civiltà classica e cristiana*
BibInt	*Biblical Interpretation*	*CH*	*Church History*
BibLeb	*Bibel und Leben*	*CiTom*	*Ciencia tomista*
BibOr	Biblica et orientalia	*ColT*	*Collectanea theologica*
BibS(N)	Biblische Studien (Neukirchen, 1951-)	ConBNT	Coniectanea biblica, New Testament
BIOSCS	*Bulletin of the International Organization for Septuagint and Cognate Studies*	ConNT	Coniectanea neotestamentica
		CRBR	*Critical Review of Books in Religion*
BJ	*Bonner Jahrbücher*	*CTM*	*Concordia Theological Monthly*
BJRL	*Bulletin of the John Rylands University Library of Manchester*	*CurTM*	*Currents in Theology and Mission*
BJS	Brown Judaic Studies		
BK	*Bibel und Kirche*	*DCG*	J. Hastings et al. (eds.), *Dictionary of Christ and the Gospels*, 2 vols. (Edinburgh, 1908)
BL	*Bibel und Liturgie*		
BLE	*Bulletin de littérature ecclésiastique*		
BN	*Biblische Notizen*	*DJG*	J. B. Green and S. McKnight (eds.), *Dictionary of Jesus and the Gospels*
BO	*Bibliotheca orientalis*		
BR	*Biblical Research*		
BRev	*Bible Review*		
BSac	*Bibliotheca sacra*	*DJPA*	M. Sokoloff, *A Dictionary of Jewish Palestinian Aramaic* (Ramat-Gan: Bar Ilan UP, 1990)
BT	*The Bible Translator*		
BTB	*Biblical Theology Bulletin*		
BTS	*Bible et terre sainte*		
BVC	*Bible et vie chrétienne*	DMOA	Documenta et Monumenta Orientis Antiqui
BW	*The Biblical World*		
BWANT	Beiträge zur Wissenschaft vom Alten und Neuen Testament	*DRev*	*Downside Review*
		DSD	*Dead Sea Discoveries*
BZ	*Biblische Zeitschrift*	*DTT*	*Dansk teologisk tidsskrift*
BZNW	Beihefte zur ZNW		
		EBib	Études bibliques
CahRB	Cahiers de la Revue biblique	EdF	Erträge der Forschung
		EHS	Europäische Hochschulschriften
CB	*Cultura bíblica*		
CBET	Contributions to Biblical Exegesis amd Theology	*EncJud*	*Encyclopaedia Judaica*, 16 vols.
CBFV	Cahiers biblique de *Foi et vie*	EPRO	Etudes préliminaires aux religions orientales dans l'empire romain
CBQ	*Catholic Biblical Quarterly*		

EdF	Erträge der Forschung	HUT	Hermeneutische
ErIsr	Eretz-Israel		Untersuchungen zur
EstBib	*Estudios bíblicos*		Theologie
EstEcl	*Estudios eclesiásticos*		
ETL	*Ephemerides theologicae*	*IBS*	*Irish Biblical Studies*
	lovanienses	*IEJ*	*Israel Exploration Journal*
ETR	*Etudes théologiques et*	*IER*	*Irish Ecclesiastical Record*
	religieuses	*IJT*	*Indian Journal of Theology*
ETS	Erfurter theologische	*IKaZ*	*Internationale katholische*
	Studien		*Zeitschrift*
EvQ	*Evangelical Quarterly*	*IKZ*	*Internationale kirchliche*
EvT	*Evangelische Theologie*		*Zeitschrift*
ExpTim	*Expository Times*	*Imm*	*Immanuel*
		Int	*Interpretation*
FB	Forschung zur Bibel	IRT	Issues in Religion and
FBBS	Facet Books, Biblical		Theology
	Series	*ITQ*	*Irish Theological Quarterly*
FoiVie	*Foi et vie*		
FRLANT	Forschungen zur	*JAAR*	*Journal of the American*
	Religion und Literatur		*Academy of Religion*
	des Alten und Neuen	Jastrow	M. Jastrow, *A Dictionary of*
	Testaments		*the Targumim, the*
FTL	Forum theologiae		*Talmud Babli and*
	linguisticae		*Yerushalmi, and the*
FZPhTh	*Freiburger Zeitschrift für*		*Midrashic Literature,* 2
	Philosophie und Theologie		vols. (London:
			Putnam, 1895–1903;
GNS	Good News Studies		repr. New York:
Greg	*Gregorianum*		Pardes, 1950)
GTA	Göttinger theologische	*JBL*	*Journal of Biblical Literature*
	Arbeiten	*JBR*	*Journal of Bible and Religion*
		JBT	*Jahrbuch für biblische*
HBT	*Horizons in Biblical*		*Theologie*
	Theology	*JES*	*Journal of Ecumenical Studies*
HDR	Harvard Dissertations in	*JETS*	*Journal of the Evangelical*
	Religion		*Theological Society*
HeyJ	*Heythrop Journal*	*JHS*	*Journal of Hellenic Studies*
HibJ	*Hibbert Journal*	*JJS*	*Journal of Jewish Studies*
HTKNT	Herders theologischer	*JQR*	*Jewish Quarterly Review*
	Kommentar zum	*JR*	*Journal of Religion*
	Neuen Testament	*JRE*	*Journal of Religious Ethics*
HTR	*Harvard Theological Review*	*JRS*	*Journal of Roman Studies*
HTS	Harvard Theological	*JSJ*	*Journal for the Study of*
	Studies		*Judaism in the Persian,*
HUCA	*Hebrew Union College*		*Hellenistic and Roman*
	Annual		*Period*

JSNT	Journal for the Study of the New Testament	NKZ	Neue kirchliche Zeitschrift
		NovT	Novum Testamentum
JSNTSup	Journal for the Study of the New Testament: Supplement Series	NovTSup	Novum Testamentum, Supplements
		NRT	La nouvelle revue théologique
JSP	Journal for the Study of the Pseudepigrapha	NTAbh	Neutestamentliche Abhandlungen
JSPSup	Journal for the Study of the Pseudepigrapha: Supplement Series	NTL	New Testament Library
		NTOA	Novum Testamentum et Orbis Antiquus
JTS	Journal of Theological Studies	NTS	New Testament Studies
JTSA	Journal of Theology for Southern Africa	NTTS	New Testament Tools and Studies
Judaica	Judaica: Beiträge zum Verständnis . . .	OBL	Orientalia et biblica lovaniensia
KBANT	Kommentare und Beiträge zum Alten und Neuen Testament	OBO	Orbis biblicus et orientalis
		ÖBS	Österreichische biblische Studien
KD	Kerygma und Dogma		
KTR	King's Theological Review (London)	OBT	Overtures to Biblical Theology
		OrChrAn	Orientali christiana analecta
LB	Linguistica Biblica		
LCC	Library of Christian Classics	OTP	J. H. Charlesworth (ed.), The Old Testament Pseudepigrapha, 2 vols.
LD	Lectio divina		
LR	Lutherische Rundschau	OtSt	Oudtestamentische Studiën
LUÅ	Lunds universitets årsskrift	PEQ	Palestine Exploration Quarterly
LumVie	Lumière et vie		
LumVieSup	Lumière et vie suppléments	PG	J. Migne (ed.), Patrologia graeca [= Patrologiae cursus completus: Series graeca], 162 vols.
ManQ	The Mankind Quarterly		
MBT	Münsterische Beiträge zur Theologie	PGL	G. W. H. Lampe (ed.), Patristic Greek Lexicon
MTS	Marburger theologische Studien	PGM	K. Preisendanz (ed.), Papyri graecae magicae
MTZ	Münchener theologische Zeitschrift	PIBA	Proceedings of the Irish Biblical Association
NBf	New Blackfriars	PL	J. Migne (ed.), Patrologia latina [= Patrologiae cursus completus: Series latina], 217 vols.
Neot	Neotestamentica		
NewDocs	G. H. Horsley and S. Llewelyn (eds.), New Documents Illustrating Early Christianity, 1981–	PRSt	Perspectives in Religious Studies

PSTJ	*Perkins (School of Theology) Journal*	SBB	Stuttgarter biblische Beiträge
PTMS	Pittsburgh Theological Monograph Series	SBL	Society of Biblical Literature
		SBLDS	SBL Dissertation Series
QD	Quaestiones disputatae	SBLMS	SBL Monograph Series
		SBLRBS	SBL Resources for Biblical Study
RAr	*Revue archéologique*		
RB	*Revue biblique*	SBLSCS	SBL Septuagint and Cognate Studies
REA	*Revue des études anciennes*		
RechBib	Recherches bibliques	SBLSP	SBL Seminar Papers
REJ	*Revue des études juives*	SBLSS	SBL Semeia Studies
ResQ	*Restoration Quarterly*	SBLTT	SBL Texts and Translations
RevExp	*Review and Expositor*		
RevistB	*Revista bíblica*	SBS	Stuttgarter Bibelstudien
RevQ	*Revue de Qumran*	SBT	Studies in Biblical Theology
RevScRel	*Revue des sciences religieuses*		
RThom	*Revue thomiste*	*ScEccl*	*Sciences ecclésiastiques*
RHPR	*Revue d'histoire et de philosophie religieuses,* 7 vols.	*ScEs*	*Science et esprit*
		Scr	*Scripture*
		SD	Studies and Documents
RHR	*Revue de l'histoire des religions*	*SE*	*Studia evangelica I, II, III* (= TU 73 [1959], 87 [1964], 88 [1964], etc.)
RIDA	*Revue internationale des droits de l'antiquité*	*SEÅ*	*Svensk exegetisk årsbok*
RivB	*Rivista biblica italiana*	*SecCent*	*Second Century*
RQ	*Römische Quartalschrift für christliche Altertumskunde und Kirchengeschichte*	*Sem*	*Semitica*
		SFSHJ	South Florida Studies in the History of Judaism
RSPT	*Revue des sciences philosophiques et théologiques*	SHAW	Sitzungen der heidelberger Akademie der Wissenschaften
RSR	*Recherches de science religieuse*	SJC	Studies in Judaism and Christianity
RST	Regensburger Studien zur Theologie	SJLA	Studies in Judaism in Late Antiquity
RTL	*Revue théologique de Louvain*	*SJT*	*Scottish Journal of Theology*
RTP	*Revue de théologie et de philosophie*	SNT	Studien zum Neuen Testament
RUO	*Revue de l'université d'Ottawa*	SNTSMS	Society for New Testament Studies Monograph Series
SANT	Studien zum Alten und Neuen Testament	SNTSU	Studien zum Neuen Testament und seiner Umwelt
SBA	Studies in Biblical Archaeology	SNTU-A	SNTSU, Series A
		SNTU-B	SNTSU, Series B

SNTW	Studies of the New Testament and Its World	TLI	J. Neusner, ed., *The Talmud of the Land of Israel*, 35 vols. (Chicago, 1982–94)
SPIB	Scripta pontificii instituti biblica		
SR	*Studies in Religion/Sciences religieuses*	TLNT	C. Sqicq, *Theological Lexicon of the New Testament*, tr. and ed. J. D.Ernest, 3 vols. (Peabody, MA: Hendrickson, 1994)
SSEJC	Studies in Scripture in Early Judaism and Christianity		
ST	*Studia theologica*	TLZ	*Theologische Literaturzeitung*
STÅ	*Svensk teologisk årsskrift*		
STDJ	Studies on the Texts of the Desert of Judah	TP	*Theologie und Philosophie*
		TPQ	*Theologisch-praktische Quartalschrift*
StPB	Studia post-biblica		
Str-B	[H. Strack and] P. Billerbeck, *Kommentar zum Neuen Testament*, 6 vols.	TQ	*Theologische Quartalschrift*
		TRE	*Theologische Realenzyklopädie*
		TRev	*Theologische Revue*
SUNT	Studien zur Umwelt des Neuen Testaments	TRu	*Theologische Rundschau*
		TS	*Theological Studies*
STZ	*Schweizerische theologische Zeitschrift*	TSAJ	Texte und Studien zum antiken Judentum
SwJT	*Southwestern Journal of Theology*	TSK	*Theologische Studien und Kritiken*
		TThSt	Trierer theologische Studien
TAPA	*Transactions of the American Philological Association*	TToday	*Theology Today*
		TTZ	*Trierer theologische Zeitschrift*
TBei	*Theologische Beiträge*		
TBl	*Theologische Blätter*	TU	Texte und Untersuchungen
TB	Theologische Bücherei		
TBT	*The Bible Today*	TVers	*Theologische Versuche*
TCGNT	B. M. Metzger, *A Textual Commentary on the Greek New Testament*, 1st ed. (1971), 2nd ed. (1994)	TvT	*Tijdschrift voor theologie*
		TynBul	*Tyndale Bulletin*
		TZ	*Theologische Zeitschrift*
TD	*Theology Digest*	UB	Die urchristliche Botschaft
TDNT	G. Kittel and G. Friedrich (eds.), *Theological Dictionary of the New Testament*, tr. G. W. Bromiley, 10 vols.		
		UBSGNT	United Bible Societies *Greek New Testament*, 3rd corrected ed. (1983), 4th ed. (1993)
TF	Theologische Forschung	UFHM	University of Florida Humanities Monograph
TGl	*Theologie und Glaube*		
Them	*Themelios*	USQR	*Union Seminary Quarterly Review*
ThViat	*Theologia viatorum*		
TJT	*Toronto Journal of Theology*		

VC	*Vigiliae christianae*		ZKG	*Zeitschrift für*
VD	*Verbum domini*			*Kirchengeschichte*
VE	*Vox evangelica*		ZKT	*Zeitschrift für katholische*
VGG	Veröffentlichungen der			*Theologie*
	Gesellschaft für		ZNW	*Zeitschrift für die*
	Geistesgeschichte			*neutestamentliche*
VSpir	*Vie spirituelle*			*Wissenschaft und die*
VT	*Vetus Testamentum*			*Kunde der älteren*
				Kirche
WBC	Word Biblical		ZRGG	*Zeitschrift für Religions-*
	Commentary			*und Geistesgeschichte*
WD	*Wort und Dienst*		ZST	*Zeitschrift für systematische*
WTJ	*Westminster Theological*			*Theologie*
	Journal		ZSSR	*Zeitschrift der Savigny*
WUNT	Wissenschaftliche			*Stiftung für*
	Untersuchungen zum			*Rechtsgeschichte*
	Neuen Testament		ZTK	*Zeitschrift für Theologie und*
				Kirche
YJS	Yale Judaica Series		ZWT	*Zeitschrift für*
				wissenschaftliche
ZDMG	*Zeitschrift der deutschen*			*Theologie*
	morgenländischen		ZPE	*Zeitschrift für Papyrologie*
	Gesellschaft			*und Epigraphik*
ZDPV	*Zeitschrift des deutschen*		ZZ	*Die Zeichen der Zeit*
	Palästina-Vereins			

D. Abbreviations for Books of the Bible with Aprocrypha

OLD TESTAMENT			NEW TESTAMENT	
Gen	1–2 Chr	Dan	Matt	1–2 Thess
Exod	Ezra	Hos	Mark	1–2 Tim
Lev	Neh	Joel	Luke	Titus
Num	Esth	Amos	John	Phlm
Deut	Job	Obad	Acts	Heb
Josh	Ps(s)	Jonah	Rom	Jas
Judg	Prov	Mic	1–2 Cor	1–2 Pet
Ruth	Eccl	Nah	Gal	1–2–3 John
1–2 Sam	Song	Hab	Eph	Jude
1–2 Kgdms	Isa	Zeph	Phil	Rev
(LXX)	Jer	Hag	Col	
1–2 Kgs	Lam	Zech		
2–4 Kgdms	Ezek	Mal		
(LXX)				

APOCRYPHA

Bar	Baruch	Jdt	Judith
Add Dan	Additions to Daniel	1-2-3-4	1-2-3-4
Pr Azar	Prayer of Azariah	Macc	Maccabees
Bel	Bel and the Dragon	Pr Man	Prayer of Manasseh
Sg Three	Song of the Three	Ps 151	Psalm 151
	Young Men	Sir	Sirach/Ecclesiasticus
Sus	Susanna	Tob	Tobit
1–2 Esd	1–2 Esdras	4 Ezra	4 Ezra
Add Esth	Additions to Esther	Wis	Wisdom of Solomon
Ep Jer	Epistle of Jeremiah		

E. Abbreviations of Old Testament Pseudepigrapha

2 Bar.	*2 Baruch (Syriac Apocalypse)*	*Sib. Or.*	*Sibylline Oracles*
3 Bar.	*3 Baruch (Greek Apocalypse)*	*T. 12 Patr.*	*Testaments of the Twelve*
Apoc. El. (H)	Hebrew *Apocalypse of*		*Patriarchs*
	Elijah	*T. Jud.*	*Testament of Judah*
Apoc. El. (C)	Coptic *Apocalypse of Elijah*	*T. Levi*	*Testament of Levi*
Jos. Asen.	*Joseph and Aseneth*	*T. Naph.*	*Testament of Naphtali*
Jub.	*Jubilees*	*T. Job*	*Testament of Job*
L.A.B.	*Liber antiquitatum*	*T. Mos.*	*Testament of Moses*
	biblicarum		*(Assumption of Moses)*
	(Pseudo-Philo)	*T. Sol.*	*Testament of Solomon*
Liv. Pro.	*Lives of the Prophets*		
Mart. Ascen. Isa.	*Martyrdom and Ascension of*		
	Isaiah		

F. Dead Sea Scrolls and Related Texts

CD	Cairo (Genizah text of	1QIsa[a,b]	First or second copy of
	the *Damascus (Document)*		Isaiah from Qumran
Ḥev	Naḥal Ḥever texts		Cave 1
Mas	Masada texts	1QpHab	*Pesher on Habakkuk* from
Mird	Khirbet Mird texts		Qumran Cave 1
Mur	Wadi Murabbaʿat texts	1QM	*Milḥāmāh* (*War Scroll*)
P	pesher (commentary)	1QS	*Serek hayyaḥad* (*Rule of the*
Q	Qumran		*Community, Manual of*
1Q, 2Q, 3Q, etc.	Numbered caves of		*Discipline*)
	Qumran	1QSa	Appendix A (*Rule of the*
1QapGen	*Genesis Apocryphon* of		*Congregation*) to 1QS
	Qumran Cave 1	1QSb	Appendix B (*Blessings*) to
1QH	*Hôdāyôt* (*Thanksgiving*		1QS
	Hymns) from Qumran		
	Cave 1		

G. Philo

Abraham	*On the Life of Abraham*	*Embassy*	*On the Embassy to Gaius*
Contempl. Life	*On the Contemplative Life*	*Migration*	*On the Migration of*
Decalogue	*On the Decalogue*		*Abraham*
Flaccus	*Against Flaccus*	*Moses*	*On the Life of Moses*
Joseph	*On the Life of Joseph*		

H. Mishnah, Talmud and Related Literature

y.	Jerusalem Talmud	*Meʿil.*	*Meʿilah*
b.	Babylonian Talmud	*Menaḥ.*	*Menahot*
t.	Tosefta	*Mid.*	*Middot*
m.	Mishnah	*Moʾed Qaṭ.*	*Moʾed Qaṭan*
ʿAbod. Zar.	*ʿAbodah Zarah*	*Ned.*	*Nedarim*
ʾAbot	*ʾAbot*	*Nid.*	*Niddah*
ʿArak.	*ʿArakin*	*Parah*	*Parah*
B. Bat.	*Baba Batra*	*Pesaḥ.*	*Pesaḥim*
B. Meṣiʿa	*Baba Meṣiʿa*	*Qidd.*	*Qiddusîn*
B. Qam.	*Baba Qamma*	*Roš. Hoš.*	*Roš Hoššanah*
Bek.	*Bekorot*	*Šabb.*	*Šabbat*
Ber.	*Berakot*	*Sanh.*	*Sanhedrin*
Beṣah	*Beṣah (= Yom Ṭob)*	*Šeb.*	*Šebiʿit*
ʿErub.	*ʿErubin*	*Šebu.*	*Šebuʿot*
ʿEd.	*ʿEduyyot*	*Šeqal.*	*Šeqalim*
Giṭ.	*Giṭṭin*	*Soṭah*	*Soṭah*
Ḥag.	*Ḥagigah*	*Sukkah*	*Sukkah*
Ḥul.	*Ḥullin*	*Taʿan.*	*Taʿanit*
Ker.	*Kerithot*	*Tamid*	*Tamid*
Ketub.	*Ketubbot*	*Yebam.*	*Yebamot*
Kil.	*Kilʾayim*	*Yoma*	*Yoma (= Kippurim)*
Meg.	*Megillah*	*Zebaḥ.*	*Zebaḥim*

I. Abbreviations of Targumic Material

Tg. Onq.	*Targum Onqelos*	*Tg. Neof.*	*Targum Neofiti I*
Frg. Tg.	*Fragmentary Targum*	*Tg. Ps.-J.*	*Targum Pseudo-Jonathan*

J. Other Rabbinic Works

ʾAbot R. Nat.	*ʾAbot de Rabbi Nathan*	*Rab.*	*Rabbah*
Midr.	*Midrash*	*Sem.*	*Semaḥot*
Pesiq. Rab.	*Pesiqta Rabbati*	*Sipra*	*Sipra*
Pesig Rab. Kah.	*Pesiqta de Rab Kahana*	*Sipre*	*Sipre*
Pirqe R. El.	*Pirqe Rabbi Eliezer*		

K. Papyri, Ostraca, and Inscriptions

BGU	*Ägyptische Urkunden aus den Königlichen Staatlichen Museen zu Berlin, Griechische Urkunden*
CBS	Catalogue of Babylonian Section in the Univ. of Pennsylvania
CIA	*Corpus Inscriptionum Atticarum*, vols. 1–3 (Berlin, 1873–97)
CIJ	*Corpus inscriptionum judaicarum*
CPJ	V. Tcherikover (ed.), *Corpus papyrorum judaicarum* (Cambridge, 1957–64)
CPL	R. Cavenaile (ed.), *Corpus papyrorum latinarum* (Wiesbaden, 1958)
GIBM	*The Collection of Greek Inscriptions in the British Museum*, 4 vols. (London, 1874–1916)
GOA	U. Wilcken (ed.), *Griechische Ostraka aus Ägypten und Nubien*, vol. 2 (Leipzig, 1899)
IG	*Inscriptiones Graecae* (Berlin, 1837)
IGR	R. Cagnat et al. (eds.), *Inscriptiones Graeca ad Res Romanas Pertinentes*, vols. 1–4 (Paris, 1911–27)
IM	O. Kern (ed.), *Die Inschriften von Magnesia am Mäander* (Berlin, 1900)
OGIS	W. Dittenberger (ed.), *Orientis graecae inscriptiones selectae*, 2 vols. (repr. Hildesheim, 1960)
O.Petr.	*Ostraca in Prof. Sir W. M. Flinders Petrie's Collection at University College London* (London, 1930)
P.Cair.Zen	C. C. Edgar (ed.), *Zenon Papyri*, 4 vols. (Cairo, 1925–31)
P.Col.Zen.	W. L. Westermann and E. S. Hasenoehrl (eds.), *Zenon Papyri*, vol. 1 (New York: Columbia UP, 1934)
P.Eger.	H. I. Bell and T. C. Skeat (eds.), *Fragments of an Unknown Gospel and Other Early Christian Papyri* (London, 1935)
P.Fay.	B. P. Grenfell et al. (eds.), *Fayûm Towns and Their Papyri* (London, 1900)
P.Flor.	G. Vitelli and D. Comparette (eds.), *Papiri Fiorentini*, 3 vols. (Milan, 1905–15)
P.Lond.	F. G. Kenyon and H. I. Bell (eds.), *Greek Papyri in the British Museum*, vols. 1–2 (London, 1893–1907)
P.Louvre	A. Jördens and K.-T. Zauzich (eds.), *Griechische Papyri aus Soknopaiu Nesos (P.Louvre I)* (Bonn, 1998)
P.Magdalen.Gr.	J. Lesquier (ed.) *Papyrus de Magdola* (1912)
P.Mich.	A. E. R. Boak et al. (eds.), *Michigan Papyri*, vols. 1–8 (Ann Arbor, MI, 1931–51)
P.Oslo	S. Eitrem and L. Amundsen (eds.), *Papyri Osloënses*, vols. 2–3 (Oslo, 1931–36)
P.Oxy.	B. P. Grenfell et al. (eds.), *The Oxyrhynchus Papyri*, 62 vols. (London, 1898–1997)
P.Ryl.	A. S. Hunt et al. (eds.), *Catalogue of the Greek Papyri in the John Rylands Library Manchester*, vols. 2, 4 (Manchester, 1915–52)
P.Şe'elim	A. Yardeni (ed.), *Nahal Şe'elim Documents* (Jerusalem, 1995)
PSI	G. Vitelli et al. (eds.), *Publicazioni della Società italiana per la Ricerca dei Papiri greci e latini in Egitto*, vols. 1–14 (Florence, 1912–57)
P.Teb.	B. P. Grenfell et al. (eds.), *The Tebtunis Papyri*, vol. 2 (London, 1907)
SB	F. Preisigke et al. (eds.), *Sammelbuch griechischer Urkunden aus Ägypten* (Strassburg, 1915–)
SEG	Supplementum epigraphicum graecum
SIG	W. Dittenberger (ed.), *Sylloge inscriptionum graecarum*, 4 vols. 3rd ed. (Leipzig, 1915–24)

Commentary Bibliography

In the text of the commentary, references to commentaries are by author's last name only.

Anderson, H. *The Gospel of Mark*. NCB. London: Oliphants, 1976. **Bacon, B. W.** *The Gospel of Mark*. New Haven, CT: Yale UP, 1925. **Bartlet, J. V.** *St Mark*. New Century Bible. Edinburgh: T. C. & E. C. Jack; New York: Oxford UP, 1922. **Blunt, A. W. F.** *The Gospel according to Saint Mark*. The Clarendon Bible. Oxford: Clarendon, 1939. **Branscomb, B. H.** *The Gospel of Mark*. The Moffatt New Testament Commentary. London: Hodder and Stoughton, 1937. **Brooks, J. A.** *Mark*. NAC 23. Nashville: Broadman, 1991. **Brown, R. E.** *The Death of the Messiah: A Commentary on the Passion Narratives in the Four Gospels*. 2 vols. ABRL. New York: Doubleday, 1994. **Carrington, P.** *According to Mark*. Cambridge: Cambridge UP, 1960. **Chadwick, G. A.** *The Gospel according to St Mark*. The Expositors' Bible. London: Hodder & Stoughton/New York: Doran, 1887. **Cranfield, C. E. B.** *The Gospel according to Saint Mark*. CGTC. Cambridge: Cambridge UP, 1963. **Ernst, J.** *Das Evangelium nach Markus*. RNT. Regensburg: Pustet, 1981. **Gould, E. P.** *A Critical and Exegetical Commentary on the Gospel according to Saint Mark*. ICC. Edinburgh: T. & T. Clark, 1896. **Gnilka, J.** *Das Evangelium nach Markus*. 2 vols. EKK 2.1–2. Zürich: Benzinger/Neukirchen-Vluyn: Neukirchener Verlag, 1978, 1979. **Grundmann, W.** *Das Evangelium nach Markus*. THNT 2. 8th ed. Berlin: Evangelische Verlagsanstalt, 1980. **Guelich, R. A.** *Mark 1–8:26*. WBC 34A. Dallas: Word, 1989. **Gundry, R. H.** *Mark: A Commentary on His Apology for the Cross*. Grand Rapids, MI: Eerdmans, 1992. **Haenchen, E.** *Der Weg Jesu: Eine Erklärung des Markus-Evangeliums und der kanonischen Parallelen*. 2nd ed. Berlin: Töpelmann, 1966. **Harrington, W. J.** *Mark*. NTM 4. Rev. ed. Wilmington, DE: Glazier, 1985. **Hooker, M. D.** *The Gospel according to Saint Mark*. BNTC. London: A. & C. Black, 1991. **Hunter, A. M.** *The Gospel according to Saint Mark*. Torch Bible Commentaries 45. London: SCM Press, 1949. **Hurtado, L. W.** *Mark*. NIBC 2. Peabody, MA: Hendrickson, 1989. **Iersel, B. M. F. van.** *Mark: A Reader-Response Commentary*. JSNTSup 164. Sheffield: Sheffield Academic Press, 1998. **Johnson, S. E.** *A Commentary on the Gospel according to St. Mark*. BNTC. London: A. & C. Black, 1972. **Juel, D. H.** *Mark*. ACNT. Minneapolis: Augsburg, 1990. **Klostermann, E.** *Das Markusevangelium*. HNT 3. 4th ed. Tübingen: Mohr-Siebeck, 1950. **Lachs, S. T.** *A Rabbinic Commentary on the New Testament: The Gospels of Matthew, Mark, and Luke*. Hoboken, NJ: Ktav, 1987. **Lagrange, M.-J.** *Évangile selon saint Marc*. Paris: Gabalda, 1929. **Lane, W. L.** *The Gospel according to Mark*. NICNT. Grand Rapids, MI: Eerdmans, 1974. **Lohmeyer, E.** *Das Evangelium des Markus*. MeyK 2. 11th ed. Göttingen: Vandenhoeck & Ruprecht, 1951. **Loisy, A.** *L'Évangile Marc*. Paris: Nourry, 1912. **Lührmann, D.** *Das Markusevangelium*. HNT 3. Tübingen: Mohr-Siebeck, 1987. **MacLear, G. F.** *The Gospel according to St Mark*. Cambridge Greek Testament for Schools and Colleges. Cambridge: Cambridge UP, 1904. **Malina, B. J.,** and **Rohrbaugh, R. L.** *Social-Science Commentary on the Synoptic Gospels*. Minneapolis: Fortress, 1992. **Mann, C. S.** *Mark*. AB 27. Garden City, NY: Doubleday, 1986. **Montefiore, C. G.** *The Synoptic Gospels*. 2 vols. 2nd ed. London: Macmillan, 1927. **Moule, C. F. D.** *The Gospel according to Mark*. Cambridge Bible Commentary on the New English Bible. Cambridge: Cambridge UP, 1965. **Nineham, D. E.** *The Gospel of St Mark*. Pelican New Testament Commentaries. New York: Penguin, 1963. **Painter, J.** *Mark's Gospel*. New Testament Readings. London: Routledge, 1997. **Pesch, R.** *Das Markusevangelium*. 2 vols. HTKNT 2.1–2. Freiburg: Herder, 1979, 1991. **Plummer, A.** *The Gospel according to St. Mark*. Cambridge Greek Testament for Schools and Colleges. Cambridge: Cambridge UP, 1914. **Radermakers, J.** *La bonne nouvelle de Jésus selon saint Marc*. Brussels: Institut d'Études Théologiques, 1974. **Rawlinson, A. E. J.** *St Mark*. 6th ed. London: Methuen, 1947. **Schmid, J.** *The Gospel according to Mark*. The Regensburg New

Testament. Staten Island, NY: Alba House, 1968. **Schmidt, D. D.** *The Gospel of Mark.* Scholars Bible 1. Sonoma: Polebridge, 1990. **Schmithals, W.** *Das Evangelium nach Markus.* 2 vols. OTNT 2.1–2. Gütersloh: Mohn, 1979. **Schniewind, J.** *Das Evangelium nach Markus.* NTD 1. 10th ed. Göttingen: Vandenhoeck & Ruprecht, 1963. **Swete, H. B.** *The Gospel according to St Mark.* 3rd ed. London: Macmillan, 1913. **Schweizer, E.** *The Good News according to Mark.* Richmond, VA: John Knox, 1970. **Stock, A.** *The Method and Message of Mark.* Wilmington, DE: Glazier, 1989. **Taylor, V.** *The Gospel according to St Mark.* 2nd ed. London: Macmillan, 1966. **Turner, C. H.** *The Gospel according to St. Mark.* London: S. P. C. K.; New York: Macmillan, 1931. **Wellhausen, J.** *Das Evangelium Marci.* 2nd ed. Berlin: Reimer, 1909. **Williamson, L.** *Mark.* Interpretation: A Bible Commentary for Teaching and Preaching. Atlanta: John Knox, 1983.

General Bibliography

Abrahams, I. *Studies in Pharisaism and the Gospels.* 2 vols. Cambridge: Cambridge UP, 1917, 1924; repr. as one vol., New York: Ktav, 1967. **Ambrozic, A. M.** *The Hidden Kingdom: A Redaction-Critical Study of the References to the Kingdom of God in Mark's Gospel.* CBQMS 2. Washington, DC: Catholic Biblical Association, 1972. **Baarlink, H.** *Anfängliches Evangelium: Ein Beitrag zur näheren Bestimmung der theologischen Motive im Markusevangelium.* Kampen: Kok, 1977. **Beasley-Murray, G. R.** *Jesus and the Kingdom of God.* Grand Rapids, MI: Eerdmans, 1986. **Becker, J.** *Jesus of Nazareth.* New York; Berlin: de Gruyter, 1998. **Benoit, P.** *The Passion and Resurrection of Jesus Christ.* London: Darton, Longman & Todd, 1969; New York: Herder and Herder, 1970. **Best, E.** *Disciples and Discipleship: Studies in the Gospel according to Mark.* Edinburgh: T. & T. Clark, 1986. ———. *Following Jesus: Discipleship in the Gospel of Mark.* JSNTSup 4. Sheffield: JSOT Press, 1981. ———. *Mark: The Gospel as Story.* SNTW. Edinburgh: T. & T. Clark, 1983. ———. *The Temptation and the Passion.* SNTS 2. 2nd ed. Cambridge: Cambridge UP, 1990. **Black, C. C.** *The Disciples according to Mark.* JSNTSup 27. Sheffield: JSOT Press, 1989. **Black, M.** *An Aramaic Approach to the Gospels and Acts.* 3rd ed. Oxford: Clarendon, 1967. **Blackburn, B.** θεῖος ἀνήρ *and the Markan Miracle Traditions.* WUNT 2.40. Tübingen: Mohr-Siebeck, 1991. **Boismard, M.-É.** *L'Évangile de Marc: Sa préhistoire.* EBib 26. Paris: Gabalda, 1994. **Boring, M. E., Berger, K.,** and **Colpe, C.** *Hellenistic Commentary to the New Testament.* Nashville: Abingdon, 1995. **Böttger, P. C.** *Der König der Juden—Das Heil für die Völker: Die Geschichte Jesu Christi im Zeugnis des Markusevangeliums.* Neukirchener Studienbücher 13. Neukirchener-Vluyn: Neukirchener Verlag, 1981. **Breytenbach, C.** *Nachfolge und Zukunftserwartung nach Markus: Eine methodenkritische Studie.* ATANT 71. Zürich: Theologischer Verlag, 1984. **Broadhead E. K.** *Teaching with Authority: Miracles and Christology in the Gospel of Mark.* JSNTSup 74. Sheffield: JSOT, 1992. **Bultmann, R.** *The History of the Synoptic Tradition.* Rev. ed. Oxford: Blackwell, 1972. **Burkill, T. A.** *Mysterious Revelation: An Examination of the Philosophy of St. Mark's Gospel.* Ithaca, NY: Cornell UP, 1963. **Burkitt, F. C.** *The Gospel History and Its Transmission.* 3rd ed. Edinburgh: T. & T. Clark, 1911. **Camery-Hoggatt, J.** *Irony in Mark's Gospel: Text and Subtext.* SNTSMS 72. Cambridge: Cambridge UP, 1992. **Casey, M.** *Aramaic Sources of Mark's Gospel.* SNTSMS 102. Cambridge: Cambridge UP, 1998. **Chilton, B. D.** *A Galilean Rabbi and His Bible: Jesus' Use of the Interpreted Scripture of His Time.* GNS 8. Wilmington, DE: Glazier, 1984. **Collins, A. Y.** *The Beginning of the Gospel: Probings of Mark in Context.* Minneapolis: Fortress, 1992. **Cook, M. J.** *Mark's Treatment of the Jewish Leaders.* NovTSup 51. Leiden: Brill, 1978. **Crossan, J. D.** *The Historical Jesus: The Life of a Mediterranean Jewish Peasant.* San Francisco: HarperCollins, 1991. 355–60. ———. *In Fragments: The Aphorisms of Jesus.* San Francisco: Harper & Row, 1983. ———. "Redaction and Citation in Mark 11:9–10 and 11:17." *BR* 17 (1972) 33–50. **Davies, W. D.,** and **Allison, D. C.** *The Gospel according to Saint Matthew.* 3 vols. ICC. Edinburgh: T. & T. Clark, 1988–97. **Dibelius, M.** *From Tradition to Gospel.* Cambridge: James Clarke, 1971. **Donahue, J. R.** *Are You the Christ? The Trial Narrative in the Gospel of Mark.* SBLDS 10. Missoula, MT: Society of Biblical Literature, 1973. **Dormeyer, D.** *Die Passion Jesu als Verhaltensmodell: Literarische und theologische Analyse der Traditions- und Redaktionsgeschichte der Markuspassion.* NTAbh 11. Münster: Aschendorff, 1974. **Evans, C. A.** *Jesus and His Contemporaries: Comparative Studies.* AGJU 25. Leiden: Brill, 1995. **Field, F.** *Notes on the Translation of the New Testament.* Cambridge: Cambridge UP, 1899. **Fitzmyer, J. A.** *The Gospel according to Luke.* AB 28 and 28A. 2 vols. Garden City, NY: Doubleday, 1981, 1985. **Fleddermann, H. T.** *Mark and Q: A Study of the Overlap Texts.* BETL 122. Leuven: Peeters and Leuven UP, 1995. **Flusser, D.** *Jesus.* Jerusalem: Magnes Press, 1997. **Fowler, R. M.** *Let the Reader Understand: Reader-Response Criticism and the Gospel of Mark.* Minneapolis:

Fortress, 1991. **France, R. T.** *Jesus and the Old Testament.* London: Tyndale, 1971. **Freyne, S.** *Galilee, Jesus and the Gospels: Literary Approaches and Historical Investigations.* Philadelphia: Fortress, 1988. **Funk, R. W.** *The Synoptic Gospels.* Vol. 1 of *New Gospel Parallels.* Philadelphia: Fortress, 1985. ——— and **Smith, M. H.,** eds. *The Gospel of Mark: Red Letter Edition.* Sonoma: Polebridge, 1991. **Geddert, T. J.** *Watchwords: Mark 13 in Markan Eschatology.* JSNTSup 26. Sheffield: JSOT Press, 1989. **Grimm, W.** *Weil ich dich liebe: Die Verkündigung Jesu und Deuterojesaja.* ANTJ 1. Bern; Frankfurt am Main: Lang, 1976. **Gundry, R. H.** *Matthew: A Commentary on His Literary and Theological Art.* Grand Rapids, MI: Eerdmans, 1982. **Hagner, D. A.** *Matthew.* 2 vols. WBC 33A and 33B. Dallas: Word, 1993, 1994. **Hengel, M.** *Studies in the Gospel of Mark.* Philadelphia: Fortress, 1985. **Hooker, M. D.** *The Son of Man in Mark: A Study of the Background of the Term "Son of Man" and Its Use in St Mark's Gospel.* London: S. P. C. K./Montreal: McGill UP, 1967. **Horsley, R. A.** *Jesus and the Spiral of Violence: Popular Jewish Resistance in Roman Palestine.* San Francisco: Harper & Row, 1987. **Horstmann, M.** *Studien zur markinischen Christologie: Mk 8,27– 9,13 als Zugang zum Christusbild des zweiten Evangeliums.* NTAbh 6. Münster: Aschendorff, 1969. **Iersel, B. M. F. van.** *Reading Mark.* Edinburgh: T. & T. Clark, 1988. **Jeremias, J.** *New Testament Theology: The Proclamation of Jesus.* Rev. ed. New York: Scribner's, 1971. **Juel, D.** *Messiah and Temple: The Trial of Jesus in the Gospel of Mark.* SBLDS 31. Missoula, MT: Scholars Press, 1977. **Kato, Z.** *Die Völkermission im Markusevangelium.* EHS 23.252. Frankfurt am Main; Bern; New York: Lang, 1986. **Kazmierski, C. R.** *Jesus, the Son of God: A Study of the Markan Tradition and its Redaction by the Evangelist.* FB 33. Würzburg: Echter, 1979. **Kee, H. C.** *Community of the New Age: Studies in Mark's Gospel.* Philadelphia: Westminster, 1977. **Keener, C. S.** *A Commentary on the Gospel of Matthew.* Grand Rapids, MI: Eerdmans, 1999. **Kelber, W.,** ed. *The Passion in Mark: Studies on Mark 14–16.* Philadelphia: Fortress, 1976. **Kertelge, K.** *Die Wunder Jesu im Markusevangelium: Eine redaktionsgeschichtliche Untersuchung.* SANT 23. Munich: Kösel, 1970. **Kingsbury, J. D.** *The Christology of Mark's Gospel.* Philadelphia: Fortress, 1983. ———. *Conflict in Mark: Jesus, Authorities, Disciples.* Minneapolis: Fortress, 1989. **Koch, D.-A.** *Die Bedeutung der Wundererzählungen für die Christologie des Markusevangeliums.* BZNW 42. Berlin: de Gruyter, 1975. **Kuhn, H.-W.** *Ältere Sammlungen im Markusevangelium.* SNTU 8. Göttingen: Vandenhoeck & Ruprecht, 1971. **Kümmel, W. G.** *Promise and Fulfilment: The Eschatological Message of Jesus.* SBT 23. London: SCM Press; Naperville, IL: Allenson, 1957. **Latourelle, R.** *The Miracles of Jesus and the Theology of Miracles.* New York: Paulist, 1988. **Linnemann, E.** *Studien zur Passionsgeschichte.* FRLANT 102. Göttingen: Vandenhoeck & Ruprecht, 1970. **Loos, H. van der.** *The Miracles of Jesus.* NovTSup 9. Leiden: Brill, 1965. **Mack, B. L.** *A Myth of Innocence: Mark and Christian Origins.* Philadelphia: Fortress, 1988. **Manson, T. W.** *The Sayings of Jesus.* London: SCM Press, 1957. ———. *The Teaching of Jesus.* 2nd ed. Cambridge: Cambridge UP, 1935. **Marcus, J.** *The Way of the Lord: Christological Exegesis of the Old Testament in the Gospel of Mark.* Louisville: Westminster John Knox, 1992. **Marshall, C. D.** *Faith as a Theme in Mark's Narrative.* SNTSMS 64. Cambridge: Cambridge UP, 1989. **Martin, R. P.** *Mark: Evangelist and Theologian.* Exeter: Paternoster; Grand Rapids, MI: Zondervan, 1972. **Marxsen, W.** *Mark the Evangelist: Studies on the Redaction History of the Gospel.* Nashville: Abingdon, 1969. **Meier, J. P.** *A Marginal Jew: Rethinking the Historical Jesus.* 2 vols. ABRL. Garden City, NY: Doubleday, 1991, 1994. **Meye, R. P.** *Jesus and the Twelve: Discipleship and Revelation in Mark's Gospel.* Grand Rapids, MI: Eerdmans, 1968. **Meyer, B. F.** *The Aims of Jesus.* London: SCM Press, 1979. **Minette de Tillesse, G.** *Le secret messianique dans l'Évangile de Marc.* LD 47. Paris: Cerf, 1968. **Mohr, T. A.** *Markus- und Johannespassion: Redaktions- und traditionsgeschichtliche Untersuchung der markinischen und johanneischen Passionstradition.* ATANT 70. Zürich: Theologischer Verlag, 1982. **Moo, D. J.** *The Old Testament in the Gospel Passion Narratives.* Sheffield: Almond, 1983. **Moore, G. F.** *Judaism in the First Centuries of the Christian Era: The Age of the Tannaim.* 3 vols. Cambridge: Harvard UP, 1927–30. **Myllykoski, M.** *Die letzten Tage Jesu: Markus und Johannes, ihre Traditionen und die historische Frage.* Vol. 1. Annales Academiae Scientiarum Fennicae B/256. Helsinki: Suomalainen Tiedeakatemia, 1991. **Neirynck, F.** *Duality in Mark: Contributions to the Study of the Markan Redaction.* BETL 31. Rev. ed. Leuven: Peeters and Leuven UP, 1988. **Nolland, J.** *Luke.* 3 vols. WBC 35A, 35B, 35C. Dallas:

Word, 1989, 1993. **Perrin, N.** *Rediscovering the Teaching of Jesus.* New York: Harper & Row, 1976. **Pesch, R.** *Das Evangelium der Urgemeinde.* Herder Bücherei 748. Freiburg: Herder, 1979. ———, ed. *Das Markus-Evangelium.* WF 411. Darmstadt: Wissenschaftliche Buchgesellschaft, 1979. **Petersen, N. R.,** ed. *Perspectives on Mark's Gospel.* Semeia 16. Missoula, MT: Scholars Press, 1979. **Pryke, E. J.** *Redactional Style in the Marcan Gospel.* SNTSMS 33. Cambridge: Cambridge UP, 1978. **Räisänen, H.** *The 'Messianic Secret' in Mark's Gospel.* Studies of the New Testament and Its World. Edinburgh: T. & T. Clark, 1990. **Reploh, K. G.** *Markus–Lehrer der Gemeinde: Eine redaktionsgeschichtliche Studie zu den Jüngerperikopen des Markusevangeliums.* SBM 9. Stuttgart: Katholisches Bibelwerk, 1969. **Rhoads, D.,** and **Michie, D.** *Mark as Story: An Introduction to the Narrative of a Gospel.* Philadelphia: Fortress, 1982. **Robbins, V. K.** *Jesus the Teacher: A Socio-Rhetorical Interpretation of Mark.* Minneapolis: Fortress, 1992. **Robinson, J. M.** *The Problem of History in Mark.* SBT 21. London: SCM Press, 1957. **Roloff, J.** *Das Kerygma und der irdische Jesus: Historische Motive in den Jesus-Erzählungen der Evangelien.* Berlin: Evangelische Verlagsanstalt, 1973. **Sabbe, M.,** ed. *L'Évangile selon Marc: Tradition et rédaction.* BETL 34. Leuven: Leuven UP, 1974. **Sanders, E. P.** *Jesus and Judaism.* London: SCM Press; Philadelphia: Fortress, 1985. **Sariola, H.** *Markus und das Gesetz: Eine redaktionskritische Untersuchung.* Annales academiae scientiarum fennicae dissertationes humanarum litterarum 56. Helsinki: Suomalainen Tiedeakatemia, 1990. **Schenk, W.** *Der Passionsbericht nach Markus: Untersuchung zur Überlieferungsgeschichte der Passionstraditionen.* Gütersloh: Mohn, 1974. **Schenke, L.** *Der gekreuzigte Christus: Versuch einer literarkritischen und traditionsgeschichtlichen Bestimmung der vormarkinischen Passionsgeschichte.* SBS 69. Stuttgart: Katholisches Bibelwerk, 1974. ———. *Studien zur Passionsgeschichte des Markus: Tradition und Redaktion in Markus 14,1–42.* FB 4. Würzburg: Echter, 1971. ———. *Die Wundererzählungen des Markusevangeliums.* SBB 5. Stuttgart: Katholische Bibelwerk, 1974. **Schille, G.** *Offen für alle Menschen: Redaktionsgeschichtliche Beobachtungen zur Theologie des Markus-Evangeliums.* AzTh 55. Stuttgart: Calwer, 1974. **Schlosser, J.** *Le règne de Dieu dans les dits de Jésus.* EBib. Paris: Gabalda, 1980. **Schmahl, G.** *Die Zwölf im Markusevangelium: Eine redaktionsgeschichtliche Untersuchung.* TThSt 30. Trier: Paulinus, 1974. **Schmidt, K. L.** *Der Rahmen der Geschichte Jesu: Literarkritische Untersuchungen zur ältesten Jesusüberlieferung.* Berlin: Trowitzsch, 1919. **Schneider, G.** *Die Passion Jesu nach den drei älteren Evangelien.* Biblische Handbibliothek 11. Munich: Kösel, 1973. **Schreiber, J.** *Theologie des Vertrauens: Eine redaktionsgeschichtliche Untersuchung des Markusevangeliums.* Hamburg: Furche, 1967. 126–45. **Schwarz, G.** *Jesus und Judas: Aramaistische Untersuchungen zur Jesus-Judas-Überlieferung der Evangelien und der Apostelgeschichte.* BWANT 123. Stuttgart: Kohlhammer, 1988. **Senior, D. P.** *The Passion of Jesus in the Gospel of Mark.* Wilmington, DE: Glazier, 1984. **Shiner, W. T.** *Follow Me! Disciples in Markan Rhetoric.* SBLDS 145. Atlanta: Scholars Press, 1995. **Söding, T.** *Glaube bei Markus: Glaube an das Evangelium, Gebetsglaube und Wunderglaube im Kontext der markinischen Basileiatheologie und Christologie.* SBB 12. Stuttgart: Katholisches Bibelwerk, 1985. **Sokoloff, M.** *A Dictionary of Jewish Palestinian Aramaic of the Byzantine Period.* Ramat-Gan: Bar Ilan University, 1990. **Standaert, B. H. M. G. M.** *L'évangile selon Marc: Composition et genre littéraire.* Nijmegen: Stichting Studentenpers, 1978. **Steichele, H.-J.** *Der leidende Sohn Gottes: Eine Untersuchung einiger alttestamentlicher Motive in der Christologie des Markusevangeliums.* Biblische Untersuchungen 14. Regensburg: Pustet, 1980. **Stock, A.** *Call to Discipleship: A Literary Study of Mark's Gospel.* GNS 1. Wilmington, DE: Glazier, 1982. **Stock, K.** *Boten aus dem Mit-Ihm-Sein: Das Verhältnis zwischen Jesus und den Zwölf nach Markus.* AnBib 70. Rome: Biblical Institute, 1975. **Stroker, W. D.** *Extracanonical Sayings of Jesus.* SBL Resources for Biblical Study 18. Atlanta: Scholars Press, 1989. **Suhl, A.** *Die Funktion der alttestamentlichen Zitate und Anspielungen im Markusevangelium.* Gütersloh: Mohn, 1965. **Taylor, V.** *The Formation of the Gospel Tradition.* London: Macmillan, 1935. ———. *Jesus and His Sacrifice: A Study of the Passion Sayings in the Gospels.* London: Macmillan, 1937. **Telford, W. R.,** ed. *The Interpretation of Mark.* IRT 7. London: S. P. C. K.; Philadelphia: Fortress, 1985. **Theissen, G.** *The Gospels in Context: Social and Political History in the Synoptic Tradition.* Minneapolis: Fortress, 1991. ———. *The Miracle Stories of the Early Christian*

Tradition. Edinburgh: T. & T. Clark; Philadelphia: Fortress, 1983. **Tolbert, M. A.** *Sowing the Gospel: Mark's World in Literary-Historical Perspective.* Minneapolis: Fortress, 1989. **Torrey, C. C.** *The Four Gospels: A New Translation.* 2nd ed. London: Hodder & Stoughton, 1947. ————. *Our Translated Gospels.* London: Hodder and Stoughton; New York: Harper & Brothers, 1936. **Trocmé, É.** *The Formation of the Gospel according to Mark.* London: S. P. C. K.; Philadelphia: Westminster, 1975. 208–40. **Tuckett, C. M.,** ed. *The Messianic Secret.* IRT 1. London: S. P. C. K.; Philadelphia: Fortress, 1983. **Via, D. O., Jr.** *The Ethics of Mark's Gospel: In the Middle of Time.* Philadelphia: Fortress, 1985. **Weeden, T. J.** *Mark: Traditions in Conflict.* Philadelphia: Fortress, 1971. **Weinacht, H.** *Die Menschwerdung des Sohnes Gottes im Markusevangelium: Studien zur Christologie des Markusevangeliums.* HUT 13. Tübingen: Mohr-Siebeck, 1972. **Weiss W.** *"Eine neue Lehre in Vollmacht": Die Streit- und Schulgespräche des Markus-Evangeliums.* BZNW 52. Berlin; New York: de Gruyter, 1989. **Westcott, B. F.,** and **Hort, F. J. A.** *The New Testament in the Original Greek: Introduction and Appendix.* 2 vols. New York: Harper & Brothers, 1882. **Williams, J. F.** *Other Followers of Jesus: Minor Characters as Major Figures in Mark's Gospel.* JSNTSup 102. Sheffield: Sheffield Academic Press, 1994. **Wrede, W.** *The Messianic Secret.* Edinburgh: T. & T. Clark, 1971. **Wright, N. T.** *Jesus and the Victory of God.* Christian Origins and the Question of God 2. London: S. P. C. K.; Minneapolis: Fortress, 1996.

J. Delobel. BETL 59. Leuven: Leuven UP, 1982. 507–15. ———. "La parabole des vignerons homicides (Mc., XII, 1–12) et l'Évangile selon Thomas." In *L'Évangile selon Marc: Tradition et rédaction*. Ed. M. Sabbe. BETL 34. Leuven: Leuven UP, 1974. 203–19. ———. "Recent Research on the Gospel of Thomas." In *The Four Gospels 1992*. FS F. Neirynck, ed. F. Van Segbroeck et al. BETL 100. Leuven: Leuven UP, 1992. 2257–62. **Denker, J.** *Die theologiegeschichtliche Stellung des Petrusevangeliums*. Bern; Frankfurt: Lang, 1975. **Dodd, C. H.** "A New Gospel." In *New Testament Studies*. Manchester: Manchester UP, 1953. 12–52. **Evans, C. A.** *Non-Canonical Writings and New Testament Interpretation*. Peabody, MA: Hendrickson, 1992. 149–54, 220–26. ———, **Webb, R. L.,** and **Wiebe, R. A.** *Nag Hammadi Texts and the Bible: A Synopsis and Index*. NTTS 18. Leiden: Brill, 1993. **Fieger, M.** *Das Thomasevangelium: Einleitung, Kommentar und Systematik*. NTAbh 22. Münster: Aschendorff, 1991. **Fitzmyer, J. A.** "The Oxyrhynchus Logoi of Jesus and the Coptic Gospel according to Thomas." In *Essays on the Semitic Background of the New Testament*. SBLSBS 5. Missoula, MT: Scholars Press, 1974. 355–433. **Fleddermann, H. T.** *Mark and Q*. **Gärtner, B.** *The Theology of the Gospel according to Thomas*. New York: Harper, 1961. **Grant, R. M.** *Gnosticism and Early Christianity*. Rev. ed. New York: Harper & Row, 1966. ———. *The Secret Sayings of Jesus*. Garden City, NY: Doubleday, 1960. **Green, J. B.** "The Gospel of Peter: Source for a Pre-Canonical Passion Narrative?" *ZNW* 78 (1987) 293–301. **Haenchen, E.** *Die Botschaft des Thomas-Evangeliums*. Berlin: Töpelmann, 1961. **Hedrick, C. W.** "Thomas and the Synoptics: Aiming at a Consensus." *SecCent* 7 (1989–90) 39–56. **Hennecke, E.,** and **Schneemelcher, W.,** eds. *New Testament Apocrypha*. 2 vols. Philadelphia: Westminster, 1963, 1965. **Hofius, O.** "Unknown Sayings of Jesus." In *The Gospel and the Gospels*. Ed. P. Stuhlmacher. Tr. J. Vriend. Grand Rapids, MI: Eerdmans, 1991. 336–60. **Jeremias, J.** "An Unknown Gospel with Johannine Elements." In *New Testament Apocrypha*. Ed. E. Hennecke and W. Schneemelcher. 2 vols. Philadelphia: Westminster, 1963, 1965. 1:94–97. ———. *Unknown Sayings of Jesus*. 2nd ed. London: S. P. C. K., 1964. **Koester, H.** *Ancient Christian Gospels: Their History and Development*. London: SCM Press; Philadelphia: Trinity Press International, 1990. ———. "Apocryphal and Canonical Gospels." *HTR* 73 (1980) 105–30. ———. "History and Development of Mark's Gospel (From Mark to *Secret Mark* and 'Canonical Mark')." In *Colloquy on New Testament Studies: A Time for Reappraisal and Fresh Approaches*. Ed. B. Corley. Macon, GA: Mercer UP, 1983. 35–57. ———. *Introduction to the New Testament*. 2 vols. Berlin; New York: de Gruyter, 1982. **Köhler, W.-D.** *Die Rezeption des Matthäusevangeliums in der Zeit vor Irenäus*. WUNT 2.24. Tübingen: Mohr-Siebeck, 1987. **Lührmann, D.** "Das neue Fragment des P Egerton 2 (P Köln 255)." In *The Four Gospels 1992*. FS F. Neirynck, ed. F. Van Segbroeck et al. BETL 100. Leuven: Leuven UP, 1992. 2238–55. **Manson, T. W.** "The Life of Jesus: A Study of the Available Materials." *BJRL* 27 (1942–43) 323–37. **Mayeda, G.** *Das Leben-Jesu-Fragment Papyrus Egerton 2 und seine Stellung in der urchristlichen Literaturgeschichte*. Bern: Haupt, 1946. **McCant, J. W.** "The Gospel of Peter: Docetism Reconsidered." *NTS* 30 (1984) 258–73. **Meier, J. P.** *The Roots of the Problem and the Person*. Vol. 1 of *A Marginal Jew: Rethinking the Historical Jesus*. New York: Doubleday, 1991. 112–66. **Ménard, J.-É.** *L'Évangile selon Thomas*. NHS 5. Leiden: Brill, 1975. ———. "La tradition synoptique et l'Évangile selon Thomas." In *Überlieferungsgeschichtliche Untersuchungen*. Ed. F. Paschke. TU 125. Berlin: Akademie, 1981. 411–26. **Merkel, H.** "Auf den Spuren des Urmarkus?" *ZTK* 71 (1974) 123–44. **Neirynck, F.** "The Apocryphal Gospels and the Gospel of Mark." In *The New Testament in Early Christianity*. Ed. J.-M. Sevrin. BETL 86. Leuven: Leuven UP, 1989. 123–75. ———. "La fuite du jeune homme en Mc 14, 51–52." *ETL* 55 (1979) 43–66. ———. "Papyrus Egerton 2 and the Healing of the Leper." *ETL* 61 (1985) 153–60. **Osborn, E.** "Clement of Alexandria: A Review of Research." *SecCent* 3 (1983) 219–44. **Quesnell, Q.** "The Mar Saba Clementine: A Question of Evidence." *CBQ* 37 (1975) 48–67. **Robinson, J. M.** "Jesus: From Easter to Valentinus (or to the Apostles' Creed)." *JBL* 101 (1982) 5–37. ———. "On Bridging the Gulf from Q to the Gospel of Thomas (or Vice Versa)." In *Nag Hammadi, Gnosticism and Early Christianity*. Ed. C. W. Hedrick and R. Hodgson. Peabody, MA: Hendrickson, 1986. 127–75. **Schaeffer, S. E.** "The Guard at the Tomb (*Gos. Pet.* 8:28–11:49 and Matt 27:62–66; 28:2–4, 11–16): A Case of Intertextuality?" In *Society of Biblical Literature 1991 Seminar Papers*.

Ed. E. H. Lovering, Jr. SBLSP 30. Atlanta: Scholars Press, 1991. 499–507. **Schrage, W.** "Evangelienzitate in den Oxyrhynchus-Logien und im koptischen Thomas-Evangelium." In *Apophoreta.* FS E. Haenchen, ed. U. Eickelberg et al. BZNW 30. Berlin: Töpelmann, 1964. 251–68. ———. *Das Verhältnis des Thomas-Evangeliums zur synoptischen Tradition und zu den koptischen Evangelienübersetzungen.* BZNW 29. Berlin: Töpelmann, 1964. **Sevrin, J.-M.** "L'Évangile selon Thomas: Paroles de Jésus et révélation gnostique." *RTL* 8 (1977) 265–92. ———. "Un groupement de trois paraboles contre les richesses dans l'Évangile selon Thomas: *EvTh* 63, 64, 65." In *Les paraboles évangéliques: Perspectives nouvelles.* Ed. J. Delorme. Paris: Cerf, 1989. 425–39. **Sieber, J. H.** "The Gospel of Thomas and the New Testament." In *Gospel Origins and Christian Beginnings.* FS J. M. Robinson, ed. J. Goehring et al. Sonoma, CA: Polebridge, 1990. 64–73. **Smith, M.** *Clement of Alexandria and a Secret Gospel of Mark.* Cambridge, MA: Harvard UP, 1973. **Snodgrass, K. R.** "The Gospel of Thomas: A Secondary Gospel." *SecCent* 7 (1989–90) 19–38. ———. "The Parable of the Wicked Husbandmen: Is the Gospel of Thomas Version the Original?" *NTS* 21 (1974–75) 142–44. **Solages, B. de.** "L'Évangile de Thomas et les évangiles canoniques: L'ordre des pericopes." *BLE* 80 (1979) 102–8. **Stroker, W. D.** *Extracanonical Sayings.* **Tuckett, C. M.** *Nag Hammadi and the Gospel Tradition.* SNTW. Edinburgh: T. & T. Clark, 1986. ———. "Q and Thomas: Evidence of a Primitive 'Wisdom Gospel'? A Response to H. Koester." *ETL* 67 (1991) 346–60. ———. "Thomas and the Synoptics." *NovT* 30 (1988) 132–57. **Vaganay, L.** *L'Évangile de Pierre.* EBib. Paris: Gabalda, 1930. **Wenham, D.,** ed. *The Jesus Tradition outside the Gospels.* Gospel Perspectives 5. Sheffield: JSOT, 1984. **Wright, D. F.** "Apocryphal Gospels: The 'Unknown Gospel' (Pap. Egerton 2) and the *Gospel of Peter.*" In *The Jesus Tradition outside the Gospels.* Ed. D. Wenham. Gospel Perspectives 5. Sheffield: JSOT, 1984. 207–32. ———. "Papyrus Egerton 2 (the Unknown Gospel)—Part of the Gospel of Peter?" *SecCent* 5 (1985–86) 129–50.

In recent years several scholars, especially those concerned with research regarding the life of Jesus, have begun serious examination of the so-called apocryphal Gospels, thinking that these writings might contain material as old or even older than that found in the NT Gospels. A few scholars even argue that some of these apocryphal Gospels antedate the New Testament Gospels and in a few cases may even have been a source of material for the NT Gospels, though this conclusion has not gone unchallenged. The issue is important, for at stake is not only the interpretation of individual passages but the larger question of which documents offer earlier and possibly more reliable information about the historical Jesus. Parallels between the Gospel of Mark and the apocryphal Gospels (including significant MS variants and the so-called *agrapha,* i.e., sayings of Jesus "not written" in the four NT Gospels) are as follows (patristic authors noted in parentheses indicate the source of quotation for a given apocryphal Gospel):

Mark 1:4–6—*Gos. Eb.* §2 (Epiphanius, *Refutation of All Heresies* 30.13.4–5)
Mark 1:9–11—*Gos. Eb.* §4 (Epiphanius, *Refutation of All Heresies* 30.13.7–8; cf. Matt 3:14–15; Luke 3:22); *Gos. Heb.* §2 (Jerome, *Comm. Isa.* 4 [on Isa 11:2]); *Gos. Naz.* §2 (Jerome, *Pelag.* 3.2)
Mark 1:16–20—*Gos. Eb.* §1 (Epiphanius, *Refutation of All Heresies* 30.13.2–3)
Mark 1:40–45—P.Eger. 2 §2
Mark 2:15–17—P.Oxy. 1224 §1; Justin Martyr, *1 Apol.* 15.8
Mark 2:18–20—*Gos. Thom.* §§27, 104
Mark 2:21–22—*Gos. Thom.* §47
Mark 2:23–28—Codex D (at Luke 6:1–5)
Mark 3:1–6—*Gos. Naz.* §10 (Jerome, *Comm. Matt.* 2 [on Matt 12:13])
Mark 3:23–27—*Gos. Thom.* §35; Clement, *Exc.* 52.1

Mark 3:28–30—*Gos. Thom.* §44

Mark 3:31–35—*Gos.Thom.* §99; *Gos. Eb.* §5 (Epiphanius, *Refutation of All Heresies* 30.13.5; *2 Clem.* 9:11)

Mark 4:2–9—*Gos. Thom.* §9 (*1 Clem.* 24:5; Justin, *Dial.* 125.1)

Mark 4:10–12—*Ap. Jas.* [NHC I,2] 7.1–10

Mark 4:11—Clement, *Miscellanies* 5.10; *Ps.-Clem. Hom.* 19.20; Theodoret, *On the Psalms* 65.16

Mark 4:13–20—*Ap. Jas.* [NHC I,2] 8.10–17

Mark 4:21—*Gos. Thom.* §33

Mark 4:22—P.Oxy. 654 §5; *Gos.Thom.* §§5, 6

Mark 4:24–25—*Gos. Thom.* §41; *Apoc. Pet.* [NHC VII,3] 83.26–84.6

Mark 4:24—*1 Clem.* 13:1–2; Poly. *Phil.* 2:3; Clement, *Miscellanies* 2.18.91

Mark 4:26–29—*Gos. Thom.* §21; *Ap. Jas.* [NHC I,2] 12.22–31

Mark 4:30–32—*Gos.Thom.* §20

Mark 6:4—P.Oxy. 1 §6; *Gos.Thom.* §31

Mark 7:1–5 + 11:27–28—P.Oxy. 840 §2

Mark 7:6–8—P.Eger. 2 §3

Mark 7:14–15—*Gos. Thom.* §14

Mark 8:17—*Acts Pet.* §10

Mark 8:27–30—*Gos. Thom.* §13

Mark 8:31–33—*Ap. Jas.* [NHC I,2] 5.31–6.11

Mark 8:31 + 9:31 + 10:33–34—Justin, *Dial.* 51.2; Ign. *Smyrn.* 3:3; *Apos. Con.* 6.30

Mark 8:34—*Gos. Thom.* §§55, 101

Mark 9:1—*Gos. Thom.* §18b

Mark 9:34 + 10:43—*Gos. Thom.* §12

Mark 9:40—P.Oxy. 1224 §2

Mark 10:13–16—*Gos. Thom.* §22

Mark 10:17–22—*Gos. Naz.* §16 (Origen, *Comm. Matt.* 15.14 [on Matt 19:16–30])

Mark 10:21—Clement, *Miscellanies* 3.6.55

Mark 10:28–30—*Ap. Jas.* [NHC I,2] 4.22–37

Mark 10:31—P.Oxy. 654 §4; *Gos. Thom.* §4

Mark 11:22–23—*Gos. Thom.* §§48, 106

Mark 12:1–12—*Gos. Thom.* §§65–66

Mark 12:13–17—*Gos. Thom.* §100; P.Eger. 2 §3

Mark 12:31—*Gos. Thom.* §25

Mark 12:34—*Gos. Thom.* §82; Origen, *Hom. Jer.* 20.3

Mark 13:5–6, 21–22, 26–27 + 14:62—*Apoc. Pet.* §1; *Ep. Apos.* §9; *Apoc. El.* 1:8, 13–14; 3:1, 4; 5:2–4

Mark 13:21—*Gos. Thom.* §113

Mark 13:28–29 + 13:22–23 + 13:6—*Apoc. Pet.* §2

Mark 14:12—*Gos. Eb.* §7 (Epiphanius, *Refutation of All Heresies* 30.22.4)

Mark 14:22—*Apos. Con.* 8.12.37

Mark 14:27–30—Fayyum Fragment

Mark 14:36—Hippolytus, *Refutation of All Heresies* 5.8.11

Mark 14:38—Tertullian, *Baptism* 20; *Didascalia Apostolorum* 2.8; *Apos. Con.* 2.8.2

Mark 14:58—*Gos. Thom.* §71

Mark 14:65—*Gos. Pet.* 3.9

Mark 15:1–5—*Acts Pil.* 3:2

Mark 15:6–15—*Acts Pil.* 4:4–5; 9:4–5

Mark 15:7—*Gos. Naz.* §20 (Jerome, *Comm. Matt.* 4 [on Matt 27:16])

Mark 15:16–20—*Gos. Pet.* 2.5–3.9; *Acts Pil.* 10:1

Mark 15:22–32—*Acts Pil.* 10:1

Mark 15:33–39—*Gos. Pet.* 5.15–20; *Acts Pil.* 11:1
Mark 15:38—*Gos. Naz.* §21 (Jerome, *Epist.* 120.8)
Mark 15:40–41—*Acts Pil.* 11:2–3a
Mark 15:42–47—*Gos. Pet.* 2.3–5; 6.21–24; *Acts Pil.* 11:3b
Mark 16:1–8—*Gos. Pet.* 9.35–13.57; *Acts Pil.* 13:1–3
Mark 16:14–18—*Acts Pil.* 14:1
Mark 16:14–15—Codex W
Mark 16:16—Clement, *Miscellanies* 6.5.43

Recently certain scholars have argued that several of the noncanonical Gospels (such as Papyrus Egerton 2, the *Gospel of Peter,* the *Gospel of the Hebrews,* and the *Gospel of Thomas*) are independent of or older than the NT Gospels. Among these scholars, J. D. Crossan is probably the most conspicuous. Crossan (*Historical Jesus,* 427–34) dates the apocryphal Gospels as follows: *Gospel of Thomas* (earliest draft: 50s C.E.), *Egerton Gospel* (= Papyrus Egerton 2 + Papyrus Köln 255: 50s C.E.), Fayum Fragment (= Papyrus Vindobonensis Greek 2325: 50s C.E.), Papyrus Oxyrhynchus 1224 (50s C.E.), *Gospel of the Hebrews* (50s C.E.), *Cross Gospel* (= a pruned version of the *Gospel of Peter:* 50s C.E.), *Gospel of the Egyptians* (60s C.E. [not to be confused with the Coptic writing of this name, NHC III,2]), *Secret Gospel of Mark* (early 70s C.E.), Papyrus Oxyrhynchus 840 (80s C.E.), *Gospel of Thomas* (= Papyrus Oxyrhynchus 1, 654, 655, and NHC II,2; later draft: 60s or 70s C.E.), Dialogue Collection (= a pruned version of the Coptic Gnostic tractate *Dialogue of the Savior* [= NHC III,5]: late [?] 70s C.E.), *Apocryphon of James* (= the Coptic Gnostic tractate NHC I,2, dating from first half of the second century C.E., but containing tradition reaching back to the 50s C.E.), *Gospel of the Nazoreans* (150s C.E.), *Gospel of the Ebionites* (150s C.E.), and *Gospel of Peter* (150s C.E.). Crossan asserts that the *Gospel of Thomas,* the *Egerton Gospel,* Papyrus Vindobonensis Greek 2325, Papyrus Oxyrhynchus 1224, the *Gospel of the Hebrews,* and the *Gospel of the Egyptians* are independent of the NT Gospels, with the *Dialogue of the Savior* and the *Apocryphon of James* containing independent traditions. He further concludes that the *Cross Gospel,* which is now imbedded in the *Gospel of Peter,* is the Passion Narrative on which all four of the NT Gospels are based (cf. Crossan, *The Cross that Spoke,* 404).

Given this chronological scheme, it is not surprising that Crossan often concludes that traditions contained in the apocryphal Gospels that parallel those of the NT Gospels are more primitive and historically superior. Often he finds the earliest, most original form of Jesus' teaching in the apocryphal Gospels. For example, Crossan (*JBL* 90 [1971] 451–65; *Historical Jesus,* 351–52) believes that the earliest version of the parable of the Wicked Vineyard Tenants (Mark 12:1–9) is preserved in *Gos. Thom.* §65. The absence of words from Isa 5:1–7 and the absence of Christology and anti-temple themes, which are thought to reflect distinctively Markan concerns, persuade Crossan that *Thomas*'s form of the parable is closest to the original. Koester (*Introduction,* 2:152), Davies (*Thomas and Christian Wisdom*), and Cameron (*Parable and Interpretation*) concur, claiming that *Thomas* was written in the first century and is uninfluenced, in its earliest form, by the NT Gospels. However, others contest this interpretation, arguing that the version of the parable in *Thomas* is no more than an edited and abridged form of the Lukan version (cf. Dehandschutter, "La parabole des vignerons homicides," 203–19; Sevrin, "Un groupement," 433–34; see *Form/Structure/Setting* on this passage).

Crossan also often prefers the versions of the narratives preserved in the apocryphal Gospels. He believes that the earliest form of the story of Jesus' baptism is found in the *Gos. Heb.* §2 (from Jerome, *Comm. Isa.* 4 [on Isa 11:2]):

> And it came to pass when the Lord was come up out of the water, the whole fount of the Holy Spirit descended upon him and rested on him and said to him: My son, in all the prophets was I waiting for thee that thou shouldest come and I might rest in thee. For thou art my rest; thou art my first-begotten Son that reignest for ever. (Cameron, *Other Gospels*, 85)

It is hard to see how Crossan can conclude that this version is the "earliest text" (*Historical Jesus,* 232). There are several indications that this version is late and secondary: (1) Referring to Jesus as "the Lord" is late (compare Luke with the earlier Mark). (2) Reference to "the whole fount" of the Holy Spirit is likely an embellishment. (3) The statement "in all the prophets was I waiting for thee that thou shouldest come and I might rest in thee" seems a pious addition. One should compare the similar Christian interpolation found in Josephus, *Ant.* 18.3.3 §64: "for the prophets of God had prophesied these and countless other marvellous things about him." (4) The remainder of this text appears to be a compilation of Christian confessional and theological materials (on *rest,* see Heb 4:1–11; on *first-begotten,* see Rom 8:29; Col 1:15, 18; on "reigning for ever," see Luke 1:33; Rev 11:15; 22:5). Mark's version is surely earlier and more primitive than that found in the *Gospel of the Hebrews.*

Perhaps the most provocative argument that Crossan (*Cross that Spoke*) has advanced is the claim that the *Gospel of Peter* contains a primitive "Cross Gospel" on which all four NT Gospels are dependent. Portions of the text read as follows (for the reader's convenience, the Markan order will be followed):

> And he delivered him to the people on the day before the unleavened bread, their feast. So they took the Lord and pushed him in great haste and said, "Let us hale the Son of God now that we have gotten power over him." And they put upon him a purple robe and set him on the judgment seat and said, "Judge righteously, O King of Israel!" And one of them brought a crown of thorns and put it on the Lord's head. And others who stood by spat on his face, and others buffeted him on the cheeks, others nudged him with a reed, and some scourged him, saying, "With such honour let us honour the Son of God." (*Gos. Pet.* 2.5b–3.9 = Mark 14:65 + 15:16–20; Funk, *New Gospel Parallels,* 272)

> And they brought two malefactors and crucified the Lord in the midst between them. But he held his peace, as if he felt no pain. And when they had set up the cross, they wrote upon it: this is the King of Israel. And they laid down his garments before him and divided them among themselves and cast the lot upon them. But one of the malefactors rebuked them, saying, "We have landed in suffering for the deeds of wickedness which we have committed, but this man, who has become the saviour of men, what wrong has he done you?" And they were wroth with him and commanded that his legs should not be broken, so that he might die in torments. (*Gos. Pet.* 4.10–14 = Mark 15:22–32 + Luke 23:39–41; Funk, *New Gospel Parallels,* 275)

> Now it was midday and a darkness covered all Judaea. And they suddenly became anxious and uneasy lest the sun had already set, since he was still alive. <For> it stands written for them: the sun should not set on one that has been put to death [cf. Deut 21:22–23]. And

one of them said, "Give him to drink gall with vinegar." And they mixed it and gave him to drink. And they fulfilled all things and completed the measure of their sins on their head. And many went about with lamps, <and> as they supposed that it was night, they went to bed (or: they stumbled). And the Lord called out and cried, "My power, O power, thou hast forsaken me!" And having said this he was taken up. And at the same hour the veil of the temple in Jerusalem was rent in two. (*Gos. Pet.* 5.15–20 = Mark 15:33–38; Funk, *New Gospel Parallels,* 277)

Now there stood there Joseph, the friend of Pilate and of the Lord, and knowing that they were about to crucify him he came to Pilate and begged the body of the Lord for burial. And Pilate sent to Herod and begged his body. And Herod said, "Brother Pilate, even if no one had begged him, we should bury him, since the Sabbath is drawing on. For it stands written in the law: the sun should not set on the one that has been put to death." (*Gos. Pet.* 2.3–5a = Mark 15:42–45; Funk, *New Gospel Parallels,* 278)

And then the Jews drew the nails from the hands of the Lord and laid him on the earth. And the whole earth shook and there came a great fear. Then the sun shone <again>, and it was found to be the ninth hour. And the Jews rejoiced and gave the body to Joseph that he might bury it, since he had seen all the good that he (Jesus) had done. And he took the Lord, washed him, wrapped him in linen and brought him into his own sepulchre, called Joseph's Garden. (*Gos. Pet.* 6.21–24 = Mark 15:45–46; Funk, *New Gospel Parallels,* 278)

Now in the night in which the Lord's day dawned, when the soldiers, two by two in every watch, were keeping guard, there rang out a loud voice in heaven, and they saw the heavens opened and two men come down from there in a great brightness and draw nigh to the sepulchre. That stone which had been laid against the entrance to the sepulchre started of itself to roll and gave way to the side, and the sepulchre was opened, and both the young men entered in. When now those soldiers saw this, they awakened the centurion and the elders—for they also were there to assist at the watch. And whilst they were relating what they had seen, they saw again three men come out from the sepulchre, and two of them sustaining the other, and a cross following them, and the heads of the two reaching to heaven, but that of him who was led of them by the hand overpassing the heavens. And they heard a voice out of the heavens crying, "Thou hast preached to them that sleep," and from the cross there was heard the answer, "Yea." Those men therefore took counsel with one another to go and report this to Pilate. And whilst they were still deliberating, the heavens were again seen to open, and a man descended and entered into the sepulchre. When those who were of the centurion's company saw this, they hastened by night to Pilate, abandoning the sepulchre which they were guarding, and reported everything that they had seen, being full of disquietude and saying, "In truth he was the Son of God." Pilate answered and said, "I am clean from the blood of the Son of God, upon such a thing have you decided." Then all came to him, beseeching him and urgently calling upon him to command the centurion and the soldiers to tell no one what they had seen. "For it is better for us," they said, "to make ourselves guilty of the greatest sin before God than to fall into the hands of the people of the Jews and be stoned." Pilate therefore commanded that the centurion and the soldiers say nothing.

Early in the morning of the Lord's day Mary Magdalene, a woman disciple of the Lord—for fear of the Jews since (they) were inflamed with wrath, she had not done at the sepulchre of the Lord what women are wont to do for those beloved of them who die—took with her her women friends and came to the sepulchre where he was laid. And they feared lest the Jews should see them, and said, "Although we could not weep and lament on that day when he was crucified, yet let us now do so at his sepulchre. But who will roll away for us the stone also that is set on the entrance to the sepulchre, that we may go in and sit beside him and do what is due?—For the stone was great,—and we fear lest any one see us. And if we cannot do so, let us at least put down at the entrance what we bring for a memorial of him and let us weep and lament until we have again gone home."

So they went and found the sepulchre open. And they came near, stooped down and saw there a young man sitting in the midst of the sepulchre, comely and clothed with a brightly shining robe, who said to them, "Wherefore are ye come? Whom seek ye? Not him that was crucified? He is risen and gone. But if ye believe not, stoop this way and see the place where he lay, for he is not here. For he is risen and is gone thither whence he was sent." Then the women fled affrighted. (*Gos. Pet.* 9.35–13.57 = Mark 16:1–8 + 15:39 + Matt 27:24 + 28:11–15 + John 20:11–12; Funk, *New Gospel Parallels*, 281)

Again, it is difficult to believe that this material, no matter how deftly pruned and reconstructed, could possibly constitute the primitive substratum of tradition on which the passion narratives of the NT Gospels are dependent. Scholars a generation ago found no independent traditions in the *Gospel of Peter* (cf. Dodd, "New Gospel," 46: "depends on all four canonical gospels, and probably not on any independent tradition"; Manson, *BJRL* 27 [1942–43] 323–37). More recently Vaganay (*L'Évangile de Pierre*), McCant (*NTS* 30 [1984] 258–73), Wright ("Apocryphal Gospels," 207–32), and R. E. Brown (*NTS* 33 [1987] 321–43) have reached similar conclusions, arguing that the *Gospel of Peter* is dependent on Matthew and possibly on the other NT Gospels. Green (*ZNW* 78 [1987] 293–301) agrees, concluding that even Crossan's pruned version, the so-called *Cross Gospel*, is little more than an embellishment based on the Gospel of Matthew (though in places the parallels seem closer to Mark). Examining the vocabulary of the *Cross Gospel*, Meier (*Roots of the Problem*, 117–18) concurs with Green's conclusion: "It is a 2d-century pastiche of traditions from the canonical Gospels, recycled through the memory and lively imagination of Christians who have heard the Gospels read and preached upon many a time." Running throughout this apocryphal Gospel is a marked apologetic that heightens Christology (e.g., frequent usage of "Lord" and "Son of God") and explains away apparent difficulties (2.3–5a: how it is that the body of Jesus would have been readily released to Joseph; 12.50–54: why the women did not weep for Jesus or complete the preparation of his body for burial, and how it was that they expected to gain access to the enclosed tomb). Finally, it should also be noted that the *Gospel of Peter* appears to be tinged with traces of anti-Semitism (5.17: "they . . . completed the measure of their sins on their head"; 12.50: "for fear of the Jews, since [they] were inflamed with wrath") and docetic Gnosticism (4.10: "But he held his peace, as if he felt no pain"; 5.19: "My power, O power! . . . and having said this he was taken up").

Another problem with Crossan's proposal that the Gospel of Mark is dependent upon the *Cross Gospel* is how to explain why the former made use of the latter's passion and not its resurrection account. The problem is resolved if we assume, as the other points of evidence suggest, that the *Gospel of Peter* (and/or the putative *Cross Gospel*) depended upon the Synoptic Gospels, which agree with the Markan narrative up to the account of the women at the empty tomb (Mark 16:1–8) and then go their separate ways because the text of Mark used by Matthew, Luke, and *Peter* did not conclude with a resurrection account. *Peter* breaks away from the Markan narrative here for the same reason that Matthew and Luke break away: there is no Markan resurrection narrative to follow. (Mark 16:9–20 was not penned until some time after the publication of Matthew and Luke-Acts.) This is certainly a more plausible explanation than one that would ask us to believe that Mark followed *Peter*'s passion account but not its resurrection account.

The *Egerton Gospel* and the *Secret Gospel of Mark* are even more problematic. The *Egerton Gospel*, which was published in 1935 by Bell and Skeat (*Fragments of an Unknown Gospel*), is extant in four fragments. The Egerton Papyrus became an item of scholarly interest when in 1946 Mayeda (*Das Leben-Jesu-Fragment Papyrus Egerton 2*) argued that it was not dependent on any of the NT Gospels. Most did not agree with this conclusion, observing that all of the fragments betray dependence on the Johannine and Synoptic Gospels (Dodd, "A New Gospel," 12–52; Jeremias, "An Unknown Gospel," 1:96; Meier, *Roots of the Problem*, 118–20; Neirynck, "Papyrus Egerton 2," 153–60; Wright, "Apocryphal Gospels," 207–32; id., *SecCent* 5 [1985–86] 129–50). Wright ("Apocryphal Gospels," 207–32; *SecCent* 5 [1985–86] 129–50) thinks that Papyrus Egerton 2 is actually a part of the *Gospel of Peter*. Let us consider the story of the cleansing of the leper (P.Eger. 2 §2 = Mark 1:40–44):

> And behold, a leper came to him and said, "Master Jesus, wandering with lepers and eating with them in the inn, I myself became a leper. If therefore [you will], I shall be clean." Accordingly the Lord said to him, "I will, be clean!" [And immediately] the leprosy left him. Jesus said to him, "Go and show yourself to the [priests], and offer for the purification as Moses has commanded, and sin no more." (Koester, *Ancient Christian Gospels*, 212)

According to Koester (*Ancient Christian Gospels*, 212–13), this form of the story is independent of the NT Gospels. Koester thinks that it is an older form of what underlies Mark 1:40–44. In favor of his assessment is the absence of the commands to secrecy (cf. Mark 1:43, 44a), which many believe to be Markan redaction. The style of address, "Master [διδάσκαλε = Rabbi] Jesus," may well reflect the convention that began to emerge in the late first century and on into the second century (cf. Meier, *Roots of the Problem*, 119–20). As in the example taken from the *Gospel of the Hebrews* above, again we find the secondary reference to Jesus as "the Lord." The Matthean form of the story omits part of the secrecy material (i.e., the charge in Mark 1:43), so its disappearance in Papyrus Egerton 2 could be due to the influence of Matthew (not to mention the possibility that the Markan secrecy theme might have been of no more interest to the author of the papyrus than it was to Matthew and Luke, who tend to mitigate it and sometimes expurgate it altogether). The concluding exhortation, "sin no more," is probably drawn from John 5:14 (or John 8:11), while the leper's explanation of how he contracted the disease is likely a fanciful embellishment of the story. It is not at all clear, therefore, that this form of the story is independent of the NT Gospels, or that it is an older and more original form.

The next example, which parallels Mark 12:13–15, once again suggests that Papyrus Egerton 2 is dependent on all four NT Gospels:

> ... and they came to him testing him with questions saying: "Teacher Jesus, we know that you have come [from God], for what you do bears witness beyond all the prophets. Tell us, is it permitted to give to the kings what pertains to their rule? Shall we give it or not?" But Jesus, knowing their intention, became angry and said, "Why do you call me teacher with your mouth and do not do what I say? Well did Isaiah prophesy concerning you when

he said, 'This people honor me with their lips, but their heart is far away from me. In vain do they worship me, [teaching] precepts of human beings.'" (P.Eger. 2 §3; Koester, *Ancient Christian Gospels,* 213–14)

Although there are parallels with Mark 12:13–15, John 3:2, Luke 6:46, and Mark 7:6–7 = Matt 15:7–9 (cf. Lührmann, "Das neue Fragment," 2249–51; Stroker, *Extracanonical Sayings,* 16), Koester (*Ancient Christian Gospels,* 214–16) does not think that this odd form of the tradition betrays dependence on the NT Gospels. This is because he does not think it likely that the author would jump from Gospel to Gospel in writing his version of the story. Indeed, Koester thinks that this Johannine-Synoptic combination probably predates the NT Gospels. Crossan (*Four Other Gospels,* 86) thinks that Mark is "directly dependent" on the text as preserved in Papyrus Egerton 2. However, there are problems with these conclusions. First, as noted above, addressing Jesus as "Teacher Jesus" probably reflects a convention that did not arise before the end of the first century and did not become commonplace until well into the second century (Dodd, "A New Gospel," 21). Second, Meier (*Roots of the Problem,* 119) thinks that the plural *kings* is secondary to the singular *Caesar* that is found in the Synoptics (and in *Gos. Thom.* §100). Third, the flattery, "what you do bears witness beyond all the prophets," may reflect John 1:34, 45 and is again reminiscent of later pious Christian embellishment that tended to exaggerate the respect that Jesus' contemporaries showed him (recall the examples in *Gos. Heb.* §2 and Josephus, *Ant.* 18.3.3 §64). Fourth, Koester's suggestion that the mixture of Johannine-Synoptic elements is primitive, while their bifurcation is secondary, is implausible. The reference to Jesus' coming from God and the witness of what he does are important components of the Fourth Gospel's distinctive Christology. Is it likely that such important Johannine concepts are to be found in pre-Synoptic traditions? On the contrary, it is much more likely that Papyrus Egerton 2 represents a conflation of Synoptic and Johannine elements rather than primitive material. Finally, mixed quotations and mixed forms of stories are not uncommon, being found in other apocryphal Gospels (cf. *Gos. Naz.* §18, which appears to be a combination of Matt 24:45–51; 25:14–30; and possibly Luke 15:30) and early Christian writers (cf. Justin, *1 Apol.* 15, where his quotation of the command to love, evidently based on memory, alternates between Matt 5 and Luke 6). Indeed, mixed quotations are common in gnostic writings (cf. *Exegesis on the Soul* [NHC II,6] 135.15–19, where Jesus utters two of the beatitudes, the first from Matt 5:4, the second from Luke 6:21a). In view of these considerations, it is probably the wiser course to view the Egerton papyrus as secondary to the NT Gospels.

The *Secret Gospel of Mark* was found in a letter purportedly written by Clement of Alexandria (ca. 150–ca. 215 C.E.). A "critical edition" and commentary of this letter and the Gospel fragments it contains have been published by M. Smith (*Secret Gospel of Mark*). Smith claims to have found and photographed the MS at Mar Saba in 1958, but did not publish his text and commentary until 1973. No one besides Smith himself has seen the MS. All we have to go on are Smith's photographs. The authenticity of the letter thus remains unconfirmed. Quesnell (*CBQ* 37 [1975] 48–67), moreover, suspects that the letter may be a (modern?) forgery (cf. Osborn, *SecCent* 3 [1983] 223–25; Merkel, *ZTK* 71 [1974] 130–36). Even if the letter is genuine, that by no means confirms either the authenticity or the reliability of the

Secret Gospel of Mark itself (on this Gospel's dependence on the NT Gospels, see Brown, *CBQ* 36 [1974] 466–85; Neirynck, *ETL* 55 [1979] 43–66).

The gnostic Gospels are hardly better candidates for early and reliable dominical traditions. Tuckett (*Nag Hammadi and the Gospel Tradition*) has found no evidence that these writings, with the possible exception of the *Gospel of Thomas*, contain Jesus traditions independent of the NT Gospels. But what of the *Gospel of Thomas?* In my judgment the oft-asserted claim that this "Gospel" contains primitive, pre-Synoptic tradition is highly questionable. Quoting or alluding to more than half of the books of the NT (Matthew, Mark, Luke, John, Acts, Romans, 1–2 Corinthians, Galatians, Ephesians, Colossians, 1 Thessalonians, 1 Timothy, Hebrews, 1 John, Revelation; cf. Evans, Webb, and Wiebe, *Nag Hammadi Texts,* 88–144), *Thomas* appears to comprise hardly more than a collage of NT and apocryphal materials that have been interpreted, often allegorically, in such a way as to advance second-century gnostic ideas (Blomberg, "Tradition and Redaction," 177–205; Brown, *NTS* 9 [1962–63] 155–77; Dehandschutter, "L'Évangile de Thomas," 507–15; id., "Recent Research," 2257–62; Fieger, *Thomasevangelium*). Moreover, the traditions contained in *Thomas* hardly reflect a setting that predates the writings of the NT, which is why Crossan attempts to extract an early version of *Thomas* from the Coptic and Greek texts that are now extant (for a more cautious attempt to extract a few sayings that might reflect primitive and independent tradition, see Chilton, "The Gospel according to Thomas," 155–75; Tuckett, *NovT* 30 [1988] 132–57).

A major problem with viewing the *Gospel of Thomas* as independent of the NT Gospels is the presence of a significant amount of material that is distinctive to Matthew ("M"), Luke ("L"), and John.

Parallels between the *Gospel of Thomas* and "M":
Matt 5:10—*Gos. Thom.* §69a
Matt 5:14—*Gos. Thom.* §32 (= P.Oxy. 1 §7)
Matt 6:2–4—*Gos. Thom.* §§6, 14 (= P.Oxy. 654 §6)
Matt 6:3—*Gos. Thom.* §62
Matt 7:6—*Gos. Thom.* §93
Matt 10:16—*Gos. Thom.* §39
Matt 11:30—*Gos. Thom.* §90
Matt 13:24–30—*Gos. Thom.* §57
Matt 13:44—*Gos. Thom.* §109
Matt 13:45–46—*Gos. Thom.* §76
Matt 13:47–50—*Gos. Thom.* §8
Matt 15:13—*Gos. Thom.* §40
Matt 18:20—*Gos. Thom.* §30 (= P.Oxy. 1 §5)
Matt 23:13—*Gos. Thom.* §§39, 102 (= P.Oxy. 655 §2)

Parallels between the *Gospel of Thomas* and "L":
Luke 11:27–28 + 23:29—*Gos. Thom.* §79
Luke 12:13–14—*Gos. Thom.* §72
Luke 12:16–21—*Gos. Thom.* §63
Luke 12:49—*Gos. Thom.* §10
Luke 17:20–21—*Gos. Thom.* §§3 (= P.Oxy. 654 §3), 113

Parallels between the *Gospel of Thomas* and John:
John 1:9—*Gos. Thom.* §24 (= P.Oxy. 655 §24)

John 1:14—*Gos. Thom.* §28 (= P.Oxy. 1 §28)
John 4:13–15—*Gos. Thom.* §13
John 7:32–36—*Gos. Thom.* §38 (= P.Oxy. 655 §38)
John 8:12; 9:5—*Gos. Thom.* §77

If *Thomas* really does represent an early, independent collection of material, then is it probable that it would contain so much M, L, and Johannine material? Perhaps sensing this problem, Koester (*Ancient Christian Gospels*, 86–107) assigns all of the L parallels and a few of the M parallels to Q. But such a move appears gratuitous. It is much more likely that the presence of M, L, and Johannine elements in *Thomas* indicates that the latter has been influenced by the NT Gospels.

Perhaps the most telling factor against seeing *Thomas* as an early and independent collection lies in the observation that features characteristic of Matthean and Lukan *redaction* are also found in *Thomas*. Two of the passages listed above as M (Matt 15:13; 13:24–30) may represent Matthean redaction (so Gundry, *Matthew*, 261–62, 306–7). Other sayings in *Thomas* that parallel the triple tradition agree with Matthew's wording (cf. Matt 15:11 = *Gos. Thom.* §34b; Matt 12:50 = *Gos. Thom.* §99), rather than with Mark's. Matthew's unique juxtaposition of alms, prayer, and fasting (Matt 6:1–18) appears to be echoed in *Gos. Thom.* §6 (= P.Oxy. 654 §6) and §14. In *Thomas* alms, prayer, and fasting are discussed in a negative light, probably reflecting gnostic antipathy toward Jewish piety, which surely argues for viewing *Thomas* as secondary to Matthew. All of this suggests that *Thomas* was influenced by the Gospel of Matthew.

De Solages (*BLE* 80 [1979] 102–8) and Crossan (*Four Other Gospels*, 35–36) contend that the order of pericopes in *Thomas*, in that it does not follow the Synoptic Gospels, is evidence that the material in this "Gospel" is independent of the Synoptics. However, there is evidence that many of the sayings in *Thomas* have been grouped together thematically, sometimes with catchwords. According to Sevrin ("Un groupement," 438–39), *Gos. Thom.* §§63, 64, and 65 have been clustered as part of the writer's polemic against wealth and materialism (which may also explain the briefer form of the parables). Meier points out, furthermore, that eclectic grouping is common in gnostic documents. He notes (*Roots of the Problem*, 161, n. 116) that "in a single saying the Naassenes bring together John 6:53–56; Matt 5:20; John 3:5; Mark 10:38; John 8:21; 13:33." To his example further examples from Nag Hammadi might be added (cf. *Dial. Sav.* [NHC III,5] §53 139.9–11, where we find quoted Matt 6:34b + 10:10b + 10:25a; *Interp. Know.* [NHC XI,1] 9.28–35, where we find quoted Matt 23:9 + 5:14a + 12:50 + 16:26a).

There is also evidence that *Thomas* was influenced by the Gospel of Luke. The Lukan evangelist alters Mark's "For there is nothing hid except to be made manifest" (Mark 4:22) to "For nothing is hid that shall not be made manifest" (Luke 8:17). It is this redacted version that is found in *Gos. Thom.* §§5–6, with the Greek parallel preserved in P.Oxy. 654 §5 matching Luke's text exactly, which counters any claim that Luke's text only influenced the later Coptic translation (Meier, *Roots of the Problem*, 136; Tuckett, *NovT* 30 [1988] 146). Elsewhere there are indications that *Thomas* has followed Luke (*Gos. Thom.* §10 influenced by Luke 12:49 [cf. Fitzmyer, *Luke*, 2:994]; *Gos. Thom.* §16 influenced by Luke 12:51–53, as well as Matt 10:34–39 [cf. Ménard, *L'Évangile selon Thomas*, 94–95, 103; Schrage, *Das Verhältnis des Thomas-Evangeliums*, 58–59]; *Gos. Thom.* §§55 and 101 influenced by Luke

14:26–27, as well as Matt 10:37 [cf. Fitzmyer, *Luke,* 2:1061; Ménard, *L'Évangile selon Thomas,* 157; Schrage, *Das Verhältnis des Thomas-Evangeliums,* 120]).

Comparison of *Thomas* with the Mark-Q overlap tradition yields similar results. Fleddermann (*Mark and Q,* 21) has identified the following fourteen parallels:

Mark + Q	*Thomas*
3:22–27 (+ Matt 12:22–30, 43–45 = Luke 11:14– 15, 17–26)	§35
3:28–30 (+ Matt 12:32 = Luke 12:10)	§44
4:21 (+ Matt 5:15 = Luke 11:33)	§33
4:22 (+ Matt 10:26 = Luke 12:2)	§5 (= P.Oxy. 654 §5) + §6b
4:25 (+ Matt 25:29 = Luke 19:26)	§41
4:30–32 (+ Matt 13:31 = Luke 13:18–19)	§20
6:7–13 (+ Matt 9:37–38; 10:7–16; 11:21–23; 10:40 = Luke 10:2–16)	§§14, 73
8:34b (+ Matt 10:38 = Luke 14:27)	§55
10:31 (+ Matt 20:16 = Luke 13:30)	§4 (= P.Oxy. 654 §4)
11:22–23 (+ Matt 17:20 = Luke 17:6)	§§48, 106
11:24 (+ Matt 7:8 = Luke 11:10)	§2 (= P.Oxy. 654 §2), §94
13:12 (+ Matt 10:34–36 = Luke 12:51–53)	§16
13:21 (+ Matt 24:26 = Luke 17:23)	§113
13:31 (+ Matt 5:18 = Luke 16:17)	§11

Fleddermann (*Mark and Q,* 217) finds that these "texts show over and over again that Thomas knew the redactional text of the Synoptic Gospels. Thomas reflects redactional Matthew seven times [§§14, 20, 33, 44, 48, 55, 106], redactional Mark four times [§§4, 20, 35, 41], redactional Luke seven times [§§5, 6b, 14, 16, 33, 55, 113], and either redactional Mark or redactional Luke once [§44]. This widespread knowledge of the redactional text of all three synoptic writers proves that Thomas depends on the synoptic Gospels."

Given the evidence, it is not surprising that Gärtner (*Theology of the Gospel according to Thomas,* 26–27, 34, 42–43), Grant (*Secret Sayings,* 113), Haenchen (*Die Botschaft,* 67–68), Meier (*Roots of the Problem,* 130–39), Schrage (*Das Verhältnis des Thomas-Evangeliums,* 1–11), Snodgrass (*SecCent* 7 [1989–90] 19–38; *NTS* 21 [1974–75] 142–44), Tuckett (*NovT* 30 [1988] 157), and others have concluded that *Thomas* is dependent upon the NT Gospels and therefore should not be viewed as an independent, pre-Synoptic source.

In view of these findings, it appears that attempts to extract pre-Synoptic and pre-Johannine forms of tradition from *Thomas* and the other apocryphal Gospels surveyed above are speculative and precarious. Even more hazardous is the assumption that the existence of pre-Synoptic Gospels has been demonstrated. Extracting primitive, first-century materials or "texts" from second-century Gospels and making generalizations about the origins and theological tendencies of small scraps of papyri make for risky scholarship at best. At worst it constitutes special pleading and an unobjective assessment of the evidence at hand. Apart from the speculative reconstructions and imaginative contextualizations of Crossan, Koester, and others, there really is no evidence that any one of the apocryphal Gospels existed prior to the NT Gospels or that any one of the extant sources contains significant portions of one that did. Moreover, the evidence of individual sayings that may represent earlier and more primitive forms of tradition than what is found in the NT Gospels is also weak and far from conclusive. Nevertheless, this latter possibility will be taken into consideration in the commentary where appropriate.

Synoptic Problem

Bibliography

Abbott, E. A. *The Corrections of Mark Adopted by Matthew and Luke.* London: Black, 1901. **Bellinzoni, A. J.** "The Gospel of Matthew in the Second Century." *SecCent* 9 (1992) 197–258. ———, ed. *The Two-Source Hypothesis: A Critical Appraisal.* Macon, GA: Mercer UP, 1985. **Boismard, M.-É.** *L'Évangile de Marc: Sa préhistoire.* EBib n.s. 26. Paris: Gabalda, 1994. ———. "Influences matthéennes sur l'ultime rédaction de l'Évangile de Marc." In *L'Évangile selon Marc: Tradition et Rédaction.* Ed. M. Sabbe. BETL 34. Leuven: Leuven UP, 1974. 93–101. ———. *Synopse des quatre évangiles.* Paris: Éditions du Cerf, 1972. ———. "Two-Source Hypothesis." *ABD* 6:679–82. ———. "The Two-Source Theory at an Impasse." *NTS* 26 (1980) 1–17. **Boring, M. E.** "The Synoptic Problem, 'Minor' Agreements, and the Beelzebul Pericope." In *The Four Gospels 1992.* FS F. Neirynck, ed. F. Van Segbroeck et al. BETL 100. Leuven: Leuven UP, 1992. 587–619. **Burkitt, F. C.** *The Gospel History and Its Transmission.* 3rd ed. Edinburgh: T. & T. Clark, 1911. **Butler, B. C.** *The Originality of St Matthew: A Critique of the Two-Document Hypothesis.* Cambridge: Cambridge UP, 1951. **Chilton, B. D.** *Profiles of a Rabbi: Synoptic Opportunities in Reading about Jesus.* BJS 177. Atlanta: Scholars Press, 1989. **Dungan, D. L.** "Mark—The Abridgement of Matthew and Luke." In *Jesus and Man's Hope.* Ed. D. G. Buttrick and J. M. Bald. 2 vols. Pittsburgh: Pittsburgh Theological Seminary, 1970. 1:51–97. ———. "The Purpose and Provenance of the Gospel of Mark according to the Two-Gospel (Owen-Griesbach) Hypothesis." In *New Synoptic Studies.* Ed. W. R. Farmer. Macon, GA: Mercer UP, 1983. 411–40. ———. *A Symposium on the Interrelations of the Gospels.* BETL 95. Leuven: Leuven UP, 1990. ———. "Two-Gospel Hypothesis." *ABD* 6:671–79. **Dunn, J. D. G.** "Matthew's Awareness of Markan Redaction." In *The Four Gospels 1992.* FS F. Neirynck, ed. F. Van Segbroeck et al. BETL 100. Leuven: Leuven UP, 1992. 1349–59. **Elliott, J. K.** "Textual Criticism, Assimilation and the Synoptic Gospels." *NTS* 26 (1980) 231–42. **Farmer, W. R.** *The Last Twelve Verses of Mark.* SNTSMS 25. Cambridge: Cambridge UP, 1974. ———. "Luke's Use of Matthew: A Christological Inquiry." *PSTJ* 40 (1987) 39–50. ———. "The Minor Agreements of Matthew and Luke against Mark and the Two Gospel Hypothesis: A Study of These Agreements in Their Compositional Contexts." In *Society of Biblical Literature 1991 Seminar Papers.* Ed. E. H. Lovering, Jr. SBLSP 30. Atlanta: Scholars Press, 1991. 773–815. ———. "Modern Developments of Griesbach's Hypothesis." *NTS* 23 (1977) 275–95. ———, ed. *New Synoptic Studies: The Cambridge Gospels Conference and Beyond.* Macon, GA: Mercer UP, 1983. ———. "State *Interesse* and Marcan Primacy: 1870–1914." In *The Four Gospels 1992.* FS F. Neirynck, ed. F. Van Segbroeck et al. BETL 100. Leuven: Leuven UP, 1992. 2477–98. ———. *The Synoptic Problem: A Critical Analysis.* New York: Macmillan, 1964. ——— et al., eds. *Outline of the Markan Composition according to the Two Gospel Hypothesis.* SBLTT 15. Atlanta: Scholars Press, 1991. **Fitzmyer, J. A.** *The Gospel according to Luke I–IX.* 63–106. ———. "The Priority of Mark and the 'Q' Source in Luke." In *Jesus and Man's Hope.* Ed. D. G. Buttrick and J. M. Bald. 2 vols. Pittsburgh: Pittsburgh Theological Seminary, 1970. 1:131–70 (repr. in J. A. Fitzmyer. *To Advance the Gospel.* New York: Crossroad, 1981. 3–40). **Fleddermann, H. T.** *Mark and Q.* **Friedrichsen, T. A.** "'Minor' and 'Major' Matthew-Luke Agreements against Mk 4,30–32." In *The Four Gospels 1992.* FS F. Neirynck, ed. F. Van Segbroeck et al. BETL 100. Leuven: Leuven UP, 1992. 649–76. **Goodacre, M.** "Fatigue in the Synoptics." *NTS* 44 (1998) 45–58. **Goulder, M. D.** *Luke: A New Paradigm.* 2 vols. JSNTSup 20. Sheffield: JSOT, 1989.

Griesbach, J. J. *Synopsis Evangeliorum Matthei Marci et Lucae una cum iis Joannis pericopis: Quae historiam passionis et resurrectionis Jesu Christi complectuntu..* 2nd ed. Halle: J. J. Curtii Haeredes, 1797. **Gundry, R. H.** "Matthean Foreign Bodies in Agreements of Luke with Matthew against Mark: Evidence that Luke Used Matthew." In *The Four Gospels 1992.* FS F. Neirynck, ed. F. Van Segbroeck. BETL 100. Leuven: Leuven UP, 1992. 1467–95. **Hawkins, J. C.** *Horae Synopticae: Contributions to the Study of the Synoptic Problem.* 2nd ed. Oxford: Clarendon, 1909. **Holtzmann, H. J.** *Lehrbuch der historisch-kritischen Einleitung in das Neue Testament.* 3rd ed. Freiburg: Mohr-Siebeck, 1892. ———. *Die synoptischen Evangelien: Ihr Ursprung und geschichtlicher Charakter.* Leipzig: Engelmann, 1863. **Jackson, H. L.** "The Present State of the Synoptic Problem." In *Essays on Some Biblical Questions of the Day.* Ed. H. B. Swete. London: Macmillan, 1909. 421–60. **Johnson, S. E.** *The Griesbach Hypothesis and Redaction Criticism.* SBLMS 41. Atlanta: Scholars Press, 1991. **Kloppenborg, J. S.** *The Formation of Q.* Philadelphia: Fortress, 1987. ———. "The Theological Stakes in the Synoptic Problem." In *The Four Gospels 1992.* FS F. Neirynck, ed. F. Van Segbroeck et al. BETL 100. Leuven: Leuven UP, 1992. 93–120. **Koester, H.** "The Text of the Synoptic Gospels in the Second Century." In *Gospel Traditions in the Second Century: Origins, Recensions, Text, and Transmission.* Ed. W. L. Petersen. Christianity and Judaism in Antiquity 3. Notre Dame, IN: Notre Dame UP, 1989. 19–37. **Lachmann, K.** "De ordine narrationum in evangeliis synopticis." *TSK* 8 (1835) 570–90 (tr. in part by N. H. Palmer. "Lachmann's Argument." *NTS* 13 [1967] 368–78, esp. 370–76). **Longstaff, T. R. W.**, *Evidence of Conflation in Mark? A Study in the Synoptic Problem.* SBLDS 28. Missoula, MT: Scholars Press, 1977. ——— and **Thomas, P. A.** *The Synoptic Problem: A Bibliography, 1716–1988.* Macon, GA: Mercer UP, 1989. **Martin, R. P.** *Mark: Evangelist and Theologian.* 29–39. **McCloughlin, S.** "Les accords mineurs Mt-Lc contre Mc et le problème synoptique." In *De Jésus aux Évangiles: Tradition et Rédaction dans les Évangiles synoptiques.* Ed. I. de la Potterie. Gembloux: Duculot, 1967. 17–40. **Meijboom, H. U.** *A History and Critique of the Origin of the Marcan Hypothesis 1835–1866.* New Gospel Studies 8. Leuven: Peeters/Macon, GA: Mercer UP, 1993. **Neirynck, F.** *Evangelica: Gospel Studies—Etudes d'évangile.* Ed. F. Van Segbroeck. BETL 60. Leuven: Leuven UP, 1982. ———. "The Griesbach Hypothesis: The Phenomenon of Order." *ETL* 58 (1982) 111–22. ———. *The Minor Agreements of Matthew and Luke against Mark with a Cumulative List.* BETL 37. Leuven: Leuven UP, 1974. **New, D. S.** *Old Testament Quotations in the Synoptic Gospels, and the Two-Document Hypothesis.* SBLCS 37. Atlanta: Scholars Press, 1993. **Niemand, C.** "Bemerkungen zur literarkritischen Relevanz der Minor Agreements." *SNTSU* 14 (1989) 25–38. **Orchard, J. B.**, and **Longstaff, T. R. W.** *J. J. Griesbach: Synoptic and Text Critical Studies 1776–1976.* SNTSMS 34. Cambridge: Cambridge UP, 1978. **Orchard, J. B.**, and **Riley, H.** *The Order of the Synoptics: Why Three Synoptic Gospels?* Macon, GA: Mercer UP, 1987. **Palmer, N. H.** "Lachmann's Argument." *NTS* 13 (1967) 368–78. **Parker, P.** *The Gospel before Mark.* Chicago: University of Chicago Press, 1953. ———. "The Posteriority of Mark." In *New Synoptic Studies: The Cambridge Gospels Conference and Beyond.* Ed. W. R. Farmer. Macon, GA: Mercer UP, 1983. 67–142. **Peabody, D. P.** *Mark as Composer.* New Gospel Studies 1. Macon, GA: Mercer UP, 1987. **Robinson, J. M.** "The Sayings of Jesus: Q." *Drew Gateway* 54 (1983–84) 26–38. ———. "The Sayings Gospel Q." In *The Four Gospels 1992.* FS F. Neirynck, ed. F. Van Segbroeck et al. BETL 100. Leuven: Leuven UP, 1992. 361–88. **Rolland, P.** *Les premiers évangiles: Un nouveau regard sur le problème synoptique.* LD. Paris: Cerf, 1984. **Sanday, W.**, ed. *Oxford Studies in the Synoptic Problem.* Oxford: Clarendon, 1911. **Sanders, E. P.** "The Argument from Order and the Relationship between Matthew and Luke." *NTS* 15 (1969) 249–61. ———. *The Tendencies of the Synoptic Tradition.* SNTSMS 9. Cambridge: Cambridge UP, 1969. ——— and **Davies, M.** *Studying the Synoptic Gospels.* London: SCM; Philadelphia: Trinity Press International, 1989. **Stanton, V. H.** *The Jewish and Christian Messiah: A Study in the Earliest History of Christianity.* Edinburgh: T. & T. Clark, 1886. **Stein, R. H.** "The Matthew–Luke Agreements against Mark: Insight from John." *CBQ* 54 (1992) 482–502. ———. *The Synoptic Problem: An Introduction.* Grand Rapids, MI: Baker, 1987. **Stoldt, H.-H.** *History and Criticism of the Marcan Hypothesis.* Macon, GA: Mercer UP, 1980. **Streeter, B. H.** *The Four*

Gospels: A Study of Origins. 2nd ed. London: Macmillan, 1930. ————. "St. Mark's Knowledge and Use of Q." In *Studies in the Synoptic Problem: By Members of the University of Oxford.* Ed. W. Sanday. Oxford: Clarendon, 1911. 165–83. **Styler, G. M.** "The Priority of Mark." In C. F. D. Moule, *The Birth of the New Testament.* 3rd ed. San Francisco: Harper & Row, 1982. 285–316. **Tuckett, C. M.** "Mark and Q." In *The Synoptic Gospels: Source Criticism and the New Literary Criticism.* Ed. C. Focant. BETL 110. Leuven: Peeters and Leuven UP, 1993. 149–75. ————. *The Revival of the Griesbach Hypothesis: An Analysis and Appraisal.* SNTSMS 44. Cambridge: Cambridge UP, 1983. ————. "Synoptic Problem." *ABD* 6:263–70. **Turner, N.** *Style.* Vol. 4 of *A Grammar of New Testament Greek.* Edinburgh: T. & T. Clark, 1976. **Walker, W. O.,** ed. *The Relationships among the Gospels: An Interdisciplinary Dialogue.* Trinity University Monograph Series in Religion 5. San Antonio, TX: Trinity UP, 1978. **Weisse, C. H.** *Die evangelische Geschichte, kritisch und philosophisch bearbeitet.* 2 vols. Leipzig: Breitkopf und Härtel, 1838. **Wenham, J.** *Redating Matthew, Mark and Luke: A Fresh Assault on the Synoptic Problem.* London: Hodder & Stoughton, 1991. **Westcott, B. F.** *An Introduction to the Study of the Gospels.* London: Macmillan, 1862. **Wilke, C. G.** "Über die Parabel von den Arbeitern im Weinberge Matth. 20.1–16." *ZWT* 1 (1826) 73–88. ————. *Der Urevangelist, oder, exegetisch-kritische Untersuchung über das Verwandtschaftsverhältnis der drei ersten Evangelien.* Dresden and Leipzig: Fleischer, 1838.

Any scholarly discussion of the Gospel of Mark must presuppose one solution or another of the so-called Synoptic Problem. The Synoptic Problem results from the observation of the extensive material overlap among the Gospels of Matthew, Mark, and Luke. Not only do these three Gospels share common content, much of which is quite close verbally, but they also present it in the same general order. These Gospels parallel one another so closely that they can be placed side by side and be "seen together," which is what is implied by the word *synoptic* (from σύνοψις). The closeness of the relationship, moreover, is only underscored when the Synoptic Gospels are compared to the Gospel of John.

This close relationship has from very early times led Christian interpreters to conclude that there is some sort of literary dependence among the Synoptic Gospels. Augustine (ca. 400 C.E.) believed that Matthew was the earliest Gospel and that Mark was an abridgement of it (cf. *Cons.* 1.2.4). Matthean priority remained the dominant view until the nineteenth century. Theories more complicated than that offered by Augustine began to emerge in the eighteenth century. In 1764 H. Owen (*Observations on the Four Gosples* [London: Payne]) tried to explain the relationship of all three Gospels arguing that Matthew was written first, that Luke used Matthew, and that Mark, last of all, used Matthew and Luke. Two years later A. F. Büsching (*Harmonie der Evangelien* [Hamburg]) came to a different conclusion arguing that Luke was first, that Matthew used Luke, and that Mark used Luke and Matthew. Returning to Owen's position J. J. Griesbach ("Inquisitio in fontes, unde evangelistae suas de resurrectione domini narrationes hauserint," repr. in *Opuscula Academica,* ed. I. P. Gabler [Jena: Frommanni, 1824–25] 2:241–56) concluded in 1783 that the Gospel of Matthew was written first, that Luke used Matthew, and that Mark abridged and conflated Matthew and Luke. This view, known as the "Griesbach Hypothesis," became the dominant scholarly view for nearly a century.

The Griesbach Hypothesis was challenged in the nineteenth century both in Germany and in England. In *An Introduction to the Study of the Gospels,* B. F. Westcott argued that written and oral sources were utilized by the evangelists independently of one another. Because some of these sources are common to two or more of the evangelists, we encounter the phenomena that have given rise to what scholars describe as the Synoptic Problem. In contrast to German scholars, Westcott did not think that it was necessary to resort to theories that view the Gospels themselves as sources. However, Westcott's solution, which could be described as a "micro-interdependence" theory, did not carry the day because it failed to explain, among other things, the Gospels' common narrative design and order. Influenced by W. Sanday's Oxford Seminar on the Gospels (see *Oxford Studies*), scholars remained convinced that the relationship involved the whole Gospels as sources. Thus the Synoptic Problem would have to be solved, it was believed, in terms of "macro-interdependence."

Westcott's approach has been lately resurrected, though in a different form, in B. D. Chilton's recently published study, *Profiles of a Rabbi*. Sympathetic to Westcott's approach and to the Jewish contextualization posited by V. H. Stanton, Chilton believes that rabbinic—not classical—literature provides the appropriate model for comparison with the Synoptic Gospels. Chilton observes the numerous examples of "synoptic" rabbinic and targumic traditions. Because the targums took shape in the synagogue, that is, in the context of worship and scriptural interpretation, Chilton suggests that "the Gospels took shape in much the same way that Targumim did" (*Profiles of a Rabbi,* 120–21). Chilton's proposal should be taken seriously, for it frees interpreters from the burden of trying to explain all the data with reference to documents and interdependence. (See also Wenham, *Redating*, who contends that the Gospels are somewhat interdependent structurally but are independent verbally.) But the Synoptic Problem entails the grouping and ordering of large blocks of material, and not simply numerous parallel pericopes. Indeed, any solution to the problem must account for the Synoptic narratives as wholes. Can Chilton's proposal do this? It is true that numbers of sayings attributed to various rabbis occur in many places. For this reason it is legitimate to speak of a "synoptic problem" in rabbinic literature. But rabbinic literature contains no extended biographical narratives. In this very important respect the parallel between rabbinic synoptic traditions and the Synoptic Gospels does not hold. Rabbinic traditions, moreover, span many centuries, whereas the Synoptic Gospels were composed within a span of two or three decades (for discussion of the possibilities and problems in comparison of the Synoptics with rabbinic literature, see the essays by L. H. Silberman, J. A. Sanders, and J. A. Fitzmyer in W. O. Walker, ed., *Relationships among the Gospels*, 195–258). Chilton's model could explain the parallels between the Synoptic Gospels and the Fourth Gospel—certainly better than the proposals that the latter is dependent upon one or more of the former. But how can it explain the narrative design and sequence common to the Synoptic Gospels? Does not this common sequence point to interdependence in a way that the lack of common sequence in the case of the Fourth Gospel points to its literary independence of the Synoptics? It seems best, notwithstanding Chilton's important insights with regard to rabbinic and targumic materials, to approach the Synoptic Problem in terms of macro-interdependence. Taking this position does not, however, preclude the possibility, even likelihood, that oral tradition continued to influence and shape the written tradition, even after the first Synoptic Gospel was published.

Evidently the first scholar to argue for Markan priority was C. G. Wilke (*ZWT* 1 [1826] 73–88). But it was K. Lachmann's observation of the intermediate position that Mark's narrative sequence occupies in relation to the narratives of Matthew and Luke that gave impetus to Markan priority. According to Lachmann, of the three Gospels, Mark was closest to the primitive narrative and sequence. Several scholars inferred from this observation that Matthew and Luke must have been dependent upon Mark. This is certainly possible, but Mark's intermediate position does not, in itself, require such an explanation. Mark's intermediate position could just as readily be explained as the result of Mark's dependence on Matthew and Luke. (The assumption that Markan priority is the only logical conclusion to be derived from the observation of Mark's intermediate position has come to be called the "Lachmann Fallacy." See Butler, *Originality of St Matthew*, 62–71. It should be noted that Lachmann himself was not guilty of this fallacy. Evidently the first scholar to advance it was Weisse, *Die evangelische Geschichte*.) Nevertheless, Lachmann's study did have the effect of undermining confidence in the tradition of Matthean priority.

The most influential and enduring challenge to Matthean priority came from H. J. Holtzmann's *Die synoptischen Evangelien*, in which it was concluded that an early form of Mark (*Urmarkus*) was written first and that Matthew and Luke, independently of one another, used this draft of Mark and another source of sayings. Holtzmann termed early Mark "Document A" and the non-Markan source common to Matthew and Luke "Document B" (which would eventually become universally known as "Q," an abbreviation for the German word *Quelle*, "source"). Hence, he called his proposal the "Two-Document Hypothesis." Not all scholars were immediately persuaded by Holtzmann's conclusion, but in the decades that followed, his solution gradually emerged as the dominant position. (For a later examination of the *Urmarkus* theory, see Parker, *Gospel before Mark*. Holtzmann himself later abandoned the *Urmarkus* hypothesis; cf. Holtzmann, *Lehrbuch*, 342–61. For an interesting, if unsympathetic, review of the early years of Markan priority, see Meijboom, *History and Critique*.)

The appearance in 1924 of the first edition of B. H. Streeter's *The Four Gospels: A Study of Origins* was largely responsible for the scholarly consensus that subsequently emerged supportive of Markan priority. Moving beyond Holtzmann, Streeter attempted to account for the material that is special to Matthew and Luke. He argued that this material was derived from written documents ("M" for what is special to Matthew, "L" for what is special to Luke). His solution was in essence a Four-Document Hypothesis (viz., Mark, "Q," "M," and "L" as the four documents utilized by Matthew and Luke). Although this solution never won universal acceptance, except perhaps for a time in England, Markan priority became the dominant view. J. C. Hawkins's earlier *Horae Synopticae* (first ed., 1898) also lent important support to Markan priority and Matthew's and Luke's use of Q.

Today the Holtzmann-Streeter hypothesis remains the most commonly held solution to the Synoptic Problem, though not without some modifications. For example, few scholars are convinced that "M" and "L" were written documents. Most tend to regard these traditions as oral, some of them stemming from the respective evangelists themselves. Moreover, some scholars are not fully persuaded that "Q" should be regarded as a written source (though see Kloppenborg's recent defense in *Formation of Q,* 41–51, as well as Fleddermann's conclusion in *Mark and Q,* 215–16). Some think that it may have been partly written and partly oral, or oral in its entirety. For this reason J. A. Fitzmyer (*Luke I–IX,* 64) thinks that it is advisable to speak of a "Two-Source Theory." (This stands in contrast to the optimism shown by J. M. Robinson [cf. *Drew Gateway* 54 (1983–84) 26–38 and "The Sayings Gospel Q"] who refers to this source as "Papyrus Q" or "Sayings Gospel Q.") Since in what form "Q" may have existed is of no pressing concern for the study of Mark, this particular matter will not be pursued further.

Recently H. T. Fleddermann (*Mark and Q*) has concluded that Q was the earliest Christian Gospel and that the Markan evangelist knew and made use of it. He finds that in every instance of the Mark-Q overlaps, the form of the tradition as preserved in Q is more primitive than what is found in Mark (*Mark and Q,* 214–16). The Markan evangelist "tones down radical Q statements. He abbreviates Q discourses. . . . He conflates Q. . . . Mark alters his source Q just as radically as Matthew and Luke change Mark" (*Mark and Q,* 216). But most scholars who hold to the two-source theory disagree, contending that Mark and Q are independent (e.g., Streeter, *The Four Gospels,* 191 [in contrast to his opinion expressed earlier in Streeter, "St. Mark's Knowledge and Use of Q"]; Taylor, 87; Grundmann, 10; Pesch, 1:30; Tuckett, "Mark and Q," 175). In my view, Fleddermann's work has demonstrated, though perhaps not to the extent that he has claimed, that the tradition of Q is more primitive than that of Mark. Fleddermann's insights here will be taken into consideration in the exegesis of the pertinent passages. But I side with the majority view that Mark did not make use of Q, especially if by Q we mean a written document (as Fleddermann does). The Markan evangelist did have access to traditions that paralleled Q in some thirty places (at least). These traditions are primitive and in most instances probably do represent forms of the tradition closer to Jesus than what we have in Mark itself. But it is doubtful that Mark had access to Q, at least to the Q to which the Matthean and Lukan evangelists had access. The fact that so little of Q appears in Mark is a weighty objection, and it is one that Fleddermann sets aside too easily.

In recent years scholarly discussion of the Synoptic Problem has intensified, with some claiming that the dominant view—Markan priority—is in danger of being overthrown. In 1964 W. R. Farmer (*Synoptic Problem*) challenged the near consensus of Markan priority. He has won a few converts (mostly in North America and in Britain; virtually no one in Germany). He and his followers continue to pound away at what are considered the weak points of Markan priority (see Farmer, ed., *New Synoptic Studies*). Their arguments fall into three basic categories. (1) The Matthean-Lukan agreements against Mark present a difficulty for Markan priority. If Matthew and Luke made use of Mark independently of one another, how are we to explain the several places where they agree against Mark? Can all of these agreements be explained as coincidental "minor agreements"? (2) Early church tradition regarded Matthew as the first of the Gospels. (3) It is argued that Markan priority was advanced in the nineteenth century for political and apologetical reasons. These points may be answered, in reverse order, as follows. (1) Arguments to the effect that nineteenth-century attempts to prove Markan priority were driven by the desire to answer the skepticism of David Strauss (cf. H.-H. Stoldt, *History and Criticism*) or were encouraged by Chancellor Bismarck in order to undermine

Roman Catholicism in Germany (cf. Farmer, "State *Interesse*") are interesting, to be sure, but not to the point. These kinds of arguments carry no more weight than criticism of Matthean priority for having been advanced by the church fathers for apologetic reasons. The Synoptic Problem is to be resolved by comparison and exegesis, not by speculations about the motives of scholars. This comment leads to the reply to the second argument. (2) Matthean priority evidently was in part championed by the early church for apologetic reasons. Of the three Synoptic Gospels it was the only one to which tradition had ascribed apostolic authorship. Arguments based on church tradition, in view of these apologetical interests, are precarious. (3) Many of the Matthean-Lukan agreements against Mark can be explained in terms of Markan priority. Many of them may have also resulted from scribal harmonization of Luke to Matthew. There is, of course, the possibility of contact between Matthew and Luke. Such contact, if there was any, does not necessarily rule out Markan priority. The major arguments against Matthean priority, and for Markan priority, will be developed shortly.

That the Synoptic Problem is indeed problematic cannot be gainsaid. Long gone are the days when it was acceptable to say that "it is no longer necessary to prove the priority of Mark" (Taylor, 11). Indeed, J. A. Fitzmyer (*Luke I–IX*, 63) has recently remarked that the Synoptic Problem is

> a problem that has thus far failed to find a fully satisfying solution. The main reason for this failure is the absence of adequate data for judgment about it. Extrinsic, historically trustworthy data about the composition of these Gospels are totally lacking, and the complexity of the traditions embedded in them, the evangelists' editorial redaction of them, and their free composition bedevil all attempts to analyze objectively the intrinsic data with critical literary methods.

Nevertheless, Fitzmyer has adopted the two-source theory as the best explanation of the extant Synoptic Gospels (see also his "Priority of Mark"). (For an attempted rebuttal, see Farmer, *New Synoptic Studies*, 501–23, and *NTS* 23 [1977] 283–93.) C. M. Tuckett (*Revival of the Griesbach Hypothesis*, 186–87) agrees with Fitzmyer, concluding that the two-source theory remains the most viable solution to the Synoptic Problem because it can "give a more coherent and consistent set of explanations of why the later changes were made." In short, the Griesbach (or Two-Gospel) Hypothesis fails to account for the changes made by Luke (in Matthew) and Mark (in Matthew and in Luke).

The following paragraphs present the principal arguments why the two-source theory has been adopted in the present commentary. There are seven basic lines of argument that support Markan priority: (1) literary style, (2) propriety, (3) agreements, (4) divergence, (5) difficulty, (6) material unique to Mark, and (7) interpretation and result.

1. Literary style. It has often been observed that Mark's literary style lacks the polish and sophistication that one regularly encounters in Matthew and Luke. Indeed, Markan style is Semitic, nonliterary, and sometimes may even be described as primitive (see Swete, xliv–l; Taylor, 55–66; Pesch, 1:23–32; Turner, *Style*, 11–30). Of course, this feature alone does not rule out the Two-Gospel Hypothesis, but one wonders why the Markan evangelist would have chosen time after time to rewrite Matthew and Luke in a cruder and less polished form. Why not simply reproduce one version or the other? Why introduce Semitic words (which are often not found in the Matthean and Lukan parallels) only to have to translate them? In a recent study P. Parker ("The Posteriority of Mark") points to numerous examples of clumsiness and inexactness on the part of the Markan evangelist, thinking that this argues that Mark was posterior to Matthew and Luke. On the contrary, it seems that his observations lend support to Markan priority. Why would Mark introduce apparent inaccuracies into his Matthean and Lukan sources? The problematic nature of these questions is brought out sharply by the odd position that C. S. Mann has taken in his commentary on Mark. Although he has followed Farmer and so believes that Mark is dependent upon Matthew and Luke (Mann, 51–66), frequently he finds examples where Mark has preserved the most primitive form of the tradition and is not dependent upon Matthew or Luke (e.g., Mann, 202: "not derived from Matthew and Luke"; 214: "a Petrine reminiscence"; 217: "not derived from Matthew . . . certainly far more vivid in style than Luke's stereotypical account . . . a traditional piece, and the style suggests reminiscence by one of the participants"; 218–19: "Mark's version, with its vivid detail, may owe far more to an original oral reminiscence than to the other evangelists"; et passim). But according to the Two-Gospel Hypothesis, Mark is supposed to be a conflation of Matthew and Luke, not of primitive materials, some of which derive from eyewitnesses (which is more consistent with theories of Markan priority). Mann does not appear to be aware of the extent to which the results of his analysis conflict with his view of the Synoptic Problem. His exegetical conclusions tend to undermine the very theory upon which he has based his commentary. In short, Mark's writing style, when compared to Matthew and Luke, supports Markan priority.

Nevertheless, when viewed in the light of the conclusions that Farmer and his supporters have drawn, Mann's exegetical results are not quite as idiosyncratic as they at first appear. Rather, his results very much reflect the theory of origins of the Synoptic Gospels, according to the Two-Gospel Hypothesis. According to Dungan ("Purpose and Provenance of the Gospel of Mark," 411–40), Farmer (*Synoptic Problem*, 279–81), and Orchard and Riley (*The Order of the Synoptics*, 263–77), the Gospel of Mark, behind which stood the Apostle Peter, was written to provide the common ground, the undisputed points of agreement, between Matthew and Luke. Mark's was a Gospel that attempted to reconcile the sharply divergent portraits of Jesus found in Matthew and Luke, the former with its Jewish emphasis, the latter with its Pauline Gentile emphasis. Given this theory, Mann's exegesis should not occasion surprise. A late, secondary Gospel, in which is imbedded early, primitive, and authentic materials, is exactly what should be expected. But is this theory plausible? Beside the dangers inherent in relying on tradition about Peter's involvement with Mark (which in any event hardly argues for posteriority), the Two-Gospel Hypothesis is faced with many difficulties. Does it explain why Mark omitted material such as the Lord's Prayer, or the Beatitudes? Surely the Lord's Prayer and the Beatitudes are "neutral." After all, they appear in both (Jewish) Matthew and (Gentile) Luke. Why would Peter elect to omit them? After all, did not Peter and the disciples ask Jesus to teach them a prayer (Luke 11:1)? Why omit the Beatitudes; were not these macarisms just as applicable to Peter's Roman church? Why omit so many of the parables? The Two-Gospel Hypothesis, complete with its speculations about Peter the reconciler, cannot explain these omissions. Additions also present a problem for the Two-Gospel Hypothesis. Can this theory account for the addition of odd material that puts the disciples—and even Jesus—in a poorer, more embarrassing light? How is Peter's putative ministry of reconciliation advanced by telling us that Jesus' family thought him mad (cf. Mark 3:20–22)? In short, the Two-Gospel Hypothesis fashions the unlikely scenario of the evangelist Mark, drawing on the mediating ministry of the Apostle Peter, creating a new Gospel out of two Gospels, which he abridges and conflates, into which he inserts two very peculiar miracles and material that seems to promote a secrecy motif, from which he omits the Beatitudes and the Lord's Prayer, and in which he emphasizes Jesus as teacher but omits the teachings themselves. Moreover, he does all of this in a cruder, more rugged, and more verbose style. Such a reconstruction seems most unlikely. Thus, the Two-Gospel Hypothesis fails to account for Markan style in a convincing manner. It is more probable that Matthew and Luke represent improvements upon Mark. (Several examples will be provided below in the discussion of agreements.)

2. *Propriety.* In comparing the Synoptics, one observes that in Mark there is frequent lack (or at least apparent lack) of propriety with respect to the disciples and Jesus. By this I mean that Jesus and the disciples are sometimes portrayed in a manner that appears either undignified or possibly at variance with Christian beliefs. For example, during the storm on the Sea of Galilee the disciples cry out, according to the Markan version, "Teacher, do you not care if we perish?" (4:38). One could infer from Mark's version a lack of respect for Jesus, especially from the perspective of a Christian who revered Jesus as the Son of God. How could the disciples have questioned Jesus' concern for them? The question of the frightened disciples is put much more politely and innocuously in Matthew, "Save, Lord, we are perishing" (8:25), and in Luke, "Master, Master, we are perishing!" (8:24). Mark's version of Jesus' reply, "Have you no faith?" (4:40), could imply that the disciples are faithless. Matthew's version, "O men of little faith" (8:26), and Luke's version, "Where is your faith?" (8:25), soften the rebuke. When Jesus walks on the water, the disciples, according to Mark, are terrified and are utterly bereft of understanding (6:49–52). But Matthew omits the part about their lack of understanding. Instead, he inserts the story of Peter walking on the water and confessing Jesus as "the Son of God" (14:26–33). A similar scene takes place following the second feeding miracle. Because the disciples do not "understand" the meaning of the loaves, they are, according to Mark, spiritually blind (8:17–21). The severity of this rebuke is greatly softened in Matthew, who concludes the episode by noting that finally "they understood" the allusion to the loaves (16:9–12). (Both of the preceding episodes are omitted by Luke.) Mark portrays the disciples negatively in the passion account as well. The disciples fall asleep (three times!), instead of praying, and are rebuked (Mark 14:37–41). Luke mitigates the picture by referring to only one occurrence of sleep and excuses the disciples by noting that they slept "for sorrow" (22:45). Mark reports that when Jesus was arrested, "all forsook him and fled" (14:50). Luke omits this detail (22:54). The curious account of the young man who fled naked (Mark 14:51–52) is omitted by both Matthew and Luke. Finally, Mark's miserable picture of Peter cursing (14:71) is omitted by Luke (22:60).

One could, of course, respond to these observations by suggesting that these negative portrayals of the disciples are part of Mark's theology. To some extent this is probably true, though it is not likely that this would explain every detail. Has Mark rewritten the essentially positive portraits of the disciples, as he finds them in Matthew and Luke, or have Matthew and Luke improved upon the negative portrait that they found in Mark?

But more importantly, it should be pointed out that in Mark there is often a lack of propriety with respect to Jesus himself. Almost always Matthew and Luke attempt to dignify or at least in some sense qualify these passages. For example, according to Mark, "the Spirit drove [Jesus] out into the wilderness" (1:12). Not only is this picture somewhat undignified, but the verb that is used is ἐκβάλλειν, the verb that is customarily used in describing the exorcism of demons (Mark 1:34, 39; 3:15, 22, 23; 6:13; 7:26; 9:18, 28, 38). According to Matthew, "Jesus was led up [ἀνάγειν] by the Spirit into the wilderness" (4:1). According to Luke, "Jesus, full of the Holy Spirit, returned from the Jordan, and was led [ἄγειν] by the Spirit" (4:1). It is hard to understand why Mark would transform these statements into the one that we find in his Gospel. Potentially embarrassing expressions of emotion on the part of Jesus are also omitted by Matthew and Luke. For example, the reference to Jesus' anger (Mark 3:5) and the reference to Jesus being "beside himself" (Mark 3:21) are omitted by Matthew and Luke. If he did not find these descriptions in his Matthean and Lukan sources, why would the Markan evangelist insert such material? The exchange between Jesus and messengers from his family provides another interesting case in point. When told that his family is outside, trying to see him, Mark narrates: "He replied, 'Who are my mother and my brothers?' And looking around on those who sat about him, he said, 'Here are my mother and my brothers!'" (3:33–34). Jesus' statement could easily be interpreted as showing disrespect toward his family. Matthew, however, is careful to note that Jesus was speaking only in reference to his "disciples" (12:49). Luke omits the potentially disrespectful rhetorical question ("Who are my mother and my brothers?"), having Jesus say only, "My mother and my brothers are those who hear the word of God and do it" (8:21). Elsewhere Christology itself seems to play a role. According to Mark, the people of Nazareth ask, "Is not this the carpenter?" (6:3). But in Matthew, the question becomes, "Is not this the son of the carpenter?" (13:55). The implication that Jesus was viewed by the people who had known him all of his life as nothing more than a carpenter probably accounts for Matthew's paraphrase of the question. Because of the unbelief of his home-folk, Jesus "could do no mighty work there" (Mark 6:5). Omitted altogether in Luke, the parallel passage reads in Matthew "he did not do many mighty works there" (13:58). It is likely that Matthew wishes to avoid the implication that Jesus' power could be hindered or thwarted. It is hard to see why Mark would have rewritten Matthew to read as it does in Mark. Finally, one might also observe that in a few passages in Mark in which Jesus is called "Teacher," he is called "Lord" in Matthew and "Master" in Luke (Mark 4:38 = Matt 8:25 = Luke 8:24; Mark 9:17 = Matt 17:15; Mark 9:38 = Luke 9:49; Mark 10:35 = Matt 20:20, where "teacher" drops out and disciples "bow" before Jesus). In these examples it seems more likely to view Matthew and Luke as enhancing Christology, rather than the reverse, that is, that Mark is downplaying Christology by replacing "Lord" with "Teacher." Such redaction is not in step with Markan Christology (as seen, for example, in Mark 1:1; 15:39).

3. Agreements. For Farmer and his supporters the agreements between Matthew and Luke against Mark (which involve content, order, or wording) provide the fatal objection to the theory of Markan priority. Farmer believes that these agreements are too extensive to be credited to coincidence and can be reasonably explained only in terms of Luke directly borrowing from Matthew. But many Synoptic scholars do not agree (see esp. Neirynck, *Minor Agreements;* id., *Evangelica*). If Mark is the source common to Matthew and Luke, one should expect the latter Gospels to agree against Mark only occasionally, not consistently. That is in fact what we find. When they do agree against Mark, almost always the agreement is minor (Hawkins, *Horae Synopticae,* 208–12; Streeter, *Four Gospels,* 293–331). These "minor agreements" usually fall into the following categories: *(a) Grammatical corrections/ improvements.* Mark's paratactic καί, "and," is often replaced with δέ, "and, but," in Matthew and Luke. Mark's historical present (which occurs some 150 times, half of which involve λέγειν, "to say") is avoided by Matthew and Luke (who usually replace λέγει/λέγουσι, "he says/they say," with εἶπεν/εἶπον, "he said/they said"). *(b) Stylistic improvements.* Sometimes Matthew and Luke agree in their improvements upon Markan style (e.g., Mark 2:12 = Matt 9:7 = Luke 5:25; Mark 4:10 = Matt 13:10 = Luke 8:9; Mark 16:8 = Matt 28:8 = Luke 24:9). These improvements sometimes take the form of choosing a more appropriate word. For example, Mark uses παίειν in describing the severing of the high priest's servant's ear (14:47). But this word is normally used to describe striking someone or something with a club or a fist, not with a sword. Matthew and Luke substitute the more appropriate πατάσσειν (Matt 26:51 = Luke 22:49). This agreement can hardly be used as evidence that Luke made use of Matthew. Indeed, this example argues for Markan priority. Why would Mark, when reading the appropriate word πατάσσειν twice in his Matthean and Lukan sources, replace it with the less appropriate παίειν? *(c) Influence of Q.* Some agreements between Matthew and Luke against Mark are probably due to the influence of Q (e.g., Mark 4:21 = Matt 5:15 // Luke 8:16 = Luke 11:33; Mark 4:22 // Matt 10:26 // Luke 8:17 = Luke 12:2; Mark 12:38–39 // Luke 20:46 = Matt 23:6 // Luke 11:43). In addition to the influence of Q, one should also take into account the influence of the "living, oral tradition" (Guelich, p. xxxiii). *(d) Influence of oral tradition as witnessed by John.* There are several instances where the Matthean-Lukan agreements against Mark are found in the Fourth Gospel as well. This is clear indication that there was tradition—probably oral—that paralleled, but did not exactly agree with, the tradition in Mark. R. H. Stein (*CBQ* 54 [1992] 482–502) has recently observed that "John witnesses to certain Gospel traditions which have parallels in the Synoptic Gospels and that at times these traditions also appear as Matthew-Luke agreements against Mark" (502). Stein identifies eight examples of this phenomenon (cf. Matt 3:11 = Mark 1:8 = Luke 3:16 = John 1:26; Matt 3:16 = Mark 1:10 = Luke 3:22 = John 1:32–33; Matt 14:13–14 = Mark 6:33 = Luke 9:10–11 = John 6:12–13; Matt 16:16 = Mark 8:29 = Luke 9:20 = John 6:69; Matt 26:34, 74 = Mark 14:30, 72 = Luke 22:34, 60 = John 13:38, 18:27; Matt 26:52 = Mark 14:47 = Luke 22:51 = John 18:10–11; Matt 27:21 = Mark 15:11–12 = Luke 23:18 = John 18:40; Matt 27:60 = Mark 15:46 = Luke 23:53 = John 19:41). *(e) Possible contact between Luke and Matthew.* Although still firmly convinced of the validity of the Two-Source Hypothesis, Gundry ("Matthean Foreign Bodies," 1467–95) finds evidence that Luke may have made use of Matthew. Some of the agreements are not minor, but complex (cf. Matt 10:1–2 = Mark 3:13–18 = Luke 6:13–14; Matt 16:21 = Mark 8:31 = Luke 9:22; Matt 17:14–20 = Mark 9:14–29 = Luke 9:37–43a; Matt 18:1 = Mark 9:33–34 = Luke 9:46–47). Because "the agreements of Matthew and Mark against Luke and of Luke and Mark against Matthew outnumber and outweigh the agreements of Matthew and Luke against Mark" (1494), Gundry concludes that the Lukan evangelist held his Markan and Q sources in higher regard than he did his Matthean source (though whether he actually possessed a written copy of Matthew, it is difficult to say). Goulder (*Luke*, 1:22–23) also holds to Markan priority but finds evidence of Luke's knowledge of Matthew. However, his explanation that Q is the product of Matthean midrash on Mark is not convincing. Finally, mention should be made of Boismard's work (see the several entries in the bibliography), which proposes a complicated variation of the two-source theory. Driving Boismard is his conviction that the two-source theory is too simple to account for several of the agreements between Matthew and Luke against Mark. He believes that a compelling solution to the Synoptic Problem must take into account not only these agreements but also the presence of Mattheanisms and Lukanisms in Mark. According to Boismard, there were three documents (A, B, and C), besides Q, which flowed into Matthean, Markan, and Lukan streams, producing respectively "intermediate Matthew," "intermediate Mark," and "Proto-Luke." Document A (intermediate Matthew's primary source) and Document C (intermediate Luke's primary source) also influenced intermediate Mark (in his more recent work, *L'Évangile de Marc*, Boismard prefers "Proto-Mark"), while Document B (intermediate Mark's primary source) also influenced intermediate Luke. Q flows into intermediate Matthew and intermediate Luke. Each of these intermediate Gospels is subsequently edited, influencing one another along the way, and eventually the Gospels emerge as the documents, more or less, that we now have. Although Boismard's theory strikes this commentator and most other Gospels scholars as overly complicated, Sanders and Davies are right in saying that he is "probably on the right track in thinking of different editions and in allowing for criss-cross copying" (*Studying*, 113). This point relates to the next one. *(f) Textual corruption.* We cannot assume that the respective texts of the extant Gospels, at least as textual critics have reconstructed them, are identical to the autographs. Textual corruption, especially involving scribal harmonization of Matthew and Luke (e.g., Mark 14:65 = Matt 26:67–68 = Luke 22:64), probably accounts for some, perhaps even many, of the agreements between these two Gospels against Mark. As H. Koester ("Synoptic Gospels," 19) has said, the assumption that "the reconstruction of the best archetype for the [Gospels] manuscript tradition is more or less identical with the assumed autograph is precarious. The oldest known archetypes are separated from the autographs by more than a century. Textual critics of classical texts know that the first century of their transmission is the period in which the most serious corruptions occur." Bellinzoni agrees, stating that "Problems such as the so-called minor agreements of Matthew and Luke against Mark may lend themselves to solutions that draw on developments in the second century when the texts of all three synoptics were reworked by church fathers in light of one another" (*SecCent* 9 [1992] 257; cf. Boismard, "Influences matthéennes"; Elliott, *NTS* 26 [1980] 231–42). *(g) Agreements in omissions.* Stoldt (*History and Criticism*, 11–17) has enumerated the agreements in omission of Matthew and Luke against Mark and asks how this can be explained in terms of these Gospels' independent usage of Mark. Stein (*Synoptic Problem,* 115–17) has responded by pointing out that Matthew and Luke have omitted a large portion of Mark's vocabulary. Therefore, a significant number of common omissions should be expected. Many of these common omissions were likely motivated by a desire to eliminate awkward or even inaccurate statements. Mark's reference to Abiathar (Mark 2:26) is difficult (since Ahimelech was the high priest at the time in question), and so we should hardly be surprised when Matthew and Luke agree in its omission. Many of the other common omissions can be readily explained. Dunn ("Matthew's Awareness of Markan Redaction," 1349–59) argues plausibly that many of the common omissions occurred when Matthew and Luke recognized and chose to omit Markan redaction. Stein rightly comments that many of the scholars who argue against Markan priority on the basis of the Matthean and Lukan agreements in omission "lose sight of the fact that the common omission of this material by Matthew and Luke makes far more sense than does Mark's addition of this material to his 'abridged' Gospel and his consequent omission of such things as the Sermon on the Mount" (*Synoptic Problem,* 117).

4. *Divergences.* Where there is no Markan parallel, Matthean and Lukan divergence is greatest. This phenomenon is explained best in reference to Markan priority, rather than Matthean. There is significant divergence in three areas involving material not found in Mark. *(a) Distribution of Q.* Probably the most important argument lies in the observation that Matthew and Luke place Q material in different locations. There are two obvious exceptions: both Matthew and Luke place the preaching of John the Baptist at the point of the story where Mark tells of the Baptist (Matt 3:1–12 = Mark 1:2–8 = Luke 3:1–17). Both Matthew and Luke insert the tradition of Jesus' three temptations at the point of the story where Mark narrates Jesus' time of testing in the wilderness (Matt 4:1–11 = Mark 1:12–13 = Luke 4:1–13). But these two exceptions hardly overthrow the point of the observation. Where else could one have expected Matthew and Luke to have inserted this Q material? Did Luke need to see Matthew in order to know where to place John's preaching and the temptations of Jesus? The remainder of Q, however, which has no obvious connections to the Markan narrative, appears in Matthew and Luke in different locations (with the exception, of course, of instances of Q "clusters"; see Kloppenborg, *Formation of Q,* 74–76). Markan priority has no difficulty explaining this. Matthew tends to lump the material into major discourses (e.g., Matt 5–7, 10, 13, 18, 24–25), but Luke has left it in its relatively scattered form (perhaps approximating the order of Q itself), with much of it appearing in his lengthy Central Section (Luke 10–18). Advocates of Matthean priority, in contrast, have great difficulty in explaining this distribution. How can one explain why Luke follows Matthew's narrative (which happens to overlap with Mark) but does not follow Matthew's arrangement of teaching material? Why would Luke break up the discourses? *(b) The Christmas story.* At many points Matthew and Luke diverge in their respective accounts of the infancy tradition: Matthew's genealogy appears at the beginning, but Luke's is outside of the infancy narrative proper; the genealogies themselves differ in many ways; Matthew cites five OT texts as "fulfilled" while Luke cites none; Luke has seven canticles, but Matthew has none; in Matthew the angel appears to Joseph, but in Luke the angel appears to Mary; in Matthew the Magi visit Jesus, but in Luke the shepherds visit him; only in

Matthew does Herod slay the infants and does the Holy Family flee to Egypt; only in Luke is Jesus dedicated in the temple; only in Luke does the boy Jesus visit the temple. The best explanation for these numerous points of divergence is that Matthew and Luke developed their respective infancy narratives independently of one another. *(c) The Easter accounts.* There is significant divergence between Matthew and Luke, at the very point in the Easter story where extant Mark ends: the Road to Emmaus episode is found only in Luke; the story of the bribed guards is found only in Matthew; the mountain commission is found only in Matthew; the "opening of the Scriptures" and the ascension are found only in Luke. If Luke had had Matthew in front of him, it would then be hard to explain why he did not make use of the mountain commission, which would have contributed to his own interests in world mission and the commissioning of the apostles (cf. Acts 1:6–11). One would also have to wonder why Luke would have failed to harmonize his account of Judas's death with the account he would have read in Matt 27:3–10 (cf. Acts 1:18–19). Again, the best explanation for these numerous points of divergence is that Matthew and Luke developed their respective resurrection narratives independently of one another.

In short, what we observe is that, as was said above, where there is no Mark to follow, this is where Matthew and Luke go their separate ways. This observation is very difficult to explain assuming Matthean priority, but it is exactly what one should expect assuming Markan priority.

5. *Difficulty.* Another indication of Markan priority is in the observation that in some instances, because of editing and the omission of Markan details, Matthew and Luke have created difficulties. Stein (*Synoptic Problem,* 70–76) and Goodacre (*NTS* 44 [1998] 45–54) have provided several examples that illustrate this feature well. *(a)* Because he has omitted Mark's description of the removal of the roof and the lowering of the paralytic (Mark 2:4), Matthew has removed the immediate reason for the editorial comment regarding the faith of the (four) men (Matt 9:2b). Matthew's readers, unfamiliar with Mark, are left to wonder why Jesus is said to have "seen their faith." *(b)* Omitting Mark's explanation of the Passover pardon (Mark 15:6–11), Luke nevertheless goes on to narrate that the people cried out for the release of Barabbas (Luke 23:18). However, the evangelist does not explain on what basis the crowd could have expected Pilate to release anyone, whether it be Jesus or Barabbas or any one else. *(c)* According to Mark 10:18 Jesus asks the man, "Why do you call me good?" In Matt 19:17 the question is slightly (but significantly) different: "Why do you ask me about what is good?" It is not hard to see why Matthew would have changed Mark's form of the question (Is Jesus implying that he is not good?). But it is not clear why Mark would have changed Matthew's form of the question. Although he changed the question, Matthew did not change the answer: "One there is who is good." This form of the answer fits better the question as it is found in Mark, in that it is in reference to the goodness of beings (such as God or Jesus), not to the subject of goodness. Accordingly, Matthew betrays his knowledge of the Markan form of the story. *(d)* According to Mark 10:35–37, James and John make a request of Jesus to sit at his right and left in his glory. The question arouses the indignation of the other disciples, so we should not be surprised that the scene is mitigated in Matthew. According to Matt 20:20–21 it is the *mother* of James and John who makes the request. But Matthew again betrays his knowledge of Mark's

version, when he has Jesus reply: "You [pl.] do not know what you [pl.] are asking" (Matt 20:22 = Mark 10:38). The plural clearly indicates that Jesus was addressing James and John, not their mother. Consequently, Mark 10:35–38 is surely what underlies Matt 20:20–22, and not the reverse.

6. *Material unique to Mark.* The small amount of material that is unique to the Gospel of Mark also supports Markan priority. This material consists of 1:1; 2:27; 3:20–21; 4:26–29; 7:2–4, 32–37; 8:22–26; 9:29, 48–49; 13:33–37; 14:51–52. In reviewing this material one should ask which explanation seems most probable, that Mark added it or that Matthew and Luke found it in Mark and chose to omit it. The nature of the material supports the latter alternative, for it seems more likely that Matthew and Luke chose to omit the flight of the naked youth (14:51–52), the odd saying about being "salted with fire" (9:48–49), the strange miracle where Jesus effects a healing in two stages (8:22–26), the even stranger miracle where Jesus puts his fingers in a man's ears, spits, and touches his tongue (7:32–37), and the episode where Jesus is regarded as mad and his family attempts to restrain him (3:20–22). If we accept the Griesbach-Farmer hypothesis, we would then have to explain why Mark would choose to add these odd, potentially embarrassing materials, only to omit the Sermon on the Mount/Plain, the Lord's Prayer, and numerous other teachings and parables found in the larger Gospels. It seems much more likely that Matthew and Luke represent attempts to make improvements upon Mark. All of the points considered in this section point in this direction. Matthew and Luke have improved upon Mark's style. They have heightened its Christology. They have enhanced the image and authority of the apostles. They have considerably augmented Jesus' teaching, but in a way that does not suggest dependence of one upon another. And they have omitted potentially confusing and embarrassing material.

7. *Interpretation and result.* The final consideration that adds weight to the probability of Markan priority has to do with the results of the respective hypotheses. The true test of any hypothesis is its effectiveness. In biblical studies a theory should aid the exegetical task. The theory of Markan priority has provided just this kind of aid. Not only has Synoptic interpretation been materially advanced because of the conclusion, and now widespread adoption, of Markan priority, but the development of critical methods oriented to Gospel research, such as form and redaction criticism, which have enjoyed success, has also presupposed Markan priority. In countless studies, whether dealing with a single pericope or treating one of the Synoptic Gospels in its entirety, it has been recognized over and over again that Matthew and Luke make the greatest sense as interpretations of Mark (Tuckett, *Revival of the Griesbach Hypothesis,* 186–87). This has been recently illustrated in a study treating explicit quotations of the OT in the Synoptic Gospels. New (*Old Testament Quotations*) has concluded that the editing and contextualization of these quotations make the best sense in terms of Matthean and Lukan dependence upon Mark. But Mark makes no sense as an interpretation of Matthew and/ or Luke. If the Griesbach-Farmer hypothesis were correct, one should expect major breakthroughs in Markan research. After all, we would now know what Mark's sources were. But Farmer's following has not cast significant light on Mark. Mann's commentary, which does presuppose the Griesbach-Farmer hypothesis, has not been successful, illustrating instead the problem encountered when attempting a verse-by-verse analysis of Mark based on an assumption of Matthean priority.

After his reexamination of the Synoptic Problem, the late S. E. Johnson concluded, "I began this study intending to keep an open mind, but the longer I worked the more I was convinced that the [Two-Source Hypothesis] is far from obsolete, and is much more easily defensible than the [Griesbach hypothesis]. Examination of the shape of the three gospels and their theology seems to me to show that in most cases the comparison confirms the judgment that Matthew and Luke are secondary to Mark, and that the Q material has a primitive theology of its own" (*Griesbach Hypothesis*, 5). Most Gospel scholars agree with Johnson.

For the seven reasons briefly sketched above, which are scarcely more than summaries of much lengthier and more detailed studies, this commentary has adopted the position that the Gospel of Mark was the first of the three Synoptics and served as the primary narrative source for Matthew and Luke. It is also concluded that Mark was the first literary attempt to record a life of Jesus and that this attempt reflects certain theological interests and motives that may account for the form that Mark's Gospel took.

Text of Mark

Bibliography

Aland, B. et al., eds. *The Greek New Testament.* 4th rev. ed. Stuttgart: Deutsche Bibelgesellschaft, 1993. ——— and **Aland, K.**, eds. *Novum Testamentum Graece.* 27th ed. Stuttgart: Deutsche Bibelgesellschaft, 1993. ——— *Synopsis Quattuor Evangeliorum.* 13th ed. Stuttgart: Deutsche Bibelgesellschaft, 1985. **Aland, K.** et al., eds. *The Greek New Testament.* 3rd corrected ed. London; New York: United Bible Societies, 1983. **Basiliano, J. C. M.,** ed. *Bibliorum Sacrorum Graecus Codex Vaticanus.* Vol. 5. *Novum Testamentum.* Rome: Congregatio de Propaganda Fide, 1868. **Beerman, G.,** and **Gregory, C. R.** *Die Koridethi Evangelien.* Leipzig: Hinrichs, 1913. **Boismard, M.-É.** *L'Évangile de Marc: Sa préhistoire.* EBib 26. Paris: Gabalda, 1994. **Clarke, K.** *Textual Optimism: The United Bible Societies' Greek New Testament and Its Evaluation of Evidence Letter-Ratings.* JSNTSup 138. Sheffield: Sheffield Academic Press, 1997. **Comfort, P. W.** *Early Manuscripts and Modern Translations of the New Testament.* Wheaton, IL: Tyndale, 1990. ———. *The Quest for the Original Text of the New Testament.* Grand Rapids, MI: Baker, 1992. **Cowper, B. H.** *Codex Alexandrinus.* London: Williams & Norgate, 1860. **Cronin, H. S.** *Codex Purpureus Petropolitanus: The Text of Codex N of the Gospels.* Cambridge: Cambridge UP, 1899. **Doudna, J. C.** *The Greek of the Gospel of Mark.* SBLMS 12. Philadelphia: SBL, 1961. **Field, F.** *Notes on the Translation of the New Testament.* Cambridge: Cambridge UP, 1899. **Huffman, N.** "Suggestions from the Gospel of Mark for a New Textual Theory." *JBL* 56 (1937) 347–59. **Hurtado, L. W.** *Text-Critical Methodology and the Pre-Caesarean Text: Codex W in the Gospel of Mark.* SD 43. Grand Rapids, MI: Eerdmans, 1981. **Kenyon, F. G.** *The Chester Beatty Biblical Papyri: Fasciculus II. The Gospels and Acts.* London: Emery Walker, 1933. ———. "Some Notes on the Chester Beatty Gospels and Acts." In *Quantulacumque.* FS K. Lake, ed. R. P. Casey et al. London: Christophers, 1937. 145–48. **Lake, K.** *The Text of the New Testament.* 6th ed. Rev. by S. Lake. London: Rivington's, 1959 [orig. 1928]. ——— and **Lake, H.** *Codex Sinaiticus Petropolitanus: The New Testament.* Oxford: Clarendon, 1911. ——— and **Lake, S.** *Family 13 (The Ferrar Group): The Text according to Mark with a Collation of Codex 28 of the Gospels.* SD 11. London: Christophers, 1941. ——— et al. "The Caesarean Text of the Gospel of Mark." *HTR* 21 (1928) 207–404. **Legg, S. C. E.** *Novum Testamentum Graece secundum Textum Westcotto-Hortianum: Euangelium secundum Marcum.* Oxford: Clarendon, 1935. **Lindsey, R. L.** *A Hebrew Translation of the Gospel of Mark.* 2nd ed.

Jerusalem: Dugith, 1973. **Linton, O.** "Evidences of a Second Century Revised Edition of St. Mark's Gospel." *NTS* 14 (1967–68) 321–55. **Metzger, B. M.** *A Textual Commentary on the Greek New Testament.* London; New York: United Bible Societies, 1971. ———. *The Text of the New Testament: Its Transmission, Corruption, and Restoration.* 3rd ed. Oxford: Oxford UP, 1992. **Neirynck, F.** "Mark in Greek." *ETL* 47 (1971) 144–98 (repr. in F. Neirynck. *Duality in Mark: Contributions to the Study of the Markan Redaction.* BETL 31. 2nd ed. Leuven: Leuven UP, 1988. 137–91). ———. "The New Nestle-Aland: The Text of Mark in N²⁶." In *Evangelica.* BETL 60. Leuven: Peeters and Leuven UP, 1982. 899–924. **Nestle, E.** *Greek New Testament: Edited with Critical Apparatus.* 26th ed. Rev. and ed. by E. Nestle and K. Aland. Stuttgart: Deutsche Bibelstiftung, 1979. **Parker, D. C.** *Codex Bezae: An Early Christian Manuscript and Its Text.* Cambridge: Cambridge UP, 1992. 215–28. **Sanders, H. A.** *Facsimile of the Washington Manuscript of the Four Gospels in the Freer Collection.* Ann Arbor, MI: University of Michigan Press, 1912. **Scrivener, F. H. A.** *Bezae Codex Cantabrigiensis.* 1864. Repr. Cambridge: Deighton, Bell; London: Bell and Daldy, 1899. **Souter, A.** *Novum Testamentum Graece.* 2nd ed. Oxford: Clarendon, 1947. **Tarelli, C. C.** "The Chester Beatty Papyrus and the Caesarean Text." *JTS* 40 (1939) 46–55. ———. "The Chester Beatty Papyrus and the Western and Byzantine Texts." *JTS* 41 (1940) 253–60. ———. "Some Further Linguistic Aspects of the Chester Beatty Papyrus of the Gospels." *JTS* 43 (1942) 19–25. ———. "Some Linguistic Aspects of the Chester Beatty Papyrus of the Gospels." *JTS* 39 (1938) 254–59. **Thompson, E. M.** *New Testament and Clementine Epistles.* Vol. 4 of *Facsimile of the Codex Alexandrinus.* London: British Museum, 1883. **Westcott, B. F.,** and **Hort, F. J. A.** *Text.* Vol. 1 of *The New Testament in the Original Greek.* Cambridge; London: Macmillan, 1881.

The Gospel of Mark is not well represented in the oldest papyri. Third-century 𝔓⁴⁵ (one of the Chester Beatty Papyri) and sixth-century 𝔓⁸⁴ (Bibliothèque de l'Université Louvain) preserve fragments of several chapters, while the fourth-century 𝔓⁸⁸ (Catholic University of Milan) preserves less than one chapter. Fifth-century P.Oxy. 3 preserves fragments of Mark 10:50–51 and 11:11–12. However, this document is not in fact a papyrus but a piece of vellum from an old codex (now assigned the number 069). Among the early codices (i.e., fourth and fifth centuries) Mark is preserved in its entirety (with the exception of 16:9–20) in ℵ A B D and almost in its entirety in C and W. Other early codices preserve much smaller portions of Mark.

The listing below identifies the earliest and most important Greek witnesses to the Gospel of Mark. With the exceptions of the eighth- and ninth-century MSS L and 33, which evidently are copies of early and reliable MSS, the witnesses that are listed date from the third through the sixth centuries.

MS	CENTURY	MARKAN CONTENTS
𝔓⁴⁵	III	4:36–40; 5:15–26; 5:38–6:3; 6:16–25, 36–50; 7:3–15; 7:25–8:1; 8:10–26; 8:34–9:9; 9:18–31; 11:27–12:1; 12:5–8, 13–19, 24–28
𝔓⁸⁴	VI	2:2–5, 8–9; 6:30–31, 33–34, 36–37, 39–41
𝔓⁸⁸	IV	2:1–26
ℵ	IV	1:1–16:8
A	V	1:1–16:20
B	IV	1:1–16:8
C	V	1:17–6:31; 8:5–12:29; 13:19–16:20
D	V	1:1–16:14 (16:15–20 added later)

L	VIII	1:1–10:15; 10:30–15:1; 15:20–16:20
N	VI	5:20–7:4; 7:20–8:32; 9:1–10:43; 11:7–12:19; 14:25–15:23, 33–42
P	VI	1:2–11; 3:5–17; 14:13–24, 48–61; 15:12–37
W	V	1:1–15:12; 15:39–16:20
Σ	VI	1:1–16:13
Φ	VI	1:1–14:62
059 + 0215	IV/V	15:20–21, 26–27, 29–38
064 + 074	VI	1:11–22; 1:34–2:12; 2:21–3:3; 3:27–4:4; 5:9–20
067	VI	9:14–22; 14:58–70
069 (= P.Oxy. 3)	V	10:50–51; 11:11–12
072	V/VI	2:23–3:5
080	VI	9:14–18, 20–22; 10:23–24, 29
083 + 0112	VI/VII	13:12–14, 16–19, 21–24; 14:29–45; 15:27–16:8; short ending; 16:9–10
087	VI	12:32–37
0143	VI	8:17–18, 27–28
0184	VI	15:36–37, 40–41
0187	VI	6:30–41
0188	IV	11:11–17
0212	III	15:40, 42 (from the *Diatessaron*)
0213	V/VI	3:2–3, 5
0214	IV/V	8:33–37
0263	VI	5:26–27, 31
0274	V	6:56–7:4; 7:6–9, 13–17, 19–23, 28–29, 34–35; 8:3–4, 8–11; 9:20–22, 26–41; 9:43–10:1, 17–22
0292	VI	6:55–7:5
33	IX	1:1–9:30; 11:12–13:10; 14:60–16:20

This commentary has relied on Barbara and Kurt Aland's *Novum Testamentum Graece* (Nestle-Aland[27]), Kurt Aland's *Synopsis Quattuor Evangeliorum* and the United Bible Societies' *Greek New Testament*, third (corrected) edition (UBSGNT[3c]) and fourth revised edition (UBSGNT[4]). Frequent reference has been made to the Chester Beatty Papyrus ($\mathfrak{P}^{45}$) and to the fourth-century codices Sinaiticus (ℵ) and Vaticanus (B). These two codices have received special attention because they represent the oldest extant copies of the complete Greek text of Mark. The Greek texts edited by Souter and Westcott and Hort, which are heavily dependent on Sinaiticus and Vaticanus, have been consulted, but the facsimiles of these codices, as well as the plates of $\mathfrak{P}^{45}$, have themselves been examined throughout the writing of the commentary.

Special Note: Have Fragments of Mark Been Found at Qumran?

Bibliography

Bernardi, J. "L'Évangile de Saint Marc et la grotte 7 de Qumrân." *ETR* 47 (1972) 453–56. **Betz, O.,** and **Riesner, R.** *Jesus, Qumran and the Vatican: Clarifications.* New York: Crossroad, 1994. **Evans, C. A.** Review of *Rekindling the Word: In Search of Gospel Truth,* by C. P. Thiede. *DSD* 4 (1997) 132–35. **Fee, G. D.** "Some Dissenting Notes on 7Q5 = Mark 6:52–53." *JBL* 92 (1973) 109–12. **Fitzmyer, J. A.** *The Dead Sea Scrolls: Major Publications and Tools for Study.* SBLRBS 20. Atlanta:

Scholars Press, 1990. **Focant, C.** "Un fragment du second évangile à Qumran: 7Q5 = Mc 6,52–53?" *RTL* 16 (1985) 447–54. **Gundry, R. H.** "No *NU* in Line 2 of 7Q5: A Final Disidentification of 7Q5 with Mark 6:52–53." *JBL* 118 (1999) 698–707. **Hemer, C. J.** "New Testament Fragments at Qumran?" *TynBul* 23 (1972) 125–28. **Mayer, B.,** ed. *Christen und Christliches in Qumran?* Eichstätter Studien n.s. 32. Regensburg: Pustet, 1992. **O'Callaghan, J.** "7Q5: Nuevas consideraciones." *SPap* 16 (1977) 41–47. ———. "¿Un fragmento del Ev. de s. Marcos en el papiro 5 de la cueva 7 de Qumran?" *Arbor* 81/316 (1972) 429–31. ———. "¿Papiros neotestamentarios en la cueva 7 de Qumrân?" *Bib* 53 (1972) 91–100. ———. *Los papiros griegos de la cueva 7 de Qumrân.* BAC 353. Madrid: Editorial católica, 1974. ———. "Verso le origini del Nuovo Testamento." *CCICr* 139 (1988) 269–72. **Parker, P.** "7Q5: Enthält das Papyrusfragment 5 aus der Höhle 7 von Qumran einen Markustext?" *Erbe und Auftrag* 48 (1972) 467–69. **Pickering, S. R.,** and **Cook, R. R. E.** *Has a Greek Fragment of the Gospel of Mark Been Found at Qumran?* Papyrology and Historical Perspectives 1. Sydney: Macquarie UP, 1989. **Reicke, B.** "Fragmente neutestamentlicher Papyri bei Qumrân?" *TZ* 28 (1972) 304. **Roberts, C. H.** "On Some Presumed Papyrus Fragments of the New Testament from Qumran." *JTS* n.s. 23 (1972) 446–47. **Rohrhirsch, F.** *Markus in Qumran? Eine Auseinandersetzung mit den Argumenten für und gegen das Fragment 7Q5 mit Hilfe des methodischen Fallibilismusprinzips.* Wuppertal; Zurich: Brockhaus, 1990. ———. "Das Qumranfragment 7Q5." *NovT* 30 (1988) 97–99. **Rosenbaum, H.-U.** "Cave 7Q5! Gegen die erneute Inanspruchnahme des Qumran-Fragments 7Q5 als Bruchstück der ältesten Evangelien-Handschrift." *BZ* 31 (1987) 189–205. **Sabourin, L.** "A Fragment of Mark at Qumran." *BTB* 2 (1972) 308–12. **Stanton, G.** *Gospel Truth? New Light on Jesus and the Gospels.* Valley Forge, PA: Trinity Press International, 1995. **Thiede, C. P.** "7 Q— Eine Rückkehr zu den neutestamentlichen Papyrusfragmenten in der siebten Höhle von Qumran." *Bib* 65 (1984) 538–59. ———. *Die älteste Evangelien-Handschrift? Das Markus-Fragment von Qumran und die Anfänge der schriftlichen Überlieferung des Neuen Testaments.* Wuppertal: Brockhaus, 1986 (ET: *The Earliest Gospel Manuscript? The Qumran Fragment 7Q5 and Its Significance for New Testament Studies.* London: Paternoster, 1992). ———. *Rekindling the Word: In Search of Gospel Truth.* Valley Forge, PA: Trinity Press International, 1995. **Vardaman, J.** "The Earliest Fragments of the New Testament?" *ExpTim* 83 (1971–72) 374–76.

In a series of studies beginning in 1972 J. O'Callaghan has argued that several small fragments from cave 7 of Qumran are actually NT writings. He thinks that he has identified fragments of Mark, Acts, Romans, 1 Timothy, James, and 2 Peter. His identifications of alleged Markan fragments are as follows:

7Q5	= Mark 6:52–53
7Q6 1	= Mark 4:28
7Q7	= Mark 12:17
7Q15	= Mark 6:48

O'Callaghan's identification of 7Q5 has been accepted by Rohrhirsch (*Markus in Qumran?*), Thiede (*Bib* 65 [1984] 538–59; *Die älteste Evangelien-Handschrift?*), and others. If O'Callaghan is correct in his identifications (see esp. O'Callaghan, *Los papiros griegos,* 44–61 [on Mark 6:52–53], 61–65 [on Mark 4:28], 66–69 [on Mark 12:17], 75–76 [on Mark 6:48]), then one could argue that Markan antiquity and priority have been conclusively established. But that is not necessarily the case. At least two problems remain. First, these fragments could be nothing more than parallels, as opposed to actual portions of the Gospel of Mark. Second, the Greek fragments of Cave 7 might not have anything to do with the Dead Sea Scrolls proper. The presence of Greek papyri in one of the caves in the Dead Sea region could be owing to Christians in later centuries and not necessarily to the Jewish sect that composed, collected, and hid the scrolls found in the other caves. So even if O'Callaghan's identifications are correct, little is gained.

Although O'Callaghan has created a sensation, many scholars have expressed grave reservations about his identifications (e.g., Focant, *RTL* 16 [1985] 447–54; Pickering and Cook, *Has a Greek Fragment;* Rosenbaum, *BZ* 31 [1987] 189–205). (The bibliography above offers only a select sampling of the secondary literature.) The difficulty lies in the tiny size of these fragments. In many of the fragments only a word or two and a few letters are extant. Firm identifications at this time are impossible. Fitzmyer (*Dead Sea Scrolls,* 168) has opined that although O'Callaghan's claims cannot simply be dismissed, "it seems most likely that the frgs. 7Q3–18 are nothing more than copies of some Old Greek translation of the OT." Betz and Riesner (*Jesus, Qumran,* 114–24) have expressed a similar opinion. Stanton (*Gospel Truth?* 20–32; the title alludes to one of Thiede's books on the subject) believes the identification of 7Q5 with Mark 6:52–53 is impossible. Some members of the international team entrusted with the publication of the Dead Sea Scrolls (in Oxford's Discoveries in the Judaean Desert series) speculate that the 7Q fragments are from *1 Enoch* or related tradition (from private communication). The condition of these fragments does not permit any firm conclusions.

When Was Mark Written?

Bibliography

Comfort, P. W. *Early Manuscripts and Modern Translations of the New Testament.* Wheaton, IL: Tyndale, 1990. ———. "Exploring the Common Identification of Three New Testament Manuscripts: $\mathfrak{P}^4$, $\mathfrak{P}^{64}$ and $\mathfrak{P}^{67}$." *TynBul* 46 (1995) 43–54. **Fredriksen, P.** "Jesus and the Temple, Mark and the War." In *Society of Biblical Literature 1990 Seminar Papers.* Ed. D. J. Lull. SBLSP 29. Atlanta: Scholars Press, 1990. 293–310. **Head, P. M.** "The Date of the Magdalen Papyrus of Matthew (*P. Magd. Gr.* 17 = P64): A Response to C. P. Thiede." *TynBul* 46 (1995) 251–85. **Hunger, H.** "Zur Datierung des Bodmer II." *Anzeiger der phil.-hist. Klasse der Österr. Akad. der Wissenschaft* 4 (1960) 12–23. **Kim, Y. K.** "Paleographical Dating of $\mathfrak{P}^{46}$ to the Later First Century." *Bib* 69 (1988) 248–57. **Marcus, J.** "The Jewish War and the *Sitz im Leben* of Mark." *JBL* 111 (1992) 441–62. **Roberts, C. H.** "An Early Papyrus of the First Gospel." *HTR* 46 (1953) 233–37. ———. *An Unpublished Fragment of the Fourth Gospel in the John Rylands Library.* Manchester: Manchester UP, 1935. **Robinson, J. A. T.** *Redating the New Testament.* London: SCM Press; Philadelphia: Westminster, 1976. **Skeat, T. C.** "The Oldest Manuscript of the Four Gospels?" *NTS* 43 (1997) 1–34. **Thiede, C. P.** "Papyrus Magdalen 17 (Gregory-Aland $\mathfrak{P}^{64}$): A Reappraisal." *ZPE* 105 (1995) 13–20 (= *TynBul* 46 [1995] 29–42). **Wenham, J.** *Redating Matthew, Mark and Luke: A Fresh Assault on the Synoptic Problem.* London: Hodder & Stoughton, 1991.

Twenty years ago J. A. T. Robinson (*Redating the New Testament*) argued that all of the NT writings were composed prior to the destruction of Jerusalem in 70 C.E. He reasoned that no NT writer could have passed over in silence such an important event. More recently J. Wenham (*Redating Matthew*), who takes early church testimony seriously, has argued that Matthew was written ca. 40, Mark ca. 45, and Luke sometime in the 50s. A major point in his argument lies in the fact that Acts ends with Paul's house imprisonment, which is to be dated ca. 62. Wenham then backtracks to the earlier Gospel of Luke, then to Mark, and then finally to Matthew, which he believes to be the oldest of the Synoptics.

Papyrologists have made important contributions to the date debate. C. H. Roberts (*An Unpublished Fragment*) and others have concluded that $\mathfrak{P}^{52}$ (= P.Rylands.Gr. 457), which consists of a single fragment of John 18, dates to ca. 125 C.E. In his recent and controversial study Thiede believes (*TynBul* 46 [1995] 39) that this date is unnecessarily late and that the famous Rylands fragment may date closer to 100 C.E. Y. K. Kim has argued that the Chester Beatty papyrus $\mathfrak{P}^{46}$, which contains fragments of Paul's letters, dates to the late first century, not to the late second. The dates of the Paulines are of no immediate relevance to the question of the date of Mark. But if Kim and Thiede are correct, we have evidence that some NT papyri may actually date to the first century. Of more relevance is the recent work of Thiede (*TynBul* 46 [1995] 29–42), who has created a sensation in his recent claim that $\mathfrak{P}^{64}$ (= P.Magdalen.Gr. 17), which consists of three small fragments of Matt 26, is also to be dated to the first century, perhaps as early as 70. This means that the first edition of Matthew was in all probability published several years earlier. Initial reaction to Thiede's contention has been mixed. In public lectures and the popular press, some scholars, such as G. N. Stanton and J. N. Birdsall, have expressed skepticism. Thiede's argument lies in the observation that the style of writing of $\mathfrak{P}^{64}$ and $\mathfrak{P}^{52}$ corresponds quite closely to that found in papyri and scrolls (such as 8ḤevXIIgr) that date to the first half of the first century C.E. But Head (*TynBul* 46 [1995] 251–85) has recently replied that the correspondence between $\mathfrak{P}^{64}$ and early papyri is not as close as Thiede has contended. He concludes that the Magdalen Papyrus probably dates toward the end of the second century. In another recent study, Skeat (*NTS* 43 [1997] 1–34) also dates $\mathfrak{P}^{64}$ to the second century. The dating of the papyri, therefore, offers no real help in dating the composition of the Gospel of Mark.

In my view Mark was probably written during the first great war with Rome (as has also been concluded by Guelich, xxxi–xxxii). If it had been written after the war and after the destruction of Jerusalem and the temple (as has recently been argued by Marcus, *JBL* 111 [1992] 441–62), one would have expected clearer allusions to these events. Of course, we do have a prediction of the temple's destruction (Mark 13:2), but it is far from clear that this is a *vaticinium ex eventu*. Hagner's point (*Matthew*, lxxiii–lxxv) about the strangeness of Matthew's concern for temple activities (e.g., 5:23–24; 17:24–27; 23:16–22), if the temple was no longer standing, is well taken. He concludes that not only was Mark written before 70 but that Matthew was too. With regard to Luke, Nolland (*Luke* 1:xxxix) is less certain. He thinks that Luke was probably written sometime between the late sixties and the late seventies.

Although Wenham's early date, briefly mentioned above, should not be dismissed out of hand, the prominence given to Jesus' various predictions of the siege of Jerusalem and of the destruction of Jerusalem throughout the Synoptics suggests that the evangelists were writing in an era of impending or outright war. They chose to emphasize Jesus' prophetic warnings because their fulfillment was sensed to be at hand. The late sixties seem to be the most prudent position.

Genre of Mark

Bibliography

Aune, D. E. "The Gospels as Hellenistic Biography." *Mosaic* 20 (1987) 1–10. ———. *The New Testament in Its Literary Environment.* Philadelphia: Westminster, 1988. ———. "The Problem of the Genre of the Gospels: A Critique of C. H. Talbert's *What Is a Gospel?*" In *Studies of History and Tradition.* Ed. R. T. France and D. Wenham. Gospel Perspectives 2. Sheffield: JSOT, 1981. 9–60. ———. *Prophecy in Early Christianity and the Ancient Mediterranean World.* Grand Rapids, MI: Eerdmans, 1983. **Baird, J. A.** *A Comparative Analysis of the Gospel Genre: The Synoptic Mode and Its Uniqueness.* Studies in the Bible and Early Christianity 24. Lewiston, NY: Mellen, 1991. **Berger, K.** "Hellenistische Gattungen im Neuen Testament." *ANRW* 2.25.2 (1984) 1231–45. **Boring, M. E.** "Christian Prophecy and the Sayings of Jesus: The State of the Question." *NTS* 29 (1983) 104–12. ———. *The Continuing Voice of Jesus: Christian Prophecy and the Gospel Tradition.* Louisville: Westminster John Knox, 1991. ———. *Sayings of the Risen Jesus: Christian Prophecy in the Synoptic Tradition.* SNTSMS 46. Cambridge: Cambridge UP, 1982. **Burridge, R. A.** *What Are the Gospels? A Comparison with Graeco-Roman Biography.* SNTSMS 70. Cambridge: Cambridge UP, 1992. **Cancik, H.** "Die Gattung Evangelium." In *Markus-Philologie: Historische, literargeschichtliche und stilistische Untersuchungen zum zweiten Evangelium.* Ed. H. Cancik. WUNT 33. Tübingen: Mohr-Siebeck, 1984. 85–113. **Chapman, D. W.** *The Orphan Gospel.* Biblical Seminar 16. Sheffield: JSOT, 1992. **Collins, A. Y.** *Is Mark's Gospel a Life of Jesus? The Question of Genre.* The Père Marquette Lecture in Theology 1990. Milwaukee: Marquette University Press, 1990 (repr. in A. Y. Collins. *The Beginning of the Gospel.* 1–38). **Crossan, J. D.** "Empty Tomb and Absent Lord." In *The Passion in Mark.* Ed. W. Kelber. 135–52. **Dihle, A.** "Die Evangelien und die biographische Tradition der Antike." *ZTK* 80 (1983) 33–49. ———. "The Gospels and Greek Biography." In *The Gospel and the Gospels.* Ed. P. Stuhlmacher. Tr. J. Vriend. Grand Rapids, MI: Eerdmans, 1991. 361–86. **Dormeyer, D.** *Evangelium als literarische und theologische Gattung.* Darmstadt: Wissenschaftliche Buchgesellschaft, 1989. **Downing, F. G.** "Contemporary Analogies to the Gospel and Acts: 'Genres' or 'Motifs'?" In *Synoptic Studies: The Ampleforth Conferences of 1982 and 1983.* Ed. C. M. Tuckett. JSNTSup 7. Sheffield: JSOT, 1984. 51–65. **Drury, J.** "What Are the Gospels?" *ExpTim* 87 (1975–76) 324–28. **Evans, C. A.** "The Hermeneutics of Mark and John: On the Theology of the Canonical Gospel." *Bib* 64 (1983) 153–72. ———. "Jesus in Gnostic Literature." *Bib* 62 (1981) 406–12. **Frankemölle, H.** *Evangelium—Begriff und Gattung: Ein Forschungsbericht.* Stuttgart: Katholisches Bibelwerk, 1988. **Guelich, R. A.** "The Gospel Genre." In *The Gospel and the Gospels.* Ed. P. Stuhlmacher. Grand Rapids, MI: Eerdmans, 1991. 173–208. **Gundry, R. H.** "Recent Investigations into the Literary Genre 'Gospel.'" In *New Dimensions in New Testament Study.* Ed. R. N. Longenecker and M. C. Tenney. Grand Rapids, MI: Zondervan, 1974. 97–114. **Hahn, F.** "Einige Überlegungen zu gegenwärtigen Aufgaben der Markusinterpretation." In *Der Erzähler des Evangeliums: Methodische Neuansätze in der Markusforschung.* Ed. F. Hahn. SBS 118–19. Stuttgart: Katholisches Bibelwerk, 1985. 171–97. **Halverson, J.** "Oral and Written Gospel: A Critique of Werner Kelber." *NTS* 40 (1994) 180–95. **Hurtado, L. W.** "Greco-Roman Textuality and the Gospel of Mark: A Critical Assessment of Werner Kelber's *The Oral and Written Gospel.*" *BBR* 7 (1997) 91–106. **Kee, H. C.** *Community of the New Age.* **Kelber, W. H.** *The Oral and Written Gospel.* Philadelphia: Fortress, 1983. **Marcus, J.** *The Way of the Lord: Christological Exegesis of the Old Testament in the Gospel of Mark.* Louisville: Westminster John Knox, 1992. **Matera, F. J.** *What Are They Saying about Mark?* New York: Paulist, 1987. 75–85. **Perrin, N.** "The Literary Gattung 'Gospel'—Some Observations." *ExpTim* 82 (1970) 4–7. **Robbins, V. K.** "Mark as Genre." In *Society of Biblical Literature 1980 Seminar Papers.* Ed. P. J. Achtemeier. SBLSP 19. Chico, CA: Scholars Press, 1980. 371–99. **Robinson, J. M.** "The Literary Composition of Mark." In *Évangile.* Ed. M. Sabbe. 11–19. ———. "On the *Gattung* of

Mark (and John)." In *Jesus and Man's Hope*. Ed. D. G. Buttrick and J. M. Bald. 2 vols. Pittsburgh: Pittsburgh Theological Seminary, 1970. 1:99–129. **Shuler, P. L.** *A Genre for the Gospels: The Biographical Character of Matthew*. Philadelphia: Fortress, 1982. **Talbert, C. H.** "Once Again: Gospel Genre." *Semeia* 43 (1988) 53–73. ———. *What Is a Gospel? The Genre of the Canonical Gospels*. Philadelphia: Fortress, 1977. **Tolbert, M. A.** *Sowing the Gospel: Mark's World in Literary-Historical Perspective*. Minneapolis: Fortress, 1989. 48–79. **Votaw, C. W.** *The Gospels and Contemporary Biographies in the Greco-Roman World*. FBBS 27. Philadelphia: Fortress, 1970. **Wills, L. M.** *The Quest of the Historical Gospel: Mark, John and the Origins of the Gospel Genre*. London; New York: Routledge, 1997.

The question of the genre of Mark has led to many proposals. (Among the items listed in the bibliography above, see especially the studies by Collins, "Is Mark's Gospel a Life of Jesus?" 1–38; Guelich, "Gospel Genre"; Kee, *Community*, 17–30; Talbert, *What Is a Gospel?*; and Votaw, *Gospels*.) Because no Jewish or Greco-Roman genre exactly matches Mark, some have concluded, and I think rightly, that the earliest Gospel is in fact a literary *novum* (so Bultmann, *History*, 374; Guelich, xix–xxii). Nevertheless, Mark does approximate the genre of biography of late antiquity. Many of its pericopes resemble in form and content pericopes found in the OT (e.g., the patriarchs, Moses, David, Elijah, and Elisha). Some scholars have found features characteristic of Greco-Roman biography as well. But the parallels are only partial (as rightly emphasized by Guelich, xxi; and Gundry, 1050). Mark's Gospel is basically an instance of biography, but biography exhibiting many unusual and unique features. Guelich (xxi) is correct, furthermore, when he says that "'Gospel' as a literary designation had more to do with the content ('good news') than the form of the document (e.g., biography or revelatory discourse)." Also important is Collins's suggestion that Mark is a blend of historical writing and apocalyptic (Collins, "Is Mark's Gospel a Life of Jesus?" 24–36 [p. 27: "an apocalyptic historical monograph"]; cf. Wills, *Quest of the Historical Gospels*, 10–12).

In Mark the word *gospel* (εὐαγγέλιον) refers to the message that Jesus proclaimed (Mark 1:14–15; 8:35; 10:29; 13:10; 14:9), not to a literary genre. It follows then that the opening words, "the beginning of the gospel of Jesus Christ" (Mark 1:1), must also refer to the message. The meaning of the word itself is probably related to the "good news" promised in Isa 40:9, 52:7, and 61:1 (see Marcus, *Way of the Lord*, 18–20). The latter passage is alluded to in Q material that in all probability derives from Jesus (Matt 11:4–6 = Luke 7:22–23; cf. Luke 4:18–19). What the word εὐαγγέλιον may have conjured up in the mind of the average inhabitant of the first-century Roman Empire will be addressed below.

Why does Mark assert that the beginning (ἀρχή) of the gospel is the preaching of John the Baptizer? Or, to put the question in a more theological light, why does the gospel begin with Jesus' public ministry? Gundry (1049–51), apparently reacting to the Bultmannian notion that the Gospel of Mark constitutes a conflation of Hellenistic ideas of heavenly redeemers and divine men with the Palestinian dominical tradition (see Bultmann, *History*, 240–41, 368–74), thinks that it is unwarranted to "credit Mark with expanding the meaning of 'gospel' to include the early ministry of Jesus in addition to the Cross and the Resurrection" (1050). Against Bultmann and his followers Gundry's objection is surely valid. But there may be an element of truth to the notion that εὐαγγέλιον has been expanded to include the pre-Easter ministry. Gundry cites Acts 2:22 and 10:36–39a as evidence that in early preaching there was interest in the earthly ministry of Jesus. But the brevity of these materials may indicate that Jesus' earthly teachings were of little consequence after all. The bulk of the Pentecost sermon is given over to the resurrection of Jesus and the scriptural apologetic that goes with it (Acts 2:23–36). In Acts 10:38–39a we find another very brief summary of Jesus' ministry. Of particular interest is the statement in Acts 2:36 that "God has made him both Lord and Christ, this Jesus whom you crucified." The implication is that it is *in the resurrection,* not at the commencement of or during his earthly ministry, that Jesus was made (or recognized as) Lord and Christ. Paul seems to say something similar in Rom 1:4 when he declares that Jesus was "designated Son of God in power according to the Spirit of holiness by his resurrection from the dead, Jesus Christ our Lord." In his summary of the gospel to the Corinthians Paul begins with Jesus' death, not with his ministry (1 Cor 15:3–5).

Robinson ("Composition of Mark"; "On the *Gattung* of Mark"), perhaps following the lead of Marxsen (*Mark the Evangelist,* 117–50), has suggested that the Markan evangelist began his narrative with the public ministry of Jesus as a corrective to a growing tendency to minimize, perhaps even ignore, the Jesus tradition in favor of the Easter proclamation. Robinson conjectures that the early church attached great importance to the risen Christ and his words but less importance to the words of the earthly, pre-Easter Jesus. Robinson thinks that the recently published gnostic finds from Nag Hammadi clarify this question and support his theory. The evidence that these writings offer may, however, be interpreted quite differently (cf. Evans, *Bib* 62 [1981] 402–12).

Admittedly, it does appear that Mark has deliberately widened the gospel message to include the public ministry of Jesus and to show that the gospel proclaimed by Christians, following Easter, was in continuity with the proclamation of Jesus himself prior to his passion. But did Mark do this, as Robinson thinks, in response to a tendency that was moving on a gnosticizing trajectory? Or, quite apart from the issue of Gnosticism and questionable assumptions that often attend employment of gnostic sources (such as dating gnosticizing tendencies to the middle of the first century, or even earlier), was Mark attempting to validate the earthly life of Jesus in terms of the early church's kerygma?

An apologetic thrust is probable, but it is driven by concerns considerably different from those proposed by Robinson. The evangelist is not hoping to show that Jesus' life and teaching were of kerygmatic significance, in the face of incipient gnosticizing interested only in the esoteric revelations of the resurrected and exalted Christ. The evangelist is attempting to convince Christians in a Roman society that Jesus, rejected by the religious authorities of Jerusalem and executed by Pilate, was nevertheless Israel's Messiah and the world's Savior. The Markan evangelist must begin with the preaching of John the Baptist in order to clarify Jesus' relationship to this popular prophet; and he must begin with Jesus' public ministry in Galilee in order to demonstrate that Jesus was indeed the "Son of God." Jesus was declared as such from the moment his earthly ministry commenced (1:11) and at the moment it ended in death on the cross (15:39). In relating the recognition of the Roman centurion that Jesus was the "Son of God" in his death, Mark has shown that Jesus was truly the Messiah and Son of God (1:1) and that his execution was not defeat but victory.

A different approach to this problem has been proposed by Kelber (*Oral and Written Gospel*). Accepting Boring's conclusion (*Sayings of the Risen Jesus*) that much of the synoptic dominical tradition arose through Christian prophecy, Kelber thinks that the Markan Gospel represents an attempt to check the growing Q tradition, a tradition that the evangelist views with misgivings. This Q tradition, he thinks, was being expanded and advanced by a community of Christian prophets who spoke in the name of Jesus. Mark hoped to replace the prophetic "Christology of presence" with a written "Christology of absence."

But there are significant problems with the views of Boring and Kelber. Boring's claims that much of the synoptic dominical tradition originated in Christian prophecy lack adequate evidence and rest on questionable assumptions (see Aune, *Prophecy in Early Christianity*). If much of Q originated in a post-Easter setting, then why is none of it cast as post-Easter sayings? Why is *all of it* placed in a pre-Easter setting, especially if it is the words of the risen Jesus that are so highly treasured by the Q community? It is interesting in this connection to compare the Christian gnostic writings. In these writings the preferred genre is the risen Jesus who appears to his disciples (usually on a mountain). Even sayings that derive from the pre-Easter ministry often appear in these fictional post-Easter settings. It is in the post-Easter setting that the risen Jesus can disclose to his disciples new knowledge and truths that supersede what he had taught them "in the flesh." Such comparison suggests that whereas the gnostic "Gospels" and "apocalypses" contain material created or heavily edited in the post-Easter period, by contrast the Synoptic Gospels (including Q) contain pre-Easter material. Kelber's claims are equally problematic. His observation of the relative paucity of teaching material in Mark need not be explained as evidence of Mark's hostility toward Q. It could as easily be explained as evidence of Mark's lack of acquaintance with Q. Kelber's ideas of orality and the differences between oral societies and written societies are problematic at many points (see Hurtado, *BBR* 7 [1997] 91–106). And finally, his attempt to explain the Markan version of the passion as largely the creation of the evangelist is unconvincing and at certain points improbable (see Halverson, *NTS* 40 [1994] 180–95).

Theology of Mark

Bibliography

Achtemeier, P. J. "Gospel Miracle Tradition and the Divine Man." *Int* 26 (1972) 174–97. **Aune, D. E.** "The Problem of the Messianic Secret." *NovT* 11 (1969) 1–31. **Bauckham, R.** "The Son of Man: 'A Man in My Position' or 'Someone'?" *JSNT* 23 (1985) 23–33. **Best, E.** *Following Jesus: Discipleship in Mark's Gospel.* JSNTSup 4. Sheffield: JSOT, 1981. **Betz, H. D.** "Jesus as Divine Man." In *Jesus and the Historian.* FS E. C. Colwell, ed. F. T. Trotter. Philadelphia: Westminster, 1968. 114–33. **Betz, O.** "The Concept of the So-Called 'Divine Man' in Mark's Christology." In *Studies in New Testament and Early Christian Literature.* FS A. Wikgren, ed. D. E. Aune. Leiden: Brill, 1972. 229–40. ———. *Die Menschensohnworte Jesu und die Zukunftserwartung des Paulus (Daniel 7,13–14).* Vol. 2 of *Jesus und das Danielbuch.* ANTJ 6.2. Frankfurt am Main: Lang, 1985. **Bieler, L.** *Theios Aner: Das Bild des "Göttlichen Menschen" in Spätantike und Frühchristentum.* 2 vols. Vienna: Höfels, 1935–36. **Bietenhard, H.** "'Der Menschensohn'—ὁ υἱὸς τοῦ ἀνθρώπου: Sprachliche und religionsgeschichtliche Untersuchungen zu einem Begriff der synoptischen Evangelien." *ANRW* 2.25.1 (1982) 265–350. **Black, M.** "Aramaic Barnasha and the 'Son of Man.'" *ExpTim* 95 (1983–84) 200–206. ———. "Jesus and the 'Son of Man.'" *JSNT* 1 (1978) 4–18. ———. "The Messianism of the Parables of Enoch: Their Date and Contributions to Christological Origins." In *The Messiah: Developments in Earliest Judaism and Christianity.* Ed. J.

H. Charlesworth. Minneapolis: Fortress, 1992. 145–68. **Blackburn, B.** "Miracle Working ΘΕΙΟΙ ΑΝΔΡΕΣ in Hellenism (and Hellenistic Judaism)." In *The Miracles of Jesus*. Ed. D. Wenham and C. L. Blomberg. Gospel Perspectives 6. Sheffield: JSOT, 1986. 185–218. ————. θεῖος ἀνήρ *and the Markan Miracle Traditions*. WUNT 2.40. Tübingen: Mohr-Siebeck, 1991. **Bornkamm, G.** *Jesus of Nazareth*. Tr. I. McLuskey and F. McLuskey, with J. M. Robinson. New York: Harper & Row, 1960. **Borsch, F. H.** "Further Reflections on 'The Son of Man': The Origins and Development of the Title." In *The Messiah: Developments in Earliest Judaism and Christianity*. Ed. J. H. Charlesworth. Minneapolis: Fortress, 1992. 130–44. **Bowker, J.** "The Son of Man." *JTS* n.s. 28 (1977) 19–48. **Broadhead, E. K.** *Teaching with Authority: Miracles and Christology in the Gospel of Mark*. JSNTSup 74. Sheffield: JSOT, 1992. **Burkett, D.** *The Son of Man in the Gospel of John*. JSNTSup 56. Sheffield: JSOT, 1991. **Caragounis, C. C.** *The Son of Man: Vision and Interpretation*. WUNT 38. Tübingen: Mohr-Siebeck, 1986. **Casey, P. M.** "Aramaic Idiom and Son of Man Sayings." *ExpTim* 96 (1984–85) 233–36. ————. "General, Generic, and Indefinite: The Use of the Term 'Son of Man' in Aramaic Sources and in the Teaching of Jesus." *JSNT* 29 (1987) 21–56. ————. *Son of Man: The Interpretation and Influence of Daniel 7*. London: S. P. C. K., 1979. **Chilton, B. D.** *The Isaiah Targum*. ArBib 11. Wilmington, DE: Glazier, 1987. ————. "The Son of Man: Human and Heavenly." In *The Four Gospels 1992*. FS F. Neirynck, ed. F. Van Segbroeck et al. BETL 100. Leuven: Leuven UP, 1992. 203–18. **Collins, A. Y.** "The Origins of the Designation of Jesus as 'Son of Man.'" *HTR* 80 (1987) 391–407. **Coppens, J.** "Les logia du Fils de l'Homme dans l'Évangile de Marc." In *L'Évangile selon Marc: Tradition et rédaction*. Ed. M. Sabbe. BETL 34. Leuven: Leuven UP, 1974. 487–528. **Dalman, G. H.** *The Words of Jesus*. Tr. D. M. Kay. Edinburgh: T. & T. Clark, 1902. **Donahue, J. R.** *Are You the Christ? The Trial Narrative in the Gospel of Mark*. SBLDS 10. Missoula, MT: Scholars Press, 1973. **Dunn, J. D. G.** "The Messianic Secret in Mark." *TynBul* 21 (1970) 92–117. ————. "'Son of God' as 'Son of Man' in the Dead Sea Scrolls? A Response to John Collins on 4Q246." In *The Scrolls and the Scriptures: Qumran Fifty Years After*. Ed. S. E. Porter and C. A. Evans. Roehampton Institute London Papers 3. JSPSup 26. Sheffield: Sheffield Academic Press, 1997. 198–210. **Fitzmyer, J. A.** "Another View of the 'Son of Man' Debate." *JSNT* 4 (1979) 58–68. ————. "The Contribution of Qumran Aramaic to the Study of the New Testament." In *A Wandering Aramean: Collected Aramaic Essays*. SBLMS 25. Missoula, MT: Scholars Press, 1979. 85–113. ————. *The Genesis Apocryphon of Qumran Cave I: A Commentary*. BibOr 18A. Rome: Biblical Institute, 1971. ————. "The New Testament Title 'Son of Man' Philologically Considered." In *A Wandering Aramean*. 143–60. **Fuller, R. H.** "The Son of Man: A Reconsideration." In *The Living Text*. FS E. W. Saunders, ed. D. E. Groh and R. Jewett. Lanham, MD: UP of America, 1985. 207–17. **Grimm, W.** *Jesu Einspruch gegen das Offenbarungssystem Daniels (Mt 11,25–27; Lk 17,20–21)*. Vol. 1 of *Jesus und das Danielbuch*. ANTJ 6.1. Frankfurt am Main: Lang, 1984. **Haenchen, E.** *Die Botschaft des Thomas-Evangeliums*. Berlin: Töpelmann, 1961. **Hamerton-Kelly, R. G.** "Sacred Violence and the Messiah: The Markan Passion Narrative as a Redefinition of Messianology." In *The Messiah: Developments in Earliest Judaism and Christianity*. Ed. J. H. Charlesworth. Minneapolis: Fortress, 1992. 461–93. **Hare, D. R. A.** *The Son of Man Tradition*. Minneapolis: Fortress, 1990. **Held, H. J.** "Der Christusweg und die Nachfolge der Gemeinde: Christologie und Ekklesiologie im Markusevangelium." In *Kirche*. FS G. Bornkamm, ed. D. Lührmann and G. Strecker. Tübingen: Mohr-Siebeck, 1980. 79–93. **Hengel, M.** "Christological Titles in Early Christianity." In *The Messiah: Developments in Earliest Judaism and Christianity*. Ed. J. H. Charlesworth. Minneapolis: Fortress, 1992. 425–48. ————. *Studies in Early Christology*. Edinburgh: T. & T. Clark, 1995. **Higgins, A. J. B.** *Jesus and the Son of Man*. Philadelphia: Fortress, 1964. ————. *The Son of Man in the Teaching of Jesus*. SNTSMS 39. Cambridge: Cambridge UP, 1980. **Holladay, C. H.** *Theios Aner in Hellenistic Judaism*. SBLDS 40. Missoula, MT: Scholars Press, 1977. **Hooker, M. D.** "Is the Son of Man Problem Really Insoluble?" In *Text and Interpretation: Studies in the New Testament*. FS M. Black, ed. E. Best and R. M. Wilson. Cambridge: Cambridge UP, 1979. 155–68. ————. *The Son of Man in Mark*. London: S. P. C. K., 1967. **Horbury, W.** "The Messianic Associations of 'the Son of Man.'" *JTS* n.s. 36 (1985) 34–55. **Horstmann, M.** *Studien zur markinischen*

Christologie. 2nd ed. NTAbh 6. Münster: Aschendorff, 1969. **Jeremias, J.** *New Testament Theology.* **Jonge, M. de.** *Christology in Context.* Philadelphia: Westminster, 1988. **Juel, D.** *Messiah and Temple.* ———. "The Origin of Mark's Christology." In *The Messiah: Developments in Earliest Judaism and Christianity.* Ed. J. H. Charlesworth. Minneapolis: Fortress, 1992. 449–60. **Kazmierski, C. R.** *Jesus, the Son of God: A Study of the Markan Tradition and Its Redaction by the Evangelist.* FB 33. Würzburg: Echter, 1979. **Kilgallen, J. J.** "The Messianic Secret and Mark's Purpose." *BTB* 7 (1977) 60–65. **Kim, S.** *"The 'Son of Man'" as the Son of God.* WUNT 30. Tübingen: Mohr-Siebeck, 1983. **Kingsbury, J. D.** *Christology.* ———. *Conflict in Mark.* ———. "The 'Divine Man' as the Key to Mark's Christology—The End of an Era?" *Int* 35 (1981) 243–57. **Koester, H.** "The Divine Human Being." *HTR* 78 (1985) 243–52. **Koskenniemi, E.** "Apollonius of Tyana: A Typical θεῖος ἀνήρ?" *JBL* 117 (1998) 455–67. **Leivestad, R.** "Der apokalyptische Menschensohn: Ein theologisches Phantom." *ASTI* 6 (1968) 49–105. ———. "Exit the Apocalyptic Son of Man." *NTS* 18 (1972) 243–67. ———. "Jesus—Messias—Menschensohn: Die jüdische Heilandserwartungen zur Zeit der ersten römishen Kaiser und die Frage nach dem messianischen Selbstbewusstsein Jesu." *ANRW* 2.25.1 (1982) 220–64. **Lindars, B.** *Jesus Son of Man: A Fresh Examination of the Son of Man Sayings in the Gospels.* London: S. P. C. K., 1983. ———. "Re-Enter the Apocalyptic Son of Man." *NTS* 22 (1975) 52–72. **Longenecker, R. N.** "The Messianic Secret in the Light of Recent Discoveries." *EvQ* 41 (1969) 207–15. **Luz, U.** "The Secrecy Motif and the Marcan Christology." In *The Messianic Secret.* Ed. C. M. Tuckett. 75–96. **Mack, B. L.** *Myth of Innocence.* **Marcus, J.** *The Way of the Lord: Christological Exegesis of the Old Testament in the Gospel of Mark.* Louisville: Westminster John Knox, 1992. **Martin, R. P.** *Mark: Evangelist and Theologian.* 84–162. ———. "The Theology of Mark's Gospel." *SwJT* 21 (1978) 23–36. **Moule, C. F. D.** "On Defining the Messianic Secret in Mark." In *Jesus und Paulus.* FS W. G. Kümmel, ed. E. E. Ellis and E. Grässer. Göttingen: Vandenhoeck & Ruprecht, 1975. 239–52. ———. *The Origin of Christology.* Cambridge; New York: Cambridge UP, 1977. **Müller, M.** *Der Ausdruck "Menschensohn" in den Evangelien: Voraussetzungen und Bedeutung.* ATD 17. Leiden: Brill, 1984. **Müller, U. B.** "Die christologische Absicht des Markusevangeliums und die Verklärungsgeschichte." *ZNW* 64 (1973) 159–93. ———. *Messias und Menschensohn in jüdischen Apokalypsen und in der Offenbarung des Johannes.* SNT 6. Gütersloh: Mohn, 1972. **Otto, R.** *The Kingdom of God and the Son of Man: A Study in the History of Religion.* London: Lutterworth, 1938. **Perrin, N.** "The Christology of Mark: A Study in Methodology." In *A Modern Pilgrimage in New Testament Christology.* Philadelphia: Fortress, 1974. 104–21. ———. "The Creative Use of the Son of Man Traditions by Mark." In *A Modern Pilgrimage in New Testament Christology.* Philadelphia: Fortress, 1974. 84–93. **Pesch, R.** "Anfänge des Evangeliums Jesu Christi." In *Die Zeit Jesu.* FS H. Schlier, ed. G. Bornkamm and K. Rahner. Freiburg: Herder, 1970. 108–44. ———. "Das Messiasbekenntnis des Petrus (Mk 8,27–30)." *BZ* 17 (1973) 178–95; 18 (1974) 20–31. **Räisänen, H.** *The 'Messianic Secret' in Mark's Gospel.* Studies of the New Testament and Its World. Tr. C. M. Tuckett. Edinburgh: T. & T. Clark, 1990. **Sahlin, H.** "Zum Verständnis der christologischen Anschauung des Markusevangeliums." *ST* 31 (1971) 1–19. **Schreiber, J.** "Die Christologie des Markusevangeliums." *ZTK* 58 (1961) 154–83. **Schwarz, G.** *Jesus "Der Menschensohn."* Stuttgart: Kohlhammer, 1986. **Schweizer, E.** "Menschensohn und eschatologischer Mensch im Frühjudentum." In *Jesus und der Menschensohn.* FS A. Vögtle, ed. R. Pesch. Freiburg: Herder, 1975. 100–16. ———. "The Question of the Messianic Secret in Mark." In *The Messianic Secret.* Ed. C. M. Tuckett. 65–74. ———. "Towards a Christology of Mark?" In *God's Christ and His People.* FS N. A. Dahl, ed. J. Jervell and W. A. Meeks. Oslo: Universitetsforlaget, 1977. 29–42. **Strecker, G.** "The Theory of the Messianic Secret in Mark's Gospel." In *The Messianic Secret.* Ed. C. M. Tuckett. 49–64. **Swetnam, J.** "On the Identity of Jesus." *Bib* 65 (1984) 412–16. **Tannehill, R. C.** "The Gospel of Mark as Narrative Christology." *Semeia* 16 (1979) 57–95. **Taylor, V.** "Important and Influential Foreign Books: W. Wrede's *The Messianic Secret in the Gospels.*" *ExpTim* 65 (1953–54) 246–50. ———. "The 'Son of Man' Sayings Relating to the Parousia." *ExpTim* 58 (1946–47) 12–15 (repr. in V. Taylor. *New Testament Essays.* London: Epworth, 1970. 119–26). ———. "Unsolved New Testament Problems: The Messianic Secret in Mark." *ExpTim* 59 (1948–49) 146–51. **Tiede, D. L.** *The Charismatic Figure as Miracle Worker.* SBLDS 1. Missoula, MT: SBL, 1972. **Tödt, H. E.** *The Son of Man in the Synoptic Tradition.* Tr. D. M. Barton. Philadelphia: Westminster, 1965. **Trocmé, E.** "Is There a Markan Christology?" In *Christ and Spirit in the New Testament.* FS C. F. D. Moule, ed. B. Lindars and S. S. Smalley. Cambridge: Cambridge UP, 1973. 3–13. **Tuckett, C. M.** "The Present Son of Man." *JSNT* 14 (1982) 58–81. **VanderKam, J. C.** "Righteous One, Messiah, Chosen One, and Son of Man in 1 Enoch 37–71." In *The Messiah: Developments in Earliest Judaism and Christianity.* Ed. J. H. Charlesworth. Minneapolis: Fortress, 1992. 169–91. **Vermes, G.** *Jesus the Jew.* London: Collins, 1973. ———. "The Present State of the 'Son of Man' Debate." *JJS* 29 (1978) 123–34. ———. "The 'Son of Man' Debate." *JSNT* 1 (1978) 19–32. ———. "The Use of נשא בר/בר נשא in Jewish Aramaic." In M. Black, *An Aramaic Approach.* 310–28. **Vielhauer, P.** "Erwägungen zur Christologie des Markusevangeliums." In *Zeit und Geschichte.* FS R. Bultmann, ed. E. Dinkler. Tübingen: Mohr-Siebeck, 1964. 155–69. **Walker, W. O.** "The Son of Man: Some Recent Developments." *CBQ* 45 (1983) 584–607. **Weber, R.** "Christologie und 'Messiasgeheimnis.'" *EvT* 43 (1983) 108–25. **Weeden, T. J.** "The Heresy That Necessitated Mark's Gospel." *ZNW* 59 (1968) 145–58. ———. *Mark—Traditions in Conflict.* **Weinacht, H.** *Die Menschwerdung des Sohnes Gottes im Markusevangelium: Studien zur Christologie des Markusevangeliums.* HUT 13. Tübingen: Mohr-Siebeck, 1972. **Witherington, B.** *The Christology of Jesus.* Minneapolis: Fortress, 1990. **Wrede, W.** *Messianic Secret.*

Any assessment of Mark's theology is entangled by several complicated and, in various ways, related issues. Since in all probability Mark's Gospel is the earliest of the NT and extracanonical Gospels, the appearance in Mark of certain features, such as the so-called messianic secret and the hotly debated "son of man" material, requires explanation. The questions naturally arise, Did the Markan evangelist or his community create the secrecy idea or the "son of man" sayings? And, if he or his community did, what purpose(s) were they to serve? The debate surrounding the "divine man" of Greco-Roman traditions also requires investigation. Was there such a concept, and, if so, is Mark's Christology in any significant way shaped by it?

1. Messianic secret. The messianic secret became an item of scholarly discussion following the publication in 1901 of W. Wrede's *Das Messiasgeheimnis in den Evangelien* (ET: *The Messianic Secret*), a book that was mostly concerned with Mark's theology. Wrede believed that this motif dominated the whole of Mark's presentation. The secrecy theme, as Wrede understood it, manifests itself in Jesus' prohibitions against making him known (e.g., 1:25, 34; 3:12; 5:43; 7:36; 8:26, 30; 9:9), in the disciples' failure to understand Jesus' teaching (e.g., 4:40–41; 6:52; 7:17–18; 8:14–21), and in the presentation of Jesus' teaching (such as the parables) as enigmatic and mysterious (e.g., 4:10–13, 33–34). Wrede concluded that this secrecy theme had been developed to explain why prior to the crucifixion no one, not even his disciples, had thought of Jesus in messianic terms. The belief that Jesus was the Messiah was a result of Easter faith (cf. Acts 2:36; Rom 1:4), Wrede averred, not of his pre-Easter teachings. Nevertheless, Easter faith increasingly led early Christians to believe that the Jesus who was now Messiah by virtue of his resurrection must have always been Messiah.

Wrede's stunning hypothesis has had a lasting influence in Markan studies. Major German form critics, such as Bultmann and Dibelius, adopted it in their respective interpretations of the formation of the Synoptic tradition. Though disagreeing at different points, over the years many other scholars have agreed with Wrede that the messianic secret was the key against which the theology of the

Markan evangelist should be understood. Characteristic of the thinking of Bultmann's pupils is the following statement by Bornkamm: ". . . behind the doctrinal teaching concerning the Messianic secret there still dimly emerges the fact that Jesus' history was originally a non-Messianic history, which was portrayed in the light of the Messianic faith of the Church only after Easter" (*Jesus,* 172).

In recent years, however, a new consensus has emerged that is on the whole critical of Wrede's arguments (cf. Aune, *NovT* 11 [1969] 1–31; Dunn, *TynBul* 21 [1970] 92–117; Gundry, 1; Kingsbury, *Christology,* 13–23; Luz, "Secrecy Motif," 75–96; Martin, *Mark: Evangelist and Theologian,* 91–106; Räisänen, *The 'Messianic Secret,'* 242–58; Trocmé, "Markan Christology," 3–13; Weeden, *ZNW* 59 [1968]145–58). Although some components of the secrecy theme may actually derive from Jesus himself (as argued by Aune, *NovT* 11 [1969]30–31; Taylor, passim), most agree that the Markan evangelist himself contributed to the theme in important ways in order to advance his theology. Recently Kingsbury has argued that the secrecy theme has less to do with the more general question of Jesus' messiahship than it has to do with the more specific question of Jesus' divine sonship (Kingsbury, *Christology,* 14–21; cf Haenchen, *Die Botschaft,* 133; Luz, "Secrecy Motif," 85–86; Martin, *Mark: Evangelist and Theologian,* 104; Moule, "Messianic Secret," 242–43; Vielhauer, "Erwägungen," 157–59). He contends that "Mark guides the reader through a progressive unveiling of Jesus' identity" (*Christology,* 20). Kingsbury's analysis is probably correct (cf. Kingsbury, *Christology,* 140–55; Martin, *Mark: Evangelist and Theologian,* 105), as can be seen by a brief overview of key passages. In the opening verse of Mark's Gospel, Jesus is identified as "the Christ, the Son of God" (1:1). The y voice at the baptism and transfiguration confirms Jesus as God's Son (1:11; 9:7). The parable of the Wicked Vineyard Tenants hints of Jesus' sonship (12:6). Even as God's Son, Jesus does not know the time of the eschaton (13:32). Jesus openly affirms the question of the high priest, "Are you the Christ, the Son of the Blessed?" (14:61–62). And finally, the centurion recognizes Jesus as "Son of God" (15:39).

Mark's secrecy motif evidently serves what may be described as a catechetical function. The evangelist leads his readers/hearers to consider who Jesus is. The evangelist identifies him initially: Jesus is the Christ and Son of God (1:1). The Father confirms this identity at the inception of Jesus' ministry, characterized by miracles (1:11), and at the inception of the final phase of his ministry, characterized by anticipation of the passion (9:7). The demons recognize Jesus' identity with great fear (1:23–27; 3:11; 5:7–13). But people are much slower to recognize who Jesus is. Jesus' critics plot his destruction (3:1–6). His family believes him mad and seeks to restrain him (3:21–22, 32). His disciples often do not understand his teaching (4:10, 13; 6:52; 7:17–18; 8:14–21; 9:10, 32). They ask among themselves, "Who then is this?" (4:41). Midway through the story, Peter recognizes that Jesus is indeed the Christ (8:29), but evidently does not recognize the suffering dimension that is a necessary part of it (8:31–33). Jesus now begins to reveal the need for the passion and resurrection (8:31, 34–38; 9:9, 30–32; 10:32–34). There are hints in the Passion Narrative regarding Jesus' identity and authority (11:7–10, 27–33; 12:10–12, 35–37; 14:27). The titles found in Mark's incipit finally are given utterance by the high priest, Jesus' principal antagonist: "Are you the Christ, the Son of the Blessed?" (14:61). Jesus answers unequivocally: "I am" (14:62). Although the high priest and his priestly colleagues reject Jesus' claim (14:63–64; 15:29–32), the Roman centurion, impressed by the manner of Jesus' death, recognizes Jesus as "Son of God" (15:39). In essence, Mark has tried to convince his readers that in his death Jesus' divine sonship (which includes messiahship) has been confirmed. He has not been defeated by mighty Rome; on the contrary, mighty Rome has recognized his divinity in the very manner of his death.

2. *Divine-man Christology.* If the focus of Mark's Christology has to do with Jesus' divine sonship, against what background should such a theology be seen? Throughout most of this century this question has been answered by appealing to Greco-Roman traditions. One very popular explanation appeals to the concept of the "divine man," or θεῖος ἀνήρ, as it would appear in Greek. Several scholars since Wrede have proposed that the early church interpreted Jesus in terms of this Hellenistic concept (see esp. the highly influential Bieler, *Theios Aner*). Betz defines the "divine man": "Only the Divine Man is man in the full sense; then his humanity becomes the epiphany of the divine. He is exceptionally gifted and extraordinary in every respect. He is in command both of a higher, revelational wisdom and of the divine power (δύναμις) to do miracles. . . . Chronologically, we can detect the Divine Man Christology at the earliest in the pre-Synoptic narrative materials, especially in the various kinds of legends and miracle stories" ("Divine Man," 116–17). Betz ("Divine Man," 117–19) then lists virtually every miracle that is narrated in Mark, along with the various titles with which Jesus is addressed (e.g., "Son of David," "Son of the Most High," "Holy One of God," "Lord," "Master").

Early on, some scholars thought that the evangelists adopted this category in a positive fashion. Later, other scholars became convinced that θεῖος ἀνήρ Christology had come to be viewed by the Markan evangelist as a heresy that needed to be opposed (so Weeden and others). The "Son of God" title was part of this heresy. Perrin suggested that Mark attempted to displace "Son of God" with "Son of Man" (Perrin, "The Creative Use of the Son of Man Traditions by Mark").

But there are many problems with this line of reasoning. For one, there was no clearly defined θεῖος ἀνήρ concept in the Greco-Roman world. Moreover, it is not at all clear that the Christology of the Synoptic tradition had its origin outside of the Jewish-Palestinian environment. References to "the Son of God" and "Son of the Most High"—the very designations for Jesus in the Gospel of Mark—in 4Q246 suggest that such titles were very much at home in first-century Palestinian Judaism (see Fitzmyer, "Contribution of Qumran Aramaic," 102–7; S. Kim, *"The 'Son of Man'" as the Son of God*). The need to find an extraneous source for these titles, such as in Greco-Roman mythology, becomes superfluous. Moreover, Holladay (*Theios Aner in Hellenistic Judaism*) has argued convincingly that there is no evidence of a tendency in early Judaism to divinize its heroes or to exaggerate their miraculous deeds (see more recently, Koskenniemi, *JBL* 117 [1998] 455–67). The θεῖος ἀνήρ concept, therefore, probably has little to offer to analysis of Markan Christology.

3. *Son of God.* Perrin and others have argued that "Son of God" was the preferred title for Jesus among early Christians whose Christology was informed by θεῖος ἀνήρ ideas. It is further argued that the Markan evangelist, who disliked this title but could not discard it given its popularity in Christian circles, redefined Jesus the "Son of God" in terms of Jesus the "Son of Man" (see discussion below). Unable to deny the miracle stories, which the proponents of the false Christology empha-

sized, the Markan evangelist placed them into a new context. The miracles create excitement and prompt Peter to confess Jesus as the Christ, but they fail to reveal to Peter and the disciples the need for the passion. The passion, highlighted by predictions of Jesus the "Son of Man's" coming suffering, was intended to correct this Christology.

But such an interpretation is questionable. Far from viewing "Son of God" as a false christological title, it seems to be Mark's preferred title. Perrin's interpretation raises many questions. Did the evangelist use it in Mark 1:1 as a concession to his opponents, as a way to persuade them to hear him out? Why would the evangelist introduce his entire narrative this way, which by doing so would only support those whom he hoped to correct? Why would the evangelist have the heavenly voice declare that Jesus is God's Son (Mark 1:11)? In this case it is God himself who confirms the title "Son of God." Would Mark concede this much to a Christology that he regarded as false? If "Son of God" is the confession of the false Christology, why does the Roman centurion employ it (Mark 15:39)? Why not have the centurion say, following Perrin's line of reasoning, "Truly this man was the Son of Man!"? It is hard to believe that Mark is criticizing the title when he identifies Jesus as the Son of God (1:1) and then at the end of his narrative has Jesus say "yes" to the high priest's question, "Are you the Son of the Blessed?" (14:61–62) and has the Roman centurion confess the same thing (15:39). And, in between these declarations, the supernatural world bears repeated witness to the divine sonship of Jesus (1:11, 24; 3:11; 5:7; 9:7). The contents of Mark simply do not support Perrin's interpretation. The title "Son of God," therefore, seems to represent the principal element of the evangelist's Christology.

4. Son of man. The enigmatic expression ὁ υἱὸς τοῦ ἀνθρώπου, "the son of man," has often occupied a prominent place in discussions of the historical Jesus and the Christologies of the NT Gospels. For this reason it will not be possible to deal with this expression in Mark apart from consideration of the problem as it touches upon these other areas. The following paragraphs will attempt to identify the most important features of this protracted and often convoluted discussion and what, in my judgment, are the most plausible results (for a full and very helpful assessment, see Hare, *The Son of Man Tradition*).

The basic problem that has hampered our understanding of the meaning of "the son of man" in the Gospels is the common assumption and frequent assertion that this epithet is a title with technical meaning, in reference to some sort of messianic apocalyptic figure. The data, however, suggest that this is not the meaning or function of this expression in the Gospels or in any early Jewish literature (though see below). To use Mark as an example, not once does "son of man" appear as a christological confession. The demons say, "You are the holy one of God" (1:24; 3:11), not "You are the Son of Man." When asked who Jesus is, Peter declares, "You are the Christ" (8:29). The blind man cries out to Jesus, "Son of David" (10:47). Jesus himself refers to the opinion that "the Messiah is the Son of David" (12:35). Jesus warns his disciples of false christs and false prophets (13:22), but never warns them of the advent of false sons of man. When Jesus dies, the centurion exclaims, "Truly this man was the Son of God" (15:39). Even in the answer to the high priest's question, "Are you the Christ, the Son of the Blessed?" (14:61), Jesus' reference to "son of man" (14:62) is not part of his self-definition.

He answers "yes" to the question, i.e., yes, he is the Christ and Son of God. His further answer asserts that Caiaphas and company will see "the son of man" (i.e., himself) seated at the right hand of God, coming with the clouds. Here, "son of man," even as an allusion to Dan 7, does not seem to have a titular meaning. "Christ" and "Son of God" are the only titles in the exchange between Caiaphas and Jesus. In other words, nowhere in Mark does someone in reference to Jesus confess, "You are the Son of Man." Of great importance also is the fact that Mark's incipit (i.e., opening line or title) reads, "The beginning of the good news of Jesus Christ, the Son of God" (1:1), not "the good news of Jesus Christ, the Son of Man." Moreover, if Mark is attempting to keep Jesus' messiahship secret, then how are we to explain Jesus' repeated and often public references to himself as "son of man"? If this is a messianic title, and Jesus is trying to keep his messianic identity secret, then why does he refer to himself as "son of man" in public and often in the presence of his enemies? (Surely it is gratuitous to claim, as Räisänen does [*"Messianic Secret,"* 224–28], that the evangelist is being inconsistent. See Kingsbury, *Christology,* 11–13.) When Peter confesses Jesus as Christ, Jesus charges him to tell no one (8:30). But nowhere is there an indication that Jesus tried to keep secret his identity as "son of man." This is indeed strange if, as some have assumed, "son of man" was a well-known title of the Messiah or some other apocalyptic figure. The absence, moreover, of a titular function of "son of man" in other early Jewish literature, including *1 Enoch* 37–71 and 4 Ezra 13 where the expression does occur, serves only to undermine further the assumption that this expression is technical or titular.

For these reasons many scholars have rightly sought after other explanations of the meaning of this expression. A century ago G. H. Dalman (*Words of Jesus,* 234–67) argued that the Hebrew (*ben ʾādām* or *ben ʾĕnôš*) and Aramaic (*bar nāš, bar nāšāʾ, bar ʾĕnôš, bar ʾenāš,* or *bar ʾĕnāšā*) terms "son of man" were generic, meaning "man" or "mankind" (or "humankind," to use inclusive language). There is evidence for the generic usage of this expression in Aramaic, as well as in Hebrew (cf. Ezek 2:1, 3, 6, 8 passim), prior to the Christian period. The plural *bĕnê ʾănāšā,* "sons of men," occurs in Dan 2:38; 5:21, while the singular, and disputed, *kĕbar ʾĕnāš,* "like a son of man," occurs in Dan 7:13. The plurals are clearly generic, while the singular is probably also. Two occurrences of the generic singular have been found at Qumran: "I shall make your descendants as numerous as the dust of the earth which no man [lit. "no son of man"] can number" (1QapGen 21:13; Fitzmyer, *Genesis Apocryphon,* 68–69, 151); "[For a man like] you (is) your sin, and for humankind [lit. "son of man"] (is) your righteousness" (11QtgJob 26:2–3 [= MT Job 35:8]; Fitzmyer, "Qumran Aramaic," 95–96). The generic function here is obvious.

The discussion became confused somewhat when Vermes (*Jesus the Jew,* 160–91; *JSNT* 1 [1978] 19–32; "Use of בר נשא/בר נש," 310–28), relying on sources that postdate the NT by two or three centuries or more, tried to show that the Aramaic terminology was often a circumlocution for the personal pronoun *I* or *me.* Although the circumlocutionary function may work in one or two instances (see the saying attributed to Rabbi Haggai in *Num. Rab.* 19.3 [on Num 19:2]; Vermes, "Use of בר נשא/בר נש," 321), the generic function still seems the best interpretation in the majority of occurrences. Even in most of the texts cited by Vermes, which he presents as examples of the circumlocutionary function of *bar nāšāʾ,* the generic function makes better sense: "It is said that Rabbi was buried wrapped in a single

sheet because, he said, 'It is not as a man [*bar nāšāʾ*] goes that he will come again.'
But the rabbis say, As a man [*bar nāšāʾ*] goes, so will he come again" (*y. Ketub.* 12.3;
Vermes, "Use of בר נשא/בר נש," 323). Surely *bar nāšāʾ* here refers to "man" (cf. J.
Neusner's tr. in *TLI* 22:345). Rabbi's generic reference, of course, includes himself.
The same seems to be the case in this example: "When Rabbi Hiyya bar Adda died,
son of the sister of Bar Kappara, Rabbi Levi received his valuables. This was because
his teacher used to say, 'The disciple of a man [*bar nāšāʾ*] is as dear to him as his son'"
(*y. Ber.* 2.7; Vermes, "Use of בר נשא/בר נש," 323). Again, it seems best to translate *bar
nāšāʾ* in a generic sense, and not as a circumlocution for *I* (cf. T. Zahavy's tr. in *TLI*
1:102). Rabbi Hiyya bar Adda taught a *principle*, viz., that a man's disciple was as dear
as a son. This should be true for all teachers, not just for Rabbi Hiyya. In other
words, Rabbi Hiyya has not referred to himself ("My disciple is as dear to me as my
son") but has made a general statement. The principle of the statement applies to
the rabbi but does not specifically refer to him. Finally Rabbi Simeon ben Yohai's
statement, in response to his observation of divine concern for a bird, provides yet
another example of the generic function of *bar nāšāʾ*: "He then said, 'Not even a
bird perishes without the will of heaven. How much less a man [*bar nāšāʾ*]'" (*y. Šeb.*
9.1; Vermes, "Use of בר נשא/בר נש," 326). Vermes's circumlocutionary interpretation
has been rightly and vigorously challenged by Fitzmyer (*JSNT* 4 [1979] 58–68; "'Son
of Man' Philologically Considered," 143–60), Chilton ("The Son of Man," 203–18),
and others (e.g., Casey, *ExpTim* 96 [1984–85] 233–36; id., *JSNT* 29 [1987] 21–56).

"Son of man" appears to function in Mark in this same basic generic sense. There
is no indication that the Markan evangelist, or his tradition, employed "son of man"
as a messianic or apocalyptic title of Jesus (Moule, *Origin of Christology*, 11–22;
Kingsbury, *Christology*, 157–76; Hare, *Son of Man*, 183–211; Hengel, *Early Christology*,
104–8). At most, "son of man" is understood as a specific reference to Jesus. While
the function of the "son of man" references in Luke-Acts appears to be about the
same (Hare, *Son of Man*, 47–78), in Matthew the picture is somewhat different. In
Matthew's Gospel "son of man" appears to be an "elevated term, pointing to the
mystery of Jesus' destiny" (Hare, *Son of Man*, 181–82). But even in Matthew, "son
of man" carries with it no specific connotations. It denotes Jesus; but apart from
Jesus himself it is void of content (Hare, *Son of Man*, 113–82). In the Fourth Gospel
the expression seems to be understood as an expression of the incarnation of the
divine Logos (Hare, *Son of Man*, 79–111), possibly influenced by Prov 30:1–4
(Burkett, *Son of Man in the Gospel of John*, 51–59).

If "son of man" in Mark (and evidently in Jesus; cf. Hare, *Son of Man*, 257–82) is
generic, why is the definite article employed? In Greek the definite article can
denote a given class. One of the son-of-man sayings illustrates this point: "Foxes
have holes, and birds of the air have nests; but the son of man has nowhere to lay
his head" (Matt 8:20 = Luke 9:58). "Foxes," "birds," and "son of man" are all
preceded by the definite article. The definite articles before foxes and birds denote
these animals by class. The articles do not identify specific animals. To translate "*the*
foxes have holes, and *the* birds of the air have nests" would be incorrect. It is thus
possible that the article that governs "son of man," whose fate is cast in parallelism
antithetical to that of foxes and birds, denotes humankind as a class rather than a
specific human.

In view of the association that the Synoptic son-of-man sayings sometimes have with Dan 7 (cf. Mark 13:26 par.; 14:62; Matt 19:28 par.), it is also possible that the definite article does indeed refer to a specific "son of man," viz., the "son of man" described in Dan 7. Moule (*Origin of Christology*, 12–16) and Chilton ("Son of Man," 215–18) suspect that this may very well be the case. But Hare (*Son of Man*, 278–80) assigns the association with Daniel to the early church. The point that lends weight to his view is the observation that the vast majority of the occurrences of the phrase "son of man" appears to constitute little more than modest self-reference on the part of Jesus. If Jesus had been alluding all along to Daniel's "son of man," why then does this tradition play such a small role in the dominical tradition as a whole? Hare's point is well taken; and he could be right.

But there are reasons nonetheless for viewing these sayings as fragments of authentic tradition. First, there is evidence in material that many regard as authentic where Jesus alludes to Dan 7. The promise to the disciples that someday they would sit at Jesus' table in the kingdom of God and "sit on [twelve] thrones judging the twelve tribes of Israel" (Q = Luke 22:30) is very likely based on Dan 7, where thrones are set up and the kingdom is granted to the saints. The Matthean evangelist, rightly sensing the allusion to Dan 7, added "the son of man shall sit on his glorious throne" (Matt 19:28). The disciples' request to sit on Jesus' right and left, when he comes in his "glory" (Mark 10:35–40), presupposes the same concept. This request, which results in rancor among the disciples (Mark 10:41–45), is hardly the creation of the early church. That the early church would have found such a request embarrassing is witnessed by the Matthean evangelist, who credits the request to the mother of the two disciples (Matt 20:20–21). Also against the likelihood that the church would have created such a tradition is Jesus' explicit admission that the granting of places in his kingdom was not his prerogative. This is hardly the stuff of post-Easter confession.

Second, there is evidence, as pointed out by Grimm (*Jesu Einspruch*) and Betz (*Die Menschensohnworte Jesu*), of Jesus correcting ideas apparently based on Daniel. This is evident in the tradition just noted. Jesus tells his disciples that to be great in his kingdom is to be a servant (Mark 10:42–44). (At this point I shall ignore the question of the authenticity of Mark 10:45; see *Form/Structure/Setting* there.) It is also evident when Jesus thanks God for disclosing to babes the mysteries of the kingdom, as opposed to the wise and discerning (compare Matt 11:25–27 and Luke 17:20–21 with Dan 2:20–23).

Third, it seems strange to think that the early church made use of Dan 7 to develop early Christology only to avoid exploiting it and then abandon it altogether. If the early church really was responsible for the Danielic son-of-man traditions in the Gospels, then why are they found only on the lips of Jesus (with two minor exceptions) and why do they play no role in the development of Christology anywhere else in the NT? These points are driven home by Hengel (*Early Christology*, 58–63).

These traditions offer a measure of support to the possibility that on occasion Jesus' use of "son of man" alluded to the being envisioned in Dan 7. Even on these rare occasions, "son of man" remains generic. It is not a title. But on these occasions it refers to a *specific* "son of man"—the "son of man" of Dan 7. Such specificity could account for the presence of the definite article. If Jesus did in fact allude to Daniel's "son of man," then he probably did so as part of his own messianic self-understanding. But because the epithet "son of man" could be used generically, hearers would not necessarily think of the figure in Dan 7 every time Jesus used it.

Before this part of the discussion is brought to a conclusion, it will be useful to comment on S. Kim's suggestion that "son of man" was employed by Jesus as a veiled reference to his claim to be "Son of God." The best evidence that Kim marshalls comes from Qumran and from a handful of LXX variants. According to 4Q246 (formerly 4Q243), an Aramaic fragment that has been identified as bearing a certain relationship to Daniel (and perhaps to 2 Sam 7 as well; cf. Dunn, "'Son of God' as 'Son of Man,'" 208–10), an awaited eschatological figure "shall be hailed (as) the Son of God, and they shall call him Son of the Most High. As comets (flash) to the sight, so shall be their kingdom. (For some) year[s] they shall rule upon the earth" (4Q246 2:1–3; Kim, *"Son of Man,"* 20; cf. Fitzmyer, "Qumran Aramaic," 92–93). If this figure is the "one like a son of man" of Dan 7:13, then we have evidence here of Daniel's "son of man" identified as the Son of God. Kim also points out an important variant in some MSS of the LXX and Syro-Hexapla in which the "son of man" is described as one "like the Ancient of Days" (Kim, *"Son of Man,"* 22–24). From the reading in 4Q246 and the LXX variant, Kim infers the existence of an exegetical tradition that had identified Daniel's "son of man" as the messianic Son of God. Kim's interpretation is plausible, but it is far from certain that Jesus' use of "son of man" always carried with it such a connotation. If Jesus did allude to Daniel's "son of man," and if he did regard himself as Israel's Messiah (which is probable— but according to his own understanding), then no doubt he would have found such a putative interpretive tradition perfectly acceptable (as is possibly the case in Mark 14:61–62). But on the evidence thus far adduced, it is probably not prudent to conclude that Jesus' regular use of "son of man" was a veiled reference to his messianic and divine status, except in those few instances were allusion to Dan 7 is probable.

Finally, there is a modicum of evidence that the son-of-man figure of Dan 7:13– 14 may have been understood in some Jewish circles as the Messiah, perhaps as early as the first century B.C.E. (or even earlier). Horbury (*JTS* n.s. 36 [1985] 34–55) appeals to the Similitudes of Enoch (i.e., *1 Enoch* 37–71), 4 Ezra 13 (i.e., 2 Esdras 13), and the fragments of Ezekiel the Tragedian (lines 67–89) for evidence of this view. Because the Similitudes and 4 Ezra probably date to the end of the first century C.E., scholars have been unwilling to argue that the messianic understanding of Daniel's "son of man" predates the time of Jesus. But Horbury argues that Ezekiel the Tragedian understands Daniel's son of man in this sense, and Ezekiel's work dates to the end of the second century B.C.E. The pertinent lines read, with Moses describing a dream to his father-in-law:

> On Sinai's peak I saw what seemed a throne
> so great in size it touched the clouds of heaven.
> Upon it sat a man of noble mien,
> becrowned, and with a scepter in one hand
> while with the other he did beckon me.
> I made approach and stood before the throne.
> He handed o'er the scepter and he bade
> me mount the throne, and gave to me the crown;
> then he himself withdrew from off the throne. . . .
> Then in terror I wakened from the dream.

And his father-in-law interprets the dream as follows:

My friend, God gave you this as a sign for good.
Would I might live to see these things transpire.
For you shall cause a mighty throne to rise,
and you yourself shall rule and govern men. . . .
Things present, past, and future you shall see.
(*Ezekiel the Tragedian* 68–89; tr. R. G. Robertson in *OTP*)

The references in the dream to "throne," "clouds of heaven," "a man," and "rule and govern" in all probability allude to Dan 7:9–14 (see also P. W. van der Horst, "Moses' Throne Vision in Ezekiel the Dramatist," *JJS* 34 [1983] 21–29). But it is not clear that the "man" (the text actually reads φῶς, "light," a poetic term for ἀνήρ, "man") in this dream and interpretation is a messianic figure. He could be, but the passage seems to suggest that Moses himself will take his seat on a heavenly throne and act as God's vice-regent. It is concluded, then, as stated above, that there is still no certain evidence that Daniel's son-of-man figure was understood as a messianic figure prior to the time of Jesus. Such interpretation may have been in its early stages in the first century B.C.E., to which the later 4 Ezra and Similitudes of Enoch, and even later rabbinic exegesis associated with Aqiba (*b. Sanh.* 38b; *b. Ḥag.* 14a), give subsequent witness (and indirect witness in the NT Gospels), but in what form it was at the time of Jesus is impossible to ascertain.

5. *Jesus and the temple.* In an important dissertation Juel (*Messiah and Temple*) discusses Mark's interest, which is largely negative, in the Jerusalem temple. This theme plays a significant role throughout the second half of the Markan Gospel (esp. chaps. 11–15). We see it in the aftermath of the triumphal entry (Mark 11:1–10), where Jesus, after "looking around" in the temple precincts (11:11), the next day curses the fig tree (11:12–14) and takes action in the temple (11:15–18), which he describes as a "cave of robbers" (v 17). Jesus' words ominously allude to the scathing oracle of Jer 7, in which the prophet pronounced doom upon the first temple. The following morning the fig tree is found withered (11:20–21). The intercalation of the fig tree and temple action is surely intended to be mutually illuminating: the fruitless fig tree symbolizes the fruitless temple establishment; both are doomed. The animosity between Jesus and the temple authorities intensifies. Ruling priests demand to know by what authority Jesus has acted (11:27–33). But Jesus does not reply in a direct manner. Again taking an indirect tack, he tells the parable of the Wicked Vineyard Tenants (12:1–11), which implies that the ruling priests, having acted corruptly, will soon lose their positions of authority. The priests perceive that the parable has been spoken against them (12:12). They then test Jesus regarding the sensitive question of paying taxes to Caesar (12:13–17); again Jesus replies in an evasive manner. Sadducees join in the fray, asking Jesus about the resurrection (12:18–27). A scribe asks about the greatest commandment (12:28–31). He is so impressed with Jesus' answer that he confesses that love for God and neighbor "is much more than all whole burnt offerings and sacrifices" (12:32–33). His subordination of the importance of the temple cultus leads Jesus to assure him that he is "not far from the kingdom of God" (12:34).

In the question about David's son (12:35–37) Jesus goes on the offensive. He raises a question about the meaning (or appropriateness) of calling the Messiah the son of David. If the Messiah is David's son, then why does David call him "Lord"? The implication is that the epithet "son of David" is an insufficient appellation for the Messiah. Does this further imply that Jesus thinks of the Messiah as having more authority, greater status, than David? And, if so, does this mean that the Messiah's authority will transcend that of the ruling priests? Jesus next warns of the scribes who "devour the houses of widows" (12:38–40). The pericope that follows, the story of the widow who cast into the temple treasury her last penny (12:41–44), in all probability is an illustration of a widow whose house (or estate) has been devoured, to the last crumb. This polemical section ends with a scene outside on the precinct steps when Jesus prophesies that "not one stone will be left on another that will not be thrown down" (Mark 13:2).

The anti-temple motif returns in the Passion Narrative itself. The ruling priests actively seek to take Jesus by stealth and have him executed (14:1–2). They bribe Judas to betray Jesus (14:10–11). During his hearing before the Jewish council Jesus is accused of threatening to destroy the temple (14:58). In response to the high priest's question (14:61: "Are you the Messiah?"), Jesus declares that he will be seen seated at the right hand of God (14:62), probably implying that he will displace the high priest as intercessor for Israel and, indeed, will appear as the high priest's judge. Caiaphas, the high priest, is outraged and calls for Jesus' death (14:63–64a). His colleagues join him in condemning Jesus (14:64b–65). The priests hand Jesus over to Pilate, the Roman prefect (15:1), and they continue to accuse Jesus (15:3). When Pilate offers to release Jesus (15:9–10), the priests stir up the crowd so that they will demand the release of Barabbas instead of Jesus (15:11–15). Finally, when Jesus hangs on the cross, the ruling priests mock him (15:31–32). But Jesus appears to get in the last word, for at the moment of his death the "veil of the temple was torn in two" (15:38). For Mark this probably signifies the first step in the fulfillment of Jesus' prophecy of the temple's destruction and the removal of the ruling priests.

6. Mark's Christology. Mark's Christology is focused on Jesus as Son of God. This is clear from the Gospel's incipit, "The beginning of the good news of Jesus Christ the Son of God" (1:1), and from the dramatic confession of the Roman centurion, "Truly this man was the Son of God" (15:39). But this identification should not be understood exclusively in reference to Greco-Roman ideas of rulers as sons of God. Israel's royal traditions also speak of the king as God's son: "The rulers are gathered against the Lord and against his Messiah. . . . The Lord said to me: 'You are my son; today I have begotten you'" (Ps 2:2, 7). The language of this psalm is echoed in one of the Dead Sea Scrolls that speak of the awaited Messiah: ". . . when God will have begotten the Messiah among them" (1QSa 2:11–12). Mark has presented Jesus as God's royal, Davidic son (rightly Kingsbury, *Christology*). This is seen in Bartimaeus's appeal to Jesus as "son of David" (10:47, 48), in the shouts of acclaim during the triumphal entry (11:10), and in the repeated reference to Jesus as the "king of the Jews" during his trial and crucifixion (15:2, 9, 12, 18, 26, 32).

The most important testimony to Jesus' divine Sonship comes from God himself, who acknowledges him at his baptism (1:11) and at the transfiguration (9:7). As God's Son, Jesus is the final messenger to Israel (Mark 12:6). Although rejected and murdered (12:7–9, 10a), he will be vindicated and will become the "head of the corner" (12:10b–11). Although as Israel's shepherd he is to be struck down (14:27), he will be raised up and will go before his disciples in Galilee (14:28). When the frightened women discover the empty tomb (16:4), they are told: "Go, tell his disciples and Peter that he is going before you to Galilee; there you will see him, as he told you" (16:7). In the resurrection of Jesus, Mark's readers are confronted with the vindicated Son of God, who continues to lead his disciples.

Purpose of Mark

Bibliography

Baarlink, H. *Anfängliches Evangelium.* **Best, E.** *Mark.* 51–54, 93–99. **Black, C. C.** *Mark: Images of an Apostolic Interpreter.* Columbia: University of South Carolina Press, 1994. **Borgen, P.** "Emperor Worship and Persecution in Philo's *In Flaccum* and *De Legatione ad Gaium* and the Revelation of John." In *Geschichte—Tradition—Reflexion.* FS M. Hengel, ed. H. Cancik, H. Lichtenberger, and P. Schäfer. 3 vols. Tübingen: Mohr-Siebeck, 1996. 3:493–509. **Bowersock, G. W.** "The Imperial Cult: Perceptions and Persistence." In *Self-Definition in the Greco-Roman World.* Vol. 3 of *Jewish and Christian Self-Definition.* Ed. B. F. Meyer and E. P. Sanders. Philadelphia: Fortress, 1982. 171–82, 238–41. **Bureth, P.** *Les titulatures impériales dans les papyrus, les ostraca et les inscriptions d'Égypte (30 a. C.–284 p. C.).* Brussels: Fondation Égyptologique Reine Élisabeth, 1964. **Burrows, M.** "The Origin of the Term 'Gospel.'" *JBL* 34 (1925) 21–33. **Deissmann, A.** *Light from the Ancient East.* London: Hodder & Stoughton/New York: Harper & Row, 1927. **Dormeyer, D.** "Mk 1,1–15 als Prolog des ersten idealbiographischen Evangeliums von Jesus Christus." *BibInt* 5 (1997) 181–211. **Foerster, W.** *Herr ist Jesus: Herkunft und Bedeutung des urchristlichen Kyrios-Bekenntnisses.* Gütersloh: Bertelsmann, 1924. **Friedrich, G.** "εὐαγγέλιον κ. τ. λ." *TDNT* 2 (1970) 707–37. **Hengel, M.** *The Son of God.* London: SCM Press/Philadelphia: Fortress, 1976. 23–32. ———. *The Zealots: Investigations into the Jewish Freedom Movement in the Period from Herod I until 70 A.D.* Edinburgh: T. & T. Clark, 1989. 99–107. **Hopkins, K.** "Divine Emperors or the Symbolic Unity of the Roman Empire." In *Conquerors and Slaves.* Cambridge: Cambridge UP, 1978. 197–242. **Horsley, G. H. R.** *New Documents Illustrating Early Christianity.* Vol. 1. North Ryde, NSW, Australia: Macquarie University, 1981. **Johnson, E. S.** "Is Mark 15.39 the Key to Mark's Christology?" *JSNT* 31 (1987) 3–22 (repr. in *The Synoptic Gospels: A Sheffield Reader.* Ed. C. A. Evans and S. E. Porter. Biblical Seminar 31. Sheffield: Sheffield Academic, 1995. 143–62). ———. "Mark 15,39 and the So-called Confession of the Roman Centurion." *Bib* 81 (2000) 406–13. **Kilgallen, J. J.** "The Messianic Secret and Mark's Purpose." *BTB* 7 (1977) 60–65. **Kingsbury, J. D.** *The Christology of Mark's Gospel.* **Kneissl, P.** *Die Siegestitulatur der römischen Kaiser: Untersuchungen zu den Siegerbeinamen der ersten und zweiten Jahrhunderts.* Hypomnemata 23. Göttingen: Vandenhoeck & Ruprecht, 1969. **Künzl, E.** *Der römische Triumph: Siegesfeiern im antiken Rom.* Munich: Beck, 1988. **Lemcio, E. E.** "The Intention of the Evangelist Mark." *NTS* 32 (1986) 187–206. **MacDonald, D. R.** *The Homeric Epics and the Gospel of Mark.* New Haven, CT: Yale UP, 2000. **Magie, D.** *De Romanorum iuris publici sacrique vocabulis.* Leipzig: Teubner, 1905. **Martin, R. P.** *Mark: Evangelist and Theologian.* 156–205. **Mastin, B. A.** "The Imperial Cult and the Ascription of the Title to Jesus." *SE* 6 [= TU 112] 1973. 352–65. **Mattingly, H.** *Coins of the Roman Empire in the British Museum.* Vol. 1: *Augustus to Vitellius.* London: British Museum, 1965. **Moule, C. F. D.** "The Intention of the Evangelists." In *New Testament Essays.* FS T. W. Manson, ed. A. J. B. Higgins. Manchester: Manchester UP, 1959. 165–79. **Nock, A. D.** "Deification and Julian." *JRS* 47 (1957) 115–23. ———. "Notes on Ruler Cult I–IV." *JHS* 48 (1928) 21–42. ———. "*Soter* and *Euergetes.*" In *The Joy of Study: Papers on New Testament and Related Subjects.* FS F. C. Grant, ed. S. E. Johnson. New York: Macmillan, 1951. 127–48. **Pleket, H. W.** "An Aspect of the Emperor Cult: Imperial Mysteries." *HTR* 58 (1965) 331–47. **Ropes,**

J. H. *The Synoptic Gospels.* Oxford: Oxford UP, 1934. 3–32. **Schmidt, T. E.** "Mark 15.16–32: The Crucifixion Narrative and the Roman Triumphal Procession." *NTS* 41 (1995) 1–18. **Schniewind, J.** *Euangelion: Ursprung und erste Gestalt des Begriffs Evangelium.* Gütersloh: Bertelsmann, 1931. **Shiner, W. T.** "The Ambiguous Pronouncement of the Centurion and the Shrouding of Meaning in Mark." *JSNT* 78 (2000) 3–22. **Standaert, B. H. M. G. M.** *L'Évangile selon Marc: Composition et genre littéraire.* Nijmegen: Stichting Studentenpers, 1978. **Syme, R.** "Imperator Caesar: A Study in Nomenclature." *Historia* 7 (1958) 172–88. **Taylor, L. R.** *The Divinity of the Roman Emperor.* APAMS 1. New York: Arno, 1931; Chico, CA: Scholars Press, 1975. **Tinh, T. T.** *Le culte des divinités en Campanei.* EPRO 27. Leiden: Brill, 1972. ———. *Le culte des divinités orientales à Herculanum.* EPRO 17. Leiden: Brill, 1971. **Versnel, H. S.** *Triumphus: An Inquiry into the Origin, Development, and Meaning of the Roman Triumph.* Leiden: Brill, 1970.

This brief section is deliberately bracketed off from the preceding longer and more involved discussion of Mark's theology. A narrower and more focused question may now be asked: Why did Mark write his Gospel? Or another way of putting it: What was his purpose? The answer to this question cannot be answered, in my opinion, apart from a proper appreciation of the political and social reality of the first-century Greco-Roman world.

Recent studies in the historical Jesus have argued that the best place to begin the task of recovering an accurate picture of what Jesus said and did is at the end, that is, Jesus' death. Jesus died on a Roman cross. The fact of this crucifixion, combined with the *titulus* that read "the King of the Jews" (Mark 15:26 and par.), provides us with an important clue to Jesus' teachings and activities and what people thought about him. Beginning with the ending, we can then work our way back to the beginning, looking for material that is consistent with this ending. In view of the nature of Jesus' death, many scholars today have correctly concluded that Jesus really did speak of the "kingdom of God," appoint the "twelve" as a symbol of the restoration of Israel, point to his miracles, especially his exorcisms, as evidence of the presence and power of the kingdom, and criticize the temple leadership, which collaborated with the Roman authorities. This mission and this message, amply attested in the Gospels, offer a compelling answer to the question, Why did Jesus die the way he did? When at the beginning of his account the Markan evangelist says that Jesus declared that the kingdom of God was at hand and that it was time to believe in the "good news" (Mark 1:15), we have every reason to believe that this is an accurate summation of Jesus' message. Just such a message would get its proclaimer executed in first-century Palestine.

It might be wise to approach the question of Mark's purpose in the same manner. Mark's narrative moves along with various declarations and questions about who Jesus is (Mark 1:1, 11, 24; 5:7; 8:27–30; 9:7; 10:47–48; 14:61–62; 15:39). At the moment that Jesus dies, the Roman centurion confesses, "Truly this man was the son of God" (Mark 15:39). This confession agrees with Mark's opening description of Jesus as the "Son of God" (1:1, at least as read by אᵃ A B D K L W Δ Π 33 and other authorities). It is natural to suspect that part of the evangelist's purpose is to show that Jesus is indeed God's son, even though he was executed at the hands of the Romans. The centurion's confession may not be the key to Mark's Christology (the claim is rightly questioned by Johnson, *JSNT* 31 [1987] 3–22; id., *Bib* 81 [2000] 406–13; Shiner, *JSNT* 78 [2000] 3–22), but it may be an important clue to Mark's purpose for writing. This confession, tumbling from the lips of a

Roman commander, helps us understand the challenge that the early Christians faced in holding and propagating their faith in the face of opposition and competition.

The centurion's confession would have struck his Roman contemporaries as strange for two important reasons: (1) Defeated and put to death, Jesus is hardly a promising candidate for such recognition. (2) Recognition of someone as "son of God" was reserved for the Roman emperor. Thus, the centurion's confession would have been viewed as potentially disloyal to Caesar. The importance of these points may be underscored by a sampling of divine epithets used in reference to the emperors from Julius Caesar to Caesar Vespasian (conveniently gathered in Bureth, *Les titulatures impériales*, 23–41; Deissmann, *Light from the Ancient East*, 338–78; Foerster, *Herr ist Jesus*, 99–118; Kneissl, *Die Siegestitulatur*, 27–57; Magie, *De Romanorum*, 62–69; Taylor, *Divinity*, 267–83).

Julius Caesar (48–44 B.C.E.). Julius Caesar was the founder of a political dynasty that would impact early Christianity profoundly. An inscription from Ephesus describes Julius Caesar as τὸν ἀπὸ Ἄρεως καὶ Ἀφροδείτης θεὸν ἐπιφανῆ καὶ κοινὸν τοῦ ἀνθρωπίνου βίου σωτῆρα (*SIG* 760), "the manifest god from Ares and Aphrodite, and universal savior of human life." The people of Carthaea honored Caesar as savior and god: Καίσαρα . . . γεγονότα δὲ σωτῆρα καὶ εὐεργέτην καὶ τῆς ἡμετέρας πόλεως, "[The Carthaean people honor] Caesar . . . who has become savior and benefactor of our city" (*IG* 12:5, 556–57); ὁ δῆμος ὁ Καρθαιέων τὸν θεὸν καὶ αὐτοκράτορα καὶ σωτῆρα τῆς οἰκουμένης Γάϊον Ἰούλιον Καίσαρα Γαΐου Καίσαρος υἱὸν ἀνέθηκεν, "The Carthaean people honor the god and emperor and savior of the inhabited world, Gaius Julius Caesar, son of Gaius Caesar." The people of Mytilene (*IG* 12:2, 165b) hailed Caesar as god (θεός), benefactor (εὐεργέτης), and founder (κτίστης). Another Mytilene inscription refers to γράμματα Καίσαρος θεοῦ, "the letters of Caesar god" (*IG* 12:2, 35b; *IGR* 4:33). References to Caesar's successors as "savior," "god," "son of god," "lord," and "benefactor" become common and formulaic.

Augustus (30 B.C.E.–14 C.E.). The most impressive and, for our purpose, instructive inscriptions and references are as follows: ἡ Καίσαρος κράτησις θεοῦ υἱοῦ, "The mastery of Caesar son of god" (P.Ryl. 601; *PSI* 1150); *Imperator Caesar divi filius Augustus*, "Emperor Caesar Augustus, son of god" (*SB* 401; BGU 628); Καίσαρος θεοῦ υἱὸς αὐτοκράτωρ, "Caesar, son of god, Emperor" (P.Teb. 382); Καίσαρος αὐτοκράτωρ θεὸς ἐκ θεοῦ, "Emperor Caesar, god from god" (*SB* 8895); Καίσαρος αὐτοκράτωρ θεοῦ υἱὸς Ζεὺς ἐλευθέριος Σεβαστός, "Emperor Caesar, son of God, Zeus the liberator, Augustus" (P.Oslo. 26; *SB* 8824); Αὐτοκράτωρ Καῖσαρ Σεβαστός σωτὴρ καὶ εὐεργέτης, "Emperor Caesar Augustus, savior and benefactor" (*SB* 8897); Ἀπόλλωνος Ἐλευθερίου Σεβαστοῦ, "Apollo Augustus, liberator" (*OGIS* 457); θεὸς Καῖσαρ, "Caesar god" (P.Oxy. 257; P.Oxy. 1266); Καῖσαρ θεός, "God Caesar" (P.Oxy. 1453; P.Lond. 192); ὁ θεὸς ἡμῶν Καῖσαρ, "Caesar our god" (P.Lond. 1912 = *CPJ* 153); θεὸς καὶ κύριος αὐτοκράτωρ Καῖσαρ, "Emperor Caesar, god and lord" (BGU 1197; BGU 1200).

Queen Dunamis of Phanagoria honored Augustus as Αὐτοκράτορα Καίσαρα θεοῦ υἱὸν θεὸν Σεβαστὸν πάσης γῆς καὶ θαλάσσης ἐπόπτην, "The Emperor, Caesar, son of god, the god Augustus, the overseer of every land and sea" (*IGR* 1:901; cf. *IGR* 4:309, 315). An inscription from Halicarnassus reads: Δία δὲ πατρῷον καὶ σωτῆρα τοῦ κοινοῦ τῶν ἀνθρώπων γένους, "Hereditary god and savior of the common race of humanity" (*GIBM* 994). A calendrical inscription from Priene (*OGIS* 458) refers to the birth of Augustus as the ἡ γενέθλιος ἡμέρα τοῦ θεοῦ, "the birthday of the god," and later refers to Augustus as τοῦ θειοτάτου Καίσαρος, "the most divine Caesar." Libations were offered up ὑπὲρ τοῦ θεοῦ καὶ Αὐτοκράτορος, "in behalf of the god and Emperor." An inscription found at Tarsus reads: Αὐτοκράτορα Καίσαρα θεοῦ υἱὸν Σεβαστὸν ὁ δῆμος ὁ Ταρσέων, "The people of Tarsus [honor] Emperor Caesar Augustus, son of god."

Tiberius (14–37 c.e.). Tiberius is called Τιβέριος Καῖσαρ Σεβαστὸς θεοῦ υἱὸς αὐτοκράτωρ, "Emperor Tiberius Caesar Augustus, son of god" (*SB* 8317), and Τιβέριος Καῖσαρ νέος Σεβαστὸς αὐτοκράτωρ θεοῦ Διὸς ἐλευθερίου, "Emperor Tiberius Caesar, new Augustus, [son] of god, Zeus the liberator" (P.Oxy. 240).

Gaius Caligula (37–41 c.e.). The people of Halasarna erect an altar to honor Gaius Caligula as a νέωι θεῶι, "new god" (*IGR* 4:1094). An inscription in Athens honors Gaius Caesar as Σεβαστοῦ υἱὸν νέον "Αρη, "Son of Augustus, a new Ares" (*CIA* 3:444). In another Athenian inscription he is called "Αρηος υἱόν, "son of Ares" (*CIA* 3:444a).

Claudius (41–54 c.e.). Claudius is given the titles Τιβέριος Κλαύδιος κύριος, "Tiberius Claudius, lord" (*SB* 4331); Τιβέριος Κλαύδιος Καῖσαρ Σεβαστὸς αὐτοκράτωρ ὁ κύριος, "Emperor Tiberius Claudius Caesar Augustus, the lord" (*GOA* 1038); θεὸς Κλαύδιος, "Claudius, god" (*PSI* 1235; P.Oxy. 713); θεὸς Καίσαρ, "Caesar, god" (P.Oxy. 808; P.Oxy. 1021); θεὸς Σεβαστός, "Augustus, god" (P.Mich. 244); and ὁ κύριος, "The lord" (O.Petr. 209).

Nero (54–68 c.e.). Nero is portrayed as Νέρων ὁ κύριος, "Nero, the lord" (P.Lond. 1215; P.Oxy. 246; *GOA* 1038); Νέρων Καῖσαρ ὁ κύριος, "Nero Caesar, the lord" (O.Petr. 288; P.Oxy. 246); Νέρων Κλαύδιος Καῖσαρ . . . ὁ σωτὴρ καὶ εὐεργέτης τῆς οἰκουμένης, "Nero Claudius Caesar . . . the savior and benefactor of the inhabited world" (*OGIS* 668); Ἀγαθὸς Δαίμων τῆς οἰκουμένης ἀρχὴ ὤν τε πάντων ἀγαθῶν, "The good god of the inhabited world, the beginning and existence of all good things" (P.Oxy. 1021); τὸν υἱὸν τοῦ μεγίστου θεῶν, "the son of the greatest of the gods" (*IM* 157b); and ὁ τοῦ παντὸς κόσμου κύριος Νέρων, "Nero, the lord of the whole world" (*SIG* 814).

Vespasian (69–79 c.e.). Vespasian is called Οὐεσπασιανὸς ὁ κύριος, "Vespasian, the lord" (P.Oxy. 1439; *SB* 1927); Οὐεσπασιανὸς αὐτοκράτωρ ὁ κύριος, "Emperor Vespasian, the lord" (*GOA* 439; *SB* 3563); θεὸς Οὐεσπασιανός, "Vespasian, god" (P.Oxy. 257; P.Oxy. 1112); and *Divus Vespasianus*, "Divine Vespasian" (*CPL* 104; P.Mich. 432).

Not only do the Gospel of Mark and other early Christian writings echo most of this language in their respective Christologies, but they also present Jesus as Caesar's rival in other ways. The whole concept of the divinity of the emperor and the honor to be accorded him are paralleled at many important points. The principal components are as follows:

1. The "good news." The emperor's reign or victory was announced as "good news" (εὐαγγέλιον or εὐαγγελίζεσθαι). The good news was celebrated as a religious event. For example, cities rejoiced and offered sacrifices to the gods upon receiving the good news (εὐαγγελίζεσθαι) of the royal heir's coming of age. The calendrical inscription from Priene, mentioned above, describes the birthday of Augustus in the following manner: ἦρξεν δὲ τῶι κόσμωι τῶν δι᾽ αὐτὸν εὐαγγελίων ἡ γενέθλιος ἡμέρα τοῦ θεοῦ, "But the birthday of the god was the beginning of the good news, on his account, for the world." A papyrus from the early third century describes the author's joy at learning of τοῦ εὐαγγελίου περὶ τοῦ ἀνηγορεῦσθαι Καίσαρα, "the good news concerning the proclaming as Caesar [of Gaius Julius Verus Maximus Augustus]" (Deissmann, *Light*, 367; for more examples, see Schniewind, *Euangelion*, 131–32). Jews knew and understood this terminology. When word spread of Vespasian's accession to the throne, "every city celebrated the good news [εὐαγγέλια] and offered sacrifices on his behalf" (Josephus, *J.W.* 4.10.6 §618). Josephus later relates: "On reaching Alexandria Vespasian was greeted by the good news [εὐαγγέλια] from Rome and by embassies of congratulation from every quarter of the world, now his own . . . . The whole empire being now secured and the Roman state saved [σώζειν] beyond expectation, Vespasian turned his thoughts to what remained in Judaea" (*J.W.* 4.11.5 §656–57).

2. *Omens and prophecies.* Often omens and prophecies preceded the accession or death of an emperor. We have Sulla's prophecy, "either by divinity or by shrewd conjecture," of Julius Caesar's eventual dictatorship (Suetonius, *Jul.* 1.3). Caesar's murder was foretold to him by "unmistakable signs" (Suetonius, *Jul.* 81.1), among which was the death of a small bird carrying a sprig of laurel (81.3). Several omens supposedly prior to, during, and shortly after the birth of Augustus were remembered, at least many years after the fact. Suetonius relates that the senate, fearing the fulfillment of the prophecy of a coming king, "decreed that no male child born that year should be reared" (*Aug.* 94.3). The parents of Augustus had portentous dreams, such that following his birth the child was regarded as the "son of Apollo" (*Aug.* 94.4). Jupiter appeared in one dream and foretold that Augustus would become the "savior of his country" (*Aug.* 94.8). On one occasion the toddler Augustus commanded noisy frogs to be silent and they obeyed (*Aug.* 94.7). The death of Augustus was preceded by many omens and signs. According to Suetonius: "His [Augustus's] death . . . and his deification after death, were known in advance by unmistakable signs" (*Aug.* 97.1). At the conclusion of a ceremony an eagle flew several times above the Emperor and then perched on a lintel of the temple, on which was inscribed the name Agrippa (*Aug.* 97.1). The story is similar to one involving another Agrippa (41–44 C.E.), the grandson of Herod the Great. The book of Acts tells of the death of the impious Jewish king (Acts 12:20–23). Josephus adds the interesting detail of the owl, which for Agrippa was a bird of omen, whose first appearance augured Agrippa's accession to the throne, and whose second appearance augured the monarch's death (*Ant.* 19.8.2 §346; cf. *Ant.* 18.6.7 §195–200). Omens were perceived that foretold Vespasian's accession (Tacitus, *Hist.* 1.10; 2.1; Josephus, *J.W.* 3.8.9 §404; Suetonius, *Vesp.* 5.2–7).

Perhaps the most interesting is the prophecy many thought was fulfilled in Vespasian. According to Suetonius, "There had spread over all the Orient an old and established belief that it was fated at that time for men coming from Judea to rule the world. This prediction, referring to the emperor of Rome, as afterwards appeared from the event, the people of Judea took to themselves; accordingly they revolted" (*Vesp.* 4.5). Josephus admits that a prophecy was a major factor in stirring up the Jewish people: "But what more than all else incited them to the war was an ambiguous oracle, likewise found in their sacred scriptures, to the effect that at that time one from their country would become ruler of the world. This they understood to mean someone of their own race, and many of their wise men went astray in their interpretation of it. The oracle, however, in reality signified the sovereignty of Vespasian, who was proclaimed Emperor on Jewish soil" (*J.W.* 6.5.4 §312–14). This Jewish prophecy seems to have been known, independently of Josephus, by Tacitus: "The majority firmly believed that their ancient priestly writings contained the prophecy that this was the very time when the East should grow strong and that men starting from Judaea should possess the world. This mysterious prophecy had in reality pointed to Vespasian and Titus, but the common people, as is the way of human ambition, interpreted these great destinies in their own favour, and could not be turned to the truth even by adversity" (*Hist.* 5.13). The prophecies reported by Suetonius and Tacitus probably had something to do with Josephus's prophecy of Vespasian's accession to the throne (*J.W.* 3.8.9 §399–402), a prophecy that is also related in Dio Cassius: "Now portents and dreams had come to Vespasian pointing to the sovereignty long beforehand . . . and Nero himself in his dreams once thought that he had brought the car of Jupiter to Vespasian's house. These portents needed interpretation; but not so the saying of a Jew named Josephus; he, having earlier been captured by Vespasian and imprisoned, laughed and said: 'You may imprison me now, but a year from now, when you have become emperor, you will release me'" (*Hist. Rom.* 66.1.2–4); in Suetonius: "and one of his high-born prisoners, Josephus by name, as he was being put in chains, declared most confidently that he would soon be released by the same man, who would then, however, be emperor" (*Vesp.* 5.6); and in Appian: "For Josephus, as he himself related it, found in the sacred writings a certain oracle signifying when some one from their country would rule the inhabited world . . . . This oracle Appian also mentions in his twenty-second book of his Roman history" (*Hist. Rom.* 22, according to Zonaras, *Epitome Hist.* 11.16). The "ambiguous oracle," to which Josephus alludes, was probably Num 24:17: "a star shall come forth out of Jacob, and a scepter shall rise out of Israel." This passage probably explains the excitement on the part of the Jewish people when on the eve of the revolt an unusual star appeared in the sky (Josephus, *J.W.* 6.5.3 §289). The passage is understood in a messianic sense in various Jewish sources (*T. Jud.* 24:1–6; 1QM 11:4–9; *Tg. Neof.* Num 24:17), including the Matthean story of the visit of the Magi (Matt 2:2, 7, 9, 10). Suetonius states that various omens attended the death of Claudius, including the appearance of a comet (*Claud.* 46).

3. *The Roman triumph.* Following a great victory a "triumph" (θρίαμβος, *triumphus*) was held, at which time the emperor's sovereignty and divine status were reaffirmed (e.g., Suetonius, *Aug.* 22). The tradition was ancient and had become part of the Greco-Roman mythology: "There was a story about Dionysius that, after subduing India, he traversed the greater part of Asia in this way, that he himself was surnamed 'Triumph' [Θρίαμβος], and that processions after victories in war were for this very reason called 'triumphs'" (Arrian, *Anab.* 6.28.2). In the same passage Arrian tells of a story, which he regards as false, in which Alexander, having conquered India, imitates Dionysius (6.28.1–3). In one of his classic poems Virgil (70–19 B.C.E.) flatters Augustus, following his victory at Actium (31 B.C.E.): "Heaven's courts have long enough grudged you to us, O Caesar, murmuring because you pay attention to earthly triumphs [*triumphos*]!" (*Georg.* 1.503–4). At the end of the work Virgil

alludes to the emperor's triumphal procession following his victory: "Thus I sang of the care of fields, of cattle, and of trees, while great Caesar thundered in war by deep Euphrates and gave a victor's laws unto willing nations, and prepared the path to Heaven [*viamque adfectat Olympo*]" (*Georg.* 4.559–62). In more prosaic terms Suetonius tells us that Augustus brought treasures from Rome, which he freely distributed during his triumph in Alexandria (*Aug.* 41.1). In Jewish history the most memorable triumph was celebrated in Rome following Titus's capture of Jerusalem in 70 C.E. (cf. Josephus, *J.W.* 7.5.4–6 §123–57). In his opening summary of the *Jewish War*, Josephus promises his readers that he will tell of the Roman victory and of Titus's "return to Italy and triumph [θρίαμβος]" (*J.W.* Prologue §29). Two stone reliefs on the inside of the Arch of Titus depict this event. Taylor comments: "With the longing of the people for a saviour went at the same time the growth of the power of individuals, chiefly the great generals, to whom was accorded the triumph that was the closest thing in Roman state ceremony to deification" (*Divinity*, 57).

4. *Hailed in divine terms.* The various inscriptions cited above illustrate well the language of the imperial cult by which the Roman emperor was viewed as divine. These expressions were not confined to public inscriptions but appear on coins, in poetry, and in didactic and polemical literature. The legend of a coin struck in honor of Augustus reads ἐπιφάνια Αὐγούστου, "manifestation of Augustus." According to Virgil, the great Roman poet, "This is he whom you have so often heard promised to you, Augustus Caesar, son of a god [*divi genus*], who shall again set up the Golden Age" (*Aen.* 6.791–93). Philo knows that Augustus was called "savior and benefactor" (Philo, *Flaccus* 74; cf. *Embassy* 148, 149). Philo's remark that Augustus "never wished anyone to address him as a god [μηδέποτε θεὸν ἑαυτὸν ἐθελῆσαι προσειπεῖν] but was annoyed if anyone used the word" (*Embassy* 154; cf. Suetonius, *Aug.* 53.1; *Tib.* 27) speaks well of Augustus but reveals the popular tendency nonetheless. Even Herod the Great, despite the risk of offending his own people, sought in various ways to promote the emperor cult in those parts of his realm that were not heavily populated with Jews (see Hengel, *Zealots*, 101–3). Suetonius (*Vit.* 2.5) tells us that Lucius Vitellius, well known for his flattery, was the first to worship Gaius Caligula as a god (*adorare ut deum*). Dio Cassius adds that Caligula called himself Zeus Latiaris and sometimes impersonated Poseidon and Apollo, as well as other gods and goddesses (*Hist. Rom.* 59.28.5–6). Caligula's blasphemous vanity was well known to Jewish writers. According to Philo the emperor imagined he had "soared above humanity and had ranked himself among the gods" (*Embassy* 218). Later Josephus adds that Caligula "wished to be considered a god and to be hailed as such" (*J.W.* 2.10.1 §184; cf. *Ant.* 18.7.2 §256; for more on Caligula, see Borgen, "Emperor Worship").

5. *Confessing Caesar as lord.* In *Georgica* the poet Virgil prays to Octavian (who later assumes the name Augustus) as the veritable lord of land and sea: "Yes, and you, O Caesar, whom which company of the gods shall claim before long is not known . . . watch over cities and care for our lands, so that the great world may receive you as the giver of increase and lord of the seasons . . . whether you come as god [*deus*] of the boundless sea and sailors worship your deity [*numen*] alone . . . or whether you add yourself as a new star to the lingering months . . . learn even now to hearken to our prayers!" (*Georg.* 1.24–42). But Jews and Christians resisted

this confession. The author of the *Psalms of Solomon* polemicizes against Pompey's arrogant claim: Ἐγὼ κύριος γῆς καὶ θαλάσσης ἔσομαι, "I shall be lord of land and sea" (2:29). Resistance led to martyrdom, both for Jews and for Christians. Josephus describes the fate of many following the capture of Jerusalem: "For under every form of torture and laceration of body, devised for the sole object of making them confess Caesar as lord [Καίσαρα δεσπότην ὁμολογήσωσιν], not one submitted nor was brought to the verge of utterance" (Josephus, *J.W.* 7.10.1 §418). Even the children refused to "name Caesar lord [Καίσαρα δεσπότην ἐξονομάσαι]" (*J.W.* 7.10.1 §419). Tacitus complains of the Jews and comments that "this flattery is not paid their kings, nor this honor given to the Caesars" (*Ann.* 5.5). Christians proved to be just as stubborn. A police captain asked Polycarp: τί γὰρ κακόν ἐστιν εἰπεῖν· κύριος Καῖσαρ; "Why is it evil to say, 'Caesar is lord'?" (*Mart. Pol.* 8:2). Polycarp refused and so was led to the arena.

6. *Healing.* Because of their divinity, it was believed that the Roman emperors could in some instances effect healing. According to Suetonius, "A man of the people, who was blind, and another who was lame, together came to [Vespasian] as he sat on the tribunal, begging for the help for their disorders which Serapis had promised in a dream; for the god declared that Vespasian would restore the eyes, if he would spit upon them, and give strength to the leg, if he would deign to touch with his heel. Though he had hardly any faith that this could possibly succeed, and therefore shrank even from making the attempt, he was at last prevailed upon by his friends and tried both things in public before a large crowd; and with success" (*Vesp.* 7.2–3).

7. *Seated or standing at God's right hand.* Being seated at the "right hand" of deity was another important part of the ritual and symbolism of the emperor cult. A coin minted in Rome in 55 C.E. depicts "divine" Claudius seated at the right hand of Augustus ("god from god"!) atop a chariot drawn by four elephants (Mattingly, *Coins of the Roman Empire,* 1:201 + pl. 38). A later sculpture depicts Hadrian, dressed as Zeus, "standing side by side with the image of Iuppiter/Zeus himself" (cf. Versnel, *Triumphus,* 69; cf. Taylor, *Divinity,* 44–45). According to Suetonius (*Cal.* 57), only days before his assassination (41 C.E.) Gaius Caligula dreamed that he "stood in heaven beside the throne of Jupiter and that the god struck him with the toe of his right foot and hurled him to the earth." This odd dream suggests that until his eviction Caligula had thought of himself as standing in heaven, next to Jupiter himself.

8. *Libations in honor of Caesar.* Beginning with Augustus, libations were to be poured out at every banquet, public and private, in honor of the emperor: καὶ ἐν τοῖς συσσιτίοις οὐχ ὅτι τοῖς κοινοῖς ἀλλὰ τοῖς ἰδίοις πάντας αὐτῷ σπένδειν ἐκέλευσαν, "and they ordered all, not only in public but also in private banquets, to pour libations to him" (Dio Cassius, *Hist. Rom.* 51.19.7). One also thinks of the eating and drinking ceremonies observed by adherents to Mithraism. To these ceremonies Justin Martyr refers, complaining that they are done in imitation of the Lord's Supper (cf. *1 Apol.* 1.66.3). It is of course entirely possible that Christian observance of the Lord's Supper was itself viewed as imitation of Mithraic practices.

9. *The emperor's "advent" and the promise of a new world order.* The anticipated arrival of the emperor was referred to as a παρουσία (Latin: *adventus*). In honor of the Roman emperors, "advent coins" were struck; e.g., a coin struck in 66 C.E. in

honor of Nero reads *adventus Augusti,* "the coming of Augustus." An inscription in honor of Hadrian speaks of the "first παρουσία of the god Hadrian" (both examples from Deissmann, *Light,* 371–72). P.Teb. 48 announces the παρουσία of the king to the forum. This manner of speaking is known to Judaism of late antiquity, as seen in Josephus, who also speaks of the "παρουσία of the king" (*Ant.* 19.8.1 §340; cf. 3 Macc 3:17; *T. Abr.* 13:4–6). The advent of the emperor was sometimes thought of as the inauguration of a new era. As already noted above, Virgil spoke of Augustus "who shall again set up the Golden Age" (*Aen.* 6.791–93). The emperor could inaugurate a new era because of his link with heaven. This idea is seen in Alexander the Great, who evidently thought of himself as a mediator between heaven and earth. According to Plutarch, Alexander "believed that he came as a heaven-sent governor [θεόθεν ἁρμοστής] to all, and as a mediator [διαλλακτής] for the whole world . . . . He brought together all people everywhere, uniting and mixing in one great loving-cup, as it were, people's lives, their characters, their marriages, their very habits of life" (*Mor.* 329c = *Alex. fort.* 1.6). Virgil's poetry in honor of Augustus reflects similar ideas.

10. Post-mortem deification. After his death the successful and respected emperor was deified, that is, enrolled among the gods. Among the most respected were Julius Caesar, whose military prowess was greatly admired, and his great-nephew and adopted son Caesar Augustus, whose remarkable, lengthy, and successful reign laid the foundation on which the Roman Empire—and the emperor cult—would rest for generations to come. According to Suetonius, "[Julius Caesar] died in the fifty-sixth year of his age, and was numbered among the gods, not only by formal decree, but also in the conviction of the common people. For at the first of the games which his heir Augustus gave in honor of his apotheosis, a comet shone for seven successive days, rising about the eleventh hour, and was believed to be the soul of Caesar, who had been taken to heaven; and this is why a star is set upon the crown of his head in his statue" (*Jul.* 88.1). A similar legend grew up around Augustus. After describing the death and cremation of the emperor, Suetonius relates: "There was an ex-praetor who took oath that he had seen the form of the Emperor, after he had been reduced to ashes, on its way to heaven" (*Aug.* 100.4).

Other Julian emperors were less successful and less honored. Because of his cruelty and lasciviousness Tiberius Caesar was not deified. Because of his greed, violence, and insanity Caligula, who was assassinated, was not deified. Despite his cowardice and many eccentricities Claudius, who was poisoned—probably by his wife—was deified. Suetonius says that "he was buried with regal pomp and enrolled among the gods, an honor neglected and finally annulled by Nero, but later restored to him by Vespasian" (*Claud.* 45). Though "longing for immortality and undying fame" (Suetonius, *Nero* 55), Nero, stabbed to death (either by his own hand or by the hand of another), was not deified because of his cruelty, incompetence, jealousy, and lack of decorum. Regarded as competent and fair-minded, Vespasian, the first of three Flavian emperors, was deified. His popular son Titus was also deified after his brief rule. But his younger brother Domitian, who was assassinated after fifteen years of cruel and paranoid rule, was not deified.

Of a more bizarre character are the stories surrounding the aftermath of Caligula's assassination. According to Suetonius (*Cal.* 59), in the vicinity of the emperor's tomb there were fearful apparitions. Indeed, "the caretakers of the gardens were disturbed by ghosts." Although what is envisioned here is negative—in keeping with Caligula's evil character—reports of ghostly appearances in the vicinity of the garden tomb are intriguing and contribute to the Roman lore surrounding their divine (or demonic) rulers.

It is important to view the history of the Julian emperors from Christianity's perspective in the late 60s, when in all probability the Gospel of Mark was written. Whereas both Julius Caesar and Caesar Augustus were greatly honored (the former mostly after his death), their successors were less successful and less honored. Tiberius was not deified; neither were Gaius and Nero. Only Claudius was deified, but his reign was hardly exemplary. The Julian dynasty was marked by increasing cruelty and tyranny, reaching its nadir and its end in Nero. Following his death, the Roman Empire was threatened with anarchy as three emperors, Galba, Otho, and Vitellius, in rapid succession (68–69 C.E.) either committed suicide or were murdered. At some point during this time the Gospel of Mark was published. In the face of what then would have appeared as a steep decline in the respect for and prospects of the Roman emperorship, with one murderer and manipulator after another trying to gain the throne, Mark's opening words, "The beginning of the good news of Jesus Christ, the Son of God," would have had the ring of a competitor's claim on the devotion and loyalty of the people of the Roman Empire. The implication of this startling proclamation would have been very clear: Nero was most certainly not the true son of God, and certainly neither were the trio of opportunistic successors who each gained office but could not hold it for more than a few months. The Roman Senate and public were not willing to deify these men. Who really was God's son? Who really interceded between heaven and earth? Who really enjoyed heaven's blessing? Was there on earth any man with a credible claim to divinity? Who among humanity could rightly be called "lord"? Who among humanity could bring salvation to a distressed and troubled world? Amid the various candidates proffered for consideration (and Romans would eventually settle on Vespasian, the general who at the time was successfully prosecuting the war in Judea), the Markan evangelist and early Christians recommended Jesus Christ to the Roman public.

In my view, the Markan evangelist presents Jesus as the true son of God and in doing so deliberatedly presents Jesus in opposition to Rome's candidates for a suitable emperor, savior, and lord. All the features that made up the emperor cult and the various customs associated with the office and title of emperor in various ways find expression in NT Christology. Most of these features are paralleled in Mark; others are paralleled elsewhere in the NT. It is clear that early Christians well understood that their confession that Jesus was "Lord," "Savior," and "Son of God" directly competed with and challenged the Roman Emperor and the cult that had grown up around the office. We may review these features in the same order as above:

1. *The "good news."* Mark asserts that the life and achievement of Jesus constitute "good news": "(This is the) beginning of the good news [εὐαγγέλιον] of Jesus Christ, Son of God [υἱοῦ θεοῦ]" (Mark 1:1). Commentators are correct to explore the possibility that εὐαγγέλιον owes its roots to בשׂר *bāśar*, "bear tidings," especially as it is employed in Second Isaiah (40:9; 52:7), but the appearance of this word in an incipit that affirms Jesus as "Son of God," in a book that is to be read and heard

in the Roman Empire, would have had an unmistakable imperial ring to it, as the parallels with the Priene inscription strongly suggest. Mark is making the claim that the good news of Jesus Christ is the genuine article. Neither Julius Caesar nor any one of his descendants can rightly be regarded as the "Son of God"; only Jesus the Messiah deserves that title.

2. *Omens and prophecies.* Christian literature, inside and outside of the NT, relates stories of omens and prophecies attending Jesus' birth, the inception of his public ministry, and his death. Although Mark does not say anything about the birth of Jesus (as do the Matthean and Lukan evangelists—complete with omens, dreams, and prophecies), omens do attend the baptism (Mark 1:10–11), the transfiguration (9:2–8), and the crucifixion and death of Jesus: daytime darkness (15:33) and the tearing of the temple veil (15:38). The most astounding omen of all was the subsequent discovery of the empty tomb and the mysterious young man who proclaimed Jesus' resurrection (16:1–8).

3. *The "triumph" of Christ.* The word θριαμβεύειν, "to lead in a triumphal procession," does not occur in the Gospels, but it does appear in 2 Cor 2:14 ("thanks be to God who always leads us in triumph") and Col 2:15 ("having disarmed the rulers and authorities, he put them on display, having triumphed over them"), which appear to be deliberate allusions to the Roman *triumphus*. For early Christians, Jesus' triumph would be celebrated at his return (see comments on παρουσία, "advent," below). In Mark, Jesus' entry into the city of Jerusalem (Mark 11:1–11) may have impressed inhabitants of the Roman world as the prelude to a triumph of sorts, but that was as far as it went. Jesus receives no honors and no acclaim. His affirmation of a close relationship with the Deity leads to cries of blasphemy and to his condemnation to death (14:61–64). Jesus finally receives a triumph, but it is a mock triumph at the hands of the Roman soldiers (see Schmidt, *NTS* 41 [1995] 1–18), who dress him in a purple robe (πορφύρα) and give him a scepter and a crown (στέφανος) of thorns (instead of a laurel wreath); then they salute him: "Hail, king of the Jews!" (15:16–20). This greeting mimicks the well-known greeting extended to the Roman emperor: *(H)ave Caesar,* "Hail, Caesar!" or *(H)ave Imperator,* "Hail, Emperor!" (e.g., Suetonius, *Claud.* 21.6: "Hail, Emperor, we who are about to die salute you"). The soldiers' mockery of Jesus stands in sharp contrast to the picture of genuine respect the Romans not long after Mark's publication would offer to Vespasian and his son Titus: "At the break of dawn, Vespasian and Titus issued forth, crowned [ἐστεφανωμένοι] with laurel and clad in the traditional purple robes [πορφύρα] . . . . Instantly acclamations rose from the troops" (Josephus, *J.W.* 7.5.4 §124–26).

4. *Hailed in divine terms.* Jesus is recognized as God's son by no less an authority than God himself (Mark 1:11; 9:7: ὁ υἱός μου, "my Son"). Perhaps even more dramatic, from the point of view of a first-century Roman, is the confession of the Roman centurion: "Truly this man was the son of God [υἱὸς θεοῦ]" (Mark 15:39). The Vulgate offers a literal translation: *vere homo hic filius Dei erat.* But in Latin inscriptions υἱὸς θεοῦ is usually translated *divi filius,* "son of deity." Even such appellations as "son of the Most High God [υἱὲ τοῦ θεοῦ τοῦ ὑψίστου]" (Mark 5:7) and "holy one of God [ὁ ἅγιος τοῦ θεοῦ]" (Mark 1:24), though clearly derived from Jewish language and background (Gen 14:18–20, 22: אל עליון *ʾēl ʿelyôn* [Hebrew], "God Most High"; 4Q246 2:1: בר עליון *bar ʿelyôn* [Aramaic], "son of the Most High"),

would not have been foreign to the Greco-Roman world. We see this in the cry of the slave girl with the familiar spirit: "These men are servants of the Most High God [τοῦ θεοῦ τοῦ ὑψίστου]" (Acts 16:17). Of course, it could be argued that the language here is not genuinely pagan, coming as it does from the pen of the Lukan evangelist. But "most high god" is attested in non-Jewish, non-Christian sources: "Epikteto fulfilled his vow to the most high god [θεῷ ὑψίστῳ]"; and "the assembled worshippers set in place this stele for god, Zeus most high [θεοῦ Διὸς ὑψίστου]" (see discussion in Horsley, *New Documents*, 1:25–29). Although this usage may ultimately derive from Jewish influence, it is nonetheless important evidence that such a form of address given Jesus would still have a familiar ring to it in the Roman world.

5. *Confessing Jesus as Lord.* Nowhere in Mark is Jesus called κύριος, "Lord," in the sense of divinity (and that probably includes Mark 2:28; 16:19, of course, is not part of the original Markan text). But Jesus is sometimes addressed as κύριος (2:28; 5:19; 7:28; 11:3), which does become a divine title in early Christian literature (Rom 1:4, 7; 4:24 passim). But the lordship of Jesus, in terms that would be well understood in the Roman world, is seen in his actions and in the impression he made on others. The question of the astonished disciples, "Who then is this, that even the wind [ἄνεμος] and the sea [θάλασσα] obey him?" (Mark 4:41), echoes the hyperbole of the emperor cult, which in turn deliberately echoed religious praise for Greco-Roman deities. In an aretalogy of Isis we read "I am mistress of rivers, winds [ἄνεμοι], and the sea [θάλασσα]" (*NewDocs* 1:19–20; cf. Diodorus Siculus 1.27.3–4). Although not in a spirit of adulation, Philo writes matter-of-factly of the time when "the Augustan house assumed the sovereignty of land and sea" (*Flaccus* 103). Elsewhere he states, "This is the Caesar who calmed the torrential storms on every side, who healed the pestilences common to Greeks and barbarians" (*Embassy* 145). One is also reminded of what is said of Antiochus IV Epiphanes (d. 164 B.C.E.), when stricken with a fatal illness: "Thus he who had just been thinking that he could command the waves of the sea, in his superhuman arrogance, and imagining that he could weigh the high mountains in a balance, was brought down to earth and carried in a litter, making the power of God manifest [φανεράν] to all" (2 Macc 9:8; the ironic reference to φανερά, "manifest" [cf. Ἐπιφανής, "Epiphanes" or "Manifest"] should not be missed).

These imperial epithets are echoed in Christian confessions of Jesus. This tendency only intensifies in later Christian literature. For example, "Awaiting the glorious appearing of our great God and Savior Jesus Christ" (Titus 2:13). The political and social difficulty and danger faced by early Christians should be evident. In the face of emperor worship, Christians were claiming that Jesus, whom God had raised from the dead, was the true "son of God," "Savior," and "Lord"— not Caesar. The claim would sound strange and treasonous at the same time— strange because Caesar had apparently defeated Jesus; treasonous because only Caesar was recognized as son of God, savior, lord, and "benefactor" (note the statement attributed to Jesus in Luke 22:25: "Those in authority over them are called 'benefactors [εὐεργέται]'").

Christian literature emphasizes Jesus' lordship in applying to him the imperial titles. In the Fourth Gospel, Jesus is the "Savior of the world" (John 4:42). According to Paul "we eagerly await a savior, the Lord Jesus Christ" (Phil 3:20). One Pauline tradent describes Jesus as "God and Savior" (Titus 2:13; cf. 2 Pet 1:1). σώζειν, "to save," is used frequently in reference to Jesus' ministry. And, as noted above, even the concept of triumph is taken up in Christology: "He disarmed the principalities and powers and made a public example of them, triumphing [θριαμβεύσας] over them in him" (Col 2:15). One thinks of the Flavian triumph, following Titus's conquest of Jerusalem, in which Jewish prisoners and trophies were paraded through the streets of Rome. (Alluding to the same imagery, Paul seems to imagine himself among God's prisoners; cf. 2 Cor 2:14: "God . . . in Christ always leads us in triumph.")

6. *Healing.* Healing miracles find prominent expression in the evangelists' portraits of Jesus' ministry. In Mark's Gospel they are especially prominent when the ratio of miracle stories to length of the Gospel is taken into account (1:21–28, 29–31, 32–34, 40–45; 2:1–12; 3:1–6, 7–12; 4:35–41; 5:1–20, 21–43; 6:35–44, 47–52, 53–56; 7:24–30, 31–37; 8:1–10, 22–26; 9:14–29; 10:46–52). Jesus' use of spittle to heal blind men (Mark 8:22–26; John 9:1–12) and a deaf-mute (Mark 7:31–37) parallels Vespasian's use of spittle to heal a blind man (Suetonius, *Vesp.* 7.2–3).

7. *Seated or standing at God's right hand.* The single most significant self-reference made by Jesus in the Markan Gospel is his assertion that the high priest would see him "seated at the right hand" of God (Mark 14:61). Although based on Ps 110:1, an OT text cited and alluded to many times in the NT, the image of sitting at God's right hand would, quite apart from familiarity with the Jewish Scriptures, evoke in the minds of Romans ideas of the emperor cult. It is not Caesar who sits next to God, the Markan evangelist avers; it is Jesus.

8. *Libations in honor of Christ.* In his final meal with his disciples Jesus shares a cup of wine. Evidently he describes it as his "blood of the covenant, which is poured out for many" (Mark 14:24). In various ways the Matthean and Lukan evangelists make explicit the link between the cup and Jesus' reference to his blood (cf. Matt 26:27b–28; Luke 22:20b), which in Mark is only implied. Paul's tradition of the Supper adds the saying, "Do this, as often as you drink it, in remembrance of me" (1 Cor 11:25). The cup in remembrance of Jesus may have suggested a parallel to the libations drunk in honor of Caesar.

9. *The hope of Jesus' advent (or Parousia) and the promise of a new world order.* Early Christians spoke of the παρουσία, "advent," of Jesus, at which time judgment would take place (Matt 24:3, 27, 37, 39; but earlier in Paul, cf. 1 Cor 15:23; 1 Thess 2:19; 3:13; 4:15; 5:23; and in other writers, cf. Jas 5:7, 8; 2 Pet 1:16; 3:4; 1 John 2:28). In Mark the word παρουσία is not employed, but the expectation of Jesus' return is emphasized in chap. 13 (esp. vv 26–27, 33–37) and plays an important part in Jesus' reply to Caiaphas: "You will see the son of man . . . coming with the clouds of heaven" (14:62). The proclamation of the coming of the kingdom of God (Mark 1:15) would relate to the Roman world as the promise of a new world order. Only the "Son of God" could make such a promise and effect such a result.

10. *Post-mortem deification.* A central component in early Christianity's proclamation of the risen Jesus is his enthronement, at God's right hand, as God's Son, who lives forever. In Mark's Gospel Jesus repeatedly foretells his death and resurrection (8:31; 9:31; 10:33–34), while he confesses to Caiaphas that he will be seen seated at God's right hand, coming with the clouds of heaven (14:62). The centurion's confession that Jesus was "truly the son of God" (15:39) is the equivalent of deification, but the discovery of the empty tomb and the (angelic?) announcement that he has risen (16:4–7) provide divine confirmation of the truth of Jesus' predictions.

It is in this context that the Markan evangelist boldly sets forth his apologetic. Despite rejection at the hands of his own people (and the most important people, as importance would have been measured at that time) and a shameful death at the hands of the most powerful people, Jesus was indeed the Son of God, humanity's true Savior and Lord. Mark's purpose is to narrate the story of Jesus in such a way that such a confession will appear compelling and plausible to Jews and Romans alike. (Mark's presentation seems to possess more affinities with the Roman imperial cult than with the old Greek stories of epic heroes like Odysseus or Hector; *pace* MacDonald, *Homeric Epics and the Gospel of Mark.*) Mark attempts this goal in the second half of his Gospel (8:27–16:8) in two principal ways: (1) he shows that Jesus was fully aware of the fate that awaited him in Jerusalem, and so instructed his fearful disciples in what lay ahead; and (2) he shows how Jesus with courage, calm, and dignity faced opposition, arrest, abuse, and a cruel death. In every way, Jesus cuts an impressive figure, a figure who had announced the impending rule of God. Implicitly Mark invites his readers to consider this rule.

Mark
8:27–16:20

V. Summons to the Discipleship of Suffering (8:27–9:50)

Bibliography

Baarlink, B. *Anfängliches Evangelium: Ein Beitrag zur näheren Bestimmung der theologischen Motive im Markusevangelium.* Kampen: Kok, 1977. 273–74. **Best, E.** *Following Jesus: Discipleship in the Gospel of Mark.* JSNTSup 4. Sheffield: JSOT Press, 1981. **Evans, C. A.** "The Hermeneutics of Mark and John: On the Theology of the Canonical 'Gospel.'" *Bib* 64 (1983) 153–72. **Faw, C. E.** "The Heart of the Gospel of Mark." *JBR* 24 (1956) 77–82. **Iersel, B. van.** *Reading Mark.* 122–41. **Kingsbury, J. D.** *Christology.* 89–107. **Lafontaine, R., and Mourlon Beernaert, P.** "Essai sur la structure de Marc, 8,27–9,13." *RSR* 57 (1969) 543–61. **Lambrecht, J.** "The Christology of Mark." *BTB* 3 (1973) 256–73. **Reedy, C. J.** "Mark 8:31–11:10 and the Gospel Ending: A Redaction Study." *CBQ* 34 (1972) 188–97. **Robbins, V. K.** "Summons and Outline in Mark: The Three-Step Progression." *NovT* 23 (1981) 97–114. **Schweizer, E.** "Zur Frage des Messiasgeheimnisses bei Markus." *ZNW* 56 (1965) 1–8. **Shiner, W. T.** *Follow Me! Disciples in Markan Rhetoric.* SBLDS 145. Atlanta: Scholars Press, 1995. **Simonsen, H.** "Mark 8,27–10,52 i Markusevangeliets komposition." *DTT* 27 (1964) 83–99. **Stein, R. H.** *The Synoptic Problem.* Grand Rapids, MI: Baker, 1987. 258–63. **Stock, A.** *Call to Discipleship: A Literary Study of Mark's Gospel.* GNS 1. Wilmington, DE: Glazier, 1982. 129–48. **Tolbert, M. A.** *Sowing the Gospel: Mark's World in Literary-Historical Perspective.* Minneapolis: Fortress, 1989. 187–92. **Venetz, H.-J.** "Widerspruch und Nachfolge: Zur Frage des Glaubens an Jesus nach Mk 8,27–10,52." *FZPhTh* 19 (1972) 111–19. **Weiss, K.** "Ekklesiologie, Tradition und Geschichte in der Jüngerunterweisung Mark. 8,27–10,52." In *Der historische Jesus und der kerygmatische Christus.* Ed. H. Ristow and K. Matthiae. Berlin: Evangelische Verlagsanstalt, 1960. 414–38. **Wrege, H.-Th.** *Die Gestalt des Evangeliums: Aufbau und Struktur der Synoptiker sowie der Apostelgeschichte.* BBET 11. Bern; Frankfurt am Main: Lang, 1978. 97–100.

Introduction

Mark 8:27–10:45 constitutes two major sections that introduce the Passion Narrative (8:27–9:50; 10:1–45). In these sections we find Jesus confessed as Messiah (8:27–30) but predicting his suffering and death (8:31–33) and teaching that his followers must be prepared to face the same fate (8:34–9:1). Jesus' solemn and disturbing asseveration receives divine confirmation in the appearance of Elijah and Moses and in the utterance of the heavenly voice (9:2–8). Following the transfiguration, Jesus predicts his passion a second time and identifies the martyred Baptist as the awaited Elijah (9:9–13). The next passage, that of healing the demon-afflicted boy (9:14–29), initially seems out of place. Why has this miracle story been reserved for this point in the narrative? Two elements in the story suggest that it is appropriate here after all. First, the disciples' failure to exorcise the demon leads Jesus to exclaim in exasperation: "O unbelieving generation, how long shall I be with you?" (9:19). The nature of his rhetorical question hints at Jesus' impending death and so is appropriate to the larger context in which Jesus speaks of his passion. Second, the exorcism leaves the boy "like a corpse; so that many were saying that he had died" (9:26). But he is not dead; Jesus takes him by the hand, "and he stood" (9:27). Thus, the conclusion of the miracle story in a certain sense foreshadows Jesus' passion.

The passion theme continues in an explicit manner with yet another passion prediction in 9:30–32. The discussion of who is the greatest (9:33–37) occasions Jesus' statement of service and so furthers the preparation for the passion. Even the exchange concerning the exorcist who was invoking Jesus' name but was not a follower of Jesus (9:38–41) appears to be tailored for the context of preparation for the passion. The disciples must maintain an attitude of humility, not only toward the young and uninfluential (such as the children in 9:36–37) but toward others outside of the community. The promise of reward for an act of mercy (9:41) anticipates the time of suffering and want that many in the early church will experience. The hint of future judgment leads to the next pericope (9:42–50), which warns believers to prepare for temptation and, in graphic pictures, to cast aside sources of temptation. The concluding statement, "be at peace with one another" (9:50), links the last three pericopes (9:33–37, 38–41, 42–50). The theme of family relations continues in chap. 10. Jesus the teacher (10:1) speaks on the permanence of marriage (10:2–12) and the need to enter the kingdom of God as children (10:13–16). Qualifications for entering the kingdom lie at the heart of the exchange between Jesus and the wealthy young man who asks about inheriting eternal life (10:17–22). Jesus then speaks on the dangers of wealth and reassures his disciples that whatever they give up in service of the gospel will be repaid to them many times over (10:23–31).

The final three pericopes in this major section recapitulate themes already touched upon. For a third time Jesus formally predicts his passion (10:32–34). The disciples once again dispute among themselves concerning who is the greatest (10:35–40, 41–45). In both pericopes Jesus teaches that suffering and service must precede glory (vv 38–39, 43–44). He himself offers the supreme example: as "son of man" he "did not come to be served but to serve, and to give his life as a ransom for many" (v 45).

Jesus' passion has been predicted, and it has been interpreted. His death is not unexpected; it is not a misadventure. It is his purpose, recognized in the most northern parts of Israel, before he turns southward and begins his fateful journey to Jerusalem. His suffering and death are his necessary service if Israel is to be ransomed. In this section Jesus' understanding of messiahship has been clarified, and, along with it, the meaning of his death has been explained. In a deliberate and noble fashion Jesus has offered his life for his people.

A. The Confession and Rebuke of Peter   (8:27–33)

Bibliography

Abrahams, I. *Studies in Pharisaism and the Gospels.* 1:136–38; 2:17–21. **Allison, D. C.** *The End of the Ages Has Come: An Early Interpretation of the Passion and Resurrection of Jesus.* Studies of the New

Testament and Its World. Edinburgh: T. & T. Clark, 1987. 137–40. **Althausen, J.** "Wer sagt denn ihr, dass ich sei? (Mk 8,29)." *LR* 27 (1977) 89–100. **Baarlink, B.** *Anfängliches Evangelium: Ein Beitrag zur näheren Bestimmung der theologischen Motive im Markusevangelium.* Kampen: Kok, 1977. 214–21. **Barrett, C. K.** *Jesus and the Gospel Tradition.* London: S. P. C. K./Philadelphia: Fortress, 1967. 35–39. **Barton, G. A.** "The Use of ἐπιτιμᾶν in Mark 8, 30 and 3, 12." *JBL* 41 (1922) 233–36. **Bastin, M.** "L'annonce de la Passion et les critères de l'historicité." *RevScRel* 50 (1976) 289–329. ———. *Jésus devant sa passion.* LD 92. Paris: Cerf, 1976. 124–38. **Bauer, J. B.** "Drei Tage." *Bib* 39 (1958) 354–58. **Bayer, H. F.** *Jesus' Predictions of Vindication and Resurrection: The Provenance, Meaning and Correlation of the Synoptic Predictions.* WUNT 2.20. Tübingen: Mohr-Siebeck, 1986. 154–66. **Beasley-Murray, G. R.** *Jesus and the Kingdom of God.* 237–47. **Beavis, M. A.** *Mark's Audience: The Literary and Social Setting of Mark 4.11–12.* JSNTSup 33. Sheffield: JSOT Press, 1989. 116–23. **Bennett, W. J., Jr.** "The Son of Man Must . . ." *NovT* 17 (1975) 113–29. **Berger, K.** *Die Auferstehung des Propheten und die Erhöhung des Menschensohnes: Traditionsgeschichtliche Untersuchungen zu Deutung des Geschickes Jesu in frühchristlichen Texte.* SUNT 13. Göttingen: Vandenhoeck & Ruprecht, 1976. 138–40. **Best, E.** *The Temptation and the Passion: The Markan Soteriology.* SNTSMS 2. Cambridge: Cambridge UP, 1965. 121–24. **Bishop, J.** "*Parabole* and *Parrhesia* in Mark." *Int* 40 (1986) 39–52. **Black, M.** *An Aramaic Approach.* 218. ———. "The 'Son of Man' Passion Sayings in the Gospel Tradition." *ZNW* 60 (1969) 1–8. **Boers, H.** "The Unity of the Gospel of Mark." *Scriptura* 4 (1981) 1–7. **Boring, M. E.** *Sayings of the Risen Jesus: Christian Prophecy in the Synoptic Tradition.* SNTSMS 46. Cambridge: Cambridge UP, 1982. **Brown, R. E.** "Peter in the Gospel of Mark." In *Peter in the New Testament: A Collaborative Assessment by Protestant and Catholic Scholars.* Ed. R. E. Brown et al. New York: Paulist/Minneapolis: Augsburg, 1973. 64–73, esp. 64–69. **Bruce, F. F.** *The Time Is Fulfilled: Five Aspects of Fulfilment of the Old Testament in the New.* Exeter: Paternoster, 1978; Grand Rapids, MI: Eerdmans, 1995. 15–32. **Bultmann, R.** "Die Frage nach dem messianischen Bewusstsein Jesu und das Petrus-Bekenntnis." *ZNW* 19 (1919–20) 165–74 (repr. in R. Bultmann. *Exegetica: Aufsätze zur Erforschung des Neuen Testaments.* Ed. E. Dinkler. Tübingen: Mohr-Siebeck, 1967. 1–9). **Burkill, T. A.** *Mysterious Revelation.* 168–87. ———. "St. Mark's Philosophy of the Passion." *NovT* 2 (1958) 245–71. **Bussby, F.** "Mark viii.33: A Mistranslation from the Aramaic?" *ExpTim* 61 (1949–50) 159. **Carmignac, J.** "Studies in the Hebrew Background of the Synoptic Gospels." *ASTI* 7 (1970) 64–93. **Catchpole, D. R.** "The 'Triumphal' Entry." In *Jesus and the Politics of His Day.* Ed. E. Bammel and C. F. D. Moule. Cambridge: Cambridge UP, 1984. 319–34. **Charlesworth, J. H.** "Has the Name 'Peter' Been Found among the Dead Sea Scrolls?" In *Christen und Christliches in Qumran?* Ed. B. Mayer. Eichstätter Studien 32. Regensburg: Pustet, 1992. 213–23. **Chilton, B. D.** "The Son of Man: Human and Heavenly." In *The Four Gospels 1992.* FS F. Neirynck, ed. F. Van Segbroeck et al. BETL 100. 3 vols. Leuven: Peeters; Leuven UP, 1992. 1:203–18. **Claudel, G.** *La confession de Pierre: Trajectorie d'une péricope évangelique.* Paris: Gabalda, 1988. 208–31, 247–307. **Colpe, C.** "Traditionsüberschreitende Argumentationen zu Aussagen Jesu über sich selbst." In *Tradition und Glaube: Das frühe Christentum in seiner Umwelt.* FS K. G. Kuhn, ed. G. Jeremias et al. Göttingen: Vandenhoeck & Ruprecht, 1971. 230–45, esp. 239–43. **Conzelmann, H.** "Das Selbstbewusstsein Jesu." In *Theologie als Schriftauslegung: Aufsätze zum Neuen Testament.* BEvT 65. Munich: Kaiser, 1974. 30–41. **Corbin, M.** "Le Christ de Dieu: Méditation théologique sur Lc 9, 18–27." *NRT* 99 (1977) 641–80. **Cullmann, O.** "L'Apôtre Pierre instrument du diable et instrument de Dieu." In *New Testament Essays.* FS T. W. Manson, ed. A. J. B. Higgins. Manchester: Manchester UP, 1959. 94–105. **Cuvillier, E.** "'Il proclamait ouvertement la Parole': Notule sur la traduction de Marc 8/32a." *ETR* 63 (1988) 427–28. **Denaux, A.** "La confession de Pierre et la première annonce de la Passion: Mc 8,27–33." *AsSeign* 2.55 (1974) 31–39. **Dinkler, E.** "Peter's Confession and the 'Satan' Saying: The Problem of Jesus' Messiahship." In *The Future of Our Religious Past.* FS R. Bultmann, ed. J. M. Robinson. New York: Harper & Row, 1971. 169–202. **Dupont, J.** "Ressuscité 'le troisième jour.'" *Bib* 40 (1959) 742–61. **Ebeling, H. J.** *Das Messiasgeheimnis und die Botschaft des Markusevangeliums.* Berlin: Töpelmann, 1939. 204–20. **Ernst, J.** "Petrusbekenntnis—Leidensankündigung—Satanswort (Mk 8,27–33): Tradition und

Redaktion." *Catholica* 32 (1978) 46–73. **Farmer, W. R.** "The Passion Prediction Passages and the Synoptic Problem: A Test Case." *NTS* 36 (1990) 558–70. **Feuillet, A.** "Les trois grandes prophéties de la passion et de la résurrection des évangiles synoptiques." *RThom* 67 (1967) 533–60; 68 (1968) 41–74. **France, R. T.** *Jesus and the Old Testament.* 125–30. ———. "The Servant of the Lord in the Teaching of Jesus." *TynBul* 19 (1968) 26–52, esp. 43–49. **Frankemölle, H.** "Jüdische Messiaserwartung und christlicher Messiasglaube: Hermeneutische Anmerkungen im Kontext des Petrusbekenntnisses Mk 8,29." *Kairos* 20 (1978) 97–109. **Glasson, T. F.** "The Uniqueness of Christ: The New Testament Witness." *EvQ* 43 (1971) 25–35. **Greig, J. C. G.** "The Problem of the Messianic Interpretation of Jesus' Ministry in the Primitive Church." *SE* 6 (1973) 197–220, esp. 206–10. **Grimm, W.** *Weil Ich dich liebe: Die Verkündigung Jesu und Deuterojesaja.* ANTJ 1. Bern; Frankfurt am Main: Lang, 1976. 201–22. **Gubler, M.-L.** *Die frühesten Deutungen des Todes Jesu: Eine motivgeschichtliche Darstellung aufgrund der neueren exegetischen Forschung.* OBO 15. Göttingen: Vandenhoeck & Ruprecht, 1977. 107–17, 230–42. **Güttgemanns, E.** *Offene Fragen zur Formgeschichte des Evangeliums: Eine methodologische Skizze der Grundlagenproblematik der Form- und Redaktionsgeschichte.* BEvT 54. Munich: Kaiser, 1970. 211–23. **Haenchen, E.** "Die Komposition von Mk vii [*sic*] 27–ix 1 und par." *NovT* 6 (1963) 81–109. **Hahn, F.** *The Titles of Jesus in Christology: Their History in Early Christianity.* Tr. H. Knight and G. Ogg. London: Lutterworth, 1969. 15–67. **Hampel, V.** *Menschensohn und historischer Jesus: Ein Rätselwort als Schlüssel zum messianischen Selbstverständnis Jesu.* Neukirchen-Vluyn: Neukirchener Verlag, 1990. 269–82. **Hasenfratz, H.-P.** *Die Rede von der Auferstehung Jesu Christi: Ein methodologischer Versuch.* FTL 10. Bonn: Linguistica Biblica, 1975. 108–14. **Hoehner, H. W.** *Herod Antipas.* SNTSMS 17. Cambridge: Cambridge UP, 1972. 317–30. **Hoffmann, P.** "Mk 8,31: Zur Herkunft und markinischen Rezeption einer alten Überlieferung." In *Orientierung an Jesus.* FS J. Schmid, ed. P. Hoffmann et al. Freiburg: Herder, 1973. 170–204. **Hooker, M. D.** *The Son of Man in Mark.* 103–16. ———. *Studying the New Testament.* London: Epworth, 1979; Minneapolis: Augsburg, 1982. 47–69. **Horsley, R. A.** "'Like One of the Prophets of Old': Two Types of Popular Prophets at the Time of Jesus." *CBQ* 47 (1985) 435–63. **Horstmann, M.** *Studien zur markinischen Christologie.* 8–31. **Howard, V. P.** "Did Jesus Speak about His Own Death?" *CBQ* 39 (1977) 515–27. **Jeremias, J.** *New Testament Theology.* 276–99. ———. "Die Drei-Tage-Worte der Evangelium." In *Tradition und Glaube: Das frühe Christentum in seiner Umwelt.* FS K. G. Kuhn, ed. G. Jeremias et al. Göttingen: Vandenhoeck & Ruprecht, 1971. 221–29. **Johnson, S. E.** *Jesus and His Towns.* GNS 29. Wilmington, DE: Glazier, 1989. 80–89. **Jonge, M. de.** "The Use of ὁ χριστός in the Passion Narratives." In *Jésus aux origines de la christologie.* Ed. J. Dupont. BETL 40. Gembloux: Duculot; Leuven: Leuven UP, 1975. 169–92. **Karrer, M.** *Der Gesalbte: Die Grundlagen des Christustitels.* FRLANT 151. Göttingen: Vandenhoeck & Ruprecht, 1990. 356–59. **Kato, Z.** *Die Völkermission im Markusevangelium: Eine redaktionsgeschichtliche Untersuchung.* Bern; Frankfurt am Main: Lang, 1986. 100–104. **Kazmierski, C. R.** "Mk 8,33—Eine Ermahnung an die Kirche?" In *Biblische Randbemerkungen.* FS R. Schnackenburg, ed. H. Merklein and J. Lange. Würzburg: Echter, 1974. 103–12. **Klein, H.** "Das Bekenntnis des Petrus und die Anfänge des Christusglaubens im Urchristentum." *EvT* 47 (1987) 176–92. **Koch, K.** "Zum Verhältnis von Christologie und Eschatologie im Markusevangelium: Beobachtungen aufgrund von Mk 8,27–9,1." In *Jesus Christus in Historie und Geschichte.* FS H. Conzelmann, ed. G. Strecker. Tübingen: Mohr-Siebeck, 1975. 395–408. **Kuthirakkattel, S.** *The Beginning of Jesus' Ministry according to Mark's Gospel (1,14–3,6): A Redaction Critical Study.* AnBib 123. Rome: Biblical Institute, 1990. 37–45. **Lindars, B.** *Jesus Son of Man: A Fresh Examination of the Son of Man Sayings in the Gospels in the Light of Recent Research.* London: S. P. C. K./Grand Rapids, MI: Eerdmans, 1983. 60–84. **Luz, U.** "Das Geheimnismotiv und die markinische Christologie." *ZNW* 56 (1965) 9–30, esp. 20–28 (ET: "The Secrecy Motif and the Marcan Christology." In *The Messianic Secret.* Ed. C. M. Tuckett. 75–96). **Maier, F. W.** *Jesus—Lehrer der Gottesherrschaft.* Würzburg: Echter, 1965. 149–52. **Malina, B. J.,** and **Rohrbaugh, R. L.** *Social-Science Commentary.* 228–32. **Martini, C. M.** "La confessione messianica di Pietro a Cesarea e l'inizio del nuovo popolo di Dio secondo il vangelo di S. Marco (8,27–33)." *Civiltà Cattolica* 118 (1967) 544–51. **Matera, F. J.** "The Incomprehension of the Disciples and Peter's

Confession (Mark 6,14–8,30)." *Bib* 70 (1989) 153–72. **Mays, J. L.** "Mark 8:27–9:1." *Int* 30 (1976) 174–78. **McArthur, H. K.** "'On the Third Day' (1 Cor 15.4b and Rabbinic Interpretation of Hosea 6.2)." *NTS* 18 (1971–72) 81–86. **Metz, J.,** and **Moltmann, J.** *Leidensgeschichte: Zwei Meditationen zu Markus 8,31–38.* Freiburg: Herder, 1974. **Meye, R. P.** *Jesus and the Twelve: Discipleship and Revelation in Mark's Gospel.* Grand Rapids, MI: Eerdmans, 1968. 73–80. **Michel, O.** "Der Umbruch: Messianität = Menschensohn: Fragen zu Markus 8,31." In *Tradition und Glaube: Das frühe Christentum in seiner Umwelt.* FS K. G. Kuhn, ed. G. Jeremias and H.-W. Stegemann. Göttingen: Vandenhoeck & Ruprecht, 1971. 310–16. **Minette de Tillesse, G.** *Le secret messianique.* 293–326, 368–80, 390–94. **Montefiore, C. G.** *The Synoptic Gospels.* 1:179–203. **Moule, C. F. D.** *Essays in New Testament Interpretation.* Cambridge: Cambridge UP, 1982. 75–90. ———. *The Origin of Christology.* Cambridge: Cambridge UP, 1977. 11–22. ———. "'The Son of Man': Some of the Facts." *NTS* 41 (1995) 277–79. **Müller, U. B.** "Die christologische Absicht des Markusevangeliums und die Verklärungsgeschichte." *ZNW* 64 (1973) 159–93. **Mundle, W.** "Die Geschichtlichkeit des messianischen Bewusstseins Jesu." *ZNW* 21 (1922) 299–311. **Oberlinner, L.** *Todeserwartung und Todesgewissheit Jesu: Zum Problem einer historischen Begründung.* SBB 10. Stuttgart: Katholisches Bibelwerk, 1980. 140–46. **Osborne, B. A. E.** "Peter: Stumbling-Block and Satan." *NovT* 15 (1973) 187–90. **Patsch, H.** *Abendmahl und historischer Jesus.* Calwer Theologische Monographien. Stuttgart: Calwer, 1972. 185–97. **Perrin, N.** "Towards an Interpretation of the Gospel of Mark." In *Christology and a Modern Pilgrimage: A Discussion with Norman Perrin.* Ed. H. D. Betz. Claremont: New Testament Colloquium, 1971. 1–78, esp. 14–30. **Perry, J. M.** "The Three Days in the Synoptic Passion Predictions." *CBQ* 48 (1986) 637–54. **Pesch, R.** *Das Evangelium der Urgemeinde.* 104–12. ———. "Das Messiasbekenntnis des Petrus (Mk 8,27–30): Neuhandlung einer alten Frage." *BZ* 17 (1973) 178–95; 18 (1974) 20–31. ———. "Die Passion des Menschensohns: Eine Studie zu den Menschensohnsworten der vormarkinischen Passionsgeschichte." In *Jesus und der Menschensohn.* FS A. Vögtle, ed. R. Pesch and R. Schnackenburg. Freiburg: Herder, 1975. 166–95. **Potterie, I. de la.** "La confessione messianica di Pietro in Marco 8,27–33." In *San Pietro.* Ed. G. Canfora. Brescia: Paideia, 1967. 59–77. **Pudussery, P. S.** *Discipleship: A Call to Suffering and Glory: An Exegetico-Theological Study of Mk 8,27–9,1; 13,9–13 and 13,24–27.* Rome: Libreria "Alma Mater," 1987. 42–140. **Quesnell, Q.** *The Mind of Mark: Interpretation and Method through the Exegesis of Mark 6,52.* AnBib 38. Rome: Biblical Institute, 1969. 129–38. **Reploh, K.-G.** *Markus—Lehrer der Gemeinde.* 89–104. **Robinson, J. A. T.** "Elijah, John and Jesus." In *Twelve New Testament Studies.* SBT 34. London: SCM Press; Naperville, IL: Allenson, 1962. 28–52. **Sandmel, S.** "'Son of Man' in Mark." In *In the Time of Harvest.* FS A. H. Silver, ed. D. J. Silver. New York: Macmillan, 1963. 355–67 (repr. in S. Sandmel. *Two Living Traditions: Essays on Religion and the Bible.* Detroit: Wayne State UP, 1972. 166–77, 349). **Saunders, D. J.** "The Confession of Peter." *TS* 10 (1949) 522–40. **Schaberg, J.** "Daniel 7.12 and the New Testament Passion-Resurrection Predictions." *NTS* 31 (1985) 208–22. **Schadewaldt, W.** "Die Zuverlässigkeit der synoptischen Tradition." *TBei* 13 (1982) 201–23, esp. 215–19. **Schenke, L.** *Studien zur Passionsgeschichte des Markus.* 244–71. **Schille, G.** "Prolegomena zur Jesusfrage." *TLZ* 93 (1968) 481–88. **Schnackenburg, R.** "Zur formgeschichtlichen Methode in der Evangelienforschung." *ZKT* 85 (1963) 16–32. **Schnider, F.** *Jesus der Prophet.* OBO 2. Freiburg: Universitätsverlag; Göttingen: Vandenhoeck & Ruprecht, 1973. 183–87. **Schreiber, J.** "Wellhausen und Wrede: Eine methodische Differenz." *ZNW* 80 (1989) 24–41, esp. 27–31. **Schürmann, H.** "Wie hat Jesus seinen Tod bestanden und verstanden? Eine methodenkritische Besinnung." In *Orientierung an Jesus.* FS J. Schmid, ed. P. Hoffmann et al. Freiburg: Herder, 1973. 325–63. **Schwarz, G.** *Jesus "der Menschensohn": Aramaistische Untersuchungen zu den synoptischen Menschensohnworten Jesu.* BWANT 119. Stuttgart: Kohlhammer, 1986. 185–87, 275–78. **Sjöberg, E.** *Der verborgene Menschensohn in den Evangelien.* Skrifter utg. av Kungl. Humanistiska vetenskapssamfundet i Lund 53. Lund: Gleerup, 1955. 100–132, 150–75. **Smith, T. V.** *Petrine Controversies in Early Christianity: Attitudes towards Peter in Christian Writings of the First Two Centuries.* WUNT 2.15. Tübingen: Mohr-Siebeck, 1985. 164–70. **Strecker, G.** "Die Leidens- und Auferstehungsvoraussagen im Markusevangelium (Mk 8,31; 9,31; 10,32–34)." *ZTK* 64 (1967)

16–39 (ET: "The Passion and Resurrection Predictions in Mark's Gospel." *Int* 22 [1968] 421–42). **Taylor, V.** *Jesus and His Sacrifice.* 85–91. ————. "The Origin of the Markan Passion-Sayings." *NTS* 1 (1954–55) 159–67 (repr. in V. Taylor. *New Testament Essays.* London: Epworth, 1970. 60–71). **Thyen, H.** *Studien zur Sündenvergeben im Neuen Testament und seinen alttestamentlichen und jüdischen Voraussetzungen.* FRLANT 96. Göttingen: Vandenhoeck & Ruprecht, 1970. 218–36. **Vögtle, A.** "Messiasbekenntnis und Petrusverheissung: Zur Komposition Mt 16, 13–23 Par." *BZ* 1 (1957) 252–72; 2 (1958) 85–103. **Walker, N.** "After Three Days." *NTS* 4 (1960) 261–62. **Willaert, B.** "La connexion littéraire entre la première prédiction de la passion et la confession de Pierre chez les synoptiques." *ETL* 32 (1956) 24–45. **Yates, J. E.** *The Spirit and the Kingdom.* London: S. P. C. K., 1963. 108–18. **Zimmermann, H.** *Jesus Christus: Geschichte und Verkündigung.* Stuttgart: Katholisches Bibelwerk, 1973. 263–67.

Translation

[27] *Jesus and his disciples went out into the villages of* [a] *Caesarea of Philip. And on the way he was asking his disciples, saying to them, "Who do people say that I am?"* [28] *They said* [b] *to him, saying, "John the Baptist, and others, Elijah, but others, one of the prophets."* [29] *And he was asking them, "But who do you say that I am?" Answering,* [c] *Peter says to him, "You are the Messiah.* [d] *"* [30] *And he* [e] *strictly charged them that they should speak to no one concerning him.* [f]

[31] *And* [g] *he began to teach them that it is necessary for the "son of man"* [h] *to suffer many things and to be rejected by the elders and the ruling priests and the scribes and to be killed and after three days* [i] *to rise up.* [32] *Now he was stating the matter plainly. And taking him aside, Peter* [j] *began to rebuke him.* [33] *But turning and seeing his disciples, he rebuked Peter* [j] *and says, "Get behind me, opponent,* [k] *for you are not thinking the things of God but the things of humans."*

Notes

[a] D omits τὰς κώμας, "the villages of."

[b] Many MSS read ἀπεκρίθησαν, "they answered."

[c] The Syriac reads *kêpā²*, "Kepha"; other Gk. MSS add Σίμων, "Simon." Syr. MSS frequently use Peter's Aram. name, "Kepha" (Aram.: אכפ כ *kêpā²*; Gk.: Κηφᾶς ["Cephas" in most Eng. translations]). Both Πέτρος, "Peter," and אכפ כ *kêpā²* mean "rock" (cf. John 1:42).

[d] Gk. ὁ χριστός, lit. "the anointed [one]." The Gk. translates the Heb. מָשִׁיחַ *māšîaḥ.* The Gk. sometimes transliterates the Heb. μεσσίας (cf. John 1:41; 4:25). See commentary on 8:29 below. ℵ and a few other authorities add ὁ υἱὸς τοῦ θεοῦ, "the Son of God," while W and others add ὁ υἱὸς τοῦ θεοῦ τοῦ ζῶντος, "the Son of the living God." Both of these variants are due to the influence of Matt 16:16.

[e] A few authorities add Ἰησοῦς, "Jesus."

[f] A few MSS add ὅτι αὐτός ἐστιν ὁ χριστός, "because he is the Christ" (cf. Matt 16:20).

[g] W and other authorities add ἀπὸ τότε, "from then on" (cf. Matt 16:21).

[h] Eng. translations frequently capitalize "Son" in the expression "Son of man" (e.g., the RSV). Capitalization, however, is misleading, for it implies that the expression is technical and perhaps approximate to the use of "Son" in "Son of God." I have chosen to leave the expression in lowercase letters, but in quotation marks to indicate the *specificity* of the expression. For more on this, see the discussion in the *Introduction.*

[i] W and other authorities read τῇ τρίτῃ ἡμέρᾳ, "on the third day." This variant is due to the influence of Matthew (cf. 16:21; 17:23; 20:19; cf. 27:64) and perhaps also to early Christian preaching, as seen in Paul (cf. 1 Cor 15:4). See *Note* d on Mark 9:31 below.

[j] The Peshitta reads *kêpā²*, "Kepha"; another Syr. tradition reads *šim⁽ôn kêpā²*, "Simon Kepha."

[k] σατανᾶ is usually transliterated "Satan," i.e., one who opposes. It will be argued in the *Comment* below that Peter has been rebuked as one who *opposes* Jesus and that Jesus did not call him "Satan."

Form/Structure/Setting

8:27–30 Peter's confession of the messiahship of Jesus has been much discussed by scholars. Opinions have ranged from the acceptance of the pericope as generally historical and reliable (Baarlink, *Anfängliches Evangelium*, 211–14; Bayer, *Jesus' Predictions*, 155–57) to its rejection as a piece of theological fiction (as in Wrede, *Messianic Secret*), developed either by the evangelist himself or tradents before him (Horstmann, *Studien zur markinischen Christologie*, 12–18), perhaps in order to explain Peter's place of priority in 1 Cor 15:3b–5 (as argued by Catchpole, "The 'Triumphal' Entry," 328). In my opinion the first option has much more to commend it than does the second. There are good reasons for holding this view.

First, the noticeable reticence in the tradition to have Jesus claim messianic status argues for the authenticity of the passage. That is, where in the Synoptic Gospels do we have Jesus proclaiming his messiahship? If early Christians were nonplussed by the paucity of messianic content (again, as Wrede supposed), then why not create unambiguous testimony in which Jesus affirms his messiahship? (The Johannine Gospel, by way of illustration, attests the possibility of the enhancement of Christology.) Mark surely wishes the reader to understand Jesus as Israel's Messiah; he says so in his incipit: "The good news of Jesus Christ, the Son of God" (Mark 1:1). But the only places where Jesus is identified as Messiah are in Peter's confession in the passage under consideration and in the high priest's question (Mark 14:61). This meager messianic content gives evidence of editorial restraint on the part of the evangelist; he has not embellished the tradition of the messiahship of Jesus, even though he may have been tempted to do so.

Second, the Jewish tradition of messianic recognition being offered by followers, not claimed by candidates, seems to be presupposed here (*pace* Bultmann, *History*, 257). One immediately thinks of the rabbinic traditions regarding Simon ben Kosiba. Perhaps best known is Rabbi Aqiba's application of Num 24:17 ("a star goes forth from Jacob") to Simon *bar kokhba*, "the star," and his solemn declaration: "This is the king Messiah!" (*y. Taʿan.* 4.5). In all probability Aqiba and other rabbis did recognize Simon as the Messiah (though the ancient editors of the talmuds and midrashim wished to leave us with a different impression). It is hard otherwise to explain the magnitude of the Bar Kokhba War (132–135 C.E.) and the great difficulty that the Romans encountered in putting down the rebellion (for Roman sources, see Fronto's *Letter to Emperor Marcus Aurelius;* Dio Cassius, *Hist. Rom.* 69.12.1–14.3; for Christian sources, see Justin, *1 Apol.* 31.5–6; Eusebius, *Hist. eccl.* 4.5.2; id., *Chronicle,* Hadrian Year 16; id., *Dem. ev.* 6.13; in a few of his letters Simon refers to himself as the "Prince of Israel [נשיא ישראל *nāśîʾ yiśrāʾēl*]"). But in the aftermath of defeat the reputation of Simon understandably suffered. The rabbinic tradition goes on to debunk the famous rabbi's interpretation: "Aqiba, grass will grow out of your cheek bones and Messiah will not have come!" The rabbinic tradition completely discredits the memory of Simon; he emerges as fraud (or "liar"), blasphemer, and tyrant (*y. Taʿan.* 4.5 = *Lam. Rab.* 2:2 §4; *Pesiq. R.* 30.3; *b. Sanh.* 93b). According to rabbinic tradition Simon also had the audacity himself to claim that he was the Messiah: "I am king Messiah" (*b. Sanh.* 93b). This self-claim, which in all probability Simon never made (on the coins he minted during the revolt he is called "Prince," never "Messiah"), is intended to provide further evidence of the falsity of Simon's messianic identity.

Third, if the Markan evangelist or tradents before him wished to create a story to illustrate or explain Peter's place of priority in 1 Cor 15:3b–5, why debunk Peter with a story about his opposition to Jesus' passion prediction? Whatever ground has been gained by the confession has been given up by this opposition.

Fourth, the tradition that Peter's confession took place in Caesarea Philippi adds verisimilitude: such a confession—the messianic recognition of the beloved rabbi of Galilee, believed by many to be a prophet—would have been provocative, perhaps disturbing, even controversial among Jesus' own following. Associating this confession with Caesarea Philippi was not the result of some sort of political or theological consideration (and certainly not, *pace* Schmithals, 381, an attempt to place Jesus' messiahship in Gentile territory) but the result of the memory that this was the place where Peter had uttered those fateful words.

But the historicity of the pericope does not mean that it has little theological or literary significance for Mark. On the contrary, the passage has been deliberately positioned as the turning point in the narrative. At 8:27–30 the evangelist takes up the most important emphasis of his narrative: the messiahship of Jesus. After some eight chapters of public ministry, highlighted by a series of astounding miracles, Jesus is now recognized by the spokesman of his followers as the Messiah. After this recognition Jesus begins to speak of his suffering and death. Mark 8:27–30 in a certain sense is both the conclusion of the first half of the Gospel and the introduction of the second. Jesus' authoritative teaching and person have led to a confession of his messiahship. Now he may begin to explain what that messiahship entails.

There is a parallel to Mark 8:27–29 in *Gos. Thom.* §13: "Jesus said to his disciples, 'Compare me to someone and tell me whom I am like.' Simon Peter said to him, 'You are like a righteous angel.' Matthew said to him, 'You are like a wise philosopher.' Thomas said to him, 'Master, my mouth is wholly incapable of saying whom you are like.'" This tradition is clearly secondary to the Synoptic Gospels. In keeping with tendencies in gnostic circles, the disciple with the most insight is not Peter but Thomas. The logion goes on to say that Jesus discloses "three words" to Thomas, which he cannot repeat to the other disciples, lest they try to stone him.

8:31–33 Throughout the critical period, scholars have expressed skepticism . with respect to Jesus' passion predictions (as in Wrede, *Messianic Secret,* 87, "the prophecies of the passion . . . contain things which Jesus cannot have known . . . cannot have prophesied"; Bultmann, *History,* 152, "have long been recognized as secondary constructions of the Church," and note 1), though Taylor resisted this critical orthodoxy (*Formation,* 150). Recently several scholars have expressed the opinion that Jesus probably did speak of his death and probably did anticipate his vindication also (e.g., Pesch, "Die Passion des Menschensohns," 189–91, appealing primarily to Mark 9:31; Hooker, 204–5). In my opinion Jesus did predict his martyrdom (even Crossan, *Historical Jesus,* 353, believes that Jesus may very well have warned his followers of the possibility of ending up on a Roman cross). In principle the idea of suffering the fate of a martyr must have been part of Jesus' thinking (as seen in dominical utterances, such as Matt 23:37 = Luke 13:33–34, and as illustrated in popular literature, such as 1 and 2 Maccabees and the *Testament of Moses*). Moreover, the fate of John the Baptist must have deeply impressed itself upon him. To assert that Jesus could not have spoken of the possibility, even probability, of his death is gratuitous and without foundation.

But Jesus' prediction has undergone a series of important developments: (1) the wording of the prediction has been drawn into closer alignment with the events of Passion Week (as seen in the specific designation of Jesus' opponents as "the elders, ruling priests, and scribes"; on the "three days" reference, see below); (2) the prediction has been removed from its original passion setting (where we find references to the eschatological "son of man") and relocated to earlier settings in the Galilean ministry; and (3) the prediction has been expanded into a series of predictions (so Pesch and many others), punctuating the final phase of the Galilean ministry. (For more discussion of the authenticity of the passion predictions, see commentary on 10:32–34 below.)

The evidence for this approach lies in the probability that Jesus approached Jerusalem not to die but to offer the holy city the opportunity to accept his message and to act upon it. (But this is not to say that Jesus was unaware of the risks of entering Jerusalem.) The so-called triumphal entry was to reach its climax at the Temple Mount, at which time the high priest would greet Jesus with the words of Ps 118:26, "We bless you from the house of the LORD." Instead, Jesus was ignored. Rebuffed, Jesus warned the ruling priesthood of its danger: the temple establishment was corrupt and had failed in its responsibilities (Mark 11:15–18); consequently it would lose its stewardship (Mark 12:1–11); the temple and city were in danger of destruction (Mark 13:2; cf. Luke 13:34–35); the "son of man" would come in judgment (Mark 13:26; 14:62).

Since the publication of K. L. Schmidt's *Der Rahmen der Geschichte Jesu*, it has been widely recognized that the pericopes that make up the Synoptic Gospels are not in chronological order. Indeed, this very point was made by Papias early in the second century: "And this is what the Elder said: 'Mark, who became Peter's interpreter, wrote accurately, but not in order [οὐ μέντοι τάξει], as many of the things said and done by the Lord as he had noted" (Eusebius, *Hist. eccl.* 3.39.15; here τάξις probably means chronological "order"; cf. BAG, 811; MM, 625, who cite P.Fay. 29.17, P.Oxy. 262.12, and *PSI* 164.17 for examples of τάξις meaning "list," which approximates "order"). Comparison of Matthew and Luke illustrates how these evangelists freely located the materials drawn from the Sayings Source (Q). Why should we assume that the Markan Gospel is any different? The passion predictions have been placed earlier in the narrative in order (1) to define Jesus' messiahship and (2) to show that Jesus' fate did not take him by surprise. Speaking of his death well in advance of turning toward Jerusalem would favorably impress Roman and Jewish readers (Suetonius, *Dom.* 15.3; Philo, *Moses* 2.51 §§290–91).

This proposal has the advantage of explaining what is otherwise a very odd feature of the narrative: if Jesus actually spoke of his death and resurrection during his Galilean ministry, how are we to account for his disciples' subsequent behavior (Hooker, 204)? But if Jesus made no such specific prediction until *after* entering Jerusalem, the behavior of the disciples now appears reasonable. They entered Jerusalem with enthusiasm and exuberance amidst shouts of "Hosanna!" But when told of impending suffering and death, Jesus' movement lost its momentum: The disciples expressed fear and confusion, at least one disciple defected (and betrayed him), all fled when he was arrested (with only the feeblest and most ineffective resistance offered), and Peter, the principal disciple, distanced himself from Jesus, denying that he even knew him.

The probability that Jesus did in fact anticipate his death is seen in his prayer in the Garden of Gethsemane: "Abba, Father, all things are possible for you. Remove this cup from me; yet not what I will, but what you will" (Mark 14:36). This scene, in which Jesus expresses his dread (cf. Mark 14:34) and in which his disciples fail to keep watch and pray with him, is so potentially embarrassing for the early church that its authenticity is virtually guaranteed (see commentary on Mark 14:32–42 below). Jesus' prayer implies that he anticipated his death and would have liked somehow to avoid it (which supports, not undermines, the authenticity of the prior passion predictions; *pace* Haenchen, 361–62 n. 1). But did Jesus anticipate his resurrection as well? Had he not anticipated it, it would have been very strange, for pious Jews very much believed in the resurrection (Dan 12:1–3; *1 Enoch* 22–27; 92–105; *Jub.* 23:11–31; 4 Macc 7:3; 4 Ezra 7:26–42; *2 Bar.* 21:23; 30:2–5; Josephus, *J.W.* 2.8.11 §154; 2.8.14 §§165–66; *Ant.* 18.1.3–5 §§14, 16, 18). One only needs to be reminded of the seven martyred sons and their mother, several of whom expressed their firmest conviction of the resurrection (2 Macc 7:14, 23, 29; cf. 4 Macc 8–17). Would Jesus have faced death and then, having earlier affirmed his belief in the resurrection (Mark 12:18–27), have expressed no faith in his own vindication? Surely not. It seems probable that Jesus would have reassured his disciples (and himself) with a confident prediction of his resurrection. The wording of the resurrection prediction also favors authenticity. As pointed out by Gundry (429–30), we should have expected ἐγείρειν, "to raise," to appear in fabricated passion predictions, since it is the verb used in the resurrection narrative itself (cf. 16:6) and in early confessional material (e.g., Rom 4:24–25; 1 Cor 15:4, 12–17), and not ἀναστῆναι, "to rise," which is the verb used in the predictions. (By the same token, the saying in Mark 14:28, which employs ἐγείρειν, is probably a Markan composition; see *Comment* on 14:28.)

However, Jesus' prediction seems not to have inspired confidence in Peter. Peter takes Jesus aside and ἤρξατο ἐπιτιμᾶν, "began to rebuke," him (Mark 8:32). The rebuke has a ring of authenticity to it. Matthew (16:22) softens it by having Peter say, "God forbid, Lord! This shall never happen to you." Luke omits it altogether. The discomfort of these later evangelists with the material argues for its authenticity. For the Markan evangelist, of course, it serves as a foil enabling Jesus to find a lesson in his suffering and apply it to his disciples and all those who in the future wish to follow him.

A parallel tradition is found in *Ap. Jas.* 5.33–6.4: "'Remember my cross and my death, and you will live!' But I [James] answered and said, 'Lord, do not mention to us the cross and death, for they are far from you.' The Lord answered and said, 'Verily I say to you, none will be saved unless they believe in my cross.'" It is interesting that it is James, not Peter, who replies to Jesus, assuring him that the cross and death "are far from" him. Jesus goes on to assure his disciples that "none of those who fear will be saved." The discourse that follows parallels the general theme of Mark 8:34–37. This version represents an admixture of second-century traditions. Throughout the *Apocryphon of James* are allusions to various NT passages.

Comment

27 ὁ Ἰησοῦς καὶ οἱ μαθηταὶ αὐτοῦ, "Jesus and his disciples." In Aramaic the name "Jesus" is rendered יֵשׁוּעַ *Yēšûaʿ*. (The name ישׁוּע has been found inscribed on a first-century ossuary.) This Aramaic form is the equivalent of the Hebrew name יְהוֹשֻׁעַ Yĕhôšua', which in English has been traditionally transliterated as "Joshua." The Aramaic name originally was transliterated into Greek as Ἰησοῦ, but later, influenced by Greek noun endings, the nominative form of the name became Ἰησοῦς, with Ἰησοῦν serving as the accusative. The Ἰησοῦ form served as both the genitive and the dative. All components of this partial declension are attested many times in the NT. (In the later rabbinic literature Jesus' name often appears simply as ישׁו Yēšû, apparently an accommodation to the Greek form of the name.) The name יֵשׁוּעַ Yēšûa' / Ἰησοῦς was very popular in Jewish families, for it recalled the great hero Joshua under whose leadership the wandering people of Israel conquered the promised land. In the Greek period, it is also possible that the name was popular because of its phonetic similarity to the famous Greek name Ἰάσων, "Jason," which sometimes was spelled Ἰήσων, thus drawing the parallel with Ἰησοῦς even closer.

Jesus is accompanied by his "disciples." In Greek μαθητής, "disciple," comes from the verb μανθάνειν, "to learn," and as such is an exact equivalent of the Hebrew תַּלְמִיד talmîd (pl. תַּלְמִידִים talmîdîm), which literally means "learner," from the verb לָמַד lāmad, "to learn" (the word talmûd, derived from this word, means "what is to be learned," or "studied"). The disciples have been referred to as such in Mark some two dozen times to this point. They have witnessed Jesus' mighty deeds, including healings and exorcisms; they have heard his teaching; they have observed disputes with critics; and they have twice assisted their master in feeding multitudes. They have in every way behaved as disciples of the Jewish masters of late antiquity (though many of the traditions and routines of the rabbinic disciples should not be read back into the Gospels).

ἐξῆλθεν . . . εἰς τὰς κώμας Καισαρείας τῆς Φιλίππου, "went out . . . into the villages of Caesarea of Philip." The evangelist tells us that Jesus and his disciples went out into the κώμας Καισαρείας τῆς Φιλίππου, "villages of Caesarea of Philip" (lit. "Philip's Caesarea," Latin Caesarea Philippi; on this form, cf. LXX Num 21:32; 32:42; Josh 10:39; 15:45; 1 Chr 2:23). This is the only mention of the city in Mark. It should not be confused with Caesarea Maritima, which was a seaport on the Mediterranean Sea (cf. Acts 8:40). Following Alexander's conquest, the city was refounded and called Paneas in honor of the god Pan. (Arabs call the city Banias.) Augustus later gave the city to Herod the Great, who built the famous White Temple. Still later the city was expanded by Herod Philip and was named Caesarea in honor of the Roman emperor. (Agrippa II would expand the city further and name it Neronia in honor of Nero. Many cities in the Roman period were named after Roman emperors.) It was at this city following the capture of Jerusalem that Titus celebrated the Roman victory.

Gundry (425–26) is probably correct in his judgment that the specificity of the topographical reference, along with the awkwardness of the reference "villages of Caesarea Philippi," argues for the historicity of the episode and its location as indicated. There is no convincing reason why Mark or tradents before him would invent this setting. Speculation that the transfiguration took place in the vicinity arose as a result of the topographical reference; the topographical reference was not inferred from the transfiguration.

καὶ ἐν τῇ ὁδῷ ἐπηρώτα τοὺς μαθητὰς αὐτοῦ, "And on the way he was asking his disciples." As a master relating to his pupils, Jesus directs an important question to his disciples. The rabbinic custom, of course, was for the disciple to ask questions of his master. Jesus holds another important conversation with his disciples ἐν τῇ ὁδῷ, "on the way," in 10:32.

τίνα με λέγουσιν οἱ ἄνθρωποι εἶναι; "Who do people say that I am?" For the evangelist Mark this is the vital question: Who is Jesus? The evangelist had introduced Jesus and his Gospel with the words "the good news of Jesus the Messiah, the Son of God" (1:1, accepting the last words as original). God himself had declared Jesus to be his Son (1:11; cf. 9:7), with the demonic world chiming in with fearful acknowledgment (1:24; 3:11; 5:7). But now Jesus is interested in ascertaining human opinion, that of the general public and then that of his own disciples.

28 Ἰωάννην τὸν βαπτιστήν, καὶ ἄλλοι, Ἠλίαν, ἄλλοι δὲ ὅτι εἷς τῶν προφητῶν, "John the Baptist; others say, Elijah; and others, one of the prophets." The disciples' report recalls the evangelist's earlier summary of opinion regarding the identity of Jesus. According to Mark 6:14 people were saying of Jesus "John the baptizer has been raised from the dead." But others were saying, "It is Elijah"; and others said, "It is a prophet, like one of the prophets of old" (6:15). Herod Antipas speculates that "John, whom I beheaded, has been raised" (6:16). Public speculation that Jesus might in some sense be "John the Baptist," whether in spirit or in some sense *redivivus* (as in Mark 6:16), pays a significant compliment to Jesus. The popular wilderness prophet had been put to death by Herod Antipas as much for political reasons (which is emphasized by Josephus, *Ant.* 18.5.2 §§116–19) as for personal reasons (which is emphasized in the account in Mark 6:17–29 and hinted at in Josephus, *Ant.* 18.5.4 §136). Jesus' ministry draws so much attention and is accompanied by such astonishing deeds of power that people wonder if God has raised up John to continue the work of preparation for the kingdom.

In what ways and to what extent the famous prophet Ἠλίας, "Elijah," of the books of Kings was understood in the first century to be part of the eschatological drama is unclear and is debated by scholars. That he was to play some role in restoration seems clear enough from passages such as Sir 48:1–14, esp. v 10: "At the appointed time, it is written, you [Elijah] are destined to calm the wrath of God before it breaks out in fury, to turn the hearts of parents to their children, and to restore the tribes of Jacob." This passage is based on Mal 4:5–6 (MT 3:23–24) and is echoed in the Dead Sea Scrolls as well (cf. 4Q558 = 4QVision). Jesus himself identifies John the Baptist as the great prophet (Mark 9:11–13).

The vaguer reference to εἷς τῶν προφητῶν, "one of the prophets," may in some way be related to eschatological ideas based on Deut 18:15–19 ("I will raise up for them a prophet like you"). In any case, it is probably in reference to an OT prophetic figure (*pace* Boring, *Sayings,* 199). According to Josephus (*J.W.* 2.13.5 §§261–63; *Ant.* 20.5.1 §§97–98; 20.8.6 §§167–68) there were others in Jesus' time who claimed to be prophets (cf. Mark 13:22), whose actions and signs were intended to recall saving moments in Israel's history. Given the number of prophetic claimants and what in all probability were contradictory messages, we should not be surprised that the Pharisees requested of Jesus a sign (Mark 8:11–12). Recall too that Jesus referred to himself as a prophet (Mark 6:4; cf. Luke 7:16, 39; 13:33; 24:19). The prophets whom Josephus so severely criticizes almost always offered the people signs of salvation to take place in the wilderness, which is consistent with the Mosaic tradition and its association with the wilderness wanderings of ancient Israel.

29 καὶ αὐτὸς ἐπηρώτα αὐτούς, ὑμεῖς δὲ τίνα με λέγετε εἶναι; "And he asked them, 'But who do you say that I am?'" Jesus now asks his disciples what *they* think.

ἀποκριθεὶς ὁ Πέτρος λέγει αὐτῷ, Σὺ εἶ ὁ Χριστός, "And answering, Peter says to him, 'You are the Messiah.'" Simon "Peter" first appeared in 1:16–18, where the fisherman left his nets and responded to Jesus' summons to discipleship. However, it is not until 3:16 that we are told that Jesus gave to Simon the name Πέτρος, "Peter," which means "rock" (see Charlesworth, "Has the Name 'Peter,'" for possible attestation of this name in the Dead Sea Scrolls). Peter would himself play a part in naming Jesus, for eventually the title Χριστός, "Christ," would function as a surname of sorts (as seen especially in Paul). Along with James and John, Peter was part of the inner circle of disciples and in the Synoptic Gospels is often portrayed as playing a leading role. So it is here, when he confesses the messiahship of Jesus.

Peter declares that Jesus is ὁ Χριστός, "the Messiah." Χριστός translates מָשִׁיחַ *māšîaḥ*, which is rendered in English "Messiah" (see *Note* d above). The word מָשִׁיחַ, "Messiah," occurs several times in the Dead Sea Scrolls, along with several other epithets that have messianic import. With the recent publication of all the photographs and virtually all the Hebrew texts (and most of the Aramaic texts) we are now in a position to assess much more accurately the messianism current in the time of Jesus. 4Q521 (= 4QMess Apoc) 2 and 4 ii 1 anticipates a time when "heaven and earth will obey his [God's] Messiah." This text goes on to tell of proclaiming the gospel to the poor, of healing, and even of resurrection of the dead (lines 8–12). The remarkable parallel with dominical tradition has not gone unobserved (cf. Matt 11:5 = Luke 7:22). But other references in the Scrolls to the Messiah presuppose a military leader who will defeat Israel's enemies. According to CD 19:10–11 the enemies of the renewed covenant "will be delivered up to the sword at the coming of the anointed [משח] of Aaron and of Israel" (cf. CD 20:1; 1QS 9:11), while 4Q252 (= 4QpGenᵃ) 1 v 3–4 speaks of "the coming of the anointed one of righteousness, the branch of David." According to other texts this Branch of David (cf. Jer 23:5; 31:15; Zech 3:8; 6:12) will engage Israel's enemies in battle, possibly slaying the Roman emperor himself (e.g., 4Q285 [= 4QMᵍ] 5 i 1–6). This portrait is consistent with the expectations of the author of the *Psalms of Solomon,* who in chaps. 17–18 longs for a Davidic Messiah who will drive Gentiles out of Israel and purify the land.

30 καὶ ἐπετίμησεν αὐτοῖς ἵνα μηδενὶ λέγωσιν περὶ αὐτοῦ, "And he strictly charged them that they should speak to no one concerning him." Why command the disciples to speak to no one about Jesus? If Peter's confession of Jesus as Christ carried with it the above connotations, Jesus' command to secrecy makes perfect sense. Moreover, in the context of Mark, much emphasis has been placed on Jesus' growing reputation and the ever-increasing popularity that has gone with it. At times Jesus has been so pressed by crowds that he has been forced to take unusual measures (such as teaching from a boat [4:1]) or simply to retire from public view (1:35; 6:31–32). If Jesus has gained such notoriety because of widespread belief that he is a prophet, what would happen if his messianic identity became common knowledge (as rightly asked by Gundry, 427)? The messianic secret is not the result of a lack of messianic content in the dominical tradition (as Wrede, *Messianic Secret,* supposed); it is part of the evangelist's strategy to heighten the awesomeness of Jesus and at the same time give definition to Jesus' messiahship (see *Introduction*).

31 καὶ ἤρξατο διδάσκειν αὐτοὺς ὅτι δεῖ τὸν υἱὸν τοῦ ἀνθρώπου πολλὰ παθεῖν, "And he began to teach them that it is necessary for the 'son of man' to suffer many things." Jesus has referred to himself as the "son of man" from the inception of his ministry (cf. 2:10, 28). Here, however, this epithet takes on special significance, for Jesus has just been recognized as the Messiah. (Kingsbury, *Christology,* 94–97, is right to insist that Jesus' self-reference "son of man" does correct the confession of Peter.) It seems that Jesus' messianic self-understanding has been informed by the mysterious heavenly figure of Dan 7:13–14. The articular form of this epithet denotes specificity, not technical or titular meaning (so Moule, *Origin of Christology,* 11–22; Chilton, "The Son of Man," 216–17). What makes us think of Dan 7, besides the obvious verbal parallel of the epithet itself, is the thematic coherence between the scene in Dan 7 and elements found in some of Jesus' son-of-man sayings. In Mark 2:10 the "son of man" has "authority [ἐξουσία] on earth" to forgive sins. "On earth" presupposes its opposite "in heaven," where Dan 7 locates the "son of man." Having received authority from heaven (Dan 7:14, which reads ἐξουσία in some Greek MSS), the "son of man" possesses authority on earth. The heavenly authority of the "son of man" is also implied by the dominical saying "the 'son of man' is lord even of the sabbath" (2:28). The suffering of the "son of man," the point that Jesus makes here in 8:31, also coheres with Dan 7's depiction of the great struggle between the saints and the forces of evil. Finally, the prize of the struggle is the kingdom (Dan 7:18, 22, 27), which God gives to the "son of man" (Dan 7:14) and which Jesus now proclaims (Mark 1:15; 4:11; 9:1). (For more discussion of the "son of man," see the *Introduction.*)

Jesus says that "it is necessary for the 'son of man' to suffer many things." Lying behind this sense of necessity (δεῖ) is the twin belief of the divine will (cf. Mark 14:36) and its concomitant, the fulfillment of Scripture (14:49). πολλὰ παθεῖν, "to suffer many things," coheres with the general tenor of Dan 7:15–27, but it also finds an interesting verbal parallel in the *Testament of Moses,* which says that Moses "suffered many things [*multa passus est*] in Egypt and at the Red Sea and in the wilderness for forty years" (3:11). Moses' suffering was the necessary prelude to the eventual deliverance of the people of Israel. The suffering of Moses, according to this early first-century pseudepigraphon, sustains the covenant and paves the way for Israel's inheritance of the promised land (see D. P. Moessner, "Suffering, Intercession and Eschatological Atonement: An Uncommon Common View in the Testament of Moses and in Luke-Acts," in *The Pseudepigrapha and Early Biblical Interpretation,* ed. J. H. Charlesworth and C. A. Evans, JSPSup 14, SSEJC 2 [Sheffield: JSOT Press, 1993] 202–27, esp. 204–15). Jesus' expectation of suffering receives further clarification in Mark 10:45, where he will say the "'son of man' came not to be served but to serve, and to give his life as a ransom for many." The assertion that the "son of man" did not come to be served qualifies the vision of Dan 7:14, which declares that all peoples and all nations "will serve" the "son of man." Although Jesus anticipates ultimate vindication for himself and the triumph of the kingdom of God, he heightens the elements of struggle in Daniel's vision (see *Comment* on 10:35–45).

καὶ ἀποδοκιμασθῆναι, "and to be rejected." Jesus also says that it is necessary for the "son of man" ἀποδοκιμασθῆναι, "to be rejected." Gundry (446) rightly sees in this word an allusion to Ps 118:22 (as opposed to Isa 53:3), which speaks of the stone "rejected" by the builders, a passage that will be cited later, at the conclusion of the parable of the Wicked Vineyard Tenants (Mark 12:1–12). Ps 118 plays an important role in Jesus' ministry in Jerusalem. He is greeted with the words of v 26 in his entry into the city (Mark 11:9–10), and he appeals to vv 22–23 as clarification of the aforementioned parable. (On the Davidic interpretation of the rejected-stone saying, see *Comment* on Mark 12:10–11.) The allusion to Ps 118:22, moreover, links the passion prediction to the Jerusalem context (where other references to Ps 118 are found), which, as has been said, is probably its original setting.

Jesus will suffer and be rejected ὑπὸ τῶν πρεσβυτέρων καὶ τῶν ἀρχιερέων καὶ τῶν γραμματέων, "by the elders and the ruling priests and the scribes." Jesus refers to the "elders" as part of his polemic against oral traditions that undermined the Law (see Mark 7:3, 5). He will be challenged by the elders in 11:27 and later arrested by them in 14:43 (cf. 14:53; 15:1). For more, see *Comment* on 11:27–33. The wording of Jesus' prediction matches the events of the narrative exactly (see all of the passages just mentioned), so that one should assume Markan editing (if not of the saying itself, then certainly in the way the Passion Narrative is told). On the "ruling priests and the scribes," see *Comment* on 11:18.

The saying concludes with the almost matter-of-fact prediction that the "son of man" is ἀποκτανθῆναι καὶ μετὰ τρεῖς ἡμέρας ἀναστῆναι, "to be killed and after three days to rise up." It has been argued above that in all probability Jesus did indeed predict his death and resurrection. The qualifying phrase, "after three days" (Mark 8:31), probably owes its inspiration to Hos 6:2, "after two days he will revive us; on the third day he will raise us up" (with Jeremias, "Die Drei-Tage-Worte der Evangelium," 226–29, but *pace* Gundry, 446, 448). The allusion to this passage in all probability derives from Jesus himself and not from the evangelist or early tradents searching for a scriptural warrant. But Jesus' allusion may have indicated no more than his expectation that his resurrection would be soon, perhaps as part of the general resurrection (see comment below on *Tg.* Hos 6:2), because the kingdom itself was soon to appear in its fullness, and with it judgment. When the tomb was found empty on the morning of the first day of the week, Jesus' followers interpreted the phrase in a literalistic fashion. The Greek, Hebrew, and Aramaic versions of this passage should be compared:

LXX Hos 6:2 reads ὑγιάσει ἡμᾶς μετὰ δύο ἡμέρας, ἐν τῇ ἡμέρᾳ τῇ τρίτῃ ἀναστησόμεθα καὶ ζησόμεθα ἐνώπιον αὐτοῦ, lit. "He will make us well after two days, on the third day we shall be raised up and shall live before him."

The MT reads יְחַיֵּנוּ מִיֹּמָיִם בַּיּוֹם הַשְּׁלִישִׁי יְקִמֵנוּ וְנִחְיֶה לְפָנָיו *yĕḥayyēnû miyyomāyim bayyôm haššĕlîšî yĕqimēnû wĕniḥyeh lĕpānāyn*, lit. "He will revive us after two days; on the third day he will raise us up that we may live before him."

Mark's Greek (μετὰ τρεῖς ἡμέρας ἀναστῆναι, "after three days to rise up"), so far as it is related to Hos 6:2, reflects the preposition of the first clause (מִן *min*/ μετά) and the substantive and adjective of the second (יוֹם הַשְּׁלִישִׁי *yôm haššĕlîšî*/τῇ ἡμέρᾳ τῇ τρίτῃ). The third clause ("that we may live before him") may very well be alluded to in the saying found in Luke 20:38 ("for all live to him"). Mark's contribution to the tradition is seen in its expansion to three predictions and in its placement at key points well before Jesus' entry into Jerusalem. The syntax of Hos 6:2, where we have both the preposition μετά, "after," in the first clause and ἐν, "on," with the dative in the second, could account for the variations in the tradition. Whereas the Markan form of the prediction reads μετὰ τρεῖς ἡμέρας ἀναστῆναι, the Matthean (16:21) and Lukan (9:22) forms read τῇ τρίτῃ ἡμέρᾳ ἐγερθῆναι, "on the third day to be raised" (cf. Acts 10:40; 1 Cor 15:4). Chronological considerations would also have led to a preference for "on the third day" as opposed to Mark's earlier "after three days" simply because Jesus was not in the tomb three full days (though see Gundry, 448).

The probability that Jesus alluded to the Hosean phrase, "on the third day he will raise us up," in his passion prediction is increased somewhat when we consider the Aramaic paraphrase found in the Targum: ביום אחיות מיתיא יקימיננא *bĕyôm ʾaḥăyôt mêtayyāʾ yĕqîmînanāʾ*, "*on the day of the resurrection of the dead* he will raise us up." The part placed in italics represents the Targum's interpretive expansion. Hosea's poetic expression of hope has become, in the Targum, fully eschatologized. It may very well be that this interpretive orientation, though, of course, not the Targum itself, which is of later vintage, was in circulation as early as the time of Jesus (so also Black, *ZNW* 60 [1969] 5; Bayer, *Jesus' Predictions*, 206–7; McArthur, *NTS* 18 [1971–72] 81–86). Jesus presupposed this understanding of the passage, and so alluded to it in his expression of confidence that he would be raised up "after three days" (or, "on the third day"), that is, "on the day of the resurrection of the dead," which, given the nearness of the kingdom, it would have been understood, must surely be at hand (Allison, *End of the Ages*, 137–39).

32 The evangelist comments in reference to the passion prediction that Jesus was "stating the matter plainly" (παρρησίᾳ). This plainness of speech probably is intended to contrast with the enigmatic dimension of the kingdom, perhaps as seen in the parables and the need sometimes to explain them to the disciples. Following the kingdom parables in Mark 4, the evangelist informs his readers that "with many such parables he was speaking the word to them as they were able to hear it; for apart from a parable he was not speaking to them, but to his own disciples he was explaining everything" (4:33–34). This curious remark is meant to clarify the earlier comment that stands between the parable of the Sower (4:3–9) and its explanation (4:13–20): "To you the mystery of the kingdom of God is given, but to those who are outside all things are in parables [ἐν παραβολαῖς]" (4:11). Most commentators agree that "in parables" here really means "in riddles" (see Guelich, 208–29), though principally in reference to the kingdom (Gundry, 200). The evangelist is saying that in referring to his death and resurrection Jesus was speaking not metaphorically but quite literally.

Although Jesus has in the plainest terms foretold his impending passion, it nevertheless causes fear and confusion among his disciples (cf. 9:10, 32; 10:32). It also provokes resistance, even from his loyalist disciples: ὁ Πέτρος . . . ἤρξατο ἐπιτιμᾶν αὐτῷ, "Peter began to rebuke him." Peter's language is harsh and borders on disrespect, for elsewhere in Mark ἐπιτιμᾶν, "to rebuke," is used in reference to the rebuking of unclean spirits (1:25; 9:25) and the threatening storm (4:39). But the word is also used in the sense of strictly enjoining someone (as in 3:12;

8:30). The report of Peter's rebuke of Jesus is meant not to discredit Peter but to underscore the surprising nature of Jesus' prediction. Given Jesus' success, given his wide popularity, and given his recognition as the Messiah, the prediction of suffering and death seems completely wrong-headed. But what the prediction, coming where it does, conveys to the reader of Mark is Jesus' prescience and a self-understanding that rises above popular expectations. Jesus is not caught up in the excitement of a public ministry that is going well; he knows what lies ahead and now begins to speak of it.

33 ὁ δὲ ἐπιστραφεὶς καὶ ἰδὼν τοὺς μαθητὰς αὐτοῦ, "turning and seeing his disciples," Jesus in turn rebukes Peter. The rebuke is severe: ὕπαγε ὀπίσω μου, σατανᾶ, "Get behind me, Satan." The command to "get behind" (ὕπαγε ὀπίσω) approximates an order to fall back into line, that is, to rejoin the other disciples (similarly Gundry, 432–33). The reader would probably infer insubordination on the part of Peter. The rebuke is particularly sharp because Jesus calls Peter "Satan." σατανᾶ transliterates the Hebrew שָׂטָן śāṭān (cf. Num 22:22, 32; Zech 3:1–2; Job 1:6–9, 12; 2:1–7; 1 Chr 21:1; 1QSb 1:8; *T. Dan* 3:6; 5:6; 6:1; *T. Gad* 4:7; *T. Asher* 6:4; *T. Job* 3:6; 4:4; 6:4; 7:1), which means "opponent." Did Jesus really call Peter "Satan"? Many epithets were applied to Satan in the literature in circulation in the NT period (such as Belial, Beliar, Mastema, Beelzebul, or Beelzebub). Jesus' use of σατανᾶ in his rebuke of Peter might have been adjectival rather than specifically identifying Peter with the Prince of Darkness. In other words, Jesus said, "Get behind me, you who oppose me!" This suggestion receives support from the explanation that follows: "for you are not thinking the things of God but the things of humans." Had Jesus meant to call Peter "Satan" in the sense of the devil, then we should expect him to have said that Peter was thinking the thoughts of the evil one or something to that effect. But Jesus' rebuke is quite serious nonetheless. Peter's thinking is anything but inspired of God; his wisdom reflects conventional human wisdom.

ὅτι οὐ φρονεῖς τὰ τοῦ θεοῦ ἀλλὰ τὰ τῶν ἀνθρώπων, "for you are not thinking the things of God but the things of humans." Mark's context defines the content of "things (or thoughts) of God" (τὰ τοῦ θεοῦ) as having to do with the necessity of Jesus' suffering and death. God's purposes will be accomplished by the obedience of his Son, even to death. The "things of humans" (τὰ τῶν ἀνθρώπων), whether Jewish or Roman, would be oriented toward conquest and assertion of power.

Explanation

Mark 8:27–33 serves as the turning point in the Markan Gospel. From the opening verse, in which Jesus is identified as "Messiah, the Son of God," to Peter's confession in 8:29 that Jesus is the Messiah and not merely a prophet or a resurrected John the Baptist, the evangelist has told a compelling story. The heavenly voice recognizes Jesus' divine sonship, the evil spirits also recognize and fear him, and with authority Jesus heals and bests his rivals and opponents. The bold assertion in 1:1 seems to be fully warranted, so that Peter's confession at the midpoint in Mark is persuasive literarily and theologically.

In sharp contrast to Peter's confession that Jesus is Israel's Messiah stands Jesus' prediction of his coming passion. Jesus' prediction qualifies the nature of his messiahship to be sure, but in the minds of many of Mark's readers it does much more; it may even nullify it. The idea of a Messiah who is rejected by the priests and who dies on a cross is unimaginable. But this is what happened. Mark 8:27–33 attempts to bring together these two seemingly contradictory elements. On the one hand, Jesus is the Messiah; yet, on the other, his destiny is to die. What resolves the tension is the prediction that Jesus will be resurrected. Thus his death on the cross is not defeat (as Jews and Romans alike would assume) but a prerequisite for accomplishment of mission and attainment to office.

That Jesus' disciples find all of this baffling is understandable. They too shared much of the popular expectation. The grievance expressed over the loss of family and material wealth (10:28–31) and the maneuvering for places of power and privilege in the anticipated new administration (10:35–45) give evidence of these lingering popular hopes. The betrayal and abandonment of Jesus upon his arrest and subsequent execution make it abundantly clear that the disciples did not embrace Jesus' vision. Only when the "son of man" was raised up "on the third day" did their thinking change.

B. Teaching on Suffering and Discipleship (8:34–9:1)

Bibliography

Bastin, M. *Jésus devant sa passion.* LD 92. Paris: Cerf, 1976. 164–67. **Bauer, J. B.** "'Wer sein Leben retten will . . .': Mk 8,35 Parr." In *Neutestamentliche Aufsätze.* FS J. Schmid, ed. J. Blinzler et al. Regensburg: Pustet, 1963. 7–10. **Baumann, R.** "Der Raum der Freiheit: Zum Wandel vom Bedingungen der Nachfolge." In *Wort Gottes in der Zeit.* FS K. H. Schelkle, ed. H. Feld and J. Nolte. Düsseldorf: Patmos, 1973. 436–50. **Baumeister, T.** *Die Anfänge der Theologie des Martyriums.* Münsterische Beiträge zur Theologie 45. Münster: Aschendorff, 1980. 82–85. **Beardslee, W. A.** "Saving One's Life by Losing It." *JAAR* 47 (1979) 57–72. ———. "Uses of the Proverb in the Synoptic Gospels." *Int* 24 (1970) 61–73. **Beasley-Murray, G. R.** *Jesus and the Kingdom of God.* 291–96. **Berger, K.** "Zu den sogenannten Sätze heiligen Rechts." *NTS* 17 (1970–71) 10–40. **Best, E.** *Following Jesus.* 19–54. **Bornkamm, G.** "Die Verzögerung der Parusie: Exegetische Bemerkungen zu zwei synoptischen Texten." In *In Memoriam E. Lohmeyer.* Ed. W. Schmauch. Stuttgart: Evangelisches Verlagswerk, 1951. 116–26, esp. 116–19. ———. "Das Wort Jesu vom Bekennen." In *Geschichte und Glaube.* BEvT 48. Munich: Kaiser, 1968. 1:25–36. **Breytenbach, C.** *Nachfolge und Zukunftserwartung nach Markus: Eine methodenkritische Studie.* ATANT 71. Zürich: Theologischer Verlag, 1984. 207–79. **Brower, K. E.** "Mark 9:1: Seeing the Kingdom in Power." *JSNT* 6 (1980) 17–41 (repr. in *The Synoptic Gospels: A Sheffield Reader.* Ed. C. A. Evans and S. E. Porter. BibSem 31. Sheffield: Sheffield Academic Press, 1995. 121–42). **Chilton, B. D.** *God in Strength: Jesus' Announcement of the Kingdom.* BibSem 8. Sheffield: JSOT Press, 1987. 251–74. **Claudel, G.** *La confession de Pierre: Trajectoire d'une péricope évangelique.* Paris: Gabalda, 1988. **Coulot, C.** *Jésus et le disciple: Étude sur l'autorité messianique de Jésus.* EBib 8. Paris: Gabalda, 1987. 47–53, 69–72, 88–90. **Crawford, B. S.** "Near Expectation in the Sayings of Jesus." *JBL* 101 (1982) 225–44. **Crossan, J. D.** *In Fragments: The Aphorisms of Jesus.* San Francisco: Harper & Row, 1983. 88–93, 131–33. **Dautzenberg, G.** *Sein Leben bewahren: ψυχή in den Herrenworten der Evangelien.*

SANT 14. Munich: Kösel, 1966. 51–82. **Derrett, J. D. M.** "Taking up the Cross and Turning the Cheek." In *Alternative Approaches to New Testament Study.* Ed. A. E. Harvey. London: S. P. C. K., 1985. 61–78. **Dinkler, E.** "Jesu Wort vom Kreuztragen." In *Neutestamentliche Studien.* FS R. Bultmann, ed. W. Eltester. BZNW 21. Berlin: Töpelmann, 1954. 110–29. **Dodd, C. H.** "Some Johannine 'Herrenworte' with Parallels in the Synoptic Gospels." *NTS* 2 (1955–56) 75–86, esp. 78–85. **Donahue, J. R.** *Are You the Christ?* 162–68. **Doncoeur, P.** "Gagner ou perdre sa ψυχή." *RSR* 35 (1948) 113–19. **Edwards, R. A.** "The Eschatological Correlative as a *Gattung* in the New Testament." *ZNW* 60 (1969) 9–20. **Fascher, E.** "Der unendliche Wert der Menschenseele: Zur Auslegung von Mark 8,36." In *Forschung und Erfahrung im Dienste der Seelsorge.* Ed. O. Söhngen et al. Göttingen: Vandenhoeck & Ruprecht, 1961. 46–57. **Fleddermann, H. T.** *Mark and Q.* 135–52. **Fletcher, D. R.** "Condemned to Die: The Logion on Cross-Bearing: What Does It Mean?" *Int* 18 (1964) 156–64. **George, A.** "'Qui veut sauver sa vie, la perdra; qui perd sa vie, la sauvera.'" *BVC* 83 (1968) 11–24. **Grässer, E.** "Nachfolge und Anfechtung bei den Synoptikern." In *Der Alte Bund im Neuen: Exegetische Studien zur Israelfrage im Neuen Testament.* WUNT 35. Tübingen: Mohr-Siebeck, 1985. 168–82. **Green, M. P.** "The Meaning of Cross-Bearing." *BSac* 140 (1983) 117–33. **Griffiths, J. G.** "The Disciples' Cross." *NTS* 16 (1969–70) 358–64. **Haenchen, E.** "Die Komposition von Mk vii [*sic*] 27–ix 1 und par." *NovT* 6 (1963) 81–109. **Hengel, M.** *Crucifixion.* London: SCM Press/Philadelphia: Fortress, 1977. **Higgins, A. J. B.** *Jesus and the Son of Man.* London: Lutterworth, 1964; Philadelphia: Fortress, 1965. 57–66. ———. *The Son of Man in the Teaching of Jesus.* SNTSMS 39. Cambridge: Cambridge UP, 1980. 80–84. **Hooker, M. D.** *The Son of Man in Mark.* 116–22. **Horstmann, M.** *Studien zur markinischen Christologie.* 34–69. **Jonge, H. J. de.** "The Sayings on Confessing and Denying Jesus in Q 12:8–9 and Mark 8:38." In *Sayings of Jesus: Canonical and Non-Canonical Essays.* FS T. Baarda, ed. W. L. Petersen et al. NovTSup 89. Leiden: Brill, 1997. 105–21. **Käsemann, E.** "Sentences of Holy Law." In *New Testament Questions of Today.* London: SCM Press; Philadephia: Fortress, 1969. 66–81. **Kattenbusch, F.** "Das Wort vom unersetzlichen Wert der Seele." *ZNW* 10 (1909) 329–31. **Kee, H. C.** "The Linguistic Background of 'Shame' in the New Testament." In *On Language, Culture and Religion.* FS E. A. Nida, ed. M. Black and W. A. Smalley. The Hague; Paris: Mouton, 1974. 133–47. **Kloppenborg, J. S.** *The Formation of Q: Trajectories in Ancient Wisdom Collections.* Studies in Antiquity and Christianity. Philadelphia: Fortress, 1987. 206–16, 230–32. **Koch, K.** "Zum Verhältnis von Christologie und Eschatologie im Markusevangelium: Beobachtungen aufgrund von Mk 8,27–9,1." In *Jesus Christus in Historie und Geschichte.* FS H. Conzelmann, ed. G. Strecker. Tübingen: Mohr-Siebeck, 1975. 395–408. **Ko Ha Fong, M.** *Crucem tollendo Christum sequi: Untersuchung zum Verständnis eines Logions Jesu in der Alten Kirche.* Münsterische Beiträge zur Theologie 52. Münster: Aschendorff, 1984. 9–25. **Kümmel, W. G.** *Promise and Fulfilment.* 25–29, 44–46. ———. "Das Verhalten Jesus gegenüber und das Verhalten des Menschensohns: Markus 8,38 par und Lukas 12,3f par Mattäus 10,32f." In *Jesus und der Menschensohn.* FS A. Vögtle, ed. R. Pesch and R. Schnackenburg. Freiburg: Herder, 1975. 210–24. **Lambrecht, J.** "The Christology of Mark." *BTB* 3 (1973) 256–73. ———. "Q-Influence on Mark 8,34–9,1." In *Logia: Les paroles de Jésus— The Sayings of Jesus.* FS J. Coppens, ed. J. Delobel. BETL 59. Leuven: Peeters; Leuven UP, 1982. 277–304. **Laufen, R.** *Die Doppelüberlieferungen der Logienquelle und des Markusevangeliums.* BBB 54. Bonn: Hanstein, 1980. 304–8, 322–25, 336–42. **Leivestad, R.** "Wer ist der Vater des Menschensohns? Einige Reflexionen über den Ausdruck 'in der Herrlichkeit seines Vaters' in Mk 8,38." In *Glaube und Gerechtigkeit.* FS R. Gyllenberg, ed. J. Kiilunen et al. Schriften der finnischen exegetischen Gesellschaft 38. Helsinki: Finnish Exegetical Society, 1983. 95–108. **Léon-Dufour, X.** "Perdre sa vie, selon l'Évangile." *Études* 351 (1979) 395–409. **Leroy, H.** "'Wer sein Leben gewinnen will . . .': Erlöste Existenz heute." *FZPhTh* 25 (1978) 171–86. **Lindars, B.** "Jesus as Advocate: A Contribution to the Christology Debate." *BJRL* 62 (1979–80) 476–97. **Luz, U.** "Theologia crucis als Mitte der Theologie im Neuen Testament." *EvT* 34 (1974) 116–41, esp. 131–39. **Maier, F. W.** *Jesus—Lehrer der Gottesherrschaft.* Würzburg: Echter, 1965. 149–52. **Mays, J. L.** "Mark 8:27–9:1." *Int* 30 (1976) 174–78. **Meinertz, M.** "'Dieses Geschlecht' im Neuen Testament." *BZ* 1 (1957) 283–89. **Metz, J.,** and **Moltmann, J.** *Leidensgeschichte: Zwei Meditationen* *zu Markus 8,31–38*. Freiburg: Herder, 1974. **Michaelis, W.** "Zeichen, Siegel, Kreuz." *TZ* 12 (1956) 505–25. **Minette de Tillesse, G.** *Le secret messianique*. 263–64, 368–73. **Moore, A. L.** *The Parousia in the New Testament*. NovTSup 13. Leiden: Brill, 1966. 125–31, 175–77. **Oberlinner, L.** *Todeserwartung und Todesgewissheit Jesu: Zum Problem einer historischen Begründung*. SBB 10. Stuttgart: Katholisches Bibelwerk, 1980. 169–71. **O'Callaghan, J.** "Nota crítica a Mc 8,36." *Bib* 64 (1983) 116–17. **Percy, E.** *Die Botschaft Jesu: Eine traditionsgeschichtliche und exegetische Untersuchung*. LUÅ 49.5. Lund: Gleerup, 1953. 170–74, 249–50. **Perrin, N.** *Rediscovering the Teaching of Jesus*. 185–91. **Pesch, R.** "Über die Autorität Jesu . . . ." In *Die Kirche des Anfangs*. FS. H. Schürmann, ed. R. Schnackenburg et al. Leipzig: St. Benno, 1977. 25–55, esp. 26–39. **Piper, R. A.** *Wisdom in the Q-Tradition: The Aphoristic Teaching of Jesus*. SNTSMS 61. Cambridge: Cambridge UP, 1989. 197–202. **Pudussery, P. S.** *Discipleship: A Call to Suffering and Glory: An Exegetico-Theological Study of Mk 8,27–9,1; 13,9–13 and 13,24–27*. Rome: Libreria "Alma Mater," 1987. 42–140. **Rebell, W.** "'Sein Leben verlieren' (Mark 8.35 parr.) als Strukturmoment vor- und nachösterlichen Glaubens." *NTS* 35 (1989) 202–18. **Reploh, K. G.** *Markus—Lehrer der Gemeinde*. 123–40. **Riesenfeld, H.** "The Meaning of the Verb ἀρνεῖσθαι." *ConNT* 11 (1947) 23–27. **Robbins, V. K.** "Interpreting the Gospel of Mark as a Jewish Document in a Greco-Roman World." In *Society and Literature in Analysis*. Vol. 5 of *New Perspectives on Ancient Judaism*. Ed. P. V. M. Flesher. Lanham, NY; London: University Press of America, 1990. 47–72, esp. 62–66. **Schenk, W.** "Der Einfluss der Logienquelle auf das Markusevangelium." *ZNW* 70 (1979) 141–65. **Schierse, F. J.** "Historische Kritik und theologische Exegese der synoptischen Evangelien, erläutert an Mk 9,1." *Scholastik* 29 (1954) 520–36. **Schlosser, J.** *Le règne de Dieu*. 323–71. **Schmahl, G.** *Die Zwölf im Markusevangelium: Eine redaktionsgeschichtliche Untersuchung*. TThSt 30. Trier: Paulinus, 1974. 117–19. **Schneider, J.** "σταυρός." *TDNT* 7:572–80. **Schülling, J.** *Studien zum Verhältnis von Logienquelle und Markusevangelium*. FB 65. Würzburg: Echter, 1991. 151–63. **Schwarz, G.** "'. . . ἀπαρνησάσθω ἑαυτόν . . . '? (Markus viii 34 Parr.)." *NovT* 17 (1975) 109–12. ⸻. *Jesus "der Menschensohn": Aramaistische Untersuchungen zu den synoptischen Menschensohnworten Jesu*. BWANT 119. Stuttgart: Kohlhammer, 1986. 238–44. ⸻. "Der Nachfolgespruch Markus 8.34b.c Parr.: Emendation und Rückübersetzung." *NTS* 33 (1987) 255–65. **Schweizer, E.** "The Son of Man." *JBL* 79 (1960) 119–29. ⸻. "Towards a Christology of Mark?" In *God's Christ and His People*. FS N. A. Dahl, ed. J. Jervell and W. A. Meeks. Oslo: Universitetsforlaget, 1977. 29–42. **Söding, T.** *Glaube bei Markus: Glaube an das Evangelium, Gebetsglaube und Wunderglaube im Kontext der markinischen Basileiatheologie und Christologie*. SBB 12. Stuttgart: Katholisches Bibelwerk, 1985. 204–9. **Strecker, G.** "Das Evangelium Jesu Christi." In *Eschaton und Historie: Aufsätze*. Göttingen: Vandenhoeck & Ruprecht, 1979. 183–228, esp. 215–20. **Tannehill, R. C.** *The Sword of His Mouth*. SBL Semeia Supplements 1. Missoula, MT: Scholars Press, 1975. 88–101. **Tödt, H. E.** *The Son of Man in the Synoptic Tradition*. NTL. London: SCM Press; Philadelphia: Westminster, 1965. **Vielhauer, P.** "Gottesreich und Menschensohn in der Verkündigung Jesu." In *Festschrift für Günther Dehn zum 75. Geburtstag*. Ed. W. Schneemelcher. Neukirchen: Verlag der Buchhandlung des Erziehungsvereins, 1957. 51–79 (repr. in P. Vielhauer. *Aufsätze zum Neuen Testament*. TBü 31. Munich: Kaiser, 1965. 55–91). ⸻. "Jesus und der Menschensohn: Zur Diskussion mit Heinz Eduard Tödt und Eduard Schweizer." *ZTK* 60 (1963) 133–77 (repr. in P. Vielhauer. *Aufsätze zum Neuen Testament*. TBü 31. Munich: Kaiser, 1965. 92–104). **Vincent, J. J.** "The Evangelism of Jesus." *JBR* 23 (1955) 266–71, esp. 267–70. **Vögtle, A.** "Exegetisches Erwägungen über das Wissen und Selbstbewusstsein Jesu." In *Gott im Welt*. FS K. Rahner, ed. J. B. Metz et al. 2 vols. Freiburg: Herder, 1964. 1:608–67, esp. 642–47. **Vorster, W. S.** "On Early Christian Communities and Theological Perspectives." *JTSA* 59 (1987) 26–34. **Wanke, J.** *"Bezugs- und Kommentarworte" in den synoptischen Evangelien: Beobachtungen zur Interpretationsgeschichte der Herrenworte in der vorevangelischen Überlieferung*. ETS 44. Leipzig: St. Benno, 1981. 96–99. ⸻. "'Kommentarworte': Älteste Kommentierungen von Herrenworte." *BZ* 24 (1980) 208–23, esp. 224–26. **Yates, J. E.** *The Spirit and the Kingdom*. London: S. P. C. K., 1963. 108–18. **Zimmermann, H.** "Christus nachfolgen: Eine Studie zu den Nachfolge-Worten der synoptischen Evangelien." *TGl* 53 (1963) 241–55.

Bibliography on Mark 9:1

Ambrozic, A. M. *The Hidden Kingdom.* 203–40. **Beasley-Murray, G. R.** *Jesus and the Kingdom of God.* 187–93. **Burkill, T. A.** *Mysterious Revelation.* 165–67. **Chilton, B. D.** *God in Strength: Jesus' Announcement of the Kingdom.* BibSem 8. Sheffield: JSOT Press, 1987. 251–74, 315–16. ———. "'Not to Taste Death': A Jewish, Christian and Gnostic Usage." In *Papers on the Gospels.* Vol. 2 of *Studia Biblica 1978.* Ed. E. A. Livingston. JSNTSup 2. Sheffield: JSOT Press, 1980. 29–36. ———. "The Transfiguration: Dominical Assurance and Apostolic Vision." *NTS* 27 (1980–81) 115–24. **Crawford, B. S.** "Near Expectation in the Sayings of Jesus." *JBL* 101 (1982) 225–44. **Giesen, H.** "Erwartete Jesus nahe das Ende der Welt? Zu Mk 1,14f; 4,11f; 9,1." In *Beiträge zur Exegese und Theologie des Matthäus- und Markus-Evangeliums.* Vol. 1 of *Glaube und Handeln.* Bern; Frankfurt am Main: Lang, 1983. 111–32, esp. 127–31. **Greeven, H.** "Nochmals Mk ix. 1 in Codex Bezae (D, 05)." *NTS* 23 (1976–77) 305–8. **Horstmann, M.** *Studien zur markinischen Christologie.* 57–69. **Kilgallen, J. J.** "Mk 9,1—The Conclusion of a Pericope." *Bib* 63 (1982) 81–83. **Künzi, M.** *Das Naherwartungslogion Markus 9,1 par.: Geschichte seiner Auslegung mit einem Nachwort zur Auslegungsgeschichte von Markus 13,30 par.* BGBE 21. Tübingen: Mohr-Siebeck, 1977. **Moir, I. A.** "The Reading of Codex Bezae (D-05) at Mark ix.1." *NTS* 20 (1973–74) 105. **Nardoni, E.** "A Redactional Interpretation of Mark 9:1." *CBQ* 43 (1981) 365–84. **Neirynck, F.** "Note on the Codex Bezae in the Textual Apparatus of the Synopsis [Mc 9,1]." In *Evangelica.* BETL 60. Leuven: Peeters; Leuven UP, 1982. 941–46. **Perrin, N.** "The Composition of Mark ix 1." *NovT* 11 (1969) 67–70. ———. *The Kingdom of God in the Teaching of Jesus.* NTL. London: SCM Press; Philadelphia: Westminster, 1963. 67–73. **Satake, A.** "Das Leiden der Jünger 'um meinetwillen.'" *ZNW* 67 (1976) 4–19. **Schlosser, J.** *Le règne de Dieu dans les dits de Jésus.* 323–71. **Söding, T.** *Glaube bei Markus: Glaube an das Evangelium, Gebetsglaube und Wunderglaube im Kontext der markinischen Basileiatheologie und Christologie.* SBB 12. Stuttgart: Katholisches Bibelwerk, 1985. 171–74. **Trocmé, E.** "Marc 9, 1: prédication ou réprimand?" *SE* 2 (1964) 259–65. **Vögtle, A.** "Exegetisches Erwägungen über das Wissen und Selbstbewusstsein Jesu." In *Gott im Welt.* FS K. Rahner, ed. J. B. Metz et al. 2 vols. Freiburg: Herder, 1964. 1:608–67, esp. 630–44. **Zeller, D.** "Prophetisches Wissen um die Zukunft in synoptischen Jesusworten." *TP* 52 (1977) 258–71.

Translation

[34]*And summoning the crowd with his disciples, he said to them, "If someone*[a] *wishes to follow*[b] *after me, let him deny himself and take up his cross and follow me.* [35]*For whoever should wish to save his life will lose it; but whoever will lose his life for the sake*[c] *of the gospel will save*[d] *it.* [36]*For what does it profit*[e] *a person to gain the whole world and lose his life?* [37]*For what should a person give in exchange for his life?* [38]*For whoever should be ashamed of me and my words*[f] *in this adulterous and sinful generation,*[g] *indeed the 'son of man' will be ashamed of him whenever he should come in the glory of his Father with*[h] *the holy angels."* [9:1]*And he was saying to them, "Truly,*[i] *I say to you that there are some of those standing here*[j] *who may not taste death until they see the kingdom of God having come in power."*

Notes

[a] א B C* D L W 33 and other authorities read εἴ τις, "if someone." A C² and other authorities read ὅστις, "whoever."

[b] א A B C² K L 33 and other authorities read ἐλθεῖν, "to come," which is accepted by UBSGNT². 𝔓⁴⁵ C* D W 0214 and other authorities read ἀκολουθεῖν, "to follow," which is accepted by Nestle-Aland²⁷, UBSGNT³ᶜ, and UBSGNT⁴ (without noting the variant).

א A B C K L W 0214 and other authorities add ἐμοῦ καί, "of me and," making the whole phrase read "for my sake and the sake of the gospel." Nestle-Aland²⁷ and UBSGNT³ᶜ accept these words, and so read "for my sake and for sake of the gospel." See discussion in *TCGNT*¹, 99. These words are omitted by 𝔓⁴⁵ D and other authorities. On the question of which reading is original, see *Comment* below.

ᵈ33 reads εὑρήσει αὐτήν, "will find it" (cf. Matt 16:25).

ᵉSome MSS read ὠφελήσει, "will it profit." The future tense coheres better with the assumed eschatological orientation of the passage.

ᶠ𝔓⁴⁵ᵛⁱᵈ W and a few authorities omit λόγους, "words," and so read "whoever is ashamed of me and my [followers]." Metzger (*TCGNT*¹, 99–100) believes that the (accidental) omission of λόγους is easier to explain than its later (deliberate) insertion in many MSS and versions.

ᵍSome MSS read ἐν τῇ γενεᾷ ταύτῃ τῇ πονηρᾷ καὶ μοιχαλίδι καὶ ἁμαρτωλῷ, "in this wicked and adulterous and sinful generation."

ʰא A B C D L 33 and many other authorities read μετά, "with," but 𝔓⁴⁵ W and a few versions read καί, "and": "in the glory of his Father and the holy angels." The latter reading probably reflects Luke 9:26 (see *TCGNT*¹, 100).

ⁱSome MSS read ἀμὴν ἀμήν, "amen, amen" (i.e., "truly, truly"), probably under Johannine influence (cf. John 1:51 passim).

ʲD and a few other authorities add μετ' ἐμοῦ, "with me." The addition is probably inspired by the transfiguration, described in the next pericope, in which Elijah and Moses join Jesus in conversation (cf. 9:4).

Form/Structure/Setting

Mark 8:34–9:1 forms a natural continuation of the preceding pericope (8:27–33). The sharp exchange between Peter and Jesus is concluded with provocative words. Not only will Jesus face suffering and death, but his disciples will also. Form-critically, it appears as a cluster of related sayings about the possibility of suffering and the Christian's need to be prepared for it and willing to accept it. The four statements in vv 35–38 (all beginning with the postpositive γάρ, "for") in effect supply a series of reasons justifying Jesus' startling assertion in v 34: "If someone wishes to come after me, let him deny himself and take up his cross and follow me."

The authenticity of the saying in v 34 is strongly supported by the observation that Jesus does not in fact take up his cross (Simon of Cyrene does; cf. 15:21). There is an approximate parallel with a Cynic saying that may suggest that speaking of the fate of the cross was proverbial (see *Comment* below). V 36 appears in a later gnostic source: "For what use is it if you gain the world and forfeit your soul?" (*Interp. Know.* [NHC XI] 9.33–35).

Bultmann (*History*, 112, 128, 151–52) and Tödt (*Son of Man*, 55–60, 224–26, 339–44) believe that Luke 12:8–9 and Mark 8:38 derive from the historical Jesus; of course, in referring to the coming "son of man," Jesus did not have *himself* in mind. Käsemann ("Sentences of Holy Law," 77–79) and Vielhauer ("Gottesreich und Menschensohn," 76–79; id., "Jesus und der Menschensohn," 101–7) do not think this son-of-man saying derives from Jesus. Is Mark 8:38 dependent on Q 12:8–9? Fleddermann (*Mark and Q*, 145–51) thinks so. De Jonge ("Sayings," 115–17) does not think so, because no Q redaction appears in Mark. He concludes that both sayings go back independently to a "common earlier tradition" (117). De Jonge is not sure if the saying goes back to Jesus (it could), but even if it does not, it accurately reflects Jesus' views regarding the coming "son of man" (119–20). He comments: "Anybody who refused to acknowledge this role by not answering adequately to the demands of God's Kingdom, would perish in the Last Judgement" (120).

On the authenticity of 9:1, see Gundry (466), as well as *Comment* below.

Comment

34 καὶ προσκαλεσάμενος τὸν ὄχλον σὺν τοῖς μαθηταῖς αὐτοῦ εἶπεν αὐτοῖς, εἴ τις θέλει ὀπίσω μου ἀκολουθεῖν, ἀπαρνησάσθω ἑαυτὸν καὶ ἀράτω τὸν σταυρὸν αὐτοῦ καὶ ἀκολουθείτω μοι, "And summoning the crowd with his disciples, he said to them, 'If someone wishes to follow after me, let him deny himself and take up his cross and follow me.'" According to Mark, Jesus summons the ὄχλος, "crowd." But who are they? According to vv 27 and 33 Jesus is with his disciples. The crowd cannot refer to the disciples because Mark says Jesus summoned "the crowd together with his disciples." Sensing this difficulty Matthew (16:24) and Luke (9:23) omit Mark's opening words. Mark has apparently added the crowd to widen the application of Jesus' words. His call for self-denial and taking up the cross is not for the apostles only but for all who would follow him. For the first-century inhabitant of the Roman Empire, taking up one's cross would call to mind the condemned person carrying his cross to the place of execution (see Hengel, *Crucifixion*, 62: "People were all too aware of what it meant to bear the cross through the city and then to be nailed to it"). Crucifixion was common enough in Palestine itself (cf. Josephus, *Ant.* 17.10.10 §295) that we need not think that Jesus' saying must have originated later and elsewhere. But the saying is strange nonetheless. In rabbinic parlance a disciple is urged to take up the yoke of Torah or the yoke of the commandments (e.g., *m. 'Abot* 3:5; *m. Ber.* 2:2), never to take up the cross. Jesus' summons would have struck a somber, if not macabre, note in the ears of his audience. However, it would also impress first-century readers and auditors, for the saying implies that Jesus knows full well what lies ahead for him and his followers.

Crossan (*Historical Jesus*, 353) leans toward accepting the authenticity of Jesus' saying about the cross, partly because of its proverbial nature and partly because it is found in a Cynic context: "If you want to be crucified, just wait. The cross will come. If it seems reasonable to comply, and the circumstances are right, then it's to be carried through, and your integrity maintained" (Epictetus, *Diatr.* 2.2.10). But in Jesus' case the cross comes not because of lifestyle or a particular worldview; it comes because of a commitment to the kingdom of God, which has arrived, and the clash with Palestine's leadership that this message will inevitably occasion.

35 ὃς γὰρ ἐὰν θέλῃ τὴν ψυχὴν αὐτοῦ σῶσαι ἀπολέσει αὐτήν· ὃς δ' ἂν ἀπολέσει τὴν ψυχὴν αὐτοῦ ἕνεκεν τοῦ εὐαγγελίου σώσει αὐτήν, "For whoever should wish to save his life will lose it; but whoever will lose his life for the sake of the gospel will save it." Jesus' saying about saving and losing one's life also finds a parallel in a later rabbinic tractate: "Everyone who preserves one thing from the Torah preserves his life, and everyone who loses one thing from the Torah will lose his life" (*'Abot R. Nat.* B §35). The saying here is proverbial (and quite rare). But the key element in Jesus' saying is the reference to the gospel (εὐαγγέλιον). The essence of the good news is the appearance of the kingdom of God (cf. Mark 1:14–15), a concept Jesus has drawn from Second Isaiah (especially Isa 40:1–9; 52:7; 61:1–2), especially as it came to be interpreted in the Aramaic-speaking synagogue. The good news is that the kingdom of God is at hand, the time of salvation is now (cf. 2 Cor 6:2). Jesus' contrasting image of saving or losing one's life underscores the point that humanity's salvation is bound up with the good news. There is no salvation apart from it, and one's response to it cannot consist of half measures (cf. John 12:25: "He who loves his life loses it, and he who hates his life in this world will keep it for eternal life"). One either embraces the gospel and lives according to its demands (even if it costs one's life), or one avoids its apparent dangers (thinking that one will save one's life by living apart from it) and perishes.

Metzger (*TCGNT*[1], 99) retains ἐμοῦ καί, "for my sake," because it is read by both Matthew (16:25) and Luke (9:24), thus possibly implying that their Markan source must also have had it. But it is also possible that the appearance of these words in Mark is due to scribal harmonization. Jesus' emphasis on the gospel—which includes taking up the cross and following Jesus who proclaims it—supports a reading without the words: losing one's life for the sake of the gospel will result in saving it. The appearance of "for my sake" probably represents a later, post-Easter christological gloss. Expanded in this way, the saying promises life for those willing to suffer and die for the gospel *and for Jesus* (who now becomes the principal content of the gospel proclamation; see Gundry, 437). This represents an important shift in meaning. But in the setting of Jesus' life (*Sitz im Leben Jesu*), a setting largely preserved here in Mark, the focus was on the gospel of God's reign, a point which will be further elaborated in 9:1.

36 τί γὰρ ὠφελεῖ ἄνθρωπον κερδῆσαι τὸν κόσμον ὅλον καὶ ζημιωθῆναι τὴν ψυχὴν αὐτοῦ; "For what does it profit a person to gain the whole world and lose his life?" Jesus' saying about gaining the world and losing one's life finds a parallel in a late first-century source: "Because of what have men lost their life and for what have those who were on the earth exchanged their soul?" (*2 Bar.* 51:15). Again, the saying is proverbial and has approximate counterparts in the Hebrew Bible: "What do people gain from all the toil at which they toil?" (Eccl 1:3 NRSV); "Truly, no ransom avails for one's life, there is no price one can give to God for it. For the ransom of life is costly, and can never suffice that one should live on forever and never see the grave" (Ps 49:7–9 NRSV). Jesus' saying is distinctive for succinctness and clarity, but not for its originality.

37 Jesus drives home his point with the rhetorical question τί γὰρ δοῖ ἄνθρωπος ἀντάλλαγμα τῆς ψυχῆς αὐτοῦ, "what should a person give in exchange for his life?" No sane person would knowingly exchange his life for any amount of wealth. Life is precious; one's eternal soul is beyond calculation (cf. Yeshua ben Sira, who once said in reference to a good wife: "there is no exchange [ἀντάλλαγμα] for a well instructed soul [ψυχή]" [Sir 26:14]; or the philosopher Menander: "Nothing is more valuable than [one's] life" [*Sentences* 843]). Yet, people in great numbers trade away their lives in the pursuit of fleeting pleasures and possessions. Jesus' appeal to wisdom (in vv 36–37) is intended to answer the question that naturally arises after his solemn warning of coming suffering and persecution. Many among his followers, including his disciples, would ask, "Why should I follow Jesus?" Jesus must provide his followers with a rationale. Following Jesus, proclaiming the kingdom, and being prepared to suffer and even die for it is the wise and prudent course to take. This argument, of course, assumes the truth of Jesus' message, namely, that the kingdom of God has really dawned and that Jesus has indeed been authorized by God to proclaim it. (On Jesus' ἐξουσία, "authority," see Comment on 11:27–33.)

38 ὃς γὰρ ἐὰν ἐπαισχυνθῇ με καὶ τοὺς ἐμοὺς λόγους ἐν τῇ γενεᾷ ταύτῃ τῇ μοιχαλίδι καὶ ἁμαρτωλῷ, καὶ ὁ υἱὸς τοῦ ἀνθρώπου ἐπαισχυνθήσεται αὐτόν, ὅταν ἔλθῃ ἐν τῇ δόξῃ τοῦ πατρὸς αὐτοῦ μετὰ τῶν ἀγγέλων τῶν ἁγίων, "For whoever should be ashamed of me and my words in this adulterous and sinful generation, indeed the 'son of man' will be ashamed of him whenever he should come in the glory of his Father with the holy angels." Taking up the cross and following Jesus are not only wise for the general reasons given in vv 36–37, but also appropriate in view of the coming judgment. Jesus may face suffering in the near future, but the day will come when he will return as the "son of man." The "son of man" will be ashamed of the one who is ashamed of Jesus and his words. This retribution is an instance of *ius talionis*, that is, "justice of equal measure." Elsewhere in the sayings of Jesus and in rabbinic sources we hear the maxim: "whatever you measure out to others will be measured out to you" (cf. Matt 7:2 = Luke 6:38; Mark 4:24; *m. Soṭa* 1:7; *Frag. Tg.* Gen 38:26). So it is in the present case; Jesus will be ashamed of anyone who was ashamed of him.

Jesus refers to the "son of man" in the third person. Did Jesus originally speak of some eschatological figure, someone other than himself? Bultmann and others so understood. The logic and force of Jesus' warning make the most sense if Jesus understood himself as the "son of man." Would the coming eschatological judge be ashamed of people who had been ashamed of someone else (i.e., Jesus)? This interpretation does not do justice to the point Jesus is making. In the wider context Jesus speaks of his own suffering and shameful treatment (vv 31 and 34). The coming of the "'son of man' . . . in the glory of his Father with the holy angels" reverses and compensates for the earlier shame and indignity. So it is in the case of the disciples. They too will face persecution, hardship, suffering, and indignities. But if they remain true to Jesus and the kingdom proclamation, then they will save their lives and, by implication, take part in the glory of the "son of man." If Jesus had in mind some other figure, then it is difficult to explain the disappearance of such an important eschatological element in his teaching. It is better to agree with the ancient witness of the Gospels and understand that Jesus has referred to himself in the third person (which he routinely does when speaking of the "son of man").

God's reign on earth will be brought to completion in the drama of the coming of the "son of man," that heavenly humanlike figure described in Dan 7:13–14, accompanied by "holy angels" (compare the "holy ones" of Dan 7:22, 25, 27). As the suffering "son of man," Jesus will be dragged before Caiaphas and the Jewish council, and then before Pilate and his brutal soldiers; later, as the returning heavenly "son of man," Jesus will enter Jerusalem as a conquering warrior.

The picture that Jesus has painted would have aroused the hopes and anticipations of his disciples. But in view of the predictions of suffering and martyrdom, doubts understandably remained. What assurance could Jesus offer that his triumphant forecast would come to pass?

9:1 Jesus assures his disciples with these words: ἀμὴν λέγω ὑμῖν ὅτι εἰσίν τινες ὧδε τῶν ἑστηκότων οἵτινες οὐ μὴ γεύσωνται θανάτου ἕως ἂν ἴδωσιν τὴν βασιλείαν τοῦ θεοῦ ἐληλυθυῖαν ἐν δυνάμει, "Truly, I say to you that there are some of those standing here who may not taste death until they see the kingdom of God having come in power." His assurance that the kingdom is sure to come, and with it the heavenly "son of man," is buttressed with yet another forecast: those standing by will not die before they have seen the arrival of the kingdom. The prediction is even more astonishing than the one in 8:38, for now we have a specific time of reference—within the lifetime of those standing by.

Jesus introduces this remarkable statement with an asseverative ἀμήν, "truly," which transliterates אָמֵן ʾāmēn, though sometimes it is translated ἐπ' ἀληθείας, "in truth" (Luke 4:25). This use of ἀμήν is distinctive to Jesus, especially in the asseverative phrase "truly, I say to you," and so at least on this score points toward authenticity (see Guelich, 177–78). A similar usage in the OT is attested only in 1 Kgs 1:36 and Jer 28:6. Chilton (*A Galilean Rabbi and His Bible*, 202) has suggested that Jesus' asseverative use of this word derives from Aramaic usage, such as we now have preserved in the later targumic tradition (cf. *Tg. Onq.* Gen 3:1; 17:19; *Tg.* Isa 37:18; 45:14, 15).

According to Chilton, the phrase "there are some of those standing here who may not taste death" refers to the immortals, that is, Enoch, Elijah, and Moses (see 4 Ezra 6:25–26; Josephus, *Ant.* 1.3.4 §85 [Enoch]; 3.5.7 §96 [Moses]; 9.2.2 §28 [Elijah and Enoch]), and the clause "until they see the kingdom of God having come in power" is an assurance that the coming of the kingdom of God is as certain as is the immortality of the immortals. The transfiguration narrative that follows (9:2–8) thus becomes a dramatic testimony to the truth of Jesus' declaration: the immortals themselves appear, thus confirming Jesus' word. (On the Semitic flavor of Mark 9:1 as a whole, see Chilton, *NTS* 27 [1980–81] 115–24.)

However, the more or less traditional understanding of this saying may yet be preferable, at least as it is understood by the Markan evangelist. If we put out of our minds Easter, Pentecost, the founding of the church, and early Christianity's end-of-the-world (*Endzeit*) speculations and try to imagine rather how Jesus' statement would have sounded to his original hearers, then its meaning might not be as elusive as has often been thought. Set in a context of itinerant ministry, with no cosmic signs portending an imminent change in the world order, with no indications that the social and political structures of Israel were on the brink of revolution, Jesus' announcement, "Truly, I say to you, there are some of those standing here who may not taste death until they see the kingdom of God having come in power," would have struck a hopeful chord. The assurance of something that will transpire before death is Semitic (cf. *Jub.* 16:16, where Abraham is told "that he would not die until he begot six more sons and he would see them before he died") and lends the saying a touch of hyperbole for emphasis. Jesus is thus strongly asserting that some of his followers will witness the power of God's kingdom (though some of his contemporaries may have scoffed at the idea). Jesus' words may very well have been in reference to his exorcisms, as seen in their close association with the kingdom in another saying: "If it is by the finger of God that I cast out demons, then the kingdom of God has come upon you" (Luke 11:20).

However, elsewhere Jesus says that "The kingdom of God is not coming with signs to be observed . . . behold, the kingdom of God is in the midst of you" (Luke 17:20–21). If there are no observable signs, then how is the kingdom's presence to be perceived? The answer probably lies in Jesus' emphasis on faith. Some have eyes that see, some do not (cf. Mark 4:11–12). Note the association of the proclamation of the arrival of the kingdom and the call to respond in faith to the good news (Mark 1:15). Accordingly, the view taken here is that Mark 9:1 represents an utterance in which Jesus assured his following that some would see the kingdom having come in power. The powerful deeds of his ministry provide the evidence of the reality of the kingdom, evidence proffered to a discouraged and questioning Baptist (cf. Matt 11:2–6 = Luke 7:18–23), provided these deeds are viewed through the eyes of faith. Doubters asserted that Jesus was aided by Satan (cf. Mark 3:22, 30), but the faithful recognized that God was at work.

Some scholars have argued that Mark 9:1 and the other sayings relating to when the kingdom of God or "son of man" would appear derive not from Jesus but from the early community trying to explain the delay of the Parousia. According to this argument, Mark 13:28–32 tries to assure Christians that the eschatological events of which Jesus spoke will take place before Jesus' generation passes away. As a post-Easter saying it is viewed as a concise summary of what is presupposed but not explicit in Jesus' teaching. But time continues to pass by; society and politics in Israel (and Rome) remain essentially unchanged. The saying in 9:1 then promises that at least some of Jesus' contemporaries will "not taste death until they see the kingdom of God having come in power." But the years continue to pass by; and Jesus' contemporaries pass from the scene. The last NT traces of this problem are seen in the Johannine Gospel, which wrestles with a tradition that had predicted that the Beloved Disciple would remain until Jesus returned (John 21:22–23), and in the second Petrine epistle (early second century), which mentions those who say: "Where is the promise of his coming? . . .all things have continued . . ." (2 Pet 3:4). It must be admitted that there is some truth to this line of argument, and it may be that the Markan evangelist understood Mark 9:1 and 13:28–32 in this way. After all, Jesus viewed the kingdom as already breaking into the human sphere, already defeating Satan, already liberating those held in his bondage. The kingdom would arrive in its fullness soon, so soon that at the Last Supper Jesus vows not to drink wine again until he does so in the kingdom of God (Mark 14:25). Nevertheless, Mark 9:1 and 13:28–32 (see *Comment*), when critically contextualized, do make sense in the life setting of Jesus *(Sitz im Leben Jesu)* and do contain authentic material.

The evangelist Mark links the saying with the astounding story of the transfiguration (9:2–8). For the evangelist, this event offers the most dramatic proof that the kingdom had indeed come in the preaching and ministry of Jesus. That it took place within "six days" of Jesus' prediction only makes the prediction more impressive (and not ludicrous, as though Jesus were predicting that some of his disciples would still be alive one week later to witness the transfiguration). But did Jesus think the kingdom of God would come in its fullness soon? This is indeed probable, as parts of the Mark 13 discourse seem to indicate and, more to the point, as the reference to the coming of the "son of man" in his glory in 8:38 seems to indicate. Elsewhere Jesus admits that he does not know the day nor the hour (13:32). Probably he assumed that the day and hour were relatively near. Of course, when Mark writes, that generation is nearing its end. Placing the prediction of 9:1 immediately before the transfiguration narrative allows the latter to become, as Gundry (469) has described it, "a stopgap-fulfilment to support Jesus' prowess at prediction."

The reference to the "kingdom of God having come" recalls Jesus' fundamental message: "The time is fulfilled; the kingdom of God has come" (Mark 1:15).

These words parallel those of Dan 7:22: "The time has arrived; the saints have received the kingdom" (author's tr.; see C. H. Dodd, *According to the Scriptures* [London: Nisbet, 1952], 67–69). According to C. H. Dodd (*The Parables of the Kingdom* [3rd ed.; London: Nisbet, 1948], 43–45) the Aramaic word מטא *mĕṭāʾ* probably underlies Daniel's ἔφθασεν (in Theodotion's Greek translation) and Mark's ἤγγικεν (see Guelich, 43–44). This language highlights the association of the expected kingdom with the task of the "son of man."

Explanation

The previous pericope (8:27–33) concluded with Jesus rebuking Peter for urging him not to speak of his passion. Jesus now summons the crowd along with his disciples to teach them that suffering is necessary. To follow Jesus, that is, to be his disciple, one must "deny oneself" and "take up" the cross. In other words, the true disciple of Jesus must be prepared to share Jesus' fate (or, in the words of 10:38–39, to drink from the same cup and to undergo the same baptism). Is it worth denying oneself, taking up a cross, and following Jesus? Yes, it is asserted; for to shrink from Jesus' cross (and so suppose that one has saved one's life) is in fact to perish, while to take up Jesus' cross (and so to lose one's life) is in fact to live. In the Roman world these words would be impressive, for Romans would themselves have been able to infer something greater from the lesser: if people were willing to die for Caesar, a dubious "son of God," would it not be wiser to be willing to die for the true "Son of God," a divine Son even recognized by a Roman centurion? (See *Comment* on 15:39.)

Gundry (434) remarks that here "discipleship plays second fiddle to Christology." He is right, for the focus is upon whether one is "ashamed" of Jesus and his words (8:38). But discipleship is an important element, even if subordinated. To be a true disciple, one must accept the fate of the Master; and the Master's fate is inextricably bound up with his identity, purpose, and mission. True discipleship cannot emerge in isolation from true Christology. The true disciple will embrace and follow the crucified Jesus because he is the heavenly "son of man" who will come in glory.

C. The Transfiguration   (9:2–8)

Bibliography

Abrahams, I. "After Six Days." *HTR* 8 (1915) 94–121. ———. *Studies in Pharisaism and the Gospels.* 2:50–55. **Bacon, B. W.** "The Transfiguration Story." *AJT* 6 (1902) 236–65. **Badcock, F. J.** "The Transfiguration." *JTS* o.s. 22 (1920–21) 321–26. **Baltensweiler, H.** *Die Verklärung Jesu.* ATANT 33. Zurich: Zwingli, 1959. **Baly, D.** "The Transfiguration Story." *ExpTim* 82 (1970) 82–83. **Bernardin, J. B.** "The Transfiguration." *JBL* 52 (1933) 181–89. **Best, E.** *Following Jesus.* 55–61. **Best, T. F.** "The Transfiguration: A Select Bibliography." *JETS* 24 (1981) 157–61. **Boobyer, G. H.** "St. Mark and the Transfiguration." *JTS* o.s. 41 (1940) 119–20.

————. St. Mark and the Transfiguration Story. Edinburgh: T. & T. Clark, 1942. **Bradley, W. P.** "The Transfiguration—Credential or Answer?" *Crozer Quarterly* 12 (1935) 57–76. **Bretscher, P.** "Exodus 4:22–23 and the Voice from Heaven." *JBL* 87 (1968) 301–11. **Burkill, T. A.** *Mysterious Revelation.* 145–64, 168–87. **Caird, G. B.** "Expository Problems: The Transfiguration." *ExpTim* 67 (1956) 291–94. **Carlston, C. E.** "Transfiguration and Resurrection." *JBL* 80 (1961) 233–40. **Chilton, B. D.** "The Transfiguration: Dominical Assurance and Apostolic Vision." *NTS* 27 (1980) 115–24. **Coune, M.** "Radieuse transfiguration: Mt 17,1–9; Mc 9,2–10; Lc 9,28–36." *AsSeign* 15 (1973) 44–84. **Crossan, J. D.** *The Cross That Spoke: The Origins of the Passion Narrative.* San Francisco: Harper & Row, 1988. **Currie, S. D.** "Isaiah 63:9 and the Transfiguration in Mark." *ASB* 82 (1966) 7–34. **Dabeck, P.** "'Siehe, es erschienen Moses und Elia' (Mt 17,3)." *Bib* 23 (1942) 175–89. **Dabrowski, E.** *La transfiguration de Jésus.* Scripta Pontificii Instituti Biblici 85. Rome: Biblical Institute, 1939. **Dalman, G.** *The Words of Jesus.* Edinburgh: T. & T. Clark, 1902. 276–80. **Dautzenberg, G.** "Elija im Markusevangelium." In *The Four Gospels 1992.* FS F. Neirynck, ed. F. Van Segbroeck et al. 3 vols. BETL 100. Leuven: Peeters; Leuven UP, 1992. 2:1077–94, esp. 1082–88. **Del Agua, A.** "The Narrative of the Transfiguration as a Derashic Scenification of a Faith Confession (Mark 9.2–8 Par.)." *NTS* 39 (1993) 340–54. **Denis, A.-M.** "Une théologie de la rédemption: La Transfiguration chez saint Marc." *VSpir* 452 (1959) 136–49. **Derrett, J. D. M.** "Peter and the Tabernacles (Mark 9, 5–7)." *DRev* 108 (1990) 37–48. **Dignath, W.** "Die Verklärung Jesu." In S. Wibbing and W. Dignath. *Taufe—Versuchung—Verklärung.* HR 3. Gütersloh: Mohn, 1966. 55–80. **Dodd, C. H.** "The Appearances of the Risen Christ: An Essay in Form Criticism of the Gospels." In *Studies in the Gospels.* Ed. D. E. Nineham. Oxford: Blackwell, 1967. 9–35. **Feuillet, A.** "Les perspectives propres à chaque évangéliste dans les récits de la transfiguration." *Bib* 39 (1958) 281–301, esp. 282–89. **Fuchs, A.** "Die Verklärung des Markus-Evangeliums in der Sicht moderner Exegese." *TPQ* 125 (1977) 29–37. **Fuller, R. H.** *The Formation of the Resurrection Narratives.* New York: MacMillan, 1971. 165–66. **Gerber, M.** "Die Metamorphose Jesu, Mark. 9,2f. par." *TZ* 23 (1967) 385–95. **Groves, W. L.** "The Significance of the Transfiguration of Our Lord." *Theology* 11 (1925) 86–92. **Hahn, F.** *The Titles of Jesus in Christology.* New York: World, 1969. **Hall, S. G.** "Synoptic Transfigurations: Mark 9,2–10 and Partners." *King's Theological Review* 10 (1987) 41–44. **Höller, J.** *Die Verklärung Jesu: Eine Auslegung der neutestamentlichen Berichte.* Freiburg: Herder, 1937. **Holzmeister, U.** "Einzeluntersuchungen über das Geheimnis der Verklärung Christi." *Bib* 21 (1940) 200–210. **Hooker, M. D.** "'What Dost Thou Here, Elijah?' A Look at St Mark's Account of the Transfiguration." In *The Glory of Christ in the New Testament: Studies in Christology.* FS G. B. Caird, ed. L. D. Hurst and N. T. Wright. Oxford: Clarendon, 1987. 59–70. **Horstmann, M.** *Studien zur markinischen Christologie.* 72–103. **Johnson, S. L., Jr.** "The Transfiguration of Christ." *BSac* 124 (1967) 133–43. **Kazmierski, C. R.** *Jesus, the Son of God.* 105–26. **Kee, H. C.** "The Transfiguration in Mark: Epiphany or Apocalyptic Vision?" In *Understanding the Sacred Text.* FS M. S. Enslin, ed. J. Reumann. Valley Forge, PA: Judson, 1972. 137–52. **Kenny, A.** "The Transfiguration and the Agony in the Garden." *CBQ* 19 (1957) 444–52. **Kingsbury, E. C.** "The Theophany *Topos* and the Mountain of God." *JBL* 86 (1967) 205–10. **Kooy, V. H.** "The Transfiguration Motif in the Gospel of John." In *Saved by Hope.* FS R. C. Oudersluys, ed. J. I. Cook. Grand Rapids, MI: Eerdmans, 1978. 64–78. **Lambrecht, J.** "The Christology of Mark." *BTB* 3 (1973) 256–73. **Liefeld, W. L.** "Theological Motifs in the Transfiguration Narrative." In *New Dimensions in New Testament Study.* Ed. R. N. Longenecker and M. C. Tenney. Grand Rapids, MI: Zondervan, 1974. 162–79. ————. "Transfiguration." *DJG* (1992) 834–41. **Lohmeyer, E.** "Die Verklärung Jesu nach dem Markus-Evangelium." *ZNW* 21 (1922) 185–215. **Marcus, J.** *The Way of the Lord: Christological Exegesis of the Old Testament in the Gospel of Mark.* Louisville: Westminster John Knox, 1992. 80–93. **Masson, C.** "La transfiguration de Jésus (Marc 9,2–13)." *RTP* 3.14 (1964) 1–14. **Mauser, U. W.** *Christ in the Wilderness: The Wilderness Theme in the Second Gospel and Its Basis in the Biblical Tradition.* SBT 39. London: SCM Press; Naperville, IL: Allenson, 1963. 110–19. **McCurley, F. R., Jr.** "'And after Six

Days' (Mark 9:2): A Semitic Literary Device." *JBL* 93 (1974) 67–81. **McGuckin, J. A.** "Jesus Transfigured: A Question of Christology." *Clergy Review* 69 (1984) 271–79. ———. "The Patristic Exegesis of the Transfiguration." *Studia Patristica* 18 (1989) 335–41. ———. *The Transfiguration of Christ in Scripture and Tradition.* Studies in the Bible and Early Christianity 9. Lewiston, NY: Mellen, 1986. **Minette de Tillesse, G.** *Le secret messianique.* 354–56. **Moiser, J.** "Moses and Elijah." *ExpTim* 96 (1984–85) 216–17. **Moulton, W. J.** "The Significance of the Transfiguration." In *Biblical and Semitic Studies.* New York: Scribner's, 1901. 159–210. **Müller, H. P.** "Die Verklärung Jesu: Eine motivgeschichtliche Studie." *ZNW* 51 (1960) 56–64. **Müller, U. B.** "Die christologische Absicht des Markusevangeliums und die Verklärungsgeschichte." *ZNW* 64 (1973) 159–93. **Murphy-O'Connor, J.** "What Really Happened at the Transfiguration?" *BRev* 3 (1987) 8–21. **Nardoni, E.** *La transfiguración de Jesús y el diálogo sobre Elías según el evangelio de San Marcos.* Buenos Aires: Ediciones de la Facultad de Teología de la Universidad Católica Argentina, 1977. **Neirynck, F.** "Minor Agreements Matthew-Luke in the Transfiguration Story." In *Orientierung an Jesus.* FS J. Schmid, ed. P. Hoffmann et al. Freiburg: Herder, 1973. 253–66. **Niemand, C.** *Studien zu den Minor Agreements der synoptischen Verklärungsperikopen: Eine Untersuchung der literarkritischen Relevanz der gemeinsamen Abweichungen des Matthäus und Lukas von Markus 9,2–10 für die synoptische Frage.* Europäische Hochschulschriften, Series 23: Theologie 352. Frankfurt am Main; New York: Lang, 1989. **Nützel, J. M.** *Die Verklärungserzählung im Markusevangelium.* FB 6. Würzburg: Echter, 1973. **Pamment, M.** "Moses and Elijah in the Story of the Transfiguration." *ExpTim* 92 (1980–81) 338–39. **Pedersen, S.** "Die Proklamation Jesu als des eschatologischen Offenbarungsträgers (Mt. xvii 1–13)." *NovT* 17 (1975) 241–64. **Pesch, R.** *Evangelium der Urgemeinde.* 112–15. **Reploh, K. G.** *Markus—Lehrer der Gemeinde.* 112–22. **Riesenfeld, H.** *Jésus transfiguré: L'Arrière-plan du récit évangélique de la transfiguration de Notre Seigneur.* ASNU 16. Copenhagen: Munksgaard, 1947. **Rivera, L. F.** "El misterio del Hijo del hombre en la transfiguración." *RevistB* 28 (1966) 19–34, 79–89. **Robinson, J. A. T.** "Elijah, John and Jesus." In *Twelve New Testament Studies.* SBT 34. London: SCM Press; Naperville, IL: Allenson, 1962. 28–52. **Robinson, J. M.** "Jesus: From Easter to Valentinus (or the Apostles' Creed)." *JBL* 101 (1982) 5–37. ———. "On the *Gattung* of Mark (and John)." In *Jesus and Man's Hope.* Ed. D. G. Buttrick. 2 vols. Pittsburgh: Pittsburgh Theological Seminary, 1970. 1:99–129. **Sabbe, M.** "La rédaction du récit de la transfiguration." In *La venue du Messie: Messianisme et eschatologie.* Ed. É. Massaux. RechBib 6. Bruges: Desclée de Brouwer, 1962. 65–100. **Schmidt, K. L.** *Rahmen.* 222–25. **Schmithals, W.** "Der Markusschluss, die Verklärungsgeschichte und die Aussendung der Zwölf." *ZTK* 69 (1972) 379–411. **Schnellbächer, E. L.** "Καὶ μετὰ ἡμέρας ἕξ (Markus 9,2)." *ZNW* 71 (1980) 252–57. **Sellin, G.** "Das Leben des Gottessohnes: Taufe und Verklärung Jesu als Bestandteile eines vormarkinischen 'Evangeliums.'" *Kairos* 25 (1983) 237–53. **Smith, M.** "The Origin and History of the Transfiguration Story." *USQR* 36 (1980) 39–44. **Steichele, H.-J.** *Der leidende Sohn Gottes: Eine Untersuchung einiger alttestamentlicher Motive in der Christologie des Markusevangeliums.* Biblische Untersuchungen 14. Regensburg: Pustet, 1980. 161–92, 280–312. **Stein, R. H.** "Is the Transfiguration (Mark 9:2–8) a Misplaced Resurrection-Account?" *JBL* 95 (1976) 79–96 (repr. in R. H. Stein. *Gospels and Tradition: Studies on Redaction Criticism of the Synoptic Gospels.* Grand Rapids, MI: Baker, 1991. 97–119). **Suhl, A.** *Die Funktion der alttestamentlichen Zitate und Anspielungen im Markusevangelium.* 104–10. **Synge, F. C.** "The Transfiguration Story." *ExpTim* 82 (1970–71) 82–83. **Taylor, V.** *The Life and Ministry of Jesus.* London: Macmillan; New York: St. Martin's, 1954. 139–49. **Thrall, M. E.** "Elijah and Moses in Mark's Account of the Transfiguration." *NTS* 16 (1970) 305–17. **Torrance, T.** "The Transfiguration of Jesus." *EvQ* 14 (1942) 214–29. **Trites, A.** "The Transfiguration of Jesus: The Gospel in Microcosm." *EvQ* 51 (1979) 67–79. **Turner, C. H.** "Ο ΥΙΟΣ ΜΟΥ Ο ΑΓΑΠΗΤΟΣ." *JTS* o.s. 27 (1925–26) 113–29. **Viviano, B. T.** "Rabbouni and Mark 9:5." *RB* 97 (1990) 207–18. **Watson, F.** "The Social Function of Mark's Secrecy Theme." *JSNT* 24 (1985) 49–69. **Weeden, T. J.** *Mark—Traditions.* 118–24. **Weinacht, H.** *Die Menschwerdung des Sohnes Gottes im Markusevangelium: Studien* zur *Christologie des Markusevangeliums.* HUT 13. Tübingen: Mohr-Siebeck, 1972. 53–60. **Weinfeld, M.** "Pentecost as Festival of the Giving of the Law." *Immanuel* 8 (1978) 7–18. **Williams, W. H.** "The Transfiguration—A New Approach?" *SE* 6 (1973) 635–50. **Wink, W.** "Mark 9:2–8." *Int* 36 (1982) 63–67. **Yates, J. E.** *The Spirit and the Kingdom.* London: S. P. C. K., 1963. 108–18. **Ziesler, J. A.** "The Transfiguration Story and the Markan Soteriology." *ExpTim* 81 (1970) 263–68.

Translation

[2]*And after six days Jesus takes along* [a]*Peter and James and John, and takes them up into a* [b]*high mountain by themselves. And* [c] *he was transformed before them,*[d] [3]*and his garments became exceedingly white as a launderer on earth cannot whiten.* [4]*And* [d] *Elijah appeared to them with Moses, and they were conversing together with Jesus.* [5]*And answering, Peter* [e] *says to Jesus, "Rabbi, it is good that we are here. Let us make* [f] *three tents: one for you, one for Moses, and one for Elijah"—*[6]*for he did not know what he should reply, because they had become greatly afraid.* [7]*And then a cloud appeared overshadowing them, and a voice came out of the cloud,*[g] *"This is my Son the beloved;* [h] *hear him!* "[i] [8]*And suddenly, looking around, they no longer saw anyone, but only Jesus with them.*

Notes

[a]The Syr. again reads *kêpāʾ*, "Kepha."
[b]א reads ὑψηλὸν λίαν, "very high."
[c]Some MSS add ἐν τῷ προσεύχεσθαι αὐτούς, "while they were praying." This reading is probably inspired by Luke 9:29, which reads ἐν τῷ προσεύχεσθαι αὐτόν, "while he [Jesus] was praying."
[d-d]Some later lectionaries add καὶ ἔλαμψεν τὸ πρόσωπον αὐτοῦ ὡς ὁ ἥλιος, "and his face shone as the sun." This addition is taken from Matt 17:2.
[e]W has εἶπεν Πέτρος, "Peter said." Some Syr. MSS read *kêpāʾ*, "Kepha."
[f]D W and other authorities read ποιήσω, "I shall make."
[g]A D L W and later authorities add λέγουσα, "saying."
[h]Some MSS add ὃν ἐξελεξάμην, "whom I chose," or ἐν ᾧ εὐδόκησα, "in whom I am pleased." The latter variant derives from Matt 17:5. The former variant may derive from Luke 9:35: οὗτός ἐστιν ὁ υἱός μου ὁ ἐκλελεγμένος, "This is my son the chosen one."
[i]"Hear him!" translates ἀκούετε αὐτοῦ. The order of these words is reversed in some MSS, possibly to agree with the order found in LXX Deut 18:15 (see *Comment* below).

Form/Structure/Setting

Carlston (*JBL* 80 [1961] 233–40), Coune (*AsSeign* 15 [1973] 50–51), McCurley (*JBL* 93 [1974] 67–81), J. M. Robinson (*JBL* 101 [1982] 5–37; "On the *Gattung* of Mark (and John)," 116–18), Schmithals (*ZTK* 69 [1972] 384–93), Watson (*JSNT* 24 [1985] 55), Weeden (*Mark—Traditions,* 118–26), and several others have ar‑ gued that Mark's account of the transfiguration was originally a resurrection appearance story. Several elements of the transfiguration account have been iden‑ tified as evidence for this hypothesis. The "cloud" is associated with Jesus' ascension (Acts 1:9). Bultmann (*History,* 259) assumed that the mountain involved was none other than the mountain from which the resurrected Jesus issued the Great Com‑ mission (Matt 28:16). The temporal notation, "after six days," is thought originally to have been in reference to Easter (i.e., six days after Easter). It is further noted that such specific temporal references are only found in the Easter narratives or in references to them (e.g., "on the third day"). In some second-century gnostic traditions the resurrection of Jesus is described in language that clearly parallels the transfiguration account: e.g., "Then a great light appeared so that the mountain shone from the sight of him who had appeared. And a voice called out to them, saying, 'Listen to my words that I may speak to you'" (*Ep. Pet. Phil.* [NHC VIII, 2] 134.9–16). Another significant example is seen here: "What then is the resurrection? It is always the disclosure of those who have risen. For if you remember reading in the Gospel that Elijah appeared and Moses was with him, do not think the resurrection is an illusion" (*Treat. Res.* [NHC I, 4] 48.3–11). The statement "Elijah appeared and Moses was with him" comes right out of Mark 9:4. Yet this gnostic text speaks of the post-Easter resurrection, not the pre-Easter transfiguration. In view of these considerations, as well as others, Carlston (*JBL* 80 [1961] 235) claims that the burden of proof rests upon those who argue that Mark 9:2–8 is not a resurrection account.

This theory, however, has been vigorously challenged by Baltensweiler (*Verklärung Jesu*), Stein (*JBL* 95 [1976] 79–96), and others. Among other things, it is pointed out that at many points the transfiguration account differs from the resurrection accounts found in the NT Gospels (cf. Dodd, "The Appearances of the Risen Christ," 25) and that some of the alleged parallels with Easter are quite dubious. For example, it is not at all clear that the earliest accounts of Jesus' resurrection involved the kind of luminosity depicted in the transfiguration or in Paul's Damascus Road encounter. Moreover, Crossan's conclusion (*Cross That Spoke*, 357–61) that Mark draws upon the *Gospel of Peter*, transforming the two heavenly beings who assist Jesus from the tomb into Moses and Elijah, is implausible on many counts, not least the thesis of the *Gospel of Peter*'s antiquity. The gnostic accounts of the risen Jesus, moreover, are clearly colored by the tradition of the transfiguration; they do not represent a primitive, pre-Synoptic tradition that later inauthentically was represented as a pre-Easter "transfiguration" tradition.

There are many features about the transfiguration that have led commentators to conclude that this episode is intended to have some sort of typological connection to Exod 24 and 33–34, passages that describe Moses' ascent up the mountain where he meets God and then descends with a shining face (so Mauser, *Christ in the Wilderness,* 110–19). The following specific parallels between Mark's account (9:2–8) and Exodus are evident: (1) the reference to "six days" (Mark 9:2; Exod 24:16), (2) the cloud that covers the mountain (Mark 9:7; Exod 24:16), (3) God's voice from the cloud (Mark 9:7; Exod 24:16), (4) three companions (Mark 9:2; Exod 24:1, 9), (5) a transformed appearance (Mark 9:3; Exod 34:30), and (6) the reaction of fear (Mark 9:6; Exod 34:30). Another suggestive item that should be mentioned is that in Exod 24:13 Joshua is singled out and taken up the mountain with Moses. Since *Joshua* in the LXX is frequently rendered Ἰησοῦς, "Jesus," the early church may have seen in Exod 24:13 a veiled prophecy, or typology, that came to fulfillment in the transfiguration where once again Moses and Jesus are together.

The transfiguration is strategically positioned in Mark's Gospel. The first phase of Jesus' ministry commenced with the heavenly acclamation, "You are my son, the beloved one. I am very pleased with you" (Mark 1:11). At every point of his subsequent ministry this sonship is affirmed, implicitly ("Who indeed is this that even the wind and the sea obey him?" [4:41]) or explicitly ("I know who you are, the Holy One of God!" [1:24]). But with the announcement of the passion a new phase in Jesus' ministry is introduced. The Markan evangelist must assure his readers that Jesus still enjoys heaven's favor and that his mission still has validity. The evangelist achieves this by a heavenly endorsement where not only do we hear God again claiming Jesus as his Son, but we witness Jesus in the company of two of ancient Israel's greatest figures: Moses and Elijah.

Comment

2 καὶ μετὰ ἡμέρας ἓξ παραλαμβάνει ὁ Ἰησοῦς τὸν Πέτρον καὶ τὸν Ἰάκωβον καὶ τὸν Ἰωάννην, "And after six days Jesus takes along Peter and James and John." The chronological notation "after six days" recalls Exod 24:16. It was after six days that God spoke out of the cloud to Moses. No other event in Jewish salvation history was remembered with greater reverence. At Sinai God met his people, or, more precisely, met Moses the spokesmen for and lawgiver to his people. Likewise, on the Mount of Transfiguration another epochal epiphany has taken place. God again has spoken to his chosen leader of Israel.

The three disciples Peter and James and John have been together, alone with Jesus, in Mark 5:37 on the occasion of raising up the daughter of Jairus. They will be together again in Mark 13:3, where they question Jesus about his startling prediction of the forthcoming destruction of the temple buildings and precincts (Mark 13:2). And finally, these three disciples will be with Jesus when he prays in Gethsemane (Mark 14:33). The impression one gains from these passages is that these three disciples formed the inner core of Jesus' following.

Jesus takes his disciples up εἰς ὄρος ὑψηλόν, "into a high mountain." Because ὄρος can mean "hill" as well as "mountain," the adjective ὑψηλόν, "high," is used to make it clear that the latter is in view. The height of the mountain implies contact with heaven (or, as Gundry, 457, puts it, "a suburb of heaven"). The heavenly voice in v 7 is therefore not out of place or unexpected. The traditional identification of the mountain with Mount Tabor is merest speculation (Schmidt, *Rahmen*, 225, and more recent commentators).

κατ' ἰδίαν μόνους, "by themselves." The evangelist Mark likes to portray Jesus and his disciples in private, usually for teaching of particular gravity (e.g., 4:34; 6:31, 32; 7:33; 9:28; 13:3). The redundant μόνους, "alone," underscores the privacy.

καὶ μετεμορφώθη ἔμπροσθεν αὐτῶν, "and he was transformed before them." According to Mark, Jesus μετεμορφώθη, "was transformed." This event, following on the heels of Jesus' confident prediction of the coming of the "son of man," may have been understood as a glimpse of Jesus' regal status "in the glory of his Father" (8:38). The evangelist underscores the glorious nature of the transfiguration. In what manner Jesus was transfigured is explained in the next verse.

3 τὰ ἱμάτια αὐτοῦ ἐγένετο στίλβοντα λευκὰ λίαν οἷα γναφεὺς ἐπὶ τῆς γῆς οὐ δύναται οὕτως λευκᾶναι, "his garments became exceedingly white as a launderer on earth cannot whiten." Jesus' "garments became exceedingly white" (στίλβοντα λευκὰ λίαν, lit. "shining white, exceedingly"). The whiteness of Jesus' garments transcends the power of the best launderer on earth. The closest parallel is probably the shining face of Moses (Exod 34:30), but the faces of other saints are described as shining (see 2 Esdras 7:97, 125; *1 Enoch* 37:7; 51:5; cf. Luke 9:29, which specifically mentions Jesus' face). The clothing of the saints also will shine (see Dan 12:3; Rev 4:4; 7:9; *1 Enoch* 62:15; *Eccl. Rab.* 1:7 §9: "he will renew their faces and will renew their garments"). But in Mark, Jesus' face does not shine (in contrast to Matt 17:2; Luke 9:29). There are stories of transfigurations of the Greco-Roman gods. One thinks of Demeter, whose transfigured person filled a house with light (*Homeric Hymns* 2.275–80). But the religious background of the transfiguration is Jewish, not Hellenistic either in a general sense (as in Hahn, *Titles*, 340–41) or pertaining to mystery religions in a more specific sense (in addition to the texts just mentioned, see also *1 Enoch* 14:20; 62:15–16; *Mart. Ascen. Isa.* 9:9).

Mark's depiction of Jesus is also reminiscent of Daniel's vision of the "Ancient of Days," whose "clothing was white as snow, and the hair of his head like pure wool" (Dan 7:9 NRSV). The "one like a son of man" approaches the Ancient of Days (i.e., God) and receives authority and kingdom (Dan 7:13–14). Perhaps in his transformation we should understand that Jesus, as the "son of man" in the presence of the Ancient of Days, has taken on some of God's characteristics (much as Moses' face began to shine with God's glory). If this is correct, then the transfiguration should be understood as a visual verification of Jesus' claim to be the "son of man" who will come in the glory of his Father with the holy angels (see Mark 8:38; Dan 7:10).

4 ὤφθη αὐτοῖς Ἡλίας σὺν Μωϋσεῖ, καὶ ἦσαν συλλαλοῦντες τῷ Ἰησοῦ, "Elijah appeared to them with Moses, and they were conversing together with Jesus." Moses and Elijah are often paired. The two witnesses of Rev 11:3–12 could very well be Moses and Elijah (on Moses compare v 6 with Exod 7:17, 19; on Elijah compare vv 5–6 with 2 Kgs 1:10). (However, Elijah is sometimes paired with Enoch; see 2 Esdras 6:26; *Apoc. El. [C]* 4:7–19, which appears to be dependent on Rev 11.) According to one rabbinic midrash, God promises in the future to bring Moses with Elijah (*Deut. Rab.* 3.17 [on Deut 10:1]). The rabbis compared Moses and Elijah at many points: "You find that two prophets rose up for Israel out of the tribe of Levi; one the first of all the prophets, and the other the last of all the prophets: Moses first and Elijah last, and both with a commission to redeem Israel. . . . You find that Moses and Elijah were alike in every respect. . . . Moses went up to heaven [cf. Exod 19:3]; and Elijah went up to heaven [cf. 2 Kgs 2:1]. . . . Moses: 'And the cloud covered him six days' [Exod 24:16]; and Elijah went up in a whirlwind [cf. 2 Kgs 2:1]" (*Pesiq. Rab.* 4.2; translation based on William G. Braude, *Pesikta Rabbati*, 2 vols., YJS 18 [New Haven, CT: Yale UP, 1968] 2:84–85). In one tradition it is said that when Elijah was born "men of shining white appearance" greeted him and wrapped him in fire" (*Liv. Pro.* 21:2). Both Moses and Elijah had revelatory experiences on mountain tops (Exod 20–34; 1 Kgs 19:8), and biblical and extrabiblical traditions of translation to heaven prior to resurrection (emphasized by Thrall, *NTS* 16 [1970] 305–17) surround them both (Josephus, *Ant.* 4.8.48 §326: "while [Moses] bade farewell to Eleazar and Joshua and was yet communicating with them, a cloud suddenly descended upon him and he disappeared"; *b. Soṭa* 13b; 2 Kgs 2:11–12; Josephus, *Ant.* 9.2.2 §28). Most importantly, both Moses and Elijah had visions of God. Perhaps it is on this basis that they qualify as witnesses to the glorious appearance of Jesus, God's son (so Baly, *ExpTim* 82 [1970] 83–83). On the passive ὤφθη, "he was seen," in the sense of "appeared," see BAG 581–82 (s.v. ὁράω).

The evangelist says that Elijah and Moses ἦσαν συλλαλοῦντες τῷ Ἰησοῦ, "were conversing together with Jesus." But the evangelist does not relate any of the conversation, or even hint at what the topic might have been. According to Luke 9:31, they "spoke of his departure [lit. *exodus*], which he was to accomplish at Jerusalem." Mark's context suggests that the conversation may have had to do with the approaching kingdom of God and Jesus' role in relation to it.

5 Ῥαββί, καλόν ἐστιν ἡμᾶς ὧδε εἶναι, "Rabbi, it is good that we are here." Addressing Jesus as ῥαββί, "Rabbi," lends the story an important element of verisimilitude, for it is not likely that in an invented story, or in an Easter appearance story, Jesus would be addressed by such a pedestrian epithet. But had some strange experience overtaken the historical, pre-Easter "Rabbi Jesus," then this is exactly how we should expect the disciples to have addressed their master. The address רבי *rabbî* appears in first-century Hebrew and Aramaic texts and inscriptions. An inscription from Jaffa (probably pre-70) reads in part: חנניה בן רבי [לעז]ר *Ḥănanyâ ben Rabbî [Laʿzā]r*, "Hananiah son of Rabbi [Laza]rus" (*CIJ* 2:895). Other examples include *CIJ* 2:249, 275–79. For more discussion, see *Comment* on 9:17 and 10:51.

ποιήσωμεν τρεῖς σκηνάς, σοὶ μίαν καὶ Μωϋσεῖ μίαν καὶ Ἠλίᾳ μίαν, "Let us make three tents: one for you, one for Moses, and one for Elijah." Why the offer to build "three tents" (τρεῖς σκηνάς)? It could be that Peter had concluded that the kingdom of God had arrived in its fullness, when some of the great events of the first exodus would be repeated (such as manna in the wilderness and God's presence among the people). To commemorate the exodus, Jews celebrated the Feast of Booths by living in small booths or huts for seven days (Lev 23:42–44; Neh 8:14–17). But the feast was also understood by many as looking ahead to the glorious day of Israel's deliverance (see Riesenfeld, *Jésus transfiguré*). The offer to build three tabernacles—one for Jesus, one for Moses, and one for Elijah—would presumably encourage the stunning consultation to continue indefinitely (though Hagner, *Matthew*, 2:493, thinks it has more to do with honoring the occasion). But, as it turns out, there is no need to detain Moses and Elijah.

6 The evangelist's comment, οὐ γὰρ ἤδει τί ἀποκριθῇ ἔκφοβοι γὰρ ἐγένοντο, "for he did not know what he should reply, because they had become greatly afraid," makes it clear that Peter's offer to build the three tabernacles (or booths) was inappropriate. Peter is not ignorant; he is simply frightened, indeed, overwhelmed by what he has just witnessed. The emphasis accordingly does not fall on Peter, but on Jesus, whose glorification is so impressive that even his closest associates are unable to assess it properly (Kazmierski, *Jesus, the Son of God*, 120–26).

7 καὶ ἐγένετο νεφέλη ἐπισκιάζουσα αὐτοῖς, καὶ ἐγένετο φωνὴ ἐκ τῆς νεφέλης, οὗτός ἐστιν ὁ υἱός μου ὁ ἀγαπητός, ἀκούετε αὐτοῦ, "And then a cloud appeared overshadowing them, and a voice came out of the cloud, 'This is my Son the beloved; hear him!'" The heavenly voice implies that Peter's request to build the tabernacles was misguided, because he and his fellow disciples are to listen to God's Son, not to Moses and Elijah. The notation that there was a νεφέλη ἐπισκιάζουσα, "cloud overshadowing," the disciples is reminiscent of the language and imagery of the OT: "And Moses was not able to enter the tent of witness, because the cloud overshadowed [ἐπεσκίαζεν] it, and the tabernacle [ἡ σκηνή] was filled with the glory of the LORD" (LXX Exod 40:35; cf. 19:19). This language is again consistent with the traces of exodus imagery lying behind the transfiguration (see also *Odes Sol.* 35:1; LXX Pss 90:4; 139:8).

The heavenly voice addresses the frightened disciples: οὗτός ἐστιν ὁ υἱός μου ὁ ἀγαπητός, "This is my Son the beloved." These words echo those spoken at Jesus' baptism (Mark 1:11), but in the present instance the address is in the third person because God is speaking to the disciples and not to Jesus. The second-person address in 1:11, σὺ εἶ ὁ υἱός μου, "You are my son," probably alludes to Ps 2:7 (בְּנִי אַתָּה *běnî 'attâ*, "you [are] my son"), even if in the LXX the word order is different (υἱός μου εἶ σύ). The substantival adjective ὁ ἀγαπητός, "the beloved," may allude to LXX Gen 22:2, where God commands Abraham: λαβὲ τὸν υἱόν σου τὸν ἀγαπητόν ὃν ἠγάπησας, "Take your son, the beloved, whom you love" (cf. Gen 22:12, 16). However, the appearance of "beloved" in the admittedly later Aramaic version of Ps 2:7 (חביב כבר לאבא לי אנת *ḥĕbîb kĕbar lĕʾabbāʾ lî ʾant*, lit. "Beloved as a son to his father to me you [are]") suggests that the language of Mark 1:11 and 9:7 may reflect an interpretive tendency that emerged in the synagogue. In any case, when "beloved" is used with "'son' or 'daughter,' it can connote uniqueness or 'only'" (Guelich, 33–34, citing Turner, *JTS* o.s. 27 [1925–26] 113–29).

ἀκούετε αὐτοῦ, "hear him!" The heavenly voice interrupts Peter (v 7) and may be partially intended as a rebuke (i.e., "listen to Jesus, not to Moses or Elijah"). The time of Moses and Elijah is over, though their support for Jesus is important. It is time to heed the words of Jesus. The heavenly voice recalls the words uttered at the time of Jesus' baptism (Mark 1:10–11) and serves as a second divine endorsement: Jesus' talk of rejection and death has not disqualified him from his messianic task. He is still God's Son, and his message, now placed in a new light, must still be heeded. Mark's ἀκούετε αὐτοῦ may echo Deut 18:15 (αὐτοῦ ἀκούσεσθε, "you shall hear him"), which, if so, would be consistent with the popular opinion earlier expressed in 8:28 that Jesus was "one of the prophets."

8 καὶ ἐξάπινα περιβλεψάμενοι οὐκέτι οὐδένα εἶδον ἀλλὰ τὸν Ἰησοῦν μόνον μεθ' ἑαυτῶν, "And suddenly, looking around, they no longer saw anyone, but only Jesus with them." The sudden disappearance of the cloud (implied) and Elijah and Moses underscores the point that it is to Jesus that the disciples are to look. Mark's redundancy adds emphasis: "they no longer saw anyone, but only Jesus with them." Only Jesus, not the great prophet Elijah or the great lawgiver Moses, can accomplish God's redemptive plan.

Explanation

The transfiguration forms an important bridge between Jesus' public ministry in Galilee and his passion in Jerusalem. The recognition of Jesus' sonship in 1:1 and 1:11 is followed by a rapid succession of stories in which the readers of Mark hear of Jesus' supernatural powers and fearful recognition by unclean spirits. For the first eight chapters of the Markan Gospel Jesus has triumphed over every foe: over demonic forces, over illness, over critics, and over nature itself. But a turning point, indeed a crisis, in the narrative is reached when Jesus announces his passion. In the minds of most, talk of death surely implied defeat and failure of mission. What is needed is a convincing and dramatic indication that Jesus continues to be God's agent of redemption. The transfiguration serves this purpose. It is intended to reassure Mark's readers that the necessity of Jesus' death does not result from a withdrawal of heavenly favor. Jesus' mission and purpose have not been compromised. God is just as much with Jesus after the announcement of his passion as he was after his baptism, and he still claims Jesus as his unique Son. Whereas the heavenly voice at the baptism might have been heard by Jesus alone, the voice at the transfiguration was heard by the disciples, who are enjoined: "Hear him!" Only Jesus can fulfill his Father's mission on earth.

D. "Why Must Elijah Come First?" (9:9–13)

Bibliography

Allison, D. C. "Elijah Must Come First." *JBL* 103 (1984) 256–58. **Arens, E.** *The HΛΘON-Sayings in the Synoptic Tradition: A Historical-Critical Investigation.* OBO 10. Göttingen: Vandenhoeck & Ruprecht, 1976. 243–48. **Baltensweiler, H.** *Die Verklärung Jesu.* ATANT 33. Zürich: Zwingli, 1959. **Bayer, H. F.** *Jesus' Predictions of Vindication and Resurrection.* WUNT 2.20. Tübingen: Mohr-Siebeck, 1986. 166–69. **Bennett, W. J., Jr.,** "'The Son of Man Must....'" *NovT* 17 (1975) 113–29. **Berger, K.** *Die Auferstehung des Propheten und die Erhöhung des Menschensohnes: Traditionsgeschichtliche Untersuchungen zu Deutung des Geschickes Jesu in frühchristlichen Texte.* SUNT 13. Göttingen: Vandenhoeck & Ruprecht, 1976. 44–48. **Best, E.** *Following Jesus.* 62–65. **Black, M.** "The Theological Appropriation of the Old Testament by the New Testament." *SJT* 39 (1986) 1–17, esp. 9–12. **Casey, M.** *Aramaic Sources of Mark's Gospel.* SNTSMS 102. Cambridge: Cambridge UP, 1998. 111–37. **Colpe, C.** "Traditionsüberschreitende Argumentationen zu Aussagen Jesu über sich selbst." In *Tradition und Glaube: Das frühe Christentum in seiner Umwelt.* FS K. G. Kuhn, ed. G. Jeremias et al. Göttingen: Vandenhoeck & Ruprecht, 1971. 239–43. **Dautzenberg, G.** "Elija im Markusevangelium." In *The Four Gospels 1992.* FS F. Neirynck, ed. F. Van Segbroeck et al. 3 vols. BETL 100. Leuven: Peeters; Leuven UP, 1992. 2:1077–94, esp. 1082–88. **Derrett, J. D. M.** "Herod's Oath and the Baptist's Head." *BZ* 9 (1965) 49–59, 233–46. **Faierstein, M. M.** "Why Do the Scribes Say That Elijah Must Come First?" *JBL* 100 (1981) 75–86. **Fitzmyer, J. A.** "More about Elijah Coming First." *JBL* 104 (1985) 295–96. **France, R. T.** *Jesus and the Old Testament.* 91–92, 123–24, 250–51. **Grimm, W.** *Weil Ich dich liebe: Die Verkündigung Jesu und Deuterojesaja.* ANTJ 1. Bern; Frankfurt am Main: Lang, 1976. 209–22. **Hampel, V.** *Menschensohn und historischer Jesus: Ein Rätselwort als Schlüssel zum messianischen Selbstverständnis Jesu.* Neukirchen-Vluyn: Neukirchener Verlag, 1990. 282–88. **Heawood, P. J.** "Mark ix. 11–13." *ExpTim* 64 (1952–53) 239. **Holzmeister, U.** "Einzeluntersuchungen über das Geheimnis der Verklärung Christi." *Bib* 21 (1940) 200–210. **Hooker, M. D.** *The Son of Man in Mark.* 122–34. **Horstmann, M.** *Studien zur markinischen Christologie.* 105–36. **Kümmel, W. G.** *Promise and Fulfilment.* 64–67. **Lambrecht, J.** "The Christology of Mark." *BTB* 3 (1973) 256–73. **Liebers, R.** *"Wie geschrieben steht": Studien zu einer besonderen Art frühchristlichen Schriftbezuges.* Berlin; New York: de Gruyter, 1993. 73–95, 369–78. **Marcus, J.** "Mark 9,11–13: 'As It Has Been Written.'" *ZNW* 80 (1989) 42–63. ———. *The Way of the Lord: Christological Exegesis of the Old Testament in the Gospel of Mark.* Louisville: Westminster John Knox, 1992. 94–110. **Martyn, J. L.** "We Have Found Elijah." In *Jews, Greeks, and Christians: Religious Cultures in Late Antiquity.* FS W. D. Davies, ed. R. Hamerton-Kelly and R. Scroggs. SJLA 21. Leiden: Brill, 1976. 181–219. **Meyer, D.** "Πολλὰ παθεῖν." *ZNW* 55 (1964) 132. **Minette de Tillesse, G.** *Le secret messianique.* 281–83. **Moo, D. J.** *The Old Testament in the Gospel Passion Narratives.* Sheffield: Almond, 1983. 89–91. **Nützel, J. M.** *Die Verklärungserzählung im Markusevangelium.* FB 6. Würzburg: Echter, 1973. 256–67. **Öhler, M.** "The Expectation of Elijah and the Presence of the Kingdom of God." *JBL* 118 (1999) 461–76. **Oke, C. C.** "The

Rearrangement and Transmission of Mark ix, 11–13." *ExpTim* 64 (1953) 187–88. **Pesch, R.**
Das Evangelium der Urgemeinde. 116–18. **Robinson, J. A. T.** "Did Jesus Have a Distinctive Use
of Scripture?" In *Christological Perspectives.* FS H. K. McArthur, ed. R. F. Berkey and S. A.
Edwards. New York: Pilgrim, 1982. 49–57. **Suhl, A.** *Zitaten.* 133–37. **Taylor, V.** *Jesus and His
Sacrifice.* 91–97. ————. "The Origin of the Markan Passion-Sayings." *NTS* 1 (1954–55)
159–67 (repr. in V. Taylor. *New Testament Essays.* London: Epworth, 1970. 60–71). **Thrall,
M. E.** "Elijah and Moses in Mark's Account of the Transfiguration." *NTS* 16 (1970) 305–
17, esp. 307–8. **Tödt, H. E.** *The Son of Man in the Synoptic Tradition.* NTL. London: SCM
Press; Philadelphia: Westminster, 1965. 152–221. **Torrey, C. C.** *Our Translated Gospels.* London: Hodder and Stoughton; New York: Harper & Brothers, 1936. **Wink, W.** *John the Baptist
in the Gospel Tradition.* SNTSMS 7. Cambridge: Cambridge UP, 1968. 13–17, 30–33. **Yates,
J. E.** *The Spirit and the Kingdom.* London: S. P. C. K., 1963. 108–18.

Translation

⁹*And when they came down from the mountain, he* [a] *commanded them that they should
not relate* [b] *to anyone what they had seen, until the "son of man" should arise from the
dead.* ¹⁰*And they kept this saying to themselves, debating what the rising from the dead* [c]
is. ¹¹*And they asked him, saying, "Why do the scribes* [d] *say, 'Elijah must come first'?"*
¹²*But he said* [e] *to them, "*[f]*Elijah,*[g] *coming first, does restore* [h] *all things; yet how is it
written about the 'son of man'?* [i] *That he should suffer many things and be despised.*[j]
¹³*But I tell you that Elijah has come, and they did to him whatever they wished, just as it
is written about him."*

Notes

[a]A few MSS add ὁ Ἰησοῦς, "Jesus" (cf. Matt 17:9).

[b]Gk. διηγήσωνται. W and other authorities read ἐξηγήσωνται, "explain."

[c]D W and a few other authorities read τί ἐστιν ὅταν ἐκ νεκρῶν ἀναστῇ, "what 'until he should arise
from the dead' meant." These authorities have rephrased and repeated the wording found in v 9.

[d]ℵ L and other authorities read οἱ Φαρισαῖοι καὶ οἱ γραμματεῖς, "the Pharisees and the scribes"
(or "scribes and Pharisees").

[e]ℵ B C L Δ and other authorities read ἔφη, "he said"; A D W and other authorities read ἀποκριθεὶς
εἶπεν, "answering he said."

[f]D adds εἰ, "if."

[g]A few late MSS add ὁ Θεσβίτης, "the Tishbite," an addition inspired by 1 Kgs 17:1.

[h]Gk. ἀποκαθιστάνει, "does restore," which is read by ℵ² A B L W 33 and other authorities and
accepted by UBSGNT³ᶜ and Nestle-Aland²⁷. Other forms are witnessed: C and a few later authorities
read ἀποκαταστήσει, "will restore," which probably reflects LXX Mal 3:23 [ET 4:6]: ἀποκαταστήσει
καρδίαν πατρὸς πρὸς υἱόν, "he will restore the heart of the father to the son"; cf. Sir 48:10: καταστῆσαι
φυλὰς Ἰακώβ, "to restore the tribes of Jacob." ℵ* and D read ἀποκαταστάνει, "does restore." Most of
the later authorities read ἀποκαθιστᾷ, "does restore."

[i]The first clause is the question; the second clause, introduced by ἵνα, "that," is the answer (so
Gundry, 464).

[j]Gk. ἐξουδενηθῇ, "be despised," is read by B D and several later authorities and accepted by
UBSGNT³ᶜ and Nestle-Aland²⁷. A C 33 and most later authorities read the synonym ἐξουδενωθῇ.

Form/Structure/Setting

Mark 9:9–13 forms a natural conclusion to the major shift in Mark's narrative.
This shift began in 8:27–30 with Peter's confession of Jesus' messianic identity
and Jesus' first prediction of his passion (8:31–33). This prediction was followed

by teaching on suffering (8:34–9:1) and the transfiguration (9:2–8). The reference to the rising of the "son of man" in v 9 takes the reader back to the first prediction of the passion, while the reference in vv 11–13 to Elijah and his treatment takes the reader back to the teaching on suffering as well as to the mysterious appearance of Elijah with Moses on the Mount of Transfiguration. These several pericopes in combination provide the turning point in the Markan Gospel, from the Galilean ministry characterized by miracles and crowds to the Judean ministry characterized by controversy in the temple precincts, arrest, suffering, and death.

The most difficult part of the pericope concerns the relationship between vv 10 and 11. In what way is the question about the meaning of the rising from the dead related to the scribes' opinion of the necessity of Elijah coming first? Another important question concerns the point of the disciples' about the meaning of "rising from the dead." What does their question mean? Do they not understand the doctrine of the general resurrection, or is their question narrower, having to do with the resurrection of the "son of man" himself?

The historical setting of this pericope is complicated. We may have combined materials here (and clumsily combined materials at that—though see the suggestion below). Perhaps in its earliest form, the Elijah question read something like this: "And they asked him, 'Why do the scribes say, "Elijah must come first"?' He said to them, 'Elijah comes first and restores all things. But I tell you that Elijah has come, and they did to him whatever they wished, just as it is written about him.'" The fate of "Elijah," who is probably to be identified with John the Baptist (as in Matt 17:13), may have been what drew the passion prediction to this context. The prediction may very well have been associated with the transfiguration story (Mark 9:2–8) and could have read something like this: "And when they had come down from the mountain, he commanded them to relate to no one what they had seen, until the "son of man" should arise from the dead. And they kept this saying to themselves, pondering what the rising from the dead meant. And he said to them, 'How is it written about the "son of man"? He should suffer many things and be despised.'" The material relating to the "son of man" may have originally belonged to the transfiguration story, while the discussion of Elijah could have originated in another context. However, another approach has recently been taken that shows how this material (9:11–13) could very well have been a unity.

Casey (*Aramaic Sources*, 121–37) has argued that Mark 9:11–13 derives from an Aramaic source and that when this is taken into account several of the perplexing exegetical problems can be solved. The English translation of Casey's Aramaic reconstruction reads as follows: "And (they were) asking him and saying, 'Why do (the) scribes say that Elijah is going to come first?' [12]And he said to them, 'Elijah comes first and turns back all, and how it is written of (a/the son of) man that he suffers much and is rejected? [13]And I tell you that, moreover, Elijah has come, and they did in the case of him whom they desired according as it is written concerning him/it'" (121–22). Casey believes that the "son of man" referred to in v 12 was originally not a reference to Jesus but a reference to John, of whom Jesus has been speaking. There is therefore no disruption in the flow of thought and no need to postulate a clumsy combination of materials dealing with Jesus' passion, on the one hand, and John's appearance as Elijah, on the other. For more on this, see *Comment* below. Casey (*Aramaic Sources*, 135–37) concludes that "Mark's Aramaic source gives us an accurate account of Jesus' teaching, even if it is an abbreviated account" and that Mark's unrevised Greek text is evidence of great antiquity and certainly priority in relation to the Gospels of Matthew and Luke.

Comment

The transfiguration, a foreshadowing of Jesus' resurrection and of the kingdom's power, is to be proclaimed when Jesus is resurrected. It is at this time that the disciples will proclaim Jesus' messiahship (as commanded by Jesus in 8:30). Mention of the resurrection of the "son of man" (v 9) prompts the disciples to ponder its meaning (v 10). From what follows we may infer that the disciples' question is as much chronological as it is logical. With regard to the latter, they wonder why Jesus must suffer and die at all. With regard to the former, they wonder when this resurrection will take place—*before* the appearance of Elijah, or *after*? Their uncertainty prompts the question about Elijah in v 11: "Why do the scribes say, 'Elijah must come first'?" The disciples' question provides Jesus with the opportunity to correct scribal opinion. He does this by interpreting scriptural promises and exegetical traditions in the light of the fate of the Baptist.

9 καὶ καταβαινόντων αὐτῶν ἐκ τοῦ ὄρους διεστείλατο αὐτοῖς, "And when they came down from the mountain, he commanded them." On the significance of the mountain setting, see *Comment* on v 2. Jesus' command ἵνα μηδενὶ ἃ εἶδον διηγήσωνται, εἰ μὴ ὅταν ὁ υἱὸς τοῦ ἀνθρώπου ἐκ νεκρῶν ἀναστῇ, "that they should not relate to anyone what they had seen, until the 'son of man' should arise from the dead," parallels the command in 8:30 to relate his messianic identity to no one. Jesus' messiahship, an aspect of which the transfiguration foreshadowed, cannot be proclaimed until Easter (for discussion of the reasons for secrecy and their essential historicity, see *Comment* on 8:30). The principal point here is that if the passion provides a vital element of Jesus' messianic identity and mission (as in 8:31–38), then the glory of the transfiguration cannot be shared until it can be proclaimed in the light of the passion, which is its proper context.

10 καὶ τὸν λόγον ἐκράτησαν πρὸς ἑαυτοὺς συζητοῦντες τί ἐστιν τὸ ἐκ νεκρῶν ἀναστῆναι, "And they kept this saying to themselves, debating what the rising from the dead is." The statement that τὸν λόγον ἐκράτησαν πρὸς ἑαυτούς, "they kept this saying to themselves," shows that the disciples heeded Jesus' command. The implication is that they did not even share the experience with the other disciples (ἐκράτησαν, "they kept," suggests that they guarded the secret closely). But they pondered the meaning of Jesus' reference to "the rising from the dead" (with the present participle συζητοῦντες, "debating," implying that they gave the matter much thought, weighing alternatives and debating the matter among themselves). If we interpret the disciples' bewilderment in the light of the subsequent question (in v 11), then it seems that they wondered in what way Jesus' death and resurrection related to Elijah's expected coming? The question is natural, for the Messiah was expected to reign on earth for a long period of time (either a full lifetime or perhaps several centuries—Jewish messianic expectations vary on the point). Matthew omits v 10, perhaps because he viewed it as superfluous, even confusing, and possibly as once again portraying the disciples as unacceptably obtuse (Luke omits the entire pericope, though he knows of it, as seen in Luke 9:36).

11 ὅτι λέγουσιν οἱ γραμματεῖς ὅτι Ἠλίαν δεῖ ἐλθεῖν πρῶτον; "Why do the scribes say, 'Elijah must come first'?" Scribal interpretation is probably based on Mal 4:5–6 (LXX 3:22–23; MT 3:23–24), which in part reads "Behold, I will send you Elijah the prophet *before* the great and terrible day of the LORD comes. And he will turn [LXX: restore] the heart of the father to the son" (RSV, adapted and emphasis added). Belief that Elijah would come at the end of days is attested in a variety of Jewish sources (e.g., Sir 48:10; 4Q558 [= 4QVision]; *Mek.* on Exod 16:33 [*Wayassaʿ* §6]; *m. ʿEd.* 8:7; cf. 1 Macc 14:41). In some texts Elijah is expected to play a role in the resurrection (*Sib. Or.* 2:187–188; *m. Soṭa* 9:15; *b. Sanh.* 113a). The scribes' question probably originated as a challenge to Jesus' proclamation of the kingdom of God: How can Jesus be right if Elijah has not yet made an appearance? We know that Elijah must come first! On the interrogative ὅτι (usually "that," but here "why"), see Field, *Notes*, 33.

12 The scribes' question is a legitimate one, and Jesus in part agrees with it: Ἠλίας μὲν ἐλθὼν πρῶτον ἀποκαθιστάνει πάντα, "Elijah, coming first, does restore all things." Here Jesus not only alludes to Malachi, but his language is reminiscent of Jesus ben Sira's praise of Elijah. Ben Sira says that the great prophet is "ready at the appointed time . . . to restore the tribes of Jacob" (Sir 48:10; cf. Luke 1:17, where the angel's speech applies Elijah language to the predicted ministry of Zechariah's son John). Sira's hope of the restoration of the tribes finds expression in Jesus' appointment of the twelve (3:13–19).

According to Torrey (*Translated Gospels*, 56–58), "Elijah, coming first, restores all things; yet how is it written . . . ?" should be "Does Elijah, coming first, restore all things? How, then, is it written . . . ?" Torrey's point is that Aramaic questions are sometimes misunderstood as declarations. Marcus has recently taken up this position. He renders Jesus' reply: "Is it true that, when he comes before the Messiah, Elijah will restore all things?" (*ZNW* 80 [1989] 47; id.,*Way of the Lord*, 99; following Wellhausen, 70). This reconstruction, however, is too daring, for the insertion of "before the Messiah" presumes too much and there is no warrant for the introduction of the interrogative "is it true that?" (see the criticisms in Casey, *Aramaic Sources*, 124). It is probably best to see the first clause as declarative, "Elijah, coming first, does restore all things," and the second as interrogative, "yet how is it written . . . ?"

πῶς γέγραπται ἐπὶ τὸν υἱὸν τοῦ ἀνθρώπου ἵνα πολλὰ πάθῃ καὶ ἐξουδενηθῇ; "how is it written about the 'son of man'? That he should suffer many things and be despised." The major interpretive difficulty lies with the reference to the "son of man" who will "suffer many things and be despised." It is almost universally assumed that the text is talking about Jesus the "son of man" and that it is part of the passion-prediction tradition. If so, then its appearance in the middle of a discussion about the fate of John the Baptist, as the expected Elijah, seems out of place. But Casey (*Aramaic Sources*, 126–37) has suggested that originally the reference was to John himself (so also Wink, *John the Baptist*, 13–17). "Son of man" is nothing more than the Aramaic idiom for "man" or "human." On that score, there is nothing about Mark 9:11–13 that necessarily refers to Jesus. The entire piece of teaching can be understood as concerned solely with John. Only in later transmission and translation of the tradition was it assumed that the reference was to Jesus. What had probably been anarthrous in Aramaic (e.g., על בר נש *ʿal bar nāš*, "about son of man") came to be rendered in Greek as articular (ἐπὶ τὸν υἱὸν τοῦ ἀνθρώπου, "about the son of man"), as referring to *the* "son of man," namely,

Jesus. If we follow Casey here, some of the interpretive problems may be solved and the need to postulate awkward redaction done away with.

Casey's "how is it written of (a/the son of) man that he suffers much and is rejected" refers to John and his recent death at the hands of Israel's leaders. Where in Scripture was such a thing foretold of the one who comes as Elijah to restore (or turn back) all? No place obvious. Hence, this is the problem for Jesus. He had explained John's ministry in terms of the expected Elijah, but before this ministry could be completed, and against all conventional expectation, John had been jailed and then cruelly executed. Although nowhere in Scripture foretelling the coming of Elijah is there mention of his suffering and martyrdom, Scripture nonetheless, Jesus reasons, must surely speak of it. Jesus' general appeal, "how is it written?" need not in fact have a specific passage in mind. It is the same vague reference as we have in Mark 14:21 ("For the 'son of man' goes as it is written of him") and Mark 14:49 ("Day after day I was with you in the temple teaching, and you did not seize me. But let the scriptures be fulfilled"). There is more than a sufficient number of passages that describe the suffering lot of humans. Casey suggests, among others, Job 14:1–2: "Man [MT: אָדָם *'ādām; Tg.:* בר נש *bar nāš*] that is born of a woman is of few days, and full of trouble. He comes forth like a flower, and withers; he flees like a shadow, and continues not. . . . Indeed his flesh suffers upon him, and his soul mourns over him" (see Casey, 127). (Casey also recommends Isa 40 and Jer 6–7.) Lying behind the slaying of the two witnesses in Rev 11:7–8 may be a tradition of a martyred Elijah.

Having said all of this, it is probable that Mark's original Greek readers would have assumed that the reference to "the 'son of (the) man' " was to Jesus. They would have interpreted Jesus' teaching as suggesting a parallel experience between himself and the recently martyred Baptist. Both had come in fulfillment of the Scriptures—John as Elijah and Jesus as *the* "son of man"—and both had been and will be treated with contempt.

13 λέγω ὑμῖν ὅτι καὶ Ἠλίας ἐλήλυθεν, καὶ ἐποίησαν αὐτῷ ὅσα ἤθελον, καθὼς γέγραπται ἐπ' αὐτόν, "I tell you that Elijah has come, and they did to him whatever they wished, just as it is written about him." Jesus agrees with the scribes that Elijah does indeed come first, but his assertion that "Elijah has come" would have surprised them. Jesus implies that Elijah is John the Baptist. (The Markan evangelist surely would have us understand that Jesus has referred to John, as the Matthean evangelist makes explicit in 17:13.) The prophecy of Scripture has been fulfilled; in the person and ministry of John, Elijah has come. But Jesus adds a significant interpretation to this prophecy by alluding to his imprisonment and martyrdom: "they did to him whatever they wished, just as it is written about him." Where exactly in Scripture Elijah's martyrdom is found is not clear (and probably for this reason Matthew omits this phrase). But Jesus' point is that John's/Elijah's fate is in keeping with the overall picture of suffering and death in which Jesus shares. It is possible that Jesus understood the struggles of Dan 7 and the suffering of Isa 53 as in some way applying to John as much as to himself (though see the passages recommended by Casey in *Comment* on v 12 above). In any case, John is Elijah and his fate adumbrates Jesus' own; hence the intertwining of materials relating to the suffering "son of man" and the coming and fate of Elijah/John.

Explanation

Mark's Greek presentation of these materials constitutes an important contribution to early Christian eschatology as well as clarification of Jesus' self-understanding and assessment of his mentor John the Baptist. The transfiguration of Jesus offered the disciples a glimpse of the glory of Jesus when he comes in the full power of the kingdom of God. But they have been told that Jesus must undergo the passion before this dream can be realized. Jesus has evidently modeled his fate after the experience of John. Just as John suffered, so Jesus must suffer also. But when he is raised up, then the disciples can proclaim his messianic identity and look forward to the fulfillment of the kingdom.

E. The Healing of the Boy with an Unclean Spirit (9:14–29)

Bibliography

Achtemeier, P. J. "Miracles and the Historical Jesus: Mark 9:14–29." *CBQ* 37 (1975) 471–91. **Aichinger, H.** "Zur Traditionsgeschichte der Epileptiker-Perikope Mk 9,14–29 par Mt 17,14–21 par Lk 9,37–43a." In *Probleme der Forschung.* Ed. A. Fuchs. SNTU-A 3. Munich: Herold, 1978. 114–43. **Best, E.** *Following Jesus.* 66–72. **Betz, H. D.** "The Early Christian Miracle Story: Some Observations on the Form Critical Problem." *Semeia* 11 (1978) 69–81. **Bolt, P. G.** "Jesus, the Daimons and the Dead." In *The Unseen World: Christian Reflections on Angels, Demons and the Heavenly Realm.* Ed. A. N. S. Lane. Carlisle: Paternoster; Grand Rapids, MI: Baker, 1996. 75–102. **Bornkamm, G.** "πνεῦμα ἄλαλον: Eine Studie zum Markusevangelium." In *Geschichte und Glaube*, Part 2. Vol. 4 of *Gesammelte Aufsätze.* BEvT 53. Munich: Kaiser, 1971. 21–36. **Brewer, D. I.** "Jesus and the Psychiatrists." In *The Unseen World: Christian Reflections on Angels, Demons and the Heavenly Realm.* Ed. A. N. S. Lane. Carlisle: Paternoster; Grand Rapids, MI: Baker, 1996. 133–48. **Carmignac, J.** "'Ah! Si tu peux! . . . Tout est possible en faveur de celui qui croit' (Marc 9:23)." In *The New Testament Age.* FS B. Reicke, ed. W. C. Weinrich. 2 vols. Macon: Mercer UP, 1984. 1:83–86. **Cranfield, C. E. B.** "St. Mark 9.14–29." *SJT* 3 (1950) 57–67. **Delorme, J.** "Dualité, dissection critique et signification: Mc 9,14–29." In *The Four Gospels 1992.* FS F. Neirynck, ed. F. Van Segbroeck et al. 3 vols. BETL 100. Leuven: Peeters; Leuven UP, 1992. 2:1095–1104. ————. "Signification d'un récit et comparaison synoptique (Marc 9,14–29 et parallèles)." In *The Synoptic Gospels.* Ed. C. Focant. BETL 110. Leuven: Peeters; Leuven UP, 1993. 531–47. **Hahn, F.** "Das Verständnis des Glaubens im Markusevangeliums." In *Glaube im Neuen Testament.* FS H. Binder, ed. F. Hahn and H. Klein. Biblisch-Theologische Studien 7. Neukirchen-Vluyn: Neukirchener Verlag, 1982. 43–67, esp. 58–61. **Howard, V. P.** *Das Ego Jesu in den synoptischen Evangelien: Untersuchungen zum Sprachgebrauch Jesu.* Marburger theologische Studien 14. Marburg: Elwert, 1975. 86–97. **Kertelge, K.** *Wunder Jesu im Markusevangelium.* 174–79. **Knoch, O.** *Dem, der glaubt, ist alles möglich: Die Botschaft der Wundererzählungen der Evangelien.* Stuttgart: Katholisches Bibelwerk, 1986. 293–307. **Koch, D.-A.** *Bedeutung der Wundererzählungen.* 114–26. **Kollmann, B.** *Jesus und die Christen als Wundertäten: Studien zu Magie, Medizin und Schamanismus in Antike und Christentum.* FRLANT 170. Göttingen: Vandenhoeck & Ruprecht, 1996. **Lang, F. G.** "Sola gratia im Markusevangelium: Die Soteriologie des Markus nach 9,14–29 und 10,17–31." In

Rechtfertigung. FS E. Käsemann, ed. J. Friedrich et al. Tübingen: Mohr-Siebeck; Göttingen: Vandenhoeck & Ruprecht, 1976. 321–38. **Latourelle, R.** *The Miracles of Jesus.* 149–54. **Léon-Dufour, X.** "L'épisode de l'enfant épileptique." In *Études d'évangile.* Parole de Dieu 2. Paris: Seuil, 1965. 183–227. **Lohse, E.** "Glaube und Wunder: Ein Beitrag zur Theologia Crucis in den synoptischen Evangelien." In *Theologia Crucis—Signum Crucis.* FS E. Dinkler, ed. C. Andresen and C. Klein. Tübingen: Mohr-Siebeck, 1979. 335–50. **Loos, H. van der.** *Miracles of Jesus.* 397–405. **Lührmann, D.** *Glaube im frühen Christentum.* Gütersloh: Mohn, 1976. 17–30. **Marshall, C. D.** *Faith as a Theme in Mark's Narrative.* SNTSMS 64. Cambridge: Cambridge UP, 1989. 110–23, 220–24. **Martin, R. P.** *Mark: Evangelist and Theologian.* **Meier, J. P.** *Marginal Jew.* 2:653–56. **Minette de Tillesse,** G. *Le secret messianique.* 89–99. **Petzke, G.** "Die historische Frage nach den Wundertaten Jesu: Dargestellt am Beilspiel des Exorzismus Mark. ix. 14–29." *NTS* 22 (1975–76) 180–204. **Reploh, K.-G.** *Markus—Lehrer der Gemeinde.* 211–21. **Rolland, P.** "Lecture par couches rédactionnelles de l'épisode de l'épileptique (Mc 9,14–29 et parallèles)." In *The Synoptic Gospels.* Ed. C. Focant. BETL 110. Leuven: Peeters; Leuven UP, 1993. 451–58. **Roloff, J.** *Kerygma und der irdische Jesus.* 143–52. **Schenk, W.** "Tradition und Redaktion in der Epileptiker-Perikope Mk 9,14–29." *ZNW* 63 (1972) 76–94. **Schenke, L.** *Die Wundererzählungen des Markusevangeliums.* SBB 5. Stuttgart: Katholische Bibelwerk, 1974. 314–49. **Schmidt, K. L.** *Rahmen.* 227–29. **Schmithals, W.** "Die Heilung des Epileptischen (Mk 9,14–29): Ein Beitrag zur notwendigen Revision der Formgeschichte." *Theologia Viatorum* 13 (1977) 211–33. **Sellew, P. H.** "Composition of Didactic Scenes in Mark's Gospel." *JBL* 108 (1989) 613–34, esp. 631–32. **Söding, T.** *Glaube bei Markus: Glaube an das Evangelium, Gebetsglaube und Wunderglaube im Kontext der markinischen Basileiatheologie und Christologie.* SBB 12. Stuttgart: Katholisches Bibelwerk, 1985. 456–84. **Sterling, G. E.** "Jesus as Exorcist: An Analysis of Matthew 17:14–20; Mark 9:14–29; Luke 9:37–43a." *CBQ* 55 (1993) 467–93. **Stock, H.** *Studien zur Auslegung der synoptischen Evangelien im Unterricht.* Gütersloh: Bertelsmann, 1959. 97–122. **Torrey, C. C.** *Our Translated Gospels.* London: Hodder and Stoughton; New York: Harper & Brothers, 1936. **Vaganay, L.** *Le problèm synoptique: Une hypothèse de travail.* Bibliothèque de théologie 3.1. Paris; Tournai: Desclée, 1954. 405–25. **Westcott, B. F.,** and **Hort, F. J. A.** *New Testament.* 2:25. **Weymann, V.,** and **Busslinger, H.** "Zum Standhalten befreit: Jesus heilt einen besessenen Knaben (Markus 9,14–29): Eine Dämonenaustreibung." In *Wunder Jesu.* Ed. A. Steiner and V. Weymann. Basel: Reinhardt; Zürich and Köln: Benziger, 1978. 89–112. **Wilkinson, J.** "The Case of the Epileptic Boy." *ExpTim* 79 (1967) 39–42. **Williams, J. F.** *Other Followers of Jesus.* 137–43.

Translation

[14]*And approaching the disciples, they* [a] *saw a great crowd around them, and scribes debating with them.* [15]*And immediately all the crowd, seeing him, were greatly amazed, and running up to him,* [b] *they greeted him.* [16]*And he asked them,* [c] *"What are you debating with them?"* [17]*And one of the crowd answered him, "Teacher, I brought to you my son, who has a mute* [d] *spirit.* [18]*And whenever it seizes him, it knocks him down; and he foams at the mouth and grinds his teeth and becomes rigid. And I asked your disciples to cast it out, but they were not able."* [e] [19]*But answering them, he* [f] *says, "O unbelieving* [g] *generation, how long shall I be with you? How long am I to bear with you? Bring him to me."* [20]*And they brought the boy* [h] *to him. And seeing him, the* [i] *spirit immediately convulsed* [j] *the boy,* [h] *and falling on the ground, he rolled about, foaming at the mouth.* [21]*And Jesus* [k] *inquired of his father, "How long has this been happening to him?" He said, "Since childhood;* [22]*indeed often it even casts him into the fire and into the water, so that it might destroy him. But if you can, help us* [l] *by having pity on us!"* [23]*But Jesus said to him, "'If you can'!* [m] *All things are possible for the one who has faith."* [24]*Immedi-*

ately the father of the boy [n] *cried out* [o] *and said, "I believe; help my unbelief!"* [p] [25]*But Jesus, seeing that a crowd was gathering, rebuked the unclean spirit, saying to it, "Mute and deaf* [q] *spirit, I command you, come out of him and never enter him again!"* [26]*And after crying and convulsing him violently, he came out;* [r] *and the boy was like a corpse, so that many were saying that he had died.* [27]*But Jesus, taking him by the hand, raised him up; and he stood.* [28]*And when he had entered the house, his disciples privately asked him, "Why were we unable to cast it out?"* [29]*And he said to them, "This kind cannot come out by any means except by prayer."* [s]

Notes

[a]A C D 33 and other authorities read εἶδεν, "he saw," with the sg. ptc. ἐλθών, "coming." This variant probably represents an attempt to smooth out a vague and confusing reading, i.e., who are the "they" who saw the crowd? They are not the disciples, nor the crowd, nor the scribes. The subject of the sg. ptc. and finite verb in all probability is Jesus.

[b]The words "to him" are implied by the ptc. προστρέχοντες, "running up to." D reads προσχαίροντες, "being glad." This word occurs nowhere else in the NT (cf. LXX Prov 8:30).

[c]A C N Σ Φ 33 and other authorities read τοὺς γραμματεῖς, "the scribes." This variant may have been caused again by a need to clarify Mark's somewhat ambiguous text. Whom did Jesus question? If his question had been addressed to his disciples, why did someone from the crowd answer? Christian scribes perhaps thought it appropriate for Jesus to interrogate hostile scribes rather than his own disciples. In any case, the context seems to suggest that Jesus questioned the crowd (as implied in v 15) while his disciples and the scribes were busy debating the problem of the demonized lad.

[d]A few MSS add καὶ κωφόν, "and deaf" (cf. v 25).

[e]D W and a few MSS add ἐκβαλεῖν αὐτό, "to cast it out," which completes the thought.

[f]Several later MSS add ὁ Ἰησοῦς, "Jesus."

[g]𝔓[45vid] W and several later MSS add καὶ διεστραμμένη, "and perverse." This addition was probably inspired by Matt 17:17.

[h]Lit. αὐτόν, "him."

[i]Some later MSS add τὸ ἀκάθαρτον, "unclean" (cf. v 25).

[j]Gk. συνεσπάραξεν, lit. "tore to pieces." D reads ἐτάραξεν, "disturbed," or "agitated," which is the more realistic, though less colorful, description.

[k]"Jesus" is not in the text (though several later MSS insert the name in various places).

[l]Some MSS add κύριε, "lord."

[m]A C[3] D 33 and many later MSS add πιστεῦσαι, "believe," which understands Jesus' reply in a very different sense. See *TCGNT* [1], 100.

[n]W reads τὸ πνεῦμα τοῦ παιδαρίου, "the spirit of the boy." Does this mean that the unclean spirit *believes?*

[o]Some MSS add μετὰ δακρύων, "with tears." See *TCGNT* [1], 100.

[p]That is, "help my weak faith!"

[q]Gk. κωφός, either "mute" or "deaf"; often the latter when used with ἄλαλον, "mute."

[r]D and later authorities add ἀπ' αὐτοῦ, "of him," which completes the thought.

[s]𝔓[45vid] א[2] A C D L W 33 and many later authorities add καὶ νηστείᾳ, "and fasting." The addition probably reflects the church's growing interest in fasting; cf. *TCGNT* [1], 101.

Form/Structure/Setting

At first blush the healing of the boy with an unclean spirit seems to fit more naturally in the context of the first half of Mark's Gospel, that is, in the part characterized by miracles (1:20–8:26). The pericope consists of the exorcism/healing, which serves as the occasion for a lesson on faith. Healings or exorcisms that occasion dialogues are found elsewhere in Mark (1:40–45; 2:1–12; 3:1–6; 5:1–14,

21–43; 7:24–30). This case is intriguing because the disciples themselves require instruction, for they had been unable to cast out the unclean spirit.

Why has the Markan evangelist placed this story here? Two details at the beginning of the story draw the pericope to its present location. First, the story presupposes that the disciples had for a time been separated. This was the case because in the transfiguration Jesus was accompanied by only Peter, James, and John. The implication is that the remainder of the disciples were not on the mountain but with a crowd of people, perhaps in a nearby village. Second, the evangelist says that "immediately all the crowd, seeing him, were greatly amazed." What amazed (ἐξεθαμβήθησαν) them? Gundry (487–88) plausibly suggests that Jesus' garments still glistened from the transfiguration experience. He may be correct, for the evangelist gives no indication that Jesus' clothing returned to its pretransfiguration appearance. In the story's present location there is nothing else to account for the crowd's reaction to Jesus' approach. Yet there is another reason, a literary and thematic one, that draws the pericope to its present position. The boy with the unclean spirit, after being terribly convulsed, lay so still, so corpselike, that people thought that he was dead, "but Jesus, taking him by the hand, raised him up; and he stood" (9:27). It is possible that the appearance of death, followed by being raised up, foreshadows the impending death and resurrection of Jesus. After all, Jesus has predicted his death and resurrection in 8:31–33, alluded to it after the transfiguration in 9:9, 12b, and will predict his passion again in the very next pericope (9:30–32). Jesus' plaintive cry, "O unbelieving generation, how long shall I be with you?" hints at the nearness of his passion and the fecklessness of his disciples on the night of his arrest.

Bultmann (*History*, 211–12) thinks our story is a composite, consisting of an account of the failure of the disciples in vv 14–20 and an account of an agitated father in vv 21–27. Evidence for this, Bultmann thinks, is found in the fading of the disciples from the scene, in the twofold description of the boy's malady (in vv 18 and 21–22), and in the twofold appearance of the crowd (in vv 15 and 25). Schmidt (*Rahmen*, 228–29) thinks the awkwardness of vv 14–15 results from a clumsy joining of materials. It is more probable, however, that the story was originally one, which the Markan evangelist has introduced and in places has edited. Mark's redundancies result largely from the addition of vv 14–15, which introduce the story, and most of the latter part of v 20, which graphically illustrates and anticipates the father's subsequent description of his son's serious condition (vv 21–22).

The Matthean and Lukan evangelists abbreviate the story (Matt 17:14–20; Luke 9:37–43a). Most of the confusing and redundant details found in Mark 9:14–15 have been omitted. Matthew enhances the theme of faith (in 17:20, by placing here material taken from Mark 11:22–23). He also increases the respect shown for Jesus, for the man kneels before Jesus and addresses him as "lord" (17:15) in place of Mark's "teacher." Luke enhances the pathos of the scene, for the child is described as the man's "only child" (9:38), who is convulsed and shattered by the spirit, which "will hardly leave him" (9:39). Moreover, the man has not merely "asked" the disciples to heal his son but has "begged" them (9:40). The Lukan version ends on a doxological note (9:43).

Comment

Jesus' healing of the boy with the unclean spirit once again offers dramatic evidence of Jesus' awesome power. What his several disciples could not achieve, Jesus could easily do. The episode also gives Jesus the opportunity to speak on the theme of faith: in the first instance, the lack of faith of his own disciples, and in the second, the lack of faith in Jesus' ability on the part of the child's father.

14 ἐλθόντες πρὸς τοὺς μαθητὰς εἶδον ὄχλον πολὺν περὶ αὐτοὺς καὶ γραμματεῖς συζητοῦντας πρὸς αὐτούς, "approaching the disciples, they saw a great crowd around them, and scribes debating with them." While Jesus had been up on the mountain in 9:2–13, a crowd had gathered around several of his disciples. An argument had erupted between them and some scribes. The argument may very well have had to do with what means were necessary to effect a successful exorcism (and apparently not with whether Jesus employed the aid of Satan, as in Mark 3:23–30). The subject is treated in a variety of sources. One immediately thinks of the man named Eleazar who followed the incantations attributed to Solomon and who could draw out demons through a person's nostrils by use of the Baaras root (see Josephus, *J.W.* 7.6.3 §§180–85; *Ant.* 8.2.5 §§46–49). Josephus explains that God gave Solomon "knowledge of the art used against demons for the benefit and healing of humans. He also composed incantations by which illnesses are relieved, and left behind forms of exorcisms with which those possessed by demons drive them out, never to return" (*Ant.* 8.2.5 §45; for an example of the rigmarole exorcists of antiquity went through, see the excerpt of the Greek Magical Papyrus discussed by A. Deissmann, *Light from the Ancient East* [New York: Harper & Row, 1927] 259–63; the opening lines of one text read: "For those possessed by daemons, an approved charm by Pibechis. Take oil made from unripe olives . . . and boil it with marjoram, saying: 'Joel, Ossarthiomi . . . come out [ἔξελθε] of such an one . . .'"). The tradition of Solomon as exorcist par excellence was widespread in late antiquity. The tradition began in 1 Kgs 4:29–34 and was enhanced in later traditions such as Wis 7:17–21 and the *Testament of Solomon*. As "son of David" (Mark 10:47, 48), Jesus would have been expected in some circles to effect cures paralleling those effected by David's famous son Solomon (see *Comment* on 10:46–52). In Mark's Gospel itself an anonymous exorcist is noted (9:38–41).

The γραμματεῖς, "scribes," have appeared before in the Markan narrative. Jesus' teaching is said to be authoritative, unlike that of the scribes (1:22). On the occasion that Jesus heals the paralyzed man, "some of the scribes were sitting there, questioning in their hearts" the legitimacy of Jesus' pronouncement of forgiveness of sins (2:6). Scribes are critical of Jesus' table fellowship with "sinners and tax collectors" (2:16). Scribes suggest that Jesus is in league with Satan (3:22). Scribes, who have come from Jerusalem, take part in the complaint that Jesus' disciples eat with unwashed hands in disregard of the tradition of the elders (7:1, 5). Only a few pericopes earlier, the scribes are named in the company of "elders and ruling priests" who will kill Jesus (8:31). In the immediately preceding pericope it is the scribes who teach that "Elijah must come first" (9:11). The scribes appear again in the third passion prediction (10:33). After the temple incident, the scribes join the ruling priests in their desire to kill Jesus (11:18). The scribes are again in the company of the ruling priests when they approach Jesus and demand by what authority he does what he does (11:27). In the temple precincts a scribe asks Jesus which commandment is the greatest (12:28). This same scribe admits that Jesus' answer is correct (12:32). Jesus openly challenges the scribes' habit of referring to the Messiah under the rubric of "son of David" (12:35). Jesus warns of avaricious scribes who prey on the poor and defenseless (12:38). The scribes take part in the plot to arrest Jesus (14:1). The thugs who arrest Jesus are said to be "from the chief priests and the scribes and the elders" (14:43). The scribes assemble with Jesus' accusers (14:53; 15:1). And finally, the scribes join in with the ruling priests in mocking Jesus on the cross (15:31; for more on the scribes, see *Comment* on 11:18).

Up to this point in the Markan narrative, the scribes are critical but not dangerous. As the review of the material just undertaken shows, the scribes become increasingly threatening as Jesus enters Judea and especially Jerusalem.

15 καὶ εὐθὺς πᾶς ὁ ὄχλος ἰδόντες αὐτὸν ἐξεθαμβήθησαν καὶ προστρέχοντες ἠσπάζοντο αὐτόν, "And immediately all the crowd, seeing him, were greatly amazed, and running up to him, they greeted him." Apparently the crowd is "greatly amazed" (according to Torrey [*Our Translated Gospels*, 11–31] the underlying Aramaic תְּוַהּוּ *tĕwahû* should have been rendered "they were *much excited*") when they see Jesus because his garments still shine. This is possible, but the Greek of Mark's text still makes perfectly good sense as it stands, especially if the amazement of the crowd is occasioned by the lingering effects of Jesus' transfiguration. Recognizing him, the crowd runs up to him and greets him. The impression one gains from this scene is that Jesus' fame and power are such that he immediately attracts crowds of people, many of them hoping for healing and blessing.

16 τί συζητεῖτε πρὸς αὐτούς; "What are you debating with them?" It is not clear to whom Jesus addressed his question. One would think that Jesus would have asked his disciples what they were discussing with the scribes. As explained in the textual note above, some MSS have Jesus direct his question to the scribes. But this seems unlikely. Why would Jesus ask a question challenging the scribes concerning what they have been discussing with his own disciples? It is more probable that Jesus is speaking to his disciples, even if someone in the crowd shouts out an answer.

17 καὶ ἀπεκρίθη αὐτῷ εἷς ἐκ τοῦ ὄχλου, διδάσκαλε, ἤνεγκα τὸν υἱόν μου πρὸς σέ, ἔχοντα πνεῦμα ἄλαλον, "And one of the crowd answered him, 'Teacher, I brought to you my son, who has a mute spirit.'" The εἷς ἐκ τοῦ ὄχλου, "one of the crowd," who answers Jesus is none other than the father of the boy who is afflicted with the unclean spirit. His anxiety overrides the details of the debate that occupy the attention of the scribes and Jesus' disciples. The father cares for none of the finer points of theology; he desperately seeks help for his son.

διδάσκαλε, "Teacher," is the dynamic equivalent of רַבִּי *rabbî*, "Rabbi" (see John 1:38). S. Cohen has collected some fifty-seven inscriptions in which *Rabbi* occurs, either in Greek or in Hebrew/Aramaic ("Epigraphical Rabbis," *JQR* 72 [1981/82] 1–17). Of these, fifty are from Palestine. He and P. W. van der Horst (*Ancient Jewish Epitaphs: An Introductory Survey of a Millennium of Jewish Funerary Epigraphy [300 B.C.E.–700 C.E.]* [Kampen: Kok Pharos, 1991] 97–98, 133–34) have concluded that the title rarely refers to an ordained person but usually refers to prominent citizens. This informal usage is consistent with what we observe with respect to Jesus. (Jesus had been called Rabbi by Peter in the earlier transfiguration episode.)

The father says ἤνεγκα τὸν υἱόν μου πρὸς σέ, "I brought to you my son." But he did not bring him directly to Jesus; rather he brought the child to the disciples who had not accompanied Jesus to the mountain. Nonetheless, Jesus will assume a measure of responsibility in the sense that if someone has reached out to his disciples, it is as though they have reached out to him (see 6:7–13, where the disciples are commissioned and granted authority over unclean spirits). This may in part explain Jesus' personal annoyance with his disciples. The father further says that his son "has a mute spirit." By this he means that the spirit impairs his son's speech.

18 ὅπου ἐὰν αὐτὸν καταλάβῃ ῥήσσει αὐτόν, καὶ ἀφρίζει καὶ τρίζει τοὺς ὀδόντας καὶ ξηραίνεται· καὶ εἶπα τοῖς μαθηταῖς σου ἵνα αὐτὸ ἐκβάλωσιν, καὶ οὐκ ἴσχυσαν, "whenever it seizes him, it knocks him down; and he foams at the mouth and grinds his teeth and becomes rigid. And I asked your disciples to cast it out, but they were not able." The effects, or symptoms, of the mute spirit resemble epilepsy (and the malady is explicitly referred to as such in Matt 17:15). Falling to the ground, foaming at the mouth, and grinding teeth are all symptomatic of the "falling down" syndrome, as people in late antiquity thought of it. One of the more famous persons with this affliction was Julius Caesar. The condition was sometimes thought to be the result of contact with spirits or deities. The case of the stricken boy falls loosely in this category, though Jesus' contemporaries regard it as demonic possession.

The father of the boy had asked Jesus' disciples to cast out the spirit, "but they were not able," or more literally, "they lacked the strength" (οὐκ ἴσχυσαν). The disciples' inability sets the stage for Jesus' superior display of strength as the "stronger one" (3:27) whom John had predicted (1:7; rightly Gundry, 488–89).

19 Jesus' outburst, ὦ γενεὰ ἄπιστος, "O unbelieving generation," underscores the need for faith, a theme touched upon elsewhere in Mark (cf. 2:5; 4:40; 5:34, 36; 10:52; 11:22–23). Perhaps more importantly, Jesus' description of his generation as "unbelieving" is meant to remind readers of the original summons to repent and "believe" in the gospel (Mark 1:15). The implication is that this generation is not simply a generation of skeptics but a generation that has failed to respond to the good news of the presence of the kingdom, a presence attested by Jesus' power over Satan and his unholy allies. Because of a lack of faith in Jesus' proclamation, gaining freedom from Satan's oppression is hindered.

Jesus' questions, ἕως πότε πρὸς ὑμᾶς ἔσομαι; ἕως πότε ἀνέξομαι ὑμῶν; "How long shall I be with you? How long am I to bear with you?" underscore how antithetical unbelief is to Jesus' message and his own faith in God. Indeed, it shows how Jesus has adopted God's viewpoint (Martin, *Mark: Evangelist and Theologian*, 118). Unbelief causes him distress and even hinders his ministry (cf. 6:5). Jesus wonders how long he must put up with this unbelief, a query that may hint at his expectation of death. However, it is also possible that Jesus anticipated a general awakening of faith in Israel and with it the appearance of the kingdom of God in its fullness.

φέρετε αὐτὸν πρός με, "bring him to me," portrays Jesus' superior power. His disciples lacked the strength, but Jesus does not. If the father will bring his afflicted son to Jesus, he will be healed.

20 ἤνεγκαν αὐτὸν πρὸς αὐτόν. καὶ ἰδὼν αὐτὸν τὸ πνεῦμα εὐθὺς συνεσπάραξεν αὐτόν, καὶ πεσὼν ἐπὶ τῆς γῆς ἐκυλίετο ἀφρίζων, "they brought the boy to him.

And seeing him, the spirit immediately convulsed the boy, and falling on the ground, he rolled about, foaming at the mouth." The reaction of the spirit to the presence of Jesus is reminiscent of the violent reactions, usually verbal, that other unclean spirits have had when they encountered him (cf. 1:23–26, 34; 3:11–12; 5:6–13). The spirit is said to have seen Jesus, and it is the spirit that is said to have convulsed the boy. The symptoms may have been those usually associated with epilepsy, but the Markan evangelist makes it clear that it was an evil spirit, something distinct from the boy himself, that caused his illness.

21   πόσος χρόνος ἐστὶν ὡς τοῦτο γέγονεν αὐτῷ; "How long has this been happening to him?" The question about how long the boy had suffered from his condition underscores the seriousness of it. ἐκ παιδιόθεν, "since childhood," Jesus is told. That is, this is no passing condition but one that has plagued the man's son from early childhood. The implication is not only that this condition is "harder to break" (Gundry, 490) but that in all probability other exorcists besides Jesus' disciples had failed in attempts to rid the boy of the spirit. Jesus' ability to cast it out is therefore all the more impressive.

22   πολλάκις καὶ εἰς πῦρ αὐτὸν ἔβαλεν καὶ εἰς ὕδατα ἵνα ἀπολέσῃ αὐτόν· ἀλλ᾿ εἴ τι δύνῃ, βοήθησον ἡμῖν σπλαγχνισθεὶς ἐφ᾿ ἡμᾶς, "indeed often it even casts him into the fire and into the water, so that it might destroy him. But if you can, help us by having pity on us!" The grim summary of what this evil spirit has done to the boy clarifies the desperation felt by the father. The demonic possession is not only disruptive and oppressive but dangerous and potentially fatal. The boy is thrown sometimes into the fire and sometimes into water, ἵνα ἀπολέσῃ αὐτόν, "so that it might destroy him." The problem is so severe that the father is not at all confident that Jesus, despite his remarkable reputation, can do anything to help. Again, this implies that others have tried and have failed. However, the boy has never been attended by Jesus.

23   ὁ δὲ Ἰησοῦς εἶπεν αὐτῷ, τὸ εἰ δύνῃ, "Jesus said to him, 'If you can'!" Jesus' exasperated response, εἰ δύνῃ, "If you can!" repeats the father's words and stems from his frustration with his generation's lack of faith. πάντα δυνατὰ τῷ πιστεύοντι, "all things are possible for the one who has faith," the converse of this statement, is also true: little is possible for him who has no faith. A further lesson on the possibility of faith will be given in 11:22–24.

24   The father responds to Jesus' teaching: πιστεύω· βοήθει μου τῇ ἀπιστίᾳ, "I believe; help my unbelief!" In a certain sense, then, Jesus provides enablement for both the father and his son: for the father, the needed faith, for the son, the needed deliverance from an evil spirit. The plea for faith, even if admittedly weak (lit. "faithlessness"), was all that was necessary. The waning faith of the father is easily explained as the result of the disciples' failure to exorcise the demon in the first place. The father may have reasoned that if Jesus' disciples could not overpower the spirit, then perhaps Jesus himself would not be able to either.

25   ἰδὼν δὲ ὁ Ἰησοῦς ὅτι ἐπισυντρέχει ὄχλος, ἐπετίμησεν τῷ πνεύματι τῷ ἀκαθάρτῳ λέγων αὐτῷ, τὸ ἄλαλον καὶ κωφὸν πνεῦμα, ἐγὼ ἐπιτάσσω σοι, ἔξελθε ἐξ αὐτοῦ καὶ μηκέτι εἰσέλθῃς εἰς αὐτόν, "But Jesus, seeing that a crowd was gathering, rebuked the unclean spirit, saying to it, 'Mute and deaf spirit, I command you, come out of him and never enter him again!'" When Jesus sees the crowd gathering (ἐπισυντρέχει, "is running together," or "is converging"), he brings the exorcism to a speedy conclusion. The press of the crowd may have interfered with what was clearly a difficult

exorcism. It is not likely that the crowd was converging upon the boy himself, perhaps to attack him, as has been suggested. Nor is it likely that secrecy plays a role, as it does elsewhere (cf. 1:25, 34, 44; 3:11–12; 5:43), for no command to secrecy is given in the present pericope; the explanation to the disciples is given "privately" (v 28), and that has nothing to do with secrecy.

Jesus commands the demon in the first person: ἐγὼ ἐπιτάσσω σοι, "I command you." In the narrative the contrast with the disciples' earlier unsuccessful attempt is thus underscored: they had given commands, which the demon had ignored; this time it is Jesus himself who is giving the commands, which the demon cannot ignore. The charge that the unclean spirit μηκέτι εἰσέλθῃς εἰς αὐτόν, "never enter him again!" parallels Josephus's claims about the success of certain exorcists of his day (see *Comment* on v 14 above). Comparison with the exorcistic lore in the *Testament of Solomon* is instructive. There, King Solomon disputes with various demons, sometimes (as in 13:1–3) complying with their requests in order to obtain the desired information. In Jesus' exorcisms demons are silenced and cast out.

26–27 κράξας καὶ πολλὰ σπαράξας ἐξῆλθεν, "After crying and convulsing him violently, he came out." The violence (as implied by πολλά, lit. "many times") serves as tangible evidence of the success of the exorcism. Jesus' command did not go unheeded but caused an upheaval. According to Josephus, the Jewish exorcist Eleazar commanded an exorcised demon to tip over a wash basin as evidence of his actual eviction (*Ant.* 8.2.5 §48). In his imaginative and apologetic biography of Apollonius of Tyana, Philostratus of Athens relates similar details (*Vit. Apoll.* 4.20, where a demon knocks over a statue as it exits a young man).

In sharp contrast to the great violence, the boy now suddenly stops moving and lies so still that τοὺς πολλοὺς λέγειν ὅτι ἀπέθανεν, "many were saying that he had died." The unusual stillness of the boy offered additional proof of the eviction of the demon, which had consistently manifested itself by throwing the boy in water and fire and, when confronted by Jesus, by violent convulsions. The evangelist does not in fact contradict the opinion of those who thought that the boy had died; perhaps he had. If so, Jesus' raising him up (κρατήσας τῆς χειρὸς αὐτοῦ ἤγειρεν αὐτόν, καὶ ἀνέστη, "taking him by the hand, raised him up; and he stood") only compounds the already astounding deed. The boy is able to stand on his own, thus demonstrating his restoration to health.

28 καὶ εἰσελθόντος αὐτοῦ εἰς οἶκον οἱ μαθηταὶ αὐτοῦ κατ᾽ ἰδίαν ἐπηρώτων αὐτόν, "And when he had entered the house, his disciples privately asked him." Elsewhere in Mark the disciples receive private instruction (cf. 4:34; 7:17–23; 13:3), and in other cases Jesus heals people in private (5:37–42; 7:33). The disciples want to know why they were unable to cast out the demon. Their question is understandable, given the fact that Jesus had earlier given them "authority over unclean spirits" (6:7).

ὅτι ἡμεῖς οὐκ ἠδυνήθημεν ἐκβαλεῖν αὐτό, "Why were we unable to cast it out?" The disciples' question implies that normally they were able to cast out demons, having been authorized earlier by Jesus to do so (6:7). On the interrogative ὅτι (usually "that," but here "why"), see Field, *Notes*, 33 (and *Comment* on 9:11).

29 Jesus explains to his disciples that τοῦτο τὸ γένος ἐν οὐδενὶ δύναται ἐξελθεῖν εἰ μὴ ἐν προσευχῇ, "this kind [of evil spirit] cannot come out by any means except by prayer." Torrey (*Our Translated Gospels*, 129–31) thinks that the phrase εἰ μὴ ἐν προσευχῇ, "except by prayer," had understood the Aramaic as אן לא *'in lā'*, "if not," when in all probability it originally read אַף לֹא, *'ap lā'*, "not even," by prayer. But this proposal does not make good sense in the present context. Is Jesus really telling his disciples that this kind of demon cannot be cast out "by any means . . . not even by prayer"? Jesus himself was able to cast it out. Or has he told his disciples that only he can cast out the difficult demons and his disciples cannot. If the latter is true, then the earlier assertion that Jesus gave his disciples "authority over the unclean spirits" (6:7) is called into question and creates an unlikely tension within the Markan narrative. On the historical level also it is not likely that Jesus, who could "cast out demons by the finger of God" (Luke 11:20), believed that there was a class of demons that his disciples could not cast out by any means, not even by prayer.

Explanation

In the healing of the boy with the unclean spirit we again witness the unmatched power of Jesus. Still exuding the radiance of his transfiguration, Jesus enters a scene of controversy and chaos, and quickly takes charge of the situation. Reauthorized by the divine voice that had commanded his disciples to "listen to him!" (9:7), Jesus commands, perhaps ironically, a deaf-mute spirit, and the spirit obeys. Jesus' power and authority are undiminished, even after the announcement of his passion in 8:31 and 9:9. The distance between Jesus and his disciples continues to widen (cf. 6:51; 8:14–21).

The story also underscores the importance of faith, for along with repentance it is the prerequisite for unleashing the power of the kingdom of God. When faith is present, God works.

F. Jesus Again Foretells His Passion   (9:30–32)

Bibliography

Achtemeier, P. J. "An Exposition of Mark 9:30–37." *Int* 30 (1976) 178–83. **Baarlink, H.** *Anfängliches Evangelium: Ein Beitrag zur näheren Bestimmung der theologischen Motive im Markusevangelium.* Kampen: Kok, 1977. 227–35. **Bastin, M.** "L'annonce de la Passion et les critères de l'historicité." *RevScRel* 50 (1976) 289–329. ———. *Jésus devant sa passion.* LD 92. Paris: Cerf, 1976. 124–38. **Bayer, H. F.** *Jesus' Predictions of Vindication and Resurrection: The Provenance, Meaning and Correlation of the Synoptic Predictions.* WUNT 2.20. Tübingen: Mohr-Siebeck, 1986. 169–71, 177–81, 188–90. **Beasley-Murray, G. R.** *Jesus and the Kingdom of God.* 237–47. **Best, E.** *Following Jesus.* 73–74. **Black, M.** "The 'Son of Man' Passion Sayings in the Gospel Tradition." *ZNW* 60 (1969) 1–8. **Briére, J.** "Le Fils de l'homme livré aux hommes: Mc 9,30–37." *AsSeign* 2.35 (1974) 42–52. **Colpe, C.** "Traditionsüberschreitende Argumentationen zu Aussagen Jesu über sich selbst." In *Tradition und Glaube: Das frühe Christentum in seiner Umwelt.* FS K. G. Kuhn, ed. G. Jeremias et al. Göttingen: Vandenhoeck & Ruprecht, 1971. 239–43. **Dupont, J.** "Ressuscité 'le troisième jour.'" *Bib* 40 (1959) 742–61. **Farmer, W. R.** "The Passion Prediction Passages and the Synoptic Problem: A Test

Case." *NTS* 36 (1990) 558–70. **Feuillet, A.** "Les trois grandes prophéties de la passion et de la résurrection des évangiles synoptiques." *RThom* 67 (1967) 533–60; 68 (1968) 41–74. **France, R. T.** *Jesus and the Old Testament.* 125–30. ———. "The Servant of the Lord in the Teaching of Jesus." *TynBul* 19 (1968) 26–52. **Grimm, W.** *Weil Ich dich liebe: Die Verkündigung Jesu und Deuterojesaja.* ANTJ 1. Bern; Frankfurt am Main: Lang, 1976. 209–22. **Gubler, M.- L.** *Die frühesten Deutungen des Todes Jesu: Eine motivgeschichtliche Darstellung aufgrund der neueren exegetischen Forschung.* OBO 15. Göttingen: Vandenhoeck & Ruprecht, 1977. 107–17. **Güttgemanns, E.** *Offene Fragen zur Formgeschichte des Evangeliums: Eine methodologische Skizze der Grundlagenproblematik der Form- und Redaktionsgeschichte.* BEvT 54. Munich: Kaiser, 1970. 211–23. **Hampel, V.** *Menschensohn und historischer Jesus: Ein Rätselwort als Schlüssel zum messianischen Selbstverständnis Jesu.* Neukirchen-Vluyn: Neukirchener Verlag, 1990. 288–300. **Hasenfratz, H.-P.** *Die Rede von der Auferstehung Jesu Christi: Ein methodologischer Versuch.* FTL 10. Bonn: Linguistica Biblica, 1975. 108–14. **Hermant, D.** "La deuxième annonce de la Passion (Histoire du texte)." *Bulletin de liaison sur l'origine des Synoptiques* 1 (1989) 14–18. **Hoehner, H. W.** *Herod Antipas.* SNTSMS 17. Cambridge: Cambridge UP, 1972. 317–30. **Hooker, M. D.** *The Son of Man in Mark.* 134–36. **Howard, V. P.** "Did Jesus Speak about His Own Death?" *CBQ* 39 (1977) 515–27. **Lindars, B.** *Jesus Son of Man: A Fresh Examination of the Son of Man Sayings in the Gospels in the Light of Recent Research.* London: S. P. C. K.; Grand Rapids, MI: Eerdmans, 1983. 60–84. **Minette de Tillesse, G.** *Le secret messianique.* 368–73. **Moo, D. J.** *The Old Testament in the Gospel Passion Narratives.* Sheffield: Almond, 1983. 92–97. **Oberlinner, L.** *Todeserwartung und Todesgewissheit Jesu: Zum Problem einer historischen Begründung.* SBB 10. Stuttgart: Katholisches Bibelwerk, 1980. 140–46. **Patsch, H.** *Abendmahl und historischer Jesus.* Calwer theologische Monographien. Stuttgart: Calwer, 1972. 185–97. **Perrin, N.** "The Use of (παρα)διδόναι in Connection with the Passion of Jesus in the New Testament." In *Der Ruf Jesu und die Antwort der Gemeinde.* FS J. Jeremias, ed. E. Lohse et al. Göttingen: Vandenhoeck & Ruprecht, 1970. 204–12 (repr. in N. Perrin. *A Modern Pilgrimage in New Testament Christology.* Philadelphia: Fortress, 1974. 94–103). **Perry, J. M.** "The Three Days in the Synoptic Passion Predictions." *CBQ* 48 (1986) 637–54. **Pesch, R.** *Evangelium der Urgemeinde.* 118–19. **Popkes, W.** *Christus traditus: Eine Untersuchung zum Begriff der Dahingabe im Neuen Testament.* ATANT 49. Zurich: Zwingli, 1967. 258–66. **Reploh, K. G.** *Markus—Lehrer der Gemeinde.* 104–7. **Schaberg, J.** "Daniel 7.12 and the New Testament Passion-Resurrection Predictions." *NTS* 31 (1985) 208–22. **Schürmann, H.** "Wie hat Jesus seinen Tod bestanden und verstanden? Eine methodenkritische Besinnung." In *Orientierung an Jesus.* FS J. Schmid, ed. P. Hoffmann et al. Freiburg: Herder, 1973. 325–63. **Strecker, G.** "Die Leidens- und Auferstehungsvoraussagen im Markusevangelium (Mk 8,31; 9,31; 10,32–34)." *ZTK* 64 (1967) 16–39 (ET: "The Passion- and Resurrection Predictions in Mark's Gospel." *Int* 22 [1968] 421–42). **Taylor, V.** *Jesus and His Sacrifice.* 85–91. ———. "The Origin of the Markan Passion-Sayings." *NTS* 1 (1954–55) 159–67 (repr. in V. Taylor. *New Testament Essays.* London: Epworth, 1970. 60–71). **Thompson, W. G.** *Matthew's Advice to a Divided Community: Mt 17,22–18,35.* AnBib 44. Rome: Biblical Institute, 1970. 40–49. **Vögtle, A.** "Todesankündigung und Todesverständnis Jesu." In *Der Tod Jesu: Deutungen im Neuen Testament.* Ed. K. Kertelge. QD 74. Freiburg: Herder, 1976. 51–113, esp. 62–64.

Translation

[30]*And leaving there, they went through Galilee. And he* [a] *was not wishing that anyone might know it;* [31]*for he was teaching his disciples and saying to them, "The 'son of man' is delivered* [b] *into human hands,* [c] *and they will kill him; and having been killed, after three days* [d] *he will rise."* [e] [32]*But they did not understand the saying, and they were afraid to ask him.*

Notes

[a]A few MSS read οὐκ ἤθελον, "they were not wishing."

[b]Gk. παραδίδοται. Some MSS put the verb in the future tense (παραδοθήσεται, "will be delivered") in agreement with the next verb (ἀποκτενοῦσιν, "will kill"), possibly under the influence of LXX Dan 7:25 (see *Comment* below).

[c]Gk. εἰς χεῖρας ἀνθρώπων, lit. "into the hands of humans." 𝔓[45vid] appears to read ἀνθρώποις, "to humans." D reads sg.: εἰς χεῖρας ἀνθρώπου, "into the hands of a human." This could be a reference either to Judas the betrayer or to Caiaphas the high priest who will order Jesus' arrest.

[d]Nestle-Aland[27] and UBSGNT[3c] follow ℵ B C* D and other authorities that read μετὰ τρεῖς ἡμέρας, "after three days." A C[3] N W and many later MSS read τῇ τρίτῃ ἡμέρᾳ, "on the third day." This variant is due to the influence of Matthew (cf. 16:21; 17:23; 20:19; cf. 27:64) and perhaps also to early Christian preaching, as seen in Paul (cf. 1 Cor 15:4). See *Note* i on Mark 8:31 above.

[e]Gk. ἀναστήσεται, "will rise," or "will arise." Some MSS read either ἐγείρεται, "is raised," or ἐγερθήσεται, "will be raised."

Form/Structure/Setting

Jesus again predicts his passion (on the first prediction, see 8:31–33). He will predict it a third time in 10:32–34. There is no objection raised this time as had been made by Peter on the first occasion (in 8:33). This time the disciples fail to understand the saying and "were afraid to ask" Jesus about its meaning. This brief passage represents another step in Jesus' instruction regarding his death. Thus far, anything having to do with his death has met with opposition or misunderstanding. This trend will continue to the very end of the Markan narrative.

The passion prediction here is probably the oldest version of an original single tradition (Lindars, *Jesus Son of Man,* 63). Traces of Aramaism and Semitism are in evidence (Bayer, *Jesus' Predictions,* 169–70). In this version we may hear echoes of Isa 53 and Dan 7 (see *Comment* on v 31), echoes that may actually derive from Jesus (also see *Comment* on 10:45). As with the first prediction, the second prediction accentuates Jesus' foreknowledge and resolve. He knows what lies ahead, he is not afraid (in sharp contrast to his disciples), and he will carry out his mission. (On the authenticity of the predictions, see *Comment* on 8:31 above.)

Comment

30 κἀκεῖθεν ἐξελθόντες παρεπορεύοντο διὰ τῆς Γαλιλαίας, "And leaving there, they went through Galilee." Jesus and his disciples are described as ἐξελθόντες, "leaving," the house in which he had privately discussed the difficult exorcism in the previous pericope (vv 14–29). The Galilean itinerary continues (until 10:1, that is, when finally Jesus turns south toward Judea). Jesus οὐκ ἤθελεν ἵνα τις γνοῖ, "was not wishing that anyone might know it," which means that for a time he and his disciples traveled "incognito" (Gundry, 502). The reason for this wish for privacy is explained in v 31.

31 ἐδίδασκεν γὰρ τοὺς μαθητὰς αὐτοῦ καὶ ἔλεγεν αὐτοῖς ὅτι ὁ υἱὸς τοῦ ἀνθρώπου παραδίδοται εἰς χεῖρας ἀνθρώπων, καὶ ἀποκτενοῦσιν αὐτόν, καὶ ἀποκτανθεὶς μετὰ τρεῖς ἡμέρας ἀναστήσεται, "for he was teaching his disciples and saying to them, 'The "son of man" is delivered into human hands, and they will kill him; and when he is killed, after three days he will rise.'" Here we have the reason for the need for secrecy; Jesus is discussing with his disciples his expectations of arrest, death, and resurrection. Such ideas flew in the face of popular messianic and eschatological hopes. Should such teaching spread among Jesus' wider following, the movement would collapse and Jesus would be challenged (much as Peter earlier had questioned Jesus' first prediction of suffering). Because of the importance of this matter, Jesus understandably discusses it with his closest followers.

The Markan evangelist says that Jesus ἐδίδασκεν, "was teaching," his disciples. This implies more than a mere announcement or prediction. It may have entailed appeals to Scripture. To what Scripture? Isa 53 has been suggested, especially as we find it in the Greek Bible. LXX Isa 53:6 reads κύριος παρέδωκεν αὐτὸν ταῖς ἁμαρτίαις ἡμῶν, "the Lord has handed him over for our sins," which does not equal the MT's "the LORD has laid on him the iniquity of us all." LXX Isa 53:12 reads παρεδόθη εἰς θάνατον ἡ ψυχὴ αὐτοῦ καὶ ἐν τοῖς ἀνόμοις ἐλογίσθη . . . καὶ διὰ τὰς ἁμαρτίας αὐτῶν παρεδόθη, "his soul was handed over to death and among the lawless he was reckoned . . . and on account of their sins he was handed over," which again does not equal the MT's "he poured out his soul to death, and was numbered with the transgressors . . . and made intercession for the transgressors." It is possible then that some early tradents heard echoes of Isa 53 in the Greek, but Dan 7 is the more probable source. In the Aramaic (i.e., the MT) Dan 7:25 reads וְיִתְיַהֲבוּן בִּידֵהּ *wĕyityahăbûn bîdēh,* "and they shall be given into his hand," while in the LXX the parallel portion reads καὶ παραδοθήσεται πάντα εἰς τὰς χεῖρας αὐτοῦ, "all shall be given into his hands." The passive (παραδίδοται εἰς τὰς χεῖρας, "is delivered into the hands") may be an instance of the "divine passive" (Bayer, *Jesus' Predictions,* 169–70, citing Jeremias), which coheres with the language and sense of Dan 7:25. The Danielic context is especially suitable, for it describes the struggle between the saints and the evil kingdom. The saints, who include the "one like a son of man" (of Dan 7:13–14), will be delivered into the hands of this evil kingdom, but only "for a time, two times, and half a time" (Dan 7:25). It is in the light of this scriptural scenario that we should understand Jesus' use of the epithet "son of man." Jesus is the human being (which is what the idiom means) to whom God has given kingdom and authority and who with the saints will contend against the kingdom of evil. Evil will prevail for a brief season, but the kingdom of God will suddenly and surely overcome it.

Consistent with this scenario is Jesus' confident prediction of being raised up μετὰ τρεῖς ἡμέρας, "after three days." Although the Scripture that underlies this confident expectation is Hos 6:2 (see *Comment* on 8:31 above), the concept of suffering, even death, and then speedy vindication is entirely consistent with what is depicted in Dan 7. The anticipation is also consistent with the proclamation of the kingdom of God, which ἤγγικεν, "is at hand" (1:15). The kingdom has broken into the human sphere and is beginning to assert itself. Evidence of its presence is the retreat of Satan and his unholy minions. However, before Satan's kingdom finally collapses, a great struggle must take place, and in this struggle there will be casualties. Among these casualties will be the "son of man" himself. But his death marks the end of Satan's kingdom, for the "son of man" will be raised up "after three days."

32 οἱ δὲ ἠγνόουν τὸ ῥῆμα, καὶ ἐφοβοῦντο αὐτὸν ἐπερωτῆσαι, "But they did not understand the saying, and they were afraid to ask him." The disciples' fear is understandable, for the death of their master may eventuate, even require, the death of the disciples. Jesus himself had made this clear enough in 8:34–37. But perhaps their greatest fear concerns the impending fate of their beloved Rabbi. Surely, they believe, he cannot be destined to die. Their reluctance ἐπερωτῆσαι, "to ask," Jesus for further clarification no doubt results from their fear that Jesus will underscore yet again the certainty of his death.

Explanation

The reader now knows that in the narrative the turn toward the passion is unavoidable. Moreover, the passion theme is seen to play an important part in Jesus' understanding of his own person and his ministry. Far from being taken by surprise after being rebuffed in Jerusalem, Jesus knows from as far away as northern Galilee what lies ahead. His destination is the holy city; his destiny is the cross. Jesus accepts his fate and his mission and teaches his disciples accordingly. Although the disciples are slow to understand and accept such grim teaching, the teaching is nevertheless necessary if they are to possess the requisite background upon which the Easter discovery is to be founded.

G. Who Is the Greatest?   (9:33–37)

Bibliography

Achtemeier, P. J. "An Exposition of Mark 9:30–37." *Int* 30 (1976) 178–83. **Best, E.** *Following Jesus.* 75–98. **Bishop, E. F. F.** "Jesus and Capernaum." *CBQ* 15 (1953) 427–37. **Black, M.** *Aramaic Approach.* 218–23. ———. "The Marcan Parable of the Child in the Midst." *ExpTim* 59 (1947–48) 14–16. **Briére, J.** "Le Fils de l'homme livré aux hommes: Mc 9,30–37." *AsSeign* 2.35 (1974) 42–52. **Catchpole, D. R.** "The Poor on Earth and the Son of Man in Heaven: A Re-Appraisal of Matthew xxv. 31–46." *BJRL* 61 (1979) 355–97. **Crossan, J. D.** *In Fragments.* 104–18, 160–63, 285–89. **Descamps, A.** "Du discours de Marc., ix, 33–50 aux paroles de Jésus." In *La formation des évangiles.* Ed. J. Cambier et al. RechBib 2. Bruges: Desclée de Brouwer, 1957. 152–77. **Di Marco, A.-S.** "Mc. 9,33–37: Analisi formale." *Orpheus* 5 (1984) 403–21. **Dodd, C. H.** "Some Johannine 'Herrenworte' with Parallels in the Synoptic Gospels." *NTS* 2 (1955–56) 75–86, esp. 81–85. **Fleddermann, H.** "The Discipleship Discourse (Mark 9:33–50)." *CBQ* 43 (1981) 57–75. ———. *Mark and Q.* 153–57. **Glasson, T. F.,** and **Benger, E. L.** "The Markan Parable of the Child in the Midst." *ExpTim* 59 (1947–48) 166–67. **Helmbold, H.** *Vorsynoptische Evangelien.* Stuttgart: Klotz, 1953. 42–49. **Hermant, D.** "La première scène d'enfants (Mt 18,1–5; Mc 9,33–37; Lc 9,46–48)." *Bulletin de liaison sur l'origine des Synoptiques* 3 (1990) 7–11. **Hoehner, H. W.** *Herod Antipas.* SNTSMS 17. Cambridge: Cambridge UP, 1972. 317–30. **Hoffmann, P.** *Jesus von Nazareth und eine christliche Moral: Sittliche perspektiven der Verkündigung Jesu.* QD 66. Freiburg: Herder, 1975. 186–230. **Kilpatrick, G. D.** "Διαλέγεσθαι and διαλογίζεσθαι in the New Testament." *JTS* n.s. 11 (1960) 338–40. **Kuhn, H.-W.** *Ältere Sammlungen im Markusevangelium.* SNTU 8. Göttingen: Vandenhoeck & Ruprecht, 1971. 32–36. **Légasse, S.** "L'exercise de l'autorité dans l'Église d'après les évangiles synoptiques." *NRT* 85 (1963) 1009–22. ———. *Jésus et l'enfant: 'Enfants,' 'Petits' et*

'*Simples*' *dans la tradition synoptique.* EBib. Paris: Gabalda, 1969. 17–36. **Lindeskog, G.** "Logia-Studien." *ST* 4 (1950) 129–89, esp. 171–77. **McDonald, J. I. H.** "Mark 9:33–50: Catechetics in Mark's Gospel." In *Papers on the Gospels.* Vol. 2 of *Studia Biblica 1978. Sixth International Congress on Biblical Studies, Oxford, 3–7 April 1978.* Ed. E. A. Livingstone. JSNTSup 2. Sheffield: JSOT, 1980. 171–77. **Minear, P. S.** *Commands of Christ.* Edinburgh: St. Andrews Press; New York and Nashville: Abingdon, 1972. 83–97. **Neirynck, F.** "Mc 9,33–50 en de overlevering van de Jezuswoorden." In *Evangelica.* BETL 60. Leuven: Peeters; Leuven UP, 1982. 811–20. ————. "The Tradition of the Sayings of Jesus: Mark 9, 33–50." *Concilium* 20 (1966) 62–74. **Pesch, R.** *Evangelium der Urgemeinde.* 119–21. **Reploh, K. G.** *Markus—Lehrer der Gemeinde.* 140–56. **Robbins, V. K.** "Pronouncement Stories and Jesus' Blessing of the Children: A Rhetorical Approach." *Semeia* 29 (1983) 43–74. **Schmidt, K. L.** *Rahmen.* 229–32. **Schnackenburg, R.** "Mk 9, 33–50." In *Synoptische Studien.* FS A. Wikenhauser, ed. J. Schmid and A. Vögtle. Munich: Zink, 1953. 184–206. **Stock, K.** *Boten aus dem Mit-Ihm-Sein: Das Verhältnis zwischen Jesus und den Zwölf nach Markus.* AnBib 70. Rome: Biblical Institute, 1975. 112–30. **Strus, A.** "Mc. 9,33–37: Problema dell'autenticità e dell'interpretazione." *RivB* 20 (1972) 589–619. **Thompson, W. G.** *Matthew's Advice to a Divided Community: Mt 17,22–18,35.* AnBib 44. Rome: Biblical Institute, 1970. 63–66, 120–51. **Vaganay, L.** "Le schématisme du discours communautaire." In *Le problèm synoptique: Une hypothèse de travail.* Bibliothèque de théologie 3.1. Paris; Tournai: Desclée, 1954. 361–404. **Wahlde, U. C. von.** "Mark 9:33–50: Discipleship: The Authority That Serves." *BZ* 29 (1985) 49–67. **Wenham, D.** "A Note on Mark 9:33–42/Matt. 18:1–6/Luke 9:46–50." *JSNT* 14 (1982) 113–18.

Translation

[33] *And they* [a] *came to Capernaum;* [b] *and when he was in the house, he asked them, "What were you discussing* [c] *on the way?"* [34] *But they were silent; for they had discussed on the way among themselves who was the greatest.* [d] [35] *And sitting down, he called the Twelve* [e] *and says to them, "If anyone wants to be first, he shall be last of all and servant* [f] *of all."* [36] *And taking a child, he put him in the midst of them; and putting his arms around him, he said to them,* [37] *"Whoever should receive one of these children in my name receives me; and whoever should receive me receives not me but the one who sent me."*

Notes

[a]Some MSS read ἦλθεν, "he came."
[b]Gk. Καφαρναούμ, read by ℵ B D W and a few later authorities. A great deal of diversity in the spelling of Capernaum may be detected in the MSS, e.g., Καπερφαρναούμ, read by Θ; Καπερναούμ, read by A C L Σ Φ and many later authorities.
[c]W and later authorities add πρὸς ἑαυτούς, "among yourselves." This detail is taken from the following verse (v 34).
[d]Lit. "greater." In Koine Gk. the comparative μείζων is often used as a superlative ("greatest").
[e]Some later MSS add μαθητάς, "disciples."
[f]Gk. διάκονος, "servant." Some later MSS read δοῦλος, "servant" or "slave."

Form/Structure/Setting

Mark 9:33–37 is the first unit of a cluster that makes up an important block of teaching material in 9:33–50. Lane (338) thinks that these units have been artificially brought together by the evangelist through catchword associations (see also Bultmann, *History,* 149; Taylor, 403), while Gundry (507–8) has countered, arguing that these associations may just as easily arise from a "stream-of-consciousness speaking on a single occasion." Perhaps, but there are some awkward joins. Moreover, the language of the introduction is Markan (for ἐπερωτᾶν, "to ask," cf. 5:9; for ἐν τῷ ὁδῷ, "on the way," cf. 8:3; for διαλογίζεσθαι, "to discuss," cf. 2:6; for σιωπᾶν, "to be silent," cf. 3:4).

The unit under consideration centers on Jesus' sayings in vv 35 and 36, which do not easily fit together and probably have been artificially joined by the evangelist. The point of the first saying has to do with proper attitudes among the disciples—to be first, one must be willing to be last and to be the servant. It is primarily this saying that the evangelist had in mind when he composed the introduction. The point of the second saying has to do with treating the weak and unimportant with compassion; to do so is to receive Jesus himself with compassion, and to receive Jesus is in fact to receive the one who sent him.

The evangelist has introduced these sayings with Jesus' question in v 33 and the editorial comment in v 34 concerning what the disciples had been discussing among themselves. This introduction may have suggested itself to the evangelist from the tradition that will be later recounted in 10:35–45.

Comment

33 καὶ ἦλθον εἰς Καφαρναούμ, "And they came to Capernaum." Capernaum has been previously mentioned in 1:21 and 2:1. Excavations at Capernaum have uncovered the ruins of several relatively simple, single-family dwellings made of black basalt stone. An older foundation of this stone may be observed lying beneath the limestone blocks that make up the ruins of what was probably a third-century synagogue. It is estimated that the older basalt foundation dates at least to the first century and therefore could very well be the remains of the Capernaum synagogue in which Jesus ministered. The οἰκίᾳ, "house," to which Jesus and the disciples came may have been Peter's (as in 1:21; cf. Taylor, 404).

τί ἐν τῇ ὁδῷ διελογίζεσθε; "What were you discussing on the way?" This question is interesting, given the fact that in the immediately preceding pericope the disciples had been "afraid to ask him" about the meaning of Jesus' death and resurrection (v 32). The reader would naturally assume that the disciples had been discussing among themselves what only moments earlier they had been afraid to ask Jesus directly.

34 οἱ δὲ ἐσιώπων, "But they were silent." Were the disciples silent because they were still afraid to ask Jesus about his passion prediction? No, it turns out that they had been discussing who among them was the greatest. The shift in narrative theme at first glance seems quite abrupt and unexpected. The reader must surely wonder how the disciples could go from being afraid to ask their master about his anticipations of death to speculations about who among them was the greatest and, perhaps, could expect the greater honors in the awaited kingdom. But the shift is less abrupt if the evangelist's point has more to do with Jesus' impressive teaching, all the more impressive since it is given in the face of anticipated death rather than with the alternating moods of the disciples. Jesus' sayings in vv 35 and 36 are in a general sense consistent with the passion prediction in v 31.

πρὸς ἀλλήλους γὰρ διελέχθησαν ἐν τῇ ὁδῷ τίς μείζων, "for they had discussed on the way among themselves who was the greatest." Their sheepish silence shows that the disciples knew that Jesus would not approve of their conversation and motives behind it. It is ironic that they chose to discuss this topic, given the grim teaching regarding Jesus' suffering and death that preceded the present pericope: "on the way to Jesus' death in Jerusalem, they talk of personal advancement" (Achtemeier, *Int* 30 [1976] 179). Was the point of the passion predictions, now two in number, lost on the disciples? The disciples compare poorly to Jesus, who alone clearly understands what lies ahead and what the costs will be.

Questions of rank and priority were not uncommon in the Mediterranean world, including Jewish Palestine. For texts emanating from this period, see 1QS 2:20–23; 5:20–24; 6:3–5, 8–10; 1QSa 2:11–22, as well as Jesus' advice in Luke 14:7–11, which alludes to wisdom traditions (cf. Prov 25:6–7; Sir 3:18, 20). For similar advice in the rabbinic tradition, see *Lev. Rab.* 1.5 (on Lev 1:1); *'Abot R. Nat.* A §25.

35 καὶ καθίσας ἐφώνησεν τοὺς δώδεκα καὶ λέγει αὐτοῖς, "And sitting down, he called the Twelve and says to them." In sitting down (καθίσας) Jesus assumes the role of teacher (cf. 12:42; Matt 5:1; 23:2; Luke 4:20; 5:3). Mark's ἐφώνησεν τοὺς δώδεκα, "he called the Twelve," underscores Jesus' authority as teacher. After all, it was hardly necessary to summon his disciples since they were already with him. Jesus' teaching, εἴ τις θέλει πρῶτος εἶναι, ἔσται πάντων ἔσχατος καὶ πάντων διάκονος, "If anyone wants to be first, he shall be last of all and servant of all," closely parallels what will be said in 10:43–44: "whoever may wish to be great among you will be your servant, and whoever may wish to be first among you will be slave of all."

In the Jewish culture of this period, πρῶτος, "first," meant rulers, aristocrats, ruling priests, and other persons of authority and influence (cf. Luke 19:47; Acts 25:2; 28:17; Josephus, *Ant.* 11.5.3 §§140–41; 18.3.3 §§63–64; 18.5.3 §121). Thus, to be ἔσχατος, "last," and διάκονος, "servant," was to be someone with no rank, no authority, no privilege—a status that humans ordinarily did not covet. But to be first in the kingdom of God (not mentioned but clearly implied) that Jesus proclaimed, one must seek to serve.

36 καὶ λαβὼν παιδίον ἔστησεν αὐτὸ ἐν μέσῳ αὐτῶν καὶ ἐναγκαλισάμενος αὐτό, "And taking a child, he put him in the midst of them; and putting his arms around him." Jesus' using a child as an example is similar to 10:13–16: ". . . whoever should not receive the kingdom of God as a child will not enter it" (see *Comment* on this passage below; the presence of the relatively rare ἐναγκαλίζεσθαι, "to put one's arms around," in both passages suggests a common tradition; so Taylor, 405). Commentators frequently point out that children were held in little regard in late antiquity. Listening to "children's talk" was thought to be a waste of time (*m. 'Abot* 3:11). By embracing the child, Jesus "is acting out a parable on what it means to be great" (Achtemeier, *Int* 30 [1976] 182). In favor of this suggestion is the observation that the Aramaic טליא *ṭalyāʾ* means both "servant" and "child" (Black, *ExpTim* 59 [1947–48] 14–15; though usually underlying "servant" is παῖς or δοῦλος, as pointed out by Fleddermann, *CBQ* 43 [1981] 64 n. 65; for examples of טליא *ṭalyāʾ* meaning "servant," cf. *b. 'Abod. Zar.* 44a; *b. Pesaḥ.* 31b; Sokoloff, *Aramaic*, 225; it should be noted that נער *naʿar* can also mean "servant" or "child" and is sometimes rendered in the LXX by διάκονος; cf. Esth 2:2; 6:3, 5). Thus, in "taking a child" Jesus is defining what he means by being a servant in his saying in v 35. One who desires to be first must be a servant, and that means service to the least powerful and least influential, such as children.

37 ὃς ἂν ἓν τῶν τοιούτων παιδίων δέξηται ἐπὶ τῷ ὀνόματί μου, ἐμὲ δέχεται·
καὶ ὃς ἂν ἐμὲ δέχηται, οὐκ ἐμὲ δέχεται ἀλλὰ τὸν ἀποστείλαντά με, "Whoever should
receive one of these children in my name receives me; and whoever should receive me receives not me but the one who sent me." Juxtaposing the saying in v
37 with the previous one in v 35 suggests that the Markan evangelist may have
understood these sayings as parallel. Seen this way, being a servant means that
one will receive a child (for the proud and haughty would have no time for a
child). But the saying in v 37 offers its own parallelism: one who receives a child
in Jesus' name receives Jesus; and in receiving Jesus one in reality has received
the one who sent him. The latter, τὸν ἀποστείλαντα, "the one who sent," Jesus, is,
of course, God. To say that receiving a child (i.e., someone who is lowly, unimportant, weak) is to receive Jesus shows that Jesus views himself as a servant. Again,
we have a parallel with Mark 10, for in 10:45 Jesus says that he has come "not to
be served, but to serve" (see *Comment* below).

δέχεσθαι, "to receive," here probably means the same thing as in 6:11. To be
received implies being welcome and being treated as a friend, even as family.
The reception of a child is qualified by the phrase "in my name." If someone
comes in the name of Jesus, he must be received, for that is equivalent to receiving Jesus himself and, by extension, to receiving God. The language here pertains
to mission, which suggests that the saying in v 37 was probably originally uttered
in a context different from the one in which the saying in v 35 was spoken (for
the latter does not seem to have anything to do with mission).

Explanation

Although the present passage does not deal with Jesus' passion or with issues
directly related to it, its teaching does stand under its shadow. Jesus predicted his
passion on two previous occasions (8:31; 9:31), both times creating fear, confusion, and even outright resistance. When he appointed and commissioned the
Twelve (in 3:13–19; 6:7–13), they were given authority to proclaim the good news
of the kingdom of God, to heal the sick, and to cast out demons. There was an
unmistakable aura of triumph about their mission and their activities. This phase
of ministry reached its climax with Peter's confident confession that Jesus was
indeed the Messiah (8:29). But with the passion predictions all has changed. To
be first (or great) has nothing to do with powers to heal or exorcise; it has to do
with service and humility. But Jesus is the model in this too, just as he had been
the model of the authority to heal and to challenge Satan. The disciples are to
adopt Jesus' values and perspectives if they are to be important in God's kingdom. More teaching of this nature will follow. The disciples have just begun to
realize what following Jesus will entail.

H. He Who Is Not against Us Is for Us (9:38–41)

Bibliography

Baltensweiler, H. "'Wer nicht gegen uns (euch) ist, ist für uns (euch)!' Bemerkungen zu Mk 9,40 und Lk 9,50." *TZ* 40 (1984) 130–36. **Catchpole, D. R.** "The Poor on Earth and the Son of Man in Heaven: A Re-Appraisal of Matthew xxv. 31–46." *BJRL* 61 (1979) 355–97. **Delorme, J.** "Jésus ensiegne ses disciples: Mc 9,38–48." *AsSeign* 2.57 (1971) 53–62. **Descamps, A.** "Du discours de Marc., ix, 33–50 aux paroles de Jésus." In *La formation des évangiles.* Ed. J. Cambier et al. RechBib 2. Bruges: Desclée de Brouwer, 1957. 152–77. **Fee, G. D.** "Modern Text Criticism and the Synoptic Problem." In *J. J. Griesbach: Synoptic and Text-Critical Studies 1776–1976.* Ed. J. B. Orchard and T. R. W. Longstaff. SNTSMS 34. Cambridge: Cambridge UP, 1978. 154–70. **Fleddermann, H.** "The Discipleship Discourse (Mark 9:33–50)." *CBQ* 43 (1981) 57–75. ———. *Mark and Q.* 157–59. **Fridrichsen, A.** "Wer nicht mit mir ist, ist wider mich." *ZNW* 13 (1912) 273–80. **Kirchschläger, W.** *Jesu exorzistisches Wirken aus der Sicht des Lukas: Ein Beitrag zur lukanischen Redaktion.* ÖBS 3. Klosterneuburg: Österreichisches Katholisches Bibelwerk, 1981. 206–11. **Kosmala, H.** "'In My Name.'" *ASTI* 5 (1967) 87–109. **Kuhn, H.-W.** *Ältere Sammlungen im Markusevangelium.* SNTU 8. Göttingen: Vandenhoeck & Ruprecht, 1971. 32–36. **Longstaff, T. R. W.** *Evidence of Conflation in Mark? A Study of the Synoptic Problem.* SBLDS 28. Missoula, MT: Scholars Press, 1977. 168–78. **Martin, R. P.** *Mark: Evangelist and Theologian.* **Morrice, W. G.** "Translating the Greek Imperative." *BT* 24 (1973) 129–34. **Neirynck, F.** "The Tradition of the Sayings of Jesus: Mark 9, 33–50." *Concilium* 20 (1966) 62–74. **Nestle, W.** "Wer nicht mit mir ist, ist wider mich." *ZNW* 13 (1912) 84–87. **Neuhäusler, E.** *Anspruch und Antwort Gottes: Zur Lehre von den Weisungen innerhalb der synoptischen Jesusverkündigung.* Düsseldorf: Patmos, 1962. 206–10. **Reploh, K. G.** *Markus—Lehrer der Gemeinde.* 140–56. **Roloff, J.** *Das Kerygma und der irdische Jesus.* 185–86. **Russell, E. A.** "A Plea for Tolerance (Mk 9.38–40)." *IBS* 8 (1986) 154–60. **Schlosser, J.** "L'exorciste étranger (Mc, 9,38–39)." *RSR* 56 (1982) 229–39. **Schmidt, K. L.** *Rahmen.* 233–37. **Schnackenburg, R.** "Mk 9, 33–50." In *Synoptische Studien.* FS A. Wikenhauser, ed. J. Schmid and A. Vögtle. Munich: Zink, 1953. 184–206. **Stock, K.** *Boten aus dem Mit-Ihm-Sein: Das Verhältnis zwischen Jesus und den Zwölf nach Markus.* AnBib 70. Rome: Biblical Institute, 1975. 112–30. **Wahlde, U. C. von.** "Mark 9:33–50: Discipleship: The Authority That Serves." *BZ* 29 (1985) 49–67. **Wenham, D.** "A Note on Mark 9:33–42/Matt. 18:1–6/Luke 9:46–50." *JSNT* 14 (1982) 113–18. **Westcott, B. F.,** and **Hort, F. J. A.** *Introduction.* **Wilhelms, E.** "Der fremde Exorzist: Eine Studie über Mark. 9,38ff." *ST* 3 (1949) 162–71.

Translation

[38]*John said [a] to him, "Teacher,[b] we saw someone casting out demons in your name, and we forbade him, because he was not following us."[c]* [39]*But Jesus said, "Do not forbid him; for there is no one who will do a miracle in my name and will soon after be able to speak evil of me.* [40]*For whoever is not against us is for us.* [41]*For whoever should give you a cup of water[d] to drink, because you bear the name of Christ,[e] truly I say to you that he will certainly not lose his reward."*

Notes

[a]Some MSS add various forms of ἀποκρίνεσθαι, "to answer," perhaps to link 9:38–41 to the preceding pericope.

^bThe Peshitta reads *rabbî,* "Rabbi," while another Syriac text reads *rabbān,* "Rabban."

^cThe wording of the latter part of John's statement varies in the MS tradition, but with no significant effect on the meaning of the passage. For discussion, see *TCGNT*¹, 101; Westcott-Hort, *Introduction,* 1:100–101; 2:25.

^dSome later MSS read ὕδατος ψυχροῦ, "cold water." This variant results from the influence of Matt 10:42.

^eThe Gk. is awkward. See *TCGNT*¹, 101. Literally it reads ἐν ὀνόματι ὅτι χριστοῦ ἐστε, "in the name because you are Christ's." In an attempt to clarify the text, some MSS add μου, "of me," after ἐν ὀνόματι, "in the name." The text then reads "in my name, because you are Christ's." Some later MSS, perhaps due to confusion resulting from abbreviations of χριστοῦ, "Christ's," read ὅτι χριστιανοί ἐστε, "because you are Christians."

Form/Structure/Setting

The present pericope consists of two parts: (1) the comments in vv 38–40 about another person casting out demons in Jesus' name and (2) the saying in v 41 about receiving a cup of water. The first part (vv 38–40) is traditional and probably derives from a setting in the life of Jesus (*Sitz im Leben Jesu*). It is not too probable that the early Christian community would invent a story about an exorcist (presumably a successful one) who was not part of Jesus' following. Indeed, our story stands in tension with the roughly parallel story in the book of Acts where the Jewish exorcists attempt to cast out an evil spirit in the name of "Jesus whom Paul preaches" (Acts 19:13–16). Bultmann (*History,* 24–25) thinks v 40 is a secondary addition (for more proposed combinations, see Schmidt, *Rahmen,* 233–37). He may be correct, for it connects to the saying in v 39 somewhat awkwardly (though see Cranfield, 311).

John, one of the "sons of thunder" (3:17), has reported to Jesus that an exorcist who was not part of their following has been observed casting out demons in Jesus' name. Although this became a common practice in the life of the early church, there is no compelling reason to conclude that this episode could not have occurred during Jesus' Galilean ministry. Jesus' success had been reported far and wide, reaching even the ears of Herod Antipas (6:14–16). The impression one gains from reports of exorcism (as in the case of Josephus, *J.W.* 7.6.3 §§180–85; *Ant.* 8.2.5 §§46–49) is that exorcists were quite pragmatic, invoking the name of Solomon and names of other supposed potentates (one might also consult the Magical Papyri). Why should not some enterprising exorcist make use of Jesus' name (but not his message) to cast out demons?

The second part (9:41) could be a post-Easter saying, though it might be a free-floating topos that does indeed derive from Jesus. Although this saying probably originated in a different setting, it complements the present pericope in an important way. However, its present wording presents some problems and may not be original (see *Comment* below).

Comment

38 ἔφη αὐτῷ ὁ Ἰωάννης, διδάσκαλε, εἴδομέν τινα ἐν τῷ ὀνόματί σου ἐκβάλλοντα δαιμόνια, "John said to him, 'Teacher, we saw someone casting out demons in your name.'" John the son of Zebedee has been mentioned by name several times in Mark (1:19, 29; 3:17; 5:37; 9:2), but this is the first time his words are recorded.

John and his brother James will later (in Mark 10) request seats at Jesus' right and left. In Mark 13 the two brothers along with Peter will ask Jesus when his words of the temple's destruction will be fulfilled. John will make his last appearance, again in the company of Peter and James, during Jesus' prayer in Gethsemane (Mark 14:33).

ἐκωλύομεν αὐτόν, ὅτι οὐκ ἠκολούθει ἡμῖν, "We forbade him, because he was not following us." John, speaking for the disciples, has taken a position against this exorcist because this person, unlike the Twelve in 6:7–13, had not been commissioned by Jesus. The disciples assumed, therefore, that this exorcist had no authority to invoke Jesus' name. (The fact that he was attempting to perform exorcisms in itself was not the occasion for the complaint.) John's concern seems legitimate, for in commissioning the disciples Jesus had in effect appointed them to act as his official ambassadors. So who was this outsider, and by what right did he think he could make use of Jesus' name and authority? The disciples' stance is similar to the one taken by Joshua when he objected to the prophesying of Eldad and Modad (Num 11:26–30).

39 μὴ κωλύετε αὐτόν, "Do not forbid him." Jesus responds to his disciples much as Moses responded to Joshua: "Are you jealous for my sake? Would that all the LORD's people were prophets, that the LORD would put his spirit upon them!" (Num 11:29). In 10:14 Jesus will command his disciples: "Let the children come to me, do not forbid [μὴ κωλύετε] them." See also 1 Cor 14:39, where Paul enjoins the Corinthians: "So, my brethren, earnestly desire to prophesy, and do not forbid [μὴ κωλύετε] speaking in tongues."

οὐδεὶς γάρ ἐστιν ὃς ποιήσει δύναμιν ἐπὶ τῷ ὀνόματί μου καὶ δυνήσεται ταχὺ κακολογῆσαί με, "For there is no one who will do a miracle in my name and will soon after be able to speak evil of me." Commentators (e.g., Str-B 2:19) sometimes appeal to *b. B. Qam.* 80b = *b. B. Bat.* 12b ("one who is in disfavor [with God] is not quickly taken into favor") as offering a parallel to Jesus' saying, but the parallel is formal only (see Lachs, 267). Lane (344) and others note the irony in that in 9:14–29 Jesus' own disciples were unable to perform an exorcism and here in 9:38 they try to prevent a man who can.

40 The saying ὃς γὰρ οὐκ ἔστιν καθ' ἡμῶν, ὑπὲρ ἡμῶν ἐστιν, "whoever is not against us is for us," is a maxim attested in Cicero (first century B.C.E.), who says to Caesar, "We have often heard you say that, while we considered all who were not with us as our enemies, you considered all who were not against you as your friends" (*Lig.* 11; as noted by Nestle, *ZNW* 13 [1912] 85). Jesus has appealed to this maxim to justify the position he has taken in v 39. But does his saying contradict the parallel saying in Q: "He who is not with me is against me" (Matt 12:30 = Luke 11:23)? This saying also appears in the context of exorcism, but its application is different. The "whoever is not against us" saying applies to a man who makes positive use of Jesus' name to carry on the fight against Satan's kingdom. The "whoever is not with me" saying refers to those who criticize and oppose Jesus' exorcisms. They are not *with* Jesus; that is, they are *against* Jesus. The man referred to in Mark 9:38 is not against Jesus but in fact is doing Jesus' work. (See also the related agraphon found in P.Oxy. 1224 §2: "He who today is far from you may tomorrow be near to you.")

41 ὃς γὰρ ἂν ποτίσῃ ὑμᾶς ποτήριον ὕδατος ἐν ὀνόματι ὅτι Χριστοῦ ἐστε, ἀμὴν λέγω ὑμῖν ὅτι οὐ μὴ ἀπολέσῃ τὸν μισθὸν αὐτοῦ, "For whoever should give you a

cup of water to drink, because you bear the name of Christ, truly I say to you that
he will certainly not lose his reward." The concluding statement is probably a
later Christian saying, perhaps originally cast in the form of a prophecy. However, if the difficult clause, ἐν ὀνόματι ὅτι Χριστοῦ ἐστε, "because you bear the
name Christ," is removed as a later gloss (as is recommended by J. C. Hawkins,
Horae Synopticae, 2nd ed. [Oxford: Clarendon, 1909] 152, and Lagrange, 249), or
emended, then the principal objection to the statement's authenticity is removed.
How should it be emended? Taylor (408) thinks that an editor replaced ἐμοί, "to
me [i.e., mine]," with Χριστοῦ, "of Christ [i.e., Christ's]" (א*, which reads ὅτι
ἐμόν ἐστε, "because you are mine," provides important textual evidence for this
suggestion), so that the original reading was ἐν ὀνόματι ὅτι ἐμοί ἐστε, "in [my]
name because you are mine." Following A. Deissmann (*Bible Studies* [Edinburgh:
T. & T. Clark, 1901] 197–98) and G. Milligan (*Selections from the Greek Papyri* [Cam-
bridge: Cambridge UP, 1912] 50), he wonders if ἐν ὀνόματι conveys the sense of
"in virtue of" or "on the ground that." If so, the saying may originally have read
"For whoever gives you a cup of water to drink, on the ground that you are mine,
will certainly not lose his reward."

Explanation

The episode of the exorcist is unusual, not least for Jesus' interesting view of the
man's activities. Contrary to the disposition of many modern Christians, who often
have rigid doctrinal requirements and expectations, Jesus appears remarkably ecumenical and accepting. The "plain meaning of the little episode in 9:38–41 is to
administer a rebuke to the Twelve who so restricted discipleship to their own company" (Martin, *Mark: Evangelist and Theologian,* 115). The story is impressive, of
course, because Jesus' name is so powerful that someone outside of his circle can
invoke it to good effect. In the previous pericope (9:33–37) Jesus spoke of receiving a child in his name. In the present pericope we are told of a man who expels
demons in his name. The power of Jesus' name would have greatly impressed Mark's
readers, for its power and usage equal that of the famous Solomon, son of David
(see *Comment* on 10:46–52), and perhaps border on the power of the name of God
himself.

The episode of the exorcist also complements the earlier story of the disciples'
discussion of who the greatest is (9:33–37). In that episode they are taught that
to be first one must be last and a servant to others. If they embrace this attitude,
then they can hardly have feelings of jealousy and rivalry for someone else through
whom God is at work. Conversely they learn that an outsider is rewarded for the
simplest act of kindness shown to one of Jesus' disciples.

I. Temptations to Sin (9:42–50)

Bibliography

Ambrozic, A. M. *The Hidden Kingdom.* 171–77. **Baarda, T. J.** "Mark ix.49." *NTS* 5 (1958–59) 318–21. **Bauer, J. B.** "'Quod si sal infatuatum fuerit': (Mt 5,13; Mc 9,50; Lc 14,34)." *VD* 29 (1951) 228–30. **Carlston, C. E.** *The Parables of the Triple Tradition.* Philadelphia: Fortress, 1975. 174–78. **Carmignac, J.** "Studies in the Hebrew Background of the Synoptic Gospels." *ASTI* 7 (1970) 64–93, esp. 68, 80–85. **Chilton, B. D.** *Galilean Rabbi.* 101–7. **Coleman, N.-D.** "Note on Mark ix 49, 50: A New Meaning for ἅλας." *JTS* o.s. 24 (1922–23) 387–96. **Crossan, J. D.** *In Fragments.* 144–52. **Cullmann, O.** "Das Gleichnis vom Salz: Zur frühesten Kommentierung eines Herrenworts durch die Evangelisten." In *Vorträge und Aufsätze 1925–1962.* Ed. K. Fröhlich. Tübingen: Mohr-Siebeck, 1966. 192–201. ———. "Que signifie le sel dans la parabole de Jésus? Les évangelistes, premiers commentateurs du logion." *RHPR* 37 (1957) 36–43. **Deatrick, E. P.** "Salt, Soil, Savior." *BA* 25 (1962) 41–48. **Delorme, J.** "Jésus enseigne ses disciples: Mc 9,38–48." *AsSeign* 2.57 (1971) 53–62. **Deming, W.** "Mark 9.41–10.12, Matthew 5.27–32, and *B. Nid.* 13b: A First Century Discussion of Male Sexuality." *NTS* 36 (1990) 130–41. **Derrett, J. D. M.** "Salted with Fire: Mark 9:42–50." *Theology* 76 (1973) 364–68. ———. "Two 'Harsh' Sayings of Christ Explained." *DRev* 103 (1985) 218–29, esp. 218–21. **Descamps, A.** "Du discours de Marc., ix, 33–50 aux paroles de Jésus." In *La formation des évangiles.* Ed. J. Cambier et al. RechBib 2. Bruges: Desclée de Brouwer, 1957. 152–77. **Fleddermann, H.** "The Discipleship Discourse (Mark 9:33–50)." *CBQ* 43 (1981) 57–75. ———. *Mark and Q.* 159–64, 166–69. **Gressmann, H.** "Mitteilungen 14: Salzdüngung in den Evangelien." *TLZ* 36 (1911) 156–57. **Hahn, F.** "Das Verständnis des Glaubens im Markusevangeliums." In *Glaube im Neuen Testament.* FS H. Binder, ed. F. Hahn and H. Klein. Biblisch-theologische Studien 7. Neukirchen-Vluyn: Neukirchener Verlag, 1982. 43–67, esp. 62–63. **Hellestam, S.** "Mysteriet med saltet." *SEÅ* 55 (1990) 59–63. **Hommel, H.** "Herrenworte im Lichte sokratischer Überlieferung." *ZNW* 57 (1966) 1–23. **Humbert, A.** "Essai d'une théologie du scandale dans les Synoptiques." *Bib* 35 (1954) 1–28. **Iersel, B. M. F. van.** "Failed Followers in Mark: Mark 13:12 as a Key for the Identification of the Intended Readers." *CBQ* 58 (1996) 244–63, esp. 252–53. ———. "Mark 9,43–48 in a Martyrological Perspective." In *Fructus Centesimus.* FS G. J. M. Bartelink, ed. A. A. R. Bastiaensen et al. Steenbrugge: Sint-Pietersabdij; Dordrecht: Kluwer, 1989. 333–41. **Jeremias, J.** *Parables.* 168–69. **Klauck, H.-J.** *Allegorie und Allegorese in synoptischen Gleichnistexten.* NTAbh 13. Münster: Aschendorff, 1978. 280–86. **Koester, H.** "Mark 9:43–47 and Quintilian 8.3.75." *HTR* 71 (1978) 151–53. **Kuhn, H.-W.** *Ältere Sammlungen im Markusevangelium.* SNTU 8. Göttingen: Vandenhoeck & Ruprecht, 1971. 32–36. **Lathan, J. E.** *The Religious Symbolism of Salt.* Theologie historique 64. Paris: Beauchesne, 1982. 221–30. **Lattke, M.** "Salz der Freundschaft in Mk 9 50c." *ZNW* 75 (1984) 44–59. **Lode, L.** "The Presentation of New Information." *BT* 35 (1984) 101–8. **Marshall, C. D.** *Faith as a Theme in Mark's Narrative.* SNTSMS 64. Cambridge: Cambridge UP, 1989. 154–59. **Michel, O.** "'Diese Kleinen'—Eine Jüngerbezeichnung Jesu." *TSK* 108 (1937–38) 401–15. **Mitton, C. L.** "Threefoldness in the Teaching of Jesus." *ExpTim* 75 (1963–64) 228–30. **Moffatt, J.** "Jesus upon 'Stumbling Blocks.'" *ExpTim* 26 (1914–15) 407–9. **Nauck, W.** "Salt as a Metaphor in Instructions for Discipleship." *ST* 6 (1952) 165–78. **Neirynck, F.** "The Tradition of the Sayings of Jesus: Mark 9, 33–50." *Concilium* 20 (1966) 62–74. **Perles, F.** "La parabole du Sel sourd." *REJ* 82 (1926) 119–23. **Reploh, K. G.** *Markus—Lehrer der Gemeinde.* 140–56. **Schmidt, K. L.** *Rahmen.* 233–37. **Schnackenburg, R.** "Mk 9, 33–50." In *Synoptische Studien.* FS A. Wikenhauser, ed. J. Schmid and A. Vögtle. Munich: Zink, 1953. 184–206. **Schwarz, G.** "Καλὸν τὸ ἅλας." *BibNot* 7 (1978) 32–35. ———. "Πᾶς πυρὶ ἁλισθήσεται (Markus 9,49)." *BN* 11 (1980) 45. **Söding,**

T. *Glaube bei Markus: Glaube an das Evangelium, Gebetsglaube und Wunderglaube im Kontext der markinischen Basileiatheologie und Christologie.* SBB 12. Stuttgart: Katholisches Bibelwerk, 1985. 175–78, 287–90. **Stock, K.** *Boten aus dem Mit-Ihm-Sein: Das Verhältnis zwischen Jesus und den Zwölf nach Markus.* AnBib 70. Rome: Biblical Institute, 1975. 112–30. **Torrey, C. C.** *Our Translated Gospels.* London: Hodder and Stoughton; New York: Harper & Brothers, 1936. **Vaganay, L.** "'Car chacun doit être salé au feu' (Marc, ix,49)." In *Mémorial J. Chaine.* Bibliothèque de la Faculté Catholique de Théologie de Lyon 5. Lyon: Facultés catholiques, 1950. 367–72. **Wahlde, U. C. von.** "Mark 9:33–50: Discipleship: The Authority That Serves." *BZ* 29 (1985) 49–67. **Westcott, B. F.,** and **Hort, F. J. A.** *Introduction.* 1:101; 2:25. **Wright, N. T.** *Jesus and the Victory of God.* 320–68. **Zager, W.** *Gottesherrschaft und Endgericht in der Verkündigung Jesu: Eine Untersuchung zur markinischen Jesusüberlieferung einschliesslich der Q-Parallelen.* BZNW 82. Berlin; New York: de Gruyter, 1996. **Zimmermann, H.** "'Mit Feuer gesalzen werden': Eine Studie zu Mk 9,49." *TQ* 139 (1959) 28–39.

Translation

[42] *"And whoever should cause to stumble one of these* [a] *little ones who believe [in me],* [b] *it is better for him if a great millstone is hung around his neck and he is cast into the sea.* [43] *And if your hand should cause you to stumble,* [c] *cut if off; it is better for you to enter into life maimed than having two hands to enter into* [d] *hell, into the unquenchable fire.* [e] [45] *And if your foot should cause you to stumble,* [f] *cut if off; it is better for you to enter into life lame than having two feet to be cast into hell.* [g] [47] *And if your eye cause you to stumble, pluck it out; it is better to enter the kingdom of God with one eye than with two eyes to be cast into hell,* [h] [48] *where 'their worm does not die, and the fire is not quenched.'* [i] [49] *For everyone will be salted with fire.* [j] [50] *Salt is good; but if the salt should become saltless,* [k] *with what will you season it? Have salt in yourselves, and be at peace with one another."*

Notes

[a]W reads ἕνα τῶν μικρῶν μου τούτων, "one of these my little ones."
[b]A B C² L W and many later MSS add εἰς ἐμέ, "in me." Both Nestle-Aland²⁷ and UBSGNT³ᶜ place these words in square brackets. The words are omitted in ℵ C*ᵛⁱᵈ and various versions. It is possible that they were imported from Matt 18:6. See discussion in *TCGNT* ¹, 101–2.
[c]A C D and several later MSS read σκανδαλίζῃ (pres. subjunc.), "should [continue to] cause to stumble." ℵ B L W and a few later authorities read σκανδαλίσῃ (aor. subjunc.), "should cause to stumble." The difference in Greek tense could be significant. The former reading (which is accepted by Nestle-Aland²⁷ and UBSGNT³ᶜ), as opposed to the latter reading, could imply habitual stumbling.
[d]D and a few later MSS read εἰς, "to be cast into," perhaps under the influence of v 45.
[e]Gk. εἰς τὴν γέενναν, εἰς τὸ πῦρ τὸ ἄσβεστον. Γέεννα transliterates the Aramaic נדהום *gêhinnām.* The word is often transliterated in English (i.e., Gehenna or Gehinnom). It is better to translate it "hell" (see *Comment* on v 48). The expression "fire of hell" (נדהום אישה *'eyššat gêhinnām*) is attested in the Targum (cf. *Frag. Tg.* Deut 32:35). Various endings are found in several MSS. Some read εἰς τὴν γέενναν, ὅπου ἐστὶν τὸ πῦρ τὸ ἄσβεστον, "to Gehenna, where there is the unquenchable fire." Others read εἰς τὴν γέενναν τοῦ πυρός, "to Gehenna of fire." ℵᵃ L and a few later MSS read simply εἰς τὴν γέενναν, "to Gehenna." ℵ B C L W and many other authorities read v 44, ὅπου ὁ σκώληξ αὐτῶν οὐ τελευτᾷ καὶ τὸ πῦρ οὐ σβέννυται, "where their worm does not die and the fire is not quenched," as it is omitted here. The verse is found in A D K and a host of later MSS. This addition derives from v 48.
[f]W and a few other MSS read the aorist subjunc. See *Note* c above.
[g]Gk. γέενναν, lit. "Gehenna" (see *Note* e above and *Comment* on v 48). Several later MSS add τοῦ πυρός, "of fire," τοῦ πυρὸς τοῦ ἀσβέστου, "of unquenchable fire," or εἰς τὸ πῦρ τὸ ἄσβεστον, "into unquenchable fire" (in place of εἰς τὴν γέενναν, "into Gehenna"). ℵ B C L W and many other authorities omit v 46, ὅπου ὁ σκώληξ αὐτῶν οὐ τελευτᾷ καὶ τὸ πῦρ οὐ σβέννυται, "where their worm does not die and the fire is not quenched," as it is omitted here. See *Note* e above.

[h]A C and many later MSS add τοῦ πυρός, "of fire."

[i]Later MSS read a variety of minor variants. The verse is a quotation of Isa 66:24.

[j]B L and a few other authorities read πᾶς γὰρ πυρὶ ἁλισθήσεται, "for everyone will be salted with fire." Nestle-Aland[27] and UBSGNT[3c] have accepted this reading; it is followed in the translation above. D and several Italian MSS read πᾶσα γὰρ θυσία ἁλὶ ἁλισθήσεται, "and every sacrifice will be salted with salt" (cf. Lev 2:13). A and several other authorities combine these readings, πᾶς γὰρ πυρὶ ἁλισθήσεται καὶ πᾶσα θυσία ἁλὶ ἁλισθήσεται, "for everyone will be salted with fire and every sacrifice will be salted with salt." Other variants are attested, such as πυρὶ ἀναλωθήσεται, "will be consumed by fire," ἐν πυρὶ δοκιμασθήσεται, "will be tested by fire," or πᾶσα δὲ οὐσία ἀναλωθήσεται, "and all [their] substance will be destroyed." On the development of these variants, see C. H. Turner, "W and θ: Studies in the Western Text of St Mark," *JTS* o.s. 17 (1916) 16–18; *TCGNT*[1], 102–3; Cranfield, 314–15.

[k]W reads ἐὰν δὲ τὸ ἅλας μωρανθῇ, "but if the salt has become insipid" (cf. Matt 5:13; Luke 14:34).

Form/Structure/Setting

The present pericope consists of teaching concerning the perils of causing people to stumble. The opening verse is often treated as originally distinct from vv 43–48 (so Bultmann, *History,* 144; cf. Schmidt, *Rahmen,* 235), but there is no good reason for this separation. Referring to "little ones" probably links with the child of 9:36 (see *Comment* below). Jesus now warns of causing little ones to stumble and then goes on to elaborate on this theme. The saying parallels a rabbinic tradition: "If in the case of trees, which neither eat nor drink nor smell, the Torah decreed that they should be burned and destroyed [cf. Deut 12:3], because they had proved to be a stumbling block, how much more so [must you destroy him] who seduces his neighbor from the path of life to that of death" (*b. Sanh.* 55a). Because of the proverbial nature of 9:42, Bultmann thinks we "have a case of the Christian Church taking over an old proverb, whose origin can no longer be recovered" (*History,* 144). Here again Bultmann applies the criterion of dissimilarity to Judaism in an unwarranted manner, for much of Jesus' teaching is proverbial and most of it parallels Jewish traditions. That it does so here is hardly grounds for crediting it to the church. What the church has added are the words εἰς ἐμέ, "in me." The original saying spoke of those "who believe," that is, who believe the gospel that Jesus and his disciples have proclaimed (cf. Mark 1:15: "Repent, and believe in the gospel")—not the kerygma of the risen Christ that the church would later proclaim.

Vv 43–48 elaborate on the theme of stumbling. Bultmann (*History,* 78) seems open to accepting them as genuine dominical tradition. I think it more than probable that this material derives from Jesus. Surely the church would emphasize the danger of hell as the result of failure to respond in faith to the Easter proclamation. The background of the sayings also points to pre-Christian origins. Van Iersel remarks that Mark "9:43–48 is best understood against the background of the story of the Maccabean brothers" (*CBQ* 58 [1996] 252). He could very well be correct, for the fearsome injuries described (amputated limbs, gouged-out eyes) parallel the horrors described in 2 Macc 6–7, which recounts the punishments inflicted upon the faithful who refused to commit apostasy during the pogroms of Antiochus IV. Once again Jesus' words resemble Jewish tradition. In a late midrashic collection we read "Do not permit your ears to listen to idle chatter, because they are first of the (body's) organs to be burned. Do not eye another's wealth, because it may cast you into heavy darkness and gloom. . . . Let not your feet hurry you to commit sin lest the Angel of Death come to meet you" (*Derek*

'*Ereṣ Zuṭa* 4.6). This parallel illustrates both the proverbial and the Jewish texture of Jesus' style of teaching.

The warnings carry with them unmistakably eschatological overtones. It is not surprising then that the North American Jesus Seminar regards this material as either outright inauthentic or at least very doubtful (cf. R. W. Funk and R. W. Hoover, eds., *The Five Gospels: The Search for the Authentic Words of Jesus* [Sonoma, CA: Polebridge Press; New York: Macmillan, 1993] 86–87). But the seminar's doubts largely arise from its misguided preference for a noneschatological Jesus (see the trenchant criticisms in Zager, *Gottesherrschaft und Endgericht;* Wright, *Jesus and the Victory of God,* 320–68).

It is not clear whether the final sayings in vv 49–50 are part of the original unit of tradition or have been drawn to the present context through the catchwords πῦρ, "fire," and ἅλας, "salt." The appearance of *fire* in v 49 may have been what drew the saying to v 48, while the word *salt* in v 49 may have been what attracted the saying found in v 50. Catchwords such as these were mnemonic aids in the preservation of the tradition (Taylor, 409–10).

Comment

42 ὃς ἂν σκανδαλίσῃ ἕνα τῶν μικρῶν τούτων τῶν πιστευόντων [εἰς ἐμέ], "whoever should cause to stumble one of these little ones who believe [in me]." ἕνα τῶν μικρῶν τούτων, "one of these little ones," probably refers to the children, one of whom Jesus had embraced in 9:36–37. How does one cause a little one to stumble? If we take our lead from 9:33–37, the cause of stumbling that Jesus has in mind may indeed be the failure to treat the little one in a way that is as important and significant as the way the powerful and influential are treated. The danger consists of those who, self-absorbed, fail to have consideration for the weaker and more vulnerable. Paul's advice to the Christians at Corinth (1 Cor 8–9; cf. Rom 14) may very well represent an extrapolation of this dominical tradition.

καλόν ἐστιν αὐτῷ μᾶλλον εἰ περίκειται μύλος ὀνικὸς περὶ τὸν τράχηλον αὐτοῦ καὶ βέβληται εἰς τὴν θάλασσαν, "it is better for him if a great millstone is hung around his neck and he is cast into the sea." The μύλος ὀνικός, "millstone" (lit. a "donkey[-driven] millstone"), of which Jesus speaks is much larger than the stones of the common handmills. The latter would be more than heavy enough to take one to the bottom quickly; the heavier stone would sink one like an anchor. Some of these stones have been uncovered in and around Capernaum. Hanging the stone around one's neck would make the situation as deadly as possible. Jesus uses hyperbolic language here to underscore the great importance of the point that he is making. Similar hyperbole is employed in vv 43–47. The image of the millstone as an instrument of judgment or punishment is found in biblical literature (in Judg 9:53 a woman crushes the head of Abimelech with a millstone [no doubt the smaller variety]; in Rev 18:21 the city of Babylon [i.e., Rome] is cast into the sea like a millstone) and in later Jewish tradition (in *b. Qidd.* 29b a millstone [רחיים *rēḥayîm*] around one's neck is employed as a metaphor of the difficulty in trying to study Torah while supporting a family).

43–47 Whereas v 42 warned against causing someone else to stumble, vv 43–47 warn against causing oneself to stumble. One has a choice: going the way of the world and risking being cast into hell, or removing the cause of temptation and entering life. There are some illustrative texts in the Greek Bible and related literature in which σκανδαλίζειν, "to cause to stumble," occurs: "Do not look intently at [lit. 'study'] a virgin, lest you stumble and incur penalties for her" (Sir 9:5); "The sinner stumbles through his lips, the reviler and the arrogant are tripped by them" (Sir 23:8); "Restrain me, O God, from sordid sin, and from every evil woman who causes the foolish to stumble" (*Pss. Sol.* 16:7). All three of these texts reflect the kind of imagery that Jesus has employed. Through one's eye one might stumble on account of lust (the first and third examples). Through one's lips one might stumble on account of rash utterances (the second example). Jesus recommends taking precautions so that one is not ensnared by such temptations. (For another example in which σκανδαλίζειν occurs, see Sir 32:15.) Of course his grotesque recommendations are not to be taken literally (as they actually have been from time to time).

The Jewishness of Jesus' illustrations is seen at several points. In 2 Macc 7:4 Antiochus IV had the hands and feet of a Jewish woman's eldest son chopped off (and inflicted similar punishment on some of his brothers). Several of these tortured and dying sons warned the tyrant of the punishment of hell that would await him. Jesus' saying, "it is better for you to enter into life maimed than to enter into hell" (Mark 9:43), follows the same form of logic, though it has nothing to do with martyrdom. Mention of the loss of eye, hand, and foot is found in the Mishnah (*m. B. Qam.* 8:1), though again a different point is being made.

The goal of self-discipline is to enter life. The more common idiom is "to have a portion in the world to come," but Jesus' phrase εἰσελθεῖν εἰς τὴν ζωήν, "to enter into life" (Mark 9:43, 45), is also paralleled in Jewish tradition: "I run to the life [חיי ḥayyê] of the World to Come" (*b. Ber.* 28b); "Which road leads [בוא bôʾ] man to the life [חיי ḥayyê] of the World to Come?" (*Gen. Rab.* 9.8 [on Gen 1:31]); "Rabbi . . . will you cause me to enter [בוא bôʾ] the life [חיי ḥayyê] of the World to Come?" (*b. ʿAbod. Zar.* 18a). Jesus' language, of course, is thoroughly hyperbolic, and his hearers would have recognized this. Resurrection to life entailed full restoration; there will be no lame and blind persons limping and groping about in heaven (cf. *Midr. Tanḥ. Bĕrēʾšît* 11.9 [on Gen 46:28]: "The blind are healed . . . the lame also are healed . . . everyone shall be healed"; *Gen. Rab.* 95.1 [on Gen 46:28]). In v 47 Jesus speaks of entering "the kingdom of God." To enter life and to enter the kingdom of God is, in Jesus' parlance, to speak of the same thing. It is perhaps for this reason that τὴν ζωήν, "life," is articular, for the life into which one enters is "the life to come."

Reference to τὸ πῦρ τὸ ἄσβεστον, "the unquenchable fire," anticipates the allusion to Isa 66:24 in v 48 and may be an attempt, as Taylor (412) suggests, to clarify to Gentile readers the meaning of the subsequent allusion to Isaiah.

48 The words ὁ σκώληξ αὐτῶν οὐ τελευτᾷ καὶ τὸ πῦρ οὐ σβέννυται, "their worm does not die, and the fire is not quenched," are taken from Isa 66:24: "And they shall go forth and look on the dead bodies of the men that have rebelled against me; for their worm shall not die, their fire shall not be quenched [LXX: ὁ γὰρ σκώληξ αὐτῶν οὐ τελευτήσει, καὶ τὸ πῦρ αὐτῶν οὐ σβεσθήσεται], and they shall be an abhorrence to all flesh." This passage is expressed in other Jewish writings of late antiquity: "Humble yourself greatly, for the punishment of the ungodly is fire and worms [ἐκδίκησις ἀσεβοῦς πῦρ καὶ σκώληξ]" (Sir 7:17); "Woe to the nations that rise up against my people! The Lord Almighty will take vengeance on them in the day of judgment; fire and worms he will give to their flesh [πῦρ καὶ σκώληκας εἰς σάρκας αὐτῶν]; they shall weep in pain for ever" (Jdt 16:17).

It is interesting to observe that the context of Isa 66:24 concerns "men that have rebelled against" God. If Jesus has the whole of the verse in mind, this would imply that he viewed causing the faithful to stumble tantamount to rebellion against God. Thus, the need to guard against causing offense becomes all the more serious and explains why Jesus employed such graphic hyperbole as amputating hands and feet and gouging out eyes. The part of Isa 66:24 that is actually quoted suggests that Gehenna is a place of endless destruction; there is no hope of relief (Gould, 180).

This teaching parallels in some ways the incident in which scribes accuse Jesus of casting out demons by the aid of Satan (3:23–30): "whoever blasphemes against the Holy Spirit never has forgiveness, but is guilty of an eternal sin—for they had said, 'He has an unclean spirit'" (vv 29–30). It is quite possible that part of the seriousness of regarding Jesus' exorcisms as having their source in Satan rather than in God lies in making these charges public and thus causing people to stumble (on 3:23–30, see Guelich, 175–80).

Jesus repeatedly refers to the danger of being cast into "hell." The word is γέεννα, "Gehenna," which approximately transliterates the Aramaic גיהנם gêhinnām, which is itself a compound word meaning "valley of Hinnom" (see Note e above). The word is common to Jewish literature (cf. 4 Ezra 7:36: "the furnace of Gehenna shall be disclosed, and opposite it the Paradise of delight"; 1 Enoch 27:2; 90:26–27; 2 Bar. 59:10; 85:13; Sib. Or. 1:103; 2:291; 4:186) and derives from the name of a valley south of Jerusalem where in great antiquity human sacrifice took place (Jer 7:31; 19:5–6; 32:35). The reforming king Josiah desecrated the place (2 Kgs 23:10). Thereafter it became a place of incinerating refuse (see G. H. Dalman, The Words of Jesus [Edinburgh: T. & T. Clark, 1902] 161–62).

The association of Gehenna with an allusion to Isa 66:24 suggests that once again Jesus' usage of Scripture, especially Isaiah, reflects familiarity with the Aramaic paraphrase as it was developing in the synagogue. In the Isaiah Targum, which in its extant form, of course, post-dates Jesus, the verse reads "And they shall go forth and look on the bodies of the sinful men who have rebelled against my Memra; for their breaths will not die and their fire shall not be quenched, and the wicked shall be judged in Gehinnom . . ." (see Chilton, Galilean Rabbi, 101–7).

On the omission of vv 44 and 46, see Notes e and g above.

49   The assertion that πᾶς γὰρ πυρὶ ἁλισθήσεται, "everyone will be salted with fire," is curious and has prompted numerous explanations as well as textual variants. Since this saying is found in its present context because of catchwords, it should be interpreted independently with respect to its setting in the life of Jesus (Sitz im Leben Jesu; rightly Cranfield, 315), though we should also ask how the Markan evangelist may have understood its meaning in the context that he has provided.

Torrey retroverts the saying into Aramaic: "Everyone [כל kōl] with fire [בְּאָשׁ baʾāš] will be salted." He believes the second Aramaic word has been misunderstood; the reading should be "Anything spoiling is salted" (Torrey, Translated Gospels, 11, 13). However, this emendation is probably unnecessary, and in any case it hardly clarifies the meaning of the saying. Taylor (413) rightly finds Torrey's translation "prosaic. A challenging word on suffering is the most probable suggestion."

We probably have an allusion to Lev 2:13: "You shall season all your cereal offerings with salt; you shall not let the salt of the covenant with your God be lacking from your cereal offering; with all your offerings you shall offer salt" (cf. Num 18:19). Correctly sensing that the saying had something to do with Lev 2:13, D adds "and every sacrifice will be salted with salt" (see *Note* j; Westcott-Hort, *Introduction* 1:101; 2:25; Swete, 213). One should also take note of Ezek 43:24, which directs the priests to sprinkle salt upon a burnt offering. Although not mentioned explicitly, fire is implied (cf. Ezra 6:9; *Jub.* 21:11; 11QTemple 20).

Although Jesus' saying is cryptic, it is probable that it originally was a meta-phor describing the process of purification, or purging, through which everyone must pass in order to gain entry into the kingdom of God (Hooker, 233). Just as every offering must be salted to meet the standards of the covenant, so must every believer be "salted." But Jesus does not say "salted with salt"; rather he says "salted with fire." This modification introduces the eschatological element of pu-rification, of which John the Baptist had spoken: "He will baptize you with Holy Spirit and with fire" (Matt 3:11 = Luke 3:16). The appearance of fire here may in part be indebted to Mal 3:2–3, a tradition that seems to have informed the Baptist's sense of call and mission: "But who can endure the day of his coming, and who can stand when he appears? For he is like a refiner's fire and like fullers' soap; he will sit as a refiner and purifier of silver, and he will purify the sons of Levi and refine them like gold and silver, till they present right offerings to the LORD." The fire spoken of here is not the same as the fire mentioned in the saying in Mark 9:48. In other words, Jesus does not salt anyone with the fire of Gehenna. But the evangelist is not remiss in placing these two sayings one after the other, for both carry with them eschatological implications. The one who becomes en-snared in the temptations of the world will be cast into Gehenna, whose fires are never quenched, but the one who submits to the purifying fire of Jesus will es-cape Gehenna (see Gould, 181).

50 The next saying about salt is probably another independent saying. καλὸν τὸ ἅλας, "salt is good," for many reasons, among them its ability to preserve. If Jesus' saying in v 49 originally referred to the salt covenant of Lev 2:13, then the goodness of salt is seen on that account.

ἐὰν δὲ τὸ ἅλας ἄναλον γένηται, ἐν τίνι αὐτὸ ἀρτύσετε; ἔχετε ἐν ἑαυτοῖς ἅλα, "if the salt should become saltless, with what will you season it? Have salt in your-selves." The idea of salt as preservative may lie behind the related saying found in Matt 5:13: "You are the salt of the earth; but if salt has lost its taste, how shall its saltness be restored? It is no longer good for anything except to be thrown out and trodden under foot by men." Salt is used for purification in 2 Kgs 2:19–23, and its mixture with incense is called "pure and holy" in Exod 30:35. In Col 4:6 salt is linked to gracious conduct: "Let your speech always be gracious, seasoned with salt, so that you may know how you ought to answer every one." This mean-ing seems to stand closest to our verse in view of the last part: "and be at peace with one another." In a rabbinic tradition salt represents wisdom: "the wisdom of the scribes will become insipid"; that is, it will lose its saltiness (*m. Soṭa* 9:15). Nauck (*ST* 6 [1952] 165–78) opts for this latter view. There really is no need to choose between these options, for salt may symbolize several of these attributes. Jesus wishes his disciples to have salt in themselves (i.e., to be wise, pure, gra-cious) and therefore "to be at peace with one another."

Again Torrey believes that the underlying Aramaic tradition has been misunderstood and improperly rendered in Greek. "Have salt in yourselves, and be at peace [אִשְׁלִמוּ *'ošlimû*] with one another" should read "Have salt in yourselves, and *hand it on* to another" (*Translated Gospels*, 11, 13–14). Torrey's clever emendation could be correct, though again it is not clear that the meaning of the passage is significantly clarified.

The final saying, εἰρηνεύετε ἐν ἀλλήλοις, "be at peace with one another," harks back to the very beginning of this chain of materials, namely, to the discussion between the disciples in vv 33–34 regarding who was the greatest among them (Turner, 47; Hooker, 233). If they take to heart Jesus' teaching in vv 35–50, they will indeed be at peace with one another and will cause neither themselves nor others to stumble.

Explanation

When it comes to giving advice, Jesus offers no platitudes. His teaching smacks of a grim realism that his disciples must take to heart. Following him is not easy; earlier it had been likened to taking up a cross and forfeiting one's life (8:34–35). Now Jesus warns his disciples of their responsibilities. Arrogance, self-absorption, insensitivity, and tyranny are all negative attitudes that frequently lie behind the desire to be first and to be the greatest (9:34). Just as frequently these attitudes cause people to stumble, especially the younger, weaker, and less influential. Far from seeking positions of power, Jesus' disciples should seek opportunities for service. Rather than causing the little ones to stumble, the disciples must help them stand and grow in faith. The matter is so important to Jesus that he describes the dire consquences in shocking hyperbole: better to drown oneself in the sea than to offend a little one; better to cut off a hand or foot, or even pluck out an eye, than to risk throwing oneself into hell over some temptation or self-induced cause of stumbling.

Chap. 9 brings to a conclusion a major shift in Mark's narrative and theological strategy. A major burden was thrust upon the evangelist the moment the passion was announced in 8:31. Until then Jesus' ministry had been marked by one astounding success after another. Sickness, the demonic world, and even nature itself yielded before him. He was, as Peter declared, the Messiah. Conventional wisdom expected this remarkable mission and ministry to end on a happy note. But no, the end will be rejection and a shameful death on the cross. Mark must show that Jesus is fully cognizant of his fate and is fully prepared for it. Not only that—Jesus must begin to prepare his disciples for the trials that lie ahead.

The evangelist has achieved this by grouping certain teachings of Jesus and certain illustrative episodes. Following his first passion prediction, Jesus rebukes Peter in no uncertain terms: opposition to his destiny of death is in fact to be on the side of Satan, not on the side of God (8:32–33). Jesus then teaches his disciples the high cost and great reward of discipleship (8:34–9:1). The transfiguration, with the heavenly voice, provides the needed confirmation that Jesus is still God's Son, to whom the disciples must listen (9:2–8). Jesus then teaches his disciples the meaning of John's fate; he was Elijah who was to come, and they should look at what happened to him (9:9–13). The disciples still have much to learn, as their lack of success in curing the demon-possessed boy showed (9:14–

29). Jesus, however, is more than sufficient even to raise one up that all thought was dead. The passion is predicted again; the disciples are uncomprehending and fearful (9:30–32). They are so uncomprehending of the gravity of the situation that they soon begin discussing privilege, wondering who among them is the greatest (9:33–34). Jesus teaches his disciples that they must be willing to be last, to be a servant, to show compassion to the weak and seemingly unimportant. To receive such a one is to receive Jesus himself, to receive even God who sent him (9:35–37). The disciples are not only to be compassionate toward the weaker of Jesus' followers, but they are to be tolerant and supportive of those outside their circle who in their own way do the work of God. Indeed, even the smallest act of compassion for the cause will be rewarded (9:38–41). Finally, chap. 9 concludes with a series of warnings to avoid causing offense toward others and even toward oneself lest one be cast into hell (9:42–48). The disciples instead are to be prepared for the challenging rigors entailed in following Jesus, and in enduring them they are to be at peace with one another (9:49–50).

VI. Journey through Perea and Judea (10:1–45)

Bibliography

Best, E. *Following Jesus.* 99–146. **Busemann, R.** *Die Jüngergemeinde nach Markus 10: Eine redaktionsgeschichtliche Untersuchung des 10. Kapitels im Markusevangeliums.* BBB 57. Bonn: Hanstein, 1983. **Dominic, A. P.** "The Threefold Call." *Review for Religious* 40 (1981) 283–96.

Form/Structure/Setting

In chap. 9 Jesus taught his disciples many things pertaining to suffering and the proper attitudes they must develop if they are to serve the kingdom and promote harmony in the community. Now Jesus turns south to Judea, crosses the Jordan, and passes through Perea. The themes of chap. 10 parallel at many points those of chap. 9. Relationships remain the principal concern: the first pericope deals with the question of divorce (vv 1–12), the second once again teaches that it is to children that the kingdom of God belongs (vv 13–16), while the third and fourth pericopes deal with the dangers and distractions of wealth (vv 17–22 and 23–31). The concluding statement in v 31, "many that are first will be last, and the last will be first," harks back to Jesus' teaching on greatness in 9:35. The third passion prediction is given in 10:32–34, which is then followed by yet another round of bickering concerning who will be granted the most important appointments in the kingdom (vv 35–45). Chap. 10 concludes with the healing of blind Bartimaeus (vv 46–52).

Mark's arrangement of material is topical. The first two pericopes are independent, but the next two pericopes (vv 17–22, 23–31) are linked by the theme of riches and rewards. These passages may have been connected in the pre-Markan tradition. The third passion prediction has been placed by the evangelist immediately prior to the disciples' second dispute over who is the greatest. This arrangement will again afford the Markan Jesus the opportunity to address the topic of values and the true meaning of discipleship.

A. Teaching about Divorce (10:1–12)

Bibliography

Baltensweiler, H. *Die Ehe im Neuen Testament: Exegetische Untersuchungen über Ehe, Ehelosigkeit und Ehescheidung.* ATANT 52. Zürich: Zwingli, 1967. 43–77. **Bammel, E.** "Markus 10,11f. und das jüdische Eherecht." *ZNW* 61 (1970) 95–101. **Banks, R. J.** *Jesus and the Law in the Synoptic Tradition.* SNTSMS 28. Cambridge: Cambridge UP, 1975. 146–59. **Berger, K.** *Die*

Gesetzesauslegung Jesu: Ihr historischer Hintergrund im Judentum und im Alten Testament. WMANT 40. Neukirchen-Vluyn: Neukirchener Verlag, 1972. 533–70. ————. "Hartherzigkeit und Gottes Gesetz: Die Vorgeschichte des antijüdischen Vorwurfs in Mc 10,5." *ZNW* 61 (1970) 1–47. ————. "Zu den sogenannten Sätzen heiligen Rechts." *NTS* 17 (1970–71) 10–40. **Berrouard, M.-F.** "L'indissolubilité du mariage dans le Nouveau Testament." *LumVie* 4 (1952) 21–40. **Best, E.** *Following Jesus.* 99–105. **Brewer, D. I.** "Jewish Women Divorcing Their Husbands in Early Judaism: The Background of Papyrus Şe'elim 13." *HTR* 92 (1999) 349–57. **Burkill, T. A.** "Two into One: The Notion of Carnal Union in Mark 10:8; 1 Kor. 6:16; Eph. 5:31." *ZNW* 62 (1971) 115–20. **Busemann, R.** *Die Jüngergemeinde nach Markus 10: Eine redaktionsgeschichtliche Untersuchung des 10. Kapitels im Markusevangeliums.* BBB 57. Bonn: Hanstein, 1983. 102–18. **Catchpole, D. R.** "The Synoptic Divorce Material as a Traditio-Historical Problem." *BJRL* 57 (1974–75) 92–127. **Coiner, H. G.** "Those 'Divorce and Remarriage' Passages (Matt. 5:32; 19:9; 1 Cor. 7:10–16), with Brief Reference to the Mark and Luke Passages." *CTM* 39 (1968) 367–84. **Condon, K.** "Apropos of the Divorce Sayings." *IBS* 2 (1980) 40–51. **Cranfield, C. E. B.** "The Church and Divorce and the Re-Marriage of Divorced Persons in the Light of Mark 10.1–12." In *The Bible and Christian Life: A Collection of Essays.* Edinburgh: T. & T. Clark, 1985. 229–34. **Crossan, J. D.** *In Fragments.* 205–13. **D'Angelo, M. R.** "Remarriage and the Divorce Saying Attributed to Jesus." In *Divorce and Remarriage.* Ed. W. D. Roberts. Kansas City: Ward and Ward, 1990. 78–106. **Daube, D.** "Precept and Example: Divorce." In *The New Testament and Rabbinic Judaism.* London: Athlone, 1956. 71–86, esp. 71–79. **Delling, G.** "Das Logion Mk x.11 (und seine Abwandlungen) im Neuen Testament." *NovT* 1 (1956) 263–74. **Delorme, J.** "Le mariage, les enfants et les disciples de Jésus. Mc 10,2–16." *AsSeign* 2.58 (1974) 42–51. **Derrett, J. D. M.** "The Teaching of Jesus on Marriage and Divorce." In *Law in the New Testament.* London: Darton, Longman & Todd, 1970. 363–88. **Descamps, A.-L.** "Les textes évangeliques sur le mariage." *RTL* 9 (1978) 259–86; 11 (1980) 5–50 (ET: "The New Testament Doctrine on Marriage." In *Contemporary Perspectives on Christian Marriage.* Ed. R. Malone and J. R. Connery. Chicago: Loyola UP, 1984. 217–73, 347–63). **Down, M. J.** "The Sayings of Jesus about Marriage and Divorce." *ExpTim* 95 (1984) 332–34. **Dungan, D. L.** *The Sayings of Jesus in the Churches of Paul: The Use of the Synoptic Tradition in the Regulation of Early Church Life.* Oxford: Blackwell, 1971. 102–24. **Dupont, J.** *Mariage et divorce dans l'évangile: Matthieu 19,3–12 et parallèles.* Bruges: Abbaye de Saint-André; Desclée de Brouwer, 1959. 15–69. **Eckel, P. T.** "Mark 10:1–16." *Int* 42 (1988) 285–91. **Egger, W.** *Frohbotschaft und Lehre.* 143–56. **Ellingworth, P.** "Text and Context in Mark 10:2, 10." *JSNT* 5 (1979) 63–66. **Fitzmyer, J. A.** "Divorce among First-Century Palestinian Jews." In *H. L. Ginsberg Volume.* Ed. M. Haran. ErIsr 14. Jerusalem: Israel Exploration Society, 1978. 103–10, 193. ————. "The Matthean Divorce Texts and Some New Palestinian Evidence." *TS* 37 (1976) 197–226 (repr. in J. A. Fitzmyer. *To Advance the Gospel: New Testament Studies.* New York: Crossroad, 1981. 79–111). **Fleddermann, H. T.** *Mark and Q.* 171–74. **Friedrich, G.** *Sexualität und Ehe: Rückfragen an das Neue Testament.* Biblisches Forum 11. Stuttgart: Katholisches Bibelwerk, 1977. 125–34. **Garland, D. E.** "A Biblical View of Divorce." *RevExp* 84 (1987) 419–32. **Geiger, R.** "Die Stellung der geschiedenen Frau in der Umwelt des Neuen Testaments." In *Die Frau im Urchristentum.* Ed. G. Dautzenberg et al. QD 95. Freiburg: Herder, 1983. 134–57, esp. 149–57. **Green, B.** "Jesus' Teaching on Divorce in the Gospel of Mark." *JSNT* 38 (1990) 67–75 (repr. in *The Historical Jesus: A Sheffield Reader.* Ed. C. A. Evans and S. E. Porter. BibSem 33. Sheffield: Sheffield Academic Press, 1995. 148–56). **Greeven, H.** "Ehe nach dem Neuen Testament." *NTS* 15 (1968–69) 365–88, esp. 376–79. **Guelich, R. A.** *The Sermon on the Mount: A Foundation for Understanding.* Waco, TX: Word, 1982. 199–211. **Haacker, K.** "Ehescheidung und Wiederverheiratung im Neuen Testament." *TQ* 151 (1971) 28–38. **Harrington, W. J.** "Jesus' Attitude toward Divorce." *ITQ* 37 (1970) 199–209. ————. "The New Testament and Divorce." *ITQ* 39 (1972) 178–87. **Herron, R. W., Jr.** "Mark's Jesus on Divorce: Mark 10:1–12 Reconsidered." *JETS* 25 (1982) 273–81. **Hirsch, E.** *Betrachtungen zu Wort und Geschichte Jesu.* Berlin: de Gruyter, 1969. 137–46. **Hoehner, H. W.** *Herod Antipas.* SNTSMS 17. Cambridge: Cambridge UP, 1972.

317–30. **Hoffmann, P.** "Jesus' Saying about Divorce and Its Interpretation in the New Testament Tradition." *Concilium* 55 (1970) 51–66. **Hübner, H.** *Das Gesetz in der synoptischen Tradition: Studien zur These einer progressiven Qumranisierung und Judaisierung innerhalb der synoptischen Tradition.* Göttingen: Vandenhoeck & Ruprecht, 1986. 40–112. **Isaksson, A.** *Marriage and Ministry in the New Temple.* Lund: Gleerup, 1965. **Jensen, J.** "Does *Porneia* Mean Fornication? A Critique of Bruce Malina." *NovT* 20 (1978) 161–84. **Katz, P.** "Mark 10:11 Once Again." *BT* 11 (1960) 152. **Kloppenborg, J. S.** "Alms, Debt and Divorce: Jesus' Ethics in Their Mediterranean Context." *TJT* 6 (1990) 182–200. **Kuhn, H.-W.** *Ältere Sammlungen im Markusevangelium.* 160–68. **Laufen, R.** *Die Doppelüberlieferungen der Logienquelle und des Markusevangeliums.* BBB 54. Bonn: Hanstein, 1980. 347–48, 357–60. **Malina, B. J.** "Does *Porneia* Mean Fornication?" *NovT* 14 (1972) 10–17. **McCaughey, J. D.** "Marriage and Divorce: Some Reflections on the Relevant Passages in the New Testament." *Colloquium* 4 (1972) 24–39. **Mueller, J. R.** "The Temple Scroll and the Gospel Divorce Texts." *RevQ* 10 (1979–81) 247–56. **Nembach, U.** "Ehescheidung nach alttestamentlichem und jüdischem Recht." *TZ* 26 (1970) 161–71. **O'Rourke, J. J.** "Explicit Old Testament Citations in the Gospels." *Studia Montis Regii* 7 (1964) 37–60. **Pesch, R.** *Freie Treue: Die Christen und die Ehescheidung.* Freiburg: Herder, 1971. 22–32. ———. "Die neutestamentliche Weisung für die Ehe." *BibLeb* 9 (1968) 208–21. **Powers, B. W.** "Marriage and Divorce: The Dispute of Jesus with the Pharisees, and Its Inception." *Colloquium* 5 (1972) 34–41. **Reploh, K.-G.** *Markus—Lehrer der Gemeinde.* 173–85. **Ruckstuhl, E.** "Hat Jesus die Unauflösigkeit der Ehe gelehrt?" In *Jesus im Horizont der Evangelien.* SBA 3. Stuttgart: Katholisches Bibelwerk, 1988. 49–68. **Sariola, H.** *Markus und das Gesetz.* 121–49. **Schaller, B.** "'Commits Adultery with Her', not 'against Her', Mk 10:11." *ExpTim* 83 (1971–72) 107–8. ———. "Die Sprüche über Ehescheidung und Wiederheirat in der synoptischen Überlieferung." In *Der Ruf Jesu und die Antwort der Gemeinde.* FS J. Jeremias, ed. E. Lohse et al. Göttingen: Vandenhoeck & Ruprecht, 1970. 226–46. **Schmidt, K. L.** *Rahmen.* 238–41. **Schneider, G.** "Jesu Wort über die Ehescheidung in der Überlieferung des Neuen Testaments." *TTZ* 80 (1971) 65–87. **Schottroff, L.** "Frauen in der Nachfolge Jesu in neutestamentlicher Zeit." In *Frauen in der Bibel.* Vol. 2 of *Traditionen der Befreiung: Sozialgeschichtliche Bibelauslegungen.* Ed. W. Schottroff and W. Stegemann. Munich: Kaiser, 1980. 91–133. **Schubert, K.** "Ehescheidung im Judentum zur Zeit Jesu." *TQ* 151 (1971) 23–27. **Schweizer, E.** "Scheidungsrecht der jüdischen Frau? Weibliche Jünger Jesu?" *EvT* 42 (1982) 294–300. **Soulen, R. N.** "Marriage and Divorce: A Problem in New Testament Interpretation." *Int* 23 (1969) 439–50. **Stein, R. H.** "'Is It Lawful for a Man to Divorce His Wife?'" *JETS* 22 (1979) 115–21, esp. 116–18. **Stenger, W.** "Zur Rekonstruktion eines Jesusworts anhand der synoptischen Ehescheidungslogien." *Kairos* 26 (1984) 194–205. **Suhl, A.** *Die Funktion der alttestamentlichen Zitate.* 72–76. **Sweet, J. P. M.** "A Saying, a Parable, a Miracle." *Theology* 76 (1973) 125–33. **Torrey, C. C.** *Our Translated Gospels.* 12–14, 93–95. **Tosato, A.** "The Law of Leviticus 18:18: A Reexamination." *CBQ* 46 (1984) 199–214. **Trilling, W.** "Zum Thema: Ehe und Ehescheidung im Neuen Testament." *TGl* 74 (1984) 390–406. **Turner, N.** "The Translation of μοιχᾶται ἐπ' αὐτήν in Mark 10:11." *BT* 7 (1956) 151–52. **Vawter, B.** "Divorce and the New Testament." *CBQ* 39 (1977) 528–42, esp. 531–36. **Via, D. O., Jr.,** *Ethics of Mark's Gospel.* 101–27. **Vouga, F.** "Die Entwicklungsgeschichte der jesuanischen Chrien und didaktischen Dialoge des Markusevangeliums." In *Jesu Rede von Gott und ihre Nachgeschichte im frühen Christentum.* FS W. Marxsen, ed. D.-A. Koch et al. Gütersloh: Mohn, 1989. 45–56. ———. *Jésus et la loi selon la tradition synoptique.* Geneva: Labor et Fides, 1988. 89–100. **Weder, H.** "Perspektive der Frauen?" *EvT* 43 (1983) 175–78. **Weiss, W.** *"Eine neue Lehre in Vollmacht."* 177–202. **Wenham, G. J.** "Gospel Definitions of Adultery and Women's Rights." *ExpTim* 95 (1983–84) 330–32. **Zimmermann, H.** *Neutestamentliche Methodenlehre: Darstellung der historish-kritischen Methode.* 7th ed. Stuttgart: Katholisches Bibelwerk, 1982. 101–12. **Zmijewski, J.** "Neutestamentliche Weisungen für Ehe und Familie." *SNTU* 9 (1984) 31–78, esp. 34–46.

Translation

[1]*And arising from there, he goes* [a] *into the region of Judea, across from the Jordan, and again crowds gather to him; and as was his custom, he again began to teach them.* [2]*And Pharisees,* [b] *approaching to test him, were asking him if it is lawful for a man to divorce his wife.* [3]*But answering, he said to them, "What did Moses command you?"* [4]*And they said, "Moses permitted [a man]* [c] *to write a bill of divorce and to release [his wife]."* [d] [5]*But Jesus said* [e] *to them, "On account of your hardness of heart he wrote this commandment* [f] *for you.* [6]*But from the beginning of creation 'male and female he* [g] *made them';* [7]*on account of this 'a man* [h] *shall leave his father and mother [and shall be joined to his wife],* [i] [8]*and the two shall be one flesh.' So that they are no longer two but one flesh.* [9]*Therefore, what God has joined together let no man divide."*

[10]*And in the house the disciples* [j] *were again asking him about this.* [11]*And he says to them, "Whoever should divorce his wife and marry another woman commits adultery against her.* [12]*And if she, divorcing her husband, marry another man, she commits adultery."* [k]

Notes

[a]The Gk. represents another instance of the historic present (ἔρχεται), of which the Markan evangelist is fond. N, followed by several versions, puts it into the past tense (ἦλθεν, "went").

[b]Metzger (*TCGNT*[1], 103–4) wonders if the words καὶ προσελθόντες Φαρισαῖοι, "and Pharisees, approaching," represent a later intrusion, perhaps from Matt 19:3. He and A. Wikgren, however, were overruled by the UBSGNT[3c] committee, which chose to include the words. The words are also read in Nestle-Aland[27].

[c]"A man" is not in the text, but it is required by the sense.

[d]"His wife" is not in the text (although some later MSS insert αὐτήν, "her"), but it is required by the sense.

[e]A D N W Σ Φ and several later MSS read καὶ ἀποκριθεὶς ὁ Ἰησοῦς, "and answering, Jesus said."

[f]One late MS reads ἐπιστολήν, "epistle."

[g]A N Σ Φ and many late MSS read ἐποίησεν ὁ θεὸς αὐτούς, "God made them."

[h]W reads ἕκαστος, "each [man]."

[i]The bracketed material is read by D W and many later MSS. It is omitted by ℵ B and other authorities. Metzger (*TCGNT*[1], 104–5) suspects that it was added under the influence of Matt 19:5 (and Gen 2:24).

[j]A D N W Σ Φ and many later MSS read οἱ μαθηταὶ αὐτοῦ, "his disciples."

[k]W reverses the order of the subjects of vv 11b–12: ἐὰν ἀπολύσῃ γυνὴ τὸν ἄνδρα αὐτῆς καὶ γαμήσῃ ἄλλον μοιχᾶται· καὶ ἐὰν ἀνὴρ ἀπολύσῃ τὴν γυναῖκα μοιχᾶται, "if a woman should divorce her husband and marry another man, she commits adultery; and if a man should divorce his wife, he commits adultery."

Form/Structure/Setting

In Mark 10:1–12 Jesus has entered Judea and encounters Pharisees who ask him if it is lawful for a man to divorce his wife. The pericope is expanded in Matt 19:1–9, is abbreviated in Luke 16:18, and reappears in a different, perhaps independent form in Matt 5:31–32. The Markan form of the story consists of five parts: (1) the Pharisees' question about divorce (v 2), (2) Jesus' counterquestion (v 3), (3) the Pharisees' response (v 4), (4) Jesus' rebuttal (vv 5–9), and (5) Jesus' further explanation to his disciples (vv 10–12).

The tradition likely derives from a setting in the life of Jesus (*Sitz im Leben Jesu*), for the legal opinion that Jesus gives creates some difficulty for the early church. Twice the Matthean evangelist (or tradents before him) finds it necessary to qualify Jesus' absolute statement. According to Matt 19:9, "whoever divorces his wife, *except for unchastity,* and marries another, commits adultery"; and Matt 5:32, "every one who divorces his wife, *except on the ground of unchastity,* makes her an adulteress." The emphasized words are those that have been added to qualify Jesus' pronouncement (and bring it more in line with Jewish law, for many believed that unchastity *required* divorce). It is not probable that the early church would have created a difficult tradition, which it then would have had to qualify. For this reason (the "criterion of embarrassment" is invoked), it is likely authentic tradition.

Another factor argues for the authenticity of the tradition. Jesus' older associate John the Baptist had also spoken out against Herod Antipas's divorce and remarriage ("and we have no reason to think that Jesus differed from John" [Gundry, 543]). According to Mark 6:18, John had said to Herod: "It is not lawful for you to have your brother's wife." Josephus also refers to Herod's marriage to Herodias: "Herodias, taking it into her head to flout the way of our fathers, married Herod, her husband's brother by the same father, who was tetrarch of Galilee; to do this she parted from a living husband" (*Ant.* 18.5.4 §136). Guelich notes, "The Baptist charged Herod with an illegal marriage based on the law of forbidden marriages that specifically excluded marrying one's brother's wife (Lev 18:16; 20:21) except for the occasion of a levirate marriage to raise children to an older brother" (331). But Josephus's comment at the end, "to do this she parted from a living husband," suggests that the divorce itself, even apart from the additional offense of marrying the wife of one's brother, was a serious breach of religious law. Of course, in this part of his narrative, we do not know whether Josephus is assuming John's position on the matter or simply expressing his own opinion. It is probable that Josephus is piling up the offenses: not only had Herod Antipas married his sister-in-law, in itself a forbidden marriage, but he had also done so while her husband was still living.

Paul's similar teaching appears to be based on Jesus' pronouncement: "To the married I give charge, not I but the Lord, that the wife should not separate from her husband (but if she does, let her remain single or else be reconciled to her husband)—and that the husband should not divorce his wife" (1 Cor 7:10–11). Most important here is Paul's belief that this ruling derives from the Lord, that is, from Jesus, and not from apostolic opinion, whether his (as in 1 Cor 7:12) or someone else's. We therefore have here an important pre-Gospel attestation of this tradition as dominical.

Finally, the way Jesus sets one Scripture (actually two: Gen 1:27 and 2:24) against another (Deut 24:1–4) without resolving the tension is highly unusual, perhaps even unique (see Bultmann, *History,* 49–50). Accordingly, Bultmann appeals to the criterion of dissimilarity: "in Mark Jesus radically rejects divorce . . . in contrast to the Law and to the Rabbis" (Bultmann, *History,* 27). Moore concurs: "All this is quite foreign to Jewish law" (*Judaism,* 2:125 n. 1). To a degree this is true, but as we shall see in the *Comment* below, the radical rejection of divorce may not have been foreign to some Jews.

Comment

Neither Philo nor Josephus, nor any rabbinic authority, bans divorce and remarriage; yet the Markan Jesus does. For this reason, Dungan has argued that "Mark's version of the question is inconceivable in a Palestinian Pharisaic milieu . . ." (*Sayings*, 233). Dungan goes on to argue for Matthean priority, since the Markan version reflects, he believes, a non-Palestinian, non-Jewish setting. Qumran, however, does provide an important parallel to Jesus' thought. Expanding on Deut 17:17 ("he shall not multiply wives for himself, lest his heart turn away"), the Temple Scroll teaches "He is not to take another wife in addition to her; no, she alone will be with him as long as she lives. If she dies, then he may take himself another wife from his father's house, that is, his family" (11QTemple 57:17–19 [M. Wise, M. Abegg, and E. Cook, *The Dead Sea Scrolls: A New Translation* (San Francisco: HarperCollins, 1996) 485]). One might object to the relevance of this passage since it is referring to Israel's king. But another text shows that the Essenes evidently did apply this teaching universally: "They [Qumran's opponents] are caught in two traps: fornication, by taking two wives in their lifetimes although the principle of creation is 'male and female he created them' [Gen 1:27] and those who went into the ark 'went into the ark two by two' [Gen 7:9]. Concerning the Leader it is written 'he shall not multiply wives to himself' [Deut 17:17]; but David had not read the sealed book of the Law . . ." (CD 4:20–5:2 [Wise, Abegg, and Cook, *Dead Sea Scrolls*, 55]). It seems then that at Qumran very strict rules applied; divorce and remarriage were not permitted. (On this interpretation, see Fitzmyer, *TS* 37 [1976] 197–226.)

Not only does the halakic ruling of the scrolls agree with Jesus' pronouncement, but appeal to Genesis is common to both. The Pharisees' question was therefore (*pace* Dungan) very much a live option in Jewish Palestine of the early first century; it certainly is not "inconceivable in a Palestinian Pharisaic milieu." Accordingly, the Pharisees wonder whether Jesus allows for divorce, as do the rabbis, or forbids it, as do the Essenes. It is quite possible that the Pharisees' question may have been occasioned by Jesus' known association with John and the assumption that he held to his views, views that may very well have been the same as those held by the Essenes. Thus, the question may not have been so innocent; it may have been a question designed to draw Jesus out and show that his view was the same as John's and therefore just as politically dangerous as John's had been (Swete, 215: "to excite the anger of Antipas"; Taylor, 417: "compromising him in the eyes of Herod"). If their question had an ulterior motive of this sort lying behind it, this could explain why the story appears where it does in that part of Mark where Jesus and his opponents engage in an escalating polemic. (Most commentators, e.g., Best, *Following Jesus*, 101, assume that the pericope had relevance for Mark's Greco-Roman audience but have difficulty explaining why it appears at this point in the Gospel.)

1 καὶ ἐκεῖθεν ἀναστὰς ἔρχεται εἰς τὰ ὅρια τῆς Ἰουδαίας [καὶ] πέραν τοῦ Ἰορδάνου, καὶ συμπορεύονται πάλιν ὄχλοι πρὸς αὐτόν, καὶ ὡς εἰώθει πάλιν ἐδίδασκεν αὐτούς, "And arising from there, he goes into the region of Judea, across from the Jordan; and again crowds gather to him; and as was his custom, he again began to teach them." The whole of this verse comes from the evangelist's pen. Characteristic vocabulary includes καὶ ἐκεῖθεν, "and from there" (6:1; 9:30),

ἀναστάς, "arising" (1:35), ἔρχεται, "he goes" (1:40; 2:3; 3:20), and εἰς τὰ ὅρια, "into the region" (5:17; 7:31). Much of this vocabulary occurs in 7:24, another Markan editorial "seam." In contrast to this opening verse, there is little evidence of Markan editing in vv 2–9. In v 1, ἐκεῖθεν, "from there," refers to the house in Capernaum (9:33) where Jesus had been teaching; ἀναστάς, "arising," presupposes Jesus' having taken a seat in 9:35. Thus, the evangelist brings to an end the teaching section found in 9:35–50 and at the same time prepares for the discussion on divorce that follows. "He began to teach" understands the imperfect verb ἐδίδασκεν (lit. "he was teaching") as inceptive.

2 καὶ προσελθόντες Φαρισαῖοι ἐπηρώτων αὐτὸν εἰ ἔξεστιν ἀνδρὶ γυναῖκα ἀπολῦσαι, πειράζοντες αὐτόν, "And Pharisees, approaching to test him, were asking him if it is lawful for a man to divorce his wife." There is some textual doubt as to the identity of those who test Jesus with the question about divorce. καὶ προσελθόντες Φαρισαῖοι, "and Pharisees, approaching," is not read in some MSS (see *Note* b above). Even if the reading is rejected, Jesus still has the question put to him in order πειράζοντες, "to test him" (the participle is purposive). As suggested above, the question of divorce had become a politically hot topic. Not only did Herodias desert and (presumably) divorce her husband (probably through the Roman courts), but Herod Antipas divorced his wife, the daughter of Aretas the king of the Nabateans, in order to marry Herodias. (Josephus tells us that when the daughter of Aretas caught wind of Herod's plan, she fled to her father.) This marital affair created a political crisis, which finally resulted in war between Galilee and the Nabatea. Had it not been for Roman intervention, Antipas likely would have lost his kingdom. In such a dangerous situation as this, it is understandable why the Galilean tetrach could not tolerate John's criticism and his popularity with the masses. Ultimately John's criticism of Herod Antipas's divorce and remarriage cost the baptizer his life.

The question put to Jesus, a one-time associate of John's, had the potential of being just as dangerous. There is some evidence that Jesus had made critical comments about Herod. Jesus explicitly refers to Herod Antipas ("that fox!"), who we are told in Luke 13:31–32 wants to kill Jesus and who fears that Jesus might actually be John raised from the dead (Mark 6:16). Jesus' reference to a "reed shaken by the wind" and "a man clothed in soft raiment" (Matt 11:7–8 = Luke 7:24–25) may have been in reference to Herod Antipas in contrast to John the prophet (Matt 11:9 = Luke 7:26). It is also possible that the "certain nobleman" in the parable of the Pounds (Luke 19:11–27) was originally a thinly veiled allusion to either Herod Antipas or to his brother Herod Archelaus (and not to Jesus himself). In the parable this figure is thieving and murderous.

ἔξεστιν, "it is lawful," is conventional in the Gospels (Mark 2:24, 26; 3:4; 6:18; 12:14 and parallels; John 5:10; 18:31), but relatively rare in the LXX. In fact, there is only one example that corresponds: "it is not lawful for us [LXX: οὐκ ἔξεστιν ἡμῖν; MT: לָא אֲרִיךְ לָנָא *lāʾ ʾărîk lanāʾ*] to behold the shame of the king" (Ezra 4:14; cf. LXX Esth 8:12g [= Add Esth 16:7]). But this example is inexact since a legal matter as such is not the subject of discussion. There are some useful parallels in Josephus (e.g., *Ant.* 3.10.5 §251: "it is lawful for all to begin harvest"; 13.8.4 §252: "it is not lawful for us to march on the Sabbath"; 20.9.1 §202). The last example is significant, though the participial form with the imperfect of εἶναι, "to be," is used: "It was not lawful for Ananus [οὐκ ἐξὸν ἦν Ἀνάνῳ] to convene the Sanhedrin without his [i.e., the governor's] consent" (on the grammatical form, see Matt 12:4). There are also some useful examples in Philo (e.g., *Posterity* 179: "a prayer that is not lawful for one of the foolish to make"; *Planting* 64: "for whom is it lawful to say, 'God is mine alone'?"; *Joseph* 43: "for us it is not lawful for a harlot even to live"; *Moses* 2.24: "in our fast it is not lawful for men to put a drink to their lips"). The idiom is not distinctly Jewish, for it appears in non-Jewish papyri (e.g., P.Mich. 507.7–8: "for it is not lawful for a woman, without an advocate, to speak before a judge"; P.Oxy. 275.22: "it not being permitted to Tryphon"; P.Oxy. 3015.4: "it is not lawful to alter a contract"; P.Ryl. 77.43: "but this was not lawful"; MM 223).

3 τί ὑμῖν ἐνετείλατο Μωϋσῆς; "What did Moses command you?" For the Jewish people, at least for those who were Torah observant, appeal to the commandments of Moses was an appeal to the highest authority on any question. In the Torah it is usually the LORD who commands (ἐντέλλεσθαι) Moses and Aaron (e.g., Exod 4:28; 7:6, 10, 20; 12:28 passim), though on occasion Moses does the commanding: "And they brought what Moses commanded before the tent of meeting" (Lev 9:5); "Moses commanded the people of Israel" (Num 34:13; cf. 32:25; 36:5); "Keep all the commandment which I command you this day" (Deut 27:1; cf. 27:11; 31:10; 33:4; note the discrepancy in Deut 31:23, where in the Hebrew it is the LORD who commands Joshua, but in the LXX it is Moses). Jesus begins his reply to the Phariseees by asking for their scriptural basis and possibly their interpretive stance. Knowing this, he can frame his own answer.

4 ἐπέτρεψεν Μωϋσῆς βιβλίον ἀποστασίου γράψαι καὶ ἀπολῦσαι, "Moses permitted *a man* to write a bill of divorce and to release *his wife*." The Pharisees summarize Deut 24:1–4:

> When a man takes a wife and marries her, if then she finds no favor in his eyes because he has found some indecency in her, and he writes her a bill of divorce and puts it in her hand and sends her out of his house, and she departs out of his house, and if she goes and becomes another man's wife, and the latter husband dislikes her and writes her a bill of divorce and puts it in her hand and sends her out of his house, or if the latter husband dies, who took her to be his wife, then her former husband, who sent her away, may not take her again to be his wife, after she has been defiled; for that is an abomination before the LORD, and you shall not bring guilt upon the land which the LORD your God gives you for an inheritance.

On the basis of this passage divorce is clearly permitted, but on what grounds? Or, if the Pharisees suspected that Jesus, like the Essenes and possibly like John, did not permit divorce at all, on what basis could he set aside what Moses had commanded?

The rabbis discussed the meaning of "some indecency [MT: עֶרְוַת דָּבָר *'erwat dābār;* LXX: ἄσχημον πρᾶγμα] in her" (Deut 24:1) and "dislikes her [lit. "hates her"; MT: שְׂנֵאָהּ *śĕnēʾāh;* LXX: μισήσῃ αὐτήν]" (24:3). The language is ambiguous. Adultery was not originally in view, for that is treated elsewhere, and in great antiquity it was treated as a capital offense (Lev 20:10: "If a man commits adultery with the wife of his neighbor, both the adulterer and the adulteress shall be put to death"; cf. Deut 22:13–27). The School of Shammai interpreted עֶרְוַת דָּבָר *'erwat dābār,* conservatively, as unchastity, while the School of Hillel interpreted the words much more elastically: "The House of Hillel says (that a man may divorce his wife) even if she has merely ruined his dinner. . . . Rabbi Aqiba says,

(He may divorce her) even if he finds another woman more beautiful than she is, as it says, 'If she finds no favor in his eyes'" (*m. Giṭ.* 9:10; cf. gemara on this passage in *b. Giṭ.* 90a–b).

5 πρὸς τὴν σκληροκαρδίαν ὑμῶν ἔγραψεν ὑμῖν τὴν ἐντολὴν ταύτην, "On account of your hardness of heart he wrote this commandment for you." Jesus sidesteps these options and instead challenges the hermeneutical assumption that because something is "permitted" it is therefore according to the will of God. Indeed, according to Mal 2:16, God "hates" divorce. Even the rabbis admitted that Heaven shed a tear every time a marriage ended in divorce (*b. Giṭ.* 90b). Jesus argues that Moses permitted divorce "on account of your hardness of heart." The idea of hard-heartedness (σκληροκαρδία) immediately brings to mind biblical language from Deuteronomy (10:16) and the prophets (Jer 4:4; Ezek 3:7). In itself this word would be perceived as a stinging rebuke, again casting Jesus in the role of a prophet. God permits divorce, not because it is his perfect will but because of human sinfulness. The purpose of the Mosaic law was to check divorce (and protect the relatively defenseless woman), not to encourage it. The religious authorities had never considered this option.

6–8 Jesus justifies his unqualified opposition to divorce and his unique interpretation of Deut 24:1–4 by an appeal to Genesis: ἀπὸ δὲ ἀρχῆς κτίσεως, "but from the beginning of creation." He refers to an implied law that is grounded in the very creation itself (cf. Mark 13:19), indeed, the very creation of man and woman. Jesus appeals to two specific texts: Gen 1:27 ("male and female he made them") in v 6 and Gen 2:24 ("a man shall leave his father and mother and the two shall be one flesh") in v 7. If the intention of the creation of the male and female is for them to be united into μία σάρξ, "one flesh," ὥστε οὐκέτι εἰσὶν δύο, "so that they are no longer two," then God's will simply cannot be that they divorce. Divorce is tantamount to an undoing of the created order. Moses' regulations, given to a stubborn and hard-hearted people, must be interpreted in this light. Jesus' argument, of course, assumes that Genesis is just as much a book of the Law as is Deuteronomy. (Paul's appeal in Galatians and Romans to Genesis to defend the idea of a covenant promise over against the Sinai covenant is in a general sense similar.)

According to Torrey (*Our Translated Gospels*, 12, 14), the Greek reading "from the beginning of creation . . ." is a misreading of the Aramaic, which originally read "in the beginning the Creator made them male and female." This is possible; however, Mark's text makes perfectly good sense as it stands.

9 Jesus' interpretation of Genesis leads him to declare that the marriage union is indissoluble: ὃ οὖν ὁ θεὸς συνέζευξεν ἄνθρωπος μὴ χωριζέτω, "what God has joined together let no man divide." The contrast between God, who creates, and human beings, who are created, should be noted (Gundry, 531). Who is *a human being* to take apart what *God* himself has put together? Divorce, then, no matter how nuanced its defense or how cleverly justified, violates God's design for human marriage. The idea of the divine as involved in some way in marriage is attested in the pagan world, as seen when the goddess Isis says: "I have brought woman and man together" (*SIG* 2:1267).

10 καὶ εἰς τὴν οἰκίαν πάλιν οἱ μαθηταὶ περὶ τούτου ἐπηρώτων αὐτόν, "And in the house the disciples were again asking him about this." V 10 is another Markan addition, though this does not mean that vv 11–12 were not part of the original story (Best, *Following Jesus*, 100). εἰς τὴν οἰκίαν, "in the house," is Markan (cf.

1:29; 3:20; 7:17, 24; 9:28). The disciples (μαθηταί) asking (ἐπηρώτων) Jesus for private instruction is typically Markan (4:10; 7:17; 9:11, 28; 13:3; sometimes when they are together in a house, Jesus asks his disciples something; cf. 9:33). The interruption here allows for Jesus to retire with his disciples and elaborate on his teaching.

11 If divorce is really not God's will but in fact stands in tension with creation itself, then in what does it result? It results in adultery: ὃς ἂν ἀπολύσῃ τὴν γυναῖκα αὐτοῦ καὶ γαμήσῃ ἄλλην μοιχᾶται ἐπ᾽ αὐτήν, "Whoever should divorce his wife and marry another woman commits adultery against her." He commits adultery ἐπ᾽ αὐτήν, "against her," in that having moved on to another woman, he is in fact still married to his first wife. He has violated one of the Ten Commandments: "You shall not commit adultery" (Exod 20:14 = Deut 5:18). Although Jesus does not refer to "traditions of men" here as he does in 7:8, the argument is similar. Having probed every loophole to accommodate what are in actuality lustful impulses, the man who divorces his wife has nullified the "commandments of God." What is said against men initiating divorce is in the next verse said against women who do the same.

12 At first blush the last part of the pronouncement against divorce, καὶ ἐὰν αὐτὴ ἀπολύσασα τὸν ἄνδρα αὐτῆς γαμήσῃ ἄλλον μοιχᾶται, "And if she, divorcing her husband, marry another man, she commits adultery," seems to fly in the face of Jewish law. A Jewish woman could not divorce her husband (Josephus, *Ant.* 15.7.10 §§259–60; 18.9.6 §§353–62; *m. Yebam.* 14:1; Abrahams, *Studies,* 1:66–72). In an oft-cited passage, Josephus sums up Jewish law and practice pertaining to divorce in reference to Salome's divorce of Costobarus: "Some time afterwards Salome had occasion to quarrel with Costobarus and soon sent him a document dissolving their marriage [ἀπολυομένη τὸν γάμον], which was not in accordance with Jewish law. For with us, it is lawful (only) for the man [ἀνδρὶ . . . ἔξεστι] to do this, and not even a divorced woman may marry again on her own initiative unless her former husband consents. Salome, however, did not choose to follow her country's law but acted on her own authority and repudiated her marriage" (*Ant.* 15.7.10 §§259–60). This makes Torrey's emendation (*Our Translated Gospels,* 93–95), "she who is divorced by her husband," for Mark's "she, divorcing her husband," unnecessary.

This understanding of Jewish law is essentially correct, but women could sue their husbands on certain grounds and force them to give them divorces (among other passages, see *m. Ketub.* 7:10: "She may say, 'Your brother I could endure; but you I cannot endure'"; the man is then compelled to give her a divorce; cf. Moore, *Judaism,* 2:125). Nevertheless, many commentators have suggested that Jesus' pronouncement against a woman divorcing her husband reflects the tradition's encounter with the Greco-Roman world where a woman could divorce her husband (e.g., Schmid, 187: v 12 was created "by the evangelist, who has in mind the gentile-Christians of Rome"; Best, *Following Jesus,* 101: "this was necessary for the Roman church in whose area wives could divorce their husbands"). Perhaps so, but Herodias's infamous desertion of her husband so that she might marry Herod Antipas provides sufficient historical backdrop to this saying (as well as Salome's earlier desertion of her husband) and may have even been the occasion for it (as suggested in the section above). Abrahams (*Studies,* 1:66) comments that Mark 10:12 "may be directed against such licentiousness" (so also

Burkitt, *Gospel History*, 98–101). He is probably correct. Moreover, Jewish Palestine itself, long before Jesus, had encountered the Greco-Roman world. Indeed, Papyrus Ṣe'elim 13 offers additional evidence that a Jewish woman could divorce her husband in late antiquity (see Brewer, *HTR* 92 [1999] 349–57). There is therefore no reason to deny the saying to Jesus. The pronouncement thus is not a comment on Jewish law, which makes no provision for a woman to divorce her husband; it is instead a comment on a recent scandal, a scandal that eventuated in John's arrest and subsequent execution. This is a point that Jesus could hardly have forgotten. Remember too that this pronouncement is part of Jesus' private teaching to his disciples; it is not part of his public dispute with the Pharisees.

Explanation

Jesus finds himself confronted with a potentially dangerous question. His reply is unequivocal: divorce and remarriage are never right in God's sight. Why did Jesus hold to such a strict view when in other areas of the Law he was so lenient, even permissive? Fitzmyer ("The Matthean Divorce Texts," 101–2) makes two very plausible suggestions. The first one (Fitzmyer here follows the lead of Isaksson, *Marriage and Ministry*, 147) draws attention to Jesus' very high standards for his followers: "Jesus taught his disciples they were chosen for and consecrated to the service of God." Fitzmyer points out that this idea is consistent with teaching elsewhere in the NT where Christians are taught to think of themselves as a spiritual temple (2 Cor 6:14–7:1; 1 Cor 3:16–17; Eph 2:18–22), an idea that may have some important parallels at Qumran (Fitzmyer draws our attention to B. Gärtner, *The Temple and the Community in Qumran and the New Testament: A Comparative Study in the Temple Symbolism of the Qumran Texts and the New Testament*, SNTSMS 1 [Cambridge: Cambridge UP, 1963]).

The second suggestion raises the possibility of the influence of royal ideas. Just as the laymen at Qumran applied the marital laws of the king (Deut 17:17) to themselves (as in 11QTemple 57:17–19 and CD 4:20–21), so Christian tradition applied priestly and royal language to Christians. Fitzmyer cites 1 Pet 2:5, 9: "Like living stones be yourselves built into a spiritual house, to be a holy priesthood.... You are a chosen race, a royal priesthood, a holy nation, God's own people ..." (Fitzmyer draws attention to J. H. Elliott, *The Elect and the Holy: An Exegetical Examination of I Peter 2:4–10 and the Phrase basileion hierateuma*, NovTSup 12 [Leiden: Brill, 1966]).

It is not necessary to decide between these two options, for the various images were easily juxtaposed by ancient writers, as can be seen in the citation from 1 Peter. Jesus' ban on divorce is consistent with his sense of mission and the rigorous demands that it placed on himself and his followers. Jesus' expectations were so high that he could say with respect to his mentor John: "Truly, I say to you, among those born of women there has risen no one greater than John the Baptist; yet he who is least in the kingdom of heaven is greater than he" (Matt 11:11 = Luke 7:28). The truly astonishing nature of this statement is not often recognized. No one born of a woman has ever been greater than John, yet the least in the kingdom is greater than he. These great ones in the kingdom must eschew divorce and the numerous temptations and entanglements that the world has to offer.

B. Entry into the Kingdom (10:13–31)

Bibliography

Abrahams, I. *Studies in Pharisaism and the Gospels.* 1:66–78, 118–20; 2:186–87, 208. **Aland, K.** *Did the Early Church Baptize Infants?* Philadelphia: Westminster, 1963. 95–99. **Ambrozic, A.** *The Hidden Kingdom.* 136–71. **Banks, R. J.** *Jesus and the Law in the Synoptic Tradition.* SNTSMS 28. Cambridge: Cambridge UP, 1975. 159–64. **Baumann, R.** "Der Raum der Freiheit: Zum Wandel vom Bedingungen der Nachfolge." In *Wort Gottes in der Zeit.* FS K. H. Schelkle, ed. H. Feld and J. Nolte. Düsseldorf: Patmos, 1973. 436–50. **Beardslee, W. A.** "Uses of the Proverb in the Synoptic Gospels." *Int* 24 (1970) 61–73. **Beasley-Murray, G. R.** *Baptism in the New Testament.* London: Macmillan, 1962. 320–29. **Berger, K.** *Die Gesetzesauslegung Jesu: Ihr historischer Hintergrund im Judentum und im Alten Testament.* WMANT 40. Neukirchen-Vluyn: Neukirchener Verlag, 1972. 396–460. **Best, E.** "The Camel and the Needle's Eye (Mk 10:25)." *ExpTim* 82 (1970–71) 83–89 (repr. in *Disciples and Discipleship,* 17–30). ———. *Following Jesus.* 106–19. ———. "Mark 10:13–16: The Child as a Model Recipient." In *Biblical Studies.* FS W. Barclay, ed. J. R. McKay and J. F. Miller. London: Collins, 1976. 119–34 (repr. in *Disciples and Discipleship,* 80–97). **Brown, R. N.** "Jesus and the Child as a Model of Spirituality." *IBS* 4 (1982) 178–92. **Busemann, R.** *Die Jüngergemeinde nach Markus 10: Eine redaktionsgeschichtliche Untersuchung des 10. Kapitels im Markusevangelium.* BBB 57. Königstein; Bonn: Hanstein, 1983. 39–102, 119–28. **Cranfield, C. E. B.** "Riches and the Kingdom of God: St. Mark 10.17–31." *SJT* 4 (1951) 302–13. **Crossan, J. D.** *In Fragments.* 108–11, 315–19. ———. "Kingdom and Children: A Study in the Aphoristic Tradition." *Semeia* 29 (1983) 75–95. **Cullmann, O.** *Baptism in the New Testament.* SBT 1. London: SCM Press, 1950. 76–80. **Dalman, G. H.** *The Words of Jesus.* Edinburgh: T. & T. Clark. 1902. 276–80. **Degenhardt, J. J.** "Was muss ich tun, um das ewige Leben zu gewinnen? Zu Mk 10,17–22." In *Biblische Randbemerkungen.* FS R. Schnackenburg, ed. H. Merklein and J. Lange. Würzburg: Echter, 1974. 159–68. **Derrett, J. D. M.** "A Camel through the Eye of a Needle." *NTS* 32 (1986) 465–70. ———. "Why Jesus Blessed the Children (Mk 10:13–16 par.)." *NovT* 25 (1983) 1–18. **Diebner, B.,** and **Diebner, B.** "Beispiele zur Bildgeschichte des sogenannten 'Kinder-Evangeliums': Markus 10,13–16." In *Die Kinder im Evangelium.* Ed. G. Krause. Praktische Schriftauslegung 10. Stuttgart; Göttingen: Klotz, 1973. 52–78. **Egger, W.** *Nachfolge als Weg zum Leben: Chancen neuerer exegetischer Methoden dargelegt an Mk 10,17–31.* ÖBS 1. Klosterneuberg: Österreichisches Katholisches Bibelwerk, 1979. ———. "Nachfolge Jesu und Verzicht auf Besitz: Mk 10,17–31 aus der Sicht der neuesten exegetischen Methoden." *TPQ* 128 (1980) 127–36. **Fleddermann, H. T.** *Mark and Q.* 174–77. **Fuchs, E.** *Jesus: Wort und Tat.* Tübingen: Mohr-Siebeck, 1971. 10–19. **Fuller, R. H.** "The Decalogue in the New Testament." *Int* 43 (1989) 243–55. **Gundry, R. H.** "Mark 10:29: Order in the List." *CBQ* 59 (1997) 465–75. **Hahn, F.** "Kindersegnung und Kindertaufe im ältesten Christentum." In *Vom Urchristentum zu Jesus.* FS J. Gnilka, ed. H. Frankemölle and K. Kertelge. Freiburg: Herder, 1989. 497–507, esp. 499–502. **Harnisch, W.** "Die Berufung des Reichen: Zur Analysen von Markus 10,17–31." In *Festschrift für Ernst Fuchs.* Ed. G. Ebeling et al. Tübingen: Mohr-Siebeck, 1973. 161–76. **Hommel, H.** "Herrenworte im Lichte sokratischer Überlieferung." *ZNW* 57 (1966) 1–23. **Iersel, B. M. F. van.** "Failed Followers in Mark: Mark 13:12 as a Key for the Identification of the Intended Readers." *CBQ* 58 (1996) 244–63, esp. 253–54. **Jeremias, J.** *Infant Baptism in the First Four Centuries.* London: SCM Press, 1960. 48–55. **Klein, G.** "Bibelarbeit über Markus 10,13–16." In *Die Kinder im Evangelium.* Ed. G. Krause. Praktische Schriftauslegung 10. Stuttgart; Göttingen: Klotz, 1973. 12–30. ———. "Jesus und die Kinder: Bibelarbeit über Markus 10,13–16." In *Ärgernisse: Konfrontationen mit dem Neuen Testament.* Munich: Kaiser, 1970. 58–81. **Köbert, R.** "Kamel und Schiffstau: Zu Markus 10,25 (Par.) und Koran 7,40/38." *Bib* 53 (1972) 229–33. **Koch, K.** "Der Schatz im Himmel." In *Leben angesichts des Todes.* Ed. B. Lohse and H. P. Schmidt. Tübingen: Mohr-Siebeck, 1968. 47–60. **Krause, G.** "Jesus der Kinderfreund: Reflexionen und Meditationen zum heutigen Verständnis." In *Die Kinder im Evangelium.* Ed. G. Krause. Praktische Schriftauslegung 10. Stuttgart; Göttingen: Klotz, 1973. 79–112, esp. 95–109. **Kuhn, H.-W.** *Ältere Sammlungen im Markusevangelium.* 146–51. ———. "Nachfolge nach Ostern." In *Kirche.* FS G. Bornkamm, ed. D. Lührmann and G. Strecker. Tübingen: Mohr-Siebeck, 1980. 105–32. **Lang, F. G.** "*Sola gratia* im Markusevangelium: Die Soteriologie des Markus nach 9,14–29 und 10,17–31." In *Rechtfertigung.* FS E. Käsemann, ed. J. Friedrich et al. Tübingen: Mohr-Siebeck; Göttingen: Vandenhoeck & Ruprecht, 1976. 321–38. **Légasse, S.** *L'appel du riche (Marc 10,17–31 et parallèles): Contribution à l'étude des fondements scripturaires de l'état religieux.* Paris: Beauchesne, 1966. 19–96. ———. "Jésus a-t-il annoncé la conversion finale d'Israël? (À propos de Marc x.23–7)." *NTS* 10 (1963–64) 480–87. ———. *Jésus et l'enfant: "Enfants," "petits" et "simples" dans la tradition synoptique.* EBib. Paris: Gabalda, 1969. 37–40, 187–95, 210–14. **Lindemann, A.** "Die Kinder und die Gottesherrschaft: Markus 10,13–16 und die Stellung der Kinder in der späthellenistischen Gesellschaft und im Urchristentum." *WD* 17 (1983) 77–104. **Lohse, E.** "Jesu Bussruf an die Reichen: Markus 10,25 Par." In *Glaube und Eschatologie.* FS W. G. Kümmel, ed. E. Grässer and O. Merk. Tübingen: Mohr-Siebeck, 1985. 159–63. **Malone, D.** "Riches and Discipleship: Mark 10,23–31." *BTB* 9 (1979) 78–88. **Minear, P. S.** *Commands of Christ.* Edinburgh: St. Andrews; Nashville and New York: Abingdon, 1972. 98–112. **Minette de Tillesse, G.** *Le secret messianique.* 149–52, 261–63. **Neuhäusler, E.** *Anspruch und Antwort Gottes: Zur Lehre von den Weisungen innerhalb der synoptischen Jesusverkündigung.* Düsseldorf: Patmos, 1962. 173–85. **Patte, D.** "Entering the Kingdom like Children: A Structural Analysis." In *Society of Biblical Literature 1982 Seminar Papers.* Ed. K. Richards. SBLSP 21. Chico, CA: Scholars Press, 1982. 371–96. ———. "Jesus' Pronouncement about Entering the Kingdom like a Child: A Structural Exegesis." *Semeia* 29 (1983) 3–42. **Perrot, C.** "La lecture d'un texte évangélique: Essai méthodologique à partir de Mc x,13–16." In *Recherches actuelles II.* Ed. H. Bouillard et al. Le point théologique 2. Paris: Beauchesne, 1972. 51–130. **Reploh, K. G.** *Markus—Lehrer der Gemeinde.* 186–210. **Ringehausen, G.** "Die Kinder der Weisheit: Zur Auslegung von Mk 10:13–16 par." *ZNW* 77 (1986) 33–63. **Robbins, V. K.** "Pronouncement Stories and Jesus' Blessing of the Children: A Rhetorical Approach." *Semeia* 29 (1983) 43–74. **Sanders, E. P.** "Mark 10.17–31 and Parallels." In *Society of Biblical Literature Seminar Papers.* Ed. J. L. White et al. 2 vols. SBLSP 10. Missoula, MT: Society of Biblical Literature, 1971. 1:257–70. ———. "Priorités et dépendancies dans la tradition synoptique." *RSR* 60 (1972) 519–40, esp. 520–30. **Sariola, H.** *Markus und das Gesetz.* 153–82. **Satake, A.** "Das Leiden der Jünger 'um meinetwillen.'" *ZNW* 67 (1976) 4–19. **Sauer, J.** "Der ursprüngliche 'Sitz im Leben' von Mk 10 13–16." *ZNW* 72 (1981) 27–50. **Schilling, F. A.** "What Means the Saying about Receiving the Kingdom of God as a Little Child (τὴν βασιλείαν τοῦ θεοῦ ὡς παιδίον)? Mk x. 15; Lk xviii. 17." *ExpTim* 77 (1965–66) 56–58. **Schlosser, J.** *Le règne de Dieu dans les dits de Jésus.* 2:477–507, 541–69. **Schmidt, K. L.** *Rahmen.* 241–44. **Schmidt, T. E.** "Mark 10.29–30; Matthew 19.29: 'Leave Houses . . . and Region'?" *NTS* 38 (1992) 617–20. **Schroeder, H.-H.** *Eltern und Kinder in der Verkündigung Jesu: Eine hermeneutische und exegetische Untersuchung.* TF 53. Hamburg: Reich, 1972. 125–32. **Söding, T.** *Glaube bei Markus.* 175–78, 204–9. **Stegemann, W.** "Lasset die Kinder zu mir kommen: Sozialgeschichtliche Aspekte des Kinderevangeliums." In *Methodische Zugänge.* Vol. 1 of *Traditionen der Befreiung: Sozialgeschichtliche Bibelauslegungen.* Ed. W. Schottroff and W. Stegemann. Munich: Kaiser, 1980. 114–44. **Stonehouse, N. B.** *Origins of the Synoptic Gospels: Some Basic Questions.* Grand Rapids, MI: Eerdmans, 1963; London: Tyndale, 1964. 93–112. **Suhl, A.** *Die Funktion der alttestamentlichen Zitate.* 77–78. **Tannehill, R. C.** *The Sword of His Mouth.* SBLSS 1. Missoula, MT: Scholars Press; Philadelphia: Fortress, 1975. 147–52. **Theissen, G.** "'Wir haben alles verlassen' (Mc. x 28): Nachfolge und soziale Entwurzelung in der jüdisch-palästinischen Gesellschaft des 1. Jahrhunderts

n. Ch." *NovT* 19 (1977) 161–96. **Venetz, H.-J.** "Theologische Grundstrukturen in der Verkündigung Jesu? Ein Vergleich von Mk 10,17–22; Lk 10,25–37 und Mt 5,21–48." In *Mélanges Dominique Barthélemy: Études bibliques offertes à l'occasion de son 60ᵉ anniversaire.* Ed. P. Casetti et al. OBO 38. Freiburg: Éditions Universitaires; Göttingen: Vandenhoeck & Ruprecht, 1981. 613–50. **Via, D. O., Jr.** *The Ethics of Mark's Gospel.* 134–55. **Vouga, F.** *Jésus et la loi selon la tradition synoptique.* Geneva: Labor et Fides, 1988. 107–20. **Walter, N.** "Zur Analyse von Mc 10,17–31." *ZNW* 53 (1962) 206–18. **Wenham, J. W.** "Why Do You Ask Me about the Good? A Study of the Relation between Text and Source Criticism." *NTS* 28 (1982) 116–25. **Westcott, B. F.,** and **Hort, F. J. A.** *Introduction.* 2:25–26. **Williams, J. F.** *Other Followers of Jesus.* 143–48. **Zager, W.** *Gottesherrschaft und Endgericht in der Verkündigung Jesu: Eine Untersuchung zur markinischen Jesusüberlieferung einschliesslich der Q-Parallelen.* BZNW 82. Berlin; New York: de Gruyter, 1996. **Zimmerli, W.** "Die Frage des Reichen nach dem ewigen Leben." *EvT* 19 (1959) 90–97.

Translation

[13]*And they were bringing to him children that he might touch them, but his disciples rebuked them.*[a] [14]*But Jesus, having observed this, was indignant and*[b] *said to them, "Permit the children to come to me. Do not forbid them; for of such ones is the kingdom of God.*[c] [15]*Truly*[d] *I say to you, whoever should not receive the kingdom of God as a child will not enter it."* [16]*And taking them into his arms, he blessed them, laying his hands on them.*[e]

[17]*And when he had gone out onto the road, one,*[f] *running up and kneeling before him, asked him, "Good teacher, what must I do that I may inherit eternal life?"* [18]*But Jesus said to him, "Why do you call me 'good'? No one is good, except one—God.*[g] [19]*You know the commandments: 'Do not commit murder; do not commit adultery;*[h] *do not steal; do not bear false witness; do not defraud;*[i] *honor your father and mother.'"* [20]*But he said to him, "Teacher, I have observed all these things since my youth."* [21]*But Jesus, looking upon him, loved him and said to him,* [j]*"You lack one thing—go, sell what you have and give to the poor, and you will have treasure in heaven; and come, follow me."*[k] [22]*But he, his face falling at this word, went away*[l] *grieving; for he had many possessions.*[m]

[23]*And looking around, Jesus says to his disciples, "How difficult will it be for those who have wealth to enter the kingdom of God!"*[n] [24]*But his disciples were marveling at his words. But Jesus, again answering, says to them, "Children, how difficult it is*[o] *to enter the kingdom of God!* [25][p]*It is easier for a camel*[q] *to pass through the eye*[r] *of a needle than for someone who is rich to enter the kingdom of God."* [26]*But they were greatly astonished, saying to themselves,*[s] *"Then who can be saved?"*[t] [27]*Looking at them, Jesus says, "With humans it is impossible, but not with God;*[u] *for all things are possible*[v] *with God."*

[28]*Peter*[w] *began to speak to him, "Behold, we left everything and have followed you."*[x] [29]*Jesus said, "Truly I say to you, there is no one who left house or brothers or sisters or mother or father*[y] *or children or fields for my sake and*[z] *for the sake of the gospel*[aa] [30]*who should not receive*[bb] *one hundredfold now in this time houses and brothers and sisters and mothers and children and fields, with persecutions,*[cc] *and in the coming age eternal life.* [31]*But many that are first will be last, and the last will be first."*[dd]

Notes

[a]To avoid the potential misunderstanding that the disciples had rebuked the children themselves, A D N W Σ Φ and other MSS read οἱ δὲ μαθηταὶ ἐπετίμων τοῖς προσφέρουσιν, "but his disciples were rebuking those who were bringing [the children]." ℵ B C L and other authorities read οἱ δὲ μαθηταὶ ἐπετίμησαν αὐτοῖς, "but his disciples rebuked them." See Metzger, TCGNT[1], 105.

[b]W and a few later MSS add ἐπιτιμήσας, "having rebuked [them]."

[c]W reads ἡ βασιλεία τῶν οὐρανῶν, "kingdom of the heavens" (cf. Matt 19:14).

[d]Some later MSS read ἀμὴν ἀμήν, "truly, truly," which probably reflects Johannine influence (cf. John 1:51 passim).

[e]D W and a few later authorities read ἐτίθει τὰς χεῖρας ἐπ᾽ αὐτὰ καὶ εὐλόγει αὐτά, "he was placing his hands upon them and was blessing them." A and several later authorities read the same way, but using the present tense.

[f]A W and several later MSS read ἰδού τις πλούσιος, "Behold, a certain one who was rich."

[g]Gk. εἷς ὁ θεός. D reads μόνος εἷς θεός, "only one—God."

[h]D and a few later MSS add μὴ πορνεύσῃς, "do not commit fornication"; see Westcott-Hort, Introduction 2:25–26.

[i]Many MSS omit μὴ ἀποστερήσῃς, "do not defraud" (cf. Exod 20:17; Deut 24:14; Sir 4:1), probably because this prohibition is not obviously one of the Ten Commandments. Matthew (19:18) and Luke (18:20) omit it also. See Metzger, TCGNT[1], 105.

[j]W Σ and other later MSS read εἰ θέλεις τέλειος εἶναι ἕν σε ὑστερεῖ, "If you wish to be perfect, you lack one thing. . . ."

[k]A W and several later authorities add ἄρας τὸν σταυρόν, "having taken up the [or 'your'] cross."

[l]W adds ἀπ᾽ αὐτοῦ, "from him."

[m]D, supported by several Latin and old Italian MSS, reads πολλὰ χρήματα, "much money" or "much wealth."

[n]Some MSS place the equivalent of v 25 between vv 23 and 24. But there are some variants. For example, D reads τάχιον κάμηλος διὰ τρυμάλιδος ῥαφίδος διελεύσεται ἢ πλούσιος εἰς τὰν βασιλείαν τοῦ θεοῦ, "a camel will pass through the eye of a needle more quickly than will a rich man [enter] the kingdom of God." See Metzger, TCGNT[1], 105–6.

[o]Some MSS qualify Jesus' statement, limiting the difficulty of entering the kingdom to certain types of persons, such as those who are wealthy. For example, A C D and others read τοὺς πεποιθότας ἐπὶ χρήμασιν, "for those who trust in money." W reads πλούσιοι, "for one who is rich." See Metzger, TCGNT[1], 106; Westcott-Hort, Introduction, 2:26.

[p]Some MSS omit v 25 (see Note n above).

[q]In place of κάμηλον, some later authorities read κάμιλον, "rope." A rope is more closely related to a needle than is a camel! In later Gk. the letters η and ι came to be pronounced quite similarly. The same variant appears in later MSS in Luke 18:25.

[r]ℵ* reads τρήματος, "hole."

[s]πρὸς ἑαυτούς, "to themselves," is read by A D N W Σ Φ and many later MSS. It is accepted by Nestle-Aland[27] and UBSGNT[3c]. A few later authorities read πρὸς ἀλλήλους, "to one another." ℵ B C and a few other authorities read πρὸς αὐτόν, "to him" (which is accepted by the RSV but placed in a note in the NRSV). Metzger (TCGNT[1], 106) believes that this latter reading is an "Alexandrian correction."

[t]Lit. "And who is able to be saved?" W reads καὶ τίς δυνήσεται σωθῆναι, "And who will be able to be saved?"

[u]D reads παρὰ δὲ τῷ θεῷ δυνατόν, "but with God it is possible."

[v]A few late MSS add τῷ πιστεύοντι, "for the one who believes."

[w]Syr. reads Kêpā᾽, "Kepha [= Cephas]."

[x]ℵ and a few other authorities add τί ἄρα ἔσται ἡμῖν, "What will there then be for us?" This addition derives from Matt 19:27.

[y]A C N Σ Φ and later authorities add ἢ γυναῖκα, "or wife" (cf. Luke 18:29).

[z]ℵ omits ἕνεκεν ἐμοῦ καί, "for my sake and."

[aa]A few late authorities read ἕνεκεν τοῦ εὐαγγελίου μου, "for the sake of my gospel." A B* and a few other authorities omit the second ἕνεκεν, "for the sake of."

[bb]A few late authorities read κληρονομήσῃ, "inherit." D rewrites v 30 in an attempt to smooth out the awkward syntax. See Metzger, TCGNT[1], 106–7.

[cc]A few late authorities read μετὰ διωγμόν, "after persecution."

[dd]Clement of Alexandria (Salvation of the Rich 4) quotes vv 29–31 as follows with some interesting

variants: ἀποκριθεὶς δὲ ὁ Ἰησοῦς [λέγει]· ἀμὴν ὑμῖν λέγω, ὃς ἂν ἀφῇ τὰ ἴδια καὶ γονεῖς καὶ ἀδελφοὺς καὶ χρήματα ἕνεκεν ἐμοῦ καὶ ἕνεκεν τοῦ εὐαγγελίου, ἀπολήψεται ἑκατονταπλασίονα. νῦν ἐν τῷ καιρῷ τούτῳ ἀγροὺς καὶ χρήματα καὶ οἰκίας καὶ ἀδελφοὺς ἔχειν μετὰ διωγμῶν εἰς ποῦ; ἐν δὲ τῷ ἐρχομένῳ ζωή[ν] ἐστιν αἰώνιος. [ἐν δὲ] ἔσονται οἱ πρῶτοι ἔσχατοι καὶ οἱ ἔσχατοι πρῶτοι, "And answering, Jesus [says], 'Truly I say to you, whoever forsakes his home and parents and brothers and money for my sake and for the sake of the gospel will receive back one hundredfold. And to what end [does he expect] to have now in this time fields and riches and houses and brothers, with persecutions? But in the coming [age] there is eternal life. [And in] [the coming age] the first will be last and the last first.'"

Form/Structure/Setting

Mark 10:13–31 consists of three units of material: (1) the reception and blessing of children (vv 13–16); (2) the dialogue with the rich man (vv 17–22); and (3) Jesus' teaching on the danger of riches (vv 23–31). The latter two units belong together; the first one was originally independent and bears some relationship to 9:35–37. The appearance of παιδίον, "child" (9:36, 37; 10:15), and ἐναγκαλισάμενος, "taking [them] into his arms" (9:36; 10:16), in both passages should be noted, especially the latter word, for only in these two passages in Mark does this word make an appearance in the NT. However, when all is considered, it seems best to view 9:35–37 and 10:13–16 as having been derived from two separated episodes, which in their transmission and in the evangelist's editing have been drawn together somewhat.

What links these units is the theme of entry into the kingdom. Children will gladly and without conditions take the opportunity, but those caught up in the cares of the world often hesitate. The contrast is startling: children whose futures were uncertain (given the high mortality rate among infants and young children) and who were not especially valued in late antiquity will readily enter the kingdom, so adults should follow their example. The wealthy, despite the assumption of conventional wisdom that wealth is a sign of divine blessing (as v 26 assumes) and despite the professed care to observe the commandments, often find it very difficult to enter the kingdom, so Jesus' disciples should beware.

A parallel to Mark 10:13–16 appears in *Gos. Thom.* §22:

> Jesus saw infants being nursed. He said to this disciples, "These infants being nursed are like those who enter the kingdom." They said to him, "If we become children, shall we enter the kingdom?" Jesus said to them, "When you make the two one, and when you make the inside like the outside and the outside like the inside, and the above like the below, and when you make the male and the female one and the same, so that the male not be male nor the female female, and when you put eyes in place of an eye, and a hand in place of a hand, and a foot in place of a foot, and a likeness in place of a likeness; then you will enter [the kingdom]."

Every indication is that this tradition is a secondary reworking of Synoptic material (cf. H. C. Kee, "'Becoming a Child' in the Gospel of Thomas," *JBL* 82 [1963] 307–14). The focus in the *Gospel of Thomas* is ontological and reflects Gnosticism's preoccupation with cosmogony. Some of the elements are reminiscent of NT passages: "when you make the two one" may reflect Eph 2:15, "that he might create in himself one new man in place of the two"; "when you make the inside like the outside and the outside like the inside" may reflect Matt 23:25–26, "you cleanse the outside of the cup and of the plate, but inside they are full of extortion and rapacity. . . . First cleanse the inside of the cup and of the plate, that the outside also may be clean"; "so that the male not be male nor the female female" may reflect Gal 3:28, "there is neither male nor female; for you are all one in Christ Jesus"; "and the above like the below" may reflect John 8:23, "He said to them, 'You are from below, I am from above'"; and the references to "eye," "hand," and "foot" may echo Mark 9:43–47 ("hand," "foot," and "eye").

There are other parallels as well. Echoing Mark 10:14–15, the *Gospel of Truth* affirms: "After all these, there came the little children also, those to whom the knowledge of the Father belongs" ([NHC I, 3] 19.27–30). Another adaptation appears in *Gos. Thom.* §46: "Yet I have said, whichever one of you comes to be a child will be acquainted with the kingdom and will become superior to John" (the reference to John alludes to Matt 11:11 = Luke 7:28).

Bultmann (*History*, 32) and Taylor (*Formation*, 72, 148) have classified Mark 10:13–16 as a pronouncement story. Bultmann wonders if the story was not inspired by 2 Kgs 4:27: "And when she came to the mountain to the man of God, she caught hold of his feet. And Gehazi came to thrust her away. But the man of God said, 'Let her alone, for she is in bitter distress; and the LORD has hidden it from me, and has not told me.'" He also cites a rabbinic story about ʿAqiba: "On approaching him [ʿAqiba] she [ʿAqiba's wife] fell on her face and kissed his feet. His disciples were about to thrust her aside, when [Rabbi ʿAqiba] cried to them, 'Leave her alone, mine and yours are hers [i.e., my knowledge and your knowledge are thanks to her]'" (*b. Ketub.* 63a; *b. Ned.* 50a). These parallels are at most formal; the details do not call for even a limited material linkage.

Bultmann (*History*, 21–22) and Taylor (*Formation*, 66) view Mark 10:17–22 as a pronouncement story. Bultmann suspects that the evangelist has added vv 23–27 (in which is embedded vv 23, 25, "an old apophthegm which Mark probably found already joined with vv 17–22" [*History*, 22] about the difficulty of the rich to enter the kingdom of God), vv 28–30 (a saying about rewards), and v 31 (the saying about the reversal of the first and last). With respect to v 31 Bultmann is probably correct, for the antinomy of the last and first occurs, in addition to Mark 10:31, in Matt 20:8, 16 (parable of the Laborers); Mark 9:35; and Luke 13:30. The impression one is left with is that this is a free-floating topos; so also the antinomy of the least and the greatest, as in Luke 9:48. Bultmann may also be correct about the apophthegm (vv 23, 25) embedded in vv 23–27. This material is consistent with other teachings many regard as authentic (e.g., Matt 6:24 = Luke 16:13; Luke 14:15–24; 16:19–31). Mark probably added "his disciples were marvelling at his words" (v 24), but the saying in v 24, "Children, how difficult it is to enter the kingdom of God," is probably dominical as well, though in this case it may have arisen as a variant of the saying in v 23. Ambrozic (*Hidden Kingdom*, 158–71) thinks vv 17–22b constituted the original unit of tradition, to which vv 24bc and 26–27 were added in the pre-Markan phase of development, which was then supplemented further with vv 22c, 23–24a, and 25 by the evangelist. For other assessments of the compositional history of this unit, see Pesch (2:136) and Best (*ExpTim* 83 [1970–71] 83–89; *Following Jesus*, 111). The exchange in vv 26–27 is probably secondary, for it seems to interrupt the flow from vv 23–25 to vv 28–30 (though many scholars, e.g., Cranfield, 325, view these latter verses as secondary as well). However, vv 26–27 probably represent genuine dominical tradition. It is hard to see how the early church would create a saying in which the apostles express doubt about salvation and in which Jesus says nothing about faith or about his mission.

The concluding unit (vv 28–31) was probably originally independent of its present context (Best, *Following Jesus,* 112–13), though there is no compelling reason to deny it to Jesus. This means, of course, that "the gospel" referred to in v 29 is the good news of the kingdom of God, that is, Jesus' message, not the good news of Easter (which is how the early church doubtlessly came to understand it). Moreover, the eschatology of v 30 seems more consistent with a setting in the life of Jesus (*Sitz im Leben Jesu*) than with the eschatology of the early church (for more on this point, see *Comment*).

Comment

13 προσέφερον αὐτῷ παιδία ἵνα αὐτῶν ἅψηται· οἱ δὲ μαθηταὶ ἐπετίμησαν αὐτοῖς, "They were bringing to him children that he might touch them, but his disciples rebuked them." We are not told who were bringing (προσέφερον) children to Jesus "that he might touch [ἅψηται] them"; presumably it was their parents, hoping for some benefit or blessing. In late antiquity it was believed that touching a holy man, even his clothing, or being touched by him would confer blessing, perhaps healing (cf. Mark 5:28). The disciples, however, rebuke (ἐπετίμησαν) them for trying to do this (Gundry, 544, rightly understands the imperfect προσέφερον as conative: "were trying to bring"). ἐπιτιμᾶν, "to rebuke," is frequently used by the evangelist. It is found in 8:32, where Peter rebukes Jesus for predicting his death, and in 8:33, where Jesus rebukes Peter for opposing the things of God. Jesus rebukes the unclean spirits in 1:25 and 9:25 and rebukes the storm in 4:39. Closer to the present context, the crowd will rebuke blind Bartimaeus in 10:48. Mark does not explain whom the disciples rebuked (the parents or the children?), nor does he give any reason for their opposing the approach of the children. The evangelist's readers would probably have assumed that the children would have been viewed as disruptive and as a distraction. After all, Jesus had more important things to do and more important people to meet; he did not have time for children—or so they thought.

14 ἰδὼν δὲ ὁ Ἰησοῦς ἠγανάκτησεν καὶ εἶπεν αὐτοῖς· ἄφετε τὰ παιδία ἔρχεσθαι πρός με, μὴ κωλύετε αὐτά, "But Jesus, having observed this, was indignant and said to them, 'Permit the children to come to me. Do not forbid them.'" Jesus is indignant (ἠγανάκτησεν) over his disciples' behavior. The disciples themselves will a bit later be indignant at James and John for requesting the prime seats in Jesus' new government (10:41), and they will again be indignant when the woman anoints Jesus' head with expensive perfume (14:4). Jesus commands his disciples, "Permit the children to come to me." Without a conjunction, Jesus adds: "Do not forbid them," or as the negated present imperative (μὴ κωλύετε) implies, "stop forbidding them." Compare also 9:39, where in reference to the exorcist who was making use of Jesus' name Jesus commands his disciples: μὴ κωλύετε αὐτόν, "stop forbidding him." In Luke 11:52 Jesus says, "Woe to you lawyers! For you have taken away the key of knowledge; you did not enter yourselves, and you hindered [ἐκωλύσατε] those who were entering." In Luke 23:2 Jesus is accused of "forbidding [κωλύοντα]" the Jewish people to pay Roman taxes.

Jesus explains why the disciples should not forbid children to come to him:

τῶν γὰρ τοιούτων ἐστὶν ἡ βασιλεία τοῦ θεοῦ, "for of such ones is the kingdom of God." The genitive τῶν . . . τοιούτων, "of such ones," is possessive; that is, the kingdom of God *belongs* to such people as children (Taylor, 423; Gundry, 544). They therefore have every right to approach Jesus and be blessed by him. Jesus' views were not necessarily unique, for in later rabbinic literature there are some approximate parallels. According to *b. Sanh.* 110b Israelite children will enter the world to come: "Rabbi 'Aqiba said: 'They [the children] will enter the world to come, as it is written, "The Lord preserves the simple" [Ps 116:6].'" On the diction הָעוֹלָם הַבָּא *hā'ôlām habbā'*, "the world [*or* age] to come," compare Jesus' statement in v 30 (τῷ αἰῶνι τῷ ἐρχομένῳ, "the coming age"); the terminology is identical. In some rabbinic traditions, children are regarded as pure, even without sin (*b. Yoma* 22b; *b. Nid.* 30b); "children meet the Divine Presence" (*Kallah Rab.* 2.9); indeed, God's Presence follows them (*Qoh. Rab.* 1:5 §32). On Jewish traditions regarding blessing and laying hands on children, see Abrahams, *Studies* 1:118–20.

15 ἀμὴν λέγω ὑμῖν, ὃς ἂν μὴ δέξηται τὴν βασιλείαν τοῦ θεοῦ ὡς παιδίον, οὐ μὴ εἰσέλθῃ εἰς αὐτήν, "Truly I say to you, whoever should not receive the kingdom of God as a child will not enter it." Jesus teaches that people are to receive the kingdom much as children receive things (Best, *Following Jesus*, 107–8). The child is not being idealized (as is often thought in the Western world), for the child was not held in high regard in late antiquity. Indeed, parents had the power of life and death over the very young (cf. P.Oxy. 744.8–10: "If you bear a child: if it is a boy, keep it; if it is a girl, throw it out"; though this is a pagan practice, not a Jewish one). Rather, Jesus' point is that one should accept the kingdom and be obedient to its summons in the same way children will without question obey adults and do what they are told.

δέξασθαι τὴν βασιλείαν τοῦ θεοῦ, "to receive the kingdom of God," is to submit to the authority of God's rule. Adults, assumed to possess power and authority of their own, will not be able to enter the kingdom, for their own authority will clash with that of God's. For this reason the person who wishes to receive the kingdom must receive it "as a child does," that is, without presumptions of self-importance and self-empowerment. Finally, παιδίον, "child," should not be understood as the direct object (as recommended by W. Clarke, *New Testament Problems* [New York: Macmillan, 1929] 37–38); this sense conflicts with the meaning of v 14, in which Jesus says the kingdom belongs to children.

16 ἐναγκαλισάμενος αὐτά, "taking them into his arms." Jesus does not merely touch the children, which in v 13 was the stated purpose of those bringing them to him; he embraces them. In 9:36 Jesus had taken a child into his arms. The embrace is a public demonstration of children's acceptance and value in the kingdom.

αὐτὰ κατευλόγει, "he blessed [lit. historic present, 'blesses'] them." The personal pronoun αὐτά, "them," serves double duty as the direct object of ἐναγκαλισάμενος, "taking [them] into his arms," and of κατευλόγει, "he blesses." The evangelist uses the intensive form κατευλογεῖν, "to bless," which occurs nowhere else in the NT. In the LXX it is found only in Tob 11:1, where Tobias blesses Raguel, and in Tob 11:17, where Tobit blesses his new daughter-in-law Sarah. The more common word is the simple form εὐλογεῖν.

τιθεὶς τὰς χεῖρας ἐπ' αὐτά, "laying his hands on them." Elsewhere in this Gospel Jesus lays hands on persons: in 5:23 a distraught father implores Jesus to lay his hands on his seriously ill daughter; in 6:5 Jesus lays "hands upon a few sick people and healed them"; Jesus lays his hands upon the blind man in 8:23–25 in order to restore his sight. There is precedent for Jesus' actions. In Gen 48:15–15 the patriarch Jacob (a.k.a. Israel) lays his hands upon the heads of Ephraim and Manasseh and then blesses their father Joseph. Laying hands on someone to heal is attested in 1QapGen 20:28–29, where Abram prays, lays his hands on Pharaoh's head, and drives out an evil spirit (on this passage, see D. Flusser, "Healing through the Laying-On of Hands in a Dead Sea Scroll," *IEJ* 7 [1957] 107–8). In Mark 10:16, however, blessing is the intent rather than healing. Nevertheless, the idea that divine power exuded from Jesus (whether to heal or to benefit in some other way) is probably an underlying assumption.

17 διδάσκαλε ἀγαθέ, "good teacher." There are no examples from the first century or earlier of anyone being called "good teacher" as we have here, though the Talmud offers a potential parallel. In a dream, Rabbi Eleazar of Hagronya (mid–fourth century C.E.) is addressed: "Good greetings to the good teacher [רב טב *rab ṭab*] from the good Lord who from his bounty dispenses good to His people" (*b. Taʿan.* 24b; cf. Dalman, *Words,* 337). However, given the exaggerated use of "good" throughout this curious address, it is probably not prudent to make any generalizations. The tradition is, moreover, quite late. The additional element of kneeling (γονυπετήσας) before Jesus, which is not usual for greeting a teacher, suggests that the title "good teacher" is also unusual. There is no reason to believe that the man who approached Jesus was being ostentatious in his otherwise unusual, perhaps even extraordinary, show of respect.

τί ποιήσω ἵνα ζωὴν αἰώνιον κληρονομήσω; "What must I do that I may inherit eternal life?" This question and the discussion of the commandments that follows bears an uncertain relationship to Luke 10:25–28:

> And behold, a lawyer stood up to put him to the test, saying, "Teacher, what shall I do to inherit eternal life [διδάσκαλε, τί ποιήσας ζωὴν αἰώνιον κληρονομήσω]?" He said to him, "What is written in the law? How do you read?" And he answered, "You shall love the Lord your God with all your heart, and with all your soul, and with all your strength, and with all your mind; and your neighbor as yourself." And he said to him, "You have answered right; do this, and you will live."

It is clear from this exchange that Jesus believed that keeping the true spirit of the Law guarantees eternal life. This point is driven home in the parable of the Good Samaritan as the identity of one's neighbor is further clarified (Luke 10:29–37). Jesus' answer, τοῦτο ποίει καὶ ζήσῃ, "do this, and you will live," alludes to Lev 18:5, אֲשֶׁר יַעֲשֶׂה אֹתָם הָאָדָם וָחַי בָּהֶם *ʾăšer yaʿăśeh ʾōtām hāʾādām wāḥay bāhem,* "which the person shall do and live by them," though with the exegetical nuance preserved in some of the later Aramaic paraphrases of the Pentateuch: "by doing which, he shall live by them in eternal life" (*Tg. Onq.* Lev 18:5); "by doing which, he shall live by them in eternal life and shall be assigned a portion with the righteous" (*Tg. Ps.-J.* Lev 18:5). Thus, Jesus appears to agree with the Torah, at least as it was understood in the synagogue. Obedience to the Law, if it includes love of one's neighbor, will result in eternal life. We shall find that this is Jesus' principal point here in Mark 10:17–22 as well. (On apparent obedience of the Law and oral traditions to the detriment of others, see Mark 7:1–13.)

18 τί με λέγεις ἀγαθόν; "Why do you call me 'good'?" The word order places the emphasis on the με, "me": "Why *me* do you call 'good'?" The oddness of Jesus' counterquestion has always puzzled Christian interpreters. The Matthean evangelist alters the exchange: the man asks Jesus, "What *good deed* must I do to have eternal life?" and Jesus responds, "Why do you *ask me about what is* good?" (Matt 19:16–17). The point Jesus is trying to make is partially clarified by his assertion that οὐδεὶς ἀγαθὸς εἰ μὴ εἷς ὁ θεός, "no one is good, except one—God." Jesus reacts to the unusual epithet "good teacher" because of his radical view of God's unique goodness. God is the source of all goodness. He fills the hungry with "good" things (Luke 1:53). He gives δόματα ἀγαθά, "good gifts," to his children (Matt 7:11= Luke 11:13). "Every good endowment and every perfect gift is from above, coming down from the Father of lights" (Jas 1:17). Jesus has come to announce the arrival of the kingdom of the God of Israel (Mark 1:14–15), the God who is the giver of all good things. Jesus' purpose is not to draw attention to himself, though his person and ministry are of such an extraordinary nature that that very thing happens; his purpose is to draw attention to the God who saves and heals, forgives and restores, and gives eternal life. Jesus is not implying that he is somehow imperfect or less than good, but only that the focus must be on God. For it is God who has made a covenant with Israel that must be honored; it is God's commandments that must be obeyed. Has the man obeyed them?

19 Jesus perceives that the man is educated and Torah-observant, so he says, τὰς ἐντολὰς οἶδας, "You know the commandments." Jesus is not asking him if he knows them; he assumes that he does and so draws attention to them as the starting point of their dialogue. τὰς ἐντολὰς, "the commandments," or מִצְוֹת miṣwōt, were foundational to the Sinai covenant (see R. H. Charles, *The Decalogue*, 2nd ed. [Edinburgh: T. & T. Clark, 1926]). The first four commandments cited by Jesus here come from the second table of the Ten Commandments (Exod 20:13–16 = Deut 5:17–20). The command μὴ ἀποστερήσῃς, "do not defraud," is a variation of the prohibition against theft and may have been intended as a substitute for the commandment against coveting (Swete, 224). Nineham (274) makes the plausible suggestion that because the man who questions Jesus is wealthy, he probably does not covet (another of the Ten Commandments), but he may very well have defrauded the poor, perhaps in holding back wages (Field, *Notes*, 33–34). This could account for the absence of the prohibition against coveting and the appearance in its place of a prohibition against defrauding, which strictly speaking is not one of the Ten Commandments. The last commandment cited by Jesus enjoins one to honor one's parents (Exod 20:12 = Deut 5:16), and it is the last commandment of the first table of the Ten Commandments. Jesus referred to this commandment earlier in his scathing criticism of the Pharisees and scribes, who "leave the commandment of God, and hold fast the tradition of men" (Mark 7:8). They do this, Jesus explains, through the tradition of Qorban and the consequent negligence in the care of one's parents (7:9–13; see Guelich, 363–71). (On economic defrauding of the poor, cf. Jas 5:4; on lawsuits and defrauding in the early church, cf. 1 Cor 6:7–8.) The appearance of the command to honor one's parents at the end of the list may have been due to the fact that it is the first commandment to promise long life (Exod 20:12: "Honor your father and your mother, that your days may be long"; Gundry, 561) and so ends on the note with which the man's question began.

Jesus' innovative reference to defrauding may also allude to Exod 21:10: "And if he take another [wife] to himself, he shall not defraud [LXX: ἀποστερήσει; MT: יִגְרָע *yigrā‛*] her of necessities, clothing, and company [*or* conjugal rights]" (cf. 1 Cor 7:5). Given Jesus' strict teaching regarding divorce in the not-too-distant context (Mark 10:2–9), it is distinctly possible that the defrauding he has in mind here concerns the treatment of women.

For Jesus' understanding of the commandments, one must review the "antitheses" of Matt 5:21–48. The first so-called antithesis concerns murder. It is not enough to refrain from committing murder; one must not hold one's brother in contempt (Matt 5:21–26): "Whoever says [to his brother], 'You fool!' shall be liable to the Gehenna of fire" (v 22). The second antithesis concerns adultery. Again, it is not enough to refrain from the physical act of adultery; one must not look lustfully upon another woman (which is often the motivation for seeking divorce; Matt 5:27–32). The third antithesis concerns false oaths (Matt 5:33–37), which at points ("let what you say be simply 'Yes' or 'No'") may relate to the commandment against perjury. In all these various antitheses Jesus argues for the spirit of the law, not merely the literal observance of it. Hatred and lust are tantamount to murder and adultery. The young man in Mark 10:17–22 may have kept these commandments on a literal level, but whether he did so on the level that Jesus demands remains to be seen.

20 διδάσκαλε, ταῦτα πάντα ἐφυλαξάμην ἐκ νεότητός μου, "Teacher, I have observed all these things since my youth." This time the man addresses Jesus simply as "teacher," omitting the adjective "good," which is not necessarily a result of his misunderstanding of the point Jesus had tried to make in quizzing him about the address "good teacher" (as Gundry, 553, suggests). The man is indeed Torah-observant. He is not from the rabble, the sinful, the outcast, with whom Jesus frequently associated and had fellowship. He will be found instead regularly attending the synagogue, perhaps even participating in the service from time to time. The word ἐφυλαξάμην, "I have observed" or "I have guarded," would have added emphasis to his claim of being Torah-observant. He has carefully guarded the laws of Torah, which is much more than merely knowing the contents of the Law. φυλάσσειν, "to observe, guard," is frequently used in reference to obeying the Law (e.g., LXX Exod 12:17, 24; 13:10; 15:26; 19:5; 20:6; passim). The nuance "guard" implies taking care not to do what the commandments forbid (Gundry, 562).

The phrase ἐκ νεότητός μου, "since my youth," is found in other contexts describing the faithful observance of the laws and customs of one's people. The Lukan Paul in Acts says, "My manner of life from my youth [ἐκ νεότητος], spent from the beginning among my own nation and at Jerusalem, is known by all the Jews" (Acts 26:4). The language harks back to Scripture itself. The dying Jacob blesses his sons by "the God who continues to nourish me from my youth [ἐκ νεότητος] until this day" (LXX Gen 48:15). But moral disposition is also described as present from one's youth, either for evil (LXX Gen 8:21: "for the imagination of a person is diligently devoted to evil things from his youth [ἐκ νεότητος]") or for good (LXX 1 Kgdms 12:2: "I have gone about before you from my youth [ἐκ νεότητός μου] and until this day"). The man's testimony, therefore, would have been taken very seriously and would have been understood as an affirmation of his faithfulness—as he understood it—in keeping with the covenant. He is, accordingly, a faithful, Torah-observant Jew, who wants to be certain of his inheritance of eternal life. Could Jesus give him the desired assurance?

21 ἐμβλέψας αὐτῷ, "looking upon him," suggests that Jesus studied the man carefully for a moment (Swete, 225), and ἠγάπησεν αὐτόν, "loved him," may suggest that Jesus actually hugged him or took him by the shoulders as a sign of affection (that is, the verb refers to overt action, not simply to an inner emotion; for the possibility, see Field, *Notes,* 34: "caressed him"; Gundry, 554). There is no need to conjecture with Lachs (331) that Mark's ἠγάπησεν erroneously takes רחם as Aramaic *rĕḥēm* meaning "loved," rather than as Hebrew (*piʿēl*) *riḥam* meaning "pitied." If there is a Semitic substratum here at all, we should expect it to be Aramaic.

ἕν σε ὑστερεῖ, "You lack one thing" (lit. "one [thing] is lacking with respect to you"; see BDF §180 [5]). As suggested in the *Comment* on v 17 above, Jesus agrees that obedience to the Law secures eternal life, but this Law includes compassion for people. Just as in the Lukan version of this exchange (Luke 10:25–28 + the parable in vv 29–37), the emphasis falls on ethics. If a person truly loves his neighbor as himself, he has fulfilled the Law (so Luke). If a person has truly kept the commandments, which entails compassion for and generosity toward the poor, he has fulfilled the Law (so Mark). Rabbinic literature speaks of the "completely righteous person" (צדיק גמור *ṣaddîq gāmûr*) who keeps all the commandments (cf. *b. Ber.* 7b; *b. Roš Haš.* 16b: "The completely righteous ones [צדיקים גמורים *ṣaddîqîm gĕmûrîm*] will be inscribed as entitled to eternal life [חיי עולם *ḥayyê ʿôlām*]"). The man does not quite qualify for this status.

ὕπαγε, ὅσα ἔχεις πώλησον καὶ δὸς [τοῖς] πτωχοῖς, "Go, sell what you have and give to the poor." There is actually little explicit teaching in the Gospels concerning the poor, at least beyond conventional almsgiving among Torah-observant Jews. There is no indication that care for the poor was a distinctive feature in Jesus' agenda. That Jesus and his disciples practiced charity seems probable. One thinks of the complaint that arose when the woman anointed Jesus' head with costly perfume: "This ointment might have been sold for more than three hundred denarii, and [the money] given to the poor" (Mark 14:5). Jesus rebuffs his disciples and commends the woman for her kindness, adding, "you always have the poor with you, and whenever you should wish you can do something good for them" (Mark 14:7). At a banquet Jesus recommends that his more fortunate table companions invite to dinner the poor and disabled, those who cannot repay (Luke 14:12–14). Jesus is also critical of the exploitation of the poor (as seen in Mark 12:38–44). Of course, his "good news" specifically targets "the poor" (Matt 5:3 = Luke 6:20; Matt 11:5 = Luke 7:22). The πτωχοί, "poor," of course, could very well refer to those to whom Jesus himself was ministering. Jesus' teaching on this subject is otherwise sketchy.

The idea of liquidating one's assets to join a community is seen at Qumran, or at least in some of the Dead Sea Scrolls, notably the Community Rule scrolls (1QS and 4QS). According to Josephus (*J.W.* 2.8.3 §122), the Essenes "despise riches" and "surrender their property to the order." Early church practice was somewhat similar: "And all who believed were together and had all things in common; and they sold their possessions and goods and distributed them to all, as any had need" (Acts 2:44–45). The Qorban vow (see Mark 7:9–13) could place all of one's estate into a trust, administered by the temple establishment (see *m. Ned.* 5:6). Jesus' requirement that the rich man give away his wealth to the poor, rather than to a particular community (such as among the Essenes) or institution (such as the temple), is distinctive.

If the man will heed Jesus' advice, he will have θησαυρὸν ἐν οὐρανῷ, "treasure in heaven." Jesus' advice here is the same as that which he gives his disciples in the Sermon on the Mount (Matt 6:19–21):

> Do not lay up for yourselves treasures on earth, where moth and rust consume and where thieves break in and steal, but lay up [θησαυρίζετε] for yourselves treasures in heaven [θησαυροὺς ἐν οὐρανῷ], where neither moth nor rust consumes and where thieves do not break in and steal. For where your treasure is, there will your heart be also.

The idea of laying up treasure in heaven is not distinctive to Jesus; it is a commonplace in Jewish religious literature (see Koch, "Schatz im Himmel"). The most important examples include Tob 4:8–9: "If you have many possessions, make your gift from them in proportion; if few, do not be afraid to give according to the little you have. So you will be laying up a good treasure [θησαυρίζεις] for yourself against the day of necessity"; *Pss. Sol.* 9:5: "He that does righteousness lays up [θησαυρίζει] for himself life with the Lord"; *2 Bar.* 24:1: "For behold! The days come and the books shall be opened in which are written the sins of all those who have sinned, and again also the treasures in which the righteousness of all those who have been righteous in creation is stored"; Sir 29:10–12: "Lose your silver for the sake of a brother or a friend, and do not let it rust under a stone and be lost. Lay up your treasure [θησαυρόν] according to the commandments of the Most High, and it will profit you more than gold. Store up almsgiving in your treasury, and it will rescue you from all affliction."

But the true test of fidelity to God's will is whether the man will respond to Jesus' summons: δεῦρο ἀκολούθει μοι, "come, follow me." The summons is imperative in view of the dawning of the kingdom of God. There really are no other options, such as following another rabbi. Jesus' summons, ἀκολούθει μοι, "follow me," is the same that he used when he called his disciples (Mark 2:14; 8:34; John 1:43; 12:26; 21:19, 22; examples from Q will be considered in the *Comment* on v 22 below). Imperatival examples are found in Greek literature, e.g., the reaction of Diogenes of Sinope to a prospective pupil: "he commanded him to follow [ἐκέλευσεν ἀκολουθεῖν]" (Diogenes Laertius 6.36); and the famous account of Socrates' summoning of Xenophon: "Follow me [ἕπου] and learn [μάνθανε]" (Diogenes Laertius 2.48). There are examples in the rabbinic literature of disciples following after their teachers (e.g., *Sipre Deut.* §305 [on Deut 31:14]; *Mek.* on Exod 31:12 [*Šabb.* §1]; cf. 1 Kgs 19:20–21: וְאֵלְכָה אַחֲרֶיךָ . . . וַיֵּלֶךְ אַחֲרֵי אֵלִיָּהוּ *wĕʾēlkā ʾaḥăreykā . . . wayyēlek ʾaḥărê ʾēliyyāhû*, "'I shall come after you' . . . and he went after Elijah"). Following entailed more than mere theological instruction; it involved imitating the teacher's very way of life.

22 ὁ δὲ στυγνάσας ἐπὶ τῷ λόγῳ, "But he, his face falling at this word." Mark's στυγνάζειν, "to have one's face fall," is rare, occurring only once elswhere in the NT (Matt 16:3: "It will be stormy today, for the sky is red and threatening [στυγνάζων]"). In the LXX στυγνάζειν only occurs in Ezekiel with the meaning of "to be appalled" (Ezek 27:35; 28:19; 32:10). Perhaps the best example is found in LXX Dan 2:12: "The king became gloomy [στυγνός] and sorrowful [περίλυπος]." Cognates of both of these words appear in our passage. The translation "his face falling" may not be strong enough (and would not be in the case of the Daniel passage), though other English expressions seem overdone (e.g., "his face clouding over," "becoming gloomy," or the like). Mark's graphic description lends his narrative vivid color.

In response to Jesus' word the man ἀπῆλθεν λυπούμενος, "went away grieving [or pained]." Mark's γάρ, "for," explains why the man reacted so quickly and negatively to Jesus' requirement: ἦν . . . ἔχων κτήματα πολλά, "he had many possessions." The implication is obvious: the requirement to sell all and give to the poor would hit him hard. After all, there is little pain in giving away little or nothing. For the wealthy, the thought of poverty is frightening. Jesus asked the man to decide between wealth in this life and wealth in heaven. The man would prefer to have both. Jesus is suggesting that he cannot. Thus, the man is pained.

Jesus summoned others who did not choose to follow him (Matt 8:18–22 = Luke 9:57–62). In every case, property or the security of home and family seemed to stand in the way. Jesus' demand to leave all behind was unusual in its stringency when compared either to the model of Elijah's call of Elisha or to the lifestyles of the rabbis and their pupils. In the case of Elijah and Elisha, the former allowed the latter to go home and bid his family farewell (cf. 1 Kgs 19:19–21), while in the case of the rabbis they and their students had "secular" vocations (cf. Paul of Tarsus, the tent maker). The difference between Jesus and these other examples was the eschatological urgency under which he labored. There was no time for tasks that distracted from the proclamation of the kingdom.

23–24 The failure of what perhaps had looked like a promising recruit prompts Jesus to look over his disciples and proclaim, πῶς δυσκόλως οἱ τὰ χρήματα ἔχοντες εἰς τὴν βασιλείαν τοῦ θεοῦ εἰσελεύσονται, "How difficult will it be for those who have wealth to enter the kingdom of God!" Mark's adverb (δυσκόλως, "with difficulty") appears in the parallels in Matthew and Luke (Matt 19:23 = Luke 18:24) and nowhere else in the NT. The adjectival form δύσκολον, "difficult" (in v 24), appears nowhere else in the NT. The adverbial form does not occur in the LXX; the adjectival form occurs but once (LXX Jer 30:2 [cf. MT 49:8]: "Dig deep for sitting, you who dwell in Dedan, because he has done troublesome things [δύσκολα ἐποίησεν]; I brought [calamity] upon him in the time in which I visited him"). The papyri (MM, 173) suggest that the word means "difficult," not "impossible."

Because wealth (τὰ χρήματα) competes for loyalty to God, those who have it will find it very difficult to receive God's rule. Jesus' pronouncement here is in step with his teaching elsewhere about the need to choose between love of God and love of money (χρῆμα, "money" = μαμωνᾶς, "mammon"): "No one can serve two masters; for either he will hate the one and love the other, or he will be devoted to the one and despise the other. You cannot serve God and mammon" (Matt 6:24 = Luke 16:13).

εἰς τὴν βασιλείαν τοῦ θεοῦ εἰσελεύσονται, "to enter the kingdom of God." On the theologoumenon of "entering the kingdom of God," see *Comment* on 9:47 and on 10:15. Apart from these Markan texts and their synoptic parallels, Jesus speaks of entering (or not entering) the kingdom of God in Matt 5:20; 7:21; 23:13; and John 3:5. From a Jewish point of view there is great irony in seeing wealth as an obstacle to entering the kingdom of God. Part of the hope for the kingdom centered on the abolition of poverty, sickness, and hunger. In the kingdom of God all will be wealthy, healthy, and well fed. But too much health and wealth in the present age acts as a distraction and deterrent from preparation for the kingdom. When it comes, many who are wealthy will not be able to enter.

In v 24 Jesus' μαθηταὶ ἐθαμβοῦντο ἐπὶ τοῖς λόγοις αὐτοῦ, "disciples were marveling at his words," so Jesus repeats them for emphasis. Wealth, after all, was often understood as an indicator of covenant blessing, not as an obstacle to covenant fulfillment. However, in repeating his words, Jesus says nothing about the difficulty *of the rich* to enter the kingdom of God. All Jesus says the second time is πῶς δύσκολόν ἐστιν εἰς τὴν βασιλείαν τοῦ θεοῦ εἰσελθεῖν, "how difficult it is to enter the kingdom of God." As will be seen below, entry into the kingdom is a feat difficult for all, rich and poor alike. Mark had used θαμβεῖσθαι, "to be amazed, marvel," earlier in 1:27 ("they were all amazed"), where the crowd had been astounded at Jesus' powerful teaching whereby with authority he commanded the unclean spirits and they obeyed. Jesus' words in 10:23–24 are just as amazing.

25 εὐκοπώτερόν ἐστιν κάμηλον διὰ [τῆς] τρυμαλιᾶς [τῆς] ῥαφίδος διελθεῖν ἢ πλούσιον εἰς τὴν βασιλείαν τοῦ θεοῦ εἰσελθεῖν, "It is easier for a camel to pass through the eye of a needle than for someone who is rich to enter the kingdom of God." To underscore just how difficult it is for people to enter the kingdom of God, Jesus likens it to a camel trying to pass through the eye of a needle. When Jesus says τρυμαλιᾶς ῥαφίδος, "eye of a needle," he means just that. He is not talking about a small gate somewhere in the walls of Jerusalem through which camels may have passed with great difficulty. The so-called Needle Gate that the locals show to gullible pilgrims to the Holy Land cannot be dated any earlier than the Middle Ages (usually to Theophylact). In the parallel, Luke uses the word βελόνη, which is a classical Attic word and may mean a surgeon's needle (as in MM, 108, though that nuance is disputed). Some have recommended reading κάμιλον, "rope" or "cable," instead of κάμηλον, "camel," as if to say that entry into the kingdom is difficult, but not impossible (see Köbert, *Bib* 53 [1972] 229–33). However, similar extreme comparisons are found in rabbinic literature (*b. Ber.* 55b, which speaks of "a palm of gold or an elephant which goes through the eye of a needle"; *b. B. Meṣiʿa* 38b; *Song Rab.* 5:2 §2: "The Holy One, blessed be He, said to Israel: 'My sons, present to me an opening no bigger than the eye of a needle, and I will widen it into openings through which wagons and carriages can pass'"). There really is no need to reduce the severity of the comparison. The last rabbinic parable anticipates the point that Jesus will make in v 27.

26 In response to Jesus' pronouncement, "How difficult it is to enter the kingdom of God" (v 24), and remarkable analogy, "It is easier for a camel to pass through the eye of a needle than for someone who is rich to enter the kingdom of God" (v 25), the stunned disciples ask, καὶ τίς δύναται σωθῆναι, "Then who can be saved?" The question grows out of the assumption that wealth was a sign of divine blessing while disease and poverty were signs of judgment. It was further assumed that because God was fair, the blessed surely were righteous while the judged surely were sinners. These generalizing assumptions (and exceptions, of course, would be allowed) are rooted in Deuteronomy, which promises blessings for obedient Israel but judgment for disobedient Israel (see the summary in Deut 30), and one can certainly interpret these promises and threats from this perspective. Jesus' teaching, however, frequently clashed with these assumptions.

One immediately thinks of the parable of the Great Banquet (Luke 14:15–24), in which against all expectation the poor, the blind, and the crippled enter the banquet hall and enjoy the supper, not the wealthy and apparently blessed. The parable of the Rich Man and Lazarus (Luke 16:19–31) teaches the same lesson.

σωθῆναι, "be saved," is no more a technical Christian term here (and hence inauthentic) than it is in the OT. In the Prophets (in the LXX) alone the word occurs eighty-five times. The following are only three instances: "But I will have pity on the house of Judah, and I will save them" (Hos 1:7 NRSV); "Then everyone who calls on the name of the LORD shall be saved" (Joel 2:32 NRSV); "But Israel is saved by the LORD with everlasting salvation" (Isa 45:17). Christian usage of σώζειν, "to save," and σωτηρία, "salvation," probably grew out of the prophetic tradition and reflects Jesus' emphases (Gundry, 565–66). Paul himself is an early witness to the importance of Joel 2:32 (Rom 10:13; cf. Acts 2:21).

27 ἐμβλέψας αὐτοῖς ὁ Ἰησοῦς λέγει, παρὰ ἀνθρώποις ἀδύνατον, ἀλλ᾽ οὐ παρὰ θεῷ· πάντα γὰρ δυνατὰ παρὰ τῷ θεῷ, "Looking at them, Jesus says, 'With humans it is impossible, but not with God; for all things are possible with God.'" By ἐμβλέψας αὐτοῖς, "looking at them," Jesus lends emphasis to his teaching. He then answers their question. According to Jesus, people cannot save themselves; only God can (see Philo, *Moses* 1.31 §174: "What is impossible to all created beings is possible to [God] only"; *Virtues* 5 §26: πάντα γὰρ θεῷ δυνατά, "for all things are possible with God"; cf. *Creation* 47; *Abraham* 175; *Spec. Laws* 4.127). This theology can be traced to Torah itself: "Is anything too hard for the LORD?" (Gen 18:14; LXX: μὴ ἀδυνατεῖ παρὰ τῷ θεῷ ῥῆμα, "Is a thing impossible for God?"; cf. LXX Job 10:13; 42:2: οἶδα ὅτι πάντα δύνασαι, ἀδυνατεῖ δέ σοι οὐθέν, "I know that you can [do] all things, and nothing is impossible for you"). The reference in the Genesis passage is to Sarah's conception and birthing of a child. Given her advanced age, the promise seemed impossible.

Jesus' assertion that humanity cannot save itself does not stand in tension with rabbinic teaching (as is sometimes erroneously assumed). Keeping the Law is required, to be sure, but divine enablement is assumed. In the words of a rabbinic dictum: "If a man commences to purify himself, he is assisted from heaven" (H. Freedman and M. Simon, eds., *Midrash Rabbah* [London: Soncino, 1983] 9:232 n. 4).

28 Perhaps out of self-justification, even self-pity, Peter exclaims, ἰδοὺ ἡμεῖς ἀφήκαμεν πάντα καὶ ἠκολουθήκαμέν σοι, "Behold, we left everything and have followed you." Peter's point is that they have in fact done what Jesus asked the rich man to do: they have given up property and have followed him (*pace* Schmid, 190, Peter's reaction is perfectly plausible). Jesus' startling saying about the difficulty of a camel trying to pass through the eye of a needle may have jarred the disciples. Surely their sacrifices have been sufficient. Jesus' reply in the next verse suggests that Peter's exclamation may have carried with it a note of complaint: since the disciples have left everything to follow Jesus, what will be their reward?

29–30 Jesus assures his disciples that whatever they have given up for his sake and for the sake of the gospel will be paid back a hundredfold in this life (see *T. Job* 4:6–9). But his followers must also understand that persecutions will accompany these earthly rewards. As their ultimate reward in the age to come they will receive eternal life (v 31). In what way will Jesus' followers receive in this life houses, brothers, sisters, and land? All of these things will be gained through the new community that Jesus has begun to establish. Whatever is left behind, owing to the demands of the ministry or flight from persecution, Jesus' followers may look forward to receiving through Christian hospitality. However, there is also the anticipation of a restored Israel in the lifetime of Jesus and his disciples. That is, they may have given up many things to proclaim the good news of the kingdom, and they may suffer, but when the kingdom comes all will be restored a hundred times over. Not only that, but ἐν τῷ αἰῶνι τῷ ἐρχομένῳ, "in the coming age" (a Jewish, rabbinical term, not an ecclesiastical one), Jesus' disciples may look for ζωὴν αἰώνιον, "eternal life" (the very thing that the wealthy man had sought but could not obtain).

In the time of the evangelist Mark and his community, the phrase μετὰ διωγμῶν, "with persecutions," may have reflected the harsh persecutions inflicted on Christians by Nero following the disastrous fire that destroyed half of the city of Rome. But the prophecy may very well derive from Jesus himself and reflect his expectations of struggle and violent opposition before the kingdom of God finally obliterates evil.

31 Jesus' saying, πολλοὶ δὲ ἔσονται πρῶτοι ἔσχατοι καὶ [οἱ] ἔσχατοι πρῶτοι, "but many that are first will be last, and the last will be first," finds expression elsewhere in the Gospels (Matt 20:16; Luke 13:30) and in noncanonical traditions, e.g., "For many who are first will become last, and they will become one and the same" (*Gos. Thom.* §4; P.Oxy. 654.3: πολλοὶ ἔσονται π[ρῶτοι ἔσχατοι καὶ] οἱ ἔσχατοι πρῶτοι, "many that are first will be last, and the last will be first"). In the context in Mark 10:28–31 it refers to being included in or excluded from the kingdom of God.

Explanation

Mark 10:13–31 teaches important truths about entry into the kingdom of God. Paradoxically, the least powerful, least wealthy, least influential have a greater prospect of entering the kingdom than do those who are most powerful, wealthy, and influential. The children who approach Jesus exemplify the former. They not only exemplify those who more readily enter; they are identified by Jesus as role models for others to follow. Whoever is to enter the kingdom must receive as a child would—without calculation and without hedging. In marked contrast to the example of the child, there appears a wealthy man who wishes assurance of eternal life. Tragically, he exemplifies the latter category of persons. Although his intentions are good and he is by all appearances a Torah-observant man, his loyalty to wealth proves too great an obstacle. He cannot give it up, and he cannot follow Jesus.

The disciples too begin to wonder if they have what it takes. They do not, for humans cannot save themselves; only God can. Herein lies the foundation of Christian theology's historic emphasis on salvation by God's action alone (as summed up succinctly in Eph 2:8–9). People cannot enter the kingdom of God without God's enabling power. But pursuit of the kingdom of God is not without costs. Jesus' disciples, and many Christians since, have given up everything to follow Jesus. They have left behind family and property. They have sacrificed what the rich man was unwilling to sacrifice. If salvation is of God and not of the believer, is such sacrifice necessary? Is it efficacious? It certainly is, for whatever is given away will be repaid many times over, while obedience to Jesus' summons will result in eternal life. It may not seem that way now, but the believer is to know that many who are now first in importance and power will someday be last, while those who lack wealth and standing in society today will someday have it all.

C. The Third Prediction of the Passion (10:32–34)

Bibliography

Bastin, M. "L'annonce de la passion et les critères de l'historicité." *RevScRel* 50 (1976) 289–329. ———. *Jésus devant sa passion.* LD 92. Paris: Cerf, 1976. 124–38. **Bauer, J. B.** "Drei Tage." *Bib* 39 (1958) 354–58. **Bayer, H. F.** *Jesus' Predictions of Vindication and Resurrection: The Provenance, Meaning and Correlation of the Synoptic Predictions.* WUNT 2.20. Tübingen: Mohr-Siebeck, 1986. 171–74. **Beasley-Murray, G. R.** *Jesus and the Kingdom of God.* 237–47. **Best, E.** *Following Jesus.* 120–22. **Busemann, R.** *Die Jüngergemeinde nach Markus 10: Eine redaktionsgeschichtliche Untersuchung des 10. Kapitels im Markusevangelium.* BBB 57. Königstein; Bonn: Hanstein, 1983. 129–45. **Caragounis, C.** *The Son of Man.* WUNT 38. Tübingen: Mohr-Siebeck, 1986. 190–201. **Clark, D. J.** "After Three Days." *BT* 30 (1979) 340–43. **Colpe, C.** "Traditionsüberschreitende Argumentationen zu Aussagen Jesu über sich selbst." In *Tradition und Glaube: Das frühe Christentum in seiner Umwelt.* FS K. G. Kuhn, ed. G. Jeremias et al. Göttingen: Vandenhoeck & Ruprecht, 1971. 230–45, esp. 239–43. **Dupont, J.** "Ressuscité 'le troisième jour.'" *Bib* 40 (1959) 742–61. **Farmer, W. R.** "The Passion Prediction Passages and the Synoptic Problem: A Test Case." *NTS* 36 (1990) 558–70. **Feuillet, A.** "Les trois grandes prophéties de la passion et de la résurrection des évangiles synoptiques." *RevThom* 67 (1967) 533–60; 68 (1968) 41–74. **France, R. T.** *Jesus and the Old Testament.* 125–30. ———. "The Servant of the Lord in the Teaching of Jesus." *TynBul* 19 (1968) 26–52, esp. 43–49. **Grimm, W.** *Weil Ich dich liebe: Die Verkündigung Jesu und Deuterojesaja.* ANTJ 1. Bern; Frankfurt am Main: Lang, 1976. 209–22. **Gubler, M.-L.** *Die frühesten Deutungen des Todes Jesu: Eine motivgeschichtliche Darstellung aufgrund der neueren exegetischen Forschung.* OBO 15. Göttingen: Vandenhoeck & Ruprecht, 1977. 107–17. **Güttgemanns, E.** *Offene Fragen zur Formgeschichte des Evangeliums: Eine methodologische Skizze der Grundlagenproblematik der Form- und Redaktionsgeschichte.* BEvT 54. Munich: Kaiser, 1970. 211–23 (ET: *Candid Questions concerning Gospel Form Criticism: A Methodological Sketch of the Fundamental Problematics of Form and Redaction Criticism.* Tr. W. G. Doty. Pittsburgh: Pickwick Press, 1979). **Hasenfratz, H.-P.** *Die Rede von der Auferstehung Jesu Christi: Ein methodologischer Versuch.* FTL 10. Bonn: Linguistica Biblica, 1975. 108–14. **Hooker, M. D.** *The Son of Man in Mark.* 137–40. **Lindars, B.** *Jesus Son of Man: A Fresh Examination of the Son of Man Sayings in the Gospels in the Light of Recent Research.* London: S. P. C. K.; Grand Rapids, MI: Eerdmans, 1983. 60–84. **McKinnis, R.** "An Analysis of Mark x 32–34." *NovT* 18 (1976) 81–100. **Meye, R. P.** *Jesus and the Twelve: Discipleship and Revelation in Mark's Gospel.* Grand Rapids, MI: Eerdmans, 1968. 159–64. **Minette de Tillesse, G.** *Le secret messianique.* 368–73. **Moo, D. J.** *The Old Testament in the Gospel Passion Narratives.* Sheffield: Almond, 1983. 92–97. **Oberlinner, L.** *Todeserwartung und Todesgewissheit Jesu: Zum Problem einer historischen Begründung.* SBB 10. Stuttgart: Katholisches Bibelwerk, 1980. 140–46. **Patsch, H.** *Abendmahl und historischer Jesus.* Calwer theologische Monographien. Stuttgart: Calwer, 1972. 185–97. **Perrin, N.** "Towards an Interpretation of the Gospel of Mark." In *Christology and a Modern Pilgrimage: A Discussion with Norman Perrin.* Ed. H. D. Betz. Claremont, CA: New Testament Colloquium, 1971. 1–78, esp. 14–30. **Perry,**

J. M. "The Three Days in the Synoptic Passion Predictions." *CBQ* 48 (1986) 637–54. **Pesch, R.** *Evangelium der Urgemeinde.* 122–24. ———. "Die Passion des Menschensohns: Eine Studie zu den Menschensohnsworten der vormarkinischen Passionsgeschichte." In *Jesus und der Menschensohn.* FS A. Vögtle, ed. R. Pesch and R. Schnackenburg. Freiburg: Herder, 1975. 166–95, esp. 179–81. **Reploh, K. G.** *Markus—Lehrer der Gemeinde.* 107–11. **Schulz, A.** *Nachfolgen und Nachahmen: Studien über das Verhältnis des neutestamentlichen Jüngerschaft zur urchristlichen Vorbildethik.* SANT 6. Munich: Kösel, 1962. 49–54. **Schwarz, G.** *Jesus "der Menschensohn": Aramaistische Untersuchungen zu den synoptischen Menschensohnworten Jesu.* BWANT 119. Stuttgart: Kohlhammer, 1986. 283–87. ———. *Jesus und Judas: Aramaistische Untersuchungen zur Jesus-Judas-Überlieferung der Evangelien und der Apostelgeschichte.* BWANT 123. Stuttgart: Kohlhammer, 1988. 98–103. **Selvidge, M. J.** "'And Those Who Followed Feared' (Mark 10:32)." *CBQ* 45 (1983) 396–400. **Stock, K.** *Boten aus dem Mit-Ihm-Sein.* 130–45. **Strecker, G.** "Die Leidens- und Auferstehungsvoraussagen im Markusevangelium (Mk 8,31; 9,31; 10,32–34)." *ZTK* 64 (1967) 16–39 (ET: "The Passion and Resurrection Predictions in Mark's Gospel." *Int* 22 [1968] 421–42). **Taylor, V.** *Jesus and His Sacrifice.* 85–91. ———. "The Origin of the Markan Passion-Sayings." *NTS* 1 (1954–55) 159–67 (repr. in V. Taylor. *New Testament Essays.* London: Epworth, 1970. 60–71). **Torrey, C. C.** *Our Translated Gospels.* London: Hodder and Stoughton; New York: Harper & Brothers, 1963. 151–53. **Via, D. O., Jr.** *The Ethics of Mark's Gospel.* 156–68. ———. "Mark 10:32–52—A Structural, Literary and Theological Interpretation." In *Society of Biblical Literature 1979 Seminar Papers.* Ed. P. J. Achtemeier. 2 vols. SBLSP 18. Missoula, MT: Scholars Press, 1979. 2:187–203. **Wink, W.** "Jesus as Magician." *USQR* 30 (1974–75) 3–14. **Zimmermann, H.** *Jesus Christus: Geschichte und Verkündigung.* Stuttgart: Katholisches Bibelwerk, 1973. 259–67. **Zmijewski, J.** "Überlieferungen zum Verhältnis von Theologie und christlicher Glaubenspraxis anhand des Neuen Testaments." *TGl* 72 (1982) 40–78, esp. 51–54.

Translation

[32]*And they were on the road ascending to Jerusalem, and Jesus was going on ahead of them; and they were amazed, but those following were afraid.*[a] *And again*[b] *taking the Twelve*[c] *aside, he began to tell them about what was going to happen to him:* [33] *"Behold, we are going up*[d] *to Jerusalem, and the 'son of man' will be handed over to the ruling priests and to the scribes, and they will condemn him to death and will hand him over to the Gentiles.* [34]*And they will mock him, and spit upon him, and scourge him, and kill him; and after three days*[e] *he will rise up."*[f]

Notes

[a]D and a few later authorities omit the odd clause οἱ δὲ ἀκολουθοῦντες ἐφοβοῦντο, "but those following were afraid."

[b]Several later MSS omit πάλιν, "again," perhaps because the occasion when Jesus last took his disciples aside is not obvious.

[c]A few later MSS read τοὺς δώδεκα μαθητὰς αὐτοῦ, "his twelve disciples."

[d]A few later MSS read ἀναβαίνωμεν, "let us go up."

[e]ℵ B C D L and other authorities read μετὰ τρεῖς ἡμέρας, "after three days." A N W Σ Φ and many later authorities read τῇ τρίτῃ ἡμέρᾳ, "on the third day." The second reading probably derives from Matt 20:19 (cf. Luke 18:33). See *Note* i on Mark 8:31 above.

[f]Gk. ἀναστήσεται. A few later MSS read ἐγερθήσεται, "he will be raised" (cf. Matt 20:19).

Form/Structure/Setting

Jesus now predicts his passion for the third time. This prediction is much more detailed than the previous two (see 8:31; 9:31; see also the partial predictions in 9:9, 12). The fear and amazement of those accompanying Jesus heighten the sense of drama. Everything about Jesus has astounded his contemporaries, from his miracles and exorcisms to his solemn pronouncements and predictions of his passion.

This third and climactic prediction summarizes the principal features of the passion of Jesus. His condemnation to death as the "son of man" at the hands of the high priest and ruling priests occurs in Mark 14:55–65. Jesus will be handed over to the Gentiles in Mark 15:1. The Gentiles will mock Jesus in Mark 15:20. They will spit upon him in Mark 15:19 (the ruling priests also will spit on him in 14:65), and they will flog him in Mark 15:15. As on the earlier occasions, Jesus predicts that "after three days he will rise." The third prediction of Jesus' passion bears the most obvious marks of post-Easter editing. The individual elements of the prediction and their counterparts in the passion are as follows (see also the convenient tabulations in Taylor, 436, and Bayer, *Jesus' Predictions*, 172):

παραδοθήσεται	
"he will be handed over"	Mark 14:41–44; cf. 1 Cor 11:23
τοῖς ἀρχιερεῦσιν καὶ τοῖς γραμματεῦσιν	
"to the ruling priests and to the scribes"	Mark 11:18, 27; 14:1, 10, 43, 55
κατακρινοῦσιν αὐτὸν θανάτῳ	
"they will condemn him to death"	Mark 14:64; 1 Cor 15:3
παραδώσουσιν αὐτὸν τοῖς ἔθνεσιν	
"they will hand him over to the Gentiles"	Mark 15:1, 10, 15; Acts 2:23; 3:13
ἐμπαίξουσιν αὐτῷ	
"they will mock him"	Mark 15:20, 31
ἐμπτύσουσιν αὐτῷ	
"they will spit upon him"	Mark 14:65; 15:19
μαστιγώσουσιν αὐτὸν καὶ ἀποκτενοῦσιν	
"they will scourge him, and kill him"	Mark 15:15, 24; John 19:1
μετὰ τρεῖς ἡμέρας ἀναστήσεται	
"after three days he will rise up"	Matt 27:63; Mark 16:6; 1 Cor 15:4

Some of these elements are quite primitive and go back to the earliest kerygma and, as argued in the *Comment* on 8:31 above, to Jesus himself. The verb παραδιδόναι, "to hand over" or "to betray," and the substantival form ὁ παραδιδούς, "betrayer," are part of this primitive tradition, as are ἀποκτείνειν, "to kill"/θάνατος, "death," and μετὰ τρεῖς ἡμέρας, "after three days," he will be raised up. These are not Markan elements. Delivering Jesus to the ruling priests and the Gentiles is also likely traditional and quite primitive. Scourging could also be traditional. But mocking and spitting could be details added by Mark, perhaps inspired by Isa 50:6: "I gave my back to the smiters [LXX: μάστιγας, "whips"], and my cheeks to those who pulled out the beard; I hid not my face from shame and spitting [LXX: ἀπὸ αἰσχύνης ἐμπτυσμάτων, "from shame of being spit upon"]"; and Ps 22:7 [MT 22:8; LXX 21:8]: "All who see me mock [MT: יַלְעִגוּ *yalʿigû;* LXX: ἐξεμυκτήρισαν] at me, they make mouths at me, they wag their heads." Because many of the details could be easily predicted (the juridical process and the rough treatment of those regarded as criminals were no secret) and because the events of the passion do not correspond chronologically to the prediction (and we would expect such correspondence in a *vaticinium ex eventu*), there is no compelling reason not to believe that the essence of the prediction derives from Jesus (see Cranfield, 334–35; Bayer, *Jesus' Predictions*, 173–74).

Comment

32 ἦσαν δὲ ἐν τῇ ὁδῷ, "And they were on the road," probably refers to Jesus' general following since the evangelist has already told his readers in v 17 that Jesus was on the road and in v 23 that he was with his disciples. τοὺς δώδεκα, "the Twelve," should be understood as a distinct group in the company of this larger following (Swete, 233; Gould, 197; MacLear, 139; Plummer, 245; Lagrange, 275; Taylor, 437; Gundry, 570).

ἀναβαίνοντες εἰς Ἱεροσόλυμα, "ascending to Jerusalem." It was a commonplace among Jews to speak of "ascending" or "going up" to Jerusalem, though it is not the highest point in Israel. (In fact, the Temple Mount itself is not the highest point in Jerusalem, for both the Mount of Olives and Mount Scopus are higher.) The picture of "going up" to Jerusalem or to the temple becomes a quasi theologoumenon (cf. 1 Sam 1:21–24; 2:28; 2 Kgs 19:14; 20:5, 8; 23:2; Pss 24:3; 68:18; 122:4; 3 Macc 3:16; John 2:13; 5:1; 11:55; Acts 11:2; 25:1, 9). Although not the first reference in Mark to the Holy City, it is the first time that Jerusalem is specifically mentioned as Jesus' destination. Mark writes Ἱεροσόλυμα, which is Matthew's preferred form, though in a Q saying (Matt 23:37 = Luke 13:34) it appears as Ἱερουσαλήμ (an archaic form), which is Luke's preferred form. Ἱεροσόλυμα was the common form in the time of Mark's writing (cf. Philo, Josephus, Diodorus, Plutarch, et al.). The basic form in the MT is יְרוּשָׁלַיִם *yĕrûšālayim*, though there are variations in vocalization. For more on the form of the word, see J. Jeremias, "ΙΕΡΟΥΣΑΛΗΜ/ ΙΕΡΟΣΟΛΥΜΑ," *ZNW* 65 (1974) 273–76.

Although not emphasized, Jerusalem is important to the Markan evangelist, appearing in 1:5 in reference to John's ministry of baptism ("and there went out to him all the country of Judea, and all the people of Jerusalem; and they were baptized by him in the river Jordan"). Jesus' reputation spreads throughout Galilee and beyond, and even reaches Jerusalem (3:8), from which come religious authorities to review and then criticize Jesus (3:22; 7:1). With these hints of trouble to come, the attentive reader of Mark is not surprised that the passion of Jesus will take place in the Holy City (for more on the city of Jerusalem, see *ABD* 3:747–66; J. Jeremias, *Jerusalem in the Time of Jesus* [Philadelphia: Fortress, 1969]).

ἦν προάγων αὐτοὺς ὁ Ἰησοῦς, "Jesus was going on ahead of them." That Jesus ἦν προάγων, "was going on ahead," of his disciples may carry some significance, for in 14:28 he promises his troubled disciples προάξω ὑμᾶς, "I will go before you," in Galilee after he has been raised from the dead. When the frightened women find the empty tomb, the young man tells them to "tell his disciples and Peter, 'He is going before [προάγει] you in Galilee. There you will see him, just as he told you'" (16:7). Jesus' going before his disciples may therefore be intended to underscore his role as leader and first to face the danger. Cranfield (335) comments that this portrayal may have been intended as a comfort to Christians in

Rome who at the time of Mark's publication were experiencing a similar fearful and uncertain future. (Gundry, 574, doubts that there is any significance.)

ἐθαμβοῦντο, "they were amazed." In 1:27 ἐθαμβήθησαν ἅπαντες, "all were amazed," at Jesus' powerful and authoritative teaching. Perhaps the same sense is intended here, for Jesus has just astounded his following with his teaching about who will enter the kingdom and how it can be done (10:13–31). But the evangelist may also wish the reader to understand that an aura of divine power attends Jesus (so Gundry, 570–71), who not long before had been transformed in such a dramatic fashion (9:2–8; and 9:15 for the crowd's astonishment at "seeing him" as he approached his disciples). Torrey (*Our Translated Gospels*, 151–53) speculates that originally the verb "amazed/distressed" was singular, not plural. He thinks the text should read, "and Jesus was going before them, and he was in deep distress." The suggestion is plausible, but impossible to confirm.

οἱ δὲ ἀκολουθοῦντες ἐφοβοῦντο, "but those following were afraid," of what lay before them (9:32) as well as afraid of what Jesus might say or do next. The fear here should be understood in the OT sense of awe that overwhelms humans in the presence of the divine. Elsewhere in Mark the disciples are afraid when in the presence of the numinous. For example, we see this clearly in 4:41: "And they were filled with awe, and said to one another, 'Who then is this, that even wind and sea obey him?'"; 5:15: "And they came to Jesus, and saw the demoniac sitting there, clothed and in his right mind, the man who had had the legion; and they were afraid"; 5:33: "But the woman, knowing what had been done to her, came in fear and trembling and fell down before him, and told him the whole truth"; and 6:50: "for they all saw him, and were terrified. But immediately he spoke to them and said, 'Take heart, it is I; have no fear.'" In all these cases the disciples or others are afraid when brought into the presence of some mighty deed—commanding the wind and sea, healing the demoniac, healing the woman (unconsciously no less!), and walking on the sea. Here in 10:32 the readers of Mark would understand that the awesomeness of Jesus is once again a cause of fear.

καὶ παραλαβὼν πάλιν τοὺς δώδεκα, "and again taking the Twelve aside." On other occasions Jesus takes aside (παραλαμβάνειν) the Twelve for private instruction. In Mark 9:2 "Jesus takes along [παραλαμβάνει] Peter and James and John, and takes them up into a high mountain by themselves"; and in Mark 14:33 "he takes along [παραλαμβάνει] Peter and James and John with him." In still other passages Jesus and his disciples have been alone (e.g., 4:34; 7:17; 9:28; 13:3). This is why Mark says πάλιν, "again." In the present passage Jesus' words would have been controversial, and doubtless many in the crowd accompanying him would have reacted the same way that Peter reacted the first time Jesus predicted his passion (back in 8:31–32). Jesus wants no disputing, no wrangling; he wants a private moment with his closest colleagues and companions.

ἤρξατο αὐτοῖς λέγειν τὰ μέλλοντα αὐτῷ συμβαίνειν, "he began to tell them about what was going to happen to him." Once again Jesus tells his disciples what lies ahead. The directness of Jesus' prediction is remarkable. He does not tell the disciples what he suspects might happen; he tells them what will in fact happen. The use of συμβαίνειν in the sense of what "happens" is common in the LXX (e.g., Gen 41:13; 42:4, 29; 44:29; Exod 1:10; 3:16; Job 1:22; Esth 6:13; 1 Macc 4:26). The certain knowledge of what lies before would have impressed Mark's readers—believers and skeptics alike—with the courage and divine foresight of Jesus. No ordinary man could behave in this manner.

33–34 Jesus predicts that the Gentiles will μαστιγώσουσιν, "scourge," him (with a μάστιξ, "whip"), but the evangelist in 15:15 uses the Latin loanword φραγελλοῦν, "to scourge" (with a φραγέλλιον or *flagellum,* "whip"). This lack of agreement between prediction and subsequent narrative favors the independence, if not authenticity, of the prediction. The prediction has been edited, but it has not been created *ex nihilo.* A similar point can be made with regard to the evangelist's failure to state in 16:1 that Sunday was the "third" day (in contrast to the Matthean evangelist, who in 27:63 has the ruling priests refer to Jesus' prediction that after "three days" he will rise again). That is, if μετὰ τρεῖς ἡμέρας, "after three days," is a *vaticinium ex eventu,* then why not make its fulfillment explicit? Most of Mark's readers would know for certain that, according to the Gospel's narrative, Jesus actually arose "after three days."

Explanation

For the third time Jesus has formally predicted his passion—this time with an amazing amount of detail. Mark's readers will have been impressed by Jesus' foreknowledge and courage, especially seen in contrast to the fear of those who were accompanying him. Implicit in his prediction is his faith in God, whose sovereign rule and redemptive purpose he has from the beginning of his ministry proclaimed and demonstrated with power. Jesus' rejection at the hands of his people and his execution at the hands of Israel's Roman overlords will not take him by surprise. He knows these things are coming and he is preparing his disciples for them. His foreknowledge and courage counter the embarrassment and sting for Mark's readers of what happened in Jerusalem nearly four decades earlier.

In the passage that follows (10:35–45) Jesus will once again teach his disciples the need for humility and service. This teaching will be directly linked to his coming passion, as he explains that he has come not "to be served but to serve, and to give his life as a ransom for many" (10:45). In other words, his mission has not failed; it has succeeded in that Jesus has accomplished the purpose of his ministry.

D. James and John's Request (10:35–45)

Bibliography

Arens, E. *The HΛΘON-Sayings in the Synoptic Tradition: A Historico-Critical Investigation.* OBO 10. Göttingen: Vandenhoeck & Ruprecht, 1976. 117–61. **Bastin, M.** *Jésus devant sa passion.* LD 92. Paris: Cerf, 1976. 156–61. **Beardslee, W. A.** "Use of the Proverb in the Synoptic Gospels." *Int* 24 (1970) 61–73. **Bernard, J. H.** "A Study of Mk x.38, 39." *JTS* o.s. 28 (1927) 262–70. **Best, E.** *Following Jesus.* 123–33. ———. *The Temptation and the Passion: The Markan Soteriology.* SNTSMS 2. Cambridge: Cambridge UP, 1965. 152–57. **Braumann, G.** "Leidenskelch und

Todestaufe (Mc 10,38f.)." *ZNW* 56 (1965) 178–83. **Busemann, R.** *Die Jüngergemeinde nach Markus 10: Eine redaktionsgeschichtliche Untersuchung des 10. Kapitels im Markusevangelium.* BBB 57. Königstein; Bonn: Hanstein, 1983. 145–61. **Casey, M.** *Aramaic Sources of Mark's Gospel.* 193–218. **Chordat, J.-L.** *Jésus devant sa mort dans l'évangile de Marc.* LD 21. Paris: Cerf, 1970. 59–73. **Clark, K. W.** "The Meaning of (kata)kyrieyein." In *Studies in New Testament Language and Texts.* Ed. J. K. Elliott. Leiden: Brill, 1980. 100–105. **Cranfield, C. E. B.** "The Cup Metaphor in Mark xiv.36." *ExpTim* 59 (1948) 137–38. **Crossan, J. D.** *In Fragments.* 285–93. **Cullmann, O.** "Courants multiples dans la communauté primitive: A propos du martyre de Jacques fils de Zébédée." *RSR* 60 (1972) 55–69. **Delling, G.** "βάπτισμα βαπτισθῆναι." *NovT* 2 (1957–58) 92–115. **Derrett, J. D. M.** "Christ's Second Baptism (Lk 12:50; Mk 10:38–40)." *ExpTim* 100 (1988–89) 294–95. **Downing, F. G.** "Jesus and Martyrdom." *JTS* n.s. 14 (1963) 279–93. **Feuillet, A.** "La coupe et le baptême de la passion (*Mc,* x,35–40; cf. *Mt,* xx,20–23; *Lc,* xii,50)." *RB* 74 (1967) 356–91. **Friedrich, G.** *Die Verkündigung des Todes Jesu im Neuen Testament.* Biblisch-theologische Studien 6. Neukirchen-Vluyn: Neukirchener Verlag, 1982. **George, A.** "La service du royaume (Marc 10,35–45)." *BVC* 25 (1959) 15–19. **Goguel, M.** "La demand des premiers places dans le Royaume messianique." *RHR* 123 (1941) 27–43. **Hedinger, U.** "Jesus und die Volksmenge: Kritik der Qualifizierung der *óchloi* in der Evangelienauslegung." *TZ* 32 (1976) 201–6. **Higgins, A. J. B.** "St. Mark x.36." *ExpTim* 52 (1941) 317–18, 437. **Hill, D.** "The Request of Zebedee's Sons and the Johannine δόξα-Theme." *NTS* 13 (1966–67) 281–85. **Hoffmann, P.** *Jesus von Nazareth und eine christliche Moral: Sittliche perspektiven der Verkündigung Jesu.* QD 66. Freiburg: Herder, 1975. 186–230. **Howard, V. P.** "Did Jesus Speak about His Own Death?" *CBQ* 39 (1977) 515–27, esp. 518–26. ———. *Das Ego Jesu in den synoptischen Evangelien: Untersuchungen zum Sprachgebrauch Jesu.* MTS 14. Marburg: Elwert, 1975. 97–107. **Kuhn, H.-W.** *Ältere Sammlungen im Markusevangelium.* 151–60. **Légasse, S.** "Approche de l'épisode préévangélique des fils de Zébédée (Marc x.35–40 par.)." *NTS* 20 (1973–74) 161–77. ———. "L'exercice de l'autorité dans l'Église d'après les évangiles synoptiques." *NRT* 85 (1963) 1009–22. **Lohse, E.** *Märtyrer und Gottesknecht: Untersuchungen zur urchristlichen Verkündigung vom Sühntod Jesu Christi.* FRLANT 64. Göttingen: Vandenhoeck & Ruprecht, 1955. 117–22. **Loisy, A.** *Les évangiles synoptiques.* 2 vols. Paris: Ceffonds, 1907. **Muddiman, J. B.** "The Glory of Jesus, Mark 10:37." In *The Glory of Christ in the New Testament: Studies in Christology.* FS G. B. Caird, ed. L. D. Hurst and N. T. Wright. Oxford; New York: Clarendon, 1987. 51–58. **Oberweis, M.** "Das Martyrium der Zebedaiden in Mk 10.35–40 (Mt 20.20–3) und Offb 11.3–13." *NTS* 44 (1998) 74–92. **Patsch, H.** *Abendmahl und historischer Jesus.* Calwer theologische Monographien. Stuttgart: Calwer, 1972. 170–80, 205–15. **Radermakers, J.** "Revendiquer ou servir? Mc 10,35–45." *AsSeign* 2.60 (1965) 28–39. **Reploh, K. G.** *Markus— Lehrer der Gemeinde.* 156–72. **Robinson, J. A. T.** "The One Baptism." *SJT* 6 (1953) 257–74. **Schmidt, K. L.** *Rahmen.* 244–45. **Schulz, A.** *Nachfolgen und Nachahmen: Studien über das Verhältnis des neutestamentlichen Jüngerschaft zur urchristlichen Vorbildethik.* SANT 6. Munich: Kösel, 1962. 252–65. ———. *Unter dem Anspruch Gottes: Das neutestamentliche Zeugnis von der Nachahmung.* Kleine Schriften zur Theologie. Munich: Kösel, 1967. 39–45. **Seeley, D.** "Rulership and Service in Mark 10.41–45." *NovT* 35 (1993) 234–50. **Smart, J. D.** "Mark 10:35–45." *Int* 33 (1979) 288–93. **Stegemann, E. W.** "Zur Rolle von Petrus, Jakobus und Johannes im Markusevangelium." *TZ* 42 (1986) 366–74. **Stock, K.** *Boten aus dem Mit-Ihm-Sein.* 135–42. **Tannehill, R. C.** *The Sword of His Mouth.* SBLSS 1. Missoula, MT: Scholars Press, 1975. 102–7. **Taylor, V.** *Jesus and His Sacrifice.* 97–99. **Tyson, J. B.** "The Blindness of the Disciples in Mark." *JBL* 80 (1961) 261–68. **Via, D. O., Jr.** *The Ethics of Mark's Gospel.* 156–68. ———. "Mark 10:32–52—A Structural, Literary and Theological Interpretation." In *Society of Biblical Literature 1979 Seminar Papers.* Ed. P. J. Achtemeier. 2 vols. SBLSP 18. Missoula, MT: Scholars Press, 1979. 2.187–203. **Vögtle, A.** "Todesankündigungen und Todesverständnis Jesu." In *Der Tod Jesu: Deutungen im Neuen Testament.* Ed. K. Kertelge. QD 74. Freiburg: Herder, 1976. 51–113, esp. 80–88. **Wischmeyer, O.** "Herrschen als Dienen—Mk 10,41–45." *ZNW* 90 (1999) 28–44.

Bibliography on Mark 10:45

Allison, D. C. *Jesus of Nazareth: Millenarian Prophet.* Minneapolis: Fortress, 1998. 54–55. **Barrett, C. K.** "The Background of Mark 10:45." In *New Testament Essays.* FS T. W. Manson, ed. A. J. B. Higgins. Manchester: Manchester UP, 1959. 1–18. **Bastin, M.** *Jésus devant sa passion.* LD 92. Paris: Cerf, 1976. 83–100. **Beasley-Murray, G. R.** *Jesus and the Kingdom of God.* 278–83. **Betz, O.** "Jesus und Jesaja 53." In *Frühes Christentum.* Vol. 3 of *Geschichte—Tradition—Reflexion.* FS M. Hengel, ed. H. Cancik et al. Tübingen: Mohr-Siebeck, 1996. 3–20. **Bieringer, R.** "Traditionsgeschichtlicher Ursprung und theologische Bedeutung der ὑπέρ-Aussagen im Neuen Testament." In *The Four Gospels 1992.* FS F. Neirynck, ed. F. Van Segbroeck et al. 3 vols. BETL 100. Leuven: Peeters; Leuven UP, 1992. 1:219–48. **Casey, M.** *Aramaic Sources of Mark's Gospel.* 209–17. **Daube, D.** *Collaboration with Tyranny in Rabbinic Law.* Riddell Memorial Lectures, Thirty-Seventh Series, University of Newcastle upon Tyne, 1965. Oxford: Oxford UP, 1965. **Dautzenberg, G.** *Sein Leben bewahren: ψυχή in den Herrenworten der Evangelien.* SANT 14. Munich: Kösel, 1966. 98–107. **Davies, P. E.** "Did Jesus Die as a Martyr-Prophet?" *BR* 2 (1957) 19–30. **Emerton, J. A.** "The Aramaic Background of Mark X,45." *JTS* n.s. 11 (1960) 334–35. **Engnell, I.** "The 'Ebed-Jahweh Songs and the Suffering Messiah in 'Deutero-Isaiah.'" *BJRL* 31 (1948) 54–64. **Feuillet, A.** "Le logion sur la rançon." *RSPT* 51 (1967) 365–402. **France, R. T.** *Jesus and the Old Testament.* 116–21. ———. "The Servant of the Lord in the Teaching of Jesus." *TynBul* 19 (1968) 26–52, esp. 32–37. **Grelot, P.** *Les poèmes du serviteur: De la lecture critique à l'herméneutique.* LD 103. Paris: Cerf, 1981. 158–64. **Grimm, W.** *Weil ich dich liebe: Die Verkündigung Jesu und Deuterojesaja.* ANTJ 1. Bern; Frankfurt am Main: Lang, 1976. 231–77. **Gubler, M.-L.** *Die frühesten Deutungen des Todes Jesu: Eine motivgeschichtliche Darstellung aufgrund der neueren exegetischen Forschung.* OBO 15. Göttingen: Vandenhoeck & Ruprecht, 1977. 230–42. **Hahn, F.** *The Titles of Jesus in Christology: Their History in Early Christianity.* London: Lutterworth, 1969. 55–61. **Hampel, V.** *Menschensohn und historischer Jesus: Ein Rätselwort als Schlüssel zum messianischen Selbstverständnis Jesu.* Neukirchen-Vluyn: Neukirchener Verlag, 1990. 302–42. **Hengel, M.** *The Atonement: The Origins of the Doctrine in the New Testament.* Philadelphia: Fortress, 1981. 33–75. ———. *Studies in the Gospel of Mark.* 37–38. **Higgins, A. J. B.** *Jesus and the Son of Man.* London: Lutterworth; Philadelphia: Fortress, 1964. 36–50. **Hill, D.** *Greek Words and Hebrew Meanings: Studies in the Semantics of Soteriological Terms.* SNTSMS 5. Cambridge: Cambridge UP, 1967. 77–81. **Hooker, M. D.** *Jesus and the Servant: The Influence of the Servant Concept of Deutero-Isaiah in the New Testament.* London: S. P. C. K., 1959. 74–79. ———. *The Son of Man in Mark.* 140–47. **Janowski, B.** "Auslösung des verwirkten Lebens: Zur Geschichte und Struktur der biblischen Lösegeldvorstellung." *ZTK* 79 (1982) 25–59. **Jeremias, J.** "Das Lösegeld für Viele (Mk 10.45)." In *Abba: Studien zur neutestamentlichen Theologie und Zeitgeschichte.* Göttingen: Vandenhoeck & Ruprecht, 1966. 216–29. **Jonge, M. de.** "Jesus' Death for Others and the Death of the Maccabean Martyrs." In *Text and Testimony.* Ed. T. J. Baarda et al. Kampen: Kok, 1988. 142–51. **Karnetzki, M.** "Die galiläische Redaktion im Markusevangelium." *ZNW* 52 (1961) 238–72. **Kertelge, K.** "Der dienende Menschensohn (Mk 10,45)." In *Jesus und der Menschensohn.* FS A. Vögtle, ed. R. Pesch and R. Schnackenburg. Freiburg: Herder, 1975. 225–39. **Kim, S.** *The "Son of Man" as the Son of God.* WUNT 30. Tübingen: Mohr-Siebeck, 1983. 38–73. **Koch, K.** "Messias und Sündenvergebung in Jesaja 53—Targum: Ein Beitrag zu der Praxis der aramäischen Bibelübersetzung." *JSJ* 3 (1972) 117–48. **Lindars, B.** *Jesus Son of Man: A Fresh Examination of the Son of Man Sayings in the Gospels in the Light of Recent Research.* London: S. P. C. K., 1983; Grand Rapids, MI: Eerdmans, 1984. 76–81. ———. "Salvation Proclaimed. VII. Mark 10 45: A Ransom for Many." *ExpTim* 93 (1981–82) 292–95. **Maier, F. W.** *Jesus—Lehrer der Gottesherrschaft.* Würzburg: Echter, 1965. 166–70. **Moo, D. J.** *The Old Testament in the Gospel Passion Narratives.* Sheffield: Almond, 1983. 122–27. **Moulder, W. J.** "The Old Testament Background and Interpretation of Mark x. 45." *NTS* 24 (1977–78) 120–27. **Müller, M.** *Der Ausdruck "Menschensohn" in den Evangelien:*

Voraussetzungen und Bedeutung. ATD 17. Leiden: Brill, 1984. 182–86. **Page, S. H. T.** "The Authenticity of the Ransom Logion (Mark 10:45b)." In *Studies of History and Tradition in the Four Gospels.* Ed. R. T. France and D. Wenham. Gospel Perspectives 1. Sheffield: JSOT Press, 1980. 137–61. **Riesenfeld, H.** *Unité et diversité dans le Nouveau Testament.* LD 98. Paris: Cerf, 1979. 113–23, esp. 117–19. **Roloff, J.** "Anfänge der soteriologischen Deutung des Todes Jesu (Mk. x. 45 und Lk. xxii. 27)." *NTS* 19 (1972–73) 38–64. **Sabourin, L.** *Rédemption sacrificielle: Une enquête exégétique.* Studia 11. Montreal: Desclée de Brouwer, 1961. 236–49. **Schenker, A.** "Substitution du châtiment ou prix de la paix? Le don de la vie du Fils de l'homme en Mc 10,45 et par. à la lumière de l'Ancien Testament." In *La Pâque du Christ: Mystère de salut.* FS F.-X. Durwell, ed. M. Benzerath et al. LD 112. Paris: Cerf, 1982. 75–90. **Schürmann, H.** *Jesu Abschiedsrede, Lukas 22,21–38.* NTAbh 20.5. Münster: Schendorff, 1957. **Schwarz, G.** *Jesus "der Menschensohn": Aramaistische Untersuchungen zu den synoptischen Menschensohnworten Jesu.* BWANT 119. Stuttgart: Kohlhammer, 1986. 171–76. ———. *Jesus und Judas: Aramaistische Untersuchungen zur Jesus-Judas-Überlieferung der Evangelien und der Apostelgeschichte.* BWANT 123. Stuttgart: Kohlhammer, 1988. 70–77. **Simon, L.** "De la situation de l'Église au sermon: Marc 10/45." *ETR* 46 (1971) 3–11. **Strecker, G.** "The Passion and Resurrection Predictions in Mark's Gospel." *Int* 22 (1968) 421–42. **Strobel, A.** "Die Deutung des Todes Jesu im ältesten Evangelium." In *Das Kreuz Jesu: Theologische Überlegungen.* Ed. P. Rieger. Forum 12. Göttingen: Vandenhoeck & Ruprecht, 1969. 32–64. **Stuhlmacher, P.** "Existenzstellvertretung für die Vielen: Mk 10,45 (Mt 20,28)." In *Werden und Wirken des Alten Testaments.* FS C. Westermann, ed. R. Albertz et al. Göttingen: Vandenhoeck & Ruprecht, 1980. 412–27 (repr. in P. Stuhlmacher. *Versöhnung, Gesetz und Gerechtigkeit: Aufsätze zur biblischen Theologie.* Göttingen: Vandenhoeck & Ruprecht, 1981. 27–42; ET: "Vicariously Giving His Life for Many, Mark 10:45 (Matt. 20:28)." In P. Stuhlmacher. *Reconciliation, Law, and Righteousness.* Philadelphia: Fortress, 1986. 16–29). ———. *Jesus des Nazareth—Christus des Glaubens.* Stuttgart: Calwer, 1988 (ET: *Jesus of Nazareth—Christ of Faith.* Peabody: Hendrickson, 1993). **Suhl, A.** *Die Funktion der alttestamentlichen Zitate.* 114–20. **Taylor, V.** *Jesus and His Sacrifice.* 99–105, 257–61. ———. "The Origin of the Markan Passion-Sayings." *NTS* 1 (1954–55) 159–67 (repr. in V. Taylor. *New Testament Essays.* London: Epworth, 1970. 60–71). **Thyen, H.** *Studien zur Sündenvergebung im Neuen Testament und seinen alttestamentlichen und jüdischen Voraussetzungen.* FRLANT 96. Göttingen: Vandenhoeck & Ruprecht, 1970. 154–63. **Tödt, H. E.** *The Son of Man in the Synoptic Tradition.* NTL. London: SCM Press, 1965. 135–38, 202–11. **Wilcox, M.** "On the Ransom-Saying in Mark 10:45c, Matt 20:28c." In *Frühes Christentum.* Vol. 3 of *Geschichte—Tradition—Reflexion.* FS M. Hengel, ed. H. Cancik et al. Tübingen: Mohr-Siebeck, 1996. 173–86.

Translation

[35]*And James and John the sons* [a] *of Zebedee approach him, saying to him, "Teacher,* [b] *we wish that you might do for us whatever we might ask you."* [36]*And he* [c] *said to them, "What do you wish that I might do for you?"* [37]*And they said to him, "Grant us that one might sit at your right and the other at your left in your glory."* [d] [38]*But Jesus said to them, "You do not know what you ask. Are you able to drink the cup that I drink, or to be baptized with the baptism with which I am baptized?"* [39]*But they said to him, "We are able." But Jesus said to them, "The cup that I drink you will drink, and with the baptism with which I am baptized you will be baptized.* [40]*But to sit at my right or at my left is not mine to grant; but it is for those for whom* [e] *it is prepared."* [f]

[41]*And hearing of this, the ten began to be indignant at James and John.* [42]*And summoning them, Jesus says to them, "You know that those who are supposed to rule over the Gentiles lord it over them, and their great ones* [g] *have power over them.* [43]*But it is* [h] *not to be so among you; but whoever may wish to be great among you will be* [i] *your servant,*

[44] *and whoever may wish to be first among you will be slave of all.* [45] *For the 'son of man' came not to be served but to serve, and to give his life as a ransom*[j] *for many."*

Notes

[a]B C and a few later MSS read οἱ δύο υἱοί, "the two sons."

[b]Gk. διδάσκαλε. Some Syr. MSS read *rabbî,* "rabbi."

Σ Φ and a few other authorities add Ἰησοῦς, "Jesus."

[d]W reads ἐν τῇ βασιλείᾳ τῆς δόξης σου, "in the kingdom of your glory." The Sahidic Coptic reads "in the glory of your kingdom." Both of these readings reflect the influence of the parallel in Matt 20:21, which reads ἐν τῇ βασιλείᾳ σου, "in your kingdom." Lohmeyer (221) accepts this reading as original. However, it is easier to explain a change from δόξα, "glory," to βασιλεία, "kingdom," than a change from βασιλεία to δόξα, for βασιλεία explains what is meant by δόξα and conforms to Jesus' proclamation of the "kingdom of God." Cranfield (337) states that "Mark's ἐν τῇ δόξῃ σου is probably rightly interpreted by the M[atthean] ἐν τῇ βασιλείᾳ σου." Cranfield is correct, but see *Comment* below.

[e]Lit. "but [it is] for whom it has been prepared." it sa[ms] sy[s] read ἄλλοις, "[it is] for others." This variant arose from misreading ΑΛΛΟΙC as ἄλλοις, rather than ἀλλ' οἷς, "but [it is] for whom." See Metzger, *TCGNT*[1], 107. One needs to remember that in the early MSS Greek was written in upper-case letters without spacing between the words.

[f]א* Φ and a few other late MSS add ὑπὸ τοῦ πατρός μου, "by my Father." This addition derives from Matt 20:23.

[g]א C[*vid] read βασιλεῖς αὐτῶν, "their kings."

[h]Gk. ἐστίν, which is read by א B C* D L W. A C[3] N Σ Φ and many later authorities read ἔσται, "it will be." The latter reading may have derived from Matt 20:26 (but some MSS of Matthew also read ἐστίν). Copyists (including the Matthean evangelist) may have felt that the future tense was appropriate for a discussion that pertained to eschatological things. See Metzger, *TCGNT*[1], 108. It is quite possible, however, that the present tense captures more accurately the original idea. Jesus and his disciples were thinking about their places of authority within a restored Israel *of their time.* See *Comment* below.

[i]א C read ἔστω ὑμῶν διάκονος, "let him be your servant."

[j]Gk. λύτρον. W reads λούτρον, "bath," "ablution," or "libation." This variant is probably no more than a copyist's error, but it also could be an attempt to introduce the idea of the cleansing effects of Jesus' death (cf. Eph 5:26; Titus 3:5).

Form/Structure/Setting

Mark 10:35–45 comprises two basic parts: (1) the request of James and John to sit at Jesus' right and left when Jesus is established in his "glory" (vv 35–40); and (2) Jesus' teaching in response to the indignation of the other disciples when they learn of this request (vv 41–45). The logic and train of thought of these parts are much more involved, however. The episode begins with the request of the sons of Zebedee: they would like Jesus to grant them a wish (v 35). Jesus asks them what it is that they would like him to do for them (v 36). They tell him that they wish to sit at Jesus' right and left, that is, to assume positions of highest authority, second and third to Jesus himself, when the kingdom has come in its fullness (v 37). But Jesus tells them that they do not know what they ask, for there will be trials (v 38). They assure, him, however, that they are equal to the task (v 39a). Jesus then declares that they will indeed share in his trials (v 39b), but he cannot grant their request: "it is for those for whom it is prepared" (v 40). When the rest of the disciples hear of James and John's request, they are indignant (v 41). Jesus then summons his disciples and teaches them regarding humility and service (vv 42–44), concluding with his own example of offering service in place of being served (v 45).

Although source critics and form critics have traditionally argued that Mark 10:35–45 is made up of various components (e.g., see Dibelius, *From Tradition,* 51; Schmidt, *Rahmen,* 244–45; Gnilka, 2:99 [vv 35–38 are original, vv 39–40 are a later expansion]; Bultmann, *History,* 24, 69 [vv 38–39 are independent]; Lohmeyer, 222–23 [vv 38–40 reflect later leadership controversies in the early church]; this is rejected by Schmithals, 2:467), mostly pre-Markan, Gundry (581–82) has argued for the unity of the passage. Even the more conservative Taylor (*Formation,* 66) believes that the evangelist added vv 41–45 to the story of the request of the sons of Zebedee (in his commentary [439] he states that vv 41–45 "may have been the immediate sequel," though he still speaks of "signs that it was appended by Mark"), while Davies and Allison (*Matthew* 3:85) think that vv 41–44 are pre-Markan material "of uncertain origin," to which the evangelist or his tradition added v 45 (on this latter point, see also Pesch, 2:154, 164).

Other scholars have tried to dissect v 45. According to Lindars (*Son of Man,* 80), the saying was originally "A man may risk his life for the sake of the many," to which later "as a ransom" was added. C. Colpe (*TDNT* 8:455) thinks the evangelist joined the two parts of the saying. Crossan (*In Fragments,* 291) thinks the evangelist added "the son of man" to v 45a and then added v 45b. Wilcox ("On the Ransom-Saying") and Pesch (2:262–67) argue plausibly that the saying in v 45 is unified and should be taken as historical, even if it originated in a different setting. Jesus has in effect offered his life to the servants and officers of the ruling priests in exchange for the lives of his disciples. In subsequent tradition, of course, Christianity imputed a great deal of theology to the saying. But in its original, historical context the saying was primarily one of negotiation: Jesus would come quietly if his followers were permitted to go their way (see also Daube, *Collaboration*).

Notwithstanding all of the objections that have been advanced, Gundry's arguments for the original unity of vv 35–45 are to be preferred. There is nothing in this narrative that is so disjunctive or incongruous or apparently independent that requires interpreters to place it in another context. Moreover, none of this material is better accounted for in a setting after the life of Jesus (post-*Sitz im Leben Jesu*). The entire passage, including v 45 (of which much more will be said below), makes good sense as a fragment of embarrassing but authentic tradition in which Jesus' disciples disputed among themselves who was the greatest and who would receive the most important posts in the anticipated new government. Had it not been for Jesus' comments in vv 42–45, none of this material likely would have been preserved and passed on. Indeed, it is amazing that vv 35–40 were passed on, not only because of the request made by James and John but because the cup saying in v 38 stands somewhat in tension with Jesus' later prayer in 14:36 that he not have to drink this cup. But, of course, vv 35–40 form the necessary prelude to what happens and what is said in vv 41–45. Thus the entire passage hangs together. Indeed, according to Casey (*Aramaic Sources,* 193–218), the unity of the passage becomes more plainly evident when the underlying Semitic elements are fully taken into account (see *Comment* on v 45 below). The only clearly Markan addition is found in v 42a: προσκαλεσάμενος αὐτούς, "summoning them," of which the evangelist is especially fond (cf. Mark 3:13, 23 [προσκαλεσάμενος αὐτούς]; 6:7; 7:14; 8:34; 12:43).

The authenticity of the disciples' request for the seats of highest honor "is in every way credible" (Taylor, 439). Many commentators agree, noting that it is not easy to explain why the early church at any stage of its history would have invented a tradition that discredited Jesus' closest followers, notwithstanding the opportunity that the original request and the subsequent response gave Jesus to instruct his disciples (see Branscomb, 187; Klostermann, 107: "The request concerning seats of honor at the side of Jesus does not shed a favorable light on the sons of Zebedee"). Rawlinson (144) speculates, not unreasonably, that the request originally was in response to Jesus' promise that the Twelve would someday sit on thrones judging the twelve tribes of Israel (Matt 19:28 = Luke 22:28–30): James and John would have liked to sit on the thrones adjacent to the throne on which Jesus would sit (see *Comment* on vv 36–37 below). Johnson (179) surmises that the same thinking underlies the post-Easter decision of the eleven to replace the deceased Judas Iscariot, so that the full administrative quorum of twelve would be ready for the kingdom (cf. Acts 1:6, 15–26).

The Markan evangelist makes use of this tradition because it affords Jesus yet another opportunity to teach his disciples true values of the kingdom. The emphasis on a willingness to suffer (clearly implied by the references to drinking "the cup"—see *Comment* below) and to serve if one is to become great casts Jesus in an impressive light and helps offset the stigma of his crucifixion and apparent defeat. In other words, what happens to Jesus in Jerusalem is consistent with his teaching after all. This is why the evangelist orders his material in the way he does, so that Jesus' teaching on suffering and humility is emphasized.

Comment

James and John's request affords Jesus the opportunity to instruct his disciples further on the type of service appropriate for the kingdom of God. Just as the first passion prediction in 8:31 was followed by instruction in self-denial, service, and even martyrdom (8:34–9:1), and the second passion prediction in 9:31 was followed by similar instruction (9:33–37), so the third passion prediction in 10:32–34 is followed by teaching on true service and the possibility of suffering (10:38–39, 41–45). Thus, each passion prediction is followed by important teaching of what followers of Jesus should expect and how they should live (see Pesch, 2:153). If Jesus' followers are to make any headway against very long odds, they must seek to serve and not vie for positions of authority; they must be willing to suffer and not flee from persecution; they must be willing to be last and not insist on being first.

35 προσπορεύονται αὐτῷ Ἰάκωβος καὶ Ἰωάννης οἱ υἱοὶ Ζεβεδαίου λέγοντες αὐτῷ, διδάσκαλε, θέλομεν ἵνα ὃ ἐὰν αἰτήσωμέν σε ποιήσῃς ἡμῖν, "James and John the sons of Zebedee approach him, saying to him, 'Teacher, we wish that you might do for us whatever we might ask you.'" The disciples James and John have previously been mentioned together, along with Jesus and Peter, in Mark 5:37 on the occasion of raising up the daughter of Jairus. These three were with Jesus on the Mount of Transfiguration (9:2), and they will be together again in Mark 13:3 when they ask for further clarification of Jesus' prophecy of the temple's coming destruction. According to Mark 3:17 Jesus surnamed James and John *Boanerges*, that is, the "sons of thunder" (on this problematical epithet, see Guelich, 161–62). They approach Jesus, the "teacher" (διδάσκαλε—on the lips of the disciples in 4:38; 9:38; on the lips of others in 5:35; 9:17; 10:17, 20), with the request that he do for them whatever they ask. The nature of the question is remarkable, for it seems unrestricted in potential.

According to Mark, it is "James and John" who make a request of Jesus to sit at his right and left in his glory. Because their request arouses the indignation of the other disciples, we should not be surprised that the scene is mitigated by the Matthean evangelist (Rawlinson, 143–44), who in various ways seeks to put the disciples in a better light. According to Matt 20:20–21 it is the *mother* of James and John who makes the request. But Matthew betrays his knowledge of Mark's version when he has Jesus reply: "You [pl.] do not know what you [pl.] are asking" (Matt 20:22 = Mark 10:38). The plural clearly indicates that Jesus was addressing James and John, not their mother.

36–37 τί θέλετέ [με] ποιήσω ὑμῖν; . . . δὸς ἡμῖν ἵνα εἷς σου ἐκ δεξιῶν καὶ εἷς ἐξ ἀριστερῶν καθίσωμεν ἐν τῇ δόξῃ σου, "'What do you wish that I might do for you?' . . . 'Grant us that one might sit at your right and the other at your left in your glory.'" Jesus makes no hasty promise but asks James and John what they wish him to do for them. Their request is to sit at Jesus' right and left (ἐκ δεξιῶν καί . . . ἐξ ἀριστερῶν) in his glory (ἐν τῇ δόξῃ σου). The disciples wish to be appointed seats (or thrones) in the coming government (see Schniewind, 143). In effect, they are requesting the top positions in the new kingdom that they anticipate will be established soon. It is not clear that the phrase ἐν τῇ δόξῃ, "in glory," means the Parousia (as assumed by some commentators, e.g., Wellhausen, 84; Blunt, 220; Taylor, 440; Schmid, 198; Mann, 412), as it probably does in 8:38 and in 13:26 (see *Comment* on 13:24–27). From a post-Easter point of view, any reference to Jesus' δόξα, "glory," would be understood in the sense of the Parousia. But in the setting in the life of Jesus (*Sitz im Leben Jesu*), the question refers to the coming kingdom of God on earth, that is, the restored Israel in which the great prophecies (especially of Isaiah) will be fulfilled, when all nations will come to Jerusalem to worship the Lord (cf. Mark 11:17, where Jesus alludes to Isa 56:7). It will be at that time that Jesus' δόξα will be recognized throughout Israel and throughout the world, when foreigners far and wide will seek to hear and see one who is greater than Jonah and wiser than Solomon (cf. Matt 12:41–42, again appealing to sources outside of Mark). Here δόξα refers to Jesus' honor, dignity, perhaps even splendor (cf. *TLNT*, 367–68).

In 9:1 Jesus declared that some will "see the kingdom of God having come in power." James and John in 10:35–37 are referring to this event in their lifetime. Outside of Mark (i.e., in Q), Jesus makes a very important prediction about the coming rule of the Twelve: "Truly, I say to you, in the new world, when the Son of man shall sit on his glorious throne, you who have followed me will also sit on twelve thrones, judging the twelve tribes of Israel" (Matt 19:28; cf. Luke 22:28–30). These statements grow out of Jesus' understanding of Daniel. Not only does he regard himself as the human being, or "son of man," described in Dan 7:13–14, but he understands the "thrones" (note the plural) in Dan 7:9 in conjunction with Ps 122:1–5 as promising a time of rule. The twelve tribes will be governed by the twelve disciples, while Jesus himself in the spirit of Ps 110:1 will share his Father's throne. This combination of material from Daniel and the Psalter, books that also contribute important ingredients to Jesus' understanding of the kingdom (see Chilton, "The Kingdom of God in Recent Discussion," in *Studying the Historical Jesus: Evaluations of the State of Current Research*, ed. B. D. Chilton and C.

A. Evans, NTTS 19 [Leiden: Brill, 1994] 255–80, esp. 273–79), is what lies behind Jesus' imagery. In view of statements like these, James and John's expectations are entirely understandable. (Cranfield's distinction, 337, between Jesus' kingdom and God's kingdom, as though the latter refers to the "final kingdom of God," while the former refers to the "Messiah's rule," is dubious.)

38–40 James and John's expectations were accurate so far as they went. The only thing that they had omitted from the equation was the struggle and suffering that lay ahead. Jesus' expectations of struggle were founded on the book of Daniel (and on what had happened to his colleague John the Baptist). The entire book depicts the struggle of the people of Israel and their supporting heavenly hosts against their foes, which are supported by demonic powers. Dan 7 itself played a role, for in the part of the seer's vision following the presentation of the "son of man" in vv 13–14 a great struggle between the "holy ones" and the forces of evil is described.

Jesus asks James and John if they are prepared πιεῖν τὸ ποτήριον, "to drink the cup," that he will drink and τὸ βάπτισμα . . . βαπτισθῆναι, "to be baptized with the baptism," that he will undergo. By this Jesus means suffering and possibly death. ποτήριον, "cup," used figuratively means fate with or without judgment (see Pss 11:6; 16:5; 116:13 ["cup of salvation"]); sometimes it refers to suffering and judgment, but not exclusively (against Schmid, 198–99; see Isa 51:22; Jer 25:15; Ezek 23:31–34; Ps 75:8; *Pss. Sol.* 8:14; Martin, *Mark: Evangelist and Theologian*, 118); but the actual idiom "cup of death" is targumic and is the closest parallel to the words of Jesus (see *Tg. Neof.* Gen 40:23; *Tg. Neof.* Deut 32:1; see also *Mart. Ascen. Isa.* 5:13, where Isaiah, about to be sawn in two, says to his disciples, "for me alone the Lord has mixed this cup"). Jesus will refer to this cup with dread in the Gethsemane prayer (14:36). James and John say they are able to drink this cup and to undergo the baptism that awaits Jesus (though they might not yet have been convinced that Jesus' violent fate was inevitable). Jesus assures (warns?) them that they will indeed share his fate. But the assignment of seats at his right and left is not his prerogative; it is God's. This admission that Jesus lacks the authority to make such assignments has often been cited as important evidence of the authenticity of the tradition.

In view of James' martyrdom in the early 40s (cf. Acts 12:2), some critics think that vv 38–39 are a later church formulation, a *vaticinium ex eventu* (e.g., Wellhausen, 84; Loisy, *Les évangiles synoptiques* 2:237–38; Klostermann, 107; Branscomb, 60; Bultmann, *History*, 24: "a manifest *vaticinium ex eventu*"; Lohmeyer, 223). Nonetheless, many disagree (Schmid, 199; Schweizer, 218; Anderson, 255; Brooks, 168–69; Hooker, 247; Casey, *Aramaic Sources*, 206). Jesus' anticipation that James and John will drink the cup of suffering, perhaps even martyrdom, is most probably authentic. Had it been an *ex eventu* prophecy, we should have expected something more explicit (and more accurate, since there is no credible tradition of John's martyrdom) as well as a promise of reward. The early church, moreover, had no interest in the question of who would sit next to Jesus (even Rev 3:20 is making a different point), while identifying with the death of Jesus (as in Rom 6) meant something very different. Reference to the cup has nothing to do with the cup of the Lord's Supper (Johnson, 179), as Turner (51) rightly denies; but see Juel (146–47), who finds it "tempting" (see also Lührmann, 180; Hurtado, 177: "Mark must have known that his readers would make associations with their own Christian rites"; perhaps). Mark may have known this, but it is an idea that only arose years after Easter.

The perceptive reader of Mark will not overlook the irony that although James and John requested privileged positions on Jesus' "right" and "left," when Jesus is crucified, it will be two rebels, ἕνα ἐκ δεξιῶν καὶ ἕνα ἐξ εὐωνύμων αὐτοῦ, "one on his right and one on his left," not the disciples, that will join him (Mark 15:27; see Moule, 83–84; van Iersel, 335). The reader will find that these disciples, as well as the other disciples who had expressed their indignation at James and John, simply did not have the stomach for the cup and the baptism for which they had said they were ready.

τὸ δὲ καθίσαι ἐκ δεξιῶν μου ἢ ἐξ εὐωνύμων οὐκ ἔστιν ἐμὸν δοῦναι, ἀλλ' οἷς ἡτοίμασται, "But to sit at my right or at my left is not mine to grant; but it is for those for whom it is prepared." This is a remarkable admission on Jesus' part. Equally remarkable is the survival of this restrictive saying in the dominical tradition. In Matt 19:28 = Luke 22:28–30 Jesus promises his disciples that they will sit with him on twelve thrones judging the twelve tribes of Israel. This discussion, whether or not it occurred on the same occasion, is surely part of the same topic. Jesus can assure his disciples that they will reign with him (cf. 2 Tim 2:12), but he cannot make specific appointments.

41 ἀκούσαντες οἱ δέκα ἤρξαντο ἀγανακτεῖν περὶ Ἰακώβου καὶ Ἰωάννου, "And hearing of this, the ten began to be indignant at James and John." It has been suggested that James and John were cousins of Jesus (for a recent presentation of the evidence, see J. W. Wenham, *Easter Enigma* [Grand Rapids, MI: Zondervan, 1984] 34–35). If they were in fact cousins, then it is understandable why these two disciples felt they could make such a request: as family, were they not entitled to a measure of privilege? The ten are indignant because of the patent favoritism (if not nepotism) that such a request apparently presupposed. It is interesting to note that Eusebius quotes from the sixth book of Clement's *Hypotyposes,* which says that "Peter and James and John after the ascension of the Savior did not struggle for glory, because they had previously been honored by the Savior, but chose James the Just as bishop of Jerusalem" (Eusebius, *Hist. eccl.* 2.1.3). What is interesting here is that a family member, in this case the brother of Jesus, ultimately was appointed to the highest position in the church.

42 προσκαλεσάμενος αὐτούς, "summoning them," Jesus teaches his disciples: οἴδατε ὅτι οἱ δοκοῦντες ἄρχειν τῶν ἐθνῶν κατακυριεύουσιν αὐτῶν καὶ οἱ μεγάλοι αὐτῶν κατεξουσιάζουσιν αὐτῶν, "You know that those who are supposed to rule over the Gentiles lord it over them, and their great ones have power over them." Jesus reminds his disciples of the conventions of leadership in their day: in essence it was tyranny (cf. how frequently Josephus uses the words τύραννος, "tyrant," and τυραννεῖν, "to act as tyrant," in his descriptions of Greek rulers and various Jewish rebels who hoped to seize power). In the Greco-Roman world οἱ μεγάλοι, "great ones," are those who rule over others, who κατακυριεύουσιν, "lord it over," others. These great ones were eulogized (cf. Virgil's flattery of Augustus [*Georg.* 1.24–42, 503–4; 4.559–62; *Aen.* 6.791–93]). In other words, greatness in Jesus' day was defined as power, coercive power. The more power one had, the "greater" one was. The disciples know these things through story and personal observation. Jesus' lesson would have an especially significant impact upon the disciples, given the state of Israel's subjugation at that time.

43 Jesus, however, categorically rejects the leadership style of the world: οὐχ οὕτως δέ ἐστιν ἐν ὑμῖν, "It is not to be so among you." What Jesus commands his disciples could not possibly be more at odds with conventional wisdom: ὃς ἂν θέλῃ μέγας γενέσθαι ἐν ὑμῖν ἔσται ὑμῶν διάκονος, "whoever may wish to be great among you will be your servant." διάκονος, "servant," is not as low as δοῦλος, "slave," but it clearly denotes a subordinate position, a position to which the world's "great" do not aspire. The frequent connotation of διάκονος is one who waits at table (e.g., Luke 17:8; Acts 6:2), though it often referred to other forms of menial labor. In the Greek world διακονία, "service," was the opposite of happiness, as Plato says: "How can one be happy when he has to serve [διακονεῖν] someone?" (*Gorg.* 491e). But the Jewish world had a higher appreciation of service (e.g., *Mek.* on Exod 18:12 ['Amālēq §3]; *b. Qidd.* 32b). Jesus, however, draws his contrast not between himself and Israel's religious heritage but between his style of leadership and that of the Roman world, which, of course, would include Roman influences in the land of Israel also (such as the Herodian dynasty).

44 ὃς ἂν θέλῃ ἐν ὑμῖν εἶναι πρῶτος ἔσται πάντων δοῦλος, "whoever may wish to be first among you will be slave of all." In this second line of his couplet Jesus intensifies the image: he who wishes to be great must be willing to serve; he who wishes to be first must be willing to be everyone's slave. Now Jesus uses the stronger word δοῦλος, "slave" (see MM, 170), though again it must be emphasized that service (whether διακονεῖν, "to serve," or δουλεύειν, "to serve [as slave]") was not viewed in the OT and early Judaism nearly as negatively as it was in the Greco-Roman world (on this point, see H. W. Beyer, *TDNT* 2:83).

45 καὶ γὰρ ὁ υἱὸς τοῦ ἀνθρώπου οὐκ ἦλθεν διακονηθῆναι ἀλλὰ διακονῆσαι καὶ δοῦναι τὴν ψυχὴν αὐτοῦ λύτρον ἀντὶ πολλῶν, "For the 'son of man' came not to be served but to serve, and to give his life as a ransom for many." This is by far the most remarkable and probably most disputed saying in Mark. Most commentators have tended to regard this saying as originally independent, whether authentic or not. Of course, many have regarded it as a later Christian formulation, especially in light of comparison with Luke 22:24–27 (Klostermann, 108–9, with regard to v 45b), perhaps deriving from Pauline circles (Branscomb, 190–91; Nineham, 280–81). Strecker (*Int* 22 [1968] 432 n. 30) thinks the saying is "an independent logion" that originated in "Hellenistic-Jewish Christianity." Similarly, Bultmann speaks of the saying as originating "from the redemption theories of Hellenistic Christianity" (*History,* 144) and so is a secondary formulation "of a later stage" (*History,* 155). Lohse (*Märtyrer und Gottesknecht,* 117–22) also believes that the saying is inauthentic but that it derives from the early Jewish community. Others who regard the saying as inauthentic include Pesch (2:162–64), S. K. Williams (*Jesus' Death as Saving Event: The Background and Origin of a Concept,* HDR 2 [Missoula, MT: Scholars Press, 1975] 211–12), and Roloff (*NTS* 19 [1972–73] 38–64). The authenticity of the saying is strongly defended by J. Jeremias (*TDNT* 5:706, 708, 710, 712–13, 715) and in more recent years by Stuhlmacher ("Vicariously Giving His Life," 16–29) and his student Grimm (*Weil ich dich liebe,* 231–77). Others who regard the saying as authentic include Lagrange (281–83), Rawlinson (146–48), Taylor (445–46; *NTS* 1 [1954–55] 159–67), Schürmann (*Jesu Abschiedsrede,* 85–86), Barrett ("Background"), C. Colpe (*TDNT* 8:448, 455), Cranfield (343–44), Schmid (200–201), Hooker (*Son of Man,* 140–47), Hampel (*Menschensohn und historischer Jesus,* 302–42), France (*Jesus and the Old Testament,*

116–21), Radermakers (270–71), Patsch (*Abendmahl*, 170–80, 205–11), and Gundry (587–90).

Boiled down, the controversies surrounding v 45 are three in number: (1) the unity of the saying and its relationship to vv 35–44; (2) the relationship of the saying to Second Isaiah, especially the Suffering Servant Song of Isa 52:13–53:12; and (3) the authenticity of the saying. All three of these disputed elements are in various ways related to one another. The position taken in this commentary is that the saying was originally a unit, that it was part of the whole pericope that makes up vv 35–45, that themes from Second Isaiah do indeed lie behind it, and that the saying derives from Jesus. The detailed discussion that follows will justify this position.

First, there are good reasons for allowing the saying to stand as a unity and as part of the whole dialogue between Jesus and his disciples as presented in vv 35–45. Claims made by Wellhausen (84–85) and Nineham (281) that v 45 stands in tension with vv 35/41–44 are overdrawn. Jesus enjoins his disciples to assume the roles of "servant," even "slave" (vv 43–44), if they are to be great in the kingdom of God (as implied by v 37). To take part in Jesus' glory, the disciples must be willing to endure a time of suffering (i.e., drinking the cup Jesus drinks, being baptized with his baptism), even martyrdom (as taught in vv 38–39). The ransom saying in v 45 properly connects to this teaching about suffering. The reference to serving (διακονῆσαι) links the saying to v 43, where the cognate word (διάκονος, "servant") occurs, and v 44, where a synonym (δοῦλος, "slave") occurs. The examples of being a servant or slave anticipate an allusion to the Suffering Servant of Isa 52:13–53:12. The willingness to give one's life in behalf of others does not introduce a new theme, one that is ill-suited for the present context or is "out of harmony," but rather brings the discussion to a fitting and logical conclusion (Casey, *Aramaic Sources,* 216, rightly says that v 45 "effectively . . . draws the whole passage together"). To be great in the kingdom of God will require a willingness to suffer (vv 37–38) and a willingness to serve (vv 43–44), and the prime example of one who is willing to serve and to suffer is the "son of man," who "came not to be served but to serve, and to give his life as a ransom for many" (v 45).

Second, there are good reasons to understand the ransom saying in terms of themes and images drawn from Second Isaiah, particularly the Suffering Servant Song. At one time this had been a given among scholars (e.g., Engnell, *BJRL* 31 [1948] 54, who speaks of the "indisputable role" that the Servant theme played in Jesus' self-understanding; cf. also Jeremias, "Lösegeld"), but in the wake of publications by Barrett ("Background of Mark 10:45," 1–18) and Hooker (*Jesus and the Servant*), many scholars have reconsidered this influence. However, in recent years there are signs that the pendulum is swinging back to the older opinion (cf. Moulder, *NTS* 24 [1977–78] 120–27; France, *Jesus and the Old Testament,* 116–21; Hengel, *Atonement,* 49–65; Pesch, 2:163–64; Stuhlmacher, "Vicariously Giving His Life"; id., *Jesus of Nazareth,* 49–57; Davies and Allison, *Matthew* 3:95–100; Hagner, *Matthew* 2:582–83; Painter, 150). Let us consider every element in the ransom saying that may reflect the Suffering Servant Song or some other Isaianic passage:

διακονῆσαι, "to serve": It has often been suggested that this word alludes to the Servant of Isa 52:13; 53:11 (both times עַבְדִּי *'abdî,* "my servant"). διακονεῖν, "to serve," and its cognates do not appear in the LXX. (In 1 Kgs 18:36; 2 Kgs 9:36; 10:10 Elijah is called the Lord's עֶבֶד *'ebed,* "servant," while in Josephus, *Ant.*

8.13.7 §354, Elisha is called Elijah's διάκονος, "servant.") The synonym δουλεύειν, "to serve (as slave)," appears in LXX Isa 53:11 (δουλεύοντα πολλοῖς, "serving many"; cf. MT: עֲבְדִי לָרַבִּים ʿabdî lārabbîm, "my servant, for the many"), and its cognate also appears in Mark 10:44 (πάντων δοῦλος, "slave of all"). Hooker (*Jesus and the Servant*, 74) concedes that this linguistic overlap "supports the claim that the concept of the Suffering Servant may lie behind Mark 10.45." Nevertheless, she goes on to reject the allusion, arguing that the contrast between the great men who lord it over others and the servant who gives up his life does not fit well the function of the Isaianic Servant. After all, the Servant is in fact the Lord's servant, not the servant of others. To this France (*Jesus and the Old Testament*, 118) replies by noting that in v 44 διάκονος, "servant," and δοῦλος, "slave," occur in parallelism and that διακονεῖν, "to serve," which appears in v 45, and δουλεύειν, "to serve (as slave)," which does translate עבד ʿābad, "serve," in the LXX, are synonymous. Therefore διακονεῖν may very well translate an Aramaic term that echoed עבד ʿābad (such as פלח pĕlaḥ, "serve," which in fact does translate עבד ʿābad). Davies and Allison (*Matthew* 3:96) agree, adding that "διακονῆσαι accurately describes what the ʿebed does."

δοῦναι τὴν ψυχὴν αὐτοῦ, "to give his life," closely approximates part of Isa 53:10: אִם־תָּשִׂים אָשָׁם נַפְשׁוֹ ʾim-tāśîm ʾāšām napšô, "when you place/make his life [as] a guilt offering" (NRSV, adapted), and 53:12: הֶעֱרָה לַמָּוֶת נַפְשׁוֹ heʿěrâ lammāwet napšô, "he poured out his life to death" (NRSV, adapted), or *Tg.* Isa. 53:12: מסר למותא נפשיה mĕsar lĕmôtāʾ napšêh, "he delivered up his soul to death." The language of giving (διδόναι), ransom (λύτρον), and life (ψυχή) is thoroughly biblical, e.g., LXX Exod 21:30: ἐὰν δὲ λύτρα ἐπιβληθῇ αὐτῷ, δώσει λύτρα τῆς ψυχῆς αὐτοῦ, "And if ransoms should be imposed on him, he shall give ransoms for his life"; Sir 29:15: χάριτας ἐγγύου μὴ ἐπιλάθῃ· ἔδωκεν γὰρ τὴν ψυχὴν αὐτοῦ ὑπὲρ σοῦ, "Do not forget all the kindness of your surety, for he has given his life for you"; and 1 Macc 2:50: νῦν τέκνα ζηλώσατε τῷ νόμῳ καὶ δότε τὰς ψυχὰς ὑμῶν ὑπὲρ διαθήκης πατέρων ἡμῶν, "Now, my children, show zeal for the law, and give your lives for the covenant of our fathers."

λύτρον ἀντί, "ransom for," approximates אָשָׁם ʾāšām, "guilt offering," but because λύτρον does not appear in LXX Isa 53 and never translates אָשָׁם ʾāšām in the LXX, Barrett and Hooker discount it as a possible allusion to the Suffering Servant, a point with which Casey (*Aramaic Sources*, 212) agrees. But Mark 10:45 is not a translation of any portion of Isa 52:13–53:12 (a point that is underscored by Davies and Allison, *Matthew* 3:96); it is a summary of the task of the Servant. It is true that Jesus has not said that the "son of man" has given his life as a guilt offering; rather he says that the "son of man" has given his life as a ransom. But a ransom for what? Why would a ransom be required? The last part of Isa 53:12 answers this question in saying that the Servant "bore the sin of many, and made intercession for the transgressors." Jesus' proclamation, following John's, called for repentance. Israel had not repented but instead had rejected God's messengers (in killing John and soon in killing Jesus). Jesus' life would constitute the ransom that would free Israel from divine penalty; his blood would make the hoped-for new covenant a reality (Mark 14:24).

The preposition ἀντί means "in the place of" (or "for" in the sense of exchange). On λύτρον, see MM, 382–83, and Deissmann, *Light*, 327–28. According to Deissmann (327), "when anybody heard the Greek word λύτρον, 'ransom,' in the first century, it was natural for him to think of the purchase-money for manumitting slaves." See Stuhlmacher (*Jesus of Nazareth*, 33–35, 49–54). According to Wilcox ("On the Ransom-Saying," 178), "it seems that the most promising choice of meaning is that of a payment for release of prisoners or hostages." This idea is consistent with Mark's portrait of Jesus as the one who is "stronger than" the strong man (i.e., Satan) and is thus able to rescue those whom the evil one has taken captive. The meaning of λύτρον is also consistent with the immediate context, for unlike the great men of late antiquity who lord it over others and by doing so often make slaves of them, Jesus is willing to give his life in exchange for their freedom from bondage.

πολλῶν, "many," probably alludes to לרבים *lārabbîm*, "for the many," which appears in Isa 53:11 (LXX: πολλοῖς, "many") and 12 (LXX: πολλῶν, "of many") "to describe the beneficiaries of the Servant's sacrifice" (France, *Jesus and the Old Testament*, 120). לרבים *lārabbîm* may also be alluded to in Mark 14:24, when Jesus says his blood will be ἐκχυννόμενον ὑπὲρ πολλῶν, "poured out for many." This phrase is a close approximation of the words of Isa 53:12: הֶעֱרָה לַמָּוֶת נַפְשׁוֹ . . . וְהוּא חֵטְא־רַבִּים נָשָׂא *heʿĕrâ lammāwet napšô . . . wĕhûʾ ḥēṭʾ-rabbîm nāśāʾ*, "he poured out his life to death . . . yet he bore the sin of many" (NRSV, adapted). There are at least five Jewish texts that antedate Christianity that entertain ideas about the death or suffering of a human being as providing either atonement or benefit for others. (1) One immediately thinks of the courageous sons who refused to abandon their faith in the face of severe persecution, one of whom says to Antiochus Epiphanes: "I, like my brothers, give up body and life for the laws of our fathers, appealing to God to show mercy soon to our nation and by afflictions and plagues to make you confess that he alone is God, and *through me to bring to an end the wrath of the Almighty* which has justly fallen on our whole nation" (2 Macc 7:37–38, emphasis added). (2) It is said of the deaths of righteous martyrs in 4 Maccabees: "By their endurance they conquered the tyrant, and thus their native land was purified through them" (1:11); "Be merciful to your people, and let our punishment suffice for them. Make my blood their purification, and take my life in exchange for theirs" (6:28–29). (3) God responded to Job the righteous sufferer: "God hearkened to Job's voice and forgave them their sins on account of him" (11QtgJob 38.2–3 [= Job 42:9: "and the Lord accepted Job's prayer"]). (4) In the Prayer of Azariah we read, "In our day we have no ruler, or prophet, or leader, no burnt offering, or sacrifice, or oblation, or incense, no place to make an offering before you and to find mercy. Yet with a contrite heart and a humble spirit may we be accepted, as though it were with burnt offerings of rams and bulls, or with tens of thousands of fat lambs; such may our sacrifice be in your sight today . . ." (LXX 3:38–40 = NRSV 3:15–17). (5) In the *Life of Adam and Eve*, Eve asks Adam to kill her, explaining, "Then perhaps the Lord God will bring you again into Paradise, for it is because of me that the Lord God is angry with you" (3:1). In view of these texts, it is simply inaccurate to maintain that human atonement ideas could not have been derived from Palestinian Judaism. (Another text sometimes mentioned is *T. Benj.* 3:8: "The innocent will be defiled for the lawless, and the sinless one will die for the ungodly"; but Christian editing can be detected in the immediate vicinity, so this passage may not represent pre-Christian Jewish ideas.)

Recently Grimm (*Weil ich dich liebe*, 231–77) and Stuhlmacher ("Vicariously Giving His Life," 22–26) have argued that the ransom saying may reflect the language of Isa 43:3–4: "For I am the LORD your God, the Holy One of Israel, your

Savior. I give [נָתַתִּי *nātattî*] Egypt as your ransom [כָפְרְךָ *koprĕkā*], Ethiopia and Seba in exchange for you [תַּחְתֶּיךָ *taḥtêkā*]. Because you are precious in my eyes, and honored, and I love you, I give man in return for you [וְאֶתֵּן אָדָם תַּחְתֶּיךָ *wĕ'ettēn 'ādām taḥtêkā*], peoples in exchange for your life [תַּחַת נַפְשֶׁךָ *taḥat napšekā*]." The linguistic and thematic coherence between this passage and the ransom saying is intriguing. Isaiah's כפר *kōper*, "ransom," is the equivalent of Mark's λύτρον, "ransom" (cf. Pesch, 2:164: "λύτρον . . . is based on כפר"); תחת *taḥat*, "in exchange for," corresponds to ἀντί (πολλῶν), "for (many)"; ואתן אדם *wĕ'ettēn 'ādām*, "I give man," may approximate Mark's ὁ υἱὸς τοῦ ἀνθρώπου . . . δοῦναι, "the 'son of man' . . . to give"; and נפש *nepeš*, "life," corresponds to Mark's τὴν ψυχὴν αὐτοῦ, "his life." However, Gundry (592) expresses reservations. Davies and Allison (*Matthew* 3:96) find the proposal "attractive but not demonstrable." Given the concentration of vocabulary and the thematic coherence (though admittedly not exact), it is probable that Isa 43:3–4 has contributed to the matrix out of which Jesus' saying was fashioned. It is not necessary to view Isa 53 and Isa 43 as competing alternatives; rather they may be viewed as prophetic sources out of which Jesus' mission, message, and self-understanding could be formed.

Finally, there are two important elements that reflect Dan 7:

(1) ὁ υἱὸς τοῦ ἀνθρώπου, "the son of [the] man," is an articular, specific reference to the בַּר אֱנָשׁ *bar 'ĕnāš*, "son of man," of Dan 7:13. The Aramaic is anarthrous and is neither technical nor titular. Jesus' messianic self-understanding has been informed by this mysterious heavenly figure. He is the figure to whom dominion and authority have been given. (For more discussion of the "son of man," see the *Introduction* as well as the *Comment* on 8:31.)

(2) διακονηθῆναι, "to be served." Even the "son of man" himself, contrary to what might be inferred from Dan 7:14 ("And to him was given dominion . . . that all peoples . . . should serve [Aramaic: יִפְלְחוּן *yiplĕḥûn;* LXX: λατρεύουσα; Theodotion: δουλεύσουσιν] him"), "came not to be served but to serve, and to give his life as a ransom for many" (v 45). Casey (*Aramaic Sources,* 212–17) believes that the OT background to the ransom saying has more to do with Daniel and stories of the Jewish martyrs (in the Maccabean literature) than with Isa 53 or 43, though he allows for some formal and thematic similarities ("It remains possible that Jesus was informed by Isa 53, among many other texts, as he meditated on his death"). However, the Danielic elements do not necessarily compete with or contradict the underlying elements from Isaiah. The two scriptural traditions complement each other, with the Suffering Servant of Isa 53 redefining the mission and destiny of the "son of man" of Dan 7. Indeed, the "son of man" will someday "be served," but he first must serve, even suffer and die, as the Servant of the Lord.

Elsewhere in the dominical tradition there is evidence of Jesus subverting teaching in Daniel. Jesus' Prayer of Thanksgiving is an especially interesting example: "I thank thee, Father, Lord of heaven and earth, that thou hast hidden these things from the wise and understanding and revealed them to babes; yea, Father, for such was thy gracious will" (Matt 11:25–26 = Luke 10:21). Grimm (*Jesu Einspruch gegen das Offenbarungssystem Daniels [Mt 11,25–27; Lk 17,20–21],* vol. 1 of *Jesus und das Danielbuch,* ANTJ 6.1 [Frankfurt am Main: Lang, 1984]) has suggested that Jesus has alluded to Daniel's similar prayer in Dan 2:19–23, parts of which read: "Blessed be the name of God for ever and ever, to whom belong wisdom and might . . . he gives wisdom to the wise and knowledge to those who have under-standing; he reveals deep and mysterious things" (vv 20–22). This shows that Jesus' hermeneutic was dynamic and experientially oriented. He was at once informed by Scripture but not necessarily confined by it. It also reflects the Jewish interpre-tive principle of two passages interpreting each other (*gĕzêrâ šāwâ*). Davies and Allison (*Matthew* 3:97), commenting on Matt 20:28 (the parallel to Mark 10:45), rightly state that "Daniel 7 is not rejected. Rather, it is creatively reinterpreted through combination with another Scripture." They go on to point out that ele-ments from Dan 7 and Isa 53 are combined in *1 Enoch* 37–71.

Third, Taylor ("The Origin of the Markan Passion-Sayings") argues compel-lingly for the authenticity of the ransom saying along with the other passion sayings (8:31; 9:31; 10:32–34) on the grounds that in Paul, Matthew, Luke-Acts, and the Johannine writings the Suffering Servant concept is on the wane. The popularity of the concept, as appropriate for understanding Jesus, was much earlier. Since the popularity of the epithet "son of man" also seems limited to the very earliest period of the development of the Jesus traditions, the two concepts, "servant" and "son of man," may have been in fact quite primitive, with only lingering ech-oes in later christological formulations. This makes perfect sense as it relates to the emergence and expansion of Christianity. The epithet "son of man" would have been dropped in the Greco-Roman world, for it would make no sense in either Greek (ὁ υἱὸς τοῦ ἀνθρώπου) or Latin (*filius hominis*), whereas the concept "servant" (whether παῖς, διάκονος, or δοῦλος) would be open to serious misun-derstanding, even ridicule. As Christian preaching moved beyond the confines of Jewish Palestine toward an increasingly hellenized and romanized world, the preferred titles for Jesus became ὁ κύριος, "Lord," ὁ υἱὸς τοῦ θεοῦ, "Son of God," and ὁ σωτήρ, "Savior," titles that resonated with the overtones of the imperial cult of the divine emperor. The lingering and rarely exploited fragments of tradition indebted to the language and imagery of Dan 7 (the "son of man," authority, reception of kingdom, struggle against demonic forces) and Second Isaiah (the messenger, announcing the kingdom, announcing good news, healing, the ser-vant, suffering for many) are better explained as originating in the teaching of Jesus, rather than in the early church, only to be muted, reformulated, or dropped altogether in subsequent years.

Evidence for this contention is seen in the parallel in 1 Tim 2:5–6: εἷς καὶ μεσίτης θεοῦ καὶ ἀνθρώπων, ἄνθρωπος Χριστὸς Ἰησοῦς, ὁ δοὺς ἑαυτὸν ἀντίλυτρον ὑπὲρ πάντων, "and there is one mediator between God and humans, the human being Christ Jesus, who gave himself as a ransom for all" (author's tr.). Jeremias ("Lösegeld") argued that this statement represents a later, hellenized version of the dominical ransom saying (with which Stuhlmacher, "Vicariously Giving His Life," 17–18, concurs): ἄνθρωπος, "human being," replaces the odd-sounding, Semitizing ὁ υἱὸς τοῦ ἀνθρώπου, "the son of [the] man"; ὁ δοὺς ἑαυτόν, "who gave himself," replaces δοῦναι τὴν ψυχὴν αὐτοῦ, "to give his life"; the hellenizing ἀντίλυτρον, "ransom," replaces λύτρον, "ransom"; and ὑπὲρ πάντων, "for all," re-places the Semitizing ἀντὶ πολλῶν, "for many." The form of the saying in 1 Timothy gives us a clearer idea of what form a hellenizing tradition of this sort would take and stands in noticeable contrast to the older, more Semitic form of the saying in Mark 10:45, thus seriously undermining the claims made by some that Mark 10:45 represents either a Pauline formula or some other hellenizing formula.

Finally, as Allison shows (*Jesus of Nazareth,* 64–65), the ransom saying corresponds to other sayings of Jesus, notably Luke 12:51–53 (= Matt 10:34–35 [Q]), where a saying beginning with "I come" is followed by an antithesis, a reference to suffering, and a scriptural allusion. The ransom saying of Mark 10:45, which thematically coheres with Mark 14:24, formally coheres with this saying in Q. Coherence such as this supports the claim to authenticity.

Explanation

The request made by James and John is innocent enough, but Jesus quite possibly perceives the proverbial tip of the iceberg: the all-too-human desire for honor, power, and prestige. Although Jesus does not rebuke his disciples, he does challenge them. If they want what Jesus has to offer, are they prepared to experience it? If they want to sit next to him, then are they prepared to share his fate? They say they are able (as many Christians today affirm), but do they really understand what lies ahead? On previous occasions Jesus has spoken of his suffering and death, and there was little indication that the disciples fully understood or accepted such discouraging teaching.

Jesus teaches his disciples that the places of honor are not his to appoint. But he can tell them what is expected of them. They are not to be like the "great ones" of the world, who like to rule over people. No, the disciples are to seek opportunities of service. The supreme example of this service is seen in Jesus himself, who as "son of man" does not in fact desire "to be served" (as Dan 7:14 depicts) but instead seeks "to serve and to give his life as a ransom for many." If the disciples are able to follow this example, then the places of honor will follow.

Hengel is correct to argue that Mark 10:45 and 14:24 underscore how important Jesus' atoning death is for the Markan evangelist. To conclude that no more than two references imply little interest in Jesus' death is to misunderstand the evangelist by failing to observe the contexts in which these passages occur (see Hengel, *Studies,* 37–38). The evangelist's economy should not be confused with lack of emphasis. Just as Jesus' acknowledgment as "Son of God" occurs only a few times (notably in 1:1; 14:61–62; and 15:39), so disclosure of Jesus' role as the suffering "son of man" occurs only a few times. Their relative rarity allows them to stand all the more in sharp relief.

VII. Jesus Confronts Jerusalem   (10:46–13:37)

Bibliography

Baarlink, H. *Anfängliches Evangelium.* Mansfield, M. R. *"Spirit and Gospel" in Mark.* Peabody, MA: Hendrickson, 1987. 98–123.

Introduction

The Galilean ministry and the southward journey are now over. Jesus is in Judea in the vicinity of Jerusalem, the city of opposition and passion. In the first two pericopes of this section, Jesus will be hailed as "son of David" (10:46–52), and he will enter the city of Jerusalem amid shouts of "blessed is the coming kingdom of our father David" (11:1–11). On this auspicious note of authority, Jesus will confront Jerusalem, David's city. This confrontation, seen in the temple action (11:15–18), the cursing of the fruitless fig tree (11:12–14), the threatening parable of the Wicked Tenant Farmers (12:1–12), criticisms against religious leaders (12:38–44), and an explicit prophecy of the temple's destruction (13:1–2), will generate dangerous political opposition, an opposition that will culminate in Jesus' arrest, interrogation, and crucifixion.

Running throughout this section is Jesus' commanding authority. He is portrayed as speaking with decisive expertise on several topics that are of great importance to the Jewish people: he condemns temple polity in 11:15–18, citing prophetic Scriptures; he easily checks those who would trip him up with a difficult question about paying tribute to Caesar (12:13–17); he instructs the Sadducees on the doctrine of the resurrection (12:18–27); he instructs a scribe on what the great commandment is and leads him to recognize that love of God and neighbor outweighs the temple establishment (12:28–34); he confounds popular scribal teaching regarding the Messiah as "son of David" (12:35–37); he openly criticizes the scribes and their avarice (12:38, 41–44); and he astounds his disciples with his confident prophecies of the fate of the temple, Jerusalem, and the coming generation. This authority, however, will be directly challenged in 11:27–33; and this challenge will prove to be the beginning of the process that will send Jesus to the cross.

A. Blind Bartimaeus   (10:46–52)

Bibliography

Achtemeier, P. J. "'And He Followed Him': Miracles and Discipleship in Mark 10:46–52." *Semeia* 11 (1978) 115–45. Albright, W. F. "The Names 'Nazareth' and 'Nazorean.'" *JBL* 65

(1946) 397–401. **Best, E.** *Following Jesus.* 134–45. **Betz, H. D.** "The Early Christian Miracle Story: Some Observations on the Form Critical Problem." *Semeia* 11 (1978) 69–81. **Borsch, F. H.** *Power in Weakness: New Hearing for Gospel Stories of Healing and Discipleship.* Philadelphia: Fortress, 1983. 99–109. **Budesheim, T. L.** "Jesus and the Disciples in Conflict with Judaism." *ZNW* 62 (1971) 190–209, esp. 194–99. **Burger, C.** *Jesus als Davidssohn: Eine traditionsgeschichtliche Untersuchung.* FRLANT 98. Göttingen: Vandenhoeck & Ruprecht, 1970. 42–46, 59–63. **Busemann, R.** *Die Jüngergemeinde nach Markus 10: Eine redaktionsgeschichtliche Untersuchung des 10. Kapitels im Markusevangelium.* BBB 57. Königstein; Bonn: Hanstein, 1983. 161–72. **Busse, U.** *Die Wunder des Propheten Jesus: Die Rezeption, Komposition und Interpretation der Wundertradition im Evangelium des Lukas.* FB 24. Stuttgart: Katholisches Bibelwerk, 1977. 227–34. **Butts, J. R.** "The Voyage of Discipleship: Narrative, Chreia, and Call Story." In *Early Jewish and Christian Exegesis.* FS W. H. Brownlee, ed. C. A. Evans and W. F. Stinespring. Homage 10. Atlanta: Scholars Press, 1987. 199–219. **Chapalain, C.** "Marc 10,46–52: Plan de travail." *Sémiotique et Bible* 20 (1980) 12–16. **Charlesworth, J. H.** "Solomon and Jesus: The Son of David in Ante-Markan Traditions (Mk 10:47)." In *Biblical and Humane.* FS J. F. Priest, ed. L. B. Elder et al. Homage 20. Atlanta: Scholars Press, 1996. 125–51. ———. "The Son of David: Solomon and Jesus (Mark 10.47)." In *The New Testament and Hellenistic Judaism.* Ed. P. Borgen and S. Giversen. Aarhus: Aarhus UP, 1995. 72–87. **Charlier, J.-P.** *Signes et prodiges: Les miracles dans l'Évangile.* LD 79. Paris: Cerf, 1987. 52–60. **Culpepper, R. A.** "Mark 10:50: Why Mention the Garment?" *JBL* 101 (1982) 131–32. **Dalman, G. H.** *The Words of Jesus.* Edinburgh: T. & T. Clark, 1902. **Droge, A.** "Call Stories in Greek Biographies and the Gospels." In *Society of Biblical Literature 1983 Seminar Papers.* Ed. K. H. Richards. SBLSP 22. Chico, CA: Scholars Press, 1983. 245–57. **Duling, D. C.** "Solomon, Exorcism, and the Son of David." *HTR* 68 (1975) 235–52. **Dupont, J.** "L'aveugle de Jéricho recouvre la vue et suit Jésus (Marc 10,46–52)." In *Études sur les Évangiles synoptiques.* FS F. Neirynck, ed. J. Dupont. 2 vols. BETL 70. Leuven: Leuven UP; Peeters, 1985. 1:350–67. **Fiederlein, F. M.** *Die Wunder Jesu und die Wundererzählungen der Urkirche.* Munich: Don Bosco, 1988. 79–84. **Fisher, L. R.** "Can This Be the Son of David?" In *Jesus and the Historian.* FS E. C. Colwell, ed. F. T. Trotter. Philadelphia: Westminster, 1968. 82–97. **Flusser, D.** *Jesus.* 180–86. **Fuchs, A.** *Sprachliche Untersuchungen zu Matthäus und Lukas: Ein Beitrag zur Quellenkritik.* AnBib 49. Rome: Biblical Institute, 1971. 45–170. **Hahn, F.** *The Titles of Jesus in Christology: Their History in Early Christianity.* London: Lutterworth, 1969. 253–58. **Johnson, E. S., Jr.** "Mark 10:46–52: Blind Bartimaeus." *CBQ* 40 (1978) 191–204. **Kertelge, K.** *Die Wunder Jesu im Markusevangelium.* 179–82. **Ketter, P.** "Zur Lokalizierung der Blindenheilung bei Jericho." *Bib* 15 (1934) 411–18. **Kirchschläger, W.** "Bartimäus—Paradigma einer Wundererzählung (Mk 10,46–52 par)." In *The Four Gospels 1992.* FS F. Neirynck, ed. F. Van Segbroeck et al. 3 vols. BETL 100. Leuven: Peeters; Leuven UP, 1992. 2:1105–23. **Koch, D.-A.** *Die Bedeutung der Wundererzählungen.* 126–32. **Latourelle, R.** *The Miracles of Jesus.* 155–61. **Loos, H. van der.** *The Miracles of Jesus.* 422–25. **Lövestam, E.** "Jésus Fils de David chez les Synoptiques." *ST* 28 (1974) 97–109. **Marshall, C. D.** *Faith as a Theme in Mark's Narrative.* 123–32, 139–44. **März, C.-P.** *"Siehe, dein König kommt zu Dir . . .": Eine traditionsgeschichtliche Untersuchung zur Einzugsperikope.* ETS 43. Leipzig: St. Benno, 1980. 56–61. **Meier, J. P.** *Marginal Jew.* 2.686–90. **Meye, R. P.** *Jesus and the Twelve.* 164–66. **Moore, G. F.** "Nazarene and Nazareth." In *The Beginnings of Christianity.* Ed. F. J. Foakes Jackson and K. Lake. 5 vols. 1920–1933. Repr. Grand Rapids, MI: Baker, 1979. 1:426–32. **Morrice, W. G.** "The Imperatival ἵνα." *BT* 23 (1972) 326–30. **Paul, A.** "Guérison de Bartimée: Mc 10,46–52." *AsSeign* 2.61 (1972) 44–52. **Pesch, R.** *Evangelium der Urgemeinde.* 124–26. **Porter, S. E.** "'In the Vicinity of Jericho': Luke 18:35 in the Light of Its Synoptic Parallels." *BBR* 2 (1992) 91–104. **Räisänen, H.** *The 'Messianic Secret' in Mark's Gospel.* 156–63, 229–30. **Ramsauer, H.,** and **Weitz J.** "Schülerauslegung—Theologische Auslegung." In *Theologie und Unterricht: Über die Repräsentanz des Christlichen in der Schule.* FS H. Stock, ed. K. Wegenast. Gütersloh: Mohn, 1969. 299–308. **Reploh, K. G.** *Markus—Lehrer der Gemeinde.* 222–26. **Robbins, V. K.** "The

Healing of Blind Bartimaeus (10:46-52) in the Marcan Theology." *JBL* 92 (1973) 224-43. **Roloff, J.** *Das Kerygma und der irdische Jesus.* 121-26. **Sanders, J. A.** "Ναζωραῖος in Matthew 2.23." In *The Gospels and the Scriptures of Israel.* Ed. C. A. Evans and W. R. Stegner. JSNTSup 104. Studies in Scripture in Early Judaism and Christianity 3. Sheffield: Sheffield Academic, 1994. 116-28. **Schenke, L.** *Die Wundererzählungen des Markusevangeliums.* 350-69. **Schille, G.** *Anfänge der Kirche: Erwägungen zur apostolische Frühgeschichte.* BEvT 43: Munich: Kaiser, 1966. 64-72. **Schmietenkopf, M.** "Jesus von Nazareth—der Davidssohn: Analyse von Mk 10,46-52." *Evangelische Erzieher* 21 (1969) 487-94. **Sinclair, S. G.** "The Healing of Bartimaeus and the Gaps in Mark's Messianic Secret." *St. Luke's Journal of Theology* 33 (1990) 249-57. **Söding, T.** *Glaube bei Markus.* 426-32. **Standaert, B. H. M. G. H. M.** *L'évangile selon Marc.* 119-25. **Steinhauser, M. G.** "The Form of the Bartimaeus Narrative (Mark 10.46-52)." *NTS* 32 (1986) 583-95. ———. "Part of a 'Call Story?'" *ExpTim* 94 (1982-83) 204-6. **Stock, A.** "Hinge Transitions in Mark's Gospel." *BTB* 15 (1985) 27-31. **Stock, K.** *Umgang mit theologischen Texten: Methoden, Analysen, Vorschläge.* Arbeits und Studienbucher Theologie. Zürich; Köln: Benziger, 1974. **Stoffel, E. L.** "Mark 10:46-52." *Int* 30 (1976) 288-92. **Suggit, J. N.** "Bartimaeus and Christian Discipleship (Mark 10:46-52)." *JTSA* 74 (1991) 57-63. **Trilling, W.** *Christusverkündigung in den synoptischen Evangelien: Beispiele gattungsgemässer Auslegung.* Biblische Handbibliothek 4. Munich: Kösel, 1969. 146-64. **Via, D. O., Jr.** *The Ethics of Mark's Gospel.* 156-68. ———. "Mark 10:32-52—A Structural, Literary and Theological Interpretation." In *Society of Biblical Literature 1979 Seminar Papers.* Ed. P. J. Achtemeier. 2 vols. SBLSP 18. Missoula, MT: Scholars Press, 1979. 2:187-203. **Westcott, B. F., and Hort, F. J. A.** *Introduction.* **Wilder, A. N.** *Early Christian Rhetoric: The Language of the Gospels.* New York: Harper & Row, 1964. 61-66. **Williams, J. F.** *Other Followers of Jesus.* 151-71.

Translation

⁴⁶*And they enter Jericho. And as he was going out from Jericho and his disciples and a considerable crowd, the son of Timaeus—Bartimaeus—a blind beggar was seated by the road.*ᵃ ⁴⁷*And hearing that it is Jesus the Nazarene,*ᵇ *he began to cry out and say,* "ᶜ*Son of David,*ᵈ *Jesus, have pity on me!*" ⁴⁸ᵉ*And many were rebuking him so that he should be quiet. But all the more he was crying out,* "ᶜ*Son of David,*ᶠ *have pity on me!*" ⁴⁹*And standing still, Jesus said,*ᵍ "*Call him.*" *And they call the blind man, saying to him, "Be of good cheer, arise, he calls you."* ⁵⁰*And throwing aside his cloak and getting to his feet, he went to Jesus.* ⁵¹*And answering him, Jesus said, "What do you wish that I might do for you?" And the blind man said to him, "My master,*ʰ *that I might see again."* ⁵²*And Jesus said to him, "Go, your faith has saved you." And immediately he regained his sight and began following him*ⁱ *on the way.*

Notes

ᵃThe opening words of v 46 have presented copyists and interpreters with difficulties. B* omits καὶ ἔρχονται εἰς Ἰεριχώ, "and they enter Jericho." Some MSS render the gen. abs. ἐκπορευομένου αὐτοῦ, "as he was going out," in the pl. (as it should be). A C D W and other authorities attempt to smooth out the latter part of the verse by reading Βαρτιμαῖος [D Βαριτιμίας] ὁ τυφλὸς ἐκάθητο παρὰ τὴν ὁδὸν προσαιτῶν [D ἐπαιτῶν], "Bartimaeus, the blind man, was seated beside the road begging." The entire verse is clumsy. For a study that attempts to explain v 46, comparing it with Luke 18:35, see Porter, *BBR* 2 [1992] 91-104.

ᵇGk. Ναζαρηνός. א A C Σ Φ and many later authorities read Ναζωραῖος. The latter reading has been imported from Matthew (2:23; 26:71) and especially from Luke (18:37). Mark consistently uses Ναζαρηνός (cf. Mark 1:24; 10:47; 14:67; 16:6).

ᶜOne late MS adds κύριε, "lord."

  dIn most Gk. authorities "David" is spelled Δαυείδ (as in B D). But in other authorities the name is spelled variously, e.g., Δαβίδ. א and other MSS read the abbreviation Δᾱδ. The same holds for v 48. See also 11:10; 12:35.

  eW omits v 48.

  fSome late MSS add Ἰησοῦ, "Jesus."

  gOne late MS reads ὁ Ἰησοῦς ἐκέλευσεν, "Jesus commanded" (cf. Luke 18:40).

  hGk. ῥαββουνί (or ῥαββουνεί), which is a transliteration of the Aram. רבוני *rabbûnî* (lit. "my great one," or "my lord"). D reads κύριε ῥαββί, "lord rabbi." The same variant appears in some Latin MSS: *domine rabbi.* Other later Greek MSS read κύριε, "lord." See Westcott-Hort, *Introduction* 2:26.

  iSome later MSS, among them Σ Φ, read ἠκολούθει τῷ Ἰησοῦ, "began following Jesus."

Form/Structure/Setting

As Jesus passes through Jericho accompanied by a large crowd, a blind beggar named Bartimaeus, or "son of Timaeus," cries out, asking for mercy. The crowd tries to silence him, but he continues to cry out, "Son of David, Jesus, have pity on me!" Jesus gives the blind man an audience and learns that he wishes to have his sight restored. Jesus heals him and then he follows Jesus on the way. The story is repeated by Matthew (20:29–34) and Luke (18:35–43), though in a more polished and economizing style. The story of the healing of the blind man, where Jesus is hailed as "son of David," prepares for the entrance narrative (11:1–11) in which the crowd will speak of the "coming kingdom of our father David." It is the last healing episode recounted in the Gospel of Mark.

Some commentators have suggested that the vividness of the scene reflects eyewitness testimony (e.g., Swete, 242; Branscomb, 192; Rawlinson, 148; Turner, 52; Taylor, 446–47). But the older form critics argued that the story of the blind man of Jericho was a secondary formulation, betrayed by the inclusion of details such as the location and the name of the blind man. However, the name "Bartimaeus" is probably traditional (*pace* Bultmann, *History,* 213; Dibelius, *From Tradition,* 51–52, "originally . . . a nameless beggar"), for it is not the habit of the Markan evangelist to provide names. Noting this and that the name is omitted in the Matthean and Lukan accounts, Bultmann gratuitously suggests that perhaps the name was added to Mark years after its publication. Furthermore, the twofold mention of Jericho in v 46 suggests antiquity, if not authenticity, of the episode. (Grundmann, 296, thinks that the one mention is traditional, the other Markan.) Finally, the designation of Jesus as "the Nazarene," which would distinguish him from the many others in the vicinity with the name of Jesus, smacks of authenticity, not later Christian tradition. In all probability, the story of the healing of the blind man of Jericho derives from a setting in the life of Jesus (*Sitz im Leben Jesu*).

According to the genealogies of Jesus found in Matthew (1:1–17) and Luke (3:23–38), Jesus was a descendant of King David. Some have contended that tradition of this descent arose only later in the aftermath of the early church's proclamation of Jesus as Messiah. To herald Jesus as Israel's Messiah, so the argument goes, would require Davidic descent. Moreover, it is claimed that there were no records of Davidic descent extant in the time of Jesus. This claim, however, is dubious. Eusebius reports that Vespasian (*Hist. eccl.* 3.12), Domitian (3.19–20), and Trajan (3.32.5–6) persecuted the family of David so that no royal claimant might arise and challenge the authority of Rome. Not long ago an ossuary dating from the first century B.C.E. was found in Jerusalem bearing the inscription:

שׁל בי דוד *šel bê dāwid,* "of the house of David" (the Aramaic בי *bê* is בית *bêt* in Hebrew; Flusser, *Jesus,* 180–86). According to early rabbinic literature "the family of
David" brought the wood offering of the priests to the temple on 20 Tammuz (cf.
m. Taʿan. 4:5; *t. Taʿan.* 3.5). Later rabbinic traditions claim that various rabbis (*b.
Šabb.* 56a), including Hillel himself (*y. Taʿan.* 4.2), were descendants of David.
Flusser thinks that Josephus's remark that Rabbi Simeon ben Gamaliel (grandson or great-grandson of Hillel) came from "a very illustrious family" (*Life* 191)
shows knowledge of this ancestry. Given the Flavian dynasty's antipathy toward
Jewish patriotic hopes in general and the Davidic dynasty in particular (as documented in Eusebius), we may understand Josephus's reluctance to be more specific
than he is. Indeed, the curious episode involving the eunuch Bagoas, who with
enthusiasm anticipated the appearance of a Jewish king who would grant him
the ability to marry and father children, probably reflected the hope that the
Davidic line would produce the awaited Messiah through the wife of Pheroras
(Josephus, *Ant.* 17.2.4 §§41–45). The hope of fertility in all probability reflects
Isa 56:3, part of an oracle concerned with Israel's restoration, to which Jesus also
alluded when he demonstrated in the temple precincts (cf. 11:17, where Isa 56:7
is cited).

The evidence of recognized Davidic lineage in the time of Jesus is compelling.
Early Christianity accepted Jesus' Davidic descent but apparently made little of it
(cf. Paul's remarks in Rom 1:3–4). Indeed, Jesus himself challenges the adequacy
of understanding the Messiah in terms of the epithet "son of David" (Mark 12:35–
37). In short, NT Christology is founded on other, more important traditions
than mere Davidic descent.

There is no evidence in early sources that anyone challenged Jesus' Davidic
descent. In later rabbinic polemic Jesus is said to have been fathered by a Roman
soldier, but this is little more than slander in response to Christian claims of Jesus'
miraculous conception. Bartimaeus's acclamation of Jesus as "son of David" and
the later shouts of the crowd, "blessed is the coming kingdom of our father David"
(11:10), offer important early evidence that Jesus was known by his contemporaries to have belonged to the house of David. How well kept his family's genealogical
records were, or how accurate the genealogies found in Matthew or Luke may
be, is another matter that need not detain us here.

Comment

The southward journey at last takes Jesus and his following to Jericho, some
fifteen miles northeast of Jerusalem. The next major leg of the journey will take
them to Jerusalem itself, a wearisome uphill trek. When he leaves Jericho, he is, as
almost always, accompanied by crowds of people. Among these is Bartimaeus, a
blind beggar. His cry, "Son of David, Jesus, have pity on me!" (v 47), carries with it
an unmistakable messianic ring (note the forward placement of the title of honor;
see also *T. Sol.* 20:1–2, where a distraught father addresses Solomon: "King Solomon,
son of David, have mercy on me!"). The crowd attempts to hush the man (possibly
because of the political dangers of such an epithet, but more probably because he
is viewed as a nuisance), but he is as determined as ever and continues to cry out
"Son of David, have pity on me!" (v 48). Reflecting the teaching of the immediately

preceding passage (10:40–45), Jesus demonstrates a willingness to render service to one in need. The contrast is marked: Jesus, the son of David (and, as such, Israel's "first" citizen), stopping to help a beggar of no account named son of Timaeus (a tragic example of one of Israel's "last" citizens). The idea of service is made plain by Jesus' inquiry: "What do you wish that I might do for you?" That is, does the man want alms or something else? The blind man requests his sight and Jesus grants it: "Go, your faith has saved you" (v 52).

46 Ἰεριχώ, "Jericho." Founded perhaps as early as 8,000 B.C.E., Jericho (Greek NT and LXX: Ἰεριχώ; MT: וִירֵחוֹ *yĕrîḥô*) is, so far as is known, the oldest continually inhabited city on earth. It is situated five miles to the west of the Jordan River and about fifteen miles northeast of Jerusalem. In Jesus' day the ancient site conquered by Joshua would have been not much different from the tell that Kathleen Kenyon excavated a half century ago. Nearby (at the mouth of the Wadi Qelt) is the newer city that Herod the Great enhanced and expanded with various official buildings, including a hippodrome and royal palace, the ruins of which are clearly visible today. Herod himself later died in Jericho. A century earlier the Maccabean priest-king Alexander Jannaeus had a royal residence at Jericho. Qumran is some miles to the south on the northwestern shore of the Dead Sea. For more on Jericho, see T. A. Holland and E. Netzer, *ABD* 3:723–40, esp. 737–39 for Roman and Herodian Jericho.

ἐκπορευομένου αὐτοῦ ἀπὸ Ἰεριχώ, "As he was going out from Jericho." Luke 18:35 modifies and simplifies Mark's version by saying that Jesus approached "near to Jerusalem." In other words, Jesus encountered the blind man on his way to Jericho, not on departing from it. The Lukan evangelist makes this change to accommodate Jesus' conversation with Zacchaeus in 19:1–10, which takes place *in* Jericho (Fitzmyer, *Luke* 2:1213; though see S. E. Porter, *BBR* 2 [1992] 91–104).

ὄχλου ἱκανοῦ, "considerable crowd." The evangelist once again emphasizes the size of the crowds that follow Jesus about. The point is that wherever Jesus goes, his power and charismatic persona are such that crowds of people are inevitably drawn to him.

ὁ υἱὸς Τιμαίου Βαρτιμαῖος, "the son of Timaeus—Bartimaeus." Mark usually gives the Aramaic word or phrase first, then the Greek translation second (cf. 3:17; 7:11, 34). Here he has reversed this order. The evangelist says that he is a τυφλὸς προσαίτης, "blind beggar." The nominal form προσαίτης, "beggar," does not occur in the LXX, while the verbal form (προσαιτεῖν, "to beg") does but once and in a very cynical statement: "And if their children be many, they shall be for slaughter; and if they also grow up, they shall beg [προσαιτήσουσιν]" (LXX Job 27:14). The only other beggar in the Gospels is the chap in John 9:8 who also was born blind and is described as one who was sitting and begging. It is possible that the Johannine story was influenced by the Markan story (but Bultmann, *History*, 227, thinks the Johannine story drew upon Mark 8:23). The name Βαρτιμαῖος is of Aramaic origin, perhaps from בַּר טִמְאַי, *bar ṭimʾay*, "son of Timai."

The evangelist says that Bartimaeus ἐκάθητο παρὰ τὴν ὁδόν, "was seated by the road." This was a strategic location, for it gave him ready access to the traffic to and from Jerusalem. This important trade route was traveled by merchants and the prosperous, as well as the pious on their way to Jerusalem to worship, who might be inclined to give alms.

47 Ἰησοῦς ὁ Ναζαρηνός ἐστιν, "It is Jesus the Nazarene." The substantival adjective ὁ Ναζαρηνός, "the Nazarene," functions as a description of a person from Nazareth. That Jesus was from the village of Nazareth has been mentioned already in Mark (1:9, 24). In the NT it is usually rendered Ναζαρέτ (Matt 2:23; Mark 1:9; John 1:45, 46) or Ναζαρέθ (Matt 21:11; Luke 1:26; 2:4, 39, 51; Acts 10:38), though sometimes it appears as Ναζαρά (Matt 4:13; Luke 4:16). Years ago Albright (*JBL* 65 [1946] 397–401; cf. Sanders, "Ναζωραῖος in Matthew 2.23") showed that the Hebrew צ *ṣ* could be transliterated by the Greek ζ, thus proving that Ναζαρέτ can be the Greek equivalent of נצרת *nāṣāret* and thereby, furthermore, making sense of the allusion to Isa 11:1 (i.e., to נצר *nēṣer,* "branch") in Matt 2:23. Nazareth is not mentioned in the OT, but a third-century inscription from Caesarea Maritima mentions a course of priests who lived in נצרת *nāṣāret.*

The epithet υἱὲ Δαυίδ, "son of David," has raised the question of whether there existed descendants of King David in the time of Jesus. Some scholars think not, or at least suppose that there were no Jews in the first century aware of Davidic ancestry. However, this position is probably unnecessarily skeptical, for there is some evidence to the contrary (see discussion above). The epithet "son of David" may denote a Solomonic identity (*Pss. Sol.* 17:21), for David's great son was famous for his healing powers and formulas for exorcism. In one incantation Solomon is addressed as the בר דויד *bar dāwîd,* "son of David," and is petitioned for protection against sickness (CBS 9012; cf. Charlesworth, "Solomon and Jesus," 137). Indeed, the *Testament of Solomon,* which is largely devoted to traditions about Solomon and the demonic, testifies to the widespread fame of David's son. Requesting that the "son of David" heal him may also suggest that the blind man sensed the approach of the kingdom of God (after all, this was the essence of Jesus' proclamation) and assumed that healings and other blessings were more readily at hand (cf. 4Q521 = 4QMessianic Apocalypse).

The blind man's cry, ἐλέησόν με, "have pity on me," echoes the language of the Psalter: "Have pity on me [ἐλέησόν με], Lord, for I am weak" (LXX Ps 6:3 [cf. ET 6:2]); "Have pity on me [ἐλέησόν με], Lord! Behold my humiliation from my enemies, you who lift me up from the gates of death" (LXX Ps 9:14 [cf. ET 9:13]; see also Pss 25:16 [LXX 24:16]; 26:11 [LXX 25:11]; 27:7 [LXX 26:7]; 31:9 [LXX 30:9]; 41:4 [LXX 40:4]; 41:10 [LXX 40:10]; 51:1 [LXX 50:1]; 57:1 [LXX 56:1]; 67:1 [LXX 66:1]; 86:3 [LXX 85:3]). According to *Pss. Sol.* 17:34, the Davidic Messiah will have pity on the nations that stand reverently before him. See also LXX Isa 30:19: "Jerusalem has wept bitterly, saying, 'Have pity on me [ἐλέησόν με].' He will have pity on you."

48 ἐπετίμων αὐτῷ πολλοὶ ἵνα σιωπήσῃ, "Many were rebuking him so that he should be quiet." ἐπιτιμᾶν can mean "to rebuke, scold, (strictly) charge, *or* enjoin." The patriarch Jacob rebukes Joseph for relating his dream (Gen 37:10). In Mark 1:25 and 9:25 Jesus rebukes unclean spirits and orders them to depart. In 4:39 Jesus rebukes the storm. Sometimes ἐπιτιμᾶν means to charge someone to be quiet (as in Mark 3:12; 8:30). This is the meaning here in v 48, as the word σιωπᾶν, "to be silent," makes clear. Why was the crowd enjoining the blind man to keep quiet? Their attempt to silence him roughly parallels the earlier attempt of the disciples in v 13 to prevent people from taking their children to Jesus. That is, they seemed to be saying that Jesus had more important things to do than to spend time with a blind beggar. It is also possible that the crowd tried to hush the beggar for the same reasons that Jesus on previous occasions attempted to mute loud acclamations, lest the exuberance of the crowds get out of hand.

ὁ δὲ πολλῷ μᾶλλον ἔκραζεν, "But all the more he was crying out." As a beggar, Bartimaeus had experienced a lifetime of indignities. The crowd could try to hush him all it liked; he was undeterred. (Anyone who has chanced upon a beggar in the Middle East will notice an immunity to being ignored and insulted.) Mark's ancient readers could not help but be impressed by the man's determination. Jesus' reputation was such that Bartimaeus would spare no effort to make his plight known to the great teacher and healer. Jesus was much more than a casual passerby who might fling a coin or two in his direction.

49 In reading στάς, "standing still," we should perhaps assume that Jesus has stopped walking. Then again, the sense may be "standing up," in which case we should assume that earlier Jesus had paused, sat down, and was teaching the crowd (cf. Luke 4:20: "And he closed the book, and gave it back to the attendant, and sat down" and began to teach). Standing up, he interrupts his teaching to tend to the blind man. Jesus then commands the crowd to summon the blind man.

θάρσει, ἔγειρε, φωνεῖ σε, "Be of good cheer, arise, he calls you." θάρσει, "be of good cheer" or "take heart," occurs in only one other place in Mark: when the disciples see Jesus walking on the sea, they are terrified and Jesus calls out: "Be of good cheer, it is I; have no fear" (6:50). Outside of Mark the word occurs in Matt 9:2, where Jesus speaks to the paralytic, in Matt 9:22, where Jesus speaks to the woman suffering from the hemorrhage, and in John 16:33, where Jesus proclaims to his disciples that he has "overcome the world." The word seems to be a corollary of the "good news" itself. The word appears in 1 Kgs 17:13, where Elijah comforts the starving widow. In Jdt 11:1 Holofernes says to Judith, "Be of good cheer, woman, and do not be afraid in your heart." See also Bar 4:27, 30; Tob 7:18; 11:11; 4 Macc 17:4.

50 ὁ δὲ ἀποβαλὼν τὸ ἱμάτιον αὐτοῦ ἀναπηδήσας, "And throwing aside his cloak and getting to his feet." Most probably the beggar has been sitting on part of his cloak with the rest folded over his lap into which coins could be tossed (Taylor, 449). This he now throws aside in order to get up. Gundry (594) is correct to suggest that the abrupt action of flinging aside the cloak and jumping up lends an element of drama to the event. See 2 Kgs 7:15: "So they went after them as far as the Jordan; and, lo, all the way was littered with garments [LXX ἱματίων] and equipment which the Syrians had thrown away in their haste."

ἦλθεν πρὸς τὸν Ἰησοῦν, "he went to Jesus." Though blind, he can find his way forward, probably with people guiding him to Jesus. Taylor (449) thinks that Bartimaeus approached Jesus unaided and that therefore his blindness was not total. Perhaps; but the evangelist may have assumed that his readers would have understood that the blind man would have been assisted. The severity of his blindness is unknown.

51 καὶ ἀποκριθεὶς αὐτῷ, "and answering him," refers to Bartimaeus's call for attention, not to a specific question, for no question has yet been asked.

τί σοι θέλεις ποιήσω, "What do you wish that I might do for you?" Indeed, it is Jesus who asks the question. The question here will remind the attentive reader of the question Jesus put to James and John in the previous pericope (v 36: "What do you wish that I might do for you?"). Here, as there, Jesus wishes to ascertain the nature of the request before any promise is given.

ῥαββουνί, "My master." Only here and in John 20:16 is Jesus called ῥαββουνί, which transliterates the Aramaic רַבּוּנִי rabbûnî (cf. Dalman, *Words*, 324–27, 336–40; *Tg. Neof.* Gen 23:11, 15; 24:12, 14, 18, 24, 54; in all of these examples the Hebrew אֲדֹנִי, *'ădōnî,* "my lord," is translated by רבוני, *răbōnî* [which is sometimes vocalized as *rabbûnî, ribbônî,* or *rabbônî*]). The address appears to be primarily a Palestinian phenomenon (cf. S. J. D. Cohen, "Epigraphical Rabbis," *JQR* 72 [1981–82] 1–17). L. I. Levine (*The Rabbinic Class of Roman Palestine in Late Antiquity* [New York: Jewish Theological Seminary of America, 1989] 15) remarks: "In antiquity this title was applied to anyone of high standing in the community." See *ABD* 5:600–602.

ἵνα ἀναβλέψω, "that I might see again." Bartimaeus's hope that Jesus can restore his sight may have been been based on the assumption that the "son of David" could heal (in the sense of the Solomonic tradition mentioned above) and that Jesus was the fulfillment of LXX Isa 61:1: "the Spirit of the Lord . . . has anointed [ἔχρισεν] me; he has sent me . . . to preach . . . the restoration of sight to the blind [τυφλοῖς ἀνάβλεψιν]" (Taylor, 448). It is probable that this passage from Isaiah played an important role in Jesus' understanding of his mission and his qualification to undertake it (cf. Matt 11:5 = Luke 7:22; 4:16–30). One is reminded of the scene in which the blind man approaches Emperor Vespasian for healing (Suetonius, *Vesp.* 7; Tacitus, *Hist.* 4.81; see Guelich, 428–36, on Mark 8:22–26).

52 ὕπαγε, ἡ πίστις σου σέσωκέν σε, "Go, your faith has saved you." In contrast to earlier healings (e.g., 7:33–34; 8:23–25), Jesus does not touch the blind man. He merely speaks the word and the man recovers his sight. Jesus' declaration that one's faith (πίστις) saves (σέσωκεν) appears elsewhere. One thinks of Jesus' words to the woman with the hemorrhage, "Daughter, your faith has saved you [ἡ πίστις σου σέσωκέν σε]; go in peace, and be healed of your disease" (Mark 5:34), the words spoken to the leper, "Rise and go your way; your faith has saved you [ἡ πίστις σου σέσωκέν σε]" (Luke 17:19 RSV, adapted), and the words to the "sinful" woman, "Your faith has saved you [ἡ πίστις σου σέσωκέν σε]; go in peace" (Luke 7:50). To be saved means to be delivered from whatever ails, afflicts, or threatens one. The idea of salvation, therefore, can refer to deliverance from physical danger, from spiritual oppression, or from the consequences of sin.

With the command ὕπαγε, "go," Jesus dismissed others whom he had healed (see Mark 1:44; 2:11; 5:19, 34; 7:29). Now able to see, Bartimaeus falls in with the crowd trailing Jesus. In the context of this seeming procession, the title "son of David" has the added ramification of foreshadowing the triumphal entry into Jerusalem.

Earlier Bartimaeus had been described as "seated by the road." Now that he has been healed, he ἠκολούθει [probably an inceptive imperfect] αὐτῷ ἐν τῇ ὁδῷ, "began following him [Jesus] on the road." Bartimaeus has been transformed from a helpless man who was going nowhere to a restored man who sets out on the road of discipleship.

Explanation

Jesus' compassion and power are once again demonstrated in the healing of the blind beggar Bartimaeus. In this episode Jesus puts into practice what he had just taught his disciples. He gives his time and attention to one of Israel's lowliest members of society. By giving sight to the blind man, Jesus has demonstrated that he is indeed the "son of David," anointed by the Spirit of God to proclaim good news to the poor and to open the eyes of the blind. This episode provides a fitting conclusion to the public ministry, which has run from Galilee to the journey south. Now Jesus turns to Jerusalem and to the final phase of his ministry.

B. The Triumphal Entry (11:1–11)

Bibliography

Ambrozic, A. M. *The Hidden Kingdom.* 32–45. **Bauer, W.** "The 'Colt' of Palm Sunday." *JBL* 72 (1953) 220–29. **Bishop, E. F. F.** "Hosanna: The Word of the Joyful Jerusalem Crowds." *ExpTim* 53 (1941–42) 212–14. **Blenkinsopp, J.** "The Oracle of Judah and the Messianic Entry." *JBL* 80 (1961) 55–64. ————. "The Hidden Messiah and His Entry into Jerusalem." *Scr* 13 (1961) 51–56, 81–88. **Bratcher, R. G.** "A Note on Mark xi.3 ὁ Κύριος αὐτοῦ χρείαν ἔχει." *ExpTim* 64 (1952–53) 93. **Bromboszcz, T.** "Der Einzug Jesu in Jerusalem bei Mondschein? Ein Beitrag zur Chronologie der Leidensgeschichte." *BZ* 9 (1911) 164–70. **Bruce, F. F.** "The Book of Zechariah and the Passion Narrative." *BJRL* 43 (1960–61) 336–53. **Burger, C.** *Jesus als Davidssohn: Eine traditiönsgeschichtliche Untersuchung.* FRLANT 98. Göttingen: Vandenhoeck & Ruprecht, 1970. 46–52, 63–64. **Burkill, T. A.** "Strain on the Secret: An Examination of Mark 11:1–13:37." *ZNW* 51 (1960) 31–46. **Cadoux, C. J.** *The Historic Mission of Jesus: A Constructive Re-Examination of the Eschatological Teaching in the Synoptic Gospels.* Lutterworth Library 12. London: Lutterworth, 1941. **Carmignac, J.** "Studies in the Hebrew Background of the Synoptic Gospels." *ASTI* 7 (1970) 64–93, esp. 83–84. **Catchpole, D. R.** "The 'Triumphal' Entry." In *Jesus and the Politics of His Day.* Ed. E. Bammel and C. F. D. Moule. Cambridge: Cambridge UP, 1984. 319–35. **Crossan, J. D.** "Redaction and Citation in Mark 11:9–10 and 11:17." *BR* 17 (1972) 33–50. **Dalman, G.** *The Words of Jesus.* Edinburgh: T. & T. Clark, 1902. 220–23. **Davies, T. L.** "Was Jesus Compelled?" *ExpTim* 42 (1930–31) 526–27. **Deissmann, G.** *Bible Studies.* Edinburgh: T. & T. Clark, 1901. **Derrett, J. D. M.** "Law in the New Testament: The Palm Sunday Colt." *NovT* 13 (1971) 241–58. **Duff, P. B.** "The March of the Divine Warrior and the Advent of the Greco-Roman King: Mark's Account of Jesus' Entry into Jerusalem." *JBL* 111 (1992) 53–71. **Eppstein, V.** "The Historicity of the Gospel Account of the Cleansing of the Temple." *ZNW* 55 (1964) 42–58. **Evans, C. F.** "'I Will Go before You into Galilee.'" *JTS* n.s. 5 (1954) 3–18, esp. 5–8. **Fahy, T.** "The Triumphal Entry into Jerusalem." In *New Testament Problems.* London: Burns and Oates, 1963. 126–39. **Farmer, W. R.** "The Palm Branches in John 12, 13." *JTS* n.s. 3 (1952) 62–66. **Fitzmyer, J. A.** "Aramaic Evidence Affecting the Interpretation of *Hosanna* in the New Testament." In *Tradition and Interpretation in the New Testament.* FS E. E. Ellis, ed. G. F. Hawthorne and O. Betz. Tübingen: Mohr-Siebeck; Grand Rapids, MI: Eerdmans, 1987. 110–18 (repr. in *The Dead Sea Scrolls and Christian Origins.* Studies in the Dead Sea Scrolls and Related Literature. Grand Rapids, MI: Eerdmans, 2000. 119–29). **France, R. T.** *Jesus and the Old Testament.* 103–10. **Grant, R. M.** "The Coming of the Kingdom." *JBL* 67 (1948) 297–303. **Hahn, F.** *The Titles of Jesus in Christology: Their History in Early Christianity.* London: Lutterworth, 1969. 82–84, 253–58. **Hart, H. St. J.** "Hosanna in the Highest." *SJT* 45 (1992) 283–301. **Harvey, A. E.** *Jesus and the Constraints of History.* London: Duckworth, 1982. 120–29. **Hiers, R. H.** *The Historical Jesus and the Kingdom of God: Present and Future in the Message and Ministry of Jesus.* University of Florida Humanities Monograph 38. Gainesville: University of Florida Press, 1973. 77–83. **Jack, J. W.** "Was Jesus Compelled?" *ExpTim* 43 (1931–32) 381–82. **Jacob, R.** *Les péricopes de l'entrée à Jérusalem et de la préparation de la cène: Contribution à l'étude du problème synoptique.* EBib. Paris: Gabalda, 1973. **Jeremias, J.** "ΙΕΡΟΥΣΑΛΗΜ/ ΙΕΡΟΣΟΛΥΜΑ." *ZNW* 65 (1974) 273–76. **Kennard, J. S.** "'Hosanna' and the Purpose of Jesus." *JBL* 67 (1948) 171–76. **Kilpatrick, G. D.** "Κύριος again." In *The Principles and Practice of New Testament Textual Criticism: Collected Essays.* Ed. J. K. Elliott. BETL 96. Leuven: Peeters, 1990. 216–22. **Kim, S.** "Jesus—The Son of God, the Stone, the Son of Man, and the Servant: The Role of Zechariah in the Self-Identification of Jesus." In *Tradition and Interpretation in the New Testament.* FS E. E. Ellis, ed. G. F. Hawthorne and O. Betz. Tübingen: Mohr-Siebeck; Grand Rapids, MI: Eerdmans, 1987. 134–48. **Knox, W. L.** *The Sources of the Synoptic Gospels.* Cambridge: Cambridge UP, 1953. 77–84. **Kuhn, H.-W.** "Das Reittier Jesu in der Einzugsgeschichte des Markusevangeliums." *ZNW* 50 (1959) 82–91. **Lagrange, M.-J.** *The Gospel of Jesus Christ.* 2 vols. London: Burns, Oates & Washbourne, 1947. **Lohse, E.** *Die Geschichte des Leidens und Sterbens Jesu Christi.* 3rd ed. Gütersloh: Mohn, 1973. 27–40. ———. "Hosanna." *NovT* 6 (1963) 113–19. **Mackay, W. M.** "The Contrasts of Palm Sunday." *ExpTim* 44 (1932–33) 275–77. **März, C.-P.** *"Siehe, dein König kommt zu dir . . .": Eine traditionsgeschichtliche Untersuchung zur Einzugsperikope.* ETS 43. Leipzig: St. Benno, 1980. **Mastin, B. A.** "The Date of the Triumphal Entry." *NTS* 16 (1969) 76–82. **Matera, F. J.** *The Kingship of Jesus: Composition and Theology in Mark 15.* SBLDS 66. Chico, CA: Scholars Press, 1982. 70–74. **Meikle, J.** "Was Jesus Compelled?" *ExpTim* 43 (1931–32) 288. **Michel, O.** "Eine philologische Frage zur Einzugsgeschichte." *NTS* 6 (1959) 81–82. ———. "Πῶλος." *TDNT* 6:959–61. **Minette de Tillesse, G.** *Le secret messianique.* 284–87. **Mohr, T. A.** *Markus- und Johannespassion: Redaktions- und traditionsgeschichtliche Untersuchung der markinischen und johanneischen Passionstradition.* ATANT 70. Zürich: Theologischer Verlag, 1982. 45–71. **Nesbitt, C. F.** "The Bethany Traditions in the Gospel Narratives." *JBR* 29 (1961) 119–24. **Patsch, H.** "Der Einzug Jesu in Jerusalem: Ein historischer Versuch." *ZTK* 68 (1971) 1–26. **Paul, A.** "L'entrée de Jésus à Jérusalem: Mc 11,1–10; Mt 21,1–11; Lc 19,1–11; Jn 12,12–19." *AsSeign* 2.19 (1971) 4–26. **Pesch, R.** *Evangelium der Urgemeinde.* 126–30. ——— and **Kratz, R.** "Jesus zieht ein in Jerusalem." In *Passionsgeschichte,* Part 1. Vol. 6 of *So liest man synoptisch.* Frankfurt am Main: Knecht, 1979. 64–72. **Pieper, K.** "Zum Einzug Jesu in Jerusalem." *BZ* 11 (1913) 397–402. **Pope, M.** "Hosanna—What It Really Means." *BR* 4 (1988) 16–25. **Räisänen, H.** *The 'Messianic Secret' in Mark's Gospel.* 231–35. **Ringgren, H.** "The Use of the Psalms in the Gospels." In *The Living Text.* FS E. W. Saunders, ed. D. E. Groh and R. Jewett. Lanham: UP of America, 1985. 39–43. **Ross, J. M.** "Names of God: A Comment on Mark 11:3 and Parallels." *BT* 35 (1984) 443. **Samuel, O.** "Die Regierungsgewalt des Wortes Gottes." *EvT* 3 (1936) 1–3. **Sanders, E. P.** *Jesus and Judaism.* 61–90. **Sanders, J. A.** "A New Testament Hermeneutic Fabric: Psalm 118 in the Entrance Narrative." In *Early Jewish and Christian Exegesis.* FS W. H. Brownlee, ed. C. A. Evans and W. F. Stinespring. Homage 10. Atlanta: Scholars Press, 1987. 177–90. **Sandvik, B.** *Das Kommen des Herrn beim Abendmahl im Neuen Testament.* ATANT 58. Zürich: Zwingli, 1970. 37–43. **Schenk, W.** *Der Passionsbericht.* 166–75. **Schmahl, G.** *Die Zwölf im Markusevangelium.* 96–98. **Schmauch, W.** "Der Ölberg: Exegese zu einer Ortsangabe besonders bei Matthäus und Markus." *TLZ* 77 (1952) 391–96. **Schmidt, K. L.** *Rahmen.* 295–98. **Spitta, F.** "Der Volksruf beim Einzug Jesu in Jerusalem." *ZWT* 52 (1910) 307–20. **Stock, A.** *Call to Discipleship.* 156–62. **Stock, K.** *Boten aus dem Mit-Ihm-Sein.* 145–50. ———. "Gliederung und Zusammenhang in Mk 11–12." *Bib* 59 (1978) 481–515. **Suhl, A.** *Die Funktion der alttestamentlichen Zitate.* 52–58. **Torrey, C. C.** *Our Translated Gospels.* London: Hodder and Stoughton; New York: Harper & Brothers, 1936. **Trautmann, M.** *Zeichenhafte Handlungen Jesu: Ein Beitrag zur Frage nach dem geschichtlichen Jesus.* FB 37. Würzburg: Echter, 1980. 347–78. **Vanbergen, P.** "L'entrée messianique de Jésus à Jérusalem." *Questions liturgiques et paroissiales* 38 (1957) 9–24. **Vielhauer, P.** "Ein Weg zur neutestamentlichen Christologie?" In *Aufsätze zum Neuen Testament.* TB 31. Munich: Kaiser, 1965. 141–98, esp. 150–57. **Visser 't Hooft, W. A.** "Triumphalism in the Gospel." *SJT*

38 (1985) 491–504. **Wagner, J.** *Auferstehung und Leben: Joh 11,1–12,19 als Spiegel johanneischer Redaktions- und Theologiegeschichte.* Biblische Untersuchungen 19. Regensburg: Pustet, 1988. 375–84. **Werner, E.** "'Hosanna' in the Gospels." *SJT* 38 (1985) 491–504. **Wrege, H.-Th.** *Die Gestalt des Evangeliums: Aufbau und Struktur der Synoptiker sowie der Apostelgeschichte.* BBET 11. Bern; Frankfurt am Main: Lang, 1978. 58–60.

Translation

[1]*And when they draw near to* [a] *Jerusalem,*[b] *Bethphage,*[c] *and Bethany,*[d] *at the Mount of Olives, he sends two of his disciples,* [2]*and says to them, "Go into the village* [e] *opposite you, and immediately as you enter it you will find a tethered colt on which no one has ever sat; untie it and bring*[f] *it.* [3]*If anyone says to you, 'Why are you doing this?' say, 'The Lord has need of it* [g]*and sends*[h] *it here again* [i] *immediately.'"* [4]*And they went away and found a tethered colt at the door, out in the open street; and they untied it.* [5]*And some of those standing there said to them, "What are you doing, untying the colt?"* [6]*And they spoke to them as Jesus had said; and they permitted them.* [7]*And they bring*[j] *the colt to Jesus and throw their garments upon it, and he sat upon it.* [8]*And many spread their garments* [k] *on the road, and others [spread]* [l] *tall grass, cutting it from the fields.* [9]*And those who went before and those who followed were crying out, "Hosanna!* [m] *Blessed is he who comes in the name of the Lord!* [10]*Blessed is the coming kingdom of our father David!* [n] *Hosanna in the highest!"* [o] [11]*And he* [p] *entered Jerusalem [and went]* [l] *into the temple; and looking around at everything,* [q]*the hour already being late, he went out to Bethany with the Twelve.*[r]

Notes

[a]A few later MSS add ὁ Ἰησοῦς καὶ οἱ μαθηταὶ αὐτοῦ, "Jesus and his disciples." The historic present is found several times in this pericope. Oftentimes MSS replace the present with other tense forms.

[b]Gk. Ἱεροσόλυμα, which is Mark's preferred form (cf. Mark 3:8, 22; 7:1; 10:32, 33; 11:1, 11, 15, 27; 15:41). Here at 11:1 some MSS give other forms, such as Ἱερουσαλήμ (Α Φ), which is favored by the author of Luke-Acts.

[c]The spelling of *Bethphage* varies in the MSS. Βηθφαγή is found in ℵ A C W Φ. B* reads Βηδφαγή. B³ Σ read Βηθσφαγή. Other variants include Βιθφαγή, Βηθφαγειν, Βηφαγή, Βησφαγή, and Βηθσφαγεί. D 700 simply read καὶ εἰς, "and to," for εἰς Βηθφαγή καί, "to Bethphage and," eliminating the reference to Bethphage. Cranfield (348) accepts Bethphage, though he thinks it is out of proper sequence: "Bethany would be reached before Bethphage; but Bethphage is mentioned first, possibly because it was better known, or because, Jerusalem having been mentioned first, it was natural to mention next the place that was nearer to it."

[d]The spelling of *Bethany* also varies in the MSS. Βηθανίαν is found in ℵ B* C D. Βιθανίαν is attested in some MSS. Other MSS omit the name altogether.

[e]Gk. κώμην. Some MSS read πόλιν, "city."

[f]Gk. φέρετε. Some MSS read ἀγάγετε, "lead," which is an attempt to find a more appropriate verb.

[g]What follows might not be part of Jesus' statement; cf. Matt 21:3; Metzger, *TCGNT*[1], 108–9.

[h]ἀποστέλλει, "he sends," is a "futuristic present" (Cranfield, 350); on the question of the verb's subject, see Field, *Notes,* 34–35.

[i]Klostermann (113) drops πάλιν, "again," with A W lat bo syr.

[j]Some MSS read ἄγουσιν, "lead" (see *Note* f above).

[k]Gk. ἱμάτια, "garments, clothes," as in v 7. Some MSS read χιτῶνας, "tunics," which in the pl. is roughly synonymous with ἱμάτια.

[l]*Spread* (v 8) and *and went* are added from the context. Some MSS actually have the words στιβάδας ἔκοπτον ἐκ τῶν δένδρων καὶ ἐστρώννυον εἰς τὴν ὁδόν, "cut *stibadas* [see *Comment* below] from the trees and were spreading [them] on the road."

[m]Some MSS add τῷ ὑψίστῳ, "in the highest," in conformity with v 10.

[n]In most Gk. authorities "David" is spelled Δαυείδ (as in B D). But in other authorities the name is spelled variously; e.g., N reads Δαβίδ; ℵ and other MSS read the abbreviation Δᾱδ. See 10:47; 12:35.

[o]Some MSS read εἰρήνη ἐν τοῖς ὑψίστοις, "peace in the highest," or εἰρήνη ἐν οὐρανῷ καὶ δόξα ἐν τοῖς ὑψίστοις, "peace in heaven and glory in the highest." These readings are reminiscent of the Lukan account (cf. Luke 19:38) and Lukan infancy narrative (cf. Luke 2:14).

[p]Some MSS add ὁ Ἰησοῦς, "Jesus."

[q]Gk. ὀψίας ἤδη οὔσης τῆς ὥρας, lit. "the hour already being evening." Taylor (458) reads ὀψέ, "late" (cf. 11:19; 13:35), which is strongly attested by ℵ C L Δ 892 1342.

[r]Some MSS add μαθητῶν, "disciples."

Form/Structure/Setting

Mark 11–15 is characterized by controversy between Jesus and Jerusalem's temple establishment. The entrance into the city of Jersualem (11:1–11) and the demonstration in the precincts (11:15–18) provoke the religious authorities, who demand to know by what authority Jesus does these things (11:27–33). Jesus refuses to provide them with a direct answer; instead, he answers indirectly with the parable of the Wicked Vineyard Tenants (12:1–12). Jesus is challenged with questions, some of which are designed to entrap him, such as the question regarding taxation (12:13–17). Jesus responds with further criticisms (12:38–44) and eventually predicts the temple's complete destruction (13:2). The plot thickens in chap. 14 as Jesus spends his last evening with his disciples teaching and eating a solemn meal. The evening ends in prayer, arrest, and interrogation. Chap. 15 provides an outline of the events of the following day, as Jesus is brought before Pilate the Roman governor. Jesus is condemned, crucified, and hastily prepared for burial. In most of the pericopes that make up these five chapters, either Jesus criticizes the temple establishment or the temple establishment criticizes and plots against him. The opening episode, the so-called triumphal entry, sets the stage for the drama that follows.

Jesus' entrance into Jerusalem marks the beginning of passion week. Jesus directs his disciples to enter a nearby village, where they will find a colt. They are to take possession of it, and if anyone questions them, they are to reply as Jesus has instructed them. The disciples follow Jesus' instructions, and all works out as planned. Jesus mounts the colt, and his disciples and others create a procession, with garments and branches paving the way. Amidst shouts of "Hosanna" and references to the coming kingdom of David, Jesus and his disciples wend their way into the ancient city of Jerusalem.

Bultmann (*History,* 261–62) allows that the story might contain a grain of actual reminiscence of Jesus' entrance into Jerusalem "with a crowd of pilgrims full of joy and expectation." But he regards the details of securing and riding upon an animal as "legendary," reflecting a "fairy-tale motif." Dibelius (*From Tradition,* 122) calls the entrance narrative a "cultus-legend." Taylor (*Formation,* 151) rightly responds that "No legend would have broken off the account with the anticlimax" of v 11: "and looking around at everything, the hour already being late, he went out to Bethany with the Twelve." Had the early church invented the story of the entrance, or thoroughly revised a more or less ordinary story of entrance, we should have expected a more pronounced christological element and surely a more impressive conclusion. Moreoever, nothing is made of the mysterious arrangements to secure the animal, which leaves the reader puzzled. It seems more probable that what we have here is a fragment of an authentic story, which the tradents and eventually the evangelist himself passed on but without being in full possession of the facts. Jesus was remembered to have entered the city mounted on a colt (not "ass," as Bultmann says; this is a later embellishment), amidst the acclaim of his disciples and others in the crowd. Finally, one must take into account the outcome of the whole affair, which is the eventual crucifixion of Jesus as "king of the Jews." The entrance as Mark describes it makes this outcome more intelligible. Schenk's proposal (*Passionsbericht*, 168–75) that two traditions have been combined, one apocalyptic (i.e., vv 4a, 1a, 8a, 9–10, 11ac) and the other an "entrance legend," is unconvincing and raises more questions than it answers. But other composite theories have been proposed. Ernst (318) thinks an original entrance narrative (vv 1a, 8–11) was later expanded with details about a colt and Jesus' prescience (vv 1b–7). Haenchen (373–77) takes vv 1–6 as a unit, which was later augmented by vv 7–11, all of which was inspired by OT elements. Gnilka (2:113–14) also thinks two traditions have been combined. See also Lührmann (187), who draws important pre-Markan and independent parallels with John's account on the entrance. His ideas of secondary expansion are much more modest. The complexity and contradictory nature of these subjective proposals are self-defeating and unpersuasive. Many interpreters rightly view the passage as an original unity (e.g., Taylor, 452; Catchpole, "Entry," 325).

Catchpole ("Entry," 319–21) cites twelve examples of celebrated entries, six from 1 and 2 Maccabees, and six from Josephus, of a "more or less fixed pattern of entry." Entries involving major figures include Alexander, who enters Jerusalem, is greeted with ceremony, and is escorted into the city where he participates in cultic activity (Josephus, *Ant.* 11.8.4–5 §§325–39); Apollonius, who enters Jerusalem accompanied by torches and shouts (2 Macc 4:21–22); Judas Maccabeus, who returns home from a military victory and is greeted with hymns and "praising God" (1 Macc 4:19–25; Josephus, *Ant.* 12.7.4 §312); Judas Maccabeus, again, who returns from battle and enters Jerusalem amidst singing and merrymaking, followed by sacrifice (1 Macc 5:45–54; Josephus, *Ant.* 12.8.5 §§348–49); Jonathan the brother of Judas, who is greeted by the men of Askalon "with great pomp" (1 Macc 10:86); Simon brother of Judas, who enters Gaza, expells idolatrous inhabitants, cleanses idolatrous houses, and enters the city "with hymns and praise" (1 Macc 13:43–48); Simon the brother of Judas, again, who enters Jerusalem and is met by crowds "with praise and palm branches, and with harps and cymbals and stringed instruments and with hymns and songs" (1 Macc 13:49–51); Antigonus, who with pomp enters Jerusalem, then the temple precincts, but with so much pomp and self-importance that he is criticized by some for imagining that he himself was "king" (Josephus, *J.W.* 1.3.2 §§73–74; *Ant.* 13.11.1 §§304–6); Marcus Agrippa, who enters Jerusalem, is met by Herod, and is welcomed by the people with acclamations (Josephus, *Ant.* 16.2.1 §§12–15); and Archelaus, who, hoping to confirm his kingship, journeys to and enters Jerusalem amidst acclamation of his procession (Josephus, *Ant.* 17.8.2 §§194–239).

According to Catchpole ("Entry," 321), the elements that make up this pattern include: "*(a)* A victory already achieved and a status already recognised for the central person. *(b)* A formal and ceremonial entry. *(c)* Greetings and/or acclamations together with invocations of God. *(d)* Entry to the city climaxed by entry to Temple, if the city in question has one. *(e)* Cultic activity, either positive (e.g., offering of sacrifice), or negative (e.g., expulsion of objectionable persons and the cleansing away of uncleanness)." Catchpole remarks: "Mark 11 contains all of these major and recurrent features. It also contains minor agreements with occasional features of some of the other stories, for example, the reference to the royal animal. . . . Mark's story thus conforms to a familiar pattern in respect of both its determinative shape and some of its incidental details" ("Entry," 321).

The Markan entrance narrative, in which Jesus mounts a colt, appears to be deliberately modeled after Zech 9:9: "Rejoice greatly, O daughter of Zion! . . . Lo, your king comes to you; triumphant and victorious is he, humble and riding on an ass, on a colt the foal of an ass." Other scriptural influences have been suggested, such as 1 Sam 10:2–10 (cf. Gnilka, 2:114; Pesch, 2:181–82). But this act is to be traced to Jesus (Taylor, 451), not to a community imagination inspired by the prophetic Scriptures. Mark's account (Mark 11:1–11) does not quote the passage from Zechariah, but the Matthean and Johannine accounts do (Matt 21:4–5; John 12:14–15). Mark's failure to exploit an important proof text argues both for his Gospel's priority and for the essential historicity of the account (Schweizer, 227; Cranfield, 348; Gundry, 632). The explicit and formal quotation of Zech 9:9 in Matthew and John is consistent with their scriptural apologetic, an apologetic that seems to be primarily fashioned with the synagogue in mind. Commentators are divided over the question of the original significance of the entrance with many seeing it as messianic (Gould, 205; Lagrange, 287–92; id., *The Gospel* 2:121–25; Turner, 53–54; Rawlinson, 151; Taylor, 451–53; Johnson, 186; Schweizer, 227; Schmid, 204; Moule, 86–87; Cranfield, 348; Grundmann, 301; Lane, 392–94; Pesch, 2:185; Hooker, 257) and many suggesting that the messianic significance is a later interpretation (Wellhausen, 88; Dalman, *Words,* 222; R. Otto, *Kingdom of God and the Son of Man* [Rev. ed.; London: Lutterworth, 1943] 224; Lohmeyer, 233; Branscomb, 198–200; Anderson, 260: "it is impossible to say"; Catchpole, "Entry"; Gnilka, 2:114). In my view, the act was indeed originally messianic, which in later tradition was exaggerated (cf. Klostermann, 112).

The shouts of the crowd, which allude to Ps 118:26 ("Blessed is he who comes in the name of the Lord!"), are consistent with the imagery of Jesus mounted on the royal mule, much as Solomon was shortly before the death of his father David (1 Kgs 1:32–40). The crowd interpretively adds to Ps 118:26 the words: "Blessed is the coming kingdom of our father David!" (Mark 11:10). In the Aramaic (i.e., the Targum), Ps 118:22–29 is understood to be speaking of David "who is worthy to be ruler and king." The coherence of the targum of Ps 118:22–29 with Jesus' Zechariah-inspired action of mounting the colt argues for the antiquity of the tradition, as well as its authenticity. The explicit quotation of Zech 9:9 in Matthew points to later elaboration and apologetic. The rephrasing of the shout of the crowd in Matt 21:9 draws the parallel closer to the text of Ps 118:26, chiefly through simplification of Mark's clumsy version, and explicitly identifies Jesus as the "son of David." The shouts of "Hosanna!" stand a "good chance of representing a genuine primitive Christian recollection of what was shouted to Jesus on the occasion of his entry into Jerusalem" (Fitzmyer, "Aramaic Evidence," 111).

As to redaction, the Markan evangelist probably inherited the story from his tradition pretty much as we find it. Ernst (319) thinks the evangelist edited the story to fit better his Passion Narrative (so also Lührmann, 187). Gnilka (2:114) essentially agrees, limiting redaction to the opening and closing verses. Pesch (2:176), however, finds "no trace of Markan reworking."

As to structure, commentators are in essential agreement. Taylor (451) says the narrative consists of two stories: "the Sending for the colt (1–6) and the Entry proper (7–11), but the two are so closely connected that they may be taken together." Gnilka (2:114) similarly finds two parts, which he outlines as follows: (*a*) preparation of the colt (vv 1b–7), with vv 1b–3 the assignment and vv 4–7 the completion; (*b*) the entry into the city (vv 8–11a), with gestures of greeting (v 8) and acclamation (vv 9–10). According to Pesch (2:177), v 1a provides a brief intoduction of the setting, vv 1b–6 provide description of the preparation for the ceremonial entry and the acquisition of the colt, vv 7–10 provide a description of the saddling, mounting, and joining of parade, vv 9b–10 express the climax of the narrative in hymnic shouts of praise, and v 11 offers a closing notice of Jesus' stop at the temple precincts, followed by departure for Bethany.

Comment

1 καὶ ὅτε ἐγγίζουσιν εἰς Ἰεροσόλυμα εἰς Βηθφαγὴ καὶ Βηθανίαν πρὸς τὸ ὄρος τῶν ἐλαιῶν, "And when they draw near to Jerusalem, Bethphage, and Bethany, at the Mount of Olives." On various problems having to do with the place names, see Schmidt, *Rahmen*, 295–98. Haenchen (373–74) thinks Bethphage was a later addition from Matt 21:1. Taylor (453) disagrees. Burger (*Jesus als Davidssohn*, 63) takes Bethany as traditional. Jerusalem is mentioned first (see *Comment* on 10:32) because it is the principal destination, not because the Markan evangelist does not know that Bethphage (= "house of figs") and Bethany (= "house of dates"?) would in fact be encountered before entry into the ancient city. Gnilka (2:110) thinks the evangelist added Ἰεροσόλυμα, "Jerusalem." Perhaps, but it too is likely traditional. Lane (394) plausibly suggests that the order of the place names in v 1 was probably "dictated by the reference to Jerusalem, followed by the village which was nearer to the city." He is probably correct, and if so, then Gnilka's suggestion is weakened.

The Mount of Olives is selected as the official starting point for entry into the city (Deissmann, *Bible Studies*, 208–12). This makes sense, for the Mount of Olives overlooks the city and the eastern side of the Temple Mount itself. But it also makes sense in view of Jesus' interest in acting out an agenda informed by themes and images in the prophecy of Zechariah: "On that day his feet shall stand on the Mount of Olives which lies before Jerusalem on the east" (Zech 14:4). The departure from the Mount of Olives in order to enter Jerusalem mounted upon a colt is the beginning of a series of elements drawn from Zechariah. With the exception of Mark 14:27, where a quotation is found on the lips of Jesus, the allusions to Zechariah are implicit and there is no reason to think that they represent either the theology of the evangelist or the theology of his tradition. What we have here are significant fragments of Jesus' theology, especially as it relates to his relationship to Jerusalem.

ἀποστέλλει δύο τῶν μαθητῶν αὐτοῦ, "he sends two of his disciples." Could these two disciples have been James and John, the sons of Zebedee? Or perhaps Peter and his brother Andrew? The scene here is as mysterious as the sending of the two disciples to secure the upper room for the Last Supper (Mark 14:12–16).

2 ὑπάγετε εἰς τὴν κώμην τὴν κατέναντι ὑμῶν, "Go into the village opposite you."
Identifying the intended village is difficult; Cranfield (348) thinks Bethphage is
meant (so also Turner, 53; Taylor, 453). Bethphage is the more probable, being
closer to the Mount of Olives (but Gundry, 624, opts for Bethany since it is closer
to the road leading up from Jericho; so also Burger, *Jesus als Davidssohn*, 47).

εὑρήσετε πῶλον δεδεμένον, "you will find a tethered colt." The "tethered colt"
is not necessarily an ass. πῶλος means a colt but not necessarily always the foal of
an ass (as Lohmeyer, 229 n. 5, notes). LXX Zech 9:9 reads: ἐπὶ ὑποζύγιον καὶ
πῶλον νέον, "upon a beast of burden, even a new colt." The ὑποζύγιον, "beast of
burden," is understood as an ass; hence Matthew's quotation of this prophetic
passage reads: ἐπὶ ὄνον καὶ ἐπὶ πῶλον υἱὸν ὑποζυγίου, "upon an ass, even upon a
colt, the foal of a beast of burden" (Matt 21:5, author's tr.). Gundry (626) is right
to insist that Mark's readers would understand πῶλος to refer to a young horse,
not necessarily to a young donkey (see πῶλος in BAGD; see further discussion on
this point in Kuhn, *ZNW* 50 [1959] 82–91). δεδεμένον, "tethered," may allude to
Gen 49:11 (e.g., Klostermann, 113; Lane, 395; Gnilka, 2:116), but the language is
too common to press it (so Ernst, 320).

ἐφ' ὃν οὐδεὶς οὔπω ἀνθρώπων ἐκάθισεν, "on which no one has ever sat," may be
a gloss, intended to allude to LXX Zech 9:9: πῶλον νέον, "new colt." Nineham
(295) opines that the phrase is an embellishment "to bring the story into closer
conformity with" Zech 9:9 (so also Anderson, 260). But would we not then expect Mark to say "new colt," as Gundry (627) rightly asks? The evangelist gives no
indication that he is aware of Zech 9:9, or at least gives no indication that it is
important to him. Saying that no one has sat on this animal does not mean that it
is unbroken and therefore potentially difficult to ride; it could have been used to
carry baggage. Mark's point in mentioning these details probably has to do with
Jesus' honor: that is, the animal on which Jesus rode was not a common one; it
was special. It had not been used before (for animals or things reserved for special use, see Num 19:2; Deut 21:3; 1 Sam 6:7; and in nonbiblical literature, see
Homer, *Iliad* 6.94; Horace, *Epod.* 9.22). According to *m. Sanh.* 2:5 no one may use
an animal on which a king rides (Catchpole, "Entry," 324). Thus, the "newness"
of the animal, in that no one else has used it, seems to be the point. (Could the
later evangelists be making the same point in describing the tomb in which Jesus'
body was placed as not having been used before? See Matt 27:60; Luke 23:53;
John 19:41.) Gundry (625) wonders too if having Jesus sit (presumably successfully) on an animal on which no one had yet sat was to show in yet another instance
Jesus' mastery and ability to do what others could not.

λύσατε αὐτὸν καὶ φέρετε, "untie it and bring it." The commandeering of an animal "is to be explained in relation to the system of official transport" (E. A. Judge,
NewDocs 1:43; cf. Derrett, *NovT* 13 [1971] 241–58; Pesch, 2:180). The practice is
described in some detail in SEG 1392 (18–19 C.E.). The term for this practice, called
ἀγγαρεία, "pressed transportation," is so widespread that it occurs in Hebrew as a
loan word אַנגַּרְיָא *'angaryā'* (cf. *m. B. Meṣiʿa* 6:3). In the OT the king לקח *lāqaḥ*, "takes,"
what he wants from the people (e.g., 1 Sam 8:16–18). Jesus' demand may hint at
his assumption of political authority, at least on par with Roman authority. However, the explanation may in fact be much simpler; Jesus evidently made a prior
arrangement with a sympathizer (Rawlinson, 152; Blunt, 224; Turner, 53).

3–6 ἐάν τις ὑμῖν εἴπῃ, τί ποιεῖτε τοῦτο, "If anyone says to you, 'Why are you doing this?'" The question has a biblical ring to it (cf. Exod 18:14; 1 Sam 2:23; Neh 2:19). As suggested above, the planned response points to a prior arrangement, not to an expected supernatural event (against Ernst, 319).

ὁ κύριος αὐτοῦ χρείαν ἔχει, καὶ εὐθὺς αὐτὸν ἀποστέλλει πάλιν ὧδε, "'The Lord has need of it and sends it here again immediately.'" To whom ὁ κύριος, "the Lord," refers is not easy to decide: Jesus, God, and the owner of the colt (Taylor, 454) seem to be the options. The Markan evangelist (in contrast to Luke) never calls Jesus ὁ κύριος, so it is probably not prudent to see it as a reference to Jesus (as Nineham, 295, and Gnilka, 2:117, think; Gundry, 624, 628, also argues for this view, but Mark 1:3, 7; 12:36 as alleged instances where the evangelist calls Jesus ὁ κύριος do not in a strict sense contradict Taylor's point). Taylor (455) opts for the owner of the colt, supposing that the owner was with Jesus. This option is plausible and coheres with the *Comment* on v 2 above that Jesus had made a prior arrangement with a sympathizer (Cranfield, 350, and Lane, 391–92 n. 3, agree with Taylor). ὁ κύριος would then mean the animal's "master" (probably from an Aramaic form of אדון *'ādôn*) or owner (against Grundmann, 302, the use of κύριος does not necessarily point to a Hellenistic context). Nevertheless, the κύριος of this animal may very well be God under whose authority Jesus is acting. The animal probably does belong to a sympathizer and an arrangment has been made, but the words "the Lord has need of it" could imply a sort of *qorbān*, i.e., something dedicated to God's use. But Jesus' use of the animal is only temporary; the animal will be returned. For the Markan community ὁ κύριος may very well have been understood as a reference to Jesus (Ernst, 320).

7 φέρουσιν τὸν πῶλον πρὸς τὸν Ἰησοῦν καὶ ἐπιβάλλουσιν αὐτῷ τὰ ἱμάτια αὐτῶν, "They bring the colt to Jesus and throw their garments upon it." The garments on the colt take the place of a saddle (Cranfield, 350). Gnilka (2:117) rightly understands that the placing of clothing upon the animal for Jesus to sit upon is reminiscent of a coronation (1 Kgs 1:38–40; 2 Kgs 9:13; see next paragraph). Lane (393) also is correct to point out that "it was not customary for pilgrims to enter Jerusalem riding upon an ass; the final stage of the pilgrimage was generally completed on foot."

ἐκάθισεν ἐπ' αὐτόν, "he sat upon it." With the colt adorned with the garments of disciples and followers, Jesus sits upon the animal. Riding upon the colt (which historically was probably a donkey, despite the fact that Mark does not specifically say this) is reminiscent of Solomon being made to ride his father David's mule in order to strengthen his claim to the throne (cf. 1 Kgs 1:38–48). Solomon rides the mule, he is anointed, and people shout "Long live King Solomon!" and follow along rejoicing and making a great deal of noise. The prophecy of Zech 9:9 is itself reminiscent of Solomon's ride.

8 πολλοὶ τὰ ἱμάτια αὐτῶν ἔστρωσαν εἰς τὴν ὁδόν, "Many spread their garments on the road." Spreading clothing on the road before an approaching general or monarch has biblical precedent. One immediately thinks of Jehu: "Then in haste every man of them took his garment [LXX ἱμάτιον], and put it under him on the bare steps, and they blew the trumpet, and proclaimed, 'Jehu is king'" (2 Kgs 9:13). Ernst (321) asserts that the spreading of garments is unrealistic. Why? The spreading of garments before an approaching dignitary was an act of showing honor because, for one, it *was* an unrealistic, exaggerated act. Lohmeyer (230) allows for it, but only if it was for a short distance. Perhaps, but how do we know

that Jesus' following would not repeatedly place garments on the road before him? The Markan narrative does not provide this much detail; it only claims that the act took place (see Pesch, 2:182). The practice of spreading garments before a beloved or celebrated figure was known in the Greco-Roman world. One thinks of Plutarch's account of the respect shown to Cato when he prepared to depart from his army (cf. Plutarch, *Cato Minor* 7; Lane, 396). On the well-preserved stone relief that adorns the sarcophagus of Adelphia one can see a man laying a garment, or mat, beneath the hooves of the horse (or mule?) on which Adelphia rides. Some stand by and watch while others are part of the procession.

ἄλλοι δὲ στιβάδας κόψαντες ἐκ τῶν ἀγρῶν, "Others spread tall grass, cutting it from the fields." The στιβάδας, "tall grass," cut from fields may have been reeds or stalks of grain (see MM, 589: "a litter of reeds or rushes"; note also BAGD, which forces the evidence to insist that στιβάδας must refer to leafy branches). Of these options, either tall grass or stalks of grain (which at this time of season would be scarcely distinguishable from grass) is the better choice, for rushes or reeds were not likely to have been plentiful in the drier, rugged hills surrounding Jerusalem (as they would have been along the banks of the Jordan River and the Sea of Galilee). Mark's στιβάδας are not the same as Matthew's κλάδους ἀπὸ τῶν δένδρων, "branches from the trees" (21:8), which is a Matthean improvement, or John's τὰ βαΐα τῶν φοινίκων, "the branches of palm trees" (12:13). Accordingly, Mohr's argument (*Markus- und Johannespassion*, 56) that Mark's "leafy branches" must refer to either the festival of Tabernacles or the festival of Dedication, instead of the festival of Passover, loses all force (as Gundry, 629, rightly points out). Nor is there any basis for Swete's proposal (250), perhaps influenced by John 12:12-13, that some of Jesus' following entered Jerusalem and brought back with them palm branches. The hero's welcome accorded Judas Maccabeus may have some traditional bearing on Jesus' welcome: "Therefore bearing ivy-wreathed wands and beautiful branches [κλάδους] and also fronds of palm [φοίνικας], they offered hymns of thanksgiving to him who had given success to the purifying of his own holy place" (2 Macc 10:7; cf. 1 Macc 13:51, which mentions "palm branches" [βαΐων]). The occasion is not the same, for Judas was not welcomed in any sort of royal or messianic sense; nor were branches or palm fronds present when Jesus wound his way to the Temple Mount. Nonetheless, the story of Judas may clarify aspects of the behavior of Jesus' disciples. One interesting parallel is that temple purification is associated with the respective celebrations of Judas and Jesus. Judas is honored after his purification of the temple and altar (2 Macc 10:1-3) while Jesus is honored before he takes action in the temple precincts.

9 οἱ προάγοντες καὶ οἱ ἀκολουθοῦντες, "those who went before and those who followed." Mark only means to refer to the crowd surrounding and accompanying Jesus (so Turner, 54; Cranfield, 351; Taylor, 456), not to two different groups, one coming from Jerusalem and the other going to Jerusalem (as implied by John 12:12-13).

ἔκραζον, ὡσαννά· εὐλογημένος ὁ ἐρχόμενος ἐν ὀνόματι κυρίου, "were crying out, 'Hosanna! Blessed is he who comes in the name of the Lord!'" ὡσαννά, "Hosanna," is a transliteration of the Hebrew הוֹשִׁיעָה נָּא *hôšî'â nā'*, which is part of the quotation of Ps 118:25-26: "Save now, we beseech thee, O LORD! O LORD, we beseech thee, give us success! Blessed be he who enters in the name of the LORD! We bless you from the house of the LORD" (RSV, adapted). Mark's "Hosanna! Blessed is he who comes in the name of the Lord!" thus represents the first part of each verse. The opening words, "Save now!" translate "Hosanna!" The LXX (Ps 117:26) does not transliterate but translates: σῶσον δή, "Save now!" Mark's retention of the Semitic ὡσαννά argues for the authenticity of the tradition, rather than a later Christian gleaning of the LXX. Literally, "Hosanna!" is a request for help (Burger, *Jesus als Davidssohn*, 47). Because the הוֹשִׁיעָה *hôšîʿâ* of "Hosanna!" and the Hebrew/ Aramaic form of Jesus' name (יְהוֹשׁוּעַ *yĕhôšûaʿ*/יֵשׁוּעַ *yēšûaʿ*) are derived from the verb יָשַׁע *yāšaʿ*, "save," Gundry (630) suspects that the cry "Hosanna!" was directed to Jesus rather than to God. Gundry could be correct, for shouts of "Hosanna!" to Israel's kings are found in Scripture: e.g., the woman of Tekoa cries out הוֹשִׁיעָה הַמֶּלֶךְ *hôšîʿâ hammelek*, "Save, O king!" (2 Sam 14:4), which in the LXX is rendered Σῶσον βασιλεῦ σῶσον, "Save, king, save!" (2 Kgdms 14:4); or the cry of a famished woman הוֹשִׁיעָה אֲדֹנִי הַמֶּלֶךְ *hôšîʿâ ʾădōnî hammelek*, "Save, O my lord king!" (2 Kgs 6:26), which in the LXX is rendered σῶσον κύριε βασιλεῦ (4 Kgdms 6:26). Nevertheless, the addressee of the "Hosanna!" of Ps 118:25 is God, so it is more likely that the people accompanying Jesus are crying out to God to fulfill the promised deliverance (through Jesus, God's agent of deliverance) and the kingdom of David. (For more on the meaning of "Hosanna!" see Fitzmyer, "Aramaic Evidence"; see also *Comment* on v 10 below.)

The temple element of Ps 118 must not be overlooked (see Cranfield, 351). Although the last part of v 26 is not cited or alluded to ("We bless you from the house of the LORD"), the fact that Jesus actually enters the temple precincts at the conclusion of the entry suggests that this part of the psalm was very much in mind. The importance of this point will become clear below.

10 εὐλογημένη ἡ ἐρχομένη βασιλεία τοῦ πατρὸς ἡμῶν Δαυίδ, "'Blessed is the coming kingdom of our father David!'" Lührmann (189) rightly remarks that the "kingdom of our father David" was never part of Jesus' proclamation. This is true, but it is the *crowd* that is shouting these words, not Jesus. This tension with Mark's theology, as well as the theology of Jesus (see commentary on 12:35–37), smacks of authenticity, not of a later Christian confession in which one would expect greater consistency. This popular acclamation coheres with the charges later brought against Jesus before the high priest and the Roman governor, and when executed as "king of the Jews." Some commentators have opined that the expression is un-Jewish (usually appealing to *b. Ber.* 16b: "The term 'Fathers' [אבות *ʾābôt*] is applied only to three [i.e., Abraham, Isaac, and Jacob]") and so is no more than an inauthentic analogy based on Jesus' proclamation of the kingdom in Mark 1:15 (e.g., Schmithals, 2:485; cf. Lohmeyer, 231–32: "a later addition"; Schniewind, 149). Appeal to this rabbinic tradition, as though this were the whole of the matter, is misleading. Another rabbinic tradition says that because David humbled himself and pleased God, God will make him "chief next to the three fathers [ראש לשלשת אבות *rōʾš lišlōšet ʾābôt*]" (*b. Moʿed Qat.* 16b). Moreover, just as God is a "shield of Abraham" (*ʾAmîdâ* §1), so is he a "shield of David" (*b. Pesaḥ.* 117b; *Midr. Pss.* 18.8 [on Ps 18:3]; *Midr. Sam.* 26.3 [on 2 Sam 7:9]: "God of David . . . God of Abraham, Isaac, and Jacob"). Thus the rabbinic tradition does allow for David to enjoy the status of one of Israel's "fathers." Pesch (2:185) also disputes the claim that the expression is un-Jewish. He appeals to Acts 4:25 (cf. Luke 1:32), where David is called "our father," and to Acts 2:29, where David is called "patriarch." Pesch also appeals to 4Q252 [= 4QpGenᵃ] 1 V, 3, which interprets Gen

49:10 and speaks of the *coming* of the "Branch of David." He also reminds us of Sirach's praise of the fathers: "Let us now praise famous men, and our *fathers* in their generations" (Sir 44:1, emphasis added). The encomium includes Abraham, Isaac, Jacob, Moses, Aaron, Phineas, and David (Sir 45:25; 47:1–11), as well as others. Finally, Isaiah's reference to the "eternal father" (Isa 9:6) may be a reference to David. In view of these traditions, there is no justification for regarding the expression "our father David" as un-Jewish.

Ironically at variance with critical opinion that regards "the coming kingdom of our father David" as un-Jewish, Ernst (322) thinks it *is* Jewish, a Jewish expression that Christians later reworked. He speculates that the phrase comes from the Christian community that identified the one "coming in the name of the Lord" with David's son. But this is what the *Jewish targum* of Ps 118:26 (see *Form/Structure/Setting* above) has done! Again, the phrase "the coming kingdom of our father David" points to pre-Easter Jewish origins, not post-Easter Christian origins.

The Aramaic paraphrase in the targum of Ps 118:22–29 is explicitly Davidic. David is the "boy" (not "stone") rejected by the builders and is worthy to be king. The builders are the priests, who eventually come to accept him and to hail him from the temple: "We bless you from the house of the LORD." The interpretive addition of these themes to the Aramaic form of the psalm suggests that the shouted allusions to Ps 118 at Jesus' entry to Jerusalem were not mere coincidence but were part of the theology of Jesus' following and of Jesus himself. (See commentary on 12:1–12 below.)

ὡσαννὰ ἐν τοῖς ὑψίστοις, "'Hosanna in the highest!'" Torrey (*Our Translated Gospels*, 21) suggests "God save him!" (i.e., the Messiah). Taylor (456) thinks he might be correct. But the salvation, or deliverance, for which the people shout is for Israel as a whole, not just for Israel's Messiah. These options need not be viewed as competing; rather they are complementary.

J. A. Sanders ("Psalm 118 in the Entrance Narrative") suggests that the shouts of "Hosanna!" and the shouts of blessing were antiphonal, with one group of pilgrims shouting the one and another group shouting the other. Given the distinct possibility that the interpretive tradition of the Aramaic version (i.e., the targum of the Psalms), in an early form, was in play, it is possible that some early form of the interpretive tradition of the rabbinic literature that Sanders takes into account may also have been in circulation in the first century. (Fitzmyer, "Aramaic Evidence," 115, however, is highly skeptical that any of the rabbinic messianic interpretation of Ps 118 can be traced to first-century Palestine.)

11 εἰσῆλθεν εἰς Ἱεροσόλυμα εἰς τὸ ἱερόν, "He entered Jerusalem and went into the temple." The destination of the entrance narrative is the temple, that is, the temple precincts. If Ps 118 gives us any guidance, especially as it is paraphrased in the Aramaic targum, then Jesus may very well have anticipated a priestly greeting. But none is recorded. This is admittedly speculative, but it could explain the awkward, anticlimactic ending of the entrance narrative.

περιβλεψάμενος πάντα, ὀψίας ἤδη οὔσης τῆς ὥρας, ἐξῆλθεν εἰς Βηθανίαν μετὰ τῶν δώδεκα, "Looking around at everything, the hour already being late, he went out to Bethany with the Twelve." Haenchen (378) wonders if this awkward conclusion is evidence of a combination of materials, one describing the entrance, another describing a visit to the temple precincts. On the contrary, the awkward conclusion is evidence that the triumphal entry did not conclude in the way its planners, including Jesus, had hoped. Nor does it imply that Jesus was a gawking first-time visitor to Jerusalem (rightly Lane, 398). The city of Jerusalem did not welcome the prophet—perhaps Messiah—from Galilee as had those among his following. When Jesus finally entered the temple precincts, there was no priestly greeting. Jesus was ignored. All that he could do was look over the precincts and then retire to Bethany with his disciples.

Explanation

Although the Markan entrance narrative does not cite or even allude to the prophecy of Zech 9:9, as do Matthew and John, the principal elements of this prophecy nevertheless are present in Jesus' actions and in the response of the pilgrims who walk along with him. The entry itself matches Zechariah's "Lo, your king comes"; the riding on the colt matches Zechariah's "riding upon an ass, even upon a colt" (author's tr.); and the jubilant shouts of the pilgrims match Zechariah's "Rejoice greatly, O daughter of Zion!" (Lane, 393–94).

Jesus' entry in Jerusalem marks in dramatic fashion the beginning of passion week. He is recognized in terms that hint at his royal messianic identity (riding on the colt, calls for the coming of the kingdom of David), an identity that will become explicit at the end of the week in his confession before the high priest (14:61–62) and in his crucifixion by the Romans as "king of the Jews" (15:26). Thus the passion week opens and closes with royal messianic themes. But these parallels also entail dramatic contrasts, for Jesus enters Jerusalem amidst shouts of joy and adulation, but he will exit the city amidst shouts of ridicule and torment.

The entry also sets the stage for the unfolding drama involving Jesus and the temple establishment. He enters the temple precincts and "looks around at everything," thus hinting that he has taken full stock of Jerusalem's religious condition. That he did not like all that he saw will become evident in the pericopes that follow, in which Jesus curses the fruitless fig tree, demonstrates in the precincts, criticizes various aspects of temple polity and religious practice, and then finally predicts the temple's destruction.

C. The Cursing of the Fig Tree   (11:12–14, 20–21)

Bibliography

Barrett, C. K. "The House of Prayer and the Den of Thieves." In *Jesus und Paulus.* FS W. G. Kümmel, ed. E. E. Ellis and E. Grässer. Göttingen: Vandenhoeck & Ruprecht, 1975. 13–20. **Bartsch, H.-W.** "Die Verfluchung des Feigenbaumes." *ZNW* 53 (1962) 256–60. **Best, E.** *Disciples and Discipleship.* 177–96. **Bird, C. H.** "Some γάρ Clauses in St. Mark's Gospel." *JTS* n.s. 4 (1953) 171–87. **Birdsall, J. N.** "The Withering of the Fig-Tree (Mark xi.12–14, 20–22)." *ExpTim* 73 (1962) 191. **Blomberg, C. L.** "The Miracles as Parables." In *The Miracles of Jesus.* Ed. D. Wenham and C. L. Blomberg. Gospel Perspectives 6. Sheffield: JSOT Press, 1986. 327–59, esp. 330–33. **Buchanan, G. W.** "Withering Fig Trees and Progression in

Midrash." In *The Gospels and the Scriptures of Israel.* Ed. C. A. Evans and W. R. Stegner. JSNTSup 104; SSEJC 3. Sheffield: Sheffield Academic Press, 1994. 249–69. **Bundy, W. E.** *Jesus and the First Three Gospels.* Cambridge, MA: Harvard UP, 1955. **Carmignac, J.** "Studies in the Hebrew Background of the Synoptic Gospels." *ASTI* 7 (1970) 64–93, esp. 84. **Cotter, W. J.** "'For It Was Not the Season for Figs.'" *CBQ* 48 (1986) 62–66. **Crossan, J. D.** "Aphorism in Discourse and Narrative." *Semeia* 43 (1988) 249–65. **Dalman, G.** *Arbeit und Sitte in Palästina.* 1/2. Hildesheim: Olms, 1928. 1/2:378–81. **Daniel, C.** "Esséniens, Zélotes et Sicaires et leur mention par paronymie dans le N.T." *Numen* 13 (1966) 88–115. **Derrett, J. D. M.** "Figtrees in the New Testament." *HeyJ* 14 (1973) 249–65. **Doeve, J. W.** "Purification du Temple et desséchement du figuier." *NTS* 1 (1954–55) 297–308. **Edwards, J. R.** "Markan Sandwiches: The Significance of Interpolations in Markan Narratives." *NovT* 31 (1989) 193–216. **Geddert, T. J.** *Watchwords: Mark 13 in Markan Eschatology.* JSNTSup 26. Sheffield: JSOT, 1989. 122–24. **Giesen, H.** "Der verdorrte Feigenbaum: Eine symbolische Aussage? Mk 11,12–14.20f." *BZ* 20 (1976) 95–111. **Grimm, W.** *Weil ich dich liebe: Verkündigung Jesu und Deuterojesaja.* ANTJ 1. Bern; Frankfurt am Main: Lang, 1976. 196–99. **Hiers, R. H.** "Not the Season for Figs." *JBL* 87 (1968) 394–400. **Hooker, M. D.** "Traditions about the Temple in the Sayings of Jesus." *BJRL* 70 (1988) 7–19. **Hre Kio, S.** "A Prayer Framework in Mark 11." *BT* 37 (1986) 323–28. **Kahn, J. G.** "La parabole du figuier stérile et les arbres récalcitrants de la Genèse." *NovT* 13 (1971) 38–45. **Kienle, B. von.** "Mk. 11:12–14, 20–25: Der verdorrte Feigenbaum." *BN* 57 (1991) 17–25. **Koch, D.-A.** *Die Bedeutung der Wundererzählungen.* 132–34. **Loos, H. van der.** *The Miracles of Jesus.* 688–98. **Losie, L. A.** "The Cursing of the Fig Tree: Tradition Criticism of a Marcan Pericope: Mk 11:12–14, 20–25." *Studia Biblica et Theologica* 7 (1977) 3–18. **Manson, T. W.** "The Cleansing of the Temple." *BJRL* 33 (1951) 271–82. **Marshall, C. D.** *Faith as a Theme in Mark's Narrative.* 163–74. **Meier, J. P.** *Marginal Jew.* 2:884–96. **Mohr, T. A.** *Markus- und Johannespassion.* 72–77. **Münderlein, G.** "Die Verfluchung des Feigenbaumes (Mk 11:12–14)." *NTS* 10 (1963) 89–104. **Oakman, D. E.** "Cursing Fig Trees and Robbers' Dens." *Semeia* 64 (1993) 253–72. **Pesch, R.** *Evangelium der Urgemeinde.* 131–33, 137–39. **Pryke, E. J.** *Redactional Style in the Marcan Gospel.* 126–35. **Robin, A. de Q.** "The Cursing of the Fig Tree in Mark xi: A Hypothesis." *NTS* 8 (1962) 276–81. **Roloff, J.** *Das Kerygma und der irdische Jesus.* 166–69. **Romaniuk, K.** "Car ce n'etait pas la saison des figue (Mk 11:12–14 parr)." *ZNW* 66 (1975) 275–78. **Schenk, W.** *Der Passionsbericht nach Markus.* 158–66. **Schlosser, J.** "Mc 11:25: Tradition et rédaction." In *À Cause de l'évangile: Études sur les Synoptiques et les Actes.* FS J. Dupont, ed. F. Refoulé. LD 123. Paris: Cerf, 1985. 277–301. **Schmidt, K. L.** *Rahmen.* 298–300. **Schnackenburg, R.** "The Primitive Church and Its Traditions of Jesus." *Perspective* 10 (1969) 103–24. **Schwartz, E.** "Der verfluchte Feigenbaum." *ZNW* 5 (1904) 80–84. **Schwarz, G.** "ἀπὸ μακρόθεν / ἐπὶ τῆς ὁδοῦ." *BN* 20 (1983) 56–57. **Smith, C. W. F.** "No Time for Figs." *JBL* 79 (1960) 315–27. **Söding, T.** *Glaube bei Markus.* 317–39. **Stein, R. H.** "The Cleansing of the Temple in Mark (11:15–19): Reformation or Judgment?" In *Gospels and Tradition: Studies on Redaction Criticism of the Synoptic Gospels.* Grand Rapids, MI: Baker, 1991. 21–33. **Telford, W. R.** *The Barren Temple and the Withered Tree: A Redaction-Critical Analysis of the Cursing of the Fig-Tree Pericope in Mark's Gospel and Its Relation to the Cleansing of the Temple Tradition.* JSNTSup 1. Sheffield: JSOT, 1980. 95–127. ———. "More Fruit from the Withered Fig Tree." In *Templum Amicitiae.* FS E. Bammel, ed. W. Horbury. JSNTSup 48. Sheffield: JSOT, 1991. 264–304. **Trautmann, M.** *Zeichenhafte Handlungen Jesu: Ein Beitrag zur Frage nach dem geschichtlichen Jesus.* FB 37. Würzburg: Echter, 1980. 319–46. **Violet, B.** "Die 'Verfluchung' des Feigenbaums." In *ΕΥΧΑΡΙΣΤΗΡΙΟΝ.* FS H. Gunkel, ed. H. Schmidt. Göttingen: Vandenhoeck & Ruprecht, 1923. 135–40. **Wagner, G.** "Le figuier stérile et la destruction du Temple: Marc 11/12–14 et 20–26." *ETR* 62 (1987) 335–42. **Wojciechowski, M.** "Marc 11.14 et Tg. Gn. 3.22: Les fruits de la Loi enlevés à Israël." *NTS* 33 (1987) 287–89. **Wright, N. T.** *Jesus and the Victory of God.* 421–22. **Zerwick, M.** *Untersuchungen zum Markus-Stil.* Rome: Biblical Institute, 1937.

Translation

[12]*And on the next day, when they had departed from Bethany, [Jesus]* [a] *became hungry.*[b] [13]*And seeing at a distance a fig tree having leaves, he went [to see]* [a] *if he might then* [c] *find something* [d] *on it. And coming upon it, he found nothing except leaves. For it was not the season for figs.* [14]*And answering, he said* [e] *to it, "May no one ever eat fruit from you again!" And his disciples were listening. . . .* [20]*And passing by early in the morning, they saw the fig tree withered from the roots up.* [21]*And being reminded [of Jesus' words],* [a] *Peter* [f] *says to him, "Master,* [g] *behold, the fig tree that you cursed is withered!"*

Notes

[a]Words added from the context.
[b]א omits ἐπείνασεν, "became hungry" (but the word is supplied in the margin).
[c]εἰ ἄρα, "if . . . then," introduces an indirect question; cf. BDF §440.2.
[d]D reads ἰδεῖν ἐάν τι ἔστιν, "to see if there is something."
[e]Some MSS add ὁ Ἰησοῦς, "Jesus."
[f]Some Syr. MSS read either *kêpāʾ*, "Kepha," or *šimʿôn*, "Simon." Some MSS read ἀποκριθεὶς ὁ Πέτρος λέγει αὐτῷ, "answering, Peter says to him."
[g]Gk. ῥαββί, "Rabbi."

Form/Structure/Setting

On the day following the entrance and brief visit to the Temple Mount (11:1–11), Jesus departs from Bethany and becomes hungry along the way. From a distance he sees a fig tree with leaves, so he approaches it hoping to find something to eat. He is disappointed; the tree offers nothing but leaves (which, given the season, is not too surprising). Jesus then says, "May no one ever eat fruit from you again!" His disciples overhear his words. The following day the disciples see the fig tree, which has in the meantime withered from the roots up. Remembering what Jesus had said, Peter exclaims: "Rabbi, behold, the fig tree that you cursed is withered!"

The Markan version of the cursing of the fig tree is presented in two parts (11:12–14, 20–21) and surrounds the temple action (11:15–19). Matthew's parallel version (Matt 21:18–22) is not broken up. In fact, the Matthean evangelist has smoothed out Mark's bumpy chronological sequence from the entrance narrative to the later question of authority. According to Mark, Jesus enters Jerusalem, looks around in the temple precincts, and then departs (11:1–11). The next day he returns and along the way curses the fig tree (11:12–14). He then enters Jerusalem again and this time demonstrates in the temple precincts, and afterward departs (11:15–19). The next day they return to the temple and along the way the disciples see the withered fig tree (11:20–21); Jesus then teaches his disciples regarding the need to have faith and to forgive (11:22–25; this latter element hardly fits the context). When they enter the temple precincts, Jesus is questioned by the priests, scribes, and elders (11:27–33). In Matthew this sequence of events is much simpler: Jesus enters the city (21:1–11); he immediately demonstrates in the temple, not the next day as in Mark (21:12–13); the next morning he curses the fig tree, and it instantly withers before their very eyes (21:18–20), whereupon he instructs the disciples regarding faith and prayer (21:21–22; with the teaching about forgiveness omitted); and he then enters the temple precincts, where his authority is questioned (21:23–27). Luke's sequence is also simpler: Jesus approaches the city (19:28–40); as he draws near, he weeps over Jerusalem (19:41–45, a Lukan addition); he demonstrates in the temple precincts (19:45–48); and the next day he is questioned about his authority (20:1–8). The cursing of the fig tree is conspicuously absent. The Lukan evangelist may have omitted the story because of embarrassment, in that cursing something that cannot really be guilty of anything is inconsistent with Jesus' person and teaching, or because of the somewhat similar parable of the Fruitless Fig Tree (Luke 13:6–9)—and Luke typically avoids duplication—or for both of these reasons. Mark's more awkward sequence of events has every claim to antiquity, with the smoother versions of Matthew and Luke evidence of their secondary character.

Form-critically the story of the fig tree has generally been designated either as a legend, based on its supposed origin, or as a miracle story. Bultmann (*History*, 218) rightly suspects that the story was originally a unit that subsequently was interrupted by the temple action described in 11:15–19. The difference in part stems from the unusual character of this story in the Jesus tradition. Bundy (*Jesus and the First Three Gospels*, 425) calls the action that is depicted "irrational and revolting." This is certainly an overstatement, but Jesus' action does seem petty and capricious, and begs for an explanation. Consequently, the story has been called an aetiological legend that developed around a withered fig tree found along the road from Bethany to Jerusalem (e.g., Schwartz, *ZNW* 5 [1904] 80–84; Lohmeyer, 234; Taylor, 459). Some commentators view it as a legend developed from a saying (e.g., Klostermann, 116) or parable of Jerusalem (such as Luke 13:6–9; e.g., Blunt, 226; Moule, 90, but with hesitation; Anderson, 264; against this option are Bultmann, *History*, 230–31; Taylor, 459) or from OT texts (such as Jer 8:11–13; Hos 9:10, 16; Mic 7:1; e.g., Ernst, 325; Telford, *Barren Temple*, 237). Still others attribute the development of the legend to the disciples' misunderstanding of a nonthreatening statement by Jesus, like "one, i.e. Jesus, will not eat fruit from you again," referring either to his coming death (e.g., Manson, *BJRL* 33 [1951] 280) or the coming kingdom (e.g., Bartsch, *ZNW* 53 [1962] 256–60; Schenk, *Passionsbericht*, 158–66). Finally, Haenchen (380–81) calls it a "later legend" that views a tree's failure to provide the Lord fruit when asked, whether or not it is in season, to be an affront to Jesus' dignity. In this way, one shifts the onus from Jesus to the early church, a move that only partially accounts for its uniqueness in the Jesus tradition. One might well ask why, if the early church could and did develop this kind of legend around Jesus here, we do not have similar stories in the Gospel tradition (cf. Luke 9:51–56)! But other factors will be taken into account shortly.

Purely from the standpoint of literary form, this would be considered a miracle story consisting of the usual (a) setting (11:12), (b) miraculous action (11:13–14), and (c) confirmation (11:20). The focus of Jesus' actions on a tree places it in the broad category of a nature miracle (e.g., Bultmann, *History*, 227–31; Lohmeyer, 234), but the specific nature of the action makes it a "curse" (e.g., Grundmann, 306; Lohmeyer, 234; Pesch, 2:291) or "punishment" (e.g., Lührmann, 190) miracle. Though this distinction may seem arbitrary, the story has the function of a nature miracle in the pre-Markan tradition (11:12–14,

20–24; and in Matt 21:18–22) but has the dual function of a curse miracle (11:12–14, 15–19) and a nature miracle (11:20–25) in Mark's narrative. It provides the interpretive framework for the temple scene in 11:15–19 and the basis for Jesus' teaching on prayer and "faith in God" in 11:22–25.

Determining the appropriate literary form in this case does not help in determining the original setting (*Sitz im Leben*, whether in the life of Jesus [*Sitz im Leben Jesu*] or the church [*der Kirche*]). It is the only example we have in the Gospel tradition of Jesus performing a curse miracle (in contrast, see Luke 9:51–56, where Jesus specifically forbids taking destructive action). Such miracle stories may be found in the OT and in Acts (e.g., 2 Kgs 1:4, 10–14; 2:23–24; 5:27; Acts 5:1–11; 13:6–12). But the capricious nature of Jesus' action here seems out of character with his ministry as found in the Jesus tradition. Some commentators have traced this story to the early church's transformation of Jesus' parable of the Fig Tree in Luke 13:6–9 into an actual event (cf. the patristic interpretation of the parable of the Good Samaritan). Nevertheless, the differences between Luke 13:6–9 and Mark 11:12–14, 20 in spirit (grace/curse), meaning (spiritually unproductive/deceptive show of productivity), and style (cf. Mark's vividness), together with the lack of parallels for parables becoming concrete events in the Jesus tradition, argue against this alternative (Telford, *Barren Temple*, 234–38). Others (e.g., Ernst, 325; Telford, *Barren Temple*, 237) view it as a dramatization of an OT text or texts, despite the fact that no one OT text or group of OT texts clearly emerges from the story itself. In either case, we have the further problem that the story is not only out of character with Jesus' ministry but also out of character with Jesus' ministry as depicted by the early church (not so according to Buchanan, "Withering Fig Trees"). This story may have its roots in an "acted parable" from Jesus' ministry, a prophetic or symbolic action as in Isa 20:1–6; Jer 13:1–11; and Ezek 4:1–15 (e.g., Cranfield, 355; Münderlein, *NTS* 10 [1963] 94–95; Giesen, *BZ* 20 [1976] 101–11), whose original context and/or interpretive key has been lost. Nothing in the story itself supplies the necessary interpretive clues (cf. Hiers, *JBL* 87 [1968] 394–400; Derrett, *HeyJ* 14 [1973] 249–65). The interpretive key in 11:21–24 (= Matt 21:21–22) is clearly secondary, as seen by the independent transmission of these isolated sayings (see *Comment* on 11:23, 24).

With regard to the question of source, the Markan evangelist appears to have found this story combined with the isolated sayings of 11:23–24. In other words, the evangelist found an apophthegm consisting of the fig-tree story and Jesus' sayings on mountain-moving faith and prayer. The fig-tree story itself most likely concluded with the confirmation of 11:20. The pre-Markan redactor who used this story as the basis for Jesus' teaching on faith and prayer (11:23–24) made the transition by adding Peter's response and Jesus' challenge in 11:21–22 (cf. Roloff, *Kerygma*, 168).

Mark's redactional modification of the fig-tree story appears in the introduction (see *Comment* on 11:12a), the γάρ explanatory clause in 11:13b (see *Comment*), and his use of this story as the framing device for the temple action in 11:15–19 (cf. Pesch, 1:189–90). The evangelist has used this "sandwich" device of intercalating traditions as an interpretive device before (see Guelich, 169), from which one gains an understanding of the significance of these traditions for Mark (Edwards, *NovT* 31 [1989] 216; though Meier, *Marginal Jew* 2:892, wonders if the fig-tree story had already been intercalated in Mark's source; see below).

By using this story to frame the temple action, Mark gives it a new literary setting with two results. First, not only is the story woven among Jesus' entry into Jerusalem (11:1–11), the temple action (11:15–19), and the question of authority (11:27–33), but its chronology (11:12–13) changes the narrative time frame behind these events by separating them into three distinct days (cf. Matt 21:12–22). Second, the fig-tree story (11:12–14, 20–21) now becomes the interpretive background for the temple action that gives meaning to the fate of the fig tree and Jesus' deeds and words in the temple precincts.

Placed in its historical setting of the first century, the story loses some of its more fanciful traits. The nature of a fig tree makes Jesus' search for figs much more reasonable (see *Comment* on v 13). And though readers today may find Jesus' talking to and cursing a fig tree unusual (cf. Pesch, 2:197 n. 30!), such stories, often involving fig trees, are so common in the rabbinic literature that Telford (*Barren Temple*, 237) has referred to our pericope as a "haggadic tale." One of these rabbinic traditions might be considered: "Once Rabbi Yose had day-laborers in the field. Night came and no food was brought to them and they said to his son, 'We are hungry.' Now they were resting under a fig tree and he exclaimed, 'Fig tree, fig tree, bring forth your fruit that my father's laborers may eat.' It brought forth fruit and they ate" (*b. Taʿan.* 24a). Shortly afterward Rabbi Yose remarks that the fig tree had brought forth its fruit "before its time."

Finally, Meier (*Marginal Jew* 2:986 n. 63) concludes that Mark 11:12–14, 20–21 "does not go back to some striking action of the historical Jesus that his disciples or audience took to be a miracle. . . . [T]he story has its origin in Christian teaching." Meier (*Marginal Jew* 2:894) suspects that an early tradent created the story of the cursed fig tree and wrapped it around the temple action in order to interpret Jesus' action as one of final judgment, not one of reform (see also *Marginal Jew* 2:894–96). As Telford has pointed out, parables of fig trees and vines were common in rabbinic literature and folklore. What we may have here is the retelling of one such tale (similar to the example cited in the preceding paragraph) in which Jesus appears. Wright (*Jesus and the Victory of God*, 421–22), who believes the story has some basis in fact, rightly calls attention to Jer 8:11–13 (and Mic 7:1 and its context) and suggests that Jesus' pronouncement against the fig tree was part of an attempt to apply Jeremiah's criticisms of the temple establishment to his own day. Wright could be correct, for Jesus will appeal to Jer 7:11 in his prophetic criticism of priestly policies and activities when he demonstrates in the temple precincts (in Mark 11:15–17). Buchanan ("Withering Fig Trees") has also recently weighed in in favor of the historicity of this tradition. He believes that Jesus' action is consistent with scriptural interpretation and eschatological expectations. Nevertheless, the reasons that Meier has marshalled against the historicity of this curious story are compelling. "It is a miracle," Meier (*Marginal Jew* 2:896) rightly avers, "that is in perfect continuity with punitive miracles in the OT, the Acts of the Apostles, and the NT apocrypha, but a miracle that lacks coherence with the other miracles of Jesus in the Four Gospels. Thus, the criteria of discontinuity and coherence converge . . . to form a fairly firm judgment: in all likelihood, Mark 11:12–14, 20–21 does not go back to the historical Jesus." Meier's historical judgment may be accepted, but not every aspect of his source criticism. The story of the cursing of the fig tree may very well have been created and attached to the temple demonstration, as Meier proposes, but the wrapping (or intercalation) of this story around the temple demonstration in all probability was the work of the evangelist.

Comment

12 τῇ ἐπαύριον, supply ἡμέρᾳ, "on the next day," occurs only here in Mark. The evangelist has added this detail as a transition from the entrance narrative. The introduction of this story "on the next day" between Jesus' entry (11:1–11) and the temple action (11:15–19), rather than a desire on his part to develop a "holy week" of days from Sunday to Sunday (see *Comment* on 11:20), may well have given rise to Mark's arranging of the traditional materials of 11:1–33 into "three days" (11:11/12; 11:19/20; 11:27).

ἐξελθόντων αὐτῶν ἀπὸ Βηθανίας, "when they had departed from Bethany," provides the story's setting by connecting it locally with 11:11. The only occurrence of ἐξέρχεσθαι, "to depart," with ἀπό, "from," in Mark (cf. 6x in Matthew; 13x in Luke; but with ἐκ, "from," the verb occurs 10x in Mark!) and the story's need of a setting argue strongly for at least an underlying tradition (cf. Gnilka, 2:122). This underlying tradition doubtless specified the antecedent and subject of αὐτῶν, "they," and ἐπείνασεν, "became hungry," and may have led to Mark's narrowing the focus to Jesus and the Twelve in 11:11 (cf. 11:14, 21). Bethany may well have been in the setting in the tradition, since nothing points to Bethany in the complex of tradition behind 11:1–9, 15–19, 27b–33 (see *Comment* on 11:19). This would also explain why the evangelist used it for Jesus' final destination in 11:11b (see *Comment* on 14:3).

ἐπείνασεν, "became hungry," represents the first of several apparent incongruities in this story. Would not Jesus' host have provided breakfast? Why would Jesus be hungry and not his disciples? How does the occasion of Jesus' actual hunger give rise to a symbolic action? Some commentators have considered this statement to have been added to the story at a later stage in its development (e.g., Schweizer, 230). Others resolve the incongruity by taking the statement metaphorically to mean Jesus' desire for the righteous fruit in Israel (L. Goppelt, *TDNT* 6:20; Giesen, *BZ* 20 [1976] 103; Ernst, 325). Still others (e.g., Birdsall, *ExpTim* 73 [1962] 191; Robin, *NTS* 8 [1962] 280) attribute this statement to the disciples misunderstanding Jesus' actions. Confusing a supposed citation of Mic 7:1 ("there is . . . no first-ripe fig which my soul desires") made by Jesus as he approached the tree, they thought that he meant that he was hungry.

These questions assume too much of the text (see Gundry, 637–38). First, they assume a context similar to Mark's redactional setting in which Jesus supposedly has just spent the night in Bethany as someone's guest (cf. 14:3; John 12:1–2). Removed from the present Markan setting, the story line implies nothing about an overnight or a host. Second, even the redactional "on the next day" does not specify the time of day as early morning (cf. 11:20, πρωΐ, "early in the morning"). This makes the question about Jesus' hunger and the disciples' lack of hunger moot. The statement simply provides the occasion for what follows. This is certainly the better explanation, if the origin of the story proposed above is accepted.

With many interpreters, Stein ("Cleansing," 121–33) is correct to conclude that Mark (or his predecessor) has deliberately intercalated the fig-tree episode with the cleansing of the temple (11:15–19) in order to have each interpret the other: "Mark interprets the cleansing by means of the cursing" ("Cleansing," 130). The fig tree, in full leaf but devoid of fruit, symbolizes the temple, while the temple, busy with religious activities but devoid of spiritual fruit, stands in danger of judgment. But Stein should not be followed when he concludes that Mark's editorial work is intended to show that "Jesus has rejected Israel. She has been weighed in the balances and found wanting. The kingdom will be given over to the Gentiles" ("Cleansing," 130; cf. similar statements on pp. 131–33). Stein's interpretation may be reflecting Matthew's "nation" (ἔθνει) in 21:43, which has replaced Mark's "others" (ἄλλοις) in 12:9. The judgmental thrust is not against Israel but against Israel's religious caretakers, as the parable of the Wicked Vineyard Tenants (12:1–12) makes clear. The kingdom is not to be given over to the Gentiles, but the leadership of the kingdom is to be taken from the ruling priests and given to Jesus' disciples. Jews as well as Gentiles will be invited to enter the kingdom. See also Geddert (*Watchwords*, 122–24), who correctly assesses the Markan context. He comments: "The false trail is the identification of the fig tree with Israel. . . . [T]he larger Markan context is careful to bring condemnation only on Israel's *leadership*, not on the nation as such" (*Watchwords*, 125, Geddert's emphasis).

13 ἰδὼν συκῆν, "seeing a fig tree." "One of the most important fruit-trees in the country" and often associated and cultivated with the vine in the OT, it stands proverbially for peace and security (cf. Mic 4:4; Zech 3:10) and along with its fruit has numerous figurative uses (H. Hunzinger, *TDNT* 7:752; cf. Isa 28:4; Jer 8:13; 24:1–10; 29:17; Hos 9:10; Mic 7:1; Nah 3:12; Prov 27:18; for a thorough discussion, including NT and rabbinic materials, see Telford, *Barren Temple*, 129–63). Consequently, many interpreters have viewed the tree, its fruit, and Jesus' actions symbolically, especially with reference to Israel. Yet the prevalence of fig trees in Palestine and the variety of figurative uses of the fig tree and figs in the OT caution against drawing the significance from the fig tree itself or its fruit. Consequently, those who take the story symbolically must look for clues in the details of the story or its present literary context.

ἔχουσαν φύλλα, "having leaves." The repetition of the reference to leaves in the following sentence underscores the importance of this detail. A deciduous tree, the fig tree sprouts leaves in late March and sheds its leaves in late fall. But why the double reference to its having leaves? According to come commentators (e.g., Gnilka, 2:124; Schweizer, 232), the reference simply anticipates and makes possible the observation of the tree's withering in 11:20. If, however, as Pliny the Elder noted in his *Naturalis historia* (16.49), the fig tree stands out as a tree that produces fruit before leaves (cf. Mark 13:28; B. W. Bacon, *DCG* 1:593; I. Jacob and W. Jacob, *ABD* 2:807: "leaves . . . often appear after the fruit develops"), the presence of leaves makes intelligible to Mark's readers why Jesus went to the tree in search of something to eat and adds force to the following statement about its having "nothing except leaves."

εἰ ἄρα τι εὑρήσει ἐν αὐτῇ, "if he might then find something on it." The construction of εἰ ἄρα, "if then," with the future tense expresses an indirect question using the inferential ἄρα, "then" (BDF §440.2; cf. §379). This construction underscores the reference to leaves and indicates that Jesus looked for something to eat on the basis of the tree's leaves. The fig tree produces two crops. The earlier ripens from late May into June, and the later and larger harvest ripens from the end of August into October (see Hunzinger, *TDNT* 7:753). Accordingly, several commentators have placed the traditional setting for this story, along with the entrance narrative and the temple demonstration, at the time of Tabernacles in early fall (e.g., Manson, "Cleansing," 271–82; Smith, *JBL* 79 [1960] 324; Losie, *Studia Biblica et Theologica* 7 [1977] 11–12). While the original setting for this story may have been different from that in Mark's story line, the presence of the leaves still offers the basis for Jesus' approach. The Markan evangelist locates the story in his narrative prior to Passover in early to mid-April, which "was not the season for figs."

From the perspective of Mark's readers, what might Jesus have expected to find? Two possibilities have been suggested: *(a)* "winter figs" left over from the fall harvest and ripening as spring approaches (Str-B 1:856–57, note "white figs" [בְּנוֹת שׁוּחַ *běnôt šûaḥ*] that ripen in the second and third year), or *(b)* "early figs" that develop from green knops, which appear in early spring before the leaves (פַּגָּה *paggâ;* cf. Song 2:13, which uses the term to refer to the unripe summer fig [LXX ὄλυνθος]), and ripen in later spring after the leaves appear (בְּכוּרָה, *bikkûrâ*, variously translated in the LXX as ὁ πρόδρομος, "the early fig" [lit. "the one that runs ahead"], τὸ σῦκον τὸ πρόϊμον, "the early fig," ὁ σκοπός, "the lookout, spy, scout") (Dalman, *Arbeit*, 1/2:378–81; cf. Telford, *Barren Temple*, 28 n. 16; Hunzinger, *TDNT* 7:751–52). Perhaps because the latter in their early undeveloped form have been considered inedible (e.g., Lagrange, 293), several commentators have opted for the former (e.g., Gnilka, 2:124; Grundmann, 307). Yet the double reference to the presence of leaves in 11:13 more than likely points to the latter. The presence of large unripe but edible figs under similar, though unusual, circumstances has been documented (E. F. F. Bishop, *Jesus of Palestine: The Local Background to the Gospel Documents* [London: Lutterworth, 1955] 217; cf. Taylor, 460 n. 1). Therefore, Jesus' going to a fig tree with leaves in mid-April, hoping to find something edible, does not strain the credulity of the story (cf. Haenchen, 380–81). Even if the narrative is fictive in its origin, Mark's reader would have found it plausible.

οὐδὲν εὗρεν εἰ μὴ φύλλα, "he found nothing except leaves." In the context of the story, this statement simply declares that the tree was completely barren and Jesus' quest was in vain. The tree apparently did not even have immature figs on it. Barrenness occurs in the OT as an expression of Israel's failure to produce appropriate fruit for God (e.g., Jer 8:13; Mic 1:7), as well as an expression of God's judgment (e.g., Jer 7:20; Hos 9:16). Consequently, Jesus' futile quest for fruit from the barren fig tree has been seen as a parable of his quest for the righteous or for righteousness within Israel (e.g., Birdsall, *ExpTim* 73 [1962] 191; Ernst, 325; Gnilka, 2:124; Grundmann, 307; Lane, 401; Münderlein, *NTS* 10 [1963] 100–101). The close association of the fig-tree narrative with the temple demonstration, however, suggests that this quest for righteousness should be understood in a narrower sense as a quest for righteousness at the heart and center of Israel's religious life: the temple.

ὁ γὰρ καιρὸς οὐκ ἦν σύκων, "for it was not the season for figs," apparently offers another and greater incongruity in the story. This γάρ, "for," statement appears to make a farce out of Jesus' previous and subsequent actions. So incongruous is this comment that it has been emended (e.g., οὐκ, "not" = οὔπω, "not yet"; see Telford, *Barren Temple*, 26 n. 4), viewed as a gloss (cf. Lohmeyer, 234; see Telford, *Barren Temple*, 26 n. 4), and repunctuated with a question mark (Romaniuk, *ZNW*

66 [1975] 278; see Telford, *Barren Temple,* 26 n. 4). We lack text-critical support
for either an emendation or a gloss. To repunctuate it does violence to the style
and function of Mark's γάρ explanatory clauses.

Some commentators have taken this clause as belonging to the tradition and
as a key element in the symbolic meaning of the story. For example, Hiers (*JBL*
87 [1968] 395–97, followed by Derrett, *HeyJ* 14 [1973] 253–54) contends that this
statement contains the point of the whole story since it indicates that Jesus expected fig trees to "bear fruit out of season" in keeping with his messianic
expectation that the "fertility of nature" and a "continuous harvest" would signal
the presence of the messianic age. Münderlein (*NTS* 10 [1963] 99–100) finds in
this "gloss" a remnant of an earlier interpretation of the story that keyed on the
eschatological moment (καιρός, "time") in Israel's redemptive history. And Giesen
(*BZ* 20 [1976] 105) takes καιρός in its eschatological sense to refer to Israel's
failure to use the time set for it in God's redemptive plan. Not only do these
explanations assume the symbolic character of this story in general and καιρός in
particular, but they overlook the fact that the γάρ, "for," explanatory clause represents one of Mark's characteristic redactional thumb prints (cf. Pryke, *Redactional
Style,* 126–35).

Why would the evangelist have added this comment? On first glance, this clause
may merely support the relocation of the story into its present Passover context
(e.g., Lohmeyer, 235; Smith, *JBL* 79 [1960] 316–17; Hunzinger, *TDNT* 7:756 n.
49). Despite the evangelist's reputation for literary clumsiness, this explanation
goes beyond all bounds of the imaginable by having the evangelist supposedly
explain what Jesus, a Palestinian, apparently did not know about fig trees. This in
turn makes the narrator more knowledgeable than Jesus and Jesus' ensuing action all the more capricious.

Others have followed Bird's suggestion (*JTS* n.s. 4 [1953] 171–87) that Mark's
γάρ, "for," clauses often allude to OT passages, words, or ideas. Thus, the "asser-
tive-allusive γάρ" portends a deeper meaning, a clue to the symbolic character of
this story rooted in the OT (e.g., Birdsall, *ExpTim* 73 [1962] 191; Lane, 401; Losie,
Studia Biblica et Theologica 7 [1977] 13). By reading the clause this way, one avoids
both the awkwardness of this misplaced comment and finds direct support for
taking the story symbolically (similarly, Grundmann, 307; Gnilka, 2:124). After
examining Bird's thesis and the use of γάρ in Mark, however, M. E. Thrall (*Greek
Particles in the New Testament,* NTTS 3 [Leiden: Brill, 1962], 41; similarly, Pryke,
Redactional Style, 126–27) has concluded that "there are no grounds for supposing that the use of γάρ is in itself significant from the point of view of the detection
of underlying symbolism. . . ." She notes further that any such OT symbolism, if
present, "must be deduced from the material content of the γάρ clauses and their
total context, and not from the fact that γάρ is the introductory particle" (*Greek
Particles,* 50). The lack of agreement about what OT text or texts this γάρ supposedly alludes to certainly supports her claim in this case.

A comment that Thrall (*Greek Particles,* 47) makes in passing may in fact hold
the key to our problem: "Writers who use γάρ frequently, as Mark does, are not
always logical thinkers who develop an argument stage by stage. . . . In narrative
they mention first the important or striking points in the story, and then fit in
the explanatory details afterwards by using γάρ, whether or not these details should
logically precede the main points." She then illustrates this point by noting the

illogical sequence of the γάρ, "for," clauses in Mark 6:16–18. This lack of strict sequence and even misplaced clauses may offer the clue, according to Cotter (*CBQ* 48 [1986] 65–66; followed by Meier, *Marginal Jew* 2:891–92), for understanding this clause in 11:13. Finding a similar illogical γάρ clause in Mark 16:4b, she posits that both clauses make better sense if they refer to a more distant previous statement rather than to the one immediately preceding. Just as the clause "for the stone was large" (16:4b) explains the women's anxious concern about who would roll aside the stone from the door of the tomb for them (16:3b), rather than the immediately preceding statement, "looking up they saw that the stone had been rolled away" (16:4a), so the clause "for it was not the season for figs" (11:13c) explains why Jesus went (ἦλθεν) to see "if he might then find something [edible]" on the tree (11:13a), rather than the immediately preceding statement that after coming (ἐλθών) to the tree, "he found nothing except leaves" (11:13b). If the γάρ clause were relocated, as Cotter suggests, the verse would then read: "Seeing at a distance a fig tree having leaves, he went to see if he might then find something on it (for it was not the season for figs). When he came to it, he found nothing except leaves." Thus, Mark's γάρ clause explains why Jesus had doubts about whether he might find figs rather than why the tree did not have figs.

Mark's addition of this explanation for Jesus' action reflects then a concern for chronological detail and shows that the evangelist understood the story as an actual event located in the context of Passover rather than merely as a parabolic or symbolic gesture. At the same time, this explanatory clause, viewed in the broader literary context of 11:12–19; 13:2; and 15:38, may have the deeper meaning of 1:14–15 (see Guelich, 43–44). While it was literally "not the season for figs," the evangelist may also be setting the stage for Jesus' announcement of the coming destruction of the temple whose καιρός, "season," had passed or been eclipsed by the fulfillment of καιρός, "time" (1:15; cf. 12:2), with Jesus' coming and proclamation of the kingdom of God. Consequently, καιρός may serve both a secular and a theological purpose here.

14 ἀποκριθεὶς εἶπεν αὐτῇ, "answering, he said to it," may seem strange to our world, but "talking to trees . . . is to be found in contexts familiar to the Jews of our period" (Derrett, *HeyJ* 14 [1973] 252; cf. esp. *b. Ta'an.* 24a). After examining several tales from rabbinic haggadah, Telford (*Barren Temple*, 195–96) notes that in these tales "the world is endowed with human characteristics. The trees are sensitive to the moral dimension. They can be addressed. They can give or withhold their fruit in response to human need. . . . Their blossoming or withering has moral and symbolic significance. In the world of the haggadah, the Rabbi's curse has an incontrovertible efficacy. Nature is responsive to the righteous." Though later than Jesus' day, these tales reflect a view of nature similar to that of the biblical world (cf. Num 20:8; Josh 10:12; 24:26–28; Matt 4:3; Luke 4:3). These stories also encourage us to view Mark's story of the fig tree as something akin to Jewish haggadah.

μηκέτι εἰς τὸν αἰῶνα, "ever . . . again," has been rendered "until the age [to come]" or "the eternal age" as a *terminus ad quem* (e.g., Hiers, *JBL* 87 [1968] 397) in support of the view that this statement had to do primarily with the imminent coming of the end time that would precede the next fig harvest (cf. Manson, *BJRL* 33 [1951] 280; Bartsch, *ZNW* 53 [1962] 256–60; Hiers, *JBL* 87 [1968] 397–98; Grundmann, 308). Unfortunately, εἰς τὸν αἰῶνα does not have this particular meaning anywhere else in the Gospels and does not, therefore, appear to have been an apocalyptic expression for either Jesus or the early church. Instead, this expression generally has the idiomatic meaning of "eternity," "to eternity," "eternally," or "in perpetuity" (e.g., Mark 3:29; Matt 6:13; BAGD).

μηδεὶς . . . φάγοι, "may no one . . . eat," uses the optative mood with the force of an adversative wish (BDF §384). One cannot reduce it to the level of a simple declaration comparable to Jesus' statement in 14:25 about his not drinking again from the fruit of the vine (cf. Grundmann, 308; Hiers, *JBL* 87 [1968] 397–98) since the latter uses the subjunctive of emphatic negation and a precise *terminus ad quem* ("again in the kingdom of God"). Nor can one ameliorate the pronouncement by distinguishing between the content of 11:14 and the result of 11:20, as though never again providing fruit for eating were less drastic than being withered from the roots (so Lohmeyer, 234; Münderlein, *NTS* 10 [1963] 90). This pronouncement carries all the weight of a curse, as Peter's observation in 11:21 aptly states. A barren tree is a condemned tree (cf. Matt 3:10 = Luke 3:9; 13:7).

ἐκ σοῦ . . . καρπόν, "fruit from you." The mention of καρπόν, "fruit," a common metaphor in the Scriptures, rather than figs provides further evidence for the symbolic character of this story for some commentators (e.g., Giesen, *BZ* 20 [1976] 105; Münderlein, *NTS* 10 [1963] 95–96). Yet this pronouncement is based on and results in barrenness. The absence of figs or fruit on the tree leads to the future inability of the tree to produce fruit. Therefore, the focus is on the failure of the fig tree and Jesus' judgment of it. Whether the product is referred to as τι, "something" (11:13), οὐδέν, "nothing" (11:13), καρπός, "fruit" (11:14b), or figs (not specified) is immaterial to the significance of the story.

In fact, the story, devoid of a literary context, contains no specific indications of symbolism. To be sure, trees in general, fig trees in particular, figs, fruit, productivity, and barrenness all serve in the Scriptures as metaphors for individuals, Israel as a nation, nations, their conduct, and their relationship before God. But hunger, fig trees, figs, and barren trees were also a common part of everyday life in Palestine. Apart from a word or context that suggests that the story as a whole or in part was intended to be symbolical, we have no solid basis for taking it as a symbolic activity or an acted parable. The sayings of 11:22–25 in response to Peter's observation (11:21) show that the story does not have to be taken as an acted parable or a symbolic action and certainly not with reference to Israel.

Mark, however, has made good use of this story, which frames the temple demonstration (11:15–19). Unlike the Matthean evangelist, the Markan evangelist is comfortable with the intercalation. In this presentation each story provides an interpretation for the other. As will be noted in 11:15–19, the thrust of Jesus' action and teaching in the temple is prophetic in terms of Jer 7:11–14, with its reference to the coming destruction of the temple as God's judgment, and Isa 56:7, with its reminder to the temple establishment that the temple should become what God had designed it to be, "a house of prayer for all the nations" (11:17). The prophecy of the coming destruction of the temple in Jer 7 stands in close proximity to Jer 8:13, which announces God's judgment on Israel: "there are no grapes on the vine, *nor figs on the fig tree*" (emphasis added). Mark, or more likely a pre-Markan tradent, may well have combined the stories about the fig tree and the temple demonstration to highlight the significance of Jesus' person and work (cf. 14:58; 15:29, 38) in place of the temple in God's redemptive plan.

Jesus comes and announces the destruction of the temple, illustrated by the cursing of the fig tree and inherent in the prophecy of Jer 7:11–14 (Mark 11:17), that will take place physically (Mark 13:2) and theologically (Mark 15:38).

ἤκουον οἱ μαθηταὶ αὐτοῦ, "his disciples were listening," has also been taken as a clue to the parabolic or symbolic character of this story. Finding behind the verb ἤκουον, "were listening," a latent reference to the disciples' failure to understand, which is later expressed in Peter's observation in 11:21, some commentators have taken this statement to point to a deeper, hidden meaning behind these events (Ernst, 326; Grundmann, 308; Losie, *Studia Biblica et Theologica* 7 [1977] 13; Telford, *Barren Temple*, 261). "Listening" (or "hearing") can connote special discernment in Mark (see Guelich, 195–96). Yet Peter's observation in 11:21 does not indicate any special discernment of a hidden meaning behind the symbolism of 11:12–14. Rather, Peter, one of the disciples who heard Jesus, refers to the fig tree as the one Jesus cursed. This observation demonstrates that he heard what Jesus, who had gone (ἦλθεν, "went"; ἐλθών, "coming"; 11:13) to the fig tree, had said. Therefore, "his disciples were listening" does not imply a hidden meaning reflecting the disciples' lack of understanding or need for discernment.

20 παραπορευόμενοι πρωΐ, "passing by early in the morning," sets off what follows as another day, the third day in the sequence (cf. 11:11–12, 19–20). Matthew 21:18–22 has the fig-tree story compressed into one day, thereby heightening the miraculous element (see Gundry, *Matthew*, 417) as a basis for the faith and prayer sayings (cf. Matt 21:21–22). Since the events in 11:20–21 follow those in 11:12–14, the τῇ ἐπαύριον, "on the next day," of 11:12 rather than πρωΐ, "early in the morning," may have opened this verse in the tradition (see *Comment* on v 12 above). Consequently, the πρωΐ (cf. ὀψέ, "evening," in 11:19) may reflect a further redactional adjustment (cf. 11:11, 12) arising from the intercalation of the fig-tree episode (11:12–14) between the entrance (11:1–11) and the temple demonstration (11:15–19).

The resulting three-day chronology would then be more a literary accommodation to the present order of events necessitated by the two-day chronology inherent in the traditional fig-tree story. This literary explanation of Mark's three days accounts for the absence of any mention of the end of this day in contrast to the previous two (cf. 11:11 necessitated by 11:12; 11:19 necessitated by 11:20), the comparatively long third day (supposedly from 11:20 through 13:37), and the missing day between 13:37 and 14:1. Furthermore, the absence of an end to this day suggests that Mark did not intend the reader to take all the events of 11:27–13:37 or even those to 12:34 as having necessarily occurred on this third day (cf. 14:49).

ἐξηραμμένην ἐκ ῥιζῶν, "withered from the roots up," expresses more the radical effect of Jesus' words (cf. Hos 9:16; Job 18:16; 28:9; 31:12; Ezek 19:9) than the result of a postmortem. One strains the narrative by taking it literally and then concluding that since the disciples could not actually see the roots, the expression indicates the symbolic character of the material (e.g., Ernst, 332; Giesen, *BZ* 20 [1976] 108; Gnilka, 2:134; Grundmann, 314). This verse may have concluded the miracle story at the earliest stage in the tradition by providing the confirmation of Jesus' words in 11:14. If so, v 21 represents an editorial transition that will afford Jesus the opportunity to speak on matters of faith and prayer. However, v 21 may in fact be the original conclusion to the story of the fig tree.

21 ἀναμνησθεὶς ὁ Πέτρος, "being reminded . . . Peter," occurs again in 14:72, the only two uses of this verb in Mark. Neither the expression nor Peter's role in this context necessitates Mark's redactional hand (cf. Best, *Disciples,* 171). In response Jesus addresses the disciples (αὐτοῖς, "to them," 11:22; cf. 11:14) rather than Peter personally (cf. 8:29–30). The ἀναμνησθείς, "being reminded," refers back to what the disciples heard in 11:14, as Peter's following comment shows. Both the disciples' hearing and Peter's remembering may have been added to the story when it was developed in the pre-Markan tradition from a simple miracle story that glossed the temple action into the introduction of the sayings that make up vv 22–24.

ῥαββί, ἴδε ἡ συκῆ ἣν κατηράσω ἐξήρανται, "Master, behold, the fig tree that you cursed is withered!" On the use of ῥαββί, "Master," "Rabbi," see *Comment* on 9:5 and 10:51. ἣν κατηράσω, "that you cursed," specifies what Peter had remembered having heard Jesus say and correctly interprets Jesus' adversative wish spoken to the tree (11:14) in the light of the effect. This astonished declaration serves the function of making the miracle of destruction (11:12–14) into the occasion for Jesus' teaching on faith and prayer (11:22–25). The miracle story becomes an apophthegm.

Explanation

Mark took the fig-tree story, which served in his tradition as the basis for Jesus' teaching on faith and prayer (11:12–14, 20–25), and used it as a framing device for the temple demonstration in 11:15–19. Through this intercalation, which may have been inherited from an earlier tradent, Mark shifts the accent of the episode that this combination has created. Instead of being simply a nature miracle that illustrates the power of God through faith (see 11:22–25), the fig-tree story presents a curse miracle that is a symbolic or prophetic action pointing to the coming destruction of the temple, which is confirmed by the narrative that is intercalated between the two halves of the fig-tree story.

The present literary context in Mark supplies the interpretive framework for 11:12–14, 20–21. Consequently, one cannot go beyond this context, even to the OT use of figs or fig trees, and speak of God's judgment on Israel as a nation (see *Comment* on v 12 above) or an attack on the priesthood or the temple establishment as such. Rather, the fig tree points to the temple with all its significance for the Jewish people as the locus of God's presence and redemptive activity. Despite its leaves, which seem to bear witness to life and productivity, the temple has no fruit. And just as the tree that does not bear fruit has no value except to be cut down, the temple too will be destroyed. The withering of the tree, therefore, corresponds to Jesus' hint of the temple's impending doom in 11:17 and to his explicit statement to the three disciples in 13:2. Its theological significance comes for Mark and his readers in 15:38 when the veil of the holiest of holies, the presence of God, is torn at Jesus' death.

Mark's prophetic use of the fig-tree story does not specify what the figs or fruit that were missing might be. The analogy simply declares that as the fig tree was barren, so the temple was unproductive in its role. The one has to do with figs, the other with the locus of God and God's redemptive activity for Israel. Perhaps

Mark's explanatory comment, "for it was not the season for figs," takes on added significance in terms of redemptive history. The season or time for the temple had been eclipsed with the fulfillment of time in Jesus' coming and proclamation of the kingdom of God (1:14–15).

D. *Jesus' Action in the Temple* (11:15–19)

Bibliography

Ådna, J. "The Attitude of Jesus to the Temple." *Mishkan* 17–18 (1992–93) 65–80. ———. "Jesu Kritik am Tempel: Eine Untersuchung zum Verlauf und Sinn der sogenannten Tempelreinigung Jesu, Markus 11,15–17 und Parallelen." Diss., University of Oslo, 1993. **Anderson, H.** "The Old Testament in Mark's Gospel." In *The Use of the Old Testament in the New and Other Essays.* FS W. F. Stinespring, ed. J. M. Efird. Durham: Duke UP, 1972. 280–306. **Bammel, E.** "Die Tempelreinigung bei den Synoptikern und im Johannesevangelium." In *John and the Synoptics.* Ed. A. Denaux. BETL 101. Leuven: Peeters; Leuven UP, 1992. 507–13. **Barrett, C. K.** "The House of Prayer and the Den of Thieves." In *Jesus und Paulus.* FS W. G. Kümmel, ed. E. E. Ellis and E. Grässer. Göttingen: Vandenhoeck & Ruprecht, 1975. 13–20. **Bauckham, R. J.** "Jesus' Demonstration in the Temple." In *Law and Religion.* Ed. B. Lindars. Cambridge: Clarke, 1988. 72–89. **Becker, J.** *Jesus of Nazareth.* 332–33. **Borg, M. J.** *Conflict, Holiness and Politics in the Teachings of Jesus.* Studies in the Bible and Early Christianity 5. New York; Toronto: Mellen, 1984. 171–75. **Brandon, S. G. F.** *Jesus and the Zealots: A Study of the Political Factor in Primitive Christianity.* Manchester: Manchester UP, 1967. 255–57, 330–40. **Braun, F.-M.** "L'expulsion des vendeurs du Temple (Mt., XXI,12–17,23–27; Mc., XI,15–19,27–33; Lc., XIX,45–XX,8; Jo., II,13–22)." *RB* 38 (1929) 178–200. **Broshi, M.** "The Role of the Temple in the Herodian Economy." *JJS* 38 (1987) 31–37. **Buchanan, G. W.** "An Additional Note to 'Mark 11.15–19: Brigands in the Temple.'" *HUCA* 31 (1960) 103–5. ———. "Mark 11.15–19: Brigands in the Temple." *HUCA* 30 (1959) 169–77. ———. "Symbolic Money-Changers in the Temple?" *NTS* 37 (1991) 280–90. **Burkitt, F. C.** "The Cleansing of the Temple." *JTS* o.s. 25 (1924) 386–90. **Buse, I.** "The Cleansing of the Temple in the Synoptics and in John." *ExpTim* 70 (1958–59) 22–24. **Caldecott, A.** "The Significance of the 'Cleansing of the Temple.'" *JTS* o.s. 24 (1923) 382–86. **Carmichael, J.** "Jésus-Christ et le Temple." *Nouvelle revue française* 12 (1964) 276–95. **Catchpole, D. R.** "The 'Triumphal' Entry." In *Jesus and the Politics of His Day.* Ed. E. Bammel and C. F. D. Moule. Cambridge: Cambridge UP, 1984. 319–35, esp. 330–34. **Chilton, B. D.** "Caiaphas." *ABD* 1:803–6. ———. *Galilean Rabbi.* ———. *The Temple of Jesus: His Sacrificial Program within a Cultural History of Sacrifice.* University Park, PA: Pennsylvania State UP, 1992. ———. "[ὡς] φραγέλλιον ἐκ σχοινίων (John 2.15)." In *Templum Amicitia.* FS E. Bammel, ed. W. Horbury. JSNTSup 48. Sheffield: JSOT Press, 1991. 330–44. **Cooke, F. A.** "The Cleansing of the Temple." *ExpTim* 63 (1951–52) 321–22. **Crossan, J. D.** *Historical Jesus.* 355–60. ———. "Redaction and Citation in Mark 11:9–10 and 11:17." *BR* 17 (1972) 33–50. **Culpepper, R. A.** "Mark 11:15–19." *Int* 34 (1980) 176–81. **Daube, D.** *Civil Disobedience in Antiquity.* Edinburgh: T. & T. Clark, 1972. 101–12. **Derrett, J. D. M.** "The Zeal of Thy House and the Cleansing of the Temple." *DRev* 95 (1977) 79–94. **Dienemann, M.** "Wechsler im Tempel." In *Jüdisches Lexikon.* Ed. G. Herlitz and B. Kirschner. 4 vols. Berlin: Jüdischer Verlag, 1927–30. 4.2:1350–52. **Doeve, J. W.** "Purification du Temple et dessèchement du figuier." *NTS* 1 (1954–55) 297–308. **Dowda, R. E.** "The Cleansing of the Temple in the Synoptic Gospels." Diss., Duke

University, 1972. **Edwards, J. R.** "Markan Sandwiches: The Significance of Interpolations in Markan Narratives." *NovT* 31 (1989) 193–216. **Eppstein, V.** "The Historicity of the Gospel Account of the Cleansing of the Temple." *ZNW* 55 (1964) 42–58. **Evans, C. A.** "From 'House of Prayer' to 'Cave of Robbers': Jesus' Prophetic Criticism of the Temple Establishment." In *The Quest for Context and Meaning: Studies in Intertextuality.* FS J. A. Sanders, ed. C. A. Evans and S. Talmon. Biblical Interpretation Series 28. Leiden: Brill, 1997. 417–42. ———. "Jesus' Action in the Temple and Evidence of Corruption in the First-Century Temple." In *SBL 1989 Seminar Papers.* Ed. D. J. Lull. SBLSP 28. Atlanta: Scholars Press, 1989. 522–39. ———. "Jesus' Action in the Temple: Cleansing or Portent of Destruction?" *CBQ* 51 (1989) 237–70. ———. "Jesus and the 'Cave of Robbers': Toward a Jewish Context for the Temple Action." *BBR* 3 (1993) 93–110. **Fredriksen, P.** *From Jesus to Christ: The Origins of the New Testament Images of Jesus.* London and New Haven: Yale UP, 1988. 111–14. ———. "Jesus and the Temple, Mark and the War." In *Society of Biblical Literature 1990 Seminar Papers.* Ed. D. J. Lull. SBLSP 29. Atlanta: Scholars Press, 1990. 293–310. **Gärtner, B. E.** *The Temple and the Community in Qumran and the New Testament: A Comparative Study in the Temple Symbolism of the Qumran Texts and the New Testament.* SNTSMS 1. Cambridge: Cambridge UP, 1965. 105–22. **Glusman, E. P., Jr.** "The Cleansing of the Temple and the Anointing at Bethany: The Order of Events in Mark 11/John 11–12." In *SBL 1979 Seminar Papers.* Ed. P. J. Achtemeier. 2 vols. SBLSP 18. Missoula, MT: Scholars Press, 1979. 1:113–17. **Hahn, F.** *The Titles of Jesus in Christology: Their History in Early Christianity.* London: Lutterworth, 1969. 155–56. **Hamilton, N. Q.** "Temple Cleansing and Temple Bank." *JBL* 83 (1964) 365–72. **Harland, P. J.** "Robber or Violent Man? A Note on the Word *pārîs*." *VT* 46 (1996) 530–34. **Harvey, A. E.** *Jesus and the Constraints of History.* London: Duckworth, 1982. 129–34. **Hengel, M.** *Was Jesus a Revolutionist?* FBBS 28. Philadelphia: Fortress, 1971. **Hiers, R. H.** "Purification of the Temple: Preparation for the Kingdom of God." *JBL* 90 (1971) 82–90. **Holladay, W. L.** *Jeremiah 1: A Commentary on the Book of the Prophet Jeremiah Chapters 1–25.* Hermeneia. Philadelphia: Fortress, 1986. **Hollenbach, P.** "Liberating Jesus for Social Involvement." *BTB* 15 (1985) 151–56. **Hooker, M. D.** "Traditions about the Temple in the Sayings of Jesus." *BJRL* 70 (1988) 7–19. **Horsley, R. A.** *Jesus and the Spiral of Violence.* 279–84. **Jeremias, J.** "Zwei Miszellen: 1. Antik-jüdische Münzdeutungen; 2. Zur Geschichtlichkeit der Tempelreinigung." *NTS* 23 (1977) 177–80. **Kato, Z.** *Die Völkermission im Markusevangelium.* **Kim, S.** "Die Vollmacht Jesu und der Tempel (Markus 11/12): Der Sinn der 'Tempelreinigung' und der geschichtliche und theologische Zusammenhang des Prozesses Jesu." *ANRW* 2.26.1. Forthcoming. **Lightfoot, R. H.** *The Gospel Message of St. Mark.* Oxford: Clarendon, 1950. 60–69. **Lohmeyer, E.** "Die Reinigung des Tempels." *TBl* 10 (1941) 257–64. **Lohse, E.** *Die Geschichte des Leidens und Sterbens Jesu Christi.* 3rd ed. Gütersloh: Mohn, 1973. 27–40. **Losie, L. A.** "The Cleansing of the Temple: A History of a Gospel Tradition in Light of Its Background in the Old Testament and in Early Judaism." Diss., Fuller Theological Seminary, 1984. **Manson, T. W.** "The Cleansing of the Temple." *BJRL* 33 (1950–51) 271–82. **Massyngberd Ford, J.** "Money 'Bags' in the Temple (Mk 11,16)." *Bib* 57 (1976) 249–53. **Matera, F. J.** "The Trial of Jesus." *Int* 45 (1991) 12–14. **Matson, M. A.** "The Contribution to the Temple Cleansing by the Fourth Gospel." In *Society of Biblical Literature 1992 Seminar Papers.* Ed. E. H. Lovering, Jr. SBLSP 31. Atlanta: Scholars Press, 1992. 489–506. **McNamara, M.** *Palestinian Judaism and the New Testament.* Wilmington, DE: Glazier, 1983. 185–88. **Meier, J. P.** *Marginal Jew.* 2:884–96. **Mendner, S.** "Die Tempelreinigung." *ZNW* 47 (1956) 93–112. **Meyer, B. F.** *The Aims of Jesus.* 197–202. **Miller, R. J.** "The (A)historicity of Jesus' Temple Demonstration: A Test Case in Methodology." In *Society of Biblical Literature 1991 Seminar Papers.* Ed. E. H. Lovering, Jr. SBLSP 30. Atlanta: Scholars Press, 1991. 235–52. **Neusner, J.** "The Absoluteness of Christianity and the Uniqueness of Judaism." *Int* 43 (1989) 18–31. ———. "Money-Changers in the Temple: The Mishnah's Explanation." *NTS* 35 (1989) 287–90. **Oakman, D. E.** "Cursing Fig Trees and Robbers' Dens." *Semeia* 64 (1993) 253–72. **Pesch, R.** "Der Anspruch Jesu." *Orientierung* 35 (1971) 53–56. ———. *Evangelium* *der Urgemeinde.* 134–37. **Plooij, D.** "Jesus and the Temple." *ExpTim* 42 (1930–31) 36–39. **Richardson, P.** "Why Turn the Tables? Jesus' Protest in the Temple Precincts." In *Society of Biblical Literature 1992 Seminar Papers.* Ed. E. H. Lovering, Jr. SBLSP 31. Atlanta: Scholars Press, 1992. 507–23. **Roloff, J.** *Kerygma und der irdische Jesus.* 90–98. **Roth, C.** "The Cleansing of the Temple and Zechariah xiv 21." *NovT* 4 (1960) 174–81. **Runnalls, D.** "The King as Temple Builder: A Messianic Typology." In *Spirit within Structure.* FS G. Johnston, ed. E. Furcha. PTMS 3. Allison Park, PA: Pickwick, 1983. 15–38. **Sabbe, M.** "The Cleansing of the Temple and the Temple Logion." In *Studia Neotestamentica: Collected Essays.* BETL 98. Leuven: Peeters; Leuven UP, 1991. 331–54. **Saldarini, A. J.** *Pharisees, Scribes and Sadducees in Palestinian Society: A Sociological Approach.* Wilmington, DE: Glazier, 1988. 241–76. **Salin, E.** "Jesus und die Wechsler." Appendix in A. Ben-David. *Jerusalem und Tyros: Ein Beitrag zur palästinensischen Münz- und Wirtschaftgeschichte (126 a.C.–57 p.C.).* Kleine Schriften zur Wirtschaftsgeschichte. Tübingen: Mohr-Siebeck, 1969. 49–55. **Sanders, E. P.** *Jesus and Judaism.* 61–71, 363–69. ———. "Jesus, Paul and Judaism." *ANRW* 2.25.1 (1982) 390–450. **Sariola, H.** *Markus und das Gesetz.* 211–35. **Schenk, W.** *Der Passionsbericht.* 151–58. **Schnellbächer, E. L.** "The Temple as Focus of Mark's Theology." *HBT* 5 (1983) 95–112. **Seeley, D.** "Jesus' Temple Act." *CBQ* 55 (1993) 263–83. **Söding, T.** "Die Tempelaktion Jesu: Redaktionskritik–Überlieferungsgeschichte–historische Rückfrage." *TTZ* 101 (1992) 36–64. **Spiegel, E.** "War Jesus gewalttätig? Bemerkungen zur Tempelreinigung." *TGl* 75 (1985) 239–47. **Stein, R. H.** "The Cleansing of the Temple in Mark (11:15–19)." In *Gospels and Tradition: Studies on Redaction Criticism of the Synoptic Gospels.* Grand Rapids, MI: Baker, 1991. 121–33. **Suhl, A.** *Die Funktion der alttestamentlichen Zitate.* 142–43. **Taylor, V.** *Formation.* 75–76. **Theissen, G.** "Die Tempelweissagung Jesu." *TZ* 32 (1976) 144–58 (ET: "Jesus' Temple Prophecy: Prophecy in the Tension between Town and Country." In *Social Reality and the Early Christians: Theology, Ethics, and the World of the New Testament.* Minneapolis: Fortress, 1992. 94–114). **Tilly, M.** "Kanaanäer, Handler und der Tempel in Jerusalem." *BN* 57 (1991) 30–36. **Trautmann, M.** *Zeichenhafte Handlungen Jesu: Ein Beitrag zur Frage nach dem geschichtlichen Jesus.* FB 37. Würzburg: Echter, 1980. 78–131. **Trocmé, É.** "L'expulsion des marchands du Temple." *NTS* 15 (1968) 1–22. ———. "Jésus-Christ et le Temple: Éloge d'un naif." *RHPR* 44 (1964) 245–51. **Wagner, G.** "The Cleansing of the Temple." In *Survey Bulletin.* Rüschlikon: Baptist Theological Seminary, 1967. 30–42. **Watty, W. W.** "Jesus and the Temple: Cleansing or Cursing?" *ExpTim* 93 (1981–82) 235–39. **Winkle, R. E.** "The Jeremiah Model for Jesus in the Temple." *AUSS* 24 (1986) 155–62.

Translation

[15]*And they went* [a] *into Jerusalem. And entering the temple,* [b] *he began to drive out those who were selling and those who were buying in the temple; and he overturned the tables of the money-changers and the seats of those who sold pigeons;* [16]*and he was not permitting anyone to carry a vessel through the temple.* [17]*And he was teaching and saying to them, "Is it not written, 'My house shall be called a house of prayer for all the Gentiles'? But you have made* [c] *it 'a cave of robbers.'"* [18]*And the ruling priests and the scribes* [d] *heard and were seeking how they might destroy him; for they feared him, because all the multitude* [e] *were impressed by his teaching.* [19]*And whenever* [f] *evening came, they* [g] *went out of the city.*

Notes

[a]Lit. pres. tense, "and they go"; an example of the historic pres. C reads the impf. ἤρχοντο, "they were going."

[b]D reads καὶ ὅτε ἦν ἐν τῷ ἱερῷ, "and when he was in the temple."

ᶜMany MSS read the simple aor. ἐποιήσατε, "you made."

ᵈSome MSS read οἱ ἀρχιερεῖς καὶ οἱ Φαρισαῖοι, "the ruling priests and the Pharisees." This variant probably derives from the tendency in Matthew (21:45; 27:62) and John (7:32, 45; 11:47, 57; 18:3) to link the Pharisees with the ruling priests. The Markan evangelist never does this, but he does link οἱ ἀρχιερεῖς καὶ οἱ γραμματεῖς, "the ruling priests and the scribes," several times (Mark 11:18, 27; 14:1, 43, 53). Other MSS read οἱ γραμματεῖς καὶ οἱ Φαρισαῖοι καὶ οἱ ἀρχιερεῖς, "the scribes and the Pharisees and the ruling priests," which combines the alternative readings and follows passages in which all three groups are mentioned together (see below).

ᵉSome MSS and versions read ὁ λαός, "the people."

ᶠGk. καὶ ὅταν. Some MSS read καὶ ὅτε, "and when," implying a particular departure from the city and not necessarily Jesus' custom to depart every evening. Luke's version suggests that this was Jesus' custom (cf. Luke 21:37: "And every day he was teaching in the temple, but at night he went out and lodged on the Mount called Olivet"). See Field, *Notes*, 35.

ᵍ The sg. ἐξεπορεύετο, "he went," is read by ℵ C D θ *f*¹ *f*¹³ 22 33 and other authorities. Taylor (465) takes the sg. over the pl. "since Jesus alone is mentioned in the narrative." Lagrange (297) and Rawlinson (157) also accept the sg. If the sg. was original, then the change to the pl. was to accommodate the following verse (v 20). However, it is also possible that the sg. was itself an accommodation to the actions of the singular Jesus in vv 15b–18. The pl. is probably original (so *TCGNT*¹, 109), forming an inclusio with the pl. in v 15a.

Form/Structure/Setting

The temple demonstration is one of the most remarkable actions of Jesus in the Gospel tradition. It is characterized by sudden, dramatic action, provocative teaching, and (by this point in the wider context of the Markan narrative) a not unexpected reference to deadly plotting on the part of Jesus' enemies. Jesus enters the temple precincts and "began to drive out those who were selling and those who were buying in the temple." Further, he does not permit people to carry vessels through the precincts, and finally, he appeals to various prophetic Scriptures that speak of the temple. The narrative is marked by succinctness and action, and functions as a turning point in the Markan narrative: Jesus has entered Jerusalem on a positive, promising note, but now with this action (and what prompted it is not made clear) an escalating series of accusations and charges begins to unfold. Ernst (331) divides this narrative into three parts: (*a*) the account of the cleansing (vv 15b–16), (*b*) Jesus' teaching (v 17), and (*c*) the reaction of Jesus' opponents (v 18), with "stage directions" in vv 15a and 19. Lohmeyer (235) divides the account into two parts: (*a*) report of Jesus' expulsion of the vendors (vv 15–16) and (*b*) his teaching (v 17).

Critics have variously assessed the source, or sources, of the story of Jesus' action in the temple. Both Bultmann (*History*, 36) and Dibelius (*From Tradition*, 45) see vv 15 and 18–19 as contributions of the evangelist. Bultmann supposes that the question of authority (Mark 11:27–33) followed immediately after v 16. Taylor (466) accepts vv 15b–17 as an isolated but unified tradition. Ernst (328) views vv 15b–17 as isolated tradition. Gnilka (2:127) thinks vv 15bc–16 and 18a are an isolated tradition, originally unrelated to the temple. Roloff (*Kerygma und der irdische Jesus*, 91–93) believes that vv 15–16, 18a, and 28–33 were part of older tradition and reflect the original setting, as John 2:18 indicates (more on this important point below). Schenk (*Der Passionsbericht*, 153) takes vv 15bc–16, 18ab; 14:2, 10, 11b as a traditional unit. He rejects (against Roloff) any connection with 11:28–33 based on John 2:18 as inadequately supported. Trocmé (*NTS* 15 [1968] 14–15) regards vv 15–16 and 17 as two separate traditions that have been combined by the Markan evangelist. The historicity of the Markan source(s) will be taken up below.

With regard to form, Bultmann (*History*, 36) describes the Markan narrative as a "biographical apophthegm," with v 17 a later substitute for "an older saying of Jesus which has been preserved" in John 2:16: "Stop making my Father's house a place of business" (author's tr.). Grundmann (310) holds to a similar position. Dibelius (*From Tradition*, 43, 45) calls the episode a "paradigm," with v 18 added, and regards the parallel version in John 2:14–17 as independent. Taylor (*Formation*, 75–76) classifies the pericope as a "story about Jesus" in which the interest appears to lie in the incident itself "rather than in the words of Jesus." Taylor is right, so far as Mark goes. The pericope furthers the drama of the triumphal entry and the cursing of the fig tree, while at the same time it provides the basis for the challenge to Jesus' authority that follows. Ernst (328) views the narrative as a symbolic action that rejects the ancient cultic ordinances (cf. Trautmann, *Zeichenhafte Handlungen Jesu*, 115–31). Gnilka (2:127) thinks the narrative approximates a prophetic parabolic action the setting (*Sitz im Leben*) of which was the Jewish community of Palestine.

Klostermann (117) identifies vv 15a and 18–19 as Markan redaction. Taylor (461) and Lührmann (191) agree. To this Ernst (331) adds v 17ab. Schenk (*Der Passionsbericht*, 152) identifies vv 15ab, 17–18c, and 19 as Markan redaction. Gnilka (2:127) finds Markan redaction throughout, seen primarily in terms of the relative weight that the evangelist gives the various components of the tradition: cleansing (little), teaching (more), opponents (much). Crossan (*BR* 17 [1972] 45–46) contends that the evangelist added the quotation of Isa 56:7 (Mark 11:17a) to emphasize Jesus' teaching and so to redirect the tone of the narrative away from the purely negative orientation of the allusion to Jer 7:11 (Mark 11:17b). Sanders (*Jesus and Judaism*, 364 n. 1) doubts the originality of v 16 and thinks (*Jesus and Judaism*, 66–67), along with Harvey (*Jesus*, 132), that v 17 is ill suited for the context and so probably is not authentic. Sanders thinks this because we find no criticisms against the priests in the teaching of Jesus and little evidence of such criticism in other sources. J. Becker (*Jesus of Nazareth*, 332–33) accepts v 16 but rejects v 17. These conclusions, however, rest on a failure to take into account the evidence of widespread criticism of and misgivings with respect to the first-century temple establishment and Jesus' concerns with purity, as well as various statements that imply criticism of temple polity. When these elements are considered, vv 16–17 make good sense as they stand in the Markan text. More will be said on this below. It seems best to conclude that the Markan redaction is seen in the first part of v 15, "and they went into Jerusalem," and vv 18–19, which are probably mostly, if not wholly, the work of the evangelist. This view is consistent with the results of most source and form critics. As will been shown below, it is also consistent with historical criticism.

The historicity of the tradition has been much debated. Grundmann (308) raises serious questions about how Jesus alone could have done what is depicted in Mark 11:15b–17. He thinks perhaps the story developed from a saying in which Jesus criticized the temple. Haenchen (384–86) speaks at length about the impossibility of this story as a historical event. He raises questions about the immensity of the task in terms of the presence of hundreds of animals, merchants, temple officials, temple police, and Roman authorities, as well as those loyal to the temple who were present to change their money, buy animals, and offer sacrifices. These people would not have stood by and allowed Jesus to behave as Mark describes. Similarly, Lohmeyer (235–37) speaks of the impossibility of Jesus actually doing such a thing. He speculates that the narrative arose from parenesis, which itself had grown up around the saying in v 17. Harking back to the skepticism of Haenchen and Grundmann, Schmithals (2:490–91) comments that the temple action is "unimaginable" because Jesus acted alone. What we have here, he contends, is a "miracle story" in which God and God alone is acting. Only God can "cleanse" the temple, as promised in the OT (cf. Mal 3:1–4; cf. Zech 10:3; 14:21). Schmithals (2:492) explains the story as growing out of early Christianity's emphasis upon Jesus' coming as an eschatological event: the Lord has come to his temple.

Other assessments of the story of the temple demonstration are not nearly so skeptical. Lührmann (192–93), who compares the different accounts in Mark and John, believes that despite their different respective developments, there stands behind these Gospel narratives a historical appearance of Jesus in the temple precincts. Nineham (301) agrees, cautiously opining that "while some definite historical incident may well underlie the story, St Mark's account is too brief and imprecise to enable us to be sure what it was, or to tell exactly what was in the mind of Jesus." Schweizer (231) is less tentative, asserting that "the story of the cleansing of the Temple must be based upon some historical act of Jesus." Pesch (2:189–90) understands vv 15–19 as part of the pre-Markan Passion Narrative. What is described is without parallel and so cannot have been created by the early church, especially the Palestinian community that continued to worship at the temple. Cranfield (357) thinks the vividness of the narrative points to "Petrine reminiscence."

Recent research in the historical Jesus has by and large come to accept the historicity of the temple demonstration. Sanders (*Jesus and Judaism,* 61–76, with notes on 363–69) regards the event as of vital importance for comprehending Jesus' self-understanding and what triggered the events of his passion. Meyer (*Aims,* 168–70) finds the event "solidly probable." Theissen (*TZ* 32 [1976] 146–48) finds Jesus' attitude toward the temple entirely plausible. Brown (455–60) shows how the temple demonstration coheres with the destruction-rebuilding saying in Mark 14:58 (a point also underscored by Sanders; see also Wright, *Jesus and the Victory of God,* 334–35, 418–28). Although interpreting the meaning of the event differently from most, Borg (*Conflict,* 171–75) and Crossan (*Historical Jesus,* 355–60) also accept the historicity of the temple demonstration. Apart from the predictable exception of some members of the North American Jesus Seminar (e.g., Mack, *Myth,* 292: a "Markan fabrication"; Miller, "Temple Demonstration"), the historicity of the temple demonstration is now widely accepted.

Much of the skepticism expressed by German commentators grows out of a misunderstanding of the nature and extent of Jesus' actions in the temple precincts. His actions were a *demonstration,* not a *takeover* of the temple precincts (as in Brandon's improbable scenario; cf. *Jesus and the Zealots*). At the earliest stage of the tradition, which in this instance is surely rooted in the actions and sayings of Jesus himself, the emphasis probably fell as much on the words as on the deeds. Jesus' allusions to Isaiah and Jeremiah would have been as provocative and offensive in the minds of the ruling priests as the actions themselves (see *Comment* below). But in the presence of many supportive pilgrims (presumably mostly from Galilee) there was an understandable reluctance to escalate the situation by taking immediate and public action against Jesus. As Sanders (*Jesus and Judaism,* 69–70, 75) has plausibly suggested, Jesus' actions were symbolic and quite limited (cf. Schweizer, 231: Jesus, in a "symbolic way, cleared only a limited area of the temple court"). He could not and did not bring temple traffic to a standstill. Most people in the precincts (whose dimensions were enormous—approximately 450 meters north to south and 300 meters east to west) that day would not have even noticed him. His words and actions would eventually have been passed on to anxious temple authorities.

Support for the historicity of the temple action lies in Josephus and the Gospel of John. According to Josephus (*Ant.* 18.3.3 §§63–64), Jesus was handed over to Pontius Pilate by "the first men [πρώτων ἀνδρῶν] among us." Elsewhere in Josephus these "first men" are ruling priests (*Ant.* 11.5.3 §§140–41; 18.5.3 §121; cf. Luke 19:47; Acts 25:2; 28:17). Why would Jerusalem's ruling priests hand over Jesus to the Roman governor? The most probable answer is that he had said and done things within the temple precincts (the ruling priests' domain of authority) that they found offensive and dangerous. The juridical process depicted in the Gospel of Mark is, moreover, consistent with Josephus's account of Ananias, the peasant prophet who proclaimed the doom of the city and the temple. Josephus tells us that this man was seized, beaten, and handed over by the "leading citizens" and "rulers" to the Roman governor (*J.W.* 6.5.3 §§300–309). More will be said below on this man's fate.

Support for the historicity of the temple action is also seen in John, whose version appears to be independent of Synoptic sources. I follow Meier's succinct assessment (*Marginal Jew,* 2:893). At Passover time, Jesus comes to Jerusalem with his disciples (John 2:13, 17 = Mark 11:1, 15); he enters the temple (John 2:14 = Mark 11:11, 15); he drives out merchants and money-changers (John 2:15 = Mark 11:15); and he rebukes the priestly authorities for turning the temple into a place of business (John 2:16 = Mark 11:17). Scripture citations appear in both the Johannine and Markan accounts (John 2:17 = Mark 11:17). Following the temple demonstration, Jesus is asked about his authority (John 2:18–22 = Mark 11:27–33). In John 2:18, Jesus is asked by "the Jews," "What sign do You show us, since You do these things [ταῦτα ποιεῖς]?" (NKJV). In Mark 11:28 Jesus is asked by scribes, ruling priests, and elders: "By what authority do you do these things [ταῦτα ποιεῖς]?" and "Who has given to you this authority, so that you may do these things [ταῦτα ποιῇς]?" Once stripped of their respective redactional and contextual differences, the accounts in Mark and John are remarkably similar. Independently of one another, they provide a common three-part cluster: (*a*) Jesus enters the temple precincts and demonstrates against some aspect or aspects of trade; (*b*) he speaks out against temple polity, appealing to Scripture; and (*c*) temple authorities challenge Jesus, wanting to know by what right he "does these things."

The principal reason that Sanders (*Jesus and Judaism,* 66–67, 364 n. 1) rejects the authenticity of vv 16–17 is that he doubts that Jesus' demonstration was a prophetic protest against corruption. It is at this point that Sanders's thesis is vulnerable, for there is ample evidence that Jesus' contemporaries were critical of the Jewish high priesthood and regarded it as corrupt in various ways. We find such evidence in some of the Dead Sea Scrolls, where the high priest is dubbed the "Wicked Priest" (1QpHab 1:13; 8:9; 9:9; 11:4), who has robbed the poor (1QpHab 8:12; 9:5; 10:1; 12:10), has amassed wealth (1QpHab 8:8–12; 9:4–5), and has defiled the "Sanctuary of God" (1QpHab 12:8–9). The *Testament of Moses* condemns the ruling priests (*T. Mos.* 7:6–10; tr. J. Priest in *OTP*):

> They consume the goods of the (poor), saying their acts are according to justice, (while in fact they are simply) exterminators, deceitfully seeking to conceal themselves so that they will not be known as completely godless because of their criminal deeds (committed) all the day long, saying, "We shall have feasts, even luxurious winings and dinings. Indeed, we shall behave ourselves as princes." They, with hand and mind, touch impure things, yet their mouths will speak enormous things, and they will even say, "Do not touch me, lest you pollute me in the position I occupy."

Whereas the pesher on Habakkuk dates from 100 B.C.E., and so originally targeted Hasmonean priests, the *Testament of Moses* was probably composed some time around 30 C.E. Other first-century sources criticize the ruling priests and call into question temple polity. Josephus tells of high priestly bribery (*Ant.* 20.9.4 §213; *Life* 39 §§195–96) and violence (*Ant.* 20.8.8 §§179–81; 20.9.2 §207). In *2 Baruch* the priests confess in the wake of the temple's destruction that they have been "false stewards" (*2 Bar.* 10:18). The scene is fictional, of course, but it expresses the view of the author at the end of the first century. Such an expression could scarcely have impressed readers unless many Jews did in fact view the pre-70 high priesthood as corrupt. Later rabbinic sources are very critical of the first-century ruling priests (see Evans, "Jesus' Action in the Temple and Evidence of Corruption," 531–34).

There is also significant evidence in the dominical tradition to indicate that Jesus was critical of the temple establishment. The parable of the Wicked Vineyard Tenants (Mark 12:1–9) threatens the priestly aristocracy with the loss of their position and power (see commentary on this passage). The abuses of power and privilege described in the parable of the Faithless Servant (Matt 24:45–51 = Luke 12:42–46) probably reflect how the ruling aristocracy was perceived in the minds of Palestinian peasants. Jesus' pronouncement on the half-shekel temple tax (Matt 17:24–27) may have been a "declaration of independence from the Temple and the attendant political-economic-religious establishment" (Horsley, *Jesus and the Spiral of Violence*, 282). Jesus' comment regarding the poor widow and the others who were contributing to the temple's coffers (Mark 12:41–44) was probably a lament—not a word of commendation—and an implicit criticism of the economic oppressiveness and inequity of the temple establishment (see commentary on this passage). The condemnation of the "scribes" who "devour widows' houses" (Mark 12:38–40) is probably in reference to efforts to collect gifts for the temple (see commentary on this passage). In Jesus' lament for Jerusalem (Matt 23:37–38 = Luke 13:34–35) there are significant parallels to Jeremiah, the prophet who had severely criticized Jerusalem's first temple (Jer 7:14, 34; 12:7; 22:5; 26:9), whose criticism Jesus may have had in mind when he took action in Jerusalem's second temple (Jer 7:11 in Mark 11:17). Various other details during passion week cohere with the criticisms of the priestly aristocracy. The priests demand to know by what authority Jesus acted the way he did (Mark 11:27–33). The ruling priests cannot arrest Jesus immediately because of their fear of the multitude (Mark

12:12). Jesus is arrested by servants of the ruling priests who are armed with clubs (Mark 14:43–50).

In view of such evidence, there really are no compelling grounds for rejecting the authenticity of v 17. This is the kind of critical statement that would account for the antagonism that arose between Jesus and the priestly aristocracy. Moreover, one wonders why early Christians, having been rejected by Israel's religious establishment, would invent a dominical saying in which the *temple*, as opposed to the *church*, is recognized as the place of prayer for Gentiles. The allusion to Isa 56:7 is consistent with Jesus' restorative hopes for Israel. Chilton, in reference to the conflated paraphrase of Isa 56:7 and Jer 7:11, rightly comments that a "mixing of scriptural elements in that manner is characteristic of Jesus, not of those who shaped the tradition after him" (*ABD* 1:806; on the historicity of the temple cleansing, see Chilton, *Galilean Rabbi*, 17–18; id., *Temple of Jesus*, 91–111; on the authenticity of the reference to the ἔθνη, "Gentiles," see Kato, *Völkermission*, 91–111; Pesch, 2:198–99).

The setting of the pericope plays a very important role both literarily and historically. For Mark it advances the antagonism between Jesus and his opponents. Criticisms now give way to deadly plotting to eliminate Jesus. It also gives Jesus the moral high ground. His criticism of the religious establishment is principally ethical. Jesus has not attacked the Roman administration (even though it is this authority that puts him to death); he has criticized Israel's religious leadership. On the historical level it is very probable that Jesus' action in the temple was the principal element that triggered the events that led to his death. One is reminded of another Jesus, son of Ananias, who some thirty years after the death of Jesus of Nazareth also appealed to Jer 7 in his pronouncement of woe upon the temple and the city of Jerusalem (Josephus, *J.W.* 6.5.3 §§300–309). The leading citizens of Jerusalem, by which is meant the temple authorities, took strong exception to this man's gloomy prophecies. The juridical procedure that involved the son of Ananias closely paralleled that which earlier had overtaken Jesus of Nazareth: Jewish authorities interrogated and beat both men; both men were then handed over to the Roman governor; the Roman governor interrogated and beat both men and then decided whether to release or execute them (for more on Jesus ben Ananias, see *Comment* on v 17).

Comment

In the latter part of the twentieth century, the so-called cleansing of the temple has figured prominently in critical discussion. The passage was the linchpin in S. G. F. Brandon's argument that Jesus attempted a violent takeover of the Temple Mount (*Jesus and the Zealots*). However, few have followed his line of interpretation. After a critical assessment of Brandon's hypothesis, Hengel concludes (*Was Jesus a Revolutionist?* 17–18):

In the so-called Temple-cleansing we have, apparently, a prophetic demonstration or, one could also say, provocation, in which it was not a matter of driving out all those who sold, and the money-changers—for such an action would not have been possible without a large contingent of troops and a corresponding general riot, and would inevitably have led to intervention on the part of the temple guards and the Romans. We are dealing, rather, with a demonstrative condemnation of their trade, a condemnation which was directed at the same time against the ruling temple aristocracy, which derived profit from it. . . . Such an episode did not call forth intervention on the part of the occupation forces, but it did make the hierarchy the deadly foes of Jesus.

Hengel's analysis puts us on the right track.

Sanders (*Jesus and Judaism*, 61–76), who also rejects Brandon's hypothesis, attaches a great deal of importance to the temple incident for understanding Jesus' message and the principal factors that led to his arrest and execution. But he interprets Jesus' actions very differently from the way Hengel and most other commentators have. He believes that Jesus' action was a symbolic action, or prophetic gesture (e.g., the breaking of the pot in Jer 19:10), portending the imminent destruction of the Herodian temple and its replacement with one that God would build through Jesus. The statement attributed to Jesus in Mark 14:58, Sanders believes, lies behind Jesus' real intentions. He has entered the temple precincts and overturned tables not because they are wrong or part of corrupt practices but because they are no longer needed. The "temple made with hands" is about to be replaced with the "temple not made with hands." That is, the Herodian, human-made temple will give way to the heaven-made eschatological temple. This startling announcement, Sanders argues, should be seen as part of Jesus' proclamation of the kingdom of God. However, most interpreters have rejected Sanders' novel interpretation (for an exception, see Fredriksen, "Jesus and the Temple"; id., *From Jesus to Christ*, 111–14).

Chilton has recently argued that Jesus' actions should be interpreted in the light of other public demonstrations by Jewish religious teachers. He shows (*Temple of Jesus*, 73, 100–103, 183) that Jesus' action is quite intelligible when viewed as one of several protests and demonstrations relating to the Jerusalem temple. Two of the incidents are preserved in the writings of Josephus. The first protest was directed against Alexander Jannaeus during the Feast of Tabernacles (*Ant.* 13.13.5 §§372–73). On this occasion teachers incited the people to pelt the king with lemons just as he was about to offer sacrifice. His critics said that "he was descended from captives [cf. *Ant.* 13.10.5 §292] and was unfit to hold office and to sacrifice." The second incident occurred in the final months of Herod's life, when two sages (σοφισταί), through their public teaching, persuaded several young men to cut down the golden eagle affixed to the gate of the temple (*J.W.* 1.33.2–4 §§648–55; *Ant.* 17.6.2–4 §§149–67). Both of these actions resulted in deadly retaliation on the part of the authorities. Two more incidents are related in rabbinic writings. In one Simeon ben Gamaliel sat on the temple steps protesting a policy of overcharging for doves (*m. Ker.* 1:7). We are told that the price went down immediately. In another episode Hillel's teaching regarding the proper manner of possessing and presenting sacrificial animals led to a dramatic demonstration in the temple precincts, in which animals were freely given to those who followed the teaching of Hillel instead of the teaching of Shammai (*t. Ḥag.* 2.11; *y. Ḥag.* 2.3; *y. Beṣah* 2.4; *b. Beṣah* 20a–b; on the antiquity of the tradition, cf. Philo, *Spec. Laws* 1.37 §198).

The views of Hengel and Chilton have much to commend them. It is probable that Jesus' action in the temple precincts was a prophetic protest and pronouncement against some aspect of perceived corruption, a corruption that may very well have had to do with purity concerns. The brief utterance in v 17, consisting of allusions to Isa 56:7 and Jer 7:11, is probably a small fragment of a longer prophetic pronouncement (which may also have carried with it messianic implications; on this, see *Comment* on v 17). It is also possible that at this time Jesus spoke of the temple's doom, as Jesus is accused of in Mark 14:58 and as the evangelist says Jesus predicted in Mark 13:2. It may very well be that Jesus said something based on Jer 7, complete with Jeremiah's warning of coming destruction of Jerusalem and the temple. Incensed at Jesus for presuming to criticize temple polity and for daring to speak of the temple's possible destruction, the religious authorities begin "seeking how they might destroy him" (v 18). (For arguments that Jesus threatened to destroy the temple establishment at his return as "son of man," see *Comment* on Mark 13:24–27.)

15 καὶ ἔρχονται εἰς Ἰεροσόλυμα, "and they went into Jerusalem." Coming from the Mount of Olives, Jesus would have entered through the East Gate (Pesch, 2:197), through which today there is no passage. This is, of course, assuming that Jesus and his disciples had not entered the city first via some other gate.

καὶ εἰσελθὼν εἰς τὸ ἱερόν, "and entering the temple." When Jesus went εἰς τὸ ἱερόν, "into the temple," he did not enter the *sanctuary* (ὁ ναός) but the *precincts* of the Temple Mount. Where exactly in the temple precincts Jesus encountered the money-changers and traffickers of sacrificial animals it is not easy to say. It is commonly thought that Jesus was in the so-called court of the Gentiles (e.g., Cranfield, 357; Ernst, 328), especially because of his reference to the temple as a "house of prayer for all the Gentiles" (v 17). But this is no more than a guess. According to Josephus (*Ag. Ap.* 2.8 §104),

> The outer court was open to all, foreigners included; women during their impurity were alone refused admission. To the second court all Jews were admitted and, when uncontaminated by any defilement, their wives; to the third male Jews, if clean and purified; to the fourth the priests robed in their priestly vestments. The sanctuary was entered only by the ruling priests, clad in the raiment peculiar to themselves.

If we follow Josephus here, it seems most probable that a gathering of animals, tables, and vendors would have been in the outer court, where foreigners were permitted, rather than in any of the other inner courts, to which Gentiles would not have access.

The temple precincts were (and the site still is) immense, running some 450 meters in length and approximately 300 meters in width. In the northwest corner stood the Antonia fortress, a tower that overlooked the precincts. The fortress housed up to five hundred Roman soldiers with easy access to the precincts (Josephus, *Ant.* 20.5.3 §§106–7; *J.W.* 2.12.1 §§224–27). The sanctuary was probably located somewhere near the center of the precincts, surrounded by walls and gates. Along the perimeter of the precincts were several buildings and porticoes. The precincts could be entered from all four sides. Remains of the southern steps have been excavated and can be viewed today. Remains of two arches on the western wall are also visible (i.e., the so-called Robinson and Wilson arches). Excavations are currently under way to expose more of the southern wall and steps, and the entire length of the western wall. The northern half of the western

wall may be explored by passing through a tunnel (the "Rabbis' Tunnel") beneath the Arab quarter of the Old City. One is able to view the magnificent
Herodian stones and in places the original pavement itself largely preserved as
they would have been seen in the days of Jesus.

τοὺς πωλοῦντας καὶ τοὺς ἀγοράζοντας ἐν τῷ ἱερῷ, "those who were selling and
those who were buying in the temple." There is little early and detailed information regarding the sellers and buyers of sacrificial animals within the temple
precincts. That animals were to be bought and sold for purposes of the sacrificial
offerings is completely in step with the requirements of the Law of Moses. But
trade in these animals within the precincts themselves is not specified in Scripture. Indeed, Zech 14:21 may even be a complaint against it: "Every pot in
Jerusalem and Judah shall be sacred to the LORD of hosts, so that all who sacrifice
may come and take of them and boil the flesh of the sacrifice in them. And there
shall no longer be a trader in the house of the LORD of hosts on that day." The
Johannine version of the temple incident speaks of sheep and oxen as well as of
money-changers and sellers of pigeons (John 2:15–16). It is sometimes thought
that Mark's reference to selling and buying may have implied the sale and purchase of sheep and oxen (though cf. Derrett, *DRev* 95 [1977] 83: "There is no
proof that sheep and oxen were actually sold to the public in the courts of the
Temple"; and Abrahams, *Studies* 1:82–89). There is the already mentioned rabbinic story of the student of Shammai who brought three thousand oxen to the
temple (*b. Beṣah* 20a–b; *t. Ḥag.* 2.2–3; *y. Ḥag.* 2.3; *y. Beṣah* 2.4), an account that
may provide additional evidence of the presence of trade in sacrificial animals
within the temple precincts.

τὰς τραπέζας τῶν κολλυβιστῶν . . . κατέστρεψεν, "he overturned the tables of
the money-changers." Rabbinic traditions also tell us that tables of money-changers were set up in the temple precincts (*m. Šeqal.* 1:3): "The money-changer [שולחני
šûlḥānî] takes (the money) from him and pays him from the coinage which circulates in his country in accord with the proper measure. For every kind of coin
circulates in Jerusalem on this account" (*t. Šeqal.* 2.13; cf. *m. Šeqal.* 1:3; 4:7–8; 5:3–
5). Although these traditions come from sources written more than a century
after the publication of the Gospels, there is little reason in this instance to doubt
their usefulness for general background information. All four Gospels (with the
Synoptic and Johannine versions in all probability representing distinct traditions)
describe Jesus taking action against sellers and money-changers in the temple
precincts. The scenario described by the Gospels agrees with what meager information can be gleaned from Tannaitic rabbinic traditions.

τὰς καθέδρας τῶν πωλούντων τὰς περιστεράς, "the seats of those who sold pigeons." The poor were permitted to offer less expensive pigeons or doves (instead
of larger, more expensive animals; Ernst, 329) at the temple for cleansing following childbirth (cf. Lev 5:7; 12:6–8; Luke 2:24, where Joseph and Mary offer up
pigeons following the birth of Jesus) and for cleansing following a case of leprosy
(cf. Lev 14:22; Mark 1:44, where Jesus commands the cleansed leper to show himself to the priest and to do what Moses commanded). Pigeons were also offered
for other purposes (cf. Lev 15:14, 29). The Mishnah tells of one occasion when
pigeons were being sold, apparently within the temple precincts, at many times
the normal cost. In angry protest to this exorbitant overcharge, Simeon ben
Gamaliel began to teach that women could offer a pair of pigeons for as many as

five live births or miscarriages and then be eligible to take part fully in the feasts. We are told that in response to Simeon's teaching the price for pigeons went down suddenly and dramatically (*m. Ker.* 1:7). It is possible that this story has relevance for understanding Jesus' actions in the temple precincts. If nothing else, the story provides evidence that the rabbis remembered that on occasion the temple authorities practiced extortion.

16 οὐκ ἤφιεν ἵνα τις διενέγκῃ σκεῦος διὰ τοῦ ἱεροῦ, "he was not permitting any one to carry a vessel through the temple." Why and in what sense Jesus was doing this is not entirely clear. A comment by Josephus may be pertinent: "No vessel whatever might be carried into the temple. . . . Nothing of the nature of food or drink is brought within the temple; objects of this kind may not even be offered on the altar, save those which are prepared for the sacrifices" (*Ag. Ap.* 2.8 §§106, 109). A later rabbinic tradition may also be relevant: "A man . . . may not enter into the Temple Mount with his staff or his sandal or his wallet, or with the dust upon his feet, nor may he make of it a short by-path; still less may he spit there" (*m. Ber.* 9:5). Chilton thinks Jesus' action here should be interpreted in the light of Zech 14:20–21, in which the prophet foretells the day when traders will no longer be present in the temple (*Temple of Jesus,* 135–36). The Hebrew כְּנַעֲנִי *kĕnaʿănî* of Zech 14:21 is understood as "trader" or "merchant," not as "Canaanite" (as in the LXX: Χαναναῖος). "Trader" is how the text is understood in the Targum (עביד *ʿābêd*), whose paraphrase appears to accentuate the eschatological dimension of the oracle, as well as in *b. Pesaḥ.* 50a: "How do we know that כנעי *[kĕnaʿănî]* connotes a merchant [תגר *taggār*]? . . . As it is written, 'A trader [כנען *kĕnaʿan*], in whose hands are false balances, he loves to oppress' (Hos 12:8)."

Chilton believes that Zechariah, which is itself concerned with the restoration of worship in Jerusalem, has informed Jesus' teaching and ministry at several important points. These include teaching against swearing (Zech 5:3–4; cf. Matt 5:33–37) and entering Jerusalem mounted on a donkey as an act of humility (Zech 9:9; cf. Matt 21:1–9 = Mark 11:1–10 = Luke 19:28–40 = John 12:12–19). Chilton also suspects that the targumic paraphrase of Zech 14:9, "the kingdom of the Lord shall be revealed," may represent yet another important link between Jesus and his proclamation of the kingdom and the Zechariah tradition. The saying attributed to Jesus in John 2:16, "Stop making my Father's house a place of business" (author's tr.), may also be an allusion to Zech 14:21 and so may lend additional support to Chilton's interpretation. Gnilka (2:127), however, sees no influence from Zech 14:21, or Mal 3:1 or Hos 9:15 for that matter. But Gnilka clearly underestimates the importance Israel's Scriptures held for Jesus; critics must carefully distinguish Jesus' use of Scripture from the later, apologetic use of Scripture by the early church.

17 καὶ ἐδίδασκεν, "and he was teaching." Mark's imperfect ἐδίδασκεν could be inceptive, i.e., "he began to teach." Mark is fond of this construction; the inceptive imperfect of διδάσκειν, "to teach," occurs in five other passages (1:21; 2:13; 4:2; 9:31; 10:1). Almost as often the evangelist gives the same sense with ἤρξατο διδάσκειν, "he began to teach" (cf. 4:1; 6:2, 34; 8:31).

οὐ γέγραπται, "Is it not written?" With one exception (i.e., 1:2), every occurrence of γέγραπται, "it is written," in the Gospel of Mark is found on the lips of Jesus (7:6; 9:12, 13; 14:21, 27). Three of these occurrences are introduced with ὡς, "as," or καθώς, "just/even as." One is introduced with the interrogative πῶς, "how"

(9:12), and one is introduced with the declarative ὅτι, "that" (14:27). Because the evangelist introduces the first quotation in 1:2 with καθὼς γέγραπται, "as it is written," some commentators incline to the view that these other appearances of γέγραπται do not derive from Jesus but are redactional. But why should not the custom of appealing to Scripture, "as it is written," derive from Jesus himself? The formula is not Hellenistic; it is Semitic. An exact equivalent appears in the Dead Sea Scrolls: אשר כתוב כאשר, ka'ăšer kātûb (e.g., 1QS 5:17; 8:14; CD 7:19; 4QFlor 1:12). Its origin is Semitic and Palestinian, not Septuagintal (what few examples there are in the LXX are translations of the underlying Hebrew or Aramaic). Jesus, after all, was frequently addressed as "rabbi" (which in the Greek Gospels is sometimes translated διδάσκαλος, "teacher"), and his closest followers were called μαθηταί, "disciples," that is, "learners." Surely part of what they learned was their master's understanding of Scripture. Critical scholarship has been far too skeptical with regard to the question of Jesus' use and understanding of the Scriptures of Israel.

ὁ οἶκός μου οἶκος προσευχῆς κληθήσεται πᾶσιν τοῖς ἔθνεσιν, "My house shall be called a house of prayer for all the Gentiles." This quotation is drawn from the last part of Isa 56:7, which in the LXX reads: ὁ γὰρ οἶκός μου οἶκος προσευχῆς κληθήσεται πᾶσιν τοῖς ἔθνεσιν, "For my house shall be called a house of prayer for all the Gentiles [or nations]." It is a literal rendering of the Hebrew: כִּי בֵיתִי בֵית־תְּפִלָּה יִקָּרֵא לְכָל־הָעַמִּים kî bêtî bêt-tĕpillâ yiqqārē' lĕkol-hā'ammîm, "For my house shall be called a house of prayer for all the peoples." It is therefore difficult to tell whether the Markan form of the quotation is directly dependent upon the LXX, or if it represents an independent translation of the Hebrew. If it is not the latter, then it is probable that in the transmission of the tradition in Greek the form of the quotation assimilated to the LXX. The meaning of this quotation in Jesus' teaching is considered below.

ὑμεῖς δὲ πεποιήκατε αὐτὸν σπήλαιον λῃστῶν, "but you have made it 'a cave of robbers.'" The final words, σπήλαιον λῃστῶν, "a cave of robbers," allude to the first part of Jer 7:11, part of which reads in the LXX: μὴ σπήλαιον λῃστῶν ὁ οἶκός μου οὗ ἐπικέκληται τὸ ὄνομά μου ἐπ' αὐτῷ ἐκεῖ ἐνώπιον ὑμῶν, "[Is] my house, where my name has been called upon it there, a cave of robbers before you?" Does Mark's σπήλαιον λῃστῶν derive from the LXX? Perhaps, but again this part of the Greek version renders the Hebrew literally: הַמְעָרַת פָּרִצִים הָיָה הַבַּיִת הַזֶּה אֲשֶׁר נִקְרָא־שְׁמִי עָלָיו בְּעֵינֵיכֶם ham'ărat pārîṣîm hāyâ habbayit hazzeh 'ăšer-niqrā'-šĕmî 'ālayw bĕ'ênêkem, "Has this house, where my name is called upon it, become a cave of robbers in your eyes?" (author's tr.). σπήλαιον, "cave," routinely translates מְעָרָה mĕ'ārâ, "cave," while λῃστής, "robber," had become a loanword in Aramaic (ליסטא lisṭā') and Hebrew (ליסטים lisṭês), so again the Markan form of the allusion may reflect an underlying Hebrew or Aramaic form, not necessarily the LXX. What has drawn these two passages together is the reference to "this/my house" (הַבַּיִת הַזֶּה/ὁ οἶκός μου). The formal antithetical parallelism (i.e., "house of prayer" versus "cave of robbers") smacks of Jewish, especially prophetic style (cf. Ernst, 329). The import of this allusion will be discussed below.

It is unfortunate that many commentators and critics have regarded the allusion to Isa 56:7 and Jer 7:11 as a later, inauthentic insertion into the temple pericope (e.g., Gnilka, 2:127; Haenchen, 386; Lohmeyer, 237; Lührmann, 193; Mann, 449; Nineham, 304; Roloff, *Das Kerygma und der irdische Jesus*, 93; Suhl, *Zitaten*, 142; Crossan, *BR* 17 [1972] 45; Trautmann, *Zeichenhafte Handlungen Jesu,*

87–90; and others). Sanders (*Jesus and Judaism,* 66), for example, thinks that the quotation of Jer 7:11 is not original to the Markan context because a reference to robbers is hardly appropriate. Had Jesus been complaining of corruption or a questionable temple polity, he should have spoken of swindlers or thieves. But Sanders has in this instance missed the hyperbolic nature of prophetic language. After all, when the prophet Jeremiah complained of robbers in the temple in his day, it is unlikely that he meant that people were literally being mugged in the temple precincts. Harland (*VT* 46 [1996] 532–33) and Holladay (*Jeremiah 1,* 246) believe that Jer 7:11 refers to "violent men" who shed blood in the course of their oppressive and grasping business and then participate in the cultic ceremonies. Their presence in the precincts defiles the sanctuary (see also Ezek 7:22). Given Josephus's description of violence practiced by ruling priests against the lower-ranking priests (*Ant.* 20.8.8 §§179–81; 20.9.2 §207), as well as the description of the violence of the ruling priests against Jesus himself in the Gospel tradition (Mark 14:43–50, 65), the temple establishment of Jesus' day may very well have been guilty of the very sort of crimes against which the prophet Jeremiah had complained centuries earlier. Indeed, only a little later Jesus will tell a parable in which the ruling priests are depicted as violent murderers (Mark 12:1–12). There is therefore nothing incongruous in the allusion to Jer 7:11.

Jesus' criticisms of the temple establishment cannot be adequately probed and understood apart from careful consideration of Isa 56:7 and Jer 7:11. The importance of these texts is seen in their respective literary contexts. The first one, from Isa 56, describes an eschatological scenario in which the nations of the world come to Jerusalem to worship and pray to God. Parts of the oracle read as follows:

> Thus says the LORD:
> "Keep justice, and do righteousness,
> for soon my salvation will come,
>   and my deliverance will be revealed." . . .
>
> Let not the foreigner who has joined himself to the LORD say,
>   "The LORD will surely separate me from his people." . . .
>
> For thus says the LORD: . . .
>
> "And the foreigners who join themselves to the LORD,
>   to minister to him, to love the name of the LORD". . . .
>
> "[T]hese I will bring to my holy mountain,
>   and make them joyful in my house of prayer;
> their burnt offerings and their sacrifices
>   will be accepted on my altar;
> for my house shall be called a house of prayer
>   for all peoples."
> Thus says the Lord GOD,
>   who gathers the outcasts of Israel,
> "I will gather yet others to him
>   besides those already gathered." (Isa 56:1–8)

The importance of this passage may not have been lost on the first-century priesthood. We may hear an echo of Isa 56:7 in the speech that Josephus attributes to Jesus ben Gamala, a former high priest. The temple, he says, "is revered by the world and honored by foreigners from the ends of the earth who have heard of its fame" (*J.W.* 4.4.3 §262). Do we hear in these words the apologetic of Josephus, the aristocratic priest, who implies that the temple in his day had indeed lived up to its biblical obligations? A similar apologetic may be operative in Josephus's free rendering of Solomon's prayer of dedication of the temple, especially the part that concerns Gentile access to the temple (1 Kgs 8:41–43). In this paraphrase King Solomon prays that all people "know that you yourself desired that this house should be built for you in our land, and also that we are not inhumane by nature nor unfriendly to those who are not of our country, but wish that all people equally should receive aid from you and enjoy your blessings" (*Ant.* 8.4.3 §117). The relation between Solomon's prayer of dedication and words of Isa 56 and Jer 7 will be considered shortly.

The second passage (from Jer 7) warns that the presence of the temple in the city is no guarantee that Jerusalem is safe from the Babylonian menace. Israel's sin will result in judgment, and the very temple in which the religious authorities have placed their trust will itself be destroyed. Portions of the passage read:

> The word that came to Jeremiah from the LORD: "Stand in the gate of the LORD's house, and proclaim there this word, and say, Hear the word of the LORD, all you men of Judah who enter these gates to worship the LORD. Thus says the LORD of hosts, the God of Israel, Amend your ways and your doings, and I will let you dwell in this place. Do not trust in these deceptive words: 'This is the temple of the LORD, the temple of the LORD, the temple of the LORD.'
>
> "For if you truly amend your ways and your doings, if you truly execute justice one with another, if you do not oppress the alien, the fatherless or the widow, or shed innocent blood in this place, and if you do not go after other gods to your own hurt, then I will let you dwell in this place, in the land that I gave of old to your fathers for ever. . . .
>
> "Will you steal, murder, commit adultery, swear falsely, burn incense to Baal, and go after other gods? . . . Has this house, which is called by my name, become a den of robbers in your eyes? . . . Go now to my place that was in Shiloh, where I made my name dwell at first, and see what I did to it for the wickedness of my people Israel. And now, because you have done all these things . . . I will do to the house which is called by my name, and in which you trust, . . . as I did to Shiloh." (Jer 7:1–14)

Jesus ben Ananias (active 62–69 C.E.) made use of Jer 7 to pronounce woe on Jerusalem and the temple (see Josephus, *J.W.* 6.5.3 §§300–309). The experience of this prophet of doom sheds light on the activities and eventual arrest and execution of Jesus of Nazareth. According to Josephus,

> Four years before the war . . . there came to the feast, at which is the custom of all Jews to erect tabernacles to God, one Jesus, son of Ananias, an untrained peasant, who, standing in the Temple, suddenly began to cry out, "A voice from the east, a voice from the west, a voice from the four winds, *a voice against Jerusalem* and the sanctuary, *a voice against the bridegroom and the bride,* a voice against all the people." . . . Some of the leading citizens, angered at this evil speech, arrested the man and whipped him with many blows. But he, not speaking anything in his own behalf or in private to those who struck him, continued his cries as before. Thereupon, the rulers . . . brought him to the Ro-

man governor. There, though flayed to the bone with scourges, he neither begged for mercy nor wept. . . . When Albinus the governor asked him who and whence he was and why he uttered these cries, he gave no answer to these things. . . . Albinus pronounced him a maniac and released him. . . . He cried out especially at the feasts. . . . While shouting from the wall, "Woe once more to the city and to the people and to the sanctuary," a stone . . . struck and killed him.

It is important to observe that Jesus ben Ananias evidently based his word of doom on a verse found in Jer 7: "I will make to cease from the cities of Judah and from the streets of *Jerusalem the voice* of mirth and the voice of gladness, the *voice of the bridegroom and the voice of the bride;* for the land shall become a waste" (Jer 7:34). The specific parallels are noted in italics. But the parallels between Jesus of Nazareth and Jesus ben Ananias involve more than their common dependence on Jer 7. Both entered the precincts of the temple (τὸ ἱερόν: Mark 11:11, 15, 27; 12:35; 13:1; 14:49; *J.W.* 6.5.3 §301) at the time of a religious festival (ἑορτή: Mark 14:2; 15:6; John 2:23; *J.W.* 6.5.3 §300). Both spoke of the doom of Jerusalem (Luke 19:41–44; 21:20–24; *J.W.* 6.5.3 §301), the sanctuary (ναός: Mark 13:2; 14:58; *J.W.* 6.5.3 §301), and the people (λαός: Mark 13:17; Luke 19:44; 23:28–31; *J.W.* 6.5.3 §301). Both were arrested by the authority of the priestly aristocracy—not the Roman governor (συλλαμβάνειν: Mark 14:48; John 18:12; *J.W.* 6.5.3 §302). Both were beaten by the Jewish authorities (παίειν: Matt 26:68; Mark 14:65; *J.W.* 6.5.3 §302). Both were handed over to the Roman governor (Luke 23:1: ἤγαγον αὐτὸν ἐπὶ τὸν Πιλᾶτον; *J.W.* 6.5.3 §303: ἀνάγουσιν . . . ἐπὶ τὸν . . . ἔπαρχον). Both were interrogated by the Roman governor (ἐρωτᾶν: Mark 15:4; *J.W.* 6.5.3 §305). Both refused to answer the governor (οὐδὲν ἀποκρίνεσθαι: Mark 15:5; *J.W.* 6.5.3 §305). Both were scourged by the governor (μαστιγοῦν/μάστιξ: John 19:1; *J.W.* 6.5.3 §304). Governor Pilate may have offered to release Jesus of Nazareth, but did not; Governor Albinus did release Jesus ben Ananias (ἀπολύειν: Mark 15:9; *J.W.* 6.5.3 §305).

If we focus upon the *reaction* to Jesus' activity in the temple, then it seems clear that the closest parallel is the experience of Jesus ben Ananias a generation later. The parallels with Hillel and Simeon, to which Chilton has drawn our attention (see the beginning of the *Comment* section above), are helpful in clarifying what may have motivated Jesus of Nazareth, but they are less helpful in clarifying the response of the Jewish and Roman authorities. Jesus ben Ananias evidently did not have any agenda of reform or criticism (as did Hillel and Simeon); nor did he attack the authorities (as did the crowd that pelted Alexander Jannaeus, the Hasmonean priest-king, or the young men who vandalized the golden eagle in the time of Herod the Great). His action consisted of nothing more than a dolorous prediction of the temple's impending doom.

Jesus of Nazareth, on the other hand, was apparently motivated out of concerns relating to temple polity. Evidently he took exception to the presence of the animals in the temple precincts and the attendant commercial activities. What he taught in the temple on this occasion, of which only fragments are preserved in the Gospels, may very well have paralleled the earlier teaching of Hillel, as Chilton has suggested. The comparison is apt. But the reaction of the temple authorities suggests the presence of a more serious element in Jesus' teaching and action. This element likely consists of some sort of prophetic pronouncement against the temple, probably related to Jer 7, just as the later oracle of Jesus ben Ananias would also be based on Jer 7.

The citation of these prophetic passages has led many to suppose that Jesus acted in the capacity of a prophet, perhaps an eschatological prophet (as in the interpretation offered by Sanders, who argues that Jesus in effect prophesied the imminent destruction of the building and its replacement). But there is another dimension that should be considered. Jesus' understanding of the temple and the Gentiles' relationship to it may have been informed by the prayer of Solomon, the son of David:

> Likewise when a foreigner, who is not of thy people Israel, comes from a far country for thy name's sake . . . when he comes and prays toward this house, hear thou in heaven thy dwelling place, and do according to all for which the foreigner calls to thee; in order that all the peoples of the earth may know thy name and fear thee, as do thy people Israel, and that they may know that this house which I have built is called by thy name. (1 Kgs 8:41–43 RSV)

This passage from 1 Kgs 8 parallels most of the vocabulary in the quotations of Isa 56:7 and Jer 7:11, as the following table makes clear:

Jeremiah 7	Isaiah 56	1 Kings 8
alien (v 6)	foreigners (v 6)	a foreigner (v 41)
this house (v 11)	my house (v 7)	this house (v 43)
called by my name (v 11)	shall be called (v 7)	called by thy name (v 43)
	house of prayer (v 7)	prays toward this house (v 42)
	for all peoples (v 7)	all the peoples of the earth (v 43)
	their burnt offerings and their sacrifices will be accepted (v 7)	do according to all for which the foreigner calls to thee (v 43)

These parallels are fascinating. They suggest that Jesus' indictment against the temple establishment was not simply prophetic but was inspired in part by a Solomonic understanding of the purpose of the temple. Could this be evidence that Jesus did indeed see himself as the son of David, a Solomonic figure who, like the famous patron of wisdom, could heal and exorcise demons (as Jesus does; cf. Matt 12:22–45; Mark 1:21–28, 32–34; 3:11–12, 21–30; 5:1–20; 7:24–30; 9:14–29 [see *Comment* above]), and someday would preside over a temple in which the peoples of the world would come to worship God? C. K. Barrett ("House of Prayer," 15) comments that the temple "had never served as a house of prayer *for all nations;* it was natural therefore to take the words as a prophecy" (his emphasis). As a royal messianic claimant, Jesus has called on the temple establishment to live up to this great heritage. Gundry (642) has reminded us that in the OT it was Israel's kings, not prophets, who cleansed and restored the temple: because of the negligence, even dishonesty, of the priests, King Jehoash found it necessary to apply royal pressure in order to bring about the repairs of the temple (2 Kgs 12:1–16). Years later King Josiah had to apply even sterner measures, removing and destroying foreign cultic objects from the sanctuary and temple precincts and putting to death pagan priests. His reform climaxed with a celebration of the Passover that was the grandest since the days of Samuel (2 Kgs 22:3–23:23; 2 Chr 34:3–35:19; cf. 1 Esdras 1:1–24). The author of the *Psalms of Solomon* expected a Davidic Messiah to arise and "purge Jerusalem" and make the city holy, so that nations would "come from the ends of the earth to see his glory" and to "see the glory of Lord" (*Pss. Sol.* 17:30–31).

In view of this evidence, it is quite possible that Jesus entered the temple precincts and acted with messianic authority. He alluded to prophetic traditions that had earlier alluded to Solomon's famous prayer of dedication. These prophetic traditions may have regarded the ruling priests of the first temple as failing to live up to the requirements of the implied temple covenant between God and Israel. Failing to dispense justice, this ruling priesthood was in danger of destruction according to the prophets. Jesus invoked this prophetic tradition and did so not simply as the prophet of the Eschaton but as God's messianic agent.

But the appeal to Jer 7 implies the possibility of repentance and restoration. This is seen when Jeremiah says: "If you truly amend your ways and your doings, if you truly execute justice one with another, if you do not oppress the alien, the fatherless or the widow . . . , then I will let you dwell in this place, in the land that I gave of old to your fathers for ever" (Jer 7:5–6). We probably should assume that Jesus' prophetic pronouncement in its fuller form contained such an offer of repentance. If the ruling priests mended their ways, heeded Jesus' words, and joined him in preparation for the coming kingdom of God, Jerusalem and her temple would not only be saved but could experience the inauguration of the long-awaited kingdom (Hengel, *Was Jesus a Revolutionist?* 18, rightly recognizes that the allusion to Jer 7:11 is a *warning*). Mark 11:27–33, however, makes it tragically clear that the ruling priests did not in fact react positively to Jesus' prophetic challenge.

18 καὶ ἤκουσαν οἱ ἀρχιερεῖς καὶ οἱ γραμματεῖς, "and the ruling priests and the scribes heard." The Markan evangelist will refer to "the ruling priests and the scribes" a few more times (Mark 11:27; 14:1, 43, 53). "Scribes," "Pharisees," "ruling priests," and "elders" (and sometimes "Sadducees" and "legal experts") are mentioned in the Gospels as Jesus' enemies. Most of the references are negative. These persons are either critical of Jesus' teachings and activities, or they are plotting to destroy him.

The NT contains more than sixty references to ruling priests (ἀρχιερεῖς). "Ruling priests" (Hebrew: ראשי הכהנים *rā'šê hakkōhănîm;* cf. Neh 12:7; 1QM 2:1) included the current high priest (Hebrew: כהן גדול *kōhēn gādôl;* Aramaic: כהנא רבא *kahănā' rabbā';* Greek: ὁ ἀρχιερεύς; cf. Josephus, *J.W.* 5.5.7 §230; *Ag. Ap.* 2.21 §185; Mark 14:53–65; 1QM 2:1: כוהן הראש *kôhēn hārō'š*), the "other priest" who stood ready in the event that the high priest be disqualified (כהן אחר *kôhēn 'aḥar;* cf. *m. Yoma* 1:1), retired high priests (ἀρχιερεῖς; cf. John 18:15, 18; Acts 4:6; Josephus, *J.W.* 2.20.4 §566), a captain of the temple (סגן *sāgān,* ὁ στρατηγὸς τοῦ ἱεροῦ; cf. Acts 4:1; *y. Yoma* 3.8: "The high priest [כהן גדול *kōhēn gādôl*] was not nominated to the office unless he had first been captain of the Temple [סגן *sāgān*]")—possibly the equivalent to Qumran's "deputy" priest (משנה *mišnā,* 1QM 2:1), and a treasurer of the temple (גזבר gizbār, ὁ γαζοφύλαξ τοῦ ἱεροῦ; cf. Josephus, *Ant.* 20.8.11 §194). Josephus speaks of their authority and the expectation that Jews will obey them: "With his [the high priest's] colleagues he will sacrifice to God, safeguard the laws, adjudicate in cases of dispute, punish those convicted of crime. Any who disobey him will pay the penalty as for impiety towards God himself" (*Ag. Ap.* 2.23 §194).

The "scribes" (סופרים *sôpěrîm*, γραμματεῖς) also make frequent appearances in the Gospels. They are sometimes closely linked with the priests and other persons of authority: "scribes and Pharisees" (Mark 7:1), "elders and scribes" (Mark 15:1), and "ruling priests, scribes, and elders" (Mark 11:27). We find this in the OT. One thinks of Ezra, who is described as "the priest and scribe" (הכהן הספר *hakkōhēn hassōpēr*, ὁ ἱερεὺς καὶ γραμματεύς; Neh 8:9 [= 2 Esd 18:9]; cf. 12:26 [= 2 Esd 22:26]; 1 Esd 8:8–9: "priest and reader"). The martyr Eleazar is said to have been a scribe (2 Macc 6:18) and in a later, parallel version is said to have been "a man of priestly family, learned in the law" (4 Macc 5:4). In the earliest parts of the OT we read of the "elders of the people and their scribes" (Num 11:16), while in later Scripture we hear of "scribes and Levites" (2 Chr 19:11), as well as "scribes and judges" (2 Chr 34:13). Jesus ben Sirach (ca. 180 B.C.E.) regarded sages as scribes (cf. Sir 38:24, which speaks of the σοφία γραμματέως, "the wisdom of the scribe"). In Jesus' day the role of "scribe" ranged from clerk or town recorder (cf. Josephus, *J.W.* 1.24.3 §479; Acts 19:35; for papyri, see MM, 132) to expert in the Law (cf. Mark 3:22). The latter usage of γραμματεύς, "scribe," is probably the equivalent of the νομικός, "lawyer," or νομοδιδάσκαλος, "teacher of the law" (cf. 4 Macc 5:4; Matt 22:35; Luke 5:17; 10:25). Josephus calls the scribes σοφισταί, "sophists" (*J.W.* 1.33.2 §648), ἱερογραμματεῖς, "sacred scribes" (*J.W.* 6.5.3 §291), and ἐξηγηταὶ τῶν πατρίων νόμων, "interpreters of the ancestral laws" (*Ant.* 17.6.2 §149). In what is probably a reference to scribes, Josephus says that his people "give credit for wisdom to those alone who have an exact knowledge of the law and who are capable of interpreting the meaning of the Holy Scriptures [τῶν ἱερῶν γραμμάτων]" (*Ant.* 20.11.2 §264). What seems clear is that the scribes of Jesus' day were honored and invested with authority. Thus, for Jesus to have both ruling priests and scribes seeking how they might destroy him is to be in serious trouble indeed. (For more on scribes, cf. Saldarini, *Pharisees, Scribes and Sadducees*, 241–76.)

It is important to emphasize that although Jesus' actions were directed against the animal vendors and money-changers, his criticism applied to the temple establishment in general. For it was by the authority of the ruling priests, especially the high priest himself, that these commercial activities took place in the precincts of the temple. In attacking the vendors and money-changers, Jesus had attacked the priesthood. It is for this reason that the ruling priests took a special, malevolent interest in Jesus. They would have acted immediately but did not for fear of arousing the crowds. Jesus could not have acted as he did without at least a measure of support and sympathy from the people within the precincts on that occasion.

The evangelist says that the ruling priests and the scribes ἤκουσαν, "heard," what Jesus had said. The evangelist has used this device before, as recently as in 11:14 when Jesus cursed the fig tree and "his disciples were listening [ἤκουον]." The evangelist's style lends an air of gravity to Jesus' words; they are powerful, evocative, and efficacious. What Jesus says and does moves the plot along, inexorably leading to its climax.

ἐζήτουν πῶς αὐτὸν ἀπολέσωσιν, "were seeking how they might destroy him."
Mark's ζητεῖν, "to seek," tells the Markan story as well as any verb in the Gospels.
In 1:37 all the crowd in Galilee is seeking Jesus, primarily for healing. In 3:32 it is
Jesus' own family members who seek him. In 8:11–12 questioning Pharisees seek
from Jesus a sign. With the appearance of ζητεῖν here in v 18, the nuance takes
an ominous turn. Here the ruling priests and scribes begin seeking to destroy
Jesus. In 12:12 they seek to arrest him. In 14:1 they seek for a way to arrest Jesus
by stealth. In 14:11 Judas, having reached a bargain with the ruling priests, begins seeking an opportune time to betray Jesus. After his arrest, the Sanhedrin in
14:55 begins seeking damning testimony against Jesus. And finally, in 16:6 women
mourners go to the tomb seeking Jesus.

ἐφοβοῦντο γὰρ αὐτόν, "for they feared him." Jesus has caused fear before. On a
historical level, the fear that Jesus caused was no more than that he might spark a
riot or rebellion. But in the Markan narrative world, the fear that Jesus causes the
ruling priests might not be too different from the fear he evoked in others. When
in 4:41 he calms the storm, the disciples are afraid. In 5:15 the villagers are frightened by the astounding exorcism of the demoniac. In 5:33 the healed woman falls
before Jesus afraid. In 6:50 the disciples are terrified with a great fear when Jesus
comes walking to them upon the sea. In 9:32 the Twelve are afraid to ask Jesus for
further clarification of his stunning passion prediction. In 11:32 and 12:12 Jesus'
great popularity is a cause of fear for the ruling priests. And finally, in 16:8 the
women at the tomb are afraid when they are told of Jesus' resurrection.

πᾶς γὰρ ὁ ὄχλος ἐξεπλήσσετο ἐπὶ τῇ διδαχῇ αὐτοῦ, "because all the multitude
were impressed by his teaching." Throughout the Markan narrative Jesus has astonished crowds and his disciples. In 1:22 villagers in Galilee are astonished at
Jesus' teaching. They are astonished again in 6:2 and wonder where Jesus acquired
such wisdom and power. In 7:37 the people are astonished over Jesus' ministry of
healing. And finally, in 10:26 Jesus astounds his disciples in his teaching about
the difficulty of entering the kingdom of God and being saved. The appearance
of ἐκπλήσσειν, "to impress," here in v 18 shows that Jesus continues to astonish
crowds in Jerusalem as well as in Galilee.

19 καὶ ὅταν ὀψὲ ἐγένετο, ἐξεπορεύοντο ἔξω τῆς πόλεως, "and when evening
came, they went out of the city." Earlier the evangelist told the reader that Jesus
did not spend nights in the city itself (cf. 11:11). It has been suggested that Jesus
did not remain in the city at night because it was unsafe for him to do so (Brooks,
186). This is possible. But it seems more likely that Jesus, along with thousands of
other Passover pilgrims, simply could not find lodgings, or could not afford them,
in Jerusalem.

Explanation

Not long after his entry into the city in anticipation of the Passover Feast, Jesus
entered the temple precincts and created a disturbance. He drove out sellers and
buyers of sacrificial animals and overturned tables of money-changers. His actions were symbolic; he did not bring all trafficking to a standstill. But he did
catch the attention of many, including the ruling priests (as the subsequent interrogation in Mark 11:27–33 indicates). His actions did not signify the imminent
destruction and replacement of the temple; they were meant to display disappro-

bation with respect to certain aspects of the trade. His complaint was not directed against the purchase of animals as such and certainly was not directed against the practice of sacrifice; nor was it directed against money-changing. All of these things were necessary for Israel's religion to be practiced, as commanded in the law of Moses. We cannot be certain precisely what angered Jesus. Given what we know from sources that derive from his approximate time, it is probable that Jesus complained of the presence of the animal trade within the precincts themselves, of the manner in which the animals were purchased and presented for sacrifice, and/or of certain aspects of the money-changing. Of these three options, the latter two are the most probable.

Jesus expressed profound disappointment in the failings of the temple establishment and issued a prophetic challenge. The temple was intended to be the place of prayer for the nations in fulfillment of its God-given purpose and in anticipation of its eschatological destiny. But instead, it had become a "cave of robbers" and stood in danger of judgment, even destruction. In what ways the temple functioned as a "cave of robbers" will be explored in several of the pericopes found in chaps. 12 and 14.

Jesus' action and teaching in the temple precincts were not in the least anti-Jewish. Such ideas are anachronistic and seriously misrepresent the nature and spirit of Jesus' intentions. In criticizing, even threatening, the temple, Jesus may very well have been inspired by the words of Jeremiah (so Hollenbach, *BTB* 15 [1985] 156; note the reference to "covenant" in the sayings at the Last Supper in Mark 14:24; cf. Jer 31:31). Jesus hoped for Jerusalem's salvation (what else could talk of "good news" entail?) and to that end had spoken out and acted in a prophetic manner. "Jesus must have had public sympathy on his side," Taylor (463) rightly comments, "that his action was not revolutionary and, although the contrary has been claimed [he cites W. O. E. Oesterley, *DCG* 2:713], was not an attack upon the sacrificial system." Jesus did not wish to destroy the temple or the system of sacrifice; he wished to save it, to propel it to achieve its prophetic calling and destiny.

Because the temple incident is surrounded by the ominous story of the cursing of the fig tree (Mark 11:12–14, 20–21), there is little doubt concerning what the evangelist is trying to communicate. The temple establishment faces doom if it does not change its ways. The fig tree could yield nothing edible and so fell under judgment. If the temple establishment cannot, or will not, do better, then it too will fall under judgment. How serious this judgment would be is addressed in the parable of the Vineyard Tenants (Mark 12:1–11) and Jesus' prophecy of the destruction of the temple (Mark 13:1–2).

Jesus' "cleansing of the temple" should not be interpreted as an indictment of Judaism, ancient or modern. Rather, his action in the temple is consistent with the classic tradition of Israel's prophets, who criticized the political and religious policies of the nation's leaders. Jesus acted and spoke in behalf of Israel. The restoration of Israel was his motivating concern. His criticism was directed squarely against the religious leaders, particularly the ruling priests. The reaction that ensued bears this out.

E. Lessons of Faith   (11:22–26)

Bibliography

Arichea, D. C., Jr. "'Faith' in the Gospels of Matthew, Mark, and Luke." *BT* 29 (1978) 420–24. **Berger, K.** *Die Amen-Worte Jesu: Eine Untersuchung zum Problem der Legitimation in apokalyptischer Rede.* BZNW 39. Berlin: de Gruyter, 1970. 35–70. **Best, E.** "Peter in the Gospel according to Mark." *CBQ* 40 (1978) 547–58 (repr. in *Disciples.* 162–76). **Broadhead, E. K.** "Which Mountain Is 'This Mountain'? A Critical Note on Mark 11,22–25." *Paradigms* 2 (1986) 33–38. **Buchanan, G. W.** "Withering Fig Trees and Progression in Midrash." In *The Gospels and the Scriptures of Israel.* Ed. C. A. Evans and W. R. Stegner. JSNTSup 104; SSEJC 3. Sheffield: Sheffield Academic Press, 1994. 249–69. **Clark, D. J.** "Our Father in Heaven." *BT* 30 (1979) 210–13. **Crockett, B. R.** "The Function of Mathetological Prayer in Mark." *IBS* 10 (1988) 123–39, esp. 130–35. **Crossan, J. D.** *In Fragments.* 94–96, 295–98. **Derrett, J. D. M.** "Moving Mountains and Uprooting Trees (Mk 11.22; Mt 17.20; 21.21; Lk 17.6)." *BO* 30 (1988) 231–44. **Dowd, S. E.** *Prayer, Power, and the Problem of Suffering: Mark 11:22–25 in the Context of Markan Theology.* SBLDS 105. Atlanta: Scholars Press, 1988. **Dowda, R. E.** "The Cleansing of the Temple in the Synoptic Gospels." Diss., Duke University, 1972. **Fleddermann, H. T.** *Mark and Q.* 178–86. **Gaston, L.** *No Stone on Another: Studies in the Significance of the Fall of Jerusalem in the Synoptic Gospels.* NovTSup 23. Leiden: Brill, 1970. **Hahn, F.** "Einige Überlegungen zu gegenwärtigen Aufgaben der Markusinterpretation." In *Der Erzähler des Evangeliums: Methodische Neuansätze in der Markusforschung.* Ed. F. Hahn. SBS 118–19. Stuttgart: Katholisches Bibelwerk, 1985. 171–97. ———. "Jesu Wort vom bergversetzenden Glauben." *ZNW* 76 (1985) 149–69. ———. "Das Verständnis des Glaubens im Markusevangelium." In *Glaube im Neuen Testament.* FS H. Binder, ed. F. Hahn and H. Klein. Biblisch-theologische Studien 7. Neukirchen-Vluyn: Neukirchener, 1982. 43–67. **Hasler, V.** *Amen: Redaktionsgeschichtliche Untersuchung zur Einführungsformel der Herrenworte "Wahrlich ich sage euch."* Zürich; Stuttgart: Gotthelf, 1969. 41–44, 67–68. **Jeremias, J.** *The Prayers of Jesus.* London: SCM Press, 1967. **Kienle, B. von.** "Mk. 11:12–14, 20–25: Der verdorrte Feigenbaum." *BN* 57 (1991) 17–25. **Kio, S. H.** "A Prayer Framework in Mark 11." *BT* 37 (1986) 323–28. **Knoch, O.** *Dem, der glaube, ist alles möglich: Die Botschaft der Wundererzählungen der Evangelien: Ein Werkbuch zur Bibel.* Stuttgart: Katholisches Bibelwerk, 1986. 391–400. **Koch, D.-A.** *Die Bedeutung der Wundererzählungen.* 132–34. **Losie, L. A.** "The Cursing of the Fig Tree: Tradition Criticism of a Marcan Pericope: Mk 11:12–14, 20–25." *Studia Biblica et Theologica* 7 (1977) 3–18. **Lührmann, D.** *Glaube im frühen Christentum.* Gütersloh: Mohn, 1976. 17–30. **Manson, W.** *Jesus the Messiah: The Synoptic Tradition of the Revelation of God in Christ, with Special Reference to Form-Criticism.* London: Hodder & Stoughton, 1943. 29–31. **Marshall, C. D.** *Faith as a Theme in Mark's Narrative.* 163–74. **Meier, J. P.** *Marginal Jew.* 2:884–96. **Mohr, T. A.** *Markus- und Johannespassion.* 72–77. **Ringe, S. H.** *Jesus, Liberation, and the Biblical Jubilee: Images for Ethics and Christology.* OBT 19. Philadelphia: Fortress, 1985. 77–80. **Robin, A. de Q.** "The Cursing of the Fig Tree in Mark xi: A Hypothesis." *NTS* 8 (1962) 276–81. **Roloff, J.** *Das Kerygma und der irdische Jesus.* 166–69. **Schlosser, J.** "Mc 11:25: Tradition et rédaction." In *A Cause de l'évangile: Études sur les Synoptiques et les Actes.* FS J. Dupont, ed. F. Refoulé. LD 123. Paris: Cerf, 1985. 277–301. **Schmidt, K. L.** *Rahmen.* 298–300. **Schulz, S.** *Q—Die Spruchquelle der Evangelisten.* Zürich: Theologischer Verlag, 1972. **Schwarz, G.** "πίστιν ὡς κόκκον σινάπεως." *BN* 25 (1984) 27–35. **Söding, T.** *Glaube bei Markus.* 317–39. **Strawson, W.** *Jesus and the Future Life: A Study in the Synoptic Gospels.* London: Epworth, 1959. 40–55. **Swartley, W.** *Israel's Scripture Traditions and the Synoptic Gospels: Story Shaping Story.* Peabody, MA: Hendrickson, 1994. **Telford, W. R.** *The Barren Temple and the Withered Tree: A Redaction-Critical Analysis of the Cursing of the Fig-*

Tree Pericope in Mark's Gospel and Its Relation to the Cleansing of the Temple Tradition. JSNTSup 1. Sheffield: JSOT, 1980. 49–59, 95–127. **Trautmann, M.** *Zeichenhafte Handlungen Jesu: Ein Beitrag zur Frage nach dem geschichtlichen Jesus.* FB 37. Würzburg: Echter, 1980. 319–46. **Wagner, G.** "Le figuier stérile et la destruction du Temple: Marc 11/12–14 et 20–26." *ETR* 62 (1987) 335–42. **Wanamaker, C. A.** "Mark 11:25 and the Gospel of Matthew." In *Studia Biblica 1978.* Vol. 2: *Papers on the Gospels: Sixth International Congress on Biblical Studies, Oxford 3–7 April 1978.* Ed. E. A. Livingstone. JSNTSup 2. Sheffield: JSOT Press, 1980. 329–37. **Wright, N. T.** *Jesus and the Victory of God.* 334–35. **Zeller, D.** *Die weisheitlichen Mahnsprüche bei den Synoptikern.* FB 17. Würzburg: Echter, 1977. 131–33. **Zmijewski, J.** "Der Glaube und seine Macht." In *Begegnung mit dem Wort.* FS H. Zimmermann, ed. J. Zmijewski and E. Nellessen. BBB 53. Bonn: Hanstein, 1980. 81–103.

Translation

^{22}*And answering, Jesus says to them,* ᵃ*"Have faith in God.*ᵇ ^{23}*Truly, I tell you that whoever should say to this mountain, 'Be taken up and be cast into the sea,' and he should not waver*ᶜ *in his heart but should believe that what he says happens,*ᵈ *it will be done for him.* ^{24}*For this reason I tell you, all that you pray and ask for—believe that you have received*ᵉ *it, and it will be yours.* ^{25}*And whenever you stand praying, forgive if you have something against someone, so that your*ᶠ *Father in heaven may also forgive you your transgressions.* ᵍ*[*^{26}*But if you do not forgive, neither will your Father in heaven forgive your trespasses.]"*

Notes

ᵃℵ D θ *f*¹³ 28 33ᶜ and some late MSS read εἰ ἔχετε πίστιν θεοῦ, ἀμὴν λέγω ὑμῖν . . . , "If you have faith in God, truly, I tell you . . . ." It is most likely influenced by Luke 17:6 since an ἀμήν, "truly," formula with a protasis is without parallel. The situation does not change if one renders the εἰ, "if," other than as conditional (e.g., interrogative, cf. *TCGNT*¹, 109 n. 1; or strong wish, Telford, *Barren Temple,* 98 n. 4; cf. Black, *Aramaic Approach,* 91).

ᵇSeveral later authorities omit ἔχετε εἰς θεοῦ, "Have faith in God" (cf. Telford, *Barren Temple,* 57, 68 n. 117). Nineham (305) and Lohmeyer (239) think the sentence is either a Markan addition or a later scribal gloss. See John 14:1: πιστεύετε εἰς τὸν θεόν, "Believe in God."

ᶜD* reads καὶ μὴ διακριθῆτε, "and you do not waver" (cf. Matt 21:21).

ᵈD reads ἀλλὰ πιστεύσῃ τὸ μέλλον ὃ ἂν εἴπῃ γενήσεται, "but believes that whatever he said is about to be, it will happen."

ᵉἐλάβετε, possibly a Semitism reflecting the Hebrew use of the "prophetic perfect" with its "certainty of future action" (Pesch, 2:206; *TCGNT*¹, 109–10; cf. a "futuristic aorist," BDF §333.2; Gnilka, 2:135). Other tense forms, such as λαμβάνετε, "receive," or λή(μ)ψεσθε, "will receive," are found in various MSS and are probably attempts to smooth out the syntax.

ᶠA few MSS read ὁ πατὴρ ἡμῶν, "our Father." This variant probably reflects the opening petition of the Matthean form of the Lord's Prayer (Matt 6:9), as well as Christian practice.

ᵍV 26, εἰ δὲ ὑμεῖς οὐκ ἀφίετε, οὐδὲ ὁ πατὴρ ὑμῶν ὁ ἐν τοῖς οὐρανοῖς ἀφήσει τὰ παραπτώματα ὑμῶν, "But if you do not forgive, neither will your Father in heaven forgive your trespasses," is found in A D 33 (with the omission of ὁ ἐν τοῖς οὐρανοῖς, "who is in heaven") and many later MSS. The verse is not present in ℵ B L W Δ Y 565 700 892 2427 and several other authorities. Metzger (*TCGNT*¹, 110) thinks that v 26 was inserted by a copyist in imitation of Matt 6:14–15. A fragment of 𝔓⁴⁵ resumes at Mark 11:27 (= fol. 8 verso) without a trace of v 26. But it is not possible to tell from this poorly preserved folio whether the doubtful verse had been in the text. See *Comment* below.

Form/Structure/Setting

Peter's exclamation in 11:21, "Master, behold, the fig tree that you cursed is withered!" occasions Jesus' teaching on faith, prayer, and forgiveness. The transition from the cursing of the fig tree in 11:12–14, to the eventual discovery of its destruction in 11:20–21, to teaching on faith, prayer, and *forgiveness* strikes many commentators as odd. Meier (*Marginal Jew* 2:888) comments: "one must admit that 11:22–25 as a unit is not as well integrated into the immediate context of Mark 11 and the larger context of Mark 11–15 as is the story of the cursing of the fig tree. In particular, the stipulation that forgiveness is a necessary condition for having one's prayers heard (v 25) strikes the reader as a strange commentary on Jesus' destructive curse of a tree that symbolizes the Temple." Meier (*Marginal Jew* 2:890) adds that the sayings that make up 11:20–25 "come from various sources; therefore the ending of the Marcan curse miracle [i.e. the cursing of the fig tree in 11:12–14] is not their original setting or context."

With regard to form, this pericope, as it stands in Mark's Gospel (11:22–25), is an apophthegm, a teaching narrative based on Jesus' cursing of the fig tree (Bultmann, *History*, 55). The use of the fig-tree story as a nature miracle to serve as the basis for the sayings on faith and prayer is obviously secondary, as Meier and many others have rightly pointed out. These logia stemming from Jesus' ministry circulated at one time independently of each other and of this story as isolated sayings. We find the mountain-moving faith saying (11:23) in the Q tradition (Matt 17:20; cf. Luke 17:6), in 1 Cor 13:2, and twice in *Gos. Thom.* (§§40, 106) without reference to faith. The promise for answered prayer (11:24) appears in John 14:13–14; 15:7, 16; 16:23–24 (cf. Matt 7:7–8 = Luke 11:9–10). In addition, Matt 6:14 parallels the forgiveness saying (11:25), and Matt 5:23 offers a material parallel. No two of these parallel logia, however, correspond exactly. They reflect variations arising in the process of their use and transmission in the tradition. The mountain-moving faith saying found in v 23 was "perhaps rooted in a popular proverb" and "circulated widely and independently of any larger context in first-generation Christianity" (Meier, *Marginal Jew* 2:889).

Much debate has focused on how Mark found these sayings in the tradition. Some commentators believe that he found the fig-tree story and the sayings as four, separate traditional units, which he has combined (e.g., Grundmann, 313; Haenchen, 391; cf. Lührmann, 190). Others believe that the evangelist found the miracle story combined with one (11:23, e.g., Pesch, 2:202; Telford, *Barren Temple*, 57) or more (11:23–25, e.g., Hahn, *ZNW* 76 [1985] 150; Schweizer, 232) of the sayings. Still others suggest that Mark found the miracle story and the sayings as two separate traditional units, with the latter having been combined by catchword association in the pre-Markan tradition (e.g., Ernst, 331; Gnilka, 2:123; Taylor, 465; Roloff, *Kerygma und der irdische Jesus*, 167).

The catchwords "faith" and "prayer," however, that supposedly led to the combination of 11:23–25 either in the tradition or by Mark are themselves the result of the consolidation of the traditional sayings behind 11:23–25; they did not exist in the traditional forms of 11:24 or 11:25 (see *Comment* on 11:24, 25). Therefore, these sayings were deliberately combined by a redactor to focus on prayer and its implications for the believer's relationship with God and with others. The redactor has often been identified as Mark.

Despite the arguments that Mark redactionally combined the fig-tree story with these sayings on prayer, the evidence does not stem from the hard data of vocabulary or style. The theme and context support a pre-Markan redaction (see *Comment* on 11:21–22 above). The focus of Mark's narrative in 11:1–12:40 is on Jesus and the authorities in contrast to 8:27–10:45 and 12:41–13:37 where it is on Jesus and his disciples. The teaching of the disciples on prayer in 11:22–25 comes as an interlude, a parenthesis, in the flow of this narrative. It is more likely that this interlude came as the result of Mark's use of the fig-tree story, which was already combined with Jesus' teaching on prayer (11:12–14, 22–25) and possibly with the temple demonstration (11:15–19), and which has interrupted the narrative flow of Jesus' entry into Jerusalem (11:1–11), the temple demonstration (11:15–19), and the ensuing dispute over authority (11:27b–33). This hardly seems to have been the place for the evangelist to add a section on prayer for the disciples. Rather, his faithful rendering of the tradition and the oblique, rather than primary, relationship of prayer in 11:17 to 11:23–25 deterred the evangelist from excising the teaching on faith and prayer and possibly relocating it elsewhere. Consequently, apart from some adaptation of 11:20 (see *Comment* on 11:12, 20 above), the Markan evangelist has taken over and preserved traditional material in 11:22–25.

With regard to setting, this story takes place on the third day in the sequence that began in 11:1. It is related to the previous day by the reference to the fig-tree event as well as by the motif of prayer. Peter's observation in 11:21, which was originally the end of the fig-tree miracle, i.e., its confirmation (11:20), becomes the basis for Jesus' teaching on prayer. Jesus' teaching on prayer has to do with one's relationship with God (11:22–24) and with others (11:25) and is only obliquely related to his teaching in the temple. In the temple precincts, Jesus cites Isa 56:7 regarding God's design for the temple to be "a house of prayer for all the Gentiles" in contrast to what it had in fact become—"a cave of robbers." Thus prayer is a connecting motif, although its development in 11:22–25 has nothing to do with either Isa 56:7 or the temple demonstration itself. This teaching stands closer thematically to 9:28–29. Therefore, its presence here serves as an interlude in the events of 11:1–33. Yet we shall again meet the motif of prayer in Jesus' warnings to his disciples in 13:33 and 14:38.

Comment

22 ἔχετε πίστιν θεοῦ, "have faith in God," stands out as an expression unique to the NT. Nowhere else does πίστιν θεοῦ, "faith in God," appear with θεοῦ, "God," as the objective genitive. The subjective genitive, "God's faithfulness," as in Rom 3:3 (τὴν πίστιν τοῦ θεοῦ), does not fit this context (cf. Lane, 409). Consequently, some scholars (e.g., Lohmeyer, 239; Nineham, 305; Telford, *Barren Temple*, 57, 98 n. 5) have considered the phrase to be a later scribal gloss (see *Note* b). Even should one take this unwarranted step, the object of faith obviously remains God.

The origin and meaning of this command stem in part from the following saying about mountain-moving faith. This saying comes to us in the double tradition of Mark (11:23 = Matt 21:21) and Q (Matt 17:20; cf. Luke 17:6). Mark diverges from the Q tradition in the command "Have faith in God!" No longer a part of an earlier protasis in the tradition behind 11:23, which spoke of having faith comparable to a mustard seed (cf. Matt 17:20; cf. Luke 17:6; see below), ἔχειν πίστιν, "to have faith," has been moved forward as an imperative, and the mustard seed comparison has been omitted in lieu of the specified object of faith, God (ἔχετε πίστιν θεοῦ, "have faith in God"). The imperative now stands as the introduction for what follows in 11:23–25. It summons the disciples to absolute trust in God as illustrated now by 11:23–24.

Just as Peter's observation in 11:21 provides the occasion for the sayings in 11:22–25, 11:22b, "Have faith in God!" drawn from the original tradition behind 11:23, now sets the tone for the combination of originally independent sayings in 11:23–25. The derivative character of this command ties it literarily and thematically to 11:23 and precludes its having originally concluded the fig-tree story (cf. Hasler, *Amen*, 42–43; Roloff, *Kerygma und der irdische Jesus*, 167). This literary and thematic relationship of 11:22b with 11:23–24 (cf. 11:25, where faith is not mentioned) strongly suggests a development when at least the saying of 11:23 was combined with 11:12–14, 20–21 (cf. Bultmann, *History*, 91; Zmijewski, "Glaube," 92). Since Mark has a "distinct preference for unqualified faith language" (Marshall, *Faith*, 230) without reference to an explicit object of faith (e.g., 2:5; 4:40; 5:34, 36; 6:6; 9:19, 23–24, 42; 10:52; cf. 1:15; 11:22, 31), this development most likely took place in the pre-Markan tradition. Thus Mark found the fig-tree story and the mountain-moving faith saying combined. The miracle (11:12–14, 20–21) now provided the basis for the saying (11:22–23).

23 The saying on mountain-moving faith appears in the Gospels (Matt 17:20; cf. Luke 17:6; Matt 22:21 = Mark 11:23) and in an abbreviated form in 1 Cor 13:2. By contrast, the *Gospel of Thomas* has two sayings about moving mountains (§§48, 106) without any mention of faith. Though the basic thrust remains constant, the structure and content of the forms of this saying differ considerably. Since the mountain-moving saying was obviously transmitted as an independent logion, its original setting in Jesus' ministry has been lost to us. The present contexts in Luke 17:5–6; Matt 17:19–20 (cf. Telford, *Barren Temple*, 104–9); and Mark 10:20–25 (cf. Pesch, 2:205) are secondary.

In a history-of-tradition study Hahn (*ZNW* 76 [1985] 149–69; similarly, Telford, *Barren Temple*, 95–119; cf. Zmijewski, "Glaube," 81–101) has posited an original saying consisting of the following elements: *(a)* an ἀμήν, "truly," formula, *(b)* a protasis speaking of ἔχειν πίστιν, "to have faith," comparable to a mustard seed, *(c)* a direct command to a mountain to be thrown into the sea, and *(d)* a concluding word about the effect. No one form of the saying in the Gospels entirely preserves the original logion, yet the Q form of Matt 17:20 comes closest (similarly Schweizer, 234; Pesch, 2:205; Telford, *Barren Temple*, 103; Lührmann, 195; id., *Glaube*, 20–21; cf. Zmijewski, "Glaube," 93–95; Schulz, *Q*, 465–68; Gnilka, 2:133, who favor Luke 17:6; cf. Pesch, 2:205, who favors Mark 11:23).

ἀμὴν λέγω ὑμῖν, "truly, I tell you," or "truly, I assure you." The roots of this introductory formula in the Jesus tradition (see Guelich, 177–78) and the proximity of Matt 17:20 to the earlier Q form (cf. Luke 17:6) argue for its authenticity here in Mark (cf. Berger, *Amen-Worte*, 33; Hasler, *Amen*, 43; Zmijewski, "Glaube," 91). For more on the asseverative use of ἀμήν, "truly," and its probable use by the historical Jesus, see B. D. Chilton, "'Amen': An Approach through Syriac Gospels," *ZNW* 69 (1978) 203–11; id., *Galilean Rabbi*, 202.

ὃς ἂν εἴπῃ τῷ ὄρει τούτῳ, "whoever should say to this mountain." Luke 17:6

has τῇ συκαμίνῳ [ταύτῃ], "[this] mulberry tree," whose deep tap root made removal very difficult (see Str-B 2:234; Telford, *Barren Temple*, 113–15). According to some commentators (e.g., H. Hunzinger, *TDNT* 7:289; Schulz, *Q*, 466–67; Zmijewski, "Glaube," 93–95; Fitzmyer, *Luke* 2:1142, cf. 1144!), this form represents the earlier version that was later modified in the light of the more familiar proverbial hyperbole of mountain moving. Yet the motif of the sea common to both Luke 17:6 (cf. Matt 17:20) and Mark 11:23 (= Matt 22:21) fits better with the disposal of a mountain than the transplanting of a tree, and the multiple references to a mountain (Matt 17:20; Mark 11:23; 1 Cor 13:2; *Gos. Thom.* §§48, 106) support the priority of the mountain motif (Hahn, "Glauben," 156; Fitzmyer, *Luke* 2:1144). Uprooting a notoriously deep-rooted tree, with its rabbinic parallels (Str-B 2:234; see below), represents a later, but pre-Lukan, softening of the hyperbole (cf. Matt 7:3; Mark 10:25) that misses the eschatological moment of the original saying (Telford, *Barren Temple*, 102–3; Hahn, *ZNW* 76 [1985] 156–58).

τῷ ὄρει τούτῳ, "this mountain." The proverbial character of the mountain-moving hyperbole supported by later rabbinic usage, the contextually independent transmission of this motif in the pre-Gospel tradition, and the different literary contexts for the saying in the Gospels, 1 Cor 13:2, and the *Gospel of Thomas* point to a metaphorical rather than concrete use of ὄρει, "mountain." This figurative rather than literal interpretation finds even further support if the original saying contained an eschatological allusion with roots in the OT (see below). In Mark's narrative, however, the demonstrative τούτῳ, "this," points, as Matt 21:22 shows, to a particular rather than general referent. Matt 17:21 and Luke 17:6, on the other hand, may simply reflect the influence of Mark's usage. In the narrative context of the fig tree (11:20; cf. 11:12, "after leaving Bethany"), τῷ ὄρει τούτῳ, "this mountain," could refer to the Mount of Olives (so Gundry, 649, 654; id., *Matthew*, 418) from whose eastern slopes one can see the Dead Sea. In favor of this suggestion is the ostensible setting of the saying on or near the Mount of Olives as well as the possible allusion to Zech 14:4: "On that day his feet shall stand on the Mount of Olives which lies before Jerusalem on the east; and the Mount of Olives shall be split in two from east to west by a very wide valley; so that one half of the Mount shall withdraw northward, and the other half southward" (cf. Zech 4:7: "What are you, O great mountain? Before Zerubbabel you shall become a plain"). Several commentators have taken this position (Gould, 215; Turner, 56; Rawlinson, 158; Klostermann, 118; Lohmeyer, 239 n. 2; Schmid, 211; Lane, 410; Gnilka, 2:134; Stock, 299; Dowd, *Prayer*, 72–75; Hurtado, 188; Brooks, 183; Buchanan, "Withering Fig Trees," 266).

But the mountain Jesus referred to may have been the Temple Mount—at least the Markan evangelist probably thought so, given his context for the saying. Jesus enters the temple precincts in 11:11, where he looks around, and then the following day he re-enters the precincts and condemns temple polity. Jesus will soon return and be challenged by the ruling priests, who will demand to know by what authority he has done what he has done (11:27–33). Why should not τῷ ὄρει τούτῳ, "this mountain," refer to Israel's most famous mountain, on which was situated the temple establishment with which Jesus had come into serious conflict? Of course, the reference to throwing the mountain into the sea is not to be equated with the literal destruction of the temple (as Marshall, *Faith*, 169, rightly cautions), as hinted at in 11:17 and explicitly prophesied in 13:2. But in the Markan context, where there is a protracted controversy between Jesus and the temple establishment, such an interpretation seems quite natural. It matters little which mountain—the Mount of Olives or the Temple Mount—affords the better view of the Dead Sea in the distance. Given the hyperbolic nature of the saying, it makes no difference which mountain is to be thrown into which sea (Mediterranean Sea, Dead Sea, or Sea of Galilee for that matter). Scholars who opt for the Temple Mount include C. H. Dodd (*The Parables of the Kingdom* [London: Nisbet, 1935] 63 n. 1), Dowda ("Cleansing," 250), Telford (*Barren Temple*, 119), Broadhead (*Paradigms* 2 [1986] 33–38), Marshall (*Faith*, 168–69), Swartley (*Israel's Scripture Traditions*, 160), and Wright (*Jesus and the Victory of God*, 334–35). For further discussion, see Berger, *Amen-Worte*, 46–48; Gaston, *No Stone*, 82–84.

Commentators frequently appeal to various rabbinic and Jewish parallels to the saying about moving mountains in faith. Among the frequently cited texts are *T. Sol.* 23:1, where a demon says to Solomon, "I am able to move mountains [ὄρη μεταστῆναι]"; *b. Ber.* 64a: "Rabbah was an 'uprooter of mountains' [עוקר הרים *ʿôqēr hārîm*]"; *b. Sanh.* 24a: "You would think he was uprooting mountains and grinding them against each other"; *b. B. Bat.* 3b: "I will uproot mountains"; and *Lev. Rab.* 8.8 (on Lev 6:13): "[Samson] took two mountains and knocked them one against another." None of these examples offers a close parallel beyond the general idea of moving mountains. The reference to Rabbah has to do with his skill as an interpreter, while the other examples have to do with strength (whether literal or figurative). Jesus' point that *faith* can move mountains seems to be unparalleled. More will be said about this in the following comments.

ἄρθητι καὶ βλήθητι εἰς τὴν θάλασσαν, "be taken up and be cast into the sea," sets the original saying off from a proverbial mountain-moving hyperbole that merely assures the believer of accomplishing the impossible or extraordinary (cf. Matt 17:20; 1 Cor 13:2). We have to do here with mountain removal rather than mountain moving, an activity with an OT background. This motif accompanies the promised day of salvation as part of the transformation of the cosmos (e.g., Isa 40:3–5; 45:2; 49:11; cf. 54:10; Zech 14:4–5; *Pss. Sol.* 11:4; Bar 5:7; cf. Hahn, *ZNW* 76 [1985] 157; Telford, *Barren Temple*, 116). Add to this the fact that the mountain-removing command issues from faith in the NT (11:22b; Matt 17:20; cf. Luke 17:6; Matt 22:21; similarly 1 Cor 13:2) and this independent saying takes on an eschatological hue (Hahn, *ZNW* 76 [1985] 157, 168; Telford, *Barren Temple*, 116). It admits the one who has placed his faith totally in God into participation in God's redemptive, transforming activity of the day of salvation (Hahn, *ZNW* 76 [1985] 168). As such, the original form of the saying not only brings those who had committed themselves in faith to God through Jesus' ministry into participation in God's promised redemptive activity but also reveals Jesus' own conviction that God was redemptively at work and that the promised day of salvation had dawned. Therefore, the original saying in Jesus' ministry carried an eschatological thrust (cf. Zmijewski, "Glaube," 95–96).

μὴ διακριθῇ ἐν τῇ καρδίᾳ αὐτοῦ, "should not waver in his heart," represents the opposite of "have faith in God" (v 22). A "not . . . but" (μή + subjunctive/ἀλλά + subjunctive) formula missing from the Q saying of Matt 17:20 (cf. Luke 17:6), it fills the gap left by the transforming of the conditional "if you have faith as a mustard seed" in the Q saying into the introductory command to "have faith in God" of v 22b (Hahn, *ZNW* 76 [1985] 153–54). This statement provides a negative definition for faith in God. Not merely the belief that God can or will do the impossible, faith here as elsewhere in Mark represents more than an attitude or state of mind. It means taking a risk with one's total person, one's καρδία, "heart," a commitment and a response to God in light of Jesus' ministry (see Guelich, 85–86). Jesus calls for an absolute, unconditional commitment to or trust in God.

This relationship with God leads then to the confidence—ἀλλὰ πιστεύῃ, "but should believe"—that what one says (ὃ λαλεῖ) to "this mountain" will happen (γίνεται). Here faith moves from an expression of one's life posture towards God (v 22) to one's attitude or confidence about what will happen based on that life posture before God.

ἔσται αὐτῷ, "it will be done for him," offers the concluding assurance of the results. Each of the four forms of the saying (Matt 17:20; Luke 17:6; Mark 11:23; Matt 21:21) has a similar concluding statement, but no two are alike. The assurance stems from the fact that it is God alone who makes the impossible possible, since it is God who is ultimately and redemptively at work through the one who has yielded totally to God.

Peter's astonished remark at what happened to the fig tree (v 21) now provides the occasion for Jesus to teach his disciples about what God can do through one who has faith in God (vv 22–23). Therefore, the fig-tree episode is an illustration on a smaller scale (cf. Matt 21:21, οὐ μόνον τὸ τῆς συκῆς ποιήσετε, "you will not only do what has been done to the fig tree") of God's ability to make the impossible possible through those who have totally placed their faith in God. The eschatological character of God's redemptive, mountain-removing activity in the original saying has not been totally lost, but the emphasis has shifted to what is possible for or through those of faith. This same emphasis now marks the forms of the saying in Luke 17:6; Matt 17:20; 1 Cor 13:2 (cf. *Gos. Thom.* §§48, 106).

24 This saying appears in various forms in Matt 21:22 = Mark 11:23; John 14:13–14; 15:7, 16; 16:23–24 (cf. Matt 7:7–8 = Luke 11:9–10). The other forms consist primarily of references to asking (αἰτεῖν) and receiving (λαμβάνειν: Matt 21:22; Matt 7:8 = Luke 11:10; John 15:7; 16:23; διδόναι, "to give": Matt 7:7 = Luke 11:9; John 15:16; 16:24; cf. John 14:13–14). Here the saying definitely reflects the influence of 11:23 on its structure and content: (*a*) ἀμὴν λέγω ὑμῖν, "truly, I tell you"/λέγω ὑμῖν, "I tell you" (cf. John 16:23); (*b*) πιστεύῃ ὅτι . . . γίνεται, "should believe that . . . [it] happens"/πιστεύετε ὅτι ἐλάβετε, "believe that you have received"; (*c*) ἔσται αὐτῷ, "it will be done for him"/ἔσται ὑμῖν, "it will be yours." Most telling is the location of the "receiving" element in v 24. It is now a part of a subordinate clause on the subject of faith or believing, a clause and a concept that are foreign to the other forms of the saying (cf. Matt 21:22 = Mark 11:24) and clearly a secondary adaptation to a similar clause in v 23. Therefore, instead of creating a catchword combination of vv 23 and 24 based on πίστις, "faith," or πιστεύειν, "to believe," the redactor who combined this saying with v 23 did so in order to use Jesus' teaching about mountain-removing faith (v 23) as the grounds for the assurance of answered prayer in v 24. That this redaction took place at a pre-Markan stage can be seen both in terms of the verse's style and its content. Meier (*Marginal Jew* 2:889) rightly comments that "we are dealing in these examples not with common literary sources but rather with similar yet independent streams of oral tradition of Jesus' sayings, sayings that circulated without a set context."

διὰ τοῦτο, "for this reason." The evangelist neither uses this phrase to introduce sayings (cf. Matt 6:25 = Luke 12:22, 31, 43) nor does he use it redactionally elsewhere (cf. 6:14; 12:24). It closely links what follows to the previous solemn declaration and makes the declaration of mountain-removing faith the logical basis for the assurance of answered prayer. At the same time, this promise, at least by implication, makes the command to "this mountain" in v 24 an expression of prayer through which God removes mountains.

λέγω ὑμῖν, "I tell you." The combination λέγω ὑμῖν occurs in Mark sixteen times (3:28; 8:12; 9:1, 13, 41; 10:15, 29; 11:23, 24, 33; 12:43; 13:30, 37; 14:9, 18, 25), and twelve of these occurrences are prefaced with ἀμήν, "truly." The fuller combination, ἀμὴν λέγω ὑμῖν, "truly, I tell you," occurs in v 23 above (see the discussion of ἀμήν in the *Comment* above). Although ἀμήν is the primary utterance that conveys the asseverative sense, Jesus' style of saying λέγω ὑμῖν seems to have a similar function. This manner of speaking derives from Jesus, often introducing especially important teaching.

πάντα ὅσα προσεύχεσθε καὶ αἰτεῖσθε, "all that you pray and ask for." πάντα ὅσα, "all [things] that," is rare in Mark, a traditional expression in 3:28 and 12:43–44 (cases where the introduction ἀμὴν λέγω ὑμῖν, "truly, I tell you," also appears) and perhaps redactional in 6:30. The other forms of the saying simply have a neuter object (ὅ τι, "whatever"/τι, "anything"). The expansive πάντα ὅσα, "all [things] that," may correspond to the magnitude of the mountain-removing command in v 23.

προσεύχεσθε, "you pray," stands out as part of a compound verb with αἰτεῖσθε, "you ask." αἰτεῖν, "to ask," definitely connotes prayer (cf. "in my name" or "the Father" in John 14:13, 14; 15:16; 16:24), so that the addition of προσεύχεσθαι, "to pray," underscores the prayer motif. Since αἰτεῖν appears consistently in the traditional forms of the saying, προσεύχεσθαι is most likely a secondary development to underscore the prayer motif, a motif that is the explicit link to v 25 and becomes the primary focus of the sayings in vv 23–25. But who added this verb and the related v 25? The evangelist Mark or a pre-Markan redactor? The objective data of style and vocabulary are inconclusive, so one can only speak of probabilities in terms of the thrust of vv 23–25 as a whole and Mark's present context for this material in 11:1–33. Therefore, one must first consider v 25 before answering this question.

More important is the question of how v 25 fits into Mark's narrative. Prayer in general and petitionary prayer in particular are not major themes in Mark's Gospel. Yet the use of prayer in this context is reminiscent of Jesus' answer to the disciples' question in 9:28–29, a passage that may reflect or be reflected in the use here. When the disciples are unable to exorcise the demon from the young boy, Jesus tells them, "This kind cannot come out by any means except by prayer [εἰ μὴ ἐν προσευχῇ]" (see *Comment* on 9:29 above). In other words, prayer gives expression of one's relationship with God and makes possible the impossible, if God is the agent (cf. 10:27). This is certainly implicit in Jesus' having just done what the disciples could not do by exorcising the demon in 9:20–27 as well as by cursing the fig tree (11:21–22), but it is also explicit in the references to Jesus praying in the context of his own ministry (1:35; 6:46; 14:32, 35, 39) and in the warnings given to the disciples in 13:33 and 14:38 to watch and pray.

Furthermore, the reader will have just read/heard Jesus' citation from Isa 56:7

regarding the temple as the "house of prayer" (11:17a) as well as the allusion to its impending destruction, which is implied by the citation from Jer 7:11 (11:17b), and the story of the fruitless fig tree (11:14). Prayer in this context, therefore, reflects one's relationship with God through faith by being the expression of that faith relationship (Gnilka, 2:135). In the words of Marshall, "Mark sees prayer as faith-verbalized" (*Faith*, 171). Accordingly, the exchange of the temple as a "house of prayer" for a "cave of robbers" in Jesus' charge of 11:17 indicates not only the absence of prayer but more critically the absence of faith in God (cf. 12:40). The temple, which was to be called the "house of prayer for all the Gentiles," is no longer the locus for prayer or faith (cf. 15:38–39!).

πιστεύετε, "believe." This secondary accommodation of the saying to the same motif in v 23 expresses the confidence one has in coming to God in prayer. πιστεύειν ὅτι, "to believe that," grows out of one's πίστις θεοῦ, "faith in God" (v 22b), expressed in the petitionary prayer. It is not the condition for answered prayer except in the sense that faith in God is the very basis for prayer itself. In other words, one believes that the mountain will be cast into the sea (v 23), that all one's requests will be answered (v 24), on the basis of one's relation to God through faith. Faith as a relationship rather than faith as an attitude of the mind allows God to accomplish God's redemptive work through the believer's words of prayer.

ὅτι ἐλάβετε, "that you have received it," expresses the confidence of that belief through the certainty of the future fulfillment of the request (see *Note* e above).

25 ὅταν στήκετε προσευχόμενοι, "whenever you stand praying." Standing was a common posture among the Jewish people at prayer (cf. 1 Kgs 8:14, 22; Ps 134:1; Jer 18:20; Matt 6:5; Luke 18:11, 13). In fact, it is for this reason that the famous synagogue prayer, the *Šĕmôneh 'Eśreh*, "Eighteen," or Eighteen Benedictions, is also called the *'Amîdâ*, that is, the "Standing." This setting of prayer offers the only connecting link (προσεύχεσθαι, "to pray") to the previous verse. Since προσεύχεσθε, "you pray," in v 24 represents a secondary expansion of the saying by comparison to its other parallels in the Gospels, this saying on forgiveness, assuming the presence of this prayer setting, would most likely have been combined with v 24 by the same redactor who added προσεύχεσθε to that saying. It is also possible that the redactor created the prayer setting for v 25 as a link for the two sayings, since the prayer setting is missing in the material parallel in Matt 6:14. This clause in v 25 contains two rarities that occur elsewhere in Mark: the verb στήκειν, "to stand" (cf. 3:31), and ὅταν, "whenever," with the indicative (cf. 3:11; 11:19). Furthermore, these rarities appear elsewhere in Mark's redactional material (see Guelich, 148, 181). Yet these data hardly point conclusively to Mark's redaction since the evangelist uses the much more common verb ἱστάναι, "to stand," eleven times, and ὅταν, "whenever," with the subjunctive seventeen times. In any event, this introductory setting emphasizes the prayer motif now implicit (v 23) and explicit (v 24) in all three sayings.

ἀφίετε εἴ τι ἔχετε κατά τινος, "forgive if you have something against someone." Nowhere else in Mark is there teaching on the need for people to forgive others. Jesus himself in Mark 2:1–12 pronounces the sins of the paralyzed man forgiven, which then stirs up controversy over the legitimacy of his forgiving sins (see esp. 2:5, 7, 9, 10). In 3:28–29 Jesus warns his critics that blasphemy against the Holy Spirit cannot be forgiven, while in 4:12 Jesus paraphrases Isa 6:9–10 to show that outsiders refuse to see and hear, lest they repent and be forgiven. The language in 11:25 is similar to that of Matt 6:14 (which will be considered in the next paragraph), but the general theme is reminiscent of teaching found in the first of the "antitheses" found in the Matthean Sermon on the Mount (Matt 5:21–26). There Jesus tells his disciples: "So if you are offering your gift at the altar, and there remember that your brother has something against you, leave your gift there before the altar and go; first be reconciled to your brother, and then come and offer your gift" (Matt 5:23–24). To be reconciled to one's brother implies the extension of forgiveness.

ἵνα καὶ ὁ πατὴρ ὑμῶν ὁ ἐν τοῖς οὐρανοῖς ἀφῇ ὑμῖν τὰ παραπτώματα ὑμῶν, "so that your Father in heaven may also forgive you your transgressions," appears on the surface to be reminiscent of Matt 6:7–15. ὁ πατὴρ ὑμῶν ὁ ἐν τοῖς οὐρανοῖς, "your Father in heaven," echoes the opening words of the Lord's Prayer in Matt 6:9 (cf. Luke 11:2). The mutual relationship of forgiving and being forgiven, as well as the use of παραπτώματα, "transgressions," which is *hapax legomenon* in Mark (since v 26 is a scribal gloss; see *Note* g), rounds off Matt 6:14–15. But these concepts are not limited to Matt 6:7–15. ὁ πατὴρ ὁ ἐν τοῖς οὐρανοῖς, "Father in heaven," frequently found in Matthew (cf. Luke 11:13), was a common Jewish designation for God (for examples, see Str-B 1:410–11; W. Schrenk, *TDNT* 5:979–80). The relationship between forgiving and being forgiven has a parallel in the Lord's Prayer, and a comparable forgiveness motif appears in Matt 5:7 and 18:21–35 (cf. Sir 38:2). Therefore, v 25bc may well reflect an earlier, less stylized form of the saying that now underlies Matt 6:14 (Pesch, 2:207; cf. Lohmeyer, 239; Lührmann, 195). Although the Markan tradition bears a resemblance to Matthew's M source, it is probably better to view it as an independent saying that also happened to find its way into the M tradition (Meier, *Marginal Jew* 2:889–90).

One misses the nature of the reciprocity in all these passages if God's forgiveness is somehow seen as caused or earned by one's forgiving of others. As the parable of the Unforgiving Servant in Matt 18:21–35 illustrates, one's own forgiving of others must grow out of one's being forgiven. Therefore, to be forgiven and not forgiving, to have obtained mercy and not be merciful, is in reality to have failed to experience God's gracious acceptance and makes a mockery out of prayer as understood in vv 22–24 as an expression of one's relationship to God.

This saying seems out of place in Mark's narrative. Its content has to do primarily neither with faith nor with prayer but with forgiveness. Furthermore, it has "Matthean" vocabulary and phrases, yet Matthew does not have a parallel to it in 21:21–22. Consequently, some scholars have ascribed it to a scribal gloss from Matt 6:14–15 along with the obvious gloss in v 26 (see *Note* g) (e.g., Klostermann, 119; Telford, *Barren Temple*, 50–54; cf. Bultmann, *History*, 25, 61; Lane, 410–11; Nineham, 305). This explanation seems quite reasonable, but it has no textual support at all, a fact that is all the more telling in view of the textual evidence for the omission of v 26. In fact, the presence of v 25 might well have attracted the verbally and thematically related v 26 from Matt 6:15, but the difference in language and content between vv 23–24 and v 25 make it improbable for a scribe to have inserted v 25.

The tension between v 25 and Mark's narrative setting may hold the strongest clue to its source. The non-Markan introduction of v 24 and its alignment with v 23 point to a pre-Markan combination of vv 23–24 around a prayer motif that takes the mountain-removing faith saying (v 23) as its basis. The adaptation and the emphasis on prayer would have been enhanced by the addition of προσεύχεσθε, "you pray," in v 24 to supplement αἰτεῖσθε, "you ask." This addition in turn would set the stage for the introduction of the saying on forgiveness (v 25) into a complex on prayer that taught that one's prayer not only gave expression to one's relationship to God but also had implications for one's relationship to others. Since it is highly unlikely that the Markan evangelist would have introduced this independent saying on forgiveness into his literary context, a context that speaks at most of faith and prayer (11:15–19), he most likely would have found it as part of a traditional complex of isolated sayings around the fig-tree story formed and used in the early church as a prayer catechism.

This traditional complex had a dual function for him. By framing the temple demonstration (11:15–19) with this tradition (11:12–14, 20–25), the evangelist used (a) the "curse miracle" of the fig tree (11:12–14, 20–21) to underscore Jesus' teaching about the coming destruction of the temple, implied in the allusion to Jer 7:11 (11:17b), and (b) the "prayer catechism" (11:22–25) to highlight Jesus' teaching about prayer as the expression of one's faith in God, certainly implicit in the citation of Isa 56:7 (11:17a). The motif of forgiveness (11:25) belongs to the whole but has no particular significance for this setting. Its presence here reflects again Mark's faithfulness to the tradition.

26 [εἰ δὲ ὑμεῖς οὐκ ἀφίετε, οὐδὲ ὁ πατὴρ ὑμῶν ὁ ἐν τοῖς οὐρανοῖς ἀφήσει τὰ παραπτώματα ὑμῶν, "but if you do not forgive, neither will your Father in heaven forgive your trespasses."] For reasons cited above in *Note* g, this verse is regarded as a later scribal gloss, probably in imitation of Matt 6:14–15, and not as original to the Gospel of Mark. Matt 6:14–15 reads: ἐὰν γὰρ ἀφῆτε τοῖς ἀνθρώποις τὰ παραπτώματα αὐτῶν, ἀφήσει καὶ ὑμῖν ὁ πατὴρ ὑμῶν ὁ οὐράνιος· ἐὰν δὲ μὴ ἀφῆτε τοῖς ἀνθρώποις, οὐδὲ ὁ πατὴρ ὑμῶν ἀφήσει τὰ παραπτώματα ὑμῶν, "For if you forgive men their trespasses, your heavenly Father also will forgive you; but if you do not forgive men their trespasses, neither will your Father forgive your trespasses." The RSV, the NRSV, the NASB, and most other modern translations and paraphrases omit v 26, but it is retained in the KJV and the ASV.

The scribe's gloss represents an attempt to fill out Mark's teaching on prayer and at the same time reveals his familiarity with the wider context of Matt 6:5–15, which encompasses the Lord's Prayer. In the Matthean context one finds an implicit emphasis on the need for faith: God who sees in secret will reward (6:6); God knows what people need before they ask (6:8). The Matthean cluster explicitly emphasizes the need for forgiveness, as seen in the teaching on the reciprocity of forgiving and being forgiven (6:12, 14–15). Compared to this Matthean template, the briefer Markan passage may very well have struck a later scribe as incomplete and thus in need of augmentation.

Explanation

When the Markan evangelist found the fig-tree story in the tradition, it doubtless was already combined with the sayings on mountain-removing faith (v 23) and prayer (vv 24–25), and may have been linked to the temple demonstration (11:15–19). The miracle story had become the basis for and illustration of Jesus' summmons to faith in God (11:21–22). After Peter notes the effect of Jesus' words on the fig tree (11:21), Jesus counters his astonishment (11:21) by calling the disciples to faith in God, that is, to commit their total person to God in the light of Jesus' own ministry (v 22).

By calling the disciples to faith in God in the setting of the fig tree, Jesus attributes his own astonishing work to God and offers those who put their faith in God the opportunity likewise to become participants in God's redemptive, mountain-removing activity (v 23). The OT background for mountain-moving or mountain-removing language, coming as it does in the context of God's promised day of salvation with personal and cosmic implications (e.g., Isa 40:3–5; 45:2; 49:11; cf. 54:10; Zech 14:4–5; *Pss. Sol.* 11:4; Bar 5:7), indicates that Jesus was speaking about God's promised redemptive activity in the world. One is not to trivialize this promise, as though God were merely in the earth-moving business. Yet God is in the business of removing personal and physical mountains that stand in the way of God's promised salvation. Furthermore, God moves these mountains through those who have yielded their lives in faith to God.

The faith in God (v 22), the relationship to total commitment to God, that attunes one to God and allows God to accomplish God's redemptive mountain-removing tasks through the believer provides confidence that all that the believer asks shall happen (v 24). Rather than the power of positive thinking or the power of thinking positively, Jesus offers the power of God to accomplish God's redemptive will through those whose requests are based on and have grown out of a relationship with God, those who have faith in God.

At the same time, this teaching on prayer underscores the relationship between prayer as an expression of faith in God and forgiveness of others. One cannot have a faith relationship with God without it affecting one's relationship with others. One cannot be right with and before God and be at odds with one's brother or sister.

The evangelist Mark, however, takes this traditional complex of miracle story (the cursing of the fig tree, 11:12–14, 20–21) that served as the basis for and illustration of Jesus' teaching about one's faith relationship with God as expressed in prayer (vv 22–25) and uses it to frame the temple demonstration in 11:15–19, thus dividing the traditional complex into two parts (11:12–19, 20–25). Consequently, on the one hand, the fig-tree event of 11:12–14 now serves as the interpretive framework for Jesus' action and teaching in the temple in 11:15–19. Both stories now speak of the temple's destruction—the one symbolically, the other prophetically.

On the other hand, the Markan evangelist emphasizes the motif of prayer as the expression of this fundamental relationship, faith in God, in two ways. First, he sets 11:20–25 in the interpretive context of the temple demonstration where in 11:17 Jesus announces the coming destruction of the temple because what was designed by God to be a "house of prayer for all the Gentiles" (Isa 56:7) had become a "cave of robbers" (Jer 7:11). In other words, the exposition of prayer in vv 22–24 picks up and offers the background to Jesus' reference to prayer in 11:17. The temple was no longer the place of prayer as an expression of faith in God (cf. 12:40). The Temple Mount may as well be hurled into the sea. Second, God's redemptive will and work are to be seen in Jesus and his ministry, which calls one to faith in God (11:20–22), a relationship that in turn is expressed in prayer.

F. The Question of Jesus' Authority   (11:27–33)

Bibliography

Bishop, E. F. F. "Jesus Walking or Teaching in the Temple (Mk xi.27, Jn x.23)." *ExpTim* 63 (1952) 226–27. **Black, M.** *Aramaic Approach.* 81. **Colson, F. H.** "Mark xi 27 and Parallels." *JTS* o.s. 25 (1925) 71–72. **Daube, D.** "Rabbinic Authority." In *The New Testament and Rabbinic Judaism.* London: Athlone, 1956. 205–23. **Eppstein, V.** "The Historicity of the Gospel Account of the Cleansing of the Temple." *ZNW* 55 (1964) 42–58. **Howard, V. P.** *Das Ego Jesu in den synoptischen Evangelien: Untersuchungen zum Sprachgebrauch Jesu.* Marburger theologische Studien 14. Marburg: Elwert, 1975. 107–16. **Hultgren, A. J.** *Jesus and His Adversaries: The Form and Function of the Conflict Stories in the Synoptic Tradition.* Minneapolis: Augsburg, 1979. 68–75. **Ireland, W. J., Jr.** "'By What Authority?' Toward the Construction of a Symbolic World in Mark." Diss., Southern Baptist Theological Seminary, 1987. **Jeremias, J.** *Jesus als Weltvollender.* Gütersloh: Bertelsmann, 1929. **Kim, S.** "Jesus—The Son of God, the Stone, the Son of Man, and the Servant: The Role of Zechariah in the Self-Identification of Jesus." In *Tradition and Interpretation in the New Testament.* FS E. E. Ellis, ed. G. F. Hawthorne and O. Betz. Grand Rapids, MI: Eerdmans, 1987. 134–48. ———. "Die Vollmacht Jesu und der Tempel (Markus 11/12): Der Sinn der 'Tempelreinigung' und der geschichtliche und theologische Zusammenhang des Prozesses Jesu." *ANRW* 2.26.1. Forthcoming. **Knox, W. L.** *The Sources of the Synoptic Gospels.* Cambridge: Cambridge UP, 1953. 85–92. **Kremer, J.** "Jesu Antwort auf die Frage nach seiner Vollmacht: Eine Auslegung von Mk 11,27–33." *BibLeb* 9 (1968) 128–36. **Lee, M. Y.-H.** *Jesus und die jüdische Autorität: Eine exegetische Untersuchung zu Mk 11,27–12,12.* FB 56. Würzburg: Echter, 1986. **Marshall, C. D.** *Faith as a Theme in Mark's Narrative.* 195–200. **Marucci, C.** "Die implizite Christologie in der sogenannten Vollmachtsfrage (Mk 11,27–33)." *ZTK* 108 (1986) 292–300. **Meier, J. P.** *Marginal Jew.* 2:163–67. **Mell, U.** *Die "andere" Winzer: Eine exegetische Studie zur Vollmacht Jesu Christi nach Markus 11,27–12,34.* WUNT 77. Tübingen: Mohr-Siebeck, 1995. 42–73. **Mohr, T. A.** *Markus- und Johannespassion.* 100–108. **Mudiso Mbâ Mundla, J.-G.** *Jesus und die Führer Israels: Studien zu den sogenannten Jerusalemer Streitgesprächen.* NTAbh 17. Münster: Aschendorff, 1984. 5–40. **Pesch, R.** *Evangelium der Urgemeinde.* 140–43. **Roloff, J.** *Das Kerygma und der irdische Jesus.* 93–95. **Schmidt, K. L.** *Rahmen.* 293–95. **Schnackenburg, R.** "Die Vollmacht Jesu: Zu Mk 11,27–33." *Katholische Gedanke* 27 (1971) 105–9. **Shae, G. S.** "The Question on the Authority of Jesus." *NovT* 16 (1974) 1–29. **Söding, T.** *Glaube bei Markus.* 148–49. **Taylor, V.** *The Names of Jesus.* London: Macmillan, 1953. **Tödt, H. E.** *The Son of Man in the Synoptic Tradition.* Tr. D. M. Barton. Philadelphia: Westminster, 1965. **Webb, R. L.** "John the Baptist and His Relationship to Jesus." In *Studying the Historical Jesus: Evaluations of the State of Current Research.* Ed. B. D. Chilton and C. A. Evans. NTTS 19. Leiden: Brill, 1994. 179–229. **Weiss, W.** *"Eine neue Lehre in Vollmacht": Die Streit- und Schulgespräche des Markus-Evangeliums.* BZNW 52. Berlin; New York: de Gruyter, 1989. 143–62. **Westcott, B. F., and Hort, F. J. A.** *New Testament.* 2:26.

Translation

[27]*And they again enter Jerusalem. And as he walked about in the temple, the ruling priests, scribes, and elders*[a] *approach him,* [28]*and were asking him, "By what*[b] *authority do you do these things?" and "Who has given to you this authority, so that*[c] *you may do these things?"* [29]*But Jesus said to them, "I shall ask you one thing. If you answer me,*[d] *then I shall tell you by what authority I do these things.* [30]*Was the baptism of John from*

heaven or of human origin? Answer me!" [31] *So they discussed it among themselves, saying,*[e] *"If we should say, 'from heaven,' he will say,*[f] *'[Then] why did you not believe him?'* [32] *But if we should say, 'of human origin' . . . ?"—they were afraid*[g] *of the crowd;*[h] *for all regarded*[i] *John as truly*[j] *a prophet.* [33] *And answering Jesus, they say, "We do not know." And Jesus says to them, "Neither am I telling you by what authority I am doing these things."*

Notes

[a]D and a few late MSS read οἱ πρεσβύτεροι τοῦ λαοῦ, "elders of the people" (cf. Matt 21:23).

[b]Use of ποίᾳ, "what," as equivalent of τίνι, "what" (12:28; Matt 24:42; Acts 23:34; cf. BDF §298.2).

[c]Use of ἵνα, "so that," is a Semitism for consecutive ד *dĕ* in Aram. (cf. Black, *Aramaic Approach,* 81).

[d]Impv. ἀποκρίθητέ μοι, "if you answer me" (lit. "answer me"), followed by fut. may reflect a Semitic influence that functions like a protasis in a conditional sentence; cf. K. Beyer, *Semitische Syntax im Neuen Testament,* 1/1 (Göttingen: Vandenhoeck & Ruprecht, 1961) 252.

[e]Taylor (471), followed by Cranfield (363), reads τί εἴπωμεν, "What should we say?" with D Θ Φ *f*[13] 28 565 700, but support is weak; cf. *TCGNT*[1], 110.

[f]D W and several late MSS read ἐρεῖ ἡμῖν, "he will say to us."

[g]D N W Σ and several late MSS read φοβούμεθα, "we are afraid."

[h]A D L W and several late MSS read λαόν, "people."

[i]Gk. εἶχον, lit. "were having"; a Latinism (so Taylor, 471; BAGD) that also appears in Gk. papyri. D W and a few late MSS read ᾔδεισαν, "knew"; 700 reads οἴδασι, "know"; these are secondary attempts to smooth out the construction (cf. Luke 20:6).

[j]Gk. ὄντως, lit. "really." D reads ἀληθῶς, lit. "truly."

Form/Structure/Setting

In its present setting, the question put to Jesus is clearly in response to the temple demonstration in 11:15–17. The ruling priests, scribes, and elders approach Jesus and demand to know by what authority does Jesus do these things and who gave him this authority. Jesus does not answer their question. Rather, he defiantly counters with a question of his own: he will ask them a question, and if they answer it, he will answer theirs. Without waiting for their agreement to this arrangement—the outcome of the story suggests that the ruling priests and colleagues give tacit assent—Jesus asks his interlocutors the source of John's authority. Faced with an obvious dilemma, the ruling priests refuse to answer: "We do not know." Recognizing their answer as a refusal to answer, Jesus concludes the interview with the words "Neither am I telling you by what authority I am doing these things."

In its present form this pericope follows the classic lines of a controversy narrative (cf. Shae, *NovT* 16 [1974] 10): (*a*) occasion (v 27), (*b*) question (v 28), (*c*) response (vv 29–33). Like 12:13–17, the response here, a counterquestion (11:28–29), is expanded to include a response from the questioner (v 32) followed by the climactic response of the questioned (v 33). This complex controversy narrative has two significant variations. First, we find a parenthetical discussion of the dilemma posed by the counterquestion to the adversaries (vv 30–31). Second, the climactic response does not answer the incriminating question but avoids it (v 33). These variations from the usual form have led to numerous explanations that generally seek an original pericope stemming from Jesus' ministry that has been expanded and modified to address a need of the early church.

Bultmann (*History*, 20), for example, finds the core to be vv 28–30, an apoph-thegm involving the discussion of John's baptism. More recently, Hultgren (*Jesus and His Adversaries*, 70) takes the original part of the story to have been a contro-versy narrative set in the context of the temple demonstration and consisting of vv 27b, 28b, 29a, and 30. By contrast, Shae (*NovT* 16 [1974] 1–29), in a thorough analysis of the tradition history, has posited an earlier story consisting of vv 28b, 30, and a response followed by a climactic response (replaced by later develop-ments) similar to the form of a rabbinic-school discussion (see *Comment* on v 29).

All of these scholars trace the original setting (*Sitz im Leben*) to Jesus' ministry but locate it according to their individual understanding of the thrust of the story: Bultmann (*History*, 19–20) and Shae (*NovT* 16 [1974] 14–19) place it in the the context of the discussion between John's disciples and Jesus (similarly, Gnilka, 2:137), and Hultgren (*Jesus and His Adversaries*, 72) traces it to a scene in the temple. The development into its present form, however, supposedly reflects the early church's controversy with the synagogue that sought to expose the Jews' unbelief and Jesus' authority (Gnilka, 2:137; Schweizer, 236; Shae, *NovT* 16 [1974] 19–20). The development enhanced the original story by focusing on Jesus' per-son (vv 28a, 29b, 33) and the nature of his authority as the "son of man" in order to "proclaim and teach the unique status of Jesus" (Hultgren, *Jesus and His Adver-saries*, 72–75).

A more rigorous form-critical look at this story demonstrates its integrity (Lohmeyer, 240–41; Pesch, 2:209). Too much has been made of the supposed parallel to the rabbinic school tradition (cf. *Comment* on v 29). Clearly the narra-tive is a conflict story (Cranfield, 362) with a question and counterquestion of like kind—not to find the truth but to wrestle for control—indirectly demon-strating Jesus' authority in a broader sense than the issue posed. Moreover, the nature of Jesus' reply, in which he counters with a question about the source (i.e., authority) of John's baptism—was it from heaven or of human origin?—cannot easily be explained as deriving from later Christianity. The comparison could have proved to be awkward, in that it may have implied that John's author-ity was equal to that of Jesus or, even more problematically, that Jesus' authority was in some way contingent upon John's. The lack of clear witness to Jesus, the absence of Christology, and an unusual conclusion—Jesus refusing to give an an-swer—all argue for a setting in the life of Jesus (*Sitz im Leben Jesu*). If so, the unity of the narrative is confirmed (Cranfield, 362: "The historical reliability of the narrative need not be doubted"; cf. Taylor, 469).

Comment

27 ἔρχονται πάλιν εἰς Ἱεροσόλυμα, "they again enter Jerusalem," is a redac-tional bridge following the fig-tree story (11:12–14, 20–21). After separating Jesus' entry, the temple demonstration, and the question of authority by framing the temple demonstration with the fig-tree story (see *Comment* on 11:12, 20), the evan-gelist brings Jesus and the disciples back into Jerusalem (see *Comment* on 11:19) for what follows. Mark may have constructed this entry along the lines of 11:15a (see *Comment* on 11:15) and added his characteristic πάλιν, "again" (see Guelich, 84 [on 2:1]).

καὶ ἐν τῷ ἱερῷ περιπατοῦντος αὐτοῦ, "and as he walked about in the temple," belonged to the pre-Markan tradition and provided the occasion for the authorities to encounter Jesus after his actions in the temple. Since in the pre-Markan tradition the question of Jesus' authority in 11:27–33 immediately followed Jesus' temple demonstration in 11:15–17, the question of the resumption of the commercial activity would have been moot (cf. Gnilka, 2:138; Haenchen, 393). And even though Mark has placed this encounter on the following day (cf. 11:19–20), the focus remains on Jesus' previous actions (cf. ποιεῖν ταῦτα, "to do these things," in vv 28, 29, 33). The accent on Jesus' doing these things (vv 28, 29, 33), and the use of περιπατεῖν, "to walk," in Mark's Gospel (e.g., 2:9; 5:42; 6:48, 49; 7:5; 8:24; 12:38; cf. John 10:23; P.Oxy. 840) hardly suggests the more technical use of περιπατεῖν in the sense of a peripatetic teacher (cf. Ernst, 336; Grundmann, 317). Luke 20:1–2 stems from the evangelist's own redactional interests (cf. 20:1) and has little to do with the significance of περιπατεῖν in Mark.

ἔρχονται πρὸς αὐτὸν οἱ ἀρχιερεῖς καὶ οἱ γραμματεῖς καὶ οἱ πρεσβύτεροι, "the ruling priests, scribes, and elders approach him," refers to the three groups that constituted the Sanhedrin (see *Comment* on 8:31 and 11:18). They appear again in 14:43, 55, and 15:1 on the occasion of Jesus' arrest and trial. Therefore, their appearance here, following the reaction of the ruling priests and scribes to Jesus' actions in the temple precincts (11:18), is reminiscent of the passion prediction of 8:31 and sets an ominous tone for the future developments in Mark's narrative. Hardly a formal hearing (cf. 15:1), the setting indicates an informal query most likely conducted by representatives of the Sanhedrin. Their presence and query follow naturally in the pre-Markan traditional complex of entry (11:1–9), temple demonstration (11:15–17), and the question of authority (vv 27b–33). Therefore, there is no particular reason to attribute this encounter to the evangelist's redaction (cf. Gnilka, 2:137; Schmithals, 2:505) or an earlier traditional development (e.g., Shae, *NovT* 16 [1974] 19–20).

28 Three crucial issues in determining the integrity and significance of this pericope lie in this verse. First, do the interlocutors ask the same question in two ways, or do they pose two very different questions? Second, what is meant by ἐξουσία, "authority," in this context? And third, what is/was the antecedent to ταῦτα, "these things," in Mark and in the pre-Markan tradition?

ἐν ποίᾳ ἐξουσίᾳ ταῦτα ποιεῖς, "By what authority do you do these things?" This question, repeated in Jesus' initial response in v 29 and in his final response in v 33, is the thread that now binds together this unit of question and counterquestion, response and counterresponse. The key word is ἐξουσία, "authority." This in turn depends on the referent of ταῦτα, "these things."

If this pericope arose and circulated independently, one has to construct an antecedent for ταῦτα, "these things," based on the story itself. For example, Bultmann (*History*, 20; similarly Nineham, 307) suggests that ταῦτα may originally have referred to Jesus' practice of baptism set in contrast to John's (cf. John 3:22, 26). Shae (*NovT* 16 [1974] 18), who suggests that the original setting was a dialogue between "former disciples of John" and Jesus (cf. Matt 11:2–3), posits "the entire movement that Jesus had initiated with his calling of people to join his movement and teaching about the Kingdom of God" as the referent. Ernst (336), who leaves the original setting more undefined, takes ταῦτα to refer to Jesus' person and ministry in general. In these examples, ἐξουσία has a broader, more religious or theological than legal/political character, which would be rendered by "authority" rather than "right" or "power" or "permission."

If, as has often been held and is argued above, the Markan evangelist found this story combined with the temple demonstration (11:15–17), ταῦτα in the tradition must have referred directly to what Jesus had just done in the temple precincts. The question follows logically and naturally from that event. The ruling priests had sole jurisdiction over the temple. They would have authorized the activities of the buyers, sellers, and money-changers. The Sanhedrin had a broader legislative and judicial jurisdiction (see *Comment* on 13:9; 14:55), but the high priest and his ranking priestly associates possessed ultimate authority on the Temple Mount, an authority to which in many respects even the Romans deferred. The high priest's authority over the Sanhedrin is illustrated by the late rabbinic tradition that the latter was ejected from the "Chamber of Hewn Stone" within the temple precincts, evidently by order of the high priest (cf. *b. Roš Haš.* 31a; *b. Šabb.* 15a; *b. Sanh.* 41a; for discussion of these texts on this question, see Eppstein, *ZNW* 55 [1964] 56 and n. 107). This tradition is admittedly late, and the refrain that this event took place "forty years" before the destruction of the temple must be taken with a grain of salt, but it probably does accurately reflect the actual authority of the high priest within the temple precincts. Josephus himself draws attention to the strict prohibition against trespassing in restricted areas, which resulted in summary execution (*J.W.* 5.5.2 §§193–94; note that Josephus says the inscribed warning was written "in Greek and Roman letters," implying that this warning was as much for Gentiles as for Israelites; fragments of this stone inscription have been found).

In light of the foregoing, therefore, the ruling priests, scribes, and elders were appropriately inquiring into Jesus' right legally or politically to usurp their right in matters of temple polity. Accordingly, ἐξουσία would then have the more elementary sense of "authorization," "right," or "permission" in keeping with the Hebrew and Aramaic equivalents (Str-B 1:859–62; Hultgren, *Jesus and His Adversaries,* 72). Read in its own narrative context, the question reflects more the authorities' own political agenda than a religious, theological or even christological concern (cf. Hultgren, *Jesus and His Adversaries,* 74; Shae, *NovT* 16 [1974] 19–20). To whatever extent their question anticipated a theological (e.g., a prophet from God) or even a christological (e.g., a messianic claim; cf. 14:61!) response, the answer would have given them the legal or political basis for taking action.

Since the ruling priests had exclusive jurisdiction over the temple, their question, which had no acceptable answer, was more a move to incriminate Jesus than an attempt to gain information from him (cf. Schmithals, 2:507). Either Jesus admitted his conduct was unauthorized, which would have made him publicly vulnerable, or he claimed a right superseding that of the ruling priests, a claim that would have made him politically vulnerable (cf. 14:61–64). In either case, his conduct would then have provided a basis for a more formal proceeding against him, without fear of the crowd (cf. v 32; 12:12). This setting, therefore, corresponds to the immediate, adverse reaction of the ruling priests after they had heard about Jesus' actions in the temple precincts (see 11:18a) and supports the close association of these two pericopes in the pre-Markan tradition.

τίς σοι ἔδωκεν τὴν ἐξουσίαν ταύτην, "who has given to you this authority." Commentators have usually taken this clause as the second part of a double question about the same thing (e.g., Acts 4:7), but some recent commentators have distinguished between the two questions and assigned them to different stages in the developing tradition, with this being the original question (e.g., Hultgren, *Jesus and His Adversaries*, 68–75; Shae, *NovT* 16 [1974] 10–13). Jesus does not repeat this question in the story as he does the first one (vv 29, 33), but he supposedly addresses it in v 30 with his question about the origin of John's baptism. The first question he refuses to answer at all (cf. v 33). Accordingly, one has an earlier story built around the second question (vv 27b, 28b, 29a, 30; so Hultgren, *Jesus and His Adversaries*, 70; vv 28b, 30 [lost responses]; Shae, *NovT* 16[1974] 13–14) that was developed into the more complex story now tied together by the repetition of the first question in vv 29 and 33.

One must, however, remain true to the narrative and avoid reading the second question in terms of Jesus' counterquestion in v 30 instead of as a question from the Jewish authorities. Since the ruling priests had sole jurisdiction over the temple, they alone could give authority or the right to act as Jesus did in the temple precincts. That the same authority or right was at stake in the second question as in the first is seen in the demonstrative τὴν ἐξουσίαν ταύτην, "*this* authority." Consequently, the answer to this question comes out at the same place in the narrative as the answer to the first question. Either Jesus had to admit that he had not been given the right to act by any human authority and thus was unauthorized, or he had to claim to have been given his right to act by God and thus make a prophetic or even a messianic claim for his actions.

In the first alternative, nothing in the story or in the Jesus tradition as such would suggest that Jesus was, or that the authorities would think he was, simply taking matters into his own hands. The very question assumes an authorization (cf. ἐν ποίᾳ ἐξουσίᾳ, "by what authority"; τὴν ἐξουσίαν ταύτην, "this authority"). A special kind of rabbinic authority (רשות *rāšût*, רשותא *rĕšûtā'*) granted by rabbinic ordination, assuming there is a case to be made for Jesus' ordination, which there is not (cf. Daube, "Rabbinic Authority," 205–23; Nineham, 307; Str-B 1:859–60), has no consequences here where such rabbinic authority would not have obtained above that of the ruling priests. The alternative of an appeal to a God-given right is the more appropriate expectation, especially if, as has been argued in the *Comment* on 11:1–2 and 11:15–18, Jesus' actions in his entry and in the temple precincts reflected an allusion of some kind to the promises of Zech 9:9 and 14:21. Thus this question, like the first, was aimed at Jesus incriminating himself regarding the nature of his right to do what he had done (cf. ταῦτα ποιεῖς, "you do these things"; ταῦτα ποιῇς, "you may do these things"). His claim then would have served the authorities' purpose for formally prosecuting him (cf. Str-B 1:860; Pesch, 2:210), just as at the trial before the Sanhedrin where Caiaphas, the high priest, directly asks, "Are you the Messiah, the son of the Blessed?" (14:61).

Does the evangelist's use of this story, separated now from the temple demonstration by Jesus' teaching on faith and prayer (11:20–25), change the thrust of these questions and shift the connotation of ἐξουσία from "right" to the broader, theologically loaded "authority"? Several commentators find the separation to have removed ταῦτα, "these things," from the immediate reference to the temple demonstration and consequently broadened the antecedent to refer more generally to Jesus' ministry (e.g., Gnilka, 2:138; Lührmann, 197; Hultgren, *Jesus and His Adversaries*, 71). This thesis gains support from Mark's use of ἐξουσία in the broader theological sense with reference to Jesus' ministry at the outset of his Gospel. This ἐξουσία is seen in Jesus' teaching (1:21–22, 27), exorcisms (1:23–27; cf. 3:22–30), and forgiving of sins and healing (2:1–12). And he grants this ἐξουσία to his disciples in 3:13 and 6:7.

Of course, in the pre-Markan tradition the temple demonstration was probably not separated from the question of authority, at least not to the extent that it now is in the Markan narrative. But the readers of Mark would also sense that Jesus had acted with breath-taking authority (or audacity) in his temple demonstration, as well as in his entry into the city. The question of authority would certainly draw the attention of the readers and auditors to the prior events of Mark 11, which these readers and auditors would recognize to be the only events known to the ruling priests (what would and could they have known of Jesus' Galilean ministry?). But the readers and auditors of the Markan narrative know more than the ruling priests do. They know that Jesus acted with astounding authority from the very beginning of his ministry.

The tradition of Jesus' authority, which has become a motif in the Markan narrative, has its roots in the ministry of the historical Jesus. On what basis did he believe that he was invested with divine authority? Part of this answer surely lies with Jesus' belief that he was anointed by God's Spirit (cf. the allusions to Isa 61:1–2 in the reply to the imprisoned Baptist in Matt 11:5 = Luke 7:22, which is tradition with strong claim to authenticity). But the Markan tradition seems more indebted to another source for understanding Jesus' authority. Perhaps the most important clue is found in 2:10, where Jesus says: ἵνα δὲ εἰδῆτε ὅτι ἐξουσίαν ἔχει ὁ υἱὸς τοῦ ἀνθρώπου ἀφιέναι ἁμαρτίας ἐπὶ τῆς γῆς, "but that you may know that the 'son of man' has authority on earth to forgive sins." Scholars are divided over the question of the authenticity of this verse. Bultmann (*History*, 14–16) thinks that the saying represents the early church's desire to trace the doctrine of forgiveness of sins back to Jesus, the "son of man" (with which Tödt, *Son of Man*, 130, agrees; Taylor, 200; id., *Names*, 27, disagrees). But this reasoning is questionable. For early Christian theology, forgiveness of sin came from repentance and faith in the risen Christ (cf. Acts 2:38; Rom 10:1–13), not from the historical Jesus, who spoke rarely of forgiveness of sin, and when he did, it was in the context of pre-70 Jewish faith and practice. Jesus' pronouncements of forgiveness, as well as cleanness, are fragments of teaching and controversy that derive from the pre-Easter Jesus, not the later community. The linkage of ὁ υἱὸς τοῦ ἀνθρώπου, "son of man," and ἐξουσία, "authority," is to be traced to Dan 7:13–14:

> I saw in the night visions, and behold, with the clouds of heaven there came one like a son of man [LXX: υἱὸς ἀνθρώπου], and he came to the Ancient of Days and was presented before him. And to him was given dominion [LXX: ἐξουσία] and glory and kingdom, that all peoples, nations, and languages should serve him; his dominion is an everlasting dominion [Aramaic: שָׁלְטָנֵהּ שָׁלְטָן עָלַם *šoḷṭānēh šoḷṭān 'ālam;* LXX: ἡ ἐξουσία αὐτοῦ ἐξουσία αἰώνιος], which shall not pass away, and his kingdom [Aramaic: מַלְכוּתֵהּ *malkûtēh;* LXX: ἡ βασιλεία αὐτοῦ] one that shall not be destroyed.

Jesus' references to himself as ὁ υἱὸς τοῦ ἀνθρώπου, "son of man," are inspired by this passage (see *Introduction*, "Theology of Mark"). But Jesus alludes to this passage in reference to "kingdom" (Aramaic: מַלְכוּ *malkû;* LXX: βασιλεία) and "authority" (Aramaic: שָׁלְטָן *šoḷṭān;* LXX: ἐξουσία) as well. His authorization to proclaim the kingdom (Mark 1:14–15) derives from passages in Second Isaiah (40:9; 52:7; 61:1–2) and in Dan 7. When Jesus says the "'son of man' has authority *on earth* to forgive sins" (emphasis added), he implies that having received authority as "son of man" from heaven itself (as in the vision of Dan 7:13–14), he now possesses this authority *on earth*. By virtue of this authority he may forgive sins, he may declare persons and foods clean (Mark 1:41; 7:14–15, cf. 7:19), and he may even claim to be "master of the Sabbath" (Mark 2:28). These things he may do *on earth*, because as "son of man" he has received authority to do so *from heaven*. (It must be remembered that the high priest of Jerusalem was viewed as a mediating link between heaven and earth. These ideas, therefore, would hardly seem strange to Jesus' contemporaries.) In other words, by virtue of this heavenly authority, Jesus may act in a quasi-priestly role. It is therefore only to be expected that at some point in his ministry Jesus would come into serious conflict with ruling priests. (For more on this theme, see *Comment* on 14:53–65.)

Without question, Mark's readers would have understood the deeper significance of Jesus' authority in the light of the Gospel narrative. Doubtless the matter of Jesus' authority, which introduces and marks Jesus' public ministry (1:16–8:26) and now leads directly into Jesus' mortal conflict with the authorities, represents a key theme in the evangelist's development of the Gospel as a narrative whole. Nevertheless, the narrative context of 11:27–33, despite the intercalation of the fig-tree story into the story of the temple demonstration and the ensuing interruption of the chronological sequence of the tradition (11:12–14, 15–19, 20–25, 27–33), does not disallow the temple demonstration (11:15–19) as the traditional referent of ταῦτα, "these things." The questioners and the questions of 11:27–28 grow out of the ruling priests' and scribes' reaction to Jesus' actions in the temple (11:18a). Therefore, in 11:27b–28 the ruling priests, scribes, and elders ask Jesus about his legal or political right to do these things in the temple precincts, because they wish to take action against him—both in the pre-Markan tradition and in Mark's reframing and recontextualization of it. The two questions ask the same thing, with the second explicating the first: What right did he have to do what he did? Consequently, this question is repeated in Jesus' responses of vv 29 and 33. We do not have then two separate questions reflecting different stages in the development of the tradition, or perhaps two distinct forms of one original question.

29 ὁ δὲ Ἰησοῦς εἶπεν αὐτοῖς, "but Jesus said to them." Jesus responds with a counterquestion, a style that has frequently been compared to parallels in rabbinic discourse (Str-B 1:861). In these parallels, a person poses a debatable point to a colleague who counters with a question on which both the interlocutor and his colleague agree. This approach provides not only the basis for the interlocutor's response but also the basis for his colleague's climactic response (Shae, *NovT* 16 [1974] 13–14). We find a helpful example in *b. Sanh.* 65b:

And this question was asked by Turnus Rufus (Tineius Rufus, a Roman governor of Judea) of Rabbi Aqiba: "Wherein does this day (the Sabbath) differ from any other?" He replied: "Wherein does one differ from another?" Rufus replied: "Because my Lord (the Emperor) wishes it." "The Sabbath too," Aqiba rejoined, "then, is distinguished because the Lord wishes so." (slightly adapted translation from J. Schachter, in *The Babylonian Talmud: Seder Nezkin*, ed. I. Epstein [London: Soncino, 1935] ad loc.)

This pattern exists in Mark 10:2–9 and in 12:13–17. Since the story as it now stands in Mark 11:27–33 does not exactly fit this form of a rabbinic school discussion or teaching narrative either in content (the authorities obviously do not share Jesus' view of John the Baptist) or in structure (cf. the reasoning in vv 31–32a), it has often been viewed as having been greatly modified by the Markan evangelist. For some, the rabbinic form is the paradigm for reconstructing the underlying tradition and its historical setting in Jesus' ministry (e.g., Shae, *NovT* 16 [1974] 13–14). The result is a totally different story, one that includes different characters (e.g., John's disciples or unspecified interlocutors), a different referent (e.g., Jesus' ministry in general or Jesus' baptism), and different responses on the part of the interlocutors and Jesus. Here we have a case where a given form controls the content. The use of a counterquestion or even the topoi of a rabbinic school discussion, however, need not point directly to a particular form, especially if the account was intended to be a narrative report (e.g., Pesch, 2:209) set as a controversy story rather than as a teaching narrative. As it stands, the story fits quite congruently into its traditional and even redactional narrative framework.

ἐπερωτήσω ὑμᾶς ἕνα λόγον, "I shall ask you one thing." Jesus' counterquestion to the temple authorities is itself an implicit statement of authority more broadly understood. The questioned becomes the questioner and takes control of the discussion. This role reversal also marks the subsequent controversies over paying Roman taxes (12:13–17) and the resurrection (12:18–27). ἕνα λόγον, "one thing" (lit. "one word" or "one item"), puts all the weight of the discussion on one point and accents the significance of the following question as the condition for Jesus' own response (cf. v 33).

καὶ ἀποκρίθητέ μοι καὶ ἐρῶ ὑμῖν, "if you answer me, then I shall tell you," uses the Semitic construction of an imperative for the protasis, or the conditional clause, and makes Jesus' response to the ruling priests' question about his right to do these things dependent on their answer to him. As will be seen in v 33, their failure to meet this condition becomes the basis for Jesus' refusal to answer their question. Such a brusque response corresponds to the tone of the authorities' question and the obvious setting of conflict. Furthermore, by making his response dependent on theirs, Jesus again demonstrates his implicit authority, which challenges that of the representatives of the Sanhedrin, the highest authority in Judaism at that time.

ἐν ποίᾳ ἐξουσίᾳ ταῦτα ποιῶ, "by what authority I do these things." Jesus repeats the crucial part of the question put to him by his interlocutors. His reply is an abridgment of the twofold question that had asked by what authority he acted and who gave him this authority. If the ruling priests answer Jesus, then he will tell them by what authority he does what he does and who gave this authority to him. Mark's readers and auditors know that it is by the power and authority of God's Spirit that Jesus does what he does and that the one who gave him this authority is God (or "heaven"; see vv 30–31).

30 τὸ βάπτισμα τὸ Ἰωάννου ἐξ οὐρανοῦ ἦν ἢ ἐξ ἀνθρώπων; "Was the baptism of John from heaven or of human origin?" Jesus asks a related but different question. The authorities had asked about his right. Jesus is not implying that his authority is in some way to be traced back to John (e.g., Lohmeyer, 242 n. 3; Grundmann, 316), as if to say that if God authorized John, and John authorized Jesus, then Jesus would indeed have the authority to do what he does. Jesus' ques-

tion about John's authority is parallel, not consecutive. Just as John's authority
may be traced to God, so Jesus' authority may be traced directly to God (and not
necessarily to his baptism, as suggested by Shae, *NovT* 16 [1974] 27–28). Jesus
confronts his questioners with a question of like kind, his own form of self-incriminating question, as seen in the reflections that follow in vv 31–32.

At the same time, Jesus' question about John's baptism is also a question about
John and raises the level of discussion from his right to do what he has done to a
much more fundamental question. John's baptism is not simply an academic or
randomly selected topic. The tradition makes clear that Jesus himself had gone
to John for baptism, thereby recognizing John's baptism to be of God (see Guelich,
33–34 [on 1:11]), and that Jesus saw John as one whose preaching and baptism
set him apart as a divinely ordained prophet calling for repentance in light of the
coming of God's sovereign rule (e.g., Matt 11:11, 16–19 = Luke 7:28, 31–34). Furthermore, Mark's readers would recognize John as the God-ordained forerunner
who had played that role throughout the Gospel (1:2–15; 6:14–29; 8:28; 9:12–13)
and plays it here for the first time. The authorities' rejection of John mirrors
their rejection of Jesus.

ἀποκρίθητέ μοι, "Answer me!" This demand, which borders on disrespect (it is
omitted in Matthew and Luke), underscores Jesus' authority and shows how he
has successfully turned the tables on his opponents. The ruling priests had come
to him demanding an explanation. Jesus' counterquestion has the effect of putting them on the defensive.

31 At this point the dialogue breaks off and the narrator takes over to inform
the reader/hearer of the authorities' deliberations. This change in the story's orientation has led several commentators for various reasons to attribute vv 31–32 or
vv 31–33 to a later, secondary development of an earlier, shorter story behind vv
28–30 (e.g., Bultmann, *History,* 20: "v 31 is an addition . . . there is a genuine Palestinian apophthegm in vv 28–30"; Nineham, 306; Shae, *NovT* 16 [1974] 13–14; Gnilka,
2:136; Hultgren, *Jesus and His Adversaries,* 70). Yet Jesus' counterquestion in v 30
requires a response, and there must be more to the story than is supplied in vv 28–
30 (Schmithals, 2:506; Lohmeyer, 242). Either one posits an answer from the
authorities with which Jesus agrees and which he uses as the basis for his own climactic response (so Shae, *NovT* 16 [1974] 13–19), or one supposes a reply similar
to that of v 33a. If there was a reply like v 33a, there would at least be the need for v
32 to clarify the refusal to respond. To posit a different response from that in v 33,
however, means having totally to rewrite an otherwise logical, coherent story for
no other reason than purely formal considerations.

How could these private deliberations have become known to Jesus and his
disciples, and so have entered the tradition? After all, the ruling priests only replied with "We do not know." They certainly did not lay before Jesus the options
they had considered. Their deliberations must have been inferences on the part
of Jesus, his disciples, and other interested onlookers. It would have taken little
imagination to guess what the options were and what the ruling priests therefore
discussed among themselves. The tradition of these deliberations is to be traced
to this event, even if none of the participants actually overheard what was considered by the ruling priests.

καὶ διελογίζοντο πρὸς ἑαυτούς, "so they discussed it among themselves." A similar
expression appears in 2:6 (διαλογιζόμενοι ἐν ταῖς καρδίαις, "reasoning in their

hearts") where the deliberations take place in the minds of the scribes. Here πρὸς ἑαυτούς, "among themselves," may mean "with each other" (cf. Luke 20:5, συνελογίσαντο πρὸς ἑαυτούς, "they discussed it with each other" [RSV, adapted]) or privately "in themselves" (cf. Matt 21:25, διελογίζοντο ἐν ἑαυτοῖς, "they discussed it in themselves" [author's tr.]). Since, according to the narrative (v 32b), fear of the people determines their response, the context implies at least a private discussion of their predicament.

ἐὰν εἴπωμεν, ἐξ οὐρανοῦ, "if we should say, 'from heaven.'" In rabbinic-school discussions, the counterquestion expects a response on which both parties can agree, which has led some commentators to assume that in the original story this could be the only appropriate answer to the question from Jesus' standpoint (e.g., Shae, *NovT* 16 [1974] 13–14; Gnilka, 2:136). That, of course, assumes the counterquestion to have the same function here as in a rabbinic-school discussion. Yet according to the story Jesus' question counters the challenge of the authorities' question with a challenge of his own (cf. vv 29, 33). Consequently, the purpose of the question could well have been to create a predicament just as the authorities' question had been intended to do rather than, as in a school discussion or teaching narrative, to build a basis for Jesus' climactic response.

διὰ τί [οὖν] οὐκ ἐπιστεύσατε αὐτῷ, "[Then] why did you not believe him?" Although Bultmann (*History,* 20) rejected this as being a later Hellenistic-Christian use of ἐπιστεύσατε, "believe," most commentators today concur that the use of πιστεύειν, "to believe," with the dative is neither exclusively Hellenistic Gentile nor uniquely Markan (Lohmeyer, 242 n. 5; Gnilka, 2:137 n. 6; Shae, *NovT* 16 [1974] 7). To believe αὐτῷ, "him" (= John), inevitably meant not only accepting John and his baptism as ordained of God but also demonstrating that faith by obediently submitting to his baptism of repentance (see Guelich, 18–20 [on 1:4]).

32 ἀλλὰ εἴπωμεν, ἐξ ἀνθρώπων, "but if we should say, 'of human origin' . . . ?" offers the alternatives in a broken sentence ending with a question mark. This awkward construction is smoothed out in Matt 21:26 and Luke 20:6 by finishing the sentence with an apodosis developed from the following comments in Mark regarding their fear of the crowd. The evangelist composes a similarly truncated sentence in 2:10: ἵνα δὲ εἰδῆτε ὅτι ἐξουσίαν ἔχει ὁ υἱὸς τοῦ ἀνθρώπου ἀφιέναι ἁμαρτίας ἐπὶ τῆς γῆς—λέγει τῷ παραλυτικῷ, "'But that you may know that the "son of man" has authority on earth to forgive sins'—he said to the paralyzed man. . . ."

ἐφοβοῦντο τὸν ὄχλον "they were afraid of the crowd," stands in place of the apodosis. On the surface it appears as though the sentence breaks off because it has not anywhere to go. What would be the consequence of saying that John's baptism was humanly ordained but to reject it as having any redemptive or binding significance for the authorities? This apparently was how the authorities had indeed viewed John. Were this an academic discussion, a rabbinical school debate, and the authorities answered candidly, where would Jesus have gone with his reply, assuming that their response would have been, according to form, to offer the basis for his climactic response? Obviously nowhere, since their designation of John's baptism as humanly ordained would have provided no grounds for Jesus' response to the question about his own authority to do ταῦτα, "these things." Therefore, the dialogue does not work when taken in the form of a rabbinic-school discussion or a teaching narrative. Rather than proposing a hypothetical dialogue that does work or assigning the breakdown to the development of the tradition, perhaps the dialogue should be recognized simply as a controversy narrative in which two parties pose questions aimed at placing the other in a predicament. Jesus' counterquestion is indeed a counterquestion in kind in this literary context.

Fear of the crowd provides the other horn of the dilemma for the authorities. On the one hand, they would be caught by disjunction of their confession and their actions; on the other hand, they would be caught between their conviction and their status with the crowd. Therefore, although some commentators have assigned this broken apodosis to Markan redaction (e.g., Shae, *NovT* 16 [1974] 8–9), the evangelist most likely found it in the tradition (which could be the case for 2:10 as well). The same statement does occur in 12:12 in a clearly redactional passage, but Mark would then have adopted it from the usage here. In doing so, he draws his final parallel between John and Jesus. Just as the fear of the crowd inhibits the expression of the authorities' unbelieving rejection of John in v 32, so the fear of the crowd inhibits their actions reflecting their unbelieving rejection of Jesus in 12:12.

ἄπαντες γὰρ εἶχον τὸν Ἰωάννην ὄντως ὅτι προφήτης ἦν, "for all regarded John as truly a prophet." Mark adds another of his γάρ, "for," explanatory clauses (cf. 11:13, 19) to explain why the authorities feared the crowd. Mark has already noted John's prophetic role as promised in the Scriptures (1:2–8; 9:12–13) as well as the popular perception of him as a prophet (6:15; 8:28).

One cannot take Mark's explanatory comment about John as a prophet to be Jesus' answer to the authorities' question regarding his own authority. First of all, as a Markan redaction this statement of John's prophetic role is a later addition to the story. That the crowds held John in high esteem, most likely as a προφήτης, "prophet," is implicit in the authorities' fear of responding candidly to Jesus' counterquestion. Jesus' counterquestion obviously takes into account the crowd's high view of John. One can assume, therefore, that Jesus by analogy saw his authority, like John's baptism, to have come from God. But that does not allow one to define more narrowly the nature of this authority as being prophetic. The analogy does not imply an identity or even an equation of the two principal figures. Second, for Mark and his readers Jesus was clearly more than a prophet. He was the Messiah, Son of God, whose authority in the broader sense had come from God (cf. 1:1, 11; 8:27–30; 9:2–8). This becomes clear in the parable of the Wicked Vineyard Tenants (12:1–12), which follows shortly.

33 οὐκ οἴδαμεν, "we do not know," gives the ruling priests' response to the counterquestion. By giving an evasive answer and failing to answer Jesus' challenge, the authorities sacrifice their opportunity to force Jesus to indict himself. The irony of this scene can hardly be overlooked. Ostensibly there to protect the temple as God's house from arbitrary acts of unauthorized persons and to take action against just such persons, these representatives of the Sanhedrin and the ranking priests show their true colors. Rather than defend the temple, they protect themselves. In doing so they betray their own selfish concerns and their inability to respond to and for God, who confronts them in the persons of John and Jesus. Their answer demonstrates their unbelief. At the very least, their admission, "we do not know," if taken at face value, is an embarrassing surrender of the field. If their admission is not taken at face value but is recognized for the dodge that it is, then it is an embarrassing public display of cowardice.

οὐδὲ ἐγὼ λέγω ὑμῖν, "neither am I telling you," follows according to the condition set in v 29. Because they have defaulted in their answer by not choosing between the two alternatives posed by Jesus, he is free to withhold his response to their question. Yet Jesus' refusal to respond on the grounds of his own condition reflects a position of authority in the debate at least equal to that of the authorities. This implicit authority entails his right to do ταῦτα, "these things," for Mark's reader. As it turns out, of course, Jesus will answer the question, albeit in an indirect way, in the parable of the Wicked Vineyard Tenants (12:1–12).

ἐν ποίᾳ ἐξουσίᾳ ταῦτα ποιῶ, "by what authority I am doing these things," brings us back to the original question of Jesus' authority to do ταῦτα, "these things," in the temple precincts. The dialogue has shown Jesus to have an implicit authority in the way he counters and responds to the temple authorities. This is the same authority implicit in Jesus' ministry to sinners, the sick, and the possessed, which the Markan evangelist highlights at the outset of his Gospel in 1:22, 27; 2:10. Therefore, the reader and auditor know that this implicit authority gives Jesus the right to do ταῦτα, "these things." But Jesus refuses to answer the narrower question about his right posed by the ruling priests, scribes, and elders. They say, "we do not know," implying ignorance; Jesus says, "I won't tell," implying that he has the authority to refuse the temple authorities. Of course, from their standpoint Jesus could have no legitimate right. Therefore, by shifting the focus of the debate, Jesus' refusal to answer reflects much more than simply a "messianic secret" (Haenchen, 394–95; Nineham, 307). The one question, the question of Jesus' right to do ταῦτα, "these things," is bound up with the more fundamental question, what is the nature of the authority that marks Jesus' ministry? The Markan evangelist moves to this broader question by adding the following parable of the Wicked Vineyard Tenants (12:1–12), which addresses who Jesus is and who the authorities are from the divine perspective (cf. 12:12b).

Explanation

The key to understanding the thrust of this story lies in its literary context. Removed from its present context, the issue becomes the nature and source of the authority that marks Jesus and his ministry (v 28). Is this authority of God or not? If it is, what is the nature of this authority—prophetic or messianic? It is a theological, more precisely, a christological question about the person of Jesus. Starting from this premise, however, the story itself disintegrates as a narrative unit since the pieces no longer fit together. Jesus' counterquestion (vv 29–30) to the representatives of the Sanhedrin and temple establishment (v 27) about John's baptism fails to provide a common ground for his answer to the authorities' question. They obviously did not believe John's baptism to have been divinely ordained and were now questioning Jesus' ministry as well (v 28). On what grounds then would Jesus have staked his claim? To account for this logical breakdown in the narrative, a complex history of tradition has been suggested in which a simple teaching narrative or rabbinic-school discussion has been transformed into a controversy narrative reflecting the views and struggles of the early church.

This solution, however, fails at three points. First, it fails to resolve the broken pattern or logic of the story. Simply attributing it to the early church does not make it disappear. Why should the early church have been any less sensitive to, though supposedly responsible for, the incongruities of this argument than are modern commentators? Second, it fails to recognize two levels of authority at issue in this pericope. The one level has to do with Jesus' *authority* to do "these things," the narrative thread of this story (vv 28, 29, 33); the other has to do with the broader theme of Jesus' authority, a theme that marks Jesus' ministry through-out Mark's Gospel and underlies this narrative. Finally, this solution takes this story from the traditional context that provides the necessary interpretive frame-work for its theme, Jesus' *authority* to do "these things."

Read in the context of the temple action (11:15–18), the story focuses more narrowly on Jesus' authority to do "these things," namely, to criticize the com-mercial traffic in the temple precincts. As sole authorities for the temple, the ruling priests would have perceived Jesus' actions to be a challenge to their au-thority by which this traffic had been sanctioned. Their question, therefore, would have sought to incriminate Jesus publicly or politically. Publicly, since no human being or institution besides the high priest or the ruling priests could authorize Jesus' actions in the temple precincts, the crowd would be able to see that he had no human authority for his actions. Politically, should Jesus appeal to God, then he would be accountable to the Jewish and/or Roman authorities for his pro-phetic or even messianic claims (cf. 14:61–64; 15:2–5). Thus the authorities' question would have sought incrimination rather than information. Such a ques-tion would fit more the setting of conflict than of instruction. The ruling priests' and scribes' reaction to the events in the temple precincts (11:18) provides that setting.

Jesus' counterquestion was of like kind. Instead of referring to John's baptism to serve as the grounds for his later climactic response, the usual function of counterquestions in rabbinic-school discussions, Jesus deliberately sought to place his questioners on the horns of a dilemma by asking them a self-incriminating question (vv 31–32). Furthermore, he forced the issue by making their response the condition for his response to their question (vv 29, 33). Therefore, one can-not take Jesus' counterquestion as his intended answer to the authorities' question about what *right* he had to do what he had done. In fact, Jesus not only explicitly made his answer to their question dependent on their answer (v 29), but he de-liberately refused to answer the question when they defaulted (v 33). The story ends without any attempt on Jesus' part to lay claim to or defend a claim to his *right* to do "these things."

At the same time and on a deeper level, the broader issue of Jesus' authority, the authority that has marked his ministry from the outset of Mark's Gospel and has led to his actions in the temple precincts, does run through this story. First of all, instead of simply answering their question Jesus counters the authorities by posing his own question (vv 29–30). Second, he makes their answer to his counterquestion the condition for his response to their question. In this way, Jesus takes control of the situation from the authorities and puts them on the defen-sive. Third, by posing a question about John's baptism, Jesus exposes the authorities' failure to believe John's ministry to have been God-ordained and, by implication, exposes their failure to believe his own work to have been God-or-dained, although he does not draw this analogy. Fourth, Mark has underscored this broader focus on Jesus' authority by the story line of his Gospel that has introduced and portrayed Jesus as one who teaches and acts with authority (1:22, 27; 2:10; 3:13; 6:7). Finally, Mark's use of the parable of the Wicked Vineyard Tenants (12:1–12), which follows, to identify Jesus as the beloved son of the father and the authorities as murderous vintners exposes the ultimate purpose of the authorities' question—to "destroy him" (cf. 11:18; 12:12)—and also identifies Jesus' unique authority to be that of the beloved Son sent from the Father (cf. 1:11; 9:7).

This story in Mark's Gospel, as in the pre-Markan tradition, reveals the conflict between Jesus and the Jewish authorities that eventually leads to his death. Although it surfaces over Jesus' actions in the temple precincts, the issue runs much deeper, as seen by their unbelieving rejection of the divinely ordained baptism of John and, by implication, their unbelieving rejection of Jesus' work as God-ordained. Both John's baptism and Jesus' actions in the temple summoned Israel and her leaders to repentance in the light of what God was going to do and was indeed doing redemptively in history according to God's promises (cf. Zech 9:9; 14:21; Isa 56:7) and even threats (Jer 7:11). For Mark this scenario sets in motion a process that eventually leads to the Sanhedrin's delivering Jesus to Pilate for sentencing to death as the "king of the Jews" (cf. 15:1–15).

G. The Parable of the Wicked Vineyard Tenants (12:1–12)

Bibliography

Almeida, Y. L'opérativité sémantique des récits-paraboles: Sémiotique narrative et textuelle. Bibliothèque des Cahiers de l'Institut de linguistique de Louvain 13. Paris: Cerf; Leuven: Peeters, 1978. 153–95. **Aurelio, T.** Disclosures in den Gleichnissen Jesu. RST 8. Bern; Frankfurt am Main: Lang, 1977. 191–201. **Aus, R. D.** The Wicked Tenants and Gethsemane: Isaiah in the Wicked Tenants' Vineyard, and Moses and the High Priest in Gethsemane: Judaic Traditions in Mark 12:1–9 and 14:32–42. University of South Florida International Studies in Formative Christianity and Judaism 4. Atlanta: Scholars Press, 1996. **Baarda, T.** "'The Cornerstone': An Aramaism in the Diatessaron and the Gospel of Thomas?" NovT 37 (1995) 285–300. **Baarlink, H.** Anfängliches Evangelium. 261–62. **Bammel, E.** "Das Gleichnis von den bösen Winzern (Mc 12,1–9) und das jüdische Erbrecht." RIDA 3.6 (1959) 11–17. **Barnard, L. W.** "The Testimonium concerning the Stone in the New Testament and in the Epistle of Barnabas." SE 3 [= TU 88] (1964) 306–13. **Bastin, M.** Jésus devant sa passion. LD 92. Paris: Cerf, 1976. 56–70. **Baumgarten, J. M.** "4Q500 and the Ancient Conception of the Lord's Vineyard." JJS 40 (1989) 1–6. **Bayer, H. F.** Jesus' Predictions of Vindication and Resurrection: The Provenance, Meaning and Correlation of the Synoptic Predictions. WUNT 2.20. Tübingen: Mohr-Siebeck, 1986. 90–109. **Beilner, W.** Christus und die Pharisäer: Exegetische Untersuchung über Grund und Verlauf der Auseindersetzung. Vienna: Herder, 1959. 185–92. **Berder, M.** "La pierre rejetée par les bâtisseurs": Psaume 118,22–23 et son emploi dans les traditions juives et dans le Nouveau Testament. EBib n.s. 31. Paris: Gabalda, 1996. **Best, E.** Following Jesus. 218–20. **Biser,**

E. *Die Gleichnisse Jesu: Versuch einer Deutung.* Munich: Kösel, 1965. 137–44. **Black, M.** "The Christological Use of the Old Testament in the New Testament." *NTS* 18 (1971–72) 1–14, esp. 11–14. ———. "The Parable as Allegory." *BJRL* 42 (1959–60) 273–87. **Blank, J.** "Die Sendung des Sohnes: Zur christologischen Bedeutung des Gleichnisses von den bösen Winzern Mk 12,1–12." In *Neues Testament und Kirche.* FS R. Schnackenburg, ed. J. Gnilka. Freiburg: Herder, 1974. 11–41. **Blomberg, C. L.** *Interpreting the Parables.* Downers Grove, IL: InterVarsity Press, 1990. 247–51. **Böttger, P. C.** *Der König der Juden—Das Heil für die Völker.* 27–32. **Boucher, M.** *The Parables.* New Testament Message 7. Wilmington, DE: Glazier, 1981. 146–52. **Brooke, G. J.** "4Q500 1 and the Use of Scripture in the Parable of the Vineyard." *DSD* 2 (1995) 268–94. **Brown, R. E.** "Parable and Allegory Reconsidered." *NovT* 5 (1962) 36–45 (repr. in R. E. Brown. *New Testament Essays.* Milwaukee: Bruce, 1965. 254–64). **Bruce, F. F.** "New Wine in Old Wine Skins: III. The Corner Stone." *ExpTim* 84 (1972–73) 231–35. **Burkitt, F. C.** "The Parable of the Wicked Husbandmen." In *Transactions of the Third International Congress for the History of Religions.* Ed. P. S. Allen and J. de M. Johnson. Vol. 2. Oxford: Clarendon, 1908. 321–28. **Cahill, M.** "Not a Cornerstone! Translating Ps 118,22 in the Jewish and Christian Sriptures." *RB* 106 (1999) 345–57. **Carlston, C. E.** *The Parables of the Triple Tradition.* Philadelphia: Fortress, 1975. 178–90. **Chilton, B. D.** *Galilean Rabbi.* 111–14. **Combet-Galland, C.** "La vigne et l'écriture, histoire de reconnaissances: Marc 12/1–12." *ETR* 62 (1987) 489–502. **Cornette, A.** "Notes sur la parabole des vignerons: Marc 12/5–12." *FoiVie* 84.1–2 (1985) 42–48. **Cousin, H.** "Sépulture criminelle et sépulture prophétique." *RB* 81 (1974) 375–93. **Crossan, J. D.** *Four Other Gospels: Shadows on the Contours of Canon.* Sonoma, CA: Polebridge, 1992. 31–38. ———. *The Historical Jesus.* 351–52. ———. *In Parables: The Challenge of the Historical Jesus.* San Francisco: Harper & Row, 1973. 86–96. ———. "Parable, Allegory, and Paradox." In *Semiology and the Parables.* Ed. D. Patte. Pittsburgh: Pickwick, 1976. 247–81, esp. 264–73. ———. "The Parable of the Wicked Husbandmen." *JBL* 90 (1971) 451–65. ———. "The Servant Parables of Jesus." *Semeia* 1 (1974) 17–62, esp. 17–55. ———. "Structuralist Analysis and the Parables of Jesus." *Semeia* 1 (1974) 192–221, esp. 208–9. **Dehandschutter, B.** "La parabole des vignerons homicides (Mc., XII,1–12) et l'évangile selon Thomas." In *L'Évangile selon Marc: Tradition et rédaction.* Ed. M. Sabbe. 203–19. **Derrett, J. D. M.** "Allegory and the Wicked Vinedresser." *JTS* n.s. 25 (1974) 426–32. ———. "Fresh Light on the Wicked Vinedressers." In *Law in the New Testament.* London: Darton, Longman & Todd, 1970. 286–312. ———. "The Stone that the Builders Rejected." *SE* 4 [= TU 102] (1968) 180–86 (repr. in J. D. M. Derrett. *Glimpses of the Legal and Social Presuppositions of the Authors.* Vol. 1 of *Studies in the New Testament.* Leiden: Brill, 1977. 112–17). **Dodd, C. H.** *The Parables of the Kingdom.* Rev. ed. London: Nisbet, 1936. 124–32. **Dombois, H.** "Juristische Bemerkungen zum Gleichnis von den bösen Weingärtnern (Mk. 12.1–12)." *Neue Zeitschrift für systematische Theologie und Religionsphilosophie* 8 (1966) 361–73. **Donahue, J. R.** *Are You the Christ?* 122–28. ———. *The Gospel in Parable: Metaphor, Narrative, and Theology in the Synoptic Gospels.* Philadelphia: Fortress, 1988. 52–57. **Dormandy, R.** "Hebrews 1:1–2 and the Parable of the Wicked Husbandmen." *ExpTim* 100 (1988–89) 371–75. **Drury, J.** "The Sower, the Vineyard, and the Place of Allegory in the Interpretation of Mark's Parables." *JTS* n.s. 24 (1973) 367–79. **Dschulnigg, P.** *Rabbinische Gleichnisse und das Neue Testament: Die Gleichnisse der PesK im Vergleich mit den Gleichnissen Jesu und dem Neuen Testament.* Judaica et Christiana 12. Bern; Frankfurt am Main: Lang, 1988. 108–11. **Duplantier, J.-P.** "Les vignerons meurtriers: Le travail d'une parabole." In *Les Paraboles évangéliques: Perspectives nouvelles: XIIe congrès de l'Association catholique française pour l'étude de la Bible.* Ed. J. Delorme. LD 135. Paris: Cerf, 1989. 259–70. **Eck, E. van,** and **Aarde, A. G. van.** "A Narratological Analysis of Mark 12:1–12: The Plot of the Gospel of Mark in a Nutshell." *HTS* 45 (1989) 778–800. **Ellis, E. E.** "New Directions in Form Criticism." In *Jesus Christus in Historie und Theologie.* FS H. Conzelmann, ed. G. Strecker. Tübingen: Mohr-Siebeck, 1975. 299–315. ———. "How the New Testament Uses the Old." In *New Testament Interpretation.* Ed. I. H. Marshall. Exeter: Paternoster; Grand Rapids, MI: Eerdmans, 1977.

199–219. **Evans, C. A.** "God's Vineyard and Its Caretakers." In *Jesus and His Contemporaries: Comparative Studies.* AGJU 25. Leiden: Brill, 1995. 381–406. ———. "Jesus' Action in the Temple: Cleansing or Portent of Destruction?" *CBQ* 51 (1989) 237–70, esp. 240–45. ———. "Jesus and the Dead Sea Scrolls." In *The Dead Sea Scrolls after Fifty Years.* Ed. P. W. Flint and J. C. VanderKam. Vol. 2. Leiden: Brill, 1999. 573–98. ———. "Jesus' Parable of the Tenant Farmers in Light of Lease Agreements in Antiquity." *JSP* 14 (1996) 65–83. ———. "On the Vineyard Parables of Isaiah 5 and Mark 12." *BZ* 28 (1984) 82–86. **Feldmeier, R.** "Heil im Unheil: Das Bild Gottes nach der Parabel von den bösen Winzern (Mk. 12,1–12 par.)." *TBei* 25 (1994) 5–22. **Frankemölle, H.** "Hat Jesus sich selbst verkündet? Christologische Implikationen in den vormarkinische Parabeln." *BibLeb* 13 (1972) 184–207. **Frieling, R.** *Christologische Aufsätze.* Gesammelte Schriften zum Alten und Neuen Testament 3. Stuttgart: Urachhaus, 1982. 290–300. **Funk, R. W.,** and **Hoover, R. W.,** eds. *The Five Gospels: The Search for the Authentic Words of Jesus.* Sonoma, CA: Polebridge Press; New York: Macmillan, 1993. **George, A.** "Comment Jésus a-t-il perça sa propre mort?" *LumVie* 101 (1971) 34–59. **Graffy, A.** "The Literary Genre of Isaiah 5,1–7." *Bib* 60 (1979) 400–409. **Gray, A.** "The Parable of the Wicked Husbandmen (Matthew xxi. 33–41; Mark xii. 1–9; Luke xx. 9–16)." *HibJ* 19 (1920–21) 42–52. **Greenspoon, L. J.** "The Dead Sea Scrolls and the Greek Bible." In *The Dead Sea Scrolls after Fifty Years: A Comprehensive Assessment.* Ed. P. W. Flint and J. C. VanderKam. Vol. 1. Leiden: Brill, 1998. 101–27. **Gressmann, H.** "Der Eckstein." *Palästinjahrbuch* 6 (1910) 38–46. **Gubler, M.-L.** *Die frühesten Deutungen des Todes Jesu: Eine motivgeschichtliche Darstellung aufgrund der neueren exegetischen Forschung.* OBO 15. Göttingen: Vandenhoeck & Ruprecht, 1977. 28–30, 71–83. **Guillet, J.** "Jésus et la politique." *RSR* 59 (1971) 531–44. **Güttgemanns, E.** "Narrative Analysis of Synoptic Texts." *Semeia* 6 (1976) 127–79, esp. 133–36. **Harnisch, W.** "Der bezwingende Vorsprung des Guten: Zur Parabel von den bösen Winzern (Markus 12,1ff. und Parallelen)." In *Die Sprache der Bilder: Gleichnis und Metaphor in Literatur und Theologie.* Ed. H. Weder. Gütersloh: Mohn, 1989. 22–38. ———. *Die Gleichniserzählungen Jesu: Eine hermeneutische Einführung.* Uni-Taschenbücher 1343. Göttingen: Vandenhoeck & Ruprecht, 1985. 177–200. **Hengel, M.** "Das Gleichnis von den Weingärtnern Mc 12,1–12 im Lichte der Zenonpapyri und der rabbinischen Gleichnisse." *ZNW* 59 (1968) 1–39. **Hester, J. D.** "Socio-Rhetorical Criticism and the Parable of the Tenants." *JSNT* 45 (1992) 27–57 (repr. in *New Testament Interpretation and Methods: A Sheffield Reader.* Ed. S. E. Porter and C. A. Evans. BibSem 45. Sheffield: Sheffield Academic Press, 1997. 222–51). **Hezser, C.** *Lohnmetaphorik und Arbeitswelt in Mt 20,1–16: Das Gleichnis von den Arbeitern im Weinberg im Rahmen rabbinischer Lohngleichnisse.* NTOA 15. Fribourg: Universitätsverlag, 1990. **Hirsch, E.** *Das Werden des Markusevangeliums.* Vol. 1 of *Frühgeschichte des Evangeliums.* Tübingen: Mohr-Siebeck, 1951. **Hoffmann, P.** *Jesus von Nazareth und eine christliche Moral: Sittliche Perspektiven der Verkündigung Jesu.* QD 66. Freiburg: Herder, 1975. 109–31. **Horne, E. H.** "The Parable of the Tenants as Indictment." *JSNT* 71 (1998) 111–16. **Horstmann, M.** *Studien zur markinischen Christologie.* 22–26. **Hubaut, M.** "La parabole des vignerons homicides: Son authenticité, sa visée première." *RTL* 6 (1975) 51–61. ———. *La parabole des vignerons homicides.* CahRB 16. Paris: Gabalda, 1976. **Iersel, B. M. F. van.** *"Der Sohn" in den synoptischen Jesusworten: Christusbezeichnung der Gemeinde oder Selbstbezeichnung Jesu?* NovTSup 3. Leiden: Brill, 1961. 124–45. **Jeremias, J.** "Eckstein-Schußstein." *ZNW* 36 (1937) 154–57. ———. "Κεφαλὴ γωνίας—Ἀκρογωνιαῖος." *ZNW* 29 (1930) 264–80. ———. "λίθος, λίθινος." *TDNT* 4:268–80. ———. *The Parables of Jesus.* Rev. ed. London: SCM; New York: Scribner's, 1963. 70–77. **Jülicher, A.** *Die Gleichnisreden Jesu.* 2 vols. 2nd ed. Tübingen: Mohr-Siebeck, 1910. 2:385–406. **Kazmierski, C. R.** *Jesus, the Son of God.* 127–37. **Kim, S.** "Jesus—The Son of God, the Stone, the Son of Man, and the Servant: The Role of Zechariah in the Self-Identification of Jesus." In *Tradition and Interpretation in the New Testament.* FS E. E. Ellis, ed. G. F. Hawthorne and O. Betz. Grand Rapids, MI: Eerdmans, 1987. 134–48. **Kimball, C. A.** "Jesus' Exposition of Scripture in Luke (20:9–19): An Inquiry in Light of Jewish Hermeneutics." *BBR* 3 (1993) 77–92. **Klauck, H.-J.** *Allegorie und Allegorese in synoptische Gleichnistexten.* NTAbh

13. Münster: Aschendorff, 1978. 286–316. ———. "Das Gleichnis vom Mord im Weinberg (Mk 12,1–12; Mt 21,33–46; Lk 20,9–19)." *BibLeb* 11 (1970) 118–45. **Kuhn, H.-W.** *Ältere Sammlungen im Markusevangelium.* **Kümmel, W. G.** "Das Gleichnis von den bösen Weingärtnern (Mk. 12. 1–9)." In *Aux sources de la tradition Chrétienne.* FS M. Goguel, ed. O. Cullmann and P. H. Menoud. Bibliothèque Théologique. Neuchâtel; Paris: Delachaux et Niestlé, 1950. 120–31 (repr. in W. G. Kümmel. *Heilsgeschehen und Geschichte.* Ed. E. Grässer et al. MTS 3. Marburg: Elwert, 1965. 207–17). **Lee, M. Y.-H.** *Jesus und die jüdische Autorität: Eine exegetische Untersuchung zu Mk 11,27–12,12.* FB 56. Würzburg: Echter, 1986. **Léon-Dufour, X.** "La parabole des vignerons homicides." *ScEccl* 17 (1965) 365–96 (repr. in X. Léon-Dufour. *Études d'évangile.* Parole de Dieu 2. Paris: Seuil, 1965. 303–44). **Levenson, J. D.** *The Death and Resurrection of the Beloved Son.* New Haven, CT: Yale UP, 1993. **Llewelyn, S. R.** "Business Transactions §13: Self-Help and Legal Redress: The Parable of the Wicked Tenants." *NewDocs* 6 (1992) 86–105. **Lohmeyer, E.** "Das Gleichnis von den bösen Weingärtnern (Mark. 12,1–12)." *ZST* 18 (1941) 242–59 (repr. in E. Lohmeyer. *Urchristliche Mystik: Neutestamentliche Studien.* Darmstadt: Gentner, 1956. 159–81). **Longenecker, R. N.** *The Christology of Early Jewish Christianity.* SBT 17. London: SCM; Naperville, IL: Allenson, 1970. 50–53. **Lowe, M.** "From the Parable of the Vineyard to a Pre-Synoptic Source." *NTS* 28 (1982) 257–63. **Malina, B. J.,** and **Rohrbaugh, R. L.** *Social-Science Commentary on the Synoptic Gospels.* 254–55. **Marcus, J.** *The Way of the Lord.* 111–29. **McGaughey, J. D.** "Two Synoptic Parables in the Gospel of Thomas." *ABR* 8 (1960) 24–28. **Meier, J. P.** *Marginal Jew.* 2:123–39. **Mell, U.** *Die "anderen" Winzer: Eine exegetische Studie zur Vollmacht Jesu Christi nach Markus 11,27–12,34.* WUNT 77. Tübingen: Mohr-Siebeck, 1995. 74–188. **Michaelis, W.** *Die Gleichnisse Jesu: Eine Einführung.* Die urchristliche Botschaft 31. Hamburg: Furche, 1956. 113–25. **Milavec, A.** "A Fresh Analysis of the Parable of the Wicked Husbandmen in the Light of Jewish-Christian Dialogue." In *Parable and Story in Judaism and Christianity.* Ed. C. Thoma and M. Wyschogrod. SJC. New York: Paulist, 1989. 81–117. ———. "The Identity of 'The Son' and 'The Others': Mark's Parable of the Wicked Husbandmen Reconsiderd." *BTB* 20 (1990) 30–37. ———. "Mark's Parable of the Wicked Husbandmen as Reaffirming God's Predilection for Israel." *JES* 26 (1989) 289–312. **Miller, M. P.** "Scripture and Parable: A Study of the Function of the Biblical Features in the Parable of the Wicked Husbandmen and Their Place in the History of the Tradition." Diss., Columbia University, 1974. **Minette de Tillesse, G.** *Le secret messianique.* 218–19, 287–92. **Montefiore, H. W.** "A Comparison of the Parables of the Gospel according to Thomas and of the Synoptic Gospels." *NTS* 7 (1960–61) 220–48, esp. 236–38. **Moo, D. J.** *The Old Testament in the Gospel Passion Narratives.* Sheffield: Almond, 1983. 335–37. **Moor, J. C. de.** "The Targumic Background of Mark 12:1–12: The Parable of the Wicked Tenants." *JSJ* 19 (1998) 63–80. **Mudiso Mbâ Mundla, J.-G.** *Jesus und die Führer Israels: Studien zu den sogenannten Jerusalemer Streitgesprächen.* NTAbh 17. Münster: Aschendorff, 1984. 5–40. **Mussner, F.** "Die bösen Winzer nach Matthäus 21,33–46." In *Antijudaismus im Neuen Testament? Exegetische und systematische Beiträge.* Ed. P. Eckert et al. Abhandlungen zum christlich-jüdischen Dialog 2. Munich: Kaiser, 1967. 129–34. **Newell, J. E.,** and **Newell, R. R.** "The Parable of the Wicked Tenants." *NovT* 14 (1972) 226–37. **Oberlinner, L.** *Todeserwartung und Todesgewissheit Jesu: Zum Problem einer historischen Begründung.* SBB 10. Stuttgart: Katholisches Bibelwerk, 1980. 151–53. **Oesterley, W. O. E.** *The Gospel Parables in the Light of Their Jewish Background.* London: S. P. C. K., 1936. 117–22. **O'Neill, J. C.** "The Source of the Parables of the Bridegroom and the Wicked Husbandmen." *JTS* n.s. 39 (1988) 485–89. **Panier, L.** "Analyse sémiotique: 'Pour commencer.'" *Sémiotique et Bible* 38 (1985) 1–31. **Patterson, S. J.** *The Gospel of Thomas and Jesus.* Sonoma, CA: Polebridge, 1993. 48–51, 140–43. **Pedersen, S.** "Zum Problem der vaticinia ex eventu: Eine Analyse von Mt. 21,33–46 par.; 22, 1–10 par." *ST* 19 (1965) 167–88. **Perkins, P.** *Hearing the Parables of Jesus.* New York: Paulist, 1981. 181–94. **Pesch, R.** *Evangelium der Urgemeinde.* 143–48. **Petzoldt, M.** *Gleichnisse Jesu und christliche Dogmatik.* Göttingen: Vandenhoeck & Ruprecht, 1984. 32–45. **Robinson, J. A. T.** "The Parable of the Wicked Husbandmen: A

Test of Synoptic Relationships." *NTS* 21 (1974–75) 443–61 (repr. in J. A. T. Robinson. *Twelve More New Testament Studies*. London: SCM, 1984. 12–34). **Rowlandson, J.** *Landowners and Tenants in Roman Egypt*. Oxford: Clarendon, 1996. **Sandvik, B.** *Das Kommen des Herrn beim Abendmahl im Neuen Testament*. ATANT 58. Zürich: Zwingli, 1970. 53–65. **Schenker, A.** "Gott als Vater—Söhne Gottes: Ein vernachlässigter Aspeck einer biblischen Metapher." *FZPhTh* 25 (1978) 3–55. **Schnider, F.** *Jesus der Prophet*. OBO 2. Göttingen: Vandenhoeck & Ruprecht, 1973. 152–56. **Schoedel, W. R.** "Parables in the Gospel of Thomas: Oral Tradition or Gnostic Exegesis?" *CTM* 43 (1972) 548–60, esp. 557–60. **Schrage, W.** *Das Verhältnis des Thomas-Evangeliums zur synoptischen Tradition und zu den koptischen Evangelienübersetzungen*. BZNW 29. Berlin: Töpelmann, 1964. 137–45. **Schramm, T.,** and **Löwenstein, K.** *Unmoralische Helden: Anstössige Gleichnisse Jesu*. Göttingen: Vandenhoeck & Ruprecht, 1986. 22–42. **Schwarz, G.** *Jesus und Judas: Aramaistische Untersuchungen zur Jesus-Judas-Überlieferung der Evangelien und der Apostelgeschichte*. BWANT 123. Stuttgart: Kohlhammer, 1988. 135–40. **Scott, B. B.** *Hear Then the Parable: A Commentary on the Parables of Jesus*. Minneapolis: Fortress, 1989. 237–53. **Sevrin, J.-M.** "Un groupement de trois paraboles contre les richesses dans l'Evangile selon Thomas." In *Les Paraboles évangeliques: Perspectives nouvelles*. Ed. J. Delorme. Paris: Cerf, 1989. 425–39. **Sheppard, G. T.** "More on Isaiah 5:1–7 as a Juridical Parable." *CBQ* 44 (1982) 45–47. **Snodgrass, K. R.** "The Gospel of Thomas: A Secondary Gospel." *SecCent* 7 (1989) 19–38. ———. "The Parable of the Wicked Husbandmen: Is the Gospel of Thomas Version the Original?" *NTS* 21 (1974–75) 142–44. ———. *The Parable of the Wicked Tenants: An Inquiry into Parable Interpretation*. WUNT 27. Tübingen: Mohr-Siebeck, 1983. ———. "Recent Research on the Parable of the Wicked Tenants: An Assessment." *BBR* 8 (1998) 187–215. **Steck, O. H.** *Israel und das gewaltsame Geschick der Propheten: Untersuchungen zur Überlieferung des deuteronomistischen Geschichtsbildes im Alten Testament, Spätjudentum und Urchristentum*. WMANT 23. Neukirchen-Vluyn: Neukirchener Verlag, 1967. 269–73. **Stern, D.** "Jesus' Parables from the Perspective of Rabbinic Literature: The Example of the Wicked Husbandmen." In *Parable and Story in Judaism and Christianity*. Ed. C. Thoma and M. Wyschogrod. SJC. New York: Paulist, 1989. 42–80. ———. *Parables in Midrash*. Cambridge, MA: Harvard UP, 1991. 189–97. **Strawson, W.** *Jesus and the Future Life: A Study in the Synoptic Gospels*. London: Epworth, 1959. 114–16. **Suhl, A.** *Zitate*. 138–42. **Trimaille, M.** "La parabole des vignerons meurtriers (Mc 12, 1–12)." In *Les Paraboles évangeliques: Perspectives nouvelles. XIIe congrès de l'Association catholique française pour l'étude de la Bible*. Ed. J. Delorme. LD 135. Paris: Cerf, 1989. 247–58. **Ulrich, E.** "The Septuagint Manuscripts from Qumran: A Reappraisal of Their Value." In *Septuagint, Scrolls and Cognate Writings*. Ed. G. J. Brooke and B. Lindars. SBLSCS 33. Atlanta: Scholars Press, 1992. 49–80. **Valantasis, R.** *The Gospel of Thomas*. New Testament Readings. London; New York: Routledge, 1997. 143–46. **Via, D. O., Jr.** *The Parables: Their Literary and Existential Dimension*. Philadelphia: Fortress, 1967. 128–37. **Vincent, J. J.** "The Parables of Jesus as Self-Revelation." *SE* 1 [= TU 73] (1959) 79–99, esp. 85–86. **Weder, H.** *Die Gleichnisse Jesu als Metaphern: Traditions- und redaktionsgeschichtliche Analysen und Interpretationen*. FRLANT 120. Göttingen: Vandenhoeck & Ruprecht, 1978. 147–62. **Weiser, A.** *Die Knechtsgleichnisse der synoptischen Evangelien*. SANT 29. Munich: Kösel, 1971. 49–57. **Weren, W. J. C.** "The Use of Isaiah 5,1–7 in the Parable of the Tenants (Mark 12,1–12; Matthew 21,33–46)." *Bib* 79 (1998) 1–26. **Willis, J. T.** "The Genre of Isaiah 5:1–7." *JBL* 96 (1977) 337–62. **Wrege, H.-Th.** *Die Gestalt des Evangeliums: Aufbau und Struktur der Synoptiker sowie der Apostelgeschichte*. BEvT 11. Bern; Frankfurt am Main: Lang, 1978. 60–67. **Wright, N. T.** *Jesus and the Victory of God*. 497–501. **Wyschogrod, M.,** and **Thoma, C.,** eds. *Parable and Story in Judaism and Christianity*. SJC. New York: Paulist, 1989. **Yee, G. A.** "The Form-Critical Study of Isaiah 5:1–7 as a Song and a Juridical Parable." *CBQ* 43 (1981) 30–40. **Young, B. H.** *Jesus and His Jewish Parables: Rediscovering the Roots of Jesus' Teaching*. New York: Paulist, 1989. 282–316.

Translation

[1] *And he began to speak to them in parables: "A man planted a vineyard; and he put a fence around it,*[a] *and hewed out a winepress, and built a tower, and leased it out to tenant farmers, and departed.*[b] [2] *And he sent to the tenant farmers in due course a servant, that he might receive from the farmers a portion of the fruit of the vineyard.* [3] *But taking him, they beat him and sent him away empty-handed.* [4] *And again he sent to them another servant; but they struck that one on the head,*[c] *and treated him dishonorably.*[d] [5] *So he sent another; and they killed that one, and many others, beating some and killing others.* [6] *He had yet one, a beloved son.*[e] *He sent him last to them, thinking, 'They will respect my son.'* [7] *But those tenants said to themselves,*[f] *'This is the heir; come, let us kill him, and the inheritance will be ours.'*[g] [8] *And taking him, they killed him, and cast him out of the vineyard.* [9] *What [therefore] will the owner of the vineyard do? He will come and destroy the tenants and give the vineyard to others.* [10] *Have you not even read*[h] *this Scripture:*

'A stone that the builders rejected,
This has become the head of the corner;
[11] *This came about from the Lord,*
and it is marvelous in our eyes'?"

[12] *And they were seeking to arrest him, but they feared the crowd, for they knew that he had spoken the parable to them. And leaving him, they departed.*[i]

Notes

[a]The indirect obj. is implied, but some MSS (C² N W Σ) do add αὐτῷ, "it" (cf. Matt 21:33).
[b]ἀπεδήμησεν, "departed," implies departing for another country.
[c]A C N Σ and a few later MSS add the ptc. λιθοβολήσαντες, making the passage read "casting stones, they struck that one on the head." ἐκεφαλίωσαν, "they struck on the head," is an odd verb. ℵ B L Ψ Nestle-Aland²⁷ and UBSGNT³ᶜ read ἐκεφαλίωσαν (which underlies the translation above; cf. BAG); C 33 Δ 1241 read ἐκεφαλαίωσαν, "they summed up" (cf. Sir 35:8), while ἐκεφάλωσαν (variant spelling) is read by 1424. For further discussion, see the excursus in Mell, *Die "anderen" Winzer*, 102–4. Burkitt ("Parable") recommends ἐκολάφισαν, "they buffeted," in anticipation of Mark 14:65. But this speculation is completely unattested in the MS tradition. Mell, appealing to LXX 2 Sam 10:2–5, translates "they disfigured his head-dress and treated him with contempt" (*Die "anderen" Winzer*, 104). For more on Mell's interpretation, see *Comment* below.
[d]A C N W Σ and a few later MSS read ἀπέστειλαν ἠτιμωμένον, "sent him away dishonored."
[e]A N Σ 33 and a few later MSS read υἱὸν ἀγαπητὸν αὐτοῦ, "his beloved son."
[f]Several later MSS and authorities read ἐκεῖνοι δὲ οἱ γεωργοὶ θεασάμενοι αὐτὸν ἐρχόμενον εἶπαν πρὸς ἑαυτούς, "But those tenants, seeing him coming, said to themselves."
[g]A few later MSS read ἀποκτείνωμεν αὐτὸν καὶ σχῶμεν τὴν κληρονομίαν, "let us kill him and take possession of the inheritance" (cf. Matt 21:38).
[h]Gk. ἀνέγνωτε. Several variants appear in later MSS. Some read ἔγνωτε, "have you [not] known"; or ἀπεδωκίμασαν, "have they [not] rejected"; or ἀπεδοκήμασαν, "have they [not] approved."
[i]W omits the last sentence.

Form/Structure/Setting

The parable of the Wicked Vineyard Tenants tells a story of a man who plants a vineyard, leases it to tenant farmers, and departs to foreign parts. In due course the owner of the vineyard sends a servant to collect his portion of the profits. But the tenants refuse to pay, instead beating and sending away the servant empty-handed. The owner sends more servants, who are treated worse. Finally, the owner sends his "beloved son," imagining that the tenant farmers will respect him. They do not. They kill him, thinking they might inherit the vineyard. Jesus asks his hearers to imagine what the owner will do. He then answers that the owner will come and destroy the tenants and lease the vineyard to others. The parable concludes with a quotation of Ps 118:22–23. The scene ends with the ruling priests, scribes, and elders (assumed from 11:27) wishing to arrest Jesus, but because they fear the crowd, they leave him.

The parable of the Wicked Vineyard Tenants finds itself at the center of a long-standing debate regarding Mark's parables and Mark's Christology. Is it an inauthentic Christian allegory? Or was Jesus its author? Or does the truth lie somewhere between these alternatives? If the parable does indeed go back to Jesus, what did it originally mean? Is the Markan narrative context true to the original context? If it is not, what was the original context? These questions and others drive the studies of this important parable.

Most scholars believe that the parable in some form derives from Jesus. It is frequently claimed that the parable has undergone a measure of allegorical embellishment and, thanks to the Markan evangelist, has been given a new context. The allegorical features, it is believed, have transformed the parable into an allegory of God's dealing with stubborn Israel, Israel's persecution and murder of the prophets, the final killing of God's Son Jesus, and judgment on Israel and vindication of Jesus. Some have claimed that the briefer version found in the *Gospel of Thomas,* which supposedly does not possess these allegorical elements, is closer to the original form of the parable.

In order to place the parable of the Wicked Vineyard Tenants in its proper setting in the life of Jesus, assuming that some form of it actually does derive from Jesus, and to understand properly what contributions, if any, the Markan evangelist may have made, it will be necessary to address several of the questions just raised. First, it is necessary to deal with the extant sources, asking *which source* (Mark, *Thomas,* or one of the other NT Gospels) provides the form closest to what Jesus may have uttered. Next to be considered is the parable's original *form.* This will entail questions of structure as well. Then the *original setting and meaning* of the parable must be determined, so far as this is possible. This task entails a whole series of related issues, such as the function of the allusions to Isa 5 in the opening portion of the parable and of the quotation of Ps 118:22–23 that concludes the parable. Finally, one must consider the Markan *redaction and contextualization* of this parable and in what ways he may have introduced new ideas and have given it new functions. When these issues have been addressed, it will be possible to comment upon the Markan form of the parable phrase by phrase.

A. *Source.* One century ago Jülicher (*Gleichnisreden,* 2:385–406, esp. 406) rejected the authenticity of the parable of the Wicked Vineyard Tenants as a manifest example of ecclesiastical allegorization (followed by Kümmel, "Das Gleichnis"; Haenchen, 396–405; Schweizer, 239–40). He allowed that Jesus might have spoken of a man who had a vineyard, and so perhaps fragments of such a parable may be discernible in vv 1 and 9, but little elsewhere in the pericope. Jülicher (*Gleichnisreden* 1:65–85) maintained that allegorical elements simply did not go back to Jesus. Dodd (*Parables,* 124–32) responded to Jülicher's skepticism by arguing that if the parable was stripped of its allegorical, christological features, there really were no sufficient grounds for denying it to Jesus. Dodd accepted Mark 12:1b–3, 5a, 6–9a as original. Within the parable proper Dodd omitted the second servant who was treated shamefully (v 4), the "many others" who were variously beaten and killed (v 5b), and the answer to the concluding question (v 9b). Dodd went on to suggest that the Matthean evangelist improved on the Markan version by having the hearers answer the question (Matt 21:41; cf. Mark 12:9b), which is truer to the parabolic form, adding the saying about the kingdom of God being taken away and given to a "nation producing the fruits of it" (Matt 21:43), and changing a few incidental details, such as having the son first cast out of the vineyard and then killed (Matt 21:39), which reverses Mark's sequence (Mark 12:8), perhaps to reflect Jesus' being taken out of the city of Jerusalem and then executed (cf. Heb 13:12, which says Jesus "suffered outside the gate"). The Matthean version of the parable and its setting is noticeably embellished at various other points (cf. Matt 21:33a, 35–36, 40–42, 45–46).

Jeremias (*Parables,* 77) agreed with Dodd, finding confirmation in the recently published *Gospel of Thomas.* Jeremias (*Parables,* 70) stated: "the allegorical features which already occur in Mark, but especially in Matthew, are secondary. This result has now been amply confirmed by the Gospel of Thomas." The form of the parable in *Thomas* reads (*Gos. Thom.* §§65–66):

> Jesus said: "There was a lender who owned a vineyard. He leased it to tenant farmers so that they might work it and he might collect the produce from them. He sent his servant so that the tenants might give him the produce of the vineyard. They seized his servant and beat him, all but killing him. The servant went back and told his master. The master said, 'Perhaps <they> did not know <him>.' He sent another servant. The tenants beat this one as well. Then the owner sent his son and said, 'Perhaps they will show respect to my son.' Because the tenants knew that it was he who was the heir to the vineyard, they seized him and killed him. Let him who has ears hear." Jesus said: "Show me the stone which the builders have rejected. That one is the cornerstone." (based on J. M. Robinson, ed., *The Nag Hammadi Library* [Leiden: Brill, 1977] 125–26)

It has been fashionable for some time, especially among North American scholars, to view the form of the parable in *Thomas* as more primitive than the Synoptic forms of the parable. The Jesus Seminar, for example, assigns a pink rating to *Gos. Thom.* §65, but a gray rating to Mark 12:1–8. A black rating is assigned to both *Gos. Thom.* §66 and Mark 12:9–11 (cf. Funk and Hoover, *The Five Gospels,* 100–101, 510–11; "pink" means the material goes back to Jesus, though perhaps not exactly; "gray" means it probably does not; "black" means that it definitely does not go back to Jesus). Funk and Hoover (101) comment that "Thomas is undoubtedly closer to the original version." Crossan (*JBL* 90 [1971] 451–65; *In Parables,* 86–96; *Historical Jesus,* 351–52) defends the independence and authenticity of the form of the parable in *Thomas,* regarding it as closest to the original form. Others who argue that *Thomas* preserves the oldest form of the parable include R. Mcl. Wilson (*Studies in the Gospel of Thomas* [London: Mowbray, 1960] 101–2) and J. E. Newell and R. R. Newell (*NovT* 14 [1972] 226–27).

Is the form of the parable in *Thomas* closer to what Jesus originally told? Not likely. Sevrin ("Un groupement de trois paraboles," 438–39) has demonstrated that the gnostic redactor of *Thomas* grouped together and abridged three synoptic parables as part of his gnostic polemic against materialism and wealth. In doing this he stripped the parables of all allusions to the OT and to Jewish-Christian views of salvation history. Meier (*Marginal Jew* 1:134) agrees: "Thomas' view of salvation is ahistorical, atemporal, amaterial, and so he regularly removes from the Four Gospels anything that contradicts this view." The whole point of the parable is that a wealthy lender (the antithesis of the gnostic ideal) ultimately loses everything— his profits, his property, and even his son, who was to be his heir.

Sevrin and Meier are probably correct in their interpretation of the context in *Thomas*. Another point in their support is found in the recognition that the older proposed restoration of the word *chrē[st]os*, "good man," which describes the owner of the vineyard, is probably incorrect. (This word is one of dozens of Greek loanwords in the Coptic text of the *Gospel of Thomas*.) Careful examination of the original text shows that what this restoration reads as an omicron is probably an eta. This point is conceded by Patterson (*Gospel of Thomas*, 142–43; cf. Dehandschutter, "La parabole," 218). Thus the restoration should be *chrē[st]ēs*, "lender" (as appears in the translation of *Gos. Thom.* §§65–66 above). The parable is not about a good man (who may or may not represent God) who owns a vineyard, but about a usurer who (by implication) hopes to make a profit but does not. He becomes another example of a tradesman or merchant who will not enter places of the Father (as in the moral that concludes the previous parable, log. §64, a rewritten version of the parable of the Banquet).

What has attracted scholars to the version in *Thomas* is its simpler, apparently less allegorical form. Because it is assumed that simpler forms are older and more original than more detailed forms, it is concluded by some that *Gos. Thom.* §65 attests a form of the parable that is more primitive than what is preserved in Mark, and in Matthew and Luke, which are dependent upon Mark. But this assumption immediately runs into difficulties in this case, for a similar simpler, apparently less allegorical form is found in Luke 20:9–17. The Lukan version omits most of the words and phrases from Isa 5:1–2. Luke retains Mark's ἀμπελῶνα ἄνθρωπος ἐφύτευσεν, "a man planted a vineyard" (although changing the order of the words), but omits "and he put a fence around it, and hewed out a winepress, and built a tower." Luke omits from v 4 Mark's puzzling ἐκεφαλίωσαν, "struck on the head." Luke also omits most of Mark's v 5: "So he sent another; and they killed that one, and many others, beating some and killing others." Luke simplifies Mark's v 6 by having the owner say "I will send my beloved son; it may be they will respect him" (Luke 20:13). Finally, Luke omits Ps 118:23, which is also absent in *Gos. Thom.* §66.

The comparison of Mark and Luke provides a clear example of abbreviation of the dominical tradition, not expansion and embellishment. Unless one wants to argue that in this case Luke preserves an earlier, more primitive form of the parable, it would seem that we have here a case where an editor has streamlined the version he inherited from the tradition. If the Lukan evangelist can do it, so can the redactor of *Thomas*. Moreover, there is evidence elsewhere in *Thomas* of Lukanisms (cf. J. H. Charlesworth and C. A. Evans, "Jesus in the Agrapha and Apocryphal Gospels," in *Studying the Historical Jesus: Evaluations of the State of Current Research*, ed. B. D. Chilton and C. A. Evans, NTTS 19 [Leiden: Brill, 1994] 496–503). For these reasons some scholars have concluded that the form of the parable of the Wicked Vineyard Tenants in *Thomas* is an edited and abridged form of the Lukan version of the parable (cf. Dehandschutter, "La parabole," 203–19; Sevrin, "Un groupement de trois paraboles," 433–34). In recent studies Snodgrass (*NTS* 21 [1974–75] 142–44; *SecCent* 7 [1989] 19–38) has concluded that the evidence is compelling, perhaps even "overwhelming," that the version of the parable of the Wicked Vineyard Tenants in *Thomas* is secondary.

Finally, when the context in *Thomas* is carefully considered, the reason for the absence of an equivalent to Mark's v 9 becomes apparent. The conclusion of the parable proper has Jesus ask and answer: "What will the owner of the vineyard do? He will come and destroy the tenants and give the vineyard to others." This conclusion is completely unacceptable to the redactor of *Thomas*. The lender (not a "good man") is supposed to suffer loss. He may own a vineyard, lease it out, and expect profits, but he has another thing coming. His plans do not come to fruition. He sends one servant after another; they all come back empty-handed. He decides to send his son, thinking that it is all a misunderstanding. The lender just doesn't get it; he is in denial. He cannot see the writing on the wall. His efforts are doomed to failure. This is the message of *Thomas:* "Tradesmen and merchants shall not enter the places of my Father" (conclusion of log. §64). For this reason the Markan ending will simply not work, for it teaches that the owner of the vineyard will be vindicated, he will have justice; the ongoing rebellion and criminal acts of the tenant farmers will not go unanswered forever. The rejected stone quotation fits this pattern as well. Having dropped Mark's v 9 (or, better, Luke 20:15b–16), the redactor of *Thomas* continues to follow the Lukan tradition by making use of the quotation of Ps 118:22, but he creates a new nuance: "Jesus said: 'Show me the stone which the builders have rejected. That one is the cornerstone.'" That is, the way of life rejected by tradesmen, merchants, and lenders is the way to truth and knowledge. Thus the version in *Thomas* can be and should be explained as a purposefully reworked version of the Lukan parable. Furthermore, the version in *Thomas* does not really provide solid evidence that the original form of the parable lacked a concluding quotation of Ps 118:22–23.

The conclusion that must be drawn from this discussion is that the Gospel of Mark preserves for us the oldest, most primitive form of the tradition (though some, e.g., Snodgrass, *Parable of the Wicked Tenants,* contend that the Matthean version reflects an older form). It will be shown in the further discussion below that some of the items that scholars have identified as pointing to later embellishment, such as the presence of words and phrases from Isa 5:1–2 and the formal quotation of Ps 118:22–23, present, on the contrary, evidence of antiquity and authenticity. It will also be shown that the Markan form of the parable fits squarely within a pre-Easter setting in the life of Jesus (*Sitz im Leben Jesu*) and the cultural and religious context of first-century Jewish Palestine.

B. Form. The form of the Markan version of the parable of the Wicked Vineyard Tenants is triadic: *(a)* God, who has blessed his people with every gift, is patient and longsuffering, even in the face of obduracy and rebellion; *(b)* the day will come, however, when God will judge those who oppose his will; and *(c)* despite the rebellion of his people, God's purposes will be fully accomplished; that which his stewards tried to oppose and destroy, God has confirmed (cf. Blomberg, *Interpreting,* 247–51). The third element is lost in the form of the parable in *Thomas;* but as argued above, the redactor of the *Thomas* tradition very probably deliberately excised the parable's conclusion. In *Thomas* the parable is dyadic: *(a)* a lender tries to make money on an investment in a vineyard; *(b)* the venture ends in disaster.

Scholars have frequently complained of the irrational behavior of the characters in the parable of the Wicked Vineyard Tenants. The owner of the vineyard seems particularly inept. Why on earth would he repeatedly send servants? Why send his beloved son to face such danger? Hirsch (*Frühgeschichte,* 129) exclaims that the owner of the vineyard acts throughout like a total idiot (*ein Verrückter*). But the behavior of the tenant farmers themselves is hardly saner. Did they really think they could violate the terms of the lease, commit assault and murder, and then inherit the vineyard? Because of these improbabilities, some think that what might have been a more realistic, original parable has become embellished. What had once made a simple, single point now has become a complicated allegory that no longer realistically reflects living conditions in first-century Palestine. It reflects instead "the 'blessed idiocy' of grace" (Carlston, *Parables,* 185). But objections such as these fail to understand the nature of the Jewish *māšāl,* "parable," which often portrays characters behaving in absurd ways.

The parable of the Wicked Vineyard Tenants immediately calls to mind several rabbinic parables. See, for instance, the opening part of a parable attributed to Rabbi Simeon ben Halafta: "To what may this be compared? To one man living in Galilee and owning a vineyard in Judea, and another man living in Judea and owning a vineyard in Galilee" (*Midr. Tanḥ.* B *Qĕdôšîm* §6 [on Lev 19:2]). One also thinks of the parable applied to Egypt, which had once enslaved Israel: "They were like robbers who had broken into the king's vineyard and destroyed the vines. When the king discovered that his vineyards had been destroyed, he was filled with wrath, and descending upon the robbers, without help from anything or anyone, he cut them down and uprooted them as they had done to his vineyard" (*Exod. Rab.* 30.17 [on Exod 21:18]; tr. S. M. Lehrman, "Exodus," in *Midrash Rabbah,* ed. H. Freedman and M. Simon, 10 vols. [London and New York: Soncino, 1983] 3:367). Another parable, attributed to Rabbi Simeon ben Yoḥai (ca. 140 C.E.), equates Israel to a vineyard and appeals to Isa 5:7:

> Rabbi Simeon ben Yoḥai said: "Why was Israel likened to a vineyard? In the case of a vineyard, in the beginning one must hoe it, then weed it, and then erect supports when he sees the clusters [forming]. Then he must return to pluck the grapes and press them in order to extract the wine from them. So also Israel—each and every shepherd who oversees them must tend them [as he would tend a vineyard]. Where [in Scripture] is Israel called a vineyard? In the verse, 'For the vineyard of the Lord of Hosts is the House of Israel, and the seedlings he lovingly tended are the men of Judah' [Isa 5:7]." (*Midr. Prov.* 19:21; translation based on B. L. Visotzky, *The Midrash on Proverbs,* YJS 27 [New Haven, CT; London: Yale UP, 1992] 89)

The parable of the Unworthy Tenants (*Sipre Deut.* §312 [on Deut 32:9]) is sometimes cited as an illustrative parallel. In it is an example of problems between the owner of a vineyard (= God) and the tenants of his vineyard:

> A parable: A king had a field which he leased to tenants. When the tenants began to steal from it, he took it away from them and leased it to their children. When the chil-

dren began to act worse than their fathers, he took it away from them and gave it to the grandchildren. When these too became worse than their predecessors, a son was born to him. He then said to the grandchildren, "Leave my property. You may not remain in it. Give me back my portion, so that I may repossess it." (translation based on R. Hammer, *Sifre: A Tannaitic Commentary on the Book of Deuteronomy,* YJS 24 [New Haven, CT; London: Yale UP, 1986] 318)

The *māšāl* (i.e., story) is followed by a brief *nimšāl* (i.e., lesson) underscoring the worthiness of the patriarchs. The *nimšāl* concludes with a quotation of Gen 25:27: "And Jacob was a perfect man, dwelling in tents." The remainder of *Sipre Deut.* §312 buttresses this conclusion with a series of loosely related Scriptures and comments.

Another parable that has nothing to do with a vineyard or farming nevertheless well illustrates betrayal of a trust and the exaggerated naïveté of the protagonist. This parable exemplifies the point that has been made that parables sometimes portray people behaving in extraordinary ways:

> The parable, as told by Rabbi Yose the Galilean, concerned a mortal king who had set out for a city far across the sea. As he was about to entrust his son to the care of a wicked guardian, his friends and servants said to him: My lord king, do not entrust your son to this wicked guardian. Nevertheless the king, ignoring the counsel of his friends and servants, entrusted his son to the wicked guardian. What did the guardian do? He proceeded to destroy the king's city, have his house consumed by fire, and slay his son with the sword. After a while the king returned. When he saw his city destroyed and desolate, his house consumed by fire, his son slain with the sword, he pulled out the hair of his head and his beard and broke out into wild weeping, saying: Woe is me! How <foolish> I have been, how senselessly I acted in this kingdom of mine in entrusting my son to a wicked guardian! (*S. Eli. Rab.* §28 [p. 150]; translation based on W. G. Braude and I. Kapstein, *Tanna debe Eliyyahu: The Lore of the School of Elijah* [Philadelphia: Jewish Publication Society, 1981] 369)

These parables parallel at many points the principal elements that make up Jesus' parable of the Wicked Vineyard Tenants. Rabbi Simeon's parable speaks of absentee vineyard owners. The next parable talks of an angry king who takes vengeance on men who had violated his vineyard. The third parable is based on Isa 5, as is Jesus' parable of the Wicked Vineyard Tenants. Note too how Simeon ben Yoḥai mixes his metaphors by introducing shepherds. Jesus likewise appends a proof text about builders. The fourth parable makes use of the image of unruly, rebellious tenants. The fifth parable, attributed to Yose the Galilean (second century C.E.), describes a remarkably foolish and incautious king who entrusts his son to a villain. Several details of this parable have significance for Jesus' parable, especially in view of the questions raised about its authenticity. Yose's parable portrays a man who appears utterly to lack common sense. Against the advice of friends and counselors he entrusts his son to a man known to be a wicked guardian. But the actions of the guardian are just as difficult to comprehend. We are not told that he stole anything or profited in any way by his actions. He destroys the king's city, burns down his house, and murders his son. What could he possibly have hoped to gain? Did he imagine that he could get away with these crimes? Would not every hearer of this parable suppose that the king would send troops after the guardian and have him executed? These are the same kinds of questions critics have raised against the logic, if not authenticity, of the parable of the Wicked Vineyard Tenants (see the discussion in Carlston, *Parables*, 183–84). How could the owner of the vineyard be so foolish and so reckless with the lives of his servants and especially the life of his son? What could the tenants realistically have hoped to gain? Did they not know that the owner had the power to come and destroy them? Did they really imagine that they could inherit the vineyard?

Questions such as these do not constitute valid objections to the authenticity of parables, whether Gospel or rabbinic. The incomprehensible folly of the king in Yose's parable should not cast doubt on the question of its authenticity (note too that Yose applies the parable to God's trusting Nebuchadnezzar!). Nor should the folly of the vineyard owner and the vineyard tenants cast doubt on the authenticity of Jesus' parable. These parables do indeed provoke these kinds of questions—for ancient hearers as well as modern. But the shocking details and the questions they raise are supposed to lead the hearers to grasp and apply the intended lesson. Furthermore, all of the rabbinic parables reviewed above are to some extent allegorical, with the king or owner of the field or vineyard often representing God, the field or vineyard representing either the people or land of Israel, and tenants representing Gentiles or other unworthy people, and the king's or owner's son representing the people of Israel or the patriarchs. These are stock images, drawn from a common Jewish religious "thesaurus" (Scott, *Hear Then the Parable*, 18).

It is concluded, then, that the form of the parable of the Wicked Vineyard Tenants is true to the parabolic form found in Judaism of late antiquity. There is nothing in it that requires us to see the hand of later Christian allegorizers trying to give it a new form and a new meaning. On the contrary, there are elements present in this parable that tell against its origin in the church.

C. Original setting and meaning. For those scholars who reject the Markan context, the concluding quotation of Ps 118:22–23, and the opening words and phrases from Isa 5:1–2, the original meaning of the parable of the Wicked Vineyard Tenants proves elusive. Concluding that Jesus was not the author of the parable and that the Markan (and synoptic) context is secondary, Carlston (*Parables*, 178–90) is left to speculate concerning what the point of it was for the early church, which created it. Carlston (*Parables*, 188–90) can think of three possible meanings: (*a*) "It could mean that God will turn from the Jews who killed his Son and heir . . . to others who are more worthy of God's vineyard, i.e., to those who believe the gospel." But what then would the vineyard mean to the early church? Israel? The land of Israel? What the church eventually came to believe of itself was that it had inherited Israel's status as God's chosen people (notwithstanding Rom 11). Does giving the vineyard to others mean this? It is hard to see how. Carlston speaks of others "who are more worthy of God's vineyard." But that is not what the parable is talking about. The issue is not what the vineyard is but who will care for the vineyard. (*b*) "The parable could also imply that Jesus foresaw God's turning from the Jews to the Gentiles." But again, how does the parable convey this idea? God turns away from the farmers to whom the vineyard had been entrusted. And if the concluding quotation is considered, the point that the parable tries to make receives a climactic scriptural confirmation: what the builders rejected, God has established. (*c*) "Finally, the parable could be understood to reflect a regular principle in the divine economy: just as God has turned from the Jews to the Gentiles, so he will always turn from those who do not produce 'fruit' to those who do." The third interpretive proposal is only slightly more convincing than the first two. The second half of the interpretation is correct: God will turn away from those who do not produce fruit. According to the Markan (and synoptic) context of the parable, God turns away from the builders, that is, the religious authorities. In their place he will appoint others to care for the vineyard. But the first part of Carlston's third interpretation suffers the same fate as the first two interpretations. God has turned away not from the vineyard but from those who care for it. If the early church was scripturally skilled enough to choose the appropriate scriptural testimony (i.e., Isa 5:1–7) to identify the vineyard and create a *heilsgeschichtliche* (history-of-salvation) allegory, summarizing Israel's history of rejecting the prophets and finally God's Son, then the parable cannot be interpreted as though the early church forgot the significance of the vineyard. One cannot have it both ways. It is not plausible that the church invented a parable that attempted to clarify its place in God's divine plan (e.g., because of persistent rejection of the prophets and God's Son, God has rejected Israel, his vineyard, in favor of the church), but then told the parable in such a misleading way that it seemed to be talking about those who cared for the vineyard. All attempts to interpret the parable as a creation of the church suffer shipwreck on the rock of the parable's basic story line: the focus is not on the identity of the vineyard, which is presupposed and remains constant; the focus is on the conflict between those who care for the vineyard and the owner of the vineyard whom the tenant farmers do not respect and will not obey.

It is not surprising, then, that most interpreters today accept the parable as authentic. What is still widely rejected is the Markan (or synoptic) contextualization of the parable, including the allusions to Isa 5:1–7 and the concluding quotation of Ps 118:22–23. But these scholars run into the same interpretive difficulties that plague the interpretive proposals of Carlston and others who view the parable as a creation of the early church. Scott (*Hear Then the Parable*, 252–53) opines: "Since the parable provides no ready identification models, no clear metaphorical referencing, an audience is left in a precarious position: *In the plot the kingdom fails and the inheritance is in doubt*" (Scott's emphasis). Scott's proposal is extraordinary, for it contradicts both context and content. He says there are "no ready identification models." But, of course, there are: the biblical tradition in general (i.e., the history of Israel's suffering prophets, Israel's stubborn sinfulness, etc.) and the allusions to Isa 5:1–7 in particular. He believes the parable leaves the auditor in a precarious position because the "kingdom fails and the inheritance is in doubt." There is no doubt about the kingdom and the inheritance if the quotation of Ps 118:22–23 is allowed to stand, which as a scriptural quotation would be an intrinsic part of the *nimšāl* of the parable (see above).

Malina and Rohrbaugh (255) have doubts about the Markan context. They wonder if the parable originally had been "a warning to landowners expropriating and exporting the produce of the land." What such a parable could possibly have meant in the context of Jesus' ministry is not clear, nor do Malina and Rohrbaugh venture an opinion. Funk and Hoover (*Five Gospels*, 101), following the lead of the version in *Thomas*, think "Jesus' version was a disturbing and tragic tale, but it was told without specific application." The Jesus Seminar's recommendation, succinctly summarized in the *Five Gospels,* bears the stamp of Crossan's earlier work (*In Parables,* 96): "It is a deliberately shocking story of successful murder." (See the ongoing evolution in Crossan's attempts to find a compelling original meaning that is bereft of the synoptic context.) Having taken the parable out of its Markan/synoptic context, these interpreters have no idea what the parable originally meant.

Despite valiant and ultimately fruitless efforts to find significant meaning in the parable of the Wicked Vineyard Tenants when the synoptic context is denied, or when authenticity is denied, all that is left is banality. Either we have a clumsy attempt at Christian *Heilsgeschichte* (history of salvation), or we have a warning against exporting the land's produce, or a tragedy, or maybe even a shocking story of successful murder. These decontextualized approaches leave us with a parable for which there is no real justification for preservation or retelling.

Because he attributes the parable's allusions to Isa 5 entirely to the LXX, and can find no Semitisms, Mell (*Die "anderen" Winzer,* 97–117) believes that the parable of the Wicked Vineyard Tenants derives from the Hellenistic church and not from Jesus himself. But there are several non-Septuagintal features, Semitic features, and important points of coherence with Jewish interpretation, attested in the later Targums and Tosefta and the much earlier Qumran documents 4Q500 (= 4QBenediction) and 4Q162 (= 4QpIsa[b]). If we take a fresh look at the parable and try to see it through pre-Easter Jewish (not Christian) eyes, we will find a parable that makes good sense in the context of Jesus' ministry. Redaction and a measure of recontextualization will also be detected, to be sure, but we shall see that the synoptic context is plausible and meets some of the important criteria used for establishing the authenticity of dominical tradition. The following four points argue for a setting in the life of Jesus (*Sitz im Leben Jesu*) rather than a setting in the life of the early church (*Sitz im Leben der alten Kirche*).

1. The Semitic character of the parable. Lee (*Jesus und die jüdische Autorität,* 80; chiefly following Kümmel, "Gleichnis," 211 n. 20; Hengel, *ZNW* 59 [1968] 7–8 n. 31) has identified more than one dozen Semitic elements in the parable of the Wicked Vineyard Tenants: (*a*) ἄνθρωπος, "man," in the sense of τὶς, "someone" (v 1b; cf. Pesch, 2:215), (*b*) the partitive use of ἀπό, "a portion from" (v 2), (*c*) the pleonastic λαβόντες, "taking" (vv 3 and 8), (*d*) ἀπέστειλαν κένον, "sent [him] away empty-handed" (v 3; cf. Gen 31:42; Deut 15:13; 1 Sam 6:3), (*e*) asyndeton in ἀπέστειλαν, "he sent" (v 6) and τί ποιήσει, "what will he do?" (v 9), (*f*) the superfluous demonstrative pronoun ἐκεῖνοι οἱ γεωργοί, "those tenants" (v 7), (*g*) the Semitic *dativus ethicus* πρὸς ἑαυτοὺς εἶπαν, "they said to themselves" (v 7), (*h*) ὁ κληρονόμος, "the heir" (v 7; cf. Gen 15:3–4), (*i*) jussive + καί, "and" + future sentence construction (v 7), (*j*) ὁ κύριος τοῦ ἀμπελῶνος, "the owner of the vineyard" (v 9), (*k*) ἐλεύσεται, "he will come" (v 9) in the sense of "to come back," (*l*) the frequent use of the paratactic καί, "and," (*m*) εἰς, "to" (v 10b) corresponding to the Hebrew לְ *lĕ* (cf. Taylor, 476), and (*n*) αὕτη, "this" (v 11), corresponding to the Hebrew זֹאת *zōʾt* (Swete, 272; Taylor, 476).

2. The presence of allusions to Isa 5:1–7. There may be some assimilation to the LXX, but some of Mark's text cannot be so explained, for there are elements that are present only in the Hebrew or the Aramaic. The words in the Markan form of the parable that have been drawn from Isaiah's Song of the Vineyard (Isa 5:1–7) may be compared to their counterparts in the LXX and MT:

Mark 12:1	ἀμπελῶνα, "vineyard"
Isa 5:1–2 LXX	ἀμπελῶνι/ἀμπελών/ἄμπελον, "concerning [his] vineyard/vineyard/vine"
Isa 5:1–2 MT	שׂרק/כֶּרֶם/לְכַרְמוֹ *lĕkarmô/kerem/śōrēq*, "concerning his vineyard/vineyard/choice vine"
Mark 12:1	ἐφύτευσεν, "he planted"
Isa 5:2 LXX	καὶ ἐφύτευσα, "and I planted"
Isa 5:2 MT	וַיִּטָּעֵהוּ *wayyiṭṭāʿēhû*, "and he planted it"
Mark 12:1	καὶ περιέθηκεν φραγμόν, "and he put a fence around it"
Isa 5:2 LXX	καὶ φραγμὸν περιέθηκα, "and I put a fence around it"
Isa 5:5 MT	הָסֵר מְשׂוּכָתוֹ *hāsēr mĕśûkātô*, "removing its fence"
Mark 12:1	καὶ ὤρυξεν ὑπολήνιον, "and he hewed out a vat [beneath a winepress]"
Isa 5:2 LXX	καὶ προλήνιον ὤρυξα, "and I hewed out a vat [before a winepress]"
Isa 5:2 MT	וְגַם־יֶקֶב חָצֵב *wĕgam-yeqeb ḥāṣēb*, "and also he hewed out a wine vat"
Mark 12:1	καὶ ᾠκοδόμησεν πύργον, "and he built a tower"
Isa 5:2 LXX	καὶ ᾠκοδόμησα πύργον, "and I built a tower"
Isa 5:2 MT	וַיִּבֶן מִגְדָּל *wayyiben migdāl*, "and he built a tower"
Mark 12:7	ἀποκτείνωμεν, "let us kill"
Isa 5:7 MT	מִשְׂפָּח *miśpāḥ*, "bloodshed"
Mark 12:9	τί ποιήσει ὁ κύριος, "what will the owner do?"
Isa 5:4 LXX	τί ποιήσω, "what will I do?"
Isa 5:5 MT	אֵת אֲשֶׁר־אֲנִי עֹשֶׂה *ʾēt ʾăšer-ʾănî ʿōśeh*, "what I will do"
Mark 12:9	καὶ ἀπολέσει, "and he will destroy"
Isa 5:5–6 MT	וְהָיָה לְבָעֵר/וַאֲשִׁיתֵהוּ בָתָה *wĕhāyâ lĕbāʿēr/waʾăšîtēhû bātâ*, "and it will be devoured"/"and I will make it a waste"

Several comments are called for: (*a*) The allusions to Isa 5:1–2 in Mark 12:1–2 do not follow the word order in the LXX. Mark reads ἀμπελῶνα ἄνθρωπος ἐφύτευσεν καὶ περιέθηκεν φραγμὸν καὶ ὤρυξεν ὑπολήνιον καὶ ᾠκοδόμησεν πύργον, "a vineyard a man planted; and he put around it a fence, and hewed out a vat [beneath a winepress], and built a tower," while the LXX reads καὶ φραγμὸν περιέθηκα καὶ ἐχαράκωσα καὶ ἐφύτευσα ἄμπελον σώρηχ καὶ ᾠκοδόμησα πύργον ἐν μέσῳ αὐτοῦ καὶ προλήνιον ὤρυξα ἐν αὐτῷ, "and a fence I put around it, and I dug a trench, and I planted a *sōrēch* vine, and I built a tower in its midst, and a vat [before a winepress] I hewed out in it." (*b*) Mark says, "a vineyard a man planted," but the LXX says, "I planted a *sōrēch* vine." (*c*) Mark's third-person verbs ("he planted," "he put around," "he hewed out," and "he built") agree with the third-person verbs in the MT, not with the first-person verbs in the LXX ("I put around," "I dug," "I planted," "I built," "I hewed out"). (*d*) Whereas the LXX renders יֶקֶב *yeqeb* as προλήνιον, "vat [before a winepress]," Mark reads ὑπολήνιον, "vat [beneath a winepress]." In the LXX יֶקֶב *yeqeb* is frequently translated ληνός, "wine vat." Three times it is rendered ὑπολήνιον (Isa 16:10; Hag 2:16; Zech 14:10); only once, here in Isa 5:2, is it rendered προλήνιον. Had Mark's text read προλήνιον, we might have suspected direct influence of LXX Isa 5:2. Had Mark's text read ληνός, the common rendering for יֶקֶב *yeqeb*, we might have suspected general Septuagintal influence, but the appearance of ὑπολήνιον suggests independence. *(e)* In Mark 12:7–8, the tenants say, "let us kill him," and then they kill the son. In the MT (Isa 5:7) "bloodshed" (מִשְׂפָּח *miśpāḥ*) is cited as one of the reasons that judgment will befall the vineyard. There is no equivalent in the LXX, which reads only ἀνομίαν, "lawlessness." Mark's language is thus closer to the MT. *(f)* Mark's language is again closer to the MT in the description of the judgment that will come: "He will come and destroy the tenants" (v 9b). MT Isa 5:5–6 says וְהָיָה לְבָעֵר *wĕhāyâ lĕbāʿēr*, "and it will be devoured," and וַאֲשִׁיתֵהוּ בָתָה *waʾăšîtēhû bātâ*, "and I will make it a waste." The LXX only says καὶ ἔσται εἰς διαρπαγήν, "and it will be for plundering," and καὶ ἀνήσω τὸν ἀμπελῶνά μου, "and I will forsake my vineyard."

Even more important than the coherence with the Hebrew text and noncoherence with the LXX is the coherence with the interpretive and thematic tendencies in the Aramaic version of the Targum of Isa 5:1–7. Below are vv 1, 2, and 5 of the Targum, with departures from the MT placed in italics:

> *The prophet said*, I will sing now for *Israel—which is like a vineyard, the seed of Abraham, my friend—my friend's* song for his vineyard: *My people*, my beloved *Israel, I gave them a heritage* on a *high* hill *in* fertile *land*. And I *sanctified* them and I *glorified* them and *I established them as the plant of a* choice vine; and *I* built *my sanctuary* in *their* midst, and I even *gave my altar to atone for their sins; I thought that they would do good deeds, but they made their deeds evil*. . . . And now I will tell you what I *am about to do* to my *people*. I will *take up my Shekhinah from them*, and *they* shall be for *plundering;* I will break down *the place of their sanctuaries*, and *they will be* for trampling. (translation from B. D. Chilton, *The Isaiah Targum*, ArBib 11 [Wilmington, DE: Glazier, 1987] 10–11)

What is striking is the explicit cultic orientation of the Aramaic version, which is consistent with the anti–temple establishment thrust of the Markan parable. Several points of coherence may be identified: *(a)* The prophetic tone of the oracle has been accentuated by adding the opening phrase "The prophet said." As something that the prophet said, Isaiah's Song of the Vineyard more readily accommodates a later appeal to it as prophecy, as though foretelling something about a later time. A futuristic hermeneutic such as this is common in Qumran and early Christian literature. *(b)* Isaiah's Song of the Vineyard has been "parabolized": "I will sing now for Israel—which is like [דמתיל *dimtîl*] a vineyard." The Aramaic מתל/מתיל *mĕtîl/mĕtal* is the equivalent of the Hebrew משל *māšal*, which is routinely used to introduce rabbinic parables (and appears in the introductions of some of the parables cited above). In other words, according to the Targum, Israel may be likened to a parable about a vineyard. *(c)* The Aramaic paraphrase introduces "heritage" (אחסנא *ʾaḥsānāʾ*), which is cognate to the parable's "heir" (κληρονόμος) and "inheritance" (κληρονομία) (Mark 12:7). *(d)* The cultic orientation of the Aramaic version is seen at several points. The most obvious is the substitution of "sanctuary" and "altar" in v 2 for the MT's "tower" and "wine vat." When judgment comes in v 5 it will be the loss of the "Shekinah" and the "place of their sanctuaries," rather than the MT's "fence" and "wall." The cultic orientation is probably also seen in the addition of "high" in v 1: the "high" hill in fertile land is none other than the Temple Mount. Two passages in the Tosefta, *t. Meʿil.* 1.16 and *t. Sukkah* 3.15, understand Isa 5:2 the same way. According to the latter, the "tower" is the "temple," the "wine vat" is the "altar," while "and" (in *"and* hewed out a wine vat") hints at a further meaning, specifically the fructifying streams that issue forth from the altar (cf. *m. Yoma* 5:6; *m. Mid.* 3:3). The antiquity of this cultic interpretation is now partially attested by 4Q500 [= 4QBenediction], in which the fragmentary lines 3–7 read: "a wine vat [bu]ilt among stones . . . to the fate of the holy height . . . your planting and the streams of your glory . . . your vine[yard . . .]." 4Q500's holy "height" (מרום *mārôm*) agrees with the Aramaic Targum's description of the fertile hill as "high" (רם *rām*), while the "streams" agree with the "water channels" in *t. Sukkah* 3.15 (cf. Baumgarten, *JJS* 40 [1989] 1–6). Of course, the reference to the height as "holy" (קודש *qôdeš*) is an obvious allusion to the Temple Mount (cf. Ezek 20:40: "For on my holy mountain, the mountain height [בְּהַר־קָדֶשׁ בְּהַר מְרוֹם *běhar-qodšî běhar měrôm*] of Israel, says the Lord GOD, there all the house of Israel, all of them, shall serve me in the land"). Jesus' use of Isa 5:1–7 presupposes several of the principal exegetical points of reference preserved in 4Q500, which predates him, and in the Targum and Tosefta, which postdate him. It is highly doubtful that this usage of Isa 5:1–7 originated in the Greek-speaking, LXX-reading church. *(e)* There also appears to be some coherence with the LXX, specifically in v 5, where both the Greek and the Aramaic say that the vineyard "will be for plundering" (LXX: ἔσται εἰς διαρπαγήν; Tg: ויהון למיבז *wîhěwōn lěmêbaz;* cf. *DJPA* 89 [s.v. בזז *bězaz*]), which differs from the MT: "it will be devoured" (וְהָיָה לְבָעֵר *wěhāyâ lěbāʿēr*). But this does not mean that there was no pre-70 Hebrew textual tradition that also read this way. The discovery at Qumran of a Hebrew text of the OT that lies behind the LXX has changed our way of viewing the LXX's relationship to the MT (cf. Ulrich, "Septuagint Manuscripts"; Greenspoon, "Dead Sea Scrolls and the Greek Bible"). There are many examples where Hebrew manuscripts agree with the LXX over against the MT, including many cases involving Isaiah. It is simply no longer critical to say that Isa 5:1–2 in the parable of the Wicked Vineyard Tenants "is quoted from the Septuagint, which would have been done only in the Greek-speaking church" (Schweizer, 239). One more observation may be made concerning the interpretation of Isa 5 at Qumran. The fragmentary 4Q162 (= 4QpIsaᵇ) quotes Isa 5:5–6 and says "the passage means that he abandoned them" (1:2); then at the end of the column it quotes Isa 5:10 and interprets it (at the top of the next column): "the passage refers to the Last Days, when the land itself is condemned by sword and famine; so it shall be at the time when the land is punished" (2:1–2). The pesher goes on to quote Isa 5:11–14 and interprets: "These are the men of mockery who are in Jerusalem" (2:6–7). It then quotes Isa 5:24–25 and interprets: "This is the company of the men of mockery who are in Jerusalem" (2:10). What is interesting here is that the pesher appears to understand Isa 5 eschatologically and emphasizes that the villains are the "men of mockery who are in Jerusalem." This line of interpretation is entirely consistent with the Aramaic paraphrase of Isa 5 in the Targum and the function of Isa 5 in the parable of the Wicked Vineyard Tenants. One final point may be added. In 4Q270 (= 4QDᶜ) 9 ii 6 the priesthood is described as God's planting: "the sons of Aaron are the planting" (בני אהרון המטעה *běnê ʾahărôn hammaṭṭāʿâ*). In the LXX מטע *maṭṭāʿ* is translated by φύτευμα, "planting" (e.g., Isa 60:21; 61:3).

The conclusion that should be drawn from this comparative study of various textual and exegetical traditions is that the appearance of Isa 5:1–7 in the parable of the Wicked Vineyard Tenants *(a)* is consistent with the parable; indeed, the parable grows out of it; *(b)* is more easily explained as originating in a pre-Christian, synagogue-related context (in which the Isaiah Targum developed); and *(c)* probably derives from Jesus. Another point that argues for the originality of the presence of Isa 5:1–7 in the parable is that Isaiah's Song of the Vineyard is essentially the same genre as Jesus' parable of the Wicked Vineyard Tenants. Both Isaiah's song and Jesus' parable are juridical parables in that both invite the hearer to pass judgment (on themselves or on others). OT scholars have identified Isaiah's Song of the Vineyard as a form of juridical parable in which the hearers judge themselves (Willis, *JBL* 96 [1977] 337–62; Graffy, *Bib* 60 [1979] 400–409; Sheppard, *CBQ* 44 [1982] 45–47; Yee, *CBQ* 43 [1981] 30–40; cf. Evans, *BZ* 28 [1984] 82–86). Other examples include the parable of the Ewe Lamb (2 Sam 12:1b–4), in which David unwittingly pronounces judgment upon himself; the parable of the Two Brothers (2 Sam 14:4–7), in which again David unknowingly condemns his own plans; and the parable of the Escaped Prisoner (1 Kgs 20:38–43), in which Ahab passes judgment upon himself. It is interesting to note that in all three of these classic OT examples of the juridical parable the target of the parable is the leader of the Jewish people. Similarly, Jesus targets the religious leaders of the people in his day. Thus, if the allusion to Isa 5:1–2 is a later embellishment of the parable, then this would represent a remarkable piece of form-critically sensitive redaction on the part of a later Christian tradent.

3. *The concluding quotation of Ps 118:22–23.* Perhaps the most frequently heard comment about Mark's form of the parable concerns the concluding quotation of Ps 118:22–23 in Mark 12:10–11. Many scholars, including those that view the parable as authentic, regard this quotation as secondary. Years ago Oesterley (*Gospel Parables,* 121) opined that the quotation is "unnecessary for the teaching of the parable." Others expressed their skepticism more forcefully (e.g., Lohmeyer, 247: it can hardly derive from Jesus; Klostermann, 120–21: it derives from early Christian polemic, and is not conceivable as an utterance of Jesus). More recent commentators hold the same view (e.g., Nineham, 313; Schmid, 217–18; Léon-Dufour, *Études,* 332–35; Haenchen, 399–400; Horstmann, *Studien zur markinischen Christologie,* 25; Anderson, 273; Gnilka, 2:142; Hooker, 276–77), usually claiming that the concluding quotation "provides for the resurrection of Jesus outside the story" (Scott, *Hear Then the Parable,* 248; cf. Haenchen, 400). But this is to read a post-Easter Christian nuance into the meaning of the quotation, a nuance found in later Christian writings that associate the rejected stone of Ps 118:22 with other related Scriptures (e.g., Acts 4:11; Rom 9:33; Eph 2:20; 1 Pet 2:6–8; *Barn.* 6:2–4; Justin, *Dial.* 36.1). The quotation speaks of vindication despite initial rejection, even martyrdom.

Notwithstanding this widespread skepticism, there are good reasons for viewing the concluding quotation of Ps 118:22–23 as indeed part of the original parable. Black (*NTS* 18 [1971–72] 11–14) thinks it was original because of the wordplay between "son" (בֵן *bēn*) and "stone" (אֶבֶן *'eben*); so does Snodgrass (*Parable of the Wicked Tenants,* 63–65, 113–18), who has provided the most recent and compelling arguments for this position. Others who accept the wordplay include Carrington (256), Evans (*BZ* 28 [1984] 82–86; id., "God's Vineyard," 403–4), Cornette (*FoiVie* 84 [1985]

47), Bayer (*Jesus' Predictions*, 105), Kim ("Jesus—The Son of God," 135–38), Milavec (*JES* 26 [1989] 307–8), Trimaille ("La parabole," 253), Gundry (689–90), Kimball (*BBR* 3 [1993] 89), Brooke (*DSD* 2 [1995] 287–89), Wright (*Jesus and the Victory of God*, 497–501), and, with some differences, Stern ("Jesus' Parables," 66–67; id., *Parables in Midrash*, 195–96), while others who doubt its originality concede that Ps 118:22–23 was added to the conclusion of the parable in the pre-Markan, pre-Greek stage of the transmission of the tradition in light of the underlying Semitic word-play (e.g., Lee, *Jesus und die jüdische Autorität*, 174; Marcus, *Way of the Lord*, 112–13; Mell, *Die "anderen" Winzer*, 157–58 esp. n. 537). J. Lightfoot (*Horae Hebraicae et Talmudicae*, 4 vols. [Oxford: Oxford UP, 1859; Latin orig. 1658–74] 2:435) suggested the wordplay nearly 350 years ago.

Much of the discussion focuses on the Hebrew wordplay between בֵּן *bēn*, "son," and אֶבֶן *'eben*, "stone," examples of which are found elsewhere in Hebrew Scripture (e.g., Exod 28:9–10; perhaps Lam 4:1–2; Zech 9:16; cf. John 4:6–7; for additional Hebrew and Aramaic examples, see Snodgrass, *Parable of the Wicked Tenants*, 115–16; Brooke, *DSD* 2 [1995] 287–88 and n. 59) and possibly in a saying of John the Baptizer: "Do not presume to say to yourselves, 'We have Abraham as our father'; for I tell you, God is able from these stones to raise up children to Abraham" (Matt 3:9 = Luke 3:8). The "stones" to which the Baptizer referred may have been twelve stones placed beside the bank of the Jordan River after the pattern of Josh 4:2, 8–9. But important evidence that such a wordplay in fact had been entertained in the exegesis of the synagogue is found in the Aramaic version of Ps 118:22 (i.e., the Targum), which reads:

טליא שביקו ארדיכליא הות ביני בניא דישי וזכה לאתמנאה למליך ושולטן

talyāʾ šabbîqû ʾardîkĕlayyāʾ hĕwāt bênê bĕnayyāʾ dĕyišay ûzĕkâ lĕʾitmannāʾâ lĕmēlêk wĕšûlṭan

The boy which the builders abandoned was among the sons of Jesse, and he is worthy to be appointed king and ruler.

The substitution of טליא *talyāʾ* for אֶבֶן *'eben* grows out of the Hebrew בֵּן/אֶבֶן *'eben/ bēn* wordplay. More important is the observation that the entire section of this Psalm (i.e., vv 19–27) in Aramaic incorporates themes from David's life, beginning with his youth and how he was initially rejected, continuing with his acceptance as Israel's king, and ending with Samuel's offering of a sacrifice to celebrate young David's accession to the throne. The coherence of this theme with the paraphrase of Ps 118:25–26, which is alluded to in the entrance narrative (11:1–11; see *Comment* above), also revealing interpretive elements from the Aramaic version, must not be overlooked. What we have is a remarkably consistent, but very subtle, exegetical thread running throughout Jesus' entrance into and activity within the temple precincts. Is it really plausible to argue that this complicated Aramaic-based exegesis is the result of the Greek-speaking, LXX-reading church? Surely not. It is more plausible to view this as fragments of an agenda generated by Jesus, inspired by certain Scriptures, frequently interpreted in light of their understanding in the Aramaic-speaking synagogue, and passed on by his disciples (so also Brooke, *DSD* 2 [1995] 294).

But what of the observation that the quotation of Ps 118:22–23 clearly comes from the LXX? Since it is a formal quotation, it is not surprising that assimilation to the LXX has occurred. One very clear example of this is to be seen in how the Aramaic-based paraphrase of Isa 6:9–10 in Mark 4:12 is assimilated to the LXX in a formal quotation in the Matthean parallel (Matt 13:10–17). We may even speculate that here in Mark 12:10–11 the assimilation to the LXX may have obliterated an original, paraphrasing allusion to a rejected "son," though that can be no more than speculation.

4. *The synoptic narrative context.* The scriptural and interpretive elements presupposed in the parable of the Wicked Vineyard Tenants (including the concluding quotation of Ps 118:22–23) cohere with a setting in the temple precincts, precisely as the Markan evangelist has presented it (cf. Brooke, *DSD* 2 [1995] 289). The parable is consistent with the prophetic indictment of 11:17 (see *Comment* on 11:17) and functions as an implicit answer to the ruling priests' question in 11:28. It is also consistent with Jesus' prophecy of the temple's destruction (13:2) and the later accusation that he had threatened the temple (14:58; cf. 15:29). The Markan/synoptic context recommends itself, for it provides a contextual setting that allows the parable to stand unified and to be interpreted in the light of the scriptural, exegetical, and traditional elements that are found in it.

Finally, the parable originally and in its later Markan context refers obliquely to Jesus as the son. A few scholars have suggested that the son of the parable is John the Baptizer (Gray, *HibJ* 19 [1920–21] 42–52; Stern, "Jesus' Parables"; id., *Parables in Midrash,* 193–95; Mann, 462–63). In favor of this view are the immediate context, where John's authority was assumed and appealed to by Jesus (cf. 11:30–32); the reference to striking the head of one of the servants (12:4), which could be a veiled reference to John's beheading (6:27–28); and the parable's reference to a succession of servants sent to the vineyard tenants, in which John the son would be seen as the last and greatest of the prophets and messengers God sent to Israel (e.g., Matt 11:11 = Luke 7:28). But identification of the parable's son with John is improbable, for where in the tradition is John (or any prophet) referred to as God's son? It is true that John is mentioned in the dispute over Jesus' authority, but at issue in that exchange between Jesus and the ruling priests was *Jesus'* authority, not John's. The parable of the Wicked Vineyard Tenants answers the priests' question concerning *what* authority empowers Jesus to do what he does (answer: by God's authority) and the question concerning *who* gave this authority to Jesus (answer: God did). These questions are not answered by a parable that alludes to John's death. Finally, and most important, it was Herod Antipas, not the ruling priests, who put John to death. The parable, even if its present context is discounted, simply does not fit the fate of John the Baptizer. Aus's proposed identification of the parable's son with Isaiah is similarly problematic, though he allows that Jesus himself might have consciously followed the example of Isaiah (Aus, *Wicked Tenants,* 1–65). This is possible, but probably in the general sense in which Jesus identified with all prophets and messengers who suffered at the hands of God's people (cf. Matt 23:37–38 = Luke 13:34).

It is concluded that the parable of the Wicked Vineyard Tenants derives from Jesus and that its Markan/synoptic context accurately reflects the original setting and meaning. Three other specific points bear repeating: (1) The parable presupposes the identity of the vineyard with Israel. This feature is not likely an ecclesiastical creation, for it stands in tension with ecclesiastical orientation and emphases. (2) The parable presupposes Aramaic interpretive tradition, which is hard to square with the oft-heard assertion that the parable was either created by the Greek-speaking church (Schweizer, 239) or with the assertion that the allusions to Isa 5:1–7 and the quotation of Ps 118:22–23 originated in the Greek-speaking, LXX-reading church. This is not an adequate explanation. The Aramaic interpretive tradition, in the case of Isa 5, is now partially documented at Qumran (i.e., 4Q500 [= 4QBenediction]), so the claim that the Aramaic and rabbinic traditions are too late to clarify the meaning of the parable is no longer justified. (3) The parable does not refer to the resurrection, even with Ps 118:22–23. This is odd, if the parable is supposed to be either a post-Easter creation or heavily redacted, christological parable. Resurrection may be implied; after all, if the son is murdered and then established as the cornerstone, that is, recognized as Israel's king, then resurrection must be in view (cf. Acts 4:10–11). But the fact that it is at most implied and not made clear, even explicit, is odd. The early church appealed to various Scriptures, including Ps 16:8–11, to explain the resurrection of Jesus (cf. Acts 2:25–28; 13:35–37). But Ps 118:22–23 was not a primary text for explaining the resurrection. (For a review of scholarship on the parable of the Wicked Vineyard Tenants, see Snodgrass, *BBR* 8 [1998] 187–215.)

D. Redaction and contextualization. The evangelist's redaction should probably be limited to vv 1a, 5b, and 12. V 5b was probably added by the evangelist to heighten the villainy of the tenants and perhaps to make it fit the larger number of prophets and messengers sent by God to Israel (e.g., Haenchen, 399; Gundry, 685). (On vv 1a and 12, see *Comment* below.)

Contextually, the parable of 12:1–12 answers the question put to Jesus in 11:28: "By what authority do you do these things?" The answer is implicit but unmistakable: Jesus acts under God's authority. God has given this authority to Jesus because he is his Son (1:11; 9:7), the "son of man" who has approached God's throne and received authority from God (see *Comment* on 11:28). Kuhn (*Ältere Sammlungen,* 42) gives the Markan evangelist credit for this contextualization. But Gundry (682) is correct to say that ultimately it is Jesus who deserves the credit for the contextualization of this parable, for the parable was his indirect way of answering the question. The above analysis fully supports this position.

Comment

1 καὶ ἤρξατο αὐτοῖς ἐν παραβολαῖς λαλεῖν, "And he began to speak to them in parables." Elsewhere the evangelist has said that Jesus spoke in parables, though usually only one parable is recorded (cf. 3:23; 4:2, 10, 11, 13, 33). The evangelist is fond of introducing Jesus' teaching with ἤρξατο, "began to": Jesus "began to" preach (1:45), teach (4:1; 6:2, 34; 8:31), and speak concerning his passion (10:32) and future dangers (13:5).

ἀμπελῶνα ἄνθρωπος ἐφύτευσεν καὶ περιέθηκεν φραγμὸν καὶ ὤρυξεν ὑπολήνιον καὶ ᾠκοδόμησεν πύργον, "A man planted a vineyard; and he put a fence around it, and hewed out a winepress, and built a tower." As analyzed in *Form/Structure/ Setting* above, these words and phrases have been drawn from Isa 5:1–7, mostly from v 2. The claim that is sometimes made that this vocabulary reflects the LXX (and not the Hebrew) often appeals to the presence of περιέθηκεν φραγμόν, "he put a fence around it," which has a counterpart in the LXX (i.e., φραγμὸν

περιέθηκα, "I put a fence around it," in v 2) but not in the MT. But this is misleading. It is true that no fence or hedge is mentioned in v 2 in the MT, but it is
present in v 5 (מְשׂוּכָתוֹ mĕsûkātô, "its fence"). That this reference in the MT is the
equivalent of the φραγμόν, "fence," of v 2 in the LXX is clear, for the LXX translates it with φραγμόν in v 5. Thus, the parable's reference to the building of a
fence assumes the later reference to the fence's destruction in the MT.

   The LXX says that the beloved planted an ἄμπελον σώρηχ, "sōrēch vine," which
is the expanded and clarifying equivalent of the MT's שֹׂרֵק sōrēq, "choice [red-
grape] vine." Neither the MT nor the LXX says that he planted a vineyard. The
parable's ἀμπελών, "vineyard," comes from Isa 5:1: "My beloved had a vineyard
[MT: כֶּרֶם kerem; LXX: ἀμπελών] on a very fertile hill." The vineyard often symbolizes the people of Israel (as in Isa 1:8; 5:1–7; 27:2; Ezek 19:10). The prophets
Isaiah and Jeremiah speak of Israel's leaders having despoiled Israel, the Lord's
vineyard: "The LORD enters into judgment with the elders and princes of his
people: 'It is you who have devoured the vineyard, the spoil of the poor is in your
houses'" (Isa 3:14); "Many shepherds have destroyed my vineyard, they have
trampled down my portion, they have made my pleasant portion a desolate wilderness" (Jer 12:10). Passages such as these are consistent with Jesus' complaints
against the religious authorities (cf. Mark 12:38–44), as well as the employment
of Isaiah's Song of the Vineyard (Isa 5:1–7) in the construction of his own parable of the Wicked Vineyard Tenants. In the wake of the destruction of Jerusalem
and the temple in 70 C.E. the grieving author of 3 Baruch asks God, "Lord, why
have you set fire to your vineyard and laid it waste?" (1:2).

   The ἄνθρωπος, "man," who plants the vineyard is an allegorical reference to God,
which is consistent with the meaning of Isaiah's Song of the Vineyard. Likewise the
vineyard represents Israel. Other details, such as the fence, the winepress, and the
tower probably do not convey any allegorical meaning, at least not in the parable
itself, though some of these details drawn from Isa 5:1–7 are assigned religious or
quasi-allegorical values in traditions dating to Jesus' time (or slightly before) and
to later times. The winepress is understood as the altar in the Targum and in passages in the Tosefta (t. Mᵉil. 1.16; t. Sukkah 3.15). The tower is understood as the
temple, or sanctuary, in these same sources. But this symbolism is quite old, as attested explicitly in 1 Enoch 89:56–73 and implicitly in 4Q500 (= 4QBenediction; see
Baumgarten, JJS 40 [1989] 1–6; Brooke, DSD 2 [1995] 268–94).

   καὶ ἐξέδετο αὐτὸν γεωργοῖς καὶ ἀπεδήμησεν, "and leased it out to tenant farmers, and departed." The language of lease and expectation of profits is biblical:
"Solomon had a vineyard at Baal-hamon; he let out [MT: נָתַן nātan; LXX: ἔδωκεν]
the vineyard to keepers; each one was to bring for its fruit a thousand pieces of
silver" (Cant 8:11). But it is quite common in the papyri from the intertestamental
and NT periods (e.g., P.Cair.Zen. 59.257). ἐκδιδόναι is found in lease agreements
with the meaning of "to let" or "to lease" (e.g., MM, 192; BAG, 237–38).

   The γεωργοῖς, "tenant farmers," should not be thought of as peasants (against
Lane, 416; Juel, 164; Crossan, Historical Jesus, 351–52). Although it is true that
most γεωργοί, "tenant farmers," in late antiquity were indeed peasants, there were
many wealthy commercial farmers who signed lease agreements to supervise large,
profitable farms, as attested by papyri (e.g., BGU 1756; P.Col.Zen. 54; P.Cair.Zen
59.341; P.Ryl. 582; P.Ryl. 583; cf. Evans, JSP 14 [1996] 74–80). Vineyards were
often farmed commercially. Given the temple context of the parable, as well as

the high-handed behavior of the tenants (see *Comment* on v 7), we should view the γεωργοί of the parable as wealthy commercial farmers.

καὶ ἀπεδήμησεν, "and departed." ἀποδημεῖν, "to depart," does not appear in the LXX. Apart from the parallels to Mark 12:1, the word occurs twice in Matt 25:14–15 (the parable of the Talents) and Luke 15:13 (the parable of the Prodigal Son). The word describes someone going away on a journey with the implication of being absent for some time (see MM, 61; Josephus, *Ant.* 6.11.7 §227; *Ag. Ap.* 2.28 §259). No allegorical or religious meaning should be attached to the vineyard owner's departure.

2 καὶ ἀπέστειλεν πρὸς τοὺς γεωργοὺς τῷ καιρῷ δοῦλον ἵνα παρὰ τῶν γεωργῶν λάβῃ ἀπὸ τῶν καρπῶν τοῦ ἀμπελῶνος, "And he sent to the tenant farmers in due course a servant, that he might receive from the farmers a portion of the fruit of the vineyard." The terminology in this verse is typical of lease agreements and other forms of business transactions (cf. *PSI* 624; P.Ryl. 583). On ἀποστέλλειν, "to send," for payment, see MM, 69. On λαμβάνειν, "to receive," in the context of collecting payments, see MM, 369. τῷ καιρῷ, "in due course," means after the time prescribed by the lease agreement (probably three to five years). By this time the vineyard should be producing a substantial crop. The owner sends a servant to the farmers to collect ἀπὸ τῶν καρπῶν, "a portion of the fruit" (lit. "from the fruits"). We should not imagine that the owner expects the servant to return with wagons loaded with grapes or barrels of wine. Rather, the servant is to return with money from the sale of the grapes and wine. καρποί, "fruit" or "fruits," is often understood as money (MM, 321; cf. BAG, 406).

3 καὶ λαβόντες αὐτὸν ἔδειραν καὶ ἀπέστειλαν κενόν, "But taking him, they beat him and sent him away empty-handed." The rough treatment that the tenant farmers gave the owner's servant is similar to an actual event described in the Zenon archive (ca. 250 B.C.E.). Alexandros reports: "I sent a young man, a servant of mine, to Straton, and wrote to Jeddous. When they returned, they said that he had taken no notice of my letter, but had attacked them and thrown them out of the village. So I am writing to you" (P.Cair.Zen. 59.018 = *CPJ* 6). This fellow Jeddous was probably a Jewish man who lived in Judea (Ἰεδδοῦς is the Greek form for ידוע *yaddûaʿ*, "Jaddua"; cf. LXX 2 Esd 22:11 [Neh 12:11]; Josephus, *Ant.* 11.7.2 §302). What is astonishing about this is that this Jeddous mistreated the servants of Zenon, a business manager in the employ of one Apollonius, who was himself the minister of finance for Ptolemy II Philadelphus, king of the Ptolemaic empire (282–246 B.C.E.). Apparently this was not an isolated incident, for a later affidavit reads: "Seeing that in spite of Zenon's order that I should be employed in the granary, Kleitarchos and Maron and Anosis have expelled my assistants from the granary" (P.Mich. 52). On the realism of the parable of the Wicked Vineyard Tenants and the light that the Zenon papyri shed on various details, see M. Hengel, *ZNW* 59 (1968) 1–39.

4 καὶ πάλιν ἀπέστειλεν πρὸς αὐτοὺς ἄλλον δοῦλον· κἀκεῖνον ἐκεφαλίωσαν καὶ ἠτίμασαν, "And again he sent to them another servant; but they struck that one on the head, and treated him dishonorably." The meaning of ἐκεφαλίωσαν (κεφαλιοῦν) has puzzled interpreters (see the discussion of etymological and semantic difficulties outlined in Field, *Notes,* 35–36). Swete (268) wonders if it means to "hit on the cheek." Following Burkitt ("Parable of the Wicked Husbandmen"), Taylor (474) thinks perhaps it "may be a palaeographical blunder for ἐκολάφισαν, 'they buffeted.'" But this conjecture is dismissed by Lagrange (307) as banal and is rejected by Cranfield (365) for having no textual support. The meaning of the ἐκεφαλίωσαν may be suggested by καὶ ἠτίμασαν, "and treated him dishonorably," that immediately follows. If these verbs are taken together in a complementary sense, then we may assume that to suffer something done to the head is to be treated dishonorably. Taking this approach, Mell (*Die "anderen" Winzer*, 104) recommends the story of David's servants in 2 Kgdms 10:2b–5 (cf. 2 Sam 10:2b–5):

> And David sent [ἀπέστειλεν] to comfort him concerning his father by the hand of his servants [δούλων] . . . and Annon took the servants [παῖδας] of David, and shaved off their beards, and cut off their garments in the midst as far as their haunches, and sent them away [ἐξαπέστειλεν]. And they reported to David concerning the men; and he sent to meet them, for the men were greatly dishonored [ἠτιμασμένοι].

Accordingly, what may have happened to the second servant whom the owner sent was a similar disfiguring of his appearance: his turban knocked off and perhaps his beard shaved. It is not a reference to John the Baptizer, who was beheaded (against Crossan, *JBL* 90 [1971] 452).

5 καὶ ἄλλον ἀπέστειλεν· κἀκεῖνον ἀπέκτειναν, καὶ πολλοὺς ἄλλους, οὓς μὲν δέροντες, οὓς δὲ ἀποκτέννοντες, "So he sent another; and they killed that one, and many others, beating some and killing others." It is probable that the evangelist added the second half of this verse: "and many others, beating some and killing others" (so most commentators, including Gundry, 685). The third servant ("So he sent another; and they killed that one") brings to a climax the sequence of sending servants: the first was beaten and sent away empty-handed (v 3), the second was grossly dishonored (v 4), and the third was murdered (v 5a). The Markan gloss in v 5b is meant to recall the biblical tradition of Israel rejecting God's prophets and messengers. One immediately thinks of Elijah's complaining prayer: "the people of Israel have forsaken thy covenant, thrown down thy altars, and slain thy prophets with the sword" (1 Kgs 19:10; cf. v 14). But the Chronicler's pessimistic review of Israel's history perhaps offers the closest parallel in spirit: "The LORD, the God of their fathers, sent persistently to them by his messengers, because he had compassion on his people and on his dwelling place; but they kept mocking the messengers of God, despising his words, and scoffing at his prophets, till the wrath of the LORD rose against his people, till there was no remedy" (2 Chr 36:15–16). The theme of Israel's rejected prophets is given expression in the dominical tradition elsewhere, as seen in Jesus' lament over Jerusalem: "O Jerusalem, Jerusalem, killing the prophets and stoning those who are sent to you!" (Matt 23:37a = Luke 13:34a).

6 ἔτι ἕνα εἶχεν υἱὸν ἀγαπητόν, "He had yet one, a beloved son." ἔτι ἕνα εἶχεν, "he had yet one," means that the vineyard owner had yet one more he could send to the tenant farmers. This one, as it turns out, was the owner's υἱὸν ἀγαπητόν, "beloved son." Commentators are puzzled by the meaning of ἀγαπητόν, "beloved." Some think that it is a Markan gloss (e.g., Grundmann, 322–23), perhaps based on the heavenly voice at the baptism and at the transfiguration (e.g., Jeremias, *Parables*, 73). It might also be the equivalent of יחיד *yāḥîd*, lit. "only," in Hebrew or Aramaic, which in the Septuagint is frequently rendered by ἀγαπητός, "beloved." If so, the allusion might be to Gen 22:2, where God commands Abraham: "Take your son, your only son [MT: אֶת־בִּנְךָ אֶת־יְחִידְךָ *'et-binkā 'et-yĕḥîdkā;* Tg. *Neof.*: יָת בְּרָךְ יָת יְחִידָךְ *yat bĕrāk yat yĕḥîdāk;* LXX: τὸν υἱόν σου τὸν ἀγαπητόν] Isaac, whom you love." It is also possible that the adjective was suggested either to Jesus or to Mark from Isa 5:1 (MT: יְדִיד *yādîd;* LXX: ἀγαπητός/ἠγαπημένος). Gundry (686) is against this option because the beloved one in Isaiah's Song of the Vineyard is God the Bridegroom in relation to his vineyard Israel, whereas in Mark's parable the beloved one is a son in relation to his father. Of these options the most likely is the allusion to Gen 22:2. ἀγαπητόν probably does not have messianic overtones (so Taylor, 475; Cranfield, 365; but against Nineham, 312; Anderson, 272).

ἀπέστειλεν αὐτὸν ἔσχατον πρὸς αὐτοὺς λέγων ὅτι ἐντραπήσονται τὸν υἱόν μου, "He sent him last to them, thinking, 'They will respect my son.'" ἐντρέπειν, "to respect," frequently translates כָּנַע *kānaʿ,* "to humble oneself" (*nipʿal*) (e.g., 2 Kgs 22:19; 2 Chr 7:14; 12:7, 12: "And when he humbled himself, the wrath of the LORD turned from him, so as not to make a complete destruction"). The owner assumes (λέγων, lit. "saying," but here the meaning is "thinking") that by sending someone of higher rank, as opposed to servants (or slaves), the tenant farmers might be more compliant. But alas, the tenants are not so inclined. The original hearers of the parable, of course, would have been filled with suspense and would rightly have questioned the judgment of the owner. How could he have been so patient, so longsuffering? How could he have sent his son after what the tenants had done to his servants? Perhaps hidden beneath the dynamics of the parable is a *qal wāḥômer* (*a minori ad maius,* "from the smaller to the greater") argument: if the hearers are outraged at the indignities inflicted on a man who owns a vineyard, how much more should they be outraged at the continuing disrespect for God, to whom they, his vineyard, belong?

7 ἐκεῖνοι δὲ οἱ γεωργοὶ πρὸς ἑαυτοὺς εἶπαν, "But those tenants said to themselves." Elsewhere in Mark characters speak to themselves, though only here is the verb in the past tense. The other examples, most if not all from the evangelist's pen, are in the present tense (cf. 1:27; 2:8; 10:26; 11:31; 16:3). When characters speak to themselves, the hearers and readers of Mark become privy to their private thoughts.

οὗτός ἐστιν ὁ κληρονόμος· δεῦτε ἀποκτείνωμεν αὐτόν, καὶ ἡμῶν ἔσται ἡ κληρονομία, "This is the heir; come, let us kill him, and the inheritance will be ours." The tenants' nefarious plan to take possession of the vineyard has a biblical precedent in Ahab's conspiracy to steal Naboth's vineyard. The most relevant portions of this sordid tale read:

> And after this Ahab said to Naboth, "Give me your vineyard [MT: כַּרְמְךָ *karmĕkā;* LXX: τὸν ἀμπελῶνά σου], that I may have it for a vegetable garden, because it is near my house; and I will give you a better vineyard for it; or, if it seems good to you, I will give you its value in money." But Naboth said to Ahab, "The LORD forbid that I should give you the inheritance [MT: נַחֲלַת *naḥălat;* LXX: κληρονομίαν; *Tg.*: אַחְסַנָא *'aḥsānā'*] of my fathers." . . . And as soon as Ahab heard that Naboth was dead, Ahab arose to go down to the vineyard of Naboth the Jezreelite, to take possession of it. (1 Kgs 21[3 Kgdms 20]:2–3, 16)

It is possible that the villainy of the tenants, the element that is not present in Isaiah's Song of the Vineyard, was suggested by the story of King Ahab and Naboth's vineyard. The tenants' references to the son as κληρονόμος, "heir," and to the vineyard as the κληρονομία, "inheritance," cohere with the Aramaic Targum's interpretation of the vineyard as a אחסנא 'aḥsānā', "heritage." The language δεῦτε ἀποκτείνωμεν αὐτόν, "come, let us kill him," reminds us of the identical words spoken by Joseph's jealous brothers in Gen 37:20: "Come now, let us kill him [LXX: νῦν οὖν δεῦτε ἀποκτείνωμεν αὐτόν]." For more on this parallel, see Pesch, 2:219.

8 καὶ λαβόντες ἀπέκτειναν αὐτόν καὶ ἐξέβαλον αὐτὸν ἔξω τοῦ ἀμπελῶνος, "And taking him, they killed him, and cast him out of the vineyard." The idiom λαμβάνειν, "to take," and ἀποκτείνειν, "to kill," is found in LXX Josh 11:17b ("and he took all their kings, and smote them, and killed them"). The murdered son is ἐξέβαλον . . . ἔξω τοῦ ἀμπελῶνος, "cast out of the vineyard." In one of the previously mentioned papyri (see *Comment* on v 3), Alexandros reports to Zenon that his servant and colleague Straton were "thrown out [ἐγβαλεῖν] of the village" (P.Cair.Zen. 59.018 = *CPJ* 6), while in a later affidavit it is alleged that certain men ἐγβεβλήκασιν, "expelled," the assistants of Zenon's servant from the granary (P.Mich. 52). Cicero's account of collecting a debt from the leading citizens of Salamis offers a dramatic historical event (ca. 50 B.C.E.) in which troops had to be employed and in which people died: "Appius had given him some squadrons to put pressure on the people of Salamis. . . . I ordered the people . . . to pay the money. . . . I threatened to compel them" (*Att.* 5.21). These squadrons, Atticus is told in Cicero's next letter, "beset the Senate at Salamis in their own chamber, so that five members of the house died of starvation" (*Att.* 6.1). The troops were sent not against the peasants and rabble of Salamis but against the rulers of the city!

These actual episodes show how the parable of the Wicked Vineyard Tenants was potentially true to life. But as argued above, parables do not have to portray life as it actually is, or normally is. Parables often indulge in hyperbole and portray characters (even when they represent God himself!) behaving in remarkably trusting and incautious ways. So it is in the case of the parable of the Wicked Vineyard Tenants. Every detail is possible, but the story as a whole is highly improbable. The intention of the hyperbole is to accent the crimes of the tenants and to heighten the sense of outrage in the hearers of the parable.

Taylor (475) is probably correct to suggest that in casting the body of the son out of the vineyard, the tenants left it unburied. If so, then the outrage committed by the vineyard tenants is only further compounded.

9 τί [οὖν] ποιήσει ὁ κύριος τοῦ ἀμπελῶνος, "What [therefore] will the owner of the vineyard do?" Jesus' rhetorical question, which is meant to elicit a response from his hearers, echoes the deliberations at the same juncture in Isaiah's Song of the Vineyard: "And now I will tell you what I will do to my vineyard" (Isa 5:5). ὁ κύριος, "the owner," is literally "the lord." The answer, ἐλεύσεται καὶ ἀπολέσει τοὺς γεωργοὺς καὶ δώσει τὸν ἀμπελῶνα ἄλλοις, "He will come and destroy the tenants, and give the vineyard to others," is usually assumed to have been given by Jesus himself, who was contravening standard practice. Perhaps, but it is possible that this was the answer of the crowd, which neither the form of the parable the evangelist inherited nor the evangelist himself explicitly introduced as the words of the hearers. In other words, the question and the response might originally have been as follows: "What will the owner of the vineyard do?" Jesus asks. "He will come and destroy the tenants, and give the vineyard to others," the hearers respond. Jesus replies, "Have you not even read this Scripture . . . ?"

The rhetoric of the question and answer is particularly pointed, especially in light of the scriptural stories that the details of the parable would evoke in the minds of the hearers. If the story of the binding of Isaac was recalled, where God commanded Abraham to take his beloved son (Gen 22:2), the hearers may have been inclined to identify the tenants with Satan himself, who according to haggadic traditions hoped to kill Isaac and thus cut off the promised line. If the story of Naboth's vineyard was recalled (1 Kgs 21), then the hearers might have identified the tenants with the apostate King Ahab, who murdered Naboth, stole his vineyard, and later died under divine judgment. If the story of Joseph's brothers was recalled (Gen 37:18–24), then the hearers might have identified the tenants with the sinful patriarchs who wickedly conspired to commit fratricide, but whose plans were marvelously thwarted. It is not necessary to settle on any one of these stories, for elements of all three could have flitted through the minds of the hearers, offering different perspectives against which the actions of the tenants could be evaluated. The multivalent potential of the parable would only have increased its prophetic power and critical application.

The answer, ἐλεύσεται καὶ ἀπολέσει τοὺς γεωργοὺς καὶ δώσει τὸν ἀμπελῶνα ἄλλοις, "He will come and destroy the tenants and give the vineyard to others," also conveys a specific threat against the ruling priests, who in v 12 rightly perceive that Jesus had told the parable against them. Their place of power and prestige will soon come to an end. Their positions will be given to others. Giving the vineyard to others means only that Israel will be governed by people other than the ruling priests. What others Jesus had in mind is not difficult to determine. The request of James and John and the ensuing squabble among the disciples in Mark 10:35–45 make it clear that Jesus expected God to appoint righteous persons, probably from among his disciples (though Jesus himself acknowledged that this was not his decision to make), to govern Israel. In a Q tradition Jesus promises his disciples that they "will sit on twelve thrones, judging the twelve tribes of Israel" (Matt 19:28 = Luke 22:30). This judging refers not to punitive activity, as in the case of a judge who passes sentence against a criminal, but to administrative, protective activity in the sense of the judges in the book of Judges. The vineyard, that is, Israel, will be given over to new administrators who will rule over Israel with justice and integrity, in contrast to the present rulers who exploit the people (as examples later in Mark 12 will document). Matthew's interesting and secondary addition, "Therefore I tell you, the kingdom of God will be taken away from you and given to a nation producing the fruits of it" (Matt 21:43), should not be read into the Markan version. However one interprets Matthew, the Markan Jesus is not saying that Israel is about to be replaced by Gentiles.

10 οὐδὲ τὴν γραφὴν ταύτην ἀνέγνωτε, "Have you not even read this Scripture?" Jesus' question is again rhetorical. Of course, the ruling priests and scribes had read Ps 118. But had they read it with understanding? Were they aware of its implication, that having rejected the stone, God was going to establish it as the cornerstone? Jesus' question throws the ruling priests on the defensive and is similar to the question that he will later throw at the Sadducees concerning the resurrection: "For this reason are you not misled, knowing neither the Scriptures nor the power of God?" (12:24).

λίθον ὃν ἀπεδοκίμασαν οἱ οἰκοδομοῦντες, οὗτος ἐγενήθη εἰς κεφαλὴν γωνίας, "A stone that the builders rejected, / This has become the head of the corner." The quotation of Ps 118:22 follows the LXX verbatim, which is a faithful translation of the MT. Grammatically one would expect λίθον, "stone," to be in the nominative case, not the accusative, which would be translated, "this stone, which the builders rejected, has become the head of the corner." But λίθον has adopted the case of the relative pronoun ὅν, "that" (an instance of *casus pendens*). This λίθον has become the κεφαλὴν γωνίας, "head of the corner," which probably refers to either a capstone that completes an arch or a capital that sits atop a column or pinnacle of the building. It is not a foundation stone (see Jeremias, *ZNW* 29 [1930] 264–80; BAG, 431; Cahill, *RB* 106 [1999] 345–57). Jewish literature offers a variety of stone nuances; cf. 4QpIsa^d 1 i 1–7 (on Isa 54:11; "stones" = priests); *Tg. Onq.* Gen 49:24 ("stone of Israel" [MT] = "seed of Israel"); Josephus, *J.W.* 5.6.3 §272 ("stone" = "son"); also see *Midr. Ps.* 118.20 (on Ps 118:22); *Exod. Rab.* 37.1 (on Exod 27:20); *Tg.* Zech 10:4; *Pirqe R. El.* §24.

The Aramaic tradition, with which in an early form Jesus was evidently familiar, understands David as the rejected stone (*Tg.*: "the boy which the builders abandoned"; see *Form/Structure/Setting* C.3 above). Although initially rejected by the religious establishment, including the prophet-priest Samuel, David comes to be recognized and blessed from the house of the Lord by the priests (cf. *Tg.* Ps 118:19–27). It is in the light of this tradition that we should understand Jesus' employment of Ps 118:22 to conclude his parable. Jesus entered Jerusalem (11:1–11) with disciples and pilgrims shouting and singing refrains from Ps 118:25–26, with strains of the Aramaic interpretive tradition being heard: "Blessed is the coming kingdom of our father David" (see *Comment* on Mark 11:10 above). But Jesus is not greeted and blessed by the ruling priests; he is initially ignored (11:11), and then later challenged (11:27–33). Accordingly, in exasperation he asks the ruling priests, "Have you not even read this Scripture?" That is, do they not realize who he is and what is happening?

In Jewish literature οἱ οἰκοδομοῦντες, "the builders," either in positive or negative colors, may refer to religious leaders; cf. CD 4:19; 8:12, 18; Acts 4:11; 1 Cor 3:10; *Song Rab.* 1:5 §3; *Exod. Rab.* 23.10 (on Exod 15:11); *b. Ber.* 64a; *b. Šabb.* 114a.

11 παρὰ κυρίου ἐγένετο αὕτη καὶ ἔστιν θαυμαστὴ ἐν ὀφθαλμοῖς ἡμῶν, "This came about from the Lord, / and it is marvelous in our eyes." What is happening is παρὰ κυρίου . . . καὶ ἔστιν θαυμαστή, "from the Lord, and it is marvelous." The quotation of Ps 118:23 again follows the LXX verbatim, which again is a faithful translation of the MT. θαυμαστή, "marvelous," suggests that God is accomplishing something against all odds, something completely unexpected, something that mortals cannot achieve apart from divine assistance. This marvel centers on Jesus, the leader of an unimpressive group of disciples from Galilee. Through Jesus and his following, God will transform Israel and the world. The ruling priests may look down upon Jesus and his disciples and view them as little more than pests, but God has begun an amazing, marvelous work.

12 Καὶ ἐζήτουν αὐτὸν κρατῆσαι . . . ἔγνωσαν γὰρ ὅτι πρὸς αὐτοὺς τὴν παραβολὴν εἶπεν, "And they were seeking to arrest him, . . . for they knew that he had spoken the parable to them." This is the first mention in Mark of the authorities' wish to arrest (κρατῆσαι) Jesus. In 14:1 the evangelist will tell us that "the ruling priests and the scribes were seeking how, taking him by stealth, they might kill him." In 14:44 Judas will explain how he will identify Jesus so that he may be arrested. In 14:46 the arrest is then narrated, with Jesus in 14:49 chastising his captors for their cowardice and unwillingness to arrest him in public while he was teaching in the temple precincts. The authorities "knew that he had spoken the parable to them." They understood better than Jesus' sympathizers the full import of Jesus' parable. The details from Isaiah's Song of the Vineyard, the interpretive slant, and the concluding quotation of Ps 118:22–23 left no doubt concerning the point Jesus was trying to make.

καὶ ἐφοβήθησαν τὸν ὄχλον . . . καὶ ἀφέντες αὐτὸν ἀπῆλθον, "but they feared the crowd. . . . And leaving him, they departed." Though the authorities would have liked to have arrested Jesus on the spot, they could not on account of his popularity with the crowd. The dilemma the authorities faced was whether to ignore Jesus, only to have him whip up a rebellion, or to seize Jesus, only to ignite the very rebellion they feared. They withdraw for the moment. The evangelist does not say so, but the expectant reader or hearer knows that the religious authorities seek opportunities to effect the arrest of Jesus. The parable of the Wicked Vineyard Tenants ends on a note of suspense and also on a note of irony. For in plotting Jesus' destruction, they unwittingly live up to their characterization in the parable as murderers.

Explanation

Certainly one of Jesus' most important teachings, the parable of the Wicked Vineyard Tenants answers the question concerning Jesus' authority, condemns the ruling priests as unfit to hold their high office, and predicts that God's purposes will be accomplished despite deadly opposition. Not only has Jesus implicitly identified himself in this parable, but by describing himself as the son who will be murdered, he continues the passion theme and prepares for the events that will lead to his arrest and crucifixion. Mark's readers and hearers by now will have become aware of how closely Jesus' identity and passion are linked. In 8:29 Peter confessed that Jesus was the Messiah, and then in 8:31 Jesus predicted his death. In 9:7 the heavenly voice declared that Jesus was God's Son, and then in 9:9 Jesus forbade his disciples to disclose what they had seen until he had risen from the dead. Now readers and hearers learn that Jesus is the son, the last of God's servants sent to Israel's wicked leaders, and the stone that, although rejected by the religious authorities, will be established. Mark's readers and hearers will continue to be impressed by Jesus' remarkable predictive power and his firm resolve to pursue his mission, even at the cost of his life.

Milavec ("Fresh Analysis," 109) comments: "The legacy of anti-Judaism attached to the parable of the wicked husbandmen from the patristic period down to our present day cannot be judged as part of the original inspiration guiding Mark in the creation of his gospel." Milavec's point is well taken. The portrait of the ruling priests as murderers should not be interpreted as anti-Semitic or anti-Jewish. The hermeneutic that lies behind the parable, as well as other expressions of judgment found in Mark, is that of prophetic criticism. Jesus criticizes the rulers of his people in the same spirit that Israel's prophets of old criticized kings and priests and others. Jesus' stance is decidedly pro-Jewish. His demonstration in the temple precincts (11:17), in which he appealed to the grand vision of Isa 56:7, had in view Israel's glorious potential. His threatening allusion to Jer 7:11 was a warning, motivated by hopes of national and religious restoration. If the tenant farmers continue their unjust ways, they face destruction (cf. 13:2).

H. Paying Taxes to Caesar   (12:13–17)

Bibliography

Abel, E. L. "Jesus and the Cause of Jewish National Independence." *REJ* 128 (1969) 247–52. **Abrahams, I.** *Studies in Pharisaism and the Gospels.* 1:62–65. **Barrett, C. K.** "The New Testament Doctrine of Church and State." In *New Testament Essays.* London: S. P. C. K., 1972. 1–19. **Beilner, W.** *Christus und die Pharisäer: Exegetische Untersuchung über Grund und Verlauf der Auseinandersetzungen.* Vienna: Herder, 1959. 129–31. **Bell, H. I.,** and **Skeat, T. C.** *Fragments of an Unknown Gospel and Other Early Christian Papyri.* London: British Museum, 1935. 1–41. **Bennett, W. J., Jr.** "The Herodians of Mark's Gospel." *NovT* 17 (1975) 9–14. **Betz, O.** "Jesus und die Zeloten (Zur Perikope von der Kaisersteuer Mark. 12,13–17)." In *Gewalt in Jesu Namen?* Ed. P. Beyerhaus and W. Künneth. Bielefeld: Missionsverlag der Evangelisch-Lutherischen Gebetsgemeinschaften, 1987. 30–45. **Bornkamm, G.** *Jesus of Nazareth.* New York: Harper & Row, 1975. 120–24. **Brandon, S. G. F.** *The Trial of Jesus of Nazareth.* London: Batsford; New York: Stein & Day, 1968. 65–68. **Braun, W.** "Were the New Testament Herodians Essenes? A Critique of an Hypothesis." *RevQ* 14 (1989) 75–88. **Breymayer, R.** "Zur Pragmatik des Bildes: Semiotische Beobachtungen zum Streitgespräch Mk 12,13–17 ("Der Zinsgroschen") unter Berücksichtigung der Spieltheorie." *LB* 13–14 (1972) 19–51. **Bruce, F. F.** *Jesus and Christian Origins Outside the New Testament.* London: Hodder and Stoughton; Grand Rapids, MI: Eerdmans, 1974. 149. ———. "Render to Caesar." In *Jesus and the Politics of His Day.* Ed. E. Bammel and C. F. D. Moule. Cambridge: Cambridge UP, 1984. 249–63, esp. 249–51. **Bünker, M.** "Gebt dem Kaiser, was des Kaisers ist!" *Kairos* 29 (1987) 85–98. **Carmignac, J.** "Studies in the Hebrew Background of the Synoptic Gospels." *ASTI* 7 (1970) 64–93, esp. 84. **Charlesworth, J. H.,** and **Evans, C. A.** "Jesus in the Agrapha and Apocryphal Gospels." In *Studying the Historical Jesus: Evaluations of the State of Research.* Ed. B. D. Chilton and C. A. Evans. NTTS 19. Leiden: Brill, 1994. 479–533. **Crossan, J. D.** *Four Other Gospels: Shadows on the Contour of Canon.* Sonoma, CA: Polebridge, 1992. 50–57. ———. "Mark 12:13–17." *Int* 37 (1983) 397–401. **Cuvillier, E.** "Marc, Justin, Thomas et les autres." *ETR* 67 (1992) 329–44. **Daniel, C.** "Les 'Hérodiens' du Nouveau Testament sont-ils des Esséniens?" *RevQ* 6 (1967) 31–53. ———. "Nouveaux arguments en faveur de l'identification des Hérodiens et des Esséniens." *RevQ* 7 (1970) 397–402. **Daube, D.** "Four Types of Question." *JTS* n.s. 2 (1951) 45–48 (repr. in D. Daube. *The New Testament and Rabbinic Judaism.* London: Athlone, 1956. 158–69). **Derrett, J. D. M.** "Render to Caesar . . . ." In *Law in the New Testament.* London: Darton, Longman & Todd, 1970. 313–38. **Finney, P. C.** "The Rabbi and the Coin Portrait (Mark 12:15b, 16)." *JBL* 112 (1993) 629–44. **George, A.** "Jésus devant le problème politique." *LumVie* 20 (1971) 5–17. **Giblin, C. H.** "'The Things of God' in the Question concerning Tribute to Caesar (Lk 20:25; Mk 12:17; Mt 22:21)." *CBQ* 33 (1971) 510–27. **Goppelt, L.** "Die Freiheit zur Kaisersteuer: Zu Mk. 12,17 und Röm. 13,1–7." In *Ecclesia und Res Publica.* FS K. D. Schmidt, ed. G. Kretschmar and B. Lohse. Göttingen: Vandenhoeck & Ruprecht, 1961. 40–50 (repr. in L. Goppelt. *Christologie und Ethik: Aufsätze zum Neuen Testament.* Göttingen: Vandenhoeck

& Ruprecht, 1968. 208–19). **Güttgemanns, E.** "Narrative Analyse des Streitgesprächs über den 'Zinsgroschen.'" *LB* 41–42 (1977) 88–105. **Haacker, K.** "Kaisertribut und Gottesdienst (Eine Auslegung von Markus 12,13–17)." *TBei* 17 (1986) 285–92. **Hart, H. St J.** "The Coin of 'Render unto Caesar . . .'" (A Note on Some Aspects of Mark 12:13–17; Matt. 22:15–22; Luke 20:20–26)." In *Jesus and the Politics of His Day.* Ed. E. Bammel and C. F. D. Moule. Cambridge: Cambridge UP, 1984. 241–48. **Horsley, R. A.** *Jesus and the Spiral of Violence.* 306–17. **Hultgren, A. J.** *Jesus and His Adversaries: The Form and Function of the Conflict Stories in the Synoptic Tradition.* Minneapolis: Augsburg, 1979. 41–44, 75–78. **Jason, H.** "Der Zinsgroschen: Analyse der Erzählstruktur." *LB* 41–42 (1977) 49–87. **Jeremias, J.** "Papyrus Egerton 2." In *Gospels and Related Writings.* Vol. 1 of *New Testament Apocrypha.* Ed. W. Schneemelcher. Rev. ed. Cambridge: James Clarke; Louisville: Westminster John Knox, 1991. 96–99. **Kennard, J. S., Jr.** *Render to God! A Study of the Tribute Passage.* New York: Oxford UP, 1950. **Klemm, H. G.** "De censu Caesaris: Beobachtungen zu J. Duncan M. Derretts Interpretation der Perikope Mk. 12:13–17 par." *NovT* 24 (1982) 234–54. **Koester, H.** *Ancient Christian Gospels: Their History and Development.* London: SCM Press; Philadelphia: Trinity Press International, 1990. 205–16. **Kümmel, W. G.** "Das Urchristentum." *TRu* 17 (1948) 387–92. **Liese, H.** "Numisma census." *VD* 12 (1932) 289–94. **Loewe, H. M. J.** *"Render unto Caesar": Religious and Political Loyalty in Palestine.* Cambridge: Cambridge UP, 1940. **Lührmann, D.** "Die Pharisäer und die Schriftgelehrten im Markusevangelium." *ZNW* 78 (1987) 169–85. **Marxsen, W.** *"Christliche" und christliche Ethik im Neuen Testament.* Gütersloh: Mohn, 1989. 112–16 (ET: *New Testament Foundations for Christian Ethics.* Tr. O. C. Dean. Minneapolis: Fortress, 1993). **Mell, U.** *Die "andere" Winzer: Eine exegetische Studie zur Vollmacht Jesu Christi nach Markus 11,27–12,34.* WUNT 77. Tübingen: Mohr-Siebeck, 1995. 205–66. **Mudiso Mbâ Mundla, J.-G.** *Jesus und die Führer Israels: Studien zu den sogenannten Jerusalemer Streitgesprächen.* NTAbh 17. Münster: Aschendorff, 1984. 41–70. **Ogle, A. B.** "What Is Left for Caesar? A Look at Mark 12:13–17 and Romans 13:1–7." *TToday* 35 (1978–79) 254–64. **Oster, R.** "Numismatic Windows into the Social World of Early Christianity: A Methodological Inquiry." *JBL* 101 (1981) 195–223. **Owen-Ball, D. T.** "Rabbinic Rhetoric and the Tribute Passage." *NovT* 35 (1993) 1–14. **Patterson, S. J.** *The Gospel of Thomas and Jesus.* Sonoma, CA: Polebridge, 1993. 68–69. **Perkins, P.** "Taxes in the New Testament." *JRE* 12 (1984) 182–200. **Pesch, R.** *Evangelium der Urgemeinde.* 148–51. **Petzke, G.** "Die historische Jesus in der sozialethischen Diskussion: Mk 12,13–17 par." In *Jesus Christus in Historie und Theologie.* FS H. Conzelmann, ed. G. Strecker. Tübingen: Mohr-Siebeck, 1975. 223–36. **Rist, M.** "Caesar or God (Mark 12:13–17)? A Study in Formgeschichte." *JR* 16 (1936) 317–31. **Rolland, P.** "Jésus connaissait leurs pensées." *ETL* 62 (1986) 118–21. **Rowland, C.** "Render to God What Belongs to God." *NBf* 70 (1989) 365–71. **Russell, E. A.** "Church and State in the New Testament." *ITQ* 44 (1977) 192–207, esp. 197–200. **Sandelin, K.-G.** "The Jesus-Tradition and Idolatry." *NTS* 42 (1996) 412–20. **Schlette, H. R.** "Die Aussagen des Neuen Testaments über 'den Staat.'" *ARSP* 48 (1962) 179–97. **Schottroff, L.** "'Gebt dem Kaiser, was dem Kaiser gehört, und Gott, was Gott gehört': Die theologische Antwort der urchristlichen Gemeinden auf ihre gesellschaftliche und politische Situation." In *Annahme und Widerstand.* Ed. J. Moltmann. Kaiser Traktate 79. Munich: Kaiser, 1984. 15–58 (repr. in L. Schottroff. *Befreiungserfahrungen: Studien zur Sozialgeschichte des Neuen Testaments.* TB 82. Munich: Kaiser, 1990. 184–216). **Schrage, W.** *Die Christen und der Staat nach dem Neuen Testament.* Gütersloh: Mohn, 1971. 30–40. **Schwank, B.** "Ein griechisches Jesuslogion? Überlegungen zur Antwort Jesu auf die Steuerfrage (Mk 12,16–17 parr.)." In *XAPIΣTEION: Anfänge der Theologie.* FS J. B. Bauer, ed. N. Brox. Graz: Styria, 1987. 61–64. **Stauffer, E.** *Die Botschaft Jesu damals und heute.* Dalp-Taschenbücher 333. Bern: Francke, 1959. 95–118. ———. *Christ and the Caesars: Historical Sketches.* London: SCM Press, 1955. 112–37. ———. "Realistische Jesusworte." In *The New Testament Age.* FS B. Reicke, ed. W. C. Weinrich. 2 vols. Macon, GA: Mercer UP, 1984. 2:503–10, esp. 504–5. **Stenger, W.** *"Gebt dem Kaiser, was* *des Kaisers ist . . . !*" BBB 68. Frankfurt am Main: Hanstein, 1988. **Stock, A.** "Jesus, Hypocrites, and Herodians." *BTB* 16 (1986) 3–7. ———. "'Render to Caesar.'" *TBT* 62 (1972) 929–34. **Surgy, P. de.** "Rendez à César ce qui est à César, et à Dieu ce qui est à Dieu." *AsSeign* 60 (1975) 16–25. **Tagawa, K.** "Jésus critiquant l'idéologie théocratique: Une étude de Marc 12, 13–17." In *Reconnaissance à S. Dietrich.* CBFV. Paris: Foi et Vie, 1971. 117–25. **Tannehill, R. C.** *The Sword of His Mouth.* SBLSS 1. Missoula, MT: Scholars Press, 1975. 171–77. **Valantasis, R.** *The Gospel of Thomas.* New Testament Readings. London; New York: Routledge, 1997. 180–81. **Vanbergen, P.** "L'Impôt dû à César." *LumVieSup* 50 (1960) 12–18. **Viviano, B. T.** "Render unto Caesar." *TBT* 26 (1988) 272–76. **Vökl, R.** *Christ und Welt nach dem Neuen Testament.* Würzburg: Echter, 1961. 113–15. **Weiss, W.** *"Eine neue Lehre in Vollmacht": Die Streit- und Schulgespräche des Markus-Evangeliums.* BZNW 52. Berlin; New York: de Gruyter, 1989. 202–34. **Wengst, K.** *Pax Romana.* Philadelphia: Fortress, 1987. 59–61. **Westcott, B. F.,** and **Hort, F. J. A.** *New Testament.* 2:26. **Wormser, G.** "'Rendez à César . . . .'" *Nouveaux Cahiers* 3.9 (1967) 43–53.

Translation

¹³*And they* ᵃ *send to him* ᵇ *some of the Pharisees and some of the Herodians, so that they might trap him with a statement.* ¹⁴*And approaching, they say to him,*ᶜ *"Teacher, we know that you are true, and that another's opinion means nothing to you;* ᵈ *for you do not regard the position of people,*ᵉ *but you truly* ᶠ *teach the way of God. Is it lawful to pay tax to Caesar,*ᵍ *or not? Should we give, or should we not give?"* ¹⁵*But knowing their hypocrisy, he* ʰ *said to them, "Why do you test me?* ⁱ *Bring me a denarius, so that I might see it."* ¹⁶*And they brought one. And he says to them, "Of whom is this image and inscription?" And they said to him, "Caesar."* ¹⁷*Jesus said to them, "Give to Caesar the things of Caesar, but give to God the things of God." And they were amazed at him.*

Notes

ᵃThe text does not name the subject. Who sent the Pharisees and the Herodians? A few later authorities insert οἱ ἀρχιερεῖς καὶ οἱ γραμματεῖς, "the ruling priests and the scribes." Mark's context supports this conjecture (cf. 11:27). See *Comment* below.

ᵇD omits πρὸς αὐτόν, "to him." Some authorities replace πρὸς αὐτόν, "to him," with πρὸς Ἰησοῦν, "to Jesus."

ᶜD reads ἐπηρώτων αὐτὸν οἱ Φαρισαῖοι, "the Pharisees were asking him." W reads ἐλθόντες ἤρξαντο ἐρωτᾶν αὐτὸν ἐν δόλῳ λέγοντες, "approaching, they began to question him deceitfully, saying."

ᵈGk. οὐ μέλει σοι περὶ οὐδενός, lit. "it is not a care to you concerning someone."

ᵉGk. οὐ γὰρ βλέπεις εἰς πρόσωπον ἀνθρώπων, lit. "for you do not look to the face of people."

ᶠGk. ἐπ᾿ ἀληθείας, lit. "in truth." The asseverative use of אמן *'āmēn,* "truly," probably underlies this idiom (see *Comment* on Mark 9:1 above).

ᵍD and a few other authorities read δοῦναι ἐπικεφάλαιον Καίσαρι, "to pay tribute to Caesar."

ʰD and a few other authorities add Ἰησοῦς, "Jesus."

ⁱ𝔓⁴⁵ N W Σ 33 and several other authorities add ὑποκριταί, "hypocrites" (cf. Matt 22:18).

Form/Structure/Setting

The question of paying tax to Caesar and Jesus' pithy reply, "Give to Caesar the things of Caesar, but give to God the things of God," have made this story a classic. The antiquated form of the pronouncement, "Render to Caesar . . . ," has become a readily recognized and frequently utilized locution.

Form critics regard the pericope as a pronouncement story (Bultmann, *History,* 26; Taylor, *Formation,* 64–65). Bultmann and Taylor readily accept it as a genuine episode in the ministry of Jesus. The point of the story is plain enough, even if Jesus' concluding pronouncement is not so clear (see *Comment* on v 17). Pharisees and Herodians present Jesus with a difficult question; the flattery that prefaces their question is meant to bait Jesus and induce him to speak with incautious candor. Is it lawful for a Torah-observant Jew to pay tax to Caesar or not? Either yes or no would prove inflammatory to one constituency or another. The structure consists of *(a)* an opening question, served up thickly with compliments (vv 13–14); *(b)* Jesus' counterquestion and demand to bring him a denarius (v 15); *(c)* Jesus' second counterquestion and his interlocutors' reply (v 16); and *(d)* Jesus' stunning pronouncement (v 17).

The Markan version of the story probably represents our earliest source. But there are three other versions. The first is found in Egerton Papyrus 2 frag. 2 *recto:*

[42][. . . com]ing [43]to him to examine [44]him, they began testing him, say[ing]: [45]"Teacher Jesus, we know that [from God] [46]you have come, for what you are doing tes[tifies] [47]beyond all the prophets. [Therefore, tell] [48]us: Is it proper to [give [49]payment] to the kings that which pertains to their rule? Should [we pay th]em [50]or n[ot]?" But Jesus, knowing th[eir [51]th]inking, becoming ang[ry], [52]said to th[em]: "Why do you call me [53]'[Te]acher' [with y]our mouth, n[ot he]aring [54]what I [s]ay? Well did Is[aiah pr]ophesy [concerning [55]y]ou, saying: 'Th[is people] [56]with the[ir li]ps [honor] [57]me, [but their hea]rt is [far] [58]from m[e. In v]ain [they worship me.] [59]Command[ments of men . . . .'"] (for Greek text, see Bell and Skeat, *Fragments,* 10–13)

This variant of the story is clearly a secondary admixture of Johannine and synoptic elements (so Fitzmyer, *Luke* 2:1290; Jeremias, "Papyrus," 96; Charlesworth and Evans, "Agrapha," 517). It is not (against Crossan, *Four Other Gospels,* 56: "Mark 12:13–17 . . . is directly dependent on the papyrus text"; Koester, *Ancient Christian Gospels,* 207) a primitive, pre-synoptic source attesting an early stage in dominical transmission in which respective Johannine and synoptic traditions have not yet bifurcated. It is second century and betrays typical second-century features of embellishment (esp. the fragmentary story [frag. 2 *verso*] about Jesus pitching seed into the Jordan River and producing a large crop).

There is also an abbreviated form of the story in Justin: "For at that time some came to him, if one ought to pay tribute to Caesar; and he answered, 'Tell me, whose image does the coin bear?' And they said, 'Caesar's.' And again he answered them, 'Render therefore to Caesar the things that are Caesar's, and to God the things that are God's'" (*1 Apol.* 17.2; tr. from ANF 1:168). Jesus' counterquestion is closer to Luke 20:24b, but his pronouncement follows Matt 22:21c (Fitzmyer, *Luke* 2:1290). Conflation of dominical tradition is common in Justin. And, in any case, the paraphrasing manner in which Justin weaves the tradition into his argument that Christians are loyal members of the Roman Empire, as seen in their willingness to pay taxes, should caution against viewing Justin's text as pristine.

A third form of the story appears in the *Gospel of Thomas:* "They showed Jesus a gold coin and said to him, 'Caesar's men demand taxes from us.' He said to them, 'Give Caesar what belongs to Caesar, give God what belongs to God, and give me what is mine'" (§100; tr. from J. M. Robinson, ed., *The Nag Hammadi Library* [Leiden: Brill, 1977] 128). Hultgren (*Jesus and His Adversaries,* 42–44) and

Patterson (*Thomas and Jesus,* 69) try to explain away the evidence of the secondary relationship of *Thomas* to the synoptic form of the tradition, especially the
Lukan form. They hope to show that the form in *Thomas* is independent. But the
condensed version of the form in *Thomas,* in that Jesus is not asked to decide
anything, undermines the whole point of Jesus' pronouncement. Other details,
such as the silver denarius becoming a gold coin and the addition of a third clause,
"give me what is mine," smack of secondary embellishments (see Bruce, *Jesus,*
149; Fitzmyer, *Luke* 2:1290–91; Gundry, 696–97; on the meaning of the form of
the saying in *Thomas,* see Valantasis, *Gospel of Thomas,* 180–81).

The Markan evangelist situates the story in the context of Jesus' public teaching in the temple precincts immediately following the parable of the Wicked
Vineyard Tenants (12:1–12). The parable concluded with the notice that "they"
(i.e., the ruling priests, scribes, and elders; cf. 11:27) tried to arrest Jesus but
could not on account of the crowd (12:12). The appearance in the very next
pericope of the question about paying tax to Caesar functions in the Markan
context as an attempt to gather incriminating evidence against Jesus. The story
contributes to the growing suspense of the story line. In the setting in the life of
Jesus (*Sitz im Leben Jesu*) the question may have been put to Jesus in Jerusalem,
and quite possibly in the temple precincts (but Gnilka, 2:152–53, does not think
so), where Jesus was known to have taught during passion week. Of course, because Jesus encountered Pharisees (2:16, 18, 24; 3:6; 7:1–5; 8:11, 15; 10:2) and
Herodians (3:6, in the company of Pharisees) during his Galilean ministry, it is
possible that this story originally took place in Galilee but because of its obvious
political dimension was associated with the ministry in Jerusalem. Certainty is
not possible.

Comment

13 Mark's καὶ ἀποστέλλουσιν πρὸς αὐτόν τινας τῶν Φαρισαίων καὶ τῶν Ἡρῳδιανῶν,
"and they send to him some of the Pharisees and some of the Herodians," creates
the misleading impression that the Pharisees and Herodians were allies; in all
probability they were not. What the evangelist means is that a group of Pharisees
(whether or not literally sent by anyone) and a group of Herodians approached
Jesus to ask his opinion on taxation. The Pharisees and the Herodians held to
very different views on this controversial subject. The Herodians (Ἡρῳδιανοί, from
Latin *Herodiani,* meaning supporters of the Herodian rulers) believed that it was
appropriate for Jews to pay taxes to Rome directly (as in Judea in the time of
Jesus) or indirectly through the Herodian client-rulers (as in Galilee and
Gaulanitis). The Pharisees, or at least those who approached Jesus, probably viewed
the payment of taxes to Rome as idolatry. At least some Pharisees took this view
(and some perhaps did not, if the rabbinic literature is any guide; cf. *b. Pesah.*
112b; *b. B. Qam.* 113a). One should remember that Saddok the Pharisee was among
the followers of Judas of Galilee (or Gaulanitis) at the time that he refused to pay
taxes to Rome (cf. Josephus, *Ant.* 18.1.1 §§1–10; *J.W.* 2.8.1 §§117–18).

The identity of the Herodians is quite uncertain. If the proposal in the preceding paragraph is not accepted, then we have virtually nothing else to guide
us. Because Herod the Great favored the Essenes, some have suggested that the

Herodians were none other than the Essenes (e.g., Daniel, *RevQ* 6 [1967] 31–53; id., *RevQ* 7 [1970] 397–402). But this is little more than a conjecture, and the view has been criticized (e.g., Braun, *RevQ* 14 [1989] 75–88). H. W. Hoehner (*Herod Antipas*, SNTSMS 28 [Cambridge: Cambridge UP, 1972] 331–42) recommends identification with the Boethusians (as in *b. Pesaḥ.* 57a: "Woe to me because of the house of Boethus!"), while B. D. Chilton ("Jesus *ben David*," in *The Historical Jesus: A Sheffield Reader*, ed. C. A. Evans and S. E. Porter, Biblical Seminar 33 [Sheffield: Sheffield Academic, 1997] 213–14) identifies the Herodians with the "rabbinic *bene Bathyra*" (as in *b. Pesaḥ.* 66a: "they [the sons of Bathyra] did not know whether the Passover overrides the Sabbath or not"). Not persuasive is Hultgren's suggestion (*Jesus and His Adversaries*, 154–56) that the Herodians were those who viewed Herod Agrippa as Israel's Messiah. (For further discussion, see Guelich, 138–39 [on 3:6].)

ἀποστέλλουσιν, "they send," in the Markan context probably should be understood as the ruling priests, scribes, and elders who initially approached Jesus and demanded to know by what authority Jesus caused disruption in the temple (11:27–28; Gundry, 692).

ἵνα αὐτὸν ἀγρεύσωσιν λόγῳ, "so that they might trap him with a statement." The purpose of their question is to trap Jesus (note the forward position of αὐτόν, "him," thus emphasizing the object of the attempted entrapment). If Jesus' answer is satisfactory to the one group, it would be unsatisfactory to the other. More than that, a recommendation to pay taxes would most likely offend his following, who hoped for tax relief, while a recommendation not to pay taxes would bring on charges of sedition. The Pharisees and the Herodians are attempting to present Jesus with the same predicament that he had presented the ruling priests in 11:27–33. On that occasion Jesus demanded that the ruling priests give their opinion on John's authority. Was it from heaven or from humans? To answer either way was problematical. This time it is Jesus' turn. But unlike the scribes and ruling priests, who disengenuously stated, "We do not know," Jesus will turn back the ethical dilemma onto his questioners with a remarkable pronouncement (see *Comment* on v 17).

14 καὶ ἐλθόντες λέγουσιν αὐτῷ, διδάσκαλε, οἴδαμεν ὅτι ἀληθὴς εἶ καὶ οὐ μέλει σοι περὶ οὐδενός, "And approaching, they say to him, 'Teacher, we know that you are true, and that another's opinion means nothing to you.'" Compare the man who in 10:17 approached Jesus and addressed him as διδάσκαλος, "Teacher" (see *Comment* on 10:17; cf. John 3:2). The flattering words, "we know that you are true, and that another's opinion means nothing to you," are intended to cajole, perhaps even pressure, Jesus into being dangerously candid. The flattery continues.

οὐ γὰρ βλέπεις εἰς πρόσωπον ἀνθρώπων, ἀλλ᾽ ἐπ᾽ ἀληθείας τὴν ὁδὸν τοῦ θεοῦ διδάσκεις, "for you do not regard the position of people, but you truly teach the way of God." It is ironic that these emissaries of the ruling priests know (οἴδαμεν, "we know") that Jesus is ἀληθής, "true," and that he truly teaches τὴν ὁδὸν τοῦ θεοῦ, "the way of God," but that the ruling priests themselves had said in 11:33a, in reference to the question of where John's authority came from, οὐκ οἴδαμεν, "we do not know." Apparently they know things when it is expedient to know them. The reference to the way of God immediately brings to mind early Christianity's self-reference as the Way (cf. Acts 9:2; 19:9, 23; 24:14, 22), which is paralleled in the Qumran literature (e.g., 1QS 8:13–14; 9:18, 21) and which apparently derives from Isa 40:3, "prepare the way of the LORD." The πρόσωπον ἀνθρώπων, "position of people" (lit. "face of people"), is biblical diction (cf. Weiss, *"Eine neue Lehre in Vollmacht,"* 208).

ἔξεστιν δοῦναι κῆνσον Καίσαρι ἢ οὔ; δῶμεν ἢ μὴ δῶμεν, "Is it lawful to pay tax to Caesar, or not? Should we give, or should we not give?" These pointed questions confront Jesus with a dilemma. Many in the crowd, including many if not most of his own following, detested Roman taxation, for not only did it represent Jewish submission to a pagan emperor, but it also implied support, even if unwilling, of what the Roman emperor stood for (such as his sovereignty and divinity, which in various forms were stamped on the coins with which the taxes were paid). On the one hand, if Jesus were to have declared that it was not lawful (for a Torah-observant Jew) to pay taxes to Caesar, he would have won instant acclaim from most of the crowd but put himself in a precarious position in the eyes of the political authorities. Given Jesus' recent entry into the city, mounted on a colt and accompanied by shouts about the coming kingdom of David (11:1–11), many in the crowd would have expected Jesus to have declared payment of taxes to Caesar to be unlawful. If taxes were to have been paid, they should have been paid to the legitimate king of Israel, perhaps to Jesus himself. On the other hand, if Jesus were to have declared payment of taxes to Caesar to be lawful, he would surely have alienated the crowd and most of his following. Thus discredited, Jesus would have lost his influence over the people, making it easier for the ruling priests to destroy him, or perhaps to ignore him altogether.

Jesus apparently held a dim view of the half-shekel temple tax: "What do you think, Simon? From whom do kings of the earth take toll or tribute [τέλη ἢ κῆνσον]? From their sons or from others?" (Matt 17:25). Peter rightly replied "from others," to which Jesus rejoined: "Then the sons are free" (Matt 17:26). Nevertheless, Jesus directed Peter to pay the tax (Matt 17:27). It is hard to believe that Jesus thought that these free sons owed tax to Caesar. Despite the cleverness of his answer in 12:17, it is possible that he taught his disciples that in the kingdom of God no more tax would be paid to Caesar, which would account for the accusation against Jesus in Luke 23:2.

κῆνσος, "tax," is a Latin loanword (*census*) that was used in Greek, Aramaic, and Hebrew (cf. קְנָס *qĕnās*, *DJPA*, 497–98). Matthew follows Mark in using κῆνσος, but Luke uses φόρος, "tribute," in his parallel account (20:22) and uses it again in L material where Jesus is accused of forbidding the Jewish people to pay tribute (23:2). On κῆνσος in the papyri, see BAG, 431, and MM, 343. The full meaning is enrollment (ἀπογράφειν) of names and assessment of property for the purpose of levying taxes (Luke 2:1–5); the word *census* or κῆνσος alone can mean "tax." On hatred of taxes in the Herodian period, see Josephus, *Ant.* 17.11.2 §308. Following the removal of Archelaus in 6 C.E., Judas the Galilean urged Jews not to pay Roman tribute and incited a revolt (cf. Josephus, *J.W.* 2.8.1 §118; *Ant.* 20.5.2 §102). An event such as this and the passions it had aroused would still have been felt twenty-five years later when Jesus was asked about his opinion on whether to pay taxes to Caesar.

15 ὁ δὲ εἰδὼς αὐτῶν τὴν ὑπόκρισιν εἶπεν αὐτοῖς, "but knowing their hypocrisy, he said to them." Only Mark describes the stratagem as ὑπόκρισιν, "hypocrisy."

The Matthean evangelist says that Jesus was "aware of their malice" but then betrays knowledge of his Markan source by having Jesus say, "Why put me to the test, you hypocrites?" (Matt 22:18). Matthew is especially fond of the epithet (cf. Matt 6:2, 5, 16; 7:5; 15:7; 22:18; 23:13, 15, 23, 25, 27, 28, 29; 24:51; only a few of these come from Mark or Q). Jesus is not fooled by this strategem for one moment, for he immediately recognizes their hypocrisy.

τί με πειράζετε; φέρετέ μοι δηνάριον ἵνα ἴδω, "Why do you test me? Bring me a denarius, so that I might see it." By asking the Pharisees and Herodians, "Why do you test me?" Jesus seeks to expose their true motives. They say nothing, but perhaps Jesus gave them no opportunity to frame an answer. He abruptly demands that they produce a denarius. The δηνάριος, "denarius," was a silver Roman coin (*denarius*), whose value in first-century Palestine was approximately one day's wage (cf. Matt 20:2). Jesus' request to see the coin may have been tantamount to a mocking condescension, as if to say, "Hmm, let me see one of Caesar's coins." Jesus' question in v 16, "Of whom is this image and inscription?" continues the irony.

16 τίνος ἡ εἰκὼν αὕτη καὶ ἡ ἐπιγραφή; οἱ δὲ εἶπαν αὐτῷ, Καίσαρος, "'Of whom is this image and inscription?' And they said to him, 'Caesar.'" The εἰκών, "image," and ἐπιγραφή, "inscription," on the denarius would probably have been that of the current Roman emperor, Tiberius (though older Augustan coins would still have been in circulation). Jesus' point is not to draw attention to the image, as a violation of the commandment not to make images (cf. Exod 20:4), or to draw attention to the blasphemous ascription of divinity to the Roman Caesar, as a violation of the commandment not to have any other god before the Lord God (cf. Exod 20:3). His point will be made clear in the next verse. The widely held view is that the denarius that Jesus looked at had been minted by Tiberius in the 20s. Its legend probably read: TI CAESAR DIVI AVG F AVGVSTVS, "Tiberius Caesar Augustus, Son of Divine Augustus." On the coin and its meaning, see Hart, "The Coin"; and Bruce, "Render to Caesar."

17 τὰ Καίσαρος ἀπόδοτε Καίσαρι καὶ τὰ τοῦ θεοῦ τῷ θεῷ, "Give to Caesar the things of Caesar, but give to God the things of God." The precise meaning of Jesus' statement is not obvious. In fact, Jesus probably intended his statement to be ambiguous. In effect, it thrusts the problem of whether Jews should pay taxes to Caesar right back onto his interlocutors. Can they justify their views? Can the Herodians justify paying taxes to Rome (along with their other political policies)? Can the Pharisees justify a provocative policy of civil disobedience, which could, and on occasion did, lead to violence? At stake are one's loyalties and motives (Matt 6:24 = Luke 16:13: "you cannot serve God and mammon").

The ambiguity of Jesus' reply was such that no matter what one's position was on the question one could agree. For the zealot, what belonged to Caesar was nothing and what belonged to God was everything. For the moderate, what belonged to Caesar was tribute and what belonged to God was worship and fidelity to the covenant.

Justin understood Jesus' pronouncement to mean that tax was to be paid to Caesar, but worship was to given to God alone, and not Caesar (*1 Apol.* 17.2). Justin is probably close to the truth, for this position is consistent with Paul's in Rom 13 (cf. vv 1, 7: "Let every person be subject to the governing authorities. For there is no authority except from God, and those that exist have been instituted by God. . . . Pay all of them their dues, taxes to whom taxes are due, revenue to whom revenue is due, respect to whom respect is due, honor to whom honor is due"). The NT recognizes the political sphere as in some sense ordained of God for the common good.

καὶ ἐξεθαύμαζον ἐπ' αὐτῷ, "and they were amazed at him." The word ἐκθαυμάζειν, "to be amazed," occurs only here in Mark and nowhere else in the NT. However, the prefix-less θαυμάζειν, "to be amazed," appears in Mark 6:6; 15:5, 44. The Markan evangelist is quite fond of the language of amazement, especially with regard to the effect Jesus has on others, friend and foe alike. For ἐκπλήσσειν, "to amaze," see 1:22; 6:2; 7:37; for θαμβεῖν, "to amaze," see 1:27; 10:24, 32; for ἐκθαμβεῖν, "to amaze," see 9:15; 16:5–6; for ἐξιστάναι, "to amaze," see 2:12. What is so amazing about Jesus' pronouncement, which answers the difficult question, is that it does not fall into the trap. "Yes" or "no," that is, "pay tax to Caesar" or "do not pay tax to Caesar," seem to have been the only options available to Jesus. His answer, however, cuts past such simplistic alternatives. Perhaps something is owed Caesar, but what is it? There is much also that is owed God, but what is that? Jesus forces his interlocutors to answer their own question and, in doing so, to probe deeply into their motives and loyalties.

Explanation

The question of authority in 11:27–33 was potentially dangerous for Jesus, but the question of whether it is lawful for a Jew to pay taxes to Caesar is especially dangerous. A false step here and Jesus could find himself in the hands of the Roman authorities before completing his ministry in Jerusalem. But the devious and ill-intentioned question gives Jesus the opportunity to offer some positive teaching, even if his own answer exhibits similar cleverness. Jesus' deliberately ambiguous pronouncement, "Give to Caesar the things of Caesar, but give to God the things of God," sets forth a fundamental principle as opposed to a rigid rule: every person must judge for himself or herself what belongs to God and what belongs to someone or something else. Jesus' principle forces a person to discern priorities and loyalties. In the context of his ministry "the things of God" consist of obedience to the call for repentance and faith in view of the coming kingdom of God. People are called to devote themselves to "the things of God," which according to Mark involve Jesus' passion (cf. 8:33, where Jesus rebukes Peter for not thinking "the things of God"; Gundry, 694). If 8:33 does indeed clarify the meaning of 12:17, then Jesus is saying that "the things of Caesar" are the things of this world, things that will pass away in the face of the coming kingdom of God, while "the things of God" pertain to Jesus' mission, which will be accomplished on a cross in Jerusalem.

I. The Question about Resurrection (12:18–27)

Bibliography

Bamberger, B. J. "The Sadducees and the Belief in Angels." *JBL* 82 (1963) 433–35. **Bartina, S.** "Jesús y los saduceos: 'El Dios de Abraham, de Isaac y de Jacob' es 'El que hace existir' (Mt 22,23–33; Mc 12,18–27; Lc 20,27–40; Hebr 11,13–16)." *EstBib* 21 (1962) 151–60. **Baumbach, G.** "The Sadducees in Josephus." In *Josephus, the Bible, and History*. Ed. L. H. Feldman and G. Hata. Detroit: Wayne State UP, 1989. 173–95. ———. "Der sadduzäische Konservativismus." In *Literatur und Religion des Frühjudentums*. Ed. J. Maier and J. Schreiner. Würzburg: Echter, 1973. 201–13. **Belkin, S.** "Levirate and Agnate Marriage in Rabbinic and Cognate Literature." *JQR* 60 (1970) 275–329. **Burgos Nuños, M. de.** "Hemos sido creados para la vida y no para la muerte: Le enseñanza de Jesús sobre la resurrección, según Marcos 12,18–27." *CiTom* 105 (1978) 529–60. **Carton, G.** "Comme des anges dans le ciel." *BVC* 28 (1959) 46–52. **Cavallin, H. C.** "Jesus gör de döda levande." *SEÅ* 51–52 (1986–87) 40–49. **Cohn-Sherbok, D. M.** "Jesus' Defense of the Resurrection of the Dead." *JSNT* 11 (1981) 64–73 (repr. in *The Historical Jesus: A Sheffield Reader*. Ed. C. A. Evans and S. E. Porter. Biblical Seminar 33. Sheffield: Sheffield Academic, 1995. 157–66). **Daalen, D. H. van.** "Some Observations on Mark 12,24–27." *SE* 4 [= TU 102] (1968) 241–45. **Daube, D.** "On Acts 23: Sadducees and Angels." *JBL* 109 (1990) 492–97. **Davies, W. D.,** and **Allison, D. C.** *The Gospel according to Saint Matthew.* **Decock, P. B.** "Holy Ones, Sons of God, and the Transcendent Future of the Righteous in 1 Enoch and the New Testament." *Neot* 17 (1983) 70–82. **Derrett, J. D. M.** "Marcan Priority and Marçan Skill." *BO* 29 (1987) 135–39. **Dinter, P. E.** "Preaching and the Inquiring of God." *Worship* 52 (1978) 223–36. **Donahue, J. R.** "A Neglected Factor in the Theology of Mark." *JBL* 101 (1982) 563–94, esp. 575–78. **Downing, F. G.** "The Resurrection of the Dead: Jesus and Philo." *JSNT* 15 (1982) 42–50 (repr. in *The Historical Jesus: A Sheffield Reader*. Ed. C. A. Evans and S. E. Porter. Biblical Seminar 33. Sheffield: Sheffield Academic, 1995. 167–75). **Dreyfus, F.-P.** "L'argument scripturaire de Jésus en faveur de la résurrection des morts (Marc, XII,26–27)." *RB* 66 (1959) 213–25. **Ellis, E. E.** "Jesus, the Sadducees and Qumran." *NTS* 10 (1963–64) 274–79. **Epstein, L. M.** *Marriage Laws in the Bible and the Talmud.* Cambridge: Cambridge UP, 1942. **Fischer, G.** *Die himmlischen Wohnungen: Untersuchungen zu Joh 14,2f.* Europäische Hochschulschriften 23.38. Bern; Frankfurt am Main: Lang, 1975. 128–36. **Hultgren, A. J.** *Jesus and His Adversaries: The Form and Function of the Conflict Stories in the Synoptic Tradition.* Minneapolis: Augsburg, 1979. 78–82, 123–31. **Iersel, B. M. F. van.** "Nederlandse varianten can de materialistische exegese: Enkele vragen." *TvT* 18 (1978) 413–23, 420–24. **Janzen, J. G.** "Resurrection and Hermeneutics: On Exodus 3.6 in Mark 12.26." *JSNT* 23 (1985) 43–58 (repr. in *The Historical Jesus: A Sheffield Reader*. Ed. C. A. Evans and S. E. Porter. Biblical Seminar 33. Sheffield: Sheffield Academic, 1995. 176–91). **Kato, Z.** *Die Völkermission im Markusevangelium.* 112–18. **Kegel, G.** *Auferstehung Jesu—Auferstehung der Toten: Eine traditionsgeschichtliche Untersuchung zum Neuen Testament.* Gütersloh: Mohn, 1970. 67–70. **Le Moyne, J.** *Les Sadducéens.* EBib. Paris: Gabalda, 1972. 123–35. **Liebers, R.** *"Wie geschrieben steht": Studien zu einer besonderen Art frühchristlichen Schriftbezuges.* Berlin; New York: de Gruyter, 1993. 95–107. **Manns, F.** "La technique du 'Al Tiqra' dans les évangiles." *RevScRel* 64 (1990) 1–7. **Manson, T. W.** "Sadducee and Pharisee: The Origin and Significance of the Names." *BJRL* 22 (1938) 144–59. **Meier, J. P.** "The Debate on the Resurrection of the Dead: An Incident from the Ministry of the Historical Jesus?" *JSNT* 77 (2000) 3–24. **Mell, U.** *Die "andere" Winzer: Eine exegetische Studie zur Vollmacht Jesu Christi nach Markus 11,27–12,34.* WUNT 77. Tübingen: Mohr-Siebeck, 1995. 267–311. **Meyer, R.** "Σαδδουκαῖος." *TDNT* 7:35–54. **Minette de Tillesse, G.** *Le secret messianique.* 154–56. **Mudiso Mbâ Mundla, J.-G.** *Jesus und die Führer Israels: Studien* *zu den sogenannten Jerusalemer Streitgesprächen.* NTAbh 17. Münster: Aschendorff, 1984. 71–109. **Müller, K.** "Jesus und die Sadduzäer." In *Biblische Randbemerkungen.* FS R. Schnackenburg, ed. H. Merklein and J. Lange. Würzburg: Echter, 1974. 3–24. **Mussner, F.** "Jesu Lehre über das kommende Leben nach den Synoptiker." *Concilium* 6 (1970) 692–95. **Nickelsburg, G. W. E.** *Resurrection, Immortality and Eternal Life in Intertestamental Judaism.* HTS 26. Cambridge: Harvard UP, 1972. **O'Rourke, J. J.** "Explicit Old Testament Citations in the Gospels." *Studia Montis Regii* 7 (1964) 37–60. **Reiser, M.** "Das Leben nach dem Tod in der Verkündigung Jesu." *Erbe und Auftrag* 66 (1990) 381–90. **Rigaux, B.** *Dieu l'a ressuscité: Exégèse et théologie biblique.* Studii Biblici Franciscani Analecta 4. Gembloux: Duculot, 1973. 24–39. **Saldarini, A. J.** *Pharisees, Scribes and Sadducees in Palestinian Society: A Sociological Approach.* Wilmington, DE: Glazier, 1988. 79–237, 298–308. **Schiffman, L. H.** "The Sadducean Origins of the Dead Sea Scroll Sect." In *Understanding the Dead Sea Scrolls.* Ed. H. Shanks. New York: Random House, 1992. 35–49. **Schlosser, J.** *Le Dieu de Jésus: Étude exégétique.* LD 129. Paris: Cerf, 1987. 77–91. **Schubert, K.** "Die Entwicklung der Auferstehungslehre von der nachexilischen bis zur frührabbinischen Zeit." *BZ* 6 (1962) 177–214. **Schwankl, O.** *Die Sadduzäerfrage (Mk 12,18–27 parr): Eine exegetisch-theologische Studie zur Auferstehungserwartung.* BBB 66. Frankfurt am Main: Athenäum, 1987. ———. "Die Sadduzäerfrage (Mk 12,18–17) und die Auferstehungserwartung Jesu." *Wissenschaft und Weisheit* 50 (1987) 81–92. **Strawson, W.** *Jesus and the Future Life: A Study in the Synoptic Gospels.* London: Epworth, 1959. 203–10. **Suhl, A.** *Die Funktion der alttestamentlichen Zitate und Anspielungen im Markusevangelium.* 67–72. **Vouga, F.** "Controverse sur la résurrection des morts (Marc 12,18–27)." *LumVie* 179 (1986) 49–61. **Weiss, W.** *"Eine neue Lehre in Vollmacht."* 234–48. **Westcott, B. F.** and **Hort, F. J. A.** *Introduction.* 2:26. **Zeitlin, S.** "The Sadducees and the Belief in Angels." *JBL* 83 (1964) 67–71.

Translation

[18]*And the Sadducees, who say there is no resurrection, come to him, and they were questioning him, saying,* [19] *"Teacher, Moses* [a] *wrote for us that if someone's brother should die and leave behind a wife and not leave behind a child, his brother should take the wife and raise up offspring for his brother.* [20] *There were seven brothers; and the first took a wife, and dying, he left behind no offspring.* [21] *And the second took her, and he died, without leaving offspring; and the third likewise.* [b] [22] *And the seven did not leave behind offspring.* [c] *Finally, the woman also died.* [23] *In the resurrection,* [d] *whose wife will she be? For the seven* [e] *had her as wife."* [24] *Jesus said to them, "For this reason are you not misled, knowing neither the Scriptures nor the power of God?* [25] *For whenever they arise from the dead, they neither marry nor are given in marriage, but they are as angels in heaven.* [26] *But concerning the dead, that they are raised, have you not read in the book of Moses, at [the passage] of the bush, how God spoke to him, saying, 'I am the God* [f] *of Abraham, and the God of Isaac,* [g] *and the God of Jacob'?* [27] *He is not God of the dead, but of the living. You are greatly mistaken."*

Notes

[a]Gk. Μωϋσῆς (read by א B D W Σ). 𝔓[45] A C Φ read Μωσῆς, which is phonetically closer to the Heb. (מֹשֶׁה *mōšeh*). On the name and person of Moses, see *Comment* on 9:4 above.

[b]Some MSS spell out what is implied by reading καὶ ὁ τρίτος ὡσαύτως ἔλαβεν αὐτήν, "and likewise the third took her."

[c]Once again, some MSS spell out what is implied: ὡσαύτως ἔλαβον αὐτὴν οἱ ἑπτὰ καὶ οὐκ ἀφῆκαν σπέρμα, "Likewise the seven took her, but did not leave behind offspring."

[d]Many MSS read ἐν τῇ ἀναστάσει ὅταν ἀναστῶσιν, "when they are resurrected in the resurrection." The words are not found in א B C* L and a few other authorities. Both Nestle-Aland[27] and

UBSGNT[3c] read ὅταν ἀναστῶσιν, "when they are resurrected," but the words are placed in square brackets. Metzger (*TCGNT*[1], 110–11) thinks that the words are original but were omitted by early copyists (including Matthew and Luke) as superfluous. See also Westcott-Hort, *Introduction* 2:26.

[e]A few later MSS read πάντες γὰρ οἱ ἑπτά, "for all seven."

[f]Gk. ἐγὼ ὁ θεός. Some MSS read ἐγώ εἰμι ὁ θεός, "I am the God," perhaps influenced by LXX Exod 3:14: ἐγώ εἰμι ὁ ὤν, "I am the one who is."

[g]Gk. Ἰσαάκ. ℵ* D read Ἰσάκ, while some Latin MSS read *Isac.* The Heb. of Exod 3:6 reads יִצְחָק *yiṣḥāq.* Both spellings are attested in the LXX. One MS reverses the order of the second and third names: ὁ θεὸς Ἰακώβ καὶ ὁ θεὸς Ἰσαάκ, "the God of Jacob and the God of Isaac."

Form/Structure/Setting

The story concerning the question of whose wife the oft-widowed woman will be in the resurrection depicts Sadducees approaching Jesus with an absurd question, whose point is not clear. The highly improbable scenario envisioned by the question is based on the law of levirate marriage (cf. Gen 38:8; Deut 25:5–6; Ruth 4; Josephus, *Ant.* 4.8.23 §§254–56; *ABD* 4:296–97), in which a man was expected to sire children by the childless widow of his deceased brother. What makes the hypothetical situation so unlikely is that the childless woman finds herself widowed seven times over. In the resurrection, whose wife will she be? The underlying premise is that the doctrine of the resurrection is inconsistent with the teaching of the Torah, especially so when someone like Jesus adopts a strict, monogamous position that rules out divorce (see Jesus' teaching on divorce in 10:1–12, which itself is based on the Torah, Gen 1:27; 2:24). Unlike the previous question concerning payment of taxes to Caesar, this question is relatively harmless. Whatever position Jesus takes will have no significant impact either on his following or on his critics who wish him ill. Jesus' reply is clever, approximating his cleverness in responding to the more serious question of paying taxes (12:13–17), and provides him another opportunity to make an important pronouncement, in this case: "He is not God of the dead, but of the living."

Form critics label this pericope a pronouncement story presented as a controversy dialogue (Taylor, *Formation,* 65; Bultmann, *History,* 26). Bultmann thinks the story derives from the early church, perhaps out of rabbinic materials (with vv 26–27 added later). Perhaps, but there is no Christian content. Why would Christians create tradition that does not advance the kerygma or clarify any significant aspect of Christology? Indeed, are we to believe that early Christians invented a controversy dialogue, so that Jesus could make a pronouncement on the topic of the resurrection, yet without a hint of his own resurrection? This lack of specific Christian content argues for an origin in the life of Jesus (*Sitz im Leben Jesu*). Moreover, there was no debate between Christians and early rabbinic Judaism over the question of the resurrection; all sides believed in it. Thus, there is no post-Easter context or occasion that can plausibly account for the creation of the tradition. A pre-Easter origin in the life of Jesus is more probable (see Meier, *JSNT* 77 [2000] 3–24).

Yet it is difficult to see how this exchange between Jesus *and the Sadducees* is historical. There are two principal difficulties: (1) Why would Sadducees take any interest in an itinerant teacher from Galilee? If their interest was a malevolent one (which would be understandable), then why ask a question about the resurrection? If the Sadducees were afraid that Jesus posed a serious threat, then why not ask questions about the kingdom of God and other aspects of social change on which accusations could be based? (2) The question itself seems out of place. The polemic of Mark 11–12 centers on the temple establishment and policies of which Jesus is critical. The question of the resurrection fits better the earlier period of Jesus' ministry, where Sabbath law and questions of divorce and purity were discussed. But is it probable that Jesus would have encountered a Sadducee in Galilee? One way that the pericope could be accepted in its present context is to view those who questioned Jesus as scribes with Sadducean affiliation. The question then might not be out of place. Many questions were thrown at Jesus, mostly of a dangerous kind ("By what authority are you doing these things?" or "Is it lawful to pay taxes to Caesar?"), but others may have been part of the typical rabbinic-school debates in which questions about the resurrection or the greatest commandment (12:28–34) may have been raised. The evangelist Mark has gathered these various traditions, some from Jerusalem, some not, some dangerous, some not, into the present literary context.

Accordingly, what we probably have here is a piece of genuine, but reworked and recontextualized, exegesis from Jesus in support of the resurrection. Because this exegesis opposes Sadducean interpretation, the evangelist—or more likely the tradition before him—has introduced the pericope in the context of Jesus' quarrels with the temple authorities and has specifically credited the Sadducees with asking the question. A Sadducean presence in the temple-precinct controversies also rounds out the cast of opponents arrayed against Jesus.

Given the Markan context of polemic (i.e., the temple authorities vs. Jesus), the Sadducees' question regarding the resurrection may have been an attempt to draw Jesus out with respect to ideas of eschatology and restoration. In its original setting, the question probably had only to do with the resurrection as an academic point of dispute, but in the Markan context the question may be understood as having broader implications. Every group of major political and religious significance in Jerusalem will take a swing at Jesus. It is now the Sadducees' turn, and they too will be bested in the argument.

Comment

18 ἔρχονται Σαδδουκαῖοι πρὸς αὐτόν, οἵτινες λέγουσιν ἀνάστασιν μὴ εἶναι, καὶ ἐπηρώτων αὐτόν, "the Sadducees, who say there is no resurrection, come to him, and they were questioning him." Here the Sadducees make their first and only appearance in the Gospel of Mark (contrast Matthew, where they make several appearances). The name Σαδδουκαῖος, "Sadducee," may have come from the adjective צַדִּיק *ṣaddîq*, "righteous," but most scholars today believe it derives from the name צָדוֹק *ṣādôq* (Σαδδούκ), "Zadok" (2 Sam 8:17). For this reason and others having to do with overlaps in halakah, Schiffman ("Sadducean Origins") contends that the founders of the Qumran sect, who in places are called the "sons of Zadok" (בני צדוק *bĕnê ṣādôq*; e.g., CD 4:3; 1QS 5:2, 9; 1QSa 1:2; 2:3), were Sadducean, or at least an early expression of the Sadducean sect. (Not many have accepted this identification.) Given the economic, social, and political orientation of the Sadducees, we should not be surprised to see them sometimes mentioned together with ruling priests, sometimes as allies (Acts 4:1–4; 15:17–18). We should not, however, assume that all Sadducees were priests, or that most priests, even ruling priests, were Sadducees. Josephus describes only one high priest, Ananus, as a Sadducee (cf. *Ant.* 20.9.1 §199: "He followed the school of the Sadducees [αἵρεσιν . . . τὴν Σαδδουκαίων]"). For more on this point, see G. G. Porton, "Sadducees," *ABD* 5:894.

On the Sadducees' denial of the resurrection, see Acts 4:2; 23:6–8 ("the Sadducees say that there is no resurrection, nor angel, nor spirit [μὴ εἶναι ἀνάστασιν μήτε ἄγγελον μήτε πνεῦμα]; but the Pharisees acknowledge them all"); and Josephus, *Ant.* 18.1.4 §16 ("The Sadducees hold that souls [ψυχάς] perish along with bodies [σώμασι]"); *J.W.* 2.8.14 §165 ("As for the persistence of the soul [ψυχῆς] after death, penalties in Hades, and rewards, they will have none of them").

ἀνάστασις, "resurrection," occurs here and in v 23 and nowhere else in Mark. Elsewhere in the Gospels, apart from Markan parallels, the word occurs but once more, in Luke 14:14: "you will be repaid at the resurrection of the righteous" (NIV). In reference to himself, Jesus refers to being "raised up" (8:31; 9:31; 10:34; 14:28).

19 διδάσκαλε, Μωϋσῆς ἔγραψεν ἡμῖν ὅτι ἐάν τινος ἀδελφὸς ἀποθάνῃ καὶ καταλίπῃ γυναῖκα καὶ μὴ ἀφῇ τέκνον, ἵνα λάβῃ ὁ ἀδελφὸς αὐτοῦ τὴν γυναῖκα καὶ ἐξαναστήσῃ σπέρμα τῷ ἀδελφῷ αὐτοῦ, "Teacher, Moses wrote for us that if someone's brother should die and leave behind a wife and not leave behind a child, his brother should take the wife and raise up offspring for his brother." On Jesus' address as διδάσκαλε, "teacher," see *Comment* on 12:14. The Matthean and Lukan evangelists smooth out Mark's clumsy construction (Matt 22:24; Luke 20:28).

The Sadducees are referring to the levirate laws in the Pentateuch (cf. Gen 38; Deut 25:5–10). The earliest tradition in which this law appears is found in the patriarchal narratives: "Then Judah said to Onan, 'Go in to your brother's wife, and perform the duty of a brother-in-law to her, and raise up offspring for your brother'" (Gen 38:8). The law is formally spelled out in Deut 25. Levirate marriage was an ancient solution to the problem of the widowed and childless woman. In great antiquity a woman had two places: her father's house as an unmarried virgin or her husband's house, in which she would bear him children. A childless widow had no secure place in ancient society. Through levirate marriage she had the opportunity to bear children in the name of her deceased husband. The Sadducees summarize the law, which is accepted as uncontroversial.

Josephus expands the teaching of Deuteronomy in an interesting way: "When a woman is left childless on her husband's death, the husband's brother shall marry her, and shall call the child that shall be born by the name of the deceased and rear him as heir to the estate; for this will at once be profitable to the public welfare, houses not dying out and property remaining with the relatives, and it will moreover bring the women an alleviation of their misfortune to live with the nearest kinsman of their former husband" (*Ant.* 4.8.23 §§254–55).

20 ἑπτὰ ἀδελφοὶ ἦσαν· καὶ ὁ πρῶτος ἔλαβεν γυναῖκα καὶ ἀποθνῄσκων οὐκ ἀφῆκεν σπέρμα, "There were seven brothers; and the first took a wife, and dying, he left behind no offspring." Seven brothers who die and leave behind no offspring superficially recalls the seven martyred sons in 2 Macc 7 (cf. 4 Macc 8–13). These brothers also believed in the resurrection. We do not know if they were married (and we perhaps should assume that they were not). In any case, levirate marriage had nothing to do with their tragic story. Tobit's story of Sarah, the daughter of Raguel, who was married seven times (Tob 3:7–15), provides a more likely backdrop. In her case, however, not one of the marriages was consummated, for the evil demon Asmodeus slew each husband before they had come together. In the Sadducees' hypothetical example the phrase ἔλαβεν γυναῖκα, "he took a wife," implies that the marriage (as well as the subsequent six levirate marriages) was indeed consummated.

21 καὶ ὁ δεύτερος ἔλαβεν αὐτὴν καὶ ἀπέθανεν μὴ καταλιπὼν σπέρμα· καὶ ὁ τρίτος ὡσαύτως, "And the second took her and he died, without leaving offspring; and the third likewise." The sequence of levirate marriages is here described. The second and third brothers take the woman as their wife, but no child is produced.

22 καὶ οἱ ἑπτὰ οὐκ ἀφῆκαν σπέρμα. ἔσχατον πάντων καὶ ἡ γυνὴ ἀπέθανεν, "And the seven did not leave behind offspring. Finally, the woman also died." The six brothers of the original husband dutifully, each in his turn, took the widow as a wife. Yet not one was able to beget a child by her. In the end the woman died childless, having been married to all seven brothers.

23 ἐν τῇ ἀναστάσει [ὅταν ἀναστῶσιν] τίνος αὐτῶν ἔσται γυνή· οἱ γὰρ ἑπτὰ ἔσχον αὐτὴν γυναῖκα, "In the resurrection, whose wife will she be? For the seven had her as wife." The phrase ἐν τῇ ἀναστάσει, "in the resurrection," is shorthand for the resurrection of the last days and the ensuing eternal life in the kingdom of God (cf. Luke 14:14; John 11:24; *Liv. Pro.* 2:15; *t. Sanh.* 13.5 [בתחיית המתים, *bithîyat hammētîm*]). Behind the question "Whose wife will she be?" is the assumption that the laws of the Torah will be perfectly observed in God's kingdom. (Related to this is the rabbinic tradition that the Messiah will be an expert in the Torah.) If there really is a resurrection (which Sadducees doubt), then how can the law of the Torah be followed, especially if strict monogamy is observed? Sadducean logic leads to the woman being married to all seven brothers, which even biblical polygamy (as in the case of the patriarchs) does not allow. How can one affirm both the suspect doctrine of the resurrection and the eternal validity of the Torah?

24 οὐ διὰ τοῦτο πλανᾶσθε μὴ εἰδότες τὰς γραφὰς μηδὲ τὴν δύναμιν τοῦ θεοῦ; "For this reason are you not misled, knowing neither the Scriptures nor the power of God?" Jesus' rhetorical question is tinged with sarcasm. Earlier he had asked the ruling priests, scribes, and elders, "Have you not even read this Scripture?" (12:10; cf. 11:27). This time the Sadducees have got it wrong because they know μὴ . . . τὰς γραφὰς μηδὲ τὴν δύναμιν τοῦ θεοῦ, "neither the Scriptures nor the power of God." Implicit in this comment is Jesus' own understanding of divine revelation: it comes through Scripture and through the power of God. Jesus' understanding of Scripture is different from that of the scribes and other religious teachers. Elsewhere in Mark it is commented that Jesus' teaching is unlike that of the scribes, for he teaches as one who possesses authority (cf. 1:22, 27). Through his experience of the power of God at work in him, Jesus preached Scripture as fulfilled (e.g., 1:12–15; cf. Luke 4:1, 14, 21; 11:20), while this same experience guided him in his understanding of the Scripture. Experience of the power of God thus becomes for Jesus a vital part of his hermeneutic (see Chilton, *Galilean Rabbi,* 165–98, esp. 168–69). Jesus doubts that the Sadducees have ever experienced God's power and that they therefore have any insight into what Scripture reveals.

Gundry (702) thinks Jesus' reference to the τὴν δύναμιν τοῦ θεοῦ, "the power of God," is an allusion to an early form of the ʿAmîdâ ("the Standing [Prayer]" or Eighteen Benedictions; Benediction 2), where the גבורות *gĕbûrôt,* "powers [of God]," are mentioned. One is also reminded of Jesus' confession before the high priest that as "son of man" he will sit "at the right hand of Power" (14:62), where "Power" is a circumlocution for God himself.

25 ὅταν γὰρ ἐκ νεκρῶν ἀναστῶσιν οὔτε γαμοῦσιν οὔτε γαμίζονται, "For whenever they arise from the dead, they neither marry nor are given in marriage." Jesus reasons implicitly that nowhere in Scripture is there any hint that the marriage state continues after the resurrection (cf. *b. Ber.* 17a: "in the world to come there is no . . . propagation"). The Sadducees' question is therefore irrelevant.

εἰσὶν ὡς ἄγγελοι ἐν τοῖς οὐρανοῖς, "they are as angels in heaven." It is widely assumed that the Sadducees did not believe in angels (cf. Acts 23:8). But angels are in the Torah, that part of Jewish Scripture the Sadducees accepted as inspired and authoritative. Thus, Jesus' statement that the resurrected righteous ones will be as angels in heaven may not be further sarcasm (as Gundry, *Matthew,* 446) but an extension of Jesus' defense of the resurrection based on the Torah (see Davies and Allison, *Matthew* 3:227–28). Belief that humans in heaven will be angel-like is well attested in the literature of the NT period (*1 Enoch* 104:4, 6: "you are about to be making a great rejoicing like the angels of heaven . . . for you are to be partners with the good-hearted people of heaven"; *2 Bar.* 51:5, 10: "And they shall be made like angels"; *Mart. Pol.* 2; cf. 1QSb 4:24–26; 4Q511 [= 4QShir^b] 35 4; *Mek.* on Exod 14:29 [*Bešallaḥ* §7]).

26 περὶ δὲ τῶν νεκρῶν ὅτι ἐγείρονται, "But concerning the dead, that they are raised." Jesus now addresses the unspoken assumption that underlies the question in the first place. The Sadducees simply do not believe in the resurrection. The real issue underlying their question is not "Whose wife will she be?" but "Is belief in the resurrection credible?" Jesus will now address this question.

οὐκ ἀνέγνωτε ἐν τῇ βίβλῳ Μωϋσέως ἐπὶ τοῦ βάτου πῶς εἶπεν αὐτῷ ὁ θεός, "have you not read in the book of Moses, at [the passage] of the bush, how God spoke to him." Jesus had asked the Sadducees if their confusion was not due to their ignorance of the Scriptures. He now appeals to a particular Scripture, a famous one from the Torah. This is the passage where God first spoke to Moses and revealed his holy name. The implication and associations of the divine name will play a role in the defense of the resurrection. The style of reference to Scripture, ἐπὶ τοῦ βάτου, "at the bush," or "at [the passage] of the bush," is Jewish. Compare *m. 'Abot* 3:7: "it is (written) in David [בדוד, *bĕdāwid*]," by which is meant, "it is (written) in (the passage concerning) David," as well as elsewhere in the NT (e.g., Rom 9:25; 11:2; Heb 4:7).

ἐγώ ὁ θεὸς Ἀβραὰμ καὶ [ὁ] θεὸς Ἰσαὰκ καὶ [ὁ] θεὸς Ἰακώβ, "I am the God of Abraham, and the God of Isaac, and the God of Jacob." Jesus appeals to one of the most sacred and most important passages in all of Jewish Scripture. To build a compelling scriptural argument for the resurrection against Sadducean skepticism, Jesus would have to appeal to the Torah. Rabbinic literature tells of a similar defense offered by Gamaliel: "Sectarians [or heretics] asked Rabban Gamaliel: 'When do we know that the Holy One, blessed be He, will resurrect the dead?' He answered them from the Torah, the Prophets, and the Writings" (*b. Sanh.* 90b). Outside of the Torah, appeals were made to Isa 26:19; Ps 16:9–11; Job 19:26; Dan 12:1–2. The eschatological hope expressed in 4Q521 (= 4QMessianic Apocalypse) 2 ii 12 that at the time of the coming of the Messiah, whom "heaven and earth will obey," God "will make alive the dead [מתים יחיה *mētîm yiḥyeh*]" probably draws on Isa 26:19: "Your dead shall live, their bodies shall rise [יקומון נבלתי מתיך יחיו *yiḥyû mēteykā nĕbēlātî yĕqûmûn*]." Appeals to the Prophets (such as Isa 26:19) or the Writings (such as Dan 12:2 and Job 19:26) would be insufficient to the Sadducees. Can Jesus find evidence of the resurrection in the passage from the Law to which he has alluded?

Ἀβραάμ, "Abraham." The name Abraham (Heb. אַבְרָהָם *'abrāhām*), the famous founding patriarch, occurs some thirty-two times in the NT Gospels; the only occurrence in Mark is here in v 26. In material found only in Luke, Jesus addresses the woman with the curved spine as "a daughter of Abraham," whom Satan has bound (Luke 13:16), and later addresses the righteous Zacchaeus as "a son of Abraham" (Luke 19:9). In the parable of the Rich Man and Lazarus, the rich man sees his former poor neighbor resting in the bosom of Abraham (Luke 16:22–23), recalling Jewish tradition in which it was believed that Abraham guarded the roads leading either to paradise or to Hades (e.g., *b. 'Erub.* 19a; *Gen. Rab.* 48.8 [on Gen 18:1]). In the Q tradition John the Baptist enjoins the religious leaders (as in Matthew) or the people in general (as in Luke) not to presume to say to themselves, "We have Abraham as our father"; for "God is able from these stones to raise up children to Abraham" (Matt 3:9 = Luke 3:8).

Ἰσαάκ, "Isaac," and Ἰακώβ, "Jacob." The names Isaac (Heb. יִצְחָק *yiṣḥāq*) and Jacob (Heb. יַעֲקֹב *ya'ăqōb*) occur in the Synoptics almost always together and along with the name of Abraham. The names of the three patriarchs occur in a Q tradition in which the impenitent are told: "You will weep and gnash your teeth, when you see Abraham and Isaac and Jacob and all the prophets in the kingdom of God and you yourselves thrust out" (Luke 13:28). In the Matthean form of the tradition the impenitent are told that "many will come from east and west and sit at table with Abraham, Isaac, and Jacob in the kingdom of heaven" (Matt 8:11). Eating and drinking with the patriarchs is part of Jewish eschatological tradition. To be included with them is to be numbered with the elect.

The patriarchs Abraham, Isaac, and Jacob are great because of the God who called them and made a covenant with them. When God says, "I am the God of Abraham, and the God of Isaac, and the God of Jacob," he has defined himself with the names of the patriarchs. The growing eschatological speculations regarding the role of the patriarchs in protecting and comforting the elect who enjoy life in the world to come accommodate the point that Jesus makes in appealing to Exod 3:6.

27 Jesus' statement οὐκ ἔστιν θεὸς νεκρῶν ἀλλὰ ζώντων, "He is not the God of the dead but of the living," is proverbial; parallels are found in rabbinic sources: "The Torah speaks not of the dead but of the living [לא דברה תורה במתים אלא בחיים *lō' dĕbārâ tôrâ bĕmētîm 'ellā' baḥayyîm*]"; *Midr. Mišlê* on Prov 17:1). B. L. Visotzky (*The Midrash on Proverbs*, YJS 27 [New Haven, CT; London: Yale UP, 1992] 144 n. 8) explains that they are dead to the obligations of Torah (cf. Matt 8:22 = Luke 9:60). Jesus' hearers, friendly or antagonistic, would all agree that God is a God of the living. If this is true and if God identifies himself also as the "God of Abraham, and the God of Isaac, and the God of Jacob," logic suggests that someday these patriarchs will again be alive. This will take place through the resurrection. Grammar and tense play no role here (either in an assumed present tense, or transforming a past reference into a future reference; on these arguments, see Gundry, 703–4). The argument turns on an inference drawn from parallel truths. God is the God of the patriarchs; he is also the God of the living. Therefore the patriarchs, though presently dead, must someday live. Even if Jesus' argument does not exactly match one of Hillel's seven interpretive principles, it is gratuitous to assert, as Cohn-Sherbok does (*JSNT* 11 [1981] 73), that Jesus' exegesis is "defective from a rabbinic point of view." Apart from the anachronism that underlies this assertion, Jesus' argument may in fact be an example of Hillel's third principle ("Building a principle from one passage of Scripture"). Downing (*JSNT* 15 [1982] 42–50) thinks so. Downing notes too that Jesus' argument parallels very closely an argument Philo makes, whereby the three great patriarchs are spoken of as eternal (cf. Philo, *Abraham* 50–55). Downing also cites 4 Macc 7:18–19: "But as men with their whole heart make righteousness their first thought, these alone are able to master the weakness of the flesh, believing that unto God they die not, as our patriarchs, Abraham and Isaac and Jacob die not, but they live unto God" (on the last phrase, see Luke 20:38). To this we might add 4 Macc 16:25: "those who die for the sake of God live unto God, as do Abraham and Isaac and Jacob and all the patriarchs." The tradition here in 4 Maccabees complements Jesus' inference from Exod 3:6 and the truism that God is a God of the living. Especially interesting is Rabbi Hiyya's interpretation in *y. Ber.* 2.3: "You know how to recite [Scripture] but you do not know how to interpret [the verse]: 'For the living know that they will die' [Qoh 9:5] refers to the righteous who are called 'the living' even when they are dead. . . . And whence do we know that the righteous are called 'the living' even when dead? For it is written, 'This is the land which I swore to Abraham, to Isaac, and to Jacob saying' [Deut 34:4]" (cf. *b. Ber.* 18a).

πολὺ πλανᾶσθε, "You are greatly mistaken." That is, the Sadducees have wandered (the literal meaning of πλανᾶν) far from the truth. They are greatly mistaken because they know "neither the Scriptures nor the power of God" (v 24). See Mark 13:5–6, where Jesus warns his disciples against false prophets who will try to lead them astray (πλανᾶν).

Explanation

The evangelist portrays Jesus in ongoing sparring with various opponents. Ever since his arrival in Jerusalem (11:1–11), tension between Jesus and the temple establishment has been escalating. Jesus' dramatic action in the temple precincts (11:15–17) resulted in the ruling priests' desire to destroy him (11:18). This notice sets the tone for the remainder of passion week. Ruling priests, scribes, and elders approach Jesus and demand to know by what authority he is doing these things (11:27–28). The parable of the Wicked Vineyard Tenants (12:1–11) offers an implicit answer to the priests' question. They wish to arrest him but cannot on account of Jesus' popularity with the crowd (12:12). Pharisees and Herodians put to Jesus the sensitive question of paying taxes to Caesar: Should a Torah-observant Jew pay taxes or not? (12:13–17). The question was intended to make it possible to destroy Jesus. A false step here and Jesus would be subject to arrest. And finally, the question of levirate marriage in the resurrection (12:18–27) was intended to destroy Jesus' credibility in the eyes of the crowd with which he was so popular. But again Jesus stands his ground, and again his opponents' lose face.

Jesus' teaching does not simply answer effectively the ill-intentioned question of his opponents; it affords Jesus the opportunity to speak on an important topic. On what basis does Jesus believe in the resurrection? No appeal is made to Isa

26:19, Dan 12:2, Ps 16:9–11, or Job 19:26, texts that more or less support the doctrine. Jesus instead appeals to the very character and being of God himself. He is the God of the living, not the God of the dead. If he is the God of Abraham, Isaac, and Jacob—as he disclosed himself to Moses the great lawgiver—then life, not death, will surely be the destiny of all those linked to him in faith. If all God's people are destined to perish and to remain dead, then in what sense is he the God of the living? The living God will surely reign over a living people. The resurrection is accordingly a logical inference and, for those who experience the power of God, it is an experiential inference.

J. The Great Commandment (12:28–34)

Bibliography

Abrahams, I. *Studies in Pharisaism and the Gospels.* 2:197–99. **Allison, D. C.** "Mark 12.28–31 and the Decalogue." In *The Gospels and the Scriptures of Israel.* Ed. C. A. Evans and W. R. Stegner. JSNTSup 104. SSEJC 3. Sheffield: Sheffield Academic, 1994. 270–78. **Ambrozic, A. M.** *The Hidden Kingdom.* 177–81. **Banks, R. J.** *Jesus and the Law in the Synoptic Tradition.* SNTSMS 28. Cambridge: Cambridge UP, 1975. 164–73. **Baumgarten, J. M.** "Messianic Forgiveness of Sin in CD 14:19 (4Q266 10 I 12–13)." In *The Provo International Conference on the Dead Sea Scrolls.* Ed. D. W. Parry and E. Ulrich. STDJ 30. Leiden: Brill, 1999. 537–44. **Beilner, W.** *Christus und die Pharisäer: Exegetische Untersuchung über Grund und Verlauf der Auseinandersetzung.* Vienna: Herder, 1959. 131–39. **Berg, L.** "Das neutestamentliche Liebesgebot: Prinzip der Sittlichkeit." *TTZ* 83 (1974) 129–45. **Berger, K.** *Die Gesetzesauslegung Jesu: Ihr historischer Hintergrund im Judentum und im Alten Testament.* WMANT 40. Neukirchen-Vluyn: Neukirchener Verlag, 1972. 136–202. **Bornkamm, G.** "Das Doppelgebot der Liebe." In *Neutestamentliche Studien.* FS R. Bultmann, ed. W. Eltester. BZNW 21. Berlin: Töpelmann, 1954. 85–93 (repr. in G. Bornkamm. *Geschichte und Glaube,* Part 1. Vol. 3 of *Gesammelte Aufsätze.* BEvT 48. Munich: Kaiser, 1968. 37–45). **Bultmann, R.** "Aimer son prochain, commandement de Dieu." *RHPR* 10 (1930) 222–41. **Burchard, C.** "Das doppelte Liebesgebot in der frühen christlichen Überlieferung." In *Der Ruf Jesu und die Antwort der Gemeinde: Exegetische Untersuchungen.* FS J. Jeremias, ed. E. Lohse et al. Göttingen: Vandenhoeck & Ruprecht, 1970. 39–62. **Dautzenberg, G.** *Sein Leben bewahren: ψυχή in den Herrenworten der Evangelien.* SANT 14. Munich: Kösel, 1966. 114–23. **Davies, W. D.,** and **Allison, D. C.** *Gospel according to Saint Matthew.* **Derrett, J. D. M.** "'Love Thy Neighbor as a Man Like Thyself?'" *ExpTim* 83 (1971–72) 55–56. **Diezinger, W.** "Zum Liebesgebot Mk xii,28–34 und Parr." *NovT* 20 (1978) 81–83. **Donahue, J. R.** "A Neglected Factor in the Theology of Mark." *JBL* 101 (1982) 563–94, esp. 578–84. **Egelkraut, H. L.** *Jesus' Mission to Jerusalem: A Redaction Critical Study of the Travel Narrative in the Gospel of Luke, Lk 9:51–19:48.* Europäische Hochschulschriften 23.38. Bern; Frankfurt am Main: Lang, 1976. 83–91. **Ernst, J.** "Die Einheit von Gottes- und Nächstenliebe in der Verkündigung Jesu." *TGl* 60 (1970) 3–14. **Fuchs, E.** *Zur Frage nach dem historischen Jesus.* Gesammelte Aufsätze 2. Tübingen: Mohr-Siebeck, 1960. 1–20. **Fuller, R. H.** "The Double Commandment of Love: Test Case for the Criteria of Authenticity." In *Essays on the Love Commandment.* Ed. R. H. Fuller. Philadelphia: Fortress, 1978. 41–56. **Furnish, V. P.** *The Love Command in the New Testament.* Nashville: Abingdon, 1972. 25–30. ———. "Love of Neighbor in the New Testament." *JRE* 10 (1982)

327–34. **Gerhardsson, B.** "The Shema‘ in Early Christianity." In *The Four Gospels 1992*. FS F. Neirynck, ed. F. Van Segbroeck et al. 3 vols. BETL 100. Leuven: Peeters and Leuven UP, 1992. 1:275–93. **Goldstein, H.** *Gottesverächter und Menschenfeinde?* Düsseldorf: Patmos, 1980. 79–98. **Greenlee, J. H.** "Verbs in the New Testament." *BT* 3 (1952) 71–75. **Hahn, F.** "Neutestamentliche Ethik als Kriterium menschlicher Rechtsordnung." In *Rechtstaat und Christentum*. Ed. E. L. Behrendt. Munich: Behrendt, 1982. 377–79. ———. "Neutestamentliche Grundlagen einer christlichen Ethik." *TTZ* 86 (1977) 31–41. **Hamilton, G. J.** "The First Commandment: A Theological Reflection." *NB* 69 (1988) 174–81. **Hiers, R. H.** *The Historical Jesus and the Kingdom of God: Present and Future in the Message and Ministry of Jesus*. University of Florida Humanities Monograph 38. Gainesville: University of Florida Press, 1973. 89–91. **Hoyer, G. W.** "Mark 12:28–34." *Int* 33 (1979) 293–98. **Hruby, K.** "L'amour du prochain dans le pensée juive." *NRT* 41 (1969) 493–516. **Hultgren, A. J.** *Jesus and His Adversaries: The Form and Function of the Conflict Stories in the Synoptic Tradition*. Minneapolis: Augsburg, 1979. 47–50. **Kertelge, K.** "Das Doppelgebot der Liebe im Markusevangelium." In *A Cause de l'évangile: Études sur les Synoptiques et les Actes*. FS J. Dupont, ed. F. Refoulé. LD 123. Paris: Cerf, 1985. 303–22. **Kiilunen, J.** *Der Doppelgebot der Liebe in synoptischer Sicht: Ein redaktionskritischer Versuch über Mk 12,28–34 und die Parallelen*. AASF B.250. Helsinki: Suomalainen Tiedeakatemia, 1989. **Kilpatrick, G. D.** "κύριος Again." In *Orientierung an Jesus: Zur Theologie der Synoptiker*. FS J. Schmid, ed. P. Hoffmann et al. Freiburg: Herder, 1973. 214–19. **Kuhn, H.-W.** "Zum Problem des Verhältnisses der markinischen Redaktion zur israelitisch-jüdischen Tradition." In *Tradition und Glaube: Das frühe Christentum in seiner Umwelt*. FS K. G. Kuhn, ed. G. Jeremias and H.-W. Stegemann. Göttingen: Vandenhoeck & Ruprecht, 1971. 299–309. **Lapide, P. E.** *Er predigte in ihren Synagogen: Jüdische Evangelienauslegung*. Gütersloher Taschenbücher Siebenstern 1400. Gütersloh: Mohn, 1980. 77–97. **Légasse, S.** "L'énendue de l'amour interhumain d'après le Nouveau Testament: Limites et promesses." *RTL* 8 (1977) 137–59, 283–304. ———. "*Et qui est mon prochain?*" *Étude sur l'objet de l'agapè dans le Nouveau Testament*. LD 136. Paris: Cerf, 1989. 53–67. **Lohfink, N.** "Das Hauptgebot." In *Das Siegeslied am Schilfmeer: Christliche Auseinandersetzungen mit dem Alten Testament*. Frankfurt am Main: Knecht, 1965. 19–50. **Malina, B. J.**, and **Rohrbaugh, R. L.** *Social-Science Commentary on the Synoptic Gospels*. 258–60. **Marcus, J.** "The Authority to Forgive Sins upon the Earth: The Shema in the Gospel of Mark." In *The Gospels and the Scriptures of Israel*. Ed. C. A. Evans and W. R. Stegner. JSNTSup 104. SSEJC 3. Sheffield: JSOT Press, 1994. 196–211. **Mell, U.** *Die "andere" Winzer: Eine exegetische Studie zur Vollmacht Jesu Christi nach Markus 11,27–12,34*. WUNT 77. Tübingen: Mohr-Siebeck, 1995. 312–53. **Merklein, H.** *Die Gottesherrschaft als Handlungsprinzip: Untersuchung zur Ethik Jesu*. FB 34. Würzburg: Echter, 1978. 100–105. **Michel, O.** "Das Gebot der Nächstenliebe in der Verkündigung Jesu." In *Zur sozialen Entscheidung: Vier Vorträge*. Ed. N. Koch. Tübingen: Mohr-Siebeck, 1947. 53–101. **Miguéns, M.** "Amour, alpha et omega de l'existence. Mc 12,28–34." *AsSeign* 2.62 (1970) 53–62. **Miller, J. S.** "The Neighbour." *ExpTim* 96 (1984–85) 337–39. **Miller, P. D.** "The Place of the Decalogue in the Old Testament and Its Law." *Int* 43 (1989) 229–43. **Minette de Tillesse, G.** *Le secret messianique*. 149–52. **Montefiore, H. W.** "Thou Shalt Love Thy Neighbor as Thyself." *NovT* 5 (1962) 157–70. **Mudiso Mbâ Mundla, J.-G.** *Jesus und die Führer Israels: Studien zu den sogenannten Jerusalemer Streitgesprächen*. NTAbh 17. Münster: Aschendorff, 1984. 110–233. **Murray, G.** "The Questioning of Jesus." *DRev* 102 (1984) 271–75. **Mussner, F.** *Traktat über die Juden*. Munich: Kösel, 1979. 194–98 (ET: *Tractate on the Jews: The Significance of Judaism for Christian Faith*. Tr. L. Swidler. Philadelphia: Fortress, 1984. 120–23). **Neuhäusler, E.** *Anspruch und Antwort Gottes: Zur Lehre von den Weisungen innerhalb der synoptischen Jesusverkündigung*. Düsseldorf: Patmos, 1962. 114–18. **Nissen, A.** *Gott und der Nächste im antiken Judentum: Untersuchungen zum Doppelgebot der Liebe*. WUNT 15. Tübingen: Mohr-Siebeck, 1974. **O'Rourke, J. J.** "Explicit Old Testament Citations in the Gospels." *Studia Montis Regii* 7 (1964) 37–60. **Perkins, P.** *Love Commands in the New Testament*. New York: Paulist, 1982. 10–26. **Pesch, R.** "Jesus und das Hauptgebot." In *Neues*

Testament und Ethik. FS R. Schnackenburg, ed. H. Merklein. Freiburg: Herder, 1989. 99–109. **Piper, J. S.** *"Love Your Enemies": Jesus' Love Command in the Synoptic Gospels and the Early Christian Paraenesis: A History of the Tradition and Interpretation of Its Uses.* SNTSMS 38. Cambridge: Cambridge UP, 1979. 92–94. **Prast, F.** "Ein Appell zur Besinnung auf das Juden wie Christen gemeinsam verpflichtende Erbe im Munde Jesu: Das Anliegen einer alten vormarkinischen Tradition (Mk 12,28–34)." In *Gottesverächter und Menschenfeinde? Juden zwischen Jesus und frühchristlicher Kirche.* Ed. H. Goldstein. Düsseldorf: Patmos, 1979. 79–98. **Quispel, G.** "Love Thy Brother." *Ancient Society* 1 (1970) 83–93. **Sariola, H.** *Markus und das Gesetz.* 185–208. **Schmidt, K. L.** *Rahmen.* 281–83. **Schneider, G.** "Die Neuheit der christlichen Nächstenliebe." *TTZ* 82 (1973) 257–75. **Schrage, W.** *Ethik des Neuen Testaments.* Grundrisse zum Neuen Testament. NTD Ergänzungsreihe 4. Göttingen: Vandenhoeck & Ruprecht, 1982. 69–72 (ET: *The Ethics of the New Testament.* Tr. D. E. Green. Philadelphia: Fortress, 1988. 68–71). **Soares Prabhu, G. M.** "The Synoptic Love-Commandment: The Dimensions of Love in the Teaching of Jesus." *Jeevadhara* 13 (1983) 85–103. **Söding, T.** *Glaube bei Markus.* 175–78. **Spicq, C.** *Agapè dans le Nouveau Testament: Analyse des textes I.* EBib. Paris: Gabalda, 1958. 62–66. **Stauffer, E.** *Die Botschaft Jesu damals und heute.* Dalp-Taschenbücher 333. Bern: Francke, 1959. 40–48. **Stern, J. B.** "Jesus' Citation of Dt 6,5 and Lv 19,18 in the Light of Jewish Tradition." *CBQ* 28 (1966) 312–16. **Strecker, G.** "Gottes- und Menschenliebe im Neuen Testament." In *Tradition and Interpretation in the New Testament.* FS E. E. Ellis, ed. G. F. Hawthorne and O. Betz. Tübingen: Mohr-Siebeck; Grand Rapids, MI: Eerdmans, 1987. 53–67. **Suhl, A.** *Zitate.* 87–89. **Thomas, K. J.** "Liturgical Citations in the Synoptics." *NTS* 22 (1975–76) 205–14, esp. 209–12. ———. "Torah Citations in the Synoptics." *NTS* 24 (1977–78) 85–96, esp. 87–88. **Tuckett, C. M.** *The Revival of the Griesbach Hypothesis: An Analysis and Appraisal.* SNTSMS 44. Cambridge: Cambridge UP, 1983. 125–33. **Vouga, F.** "Die Entwicklungsgeschichte der jesuanischen Chrien und didaktischen Dialoge des Markusevangelium." In *Jesu Rede von Gott und ihre Nachgeschichte im frühen Christentum: Beiträge zur Verkündigung Jesu und zum Kerygma der Kirche.* FS W. Marxsen, ed. D.-A. Koch et al. Gütersloh: Mohn, 1989. 45–56, esp. 55–56. ———. *Jésus et la loi selon la tradition synoptique.* Le monde de la Bible. Geneva: Labor et Fides, 1988. 134–45. **Vurst, J. van.** "The Scribe's Insight." *TBT* 25 (1987) 37–41. **Weiss, W.** *"Eine neue Lehre in Vollmacht."* 249–66. **Williams, J. F.** *Other Followers of Jesus.* 172–76. **Wischmeyer, O.** "Das Gebot der Nächstenliebe bei Paulus: Eine traditionsgeschichtliche Untersuchung." *BZ* 30 (1986) 161–87. **Wolpert, W.** "Die Liebe zum Nächsten, zum Feind und zum Sünder." *TGl* 74 (1984) 262–82. **Zimmermann, H.** *Jesus Christus: Geschichte und Verkündigung.* Stuttgart: Katholisches Bibelwerk, 1973. 246–48.

Translation

[28]*And one of the scribes, approaching and hearing them disputing,*[a] *seeing*[b] *that he had answered them well, asked him, "Which commandment is first*[c] *of all?"* [29]*Jesus answered, "The first is*[d] *'Hear, Israel, the Lord our God is one Lord;* [30]*and you shall love the Lord your God with your whole heart, and with your whole life, and with your whole mind, and with your whole strength.'*[e] [31]*This is the second:*[f] *'You shall love your neighbor as yourself.' There is no other commandment greater than these."* [32]*And the scribe said to him, "Well said, teacher. In truth have you said 'he is one and there is no other besides him';* [33]*and 'to love him with the whole heart, and with the whole understanding,*[g] *and with the whole strength,' and 'to love the neighbor as oneself' is much more than all whole burnt offerings and sacrifices."* [34]*And Jesus, seeing that he had answered wisely, said to him, "You are not far from the kingdom of God."*[h] *And no one any longer dared to question him.*

Notes

[a]Some later authorities read ἀκούσας τῶν Σαδδουκαίων συζητούντων αὐτῷ, "having heard the Sadducees disputing with him."

[b]Gk. ἰδών, which is read by ℵ* C D L W Σ Φ. ℵ² A B 33 read εἰδώς, "knowing."

[c]One MS reads πρώτη καὶ μείζων, "first and greatest."

[d]A C Σ 33 and several later MSS read πρώτη πάντων τῶν ἐντολῶν, "The first of all of the commandments."

[e]A D W 33 and several later MSS add αὕτη πρώτη ἐντολή, "This is the first commandment."

[f]A D W 33 and several later MSS read καὶ δευτέρα ὅμοια αὕτη, "and a second is like it."

[g]Gk. συνέσεως. D and a few other MSS read δυνάμεως, "power."

[h]Under Matthean influence, a few later MSS read τῆς βασιλείας τῶν οὐρανῶν, "kingdom of heaven."

Form/Structure/Setting

The opening verse (v 28) makes clear that the question of the Great Commandment is asked shortly after the question of levirate marriage and the resurrection (12:18–27). A scribe is impressed with Jesus' ability and so asks him "Which commandment is first of all?" The pericope consists of the question (v 28), Jesus' reply (vv 29–31), the scribe's approving response (vv 32–33), and Jesus' commendation (v 34). The Markan evangelist has added the opening "And one of the scribes, approaching and hearing them disputing, seeing that he had answered them well," as well as the concluding "And no one any longer dared to question him." The evangelist may also have added most of v 33, where the scribe repeats the two commandments (on this and other points of source criticism, see G. Bornkamm, "Das Doppelgebot").

Bultmann (*History,* 54–55) classifies 12:28–34 as a "scholastic dialogue" (cf. 10:17–31) and seems undecided about its origin. On the one hand, Bultmann admits that it is "highly probable that Jesus was asked questions about the way to life, or about the greatest commandment," but he wonders, on the other hand, if the setting is fictional. He also concedes that "such a dialogue could easily contain an historical reminiscence," especially if "the special interests of the Church" are not in evidence. The latter point surely applies to 12:28–34, for it is difficult to understand how and why Jesus' affirmation of the Shema, which is neither remarkable nor specifically Christian, would have been created by an early Christian prophet or tradent. Exalting the Jewish Law is hardly what one would expect an early Christian to do (especially if Jesus had not). Even the Jesus Seminar is willing to admit that "this exchange represented Jesus' own views," though a majority of members believe that "the words, however, were those of the young church" (R. W. Funk, ed., *Mark,* 187). If the exchange is thoroughly Jewish in perspective and advanced nothing of the early church's distinctive claims, why was the tradition preserved? Pre-Markan tradents no doubt found the material useful because of the scribe's enthusiastic agreement with Jesus, which included the assertion that the double commandment "is much more than all whole burnt offerings and sacrifices" (v 33). The Markan evangelist found the material useful because it supplemented well his depiction of Jesus besting temple authorities within the temple precincts themselves. Why, even one of their own had to admit that there were principles that took precedence over the temple cultus. For a community rejected by the cultus, and therefore rejected by the synagogue of the Diaspora, the scribe's assertion would be reassuring and of some apologetic value.

The most difficult question facing interpreters concerns the relationship of Mark 12:28–34 to Matt 22:34–40 and Luke 10:25–29. Matthean and Lukan dependence upon Mark cannot account for Luke's very different form and context of the tradition, for in Luke the question is "What shall I do to inherit eternal life?" and it is the one who asks the question, not Jesus, who articulates the famous double commandment to love God and one's neighbor. Moreover, Matthean and Lukan agreements against Mark complicate the picture. The three most obvious agreements are νομικός, "lawyer," in Matt 22:35 and Luke 10:25 instead of εἷς τῶν γραμματέων, "one of the scribes," in Mark 12:28; Jesus addressed as διδάσκαλε, "teacher," in Matt 22:36 and Luke 10:25 (he is not addressed with an epithet in Mark); and the phrase ἐν τῷ νόμῳ, "in the law," in Matt 22:36 and Luke 10:26, in contrast to πάντων, "of all," in Mark 12:28. But the disagreements between Matthew and Luke resist the explanation that Q underlies the respective traditions of these Gospels. The Griesbach Two-Gospel Hypothesis does not really offer a better solution either. It is more likely that several forms of the double commandment pronouncement, or dialogue, were in circulation in the oral dominical tradition. These variant forms could easily account for the few agreements of Matthew and Luke against Mark (viz., some versions had Jesus addressed as "teacher" by a "lawyer" who wanted to know what was the greatest commandment "in the law") and the differences in other details, such as setting and occasion. Luke's version reflects the greatest departure from the Markan setting and occasion (which the Matthean evangelist follows, even if in an edited and abridged form). In Luke the question concerns eternal life, the lawyer answers his own question, Jesus affirms his answer, the lawyer calls for clarification of who his neighbor is, and Jesus responds with the famous parable of the Good Samaritan (Luke 10:29–37). The Lukan tradition probably reflects a different occasion (cf. Manson, *Sayings*, 259–60). The briefer Matthean version concludes with the rabbinic maxim "On these two commandments depend all the law and the prophets" (Matt 22:40; cf. *Sipra Lev.* §195 [on Lev 19:1–4]; *m. Ḥag.* 1:8).

Comment

The question put forth in this instance is not a trick question, nor is it designed to entrap Jesus. Unlike his response to the previous questions (12:14–15, 19–23), which Jesus countered with questions of his own, this time Jesus' answer is straightforward. The scribe asks which commandment is first (or most important) of all (v 28). Jesus replies by quoting Deut 6:4–5 as the first (vv 29–30). He then quotes part of Lev 19:18 as the second (v 31). Jesus' double commandment has some parallels in the Jewish literature of late antiquity and so may not be innovative (see *Comment* below). The scribe finds Jesus' reply succinct and compelling, commenting that to love God with all that one is and has and to love one's neighbor as oneself "is much more than all whole burnt offerings and sacrifices" (vv 32–33). His comment is a remarkable admission, suggesting that Jesus' teaching potentially renders the temple activities of the priests redundant. As such, in the Markan context it represents one more criticism of the temple establishment. Jesus commends the scribe for his answer, "You are not far from the kingdom of God" (v 34a). Having come to the point of agreeing with Jesus' answer, the scribe is now drawing closer to the kingdom.

28 καὶ προσελθὼν εἷς τῶν γραμματέων ἀκούσας αὐτῶν συζητούντων, "And one of the scribes, approaching and hearing them disputing." The γραμματεῖς, "scribes," make frequent appearances in the Markan Gospel (cf. 1:22; 2:6, 16 ["of the Pharisees"]; 3:22 ["from Jerusalem"]; 7:1, 5; 8:31; 9:11, 14; 10:33; 11:18, 27; 12:35, 38; 14:1, 43, 53; 15:1, 31; see *Comment* on 11:18 and 11:27). Almost all of these references have hostile implications for Jesus. συζητεῖν, "to dispute," is a Markan favorite (cf. 1:27; 8:11; 9:10, 14, 16). In 9:14 the scribes dispute with the disciples in the episode involving the demon-possessed boy. In the present episode the scribe joins a dispute already in progress, by which the evangelist means the Sadducees' question about the implications of levirate marriage and resurrection hope (12:18–27).

ἰδὼν ὅτι καλῶς ἀπεκρίθη αὐτοῖς, "seeing that he had answered them well." What motivated the scribe is not made clear. We should not assume that his intentions were necessarily hostile (against Gundry, 710). Had the scribe's intentions been malevolent, could we really expect him to compliment Jesus for an appeal to the Shema and the commandment to love one's neighbor? Such a summation of the Jewish Law was neither surprising nor unique to Jesus. On the contrary, the evangelist's comment that he perceived that Jesus καλῶς ἀπεκρίθη αὐτοῖς, "had answered them well," implies that the scribe was impressed, so impressed with Jesus' skill that asking his opinion on a matter was an opportunity not to be missed. Had Jesus been beaten in the debates, there would have been little reason to solicit an opinion. Had the scribe's intentions been hostile, a resounding compliment would have been unlikely.

ποία ἐστὶν ἐντολὴ πρώτη πάντων, "Which commandment is first of all?" is cognate to the question, "What must I do that I may inherit eternal life?" (Mark 10:17; cf. Luke 10:25). To ascertain the most important commandment and then to do it provided the surest hope of securing one's place among the elect and of guaranteeing life in the world to come. But this does not imply an indifferent attitude toward the other commandments. Mark's πρώτη πάντων, "first of all," means "most important." ἐντολή, "commandment," appears frequently in the LXX (some sixty times in the Pentateuch), almost always in the plural (Heb. מצוה *miṣwâ*). The commandments made up the components of Israel's covenant with God.

29 πρώτη ἐστίν, ἄκουε, Ἰσραήλ, κύριος ὁ θεὸς ἡμῶν κύριος εἷς ἐστιν, "The first is 'Hear, Israel, the Lord our God is one Lord.'" Jesus affirms that the πρώτη, "first," commandment is contained in the Shema (i.e., from the opening word "Hear," which in Hebrew is שְׁמַע *šĕmaʿ*; cf. *m.* ʾAbot 2:13), Deut 6:4–5. (The LXX is followed verbatim.) The Shema denotes three passages (Deut 6:4–9; 11:13–21; Num 15:37–41) and was to be recited every morning and evening. Although the opening words, strictly speaking, are not a commandment, the affirmation that "the Lord our God is one Lord" is implicitly an injunction to recognize and obey the only God. The only God is identified as יהוה (*YHWH*). The commandment proper that follows presupposes this identity. A comment in Josephus (*Ag. Ap.* 2.22 §190) reflects similar thinking: "What, then, are the precepts and prohibitions of our Law? They are simple and familiar. The first [πρώτη] that leads (all of the commandments) concerns God."

30 ἀγαπήσεις κύριον τὸν θεόν σου ἐξ ὅλης τῆς καρδίας σου καὶ ἐξ ὅλης τῆς ψυχῆς σου καὶ ἐξ ὅλης τῆς διανοίας σου καὶ ἐξ ὅλης τῆς ἰσχύος σου, "you shall love the Lord your God with your whole heart, and with your whole life, and with your whole mind, and with your whole strength." Jesus' affirmation of Deut 6:4b–5 is thoroughly Jewish and is, as already stated, unremarkable. The quotation more or less follows the LXX (though there are variations within the Greek tradition itself). The Markan form of the quotation adds the phrase καὶ ἐξ ὅλης τῆς διανοίας σου, "and with your whole mind," thus expanding the original three modifiers to four, and the final phrase reads ἰσχύος, "strength," instead of δυνάμεως, "might." The quotation in Matt 22:37 matches Mark's first three modifiers: "You shall love the Lord your God with your whole heart, and with your whole soul, and with your whole mind" (RSV, adapted). All four modifiers appear in Luke 10:27. Davies and Allison (*Matthew* 3:242) suspect that Matthew dropped Mark's fourth modifier in order to conform to the biblical precedent of three, while Gundry (711) plausibly suggests that the "mind" modifier may have entered the tradition as a result of reading מְאֹדֶךָ (*mĕʾōdekā*, "your might") as מַדָּעֲךָ (*maddāʿăkā*, "your mind"). However, some of the Greek tradition reads διάνοια, "mind," which could more directly account for Mark's additional modifier. The three, or four, modifiers of the command to love the Lord God are meant to convey the totality of one's being and resources. Later Jewish and Christian interpretation greatly elaborated on the respective properties of the heart, life, mind, and strength/might. The modifiers are not synonymous, to be sure. καρδία, "heart" (Heb. לֵב, *lēb*), can mean "mind" in Semitic texts (hence some LXX MSS read διάνοια). The heart is the seat of spiritual life and the inner being, among other things (BAG, 404; BDB, 523–24; *TDNT* 3:605–13). ψυχή, "life" or "soul" (Heb. נֶפֶשׁ, *nepeš*), refers to life itself, though often with reference to feelings, emotions, and desires (BAG, 901; BDB, 659–61; *TDNT* 9:617–50), and thus overlaps at points with καρδία. διάνοια, "mind," refers to understanding and intelligence (BAG, 186; *TDNT* 4:963–68) and in the LXX often translates לֵב, *lēb*, "heart." ἰσχύς, "strength," is roughly synonymous with δύναμις, "might," and both translate כֹּח *kōḥ* and חַיִל *ḥêl* among other words in the LXX (BAG, 384). ἰσχύς refers to one's ability, or to one's capacity or power to act (*TDNT* 3:397–402).

31 δευτέρα αὕτη, ἀγαπήσεις τὸν πλησίον σου ὡς σεαυτόν, "This is the second: 'You shall love your neighbor as yourself.'" Jesus' δευτέρα, "second," commandment is found in Lev 19:18b: "You shall love your neighbor as yourself." The quotation matches the LXX exactly, which in turn is an exact translation of the Hebrew (וְאָהַבְתָּ לְרֵעֲךָ כָּמוֹךָ *wĕʾāhabtā lĕrēʿăkā kāmôkā*). Appeal to Lev 19:18b to sum up one's duty to humanity finds an important parallel in a tradition ascribed to Rabbi Aqiba: "'but you shall love your neighbor as yourself.' Rabbi Aqiba says, 'This is the encompassing principle of the Law'" (*Sipra Lev.* §200 [on Lev 19:15–20]). Hillel's negative form of the Golden Rule is also relevant, in that it finds the whole of the Law summarized in a single principle: "What is hateful to you, do not do to your neighbor; that is the whole Law" (*b. Šabb.* 31a). Of course, Jesus provides not one (i.e., the first) commandment but two (i.e., a second as well). However, in this also he is not unique, for the idea of love for human beings as a complement to love for God is found elsewhere in Jewish thinkers and writers of late antiquity. According to Philo (*Decalogue* 109–10), lovers of human beings and lovers of God only attain virtue by half if they are not lovers both of human beings and of God. The idea of love of God and love of humanity is expressed in many texts (e.g., *T. Iss.* 5:2: "love the Lord and your neighbor"; *T. Iss.* 7:6: "I loved the Lord and humanity with the whole heart"; *T. Dan* 5:3: "Love the Lord with your all your life and one another with a true heart"; Philo, *Spec. Laws* 2.63: "But among the vast number of particular truths and principles [are] two main heads: one of duty to God . . . one of duty to humans"). For more on the development of the double-commandment tradition, see Allison ("Mark 12.28–31 and the Decalogue").

μείζων τούτων ἄλλη ἐντολὴ οὐκ ἔστιν, "there is no other commandment greater than these," because these two commandments summarize the Decalogue (i.e., the first part summarizes the first five commandments; the second summarizes the second five commandments), as is persuasively argued by Allison ("Mark 12.28–31 and the Decalogue"). Jesus' double-commandment summary of the Law places him squarely in the center of Jewish piety.

32 καλῶς, διδάσκαλε, "Well said, teacher." On διδάσκαλε, "teacher," see *Comment* on 9:17. The scribe is so impressed with Jesus' succinct summary of the most important commandments of the Law that he compliments Jesus with the adverb καλῶς, "well," which, of course, means "well said" or "well answered."

ἐπ' ἀληθείας εἶπες ὅτι εἷς ἐστιν καὶ οὐκ ἔστιν ἄλλος πλὴν αὐτοῦ, "In truth have you said 'he is one and there is no other besides him.'" The scribe's ἐπ' ἀληθείας, "in truth," which probably translates אָמֵן *'āmēn*, "truly," underscores his approval of Jesus' answer as well as hints at his admiration for Jesus himself. The scribe's εἷς ἐστιν καὶ οὐκ ἔστιν ἄλλος πλὴν αὐτοῦ, "he is one and there is no other besides him," combines Deut 6:4b ("he is one") and Deut 4:35 ("the Lord your God, he is God and there is no other except him") and so complements Jesus' quotation of this portion of the passage (see also similar affirmations in Exod 8:10 [LXX v 6]; Deut 4:39; 2 Sam 7:22; 1 Kgs 8:60; 2 Kgs 19:19; 2 Chr 33:13; Isa 37:20; 43:10; 44:6; 45:21). The scribe will also augment Jesus' appeal to Deut 6:5 and Lev 19:18.

33 καὶ τὸ ἀγαπᾶν αὐτὸν ἐξ ὅλης τῆς καρδίας καὶ ἐξ ὅλης τῆς συνέσεως καὶ ἐξ ὅλης τῆς ἰσχύος, "and 'to love him with the whole heart, and with the whole understanding, and with the whole strength.'" In repeating Jesus' appeal to Deut 6:5, the scribe reduces the modifiers from four (as in v 30) to three, though the second modifier is σύνεσις, "understanding," rather than ψυχή, "life/soul." The omitted modifier is the problematic third one ("with your whole mind").

καὶ τὸ ἀγαπᾶν τὸν πλησίον ὡς ἑαυτὸν περισσότερόν ἐστιν πάντων τῶν ὁλοκαυτωμάτων καὶ θυσιῶν, "and 'to love the neighbor as oneself' is much more than all whole burnt offerings and sacrifices." The combination of ὁλοκαυτωμάτων καὶ θυσιῶν, "whole burnt offerings and sacrifices," occurs more than one hundred times in the LXX, so it may be regarded as a set phrase. The scribe's confession that love of God and love of one's neighbor are "much more than all whole burnt offerings and sacrifices" reflects various great statements in the prophetic tradition. The prophet/priest Samuel tells the disobedient King Saul: "Has the LORD as great delight in burnt offerings and sacrifices [LXX: ὁλοκαυτώματα καὶ θυσίαι], as in obeying the voice of the LORD? Behold, to obey is better than sacrifice, and to hearken than the fat of rams" (1 Sam [LXX 1 Kgdms] 15:22). Hosea, the prophet to the northern tribes, declares the word of the Lord: "For I desire steadfast love and not sacrifice [LXX: θυσίαν], the knowledge of God, rather than burnt offerings [LXX: ὁλοκαυτώματα]" (Hos 6:6). See also Isa 1:11; Jer 6:20; Amos 5:22; Mic 6:6–8; Pss 40:6 (LXX 39:7); 51:16 (LXX 50:18). The scribe's en-

thusiastic endorsement of Jesus' theology is in keeping with the prophetic tradition and with Jesus' own general principles (cf. the appeals to Isa 56:7 and Jer
7:11 in Mark 11:17). This endorsement thus highlights again Jesus' competent
knowledge of Scripture and his impressive ability to engage the scribes in debate.

The scribe's assertion that "'to love the neighbor as oneself' is much more than
all whole burnt offerings and sacrifices" finds potentially two interesting parallels
from the Dead Sea Scrolls. The first comes from 1QS 9:4, which anticipates the
time when the Qumran Community will "atone for iniquitous guilt and for sinful
unfaithfulness and as good will for the earth better than the flesh of burnt offerings and the fat of sacrifices." The second comes from 4Q266 [= 4QD^a] 10 i 13, a
fragment of the Damascus Document, which looks to the time when "he [the Mes-
siah] will atone for their sin better than meal and sin offerings." Baumgarten
understands these two texts to "envision a time when the perfection of priestly and
lay institutions will become a source of atonement which will be available without
the need for ritual sacrifice" ("Messianic Forgiveness," 541–42). Baumgarten concludes that these Qumran texts may provide evidence of the expectation that at
the coming of the Messiah atonement will be effected "not through ritual sacrifice
. . . but through his illuminational presence as the embodiment of divine good will
for the earth" ("Messianic Forgiveness," 544). This perspective is consistent with
Jesus' eschatology and may shed light on his criticism of the temple establishment
in 11:15–18 (see *Comment* on 11:17). However, it is not necessary to conclude that
Jesus anticipated the cessation of sacrifice in Jerusalem.

34   καὶ ὁ Ἰησοῦς ἰδὼν ὅτι νουνεχῶς ἀπεκρίθη, "And Jesus, seeing that he had
answered wisely." Jesus is impressed with the wisdom of the scribe's answer. Mark's
adverb νουνεχῶς, "wisely," occurs only here and nowhere else in the NT or the
LXX. The word, a compound of νοῦς, "mind," and ἔχειν, "to have" or "to possess," is attested in nonbiblical literature (e.g., Aristotle, Polybius; cf. *Sib. Or.* 1:7)
and means "wisely" or "thoughtfully" (BAG, 546).

οὐ μακρὰν εἶ ἀπὸ τῆς βασιλείας τοῦ θεοῦ, "You are not far from the kingdom of
God." The accuracy of the scribe's answer indicates that he is "not far from the
kingdom of God," that is, he is close to entering the ranks of those who have
responded to the message of the kingdom. The βασιλείας τοῦ θεοῦ, "kingdom of
God," of course, has been the essence of Jesus' proclamation from the very beginning (cf. 1:14–15; 4:11, 26, 30; 9:1, 47; 10:14, 15, 23–25; 14:25). To be μακράν,
"far," from God or from the kingdom of God is language that recalls exile and
diaspora (e.g., Isa 57:19: "Peace, peace, to the far and to the near, says the LORD;
and I will heal him"; Ezek 11:15; Zech 6:15; 10:9), which according to NT theology has been rectified by Christ's mission (cf. Eph 2:13: "But now in Christ Jesus
you who once were far off have been brought near in the blood of Christ").

Why does Jesus regard the scribe as οὐ μακρὰν . . . ἀπό, "not far from," the
kingdom, rather than as having entered the kingdom? Perhaps the evangelist
expects his readers to assume that all that remains for the scribe is repentance, as
both John the Baptist and Jesus required (cf.1:14–15; 6:12). In an earlier exchange
(10:17–31), wealth had prevented another man from entering eternal life (i.e.,
the kingdom). What prevents the scribe on this occasion we are not told (or did
he later repent?). As the heavenly "son of man" (2:10, 28; 3:28; 10:45; 13:26; 14:62),
Jesus has the authority to make pronouncements regarding one's nearness to or
remoteness from the kingdom.

καὶ οὐδεὶς οὐκέτι ἐτόλμα αὐτὸν ἐπερωτῆσαι, "And no one any longer dared to question him." The evangelist has in mind the several exchanges between Jesus and critics that have run throughout chaps. 11 and 12. One challenge and question after another has been hurled at Jesus, and each one has been answered with skill and, in some instances, surprising innovation. Jesus will now take the initiative.

Explanation

In the present pericope the evangelist Mark scores two important points. The first directly concerns Jesus' summarizing of the Law in terms of the two great commandments: to love God with what one is and has and to love one's neighbor as oneself. Jesus is not presenting Israel with some new, strange doctrine. His is a call to repentance, a call that will require undistracted and unrivaled love of God and a genuine love and concern for one's fellow. This love that Scripture and Jesus command is not simply an emotion (though that is often involved); it is rather a commitment and a loyalty, which will manifest itself in obedience to the will of God and respect for and, when required, assistance for one's neighbor (e.g., the parable of the Good Samaritan in Luke 10:29–37). The highest ethic of the Law is not sacrifice or other cultic activity; it is loyalty to God and compassion for human beings.

The second point that the evangelist scores concerns the recognition, on the part of the scribe, of Jesus' sound teaching. Jesus' teaching is so persuasive that even a scribe, whose colleagues only moments earlier had been trying to trip up Jesus, acknowledges its soundness. Indeed, the scribe's enthusiastic endorsement potentially undermines the primacy of the temple establishment itself. Yes, "'to love him with the whole heart, and with the whole understanding, and with the whole strength,' and 'to love the neighbor as oneself' is much more than all whole burnt offerings and sacrifices." The scribe's remarkable pronouncement serves the Markan context well, underscoring the rightness of Jesus' message, even in the face of priestly criticism and opposition.

K. The Question about David's Son   (12:35–37)

Bibliography

Baarlink, H. *Anfängliches Evangelium.* 211–14. **Baumeister, A.** "'Setze dich zu meiner Rechten': Die Bibelauslegung Jesu." *Entschluss* 40.4 (1985) 28–29. **Beilner, W.** *Christus und die Pharisäer: Exegetische Untersuchung über Grund und Verlauf der Auseinandersetzungen.* Vienna: Herder, 1959. 197–200. **Berger, K.** "Die königlichen Messiastraditionen des Neuen Testaments." *NTS* 20 (1973–74) 1–44. **Betz, O.** "Donnersöhne, Menschenfischer und der davidische Messias." *RevQ* 3 (1961) 41–70, esp. 61–67. ———. "Die Frage nach dem messianischen Bewusstsein Jesu." *NovT* 6 (1963) 20–48. **Boobyer, G. H.** "Mark XII. 35–37 and the Preexistence of Jesus in Mark." *ExpTim* 51 (1939–40) 393–94. **Burger, C.** *Jesus als*

Davidssohn: Eine traditionsgeschichtliche Untersuchung. FRLANT 98. Göttingen: Vandenhoeck & Ruprecht, 1970. 52–59, 64–70. **Charlesworth, J. H.** "Solomon and Jesus: The Son of David in Ante-Markan Traditions (Mk 10:47)." In *Biblical and Humane.* FS J. F. Priest, ed. L. B. Elder et al. Homage 20. Atlanta: Scholars Press, 1996. 125–51. ————. "The Son of David: Solomon and Jesus (Mark 10.47)." In *The New Testament and Hellenistic Judaism.* Ed. P. Borgen and S. Giversen. Aarhus: Aarhus UP, 1995. 72–87. **Chilton, B.** "Jesus ben David: Reflections on the Davidssohnfrage." *JSNT* 14 (1982) 88–112 (repr. in *The Historical Jesus: A Sheffield Reader.* Ed. C. A. Evans and S. E. Porter. BibSem 33. Sheffield: Sheffield Academic, 1995. 192–215). **Crossan, J. D.** *In Fragments.* 260–62. **Daube, D.** *The New Testament and Rabbinic Judaism.* London: Athlone, 1956. 158–69. **Dautzenberg, G.** "Psalm 110 im Neuen Testament." In *Liturgie und Dichtung: Ein interdisziplinäres Kompendium.* Ed. H. Becker and R. Kaczynski. St. Ottilien: EOS, 1983. 141–71, esp. 149–52. **Dodd, C. H.** *According to the Scriptures: The Sub-Structure of New Testament Theology.* London: Nisbet, 1952. 119–22. **Duling, D. C.** "Solomon, Exorcism, and the Son of David." *HTR* 68 (1975) 235–52. **Dupont, J.** "Assis à la droite de Dieu: L'interprétation du Ps 110,1 dans le Nouveau Testament." In *Resurrexit: Actes du Symposion sur la résurrection de Jésus (Rome 31 mars–6 avril 1970).* Ed. E. Dhanis. Rome: Libreria Editrice Vaticana, 1974. 423–36. **Fisher, L. R.** "Can This Be the Son of David?" In *Jesus and the Historian.* FS E. C. Colwell, ed. F. T. Trotter. Philadelphia: Westminster, 1968. 82–97. **Fitzmyer, J. A.** "The Contribution of Qumran Aramaic to the Study of the New Testament." *NTS* (1973–74) 382–407, esp. 386–91 (repr. in J. A. Fitzmyer. *A Wandering Aramean: Collected Aramaic Essays.* SBLMS 25. Missoula: Scholars Press, 1979. 85–142, esp. 90–95). ————. "Der semitische Hintergrund des neutestamentlichen Kyriostitels." In *Jesus Christus in Historie und Theologie.* FS H. Conzelmann, ed. G. Strecker. Tübingen: Mohr-Siebeck, 1975. 267–98. ————. "The Son of David Tradition and Mt 22:41–46 and Parallels." *Concilium* 10.2 (1966) 40–46 (repr. in J. A. Fitzmyer. *Essays on the Semitic Background of the New Testament.* SBLSBS 5. London: Chapman, 1971; Missoula, MT: Scholars Press, 1974. 113–26). **Flusser, D.** "Familien vom 'Haus Davids' in der Zeit Jesu." In *Jesus—Qumran—Urchristentum.* Vol. 2 of *Entdeckungen im Neuen Testament.* Neukirchen-Vluyn: Neukirchener Verlag, 1999. 1579–84. **France, R. T.** *Jesus and the Old Testament.* 100–102, 163–69. **Friedrich, G.** "Messianische Hohepriesterwartung in den Synoptikern." *ZTK* 53 (1956) 265–311, esp. 286–89 (repr. in G. Friedrich. *Auf das Wort kommt es an: Gesammelte Aufsätze.* Ed. J. H. Friedrich. Göttingen: Vandenhoeck & Ruprecht, 1978. 56–102, esp. 77–79). **Funk, R. W.,** ed. *Mark.* 187–88. **Gagg, R. P.** "Jesus und die Davidssohnfrage: Zur Exegese von Markus 12,35–37." *TZ* 7 (1951) 18–30. **Gourgues, M.** *À la droite de Dieu: Résurrection de Jésus et actualisation du Psaume 110:1 dans le NT.* EBib. Paris: Gabalda, 1978. 127–42. **Hahn, F.** *The Titles of Jesus in Christology: Their History in Early Christianity.* London: Lutterworth, 1969. 103–8, 251–58. **Harvey, A. E.** *Jesus and the Constraints of History.* London: Duckworth, 1982. 120–51. **Hay, D. M.** *Glory at the Right Hand: Psalm 110 in Early Christianity.* SBLMS 18. Nashville: Abingdon, 1973. 104–21. **Hengel, M.** "'Setze dich zu meiner Rechten!' Die Inthronisation Christi zur Rechten Gottes und Psalm 110,1." In *Le Trône de Dieu.* Ed. M. Philonenko. WUNT 69. Tübingen: Mohr-Siebeck, 1993. 108–94 (ET: "'Sit at My Right Hand!' The Enthronement of Christ at the Right Hand of God and Psalm 110:1." In M. Hengel. *Studies in Early Christology.* Edinburgh: T. & T. Clark, 1995. 119–225). **Iersel, B. M. F. van.** "Fils de David et Fils de Dieu." In *La venue du Messie: Messianisme et eschatologie.* Ed. E. Massaux. RechBib 6. Brügge: Desclée de Brouwer, 1962. 113–32. ————. *"Der Sohn" in den synoptischen Jesusworten: Christusbezeichnung der Gemeinde oder Selbstbezeichnung Jesu?* NovTSup 3. Leiden: Brill, 1961. 171–73. **Johnson, S. E.** "The David-Royal Motif in the Gospels." *JBL* 87 (1968) 136–50, esp. 136–39. **Jonge, M. de.** "Jesus, Son of David and Son of God." In *Intertextuality in Biblical Writings.* FS B. M. F. van Iersel, ed. S. Draisma. Kampen: Kok, 1989. 95–104 (repr. in M. de Jonge. *Jewish Eschatology, Early Christian Christology and the Testaments of the Twelve Patriarchs.* NovTSup 63. Leiden: Brill, 1991. 135–44). **Juel, D.** *Messianic Exegesis: Christological Interpretation of the Old Testament in Early Christianity.* Philadelphia: Fortress, 1988. 135–50, esp. 141–44. **Kilpatrick, G. D.** "Κύριος again." In *Orientierung an Jesus: Zur Theologie der Synoptiker.* FS J. Schmid, ed. P. Hoffmann et al. Freiburg: Herder, 1973. 214–19. **Lindars, B.** *New Testament Apologetic: The Doctrinal Significance of Old Testament Quotations.* London: SCM; Philadelphia: Westminster, 1961. 45–51. **Loader, W. R. G.** "Christ at the Right Hand–Ps. CX. 1 in the NT." *NTS* 24 (1978–79) 199–217, esp. 214–15. **Lohse, E.** "υἱὸς Δαυίδ." *TDNT* 8:478–88. ———. "Der König aus Davids Geschlecht: Bemerkungen zur messianischen Erwartung der Synagoge." In *Abraham unser Vater: Juden und Christen im Gespräch über die Bibel.* FS O. Michel, ed. O. Betz et al. AGSU 5. Leiden: Brill, 1963. 337–45. **Lövestam, E.** "Die Davidssohnfrage." *SEÅ* 27 (1962) 72–82. ———. "Jésus Fils de David chez les Synoptiques." *ST* 28 (1974) 97–109. **Marcus, J.** *The Way of the Lord: Christological Exegesis of the Old Testament in the Gospel of Mark.* Louisville: Westminster John Knox, 1992. 130–52. **Michaelis, W.** "Die Davidssohnschaft Jesu als historisches und kerygmatisches Problem." In *Der historische Jesus und der kerygmatische Christus.* Ed. H. Ristow and K. Matthiae. 2nd ed. Berlin: Evangelische Verlagsanstalt, 1962. 317–30. **Minette de Tillesse, G.** *Le secret messianique.* 156–57, 331–33. **Moloney, F. J.** "The Re-Interpretation of Psalm VIII and the Son of Man Debate." *NTS* 27 (1980–81) 656–72. ———. "The Targum on Ps. 8 and the New Testament." *Salesianum* 37 (1975) 326–36. **Mudiso Mbâ Mundla, J.-G.** *Jesus und die Führer Israels: Studien zu den sogenannten Jerusalemer Streitgesprächen.* NTAbh 17. Münster: Aschendorff, 1984. 234–98. **Neugebauer, F.** "Die Davidssohnfrage (Mark xii. 35–7 Parr.) und der Menschensohn." *NTS* 21 (1974–75) 81–108. **Pesch, R.** *Evangelium der Urgemeinde.* 152–54. **Räisänen, H.** *The 'Messianic Secret' in Mark's Gospel.* 229–34. **Ringgren, H.** "The Use of the Psalms in the Gospels." In *The Living Text.* FS E.W. Saunders, ed. D. Groh and R. Jewett. Lanham: University Press of America, 1985. 39–43. **Schneider, G.** "Zur Vorgeschichte des christologischen Prädikats 'Sohn Davids.'" *TTZ* 80 (1971) 247–53. ———. "Der Davidssohnfrage (Mk 12,35–37)." *Bib* 53 (1972) 65–90. **Suhl, A.** "Der Davidssohn im Matthäus-Evangelium." *ZNW* 59 (1968) 57–81. ———. *Zitate.* 89–94. **Walker, W. O.** "The Origin of the Son of Man Concept as Applied to Jesus." *JBL* 91 (1972) 482–90. **Weinacht, H.** *Die Menschwerdung des Sohnes Gottes im Markusevangelium.* 134–36. **Wrede, W.** "Jesus als Davidssohn." In *Vorträge und Studien.* Tübingen: Mohr-Siebeck, 1907. 147–77.

Translation

[35]*And answering, Jesus was speaking, while teaching in the temple, "How do the scribes say, 'The Messiah* [a] *is "son of David"'?* [b] [36]*David himself said in the Holy Spirit,*
'The Lord [c] *said to my lord,*
"Sit at my right hand,
until I should place your enemies
beneath [d] *your feet."'*
[37]*David himself* [e] *calls him 'lord'; so how is he his son?" And the great crowd was hearing him with pleasure.*

Notes

[a]Gk. ὁ χριστός, lit. "the anointed [one]." The Gk. translates the Heb. מָשִׁיחַ *māšîaḥ.* The Heb. is sometimes transliterated as μεσσίας (cf. John 1:41; 4:25). See *Note* d and *Comment* on 8:29 above.

[b]In most Gk. authorities *David* is spelled Δαυείδ (as in B D). But in other authorities the name is spelled variously, e.g., Δαυίδ and Δαβίδ. ℵ and other MSS read the abbreviation Δᾱδ. The same holds for vv 36 and 37. See 10:47; 11:10.

[c]Nestle-Aland[27] and UBSGNT[3c] (following B D and a few other authorities) read κύριος, "Lord." ℵ A L Σ Φ and many later MSS read ὁ κύριος, "the Lord." It is easier to explain the addition of the article rather than its deletion or omission.

ᵈGk. ὑποκάτω (read by B D W and a few other authorities). א A L Σ Φ 33 and many later MSS read ὑποπόδιον τῶν ποδῶν σου, "a footstool for your feet," which is an assimilation to LXX Ps 109:1.

ᵉ33 and a few late MSS read αὐτὸς Δαυὶδ ἐν τῷ πνεύματι, "David himself in the Spirit."

Form/Structure/Setting

The form of the question concerning the "son of David" as an epithet of the Messiah is somewhat anomalous in the dominical tradition. It begins with a question (v 35b), is followed by a quotation of Ps 110:1 (v 36), and concludes with another question (v 37a). Because this pericope does not follow the usual pattern of Jesus' first being asked a question to which he responds with a counterquestion, some commentators doubt its authenticity. Moreover, the apparent strangeness of the point Jesus seems to be making (e.g., either that Jesus is not a Davidide or that the Messiah is not a Davidide) has only raised more questions about authenticity and the original meaning.

Bultmann (*History*, 66, 136–37) classifies Mark 12:35–37 as an apophthegm but judges it a "secondary form" and "a community product." Bultmann explains by saying the "proof that Messiah could not be David's Son could hardly have had any meaning for Jesus." On the contrary, what could or could not have had meaning for Jesus begs the question. And in any case, it is not clear that this is the point of the story; in fact, it is probable that it is not. Taylor (*Formation*, 78) calls the tradition a pronouncement story. He does not say so explicitly, but he apparently accepts it as authentic tradition. Agreeing with Bultmann, Suhl (*Zitate*, 89–94; *ZNW* 59 [1968] 57–59) thinks that Davidic descent is denied and that the tradition derives from the post-Easter community. Some recent scholars hold this view. For example, Funk (*Mark*, 187–88) avers, "When Jesus initiates a dialogue or debate, we have a good indication that we are dealing with a secondary composition. . . . [T]he church would have been inclined, subsequently, to represent Jesus as making pronouncements on a variety of topics. The direct way to this end would have been to have Jesus raise the issue himself." Such a view is a bit doctrinaire, however. There really are no compelling reasons for viewing tradition as inauthentic simply because Jesus initiates the discussion. And, in any case, why would the early church have been inclined to have Jesus make such a pronouncement? The pronouncement raises a question about the grounds for calling the Messiah the "son of David," but no answer is given. No alternative is offered; no explicit affirmation of Christology is provided. What has been clarified? What has the church gained? Casting doubt on the Davidic descent of the Messiah is hardly what we should expect the church to have done, for the church believed that the Messiah (who was Jesus, of course) *did* in fact descend from David. This is seen in Paul (Rom 1:3–4; cf. 2 Tim 2:8) and in the genealogies that the Matthean and Lukan evangelists add to their respective Gospels. Cranfield (381) is right in his opinion that it is "most unlikely that this saying is the creation of the early Church" (cf. Chilton, "Jesus *ben David*," 210).

Gagg (*TZ* 7 [1951] 18–30) wonders if 12:35–37 is all that remains of a conflict story that originally began with a challenging question (as in the question about authority in 11:27–33, the question about taxes in 12:13–17, the question about levirate marriage and belief in the resurrection in 12:18–27, and the question about the first commandment in 12:28–34). The opening question was lost; the extant and truncated tradition now consists of (1) Jesus' counterquestion, (2) the buttressing citation of Ps 110:1, and (3) the final question that teases out the tension between scribal opinion and the implications of Ps 110:1. The evangelist introduces and concludes (in vv 35a and 37b) the fragmented story (though part of v 35a may be tradition; see *Comment*). Cranfield (381–82) thinks Gagg may well be correct. It may also be supposed that the evangelist's "no one any longer dared to question him" (12:34b) consciously compensates for the loss (or deletion) of the opening challenging question. The evangelist suspected that the story began with such a question, but the question was lost (or deleted). In essence, then, the evangelist explains the omission by saying "no one any longer dared to question him." The Matthean evangelist also sensed that something was wrong with the form of the tradition and so has the Pharisees reply to Jesus' question (cf. Matt 22:41–42).

What was the original, challenging question put to Jesus? Cranfield (381) thinks it may have been whether Jesus taught that the Messiah was the son of David. The suggestion is plausible, for Jesus himself had earlier been hailed as "son of David" (10:47, 48), and in his entry into Jerusalem some of the crowd shouted, "Blessed is the coming kingdom of our father David" (11:10). Cranfield speculates further that the question may have been intended to lead Jesus into saying something self-incriminating (as in other encounters related in chap. 12). It is reasonable to suppose that the question attempted to elicit an answer whereby Jesus' messianic hopes would be defined in terms of Davidism. Like the question concerning taxes, this exchange, if answered "correctly," could have led to charges of sedition. But the question could have been more than merely a question concerning Jesus' views of the Messiah (e.g., is he Davidic, prophetic, or something else?); it could have been an attempt to get Jesus, one rumored to be anointed, to identify himself as the "son of David." Or, to put it the other way around, was Jesus, known as a Solomonic "son of David" by virtue of his ministry of exorcism and healing (on which more will be said below), an anointed son of David, that is, a royal claimant of some sort?

It is perhaps best to understand 12:35–37 as a fragment of a controversy or scholastic dialogue similar to the others found in chap. 12. This pericope is essentially in its proper context and setting, that is, in the context of debate between Jesus and the religious authorities in the temple precincts. Although we cannot ascertain why or how the opening challenging question was lost, it is clear that the point of issue concerned messianism and how this related to Davidic tradition. The intent of Jesus' reply to the challenging question was, as Chilton ("Jesus *ben David*," 210–11) has plausibly suggested, "to deflect the growing suspicion that he claimed to be the messiah." Chilton goes on to say that Jesus' "Davidic descent, his willingness to be called David's son in the context of healing, his comparison of himself with David and Solomon, his entry into Jerusalem must all have contributed to this suspicion." As such, this question and the question about paying taxes to Caesar were the two most dangerous questions put to Jesus while he taught in the temple precincts. These questions, moreover, were probably related, if not linked. For first-century Jews would have assumed that Jesus, as Israel's anointed king, would surely have forbidden the paying of taxes to Caesar. Should we pay taxes to Caesar? Jesus is asked. And, what kind of "son of David" are you? the Messiah kind? The Lukan evangelist may provide us with an independent tradition that reflects the close association of these two questions. We find this in Luke 23:2, where the religious authorities accuse Jesus before the Roman governor: "We found this man perverting our nation, and forbidding us to give tribute to Caesar, and saying that he himself is Messiah a king." The way the tradition is presented in Mark 12 gives the reader the impression that Jesus successfullly extricated himself from these questions that had been designed to entrap him. But Luke 23:2 seems to indicate that in the opinion of his critics Jesus had not.

Comment

35 καὶ ἀποκριθεὶς ὁ Ἰησοῦς ἔλεγεν διδάσκων ἐν τῷ ἱερῷ, "And answering, Jesus was speaking, while teaching in the temple." Often Jesus is teaching (διδάσκειν) in the Markan Gospel (1:21, 22; 2:13; 4:1, 2; 6:2, 6, 30, 34; 7:7; 8:31; 9:31; 10:1; 11:17; 12:14; 14:49) and often he is referred to as διδάσκαλος, "teacher" (4:38; 5:35; 9:17, 38; 10:17, 20, 35; 12:14, 19, 32; 13:1; 14:14). Beginning with the entrance narrative (11:1–11), Mark presents Jesus as frequenting the temple precincts (11:11, 15, 16, 27; 13:1; 14:49). Here in v 35 Jesus is said to be teaching ἐν τῷ ἱερῷ, "in the temple," by which is meant the precincts, not the sanctuary. At the time of his arrest Jesus will remind the officers and servants of the ruling priests that he had taught daily in the temple (14:49; cf. 1:21, where Jesus teaches in the synagogue).

The opening words, "And answering, Jesus was speaking, while teaching in the temple," seem to be mostly Markan. Gundry (717) understands ἀποκριθεὶς, "answering," as Jesus' response to the lack of further questions. But if vv 35–37 were originally preceded by a challenging question (see discussion in *Form/Structure/Setting* above), then "and answering, Jesus was speaking" may have been part of the original tradition, with only "while teaching in the temple" added by the evangelist.

πῶς λέγουσιν οἱ γραμματεῖς ὅτι ὁ Χριστὸς υἱὸς Δαυίδ ἐστιν; "How do the scribes say, 'The Messiah is "son of David"'?" "Son of David" as a messianic reference is commonplace in later rabbinic literature. Here we have an early attestation; an even earlier attestation of the epithet is found in *Pss. Sol.* 17:21: "See, Lord, and raise up for them their king, the son of David [υἱὸν Δαυίδ], to rule over your servant Israel in the time known to you, O God." See also Σολομῶν υἱὸς Δαυείδ, "Solomon, son of David," in *T. Sol.* 1:7 (ca. 100 C.E.). Jesus' question implies that there is no scriptural basis for calling the Messiah the "son of David." On the face of it, this is a curious position to adopt. While it is true that nowhere in the Scriptures of Israel is the Messiah so identified, Jeremiah promises a branch that will be raised up for David (Jer 23:5; 33:15). Here progeny is clearly envisioned. Jeremiah's prophetic hope is probably based on Isa 11:1: "There shall come forth a shoot from the stump of Jesse, and a branch shall grow out of his roots." In Zechariah "Branch" becomes a messianic epithet (cf. Zech 3:8; 6:12). In view of prophecies such as these, the scribal habit of referring to the Messiah as "son of David" seems reasonable (for rabbinic examples, see *b. ʿErub.* 43a; *b. Yoma* 10a; *b. Sukkah* 52a: "Messiah, son of David"; 52b; *b. Meg.* 17b; *b. Ḥag.* 16a; *b. Yebam.* 62a; *b. Ketub.* 112b; *b. Soṭah* 48b; *b. Sanh.* 38a; and in the midrashim, see *Gen. Rab.* 97 [on Gen 49:10]; *Exod. Rab.* 25.12 [on Exod 16:29]; *Num. Rab.* 14.1 [on Num 7:48]), even if not specifically attested in Scripture. So what is Jesus' point?

36 αὐτὸς Δαυὶδ εἶπεν ἐν τῷ πνεύματι τῷ ἁγίῳ, "David himself said in the Holy Spirit." The use of the emphatic αὐτός, "himself," is intended to show that αὐτὸς Δαυίδ, "David himself," bears witness against the sufficiency of the scribes' messianic epithet. This testimony is, moreover, prophetic, which is the import of the modifier ἐν τῷ πνεύματι τῷ ἁγίῳ, "in the Holy Spirit." The tradition of David's being inspired and prophetic reaches back to the ancient Scriptures themselves and is augmented in later literature. According to 2 Sam 23:2, David declares that "the Spirit of the LORD speaks by me, his word is upon my tongue." According to the great Psalms scroll from Qumran's eleventh cave, the "wise and learned" David, to whom the Lord had given a "discerning and enlightened spirit," composed more than four thousand songs "through prophecy that had been given to him from before the Most High" (11QPs^a 27:2–4, 11). At Qumran, the Psalms—most of which were thought to have been composed by David—were apparently understood as prophetic, for the pesharim (interpretations) are restricted to the Prophets and Psalms. David's inspiration and prophetic gift are also attested in the book of Acts (1:16; 4:25) and rabbinic literature (*b. Ber.* 4b; *b. ʿArak.* 15b; *b. Sukkah* 52a; *Song Rab.* 2:1 §3). It is also said of Solomon, David's son, that he composed his songs "in the Holy Spirit" (*Song Rab.* 1:1 §8). On the inspiration of Scripture, see Acts 28:25; 2 Tim 3:16; 2 Pet 1:21; Heb 3:7; 10:15. The evangelist may have intended "David himself said in the Holy Spirit" to contrast with "the scribes say," implying that the scribes lack the Spirit (so Gundry, 718).

εἶπεν κύριος τῷ κυρίῳ μου, "the Lord said to my lord," agrees exactly with the LXX (εἶπεν ὁ κύριος τῷ κυρίῳ μου), if ℵ A L W Θ Ψ 087 33 and other authorities are followed, which read the definite article ὁ, "the," before κύριος, "Lord." The LXX approximates the Hebrew, which uses different words for "lord": נְאֻם יְהוָה לַאדֹנִי *nĕʾum YHWH laʾdōnî*, "oracle of Yahweh to my lord." In the LXX both אֲדֹנִי *ʾădōnāy* and יהוה *YHWH* are translated κύριος. Is this evidence that the LXX has been followed, rather than the Hebrew, and if so, is this evidence that 12:35–37 is the creation of the Greek-speaking church and not authentic dominical tradition? Some scholars have so argued (Bultmann, *History*, 137; Hahn, *Titles*, 105). Fitzmyer (*Wandering Aramean*, 90) has shown that the Aramaic מָרֵא *mārēʾ*, "lord," could have been used to translate both אדני *ʾădōnāy* and יהוה *YHWH*. He thinks Jesus may very well have quoted Ps 110:1 in Aramaic (e.g., מָרָא לְמָרִאי *mārēʾ lĕmārî*), which in the Gospel tradition has been preserved in a Greek form that closely follows the LXX (see also Hengel, "'Sit at My Right Hand!'" 156 n. 81). Moreover, the Semitic form of the quotation of Ps 110:1, more than the Greek translation of the LXX, coheres with Jesus' interpretation. Jesus understands David's utterance as prophetic, spoken "in the Holy Spirit." The Hebrew נְאֻם *nĕʾum*, "oracle," is more suggestive of this understanding than the simple Greek εἶπεν, "said."

κάθου ἐκ δεξιῶν μου, "sit at my right hand." To be seated ἐκ δεξιῶν, "at the right hand," is a great honor. Mark's readers have already been introduced to this idea, as seen in James and John's ill-timed request in 10:35–40. Before Caiaphas and members of the Sanhedrin, Jesus will himself allude to Ps 110:1 (and Dan 7:13), declaring that he will be seated at the right hand of God (Mark 14:61–62; see *Comment* there, as well as Hengel, "'Sit at My Right Hand!'" 181–89). In ancient traditions, as well as in traditions both Jewish and Greco-Roman in the NT period, to be situated at the right hand of God was to enjoy the status and function of intermediary between heaven and earth, to serve as God's vice regent on earth.

ἕως ἂν θῶ τοὺς ἐχθρούς σου ὑποκάτω τῶν ποδῶν σου, "until I should place your enemies beneath your feet." The ancient psalm goes on to promise the favored king that God will defeat his enemies and make them subservient to him. For Jesus, these enemies were primarily spiritual forces. The conquest of Satan and his evil allies were of more concern to Jesus. This conquest was a prerequisite before Israel could be restored and able to inherit the blessings promised in the prophetic Scriptures. The readers of Mark have already been introduced to Jesus at war with Satan and his unclean spirits (cf. 1:21–28; 3:23–27; 5:1–20). The defeat of Satan is a certain sign of the advent of the kingdom of God (cf. Luke 10:17–20; 11:20; *T. Mos.* 10:1–3). Jesus has given his disciples the "authority to tread upon serpents and scorpions" (Luke 10:19), that is, upon evil spirits. It is probably in this light that ὑποκάτω τῶν ποδῶν σου, "beneath your feet," was understood by Jesus and his following.

37 αὐτὸς Δαυὶδ λέγει αὐτὸν κύριον, καὶ πόθεν αὐτοῦ ἐστιν υἱός, "David himself calls him 'lord'; so how is he his son?" The inspired authority on the question of the messianic epithet is αὐτὸς Δαυίδ, "David himself," not the scribes. David calls the Messiah κύριον, "lord," so in what sense then can the Messiah be David's υἱός, "son"? The point of the question rests in the assumption that to be son of someone is to be in some sense subordinate or even inferior. Is the Messiah inferior to David? In other words, is it true that the Messiah will only be a junior David? Jesus disputes this assumption on the basis of Ps 110:1: "The Lord said to my lord, 'Sit at my right hand.'" Jesus understands this to mean "The Lord (God) said to my (David's) lord (the Messiah)." Thus, David the famous king recognizes the Messiah as his lord. So in what sense is the Messiah nothing more than David's son? In no sense at all.

Two questions arise from Jesus' interpretation of Ps 110:1: (1) If the Messiah was more than merely David's son, how did Jesus think he should be identified? (2) Was Jesus distancing himself from Davidic messiahship? Both questions are answered by recognizing that Jesus evidently defined his messiahship in terms of the "son of man" described in the vision of Dan 7. Jesus saw himself as that human being (or "son of man" in Aramaic idiom) who received from God authority and kingdom (Dan 7:13–14) and who would sit on one of the thrones set up in heaven (note the plural "thrones" in Dan 7:9) at God's right hand (Ps 110:1). His authority had eclipsed that conferred upon David his ancestor, so while it may be genetically true that Jesus was the "son of David" (as hailed by blind Bartimaeus in Mark 10:47, 48, and assumed by Paul in Rom 1:3), it is not true to think that the epithet "son of David" implied subordination or inferiority in any sense. Lohmeyer (262–63) concludes that Jesus rejected Davidic messianism in favor of emphasis on the "son of man." This is partially correct. However, Jesus' self-understanding as "son of man" would not necessitate rejection of Davidic messianism, only a qualification of it (cf. O. Betz, *NovT* 6 [1963] 20–48).

Jesus has not denied the physical Davidic descent of the Messiah (and how could he in light of texts like Isa 9:2–7; 11:1–9; Jer 23:5–6; 33:14–18; Ezek 34:23–24; 37:24?). It is the scriptural legitimacy of referring to the Messiah as "son of David" that Jesus questions. There is no scriptural evidence for this manner of speaking (which in rabbinic literature becomes commonplace). In Scripture there is the anticipation that the Messiah will be recognized as *God's* son, not David's son. One immediately thinks of Ps 2:2, 7, where it is said of the Lord's "anointed

[מָשִׁיחַ *māšîaḥ*]" (v 2), "You are my son, today I have begotten you" (v 7), as well as 2 Sam 7:14, where God promises David, "I will be his father, and he shall be my son." The latter passage is cited in a messianic sense in the Dead Sea Scrolls (cf. 4Q174 [= 4QFlor] 3:7–13). In the Scrolls the Messiah is called "Branch of David" (e.g., 4Q161 [= 4QpIsaᵃ] 7 iii 22; 4Q174 [= 4QFlor] 3:11; 4Q285 [= 4QMᵍ] 5 i 3), but never "son of David."

In the Gospel of Mark, of course, the divine sonship, not Davidic sonship, of Jesus is emphasized (1:1, 11; 3:11; 5:7). Jesus is hailed "son of David" by blind Bartimaeus in 10:46–52, and in 2:23–28 Jesus compares the actions of his disciples in plucking grain on the Sabbath to the actions of David and his men in 1 Sam 21:1–6. Jesus is thus linked to David, but on what grounds? Chilton ("Jesus *ben David*") makes a compelling case for the authenticity of 12:35–37 on the basis of the association of healing and exorcism and the epithet "son of David." As a healer and exorcist, Jesus would have been associated with Solomon, the son of David. Charlesworth ("The Son of David," 87) concludes that blind Bartimaeus's cry in 10:47–48, "son of David," is a "Solomonic denotation." This is probably correct. Burger (*Jesus als Davidssohn*, 170) also observes that in the Gospel tradition, especially in Matthew, the epithet "son of David" almost always appears in contexts of healing or exorcism (e.g., Matt 9:27–31; 12:22–24; 15:21–28; 20:29–34; 21:1–11, 14–16). Rumors that Jesus was some sort of "son of David" probably arose from his ministry of healing and exorcism. The association of "Solomon, son of David" with healing and exorcism is attested in the *Testament of Solomon*, which dates to the end of the first century C.E. It is attested somewhat earlier in Josephus, who tells of one Eleazar, an exorcist who cast out demons in the name of Solomon and with recipes and secret adjurations composed by Solomon (*Ant.* 8.2.5 §46–49). D. C. Duling remarks: "The address 'Son of David' could be a link between the magical tradition about Solomon and the activity of Jesus as exorcist and healer" (*OTP* 2:960 n. d). David's great son was famous for his healing powers and formulas for exorcism. In one incantation Solomon is addressed as the "son of David" (בר דויד *bar dāwîd*) and is petitioned for protection against sickness (CBS 9012; cf. Charlesworth, "Solomon and Jesus," 137). Jesus comes to be regarded as "son of David" in reference to his ministry of exorcism and healing and perhaps in light of his outreach to the outcast and marginalized (see O. Betz, *NovT* 6 [1963] 29–30, 38–41).

The authenticity of 12:35–37 is supported by the improbability of the early church developing a tradition that could undermine the claim that Jesus was a descendant of David and therefore held a legitimate place in the messianic line, as well as the improbability that the early church would invent a saying that could be understood as in tension with the convention that the Messiah was of Davidic descent. On the likelihood that Jesus really descended from the line of David, see Meier, *Marginal Jew* 1:216–19, 238 n. 49; 240 n. 55; R. E. Brown, *The Virginal Conception and Bodily Resurrection of Jesus* (New York: Paulist, 1973) 55 n. 87.

καὶ [ὁ] πολὺς ὄχλος ἤκουεν αὐτοῦ ἡδέως, "And the great crowd was hearing him with pleasure." The crowd is impressed with Jesus' teaching and hear him ἡδέως, "gladly" or "with pleasure." Compare the report in Josephus, *Ant.* 18.3.3 §63, which says Jesus the teacher was followed by those who "receive truth with pleasure [ἡδονῇ]." On prior occasions the Markan evangelist has said that Jesus' hearers were amazed or astonished by his teaching (e.g., 1:22, 27; 2:12; 6:2; 7:37; 9:15; 10:24, 26; 11:18;

12:17). On this occasion they take pleasure in hearing someone so skilled in Scripture and the power of God (cf. 12:24).

Explanation

In Mark 11:27–12:34 Jesus has been challenged and questioned by various religious authorities. Some questions, such as whether Jews should pay taxes to Rome (12:13–17), have been designed to entrap and destroy Jesus and so have been potentially very dangerous. Nevertheless, Jesus has risen to the challenge, countering these questions with stunning answers or questions of his own. Indeed, in 12:34 the evangelist remarks that "no one any longer dared to question him," so effective have been Jesus' responses. Beginning with the present pericope Jesus goes on the offensive. In 12:35–37 he challenges the scribes' understanding of the Messiah. In 12:38–40 he will warn of hypocritical, avaricious scribes. In 12:41–44 he will lament the poverty of the widow and, by implication, the failing of the temple establishment. And in 13:1–2 he will foretell the doom of the temple.

In 12:35–37 Jesus challenges the adequacy of the scribal habit of referring to the Messiah as the "son of David." The appeal to Ps 110:1, where David himself calls the Messiah his "lord," implies that Jesus regarded the epithet "son of David" as insufficient as a reference to the Messiah. Evidently Jesus held to a higher view of the Messiah. This figure was so exalted that even the great David, the archetype of the Messiah, had "in the Holy Spirit" addressed him as "lord." On what basis does Jesus in Mark hold to such a lofty view of the Messiah? Probably because the Messiah is viewed as "son of God" who as the "son of man" figure of Dan 7:9–14 has received his kingdom and authority directly from God himself (and not from the line of David). Jesus' stunning teaching, as well as his interpretation of Ps 110:1, will come to the fore in the subsequent hearing before the high priest and the Sanhedrin. There Jesus will once again allude to Ps 110:1, only this time expressly in conjunction with Dan 7:13. At that time Jesus' understanding of Ps 110:1 and the reason why he regards "son of David" as an inadequate messianic epithet will become clear, but the ruling priests will not on that occasion hear his words "with pleasure."

L. Denunciation of Scribes   (12:38–40)

Bibliography

Abrahams, I. *Studies in Pharisaism and the Gospels.* 1:79–81. **Banks, R. J.** *Jesus and the Law in the Synoptic Tradition.* SNTSMS 28. Cambridge: Cambridge UP, 1975. 173–81. **Beilner, W.** *Christus und die Pharisäer: Exegetische Untersuchung über Grund und Verlauf der Auseinandersetzungen.* Vienna: Herder, 1959. 200–235. **Cook, M. J.** *Mark's Treatment of the Jewish Leaders.* 29–51. **Derrett, J. D. M.** "'Eating Up the Houses of Widows': Jesus's Comment on Lawyers?" *NovT* 14 (1972) 1–9 (repr. in *Studies in the New Testament.* 2 vols. Leiden: Brill, 1977–78. 1:118–27). **Fleddermann, H. T.** *Mark and Q.* 186–89. ———. "A Warning about the Scribes (Mark

12.37b–40).” *CBQ* 44 (1982) 52–67. **Geddert, T. J.** *Watchwords.* 122–24. **Jeremias, J.** "γραμματεύς." *TDNT* 1:740–42. **Keck, F.** *Die öffentliche Abschiedsrede Jesu in Lk 20,45–21,36: Eine redaktions- und motivgeschichtliche Untersuchung.* FzB 25. Stuttgart: Katholisches Bibelwerk, 1976. 36–46. **Knox, W. L.** *The Sources of the Synoptic Gospels.* Cambridge: Cambridge UP, 1953. 93–102. **Légasse, S.** "Scribes et disciples de Jésus." *RB* 68 (1961) 321–45, 481–506. **Manson, T. W.** *The Sayings of Jesus.* London: SCM Press, 1949. 228–31. **Marshall, I. H.** "How to Solve the Synoptic Problem: Luke 11,43 and Parallels." In *The New Testament Age.* FS B. Reicke, ed. W. C. Weinrich. 2 vols. Macon, GA: Mercer UP, 1984. 2:313–25. **Rengstorf, K. H.** "Die στολαί der Schriftgelehrten: Eine Erläuterung zu Mark. 12,13." In *Abraham unser Vater: Juden und Christen im Gespräch über die Bibel.* FS O. Michel, ed. O. Betz et al. AGSU 5. Leiden: Brill, 1963. 383–404. **Saldarini, A. J.** *Pharisees, Scribes and Sadducees in Palestinian Society: A Sociological Approach.* Wilmington, DE: Glazier, 1988. 144–73. ———. "Scribes." *ABD* 5:1012–16. **Schmitt, G.** "Das Zeichen des Jona." *ZNW* 69 (1978) 123–29. **Söding, T.** *Glaube bei Markus.* 355–60. **Tuckett, C. M.** *The Revival of the Griesbach Hypothesis: An Analysis and Appraisal.* SNTSMS 44. Cambridge: Cambridge UP, 1983. 134–39. **Turner, N.** *Grammatical Insights into the New Testament.* Edinburgh: T & T Clark, 1965. 55–56. **Westcott, B. F.,** and **Hort, F. J. A.** *Introduction.* 2:26.

Translation

[38]*And in his teaching he was saying,*[a] *"Beware of the scribes,*[b] *who want to walk about in long robes, and want*[c] *greetings in the market places* [39]*and the choice seats in the synagogues and the places of honor at banquets.* [40]*They devour the estates of widows,*[d] *and in pretense praying at great length, these will receive the harsher judgment."*

Notes

[a]33 adds αὐτοῖς, "to them."
[b]D adds καὶ τῶν τελωνῶν, "and tax collectors."
[c]The verb is implied. D Φ and a few late authorities add ποιεῖσθαι, "to elicit."
[d]D W and other authorities add καὶ ὀρφανῶν, "and orphans."

Form/Structure/Setting

Form critics classify 12:38–40 as a minatory saying (Bultmann, *History,* 113–14) or warning (Taylor, *Formation,* 179). The saying is made up of three principal parts: *(a)* the warning proper, "Beware of the scribes" (v 38b), *(b)* a series of descriptive phrases describing the habits and conduct of the scribes (vv 38c–40ab), and *(c)* a pronouncement of judgment (v 40c). Both Bultmann (*History,* 113) and Dibelius (*Tradition,* 236) suspect that the saying, as well as others like it, may very well be authentic.

The warning regarding the scribes emphasizes their hypocrisy and avarice. Of special concern, as the subsequent context will show (i.e., 12:41–44), is the treatment of widows. The temple establishment was supposed to have provided social protection and economic assistance to widows (Exod 22:22, 24; Deut 10:18; 14:29; 24:17, 19–21; 26:12–13; 27:19); instead, under the leadership of the scribes it had become an institution of oppression. The reference to the exploitative treatment of widows may hark back to the criticisms by the OT prophets (e.g., Isa 1:23; 10:2; Ezek 22:7; Job 22:9; 24:3).

Comment

38–39 καὶ ἐν τῇ διδαχῇ αὐτοῦ ἔλεγεν, "And in his teaching he was saying," continues the setting of Jesus' teaching in the temple precincts and is clearly Markan (Dibelius, *Tradition*, 236). On the evangelist's fondness for portraying Jesus as a teacher, see *Comment* on 12:35.

βλέπετε ἀπὸ τῶν γραμματέων, "Beware of the scribes." Earlier Jesus had warned his disciples to beware what they hear (4:24) and to beware of the Pharisees: "And he cautioned them, saying, 'Take heed, beware of [βλέπετε ἀπό] the leaven of the Pharisees and the leaven of Herod'" (Mark 8:15). Guelich (423–24) understands "the leaven of the Pharisees and the leaven of Herod" as a reference to unbelief and the failure to recognize the person and mission of Jesus. Here we have Jesus warning his disciples of false piety and worship (cf. Phil 3:2). Elsewhere in Mark Jesus warns his disciples to beware of those who would mislead them (13:5) and to be alert for coming tribulation (13:9, 23, 33). In all of these examples the evangelist uses the present imperative form of βλέπειν, "to see, beware of," rather than προσέχειν, "to pay attention to, beware of," which is common in Matthew, Luke, and the LXX (e.g., Gen 24:6; Exod 10:28; Deut 11:16; 12:30; passim).

τῶν θελόντων ἐν στολαῖς περιπατεῖν καὶ ἀσπασμοὺς ἐν ταῖς ἀγοραῖς, "who want to walk about in long robes, and want greetings in the market places." Jesus rattles off a series of scribal vanities: long robes, greetings, choice seats, and places of honor. The στολαί, "long robes," refer to those worn by priests and—probably in imitation of the priests—by religious men (Philo, *Embassy* 296; Josephus, *Ant.* 3.7.1 §151; 11.4.2 §80), especially on religious occasions (*b. Ber.* 24b; 51a; *b. Roš Haš.* 17b; *b. Meg.* 16a). Jesus says that the scribes like περιπατεῖν, "to walk about," in these robes, probably to draw attention to themselves and to be associated with the prestigious temple establishment. The exhibition results in receiving ἀσπασμοὺς ἐν ταῖς ἀγοραῖς, "greetings in the market places." In other words, the wearing of these robes is not limited to the synagogue or the temple. On the contrary, they are being worn ostentatiously in the market to attract notice and greetings (Matt 23:7 adds "and being called rabbi by men"). The custom was that those of lower rank were expected to greet those of higher rank (cf. *y. Ber.* 2.1: "a person must greet one who is greater than he in knowledge of Torah"). Contrary to this custom, Yoḥanan ben Zakkai, who was of the highest rank, initiated greetings to those of lower rank, including Gentiles (cf. *b. Ber.* 17a).

καὶ πρωτοκαθεδρίας ἐν ταῖς συναγωγαῖς, "and the choice seats in the synagogues." The scribes also liked to have the πρωτοκαθεδρίας, "choice seats" or "first seats," in the synagogues. These choice seats, not to be confused with the "seat of Moses" (Matt 23:2), were reserved for dignitaries and honored guests, especially scholars/scribes (cf. *t. Meg.* 3.21: "How did the elders sit in session? It was facing the people, with their backs toward the sanctuary"; *b. Taʿan.* 21b). The word συναγωγή, "synagogue," is attested in an ancient inscription, possibly late Ptolemaic, perhaps Roman (*CIJ* vol. 2 no. 1447; discussed by W. Horbury and D. Noy, *Jewish Inscriptions of Graeco-Roman Egypt* [Cambridge: Cambridge UP, 1992] 32–34).

καὶ πρωτοκλισίας ἐν τοῖς δείπνοις, "and the places of honor at banquets." Seating at banquets was either according to age (cf. *b. B. Bat.* 120a) or according to importance (cf. *b. Ber.* 46b; *t. Ber.* 5.5: "What is the order for reclining? When there are two couches, the greatest among them reclines at the head of the first, the second to him reclines below him"). For related dominical tradition, see Luke 14:7–14.

40 οἱ κατεσθίοντες τὰς οἰκίας τῶν χηρῶν, "They devour the estates of widows." With the charge of devouring the estates (lit. "houses") of widows the descriptive litany takes a decidedly nasty turn. Hypocrisy and vanity were one thing, but the ruin and impoverishment of those most vulnerable in ancient society was quite another. J. A. Fitzmyer (*Luke,* 2:1318) identifies six different explanations of what is meant by devouring the houses of widows: (*a*) Scribes accepted payment for legal assistance, though such payment was forbidden. (*b*) Acting in the capacity of lawyers, perhaps appointed to such office in the wills of the deceased husbands, the scribes cheated widows out of their estates. (*c*) Scribes freeloaded on the hospitality of widows. (*d*) Scribes mismanaged the estates entrusted to them. (*e*) Scribes took money from credulous women in return for the supposed benefit of intercessory prayer (as perhaps implied by the next clause in v 40). (*f*) Scribes took houses as pledges for debts that could not realistically be expected to be repaid. It is difficult to choose among these options, for Jesus' brief complaint supplies insufficient details. Fitzmyer appears to lean toward the second option.

καὶ προφάσει μακρὰ προσευχόμενοι, "and in pretense praying at great length." The scribes are capable of lengthy, perhaps even eloquent, prayers, but they are uttered προφάσει, "in pretense." These showy prayers are consistent with the scribes' ostentation in dress and their pursuit of honors and recognition. Their long prayers and implied piety would enhance their status and make it possible to take advantage of the less influential (such as widows). For a possible example of the type of prayer that Jesus has in mind, see Luke 18:11–12, where the Pharisee prays: "God, I thank you that I am not like other men, extortioners, unjust, adulterers, or even like this tax collector. I fast twice a week, I give tithes of all that I get." On the association of the robe and prayer, see *b. Meg.* 16a.

οὗτοι λήμψονται περισσότερον κρίμα, "these will receive the harsher judgment." Because the scribes exploit the poor and insult God with their phony prayers, they deserve the harsher judgment. This is to be expected, for they have failed to fulfill the Great Commandment to love God and to love one's neighbor as onself (cf. 12:28–34). The judgment that awaits the self-righteous scribes is consistent with Jesus' teaching that "every one who exalts himself will be humbled, and he who humbles himself will be exalted" (Luke 14:11; cf. Matt 23:12). According to the *Psalms of Solomon,* the Davidic Messiah is expected "to purge Jerusalem" and to "expose officials and drive out sinners" (*Pss. Sol.* 17:30, 36). Jesus' vision of judgment may have included temporal elements (such as is clearly taught in the parable of the Wicked Vineyard Tenants in 12:1–12), though his reference to κρίμα, "judgment," in this context may have been primarily eschatological.

Explanation

Jesus continues his challenging teaching in the temple precincts. He has challenged scribal teaching on messianism in 12:35–37, while here in 12:38–40 he criticizes the ethical shortcomings of the scribes. Not all scribes in Jesus' day were hypocritical and corrupt, of course, and although it is true that Jesus warns of "the scribes," and not "some scribes," the hyperbolic and generalizing language should be recognized for what it is. Josephus's anecdotes touching priestly behavior in the final years of the Second Temple make it clear that at least some scribes could easily have been guilty of the hypocrisy and unethical conduct that Jesus has described. The warning of impending judgment well suits the Markan context. Judgment was hinted at earlier in 11:17, where Jesus alluded to Jer 7:11, and in the parable of the Wicked Vineyard Tenants (12:1–12), where Jesus told the ruling priests, scribes, and elders (cf. 11:27) that they would be destroyed and the vineyard (i.e., Israel) given to others (12:9). Soon Jesus will speak explicitly of Jerusalem's doom (13:1–2). But in the next pericope Jesus will point out an example of a widow whose estate has been devoured by an exploitive and avaricious temple establishment.

M. The Widow's Offering   (12:41–44)

Bibliography

Beavis, M. A. "Women as Models of Faith in Mark." *BTB* 18 (1988) 3–9. **Berger, K.** *Die Amen-Worte Jesu: Eine Untersuchung zum Problem der Legitimation in apokalyptischer Rede.* BZNW 39. Berlin: de Gruyter, 1970. 48–49. **Berglund, A. I.** "The Treasury in God's Temple (Mk. 12:41–44)." *Credo* 5 (1959) 2–4. **Best, E.** *Following Jesus.* 155–56. **Blass, F.** "On Mark xii. 42 and xv 16." *ExpTim* 10 (1898–99) 185–87, 286–87. **Carmignac, J.** "Studies in the Hebrew Background of the Synoptic Gospels." *ASTI* 7 (1970) 64–93, esp. 78–89. **Geddert, T. J.** *Watchwords.* 122–24, 137–40. **Hasler, V.** *Amen: Redaktionsgeschichtliche Untersuchung zur Einführungsformel der Herrenworte "Wahrlich ich sage euch."* Zürich; Stuttgart: Gotthelf, 1969. 44–47. **Jeremias, J.** "Zwei Miszellen: 1. Antik-jüdische Münzdeutungen. 2. Zur Geschichtlichkeit der Tempelreinigung." *NTS* 23 (1976–77) 177–80. **LaVerdiere, E.** "The Widow's Mite." *Emmanuel* 92 (1986) 316–21, 341. **Lee, G. M.** "The Story of the Widow's Mite." *ExpTim* 82 (1971) 344. **Malbon, E. S.** "The Poor Widow in Mark and Her Poor Rich Readers." *CBQ* 53 (1991) 589–604. **März, C.-P.** *"Siehe, dein König kommt zu Dir . . .": Eine traditionsgeschichtliche Untersuchung zur Einzugsperikope.* ETS 43. Leipzig: St. Benno, 1980. 74–75. **Pesch, R.** *Evangelium der Urgemeinde.* 155–56. ———. "Jesus und das Hauptgebot." In *Neues Testament und Ethik.* FS R. Schnackenburg, ed. H. Merklein. Freiburg: Herder, 1989. 99–109, esp. 106–7. **Ramsay, W. M.** "On Mark xii. 42." *ExpTim* 10 (1898–99) 232, 336. **Sariola, H.** *Markus und das Gesetz.* 232–33. **Schmidt, T. E.** *Hostility to Wealth in the Synoptic Gospels.* JSNTSup 15. Sheffield: JSOT Press, 1987. 116–17. **Simon, L.** "Le sou de la veuve: Marc 12/41–44." *ETR* 44 (1969) 115–26. **Sperber, D.** "Mark xii 42 and Its Metrological Background: A Study in Ancient Syriac Versions." *NovT* 9 (1967) 178–90. **Stählin, G.** "χήρα." *TDNT* 9:440–65. **Standaert, B. H. M. G. M.** *L'évangile selon Marc.* 149–52. **Sugirtharajah, R. S.** "The Widow's Mite Revalued." *ExpTim* 103 (1991–92) 42–43. **Thurston, B. B.** "The Widows as the 'Altar of God.'" In *Society of Biblical Literature 1985 Seminar Papers.* Ed. K. H. Richards. SBLSP 24. Atlanta: Scholars Press, 1985. 279–89. **Tuckett, C. M.** *The Revival of the Griesbach Hypothesis: An Analysis and Appraisal.* SNTSMS 44. Cambridge: Cambridge UP, 1983. 140–44. **Wallace, D. B.** "The Relation of Adjective to Noun in Anarthrous Constructions in the New Testament." *NovT* 26 (1984) 128–67. **Williams, J. F.** *Other Followers of Jesus.* 176–78. **Wright, A. G.** "The Widow's Mites: Praise or Lament?—A Matter of Context." *CBQ* 44 (1982) 256–65.

Translation

[41]*And taking a seat*[a] *opposite the treasury, he*[b] *was watching how the crowd casts money into the offering box. And many wealthy people were casting in large sums.* [42]*And approaching, a poor*[c] *widow cast in two small coins, which make a penny.*[d] [43]*And summoning his disciples, he said to them: "Truly I tell you that this poor widow has cast in more [money]*[e] *than all who cast [money]*[e] *into the offering box;* [44]*for all of them have cast in [money]*[e] *from their abundance, but she from her want has cast in all that she has—her whole life."*

Notes

[a]W and a few other MSS read ἑστώς, "having stood."

[b]Some MSS (including 33) add ὁ Ἰησοῦς, "Jesus." The name of Jesus had not appeared in the narrative since v 35.

[c]D and a few other MSS omit πτωχή, "poor." The adj. is used in v 43. ℵ adds γυνή, "woman."

[d]The Gk. word is κοδράντης, which is borrowed from the Lat. *quadrans*. Spelling differences are found in some MSS; in some it is κοδράντες or κοδράντις. On the value of this coin, see *Comment*.

[e]I have added *money*, which is the understood direct obj. Some MSS supply a direct obj., e.g., τὰ δῶρα, "gifts" (in Gk. MSS), or *munus*, "gift" (in Lat. MSS); cf. Luke 21:4.

Form/Structure/Setting

Form critics have designated the story of the widow's offering a pronouncement story or biographical apophthegm (Bultmann, *History*, 32–33; Dibelius, *Tradition*, 261; Taylor, *Formation*, 72). Dibelius speculates that Jesus' pronouncement might originally have been part of a parable about a poor widow. But there is no need to imagine any other form or setting than the one presented in Mark. Bultmann comments that Mark 12:41–44 parallels a story in Buddhist tradition so closely that "it is difficult to avoid concluding that there was some dependence on it" (*History*, 33). But as Bultmann himself acknowledges, stories contrasting the gifts of the rich and poor are common in the Middle East of late antiquity. Bultmann's idea of dependence on a Buddhist story is farfetched and unnecessary. Lührmann's (212) suggestion that underlying the story of the widow's offering is competition between church and synagogue regarding which community cared most for widows is purely speculative and reads nuances into the story that are not present. Haenchen (432–33) doubts the historicity of the story on the grounds that Jesus would not have been able to see the respective amounts of the gifts. Like Dibelius (whom Haenchen does not cite), he thinks that "a parable of Jesus has been transformed into a historical event" (433). But the observation of gifts by treasury attendants and onlookers is noted in rabbinic tradition and is probably implied in Jesus' criticisms of those who "sound [a] trumpet before them" when they give alms (Matt 6:2).

The story of the widow's offering follows right on the heels of the denunciation of the scribes who "devour the estates of widows" (Mark 12:38–40). The context of the widow's offering suggests, therefore, that it is an example of the very thing that Jesus warned about: the οἰκία, "house," or estate of the poor widow has finally been consumed. But Gundry (728) sees a contrast between the "true godliness of a widow" and the "pretended righteousness of the scribes." The point, if we expand on Gundry's approach, lies in the contrast between the scribes, on the one hand, whose religiosity is selfish and avaricious, and the poor widow, on the other hand, whose religiosity is generous, even to the point of self-denial and hardship. That there is implicit such a contrast cannot be denied. But the reference to widows in 12:38–40 has to do with the scribes' exploitation of these defenseless persons. Is the point then really to provide a contrast between the self-righteous scribe and the devoted widow? Or is the point to provide a tragic example of how the scribes have indeed consumed the poor? This question will be pursued further in the *Comment*.

Comment

The touching story of the widow's offering has often been cited in literature, sermons, and Bible lessons as providing an exemplary model of sacrificial giving. Many commentators have taken the passage in this sense, as most recently has Gundry. But the interpretation offered by A. G. Wright (*CBQ* 44 [1982] 256–65), which Gundry (730–31) questions but Fitzmyer (*Luke* 2:1320–21) accepts, to the effect that Jesus' word was not one of praise but one of lament, is in my opinion correct. Fitzmyer joins Wright in criticizing the traditional interpretation for assuming facts not in evidence. Fitzmyer reminds us that in Mark Jesus asserts that human needs take precedence over religiosity (as seen in 3:1–5 [healing on Sabbath], 7:10–13 [the qorban tradition, by which elderly parents may be denied support from their adult children], and 12:28–34 [where loving God and neighbor is worth more than burnt offerings]). He concludes: "Given such a reaction of Jesus in other parts of the Marcan Gospel, would the Marcan Jesus become enthusiastic about and praise the widow's contribution, when it involves 'all that she had to live on'? The Corban-saying seems to set limits to the interpretation of Jesus' words in this episode" (*Luke* 2:1321). With the Markan context in mind, Wright (*CBQ* 44 [1982] 262) says: "Her religious thinking has accomplished the very thing that the scribes were accused of doing. . . . She has been taught and encouraged by religious leaders to donate as she does, and Jesus condemns the value system that motivates her action."

There is also a potentially significant parallel to our story in a later rabbinic tradition. In some ways it might offer support for Wright's line of interpretation. Jesus' comment that the widow has cast into the treasury box "her whole life [βίον]" finds an interesting parallel in an anonymous midrash: "Once a woman brought a handful of fine flour, and the priest despised her, saying: 'See what she offers! What is there in this to eat? What is there in this to offer up?' It was shown to him in a dream: 'Do not despise her! It is regarded as if she had sacrificed her own life [נפשה *napšâ*]'" (*Lev. Rab.* 3.5 [on Lev 1:17]). What is of interest here is not the exegetical point that this midrash is trying to make (that in offering a sacrifice one offers one's "life") but rather that the midrash presupposes that priests on occasion viewed small gifts with contempt. (The "handful of fine flour" in the midrash approximates the value of the two lepta brought to the temple in Mark's story.) Such an attitude is consistent with the thinking of the ruling priests with whom Jesus contended and against whom many of his contemporaries complained (for a summary of the evidence of ancient criticism directed against the temple establishment, see *Comment* on 11:15–19). If the rabbinic story ultimately derives from an ancient tradition, then Jesus may have deliberately and ironically alluded to it. In giving her last two lepta, the woman has indeed given her life! Given the Markan context, both the immediate context and the larger context of his Gospel as a whole, and given the rabbinic parallel just considered, it seems appropriate to accept Wright's interpretation.

41 καὶ καθίσας κατέναντι τοῦ γαζοφυλακίου ἐθεώρει. πῶς ὁ ὄχλος βάλλει χαλκὸν εἰς τὸ γαζοφυλάκιον, "And taking a seat opposite the treasury, he was watching how the crowd casts money into the offering box." The temple's γαζοφυλάκιον, "treasury," and various chambers are mentioned in several early texts (Neh 12:44; Josephus, *J.W.* 5.5.2 §200; 6.5.2 §282; 1 Macc 14:49; 2 Macc 3:6, 24, 28, 40). According to the Mishnah there were thirteen trumpet-shaped receptacles into which people could cast money (*m. Šeq.* 6:5). Some of these receptacles were designated for specific purposes; others were used for "freewill offerings." It could very well be that the widow pitched her coins into the latter. χαλκός, "money," actually refers to the metal itself (i.e., copper, brass, or bronze; cf. Josephus, *Ant.* 8.3.4 §76, in reference to workers "in gold, silver, and bronze"). It would be much like slang a century ago in referring to a "copper."

καὶ πολλοὶ πλούσιοι ἔβαλλον πολλά, "and many wealthy people were casting in large sums." Josephus, as well as Roman historians, remarks on the immense wealth of the Jerusalem temple. Many of those donating large sums were wealthy landowners who lived in or near Jerusalem; others were Jewish businessmen and merchants of the Diaspora who had journeyed to Jerusalem for the Passover holiday.

42 καὶ ἐλθοῦσα μία χήρα πτωχή, "and approaching, a poor widow." Might the reference to the widow remind Mark's astute readers of Jeremiah's complaints against the temple establishment of his day, in which, among other things, widows and orphans were neglected and denied justice (cf. Jer 7:6, as well as *Comment* on Mark 11:15–19)? The reference will, of course, cause the reader to recall the previous pericope where Jesus accuses the scribes of devouring the houses of widows.

ἔβαλεν λεπτὰ δύο, ὅ ἐστιν κοδράντης, "cast in two small coins, which make a penny." Mark's two "small coins" are λεπτά (sg. λεπτόν, a loanword from the Latin *lepton*). The evangelist says that the two lepta equaled a κοδράντης (also a loanword from the Latin *quadrans*), which is probably correct. It took more than one hundred lepta to equal a denarius, itself worth a day's wage. It has been said that two lepta could buy one a handful of flour or the equivalent of one meager meal (regarding this point, see *Comment* above).

43 καὶ προσκαλεσάμενος τοὺς μαθητὰς αὐτοῦ εἶπεν αὐτοῖς, "and summoning his disciples, he said to them." Often in Mark Jesus summons his disciples (3:13; 6:7; 8:1; 10:42), sometimes for the express purpose of teaching (cf. 3:23; 7:14; 8:34). On Jesus as teacher in Mark, see *Comment* on 12:35.

ἀμὴν λέγω ὑμῖν ὅτι ἡ χήρα αὕτη ἡ πτωχὴ πλεῖον πάντων ἔβαλεν τῶν βαλλόντων εἰς τὸ γαζοφυλάκιον, "Truly I tell you that this poor widow has cast in more money than all who cast money into the offering box." Prefacing his statement with ἀμήν, "truly," heightens the importance of the pronouncement. On Jesus' use of ἀμήν, see *Comment* on 9:1. The reference to ἡ χήρα αὕτη ἡ πτωχή, "this widow, the poor one," in which the adjective is delayed, emphasizes her poverty. How did Jesus know she was a widow? The most probable answer is that he could tell by her dress (cf. Luke 7:11–19, where the grieving mother is readily recognized as a widow).

44 πάντες γὰρ ἐκ τοῦ περισσεύοντος αὐτοῖς ἔβαλον, αὕτη δὲ ἐκ τῆς ὑστερήσεως αὐτῆς πάντα ὅσα εἶχεν ἔβαλεν ὅλον τὸν βίον αὐτῆς, "For all of them have cast in money from their abundance, but she from her want has cast in all that she has—her whole life." The contrast between the wealthy people's περισσεύοντος, "abundance," and the poor widow's ὑστερήσεως, "want," is noteworthy. The word translated "abundance" can also mean "surplus," while the word translated "want" can also mean "lack" or "deficiency." In other words, the woman had nothing extra. She had no margin from which she could contribute to the temple. Unlike the wealthy, whose gifts would not be missed and would not cause for them any hardship or discomfort, the widow's gift took food right out of her mouth.

How did Jesus know that the two lepta that she gave to the temple represented the last of the widow's resources? It is probable that her attire, which in itself indicated her status as a widow, made it sadly apparent that she was impoverished. It is not necessary to insist that Jesus was clairvoyant in this instance. Given her status as a widow and given her apparent poverty, as seen by her clothing and the smallness of her gift, Jesus may have only assumed that the two coins were all that she had left. Jesus' words could also be viewed as hyperbolic.

Explanation

The story of the widow's offering may provide us with an important clue for understanding the points of disagreement between Jesus and the temple establishment. In the law of Moses widows and orphans enjoyed an important measure of economic and legal protection. At Sinai Israel was commanded not to "afflict any widow or orphan" (Exod 22:22). Legislation in defense of widows and orphans was expanded and intensified in Deuteronomy. In this restatement of the covenant God describes himself as one who "executes justice for the fatherless and the widow" (Deut 10:18). Therefore, human judges must deal justly with the marginalized (cf. Deut 24:17; 27:19). Part of this justice meant that widows and orphans were to partake of the tithes (Deut 14:29; 26:12–13) and to enjoy special gleaning privileges (Deut 24:19–21). Partaking of the tithes was to be shared along with the Levites.

Were widows and orphans in Jesus' time receiving the full protection and privileges commanded in the law of Moses? The Damascus Document has what could be a very important passage in which the sons of the covenant are to "separate themselves from the sons of the Pit, and to keep themselves from the unclean riches of wickedness (acquired) through vow or anathema and by robbing the wealth of the Sanctuary, (and not) 'to rob the poor of his people that widows may be their spoil and that they might murder the fatherless' [Isa 10:2]" (CD 6:14–17 = 4Q266 [= 4QD^a] 3 iii 7–9). These angry criticisms appear to be leveled against the Jerusalem priesthood. The quotation from Isa 10 is significant, for vv 1–4 of this text make up an oracle of judgment against Israel's leaders who pass decrees that oppress widows and orphans. Note too that the reference to "vow or anathema" is closely related to the qorban tradition, of which Jesus was critical (see above). Elsewhere fragments of the Damascus Document from cave 4 speak of widows who prostitute themselves after they are widowed (cf. 4Q270 [= 4QD^e] 5 19 = 4Q271 [= 4QD^f] 1 i 12). Perhaps from this we should infer that some widows turned to prostitution out of economic desperation. The parable of the

Dishonest Judge (Luke 18:1–8a) may presuppose a callous indifference to widows' cries for justice. That the ruling priests might have neglected their legal and ethical obligations to protect and provide for widows seems probable in view of their shabby treatment of fellow Levites and lower-ranking priests (for whom the Mosaic laws, as observed above, provided assistance similar to that provided orphans and widows). According to Josephus, some ruling priests sent thugs to rob the lower-ranking priests of their fair share of the tithes and to beat those who resisted (*Ant.* 20.8.8 §181; 20.9.2 §§206–7). The rabbis remember and pass on related stories (*t. Menaḥ.* 13.18–22; *b. Pesaḥ.* 57a). If the ruling priests treated their lower-ranking colleagues so poorly and disregarded the spirit, if not the letter, of the law as it applied to them, why would they have paid any attention to widows? One should recall too how the rebels in 66 C.E. burned the house of the High Priest Ananias and then set fire to the public archives in order to destroy the records of debt (Josephus, *J.W.* 2.17.6 §§426–27).

Jesus apparently has taken up the cause of the marginalized, and widows were among the most marginalized in his society. Evidently he has leveled a prophetic complaint against the religious establishment for failing to live up to its Mosaic obligations. He has warned of the scribes whose religion devours the poor and enriches themselves. He has pointed to the poor widow who cast her last tiny coins into the temple's coffers as an example of one such person who has been consumed. We have here an important remnant of Jesus' criticisms against the temple establishment and what motivated them. In the next passage (Mark 13:1–2) Jesus will prophesy the dreadful result, to which this oppressive policy will inevitably lead.

N. The Eschatological Discourse (13:1–37)

Bibliography

Adams, E. "Historical Crisis and Cosmic Crisis in Mark 13 and Lucan's *Civil War.*" *TynBul* 48 (1997) 329–44. **Ambrozic, A. M.** *Hidden Kingdom.* 222–31. **Aune, D. E.** *Prophecy in Early Christianity and the Ancient Mediterranean World.* Grand Rapids, MI: Eerdmans, 1983. 186–87. **Baarlink, H.** *Die Eschatologie der synoptischen Evangelien.* BWANT 120. Stuttgart: Kohlhammer, 1986. 55–66. **Bacon, B. W.** "The Apocalyptic Chapter of the Synoptic Gospels." *JBL* 28 (1909) 1–25. **Beale, G. K.** "The Use of Daniel in the Synoptic Eschatological Discourse and in the Book of Revelation." In *The Jesus Tradition Outside the Gospels.* Ed. D. Wenham. Gospel Perspectives 5. Sheffield: JSOT Press, 1985. 129–53. **Beasley-Murray, G. R.** *A Commentary on Mark Thirteen.* London: Macmillan; New York: St. Martin's, 1957. ———. "The Eschatological Discourse of Jesus." *RevExp* 57 (1960) 153–66. ———. *Jesus and the Future: An Examination of the Criticism of the Eschatological Discourse, Mark 13, with Special Reference to the Little Apocalypse Theory.* London: Macmillan; New York: St. Martin's, 1954. ———. *Jesus and the Kingdom of God.* 322–37. ———. *Jesus and the Last Days: The Interpretation of the Olivet Discourse.* Peabody: Hendrickson, 1993. ———. "The Rise and Fall of the Little Apocalypse Theory." *ExpTim* 64 (1952–53) 346–49. ———. "Second Thoughts on the Composition of Mark 13." *NTS* 29 (1983) 414–20. **Black, C. C.** "An Oration at Olivet: Some Rhetorical Dimensions of Mark 13." In *Persuasive Artistry: Studies in New Testament Rhetoric.* FS G. A.

Kennedy, ed. D. F. Watson. JSNTSup 50. Sheffield: JSOT Press, 1991. 66–92. **Böttger, P. C.** *Der König der Juden.* 18–27. **Brandenburger, E.** *Markus 13 und die Apokalyptik.* FRLANT 134. Göttingen: Vandenhoeck & Ruprecht, 1984. **Breytenbach, C.** *Nachfolge und Zukunftserwartung nach Markus.* 280–330. **Bristol, L. O.** "Mark's Little Apocalypse: A Hypothesis." *ExpTim* 51 (1939–40) 301–3. **Brower, K. E.** "'Let the Reader Understand': Temple and Eschatology in Mark." In *'The Reader Must Understand': Eschatology in Bible and Theology.* Ed. K. E. Brower and M. W. Elliott. Leicester: Inter-Varsity Press, 1997. 119–43. **Brunec, M.** "Sermo Eschatologicus." *VD* 30 (1952) 214–18, 265–77, 321–31; 31 (1953) 13–20, 83–94, 156–63, 211–20, 282–90, 344–51. **Busch, F.** *Zum Verständnis der synoptischen Eschatologie: Markus 13 neu untersucht.* Gütersloh: Bertelsmann, 1938. **Collins, A. Y.** *Beginning of the Gospel.* 73–91. ———. "The Eschatological Discourse of Mark 13." In *The Four Gospels 1992.* FS F. Neirynck, ed. F. Van Segbroeck et al. 3 vols. BETL 100. Leuven: Peeters and Leuven UP, 1992. 2:1125–40. **Combet-Galland, C.** "Marc 13: Les saisons du monde." *Cahiers bibliques* 16 (1977) 45–66. **Conzelmann, H.** "Geschichte und Eschaton nach Mc 13." *ZNW* 50 (1959) 210–21 (repr. in H. Conzelmann, *Theologie als Schriftauslegung: Aufsätze zum Neuen Testament.* BEvT 65. Munich: Kaiser, 1974. 62–73). **Cothenet, É.** "Le IIe épître aux Thessaloniciens et l'apocalypse synoptique." *RSR* 42 (1954) 5–39. **Cotter, A. C.** "The Eschatological Discourse." *CBQ* 1 (1939) 125–32, 204–13. **Cousar, C. B.** "Eschatology and Mark's *Theologia Crucis:* A Critical Analysis of Mark 13." *Int* 24 (1970) 321–35. **Cranfield, C. E. B.** "St. Mark 13." *SJT* 6 (1953) 189–96, 287–303; 7 (1954) 284–303. **Dewar, F.** "Chapter 13 and the Passion Narrative in St Mark." *Theology* 64 (1961) 99–107. **Dupont, J.** "La ruine du Temple et la fin des temps dans le discours de Mc 13." In *Apocalypses et théologies de l'espérance.* Ed. L. Monloubou. LD 95. Paris: Cerf, 1977. 207–69. ———. *Les trois apocalypses synoptiques: Marc 13; Matthieu 24–25; Luc 21.* LD 121. Paris: Cerf, 1985. **Easton, B. S.** "The Little Apocalypse." *BW* 40 (1912) 130–38. **Estes, D. F.** "The Eschatological Discourse of Jesus." *RevExp* 15 (1918) 411–36. **Feuillet, A.** "Le discours de Jésus sur la ruine du Temple d'après Marc XIII et Luc XXI, 5–36." *RB* 55 (1948) 481–502; 56 (1949) 61–92. ———. "La signification fondamentale de Marc XIII: Recherches sur l'eschatologie des Synoptiques." *RThom* 80 (1980) 181–215. **Flückiger, F.** "Die Redaktion der Zukunftsrede in Markus. 13." *TZ* 26 (1970) 395–409. **Ford, D.** *The Abomination of Desolation in Biblical Eschatology.* Washington: University Press of America, 1979. **Fuller, G. C.** "The Olivet Discourse: An Apocalyptic Timetable." *WTJ* 28 (1966) 157–63. **Fusco, V.** "Le discours eschatologique lucanien: 'rédaction' et 'composition' (Lc 21,5–36 et Mc 13,1–37)." In *The Synoptic Gospels.* Ed. C. Focant. BETL 110. Leuven: Peeters and Leuven UP, 1993. 311–55. **Geddert, T. J.** *Watchwords.* **Glasson, T. F.** "Mark xiii and the Greek Old Testament." *ExpTim* 69 (1958) 213–15. **Grässer, E.** *Die Naherwartung Jesu.* SBS 61. Stuttgart: Katholisches Bibelwerk, 1973. ———. *Das Problem der Parusieverzögerung in den synoptischen Evangelien und in der Apostelgeschichte.* BZNW 22. Berlin: Töpelmann, 1957. 152–70. **Grayston, K.** "The Study of Mark XIII." *BJRL* 56 (1973–74) 371–87. **Hahn, F.** "Die Rede von der Parusie des Menschensohnes Markus 13." In *Jesus der Menschensohn.* FS A. Vögtle, ed. R. Pesch and R. Schnackenburg. Freiburg: Herder, 1975. 240–66. **Hanley, E. A.** "The Destruction of Jerusalem: Mark, Chap. 13." *BW* 34 (1909) 45–46. **Harder, G.** "Das eschatologische Geschichtsbild der sogenannten kleinen Apokalypse Markus 13." *ThViat* 4 (1952–53) 71–107. **Hartman, L.** *Prophecy Interpreted: The Formation of Some Jewish Apocalyptic Texts and of the Eschatological Discourse Mark 13 par.* ConBNT 1. Lund: Gleerup, 1966. 145–252. **Hengel, M.** "The Gospel of Mark: Time of Origin and Situation." In *Studies in the Gospel of Mark.* 1–30, esp. 14–28. **Hermann, I.** "Die Gefährdung der Welt und ihre Erneuerung: Auslegung von Mk 13,1–37." *BibLeb* 7 (1966) 305–9. **Hiers, R. H.** *The Kingdom of the God in the Synoptic Tradition.* UFHM 33. Gainesville: University of Florida, 1970. 82–85. **Hölscher, G.** "Der Ursprung des Apokalypse Mk 13." *TBl* 121 (1933) 193–202. **Hooker, M. D.** "Trial and Tribulation in Mark XIII." *BJRL* 65 (1982) 78–99. **Horsley, R. A.** "Wisdom and Apocalypticism in Mark." In *Search of Wisdom.* FS J. G. Gammie, ed. L. G. Perdue et al. Louisville: Westminster John Knox, 1993. 223–44. **Howard, J. K.** "Our

Lord's Teaching concerning His Parousia: A Study in the Gospel of Mark." *EvQ* 38 (1966) 52–58, 68–75, 150–57. **Jones, A.** "Did Christ Foretell the End of the World in Mark XIII?" *Scr* 4 (1950) 264–73. ———. "The Eschatology of the Synoptic Gospels." *Scr* 4 (1950) 222–31. **Karnetzki, M.** "Die galiläische Redaktion im Markusevangelium." *ZNW* 52 (1961) 238–72. **Kee, H. C.** *Community of the New Age.* 43–45. **Kelber, W. H.** "The History of the Kingdom in Mark: Aspects of Markan Eschatology." In *Society of Biblical Literature 1972 Seminar Papers.* Ed L. C. McGaughey. 2 vols. SBLSP 11. Missoula, MT: SBL, 1972. 1:63–95, esp. 80–85. ———. *The Kingdom in Mark: A New Place and a New Time.* Philadelphia: Fortress, 1974. 109–44. **Kermode, F.** *The Genesis of Secrecy: On the Interpretation of Narrative.* Cambridge: Harvard UP, 1979. 127–31. **Kippenberg, H. G.** "Ein Vergleich jüdischer, christlicher und der gnostischer Apokalyptik." In *Apocalypticism in the Mediterranean World and the Near East: Proceedings of the International Colloquium on Apocalypticism. Uppsala, August 12–17, 1979.* Ed. D. Hellholm. Tübingen: Mohr-Siebeck, 1983. 751–68. **Klauck, H.-J.** *Allegorie und Allegorese in synoptischen Gleichnistexten.* NTAbh 13. Münster: Aschendorff, 1978. 316–39. **Knox, W. L.** *The Sources of the Synoptic Gospels.* Cambridge: Cambridge UP, 1953. 103–14. **Kuhn, H.-W.** *Ältere Sammlungen.* 43–45. **Kümmel, W. G.** *Promise and Fulfillment.* 95–104. **Lambrecht, J.** "Die Logia-Quellen von Markus 13." *Bib* 47 (1966) 321–60. ———. "Die 'Midrasch-Quelle' von Mk 13." *Bib* 49 (1968) 254–70. ———. "Redactio sermonis eschatologici." *VD* 43 (1965) 278–87. ———. *Die Redaktion des Markus-Apokalypse: Literarische Analyse und Strukturuntersuchung.* AnBib 28. Rome: Biblical Institute, 1967. ———. "La structure de Mc., XIII." In *De Jésus aux Évangiles: Tradition et rédaction dans les Évangiles synoptiques.* FS I. Coppens, ed. I. de la Potterie. BETL 25. Gembloux: Duculot, 1967. 140–64. **Lattanzi, H.** "Eschatologici sermonis Domini logica interpretatio (Mt. 24,1–36; Mc. 13,1–37; Lc 21,5–35)." *Divinitas* 11 (1967) 71–92. **Laws, S.** "Can Apocalyptic Be Relevant?" In *What about the New Testament?* FS C. F. Evans, ed. M. D. Hooker and C. Hickling. London: SCM Press, 1975. 89–102. **Légasse, S.** "Le discours eschatologique de Marc 13 d'après trois ourages récents." *BLE* 71 (1970) 241–61. **Lightfoot, R. H.** *The Gospel Message of St. Mark.* Oxford: Clarendon, 1950. 48–59. **Lohse, E.** "Apokalyptik und Christologie." *ZNW* 62 (1971) 48–67, esp. 61–63. **Mack, B. L.** *Myth.* 325–31. **Manson, T. W.** *Sayings.* 323–37. ———. *Teaching.* 260–84. **Manson, W.** "The Son of Man and History." *SJT* 5 (1952) 113–22. **Marxsen, W.** *Mark the Evangelist.* 151–206. **Masson, C.** *L'Évangile de Marc et l'Église de Rome.* Bibliothèque théologique. Neuchâtel: Delachaux & Niestlé, 1968. 100–112. **Mateos, J.** *Marcos 13: El grupo cristiano en la historia.* Lectura del Nuevo Testamento: Estudios críticos y exegéticos 3. Madrid: Cristiandad, 1987. **McNicol, A. J.** "The Composition of the Synoptic Eschatological Discourse." In *The Interrelations of the Gospels: A Symposium Led by M.-É. Boismard, W. R. Farmer, and F. Neirynck, Jerusalem 1984.* Ed. D. L. Dungan. BETL 95. Leuven: Peeters and Leuven UP, 1990. 157–200. **Minette de Tillesse, G.** *Le secret messianique.* 420–37. **Mussner, F.** *Christ and the End of the World: A Biblical Study in Eschatology.* Contemporary Catechetics Series 2. Notre Dame, IN: Notre Dame UP, 1965. **Neirynck, F.** "Le discours anti-apokalyptique de Mc., XIII." *ETL* 45 (1969) 154–64 (repr. in F. Neirynck. *Evangelica.* BETL 60. Leuven: Peeters and Leuven UP, 1982. 598–608). ———. "Marc 13: Examen critique de l'interprétation de R. Pesch." In *L'Apocalypse johannique et l'apocalyptique dans le Nouveau Testament.* Ed. J. Lambrecht. BETL 53. Gembloux: Duculot; Leuven: Leuven UP, 1980. 369–401 (repr. in F. Neirynck. *Evangelica.* BETL 60. Leuven: Peeters and Leuven UP, 1982. 565–97). ———. "Note on the Eschatological Discourse." In *The Interrelations of the Gospels: A Symposium Led by M.-É. Boismard, W. R. Farmer, and F. Neirynck, Jerusalem 1984.* Ed. D. L. Dungan. BETL 95. Leuven: Peeters and Leuven UP, 1990. 77–80. ———. "Response to the Multiple State Hypothesis: The Eschatological Discourse." In *The Interrelations of the Gospels: A Symposium Led by M.-É. Boismard, W. R. Farmer, and F. Neirynck, Jerusalem 1984.* Ed. D. L. Dungan. BETL 95. Leuven: Peeters and Leuven UP, 1990. 108–24 (repr. in F. Neirynck. *Evangelica II.* BETL 99. Leuven: Peeters and Leuven UP, 1991. 493–509). **Neville, G.** *The Advent Hope: A Study of the Context of Mark 13.* London: Darton, Longman & Todd, 1961. **Nützel, J. M.** "Hoffnung und Treue: Zur Eschatologie des Markusevangeliums." In *Gegenwart und kommendes Reich.* FS A. Vögtle, ed. P. Fiedler and D. Zeller. SBB. Stuttgart: Katholisches Bibelwerk, 1975. 79–90, esp. 82–84. **O'Flynn, J. A.** "The Eschatological Discourse." *ITQ* 18 (1951) 277–81. **Perrot, C.** "Essai sur le discours eschatologique (Mc. XIII, 1–37; Mt. XXIV, 1–36; Lc. XXI, 5–36)." *RSR* 47 (1959) 481–514. **Pesch, R.** "Heilszukunft und Zukunft des Heils: Eschatologie und Apokalyptik in den Evangelien und Briefen." In *Gestalt und Anspruch des Neuen Testaments.* Ed. J. Schreiner and G. Dautzenberg. 2nd ed. Würzburg: Echter, 1979. 313–29, esp. 320–22. ———. "Markus 13." In *L'Apocalypse johannique et l'apocalyptique dans le Nouveau Testament.* Ed. J. Lambrecht. BETL 53. Gembloux: Duculot; Leuven: Peeters, 1980. 355–68. ———. *Naherwartungen: Tradition und Redaktion in Mk 13.* KBANT. Düsseldorf: Patmos, 1968. **Piganiol, A.** "Observations sur la date de l'apocalypse synoptique." *RHPR* 4 (1924) 245–49. **Rau, G.** "Das Markus-Evangelium: Komposition und Intention der ersten Darstellung christlicher Mission." *ANRW* 2.25.3 (1985) 2036–2257, esp. 2164–86. **Raymond, P.** "Le discours eschatologique de Mc 13." *BCPE* 21 (1969) 35–41. **Roarck, D. M.** "The Great Eschatological Discourse." *NovT* 7 (1964–65) 122–27. **Robbins, V. K.** *Jesus the Teacher.* 171–78. **Robinson, J. M.** *Problem of History.* 60–63. **Rohr, J.** "Der Sprachgebrauch des Markusevangeliums und die 'Markusapokalypse.'" *TQ* 89 (1907) 507–36. **Rousseau, F.** "La structure de Marc 13." *Bib* 56 (1975) 157–72. **Schelkle, K. H.** "Neutestamentliche Eschatologie." In *Zwischenzeit und Vollendung der Heilsgeschichte.* Vol. 5 of *Mysterium Salutis: Grundriss heilsgeschichtlicher Dogmatik.* Ed. J. Feiner and M. Löhrer. Zürich: Benziger, 1976. 723–78 (repr. in K. H. Schelkle. *Die Kraft des Wortes: Beiträge zu einer biblischen Theologie.* Stuttgart: Katholisches Bibelwerk, 1983. 147–207, esp. 157–66). ———. *Vollendung von Schöpfung und Erlösung.* Vol. 4, part 1 of *Theologie des Neuen Testaments.* KBANT. Düsseldorf: Patmos, 1974. 36–47. **Schoeps, H.-J.** "Ebionitische Apokalyptik im Neuen Testament." *ZNW* 51 (1960) 101–11, esp. 102–6 (repr. in H.-J. Schoeps. *Studien zur unbekannten Religions- und Geistesgeschichte.* VGG 3. Göttingen: Musterschmidt, 1963. 68–77, esp. 69–73). **Schottroff, L.** "Die Gegenwart in der Apokalyptik der synoptischen Evangelien." In *Apocalypticism in the Mediterranean World and the Near East: Proceedings of the International Colloquium on Apocalypticism. Uppsala, August 12–17, 1979.* Ed. D. Hellholm. Tübingen: Mohr-Siebeck, 1983. 707–28 (repr. in L. Schottroff. *Befreiungserfahrungen: Studien zur Sozialgeschichte des Neuen Testaments.* TBü 82. Munich: Kaiser, 1990. 73–95, esp. 86–88). **Schreiber, J.** *Theologie des Vertrauens.* 126–45. **Spitta, F.** "Die grosse eschatologische Rede Jesu." *TSK* 82 (1909) 348–401. **Standaert, B. H. M. G. M.** *L'évangile selon Marc.* 231–53. **Stather Hunt, B. P. W.** *Primitive Gospel Sources.* London; New York: Clarke-Philosophical Library, 1951. 63–73. **Stock, A.** *Call to Discipleship.* 171–80. **Streeter, B. H.** *The Four Gospels: A Study of Origins.* Rev. ed. London: Macmillan, 1930. 491–99. **Suhl, A.** *Zitate.* 152–57. **Tagawa, K.** "Marc 13: La tâtonnement d'un homme réaliste éveillé face à la tradition apocalyptique." *FoiVie* 76 (1977) 11–44. **Taylor, V.** "Unsolved New Testament Problems—The Apocalyptic Discourse of Mark 13." *ExpTim* 60 (1948–49) 94–98. **Theissen, G.** *Gospels in Context.* 125–65. **Theobald, M.** "Gottessohn und Menschensohn: Zur polaren Struktur der Christologie im Markusevangelium." SNTSU 13 (1988) 37–79, esp. 71–76. **Tolbert, M. A.** *Sowing the Gospel.* 257–65. **Trocmé, É.** *Formation of the Gospel according to Mark.* 208–40. **Tuckett, C. M.** "Response to the Two-Gospel Hypothesis: The Eschatological Discourse." In *The Interrelations of the Gospels: A Symposium Led by M.-É. Boismard, W. R. Farmer, and F. Neirynck, Jerusalem 1984.* Ed. D. L. Dungan. BETL 95. Leuven: Peeters and Leuven UP, 1990. 63–76. **Völter, D.** "Die eschatologische Rede Jesu und seine Weissagung von der Zerstörung Jerusalems." *STZ* 31 (1915) 180–202. **Vorster, W. S.** "Intertextuality and Redaktionsgeschichte." In *Intertextuality in Biblical Writings.* FS B. M. F. van Iersel, ed. S. Draisma. Kampen: Kok, 1989. 22–26. ———. "Literary Reflections on Mark 13:5–37: A Narrated Speech of Jesus." *Neot* 21 (1987) 203–24. **Walter, N.** "Tempelzerstörung und Synoptische Apokalypse." *ZNW* 57 (1966) 38–49. **Weeden, T. J.** "The Heresy that Necessitated Mark's Gospel." *ZNW* 59 (1968) 145–58, esp. 150–58. ———. *Mark.* 73–100. **Weinacht, H.** *Menschwerdung des Sohnes Gottes.* 89–110.

Wenham, D. "Paul and the Synoptic Apocalypse." In *Studies of History and Tradition in the Four Gospels*. Ed. R. T. France and D. Wenham. Gospel Perspectives 2. Sheffield: JSOT Press, 1981. 345–75. ———. *The Rediscovery of Jesus' Eschatological Discourse*. Gospel Perspectives 4. Sheffield: JSOT Press, 1984. ———. "'This Generation Will Not Pass . . .': A Study of Jesus' Future Expectation in Mark 13." In *Christ the Lord: Studies in Christology*. FS D. Guthrie, ed. H. H. Rowdon. Leicester: Inter-Varsity Press, 1982. 127–50.

Form/Structure/Setting

Mark 13 has been the subject of a great deal of critical discussion, primarily because of its apparent importance in the Markan Gospel (e.g., see the title of C. B. Cousar's study, "Mark's *Theologia Crucis*," *Int* 24 [1970] 321–35). The discourse has been variously described as the Eschatological Discourse (because it deals with *eschata* or "last things"), the Olivet Discourse (because its ostensible setting is the Mount of Olives), and the Little Apocalypse (because of the presence of apocalyptic elements). Since the publication of T. Colani's *Jésus-Christ et les croyances messianiques de son temps*, 2nd ed. (Strasbourg: Truettel et Wurtz, 1864), it has become a commonplace to view Mark 13 as constituting a Jewish apocalypse (for a survey of scholarship, see Beasley-Murray, *Jesus and the Last Days*, 32–79). The passage, accordingly, has been frequently designated the "Little Apocalypse" (Hölscher, *TBl* 121 [1933] 193–202; Pesch, 2:266; Taylor, 498: an edited "fly-sheet"; similarly Brandenburger, *Markus 13;* Haenchen, 438: a *fliegende Blatt* [fly sheet] of a Christian prophet; but see Beasley-Murray, *ExpTim* 64 [1952–53] 346–49; Cranfield, 387–88). Dibelius (*Tradition,* 260) classifies the discourse as a secret apocalypse, quite in keeping with Mark's inclination for the esoteric. Bultmann (*History,* 125) regards the discourse as a "Jewish Apocalypse with Christian editing" (125). Admittedly there are elements in this discourse that are frequently found in apocalyptic literature: the prediction of family discord in v 12, the prediction of persecution in v 13, the anticipation of tribulation in v 19, the celestial portents in vv 24–25 (cf. Isa 13:10), the descripton of the angels coming to gather the elect in v 27, and the promise of the coming of the "son of man" in vv 26 and 29. Nevertheless, there are elements in the eschatological discourse that are not typically found in Jewish apocalyptic literature: the setting, where a rabbi responds to a comment or question of his disciples; Jesus' repeated commands in the second person to his disciples to watch out and be prepared; and a whole series of detailed predictions tied to these warnings. Moreover, many of the typical features of apocalyptic literature are not found in Mark 13: no vision or heavenly rapture as occasion for the discourse; no review of human history, especially Israel's history; no commentary on how God has dealt with humankind and how humankind has gone from one sinful activity to another; no heavenly portraits and attendant heavenly secrets; no depictions of heavenly or earthly battles; no clash of angels and the powers of darkness; and no depiction of the final dawning of either the messianic kingdom or judgment day. The discourse is eschatological, in that it deals with "last things," and it has affinities with Jewish apocalyptic, but it is not an apocalypse (Anderson, 289–90; Cranfield, 388; Gundry, 751–52).

Mark 13 has also been compared to the Jewish farewell discourse (first by Busch, *Zum Verständnis;* see also Ernst, 366; Grundmann, 347: "an esoteric farewell address"; Klostermann, 131; Lane, 444; Lührmann, 215), as in Gen 49 (Jacob's fare-well to his sons), Deut 33 (Moses' farewell), Josh 23–24 (Joshua's farewell), 1 Sam 12 (Samuel's farewell), 1 Chron 28–29 (David's farewell), John 13–16 (Jesus' farewell), Acts 20:17–38 (Paul's farewell), and other examples in Judeo-Christian literature of late antiquity (as seen especially in the *Testaments of the Twelve Patri-archs* and other testamentary literature). Although there are general similarities, to be sure, there are also significant differences. Jesus' eschatological discourse does not review and comment on the past, which is common in the farewell dis-courses. Farewell discourses, moreover, usually are cast in a much more formal setting: the dying patriarch or the aged monarch summons his sons/people to attend his final words. Mark 13 is nothing of the sort: Jesus responds to a ques-tion and offers no moral instruction. The content of Mark 13 itself does not fit the genre of the farewell discourse, for its basic purpose is to predict the coming of the "son of man" and the events and dangers that portend it.

D. E. Aune (*Prophecy,* 186–87) thinks that Mark 13 follows the pattern of the Greco-Roman "peripatetic dialogue." These dialogues are usually situated at a temple and occur in response to an oracle. But the eschatological discourse of Mark 13 is not a dialogue; it is rather a discourse of moderate length, prompted by a question. Furthermore, the purpose is to warn more than to enlighten. Moreover, how peri-patetic is the eschatological discourse? According to v 3 Jesus sits down and then begins teaching, which is what he does elsewhere (cf. 4:1; 12:41). Aune's proposed pattern does not fit Mark 13 well and consequently adds little clarification.

Many scholars have maintained that the eschatological discourse reflects little of Jesus' teaching and really does not answer the questions that the disciples have put to Jesus. Cranfield identifies three principal objections to the authenticity of the discourse: (1) its inconsistency, as seen in the warning to be prepared for a sudden Parousia, on the one hand, and in the urging to recognize the approach-ing end through the observation of portending signs, on the other hand; (2) its inconsistency with Jesus' teaching elsewhere, especially as seen in Q, which in-sists on suddenness and unexpectedness and not portending signs; and (3) the discourse's apparent failure to answer directly the actual questions raised by the disciples. Cranfield, however, does not find these objections compelling, noting that the paradox between suddenness and portending signs may be intentional and mutually clarifying, both in the eschatological discourse itself and in the wider body of Jesus' teachings. As to the objection that the disciples' questions are not answered, Cranfield and others argue that the questions are answered. The de-struction of the temple will be portended by various signs, signs that will ultimately give indication of the coming of the "son of man," a question not raised by the disciples in the Markan version but explicitly raised in the Matthean version (cf. Matt 24:3: "Tell us, when will this be, and what will be the sign of your coming and of the close of the age?"). Grundmann (349–50), Gundry (752–53), Lane (448–50), Schniewind (168), Taylor (499: "genuine sayings of Jesus are imbed-ded in [the discourse] and adapted to later conditions"), and recently Wenham (*Rediscovery*) also believe that most of this material derives from Jesus.

Also in support of the authenticity of the discourse is the prophecy's difficult fit with actual events. True, the temple complex was eventually razed (and there are indications that it took some time: *J.W.* 6.9.1 §413: "And when, at a later pe-riod, he demolished the rest of the city and razed the walls . . ."; cf. 7.1.1 §1:

"Caesar ordered the whole city and the Temple to be razed to the ground"; *J.W.* 7.5.2 §114–15: months later Titus revisits Jerusalem, which was still being dug up by soldiers looking for buried wealth), but *fire* is the detail that was greatly emphasized (see below). Jesus' prediction in v 2 says nothing of fire. The destruction of the city of Jerusalem itself was greatly emphasized in Josephus and other writers looking back, yet Jesus says nothing about that in Mark 13. Indeed, the details in the discourse—the warnings about false messiahs, wars and rumors of war, the desolating abomination, the warning to flee to the mountains—do not fit neatly the events that transpired between 30 and 70 (on this important point, see Gundry, 754–56), though there are certainly important parallels. How well they correspond, or do not correspond, will be treated in the respective *Comment* sections.

If the discourse constitutes genuine dominical tradition, does it comprise clusters and isolated sayings of loosely related eschatological teaching (as proposed as far back as 1838 by C. H. Weisse, *Die evangelische Geschichte: Kritisch und philosophisch bearbeitet* [Leipzig: Breitkopf und Hartel, 1838]), perhaps enhanced with allusions to various OT passages? Anderson (290) doubts the unity and authenticity of much of the discourse, for "it is not in character for Jesus to string together *OT* quotations or to indulge in apocalyptic time-tabling." Gundry (753), however, rightly challenges Anderson's description of the discourse as a stringing together of quotations. There are a few phrases from Daniel in vv 14, 19, and 26 (though Daniel's influence is pervasive, as Hartman, *Prophecy Interpreted,* has shown), a composite quotation from Isaiah in vv 24–25, a few other echoes here and there, but to imply that the discourse is a string of quotations is an exaggeration. Thus, it is irrelevant to say that Jesus does not string together OT quotations elsewhere. But elsewhere he does allude to Scripture, sometimes linking and conflating passages from diverse texts (as in Mark 10:6–7, where Jesus links Gen 1:27 with Gen 2:24; or Mark 11:17, where part of Isa 56:7 is quoted, followed by an allusion to Jer 7:11; or in Mark 12:1–11, where an allusion to parts of Isa 5:1–7 at the beginning of the parable of the Wicked Vineyard Tenants is followed by a quotation of Ps 118:22–23 at the conclusion of the parable). Moreover, "timetabling," which is often found in apocalyptic literature, is hardly a fair description of the eschatological discourse, whose principal function is to warn the disciples of dangers and difficulties that lie ahead.

Contrary to his earlier position (in *Naherwartungen,* 83–96) Pesch (2:268–69) now assigns Mark 13 to the Passion Narrative, based on the logical conclusion of Jesus' third day in the temple (cf. 12:41–44); use of the genitive absolute in the pre-Markan Passion Narrative; use of ἱερόν, "temple," which is characteristic of the pre-Markan Passion Narrative (cf. 11:11, 15, 16, 27; 12:35; 14:49); and the uncharacteristic framework of the story. Jesus leaves the temple precincts and the city for the third time in three days (2:270). The question posed by the unnamed disciple is unique. All of these factors point to early, primitive tradition that is closely linked to the pre-Markan Passion Narrative. As important as Mark 13 is, however, it probably was not the conclusion of the earliest published form of Mark (as is argued by Trocmé, *Formation,* 215–40). It is Jesus' longest discourse in Mark because for the evangelist and his community it offered the most impressive evidence of Jesus' predictive power and of the remarkable relevance of his teaching.

The view taken in the present commentary is that most of the material that

makes up the eschatological discourse does derive from Jesus, though its arrangement in Mark 13 is at points artificial and reflects a measure of later updating.
For reasons that will be given in the *Comment* sections that treat Mark 13, it is
argued here that Jesus' words only partly pertain to the events and experiences
of his followers leading up to the destruction of Jerusalem and the temple. Jesus'
words primarily have in view the end of the sinful age that would eventually and
finally give way to the kingdom of God. The Markan evangelist, probably sensing
that the end of the age was in fact fast approaching in light of the Jewish war,
gave a prominent place to the eschatological discourse and edited it accordingly
(see Grundmann, 350).

Hengel (*Studies in the Gospel of Mark*, 25) provides the most helpful and succinct statement of the context and purpose in the light of which the eschatological
discourse should be read:

> The time in which the evangelist is living is coloured by the vivid experience of fearful
> persecution, an expanding mission, the danger of being led astray, and the tumult of
> war threatening the whole empire; this tumult is misunderstood by Christians as a sign
> of the end which is already dawning. Jerusalem is not yet destroyed, but it is probably
> threatened, though the evangelist has only fairly vague ideas of what is going on there.
> The climax of the time of distress is still to come, but it is to be expected relatively
> soon, when the Antichrist, whose features are already becoming evident, takes over the
> sanctuary in Jerusalem in order to desecrate and destroy it.

Nineham (339–40) identifies vv 5–27 as the discourse proper, with vv 28–37
providing a supplement. Hartman (*Prophecy Interpreted*) believes that lying behind
the eschatological discourse is a source whose primary components are vv 5b–8,
12–16, 19–22, and 24–27. Gnilka (2:180) divides the discourse into three major
divisions: vv 5b–23, vv 24–27, vv 28–37, with warnings about being misled forming an inclusion in vv 5b and 23 with βλέπετε, "watch out." V 28 begins with μάθετε,
"learn," and ends in v 37 with γρηγορεῖτε, "watch." Beasley-Murray (*ExpTim* 64
[1952–53] 346–49) divides the discourse into four sections: (1) Introduction and
Prophecy of the Temple's Doom (vv 1–4), (2) the Tribulation of Israel and the
Church (vv 5–23), (3) the Parousia of the Son of Man and the Gathering of the
People of God (vv 24–27), and (4) the Times of Fulfillment and Exhortations to
Watchfulness (vv 28–37). Gundry (733) sees two main sections: vv 5b–23, centered on what must precede the coming of the "son of man," and vv 24–37,
centered on the coming itself. Gundry's understanding is adopted here, with
pericopes identified as vv 5–13, vv 14–23, vv 24–27, vv 28–32, and vv 33–37. Commentators have offered various outlines of this material, as well as a large number
of proposals for what is traditional and what is Markan (for a sampling, see Ernst,
372–76; Gnilka, 2:179–80; Grundmann, 347; Hahn, "Die Rede von der Parusie";
Pesch, 2:265–67; Taylor, 499). Distinctions between tradition (including what derives from Jesus and what derives from early Christian tradents) and Markan
redaction will be discussed in the *Comment* sections below.

1. The Prediction of the Destruction of the Temple (13:1–2)

Bibliography

Beasley-Murray, G. R. *Jesus and the Last Days: The Interpretation of the Olivet Discourse.* Peabody: Hendrickson, 1993. 377–84. **Best, E.** *Following Jesus.* 155. **Brandon, S. G. F.** *Jesus and the Zealots: A Study of the Political Factor in Primitive Christianity.* Manchester: Manchester UP; New York: Scribner's, 1967. 230–40. **Crossan, J. D.** *In Fragments.* 302–9. **Derrett, J. D. M.** "No Stone upon Another: Leprosy and the Temple." *JSNT* 30 (1987) 3–20. **Dodd, C. H.** "The Fall of Jerusalem and the 'Abomination of Desolation.'" *JRS* 37 (1947) 47–54 (repr. in C. H. Dodd. *More New Testament Studies.* Manchester: Manchester UP; Grand Rapids: Eerdmans, 1968. 69–83). **Dupont, J.** "Il n'en sera pas laissé pierre sur pierre (Marc 13,2; Luc 19,44)." *Bib* 52 (1971) 301–20. **Evans, C. A.** "Predictions of the Destruction of the Herodian Temple in the Pseudepigrapha, Qumran Scrolls, and Related Texts." *JSP* 10 (1992) 89–147. **Fascher, E.** "Jerusalems Untergang in der urchristlichen und altkirchlichen Überlieferung." *TLZ* 89 (1964) 81–98. **Feuillet, A.** "Le discours de Jésus sur la ruine du Temple d'après Marc XIII et Luc XXI, 5–36." *RB* 55 (1948) 481–502; 56 (1949) 61–92. **Fredriksen, P.** "Jesus and the Temple, Mark and the War." In *Society of Biblical Literature 1990 Seminar Papers.* Ed. D. J. Lull. SBLSP 29. Atlanta: Scholars Press, 1990. 293–310. **Gaston, L.** *No Stone on Another: Studies in the Significance of the Fall of Jerusalem in the Synoptic Gospels.* NovTSup 23. Leiden: Brill, 1970. 8–64. **Geddert, T. J.** *Watchwords.* 133–40, 203–6. **Hengel, M.** *Studies in the Gospel of Mark.* 14–16. **Hiers, R. H.** *The Historical Jesus and the Kingdom of God: Present and Future in the Message and Ministry of Jesus.* UFHM 38. Gainesville: University of Florida Press, 1973. 91–94. **Kato, Z.** *Völkermission im Markusevangelium.* 130–36. **Kümmel, W. G.** *Promise and Fulfilment.* 99–102. **Lambrecht, J.** *Die Redaktion des Markus-Apokalypse: Literarische Analyse und Strukturuntersuchung.* AnBib 28. Rome: Biblical Institute, 1967. 65–91. **Lührmann, D.** "Markus 14,55–64: Christologie und Zerstörung des Tempels im Markusevangelium." *NTS* 27 (1981) 457–74. **Mateos, J.** *Marcos 13: El grupo cristiano en la historia.* Lectura del Nuevo Testamento: Estudios críticos y exegéticos 3. Madrid: Cristiandad, 1987. 78–142. **Meinertz, M.** "Die Tragweite der Weissagung Jesu von der Zerstörung des Tempels." *TGl* 35 (1943) 135–41. **Meyer, R.** *Der Prophet aus Galiläa: Studie zum Jesusbild der drei ersten Evangelien.* Leipzig: Hinrichs, 1940. Repr. Darmstadt: Wissenschaftliche Buchgesellschaft, 1970. 16–18. **Michel, O.** "Spätjüdisches Prophetentum." In *Neutestamentliche Studien.* FS R. Bultmann, ed. W. Eltester. Berlin: Töpelmann, 1954. 60–66. **Neirynck, F.** "Marc 13: Examen critique de l'interprétation de R. Pesch." In *L'Apocalypse johannique et l'apocalyptique dans le Nouveau Testament.* Ed. J. Lambrecht. BETL 53. Gembloux: Duculot; Leuven: Leuven UP, 1980. 369–401, esp. 397–99 (repr. in F. Neirynck. *Evangelica: Gospel Studies—Études d'Évangile.* BETL 60. Leuven: Peeters and Leuven UP, 1982. 565–97, esp. 593–95). **Pesch, R.** *Evangelium der Urgemeinde.* 157–58. ———. *Naherwartungen: Tradition und Redaktion in Mk 13.* KBANT. Düsseldorf: Patmos, 1968. 83–106. **Reicke, B.** "Synoptic Prophecies on the Destruction of Jerusalem." In *Studies in the New Testament and Early Christian Literature.* FS A. P. Wikgren, ed. D. E. Aune. NovTSup 33. Leiden: Brill, 1972. 121–34. **Sanders, E. P.** "Jesus, Paul and Judaism." *ANRW* 2.25.1 (1982) 390–450, esp. 408–11. **Sariola, H.** *Markus und das Gesetz.* 225–29. **Schlosser, J.** "La parole de Jésus sur le fin du Temple." *NTS* 36 (1990) 398–414. **Smith, S. H.** "The Literary Structure of Mark 11:1–12:40." *NovT* 31 (1989) 104–24, esp. 108–11. **Theissen, G.** "Tempelweissagung Jesu: Prophetie im Spannungsfeld von Stadt und Land." *TZ* 32 (1976) 144–58 (repr. in G. Theissen. *Studien zur Soziologie des Urchristentums.* WUNT 19. Tübingen: Mohr-Siebeck, 1979. 142–59; ET:

"Jesus' Temple Prophecy: Prophecy in the Tension between Town and Country." In *Social Reality and the Early Christians: Theology, Ethics, and the World of the New Testament.* Tr. M. Kohl. Minneapolis: Fortress, 1992. 94–114). **Vielhauer, P.** *Oikodome.* Vol. 2 of *Aufsätze zum Neuen Testament.* Ed. G. Klein. TB 65. Munich: Kaiser, 1979. 59–66. **Wenham, D.** *The Rediscovery of Jesus' Eschatological Discourse.* Gospel Perspectives 4. Sheffield: JSOT Press, 1984. 287–94. **Westcott, B. F.,** and **Hort, F. J. A.** *Introduction.* 2:26.

Translation

¹*And as he* ᵃ *went out of the temple, one of his disciples says to him, "Teacher,*ᵇ *behold, what wonderful stones and what wonderful buildings!"* ᶜ ²*And Jesus said to him, "Do you see these great buildings? Not one stone will be left here upon another that will not be thrown down."* ᵈᵉ

Notes

ᵃA few MSS read the pl. ἐκπορευομένων αὐτῶν ἐκ τοῦ ἱεροῦ, "as they went out of the temple."
ᵇGk. διδάσκαλε. Some Syr. MSS read *rabbî*, "rabbi."
ᶜD adds τοῦ ἱεροῦ, "of the temple."
ᵈGk. καταλυθῇ. Some MSS (such as ℵ* L) replace the aor. subjunctive with the fut. indic. καταλυθήσεται.
ᵉD W and few late authorities add καὶ διὰ τριῶν ἡμερῶν ἄλλος ἀναστήσεται ἄνευ χειρῶν, "And after three days another will be raised without hands." This addition was inspired by Mark 14:58 and John 2:19; cf. Westcott and Hort, *Introduction* 2:26. The addition represents an early attempt to interpret the significance of Jesus' strange saying.

Form/Structure/Setting

Jesus' startling prediction of the destruction of the temple complex elicits the disciples' question regarding when these things will take place and what will be the sign of their coming (v 4). The answer that Jesus provides (vv 5–32), including the concluding admonition to watch (vv 33–37), constitutes the eschatological discourse. However, the relationship of the prediction in v 2 to the one found on the lips of the false witnesses in 14:58 (cf. 15:29) presents difficulties. Some scholars have maintained that the prediction is but part of an original combined saying (cf. Theissen, *TZ* 32 [1976] 145); others that it is an abbreviated and edited form of the longer saying in 14:58 (cf. Pesch, *Naherwartung,* 91; Lührmann, *NTS* 27 [1981] 463–69); still others that the predictions in v 2 and 14:58 grew out of a common tradition (cf. Schlosser, *NTS* 36 [1990] 409). Ideologically the sayings are, of course, related, but stylistically and formally they appear to be distinct units of tradition (so Ernst, 369; Beasley-Murray, *Jesus and the Last Days,* 378–79).

A similar problem arises from comparison with Luke 19:44: "and [your enemies will] dash you to the ground, you and your children within you, and they will not leave one stone upon another in you." Here the city of Jerusalem is being addressed, not the temple precincts. Gaston (*No Stone,* 66–67) believes that Jesus' utterance originally had to do with the city. In his commentary, Pesch (2:271) thinks Mark 13:2 and Luke 19:44 are independent sayings. He is probably correct, for the Markan form of the saying is probably a narrow application of the wider, more encompassing Lukan prediction. Jesus is remembered to have predicted the utter demolition of Jerusalem, including the city's famous temple precincts. In the prophetic tradition concerned with the Babylonian destruction, the fate of the city and the temple are linked. In Ezek 9–11 the divine glory departs first from the temple, then from the city. Jeremiah's prophecy of the doom of the temple (Jer 7) implies doom of the city and its inhabitants as well.

The question of the authenticity of v 2 is linked to the question of whether Jesus could or would have predicted the destruction of the temple and the grand buildings that surrounded it on the Temple Mount. Surprisingly, Bultmann (*History*, 120–21) allows that the prediction in v 2 might "rest on an actual dominical saying," based on apocalyptic expectations circulating among Jews in Jesus' day; but it "is nothing more than a possibility." Lohmeyer (268) thinks that the prophecy approximates the viewpoint of Jesus. With less hesitancy, Taylor (*Formation*, 73) rightly opines that there is "no real justification for regarding this story as 'a prophecy after the event.'" Taylor is correct, and he has been followed by others. The principal factor in favor of the authenticity of this prediction is the lack of detail and precise correspondence with the event (*pace* Gnilka, 2:184; but with Grundmann, 351, "scarcely a *vaticinium ex eventu*"; Anderson, 291; Hengel, *Studies in the Gospel of Mark*, 16, "in no way presupposes the catastrophe of 70"; cf. Evans, *JSP* 10 [1992] 89–147), as is often seen in *vaticinia ex eventu* (prophecies after the event). There is no mention of the devastating fire that swept the precincts and was much emphasized in the graphic description narrated by Josephus (*J. W.* 6.2.9 §§165–68; 6.3.1 §§177–85; 6.3.2 §§190–92; 6.4.1–2 §§228–35; 6.4.5–8 §§250–70; 6.5.1–2 §§271–84; 6.6.1 §316; 6.6.2 §346; 6.6.3 §§353–55; 6.8.5 §407; 6.9.4 §434). Almost poetically, Josephus says, "You would indeed have thought that the Temple Mount [τὸν . . . τοῦ ἱεροῦ λόφον] was boiling over from its base, being everywhere one mass of flame" (*J. W.* 6.5.1 §275). And Jesus' admonition to pray that the destruction not come in winter (cf. 13:18) would, of course, be irrelevant and curious in light of the fact that the city was captured and the temple burned in August and September. (This tells against Pesch's argument [2:272–73] that Mark was written after 70 in order to show that the fulfillment of the prophecy did not mean that the end time was necessarily at hand.)

This passage (13:1–2) is one of several predictions attributed to Jesus. He predicts the destruction of the ruling priestly establishment in the parable of the Wicked Vineyard Tenants (12:1–12), the perpetual remembrance of the unnamed woman's act of devotion (14:9), his betrayal (14:17–21), his disciples' defection and Peter's denials (14:26–31), and his death and resurrection (14:27–28; cf. 8:31; 9:31; 10:32–34). But Jesus makes more general and thematic predictions, such as "the first will be last" (9:35; 10:31) and "he who exalts himself will be debased" (Matt 23:12 = Luke 14:11). Predictions such as these cohere with Jesus' principal proclamation: the coming of the kingdom of God. Implicit in such a proclamation is the certainty of dramatic changes. It is inconceivable that Jesus' understanding of the kingdom of God would not have entertained ideas of change. If the kingdom of God was truly breaking into the human sphere with a power never before seen, then the expectation of judgment upon persons and institutions that opposed this kingdom logically followed.

Jesus was not the only one to make predictions of the doom of Jerusalem or its temple. Several predictions are found in intertestamental literature:

your holy places will be made desolate [ἔσται τὰ ἅγια ὑμῶν ἔρημα]. (*T. Levi* 16:4; cf. 15:1)

destruction . . . slaughter . . . plunder . . . consumption of God's sanctuary by fire. (*T. Jud.* 23:3)

But again the kings of the peoples will launch an attack together against this land, bringing doom upon themselves, for they will want to destroy the Temple of the Great God and most excellent men when they enter the land. The abominable kings, each one with his throne and faithless people, will set them up around the city. (*Sib. Or.* 3:665)

And he [Jonah] gave a portent concerning Jerusalem and the whole land, that whenever they should see a stone crying out piteously the end was at hand. And whenever they should see all the gentiles in Jerusalem, the entire city would be razed to the ground [ἡ πόλις ἕως ἐδάφους ἀφανισθήσεται]." (*Liv. Pro.* 10:10–11 [Jonah])

And concerning the end [συντέλεια] of the Temple he [Habakkuk] predicted, "By a western nation it will happen." "At that time," he said, "the curtain [ἄπλωμα] of the Dabeir [i.e., the holy of holies] will be torn into small pieces, and the capitals of the two pillars will be taken away, and no one will know where they are; and they will be carried away by angels into the wilderness, where the Tent of Witness was set up in the beginning." (*Liv. Pro.* 12:11 [Habakkuk])

Though there are some who have expressed skepticism, many, if not most, scholars accept these traditions as authentic predictions of the temple's doom.

Josephus himself claims that he foresaw the temple's destruction:

But as . . . Josephus overheard the threats of the hostile crowd, suddenly there came back into his mind those nightly dreams, in which God had foretold to him the impending fate of the Jews and the destinies of the Roman sovereigns . . . he was not ignorant of the prophecies in the sacred books. (*J.W.* 3.8.3 §§351–52)

Who does not know the records of the ancient prophets and that oracle [χρησμόν] which threatens this poor city and is even now coming true? For they foretold that it would then be taken whenever one should begin to slaughter his own countrymen. (*J.W.* 6.2.1 §109)

Thus the Jews, after the demolition of Antonia, reduced the Temple to a square, although they had it recorded in their oracles that the city and the sanctuary would be taken when the Temple should become foursquare [τετράγωνον]. (*J.W.* 6.5.4 §311)

Josephus, moreover, tells us of another Jesus who had predicted the coming destruction:

Four years before the war . . . one Jesus, son of Ananias ['Ιησοῦς . . . τις υἱὸς Ἀνανίου] . . . who, standing in the Temple [ἱερόν], suddenly began to cry out: "A voice from the east, a voice from the west, a voice from the four winds, a voice against Jerusalem and the Sanctuary [ναόν], a voice against the bridegroom and the bride, a voice against all people. . . .

Woe to Jerusalem! . . . Woe once more to the city and to the people and to the Sanctuary [ναῷ] . . . and woe to me also." (*J.W.* 6.5.3 §301, §306, §309; cf. Jer 7:34)

What is intriguing here is that this Jesus, like Jesus of Nazareth thirty years earlier, also appealed to Jer 7 to clarify, if not justify, his prophecy of the temple's fate (cf. Mark 11:17, where Jesus alludes to Jer 7:11).

Rabbinic literature also contains traditions of predictions of the temple's destruction. Of especial importance is the story of Yoḥanan ben Zakkai:

> Forty years before the destruction of the Temple the western light went out, the crimson thread remained crimson, and the lot for the Lord always came up in the left hand. They would close the gates of the Temple by night and get up in the morning and find them wide open. Said Rabban Yohanan ben Zakkai [first century] to the Temple, "O Temple, why do you frighten us? We know that you will end up destroyed. For it has been said, 'Open your doors, O Lebanon, that the fire may devour your cedars' [Zech 11:1]." (*y. Soṭah* 6.3; cf. *b. Yoma* 39b; *'Abot R. Nat.* [A] §4)

> [When Vespasian objected to Yoḥanan ben Zakkai's greeting, "Vive domine Imperator," Yoḥanan explained:] "If you are not the king, you will be eventually, because the Temple will only be destroyed by a king's hand; as it is said, 'And Lebanon shall fall by a mighty one' [Isa 10:34]." (*Lam. Rab.* 1:5 §31)

These Scriptures were thought to pertain to the doom of the temple because of the tradition that linked Lebanon with the temple.

Best (*Following Jesus*, 155) rightly calls our attention to the links among three pericopes: the warning of the avaricious scribes (12:38–40), the widow's last penny (12:41–44), and the prediction of the temple's destruction (13:1–2). The scribes are part of, and the impoverished widow is contributing to, a temple establishment that soon will be destroyed. The prediction of the destruction lends gravity to the earlier pericopes, suggesting that they provide the grounds, or at least contribute to the grounds, of the prophecy itself.

Comment

1 καὶ ἐκπορευομένου αὐτοῦ ἐκ τοῦ ἱεροῦ, "And as he went out of the temple." Jesus has been teaching in the temple precincts throughout chaps. 11 and 12 with increasing hostility developing between himself and the ruling priests. Jesus in all probability exits through the eastern gate of the city, descends to the foot of the Mount of Olives, and then ascends to the point where he and his disciples can turn and look down upon the beautiful complex of buildings on the Temple Mount. Ernst (369) and Grundmann (350) think that Jesus' leaving the temple precincts signifies a final break with the temple. This is an overinterpretation, however. Jesus' departure, as it turns out in the Markan narrative, signifies an end of his teaching in the precincts. Taylor (500) remarks that the genitive absolute (ἐκπορευομένου αὐτοῦ, "as he went out") provides the link by which the evangelist is able to connect the present scene to the larger temple narrative context (11:27–12:44).

λέγει αὐτῷ εἷς τῶν μαθητῶν αὐτοῦ, "one of his disciples says to him." On previous occasions the comment or question of a disciple elicited a didactic response from Jesus (4:10; 7:17; 9:28–29, 38–39; 10:13–16, 35–40). On this occasion, however, the comment is merely an observation and, from the disciple's point of view, purely an innocent one.

διδάσκαλε, ἴδε ποταποὶ λίθοι καὶ ποταπαὶ οἰκοδομαί, "Teacher, behold, what wonderful stones and what wonderful buildings!" The disciple is impressed by the grandeur and beauty of the Herodian temple. Although the unloved monarch Herod the Great had been dead for some thirty-five years, his massive rebuilding and expansion of the temple precincts were still under way and would continue for decades to come (see the description of the temple in Josephus, *J.W.* 5.5.1–8 §§184–247; *Ant.* 15.11.3 §§391–402). The disciple's comment may have been little more than that of an awestruck tourist (see Lohmeyer, 268), but behind it may have lain excitement at the prospect of taking possession of these grand buildings when the kingdom of God arrived in its fullness and the current inmates were evicted.

2 βλέπεις ταύτας τὰς μεγάλας οἰκοδομάς, "Do you see these great buildings?" Recent excavations at the southwest corner of the pavement below the Temple Mount have clearly exposed the stones that were cast down. The original, specific placement of some of these stones has been identified (such as part of the lintel of what may have been Barclay's Gate and the stone bearing the inscription [לבית התקיעה להכ] *lĕbêt hattĕqîʿâ lhk[ ]*, "to the place of trumpeting," which was at one time at the top of the Temple Mount wall). The enormous weight of these stones and the force with which they impacted the pavement below actually caused the pavement in one place to collapse into the subterranean passages below. The purpose of these passages and their full extent are now being explored. The enormous quantity of the building material that has been cleared away (and some of it has deliberately been left *in situ*) impresses one with the magnitude of the task of demolition ordered by Titus (cf. *J.W.* 7.1.1 §§1–4: κελεύει Καῖσαρ ἤδη τήν τε πόλιν ἅπασαν καὶ τὸν νεὼν κατασκάπτειν, "Caesar now orders [the army] to raze all the city and the sanctuary to the ground"), which followed the capture of Jerusalem and the fiery destruction of the sanctuary and adjacent buildings. Although it is possible that this demolition was completed in a few months, it is probable that it took considerable time, perhaps even years. The assumption held by some commentators that Mark wrote in 71 C.E., shortly after the destruction of Jerusalem and the temple, is problematic. The most impressive feature of the destruction of the city and the temple was its destruction by fire (cf. *J.W.* 6.4.5 §250). The razing of the buildings came later. An *ex eventu* (after the event) prophecy, formulated only months after the capture of the city, would in all probability have described the fire, not the razing that in any case might not have been completed at the time of writing. Indeed, the complete and total razing of the temple complex, as Jesus' prophecy seems to envision, never was entirely fulfilled. Portions of all four supporting walls of the Temple Mount remain to this day, and some of the structures may not have been pulled down and may have been put to secondary use as late as the time of Hadrian. Had Mark 13:2 predicted the fiery destruction of the temple and city and the putting to the sword of the last of the defenders, we would have better reason to suspect that the prediction had indeed been composed in 70 or 71. As it stands, however, it is more prudent to view it as a genuine prediction of the grim fate of the temple and its supporting buildings, modeled after language found in Scripture.

The excavation of the Western Wall has uncovered many massive Herodian stones relatively untouched by the ravages of time. One stone has gained attention, owing to its enormous dimensions. It is more than 15 meters in length and 2.5 meters in height. Because its width is unknown, estimations of its weight vary, ranging from 420 tons to 600 tons. This stone is especially remarkable because it is not set at the base but has been set on the second tier above the pavement. Unfortunately, this stone has been marred by several holes chiseled into it for the anchors that at one time held a thick layer of plaster in place, as part of a large cistern in a later period. Nevertheless, this stone and countless others, complete with their characteristic borders, attest the magnificence and beauty to which one of the disciples meant to call Jesus' attention.

οὐ μὴ ἀφεθῇ ὧδε λίθος ἐπὶ λίθον ὃς οὐ μὴ καταλυθῇ, "Not one stone will be left here upon another that will not be thrown down." Jesus' reply could not have been more startling. The disciples knew of Jesus' criticism of the priestly establishment. They knew of his threat that their stewardship was in danger of being taken away and given to others. But the destruction of the temple itself would have surprised them. (The story of Jesus weeping over the city and predicting its doom is found in Luke 19:41–44, not in Mark. In the Markan story there has not been a hint of the destruction of either the city or the temple.)

"Not one stone . . . upon another" probably alludes to LXX 2 Kgdms 17:13 (cf. 2 Sam 17:13): "all Israel will take ropes to that city, and we will drag it into the river, so that not even a stone is left there [ὅπως μὴ καταλειφθῇ ἐκεῖ μηδὲ λίθος]" (cf. LXX Hag 2:15, "stone upon stone [λίθον ἐπὶ λίθον]," in rebuilding the temple). Haggai, along with Zechariah, was a prophet of diarchic (two-ruler) restoration. Could Jesus' allusion have been ironic? Jerusalem's rejection of him would lead to the dismantling of the temple. Micah predicted that Jerusalem would become a "heap of ruins" (Mic 3:12; cf. Jer 26:17–19), while an angry God said through Amos: "Smite the capitals until the thresholds shake" (9:1). Allusive usage of the language of the prophets is typical of Jesus (e.g., Isa 56:7 and Jer 7:11 in Mark 11:17; Isa 5:1–7 in Mark 12:1–9) and will be especially in evidence in the eschatological discourse itself. Rabbi Eliezer is said to have alluded to Ps 137:7 ("Rase it, rase it! Down to its foundations!") in his prediction of the temple's destruction: "Let your witness, the Temple, give you the proof. Our fathers have removed the roof beams; but we have broken the walls" (*y. Yoma* 1.1 [38c]).

Jesus' prophecy is so stunning because it was occasioned by the disciple's admiration of the massive stones and large, impressive buildings. Such sturdy stonework and impressive architecture surely inspired a sense of permanence, not impending catastrophe. But contrary to all expectations, Jesus speaks of the temple's complete destruction, "not one stone . . . upon another that will not be thrown down." It is no wonder that the bewildered disciples call for further clarification.

Explanation

Jesus' surprising prediction of the complete and total destruction of the temple precincts marks an important turning point both in the evangelist's narrative and in the unfolding events in the life of Jesus. Gone now are hopes that the city will repent; gone are the hopes that the ruling priests will welcome the message of the kingdom and its messenger. The verbal sparring in the precincts is now at an end. The dire consequences are spelled out to the disciples in the balance of Mark 13 and in many places in Mark 14. Having rejected the one who came to the city and the temple "in the name of the Lord," the city and her temple authorities have sealed their fate.

Jesus' prediction becomes the hinge on which the Passion Narrative turns. In chaps. 11–12 Jesus challenges and criticizes the people and authorities of Jerusalem. But his message and person are rebuffed. His entry is ignored, his authority is challenged, his life is threatened. In chaps. 13–14 Jesus gives his final post–public ministry teaching to his disciples. By predicting the doom of the temple, Jesus makes clear to his disciples that he is fully prescient of what lies ahead, and by reporting this the evangelist makes Jesus' prior knowledge clear to his readers, as they live on the eve of the prophecy's fulfillment. Jesus' arrest will not take him by surprise; indeed, the very betrayal of Judas and denial of Peter will also be foretold. Now Jesus must disclose to his disciples what is in store for them and for an unbelieving Israel.

2. The Coming Woes   (13:3–13)

Bibliography

Barrett, C. K. *The Holy Spirit and the Gospel Tradition.* London: S. P. C. K., 1966. 130–32. **Baumeister, T.** *Die Anfänge der Theologie des Martyriums.* MBT 45. Münster: Aschendorff, 1980. 86–89, 101–7. **Beasley-Murray, G. R.** *Jesus and the Last Days: The Interpretation of the Olivet Discourse.* Peabody, MA: Hendrickson, 1993. 384–407. **Boismard, M.-É.** *L'Évangile de Marc.* 182–89. **Boring, M. E.** *The Continuing Voice of Jesus: Christian Prophecy and the Gospel Tradition.* Louisville: Westminster John Knox, 1991. 236–42. **Bosch, D.** *Die Heidenmission in der Zukunftsschau Jesu: Eine Untersuchung zur Eschatologie der synoptischen Evangelien.* ATANT 36. Zürich: Zwingli, 1959. 132–74. **Brandenburger, E.** *Markus 13 und die Apokalyptik.* FRLANT 134. Göttingen: Vandenhoeck & Ruprecht, 1984. 30–35, 47–49, 95–104, 147–61. **Collins, A. Y.** "The Eschatological Discourse of Mark 13." In *The Four Gospels 1992.* FS F. Neirynck, ed. F. Van Segbroeck et al. 3 vols. BETL 100. Leuven: Leuven UP, 1992. 1125–40. **Conzelmann, H.** "Geschichte und Eschaton nach Mc 13." *ZNW* 50 (1959) 210–21 (repr. in H. Conzelmann. *Theologie als Schriftauslegung: Aufsätze zum Neuen Testament.* BEvT 65. Munich: Kaiser, 1974. 62–73). **Daniélou, J.** "Apocalyptique juive et messianisme chrétien." *Quatre Fleuves* 2 (1974) 10–21. **Danker, F. W.** "Double-entendre in Mark XIII 9." *NovT* 10 (1968) 162–63. **Daube, D.** "The 'I am' of the Messianic Presence." In *The New Testament and Rabbinic Judaism.* London: Athlone, 1956. 325–29. **Dautzenberg, G.** "Das Wort von der weltweiten Verkündigung des Evangeliums (Mk 13,10) und seine Vorgeschichte." In *Christus bezeugen.* FS W. Trilling, ed. K. Kertelge et al. ETS 59. Leipzig: St. Benno, 1989; Freiburg: Herder, 1990. 150–65. ———. "Die Zeit des Evangeliums: Mk 1,1–15 und die Konzeption des Markusevangeliums." *BZ* 21 (1977) 219–34; 22 (1978) 76–91. **Donahue, J. R.** *Are You the Christ?* 212–22. **Dupont, J.** "Il n'en sera pas laissé pierre sur pierre (Mc 13,2; Lc 19,44)." *Bib* 52 (1971) 301–20. ———. "La persécution comme situation missionaire (Marc 13, 9–11)." In *Die Kirche des Anfangs.* FS H. Schürmann, ed. R. Schnackenburg et al. Leipzig: St. Benno, 1977; Freiburg: Herder, 1978. 97–114. ———. "La ruine du temple et la fin des temps dans le discours de Marc 13." In *Apocalypses et theologie de l'espérance*. Ed. L. Monloubou. LD 95. Paris: Cerf, 1977. 207–69. **Evans, C. A.** "Mishna and Messiah 'in Context': Some Comments on Jacob Neusner's Proposals." *JBL* 112 (1993) 267–89. ———. "Predictions of the Destruction of the Herodian Temple in the Pseudepigrapha, Qumran Scrolls, and Related Texts." *JSP* 10 (1992) 89–147. **Farrer, A. M.** "An Examination of Mark XIII.10." *JTS* n.s. 7 (1956) 75–79. **Fleddermann, H. T.** *Mark and Q*. 191–99. **Fuchs, A.** *Sprachliche Untersuchungen zu Matthäus und Lukas: Ein Beitrag zur Quellenkritik*. AnBib 49. Rome: Biblical Institute, 1971. 171–89. **Gaston, L.** *No Stone on Another: Studies in the Significance of the Fall of Jerusalem in the Synoptic Gospels*. NovTSup 23. Leiden: Brill, 1970. 8–64. **Geddert, T. J.** *Watchwords*. 199–221. **Gils, F.** *Jésus prophète d'après les évangiles synoptiques*. OBL 2. Louvain: Publications Universitaires, 1957. 115–17. **Graham, H. R.** "A Markan Theme: Endurance in Time of Persecution." *TBT* 23 (1985) 297–304. ———. "A Passion Prediction for Mark's Community: Mark 13:9–13." *BTB* 16 (1986) 18–22. **Grässer, E.** *Das Problem der Parusieverzögerung in den synoptischen Evangelien und in der Apostelgeschichte*. BZNW 22. Berlin: Töpelmann, 1957. 158–61. **Grelot, P.** "Michée 7,6 dans les évangiles et dans la littérature rabbinique." *Bib* 67 (1986) 363–77. ———. *Les paroles de Jésus Christ*. Introduction à la Bible: Édition nouvell. Le Nouveau Testament 7. Paris: Desclée, 1986. 42–44. **Haiduk, A.** "'Ego eimi' bei Jesus und seine Messianität." *ThViat* 6 (1963) 55–60. **Hallbäck, G.** "Der anonyme Plan: Analyse von Mk 13,5–37 im Hinblick auf die Relevanz der apokalyptischen Rede für die Problematik der Aussage." *LB* 49 (1981) 28–53. **Hare, D. R. A.** *The Theme of Jewish Persecution of Christians in the Gospel according to St. Matthew*. SNTSMS 6. Cambridge: Cambridge UP, 1967. **Harrisville, R. A.** "Jesus and the Family." *Int* 23 (1969) 425–38. **Hengel, M.** *Studies in the Gospel of Mark*. 21–28. **Howard, V. P.** *Das Ego Jesu in den synoptischen Evangelien: Untersuchungen zum Sprachgebrauch Jesu*. MTS 14. Marburg: Elwert, 1975. 116–23. **Iersel, B. M. F. van.** "Failed Followers in Mark: Mark 13:12 as a Key for the Identification of the Intended Readers." *CBQ* 58 (1996) 244–63. **Kato, Z.** *Völkermission im Markusevangelium*. 137–51. **Kilpatrick, G. D.** "The Gentile Mission in Mark and Mark xiii.9–11." In *Studies in the Gospels*. FS R. H. Lightfoot, ed. D. E. Nineham. Oxford: Blackwell, 1955. 145–58 (repr. in *The Principles and Practice of New Testament Textual Criticism: Collected Essays*. Ed. J. K. Elliott. BETL 96. Leuven: Peeters and Leuven UP, 1990. 284–98). ———. "Mark xiii 9–10." *JTS* n.s. 9 (1958) 81–86 (repr. in *The Principles and Practice of New Testament Textual Criticism: Collected Essays*. Ed. J. K. Elliott. BETL 96. Leuven: Peeters and Leuven UP, 1990. 299–304). **Kolenkow, A. B.** "Beyond Miracles, Suffering and Eschatology." In *Society of Biblical Literature 1973 Seminar Papers*. Ed. G. W. MacRae. 2 vols. SBLSP 12. Cambridge, MA: SBL, 1973. 2:155–202, esp. 172–83. **Kühschelm, R.** *Jüngerverfolgung und Geschick Jesu: Eine exegetisch-bibeltheologische Untersuchung der synoptischen Verfolgungsankündigungen Mk 13,9–13 par und Mt 23,29–36 par*. ÖBS 5. Klosterneuberg: Österreichisches Katholisches Bibelwerk, 1983. 163–84, 260–72. **Lambrecht, J.** *Die Redaktion der Markus-Apokalypse: Literarische Analyse und Strukturuntersuchung*. AnBib 28. Rome: Biblical Institute, 1967. 65–144. **Laufen, R.** *Die Doppelüberlieferungen der Logienquelle und des Markusevangeliums*. BBB 54. Königstein; Bonn: Hanstein, 1980. 363–65, 374–84. **Manson, W.** "The Ego Eimi of the Messianic Presence in the New Testament." In *Jesus and the Christian*. London: Clarke; Grand Rapids, MI: Eerdmans, 1967. 174–83. **Marshall, C. D.** *Faith as a Theme*. 144–51. **Martin, R. P.** *Mark: Evangelist and Theologian*. 222–24. **Mateos, J.** *Marcos 13: El grupo cristiano en la historia*. Lectura del Nuevo Testamento: Estudios críticos y exegéticos 3. Madrid: Cristiandad, 1987. 193–281. **Minette de Tillesse, G.** *Le secret messianique*. 405–9. **Mosley, A. W.** "Jesus' Audiences in the Gospels of St Mark and St Luke." *NTS* 10 (1963–64) 139–49. **Neirynck, F.** "Le discours anti-apocalyptique de Mc 13." *ETL* 45 (1969) 154–64 (repr. in F. Neirynck. *Evangelica*. BETL 60. Leuven: Leuven UP, 1982. 598–608). ———. "Marc 13: Examen critique de l'interpretation de R. Pesch." In *L'Apocalypse johannique et l'apocalyptique dans le Nouveau Testament*. Ed. J. Lambrecht. BETL 53. Leuven: Leuven UP, 1980. 369–401 (repr. in F. Neirynck. *Evangelica*. BETL 60. Leuven: Leuven UP, 1982. 565–97). **Pesch, R.** *Naherwartungen: Tradition und Redaktion in Mk. 13*. Düsseldorf: Patmos, 1968. 107–12, 118–

37. **Popkes, W.** *Christus traditus: Eine Untersuchung zum Begriff der Dahingabe im Neuen Testament.* ATANT 49. Zürich: Zwingli, 1967. 145–48. **Pudussery, P. S.** *Discipleship: A Call to Suffering and Glory: An Exegetico-Theological Study of Mk 8,27–9,1; 13,9–13 and 13,24–27.* Rome: Libreria "Alma Mater," 1987. 141–97. **Riddle, D. W.** "The Martyr Motif in the Gospel according to Mark." *JR* 4 (1924) 397–410. ———. "Die Verfolgungslogien in formgeschichtlicher und soziologischer Beleuchtung." *ZNW* 33 (1934) 271–89. **Robbins, V. K.** "*Dynameis* and *Semeia* in Mark." *BR* 18 (1973) 5–20. **Satake, A.** "Das Leiden der Jünger 'um meinetwillen.'" *ZNW* 67 (1976) 4–19. **Schmauch, W.** "Der Ölberg: Exegese zu einer Ortsangabe besonders bei Matthäus und Markus." *TLZ* 77 (1952) 391–96. **Schottroff, L.** "Frauen in der Nachfolge Jesu in neutestamentlicher Zeit." In *Frauen in der Bibel.* Vol. 2 of *Traditionen der Befreiung: Sozialgeschichtliche Bibelauslegung.* Ed. W. Schottroff and W. Stegemann. Munich: Kaiser, 1980. 91–133 (repr. in L. Schottroff. *Befreiungserfahrungen: Studien zur Sozialgeschichte des Neuen Testaments.* TB 82. Munich: Kaiser, 1990. 96–133; ET: "Women as Disciples of Jesus in New Testament Times." In *Let the Oppressed Go Free: Feminist Perspectives on the New Testament.* Louisville: Westminster John Knox, 1993). **Schroeder, H.-H.** *Eltern und Kinder in der Verkündigung Jesu: Eine hermeneutische und exegetische Untersuchung.* TF 53. Hamburg: Reich, 1972. 133–56. **Söding, T.** *Glaube bei Markus.* 201–4. **Strecker, G.** "Das Evangelium Jesu Christi." In *Jesus Christus in Historie und Theologie.* FS H. Conzelmann, ed. G. Strecker. Tübingen: Mohr-Siebeck, 1975. 503–48. ———. "Literarkritische Überlieferungen zum εὐαγγέλιον-Begriff im Markusevangelium." In *Neues Testament und Geschichte: Historisches Geschehen und Deutung im Neuen Testament.* FS O. Cullmann, ed. H. Baltensweiler and B. Reicke. Tübingen: Mohr-Siebeck; Zürich: Theologischer Verlag, 1972. 91–104 (repr. in G. Strecker. *Eschaton und Historie: Aufsätze.* Göttingen: Vandenhoeck & Ruprecht, 1979. 76–89, esp. 77–79, 85–88). **Such, W. A.** "The Significance of τὸ σημεῖον in Mark 13:4." *IBS* 13 (1991) 134–54. **Thompson, J. W.** "The Gentile Mission as an Eschatological Necessity." *ResQ* 14 (1971) 18–27. **Thompson, W. G.** "An Historical Perspective in the Gospel of Matthew." *JBL* 93 (1974) 243–62, esp. 250–56. **Verheyden, J.** "Persecution and Eschatology. Mk 13,9–13." In *The Four Gospels 1992.* FS F. Neirynck, ed. F. Van Segbroeck et al. 3 vols. BETL 100. Leuven: Leuven UP, 1992. 1141–59. **Vorster, W. S.** "Literary Reflections on Mark 13:5–37: A Narrated Speech of Jesus." *Neot* 21 (1987) 203–14. **Walter, N.** "Tempelzerstörung und synoptische Apokalypse." *ZNW* 57 (1966) 38–49. **Wenham, D.** *The Rediscovery of Jesus' Eschatological Discourse.* Gospel Perspectives 4. Sheffield: JSOT Press, 1984. 219–85, 294–304. **Westcott, B. F.,** and **Hort, F. J. A.** *Introduction.* 2:26. **Wrege, H.-Th.** *Die Gestalt des Evangeliums: Aufbau und Struktur der Synoptiker sowie der Apostelgeschichte.* BBET 11. Bern; Frankfurt am Main: Lang, 1978. 68–74. **Yates, J. E.** *The Spirit and the Kingdom.* London: S. P. C. K., 1963. 94–98.

Translation

[3] *And when he had sat down on the Mount of Olives, opposite the temple, Peter,[a] James, John, and Andrew were questioning[b] him in private,* [4] *"Tell us, when will these things be, and what will be the sign when all these things are about to be accomplished?"* [5] *And Jesus began to speak to them, "Watch out, lest someone mislead[c] you.* [6] *Many will come in my name, saying, 'I am he';[d] and they will deceive many.* [7] *Whenever you hear of wars and rumors of wars,[e] do not be alarmed;[f] it must come to pass, but the end is not yet.* [8] *For nation will be raised up against nation, and kingdom against kingdom. There will be earthquakes in various places. There will be famines.[g] These things are the beginning of birth pains.* [9] *But watch out for yourselves; they will deliver you up to councils, and in synagogues you will be beaten, and before governors and kings you will be made to stand[h] for my sake, to [give] testimony to them.* [10] *And to all the nations[i] it is necessary first for the gospel to be proclaimed.[i]* [11] *And when, delivering you up, they lead you*

[to trial],[j] *do not worry about what you should say.*[k] *But whatever is given you in that hour*[1] *speak; for you are not the ones who are speaking, but the Holy Spirit.* [12]*And brother will deliver brother to death, and a father his child; and children will rise up against parents*[m] *and will put them to death.*[n] [13]*And you will be hated by all on account of my name. But the one who endures to the end—this one*[o] *will be saved.*"

Notes

[a]Syr. MSS read *kêpā*ʾ, "Cephas."

[b]Gk. ἐπηρώτα, lit. "was questioning." The sg. form of the verb sometimes appears with a string of sg. subjects (e.g., Mark 1:36; John 2:2, 12; 1 Tim 1:20; LXX Lev 25:54; cf. Gundry, 759).

[c]Gk. πλανήσῃ, "mislead" or "lead astray." Some MSS read ἀπατήσῃ, "deceive" or "trick."

[d]Gk. ἐγώ εἰμι, lit. "I am"; "he" is implied. W and many later MSS read ἐγώ εἰμι ὁ χριστός, "I am the Messiah." This variant reflects Mark 13:21. A few late MSS expand the claims of the deceivers to read ἐγώ εἰμι καὶ ὁ καιρὸς ἤγγικεν, "I am he. The time has come!" (cf. Luke 21:8).

[e]Some late MSS read ἀκοὰς ἀναρχίας, "rumors of anarchy."

[f]D and a few later MSS read θορυβεῖσθε, "perturbed." Other late MSS read πτοηθῆτε, "agitated" (cf. Luke 21:9).

[g]A W Φ 33 and several later MSS add καὶ ταραχαί, "and riots." Σ and a few later MSS add καὶ λοιμοὶ καὶ ταραχαί, "and plagues and riots." Westcott and Hort (*Introduction* 2:26) suspect καὶ ταραχαί, "and riots," was added "for the sake of rhythm." Field (*Notes*, 37) agrees but thinks the words καὶ λοιμοί, "and plagues," originally followed, even if there is no MS evidence. He cites the parallel in Luke 21:11.

[h]33 and several later MSS read ἀχθήσεσθε, "you will be led" (cf. Matt 24:18).

[i]D reads πρῶτον δεῖ κηρυχθῆναι τὸ εὐαγγέλιον ἐν πᾶσι τοῖς ἔθνεσιν, "It is necessary first for the gospel to be proclaimed among all the nations."

[j]The words in brackets have been added to the text because the verb ἄγωσιν, "they lead," implies that Jesus' followers will be led *to trial*.

[k]A Φ and several later MSS add μηδὲ μελετᾶτε, "or what to practice."

[l]A few later MSS read ἡμέρᾳ, "day."

[m]A few later MSS add καὶ οἱ γονεῖς ἐπὶ τὰ τέκνα, "and parents against children."

[n]Gk. θανατώσουσιν αὐτούς. The translation "will put them to death" is preferred to "will kill them" (Cranfield, 401).

[o]Gk. οὗτος. Some MSS read οὗτως, "in this manner": "But the one who endures to the end will in this manner be saved."

Form/Structure/Setting

Mark 13:3–13 is made up of three components: (1) the setting and question of the disciples (vv 3–4), (2) a warning against deception (vv 4–8), and (3) a warning against persecution and various trials (vv 9–13). The disciples, identified as Peter, James, John, and Andrew, have asked Jesus about his startling prediction of the temple's destruction (in v 2). But Jesus does not directly answer their questions concerning "when will these things be" or "what will be the sign when all these things are about to be accomplished." Jesus instead warns of deception and persecution. However, the disciples' questions have been answered implicitly. When will these things be? What will be the signs? When the deceivers are saying, "I am he"; when the disciples hear of "wars and rumors of wars"; when the disciples have endured persecutions and the gospel has been proclaimed to all nations; and when families are divided on account of Jesus.

The destruction of the temple and the collapse of the priestly establishment will accompany a period of unprecedented spiritual and social decline. The chaos and persecution that is described in this discourse resembles at many points the Mishnah's depressing depiction of spiritual decline and social breakdown (cf. *m. Soṭah* 9:9–15) and is in fact somewhat typical of eschatological and apocalyptic scenarios. It was anticipated that redemption and restoration would be preceded by a period of steep moral decline and religious apostasy (cf. 2 Thess 2:1–12; Rev 6–18).

Comment

3 καὶ καθημένου αὐτοῦ εἰς τὸ ὄρος τῶν ἐλαιῶν κατέναντι τοῦ ἱεροῦ, "And when he had sat down on the Mount of Olives, opposite the temple." The location described here is a favorite of pilgrims, affording a commanding view of the Temple Mount across the Kidron Valley. Jesus' taking his seat (καθημένου αὐτοῦ) is reminiscent of his sitting down to deliver the Sermon on the Mount (cf. Matt 5:1). Elsewhere in Mark a crowd sits near Jesus (3:32), or Jesus sits in a boat and teaches the crowd (4:1). But here, as in Matt 5:1, the very hillside becomes "the Teacher's chair" (Swete, 297). Delivery of the eschatological discourse in full view of the temple precincts (κατέναντι τοῦ ἱεροῦ) lends poignancy to the scene and helps keep the image of the "wonderful stones" and "wonderful buildings" (v 1) in the readers' and auditors' mind's eye.

ἐπηρώτα αὐτὸν κατ' ἰδίαν Πέτρος καὶ Ἰάκωβος καὶ Ἰωάννης καὶ Ἀνδρέας, "Peter, James, John, and Andrew were questioning him in private." Many times in Mark (4:34; 6:31–32; 9:2, 28) Jesus provides his disciples with private instruction or simply privacy (κατ' ἰδίαν). Sometimes it is just the three leading disciples Peter, James, and John (as in the transfiguration). But here in v 3 it is the two sets of brothers—Peter and Andrew, James and John, who were the first disciples called (cf. 1:16–20). Ernst (370) wonders if Andrew was added so that the narrative might end where the ministry began; but this is hardly the final scene in the Markan narrative. Gnilka's suggestion (2:183) that the evangelist has introduced a fourth disciple because of the eschatological character of the discourse (as opposed to earthly teaching, where three disciples suffice) seems farfetched.

The pronouncement of judgment upon Jerusalem from the vantage point of the Mount of Olives has biblical (cf. Ezek 11:23; 43:2; Zech 14:3–4) and traditional precedents (cf. *T. Naph.* 5:1–2, where it is said that the patriarch Naphtali has seen the sun and moon stand still "on the Mount of Olives"). The setting thus carries with it ominous connotations.

4 εἰπὸν ἡμῖν πότε ταῦτα ἔσται καὶ τί τὸ σημεῖον ὅταν μέλλῃ ταῦτα συντελεῖσθαι πάντα, "Tell us, when will these things be, and what will be the sign when all these things are about to be accomplished?" These questions do not constitute a tautology. The first one asks when (πότε) the destruction of the temple precincts will take place. ταῦτα, "these things," implies the expectation, rightly so, that the destruction of the temple will be attended by other upheavals, for the temple's destruction cannot be an isolated event. There would have to be a war and an assault on the city, or a natural catastrophe. The second question inquires after τὸ σημεῖον, "the sign," that will provide a reliable indication of when μέλλῃ ταῦτα συντελεῖσθαι πάντα, "all these things are about to be accomplished." The request for a sign is thoroughly Jewish (cf. Paul's assertion in 1 Cor 1:22). Earlier in Mark, the Pharisees sought a sign from Jesus, and were refused (8:11–12). But the disciples here are not asking for a sign whereby the validity of Jesus' message might be confirmed; they wish to be forewarned. Later in the eschatological discourse (v 22) Jesus warns of the false messiahs and false prophets who will show signs and wonders.

The question that is attributed to the disciples is probably genuine, but it and the answer that follows have been edited and updated. Jesus' teaching about the end of the age, which is closely related to the fate of Jerusalem and her temple, seems to have been brought up to date during the turbulent and uncertain 50s and 60s. But these parallels are not so close as to require that Jesus' sayings be seen either as generated by these events or as fulfilled in them.

The disciples' specific question, τί τὸ σημεῖον [ἔσται], "what will be the sign?" reflects Jewish concern with signs (σημεῖον or אוֹת 'ôt) as evidence either of the truth of a prophet's utterance or as warning of impending events. These nuances are attested in the OT; for the former, see Exod 3:12: "this shall be the sign [אוֹת 'ôt; LXX: σημεῖον] for you, that I have sent you"; for the latter, see Isa 7:11: "Ask a sign of the LORD your God; let it be deep as Sheol or high as heaven." In *2 Baruch*, written a generation or so after the publication of Mark, the Lord tells Baruch, with respect to the approaching "end of days": "This then will be the sign" (*2 Bar.* 25:2 [preserved only in Syriac]). The disciples' question and Jesus' response to it follow the general pattern in 4 Ezra 4:52: "He answered me and said, 'Concerning the signs about which you ask me, I can tell you in part.'"

5 βλέπετε μή τις ὑμᾶς πλανήσῃ, "Watch out, lest someone mislead you." Earlier in Mark Jesus had said that the Sadducees were quite misled in their thinking about the resurrection (12:24, 27). In the next verse Jesus will predict that many will be misled. In John 7:12 some in the crowd think Jesus is misleading the nation (cf. John 7:47). On the use of πλανᾶν, "to mislead," elsewhere in reference to religious error, see 1 Cor 6:9; 15:33; Gal 6:7; 2 Tim 3:13; 1 John 1:8; 2:26; Rev 2:20; 12:9. On the OT background, see Deut 11:28; Ps 94(95):10; Wis 5:6; 17:1; 2 Macc 7:18. See examples in Josephus (*J.W.* 1.10.6 §209; *Ant.* 10.1.3 §19). For a parallel to μή τις ὑμᾶς πλανήσῃ, "lest someone mislead you," see *Apoc. El. (C)* 1:14: "Don't let those people lead you astray" (also see *Comment* on v 6).

The warning about being misled introduces some of the later, updated material. The warning hardly applies to the disciples themselves. After all, who would mislead them? Did Jesus think that a false prophet or false Messiah could arise and fool his own disciples, soon to be apostles? No, but false figures could and did deceive Christians and Jews in the decades leading to the great war with Rome. Josephus tells of many self-proclaimed prophets and would-be deliverers. His critical language parallels the critical language found in Mark 13 and parallels.

6 πολλοὶ ἐλεύσονται ἐπὶ τῷ ὀνόματί μου, "Many will come in my name." On the expectation of πολλοί, "many," see *Apoc. El. (C)* 1:13 ("deceivers . . . will multiply in the last times"; cf. 2 Tim 4:1–5). Coming in Jesus' name means coming in Jesus' authority. On the OT background of speaking or acting "in the name of the Lord [בְּשֵׁם־יהוה, běšēm YHWH]," see Deut 18:5, 7, 20, 22; for the expression "in the name of David," see 1 Sam 25:9. But those who will come in Jesus' name will also say ἐγώ εἰμι, καὶ πολλοὺς πλανήσουσιν, "'I am he'; and they will deceive many." The meaning of this claim is uncertain. The impostor may be claiming that Jesus sent him ("in my name"; Klostermann, 133) or that he is the Messiah (i.e., the name or title that truly and only belongs to Jesus; Lane, 457). But when the imposter says ἐγώ εἰμι, "I am he," he may be claiming to be Jesus himself (Pesch,

2:279; a view Haenchen, 437, regards as unthinkable) or the Messiah. (No allusion to the divine name is intended here.) The most probable interpretation is that the impostor claims to be the Messiah; that is, he will come in the Messiah's name, claiming to be "he," that is, the Messiah (so Haenchen, 437). Jesus' later warning in v 21, "behold, here is the Messiah," supports this interpretation (see Cranfield, 395; Beasley-Murray, *Jesus and the Last Days*, 391–94).

Josephus's catalogue of false kings (some of whom were probably messianic claimants) may also provide support for this interpretation. According to him, there were several men at the time of Herod's death in 4 B.C.E. and the great rebellion in 66–70 C.E. who "donned the diadem" and began acting like monarchs. Although it is impossible to prove, it is quite possible that some of these men regarded themselves as Israel's awaited Messiah and deliverer from the oppressive hand of the Romans. These men include Judas (of Sepphoris, Galilee), son of Hezekiah the "brigand-chief" (4 B.C.E.; *Ant.* 17.10.5 §§271–72; *J.W.* 2.4.1 §56), who plundered the royal arsenal and attacked other kingly aspirants; Simon of Perea (4 B.C.E.; *Ant.* 17.10.6 §§273–76; *J.W.* 2.4.2 §§57–59), a former royal servant and a man of imposing size and strength who assumed the "diadem" and plundered the royal palace and several estates of the wealthy; Athronges the shepherd of Judea (4–2 B.C.E.; *Ant.* 17.10.7 §§278–84; *J.W.* 2.4.3 §§60–65), a man of great stature and great strength who, "donning the diadem," assumed the title of "king"; Menahem son of Judas of Galilee (66 C.E.; *J.W.* 2.17.8–9 §§433–48), who rode into Jerusalem as a "veritable king" and murdered Ananias the high priest; Simon bar-Giora (68–70 C.E.; *J.W.* 4.9.3–8 §§503–44; 4.9.10 §§556–65; 4.9.11–12 §§573–84; 5.1.3–4 §§11–26; 5.6.1 §§248–54; 5.6.3 §§266–67; 5.7.3 §309; 5.13.1–2 §§527–40; 7.2.2 §§26–36; 7.5.6 §154), "regarded with reverence and awe," who wore a purple robe in a dramatic appearance before the Romans in the midst of the smoking ruins of the temple.

7 ὅταν δὲ ἀκούσητε πολέμους καὶ ἀκοὰς πολέμων, "Whenever you hear of wars and rumors of wars." The "wars and rumors [or sounds, or reports] of wars" remind us of the riots and battles that initiated the great war with Rome, as well as the political turbulence that overtook Rome itself in the aftermath of Nero's death (Hengel, *Studies in the Gospel of Mark*, 22; Ernst, 373–74). It is consistent with the eschatological perspective of Jer 51:46, "Let not your heart faint, and be not fearful at the report heard in the land, when a report comes in one year and afterward a report in another year, and violence is in the land, and ruler is against ruler," and Dan 11:44, "tidings from the east and the north shall alarm him, and he shall go forth with great fury to exterminate and utterly destroy many," as well as the author of *2 Baruch:* "slaughter . . . drawing of the sword" (*2 Bar.* 27:3, 5). There is an interesting parallel in later rabbinic tradition about "sounds and wars" heralding the age to come: "there will be rumors [קולות *qôlôt* = ἀκοαί] (of war) and . . . there will be wars [מלחמות *milḥāmôt* = πόλεμοι]" (*Pesiq. Rab Kah.* 5.9; cf. *m. Soṭah* 9:15; *Pesiq. Rab.* 15.14/15; *Song Rab.* 2:13 §4; Evans, *JBL* 112 [1992] 286; Pesch 2:280). Luke's use of the phrase πολέμους καὶ ἀκαταστασίας, "wars and insurrections" (21:9), is probably an attempt to draw closer the parallel between Jesus' prophecy and the Jewish insurrection against Rome.

μὴ θροεῖσθε· δεῖ γενέσθαι, ἀλλ᾽ οὔπω τὸ τέλος, "do not be alarmed; it must come to pass, but the end is not yet." Jesus assures his disciples that these terrible things will surely come to pass, but the end of the human era is not yet. The Markan evangelist very probably saw these words as directed to Christians during the Jewish war since they had been led to think that the war was a certain sign of the imminent return of Jesus. The idea that some things δεῖ γενέσθαι, "must come to pass," is drawn from apocalyptic (Lührmann, 219; Pesch, 2:279–80): "but there is a God in heaven who reveals mysteries, who has shown to King Nebuchadnezzar what must be [δεῖ γενέσθαι] in the last days. . . . You, O king, having lain in your bed, have seen all that must be [δεῖ γενέσθαι] in the last days, and the one who reveals mysteries has shown to you what must be [δεῖ γενέσθαι]" (LXX Dan 2:28–29). The same idea appears in the first passion prediction in Mark: "the 'son of man' must suffer many things" (8:31). Earlier in Mark δεῖ, "it must," appeared in reference to Elijah who "must" come (9:11); the word will appear again in the eschatological discourse in vv 10 and 14. τὸ τέλος, "the end," implies the goal toward which history is moving. For both Jesus and the Markan community, this end is the appearance of the "son of man" and the full establishment of the kingdom of God.

8 ἐγερθήσεται γὰρ ἔθνος ἐπ' ἔθνος καὶ βασιλεία ἐπὶ βασιλείαν, "For nation will be raised up against nation, and kingdom against kingdom." The expectation of global warfare and chaos is well entrenched in the prophetic and eschatological traditions. Many examples come to mind: "And I will stir up Egyptians against Egyptians, and they will fight, every man against his brother and every man against his neighbor, city against city, kingdom against kingdom" (Isa 19:2); "And they shall plan to make war against one another, city against city, place against place, people against people, and kingdom against kingdom" (4 Ezra 13:31); "and nation shall rise up to fight against nation, with swords in their hands" (4 Ezra 15:15; cf. *Sib. Or.* 3:636: "peoples will ravage peoples"); "king will lay hold of king and take away territory" (*Sib. Or.* 3:635). This detail roughly parallels the events that led up to and included the great Jewish revolt against the Roman Empire. However, there were no major wars prior to the Jewish revolt. One thinks of the minor war between Herod Antipas and his father-in-law Aretas the king of Nabatea (cf. Josephus, *Ant.* 18.5.1–3 §§109–25). Roman intervention saved Herod, whose army had been destroyed by the Nabateans. Also, there were ongoing border clashes and political intrigue with the Parthians in the northeastern part of the Roman Empire (e.g., in the rule of Tiberius [cf. Josephus, *Ant.* 18.4.4 §§96–100]; conflict between Parthians and Babylonians [cf. *Ant.* 18.9.1–7 §§310–70]; and Vardanes's war with Rome [cf. *Ant.* 20.3.4–20.4.2 §§69–91]). One must remember also the internal strife and near civil war through which Rome passed in the wake of the death of Nero. One emperor followed another in rapid succession in 68–69 C.E. At the beginning of the Jewish revolt villages and cities attacked one another as people took sides prior to the war between Israel and Rome. Toward the end of the Jewish war some German tribes rebelled, imagining that "every quarter of the world beneath [the Roman Empire's] sway was seething and quivering with excitement" (Josephus, *J.W.* 7.4.2 §79; 7.4.3 §§89–95). Even if Jesus' words only vaguely approximated the events between Easter and the Jewish revolt, from Mark's perspective these village skirmishes, as well as the full-scale war itself, may have been understood as the beginnings of the events that Jesus foretold.

ἔσονται σεισμοὶ κατὰ τόπους, "There will be earthquakes in various places." In the OT, earthquakes are sometimes associated with God's coming in judgment (e.g., Mic 1:3–4; Hab 3:6, 10). According to *2 Baruch*, the last days will be divided up into twelve parts: "in the first part (will be) the beginning of commotions . . . in the sixth part (will be) earthquakes and terrors" (*2 Bar.* 27:2, 7· ʿf. 4 Ezra 6:13–15; 9:3; *T. Mos.* 10:4). Again, events in the decades immediately preceding the Jewish revolt only roughly parallel this part of Jesus' prophecy. There were earthquakes at Laodicea in 61 C.E. and at Pompeii in 62 C.E. But the eruption of Mount Vesuvius, which buried Pompeii and Herculaneum (on the west side of the Italian peninsula near the Bay of Naples), did not occur until 79 C.E., some years after the publication of the Gospel of Mark. Corinth and Cyprus also suffered earthquakes in the 70s C.E.

Anticipation of earthquakes was part of apocalyptic, with roots in the Hebrew Scripture itself: "And the valley of my mountains shall be stopped up, for the valley of the mountains shall touch the side of it; and you shall flee as you fled from the earthquake [LXX: σεισμός] in the days of Uzziah king of Judah. Then the LORD your God will come, and all the holy ones with him" (Zech 14:5). Given Jesus' interest in the prophecy of Zechariah, it is possible that this very text inspired this part of his prophecy. But was it fulfilled in any sense in the years leading up to the Jewish revolt? For other oracles that speak of earthquakes and noise, see Isa 29:6, "you will be visited by the LORD of hosts with thunder and with earthquake [LXX: σεισμός] and great noise"; Jer 10:22, "Hark, a rumor! Behold, it comes! —a great commotion [LXX: σεισμός] out of the north country to make the cities of Judah a desolation" (cf. Jer 23:19; 29:3). Eschatological expections in later Jewish texts anticipated earthquakes (e.g., *m. Ber.* 9:2; *Sib. Or.* 1:187; 3:405, 449, 452, 459). Gentiles also had their own oracles of coming earthquakes (e.g., Ovid, *Metam.* 15.798; Livy 32.8.3; Appian, *Civil Wars* 1.9.83).

ἔσονται λιμοί, "There will be famines." The expectation and fear of famine was yet another stock component in eschatology and apocalyptic. Once again we find a close parallel in *2 Baruch:* "In the fifth part (will be) famine and the withholding of rain" (*2 Bar.* 27:6). The threat of famine is heard in prophetic oracles of Israel's classical prophets: "Therefore thus says the LORD of hosts: 'Behold, I will punish them; the young men shall die by the sword; their sons and their daughters shall die by famine'" (Jer 11:22); "And the people to whom they prophesy shall be cast out in the streets of Jerusalem, victims of famine and sword, with none to bury them" (Jer 14:16; cf. Jer 18:21; 24:10; 32:24; Ezek 5:16–17; Amos 4:6–9; Bar 2:25; *Pss. Sol.* 17:18–19). Anticipation of famine in the end times appears in the rabbinic literature also (e.g., *b. Ber.* 55a; *Pesiq. Rab Kah.* 5.9; *Gen. Rab.* 25.3 [on Gen 5:29]; 40.3 [on Gen 12:10]; 64.2 [on Gen 26:1]; *Ruth Rab.* 1.4 [on Ruth 1:1]). Judea was struck by famine in ca. 46 C.E. (cf. Josephus, *Ant.* 20.2.5 §§51–53; Acts 11:27–30). Toward the end of Nero's rule there was unrest in Rome over food shortages (Hengel, *Studies in the Gospel of Mark,* 23).

ἀρχὴ ὠδίνων ταῦτα, "These things are the beginning of birth pains." In biblical literature "birth pains" (or "birth pangs") are frequently taken in a figurative sense, meaning great fear and trembling (cf. Exod 15:14; Deut 2:25; Isa 13:8; 21:3; 26:17; Jer 4:31; 6:24; Hos 13:13; Mic 4:9; Nah 2:11 [LXX 10]). The idea also appears in Paul (cf. 1 Thess 5:3). All of ταῦτα, "these things"—the men who claim to be the Messiah (v 6), the wars and the rumors of war (v 7), the strife between nations (v 8a), and the earthquakes and famines (v 8b)—are but ἀρχὴ ὠδίνων, "the beginning of birth pains." Much more—and much worse—is still to come. However, the image of birth pains may hint at the new social order that is about to emerge.

Rabbinic literature sometimes speaks of the "birth pain of the Messiah": "He who observes (the practice of) three meals on the Sabbath is saved from three evils: the birth pain of the Messiah [מחבלו של משיח, *mēheblô šel māšîaḥ*], the retribution of Gehenna, and the wars of Gog and Magog" (*Mek.* on Exod 16:28–36 [*Wayyassaʿ* §6]; and *b. Šabb.* 118a; cf. *b. Sanh.* 98b: "What must a man do to be spared the birth pain of the Messiah?"). The rabbinic idea of the birth pain of the Messiah is not identical to Jesus' reference to birth pains here in v 8 (as emphasized by Gundry, 763). Nevertheless, the association of the Messiah's arrival with the judgment of Gehenna and the final wars of Gog and Magog, stock components in the final eschatological scenario, is surely related in some way to Jesus' prophecy.

9 βλέπετε δὲ ὑμεῖς ἑαυτούς· παραδώσουσιν ὑμᾶς εἰς συνέδρια, "But watch out for yourselves; they will deliver you up to councils." When συνέδριον, "council," is sometimes translated "Sanhedrin," it is usually in reference to the Jewish Sanhedrin. In the plural (συνέδρια) it refers to councils in general, whether Jewish or Gentile. Jesus' disciples make appearances before the Jewish Sanhedrin (Acts 4:5–22; 5:27–41; 6:12; 22:30; 23:1; 24:20; Josephus, *Ant.* 20.9.1 §200 [in reference to James, the brother of Jesus]; *Life* 368). Josephus tells us that when Rome took control of Jerusalem in 63 B.C.E., Gabinius "set up five councils [συνέδρια], and divided the nation into as many districts" (*Ant.* 14.5.4 §91). For further examples of συνέδριον in reference to Gentile councils, see Josephus, *Ant.* 17.11.1–4 §§299–317, where Augustus convenes "a council [συνέδριον] of his own friends and the leading Romans in the temple of Apollo" to consider the claims of Archelaus and his brothers (cf. *Ant.* 20.3.2 §61; and MM, 604). Many of Mark's readers would think of the Neronian persecutions that Christians only recently had experienced (Pesch, 2:288).

καὶ εἰς συναγωγὰς δαρήσεσθε, "and in synagogues you will be beaten." The disciples will be delivered up to councils, and in synagogues they will be beaten. For support of this sense, see Cranfield, 397. Taylor (506) rightly notes that the preposition "εἰς is freely used for ἐν in the Koine." However, some commentators and translations recommend different punctuation: e.g., the disciples will be delivered up, and in councils and in synagogues, they will be beaten (see Pesch, 2.284). Gundry (765), however, links "and in synagogues" with the previous phrase, "they will deliver you up to councils." The advantage to this interpretation is that the preposition εἰς both times means "to": "they will deliver you up to councils and to synagogues." It is not easy to decide between these competing options. Syntax aside, the picture is clear enough: the disciples may expect to be delivered up to councils and synagogues, and in councils and synagogues they will be beaten.

In some of the stories in the book of Acts the disciples are beaten (Acts 5:40; 16:19–23, 37), even stoned (Acts 7:58; 14:19). Jesus has in effect warned his disciples that they will be treated as heretics and as disturbers of the Jewish community. Because of these accusations they may anticipate discipline.

καὶ ἐπὶ ἡγεμόνων καὶ βασιλέων σταθήσεσθε, "and before governors and kings you will be made to stand." There is little information indicating that the disciples of Jesus stood before governors and kings. However, Paul stood before the Roman governors Felix and Festus (in Acts 24:10–27; 25:1–12; 26:24–32) and before king Agrippa (in Acts 25:23–26:32). Jesus' prophecy may have been inspired in part by the fate of his mentor John the Baptist, who was brought before Herod Antipas (6:20). In the NT, ἡγεμών, "governor," is normally used in reference to the Roman governor (either a prefect, as Pilate was, or a procurator, as Fadus, Felix, and Festus were); see 1 Pet 2:13–14. Jesus' followers "will be made to stand" (σταθήσεσθε) before officials (see Acts 24:20; 25:10; 1 Pet 4:16).

ἕνεκεν ἐμοῦ εἰς μαρτύριον αὐτοῖς, "for my sake, to [give] testimony to them." Even the idea of going forth to give testimony seems to be part of the eschatological tradition, as seen in 2 Bar. 13:3: "you will surely be preserved until the end of times to be for a testimony." As in Mark 8:35 (see Comment there), the appearance of ἕνεκεν ἐμοῦ, "for my sake," probably represents a later, post-Easter christological gloss (though for arguments for its authenticity, see Gundry, 766). The μαρτύριον, "testimony" or "witness," is none other than τὸ εὐαγγέλιον, "the gospel," of the kingdom mentioned in the next verse. This material reflects the life of the early church in the years leading up to the Jewish revolt (Haenchen, 441). However, Lohmeyer (274) goes too far in describing this material as a collection of martyr sayings derived from several sources. In Matthew, most of this verse appears in the Missionary Discourse (cf. Matt 10:17–18).

10 καὶ εἰς πάντα τὰ ἔθνη πρῶτον δεῖ κηρυχθῆναι τὸ εὐαγγέλιον, "And to all the nations it is necessary first for the gospel to be proclaimed." Some commentators (e.g., Kilpatrick, "Gentile Mission") connect the first part of this verse to v 9: "to give testimony to them and to all the nations." V 10 would then read "It is necessary first for the gospel to be proclaimed." But few have followed this arrangement (see criticism in Gundry, 768). V 10 in any event is probably an editorial insertion (Taylor, 507; Cranfield, 399–400; Pesch, 2:284; see discussion in Beasley-Murray, Jesus and the Last Days, 402–3).

Jesus says that the gospel must first be proclaimed to all the nations. To what does πρῶτον, "first," refer? This chronological reference takes the reader back to v 7: "but the end is not yet." That is, before the end can come the gospel must first be proclaimed to all the nations (cf. v 8: "the beginnings of birth pains"; v 13: "the one who endures to the end"). πάντα τὰ ἔθνη, "all the nations," may be hyperbolic and probably reflects a somewhat limited geographical perspective: the Roman Empire and the peoples just beyond its borders. This expectation, therefore, does not stand in tension with Jesus' expectation that all of these things will be accomplished in one generation (v 30). Nor is this expectation inauthentic to the dominical tradition. Jesus' interest in Gentiles coming to faith is strongly hinted at in his words uttered in the demonstration in the temple (11:17, quoting part of Isa 56:7). Moreover, interest in Gentile outreach is rooted in the OT itself (cf. Isa 42:6; 49:6, 12; 52:10; 57:1–8; 60:6; Ps 96) and is reflected in intertestamental writings (cf. Pss. Sol. 8:17, 43; 11:1).

τὸ εὐαγγέλιον, "the gospel," is shorthand for the gospel of the kingdom of God (cf. 1:14–15). The gloss in v 9 ("for my sake") redirects the emphasis to the proclamation of Jesus himself, his resurrection, and his promise of return. The good news of the kingdom is the joyous proclamation that the kingdom of Satan is coming to an end. Satan is now bound (3:27); liberation is now possible. The negative side of the good news is the coming judgment of God. Hence repentance is required; hence the gospel is not always welcome, especially to those who have no desire for the human situation to change. The disciples may therefore expect serious opposition.

Lohmeyer's suggestion (272 and n. 4) that κηρυχθῆναι, "to be proclaimed," means a proclamation from heaven by a divine voice (as in Rev 14:6–7) is implausible and does not conform to the usage of κηρύσσειν, "to proclaim," elsewhere in Mark (1:4, 7, in reference to John's preaching; 1:14, 38–39, in reference to Jesus' preaching; 3:14; 6:12, in reference to the disciples' preaching; 14:9, in reference to the general mission of the church).

11 καὶ ὅταν ἄγωσιν ὑμᾶς παραδιδόντες, μὴ προμεριμνᾶτε τί λαλήσητε, "And when, delivering you up, they lead you [to trial], do not worry about what you should say." Jesus' advice picks up where v 9 left off: "they will deliver you up to councils . . . and before governors and kings you will be made to stand . . . to [give] testimony to them." When the disciples are brought before the councils and are made to stand before governors and kings, they are not to worry about what to say. These unlettered and academically untrained men (cf. Acts 4:13) need such assurance.

ἀλλ᾽ ὃ ἐὰν δοθῇ ὑμῖν ἐν ἐκείνῃ τῇ ὥρᾳ τοῦτο λαλεῖτε, "But whatever is given you in that hour speak." The disciples need not worry, because they are only to speak whatever is given to them ἐν ἐκείνῃ τῇ ὥρᾳ, "in that hour," that is, at the time they are brought to trial or are made to stand before the authorities. Jesus' assurance may have recalled God's promise to Moses to enable him to speak before Pharaoh (cf. Exod 4:10–17; esp. v 12: "Go, and I will be with your mouth and teach you what you shall speak [LXX: ὃ μέλλεις λαλῆσαι]"; also see Jer 1:9).

οὐ γάρ ἐστε ὑμεῖς οἱ λαλοῦντες ἀλλὰ τὸ πνεῦμα τὸ ἅγιον, "for you are not the ones who are speaking, but the Holy Spirit." The disciples will be given the words that the Holy Spirit of God will speak (which refers to their defense, not to the proclamation of the gospel; so Lane, 463). The speaking in tongues described in Acts 2 may offer an analogy, where clearly it is the Spirit that gives the disciples utterance. Then in Acts 4 and 5 the disciples are brought before Jewish authorities in Jerusalem, where now they must defend themselves. Caiaphas and other ruling priests are unable to reply to Peter and the apostles, even though the latter are recognized as "uneducated, common men" (Acts 4:13–14). For examples of being filled with the Spirit and then speaking, see Acts 2:4; 4:8, 31; 13:9. The belief that God will assist the righteous in proclaiming truth is attested in *Ahiqar* 115: "If he is beloved of the gods, they will give him something worthwhile to say." Although this work is ancient (and its pagan character is in evidence in the proverb just cited), it was in circulation in the first century C.E. and was popular in Jewish circles. Ernst (377) is right to suspect that lying behind the assurances in v 11 is a Jewish martyr ideology. Once again much of this verse appears in Matthew's Missionary Discourse (cf. Matt 10:20).

12 καὶ παραδώσει ἀδελφὸς ἀδελφὸν εἰς θάνατον καὶ πατὴρ τέκνον, καὶ ἐπαναστήσονται τέκνα ἐπὶ γονεῖς καὶ θανατώσουσιν αὐτούς, "And brother will deliver brother to death, and a father his child; and children will rise up against parents, and will put them to death." The opposition that the apostles will face will be more than merely political and social; they, and those who respond in faith and obedience to the gospel, will face opposition from family. The Matthean evangelist transfers this saying to his Missionary Discourse (cf. Matt 10:21), perhaps under the influence of Q: "For I have come to set a man against his father, and a daughter against her mother, and a daughter-in-law against her mother-in-law" (Matt 10:35; cf. Luke 12:52–53; *Gos. Thom.* §16b). Jesus' words allude to Mic 7:6, "for the son treats the father with contempt, the daughter rises up against her mother, the daughter-in-law against her mother-in-law; a man's enemies are the men of his own house," with perhaps influence from Isa 19:2, "and they will fight, every man against his brother and every man against his neighbor, city against city, kingdom against kingdom."

The tradition of the divided family became a fixture in eschatological expectation. According to *1 Enoch* 100:1–2, "In those days, the father will be beaten together with his sons, in one place; and brothers shall fall together with their friends, in death . . . for a man shall not be able to withhold his hands from his sons nor from (his) sons' sons in order to kill them. Nor is it possible for the sinner to withhold his hands from his honored brother. From dawn until the sun sets, they slay each other." Other old tradition includes *Jub.* 23:19, "some of these will strive with others, youths with old men and old men with youths, the poor with the rich," and 4 Ezra 6:24, "and friends shall make war on friends like enemies" (cf. 4 Ezra 5:9). The parallel in *3 Bar.* 4:17, "Brother does not have mercy on brother, nor father on son, nor children on parents," is probably based on the Gospels themselves. Josephus may also allude to this tradition when he says that the ancient prophets foretold that desolation was at hand when "one should begin to slaughter his own countrymen" (*J.W.* 6.2.1 §109). Elsewhere, money is said to be the cause of family strife: "children become the enemies of their parents, and brothers (the enemies) of their kinsmen" (Ps.-Phoc. 47). But religion is the real dividing point. On account of Aseneth's new faith in the God of the Jews, her parents come to hate her (*Jos. Asen.* 11:3–5). In the Mishnah we find an interesting passage that speaks of the "footsteps of the Messiah" (i.e., when the Messiah comes; cf. *Tg. Ps.* 89:52; *Song Rab.* 2:13 §4), where Mic 7:6 is quoted: "With the footsteps of the Messiah presumption shall increase . . . the empire shall fall into heresy . . . the council-chamber shall be given to fornication. Galilee shall be laid waste . . . the wisdom of the scribes shall become insipid . . . children shall shame the elders, and the elders shall rise up before the children, 'for the son dishonors the father, the daughter rises up against her mother'" (*m. Soṭah* 9:15). Hengel (*Studies in the Gospel of Mark*, 23–24) reminds us of the cruel tortures Christians experienced at the hands of Nero and how family members were coerced into betraying one another (cf. Tacitus, *Ann.* 15.44.4: "they first arrested those who openly confessed [that they were Christians] and then on their evidence an enormous crowd . . . was condemned").

13 καὶ ἔσεσθε μισούμενοι ὑπὸ πάντων διὰ τὸ ὄνομά μου, "And you will be hated by all on account of my name." So controversial is the gospel that Jesus' disciples may expect to be μισούμενοι ὑπὸ πάντων, "hated by all." This πάντων, "all," refers to every segment of society: authorities, citizens, and even members of one's own family. διὰ τὸ ὄνομά μου, "on account of my name," recalls the earlier warnings about those who will come in Jesus' name and will claim that they are he (v 6), that is, the Messiah. The gospel of the true Messiah will cause division, strife, and hatred (cf. Matt 10:34: "I have not come to bring peace, but a sword").

Observing that the wording, "and you will be hated by all on account of my name," is identical in all three Synoptics (though with textual uncertainties in Matt 24:9, where τῶν ἐθνῶν, "nations," is read by some MSS, i.e., "hated by all nations"), Swete (303) surmises that the saying was well known in the early community and had become a commonplace in Greek-speaking Christianity. Although the saying has become formulaic and probably has moved somewhat away from its original form, there is no compelling reason to deny its essence to Jesus.

ὁ δὲ ὑπομείνας εἰς τέλος οὗτος σωθήσεται, "But the one who endures to the end—this one will be saved." εἰς τέλος, "to the end," here is not the eschatological end (as in v 7: τὸ τέλος, "the end"; *pace* Ernst, 377–78), but has the adverbial meaning "finally" or "completely" (Swete 303–4; Taylor, 510; Cranfield, 401, who cites John 13:1; 1 Thess 2:16; 2 Chr 31:1). Lohmeyer (274) thinks that τέλος, "end," refers to both aspects. In any case, the point has to do with enduring and not quitting or abandoning the faith. A similar idea is expressed in 4 Ezra 6:25: "whoever remains after all that I have foretold to you shall be saved and shall see my salvation and the end of my world." σωθήσεται, "will be saved," in this instance refers to eschatological salvation (as in 10:26) and not, for example, to escaping the disaster that overtook the Jewish people in 66–74 C.E.

Gnilka (2:192), whose view falls between the two positions above, thinks that in the original source the saying referred to one's death (similarly in Pesch, 2:287) but that in Mark it means the final deliverance. He ascribes vv 11–13, which he calls a collection of persecution texts, to a Christian prophet, not to Jesus. But are there really compelling reasons to attribute this material, however edited it may be, to a Christian prophet rather than to Jesus? If Jesus predicted doom for Jerusalem and her temple, surely he had predictions and warnings for his disciples.

Explanation

Shaken by the prediction of the temple's destruction (v 2), the disciples privately inquire of Jesus "when will these things be, and what will be the sign when all these things are about to be accomplished?" (v 4). Jesus answers their questions with a staggering string of predictions and warnings. He begins with a warning of deceivers who will claim his messianic authority. Following the appearance of these impostors will be wars and rumors of war. But Jesus' disciples are not to be unduly alarmed; these must happen, but the end time is yet to come. This is because there are many more events that must take place: nations and kingdoms at war, earthquakes, and famines are among the "beginning of birth pains." These birth pains signify the crumbling of the old order as it gives way to the kingdom of God, which will finally manifest itself in its fullness.

As the disciples await the unfolding of these events, they must look to themselves and be ready. For they will be delivered up to councils; in synagogues, which for Jews should be places of refuge and community, they will be beaten. Indeed, they will be brought before governors and kings. But they need not worry about what to say; they need only speak what is given to them at that time, for it will be God's Holy Spirit that will be speaking through them. Even more disheartening than political opposition and persecution will be family wrath and betrayal. Proclamation of the gospel will not make the apostles popular; on the contrary, they will be hated by all on account of the one who has sent them.

Although not a blueprint for the Christian mission, the first part of the eschatological discourse has over the centuries inspired many Christian missionaries and sustained them through difficult times in places where the gospel has faced vigorous, sometimes even violent, resistance. What is reassuring in all of this is the knowledge that no matter how severe the persecution, no matter how frightening world events, the believer may take comfort in knowing that God's plan is working itself out according to his will and that his Son Jesus has disclosed much of it to his followers. For him or her who is instructed in the teaching of Jesus there should be no surprises as the present age comes to a close.

3. The Great Tribulation (13:14–23)

Bibliography

Bach, R. *Die Aufforderung zur Flucht und zum Kampf im alttestamentlichen Prophetenspruch.* WMANT 9. Neukirchen-Vluyn: Neukirchener, 1962. 15–50. **Bacht, H.** "Wahres und falsches Prophetentum." *Bib* 32 (1951) 237–62. **Beasley-Murray, G. R.** *Jesus and the Last Days: The Interpretation of the Olivet Discourse.* Peabody: Hendrickson, 1993. 407–22. **Best, E.** "The Gospel of Mark: Who Was the Reader?" *IBS* 11 (1989) 124–32. **Boring, M. E.** *The Continuing Voice of Jesus: Christian Prophecy and the Gospel Tradition.* Louisville: Westminster John Knox, 1991. 236–42. **Brandenburger, E.** *Markus 13 und die Apokalyptik.* FRLANT 134. Göttingen: Vandenhoeck & Ruprecht, 1984. 49–54, 95–104, 147–61. **Clements, R. E.** "Apocalyptic, Literacy, and the Canonical Tradition." In *Eschatology and the New Testament.* FS G. R. Beasley-Murray, ed. W. H. Gloer. Peabody: Hendrickson, 1988. 15–27. **Daube, D.** "The Abomination of Desolation." In *The New Testament and Rabbinic Judaism.* London: Athlone, 1956. 418–37. **Daumoser, I.** *Berufung und Erwählung bei den Synoptikern: Ein Beitrag zur biblischen Theologie des Neuen Testaments.* Meisenheim: Hain; Stuttgart: Katholisches Bibelwerk, 1954. 215–34. **Dennison, W. D.** "Miracles as 'Signs.'" *BTB* 6 (1976) 190–202. **Dexinger, F.** "Ein 'Messianisches Szenarium' als Gemeingut des Judentums in nachherodianischer Zeit." *Kairos* 17 (1975) 249–78. **Dodd, C. H.** "The Fall of Jerusalem and the 'Abomination of Desolation.'" *JRS* 37 (1947) 47–54 (repr. in C. H. Dodd. *More New Testament Studies.* Manchester: Manchester UP; Grand Rapids, MI: Eerdmans, 1968. 69–83). **Elliott-Binns, L. E.** *Galilean Christianity.* SBT 16. London: SCM Press; Naperville, IL: Allenson, 1956. **Evans, C. A.** "Predictions of the Destruction of the Herodian Temple in the Pseudepigrapha, Qumran Scrolls, and Related Texts." *JSP* 10 (1992) 89–147, esp. 110–14. **Farrer, A. M.** *A Study in St. Mark.* Westminster: Dacre, 1951; New York: Oxford UP, 1952. 360–66. **Fee, G. D.** "A Text-Critical Look at the Synoptic Problem." *NovT* 22 (1980) 12–28, esp. 17–23. **Fleddermann, H. T.** *Mark and Q.* 199–201. **Flusser, D.** "Prophetische Aussagen Jesu über Jerusalem." In *Jesus—Qumran—Urchristentum.* Vol. 2 of *Entdeckungen im Neuen Testament.* Neukirchen-Vluyn: Neukirchener Verlag, 1999. 152–78. **Focant, C.** "La chute de Jérusalem et la datation des évangiles." *RTL* 19 (1988) 17–37. **Ford, D.** *The Abomination of Desolation in Biblical Eschatology.* Washington, DC: University Press of America, 1979. **France, R. T.** *Jesus and the Old Testament.* 72–73, 89–90. **Gaston, L.** *No Stone on Another: Studies in the Significance of the Fall of Jerusalem in the Synoptic Gospels.* NovTSup 23. Leiden: Brill, 1970. 8–64. **Geddert, T. J.** *Watchwords.* 206–15. **Gunther, J. J.** "The Fate of the Jerusalem Church: The Flight to Pella." *TZ* 29 (1973) 81–84. **Guy, H. A.** "Mark xiii.14: ὁ ἀναγινώσκων νοείτω." *ExpTim* 65 (1953–54) 30. **Hallbäck, G.** "Der anonyme Plan: Analyse von Mk 13,5–37 im Hinblick auf die Relevanz der apokalyptischen Rede für die Problematik der Aussage." *LB* 49 (1981) 28–53. **Hengel, M.** *Studies in the Gospel of Mark.* 16–20. **Hiers, R. H.** "Why Will They Not Say, 'Lo, here!' or, 'There!'?" *JAAR* 35 (1967) 379–84. **Jenks, G. C.** *The Origins and Early Development of the Antichrist Myth.* BZNW 59. Berlin: de Guyter, 1990. Esp. 199–207. **Jonge, M. de.** "The Earliest Christian Use of *Christos:* Some Suggestions." *NTS* 32 (1986) 321–43, esp. 324–29. **Kato, Z.** *Völkermission im Markusevangelium.* 137–51. **Kertelge, K.** *Wunder Jesu im Markusevangelium.* 27–29. **Kister, M.,** and **Qimron, E.** "Observations on 4QSecond Ezekiel (4Q385 2–3)." *RevQ* 15 (1992) 595–602. **Koester, C.** "The

Origin and Significance of the Flight to Pella Tradition." *CBQ* 51 (1989) 90–106. **Kolenkow, A. B.** "Beyond Miracles, Suffering and Eschatology." In *Society of Biblical Literature 1973 Seminar Papers.* Ed. G. W. MacRae. 2 vols. SBLSP 12. Cambridge: SBL, 1973. 2:155–202, esp. 172–83. **Lambrecht, J.** *Die Redaktion des Markus-Apokalypse: Literarische Analyse und Strukturuntersuchung.* AnBib 28. Rome: Biblical Institute, 1967. 114–73. **Laufen, R.** *Die Doppelüberlieferungen der Logienquelle und des Markusevangeliums.* BBB 54. Königstein; Bonn: Hanstein, 1980. 363–65, 374–84. **Lüdemann, G.** "The Successors of Pre-70 Jerusalem Christianity: A Critical Evaluation of the Pella-Tradition." In *The Shaping of Christianity in the Second and Third Centuries.* Vol. 1 of *Jewish and Christian Self-Definition.* Ed. E. P. Sanders. Philadelphia: Fortress, 1990. 161–73, 245–54. **Manson, T. W.** *Sayings.* 329–31. **Marshall, C. D.** *Faith as a Theme.* 144–51. **Martin, R. P.** *Mark: Evangelist and Theologian.* 172–74. **Mateos, J.** *Marcos 13: El grupo cristiano en la historia.* Lectura del Nuevo Testamento: Estudios críticos y exegéticos 3. Madrid: Cristiandad, 1987. 283–372. **McCasland, S. V.** "Signs and Wonders." *JBL* 76 (1957) 149–52. **Michel, O.** "Spätjüdisches Prophetentum." In *Neutestamentliche Studien.* FS R. Bultmann, ed. W. Eltester. BZNW 21. Berlin: Töpelmann, 1954. 60–66. **Munck, J.** "Jewish Christianity in the Post-Apostolic Times." *NTS* 6 (1959–60) 103–16. **Neirynck, F.** "Marc 13: Examen critique de l'interprétation de R. Pesch." In *L'Apocalypse johannique et l'apocalyptique dans le Nouveau Testament.* Ed. J. Lambrecht. BETL 53. Gembloux: Duculot; Leuven: Leuven UP, 1980. 369–401, esp. 370–75, 381–90 (repr. in F. Neirynck. *Evangelica.* BETL 60. Leuven: Peeters and Leuven UP, 1982. 565–97, esp. 566–71, 577–86). ———. "Response to the Multiple State Hypothesis: The Eschatological Discourse." In *The Interrelations of the Gospels: A Symposium Led by M.-É. Boismard, W. R. Farmer, and F. Neirynck, Jerusalem 1984.* Ed. D. L. Dungan. BETL 95. Leuven: Peeters and Leuven UP, 1990. 108–24, esp. 114–16 (repr. in F. Neirynck. *Evangelica II.* BETL 99. Leuven: Peeters and Leuven UP, 1991. 493–509, esp. 499–501). **Pedersen, S.** "Zum Problem der vaticinia ex eventu (Eine Analyse von Mt. 21,33–46 par.; 22,1–10 par.)." *ST* 19 (1965) 167–88. **Pesch, R.** *Naherwartungen: Tradition und Redaktion in Mk 13.* KBANT. Düsseldorf: Patmos, 1968. 112–17, 154–57. **Reicke, B.** "Synoptic Prophecies on the Destruction of Jerusalem." In *Studies in New Testament and Early Christian Literature.* FS A. P. Wikgren, ed. D. E. Aune. NovTSup 33. Leiden: Brill, 1972. 121–34. **Reiling, J.** "The Use of ΨΕΥΔΟΠΡΟΦΗΤΗΣ in the Septuagint, Philo and Josephus." *NovT* 13 (1971) 147–56. **Rigaux, B.** "βδέλυγμα τῆς ἐρημώσεως (Mc 13,14; Mt 24,15)." *Bib* 40 (1959) 675–83. **Robbins, V. K.** "*Dynameis* and *Semeia* in Mark." *BR* 18 (1973) 5–20. **Rokeah, D.** "The Elect and the Pangs of the Messiah." *Tarbiz* 38 (1968–69) 395–96. **Schille, G.** *Offen für alle Menschen.* 24–28. **Schoeps, H. J.** "Ebionitische Apokalyptik im Neuen Testament." *ZNW* 51 (1960) 101–11, esp. 102–6. **Shaw, R. H.** "A Conjecture on the Signs of the End." *ATR* 47 (1965) 96–102. **Simon, M.** "La migration à Pella: Légende ou réalité?" *RSR* 60 (1972) 37–54. **Snoy, T.** "Les miracles dans l'évangile de Marc." *RTL* 3 (1972) 449–66, esp. 464–66. **Söding, T.** *Glaube bei Markus.* 340–43, 391–97. **Sowers, S. G.** "The Circumstances and Recollection of the Pella Flight." *TZ* 26 (1970) 305–20. **Stuhlmann, R.** *Das eschatologische Mass im Neuen Testament.* FRLANT 132. Göttingen: Vandenhoeck & Ruprecht, 1983. 53–59. **Thoma, C.** "Auswirkungen des jüdischen Krieges gegen Rom (66–70/73 n.Chr.) auf das rabbinischen Judentum." *BZ* 12 (1968) 30–54, 186–210. **Vorster, W. S.** "Literary Reflections on Mark 13:5–37: A Narrated Speech of Jesus." *Neot* 21 (1987) 203–14. **Weeden, T. J.** "The Heresy that Necessitated Mark's Gospel." *ZNW* 59 (1968) 145–58, esp. 150–55. **Wenham, D.** *The Rediscovery of Jesus' Eschatological Discourse.* Gospel Perspectives 4. Sheffield: JSOT Press, 1984. 135–46, 175–218. **Wrege, H.-Th.** *Die Gestalt des Evangeliums: Aufbau und Struktur der Synoptiker sowie der Apostelgeschichte.* BET 11. Bern; Frankfurt am Main: Lang, 1978. 68–74.

Translation

[14] *"Whenever you see 'the abomination of desolation'* [a] *standing where* [b] *he must not— let the one who is reading understand* [c] *—then let those who are in Judea flee to the*

mountains.[d] [15]*But let him who is on the housetop not come down,*[e] *nor enter to take anything out of his house.* [16]*And let him who is in the field not return to take his coat.*[f] [17]*But woe to those women who are pregnant and to those who nurse in those days.* [18]*But pray that it might not happen in winter.*[g] [19]*For those days will be such a tribulation as has never happened from the beginning of creation,*[h] *which God created, until now, nor ever will be.* [20]*And unless the Lord* [i] *had shortened the days,*[j] *no human would survive;*[k] *but on account of the elect, whom he chose, he shortened the days.*[j]

[21] *"And then if someone should say to you, 'Behold, here is the Messiah!'*[l] *Behold, there!'—do not believe it.* [22]*For false messiahs and false prophets will be raised up and will offer*[m] *signs and wonders in order to deceive, if possible, the elect.* [23]*But you, beware; I have told you all things in advance."*

Notes

[a]Α Σ Φ and many later MSS add τὸ ῥηθὲν ὑπὸ Δανιὴλ τοῦ προφήτου, "which was spoken by the prophet Daniel." ℵ B D L W and other authorities lack these words.

[b]A few late MSS read ἐν τόπῳ ἁγίῳ, "standing in the holy place" (cf. Matt 24:15).

[c]D adds τι ἀναγινώσκει, "what he reads."

[d]A few late MSS read φευγέτωσαν εἰς τὴν ἔρημον, "flee to the wilderness."

[e]A D W Σ Φ and several later MSS add εἰς τὴν οἰκίαν, "into the house."

[f]W and a few late MSS read the pl. τὰ ἱμάτια, "clothes."

[g]ℵ[c] Α Σ Φ and several later MSS read προσεύχεσθε δὲ ἵνα μὴ γένηται ἡ φυγὴ ὑμῶν χειμῶνος, "but pray that your flight not be in winter." Some MSS read προσεύχεσθε δὲ ἵνα μὴ γένηται ταῦτα χειμῶνος, "but pray that these things not happen in winter." L agrees with this variant and adds ἢ σαββάτου, "or on the Sabbath" (cf. Matt 24:20).

[h]A few late MSS add κόσμου, "of the world" (cf. Matt 24:21).

[i]Several later authorities read ὁ θεός, "God."

[j]Σ and a few later MSS read τὰς ἡμέρας ἐκείνας, "those days" (cf. Matt 24:22).

[k]Lit. "all flesh would not be saved."

[l]W reads ὁ κύριος, "the Lord."

[m]Gk. δώσουσιν, lit. "they will give." D and several later MSS read ποιήσουσιν, "they will do."

Form/Structure/Setting

Mark 13:14–23 offers many parallels to the events immediately leading up to and involved in the Jewish revolt in 66–74 C.E. The "'abomination of desolation' standing where he must not" is sometimes linked to Titus's entrance into the sanctuary of the Jerusalem temple. The flight to the mountains is sometimes linked to the legend of the Christians' flight to Pella. The extremity of human destruction is seen in the devastating loss of life during the final taking of Jerusalem in the summer of 70. The "false messiahs and false prophets" are often thought to refer to the various would-be kings and prophets described by Josephus, people who in fact did deceive many. It is probable that most readers of Mark would see the events of the 60s and 70s in these verses. The Markan evangelist himself probably understood this material in this way and edited it accordingly (see Gnilka, 2:193, for discussion of the components that make up vv 14–23).

But again, there are elements in this tradition that do not square easily with the events as we know them (Hengel, *Studies in the Gospel of Mark,* 16). By the time Titus stood in the sanctuary, there no longer was any realistic opportunity to flee to the mountains (Haenchen, 444). Besides, the saying refers to those in Judea, not Jerusalem. The urgency of vv 15–16 hardly makes any sense in the light of such a scenario. What Jew in the environs of Jerusalem was out working in the field in the summer of 70? Why have Jesus urge his disciples to pray that it not happen in winter, if at the time of the composing this material, everyone knew that Jerusalem was captured in the summer? Incongruities such as these should caution against seeing this material as deriving from Christian prophets, or the evangelist himself, in response to the events of the 60s and 70s.

Mark's ordering and editing of the material in all probability does reflect some of these events, and the evangelist may very well have felt that much or even most of Jesus' discourse had come to fulfillment in these events, but the nature of the material suggests that most of it reaches back to Jesus himself. Cranfield (402) opines prudently with respect to this material: "It seems then that neither an exclusively historical nor an exclusively eschatological interpretation is satisfactory, and that we must allow for a double reference, for a mingling of historical and eschatological."

Up to now, Jesus has mostly spoken in generalities. Wars, rumors of war, earthquakes, famine, persecutions, family strife, and the like will characterize the future. But in v 14 Jesus becomes much more specific. He warns his disciples that they will see "the abomination of desolation." He does not explain what is meant by this designation, but he does say that it will be "standing where he must not." Again this is not explained, but the evangelist believes his readers should be able to understand it and so enjoins them to do so. What is envisioned here is some specific event that will signal the imminent approach of the end time (cf. v 7). Perhaps this is the very sign that the disciples requested in v 4, the sign that "all these things are about to be accomplished."

Mark 13:14–23 falls into two principal parts: (1) warnings surrounding the "abomination of desolation" (vv 14–20), and (2) another warning against false prophets and false messiahs who will deceive many, possibly even Jesus' own followers (vv 21–23). Mark 13:14–23 brings to a conclusion Jesus' series of warnings and prepares for the cataclysmic elements in the final pericopes that make up the eschatological discourse.

Klostermann (135) regards vv 14–23 as a unit (Grundmann, 356, calls it "an apocalyptic fly sheet"; but see Haenchen, 443), entitling it "the Tribulation" (*die Drangsal*). Lohmeyer (274–75) lumps together vv 14–27, calling it "the End" (*das Ende*).

Comment

14 ὅταν δὲ ἴδητε τὸ βδέλυγμα τῆς ἐρημώσεως ἐστηκότα ὅπου οὐ δεῖ, "Whenever you see 'the abomination of desolation' standing where he must not." The exact words τὸ βδέλυγμα τῆς ἐρημώσεως, "abomination of desolation," derive from LXX Dan 12:11: "From [the time] when the continual sacrifice is taken away and the abomination of desolation [τὸ βδέλυγμα τῆς ἐρημώσεως] is prepared to be given, [there shall be] a thousand two hundred and ninety days." Close approximations are also found in LXX Dan 11:31: "Forces [lit. arms] from him shall be established and profane the holy place of fear and take away the sacrifice and give the abomination of desolation [βδέλυγμα ἐρημώσεως]." See also Dan 9:27. Daniel's language may have been inspired by Jer 44:22 (LXX 51:22): "The LORD could no longer bear your evil doings and the abominations [LXX: βδελυγμάτων] which you committed; therefore your land has become a desolation [LXX: ἐρήμωσιν] and a waste and a curse, without inhabitant, as it is this day." The Danielic abomination is alluded to in 1 Macc 1:54: "Now on the fifteenth day of Chislev, in the one hundred and forty-fifth year, they erected an abomination of desolation [βδέλυγμα ἐρημώσεως] upon the altar of burnt offering. They also built altars in the surrounding cities of Judah."

The Hebrew that underlies τὸ βδέλυγμα τῆς ἐρημώσεως, "the abomination of desolation," is שִׁקּוּץ שֹׁמֵם *šiqqûs šōmēm*), which literally means "an (or the) abomination that makes desolate" (so the RSV). It is "a derogatory pun on בַּעַל שָׁמַיִם [*ba'al šāmayim*], the Syrian counterpart of Zeus Olympius," and may allude to Antiochus Epiphanes IV's renaming of the Jerusalem temple in honor of Olympian Zeus (2 Macc 6:2), as J. J. Collins (*Daniel*, Hermeneia [Minneapolis: Fortress, 1993] 357) explains. שָׁמֵם *šāmēm* occurs some ninety-five times in the Hebrew Bible and usually means "be desolate" or "be uninhabited." It is frequently translated in the LXX with forms of ἔρημος, "desolate," ἐρήμωσις, "desolation," ἐρημοῦν, "to desolate," or ἀφανίζειν, "to destroy," and its various cognates. שִׁקּוּץ *šiqqûs* occurs some twenty-eight times in the Hebrew Bible and usually means "abomination." It is frequently translated in the LXX with forms of βδελύσσειν/βδελύττειν, "to make abominable," βδέλυγμα, "abomination," βδελυγμός, "abomination," or εἴδωλον, "idol," or μίασμα, "defilement" or "pollution." All of these occurrences are in reference to pagan worship or to one form of idolatry or another (e.g., Deut 29:17; 1 Kgs 11:5, 7; 2 Kgs 23:13, 24; Isa 66:3; Jer 4:1; 7:30, "they have set their abominations in the house which is called by my name"; 13:27; 16:18; 32:34, "They set up their abominations in the house which is called by my name"; Ezek 5:11, "you have defiled my sanctuary with all your detestable things and with all your abominations"; Zech 9:7; 2 Chr 15:8; in addition to the occurrences in Daniel).

It was the action of Antiochus IV in 167 B.C.E. that gave rise to the dubious sobriquet "abomination of desolation." Most Jewish readers in the time Daniel was published would have recognized its meaning. When this sobriquet is used in the later report of 1 Maccabees, it is made more specific: the "abomination of desolation" was set up on the altar itself. Its precise identity, however, is disputed. According to Josephus (*Ant.* 12.5.4 §253), the abomination of Antiochus was a pagan altar on which swine were sacrificed. According to Dan 11:29–32, Antiochus's withdrawal from Egypt in 168 B.C.E. led to his plundering of the temple in Jerusalem and the setting up the abomination of desolation. This is a retelling of the event earlier described in Dan 9. For four principal options, see Collins, who is inclined to understand it as an altar (*Daniel*, 357–58; cf. 1 Macc 4:43; 2 Macc 6:5; Jerome, *Commentary* on Dan 11:31). Precisely what it was is not important for our purposes. It came to symbolize an unspeakable affront to the sanctity of God's house and to God himself.

Did any event in the first century fulfill Jesus' prophecy? At least four candidates have been suggested. (1) The prefect of Judea, Pontius Pilate, became notorious in his attempt to have Roman soldiers march with their standards (to which were attached busts of Tiberius Caesar) into Jerusalem (*J.W.* 2.9.2–3 §§169–74; *Ant.* 18.3.1 §§55–59). Pilate was forced to back down in order to avert an uprising. This event occurred early in Pilate's tenure and would have been known to Jesus and his disciples. (2) Caligula's attempt to place his image in the temple has been suggested (e.g., Bacon, 93, 99; T. W. Manson, *Sayings*, 329–30; Ernst,

380, Grundmann, 358, and Gnilka, 2:194, think that in Mark's *Vorlage* [pre-Markan tradition] Caligula may have been understood). According to Josephus, Gaius Caligula ordered the Syrian legate Petronius "to set up a statue [ἀνδριάντα] of Gaius in the Temple of God" (*Ant.* 18.8.2 §261; cf. *Ant.* 18.8.3 §271: "they besought him . . . not to pollute the city by setting up a statue"). The horror with which the Jewish population received this news makes it clear that had Petronius done this (and as it turned out, he did not), it would in all probability have been regarded as "an abomination of desolation." Indeed, the death of Caligula shortly after his angry letter to Petronius may even suggest a parallel with the fate of the impious Antiochus, who died not long after his profanation of the temple. (3) Lane (469) and Sowers (*TZ* 26 [1970] 305–20) think that Phanni, the high priest appointed by the Zealots in 67–68 C.E. (Josephus, *J.W.* 4.3.6–8 §§147–57), was the abomination, because he was not qualified to serve in the holy of holies. Josephus describes it as impious and outrageous. Seeing this, Lane thinks, Christians would have realized that it was time to flee the city. (4) Yet another proposal is Titus's entrance into the temple in the summer of 70 C.E. Lührmann (221–22) and Pesch (2:291) think that this Roman occupation of the temple is the desolating abomination. According to Josephus, Titus and his generals walked into the sanctuary and viewed the "holy place of the sanctuary [τοῦ ναοῦ τὸ ἅγιον] and all that it contained" (*J.W.* 6.4.7 §260). Later the Romans "carried their standards into the temple court and, setting them up opposite the eastern gate, there sacrificed to them, and with rousing acclamations hailed Titus as imperator" (*J.W.* 6.6.1 §316).

None of these events, however, fits well the context of Jesus' warning in v 14. Pilate's attempted sacrilege did not take place. The temple was not in any way desecrated or left desolate. Caligula's order to erect his statue was never carried out, so again there was no abomination and the temple was not left desolate. Josephus's discussion of Phanni's appointment as high priest reflects Josephus's own bias against the Zealots, as well as his bias in favor of the non-Zadokite priestly aristocracy. It is very probable that many Jews, including Christians, would not have viewed Phanni's appointment as an outrage and certainly not as the "abomination that makes desolate" (note well *J.W.* 4.3.9 §160, where according to Josephus, the priestly aristocracy found it necessary to upbraid the people for their apathy against the Zealots!). And finally, Titus's stroll through the sanctuary occurred after the temple had already been seriously damaged and was in fact in flames, and after Jewish sacrifices had ceased. Moreover, the "abomination of desolation" of which Daniel speaks and to which Jesus alludes envisioned the cessation of sacrifice in the Jerusalem temple, not its destruction (Gundry, 741). Thus, none of the four events often cited as an explanation actually offers a parallel to v 14.

Jesus' warning probably reflects Danielic tradition, from which he prophesies a future abomination in God's house. Daniel is clearly oriented to the great crisis brought on by Antiochus IV. Jesus' appeal to Daniel's "abomination of desolation" should be understood in a typological sense. That is, the crisis of long ago, which threatened to bring Judaism and Israel's national life to an end, will once again threaten Israel and Jesus' followers. Jesus says this abomination will be ἑστηκότα ὅπου οὐ δεῖ, "standing where he must not." The masculine gender of the participle ἑστηκότα, "standing" (in contrast to the neuter βδέλυγμα, "abomination"), may suggest that the abomination is a statue or image of a pagan deity

or deified man. Probably related to this tradition is the Pauline prediction in 2
Thess 2:3–4: "for that day will not come, unless . . . the man of lawlessness is
revealed . . . so that he takes his seat in the temple of God, proclaiming himself to
be God." Caligula's attempt to have his image erected in the temple and Titus's
entrance into the sanctuary no doubt conjured up in the minds of the evangelist
and his readers analogies to Jesus' prophecy. But the prophecy itself has not yet
been fulfilled. Haenchen (445–48) is largely correct to see in the prophecy, deliberately framed in cryptic terms, the anticipation of some form of emperor
worship within the Jewish temple, analogous to what Antiochus IV attempted and
what the Roman emperors expected. The figure about which Jesus warns his disciples is that which early Christianity came to call ὁ ἀντίχριστος, "the antichrist"
(so Lohmeyer, 275; Taylor, 511; Hengel, *Studies in the Gospel of Mark*, 25–28), that
is, that figure who fraudulently assumes the place of the true Christ (ἀντί in the
sense of "instead of") and opposes the work of God and of his Christ (ἀντί in the
sense of "against"). Such expectation may very well have been tempered by ideas
and rumors of Nero *redivivus* (e.g., Suetonius, *Nero* 6.57).

ὁ ἀναγινώσκων νοείτω, "let the one who is reading understand." This paren-
thetic comment is Markan (see his other insertions in 2:10; 3:30; 7:11, 19) and
may be intended to alert readers to Dan 12:5–13, a passage in which Daniel asks
an angel "How long shall it be till the end of these wonders?" just as the disciples
had earlier asked Jesus "When will these things be?" (Mark 13:4). To understand
what is happening, the evangelist advises his readers, one must read Daniel. The
answer provided in Daniel entails, among other things, the appearance of the
abomination that will leave the temple desolate (Dan 12:11; cf. v 10, where it is
promised that those with insight "will understand"). Thus the parallel with Mark
13:4–14 is structurally and thematically quite close.

τότε οἱ ἐν τῇ Ἰουδαίᾳ φευγέτωσαν εἰς τὰ ὄρη, "then let those who are in Judea
flee to the mountains." When the "abomination of desolation" is observed, then
it is time to flee; disaster is near. When Jesus' followers see this desecrating thing
set up, which makes it impossible for the faithful to worship in the temple precincts and continue with proper sacrifice (hence the idea of ἐρημώσεως,
"desolation," i.e., deserted), they will know that it is time to flee to the mountains. The tradition that Christians fled to Pella in answer to Jesus' warning (cf.
Eusebius, *Hist. eccl.* 3.5.3; Epiphanius, *De mensuris et ponderibus* 15) is fraught with
problems (but is accepted by Pesch, 2:293, and others), not least of which is the
fact that Pella hardly qualifies as the mountains but was a major city (one of the
Decapolis; cf. Pliny, *Nat.* 5.74) that lay on a thoroughfare (for critical review of
the problems, see Koester, *CBQ* 51 [1989] 90–106; Gundry, 774). Hengel (*Studies
in the Gospel of Mark*, 16–18) is correct to emphasize that Jesus could not have
meant flight from the city during the Roman siege, which would have meant running into the hands of the enemy. The Markan tradition is primitive, probably
authentic.

Grundmann's (359) interpretation that the command to flee has taken on a
symbolic meaning whereby Judea is understood as the place of opposition to Jesus,
Galilee is the land of refuge (where Jesus had taught and had performed his
mighty works), and the warning to flee means Christians are to flee from Judaism
(i.e., Judea) to Galilee, the land of Christ, is simply unwarranted allegory (see
also Pesch, *Naherwartungen*, 145–47).

15 ὁ [δὲ] ἐπὶ τοῦ δώματος μὴ καταβάτω μηδὲ εἰσελθάτω ἀραί τι ἐκ τῆς οἰκίας αὐτοῦ, "But let him who is on the housetop not come down, nor enter to take anything out of his house." The danger will be so great that people should flee without stopping to gather up possessions. Again, this detail does not square well with the events of the 60s and 70s. Jesus' point is that one must flee immediately and in great haste. The Jewish war had been waged for three years before Jerusalem was besieged. The approach of the Roman army was slow, the opportunity to escape prolonged. No, Jesus' warning means that when the "abomination of desolation" is set up where he must not stand, "the End" is now at hand (Gnilka, 2:195); the danger is great; the city must be abandoned without a moment's delay. Why would anyone be on the rooftop of his house? It was the custom in Jewish Palestine of late antiquity to use the flat roof of one's house for prayer or worship (Jer 19:13; Zeph 1:5; Acts 10:9), sleep (1 Sam 9:25), storing or drying fruit (Josh 2:6), proclaiming news (Isa 15:3; 22:1; Matt 10:27), or celebrating festivals (Neh 8:16). Outside stairs or ladders made it possible for one to descend from the roof without entering the house itself.

16 καὶ ὁ εἰς τὸν ἀγρὸν μὴ ἐπιστρεψάτω εἰς τὰ ὀπίσω ἆραι τὸ ἱμάτιον αὐτοῦ, "And let him who is in the field not return to take his coat." It is one thing to be warned not to enter one's house and try to pack up valuables and goods in preparation of a move or a long journey (the probable import of the words in v 15). But no, the danger is so great, the urgency so pressing, one must not even run to the house to take one's coat. This is akin to fleeing from a burning building: better to flee and later be uncomfortable than to run back and risk death. The language of vv 15–16 is vaguely reminiscent of Lot's escape from Sodom (Gen 19:17; cf. Luke 17:28–30).

17 οὐαὶ δὲ ταῖς ἐν γαστρὶ ἐχούσαις καὶ ταῖς θηλαζούσαις ἐν ἐκείναις ταῖς ἡμέραις, "But woe to those women who are pregnant and to those who nurse in those days." It will be the worst possible time for pregnant and nursing women. An expectant woman or a woman with a nursing infant cannot drop her burden and run, as implied in the instructions in vv 15–16. She will face an awful dilemma and therefore even greater danger. In OT literature pregnant and nursing women sometimes figure in oracles and descriptions of national disasters or times of divine judgment (e.g., Deut 32:25; 2 Kgs 8:12; 15:16; Jer 44:7; Lam 2:11; 4:4; Hos 13:16; Amos 1:13; 4 Ezra 6:21). We are reminded of the Lukan tradition, where Jesus on his way to the cross tells the wailing women: "Daughters of Jerusalem, do not weep for me, but weep for yourselves and for your children. For behold, the days are coming when they will say, 'Blessed are the barren, and the wombs that never bore, and the breasts that never gave suck!'" (Luke 23:28–29). This negative macarism (beatitude) stands in stark contrast to the beatitude that one woman had earlier addressed to Jesus: "Blessed is the womb that bore you, and the breasts that you sucked!" (Luke 11:27). The word οὐαί, "woe," recalls the woes of the prophets pronounced on a sinful and disobedient people (e.g., Isa 3:11, "Woe to the wicked!"; 30:1; 31:1; Jer 4:13; 13:27, "Woe to you, O Jerusalem!"; Ezek 13:18, "Woe to the women"; Hos 7:13; 9:12; Amos 5:18, "Woe to you who desire the day of the LORD!").

18 προσεύχεσθε δὲ ἵνα μὴ γένηται χειμῶνος, "But pray that it might not happen in winter." Jesus' followers should pray that it (i.e., the "abomination of desolation") not happen in the winter (v 18) when travel is more difficult and keeping warm in the countryside is a problem. Winter rains would have made the wadis more difficult to cross (Cranfield, 403; Pesch, 2:293). χειμῶνος can mean stormy weather, as well as winter (Taylor, 513). The addition of ἢ σαββάτου, "or on the sabbath," in Codex L (see *Note* g above), probably a harmonization with Matt 24:20, testifies to the Jewish character of the tradition and of the early church, for Jewish Christians "would be hindered by their scruples from escaping beyond the immediate vicinity of Jerusalem" (Swete, 307, with citation of 1 Macc 2:32–38; Acts 21:20–21).

19 ἔσονται γὰρ αἱ ἡμέραι ἐκεῖναι θλῖψις οἵα οὐ γέγονεν τοιαύτη ἀπ' ἀρχῆς κτίσεως ἣν ἔκτισεν ὁ θεὸς ἕως τοῦ νῦν καὶ οὐ μὴ γένηται, "For those days will be such a tribulation as has never happened from the beginning of creation, which God created, until now, nor ever will be." The tribulation will be so great that it will eclipse all crises of biblical history, which is quite a claim when we remember the flood, the Babylonian captivity, and the war with Antiochus. The language itself echoes Daniel: "And there shall be a time of trouble [LXX: ἐκείνη ἡ ἡμέρα θλίψεως, 'that day of tribulation'], such as never has been since there was a nation till that time" (Dan 12:1), and may also reflect acquaintance with the *Testament of Moses,* as seen in the reference to κτίσεως, "creation" (which is lacking in the Danielic parallel): "And there will come upon them . . . punishment and wrath such as has never happened to them from the creation till that time when he stirs up against them a king of the kings of the earth" (*T. Mos.* 8:1). This great king has been variously interpreted as Antiochus IV, Pompey, or one of the Roman emperors. Elsewhere in Jewish tradition (e.g., *m. Soṭa* 9:15) great tribulation was expected to precede the coming of the Messiah. The redundant κτίσεως ἣν ἔκτισεν ὁ θεός, "creation, which God created," is Semitic (for other examples in Mark, see 2:19; 4:30; 7:13; 11:28; 12:14, 23; 13:20) and probably points to pre-Markan tradition (probably to Jesus himself) and not to the evangelist. This "tribulation as has never happened from the beginning of creation" contrasts with the earlier "beginning of birth pains" in v 8. Vv 5–8 had been only the beginning of troubles; now the really serious trouble has arrived.

20 καὶ εἰ μὴ ἐκολόβωσεν κύριος τὰς ἡμέρας, οὐκ ἂν ἐσώθη πᾶσα σάρξ, "And unless the Lord had shortened the days, no human would survive." Indeed, it will be so bad that no one could survive had not God shortened the period (see discussion below). οὐκ ἂν ἐσώθη πᾶσα σάρξ, "no human would survive," literally translated is "all flesh would not be saved" (see *Note* k above) and reflects Semitic idiom (e.g., Gen 9:11: "never again shall all flesh be cut off by the waters of a flood"; Isa 40:5: "all flesh shall see it together "). Unless we view this statement as unbridled hyperbole, the warning that the period of tribulation will be so severe that unless shortened it will extinguish human life argues that the prophecy portends more than the Jewish war. To be sure, this war threatened all Jewish lives in Jerusalem (though, as it turned out, many thousands survived), but the fate of the whole of humanity did not hang in the balance.

ἀλλὰ διὰ τοὺς ἐκλεκτοὺς οὓς ἐξελέξατο ἐκολόβωσεν τὰς ἡμέρας, "but on account of the elect, whom he chose, he shortened the days." On the days being shortened, see 4Q385 (= 4QpsEzᵃ) frg. 3, lines 3–5: "the days hasten in order that the children of Israel may inherit. . . . I shall cut short [גודד *gôdēd*] the days and the years" (Kister and Qimron, *RevQ* 15 [1992] 600). גודד *gôdēd* approximates συντέμνειν, "to cut short," which appears in *Barn.* 4:3 (which in turn alludes to

Dan 9:24 [Theodotion]). The concept is probably dependent on Isa 60:21–22: "Your people shall all be righteous; they shall possess the land for ever. . . . I am the LORD; in its time I will hasten it." Mark uses the synonym κολοβοῦν, which literally means to "to cut short" or "to curtail." The idea of God shortening time is found in some pseudepigraphal texts (e.g., *1 Enoch* 80:2; *L.A.B.* 19:13; *2 Bar.* 20:1; 54:1; 83:1) and perhaps in some rabbinic texts (e.g., *b. Ketub.* 111a [dying before one's time]; *b. B. Meṣiʿa* 85b [Messiah coming before his time]; *Tg. Neof.* Gen 28:10 ["the hours of the day were shortened"]), but these parallels are inexact. God shortens the days διὰ τοὺς ἐκλεκτοὺς οὓς ἐξελέξατο, "on account of the elect, whom he chose." In the OT the elect are the people of the covenant (e.g., Ps 105:6; Isa 42:1; 43:20; 65:9–11; cf. *1 Enoch* 1:1). The redundant ἐκλεκτοὺς οὓς ἐξελέξατο, "elect, whom he chose [or elected]," is another example of Semitic style (see *Comment* on v 19).

21 καὶ τότε ἐάν τις ὑμῖν εἴπῃ, ἴδε ὧδε ὁ Χριστός, ἴδε ἐκεῖ, μὴ πιστεύετε, "And then if someone should say to you, 'Behold, here is the Messiah! Behold, there!'— do not believe it." The warning about false messiahs and false prophets is repeated (see v 6 above; Lührmann, 223). The disciples are not to believe these claims, because when the real Messiah does come, "they will see 'the son of man coming in clouds,' with great power and glory" (v 26). No secret disclosures will be necessary.

22 ἐγερθήσονται γὰρ ψευδόχριστοι καὶ ψευδοπροφῆται καὶ δώσουσιν σημεῖα καὶ τέρατα πρὸς τὸ ἀποπλανᾶν, εἰ δυνατόν, τοὺς ἐκλεκτούς, "For false messiahs and false prophets will be raised up and will offer signs and wonders in order to deceive, if possible, the elect." This time Jesus warns of false prophets, as well as false messiahs. These false prophets may come on their own, or they may accompany various false messiahs. A remarkable parallel, one that alludes to the myth of the returning Nero, is worth noting: "Then Beliar will come from the Sebastenoi [i.e., from the line of Augustus, in reference to Nero *redivivus*] . . . and he will raise up the dead, and perform many signs [σήματα πολλά] for men . . . he will, indeed, also lead men astray [πλανᾷ], and he will lead astray [πλανήσει] many faithful, chosen [ἐκλεκτούς] Hebrews" (*Sib. Or.* 3:63–69). ψευδοπροφῆται, "false prophets," are mentioned in the LXX (e.g., Jer 6:13; 33:7 [26:7]; 33:8 [26:8]; 33:11 [26:11]; 33:16 [26:16]; 34:9 [27:9]; 35:1 [28:1]; 36:1 [29:1]; Zech 13:2).

These false messiahs and false prophets will offer σημεῖα καὶ τέρατα, "signs and wonders," a phrase that echoes OT tradition, especially Deut 13:1(2) (see Gnilka, 2:198), which expressly warns of the false prophet who hopes to gain acceptance through signs: "If a prophet arises among you, or a dreamer of dreams, and gives you a sign or a wonder [LXX: σημεῖον ἢ τέρας]" (cf. *Tg. Neof.* Deut 13:2, which reads, "if a false prophet arise"). The plural combination of "signs and wonders" is common in the OT (e.g., Deut 28:46; 29:3[4]; 34:11; Isa 8:18). Those prophets whom Josephus regarded as false prophets or impostors also offered signs (e.g., *J.W.* 2.13.4 §259; 7.11.1 §§437–38). Grundmann (360) wonders if Simon Magus (cf. Acts 8:9–24) could be in view. First-century Christians may have thought of him, but in the context of Jesus' prophecy much more sinister figures are in view, figures who will appear as the end time draws near. According to 2 Thess 2:9, the coming of the "man of lawlessness" will be marked by "false signs and wonders [σημείοις καὶ τέρασιν ψεύδους]" (Schmid, 240). It is ironic in that these false prophets will offer signs, the very thing that Jesus himself refused to do (Mark 8:11–12; R. P. Martin, *Mark: Evangelist and Theologian*, 172).

23 ὑμεῖς δὲ βλέπετε· προείρηκα ὑμῖν πάντα, "But you, beware; I have told you all things in advance." Jesus' followers have been warned; they have been told all in advance. Now they must be on their guard (Swete, 310). προείρηκα, "I have told . . . in advance," echoes the prophetic oracle: προείρηκεν Ἡσαΐας, "Isaiah has spoken in advance" (Rom 9:29; cf. Acts 1:16: "the Holy Spirit spoke in advance" in the Scripture concerning the defection of Judas). This provides the disciples the only comfort in what is a frightening and discouraging prophecy. Ernst (383–84), Gnilka (2:195), Pesch (2:300), and Taylor (516) regard this version as the product of Markan redaction, looking back at vv 5–22. But the warning, so emphatically addressed to the disciples, very naturally concludes the prediction of the false messiahs and false prophets that immediately precedes.

Explanation

Jesus has provided his disciples with more information than in all probability they cared to hear. They have been warned of a spiraling series of dangers and threats. The key event is not the destruction of the temple, the very thing they had asked about in the first place, but seeing "'the abomination of desolation' standing where he must not." Mark knows his readers will understand what or who this is. Today we are not so sure. In keeping with other eschatological material, such as in Revelation or in Paul (especially 1 Thess 4–5 and 2 Thess 2), it has been concluded that the figure of whom Jesus warns is the antichrist. Jesus did not use this epithet, but his warning of false messiahs (christs) may very well have suggested this grim title to his followers. Various false and evil figures in the first century may have been in view in parts of the eschatological discourse, but none of these figures fully answers the terrifying description of this person who will stand where he must not (probably in the temple of God) and pose such great danger that all in Judea must immediately flee.

Christians today are tempted to match the details of the eschatological discourse to current events and happenings throughout the world. Proposed correspondences invariably prove inaccurate and sometimes occasion embarrassment. It is enough to be reminded that until the kingdom of God has come in its fullness, evil still poses a danger and may some day rise up in an unprecedented manifestation. God's people have been warned. They are to be prepared, but they are also to be encouraged; Jesus has foreseen and foretold all.

4. The Coming of the Son of Man   (13:24–27)

Bibliography

Adams, E. "Historical Crisis and Cosmic Crisis in Mark 13 and Lucan's *Civil War.*" *TynBul* 48 (1997) 329–44. **Beasley-Murray, G. R.** *Jesus and the Last Days: The Interpretation of the Olivet Discourse.* Peabody: Hendrickson, 1993. 422–34. **Boring, M. E.** *The Continuing Voice of Jesus: Christian Prophecy and the Gospel Tradition.* Louisville: Westminster John Knox, 1991.

235, 240–42. **Brandenburger, E.** *Markus 13 und die Apokalyptik.* FRLANT 134. Göttingen: Vandenhoeck & Ruprecht, 1984. 54–73, 95–104. **Caragounis, C. C.** *The Son of Man: Vision and Interpretation.* WUNT 38. Tübingen: Mohr-Siebeck, 1986. 204–7. **Casey, P. M.** *Son of Man: The Interpretation and Influence of Daniel 7.* London: S. P. C. K., 1979. 165–78. **Coke, P. T.** "The Angels of the Son of Man." SNTSU 3 (1978) 91–98. **Coppens, J.** *Le Fils de l'homme néotestamentaire.* Vol. 3 of *La relève apocalyptique du messianisme royal.* Ed. F. Neirynck. BETL 55. Leuven: Peeters and Leuven UP, 1981. 126–30. **Daumoser, I.** *Berufung und Erwählung bei den Synoptikern: Ein Beitrag zur biblischen Theologie des Neuen Testaments.* Meisenheim: Hain; Stuttgart: Katholisches Bibelwerk, 1954. 215–34. **Donahue, J. R.** *Are You the Christ?* 168–72. **Draper, J. A.** "The Development of the 'Sign of the Son of Man' in the Jesus Tradition." *NTS* 39 (1993) 1–21. **France, R. T.** *Jesus and the Old Testament.* 63–64, 74, 140, 227–39. **Geddert, T. J.** *Watchwords.* 226–31. **Giesen, H.** "Christliche Existenz in der Welt und der Menschensohn: Versuch einer Neuinterpretation des Terminwortes Mk 13,30." SNTSU 8 (1983) 18–69, esp. 40–50. **Grelot, P.** *Les Paroles de Jésus.* Introduction à la Bible: Édition nouvelle. Le Nouveau Testament 7. Paris: Desclée, 1986. 121–25. **Hallbäck, G.** "Der anonyme Plan: Analyse von Mk 13,5–37 im Hinblick auf die Relevance der apokalyptischen Rede für die Problematik der Aussage." *LB* 49 (1981) 28–53. **Hampel, V.** *Menschensohn und historischer Jesus: Ein Rätselwort als Schlüssel zum messianischen Selbstverständnis Jesu.* Neukirchen-Vluyn: Neukirchener, 1990. 165–68. **Hartman, L.** "La parousie du Fils de l'homme: Mc 13,24–32." *AsSeign* 2.64 (1969) 47–57. **Hatina, T. R.** "The Focus of Mark 13:24–27—The Parousia, or the Destruction of the Temple?" *BBR* 6 (1996) 43–66. **Hooker, M. D.** *Son of Man in Mark.* 148–59. **Kato, Z.** *Völkermission im Markusevangelium.* 137–51. **Kazmierski, C. R.** *Jesus, the Son of God.* 139–50. **Kolenkow, A. B.** "Beyond Miracles, Suffering and Eschatology." In *Society of Biblical Literature 1973 Seminar Papers.* Ed. G. W. MacRae. 2 vols. SBLSP 12. Cambridge, MA: SBL, 1973. 2:155–202, esp. 172–83. **Lambrecht, J.** *Die Redaktion des Markus-Apokalypse: Literarische Analyse und Strukturuntersuchung.* AnBib 28. Rome: Biblical Institute, 1967. 173–93. **Lindars, B.** *Jesus Son of Man: A Fresh Examination of the Son of Man Sayings in the Gospels in the Light of Recent Research.* London: S. P. C. K., 1983; Grand Rapids, MI: Eerdmans, 1984. 88–93, 108–10. **Mateos, J.** *Marcos 13: El grupo cristiano en la historia.* Lectura del Nuevo Testamento: Estudios críticos y exegéticos 3. Madrid: Cristiandad, 1987. 283–372. **Merklein, H.** "Untergang und Neuschöpfung: Zur theologischen Bedeutung neutestamentlicher Texte vom 'End' der Welt." In *Biblische Randbemerkungen.* FS R. Schnackenburg, ed. H. Merklein and J. Lange. Würzburg: Echter, 1974. 349–60. **Minear, P. S.** "Some Archetypal Origins of Apocalyptic Predictions." *Horizons* 1 (1979) 105–35. ———. *To Die and to Live: Christ's Resurrection and Christian Vocation.* New York: Seabury, 1977. 123–49. **Minette de Tillesse, G.** *Le secret messianique.* 368–73. **Müller, M.** *Der Ausdruck "Menschensohn" in den Evangelien: Voraussetzungen und Bedeutung.* ATD 17. Leiden: Brill, 1984. 91–97. **Mussner, F.** "Die Wiederkunft des Menschensohnes nach Markus 13,24–27 und 14,61–62." *BK* 16 (1961) 105–7. **Neirynck, F.** "Marc 13: Examen critique de l'interprétation de R. Pesch." In *L'Apocalypse johannique et l'apocalyptique dans le Nouveau Testament.* Ed. J. Lambrecht. BETL 53. Gembloux: Duculot; Leuven: Leuven UP, 1980. 369–401, esp. 391–93 (repr. in F. Neirynck. *Evangelica.* BETL 60. Leuven: Peeters and Leuven UP, 1982. 565–97, esp. 587–89). **Nützel, J. M.** "Hoffnung und Treue: Zur Eschatologie des Markusevangeliums." In *Gegenwart und kommendes Reich.* FS A. Vögtle, ed. P. Fiedler and D. Zeller. SBB. Stuttgart: Katholisches Bibelwerk, 1975. 79–90, esp. 82–84. **Perrin, N.** *Rediscovering the Teaching of Jesus.* 173–81. **Pesch, R.** "Der Menschensohn wird kommen (Mk 13,24–32)." *Am Tisch des Wortes* 144 (1974) 55–61. ———. *Naherwartungen: Tradition und Redaktion in Mk 13.* KBANT. Düsseldorf: Patmos, 1968. 157–75. **Pudussery, P. S.** *Discipleship: A Call to Suffering and Glory: An Exegetico-Theological Study of Mk 8,27–9,1; 13,9–13 and 13,24–27.* Rome: Libreria "Alma Mater," 1987. 198–238. **Radcliffe, T.** "'The Coming of the Son of Man': Mark's Gospel and the Subversion of the Apocalyptic Imagination." In *Language, Meaning and God.* FS H. McCabe, ed. B. Davies. London: Chapman, 1987. 167–89. **Sabourin, L.** "The Biblical Cloud: Terminology and Traditions." *BTB* 4 (1974) 290–311.

Schille, G. *Offen für alle Menschen.* 24–28. **Schnackenburg, R.** "Kirche und Parusie." In *Gott in Welt.* FS K. Rahner, ed. J. B. Metz et al. 2 vols. Freiburg: Herder, 1964. 1:551–78. **Schwarz, G.** *Jesus "der Menschensohn": Aramaistische Untersuchungen zu den synoptischen Menschensohnworten Jesu.* BWANT 119. Stuttgart: Kohlhammer, 1986. 147–51. **Seitz, O. F. J.** "The Future Coming of the Son of Man: Three Midrashic Formulations in the Gospel of Mark." *SE* 6 [= TU 112] (1973) 478–94, esp. 488–90. **Simonis, W.** *Jesus von Nazareth: Seine Botschaft vom Reich Gottes und der Glaube der Urgemeinde: Historische-kritische Erhellung der Ursprünge des Christentums.* Düsseldorf: Patmos, 1985. 141–43. **Taylor, V.** "The 'Son of Man' Sayings Relating to the Parousia." *ExpTim* 58 (1946–47) 12–15 (repr. in V. Taylor. *New Testament Essays.* London: Epworth, 1970. 119–26). **Tödt, H. E.** *Der Menschensohn in der synoptischen Überlieferung.* Gütersloh: Mohn, 1959. 30–33 (ET: *The Son of Man in the Synoptic Tradition.* New Testament Library. Philadelphia: Westminster, 1965. 33–36). **Tolbert, M. A.** *Sowing the Gospel.* 265–69. **Towner, W. S.** "An Exposition of Mark 13:24–32." *Int* 30 (1976) 292–96. **Vögtle, A.** *Das Neue Testament und die Zukunft des Kosmos.* KBANT. Düsseldorf: Patmos, 1970. 28–31, 67–71. **Vorster, W. S.** "Literary Reflections on Mark 13:5–37: A Narrated Speech of Jesus." *Neot* 21 (1987) 203–14. **Weeden, T. J.** *Mark.* 126–37. **Wenham, D.** *The Rediscovery of Jesus' Eschatological Discourse.* Gospel Perspectives 4. Sheffield: JSOT Press, 1984. 304–26. **Wrege, H.-Th.** *Die Gestalt des Evangeliums: Aufbau und Struktur der Synoptiker sowie der Apostelgeschichte.* BBET 11. Bern; Frankfurt am Main: Lang, 1978. 68–74.

Translation

²⁴ *"But in those days, after that tribulation, 'the sun will be darkened, and the moon will not give its light,* ²⁵ *and the stars will fall from heaven, and the powers in the heavens will be shaken.'* ²⁶ *And then they will see 'the son of man coming in clouds,'* ᵃ *with great power and glory.* ᵇ ²⁷ *And then he will send his* ᶜ *angels* ᵈ *and will gather together [his] elect from the four winds, from the corner of the earth to the corner of heaven."*

Notes

ᵃW and many later authorities read ἐν νεφέλῃ, "in a cloud." D and Syr. authorities read ἐπὶ τῶν νεφελῶν, "on the clouds." The variants probably reflect some of the textual uncertainty that involves LXX Dan 7:13, where various authorities read "in [ἐν] the clouds," "on [ἐπί] the clouds," and "with [μετά] the clouds." See *Note* j and *Comment* on Mark 14:62.

ᵇA and several later MSS read μετὰ δυνάμεως καὶ δόξης πολλῆς, "with power and great glory" (cf. Matt 24:30; Luke 21:27).

ᶜGk. τοὺς ἀγγέλους, lit. "the angels." The definite art. can imply the gen. of possession or description. Several early MSS (ℵ A C Σ Φ) add αὐτοῦ, "his."

ᵈA few late MSS add μετὰ σάλπιγγος μεγάλης, "with a loud trumpet call." This addition was inspired by Matt 24:31.

Form/Structure/Setting

Mark 13:24–27 is made up of three brief units: (1) cosmic signs that follow the tribulation (vv 24–25); (2) the appearance of the "son of man coming in clouds" (v 26); and (3) the sending of the angels to gather the elect from all parts of the world (v 27). The pericope forms the climax to what has preceded and is followed by final parables and admonitions to watch.

Form-critical assessment of the passage typically views this material as apocalyptic and primitive, but not as deriving from Jesus. Bultmann (*History*, 122) views vv 26–27 as an apocalyptic son-of-man tradition that "was simply identified with

Jesus." Taylor (519) thinks it highly unlikely that Jesus uttered v 26. Klostermann (137) sees vv 24–27 as the final act of the Markan apocalypse. Gnilka (2:199) believes Mark has taken this material from his *Vorlage* (pre-Markan tradition). Grundmann (361) sees it as the concluding pericope in Mark's *Vorlage*, but not as deriving from anything that Jesus said (so also A. Vögtle, *Neue Testament und die Zukunft,* 69–70). Pesch (2:301) agrees that vv 24–27 belong to Mark's *Vorlage*, but suggests that this material has been separated from the previous material in the *Vorlage* by the evangelist's insertion of v 23 (see *Comment* above on this point). Pesch (2:302) views vv 24–27 as an apocalyptic prophecy with a midrashic combination of several OT texts (also Ernst, 385). Ernst (385) also sees vv 24–27 as the climax of the discourse. Lohmeyer (279) regards vv 24–27 as a fragment. G. R. Beasley-Murray (*Last Days,* 422) agrees, saying that it "circulated at one time as a unit." According to Lührmann (224), whereas vv 7–23 surveyed historical events, vv 24–27 actually pertains to the future; here for the first time the discourse addresses events of the end time. However, it has been argued above that vv 14–23 also contain material that is futuristic and as yet unfulfilled.

Ernst (385) asserts that it is impossible to relate vv 24–27 to the destruction of Jerusalem, particularly because of the cosmic catastrophes. But Hatina (*BBR* 6 [1996] 43–66) has recently attempted to meet this objection by pointing out the parallels of cosmic language used by the classic prophets of the OT to describe the destruction of infamous cities, implying that Jesus' use of such language here would indicate that he is prophesying Jerusalem's destruction. This debate will be pursued further in the *Comment*.

Comment

24–25 ἀλλὰ ἐν ἐκείναις ταῖς ἡμέραις μετὰ τὴν θλῖψιν ἐκείνην, "But in those days, after that tribulation." ἐν ἐκείναις ταῖς ἡμέραις, "in those days," is biblical language and frequently introduces eschatological oracles (e.g., Jer 3:16; 5:18; 31:29; 33:15–16; Joel 3:2[2:29]; 4[3]:1; Zech 8:23). The expression has appeared twice already in the eschatological discourse (vv 17, 19). It is found also in 2:20 in answer to the question regarding the failure of Jesus' disciples to fast: "The days will come, when the bridegroom is taken away from them, and then they will fast in that day."

τὴν θλῖψιν ἐκείνην, "that tribulation," refers to the events described in vv 14–23, the tribulation that began with the "abomination of desolation." θλῖψις, "tribulation," occurs frequently in the OT (LXX) prophets (e.g. Isa 8:22; Jer 10:18; Mic 2:12; Hab 3:16; Zeph 1:15; Zech 8:10), lending itself usefully to a description of the terrifying future scenario Jesus envisions.

ὁ ἥλιος σκοτισθήσεται, καὶ ἡ σελήνη οὐ δώσει τὸ φέγγος αὐτῆς, καὶ οἱ ἀστέρες ἔσονται ἐκ τοῦ οὐρανοῦ πίπτοντες, καὶ αἱ δυνάμεις αἱ ἐν τοῖς οὐρανοῖς σαλευθήσονται, "the sun will be darkened, and the moon will not give its light, and the stars will fall from heaven, and the powers in the heavens will be shaken." Various cosmic signs are said to portend the coming of the "son of man": The "sun will be darkened, and the moon will not give its light, and the stars will fall from heaven" (vv 24–25) alludes to part of LXX Isa 13:10: "For the stars of heaven [οἱ γὰρ ἀστέρες τοῦ οὐρανοῦ] and Orion and all the order of heaven will not give their light; and when the sun rises, it will be dark [σκοτισθήσεται τοῦ ἡλίου ἀνατέλλοντος], and the moon will not shed its light [ἡ σελήνη οὐ δώσει τὸ φῶς αὐτῆς]" (see also Isa 34:4, where we read of the fall of the host of heaven [πάντα τὰ ἄστρα πεσεῖται]). Isaiah's oracle concerns the destruction of Babylon. Gundry (782) remarks that the darkening of the sun and the failure of the moon to provide light constitute an undoing of the fourth day of creation (Gen 1:14–19). He may well be correct, for in v 19 the tribulation was described as "a tribulation as has never happened from the beginning of creation."

σαλευθήσονται, "will be shaken," is not found in the OT passages cited above from the LXX, but this verb does occur in passages that describe fearful theophany (Beasley-Murray, *Last Days,* 424). The picture of heaven and earth shaken by God's appearance (cf. Judg 5:5; Amos 9:5; Mic 1:4; Hab 3:6; Nah 1:5; Pss 18:7; 114:7; Job 9:6) only heightens the drama envisioned here. Beasley-Murray (*Last Days,* 424–25) argues that it is the theophany that causes the sun to grow dark and the moon to fail to give its light. According to the *Testament of Moses,* when the kingdom of God appears (*T. Mos.* 10:1), "the earth will tremble, even to its ends shall it be shaken, and the high mountains will be made low. Yes, they will be shaken . . . the sun will not give light, and in darkness the horns of the moon will flee" (*T. Mos.* 10:4–5). Similarly, in the *Sibylline Oracles* we find, "I will tell you a very clear sign, so that you may know when the end of all things comes to pass on earth . . . upon the earth all the light of the sun is eclipsed in the middle from heaven, and the rays of the moon appear and return to the earth" (*Sib. Or.* 3:796–803; cf. *T. Levi* 4:1: "when the sun is extinguished"; *1 Enoch* 57:2: "the holy ones in heaven took notice of it and the pillars of the earth were shaken").

Hatina (*BBR* 6 [1996] 53–59) has argued that these cosmic portents should be interpreted in the light of the fuller contexts of the prophetic passages to which they allude. Isa 13:10 is part of an oracle (Isa 13:9–11) that prophesies the coming "day of the Lord," at which time wicked Babylon will be punished. All that is envisioned is the destruction of the city, yet hyperbolic cosmic language is employed. Hatina also notes that the allusion to Isa 34:4 recalls the oracle against Edom (Isa 34:4–5), which again employs cosmic language in foretelling the judgment that will befall it. Hatina notes further that oracles in Ezek 32:7–8; Joel 2:10, 31; 3:15; and Amos 8:9 describe cosmic portents in foretelling judgment upon various cities and kingdoms. From this it is concluded that Mark 13:24–27 is another example of the usage of such language to foretell a city's doom, but this time the city is Jerusalem itself. This interpretation would then show that Jesus did in fact answer the disciples' question concerning his prediction of the temple's destruction (vv 2, 4). Such an interpretation may also cohere with Mark 14:62, where Jesus predicts that Caiaphas and company will "see 'the son of man' seated 'at the right hand' of the Power and 'coming with the clouds of heaven.'" That is, in the destruction of Jerusalem, they will see the coming of the "son of man," as the next verse describes.

Although this interpretation is suggestive and could be correct, it leaves important questions unanswered and connects with great difficulty to the material that precedes. As has already been argued, there are too many details in vv 5–23 that do not fit the events between Pentecost and the Jewish revolt. There was no appearance of the "abomination of desolation," nor was there a tribulation so terrible that all of humanity came close to annihilation. Of course, it is possible that Jesus himself expected to return as "son of man" at the time of Jerusalem's destruction, in which case vv 24–27 would then be a metaphorical description of this event. But the eschatological tenor of vv 14–23 looks to events beyond the catastrophe of 70 C.E. to the appearance of an antichrist figure who will stand in the temple of God, who will be accompanied by false prophets, and who will inaugurate a period of tribulation unprecedented in human history. It is μετὰ τὴν θλῖψιν ἐκείνην, "after that tribulation," that the "son of man" will come. Furthermore, Beasley-Murray (*Last Days*, 425) has argued that vv 24–27 are theophanic. Accordingly, God's appearance does not destroy the cosmos; it frightens it. Beasley-Murray states: "when the language of theophany is used in relation to the parousia, there is no suggestion that the Son of man comes to destroy the world; the function of this ancient mythological language is purely to highlight the glory of that event and set it in its proper category: it represents the divine intervention for judgment and salvation." Meting out judgment and salvation on earth will be the task of the coming "son of man."

26 καὶ τότε ὄψονται τὸν υἱὸν τοῦ ἀνθρώπου ἐρχόμενον ἐν νεφέλαις μετὰ δυνάμεως πολλῆς καὶ δόξης, "And then they will see 'the son of man coming in clouds,' with great power and glory." The phrase τὸν υἱὸν τοῦ ἀνθρώπου, "son of man," is drawn from Dan 7:13 and apparently was the key to Jesus' messianic self-understanding (see *Comment* on 8:31, as well as *Comment* on 2:10 in Guelich, 89–94).

The combination δυνάμεως . . . καὶ δόξης, "power and glory," is found in the OT (e.g., Ps 62:3[63:2]; with synonyms, see 1 Chr 29:11; Dan 2:37; 4:30). The first two passages speak of God's power and glory, but the second two refer to a human king. The ὄψονται, "they will see," anticipates Jesus' reply to Caiaphas and those who gathered to find evidence against him: "you will see [ὄψεσθε] the 'son of man'" (14:62).

27 καὶ τότε ἀποστελεῖ τοὺς ἀγγέλους, "And then he will send his angels." The assertion that the "son of man" will send his angels is astounding and only underscores the heavenly authority that has been invested in this individual (cf. Dan 7:14: "And to him was given dominion and glory and kingdom, that all peoples, nations, and languages should serve him"), for throughout the OT it is God who commands and directs the angels of heaven. In Mark 8:38 Jesus had said that the "son of man" would "come in the glory of his Father with the holy angels." According to Matt 13:41, "The Son of man will send his angels, and they will gather out of his kingdom all causes of sin and all evildoers."

καὶ ἐπισυνάξει τοὺς ἐκλεκτοὺς [αὐτοῦ] ἐκ τῶν τεσσάρων ἀνέμων ἀπ' ἄκρου γῆς ἕως ἄκρου οὐρανοῦ, "and will gather together [his] elect from the four winds, from the corner of the earth to the corner of heaven." The glorious and powerful "son of man" will send forth his angels (or messengers) to gather the elect who have been scattered to the four winds (on the salvation of the elect and the appearance of the "son of man," see *1 Enoch* 62:13–14). The allusion is to Zech 2:6 (MT 2:10), which is part of an oracle that foretells the gathering of Israel's exiles. The gathering of the exiles is a messianic task (see *Pss. Sol.* 8:28; 11:1–4; 17:21–28; *Tg.* Isa 53:8; *Tg.* Hos 14:8; *Tg.* Mic 5:1–3), an idea that coheres with both the literary context in Mark and the ministry of Jesus, as seen in his appointment of the Twelve (see Mark 3:13–19; Grundmann, 101; Cranfield, 127; Schweizer, 81; Meyer, *Aims*, 153–54; Sanders, *Jesus and Judaism*, 95–106), in the expectation of the gathering of the scattered people of Israel (Matt 8:11 = Luke 13:28–29; cf. Isa 11:12; 27:12–13; 60:1–9), and in his promise that the Twelve would sit on twelve thrones judging the twelve tribes of Israel (Matt 19:28 = Luke 22:30).

There is nothing mysterious about the meaning of "the four winds, from the corner of the earth to the corner of heaven." It is pleonastic language and simply means that God's elect will be gathered, no matter how scattered and far-flung they may be (Swete, 313; Lambrecht, *Redaktion des Markus-Apokalypse,* 189; cf. Philo, *Cherubim* 99; *Migration* 181).

There may be an important parallel here with the *Testament of Moses,* an early first-century pseudepigraphon. We read that a second punishment will befall God's people, so severe that it will "exceed the former one" (*T. Mos.* 9:2, in reference to the Babylonian destruction and exile); "Then [God's] kingdom will appear throughout his whole creation" (*T. Mos.* 10:1). The sequence here is the same as in Mark 13: terrible tribulation followed by the appearance of God's kingdom. The only difference is that in Mark the kingdom is consummated through the coming of the "son of man," the person to whom God entrusts the kingdom.

The idea of someone dying and then returning in kingly power is not without parallel in late antiquity. Some believed that Nero, who died in 68 C.E., would return or even had returned. For fear of him, and in some cases out of love for him, some people prepared for his return (see Suetonius, *Nero* 6.57).

Explanation

Jesus has taught his disciples that following the unprecedented tribulation of vv 14–23 a series of heavenly portents will take place signaling the glorious and powerful coming of the "son of man." Then the tribulation will be over; then the elect will be gathered from every part of the planet. No matter how fearful and uncertain events become, the disciples may rest assured that the "son of man," God's agent, will assuredly make a sudden and decisive appearance. When this will take place is uncertain, and in fact in v 32 Jesus will inform his disciples that no one, not even he, knows when that day will be; but the fact of its coming is the important point, and in light of that fact the disciples must be watchful, discerning, and prepared.

5. The Lesson of the Fig Tree   (13:28–32)

Bibliography

Bauckham, R. "Synoptic Parousia Parables and the Apocalypse." *NTS* 23 (1976–77) 162–76. **Bayer, H. F.** *Jesus' Predictions of Vindication and Resurrection: The Provenance, Meaning and Correlation of the Synoptic Predictions.* WUNT 2.20. Tübingen: Mohr-Siebeck, 1986. 244–49. **Beasley-Murray, G. R.** *Jesus and the Last Days: The Interpretation of the Olivet Discourse.* Peabody: Hendrickson, 1993. 434–53. **Berger, K.** *Die Amen-Worte Jesu.* BZNW 39. Berlin: de Gruyter, 1970. 68–69. **Boring, M. E.** *The Continuing Voice of Jesus: Christian Prophecy and the Gospel Tradition.* Louisville: Westminster John Knox, 1991. 236–42. **Brandenburger, E.** *Markus 13 und die Apokalyptik.* FRLANT 134. Göttingen: Vandenhoeck & Ruprecht, 1984. 104–25. **Carlston, C. E.** *The Parables of the Triple Tradition.* Philadelphia: Fortress, 1975. 190–97.

Cranfield, C. E. B. "Thoughts on New Testament Eschatology." *SJT* 35 (1982) 497–512, esp. 502–4 (repr. in C. E. B. Cranfield. *The Bible and Christian Life: A Collection of Essays.* Edinburgh: T & T. Clark, 1985. 105–26, esp. 112–15). **Crawford, B. S.** "Near Expectation in the Sayings of Jesus." *JBL* 101 (1982) 225–44. **Derrett, J. D. M.** "Figtrees in the New Testament." *HeyJ* 14 (1973) 249–65. **Dupont, J.** "La parabole du figuier qui bourgeonne (Mc, XIII, 28–29 et par.)." *RB* 75 (1968) 526–48. **Fascher, E.** *Frage und Antwort: Studien zur Theologie und Religionsgeschichte.* Berlin: Evangelische Verlagsanstalt, 1968. 68–84. ———. "'Von jenem Tage aber und von der Stunde weiss niemand . . .': Der Anstoss in Mark 13,32 (Matth. 24,36)." In *Ruf und Antwort.* FS E. Fuchs. Leipzig: Kohler und Amelang, 1964. 475–83. **Fleddermann, H. T.** *Mark and Q.* 201–6. **Fletcher-Louis, C. H. T.** "The Destruction of the Temple and the Relativization of the Old Covenant: Mark 13:31 and Matthew 5:18." In *'The Reader Must Understand': Eschatology in Bible and Theology.* Ed. K. E. Brower and M. W. Elliott. Leicester: Inter-Varsity Press, 1997. 145–69. **Fuchs, E.** "Verheissung und Erfüllung (Untersuchungen zur eschatologischen Verkündigung Jesu von W. G. Kümmel)." In *Zur Frage nach dem historischen Jesus.* Gesammelte Aufsätze 2. Tübingen: Mohr-Siebeck, 1960. 66–78. **Gaston, L.** *No Stone on Another: Studies in the Significance of the Fall of Jerusalem in the Synoptic Gospels.* NovTSup 23. Leiden: Brill, 1970. 453–54. **Geddert, T. J.** *Watchwords.* 107–9, 239–53. **Giesen, H.** "Christliche Existenz in der Welt und der Menschensohn: Versuch einer Neuinterpretation des Terminwortes Mk 13,30." SNTSU 8 (1983) 18–69. **Gnilka, J.** "'Parusieverzögerung' und Naherwartung in den synoptischen Evangelien und in der Apostelgeschichte." *Catholica* 13 (1959) 277–90. **Grässer, E.** *Die Naherwartung Jesu.* SBS 61. Stuttgart: Katholisches Bibelwerk, 1973. ———. *Das Problem der Parusieverzögerung in den synoptischen Evangelien und in der Apostelgeschichte.* BZNW 22. Berlin: Töpelmann, 1957. 128–31. **Grimm, W.** *Weil ich dich liebe.* 177–82. **Hahn, F.** "Die Rede von der Parusie des Menschensohnes Markus 13." In *Jesus und der Menschensohn.* FS A. Vögtle, ed. R. Pesch and R. Schnackenburg. Freiburg: Herder, 1975. 240–66. **Hasler, V.** *Amen: Redaktionsgeschichtliche Untersuchung zur Einführungsformel der Herrenworte "Wahrlich ich sage euch."* Zürich; Stuttgart: Gotthelf, 1969. 47–49. **Iersel, B. M. F. van.** *"Der Sohn" in den synoptischen Jesusworten: Christusbezeichnung der Gemeinde oder Selbstbezeichnung Jesu?* NovTSup 3. Leiden: Brill, 1961. 117–23. **Jeremias, J.** *The Parables of Jesus.* Rev. ed. New York: Scribner's, 1963. 119–20. **Kato, Z.** *Völkermission im Markusevangelium.* 137–51. **Kazmierski, C. R.** *Jesus, the Son of God.* 139–50. **Klauck, H.-J.** *Allegorie und Allegorese in synoptische Gleichnistexten.* NTAbh 13. Münster: Aschendorff, 1978. 316–25. **Kümmel, W. G.** "Eschatological Expectation in the Proclamation of Jesus." In *The Future of Our Religious Past.* FS. R. Bultmann, ed. J. M. Robinson. London: SCM Press; New York: Harper & Row, 1971. 29–48. ———. *Promise and Fulfilment.* 88–104. **Künzi, M.** *Das Naherwartungslogion Markus 9,1 par.: Geschichte seiner Auslegung mit einem Nachwort zur Auslegungsgeschichte von Markus 13,30 par.* BGBE 21. Tübingen: Mohr-Siebeck, 1977. **Lambrecht, J.** *Die Redaktion des Markus-Apokalypse: Literarische Analyse und Strukturuntersuchung.* AnBib 28. Rome: Biblical Institute, 1967. 193–227. **Lebreton, J.** "L'ignorance du jour du jugement." *RSR* 9 (1918) 281–89. **Lindars, B.** *Jesus Son of Man: A Fresh Examination of the Son of Man Sayings in the Gospels in the Light of Recent Research.* London: S. P. C. K., 1983; Grand Rapids, MI: Eerdmans, 1984. 112–14. **Linnemann, E.** "Hat Jesus Naherwartung gehabt?" In *Jésus aux origines de la christologie.* Ed. J. Dupont. BETL 40. Gembloux: Duculot, 1975. 103–10. **Lohfink, G.** *Naherwartung—Auferstehung—Unsterblichkeit.* QD 71. Freiburg: Herder, 1975. 38–81. **Lövestam, E.** "The ἡ γενεὰ αὕτη Eschatology in Mk 13,30 parr." In *L'Apocalypse johannique et l'apocalyptique dans le Nouveau Testament.* Ed. J. Lambrecht. Gembloux: Duculot, 1980. 403–13. ———. *Jesus and "This Generation": A New Testament Study.* ConBNT 25. Stockholm: Almqvist & Wiksell, 1995. ———. *Spiritual Wakefulness in the New Testament.* LUÅ 1.55/3. Lund: Gleerup, 1963. **Löw, I.** "Zum Feigengleichnis." *ZNW* 11 (1910) 167–68. **Mateos, J.** *Marcos 13: El grupo cristiano en la historia.* Lectura del Nuevo Testamento: Estudios críticos y exegéticos 3. Madrid: Cristiandad, 1987. 373–441. **McNicol, A. J.** "The Lesson of the Fig Tree in Mark 13:28–32: A Comparison between Two Exegetical Methodologies." *ResQ* 27 (1984) 193–207. **Meinertz, M.** "Dieses Geschlecht." *BZ* 1 (1957) 283–89. **Moore, A. L.** *The Parousia in the New Testament.* NovTSup 13. Leiden: Brill, 1966. 131–36, 177–81. **Müller, K.** "Jesu Naherwartung und die Anfänge der Kirche." In *Die Aktion Jesu und die Re-Aktion der Kirche.* Würzburg: Echter, 1972. 9–30. **Mussner, F.** "Wer ist 'dieses Geschlecht' in Mk 13,30 parr.?" *Kairos* 29 (1987) 23–28. **Nolan, B. M.** "Some Observations on the Parousia and New Testament Eschatology." *ITQ* 36 (1969) 283–314. **Nützel, J. M.** "Hoffnung und Treue: Zur Eschatologie des Markusevangeliums." In *Gegenwart und kommendes Reich.* FS A. Vögtle, ed. P. Fiedler and D. Zeller. SBB. Stuttgart: Katholisches Bibelwerk, 1975. 79–90, esp. 89–90. **Oberlinner, L.** "Die Stellung der 'Terminworte' in der eschatologischen Verkündigung des Neuen Testaments." In *Gegenwart und kommendes Reich.* FS A. Vögtle, ed. P. Fiedler and D. Zeller. SBB. Stuttgart: Katholisches Bibelwerk, 1975. 51–66, esp. 62–64. **Patsch, H.** *Abendmahl und historischer Jesus.* Calwer theologische Monographien A.1. Stuttgart: Calwer, 1972. 123–24. **Perez Fernández, M.** "'Prope est aetas' (Mc 13,28; Mt 24,32; Lc 21,29)." *VD* 46 (1968) 526–48. **Perrin, N.** *Rediscovering the Teaching of Jesus.* 199–202. **Pesch, R.** *Naherwartungen: Tradition und Redaktion in Mk 13.* KBANT. Düsseldorf: Patmos, 1968. 175–95. **Rau, E.** *Reden in Vollmacht: Hintergrund, Form und Anliegen der Gleichnisse Jesu.* FRLANT 149. Göttingen: Vandenhoeck & Ruprecht, 1990. 157–63. **Riedlinger, H.** *Geschichtlichkeit und Vollendung des Wissens Christi.* QD 32. Freiburg: Herder, 1966. 29–41. **Schlosser, J.** *Le Dieu de Jésus: Étude exégétique.* LD 129. Paris: Cerf, 1987. 127–30. **Schütz, R.** "Das Feigengleichnis der Synoptikern." *ZNW* 10 (1909) 333–34. ⸻. "Zum Feigengleichnis." *ZNW* 12 (1911) 88. **Scott, B. B.** *Hear Then the Parable: A Commentary on the Parables of Jesus.* Minneapolis: Fortress, 1989. 338–42. ⸻. *Jesus, Symbol-Maker for the Kingdom.* Philadelphia: Fortress, 1981. 77–79. **Telford, W. R.** *The Barren Temple and the Withered Tree: A Redaction-Critical Analysis of the Cursing of the Fig-Tree Pericope in Mark's Gospel and Its Relation to the Cleansing of the Temple Tradition.* JSNTSup 1. Sheffield: JSOT Press, 1980. 213–18. **Vögtle, A.** "Exegetische Erwägungen über das Wissen und Selbstbewusstsein Jesu." In *Gott in Welt.* FS K. Rahner, ed. J. B. Metz et al. 2 vols. Freiburg: Herder, 1964. 1:608–67 (repr. in A. Vögtle. *Das Evangelium und die Evangelien: Beiträge zur Evangelienforschung.* KBANT. Düsseldorf: Patmos, 1971. 296–344, esp. 317–28, 332–34). ⸻. *Das Neue Testament und die Zukunft des Kosmos.* KBANT. Düsseldorf: Patmos, 1970. 99–107. ⸻. "'Theo-logie' und 'Eschato-logie' in der Verkündigung Jesu." In *Neues Testament und Kirche.* FS R. Schnackenburg, ed. J. Gnilka. Freiburg: Herder, 1974. 371–98. **Vorster, W. S.** "Literary Reflections on Mark 13:5–37: A Narrated Speech of Jesus." *Neot* 21 (1987) 203–14. **Wenham, D.** *The Rediscovery of Jesus' Eschatological Discourse.* Gospel Perspectives 4. Sheffield: JSOT Press, 1984. 326–34. **Winandy, J.** "Le Logion de l'ignorance (Mc, XIII, 32; Mt., XXIV, 36)." *RB* 75 (1968) 63–79. **Wrege, H.-Th.** *Die Gestalt des Evangeliums: Aufbau und Struktur der Synoptiker sowie der Apostelgeschichte.* BBET 11. Bern; Frankfurt am Main: Lang, 1978. 68–74. **Zeller, D.** "Prophetisches Wissen um die Zukunft in synoptischen Jesusworten." *TP* 52 (1977) 258–71.

Translation

[28] "And from the fig tree learn the parable: As soon as its branch should become tender and sprout leaves, you know[a] that summer is near.[b] [29] So also you know,[a] whenever you should see these things[c] happening, that he is near,[d] at the gates. [30] Truly,[e] I say to you that this generation will not pass away until all these things should take place. [31] Heaven and earth will pass away, but my words will not pass away. [32] But of that day or[f] hour no one knows, neither the angels[g] in heaven, nor the Son, only the Father."[h]

Notes

[a]Gk. γινώσκετε. γινώσκεται, "it is known," is read by B² D L W and other authorities in v 28, and by A D L and a few other MSS in v 29. The variant seems to change the sense to "that summer is near is known."

[b]D adds ἤδη, "already" (cf. Luke 21:30).

[c]D and a few other authorities read πάντα ταῦτα, "all these things."

[d]Gk. ἐγγύς ἐστιν, which can mean the sg., "he is near," or the pl., "they are near," i.e., "these things happening are near."

[e]Gk. ἀμήν. A few late MSS read, after the Johannine fashion, ἀμὴν ἀμήν, "truly, truly."

[f]Gk. ἤ (read by A B C L Σ Φ). ℵ D W and many later MSS and authorities read καί, "and" (i.e., "of that day and hour").

[g]B and a few authorities read ἄγγελος, "an angel."

[h]A few late MSS add μόνος, "alone," or read ὁ πατήρ μου μόνος, "my Father alone" (cf. Matt 24:36).

Form/Structure/Setting

The evangelist appends the parable of the Fig Tree to his eschatological discourse to illustrate the somewhat paradoxical truth that signs indicate the nearness of the events that Jesus has described, but one still cannot with any certainty predict the "day or hour." Bultmann (*History,* 123, 125, 173) thinks this parable (or similitude) is primitive and Jewish, though he is not sure if it derives from Jesus (on p. 123 he seems to lean in favor of authenticity; on p. 125 against). Taylor (520) thinks the parable is authentic (so also Klostermann, 137; Lohmeyer, 280–81; Schniewind, 175; Grundmann, 170; Schweizer, 278; Anderson, 299) but was originally uttered in a different context. The evidence for this is twofold: (1) the parable seems to point to the beginning of the birth pains, not to the final, climactic coming of the "son of man." Moreover, (2) it is not clear what or who is "near, at the gates." "These ambiguities," Taylor says, "strongly suggest that the parable is used by the compiler for a purpose for which it was not originally intended." The original point of the parable may have had to do with the nature of the kingdom of God, much in the same sense as the parable of the Mustard Seed. Lohmeyer (280) thinks the parable originally began "The kingdom of God is like a tree, as soon as its branch . . ." (see also Ernst, 389; Gnilka, 2:205: the parable may have been used by Jesus to illustrate the inbreaking of the kingdom of God).

The parable of the Fig Tree is linked to the following sayings through catchwords (Taylor, 519; Nineham, 358): ταῦτα γινόμενα, "these things happening" (v 29), and ταῦτα πάντα γένηται, "all these things should take place" (v 30); παρέλθη, "pass away" (v 30), and παρελεύσονται, "pass away" (v 31); ἀγρυπνεῖτε, "be alert" (v 33), and γρηγορεῖτε, "watch" (vv 35, 37); and ἐπὶ θύραις, "at the gates" (v 29), and θυρωρῷ, "doorkeeper" (v 34). The evangelist has apparently combined related traditions, vv 28–29, vv 30–31, and v 32, in order to provide an admonitory conclusion to the eschatological discourse (Gnilka, 2:205). In its present context, the parable of the Fig Tree serves to illustrate the need for watchfulness and provides assurance that the disciples, if watching carefully, will perceive the signs that indicate that the end time is fast approaching.

Comment

Jesus urges his disciples to be perceptive of the signs portending the time when the "son of man" will return (which is what is implied by "he is near, at the gates"). The saying "this generation will not pass away until all these things should take place" (v 30) is consistent with the similar prediction in 9:1 ("there are some of those standing here who may not taste death until they see the kingdom of God having come in power"), even if this pronouncement is partially fulfilled in the transfiguration (9:2–8). Jesus' generation expected to see the things prophesied in the discourse. These predictions were partially fulfilled in the events of the first century. That generation saw the destruction of the temple and some of the signs, or at least events that paralleled the signs, that would portend the coming of the "son of man." But Jesus' generation did not see the coming of the "son of man," nor did it see the consummation of the kingdom of God. When will these things take place? The qualification in v 32, where even Jesus is excluded, answers our question in part: "of that day or hour no one knows." As in the case with many of the prophecies of the OT prophets, some things have come to pass, some things yet remain.

28 ἀπὸ δὲ τῆς συκῆς μάθετε τὴν παραβολήν· ὅταν ἤδη ὁ κλάδος αὐτῆς ἁπαλὸς γένηται καὶ ἐκφύῃ τὰ φύλλα, γινώσκετε ὅτι ἐγγὺς τὸ θέρος ἐστίν, "And from the fig tree learn the parable: As soon as its branch should become tender and sprout leaves, you know that summer is near." The original context of the parable might now be obscure, but the basic meaning is clear enough: when one sees the green buds form and begin to sprout leaves, one knows that summer is on its way. (τὸ θέρος can mean "the harvest," but the harvest is not near when the trees are just beginning to bud and sprout leaves; hence the translation "summer.") The original lesson had to do either with the approach of the kingdom (Ernst, 390)—i.e., evidence of the kingdom, such as Jesus' ministry, suggested that the kingdom was fast approaching—or perhaps with the approach of the end time in the sense of seeing the beginning of the birth pains (v 8) and knowing that the tribulation was on its way.

One may wonder if the parable of the Fig Tree relates in some way to the cursing of the fig tree in Mark 11:12–14, 20–21. The cursed fig tree had produced leaves, thus indicating the approach of summer and the possibility of early figs. But as it turned out, this fig tree offered a false sign and so did not teach the lesson of the fig tree in the parable of the Fig Tree!

29 οὕτως καὶ ὑμεῖς, ὅταν ἴδητε ταῦτα γινόμενα, γινώσκετε ὅτι ἐγγύς ἐστιν ἐπὶ θύραις, "So also you know, whenever you should see these things happening, that he is near, at the gates." Some think that this verse is entirely redactional (Pesch, *Naherwartungen,* 179; Lambrecht, *Redaktion des Markus-Apokalypse,* 199), but it is probably better to view it as a piece of reworked tradition that provides the parable of the Fig Tree with a meaning that fits the present context. The parable of the budding fig tree now concerns the coming of the "son of man." Therefore the implied subject of ἐστίν, "is," is either "he," that is, the "son of man," or "it," in reference to the "coming" of the "son of man" (v 26). For examples from the LXX of ἐπὶ θύραις, "at the gates" (or "door[s]"), see Gen 19:11; Prov 9:14; Wis 19:17.

30 ἀμὴν λέγω ὑμῖν ὅτι οὐ μὴ παρέλθῃ ἡ γενεὰ αὕτη μέχρις οὗ ταῦτα πάντα γένηται, "Truly, I say to you that this generation will not pass away until all these things should take place." Lövestam (*Jesus and "This Generation,"* 102) has argued that the phrase ἡ γενεὰ αὕτη, "this generation," which in the NT is almost always found on the lips of Jesus (for elsewhere in Mark, see 8:12), is taken from the Hebrew phrase הַדּוֹר הַזֶּה *haddôr hazzeh* (cf. Gen 7:1). The expression is almost always in a negative or judgmental context, whether in the OT or in Jesus' usage. Given its multiple attestation in the dominical tradition and its absence in the diction of the early church, Lövestam believes that it is "firmly established" that this phrase derives from Jesus (*Jesus and "This Generation,"* 102). Lövestam further concludes that Jesus' usage of this language implies that he understood himself as an eschatological redeemer. Perhaps, but the linguistic, contextual, and traditional evidence may not bear the weight of this conclusion. Jesus' usage of the phrase does, however, suggest at the very least that he understood his mission and message to be of the utmost importance for Israel and that rejection of his message would have dire consequences for his people. This idea coheres with Mark's eschatology and finds its specific application in the prophesied doom of Jerusalem and her temple. Because "this generation" demands signs (8:11–12) instead of responding in faith, it will come under divine judgment (cf. Matt 23:36 = Luke 11:51; Beasley-Murray, *Last Days*, 447).

In context, the phrase ταῦτα πάντα, "all these things," refers to the various predictions of the eschatological discourse (vv 5–27; Gnilka, 2:205), the events leading up to and including the coming of the "son of man" (see Hahn, "Die Rede von der Parusie," 247). Jesus expects that all of these things will take place within the span of a single generation (Grundmann, 365; Lane, 480; Gnilka, 2:206). On ἀμήν, "truly," see *Comment* on 9:1.

31 ὁ οὐρανὸς καὶ ἡ γῆ παρελεύσονται, οἱ δὲ λόγοι μου οὐ μὴ παρελεύσονται, "Heaven and earth will pass away, but my words will not pass away." Interpreters are divided over the origin of this saying, with some contending that it is the original conclusion of the eschatological discourse (e.g., Hahn, "Die Rede von der Parusie," 243; Pesch, 2:304, 309) and others contending that it was an isolated saying (e.g., Wellhausen, 107; Rawlinson, 192; Schniewind, 176; Lohmeyer, 280, Taylor, 521; Cranfield, 410; Grundmann, 260). Given the composite nature of the discourse, especially its final parts, it is impossible to decide this question with any degree of certainty.

Contrasts between God's eternal word and the temporal, created order are found in the OT (e.g., Isa 40:6–8; 51:6; Ps 102:25–27). But it is only God's word that is regarded as eternal, never a mortal's. In later Jewish writings the eternity of the Torah is emphasized (e.g., Bar 4:1; Wis 18:4; 4 Ezra 9:36–37). The remarkable quality of Jesus' saying is underscored further when we remember that on another occasion Jesus used similar language with respect to the Torah itself: "Truly I say to you, until heaven and earth pass away, not one yod or tittle will pass from the Torah until all is fulfilled" (Matt 5:18 [author's tr.]; cf. Luke 16:17; on the relationship of the Matthean and Lukan forms of Q, see Lambrecht, *Redaktion des Markus-Apokalypse*, 220). Ernst (390) thinks that the saying was constructed by an early Christian prophet based on OT texts like Isa 40:8. Some contend that the Markan saying is dependent on Q (e.g., Lambrecht, *Redaktion des Markus-Apokalypse*, 221; Schweizer, 279). But against this view, which rests on grave doubts that Jesus would have viewed his words as on a par with those of the Torah, Beasley-Murray (*Last Days*, 451) replies that Jesus may very well have viewed his message, which he had received from God, as having the same authority as the Torah that God had given to Moses. We must remember that some of the controversies in which Jesus became embroiled revolved around the question of Jesus' authority in relationship to that of the Torah (e.g., Mark 2:23–28; 3:1–6; cf. Matt 5:21–48). Kümmel (*Prophecy and Fulfilment*, 91) finds no reason to view this saying as a creation of the early church.

To what do Jesus' λόγοι, "words," refer? They may refer to all that has preceded (vv 5–30). They may even refer to his teaching as a whole (so Cranfield, 410; Gnilka, 2:206; especially if this is the utterance of a later Christian prophet; less probably if it is an authentic dominical saying). But they may only refer to the preceding verse, in which Jesus asseverates, "Truly, I say to you that this generation will not pass away until all these things should take place" (v 30). In support of this unqualified prediction, Jesus adds another asseveration in v 31: "Heaven and earth will pass away, but my words will not pass away." In a general sense, then, v 31 does apply to Jesus' general proclamation of the kingdom (Lohmeyer, 282), but in its present context the primary reference seems to be to v 30.

32 περὶ δὲ τῆς ἡμέρας ἐκείνης ἢ τῆς ὥρας οὐδεὶς οἶδεν, οὐδὲ οἱ ἄγγελοι ἐν οὐρανῷ οὐδὲ ὁ υἱός, εἰ μὴ ὁ πατήρ, "But of that day or hour no one knows, neither the angels in heaven, nor the Son, only the Father." According to this saying no one knows, not even "the Son," when the eschatological "that day" will come. The inclusion of the Son with those who do not know was an embarrassment for early Christians (not surprisingly, some MSS omit the words in the Matthean parallel, Luke omits the verse altogether, and John makes it clear that Jesus knew everything; cf. John 5:6; 6:6; 8:14; 9:3; 11:11–15; 13:1–3, 11). All of this suggests that the saying in Mark 13:32 goes back to Jesus and not to the early community (see Meier, *Marginal Jew*, 169). Bultmann (*History*, 123) regards this verse as a Jewish saying, to which a later Christian tradent added the words οὐδὲ ὁ υἱός, εἰ μὴ ὁ πατήρ, "nor the Son, only the Father" (cf. Ernst, 390, who suggests that the simple "no one knows" was expanded into a tripartite denial: "no one knows, neither the angels in heaven, nor the Son"). These suggestions are wholly implausible. Why would a Christian have had Jesus admit that he, right along with the angels, did not know the day or hour and then append this saying to a verse where Jesus has just stated that his word has the same permanence as the word of God? Such an admission strongly recommends authenticity, not inauthenticity (Cranfield, 410–11; Grundmann, 366).

In Jewish Scripture and tradition it is believed that God knows everything, including the future (e.g., Isa 46:10; Zech 14:7; 4 Ezra 4:51–52; 2 Bar. 21:8). There are also traditions that declare that humans, or even angels, do not and cannot know the future (see 4 Ezra 4:44–52, where Ezra asks if he will be alive in the last days and the angel tells him, "I do not know"; *Pss. Sol.* 17:21, where the psalmist petitions God to "raise up for them their king, the son of David, to rule over your servant Israel in the time known to you, O God"; see also *2 Bar.* 21:8, which in a prayer to God says: "You alone know the end of times before it has arrived"). In a discussion of the length of the Messiah's reign (*b. Sanh.* 99a), Rabbi Simon ben Laqish comments that Isa 63:4, "For the day of vengeance was in my heart, and my year of redemption has come," implies that God has not revealed his eschatological plans to the angels, for knowledge of this day is in God's heart only—in no one else's. According to *Mek.* on Exod 16:28–36 [*Wayyassa'* §6], "No one knows when the kingdom of the house of David will be restored to its former position, nor when this wicked kingdom [i.e., Rome] will be uprooted." Gnilka (2:206) wonders if ἢ τῆς ὥρας, "or hour," is an addition intended to counter eschatological enthusiasm and a tendency to make predictions. Perhaps.

τῆς ἡμέρας ἐκείνης, "that day," the only use of this OT idiom in the Synoptics (e.g., Isa 2:12; Jer 46:10; Ezek 13:5; Amos 5:18–20; Zeph 1:7; Zech 14:1), underscores the suddenness of the coming of the end time (Lohmeyer, 283; Taylor, 522) and refers to the coming of the "son of man," who will be accompanied by angels (Lührmann, 225; Pesch, 2:310).

If Jesus and the angels of God do not know when the end time will come, then certainly his disciples or any self-styled prophets do not know (see v 33). Because the date cannot be discovered, there is all the more need to be watchful and prepared. The Markan evangelist wishes to hold fast to eschatological expectation but at the same time to sharpen the warning against calculating the end time (Pesch, 2:311).

Explanation

As his eschatological discourse draws toward its conclusion, Jesus appends a series of parables, warnings, and admonitions. The approaching end time may be likened to the budding fig tree at the beginning of summer. The sprouting leaves indicate that the end time is approaching. But the exact end time cannot be predicted. No human can make this prediction, not even angels or Jesus the Son himself. Therefore, the end time is also like a man on a journey, who returns suddenly and without announcement (v 34; see below). Accordingly, Jesus' followers must be watchful and expectant.

But as stunning as Jesus' predictions throughout the eschatological discourse have been, he surprises his disciples with the declaration, "heaven and earth will pass away, but my words will not pass away." Jesus views his message, in this case specifically his teaching on the certainty of the fulfillment of his prophecy that all will be fulfilled in the lifetime of "this generation," as on par with the Torah itself, with God's very words. Mark's readers, aware that General Titus had besieged the city of Jerusalem and that therefore Jesus' doleful prophecy of the doom of the holy city and its famous temple were on the verge of literal fulfillment, would have been awestruck by Jesus' predictive power and confidence of the ultimate fulfillment of the divine plan. As frightening as the times were, followers of Jesus could take comfort in their Master's words.

6. The Need to Watch (13:33–37)

Bibliography

Aejmelaeus, L. *Wachen vor dem Ende: Die traditionsgeschichtlichen Wurzeln von 1. Thess 5:1–11 und Luke 21:34–36.* Schriften der finnischen exegetischen Gesellschaft 44. Helsinki: Finnish Exegetical Society, 1985. 100–102, 131–37. **Armstrong, E. A.** *The Gospel Parables.* London: Hodder & Stoughton, 1967; New York: Sheed & Ward, 1969. 78–79, 123–24. **Bauckham, R. J.** "Synoptic Parousia Parables and the Apocalypse." *NTS* 23 (1976–77) 162–76. ———. "Synoptic Parousia Parables Again." *NTS* 29 (1983) 129–34. **Beasley-Murray, G. R.** *Jesus and the Last Days: The Interpretation of the Olivet Discourse.* Peabody: Hendrickson, 1993. 453–75. **Best, E.** *Following Jesus.* 152–55. **Biser, E.** *Die Gleichnisse Jesu: Versuch einer Deutung.* Munich: Kösel, 1965. 127–28. **Bouttier, M.** "Les paraboles du maître dans la tradition synoptique." *ETR* 48 (1973) 175–95. **Brandenburger, E.** *Markus 13 und die Apokalyptik.* FRLANT 134. Göttingen: Vandenhoeck & Ruprecht, 1984. 125–30. **Carlston, C. E.** *The Parables of the Triple Tradition.* Philadelphia: Fortress, 1975. 197–202. **Crossan, J. D.** "The Servant Parables of Jesus." In *Society of Biblical Literature 1973 Seminar Papers.* Ed. G. W. MacRae. SBLSP 12. Cambridge, MA: SBL, 1973. 94–118 (repr. in *Semeia* 1 [1974] 17–62, esp. 20–21). **Didier, M.** "La parabole des talents et des mines." In *De Jésus aux Évangiles: Tradition et rédaction dans les Évangiles synoptiques.* FS J. Coppens, ed. I. de la Potterie. 2 vols. BETL 25. Gembloux: Duculot, 1967. 2:248–71. **Dodd, C. H.** *The Parables of the Kingdom.* Rev. ed. London: Nisbet, 1936. 160–67. **Dschulnigg, P.** *Sprache, Redaktion und Intention des Markus-Evangeliums: Eigentümlichkeiten der Sprache des Markus-Evangeliums und ihre Bedeutung für die Redaktionskritik.* SBB 11. Stuttgart: Katholisches Bibelwerk, 1988. 377–80. **Dupont, J.** "La parabole du maître qui rentre dans la nui." In *Mélanges bibliques.* FS B. Rigaux, ed. A. L. Descamps and A. de Halleux. Gembloux: Duculot, 1970. 89–116. **Eckstein, R.** "Vom rechten Warten: Markus 13,33–37." In *Gleichnisse aus Altem und Neuem Testament.* Ed. C. Bourbeck. Stuttgart: Klotz, 1971. 145–48. **Fleddermann, H. T.** *Mark and Q.* 206–8. **Geddert, T. J.** *Watchwords.* 90–111. **Giesen, H.** "Christliche Existenz in der Welt und der Menschensohn: Versuch einer Neuinterpretation des Terminwortes Mk 13,30." SNTSU 8 (1983) 18–69, esp. 56–62. **Harrington, W. J.** *A Key to the Parables.* New York: Paulist, 1964. 142–44. **Hasler, V.** *Amen: Redaktionsgeschichtliche Untersuchung zur Einführungsformel der Herrenworte "Wahrlich ich sage euch."* Zürich; Stuttgart: Gotthelf, 1969. 47–49. **Jeremias, J.** *The Parables of Jesus.* Rev. ed. New York: Scribner's, 1963. 53–55. **Joüon, P.** "La parabole du portier qui doit veiller, Mc 13,33–37, et la parabole des serviteurs qui doivent veiller." *RSR* 30 (1940) 365–68. **Kato, Z.** *Völkermission im Markusevangelium.* 151–54. **Klauck, H.-J.** *Allegorie und Allegorese in synoptische Gleichnistexten.* NTAbh 13. Münster: Aschendorff, 1978. 326–38. **Kosmala, H.** "The Time of the Cock-Crow." *ASTI* 2 (1963) 118–20. **Lambrecht, J.** *Die Redaktion des Markus-Apokalypse: Literarische Analyse und Strukturuntersuchung.* AnBib 28. Rome: Biblical Institute, 1967. 228–56. **Lövestam, E.** "Le portier qui veille la nuit." *AsSeign* 2.5 (1969) 44–55. ———. *Spiritual Wakefulness in the New Testament.* LUÅ 1.55/3. Lund: Gleerup, 1963. 78–91. **Manson, T. W.** *Teaching.* 260–65. **Mateos, J.** *Marcos 13: El grupo cristiano en la historia.* Lectura del Nuevo Testamento: Estudios críticos y exegéticos 3. Madrid: Cristiandad, 1987. 373–441. **Michaelis, W.** *Die Gleichnisse Jesu: Eine Einführung.* UB 32. Hamburg: Furche, 1956. 81–86. **Minear, P. S.** *Commands of Christ.* Edinburgh: St. Andrews; Nashville and New York: Abingdon, 1972. 153–57. **Minette de Tillesse, G.** *Le secret messianique.* 414–20. **Pesch, R.** *Naherwartungen: Tradition und Redaktion in Mk 13.* KBANT. Düsseldorf: Patmos, 1968. 195–202. **Roloff, J.** "'Siehe, ich stehe vor der Tür und klopfe an': Beobachtungen zur Überlieferungsgeschichte von Offb 3,20." In *Vom Urchristentum zu Jesus.* FS J. Gnilka, ed. H. Frankemölle and K. Kertelge. Freiburg: Herder, 1989. 455–58. **Scott, B. B.** *Hear Then the Parable: A Commentary on the Parables of Jesus.* Minneapolis: Fortress, 1989. 212–13. **Strawson, W.** *Jesus and the Future Life: A Study in the Synoptic Gospels.* London: Epworth, 1959. 116–17. **Strobel, A.** *Untersuchungen zum eschatologischen Verzögerungsproblem auf Grund der spätjüdisch-urchristlichen Geschichte von Habakuk 2,2 ff.* NovTSup 2. Leiden: Brill, 1961. 222–23. **Trotti, J. B.** "Mark 13:32–37." *Int* 32 (1978) 410–13. **Vorster, W. S.** "Literary Reflections on Mark 13:5–37: A Narrated Speech of Jesus." *Neot* 21 (1987) 203–14. **Weder, H.** *Die Gleichnisse Jesu als Metaphern: Traditions- und redaktionsgeschichtliche Analysen und Interpretationen.* FRLANT 120. Göttingen: Vandenhoeck & Ruprecht, 1978. 162–68. **Weiser, A.** *Die Knechtsgleichnisse der synoptischen*

Evangelien. SANT 29. Munich: Kösel, 1971. 131–53. ———. "Von der Predigt Jesu zur Erwartung der Parusie." *BibLeb* 12 (1971) 25–31. **Wenham, D.** *The Rediscovery of Jesus' Eschatological Discourse*. Gospel Perspectives 4. Sheffield: JSOT Press, 1984. 15–100. **Wrege, H.-Th.** *Die Gestalt des Evangeliums: Aufbau und Struktur der Synoptiker sowie der Apostelgeschichte*. BBET 11. Bern; Frankfurt am Main: Lang, 1978. 68–74.

Translation

[33] *"Watch out,[a] be alert;[b] for you do not know[c] when the time is.* [34] *[It is][d] like a man on a journey, leaving his home and giving authority to his servants, to each one his work, and he gave orders to the doorkeeper that he should keep watch.* [35] *Watch, therefore—for you do not know[c] when[f] the lord of the house comes, whether it be evening, or the middle of the night, or at cockcrowing, or early in the morning—*[36] *lest coming suddenly, he should find you[g] sleeping.* [37] *But what I say to you, I say to all: Watch!"*

Notes

[a]D and a few late authorities add οὖν, "therefore."
[b]א C L W and many later MSS and authorities add καὶ προσεύχεσθε, "and pray."
[c]W adds εἰ μὴ ὁ πατὴρ καὶ ὁ υἱός, "except the Father and the Son."
[d]Words in brackets have been added.
[e]A few late Lat. MSS add *quia nescitis*, "what you need."
[f]A few late MSS read ποίᾳ ὥρᾳ, "at what hour."
[g]A few late MSS read ἡμᾶς, "us."

Form/Structure/Setting

Bultmann (*History*, 119) comments that Mark 13:33–37 is "not an organized composition." He regards v 33 as a Markan editorial formulation, but he allows that vv 34–35a may be an element from ancient tradition, with v 35b an allegorical expansion (*History*, 174). Dibelius (*Tradition*, 212–13) regards v 35 as traditional, though he does differentiate between the two halves. Taylor (524) regards the passage as "a homiletical echo of several parables" (see *Comment* on v 34). It is not clear why Bultmann regards vv 33–37 as unorganized. That the material has been edited and contextualized by the evangelist is probable (with v 37 the most likely candidate; Schmid, 245). But what we have here looks for the most part like a genuine parable (beginning abruptly with ὡς, "as" or "like," is typical of Jewish parables), prefaced, interrupted, and concluded with the exhortation to "watch!" The style smacks of the originality and spontaneity characteristic of authentic dominical tradition. Bultmann's comment (*History*, 174) that v 35 is ill-suited to the parable, because it implies that all the servants stay up the whole night, demands too much verisimilitude of the parable. Of course, in the real world servants would keep shifts and thus take turns; all would not stay up all night. But such appeal to reality would then spoil the parable (as it would spoil other parables). Whatever the reason, the servants are expected to be awake and ready to serve their master whenever he should appear, regardless of the hour. The appearance of the admittedly pleonastic "whether it be evening, or the middle of the night, or at cockcrowing, or early in the morning" adds vividness and color to the parable and drives home the point: at no time is it safe to cease being on the alert.

Manson (*Teaching,* 262 n. 1) thinks that vv 32–37 may "represent the original answer of Jesus to the question put to him in v 4." He suggests then that the "Little Apocalypse" would run from v 5 to v 31. Aside from the classification of vv 5–31 as an apocalypse (for reservations concerning this position, see *Form/Structure/Setting* for 13:1–37), Manson's proposal has merit, but there really is no compelling reason to regard vv 5–31(32) as out of place and as not part of Jesus' answer to the question of his disciples. Apart from the prediction of the destruction of the temple (v 2) and the warnings to be watchful (vv 9, 23, and the passage under discussion) because the event will come suddenly and unexpectedly, does Jesus have nothing else to say about the future? Is it not more probable that Jesus, who from the outset of his ministry proclaimed the coming kingdom of God and the complete change of the social order, in fact envisioned many things to lie ahead? When asked when "these things" will happen and what will be the sign that they are about to be accomplished (v 4), Jesus answers, but not directly or immediately. Some of this indirectness may very well result from the growth of the tradition in being handed down and, of course, from the evangelist's editing, especially in light of the Jewish revolt and the Roman threat to Jersualem in 69 C.E. But the eschatological discourse as a whole is coherent and probably does represent a substantial block of authentic dominical tradition.

Ernst (392) describes vv 33–37 as an eschatological parenesis based on a three-fold summons to watchfulness. But it is better to describe this unit as a parable that emphasizes the need for watchfulness. The threefold summons to watchfulness does not undermine the integrity of the parable itself. Pesch (2:313) rightly regards the parable as traditional, though he regards v 33 as largely redactional (as v 28a is to the parable of v 28b; see also Schmid, 245). The parable concludes the discourse (Lohmeyer, 284), but in bringing it to a conclusion it also answers the disciples' question.

Comment

33 βλέπετε, ἀγρυπνεῖτε· οὐκ οἴδατε γὰρ πότε ὁ καιρός ἐστιν, "Watch out, be alert; for you do not know when the time is." Because the disciples do not know the time of the end and the appearing of the "son of man," they must watch and be alert. The καιρός, "time," has to do with the final climax, the great danger of the "abomination of desolation" (v 14), the sudden appearance of the "son of man" (v 26). Gnilka (2:209) thinks ἀγρυπνεῖτε, "be alert," which basically means "do not sleep," is a wisdom term (cf. LXX Job 21:32; Prov 8:34; Wis 6:15; Sir 36:16; and in the NT, cf. Luke 21:36; Eph 6:18; Heb 13:17). Perhaps, but the word occurs meaning no more than keeping watch or guarding something (LXX 2 Sam 12:21; Ezra 8:29; Ps 126[127]:1; Job 21:32). Lohmeyer (284) is right to point out that ἀγρυπνεῖτε is traditional, for one would expect the evangelist to use a favorite like γρηγορεῖτε, "watch." Pesch (2:314) agrees that it is traditional and wonders if it was not the original introduction to the parable.

34 ὡς ἄνθρωπος ἀπόδημος ἀφεὶς τὴν οἰκίαν αὐτοῦ καὶ δοὺς τοῖς δούλοις αὐτοῦ τὴν ἐξουσίαν ἑκάστῳ τὸ ἔργον αὐτοῦ καὶ τῷ θυρωρῷ ἐνετείλατο ἵνα γρηγορῇ, "[It is] like a man on a journey, leaving his home and giving authority to his servants, to each one his work, and he gave orders to the doorkeeper that he should keep watch." The parable of the man who goes on a journey is reminiscent of the longer parable in Matt 24:45–51 or in Luke 12:35–40 and may even be an abbreviated form of one of them (abbreviated either by the evangelist or by Jesus himself). No reason is given for why the man who leaves on a journey requires his servants to be so vigilant. This information is not necessary for the hearer to appreciate the point of the parable. The man has asked his servants to keep watch. He expects them to do so.

Lohmeyer (285) thinks the plural δούλοις, "servants," points to Mark's community. But why should not the plural δούλοις point to the disciples themselves, to whom Jesus first addressed the parable? Naturally, later readers and hearers of the Markan Gospel would be inclined to identify with the servants of the parable. But there is no reason to view the plural δούλοις as an indicator of secondariness. Swete (317) wonders if the servants are the apostles and the doorkeeper is the apostolate (appealing to John 10:3). Indeed, Turner (65) wonders if Peter himself is intended. This is unwarranted allegorization. *Pace* Lührmann (225), the parable has not been allegorized to reflect the situation of the community. There was no need to allegorize it; for the parable's application to Jesus' disciples was such that it easily continued to apply to any follower of Jesus.

35 γρηγορεῖτε οὖν· οὐκ οἴδατε γὰρ πότε ὁ κύριος τῆς οἰκίας ἔρχεται, "Watch, therefore—for you do not know when the lord of the house comes." The man of v 34 is now identified as ὁ κύριος τῆς οἰκίας, "the lord of the house," but his delegation of authority to αὐτοῦ, "his," servants and his giving orders to the doorkeeper had already made it clear that he was the master. Jesus interrupts his parable to enjoin his disciples to watchfulness, and then alters what should have been the third person, "for *they* do not know when the lord of the house comes," to the second person "for *you* do not know when the lord of the house comes." This admonitory interference with the form of the parable points to the vividness and the urgency of the telling as well as to its applicability. Jesus wants to make sure that the point is not lost on his disciples: "You do not know when the lord of the house comes"; therefore "watch!"

ἢ ὀψὲ ἢ μεσονύκτιον ἢ ἀλεκτοροφωνίας ἢ πρωΐ, "whether it be evening, or the middle of the night, or at cockcrowing, or early in the morning." The four watches of the night correspond with Roman custom (Josephus, *Ant.* 5.6.5 §223, "at about the fourth watch"; Taylor, 524; Cranfield, 412). These details are not secondary, nor do they have allegorical meaning. They underscore the point of the parable, that is, the need to be alert at all times. No time is slack time.

36 μὴ ἐλθὼν ἐξαίφνης εὕρῃ ὑμᾶς καθεύδοντας, "lest coming suddenly, he should find you sleeping." To be discovered sleeping is to be caught at having failed to heed the master's orders; it is dereliction of duty at the very least and may also indicate disloyalty. Embarrassingly, the disciples will be caught sleeping while Jesus prays in the Garden of Gethsemane (14:32–39). Despite being admonished to "watch and pray" (14:34, 38), the disciples three times drift off to sleep (14:37, 40, 41). The narrative does not say so, but the reader will wonder if the disciples' pathetic behavior when Jesus is arrested (14:43–52) is not due to their failure to watch and pray, as Jesus earlier had enjoined them. Instead of being alert and watchful, they doze. When the danger suddenly comes upon them, they panic and desert their master. Thus the disciples provide a mindful lesson for Mark's readers, a lesson that well illustrates the concluding teaching and justifies fully the repeated admonitions to be alert and watchful.

37 ὃ δὲ ὑμῖν λέγω πᾶσιν λέγω, γρηγορεῖτε, "But what I say to you, I say to all: Watch!" This verse may very well be a later addition, designed to make Jesus' warnings applicable to all in the community and not just to the disciples themselves (Cranfield, 412: "The command to watch is addressed not only to the four, but also the the rest of the Twelve, to Mark's readers in the Church of Rome, and to the whole Church throughout the Last Times"). As a final admonition to watch, v 37 brings the eschatological discourse as a whole to an emphatic conclusion.

Explanation

Jesus' warning to take heed is illustrated with a parable of watchfulness and lessons that can be drawn from it (vv 33–37). Taken with v 32, where Jesus asserts that no one knows the day or the hour of the coming of the "son of man," the principal lesson here is that Christians are to be watchful and prepared, not caught up in attempts to calculate the time of the Parousia. It is enough to know that that day will eventually and finally come, but it cannot be predicted. Christians are to be about their Master's work, faithfully observing his word, alert and watchful.

VIII. The Passion and Resurrection of Jesus (14:1–16:20)

Bibliography on Passion Narratives

Aletti, J. N. "Mort de Jésus et théorie du récit." *RSR* 73 (1985) 147–60. **Allison, D. C.** *The End of the Ages Has Come: An Early Interpretation of the Passion and Resurrection of Jesus.* Philadelphia: Fortress, 1985. **Avanzo, M.** "El arresto, el juicio y la condena de Jesús: Historia y presente." *RevistB* 35 (1973) 131–50. **Bammel, E.,** ed. *The Trial of Jesus.* FS C. F. D. Moule. SBT 13. London: SCM Press; Naperville, IL: Allenson, 1970. **Bartsch, H.-W.** "Die Bedeutung des Sterbens Jesu nach den Synoptikern." *TZ* 20 (1964) 87–102. ———. "Historische Erwägungen zur Leidensgeschichte." *EvT* 22 (1962) 449–59. ———. "Die Ideologiekritik des Evangeliums dargestellt an der Leidensgeschichte." *EvT* 34 (1974) 176–95. **Bastin, M.** *Jésus devant sa Passion.* LD 92. Paris: Cerf, 1976. **Beauchamp, P.** "Narrativité biblique du récit de la passion." *RSR* 73 (1985) 39–59. **Beilner, W.** *Christus und die Pharisäer: Exegetische Untersuchung über Grund und Verlauf der Auseinandersetzungen.* Vienna: Herder, 1959. 235–38. **Benoit, P.** *Passion and Resurrection.* **Bertram, G.** *Die Leidensgeschichte Jesu und der Christuskult: Eine formgeschichtliche Untersuchung.* FRLANT 15. Göttingen: Vandenhoeck & Ruprecht, 1922 (repr. in *Zur Formgeschichte des Evangeliums.* Ed. F. Hahn. Wege der Forschung 81. Darmstadt: Wissenschaftliche Buchgesellschaft, 1985. 273–97). **Betz, O.** "Probleme des Prozesses Jesu." *ANRW* 2.25.1 (1982) 565–647, esp. 613–44. **Binz, S. J.** *The Passion and Resurrection Narratives of Jesus: A Commentary.* Collegeville: Liturgical Press, 1989. **Biser, E.** "Die älteste Passionsgeschichte." *Geist und Leben* 56 (1983) 111–18. **Bishop, E. F. F.** "With Jesus on the Road from Galilee to Calvary: Palestinian Glimpses into the Days around the Passion." *CBQ* 11 (1949) 428–44. **Bligh, J.** "Typology in the Passion Narratives: Daniel, Elijah, Melchizedek." *HeyJ* 6 (1965) 302–9. **Borgen, P.** "John and the Synoptics in the Passion Narrative." *NTS* 5 (1958–59) 246–59. **Bornhäuser, K.** *The Death and Resurrection of Christ.* London: Independent, 1958. **Bovon, F.** *Les derniers jours de Jésus: Textes et événements.* Neuchâtel; Paris: Delachaux et Niestlé, 1974. **Brown, R. E.** *A Crucified Christ in Holy Week: Essays on the Four Gospel Passion Narratives.* Collegeville: Liturgical Press, 1986. ———. "The *Gospel of Peter* and Canonical Gospel Priority." *NTS* 33 (1987) 321–43. **Bruce, F. F.** "The Book of Zechariah and the Passion Narrative." *BJRL* 43 (1960–61) 336–53. **Bultmann, R.** *History of the Synoptic Tradition.* 275–91, 440–44. **Calloud, J.** "Entre les écritures et la violence: La passion du témoin." *RSR* 73 (1985) 111–28. **Cambe, M.** "Les récits de la Passion en relation avec différents textes du IIᵉ siècle." *Cahiers bibliques* 21 (1982) 12–24. **Carmichael, J.** *The Death of Jesus.* New York: Harper & Row, 1966. **Catchpole, D. R.** *The Trial of Jesus: A Study in the Gospels and Jewish Historiography from 1770 to the Present Day.* StPB 18. Leiden: Brill, 1971. **Caza, L.** *"Mon Dieu, mon Dieu, pourquoi m'as-tu abandonné?" Comme bonne nouvelle de Jésus Christ, Fils de Dieu, comme bonne nouvelle de Dieu, pour la multitude.* Recherches 24. Paris: Cerf; Montreal: Bellarmin, 1989. 297–310. **Chabrol, C.** "An Analysis of the 'Text' of the Passion." In *The New Testament and Structuralism.* Ed. A. M. Johnson, Jr. PTMS 11. Pittsburgh: Pickwick, 1976. 145–86. **Conzelmann, H.** "History and Theology in the Passion Narratives of the Synoptic Gospels." *Int* 24 (1970) 178–97. **Cousin, H.** *Le prophète assassiné: Histoire des textes évangélique de la Passion.* Paris: Delarge, 1976. **Crespy, G.** "Recherche sur le signification politique de la mort du Christ." *LumVie* 20 (1971) 110–21. **Crossan, J. D.** *The Cross That Spoke: The Origins of the Passion Narrative.* San Francisco: Harper & Row, 1988. **Czerski, J.** "Die Passion Christi in den synoptischen Evangelien im Lichte der historisch-literarischen Kritik." *ColT* 46 (1976) 81–96. **Dahl, N. A.** "Der gekreuzigte Messias." In *Der* *historische Jesus und der kerygmatische Christus: Beiträge zum Christusverständnis in Forschung und Verkündigung.* Ed. H. Ristow and K. Matthiae. Berlin: Evangelische Verlagsanstalt, 1960. 149–69, esp. 154–57 (ET: "The Crucified Messiah." In N. A. Dahl. *The Crucified Messiah and Other Essays.* Minneapolis: Augsburg, 1974. 10–36, esp. 17–20). **Delling, G.** *Der Kreuztod Jesu in der urchristlichen Verkündigung.* Berlin: Evangelische Verlagsanstalt, 1971; Göttingen: Vandenhoeck & Ruprecht, 1972. **Delorme, J.** "Sémiotique du récit et récit de la passion." *RSR* 73 (1985) 85–109. **Dibelius, M.** *From Tradition to Gospel.* 178–217. ———. "Das historische Problem der Leidensgeschichte." *ZNW* 30 (1931) 193–201. ———. "La signification religieuse des récits évangéliques de la passion." *RHPR* 13 (1933) 30–45. **Dillon, R. J.** "The Psalms of the Suffering Just in the Accounts of Jesus' Passion." *Worship* 61 (1987) 430–40. **Dodd, C. H.** "The Historical Problem of the Death of Jesus." In *More New Testament Studies.* Manchester: Manchester UP; Grand Rapids, MI: Eerdmans, 1968. 84–101. **Dormeyer, D.** "Die Passion Jesu als Ergebnis seines Konflikts mit führenden Kreisen des Judentums." In *Gottesverächter und Menschenfeinde? Juden zwischen Jesus und frühchristlicher Kirche.* Ed. H. Goldstein. Düsseldorf: Patmos, 1979. 211–38. **Downing, J.** "Jesus and Martyrdom." *JTS* n.s. 14 (1963) 279–93. **Evans, C. A.** "From Public Ministry to the Passion: Can a Link Be Found between the (Galilean) Life and the (Judean) Death of Jesus?" In *Society of Biblical Literature 1993 Seminar Papers.* Ed. E. H. Lovering, Jr. SBLSP 32. Atlanta: Scholars Press, 1993. 460–72 (rev. and repr. in C. A. Evans. *Jesus and His Contemporaries: Comparative Studies.* AGJU 25. Leiden: Brill, 1995. 301–18). **Evans, C. F.** "The Passion of Christ." In *Explorations in Theology 2.* London: SCM Press, 1977. **Feigel, F. K.** *Der Einfluss des Weissagungsbeweises und anderer Motive auf die Leidensgeschichte: Ein Beitrag zur Evangelien Kritik.* Tübingen: Mohr-Siebeck, 1910. **Finegan, J.** "A Quest for the History behind the Passion." *JBT* 16 (1962) 102–4. ———. *Die Überlieferung der Leidens- und Auferstehungsgeschichte Jesu.* BZNW 15. Giessen: Töpelmann, 1934. **Flesseman, E. van.** "Die Interpretation der Passionsgeschichte vom Alten Testament aus." In *Zur Bedeutung des Todes Jesu.* Ed. F. Viering. Gütersloh: Mohn, 1967. 79–96. **Flusser, D.** *Die letzten Tage Jesu in Jerusalem: Das Passionsgeschehen aus jüdischer Sicht: Bericht über neueste Forschungsergebnisse.* Stuttgart: Calwer, 1982. **Fuller, R. H.** *The Mission and Achievement of Jesus.* SBT 12. London: SCM Press, 1954. 51–78. **Galvin, J. P.** "Jesus' Approach to Death: An Examination of Some Recent Studies." *TS* 41 (1980) 713–44. **Garland, D. E.** *One Hundred Years of Study on the Passion Narratives.* National Association of Baptist Professors of Religion Bibliographic Series 3. Macon, GA: Mercer UP, 1989. **Genest, O.** "Le discours de l'exégèse biblique sur la mort de Jésus." In *Essais sur la mort.* Ed. G. Couturier et al. Héritage et Projet 29. Montreal: Fides, 1985. 123–76. **Geoltrain, P.** "Les récits de la Passion dans les Synoptiques." *FoiVie* 65 (1966) 41–49. **George, A.** "Comment Jésus a-t-il perçu sa propre mort?" *LumVie* 101 (1971) 34–59. **Girard, R.** "The Gospel Passion as Victim's Story." *Cross Currents* 36 (1986–87) 28–38. **Gnilka, J.** *Jesus Christ nach frühen Zeugnissen des Glaubens.* Biblische Handbibliothek 8. Munich: Kösel, 1970. 95–110. ———. *Jesus von Nazareth: Botschaft und Geschichte.* HTKNTSup 1. Freiburg: Herder, 1990. 268–318. **Goguel, M.** "Juifs et Romains dans l'histoire de la passion." *RHR* 62 (1910) 165–82, 295–322. **Gourgues, M.** *Le Crucifié: Du scandale à l'exaltation.* Jésus et Jésus Christ 38. Paris: Desclée; Montreal: Bellarmin, 1989. Esp. 29–74. **Green, J. B.** *The Death of Jesus: Tradition and Interpretation in the Passion Narrative.* WUNT 2.33. Tübingen: Mohr-Siebeck, 1988. 221–313. ———. "Passion Narrative." *DJG.* 601–4. **Gubler, M.-L.** *Die frühesten Deutungen des Todes Jesu: Eine motivgeschichtliche Darstellung aufgrund der neueren exegetischen Forschung.* OBO 15. Göttingen: Vandenhoeck & Ruprecht, 1977. 100–107. **Guillet, J.** "Les récits de la Passion." *LumVie* 23 (1974) 6–17. **Harvey, A. E.** *Jesus and the Constraints of History.* The Bampton Lectures, 1980. London: Duckworth, 1982. **Haufe, G.** "Der Prozess Jesu im Lichte der gegenwärtigen Forschung." *ZZ* 22 (1968) 93–101. **Haulotte, E.** "Du récit quadriforme de la Passion au concept de Croix." *RSR* 73 (1985) 187–228. **Hendrickx, H.** *The Passion Narratives of the Synoptic Gospels.* Rev. ed. London: Chapman, 1984. **Hillmann, W.** *Aufbau und Deutung der synoptischen Leidensberichte: Ein Beitrag zur Kompositionstechnik und*

Sinnbedeutung der drei älteren Evangelien. Freiburg: Herder, 1941. **Horbury, W.** "The Passion Narratives and Historical Criticism." *Theology* 75 (1972) 58–71. **Horsley, R. A.** "The Death of Jesus." In *Studying the Historical Jesus: Evaluations of the State of Current Research.* Ed. B. D. Chilton and C. A. Evans. NTTS 19. Leiden: Brill, 1994. 395–422. **Innitzer, T.** *Kommentar zur Leidens- und Verklärungsgeschichte Jesu Christi.* 4th ed. Vienna: Herder, 1948. **Isaac, J.** "Problèmes de la Passion d'après deux études récentes." *Revue historique* 85 (1961) 119–38. **Janssen, F.** "Die synoptischen Passionsberichte: Ihre theologische Konzeption und literarische Komposition." *BibLeb* 14 (1973) 40–57. **Jeremias, J.** *The Eucharistic Words of Jesus.* Philadelphia: Fortress, 1977. **Jonge, M. de.** "Jesus' Death for Others and the Death of the Maccabean Martyrs." In *Text and Testimony.* FS A. F. J. Klijn, ed. T. J. Baarda et al. Kampen: Kok, 1988. 142–51. ———. "The Use of Ο ΧΡΙΣΤΟΣ in the Passion Narratives." In *Jésus aux origines de la christologie.* Ed. J. Dupont. BETL 40. Leuven: Leuven UP, 1975. 169–92. **Kertelge, K.,** ed. *Der Prozess gegen Jesus: Historische Rückfrage und theologische Deutung.* QD 112. Freiburg; Basel: Herder, 1988. **Knox, W. L.** *The Sources of the Synoptic Gospels.* Cambridge: Cambridge UP, 1953. 115–47. **Kraft, H.** *Die Entstehung des Christentums.* Darmstadt: Wissenschaftliche Buchgesellschaft, 1981. 180–203. **Kremer, J.** *Das Ärgernis des Kreuzes: Eine Hinführung zum Verstehen der Leidensgeschichte.* Stuttgart: Katholisches Bibelwerk, 1969. **Kümmel, W. G.** "Jesusforschung seit 1965: VI. Der Prozess und der Kreuzestod Jesu." *TRu* 45 (1980) 293–337. **Lacomora, A.,** ed. *The Language of the Cross.* Chicago: Franciscan Herald Press, 1977. **Lange, H. D.** "The Relationship between Psalm 22 and the Passion Narrative." *CurTM* 43 (1972) 610–21. **Leenhardt, F. J.** *La mort et le testament de Jésus.* Essais bibliques 6. Geneva: Labor et Fides, 1983. **Lehmann, M.** *Synoptische Quellenanalyse und die Frage nach dem historischen Jesus: Kriterien der Jesusforschung untersucht in Auseinandersetzung mit Emmanuel Hirschs Frühgeschichte des Evangeliums.* BZNW 38. Berlin: de Gruyter, 1970. 103–12. **Lentzen-Deis, F.** "Passionsbericht als Handlungsmodell? Überlegungen zu Anstössen aus der 'pragmatischen' Sprachwissenschaft für die exegetischen Methoden." In *Der Prozess gegen Jesus: Historische Rückfrage und theologische Deutung.* Ed. K. Kertelge. QD 112. Freiburg; Basel: Herder, 1988. 191–232. **Léon-Dufour, X.** "Autor de la mort de Jésus." *RSR* 66 (1978) 113–24. ———. "Autor des récits de la Passion." *RSR* 48 (1960) 489–507. **Limbeck, M.,** ed. *Redaktion und Theologie des Passionsberichtes nach den Synoptikern.* Wege der Forschung 481. Darmstadt: Wissenschaftliche Buchgesellschaft, 1981. **Linnemann, E.** *Studien zur Passionsgeschichte.* FRLANT 61. 2nd ed. Göttingen: Vandenhoeck & Ruprecht, 1953. 57–64. **Lohse, E.** *History of the Suffering and Death of Jesus Christ.* Philadelphia: Fortress, 1967. **Lunn, A. J.** "Christ's Passion as Tragedy." *SJT* 43 (1990) 308–20. **Manson, W.** *Jesus the Messiah: The Synoptic Tradition of the Revelation of God in Christ.* 2nd ed. London: Hodder & Stoughton, 1952. 121–46. **Marin, L.** *The Semiotics of the Passion Narrative: Topics and Figures.* PTMS 25. Pittsburgh: Pickwick, 1980. **Martinez, E. R.** *The Gospel Accounts of the Death of Jesus.* Rome: Gregorian UP, 1970. **Matera, F. J.** *Passion Narratives and Gospel Theologies.* New York: Paulist, 1986. **McCafferey, U. P.** "Psalm Quotations in the Passion Narratives of the Gospels." *Neot* 14 (1981) 73–89. **Meyer, E.** *Ursprung und Anfänge des Christentums.* Vol. 1: *Die Evangelien.* 1921. Repr. Darmstadt: Wissenschaftliche Buchgesellschaft, 1962. 161–211. **Michl, J.** "Der Tod Jesu: Ein Beitrag zur Frage nach Schuld und Verantwortung eines Volkes." *MTZ* 1 (1950) 5–15. **Mode, E.** "Der Passionsweg Jesu Christi: Vom 'Hosianna' zum 'Kreuzige.'" *Forum Katholische Theologie* 7 (1991) 61–72. **Moo, D. J.** *Old Testament in the Gospel Passion Narratives.* **Morgan, R.** "'Nothing more negative . . .': A Concluding Unscientific Postscript to Historical Research on the Trial of Jesus." In *The Trial of Jesus.* FS C. F. D. Moule, ed. E. Bammel. SBT 13. London: SCM Press; Naperville, IL: Allenson, 1970. 135–46. **Moule, C. F. D.** "The Gravamen against Jesus." In *Jesus, the Gospels, and the Church.* FS W. R. Farmer, ed. E. P. Sanders. Macon, GA: Mercer UP, 1987. 177–95. **Navone, J.,** and **Cooper, T.** *The Story of the Passion.* Rome: Gregorian UP, 1986. **Nickelsburg, G. W. E.** "Passion Narratives." *ABD* 5:172–77. **Pedersen, S.** "Die Gotteserfahrung bei Jesus." *ST* 41 (1987) 127–56, esp. 143–49. **Pesch, R.** "Die

Überlieferung der Passion Jesu." In *Rückfrage nach Jesus.* Ed. K. Kertelge. QD 63. Freiburg: Herder, 1974. 148–73. **Prigent, P.** "Les récits évangéliques de la Passion et l'utilisation des 'Testimonia.'" *RHR* 161 (1962) 130–32. **Radl, W.** "Der Tod Jesu in der Darstellung der Evangelien." *TGl* 72 (1982) 432–46. **Ramsey, A. M.** *The Narratives of the Passion.* Contemporary Studies in Theology 1. London: Mowbray, 1962 (= "The Narratives of the Passion." *SE* 2 [= TU 87] [1964] 122–34). **Richardson, P.** "The Israel-Idea in the Passion Narratives." In *The Trial of Jesus.* FS C. F. D. Moule, ed. E. Bammel. SBT 13. London: SCM Press; Naperville, IL: Allenson, 1970. 1–10. **Ricoeur, P.** "Le récit interprétatif: Exégèse et théologie dans les récits de la Passion." *RSR* 73 (1985) 17–38. **Riedl, J.** "Die evangelische Leidensgeschichte und ihre theologische Aussage." *BL* 41 (1968) 70–111. **Rivkin, E.** *What Crucified Jesus? The Political Execution of a Charismatic.* London: SCM Press, 1986. **Rose, A.** "L'influence des psaumes sur les annonces et les récits de la Passion et de la Résurrection dans les Évangiles." In *Le Psautier, ses origines, ses problèmes litteraires, son influence: Études presentées au XIIe Journées bibliques (29-31 aout 1960).* Ed. R. de Langhe. OBL 4. Louvain: Publications Universitaires, 1962. 297–356. **Ruppert, L.** *Jesus als der leidende Gerecht? Der Weg Jesu im Lichte eines alt- und zwischentestamentlichen Motivs.* SBS 59. Stuttgart: Katholisches Bibewerk, 1972. **Sanders, E. P.** *Jesus and Judaism.* 294–318. **Schelkle, K. H.** *Die Passion Jesu in der Verkündigung des Neuen Testaments: Ein Beitrag zur Formgeschichte und zur Theologie des Neuen Testaments.* Heidelberg: Kerle, 1949. **Schenk, W.** "Der derzeitige Stand der Auslegung der Passionsgeschichte." *Der evangelische Erzieher* 36 (1984) 527–43. ———. "Leidensgeschichte Jesu." *TRE* 20 (1990) 714–21. **Schille, G.** "Das Leiden des Herrn: Die evangelische Passionsgestradition und ihr 'Sitz im Leben.'" *ZTK* 52 (1955) 161–205 (repr. in *Redaktion und Theologie des Passionsberichtes nach den Synoptikern.* Ed. M. Limbeck. Wege der Forschung 481. Darmstadt: Wissenschaftliche Buchgesellschaft, 1981. 154–204). **Schmauch, W.** "Auslegungsprobleme der Leidensgeschichte." In *Zu Achten aufs Wort.* Göttingen: Vandenhoeck & Ruprecht, 1967. 56–64. **Schmid, J.** "Die Darstellung der Passion Jesu in den Evangelien." *Geist und Leben* 27 (1954) 6–15. **Schmidt, K. L.** *Rahmen der Geschichte Jesu.* 303–9. **Schneider, G.** *Passion Jesu.* ———. "Das Problem einer vorkanonischen Passionserzählung." *BZ* 16 (1972) 222–44. **Schürmann, H.** "Jesu ureigener Tod im Licht seiner Basileia-Verkündigung." In *Gottes Reich—Jesu Geschick: Jesu ureigener Tod im Licht seiner Basileia-Verkündigung.* Freiburg: Herder, 1983. 11–18. **Sloyan, G. S.** *Jesus on Trial: The Development of the Passion Narratives and Their Historical and Ecumenical Implications.* Philadelphia: Fortress, 1973. **Soards, M. L.** "Oral Tradition Before, In, and Outside Canonical Passion Narratives." In *Jesus and the Oral Gospel Tradition.* Ed. H. Wansbrough. JSNTSup 64. Sheffield: JSOT Press, 1991. 334–40. **Speidel, K. A.** *Das Urteil des Pilatus: Bilder und Berichte zur Passion Jesu.* Stuttgart: Katholisches Bibelwerk, 1976. **Stanton, G. N.** *The Gospels and Jesus.* Oxford Bible Series. Oxford; New York: Oxford UP, 1989. 248–70. **Strobel, A.** *Die Stunde der Wahrheit: Untersuchungen zum Strafverfahren gegen Jesus.* WUNT 21. Tübingen: Mohr-Siebeck, 1980. **Suggs, M. J.** "The Passion and Resurrection Narratives." In *Jesus and Man's Hope.* Ed. D. G. Miller and D. Y. Hadidian. 2 vols. Pittsburgh: Pittsburgh Theological Seminary, 1971. 2:323–38. **Surkau, H. W.** *Martyrien in jüdischer und frühchristlicher Zeit.* FRLANT 54. Göttingen: Vandenhoeck & Ruprecht, 1938. 82–105. **Taylor, V.** *Formation.* 44–62. ———. "Modern Issues in Biblical Studies: Methods of Gospel Criticism." *ExpTim* 71 (1959–60) 68–72. **Theissen, G.** *Gospels in Context.* 166–99. **Trilling, W.** "Die Passion Jesu in der Darstellung der synoptischen Evangelien." In *Vielfalt und Einheit im Neuen Testament: Zur exegese und Verkündigung des Neuen Testaments.* Unterweisen und Verkünden 3. Zürich; Köln: Benziger, 1968. 83–111. **Trocmé, É.** *The Passion as Liturgy: A Study in the Origin of the Passion Narratives in the Four Gospels.* London: SCM Press, 1983. 7–19. **Vanhoye, A.** *La Passion selon les quatres Évangiles.* Lire la Bible 55. Paris: Cerf, 1981. ———. "Les récits de la Passion dans les évangiles synoptiques." *AsSeign* 2.19 (1971) 38–67. ———. *Structure and Theology of the Accounts of the Passion in the Synoptic Gospels.* Bible Today Supplementary Studies 1. Collegeville, MN: Liturgical Press, 1967.

Viering, F., ed. *Das Kreuz Jesu Christi als Grund des Heils.* Gütersloh: Mohn, 1967. **Weber, H.-R.** *The Cross: Tradition and Interpretation.* Grand Rapids, MI: Eerdmans, 1979. **Wilson, W. R.** *The Execution of Jesus: A Judicial, Literary, and Historical Investigation.* New York: Scribner's, 1970. **Wrege, H.-T.** "Die Passionsgeschichte." In *Die Gestalt des Evangeliums.* BET 11. Frankfurt am Main; Bern: Lang, 1978. 49–96. **Zehrer, F.** "Jesus, der leidende Gerechte, in der Passion." *BL* 47 (1974) 104–11. ———. *Das Leiden Christi nach den vier Evangelien: Die wichtigsten Passionstexte und ihre hauptsachlichen Probleme.* Vienna: Mayer, 1980. ———. "Sinn und Problematik der Schriftverwendung in der Passion." *TPQ* 121 (1973) 18–25. **Zmijewski, J.** "Überlieferungen zum Verhältnis von Theologie und christlicher Glaubenspraxis anhand des Neuen Testaments." *TGl* 72 (1982) 40–78, esp. 45–47.

Bibliography on the Markan Passion Narrative

Allison, D. C. *The End of the Ages Has Come: An Early Interpretation of the Passion and Resurrection of Jesus.* Philadelphia: Fortress, 1985. 26–39. **Anderson, C. P.** "The Trial of Jesus as Jewish-Christian Polarization: Blasphemy and Polemic in Mark's Gospel." In *Paul and the Gospels.* Vol. 1 of *Anti-Judaism in Early Christianity.* Ed. P. Richardson. Waterloo, Ontario: Wilfrid Laurier UP, 1986. 107–25. **Barrett, C. K.** *Jesus and the Gospel Tradition.* London: S. P. C. K., 1967; Philadelphia: Fortress, 1968. 35–67. **Bartsch, H.-W.** "Historische Erwägungen zur Leidensgeschichte." *EvT* 22 (1962) 449–59. ———. "Der ursprüngliche Schluss der Leidensgeschichte: Überlieferungs-geschichtliche Studien zum Markus-Schluss." *TZ* 27 (1971) 241–54 (repr. in *L'Évangile selon Marc: Tradition et rédaction.* Ed. M. Sabbe. BETL 34. Gembloux: Duculot; Leuven: Leuven UP, 1974. 411–33). **Best, E.** *Mark: The Gospel as Story.* 66–71. ———. *The Temptation and the Passion.* **Black, C. C.** *Disciples according to Mark.* **Blinzler, J.** "Jesusverkündigung im Markusevangelium." In *Jesus in den Evangelien.* Ed. W. Pesch. SBS 45. Stuttgart: Katholisches Bibelwerk, 1970. 71–104, esp. 95–104. **Boomershine, T. E.** "Mark the Storyteller: A Rhetorical-Critical Investigation of Mark's Passion and Resurrection Narrative." Diss., Union Theological Seminary, New York, 1974. **Broadhead, E. K.** *Prophet, Son, Messiah: Narrative Form and Function in Mark 14–16.* JSNTSup 97. Sheffield: JSOT Press, 1994. **Buckley, E. R.** "The Sources of the Passion Narrative in St. Mark's Gospel." *JTS* o.s. 34 (1932–33) 138–44. **Burkill, T. A.** "St. Mark's Philosophy of the Passion." *NovT* 2 (1958) 245–71. **Bussmann, W.** *Synoptischen Studien.* 3 vols. Halle: Waisenhaus, 1925–31. 1:192–205. **Chordat, J.-L.** *Jésus devant sa mort dans l'évangile de Marc.* Lire la Bible. Paris: Cerf, 1970. **Cook, M. J.** *Mark's Treatment of the Jewish Leaders.* **Culpepper, R. A.** "The Passion and Resurrection in Mark." *RevExp* 75 (1978) 483–600. **Danker, F. W.** "The Literary Unity of Mark 14:1–25." *JBL* 85 (1966) 467–72. **Delling, G.** *Der Kreuzestod Jesu in der urchristlichen Verkündigung.* Berlin: Evangelische Verlagsanstalt, 1971; Göttingen: Vandenhoeck & Ruprecht, 1972. 57–74. **Dewar, F.** "Chapter 13 and the Passion Narrative in St Mark." *Theology* 64 (1961) 99–107. **Donahue, J. R.** *Are You the Christ?* ———. "Introduction: From Passion Traditions to Passion Narrative." In *The Passion in Mark: Studies on Mark 14–16.* Ed. W. Kelber. Philadelphia: Fortress, 1976. 1–20, esp. 8–16. **Dormeyer, D.** *Passion Jesu als Verhaltensmodell.* ———. *Der Sinn des Leidens Jesu: Historisch-kritische und textpragmatische Analysen zur Markuspassion.* SBS 96. Stuttgart: Katholisches Bibelwerk, 1979. **Ernst, J.** "Die Passionserzählung des Markus und die Aporien der Forschung." *TGl* 70 (1980) 160–80. **Evans, C. F.** *The Beginning of the Gospel: Four Lectures on St Mark's Gospel.* London: S. P. C. K., 1968. 63–82. ———. "The Passion of Christ." In *Explorations in Theology 2.* London: SCM Press, 1977. 1–66, esp. 34–49. **Feneberg, F.** "Formgeschichte und historischer Jesus." In *Das Leben Jesu im Evangelium.* Ed. W. Feneberg. QD 88. Freiburg: Herder, 1980. 19–183, esp. 128–71. **Fenton, J. C.** "The Passion Narrative in St Mark's Gospel." In *The Reality of God.* FS T. Baker, ed. J. Butterworth. London: Severn House, 1986. 21–32. ———. *Preaching the Cross: The Passion and Resurrection according to St Mark with an Introduction and Notes.* London: S. P. C. K., 1958. **Funk, R. W.** *The Poetics of Bibli-*

cal Narrative. Sonoma: Polebridge, 1988. 245–62. **Genest, O.** *Le Christ de la Passion: Perspective structurale: Analyse de Marc 14,53–15,47 des parallèles bibliques et extra-bibliques.* Tournai: Desclée, 1978. **Green, J. B.** *The Death of Jesus: Tradition and Interpretation in the Passion Narrative.* WUNT 2.33. Tübingen: Mohr-Siebeck, 1988. 136–56. **Hamerton-Kelly, R. G.** "Sacred Violence and the Messiah: The Markan Passion Narrative as a Redefinition of Messianology." In *The Messiah: Developments in Earliest Judaism and Christianity.* Ed. J. H. Charlesworth. Minneapolis: Fortress, 1992. 461–93. **Heil, J. P.** "Mark 14,1–52: Narrative Structure and Reader-Response." *Bib* 71 (1990) 305–32. ———. "Mark 14,53–16,8: Narrative Structure and Reader-Response." *Bib* 73 (1992) 331–58. **Houlden, J. L.** *Backward into Light: The Passion and Resurrection of Jesus according to Matthew and Mark.* London: SCM Press, 1987. **Iersel, B. M. F. van.** "Jesus' Way of Obedience according to Mark's Gospel." *Concilium* 139 (1980) 25–33. **Jeremias, J.** "A Comparison of the Marcan Passion Narrative with the Johannine." In *The Eucharistic Words of Jesus.* Philadelphia: Fortress, 1977. 89–96. **Johns, E.,** and **Major, D.** *Witness in a Pagan World: A Study of Mark's Gospel.* London: Lutterworth, 1980. 128–38. **Juel, D. H.** "The Function of the Trial of Jesus in Mark's Gospel." In *Society of Biblical Literature 1975 Seminar Papers.* Ed. G. W. MacRae. 2 vols. SBLSP 14. Missoula, MT: Scholars Press, 1975. 2:83–104. ———. *Messiah and Temple.* **Keck, L. E.** "Mark and the Passion." *Int* 31 (1977) 432–34. **Kelber, W.** "Conclusion: From Passion Narrative to Gospel." In *The Passion in Mark: Studies on Mark 14–16.* Ed. W. Kelber. Philadelphia: Fortress, 1976. 153–80. ———. *Mark's Story of Jesus.* Philadelphia: Fortress, 1979. 71–87. ———. *The Oral and Written Gospel.* Philadelphia: Fortress, 1983. 184–99. ———, ed. *The Passion in Mark: Studies on Mark 14–16.* Philadelphia: Fortress, 1976. ———, **Kolenkow, A. B.,** and **Scroggs, R.** "Reflections on the Question: Was There a Pre-Markan Passion Narrative?" In *Society of Biblical Literature 1971 Seminar Papers.* Ed. J. L. White et al. 2 vols. SBLSP 10. Missoula, MT: SBL, 1971. 2:503–85. **Kingsbury, J. D.** "The Religious Authorities in the Gospel of Mark." *NTS* 36 (1990) 42–65. **Kolenkow, A. B.** "Healing Controversy as a Tie between Miracle and Passion Material for a Proto-Gospel." *JBL* 95 (1976) 623–38. **Kuhn, H.-W.** *Ältere Sammlungen.* 220–25. **Kuhn, K. G.** "Jesus in Gethsemane." *EvT* 12 (1952–53) 260–85. **Lambrecht, J.** *Die Redaktion der Markus-Apokalypse: Literarische Analyse und Strukturuntersuchung.* AnBib 28. Rome: Biblical Institute, 1967. 55–60. **Léon-Dufour, X.** "Mt et Mc dans le récit de la Passion." *Bib* 40 (1959) 684–96. **Lull, D. J.** "Interpreting Mark's Story of Jesus' Death: Toward a Theology of Suffering." In *Society of Biblical Literature 1985 Seminar Papers.* Ed. K. H. Richards. SBLSP 24. Atlanta: Scholars Press, 1985. 1–12. **Luz, U.** "Theologia Crucis als Mitte der Theologie im Neuen Testament." *EvT* 34 (1974) 116–41. **Mack, B. L.** *A Myth of Innocence.* 247–312. **Malbon, E. S.** "The Jewish Leaders in the Gospel of Mark." *JBL* 108 (1989) 259–81. **Mann, D.** *Mein Gott, mein Gott, warum hast du mich verlassen? Eine Auslegung der Passionsgeschichte nach Markus.* Neukirchen-Vluyn: Neukirchener Verlag, 1980. **Mansfield, M. R.** *"Spirit and Gospel" in Mark.* Peabody: Hendrickson, 1987. 125–44. **Matera, F. J.** *The Kingship of Jesus: Composition and Theology in Mark 15.* SBLDS 66. Chico, CA: Scholars Press, 1982. **Maurer, C.** "Knecht Gottes und Sohn Gottes im Passionsbericht des Markusevangeliums." *ZTK* 50 (1953) 1–38 (repr. in *Redaktion und Theologie des Passionsberichtes nach den Synoptikern.* Ed. M. Limbeck. Wege und Forschung 481. Darmstadt: Wissenschaftliche Buchgesellschaft, 1981. 112–53). **McVann, M.** "The Passion in Mark: Transformation Ritual." *BTB* 18 (1988) 96–101. **Milling, F. H.** "History and Prophecy in the Marcan Passion Narrative." *IJT* 16 (1967) 42–53. **Mohr, T. A.** *Markus- und Johannespassion.* **Myllykoski, M.** *Die letzten Tage Jesu.* Esp. 1:18–21. **Navone, J.** "Mark's Story of the Death of Jesus." *NBf* 65 (1984) 123–35. **Neirynck, F.** "L'Évangile de Marc II: À propos de R. Pesch, *Das Markusevangelium, 2 Teil.*" *ETL* 55 (1979) 1–42, esp. 8–27 (repr. in F. Neirynck. *Evangelica.* BETL 60. Leuven: Peeters and Leuven UP, 1982. 520–64, esp. 527–46). **Nickelsburg, G. W. E.** "The Genre and Function of the Markan Passion Narrative." *HTR* 73 (1980) 153–84. **Oberlinner, L.** "Die Botschaft vom Kreuz als die Botschaft vom Heil nach Markus." *BL* 61 (1988) 56–65. **Oswald, J.** "Die Beziehungen zwischen Psalm 22 und dem vormarkinischen Passionsbericht." *ZKT* 101 (1979) 53–66. **Patte, D.,** and **Patte, A.** *Structural Exegesis: From Theory to Practice. Exegesis of Mark 15* *and 16.* Philadelphia: Fortress, 1978. **Pesch, R.** *Evangelium der Urgemeinde.* ———. "Die Passion des Menschensohnes: Eine Studie zu den Menschensohnworten der vormarkinischen Passionsgeschichte." In *Jesus und der Menschensohn.* FS A. Vögtle, ed. R. Pesch et al. Freiburg: Herder, 1975. 166–95. ———. "Der Schluss der vormarkinischen Passionsgeschichte und des Markusevangeliums: Mk 15,42–16,8." In *L'Évangile selon Marc: Tradition et rédaction.* Ed. M. Sabbe. BETL 34. Gembloux: Duculot; Leuven: Leuven UP, 1974. 365–409. **Piper, O. A.** "God's Good News: The Passion Story according to Mark." *Int* 9 (1955) 165–82. **Rau, G.** "Das Markus-Evangelium: Komposition und Intention der ersten Darstellung christlicher Mission." *ANRW* 2.25.3 (1985) 2036–2257, esp. 2186–2227. **Riches, J. K.** "The Dense and Driven Passion: The Story according to Mark." *Furrow* 33 (1982) 195–202. **Sahlin, H.** "Zum Verständnis der christologischen Anschauung der Markusevangeliums." *ST* 31 (1977) 1–19, esp. 3–15. **Schenk, W.** "Die gnostisierende Deutung des Todes Jesu und ihre kritische Interpretation durch den Evangelisten Markus." In *Gnosis und Neues Testament.* Ed. K. W. Tröger. Gütersloh: Mohn, 1963. 231–43. ———. *Passionsbericht nach Markus.* **Schenke, L.** *Der gekreuzigten Christus.* ———. *Studien zur Passionsgeschichte des Markus.* **Schlier, H.** *Die Markuspassion.* Kriterien 32. Einsiedeln: Johannes, 1974. **Schmidt, K. L.** *Rahmen.* 303–9. **Schneider, G.** *Verleugnung, Verspottung und Verhör Jesu nach Lukas 22,54–71: Studien zur lukanischen Darstellung der Passion.* SANT 22. Munich: Kösel, 1969. 26–46. **Schreiber, J.** *Der Kreuzigungsbericht des Markusevangeliums: Mk 15,20b–41: Eine traditionsgeschichtliche und methodenkritische Untersuchung nach William Wrede (1859–1906).* BZNW 48. Berlin; New York: de Gruyter, 1986. ———. *Die Markuspassion: Wege zur Erforschung der Leidensgeschichte Jesu.* Hamburg: Furche, 1969. ———. *Theologie des Vertrauens.* 22–86. **Senior, D. P.** "Crucible of Truth: Passion and Resurrection in the Gospel of Mark." *Chicago Studies* 25 (1986) 21–34. ———. *Passion of Jesus in the Gospel of Mark.* 139–56. **Smith, R. H.** "Darkness at Noon: Mark's Passion Narrative." *CTM* 44 (1973) 325–38. **Soards, M. L.** "Appendix IX: The Question of a Pre-Markan Passion Narrative." In R. E. Brown. *The Death of the Messiah: A Commentary on the Passion Narratives in the Four Gospels.* 2 vols. ABRL. New York: Doubleday, 1994. 2:1492–1524. **Standaert, B. H. J. G. M.** *L'évangile selon Marc.* 70–82. **Stock, A.** *Call to Discipleship.* 191–202. ———. "Literary Criticism and Mark's Mystery Play." *TBT* 100 (1979) 1909–15. **Taylor, V.** *The Passion Narrative of St Luke: A Critical and Historical Investigation.* Ed. O. E. Evans. SNTSMS 19. Cambridge: Cambridge UP, 1972. 39–115. **Telford, W. R.** "Introduction: The Gospel of Mark." In *The Interpretation of Mark.* Ed. W. R. Telford. IRT 7. London: S. P. C. K.; Philadelphia: Fortress, 1985. 1–42. **Temple, S.** "The Two Traditions of the Last Supper, Betrayal, and Arrest." *NTS* 7 (1960–61) 77–85. **Trocmé, É.** *Formation of the Gospel according to Mark.* 224–40. **Vellanickal, M.** "The Passion Narrative in the Gospel of Mark (Mk. 14:–15:47)." *Biblebhashyam* 9 (1983) 258–78. **Weinacht, H.** *Menschwerdung des Sohnes Gottes.* 61–69. **White, J. L.** "The Way of the Cross: Was There a Pre-Markan Passion Narrative?" *Forum* 3.2 (1987) 35–49. **Wiéner, C.** "Le mystère pascal dans le deuxième évangile: Recherches sur la construction de Marc 14–16." In *La pâque du Christ: Mystère de salut.* FS F.-X. Durrwell, ed. M. Benzerath et al. LD 112. Paris: Cerf, 1982. 131–45. **Wrege, H.-T.** *Die Gestalt des Evangeliums: Aufbau und Struktur der Synoptiker sowie der Apostelgeschichte.* BET 11. Bern; Frankfurt am Main: Lang, 1978. 49–96. **Zeller, D.** "Die Handlungsstruktur der Markuspassion: Der Ertrag strukturalistischer Literaturwissenschaft für die Exegese." *TQ* 159 (1979) 213–27. **Zwick, R.** *Montage im Markusevangelium: Studien zur narrativen Organisation der ältesten Jesuserzählung.* SBB 18. Stuttgart: Katholisches Bibelwerk, 1989. 329–473.

Bibliography on Chronology of the Passion and Date of the Crucifixion

Beckwith, R. T. "Cautionary Notes on the Use of Calendars and Astronomy to Determine the Chronology of the Passion." In *Chronos, Kairos, Christos.* FS J. Finegan, ed. J. Vardaman and E. M. Yamauchi. Winona Lake, IN: Eisenbrauns, 1989. 183–205. ———. "The Day, Its

Divisions and Its Limits, in Biblical Thought." *EvQ* 43 (1971) 218–27. **Benoit, P.** "The Date of the Last Supper." In *Jesus and the Gospel.* 2 vols. London: Darton, Longman and Todd; New York: Herder and Herder, 1973. 1:87–93. **Black, M.** "The Arrest and Trial of Jesus and the Date of the Last Supper." In *New Testament Essays.* FS T. W. Manson, ed. A. J. B. Higgins. Manchester: Manchester UP, 1959. 19–33. **Blinzler, J.** *Der Prozess Jesu: Das jüdische und das römische Gerichtsverfahren gegen Jesus auf Grund der ältesten Zeugnisse dargestellt and beurteilt.* 4th ed. Regensburg: Pustet, 1969. 101–26, 416–22. ———. "Qumran-Kalender und Passionschronologie." *ZNW* 49 (1958) 238–51. **Bokser, B. M.** "Was the Last Supper a Passover Seder?" *BRev* 3.2 (1987) 24–33. **Braun, H.** *Qumran und das Neue Testament.* 2 vols. Tübingen: Mohr-Siebeck, 1966. 2:29–54. **Brown, R. E.** "The Date of the Last Supper." *TBT* 11 (1964) 727–33. **Carmignac, J.** "Les apparitions de Jésus resuscité et le calendrier biblico-qumrânien." *RevQ* 7 (1971) 483–504. ———. "Comment Jésus et ses contemporains pouvaient-ils célébrer la Pâque à une date no officelle?" *RevQ* 5 (1964–66) 59–79. **Chenderlin, F.** "Distributed Observance of the Passover—A Hypothesis." *Bib* 56 (1975) 369–93; 57 (1976) 1–24, esp. 3–9. **Christie, W. M.** "Did Christ Eat the Passover with His Disciples?" *ExpTim* 43 (1932) 515–19. **Chwolson, D.** *Das letzte Passamahl Christi und der Tag seines Todes.* 2nd ed. Leipzig: Haessel, 1908. **Cichorius, C.** "Chronologisches zum Leben Jesu." *ZNW* 22 (1923) 16–20. **Daly, R.** "The Eucharist and Redemption: The Last Supper and Jesus' Understanding of His Death." *BTB* 11 (1981) 21–27. **Davison, A.** "The Crucifixion, Burial, and Resurrection of Jesus." *PEFQS* 38 (1906) 124–29. **Dockx, S.** "Le 14 Nisan de l'an 30." In *Chronologies neotestamentaires et vie de l'Église primitive: Recherches exégétiques.* Gembloux: Duculot, 1976. 21–29. ———. "Chronologie du dernier jour de la vie de Jésus." In *Chronologies neotestamentaires et vie de l'Église primitive: Recherches exégétiques.* Gembloux: Duculot, 1976. 31–43. **Doyle, A. D.** "Pilate's Career and the Date of the Crucifixion." *JTS* n.s. 42 (1941) 190–93. **Dugmore, C. W.** "A Note on the Quartodecimans." In *Studia patristica IV.* TU 79. Berlin: Akademie, 1961. 410–21. **Feld, H.** *Das Verständnis des Abendmahls.* EdF 50. Darmstadt: Wissenschaftliche Buchgesellschaft, 1976. 39–48. **Fotheringham, J. K.** "Astronomical Evidence for the Date of the Crucifixion." *JTS* o.s. 12 (1910) 120–27. ———. "The Evidence of Astronomy and Technical Chronology for the Date of the Crucifixion." *JTS* o.s. 35 (1934) 146–62. **France, R. T.** "Chronological Aspects of 'Gospel Harmony.'" *VE* 16 (1986) 33–59. **Gaechter, P.** "Eine neue Chronologie der Leidenswoche?" *ZKT* 80 (1958) 555–61. **Gilmore, A.** "The Date and Significance of the Last Supper." *SJT* 14 (1961) 256–69. **Grappe, C.** "Essai sur l'arrière-plan des récits de la dernière nuit de Jésus." *RHPR* 65 (1985) 105–25. **Heawood, P. J.** "The Time of the Last Supper." *JQR* 42 (1951–52) 37–44. **Hinz, W.** "Chronologie des Lebens Jesu." *ZDMG* 139 (1989) 301–8. ———. "Jesu Sterbedatum." *ZDMG* 142 (1992) 53–56. **Hoehner, H. W.** *Chronological Aspects of the Life of Christ.* Contemporary Evangelical Perspectives. Grand Rapids: Zondervan, 1977. 65–114. **Hölscher, G.** *Die Hohenpriesterliste bei Josephus und die evangelische Chronologie.* SHAW 30. Heidelberg: Winters, 1940. **Holzmeister, U.** "Neuere Arbeiten über das Datum der Kreuzigung Christi." *Bib* 13 (1932) 93–103. **Humphreys, C. J.,** and **Waddington, W. G.** "Astronomy and the Date of the Crucifixion." In *Chronos, Kairos, Christos.* FS J. Finegan, ed. J. Vardaman and E. M. Yamauchi. Winona Lake, IN: Eisenbrauns, 1989. 165–81. ———. "Dating the Crucifixion." *Nature* 306 (1983) 743–46. ———. "The Jewish Calendar, a Lunar Eclipse and the Date of Christ's Crucifixion." *TynBul* 43 (1992) 331–51. **Husband, R. W.** "The Year of the Crucifixion." *TAPA* 46 (1915) 5–27. **Jaubert, A.** "Le calendrier des Jubilés et de la secte de Qumrân: Ses origines bibliques." *VT* 3 (1953) 250–64. ———. "Le calendrier des Jubilés et les jours liturgiques de la semaine." *VT* 7 (1957) 35–61. ———. "La date de la dernière Cène." *RHR* 146 (1954) 140–73. ———. *The Date of the Last Supper.* Staten Island, NY: Alba House, 1965. ———. "Jésus et le calendrier de Qumrân." *NTS* 7 (1960–61) 1–30. ———. "Le mercredi où Jésus fut livré." *NTS* 14 (1967–68) 145–64. **Johnston, L.** "The Date of the Last Supper." *Scr* 9 (1957) 108–15. **King, C.** "The Outlines of New Testament Chronology." *CBQ* 7 (1945) 129–53. **Kokkinos, N.** "Crucifixion in A.D. 36: The Keystone for Dating the Birth of Jesus." In *Chronos, Kairos, Christos.* FS J. Finegan, ed. J. Vardaman and E. M.

Yamauchi. Winona Lake, IN: Eisenbrauns, 1989. 133–63. **Kraeling, C. H.** "Olstead's Chronology of the Life of Jesus." *ATR* 24 (1942) 334–54. **Lake, K.** "The Date of Herod's Marriage with Herodia, and the Chronology of the Gospels." *Exp* 4 (1912) 462–77. **MacRae, G. W.** "A New Date for the Last Supper." *AER* 138 (1958) 294–302. **Mahoney, J.** "The Last Supper and the Qumran Calendar." *ClerRev* 48 (1963) 216–32. **Maier, P. L.** "Sejanus, Pilate, and the Date of the Crucifixion." *CH* 37 (1968) 3–13. **Mann, C. S.** "The Chronology of the Passion and the Qumran Calendar." *CQR* 160 (1959) 446–56. **Mastin, B. A.** "The Date of the Triumphal Entry." *NTS* 16 (1969–70) 76–82. **Meier, J. P.** *Marginal Jew.* 1:372–433. **Montefiore, H. W.** "When Did Jesus Die?" *ExpTim* 72 (1960–61) 53–54. **Mulder, H.** "John xviii 28 and the Date of the Crucifixion." In *Miscellanea Neotestamentica II.* Ed. T. Baarda et al. NovTSup 48. Leiden: Brill, 1978. 87–106. **O'Flynn, J. A.** "The Date of the Last Supper." *ITQ* 25 (1958) 58–63. **Ogg, G.** "The Chronology of the Last Supper." In *Historicity and Chronology in the New Testament.* Ed. D. E. Nineham et al. London: SCM Press, 1965. 92–96. ———. "Review of Mlle Jaubert, *La Date de la Cène.*" *NovT* 3 (1959) 149–60. **Olmstead, A. T.** "The Chronology of Jesus' Life." *ATR* 24 (1942) 1–26. **Power, E.** "John 2,20 and the Date of the Crucifixion." *Bib* 9 (1928) 257–88. **Ruckstuhl, E.** *Chronology of the Last Days of Jesus: A Critical Study.* Rome; New York: Desclée, 1965. ———. "Zur Chronologie der Leidensgeschichte Jesu." SNTSU 10 (1985) 27–61; 11 (1986) 97–129 (repr. in E. Ruckstuhl. *Jesus im Horizont der Evangelien.* SBA 3. Stuttgart: Katholisches Bibelwerk, 1988. 101–39, 141–76 [with supplement on pp. 177–84]). **Saldarini, A. J.** *Jesus and Passover.* New York: Paulist, 1984. **Sanders, E. P.** *The Historical Figure of Jesus.* London: Penguin, 1993. 66–73. **Schaumberger, J.** "Der 14. Nisan als Kreuzigungstag und die Synoptiker." *Bib* 9 (1928) 57–77. **Shepherd, M. H.** "Are Both the Synoptics and John Correct about the Date of Jesus' Death?" *JBL* 80 (1961) 123–32. **Skehan, P. W.** "The Date of the Last Supper." *CBQ* 20 (1958) 192–99. **Smallwood, E. M.** "The Date of the Dismissal of Pontius Pilate from Judaea." *JJS* 5 (1954) 12–21. **Smith, B. D.** "The Chronology of the Last Supper." *WTJ* 53 (1991) 29–45. **Story, C. I. K.** "The Bearing of Old Testament Terminology on the Johannine Chronology of the Final Passover of Jesus." *NovT* 31 (1989) 316–24. **Strobel, A.** "Die Termin des Todes Jesu: Überschau und Lösungsvorschlag unter Einschluss des Qumrankalenders." *ZNW* 51 (1960) 69–101. ———. *Ursprung und Geschichte des frühchristlichen Osterkalenders.* TU 121. Berlin: Akademie, 1977. 109–21. **Thiele, E. R.** "The Day and Hour of Passover Observance in New Testament Times." *ATR* 28 (1946) 163–68. **Torrey, C. C.** "The Date of the Crucifixion according to the Fourth Gospel." *JBL* 50 (1931) 227–41. ———. "In the Fourth Gospel the Last Supper Was the Paschal Meal." *JQR* 42 (1951–52) 237–50. **Turner, H. E. W.** "The Chronological Framework of the Ministry." In *Historicity and Chronology in the New Testament.* Ed. D. E. Nineham et al. London: SCM Press, 1965. 59–74. **Vogt, E.** "Une lumière nouvelle sur la semaine de la passion." *Christus* 4 (1956) 413–21. **Walker, N.** "Concerning the Jaubertian Chronology of the Passion." *NovT* 3 (1959) 317–20. ———. "The Dating of the Last Supper." *JQR* 47 (1957) 293–95. ———. "Pauses in the Passion Story and Their Significance for Chronology." *NovT* 6 (1963) 16–19. ———. "Yet Another Look at the Passion Chronology." *NovT* 6 (1963) 286–89. **Walther, J. A.** "The Chronology of the Passion Week." *JBL* 77 (1958) 116–22. **Zeitlin, S.** "The Beginning of the Jewish Day during the Second Commonwealth." *JQR* 36 (1945–46) 403–14. ———. "The Date of the Crucifixion according to the Fourth Gospel." *JBL* 51 (1932) 263–71. ———. "The Dates of the Birth and the Crucifixion of Jesus." *JQR* 55 (1964) 1–22. ———. "The Time of the Passover Meal." *JQR* 42 (1951–52) 45–50.

Introduction

The Markan Passion Narrative "is the most closely articulated in the Gospel" (Taylor, 524). Nothing else in Mark compares with it; even the day in Capernaum consists of no more than a few brief pericopes (1:21–34, plus perhaps 1:35–45). The Passion Narrative, in contrast, provides a series of closely related events, many

of which are clearly associated with Jerusalem and its environs, especially the
temple precincts. Form critics have long recognized the cohesion of this material
(cf. Dibelius, *Tradition*, 178–217; Schmidt, *Rahmen*, 303–6; Bultmann, *History*, 262–
84; Taylor, *Formation*, 44–62). Although in recent years some voices have been
raised against it (e.g., Donahue, *Are You the Christ?*; id., "From Passion Traditions
to Passion Narrative"; Kelber, *Oral and Written Gospel*; id., "From Passion Narrative to Gospel"; Mack, *Myth of Innocence*; Matera, *Passion Narratives*; and Schille,
ZTK 52 [1955] 161–205), most scholars still believe that underlying Mark 14–15
is a pre-Markan Passion Narrative (see esp. Pesch, *Evangelium der Urgemeinde*; id.,
"Der Schluss der vormarkinischen Passionsgeschichte"; id., "Die Überlieferung
der Passion Jesu"), or, in the case of K. G. Kuhn (*EvT* 12 [1952–53] 260–85) and
others (especially with regard to Gethsemane; see *Comment* section for 14:32–42),
two passion sources (more on this below).

Proposals regarding what is source and what is redaction are numerous and
frequently contradictory. Dibelius (*Tradition*, 178–217) believes that the evangelist added five stories to his passion source: the anointing (14:3–9), the preparation
for the Passover (14:12–16), portions of the Gethsemane story (14:39–42), portions of the hearing before the priests (14:59–65), and the narrative of the empty
tomb (16:1–8). Bultmann (*History*, 262–84) believes that the evangelist added details and stories about Peter—the journey to the home of the high priest and the
denials—as well as whole pericopes such as the plot of the priests (14:1–2), the
anointing (14:3–9), the treachery of Judas (14:10–11), the institution of the Lord's
Supper (14:22–25), Gethsemane (14:32–42), the hearing before the priests (14:55–
64), the mocking of the soldiers (15:16–20a), the women at the cross (15:40–41),
and the burial (15:42–47). Taylor (653–54) identifies the primitive "Roman tradition" of the Passion Narrative as consisting of 14:1–2, 10–11, 17–21, 26–31, 43–46,
53a; 15:1, 3–5, 15, 21–24, 26, 29–30, 34–37, 39, 42–46. Taylor (653–64) believes
that the Markan Passion Narrative came into existence in two basic stages: first,
there was a continuous Roman, non-Semitic summarizing source; second, this
source was supplemented with several noncontinuous primitive stories that betray many Semitizing features. Taylor concludes that "the Roman story of the
Cross was expanded by the aid of Petrine tradition and the necessary editorial
supplements" (663–64). For a recent assessment of passion traditions that also
takes into account extracanonical Gospels and sources, see M. L. Soards, "Oral
Tradition."

The passion of Jesus comes to a speedy climax. It is introduced with the notation "it was now two days before the Passover and the Feast of Unleavened Bread"
(14:1a) and the sinister comment "the ruling priests and the scribes were seeking
how, taking him by stealth, they might kill him" (14:1b). With these opening verses
the stage is set: the reader knows the season—Passover, the sacred festival celebrating the deliverance from Egypt—and is introduced to the guiding theme of
the murderous plottings of the antagonists—the priests who oversee the Passover
festival. A whole series of significant events begin to unfold quickly. Jesus is
anointed by a woman (14:3–9), Judas decides to betray him (14:10–11), Jesus
and the disciples observe the Passover (14:12–26), Jesus prays (14:27–42), and
Jesus is arrested (14:43–52). The passion comes to an end with Jesus before the
high priest and members of the Jewish council (14:53–65), Peter's denials (14:66–
72), Jesus before Pilate (15:1–15), and the crucifixion (15:16–41) and burial

(15:42–47). Mark's narrative then concludes with the drama of the discovery of the empty tomb and the message that Jesus has risen (16:1–8).

Mark's Passion Narrative portrays Jesus as in control of his destiny. His actions are deliberate and compelling. He knows that he will be put to death and that his death will be "for many" (14:24; cf. 10:45). Although he has no desire to die, he is willing to accept his fate (14:34–36). Rome must acknowledge that Jesus, even in death, "was truly the son of God" (15:39). Jesus cuts an impressive figure, one that should elicit respect and admiration from the Roman world (for a major study of the passion narratives of the Gospels, see Brown, *Death of the Messiah* [*Commentary Bibliography* above]).

A. The Plot to Kill Jesus   (14:1–2)

Bibliography

Burchard, C. "Fussnoten zum neutestamentlichen Griechisch: 1. Mc 14,2 parr." *ZNW* 61 (1970) 157–71, esp. 157–58. **Carmignac, J.** "Comment Jésus et ses contemporains pouvaient-ils célébrer la Pâque à une date no officelle?" *RevQ* 5 (1964–66) 59–79. **Dormeyer, D.** *Passion Jesu als Verhaltensmodell.* 66–72. ———. *Der Sinn des Leidens Jesu: Historisch-kritische und textpragmatische Analysen zur Markuspassion.* SBS 96. Stuttgart: Katholisches Bibelwerk, 1979. 34–48. **Hedinger, U.** "Jesus und die Volksmenge: Kritik der Qualifizierung der óchloi in der Evangelienauslegung." *TZ* 32 (1976) 201–6. **Kremer, J.** *Das Ärgernis des Kreuzes: Eine Hinführung zum Verstehen der Leidensgeschichte.* Stuttgart: Katholisches Bibelwerk, 1969. 11–16. **Lentzen-Deis, F.** "Passionsbericht als Handlungsmodell? Überlegungen zu Anstössen aus der 'pragmatischen' Sprachwissenschaft für die exegetischen Methoden." In *Der Prozess gegen Jesus: Historische Rückfrage und theologische Deutung.* Ed. K. Kertelge. QD 112. Freiburg; Basel: Herder, 1988. 191–232, esp. 203–21. **März, C.-P.** *"Siehe, dein König kommt zu Dir . . .": Eine traditionsgeschichtliche Untersuchung zur Einzugsperikope.* ETS 43. Leipzig: St. Benno, 1980. 76–80. **Matera, F. J.** *Passion Narratives and Gospel Theologies.* New York: Paulist, 1986. 12–17. **Mohr, T. A.** *Markus- und Johannespassion.* 159–60. **Pesch, R.** *Evangelium der Urgemeinde.* 159–60. **Schenk, W.** *Passionsbericht nach Markus.* 143–51. **Schenke, L.** *Studien zur Passionsgeschichte des Markus.* 12–66. **Schlier, H.** *Die Markuspassion.* Kriterien 32. Einsiedeln: Johannes, 1974. 11–21. **Schwarz, G.** *Jesus und Judas.* 141–48. **Senior, D. P.** *Passion of Jesus.* 139–56. 42–49. **Turner, N.** *Grammatical Insights into the New Testament.* Edinburgh: T. & T. Clark, 1965. 66–67. **Walker, N.** "Concerning the Jaubertian Chronology of the Passion." *NovT* 3 (1959) 317–20.

Translation

[1] *It was now two days before the Passover and the Festival of Unleavened Bread.*[a] *And the ruling priests and the scribes* [b] *were seeking how, taking him* [c] *by stealth,* [d] *they might kill him;* [2] *for they were saying, "Not during the feast, lest there will be a riot of the people."* [e]

Notes

[a] Lit. "After two days was the festival of the Passover and the Unleavened Bread." μετὰ δύο ἡμέρας,

"after two days" = ἐν τῇ τρίτῃ ἡμέρᾳ, "on the third day." D omits καὶ τὰ ἄζυμα, "and the Feast of Unleavened Bread."

[b]W reads οἱ Φαρισαῖοι, "Pharisees," in place of οἱ γραμματεῖς, "scribes."

[c]A few late MSS read τὸν Ἰησοῦν, "Jesus" (cf. Matt 26:4).

[d]Gk. ἐν δόλῳ, lit. "with trickery."

[e]A few late MSS read θόρυβος ἐν τῷ λαῷ, "a riot among the people" (cf. Matt 26:5).

Form/Structure/Setting

Mark 14:1–2 introduces the Passion Narrative with an ominous note. This brief pericope consists of three parts: (1) the notation of the Passover and Unleavened Bread festivals (v 1a); (2) the report that the rulings priests and the scribes were seeking to seize Jesus by stealth and kill him (v 1b); and (3) the explanation of why stealth was necessary, as opposed to an open show of force (v 2): the ruling priests do not want to provoke the people.

The evangelist observes that it is just two days before the Passover and the Festival of Unleavened Bread. The ruling priests wish to arrest Jesus, but not during the festival itself, lest it spark a riot. It would be bad enough for any Jew to be seized and handed over to the Romans, but to arrest a popular prophet and preacher like Jesus, whom some among his following believed to be the awaited Messiah, would be especially risky.

Comment

1 ἦν δὲ τὸ πάσχα καὶ τὰ ἄζυμα μετὰ δύο ἡμέρας, "It was now two days before the Passover and the Festival of Unleavened Bread." The Passover was the great festival in which Jews remembered and celebrated their rescue from slavery in Egypt (see Exod 12). It was celebrated on 14 or 15 Nisan (April/May) and was followed by the Feast of Unleavened Bread, which was celebrated on 15–21 Nisan. These holidays were usually thought of as the week of Passover. Passover week was especially worrisome for the Romans and their aristocratic and priestly Jewish collaborators. Recalling God's great act of salvation in history could inspire thoughts of revolt from Rome. μετὰ δύο ἡμέρας, "two days before" (or lit. "after two days"; see *Note* a above), suggests that the day in question is 12 or 13 Nisan (Cranfield, 414).

τὸ πάσχα, "the Passover," transliterates the Aramaic פסחא *pishā'*, rather than the Hebrew פסח *pesaḥ*, which in the LXX is transliterated φασέκ and φασέχ. In Jesus' day פסחא was probably vocalized *pashā'*, as seen by the Greek spelling of the transliteration. τὰ ἄζυμα, "Unleavened Bread," translates the Hebrew מצות *maṣṣôt*. See Exod 12:15: "seven days you shall eat unleavened bread."

καὶ ἐζήτουν οἱ ἀρχιερεῖς καὶ οἱ γραμματεῖς πῶς αὐτὸν ἐν δόλῳ κρατήσαντες ἀποκτείνωσιν, "And the ruling priests and the scribes were seeking how, taking him by stealth, they might kill him." οἱ ἀρχιερεῖς καὶ οἱ γραμματεῖς, "the ruling priests and the scribes," first appear together in two of Jesus' passion predictions (8:31; 10:33). They plot his destruction after the temple demonstration (11:18). They later approach him in the temple precincts, demanding to know by what authority he does the things he does (11:27). Later they will participate in Jesus' arrest (14:43) and will be present at his hearing before the high priest and the council (14:53; 15:1). They will also mock Jesus as he hangs on the cross (15:31). For more on the ruling priests and the scribes, see *Comment* on 11:18.

ἐν δόλῳ literally means "with trickery" or "with deceit," but in the Markan context the point seems to be stealth. That is, the ruling priests and the scribes are not resorting to trickery in the sense that they hope to entrap Jesus (earlier they have tried that without success) or in some way to fool him. Here ἐν δόλῳ means that they hope to take him into custody by surprise and without a public show of force.

2 The cautionary comment μὴ ἐν τῇ ἑορτῇ, μήποτε ἔσται θόρυβος τοῦ λαοῦ, "Not during the feast, lest there will be a riot of the people," reflects a history of Passover disturbances. One such incident described by Josephus offers a helpful example:

> At this time [4 B.C.E.] there came round the festival during which it is the ancestral custom of the Jews to serve unleavened bread. It is called Passover, being a commemoration of their departure from Egypt. They celebrate it with gladness, and it is their custom to slaughter a greater number of sacrifices at this festival than at any other, and an innumerable multitude of people come down from the country and even from abroad to worship God. Now the fomentors of disorder, who were mourning for Judas and Matthias, the interpreters of the laws, stood together in the temple and provided the dissidents with plenty of food, for they were not ashamed to beg for it. And Archelaus, fearing that something dangerous might grow out of their fanaticism, sent a cohort of legionaries under a tribune to suppress the violence of the rebels before they should infect the whole crowd with their madness. (*Ant.* 17.9.3 §§213–15)

Another serious uprising during Passover took place in Jerusalem when Cumanus was procurator (49 C.E.). As Jewish pilgrims made their way into the temple precincts a Roman soldier exposed his buttocks to the crowd and flatulated. A riot ensued in which many died (*J.W.* 2.12.1 §§224–27; *Ant.* 20.5.3 §§105–12). The caution of the ruling priests and the scribes is thus entirely plausible and sensible. They wish to take Jesus, but they wish to do so only if a serious disturbance can be avoided.

θόρυβος, "riot," can also mean "commotion," as in 5:38. Examples in the LXX that approximate the meaning "riot" include Jer 30:18(49:2); Ezek 7:7; Jdt 6:1.

Explanation

The notation that the Passover and Festival of Unleavened Bread are but two days away and that at the same time the ruling priests and the scribes have begun in earnest to seek an expeditious way to eliminate Jesus lend an element of drama and tension to the evangelist's narrative. Of course, the reader can hardly be surprised. Three times Jesus has formally predicted his passion, and in two of those predictions the ruling priests and the scribes have been mentioned. In the immediate context (13:33–37) Jesus has just warned his disciples of impending persecution and the need to be alert and watchful for the coming danger. Notice of the priests' and scribes' plotting follows naturally, almost expectedly.

The report of the ruling priests and scribes' murderous intentions sets the tone for the Passion Narrative that will now unfold. Every pericope from here on must be interpreted in the light of these intentions. Jesus must complete his ministry, and he must do it before his enemies have their way with him. His enemies cannot simply go out and arrest him in broad daylight, however, for Jesus is popular with the people. To act in this manner may very well precipitate one of the things they fear most: a riot of the people. Therefore, if they are to destroy Jesus, they must use stealth. In behaving this way, they live up to some of the very criticisms that Jesus had leveled against them during his teaching in the temple precincts.

The religious backdrop of the plot to arrest Jesus is the Passover. Although the Markan evangelist makes little of it, at least little that is apparent, the irony must have surely impressed itself upon his readers and hearers. Jesus has entered Jerusalem at the time of the Passover to announce the kingdom of God and to call the nation to repentance. His goal is Israel's restoration and liberation from the dominion of Satan. His hope is to renew the covenant. His message accords well with this festival, and the timing of his arrival in Jerusalem is in all probability calculated. Yet the ruling priests and the scribes will have none of it (chaps. 11–12). During this Passover season they will busy themselves with plans to do away with the one who hopes to bring Israel the final, eschatological Exodus.

B. The Anointing at Bethany   (14:3–9)

Bibliography

Barrett, C. K. "Important Hypotheses Reconsidered Pt 5: Spirit and the Gospel Tradition." *ExpTim* 67 (1956–57) 142–45. **Barton, S. C.** "Mark as Narrative: The Story of the Anointing Woman (Mk 14:3–9)." *ExpTim* 102 (1991) 230–34. **Bastin, M.** *Jésus devant sa passion.* LD 92. Paris: Cerf, 1976. 146–50. **Bauer, J. B.** "Ut quid perditio ista?—Zu Mk 14,4f und Parr." *NovT* 3 (1959) 54–56. **Beavis, M. A.** "Women as Models of Faith in Mark." *BTB* 18 (1988) 3–9. **Berger, K.** *Die Amen-Worte Jesu: Eine Untersuchung zum Problem der Legitimation in apokalyptischer Rede.* BZNW 39. Berlin: de Gruyter, 1970. 50–54. **Bevan, T. W.** "The Four Anointings." *ExpTim* 39 (1927–28) 137–39. **Black, M.** *Aramaic Approach.* 223–25. **Blackwell, J. N.** *The Passion as Story: The Plot of Mark.* Philadelphia: Fortress, 1986. 15–24. **Blank, J.** "Frauen in den Jesusüberlieferungen." In *Die Frau im Urchristentum.* Ed. G. Dautzenberg et al. QD 95. Freiburg: Herder, 1983. 9–91, esp. 22–28. **Broadhead, E. K.** "Mark 14,1–9, a Gospel within a Gospel." *Paradigms* 1.1 (1985) 32–41. ———. *Prophet, Son, Messiah: Narrative Form and Function in Mark 14–16.* JSNTSup 97. Sheffield: JSOT Press, 1994. 29–50. **Coakley, J. F.** "The Anointing at Bethany and the Priority of John." *JBL* 107 (1988) 241–56. **Cousin, H.** "Sépulture criminelle et sépulture prophétique." *RB* 81 (1974) 375–93. **Danker, F. W.** "The Literary Unity of Mark 14:1–25." *JBL* 85 (1966) 467–72. **Daube, D.** "The Anointing at Bethany and Jesus' Burial." *ATR* 32 (1950) 186–99 (repr. in D. Daube. *The New Testament and Rabbinic Judaism.* London: Athlone, 1956. 310–24). **Deichgräber, R.** "Die Gemeinderegel (1QS) X 4." *RevQ* 2 (1960) 277–80, esp. 279–80. **Derrett, J. D. M.** "The Anointing at Bethany." *SE* 2 [= TU 87] (1964) 174–82 (repr. in J. D. M. Derrett. *Law in the New Testament.* London: Darton, Longman & Todd, 1970. 266–75). **Dormeyer, D.** *Passion Jesu als Verhaltensmodell.* 73–82. **Egger, W.** *Methodenlehre zum Neuen Testament: Einführung in linguistische und historisch-kritische Methoden.* Freiburg: Herder, 1987. 176–81. **Elliott, J. K.** "The Anointing of Jesus." *ExpTim* 85 (1974) 105–7. **Feuillet, A.** "Les deux onctions faites sur Jésus, et Marie-Madeleine." *RThom* 75 (1975) 357–94. **Fonck, L.** "Cena

Bethanica." *VD* 8 (1928) 65–74, 97–105. **Geddert, T. J.** *Watchwords.* 137–40. **Goetz, K. G.** "Zur Salbung Jesu in Bethanien." *ZNW* 4 (1903) 181–85. **Grassi, J. A.** "The Secret Heroine in Mark's Drama." *BTB* 18 (1988) 10–15. **Greenlee, J. H.** "Εἰς μνημόσυνον αὐτῆς, 'For her Memorial': Mt xxvi.13, Mk xiv.9." *ExpTim* 71 (1959–60) 245. **Grubb, E.** "The Anointing of Jesus." *ExpTim* 26 (1914–15) 461–63. **Hasenfratz, H.-P.** *Die Rede von der Auferstehung Jesu Christi: Ein methodologischer Versuch.* FTL 10. Bonn: Linguistica Biblica, 1975. 125–27. **Hasler, V.** *Amen: Redaktionsgeschichtliche Untersuchung zur Einführungsformel der Herrenworte "Wahrlich ich sage euch."* Zürich; Stuttgart: Gotthelf, 1969. 44–47. **Heil, J. P.** "Mark 14:1–52: Narrative Structure and Reader-Response." *Bib* 71 (1990) 305–32. **Hiers, R. H.** *The Historical Jesus and the Kingdom of God: Present and Future in the Message and Ministry of Jesus.* UFHM 38. Gainesville: University of Florida Press, 1973. 94–96. **Hirsch, E.** *Betrachtungen zu Wort und Geschichte Jesu.* Berlin: de Gruyter, 1969. 215–23. **Holst, R.** "The One Anointing of Jesus: Another Application of the Form-Critical Method." *JBL* 95 (1976) 435–46. **Holtzmann, O.** "Zur Salbung Jesu in Bethanien." *ZNW* 4 (1903) 181. **Holzmeister, U.** "Die Magdalenenfrage in der christlichen Überlieferung." *ZKT* 46 (1922) 402–22, 556–84. **Jeremias, J.** "Markus 14,9." *ZNW* 44 (1952–53) 103–7. ———. "Die Salbungsgeschichte Mc 14,3–9." *ZNW* 35 (1936) 77–82. **Kato, Z.** *Völkermission im Markusevangelium.* 155–61. **Kilpatrick, G. D.** "ἐπάνω Mark xiv 5." *JTS* o.s. 42 (1941) 181–82. **Köbert, R.** "Nardos Pistike—Kostnarde." *Bib* 29 (1948) 279–81. **Lagrange, M.-J.** "Jésus a-t-il été oint plusieurs fois et par plusieurs femmes?" *RB* 9 (1912) 504–32. **Legault, A.** "An Application of the Form-Critique Method to the Anointings in Galilee (Lk 7,36–50) and Bethany (Mt 26,6–13; Mk 14,3–9; Jn 12,1–8)." *CBQ* 16 (1954) 131–45. **Linder, G.** "Zur Salbung Jesu in Bethanien." *ZNW* 4 (1903) 179–81. **Mack, B. L.** "The Anointing of Jesus: Elaboration within a Chreia." In B. L. Mack and V. K. Robbins. *Patterns of Persuasion in the Gospels.* Sonoma: Polebridge, 1989. 85–106, esp. 92–100. ———. *Myth of Innocence.* 199–202, 309–12. **Martin, R. P.** *Mark: Evangelist and Theologian.* 222–24. **März, C.-P.** "Zur Traditionsgeschichte von Mk 14,3–9 und Parallelen." SNTSU 6–7 (1981–82) 89–112. **Maunder, C. J.** "A Sitz im Leben for Mark 14:9." *ExpTim* 99 (1987–88) 78–80. **Mohr, T. A.** *Markus- und Johannespassion.* 129–47. **Munro, W.** "The Anointing in Mark 14:3–9 and John 12:1–8." In *Society of Biblical Literature 1979 Seminar Papers.* Ed. P. J. Achtemeier. 2 vols. SBLSP 18. Missoula, MT: Scholars Press, 1979. 1:127–30. **Myllykoski, M.** *Die letzten Tage Jesu.* 1:185–91. **Naber, S. A.** "ΝΑΡΔΟΣ ΠΙΣΤΙΚΗ." *Mnemosyne* 30 (1902) 1–15. **Nesbitt, C. F.** "The Bethany Traditions in the Gospel Narratives." *JBR* 29 (1961) 119–24. **Nestle, E.** "Die unverfälschte köstliche Narde." *ZNW* 3 (1902) 169–71. **Patsch, H.** *Abendmahl und historischer Jesus.* CTM A.1. Stuttgart: Calwer, 1972. 198–99. **Pesch, R.** *Evangelium der Urgemeinde.* 160–62. ———. "Die Salbung Jesu in Bethanien (Mk 14,3–9): Eine Studie zur Passionsgeschichte." In *Orientierung an Jesus: Zur Theologie der Synoptiker.* FS J. Schmid, ed. P. Hoffmann et al. Freiburg: Herder, 1973. 267–85. **Platt, E. E.** "The Ministry of Mary of Bethany." *TToday* 34 (1977) 29–39. **Preuschen, E.** "Die Salbung Jesu in Bethanien." *ZNW* 3 (1902) 252–53. ———. "Zur Salbung Jesu in Bethanien." *ZNW* 4 (1903) 88. **Roloff, J.** *Kerygma und der irdische Jesus.* 210–23. **Sahlin, H.** "Zwei Fälle von harmonisierendem Einfluss des Matthäus-Evangeliums auf das Markus-Evangelium." *ST* 13 (1959) 166–79, esp. 172–79. **Schedl, C.** "Die Salbung Jesu in Betanien." *BL* 54 (1981) 151–62. **Schenk, W.** *Passionsbericht nach Markus.* 175–80. **Schenke, L.** *Studien zur Passionsgeschichte des Markus.* 67–118. **Schille, G.** *Das vorsynoptische Judenchristentum.* AVTRW 48. Berlin: Evangelische Verlagsanstalt, 1970. 75–76. **Schnider, F.** "Christusverkündigung und Jesuserzählungen: Exegetische Überlieferungen zu Mk 14,3–9." *Kairos* 24 (1982) 171–79. **Schottroff, L.** "'Was sie tun konnte, hat sie getan': Die Salbung in Bethanien (Mk 14,3–8)." In L. Schottroff and D. Sölle. *Hannas Aufbruch.* Gütersloh: Gütersloher Verlagsanstalt, 1990. 142–54. **Söding, T.** *Glaube bei Markus.* 199–201. **Stock, K.** *Boten aus dem Mit-Ihm-Sein.* 150–54. **Storch, R.** "'Was soll diese Verschwendung?': Bemerkungen zur Auslegungsgeschichte von Mk 14,4f." In *Der Ruf Jesu und die Antwort der Gemeinde.* FS J. Jeremias, ed. E. Lohse et al. Göttingen: Vandenhoeck & Ruprecht, 1970. 247–58. **Sybel, L.**

von. "Die Salbungen: Mt 26,6–13, Mc 14,3–9, Lc 7,36–50, Joh 12,1–8." *ZNW* 23 (1924) 184–93. **Torrey, C. C.** *Four Gospels.* 101. ———. *Our Translated Gospels.* 96. **Westcott, B. F.,** and **Hort, F. J. A.** *Introduction.* 2:26. **Williams, J. F.** *Other Followers of Jesus.* 180–82. **Wood, J. A.** "The Anointing at Bethany and Its Significance." *ExpTim* 39 (1927–28) 475–76.

Translation

³*And when he* ᵃ *was at Bethany in the house of Simon the leper, as he reclined, a woman came, having an alabaster flask of ointment of pure nard, very costly. Breaking* ᵇ *the flask, she poured it over his head.* ⁴*But there were some who were indignant, [saying]* ᶜ *to themselves, "To what end was this waste of ointment?* ⁵*For this ointment could have been* ᵈ *sold for more than three hundred denarii, and [the money] given to the poor."* *And they were reproaching her.* ᵉ ⁶*But Jesus said,* ᶠ *"Leave her alone. Why do you give her trouble? She has done a beautiful thing to me.* ᵍ ⁷*For you always have the poor with you, and whenever you should wish, you can do something good for them; but me you do not always have.* ⁸*What she has she has done;* ʰ *she has anointed my body beforehand for burial.* ⁱ ⁹*But truly, I say to you, wherever in all the world the good news should be proclaimed, what this woman has done will also be spoken of in her memory."*

Notes

ᵃD reads τοῦ Ἰησοῦ, "Jesus" (cf. Matt 26:6).

ᵇD reads καὶ θραύσασα, "and shattering."

ᶜThe word in brackets has been added. A C² W Σ Φ and a few later MSS add καὶ λέγοντες, "and saying." These words are not found in ℵ B C* L and other authorities. D reads οἱ δὲ μαθηταὶ αὐτοῦ διεπονοῦντο καὶ ἔλεγον, "but his disciples were worked up and were saying."

ᵈGk. ἠδύνατο . . . τοῦτο τὸ μύρον πραθῆναι, lit. "it was possible for this ointment to be sold." L W and a few later MSS read the verb with the more conventional augment (ἐδύνατο).

ᵉA few later MSS add πολλά, "much."

ᶠD W and a few late MSS add αὐτοῖς, "to them."

ᵍGk. ἐν ἐμοί, lit. "in me," or "with me." The choice of prep. is a bit odd. A few later MSS substitute more appropriate preps., reading either εἰς ἐμέ, "to me," or ἐπ᾽ ἐμοί, "for me" or "in my behalf."

ʰGk. ὃ ἔσχεν ἐποίησιν. See *Comment* below.

ⁱA few late MSS read εἰς τὸν ἐνταφιασμόν μου, "my burial."

Form/Structure/Setting

Mark 14:3–9 is a story of a woman who anoints Jesus. The story is an insertion between vv 1–2 and vv 10–11, verses that narrate the ruling priests' plotting against Jesus and Judas Iscariot's agreement with the priests to hand Jesus over to them (so Schweizer, 290, and many others). According to Schnider (*Kairos* 24 [1982] 171–79), 14:3–9 contains three scenes: (1) the woman's action in anointing Jesus (v 3), (2) the evaluation of this deed by "some" (vv 4–5), and (3) the threefold evaluation by Jesus (vv 6–7, 8, 9). On the evangelist's editorial activity in chap. 14, with special attention to his tendency to intercalate materials, see Heil, *Bib* 71 (1990) 305–32.

Interpreters are confronted with two principal questions: (1) What relationship does this passage have with the other stories in which women anoint Jesus (Luke 7:36–50; John 12:1–8)? (2) In what sense was Jesus anointed in the passage under consideration? The Lukan version of the sinful woman is probably a different story, which was influenced by the details of the passion-week anointing through transmission of the dominical tradition in which overlap occurred. The Lukan evangelist himself may have borrowed some details from his Markan source (and the Lukan evangelist does narrate a later passion-week anointing). There are numerous differences that suggest that originally there were two separate anointing stories (see the summary in Fitzmyer, *Luke* 1:684–85). In Luke's version the event takes place in Galilee rather than in Judea; Jesus' feet are anointed instead of his head; and it occurs in the presence of a Pharisee rather than among the disciples. There are indications that this story is rooted in early, Aramaic tradition (Taylor, 531; Cranfield, 417; Gundry, 811).

The meaning of the passion-week anointing is also a matter of debate. Anointing was a custom at feasts (Pss 23:5; 141:5; *b. Ḥul.* 94a; cf. Lane, 492–93). But was the woman's action nothing more than a holiday anointing? Although Pesch (2:332) expresses doubt, I am inclined to agree with Elliott (*ExpTim* 85 [1974] 105–7) and Platt (*TToday* 34 [1977] 29–39) that the anointing of Jesus in Mark 14:3–9 was intended to be messianic. Hooker (329) sees in the woman's action "the symbol of Jesus' messianic anointing," while Johnson (224) regards it as "a secret anointing for kingship" (cf. 1 Kgs 1:38–40; 2 Kgs 9:1–13). The woman's act of anointing could have connoted, and probably did connote, both ideas—a holiday anointing that implied even more because Jesus was the Lord's Anointed.

Hooker (327–28) thinks Jesus is anointed for burial beforehand, perhaps because his body will not be available afterward, as the women will discover in 16:1. However, it is not likely that the story is designed to compensate for the lack of anointing of Jesus' body at the time of his burial (as also proposed by Branscomb, 246; Nineham, 372; and rightly opposed by Taylor, 533). Had the evangelist wished to compensate in this manner, why did he not simply add a sentence to 15:46 or 15:47, saying that Jesus had been anointed? The anointing of Jesus' head some time before his death would scarcely have been recognized as a substitution or compensation for lack of anointing at the time of burial.

Comment

3 Καὶ ὄντος αὐτοῦ ἐν Βηθανίᾳ ἐν τῇ οἰκίᾳ Σίμωνος τοῦ λεπροῦ, "And when he was at Bethany in the house of Simon the leper." Bethany has been previously identified as the village in which Jesus had taken up residence for the week of Passover (cf. 11:1, 11). This Bethany is not to be confused with the "Bethany beyond the Jordan" (cf. John 1:19–28), which in fact may have been the region of Batanea. The Bethany of Mark 14:3 (cf. 11:1, 11, 12) was three kilometers east of Jerusalem and may have accommodated quarters for lepers, as is apparently documented in 11QTemple[a] 46:16–18: "And you shall make three places to the east of the city, separated from one another, to which shall come the lepers and those afflicted with discharge." This does not mean that Simon was still leprous on the occasion of Jesus' visit; this is quite improbable (for the disciples and the unnamed woman would scarcely have gone into this man's house for a meal). This Simon had been a leper, but now was cleansed, perhaps by Jesus. Reference to "Simon the leper" has occasioned speculation. Torrey (*Four Gospels,* 101; *Our Translated Gospels,* 96) suggests that the description of Simon as τοῦ λεπροῦ, "the leper," has resulted from mistranslating the Aramaic גרבא *gārābā'*, a "jar-merchant." The same consonants can be vocalized as *garbā'*, meaning λεπρός, "leper." Black (*Aramaic Approach*, 9), however, points out that *garbā'* is the usual vocalization, that it always means "leper," and that there is no lexical evidence for *gārābā'* meaning "jar-merchant."

κατακειμένου αὐτοῦ ἦλθεν γυνὴ ἔχουσα ἀλάβαστρον μύρου νάρδου πιστικῆς πολυτελοῦς, "as he reclined, a woman came, having an alabaster flask of ointment of pure nard, very costly." κατακειμένου αὐτοῦ, "as he reclined," implies that Jesus, along with his disciples, was eating. With Jesus thus reclined, it would not have been difficult for a woman to approach him (probably from behind) to anoint his head. The evangelist says that this unnamed woman had ἀλάβαστρον μύρου νάρδου πιστικῆς, "an alabaster flask of ointment of pure nard." The very best perfumes and other precious unguents were often contained in alabaster vessels (cf. Pliny the Elder, *Nat.* 13.3.19). Nard was among the most costly ointments. Black (*Aramaic Approach*, 223–25) wonders if Mark's πιστικῆς is simply a transliteration of the Aramaic פסתקא *pîstĕqā'*, which means "pistachio nut." Cranfield (415) agrees, noting that the oil of the pistachio nut "was used as a base for perfumes." Perhaps this is plausible, but as Gundry (812) points out, had the reference been to the pistachio nut, we should have expected πιστάκιον. Accordingly, πιστικῆς is probably best understood as "genuine" (i.e., "faithful"), or in this context "pure."

συντρίψασα τὴν ἀλάβαστρον κατέχεεν αὐτοῦ τῆς κεφαλῆς, "Breaking the flask, she poured it over his head." The neck of the perfume bottle was sometimes snapped off. In this case, the breaking of the flask and the pouring imply that no portion of the ointment was held back; all was poured out on Jesus' head. The extravagance of the woman's action is thus underscored. The action that is described here is reminiscent of 2 Kgs 9:6, where Elisha commands the young man to anoint Jehu king of Israel: "the young man poured [LXX 4 Kgdms 9:6: ἐπέχεεν] oil on his head, saying to him, 'Thus says the LORD the God of Israel, "I anoint you king over the people of the LORD, over Israel."'" See also Exod 29:7; 1 Sam 10:1; 2 Kgs 9:3; Ps 133:2. Cranfield (415) comments that it is "not likely that the woman thought of herself as anointing the Messiah, but Mark doubtless intended his readers to recognize the messianic significance of her actions." Why would the woman not think of her action as a messianic anointing? Her action was spontaneous and impromptu and would not have been interpreted in any official sense, to be sure, but anointing the head of one whom she and the disciples regarded as Israel's Messiah would in all probability have been perceived in a messianic sense.

4 ἦσαν δέ τινες ἀγανακτοῦντες, "But there were some who were indignant." The Matthean evangelist says it was the Twelve, but the Markan narrative simply has τινές, "some." Because the Markan evangelist does not spare the Twelve elsewhere, Taylor (532) thinks that we should not assume that the Twelve are meant here. But the words of vv 6–9 make the most sense if they are addressed to the Twelve (Cranfield, 415–16). Earlier Jesus had been indignant at his disciples for discouraging children to come to him (10:14), while later the disciples themselves had become indignant at James and John over their request to sit at Jesus' right and left (10:41).

πρὸς ἑαυτούς, εἰς τί ἡ ἀπώλεια αὕτη τοῦ μύρου γέγονεν, "[saying] to themselves, 'To what end was this waste of ointment?'" ἀπώλεια, meaning "waste" or "loss" (instead of "destruction"), is attested in the papyri (see MM, 73). The disciples' indignation is not petty, but it is oafish and betrays their lack of sensitivity for the woman in view of her great sacrifice.

5 ἠδύνατο γὰρ τοῦτο τὸ μύρον πραθῆναι ἐπάνω δηναρίων τριακοσίων καὶ δοθῆναι τοῖς πτωχοῖς, "For this ointment could have been sold for more than three hundred denarii, and [the money] given to the poor." On the evening of Passover the poor were remembered (cf. *m. Pesaḥ.* 9:11; 10:1; Jeremias, *ZNW* 35 [1936] 77–82; Lane, 493). Perhaps of more pressing concern to the disciples were the financial needs of a new government that some still hoped would be inaugurated soon. Money would be needed for the poor as well as for other expenses. Kilpatrick (*JTS* o.s. 42 [1941] 181) wonders if ἐπάνω, "for more than," was added to allow for post-70 inflation. Perhaps this is true. A late rabbinic tradition informs us that the daughter of Naqdimon ben Gorion sometimes spent as much as four hundred denarii for ointments and perfumes (cf. *b. Ketub.* 66b).

καὶ ἐνεβριμῶντο αὐτῇ, "And they were reproaching her." The Markan evangelist used ἐμβριμᾶσθαι, "to reproach," in 1:43, where Jesus sternly charged the cleansed leper to show himself to the priest and to fulfill what Moses had commanded with respect to recovered lepers. Thus, the disciples here may have been giving the woman orders, as it were (i.e., "Stop this waste; we need the money").

6 ὁ δὲ Ἰησοῦς εἶπεν, ἄφετε αὐτήν· τί αὐτῇ κόπους παρέχετε, "But Jesus said, 'Leave her alone. Why do you give her trouble?'" Danker (*JBL* 85 [1966] 467–72) and Lane (493) think Ps 41 (e.g., v 1: "Blessed is he who considers the poor") underlies the scene and Jesus' words. Lane (494) thinks the woman's deed is an act of charity, for Jesus is "the poor man *par excellence*" (Lane, 494). Her deed is an act of charity toward the poor. But is it? Does this line of interpretation accord adequately with what Jesus says? Her act to him is set in *contrast* to opportunities to assist the poor.

καλὸν ἔργον ἠργάσατο ἐν ἐμοί, "She has done a beautiful thing to me." καλὸν ἔργον, "beautiful thing," "beautiful work," is a technical term for charity according to Daube ("Anointing at Bethany," 315–16). The emphasis falls on her extravagance, on her gift, but not in the sense that she has bestowed a gift on Jesus the poor man. She has recognized Jesus as the Messiah and has expressed her faith in him and love for him in an extravagant manner. The issue of the poor resides in the minds of the disciples, not in the mind of the woman.

7 πάντοτε γὰρ τοὺς πτωχοὺς ἔχετε μεθ᾽ ἑαυτῶν καὶ ὅταν θέλητε δύνασθε αὐτοῖς εὖ ποιῆσαι, "For you always have the poor with you, and whenever you should wish, you can do something good for them." Jesus' words allude to Deut 15:11: "For the poor will never cease out of the land; therefore I command you, You shall open wide your hand to your brother, to the needy and to the poor, in the land" (Lane, 494; Schweizer, 291; Taylor, 532). The opportunities to minister to the poor will never end (perhaps even into the messianic age according to *b. Šabb.* 63a). By saying this, Jesus is not implying that the needs of the poor are unimportant and can be attended to when it is convenient. The point of his comment is seen in the next sentence.

ἐμὲ δὲ οὐ πάντοτε ἔχετε, "but me you do not always have." The opportunities to minister to Jesus are very limited and soon will be gone. Jesus' reasoning here is similar to that offered a frustrated Martha in Luke 10:38–42. Against Barrett (*ExpTim* 67 [1956–57] 143–44), Cranfield (417) finds in this comment evidence that Jesus did envisage an interval, even if brief, between his death and the Parousia (see also *Comment* on 14:25).

8 ὃ ἔσχεν ἐποίησεν, "What she has she has done." That is, what means the woman has at her disposal, she has employed. This does not mean that she spent all she had (as in Mark 12:44); it means that she has done the only service within her power (Taylor, 532; Hooker, 330).

προέλαβεν μυρίσαι τὸ σῶμά μου εἰς τὸν ἐνταφιασμόν, "she has anointed my body beforehand for burial." The use of προέλαβεν μυρίσαι, "she has anointed . . . beforehand," may be another Aramaism (Taylor, 533). Jesus' grim words allude to the Jewish custom of anointing the body as part of the preparation for burial (e.g., *m. Šabb.* 23:5: "They make ready all that is needful for the dead, and anoint it [the corpse] and wash it").

9 ἀμὴν δὲ λέγω ὑμῖν, ὅπου ἐὰν κηρυχθῇ τὸ εὐαγγέλιον εἰς ὅλον τὸν κόσμον, "But truly, I say to you, wherever in all the world the good news should be proclaimed." Jeremias (*ZNW* 44 [1952–53] 103–7) argues that Jesus' saying pertains to the final judgment, not to the church's mission. But this is doubtful. It probably does refer to the church's mission. If so, is it a later gloss (so Bultmann, *History,* 36–37; Klostermann, 158; [apparently] Johnson, 224; Schweizer, 290; Hooker, 330)? Or is it dominical (so Bartlet, 375; Rawlinson, 198; Blunt, 247; Lane, 494–95; Taylor, 534; Cranfield, 417–18; Martin, *Mark: Evangelist and Theologian,* 202)? For arguments in favor of authenticity, see Taylor and Cranfield. The hyperbole of the statement is characteristic of Jesus, while the absence of the woman's name, a fact that stands somewhat in tension with the point of the saying (as seen in the next clause), argues against later pseudepigraphy.

καὶ ὃ ἐποίησεν αὕτη λαληθήσεται εἰς μνημόσυνον αὐτῆς, "what this woman has done will also be spoken of in her memory." The language may recall the words of blessing that Joseph pronounces on Aseneth: "Blessed are you by the Most High God, and blessed (is) your name for ever" (*Jos. Asen.* 19:8). Rabbinic literature has memorial blessings: e.g., "may he be remembered for good" (*b. B. Bat.* 21a), or "remember him for praise" (*Tanḥ. Haʾăzînû* §1), or "his memory was kept in honor" (*m. Yoma* 3:9). Jeremias (*ZNW* 44 [1952–53] 103–7) thinks that Jesus means that what the woman has done will be remembered before God's throne on the day of judgment. But remembering in the passion context carries with it the connotation of what humans are to remember (cf. 1 Cor 11:25; Cranfield, 418), not what God is to remember. It is unnecessary and convoluted to link this saying to Mary's discovery of the empty tomb and announcement of the resurrection (*pace* Maunder, *ExpTim* 99 [1987–88] 78–80). The woman does, however, serve in the Markan Gospel as a model of faith (Beavis, *BTB* 18 [1988] 3–9; Grassi, *BTB* 18 [1988] 10–15).

Explanation

In one of the most poignant stories in the Gospels we witness an act of remarkable generosity, devotion, and faith on the part of the woman who anointed the head of Jesus with an ointment that was worth a small fortune. This woman's selfless act stands in stark contrast to Judas's act of treachery and greed that will be described in the passage that immediately follows (Barton, *ExpTim* 102 [1991] 230–34). But her act and the attitude that prompted it also stand in noticeable contrast to the thinking and behavior of the disciples at the very moment of her deed. She was concerned with no one but Jesus; the disciples were concerned with their responsibilities and the pressing needs of their ministry. These worries blinded them to the uniqueness of the moment, to an unparalleled opportunity. What they saw as waste and loss was in fact a priceless deed, whose value would endure as long as the gospel was proclaimed. We may infer from the story that the success of the preaching of the gospel, "wherever in all the world the good news should be proclaimed," will be due to faith and devotion like hers. In this she becomes an example for the Twelve themselves and for all Christians in later times. This episode in many ways encapsulates the essence of the passion story itself.

C. *Judas's Agreement to Betray Jesus* *(14:10–11)*

Bibliography

Arbeitman, Y. "The Suffix of Iscariot." *JBL* 99 (1980) 122–24. **Bacon, B. W.** "What Did Judas Betray?" *HibJ* 19 (1920–21) 476–93. **Barton, S. C.** "Mark as Narrative: The Story of the Anointing Woman (Mk 14:3–9)." *ExpTim* 102 (1991) 230–34. **Baumbach, G.** "Judas— Jünger und Verräter Jesu." *ZZ* 17 (1963) 91–98. **Buchheit, G.** *Judas Iskarioth (Legende–Geschichte–Deutung)*. Gütersloh: Rufer, 1954. **Cullmann, O.** "Der zwölfte Apostel." In *Vorträge und Aufsätze 1925–1962*. Ed. K. Fröhlich. Tübingen: Mohr-Siebeck; Zürich: Zwingli, 1966. 214–22. **Dormeyer, D.** *Die Passion Jesu*. 82–85. **Ehrman, A.** "Judas Iscariot and Abba Saqqara." *JBL* 97 (1978) 572–73. **Enslin, M. S.** "How the Story Grew: Judas in Fact and Fiction." In *Festschrift to Honor F. Wilber Gingrich*. Ed. E. H. Barth and E. E. Cocroft. Leiden: Brill, 1972. 123–41. **Gärtner, B.** *Iscariot*. FBBS. Philadelphia: Fortress, 1971. **Goldschmidt, H. L.** "Das Judasbild im Neuen Testament aus jüdischer Sicht." In H. L. Goldschmidt and M. Limbeck. *Heilvoller Verrat? Judas im Neuen Testament*. Stuttgart: Katholisches Bibelwerk, 1976. 9–36. **Harris, J. R.** "Did Judas Really Commit Suicide?" *AJT* 4 (1900) 490–513. **Haugg, D.** *Judas Iskarioth in den neutestamentlichen Berichten*. Freiburg: Herder, 1930. **Hein, K.** "Judas Iscariot: Key to the Last-Supper Narratives?" *NTS* 17 (1970–71) 227–32. **Jens, W.** *Der Fall Judas*. Stuttgart: Katholisches Bibelwerk, 1975. **Klassen, W.** "Judas Iscariot." *ABD* 3:1091–96. ———. *Judas: Betrayer or Friend of Jesus?* Minneapolis: Fortress, 1996. **Klauck, H.-J.** *Judas—Ein Jünger des Herrn*. QD 111. Freiburg; Basel: Herder, 1987. 33–48. **Laeuchli, S.** "Origen's Interpretation of Judas Iscariot." *CH* 22 (1953) 253–68. **Lapide, P. E.** "Verräter oder verraten? Judas in evangelischer und jüdischer Sicht." *Lutherische Monatshefte* 16 (1977) 75–79. **Limbeck, M.** "Das Judasbild im Neuen Testament aus christlicher Sicht." In H. L. Goldschmidt and M. Limbeck. *Heilvoller Verrat? Judas im Neuen Testament*. Stuttgart: Katholisches Bibelwerk, 1976. 37–101. **Linnemann, E.** *Studien zur Passionsgeschichte*. 47–50. **Lüthi, K.** *Judas Iskarioth in der Geschichte der Auslegung*. Zürich: Zwingli, 1955. ———. "Das Problem des Judas Iskarioth—Neu untersucht." *EvT* 16 (1956) 98–114. **Morin, J.-A.** "Les deux derniers des Douzes: Simon le Zélote et Judas Iskariôth." *RB* 80 (1973) 332–58. **Pesch, R.** *Evangelium der Urgemeinde*. 162–64. **Plath, M.** "Warum hat die urchristliche Gemeinde und die Überlieferung der Judas Erzählung Wert gelegt?" *ZNW* 17 (1916) 178–88. **Popkes, W.** *Christus Traditus: Eine Untersuchung zum Begriff der Dahingabe im Neuen Testament*. ATANT 49. Zürich: Zwingli, 1967. 174–81. **Preisker, H.** "Der Verrat des Judas und das Abendmahl." *ZNW* 41 (1942) 151–55. **Roquefort, D.** "Judas: Une figure de la perversion." *ETR* 58 (1983) 501–13. **Sanders, E. P.** *Jesus and Judaism.* 309. **Schenk, W.** *Der Passionsbericht.* 143–51. **Schenke, L.** *Studien zur Passionsgeschichte des Markus.* 119–40. **Schläger, G.** "Die Ungeschichtlichkeit des Verräters Judas." *ZNW* 15 (1914) 50–59. **Schmahl, G.** *Die Zwölf im Markusevangelium.* 98–100. **Schwarz, G.** *Jesus und Judas.* 176–82. **Smith, W. B.** "Judas Iscariot." *HibJ* 9 (1911) 532–35. **Stein-Schneider, H.** "À la recherche du Judas historique." *ETR* 60 (1985) 403–24. **Stock, K.** *Boten aus dem Mit-Ihm-Sein.* 150–54. **Torrey, C. C.** "The Name 'Iscarioth.'" *HTR* 36 (1943) 51–62. **Trudinger, L. P.** "Davidic Links with the Betrayal of Jesus." *ExpTim* 86 (1974–75) 278–79. **Vogler, W.** *Judas Iskarioth: Untersuchungen zu Tradition und Redaktion von Textes des Neuen Testaments und ausserkanonischer Schriften.* 2nd ed. Theologische Arbeiten 42. Berlin: Evangelische Verlagsanstalt, 1985. 39–43. **Wagner, H.,** ed. *Judas Iskariot: Menschliches oder heilsgeschichtliches Drama?* Frankfurt: Knecht, 1985. **Wrede, W.** "Judas Ischarioth in der urchristlichen Überlieferung." In *Vorträge und Studien.* Tübingen: Mohr-Siebeck, 1907. 127–46.

Translation

[10]*And Judas Iscariot,*[a] *one of the Twelve,*[b] *went away to the ruling priests, so that he might hand him*[c] *over to them.* [11]*When they heard, they were pleased and promised to give him money; and he was seeking how he might hand him over*[d] *at an opportune moment.*

Notes

[a]Ἰσκαριώθ, "Iscarioth," is read by א* B C*[vid]. ὁ Ἰσκαριώθ, "the Iscarioth," is read by א[c] L and other authorities. Ἰσκαριώτης, "Iscariot," is read by A C² W Φ and many other authorities. Finally, Σκαριώτης, "Scariot," is read by D and some old Italian MSS (with further variations). Syr. MSS read *skariōta'*. Augustine reads *Scarioth*. The textual variants reflect the uncertainty of the derivation of this name (see discussion below).

[b]A omits ὁ εἷς τῶν δώδεκα, "one of the Twelve," lit. "the one of the Twelve." See *Comment.*

[c]A few Latin versions read *Iesum*, "Jesus."

[d]A few later MSS and authorities add αὐτοῖς, "to them" (cf. Luke 22:6).

Form/Structure/Setting

Mark 14:10–12 is the second half of the interrupted unit of tradition (see Bultmann, *History*, 262–63) that relates the ruling priests' plot to arrest Jesus by stealth (14:1–2). The evangelist says in v 1 that they "were seeking how" they might accomplish this. In v 10 Judas Iscariot has answered the call. By inserting the story of the woman who anoints Jesus' head (14:3–9), the evangelist creates a vivid contrast between the devotion and faith of the unnamed woman, on the one hand, and the faithlessness and treachery of the named disciple, "Judas Iscariot, one of the Twelve," on the other (S. C. Barton, *ExpTim* 102 [1991] 230–34).

We have here an ancient bit of tradition that was surely a cause of embarrassment for the early church. For this reason it is probably not a creation of Christian tradents. The explanations that "Satan entered into Judas" (Luke 22:3; John 13:27) and that Judas's action fulfilled Scripture (John 13:18, quoting Ps 41:9) were attempts to mitigate this embarrassment. That one of the Twelve, to whom were promised "twelve thrones" on which they would sit and administer the twelve tribes of Israel (Matt 19:28 = Luke 22:28–30), could have betrayed Jesus was appalling and disturbing to the early church.

Judas's betrayal also attests the awareness of the political dangers that Jesus and his following faced. After all, Judas does not merely defect (as apparently some of Jesus' following did; cf. John 6:66–71) or run away (as "all" with Jesus did when he was arrested; cf. Mark 14:50); Judas gives up his friend and master to his enemies, knowing that they are seeking Jesus' life. Judas's betrayal of Jesus enables the disillusioned disciple to make a clean break and to distance himself from the Galilean proclaimer of the kingdom who had dared to criticize the integrity of the temple establishment and to predict its destruction.

Comment

10 καὶ Ἰούδας Ἰσκαριὼθ ὁ εἷς τῶν δώδεκα, "And Judas Iscariot, one of the Twelve." Judas Iscariot is identified here as ὁ εἷς τῶν δώδεκα, lit. "the one of the Twelve." He is not simply "one of the Twelve"; he is "the" one of the Twelve whose name was mentioned in Mark 3:14 and 19: "he appointed twelve, to be with him . . . Judas Iscariot, who betrayed him." The definite article reminds the reader of this earlier introduction of Judas, named with the Twelve, sent out by Jesus to preach, and given authority. It also anticipates 14:20, where Judas will be alluded to as "one of the Twelve" (Cranfield, 419). Thus the reader is reminded emphatically that this Judas had been one of Jesus' intimates from the very beginning.

ἀπῆλθεν πρὸς τοὺς ἀρχιερεῖς ἵνα αὐτὸν παραδοῖ αὐτοῖς, "went away to the ruling priests, so that he might hand him over to them." Since entering Jerusalem, the ἀρχιερεῖς, "ruling priests," have been Jesus' principal and most dangerous opponents (cf. 11:18, 27). παραδιδόναι, "to hand over," is not exactly "to betray" (for which one might expect a form of προδιδόναι, "to betray," or καταμηνύειν, "to inform against"). Klassen ("Judas Iscariot"; id., *Judas*) attempts to make this important distinction, but it is inconceivable that the disciples and the early church could have viewed Judas's actions as anything other than a betrayal.

With what did Judas supply the ruling priests? Mark 14:1–2 and 11 make it clear that stealth was a major factor. Judas succeeds in this when he leads agents of the priests to Gethsemane (14:43). But he probably also divulged to the ruling priests the essence of Jesus' proclamation and self-understanding (as argued by Sanders, *Jesus and Judaism*, 309). The questions raised against Jesus during the hearing before the high priest and members of the council (14:55–61) suggest this. The claim of the false witnesses that Jesus said something about destroying the temple "made with hands" and building a new one "not made with hands" (language that alludes to Dan 2) probably relates in some way to Jesus' message of the coming kingdom and the demise of the present administration in Jerusalem, while the high priest's pointed question, "Are you the Messiah, the son of the Blessed?" (14:61), suggests that he was aware of Jesus' messianic self-understanding. It is thus probable that Judas supplied the ruling priests with more than a convenient time and place to arrest Jesus.

11 οἱ δὲ ἀκούσαντες ἐχάρησαν καὶ ἐπηγγείλαντο αὐτῷ ἀργύριον δοῦναι, "When they heard, they were pleased and promised to give him money." The ruling priests were both pleased and relieved. A quiet arrest was essential; otherwise a preemptive strike against Jesus might instigate a riot, the very thing the priests hoped to avoid. They promised to give Judas money. He would be paid when he "delivered the goods." The information that he supplied the ruling priests would certainly be useful when charges were brought, but securing a quiet and timely arrest of Jesus was of the utmost importance. When Judas accomplished this, then he would receive the money.

καὶ ἐζήτει πῶς αὐτὸν εὐκαίρως παραδοῖ, "and he was seeking how he might hand him over at an opportune moment." The Matthean evangelist paraphrases his Markan source so that Judas asks the ruling priests, "What will you give me if I deliver him to you?" (Matt 26:15). As Hagner (*Matthew*, 761) suggests, the introduction of this question is intended to give Judas a motive for the betrayal; he wants money. This is consistent with the Fourth Evangelist's claim that Judas used to pilfer from the money box (John 12:6). But Mark says none of this. Mark's readers might infer that Judas has given up on Jesus, who continues to speak of his death. The insertion of the anointing story (14:3–9) between the notice of the ruling priests' desire to find a way to take Jesus by stealth (14:1–2) and the description of Judas's perfidy (14:10–11) seems to support this inference. (Gundry, 819–20, is correct to say that Mark does not explicitly mention unease on the part of Judas, but surely readers would infer this.) When the woman anoints Jesus and so recognizes his messianic identity, how does Jesus respond? He interprets her extravagant deed as preparation for burial. With this, Judas "went away to the ruling priests, so that he might hand him over to them" (14:10). Perhaps from Judas's perspective, it is Jesus who has betrayed the cause. Having given up on the hope of inaugurating the kingdom of God now and establishing a new government in Jerusalem (in which Judas may play a part), Jesus seems determined to pursue a reckless and pointless course of martyrdom. Judas will have none of it; he wants out.

Explanation

Judas Iscariot has had enough. Jesus' insistence on dying has demoralized him. We may speculate that he had joined Jesus in the first place because he, too, longed for the appearance of the kingdom of God. But things have not gone well in Jerusalem. The ruling priests have not welcomed Jesus; on the contrary, they are actively opposing him. Jesus himself now speaks of martyrdom. This is not what Judas had anticipated. It is time to cut his losses and get out. He decides to surrender Jesus to the ruling priests. They promise Judas money in exchange for arranging a quiet and effective arrest. Though they want him out of the way, they do not want to incite violence.

Some scholars have tried to make Judas's deed into something other than a betrayal of Jesus. But these proposals struggle against the evidence. In the world of late antiquity, traitors were despised (Babrius 138.7–8; Livy 1.11.6–7; 5.27.6–10); to betray one's own people for a bribe was considered a terrible crime and a cause for great shame (cf. Demosthenes, *Rhod. lib.* 23; *Cor.* 46–49). There is no hint in Christian tradition that Judas's deed could be interpreted in any but the darkest light. However, just as we should not exculpate or even lionize Judas and try to find something positive in his deed, neither should we demonize him. Judas Iscariot exemplifies human weakness, and all Christians should know that the discouragement and temptation that overtook him could overtake them as well.

D. The Passover with the Disciples (14:12–21)

Bibliography

Allen, W. C. "The Last Supper Not a Passover Meal." *ExpTim* 20 (1908) 377. **Arnott, A. G.** "The First Day of Unleavened . . . ,' Mt 26.17, Mk 14.12, Lk 22.7." *BT* 35 (1984) 235–38. **Bokser, B. M.** "Was the Last Supper a Passover Seder?" *BR* 3.2 (1987) 24–33. **Casey, M.** *Aramaic Sources.* 219–52. ———. "The Date of the Passover Sacrifices and Mark 14:12." *TynBul* 48 (1997) 245–47. **Chenderlin, F.** "Distributed Observance of the Passover: A Hypothesis." *Bib* 56 (1975) 369–93. ———. "Distributed Observance of the Passover: A Preliminary Test of the Hypothesis." *Bib* 57 (1976) 1–24. **Christensen, J.** "Le fils de l'homme s'en va, ainsi qu'il est écrit de lui." *ST* 10 (1956) 28–39. **Chwolson, D.** *Das letzte Passamahl Christi und der Tag seines Todes.* 2nd ed. Leipzig: Hässel, 1908. **Derrett, J. D. M.** "The Upper Room and the Dish." *HeyJ* 26 (1985) 373–82 (repr. in J. D. M. Derrett. *Studies in the New Testament.* 5 vols. Leiden: Brill, 1989. 5:119–28). **Dockx, S.** "Le récit du repas pascal: Marc 14,17–26." *Bib* 46 (1965) 445–53. **Dormeyer, D.** *Die Passion Jesu.* 88–100. **Field, F.** *Notes.* 39. **Fleddermann, H. T.** *Mark and Q.* 164–66. **Hasler, V.** *Amen: Redaktionsgeschichtliche Untersuchung zur Einführungsformel der Herrenworte "Wahrlich ich sage euch."* Zürich; Stuttgart: Gotthelf, 1969. 49–54. **Heawood, P. J.** "The Time of the Last Supper." *JQR* 42 (1951–52) 37–44. **Heil, J. P.** "Mark 14:1–52: Narrative Structure and Reader-Response." *Bib* 71 (1990) 305–32. **Hein, K.** "Judas Iscariot: Key to the Last-Supper Narratives?" *NTS* 17 (1970–71) 227–32. **Hiers, R. H.** *The Historical Jesus and the Kingdom of God: Present and Future in the Message and Ministry of Jesus.* UFHM 38. Gainesville: University of Florida, 1973. 96–101. **Hooker, M. D.** *The Signs of a Prophet: The Prophetic Actions of Jesus.* Harrisburg, PA: Trinity Press International, 1997. 48–54. **Jacob, R.** *Les péricopes de l'entrée à Jérusalem et de la préparation de la cène: Contribution à l'étude du problème synoptique.* EBib. Paris: Gabalda, 1973. **Jaubert, A.** "La date de la dernière Cène." *RHR* 146 (1954) 140–73. ———. *The Date of the Last Supper.* Staten Island, NY: Alba House, 1965. **Jeremias, J.** *The Eucharistic Words of Jesus.* London: SCM Press, 1966; Philadelphia: Fortress, 1977. **Johnston, L.** "The Date of the Last Supper." *Scr* 9 (1957) 108–15. **Klassen, W.** *Judas: Betrayer or Friend of Jesus?* Minneapolis: Fortress, 1996. **Klauck, H.-J.** *Judas—Ein Jünger des Herrn.* QD 111. Freiburg; Basel: Herder, 1987. 55–63. **Kosmala, H.** "Der Ort des letzten Mahles Jesu und das heutigen Coenaculum." *Jud* 17 (1961) 43–47. **Kremer, J.** *Das Ärgernis des Kreuzes: Eine Hinführung zum Verstehen der Leidensgeschichte.* Stuttgart: Katholisches Bibelwerk, 1969. 17–21. **MacRae, G. W.** "A New Date for the Last Supper." *AER* 138 (1958) 294–302. **Mahoney, J.** "The Last Supper and the Qumran Calendar." *Clergy Review* 48 (1963) 216–32. **Marcus, J.** *Way of the Lord.* 172–79. **März, C.-P.** "Siehe, dein König kommt zu Dir . . .": Eine traditionsgeschichtliche Untersuchung zur Einzugsperikope.* ETS 43. Leipzig: St. Benno, 1980. 81–86. **Mohr, T. A.** *Markus- und Johannespassion.* 150–84. **Moo, D. J.** *Old Testament in the Gospel Passion Narratives.* 235–40. **O'Flynn, J. A.** "The Date of the Last Supper." *ITQ* 25 (1958) 58–63. **Ogg, G.** "The Chronology of the Last Supper." In *Historicity and Chronology in the New Testament.* Ed. D. E. Nineham et al. S. P. C. K. Theological Collections 6. London: S. P. C. K., 1965. 75–96. ———. Review of *La Date de la Cène,* by A. Jaubert. *NovT* 3 (1959) 149–60. **Pesch, R.** *Das Abendmahl und Jesu Todesverständnis.* QD 80. Freiburg: Herder, 1978. ———. *Evangelium der Urgemeinde.* 165–68. ———. "The Gospel in Jerusalem: Mark 14:12–26 as the Oldest Tradition of the Early Church." In *The Gospel and the Gospels.* Ed. P. Stuhlmacher. Grand Rapids, MI: Eerdmans, 1991. 106–48. **Pickl, J.** *The Messias.* St. Louis: Herder, 1946. **Robbins, V. K.** "Last Meal: Preparation, Betrayal, and Absence." In *The Passion in Mark: Studies on Mark 14–16.* Ed. W. Kelber. Philadelphia: Fortress, 1976. 21–40. **Ruckstuhl, E.** *Die Chronologie des letzten Mahles und des Leidens Jesu.* Zürich: Schweizerischen Katholischen Bibelbewegung,

1963. **Saldarini, A. J.** *Jesus and Passover.* New York: Paulist, 1984. **Schenk, W.** *Der Passionsbericht nach Markus.* 182–89. **Schenke, L.** *Studien zur Passionsgeschichte des Markus.* 152–285. **Schmahl, G.** *Die Zwölf im Markusevangelium.* 100–102. **Schwarz, G.** *Jesus und Judas.* 162–67. **Senn, F. C.** "The Lord's Supper, Not the Passover Seder." *Worship* 60 (1986) 362–68. **Shepherd, M. H., Jr.** *Paschal Liturgy and the Apocalypse.* London: Lutterworth, 1960. **Skehan, P. W.** "The Date of the Last Supper." *CBQ* 20 (1958) 192–99. **Smith, B. D.** "The Chronology of the Last Supper." *WTJ* 53 (1991) 29–45. ———. *Jesus' Last Passover Meal.* Lewiston; Queenston: Mellen, 1993. ———. "The More Original Form of the Words of Institution." *ZNW* 83 (1992) 166–86. **Stock, K.** *Boten aus dem Mit-Ihm-Sein.* 150–61. **Strobel, A.** "Die Termin des Todes Jesu: Überschau und Lösungsvorschlag unter Einschluss des Qumrankalenders." *ZNW* 51 (1960) 69–101. ———. *Ursprung und Geschichte des frühchristlichen Osterkalenders.* TU 121. Berlin: Akademie, 1977. 46–53. **Suhl, A.** *Zitate.* 51–52. ———. "Der Termin Jesu." *ZNW* 51 (1960) 69–101. **Torrey, C. C.** "In the Fourth Gospel the Last Supper Was the Paschal Meal." *JQR* 42 (1951–52) 237–50. **Vogler, W.** *Judas Iskarioth: Untersuchungen zu Tradition und Redaktion von Textes des Neuen Testaments und ausserkanonischer Schriften.* 2nd ed. Theologische Arbeiten 42. Berlin: Evangelische Verlagsanstalt, 1985. 43–47. **White, J. L.** "Beware of Leavened Bread: Markan Imagery in the Last Supper." *Forum* 3.4 (1987) 49–63. **Zeitlin, S.** "The Last Supper as an Ordinary Meal in the Fourth Gospel." *JQR* 42 (1951–52) 257–60. ———. "The Time of the Passover Meal." *JQR* 42 (1951–52) 45–50.

See also *Bibliography* for Mark 14:1–16:20.

Bibliography on Mark 14:21

Bastin, M. *Jésus devant sa passion.* LD 92. Paris: Cerf, 1976. 144–46. **Crossan, J. D.** *In Fragments.* 144–51. **Grimm, W.** *Weil ich dich liebe.* 209–22. **Higgins, A. J. B.** *Jesus and the Son of Man.* Philadelphia: Fortress, 1964; London: Lutterworth, 1965. 50–52. **Hooker, M. D.** *Jesus and the Servant: The Influence of the Servant Concept of Deutero-Isaiah in the New Testament.* London: S. P. C. K., 1959. 79–80. ———. *Son of Man in Mark.* 159–61. **Lindars, B.** *Jesus Son of Man: A Fresh Examination of the Son of Man Sayings in the Gospels in the Light of Recent Research.* London: S. P. C. K., 1983; Grand Rapids, MI: Eerdmans, 1984. 74–76. **Moo, D. J.** *Old Testament in the Gospel Passion Narratives.* 106–9. **Schwarz, G.** *Jesus "der Menschensohn": Aramaistische Untersuchungen zu den synoptischen Menschensohnworten Jesu.* BWANT 119. Stuttgart: Kohlhammer, 1986. 268–74. ———. *Jesus und Judas.* 110–15. **White, J. L.** "Beware of Leavened Bread: Markan Imagery in the Last Supper." *Forum* 3.4 (1987) 49–63.

Translation

[12]*And on the first*[a] *day of Unleavened Bread, when they were slaughtering the Passover lamb, his disciples say to him, "Where do you wish that we go to prepare,*[b] *so that you may eat the Passover?"* [13]*And he sends two of his disciples, and says to them, "Go into the city,*[c] *and a man carrying a jar of water will meet you; follow him.* [14]*And wherever he might go, say to the owner of the house, 'The teacher*[d] *says, "Where is my guest room, where I may eat the Passover with my disciples?"'* [15]*And he will show you a large upper room,*[e] *furnished [and] ready; and there prepare for us."*[f] [16]*And the disciples*[g] *went out*[h] *and entered the city, and they found [things] as he*[i] *had told them, and they prepared the Passover.*

[17]*And when it was evening, he comes with the Twelve.* [18]*And while they were reclining and eating, Jesus said, "Truly,*[j] *I say to you, one of you will betray me, one who is eating with me."* [19]*They began to be grieved*[k] *and to say to him, one by one, "It is not I, is*

it?"[1] [20]*But he said to them, "One of the Twelve, one who dips*[m] *into the bowl*[n] *with me.*[o] [21]*For the 'son of man' goes,*[p] *just as it is written concerning him; but woe to that man through whom the 'son of man' is betrayed—better for him if that man had not been born."*

Notes

[a]A few late MSS read τρίτῃ, "third."

[b]Lit. "Where do you wish that we, going, might prepare?" D and several late MSS add σοι, "for you."

[c]A few late MSS add τὴν κατέναντι ὑμῶν, "that is opposite you" (cf. Mark 11:2).

[d]Gk. ὁ διδάσκαλος. Many Latin MSS read *magister noster,* "our teacher." Syr. MSS read *rabbān,* "master," or "teacher."

[e]D reads ἀνάγαιον οἶκον . . . μέγαν, "a large upper house," as it also does in Luke 22:12 D (but omitting the μέγαν). Black (*Aramaic Approach,* 246) suspects that confusion over interpretation of the underlying Aramaic accounts for this variant.

[f]Φ and a few late MSS read ὑμῖν, "for you." Some authorities add τὸ πάσχα, "the Passover."

[g]A C D W Σ Φ and several late authorities read οἱ μαθηταὶ αὐτοῦ, "his disciples."

[h]W and a few late MSS add ἑτοιμάσαι, "to prepare," or ἑτοιμάσαι αὐτῷ, "to prepare for him."

[i]A few late MSS read ὁ Ἰησοῦς, "Jesus."

[j]Gk. ἀμήν. A few Syr. MSS read *'āmēn 'āmēn,* "truly, truly." This variant reflects Johannine influence.

[k]A few late MSS add καὶ ἀδημονεῖν, "and to be anguished" (cf. Matt 26:37).

[l]D Σ Φ and several later MSS add καὶ ἄλλος· μήτι ἐγώ, "and another, 'It is not I, is it?'" Some late MSS add ῥαββί, "rabbi," or κύριε, "lord."

[m]A and a few late authorities add τὴν χεῖρα, "the hand" (cf. Matt 26:23).

[n]B C*vid and a few late MSS read εἰς τὸ ἓν τρύβλιον, "into the one bowl."

[o]A few late MSS add οὗτός με παραδώσει, "he will betray me" (cf. Matt 26:23).

[p]D W and a few late authorities read παραδίδοται, "is betrayed."

Form/Structure/Setting

The securing of the upper room and the meal at which Jesus announces his betrayal constitute two principal components (vv 12–16 and vv 17–21) of this pericope with various minor subunits. Six discrete steps make up the progression of these components: (1) the announcement of time and occasion (v 12), (2) the sending and instructing two disciples (vv 13–15), and (3) the accomplishment of the mission (v 16); (4) the announcement of betrayal (vv 17–18), (5) the disciples' sorrowful reaction (v 19); and (6) Jesus' asseveration and pronouncement of woe upon the betrayer (vv 20–21). In typical Markan fashion, the pace of the narrative moves quickly and dramatically.

According to Bultmann (*History,* 263–64) the story of the securing of the upper room is a legend, driven by a "fairy-tale motif." Nineham (376) regards it as a late addition to the Passion Narrative. Some wonder if the story is a fabrication based on 1 Sam 10:1–5, where after his anointing Saul meets three men, receives food, and then enters a city (see *Comment* on 14:3). However, Cranfield (420) does not think this parallel justifies regarding the passage as legendary. Others argue for the story's historicity (e.g., Lagrange, 371–75; Bartlet, 378–80; Turner, 67; and others). Indeed, Pesch ("The Gospel in Jerusalem"; id., *Das Abendmahl,* 69–90) has argued that 14:12–26 constitutes an ancient, pre-Markan passion tradition.

The preparations and prior arrangement remind us of the entry into Jerusalem in 11:1–6. Are the two stories really a doublet, that is, two versions of what originally was a single story? Taylor (536) has identified the most important verbal agreements:

11:1–6	*14:13–16*
¹ἀποστέλλει δύο τῶν μαθητῶν αὐτοῦ "he sends two of his disciples"	¹³ἀποστέλλει δύο τῶν μαθητῶν αὐτοῦ "he sends two of his disciples"
²καὶ λέγει αὐτοῖς "and says to them"	καὶ λέγει αὐτοῖς "and says to them"
ὑπάγετε εἰς τὴν κώμην "Go into the village"	ὑπάγετε εἰς τὴν πόλιν "Go into the city"
³εἴπατε "say"	¹⁴εἴπατε "say"
ὁ κύριος "the Lord"	ὁ διδάσκαλος "the teacher"
⁴καὶ ἀπῆλθον καὶ εὗρον "and they went away and found"	¹⁶καὶ ἐξῆλθον . . . καὶ εὗρον "and . . . went out . . . and . . . found"
⁶καθὼς εἶπεν ὁ Ἰησοῦς "as Jesus had said"	καθὼς εἶπεν αὐτοῖς "as he had told them"

Taylor rightly infers from these agreements that both stories were composed by the same author (probably the Markan evangelist), but the similarities do not compel us to conclude that the stories are a doublet. Mark has a tendency to be formulaic and repetitive (compare the narratives of the Deaf Mute in 7:31–37 and the Blind Man at Bethsaida in 8:22–26). Moreover, the differences in setting and purpose are much greater than the formal agreements listed above. Taylor concludes that the "evidence suggests that each narrative is composed by Mark on the basis of tradition" (536; see also Pesch, 2:341). Indeed, Cranfield (423) suspects that vv 18–21 may constitute an independent unit, inserted between vv 17 and 22. The repetition in vv 18 and 22 ("and while they were . . . eating") supports this suggestion. The Markan evangelist is fond of intercalation (e.g., 11:11, 15; 11:12–13, 20), though not every example necessarily derives from the evangelist; some may be traditional (see *Comment* on 14:54, 67; for discussion of intercalations in chap. 14, see Heil, *Bib* 71 [1990] 305–32).

The major historical and interpretive question is whether this meal was a Passover meal. Major scholars have weighed in on both sides of the debate. The Gospels themselves appear divided on the question. Mark 14:12 ("prepare, so that you may eat the Passover"), followed by Matthew (26:17) and Luke (22:8), apparently understands the Last Supper (14:17–25) as a Passover meal, while John 18:28 (cf. John 19:14, 31, 42) seems to imply that the Last Supper took place the day before Passover and that Jesus in fact died on Passover, 15 Nisan. Chronological discrepancies between the Synoptic Gospels and the Johannine Gospel are not unusual (compare the respective settings of the action in the temple), nor are discrepancies between the Synoptics themselves (compare Mark and Matthew on when Jesus cursed the fig tree and took action in the temple). But a discrepancy concerning the relationship of the Passover to the actual day on which Jesus died is somewhat surprising. Cranfield (420–22) and many others prefer the synoptic chronology, while suggesting that the Johannine chronology reflects a theological interest, that is, a desire to present Jesus as the Passover lamb, slain on Passover

(John 1:29; 19:36). However, Paul also speaks of Jesus as the sacrificed Passover lamb (1 Cor 5:7). Paul's language may be theological, but it may also reflect an early, pre-Johannine chronology. If so, perhaps the Johannine chronology in this instance should be preferred to the synoptic chronology. Jesus may very well have intended to eat the Passover with his disciples, but as it turned out, his last meal with them was a meal on the day before, in which he foretold his betrayal and uttered the words of institution. Given the chronological uncertainties that Mark creates in chap. 11, one should be cautious about assuming that his timetable is superior to John's.

The positions may be conveniently reviewed under three headings: (1) theories of calendar discrepancy, (2) arguments in favor of Markan (or synoptic) chronology, and (3) arguments in favor of Johannine chronology. (1) With regard to theories of calendar discrepancy, Shepherd (*Paschal Liturgy*, 36–37) wonders if in the year Jesus was crucified, Palestinian Jews celebrated Passover on Saturday, whereas Diaspora Jews celebrated it on Friday, perhaps accounting for the discrepancy between the Synoptic Gospels and the Fourth Gospel (see Pickl, *Messias*, 120–22, for a similar view). Billerbeck (Str-B 2:812–13) speculates that Passover was celebrated on two days, reflecting a dispute between Pharisees and Sadducees. Similarly, Chwolson (*Passamahl Christi*) contends that the lambs were slaughtered on 13 and 14 Nisan and that the Passover meal itself was observed on 14 and 15 Nisan (see more recently Chenderlin, *Bib* 56 [1975] 369–93). Jaubert (*Date of the Last Supper*) argues that Jesus kept the Passover according to the Essene calendar (see also Strobel, *ZNW* 51 (1960) 69–101). However, this theory assumes too much and cannot be proven. Few accept it today. The problem with all these theories is that they lack hard evidence and are speculative.

(2) In favor of Markan chronology, Jeremias (*Eucharistic Words*, 41–62) emphatically defends the Last Supper as a Passover meal and marshalls fourteen reasons in support of this identification. Agreeing with Jeremias, Lane (497) summarizes the evidence as follows: (a) Jesus returned to Jerusalem in the evening for the meal (14:17) instead of eating in Bethany, where he had been residing since arriving in the vicinity of Jerusalem. This is significant, for the Passover meal had to be eaten within the city's walls (cf. Deut 16:2; *m. Pesaḥ.* 7:9; Nineham, 374). (b) The fact that the meal was an *evening* meal suggests that it was a Passover meal (cf. Exod 12:8; *Jub.* 49:12). (c) Reclining (14:18) satisfies the requirement for the Passover meal, for it signifies the posture of free persons (cf. *m. Pesaḥ.* 10:1). (d) Breaking bread after serving a bowl (14:18–20, 22) is consistent with Passover meal practice. (e) Serving wine was customary for the Passover meal (*m. Pesaḥ.* 10:1). (f) The interpretive elements along with the meal suggest a Passover meal. (g) The singing of a hymn at the conclusion of the meal also supports a Passover interpretation. Moreover, Lane (498) attempts to resolve the discrepancy between Mark and John by suggesting that John's παρασκευὴ τοῦ πάσχα in 19:14 should be translated "the Friday of the Passover week" rather than "the preparation of the Passover" (on this, see Matt 27:62; Mark 15:42; Luke 23:54; John 19:31; *Did.* 8). But this suggestion has difficulties. In a recent, specialized study Smith (*WTJ* 53 [1991] 29–45; id., *Last Passover Meal*) has reviewed the evidence, and he too finds in favor of the synoptic chronology (and also tries to harmonize it with the chronology of the Fourth Gospel). In view of the evidence that Jeremias and others have cited, many commentators have opted for the

Markan chronology. However, much of the evidence actually proves little. Schweizer (297) asserts that "there is nothing which would indicate whether it was the Passover meal or a formal dinner on the preceding evening." In the list above, items *b–e* do not constitute exclusive evidence of a Passover meal (though see the argument in Casey, *Aramaic Sources,* 229). Items *f* and *g* offer weak support at best. The best evidence is item *a,* but even it is not conclusive.

(3) Because there is no reference to the roasted lamb or to the bitter herbs, other commentators do not think the Last Supper was a Passover meal. Therefore, some prefer the Johannine chronology. Ogg ("Chronology") reviews Jeremias's fourteen reasons in support of the Last Supper as a Passover meal and judges every one of them to be weak, ambiguous, or inconclusive and therefore insufficient to overturn the Johannine chronology. He concludes that Mark's chronology represents a deviation from the older tradition (as attested in 1 Cor 5:7) that Jesus was crucified on Passover. He argues that *(a)* Mark 14:22–25 is an independent tradition, in which no mention of Passover is found; *(b)* Mark 14:12–16 is a later insertion to place 14:22–25 in the context of a Passover meal; *(c)* John clearly understands the Last Supper as one day before the Passover; and *(d)* to arrest Jesus on the day of Passover itself would have presented the ruling priests and their agents with legal problems (if Mishnaic legislation is any guide; on this point, see B. Weiss, *The Life of Christ,* vol. 3 [Edinburgh: T. & T. Clark, 1884] 274). Moreover, Ogg finds the linguistic arguments that attempt to understand the reference to παρασκευὴ τοῦ πάσχα in John 19:14 as "the Friday of the Passover week" unpersuasive. He therefore concludes that the Last Supper was a meal before the day of Passover and that the Johannine chronology is to be preferred. Turner (67), Taylor (664–67), Johnson (228), Hooker (333; id., *Signs of a Prophet,* 115–16 n. 59), Brown (2:915–16; id., *John* 2:555–56), and others (e.g., Allen, *ExpTim* 20 [1908] 377; Bokser, *BR* 3.2 [1987] 24–33; Senn, *Worship* 60 [1986] 362–68) have come to this conclusion. With some hesitation, this commentary has taken this position. One should also take Luke 22:15–16 into account, for the distinctly Lukan saying of v 15 and the variant form of the saying in v 16 (compare Mark 14:25) seem to suggest that Jesus' desire to eat the Passover went unfulfilled: "I have earnestly desired to eat this passover with you before I suffer; for I tell you I shall not eat it until it is fulfilled in the kingdom of God." And finally, it might be added that arresting Jesus *before* Passover, not on the *day* of Passover itself, would have better served the interests of the authorities. Thoughts of liberation from foreign domination would reach their highest pitch on the day of Passover. But if the proclaimer of the kingdom of God, who perhaps was himself the Lord's Anointed, was safely in custody, then he could hardly rally his followers and ignite his movement. Surely the authorities intended to take Jesus before the day of Passover, not the evening of the day itself.

Having taken this position, we should not conclude that Passover ideology was therefore absent from the thoughts or table talk of Jesus and his companions during the Last Supper. The Markan tradition, even if confused and edited, indicates that Jesus had made plans to eat the Passover with the Twelve. Passover themes very probably contributed to their conflicting hopes and fears: hopes that soon the kingdom of God would manifest itself fully; fears that Jesus' predictions of his death would all too soon be fulfilled. Turner (67) plausibly suggests that in the passage of time, early Christians increasingly associated the Last Supper with Passover, which may then account for the Markan chronology.

Comment

12 καὶ τῇ πρώτῃ ἡμέρᾳ τῶν ἀζύμων, "And on the first day of Unleavened Bread." The reference is to the Passover day itself (see *Comment* section for 14:1–2). By introducing in this way the story of securing the upper room and the meal that follows, the evangelist presents the Last Supper as a Passover meal (see discussion of this issue in *Form/Structure/Setting* above).

ὅτε τὸ πάσχα ἔθυον, "when they were slaughtering the Passover lamb." Casey (*Aramaic Sources,* 223) argues that the subject of the verb ἔθυον, "they were slaughtering," refers not to the crowd in general (*pace* Taylor, 537, and Gundry, 820, who see it as a customary imperfect tense) but to Jesus and his disciples, who are depicted as having slaughtered the "Passover lamb" (which is the meaning of πάσχα) in the temple precincts. Given the meaning of the question that the disciples will shortly ask Jesus, Casey is probably correct. According to Jewish convention, Jesus would have slit the animal's throat, its blood would have been drained into a silver or gold basin held by a priest, and the priest would have taken the basin to the altar where he would have sprinkled the blood at the base of the altar (cf. *Tg. Onq.* Exod 24:8: "Moses took the blood and sprinkled it on the altar to atone for the people"). Throughout the course of the day thousands of lambs would have been slaughtered in this fashion. The Greek θύειν τὸ πάσχα, "to slaughter the Passover lamb," is taken from the LXX (e.g., Exod 12:21; Deut 16:2; see G. B. Gray, *Sacrifice in the Old Testament* [Oxford: Clarendon, 1925] 376–82).

Having finished the flaying of the lamb, the disciples ask Jesus, ποῦ θέλεις ἀπελθόντες ἑτοιμάσωμεν ἵνα φάγῃς τὸ πάσχα, "Where do you wish that we go to prepare, so that you may eat the Passover?" In ancient times, if biblical legislation was observed literally, the Passover lamb would have been cooked and eaten within the temple precincts themselves (inferred from Deut 16:7, "the place which the LORD your God will choose"). In late antiquity, the much larger population made this impossible. After the slaughter and the sprinkling of blood on the altar, the celebrant and his family would retire to a private setting within the city of Jerusalem to cook and eat the Passover lamb (cf. *Sipre Num.* §69 [on Num 9:10]: "What is the place in which it must be eaten? Within the gate of Jerusalem"; *t. Pesaḥ* 8.2). The implication of the disciples' question is that the Passover lamb has just been slaughtered, so there is now need to retire to suitable quarters. They are asking where those quarters are.

13 Jesus has made prior arrangements, so ἀποστέλλει δύο τῶν μαθητῶν αὐτοῦ, "he sends two of his disciples." Jesus sends his disciples ahead to take care of the Passover meal preparation (in Mark's presentation the Last Supper is understood to have been a Passover meal).

These disciples, not the Twelve (who remain with Jesus; see v 17), are told, ὑπάγετε εἰς τὴν πόλιν, καὶ ἀπαντήσει ὑμῖν ἄνθρωπος κεράμιον ὕδατος βαστάζων· ἀκολουθήσατε αὐτῷ, "Go into the city, and a man carrying a jar of water will meet you; follow him." In a manner reminiscent of the arrangements for securing a colt for his entry (see 11:1–6 and the columns of parallels in *Form/Structure/Setting* above), Jesus again has made arrangements—evidently unknown to the disciples whom he has sent—for observing the Passover in a private room. The clandestine rendezvous with the man carrying a jar of water may have had to do with precautions that Jesus felt were necessary. He knew he was a wanted man.

But he was also determined to eat the Passover meal, and to do that he had to find a room in the city (i.e., in Jerusalem). Casey (*Aramaic Sources,* 227) wonders why Jesus would say, "Go into the city," since technically he and his disciples were already in the city. It is probable that a distinction between the (sacred) temple precincts and the (mundane) city proper is assumed. The two unnamed disciples are to leave the temple precincts (whose eastern wall serves as the eastern wall of the city) and go into the heart of the city that lay largely to the west of the Temple Mount. These arrangements tell against the view that the securing of the upper room is to be understood as a miracle.

The sign of the man carrying the water jug is somewhat reminiscent of the sign of the three men going up to Bethel, one of whom was carrying a wineskin, which was given to Saul (1 Sam 10:1–5, esp. vv 2, 3, and 5; Cranfield, 420). The parallel is interesting also because the OT story begins with Samuel's anointing of Saul. Lagrange (373) rightly remarks that in the culture of Jesus' day, men normally carried water in skins, while women carried water in jars. Therefore, this anomaly may have been deliberate as part of the sign. The unnamed disciples are to follow this man, and he will lead them to the house where the Passover meal will be eaten.

14 τῷ οἰκοδεσπότῃ, "the owner of the house." The disciples may expect to meet the "owner" or "master [lit. 'despot'] of the house." A password will be needed, again suggesting that these arrangements have security concerns in mind. The disciples are to say to the owner of the house: ὁ διδάσκαλος λέγει, ποῦ ἐστιν τὸ κατάλυμά μου ὅπου τὸ πάσχα μετὰ τῶν μαθητῶν μου φάγω, "The teacher says, 'Where is my guest room, where I may eat the Passover with my disciples?'" ὁ διδάσκαλος, "the teacher," refers, of course, to Jesus. It is deliberately anonymous in keeping with the desire for precaution. The question itself completes the identification. The reference to Jesus as the teacher also tells against interpreting the episode as a miracle (Bartlet, 379–80). The owner of the house now knows that these men are from Jesus of Nazareth and that they are here to make Passover preparations, perhaps with the owner's assistance. κατάλυμα often means "place of lodging" (the equivalent of an inn or boarding house; cf. LXX Jer 14:8; Luke 2:7). But it can also mean "guest room," as it does here and in LXX 1 Sam 1:18.

15 καὶ αὐτὸς ὑμῖν δείξει ἀνάγαιον μέγα ἐστρωμένον ἕτοιμον, "And he will show you a large upper room, furnished [and] ready." The disciples will be shown an ἀνάγαιον μέγα, "large upper room." The room is μέγα, "large," because Jesus, the Twelve, other disciples (such as the two unnamed disciples who have been sent ahead to make preparations), and women (as we may rightly infer from passages such as Luke 10:38–42) will be present. If the meal were indeed a Passover meal, then we might even expect the presence of children, who would ask the prompting questions of what the Passover means. ἐστρωμένον ἕτοιμον, "furnished [and] ready," implies a room with carpet and upholstered couches (so Swete, 330; Bartlet, 380; Rawlinson, 201; Lohmeyer, 299; cf. Field, *Notes,* 39). στρωννύειν, "to furnish," has this meaning in Jewish and Hellenistic sources. However, Taylor (538) notes that this word can mean much more modest furnishings, even "bare necessities."

ἐκεῖ ἑτοιμάσατε ἡμῖν, "there prepare for us." The disciples are to prepare the room and food for the meal that will be served later in the evening when Jesus, the Twelve, and the other disciples will gather. It is not said if the jug-carrying man who is expected to show the disciples the upper room will have a part in this preparation. With respect to ἡμῖν, "for us," Swete (330–31) observes that Jesus seldom uses the inclusive first-person plural (for another example, see 9:40: "whoever is not against us is for us").

16 εὗρον καθὼς εἶπεν αὐτοῖς, "they found [things] as he had told them." The disciples did not simply find the room as Jesus had told them; they found everything as he had told them—the man carrying the jar of water, his leading them to the house, the cooperation of the owner, and the room, furnished and ready. Again Jesus is portrayed as master of the situation.

καὶ ἡτοίμασαν τὸ πάσχα, "and they prepared the Passover." From this it is clear that the evangelist understands the Last Supper as a Passover meal. On the derivation of πάσχα, "Passover," see *Comment* on 14:1. Preparation for the Passover meal entailed roasting the lamb and providing unleavened biscuits, bitter herbs, sauce, water, and wine. The room itself would require special furnishings (such as couches and lamps).

17 καὶ ὀψίας γενομένης ἔρχεται μετὰ τῶν δώδεκα, "And when it was evening, he comes with the Twelve." If the Last Supper was a Passover meal, then the ὀψίας, "evening," begins 15 Nisan, the night of Passover (cf. Exod 12). After the preparations of vv 12–16 one should expect a fuller account of a Passover meal. Indeed, there is nothing about the supper itself that requires us to view it as a Passover meal. The supper itself unfolds in two stages: (1) the prediction of the betrayal by εἷς, "one," of the Twelve in vv 17–21, and (2) the words of institution in vv 22–25. Bultmann (*History*, 265) maintains that vv 17–21 and vv 22–25 "were not originally contiguous." Taylor (539) suspects that he is correct in this judgment. (But there is little justification to say with Bultmann that vv 22–25 constitute the "cult legend of the Hellenistic circles about Paul"; see below.)

The restraint in the narrative and sayings argues for the originality of the tradition. Judas is not named or rebuked. There is no mention of money or mention of those to whom Judas will betray Jesus. How does Jesus know? Again, we may suspect that his knowledge derives from various friendly sources in Jerusalem (as the preparations for the entry into the city and securing the upper room would indicate), sources outside his immediate circle. Jesus has evidently heard that the ruling priests have struck a bargain with one of his disciples.

18 καὶ ἀνακειμένων αὐτῶν καὶ ἐσθιόντων, "And while they were reclining and eating." Jesus and his disciples have now reclined on the couches and have begun to eat the Passover meal (though compare Exod 12:11, which requires Israelites to eat while standing). The use of the genitive absolute, however, implies that the reclining and eating merely serve as the backdrop to the main point of the sentence, which is Jesus' startling prediction of betrayal.

ἀμὴν λέγω ὑμῖν ὅτι εἷς ἐξ ὑμῶν παραδώσει με ὁ ἐσθίων μετ' ἐμοῦ, "Truly, I say to you, one of you will betray me, one who is eating with me." The idea that one who shares another's food will then become a betrayer was viewed with loathing and outrage in late antiquity. Jesus' words, ὁ ἐσθίων μετ' ἐμοῦ, "one who is eating with me," probably echo Ps 41:9, "Even my bosom friend in whom I trusted, who ate of my bread, has lifted his heel against me," as Cranfield (423) thinks (see also Casey, *Aramaic Sources*, 229–32; Marcus, *Way of the Lord*, 178). In the Johannine version, the reference to the lament Psalm is explicit (cf. John 13:18). We find here an interesting parallel with the Hymn Scroll, whose author makes a similar complaint: "Ev[en those who a]te my bread have lifted up their heel against me, and all those who have committed themselves to my counsel speak perversely against me with unjust lips. The men of my [coun]cil rebel and grumble round about" (1QH 13:23–25 [*olim* 5:23–25]). The allusion to Ps 41:9 is clear. The antithesis of sharing food and then engaging in treachery seems to have become proverbial. See also the *Sentences of the Syriac Menander:* "He with whom you had a meal, do not walk with him in a treacherous way" (215–16).

While reclining at table and eating, Jesus predicts that one of his disciples will betray him (vv 18–19). Mark again emphasizes Jesus' predictive power. He has predicted his death on several occasions, he has only recently predicted that the woman's pouring of perfume on his head would be preparation for his burial, and now he startles his disciples by predicting the betrayal. Predicting the betrayal softens the embarrassment and disgrace for Jesus, namely, that one of his own disciples would give him up. Far from being a discreditable reflection on Jesus, it becomes a credit to him, because he foresaw it (unlike Julius Caesar, for example, who entered the Senate chambers and much to his surprise was attacked by his colleagues).

19 ἤρξαντο λυπεῖσθαι, "They began to be grieved." The only other occurrence in Mark of λυπεῖν, "to grieve," is found in 10:22, where the rich man turns away in sorrow, unable to give away his wealth and follow Jesus. The reaction of the disciples is only natural. They have been with Jesus throughout the course of most of his public ministry. They have witnessed firsthand his astounding deeds and have heard his provocative, hope-inspiring proclamation of the kingdom of God. This message and its powerful attestation through exorcism and healing were delegated to them (6:7–13) so that they could take an active role in his ministry. But now on the eve of Passover when the Jewish people remember God's greatest act of deliverance in the nation's history, they are horrified to learn that one of their own number will betray their master.

καὶ λέγειν αὐτῷ εἷς κατὰ εἷς, μήτι ἐγώ, "and to say to him, one by one, 'It is not I, is it?'" Mark's grammatically awkward εἷς κατὰ εἷς, "one by one," is Semitic (probably the equivalent of חד חד *had had;* cf. Casey, *Aramaic Sources,* 231). Shocked, the disciples each in turn ask, "It is not I, is it?" They are too stunned by Jesus' charge even to begin to suspect or accuse someone else; each looks to himself (Taylor, 541). The negative μήτι, "It is not . . . is it?" shows that the disciples expect, or hope for, assurance from Jesus that "no, it is not you." Besides shock, the reaction of the disciples shows that they do not know that Judas is the betrayer. Indeed, each disciple may even wonder if he himself will succumb to the temptation to betray Jesus and so escape the dangers that by now they know they face.

Both Matthew and John embellish the story. Mark's "one by one, 'It is not I, is it?'" gives rise to Matt 26:25: "Judas, who betrayed him, said, 'Is it I, Master?' He said to him, 'You have said so'"; and to John 13:25–26: "'Lord, who is it?' Jesus answered, 'It is he to whom I shall give this morsel when I have dipped it.' So when he had dipped the morsel, he gave it to Judas." These embellishments enhance the evidence of Jesus' knowledge. In Mark's account the reader is not sure if Jesus knows that it is Judas Iscariot; all that Jesus knows is that it is "one of the Twelve" (v 20). But in Matthew and John Jesus knows exactly which one of the Twelve it is.

20 εἷς τῶν δώδεκα, ὁ ἐμβαπτόμενος μετ' ἐμοῦ εἰς τὸ τρύβλιον, "One of the

Twelve, one who dips into the bowl with me." Confirming the disciples' worst fears, Jesus declares that the betrayer is one of the Twelve (as opposed to one of those of the larger following), a friend who shares food with Jesus. In v 15 it was suggested that a large upper room was secured because the group that was expected to attend was more than simply Jesus and the Twelve. Jesus' reply here supports that view. Had he and the Twelve been the only ones present, his declaration, "one of the Twelve," would have sounded a bit odd. But in a room of many disciples, Jesus' statement would be especially shocking. For he would be saying, in effect, "not just one of my disciples, but one of the Twelve; indeed, one who dips into the bowl with me." The implied contrast between one of the Twelve and one of the rest of his following would only heighten the shock of the betrayal. Reference to the bowl does not identify the betrayer (as in John 13:26–30); it "stresses the enormity of the act" (Taylor, 541). For an OT example of dipping food into a bowl, see Ruth 2:14. If this meal were a Passover meal (and it may not have been), then the τρύβλιον, "bowl," would probably be the bowl (not "dish"; cf. MM, 643) that "contains the sauce . . . in which the bitter herbs were dipped" (Cranfield, 424).

In v 18 Jesus startled his disciples by saying that one of them would betray him, "one who is eating with me." Betrayal by a friend, a friend with whom one eats, is appalling. But here in v 20, Jesus intensifies the odium by saying that the betrayer is one who shares the food from the very bowl into which Jesus himself dips his fingers.

21 ὅτι ὁ μὲν υἱὸς τοῦ ἀνθρώπου ὑπάγει καθὼς γέγραπται περὶ αὐτοῦ, "For the 'son of man' goes, just as it is written concerning him." The "son of man" will suffer the fate that awaits him, a fate foretold in Scripture. The Markan Gospel does not tell its readers what Scripture is in view. When Jesus is arrested in 14:49, he says, "that the Scriptures should be fulfilled." Again, we are not told what Scriptures are in view. However, in 14:27 Jesus will paraphrase Zech 13:7: "I will strike the shepherd, and the sheep will be scattered." Jesus may also have had in mind Ps 41:9, which has been alluded to earlier in 14:18, and Isa 53, which is echoed here and there in the Gospels (see *Comment* on Mark 10:45). But here in v 21 Jesus links what is written to the "son of man." According to Dan 7, the holy ones of God will engage the powers of evil in a fierce struggle. Evil will prevail over the saints for a time and will wear them out (Dan 7:21, 25). The handing over of the "son of man" to those who seek his life coheres with this scenario. It is also possible, given Jesus' interest in Daniel, that Dan 9:26 ("an anointed one shall be cut off") was in mind. Jesus' vague reference to what is written in Scripture of the "son of man" supports the authenticity of the utterance (as also in 14:49). Early Christian scriptural apologetic supplied proof texts; none is provided here.

Christensen (*ST* 10 [1956] 1–24) appeals to *Tg.* Ezek 12:1–16 as attesting an interpretive scriptural background to Jesus' words. However, there really is little in this passage, either in Hebrew or Aramaic (or Greek), that substantiates this proposal. Even the epithet "son of man" in *Tg.* Ezek 12:2 is בר אדם *bar ʾādām*, not בר אנוש *bar ʾĕnôš*. Thus, the one essential element is missing.

Casey (*Aramaic Sources*, 233–36; *pace* Gundry, 838) sees behind ὑπάγει, "goes," the Aramaic אזל *ʾăzal*, citing the saying of Rabbi (probably Judah the Prince) in *y. Kil.* 9.4: "It is not as a son of man goes [אזל *ʾăzal*] that he (will) come (again)" (cf. *y. Ketub.* 12.3; *Gen. Rab.* 100.2 [on Gen 49:33]). Here אזל *ʾăzal*, "goes," clearly re-

fers to one's passing; that is, a man will not return to life in the same apparel in
which he had been buried.

οὐαὶ δὲ τῷ ἀνθρώπῳ ἐκείνῳ δι' οὗ ὁ υἱὸς τοῦ ἀνθρώπου παραδίδοται, "woe to that
man through whom the 'son of man' is betrayed." The scene concludes with a
dolorous woe pronounced upon the man who betrays the "son of man." οὐαί, "woe,"
reflects the Hebrew אוֹי 'ôy, which appears almost a hundred times in the OT: e.g.,
"Woe to the wicked! It shall be ill with him, for what his hands have done shall be
done to him" (Isa 3:11); "Woe to those who devise wickedness and work evil upon
their beds!" (Mic 2:1). Jesus' pronouncement of woe upon his betrayer is one of
two appearances of οὐαί, "woe," in the Gospel of Mark (cf. 13:17: "Woe to those
women who are pregnant and to those who nurse in those days!"). Elsewhere in
the Gospels of Matthew and Luke Jesus pronounces woe on the cities of Chorazin
and Bethsaida (Matt 11:21 = Luke 10:13) and the scribes and Pharisees (Matt 23:13,
15–16, 23, 25, 27, 29 = Luke 11:42–44, 46–47, 52), and, in contrast to the beatitudes, he pronounces woe on the rich, well fed, and popular (Luke 6:24–26).

καλὸν αὐτῷ εἰ οὐκ ἐγεννήθη ὁ ἄνθρωπος ἐκεῖνος, "better for him if that man
had not been born." Jesus may very well be betrayed into the hands of those who
will put him to death, but his betrayer faces a fate far worse. In his case it would
have been better for him never to have been born. This kind of expression is
attested in other Jewish texts, e.g., "when the Righteous One shall appear . . . it
would have been better for them [i.e., those who denied the name of the Lord]
not to have been born" (*1 Enoch* 38:2; cf. *2 Enoch* 41:2; *m. Ḥag.* 2:1). The sin of
the betrayal approximates the unforgivable sin of Mark 3:28–29, while Jesus' saying is similar in form and content to the Q saying "Woe to the world for temptations
to sin! For it is necessary that temptations come, but woe to the man by whom
the temptation comes!" (Matt 18:7; cf. Luke 17:1–2). Johnson (230) wonders if
the Markan saying is drawn from this Q saying. *Pace* White (*Forum* 3.4 [1987] 49–
63), there is no need to view the woe oracle as a creation inspired by Ps 41:9.

Explanation

Once again Jesus is portrayed as the master of the situation, indeed, as the
master of his fate. Having killed the Passover lamb, he sends two of his disciples
from the Temple Mount into the city with instructions on how to find and prepare the room in which the Passover meal will be eaten. All turns out as Jesus has
instructed. The room and the food are prepared; later in the evening Jesus and
the Twelve join the others. But this particular Passover meal is no ordinary one.
The Markan narrative omits mention of the recounting of the exodus story and
the original Passover night, and says nothing of the lamb or the bitter herbs. The
evangelist narrates only Jesus' startling words. In the midst of the observance of
the most important Jewish holiday, Jesus stuns his disciples with his declaration,
"one of you will betray me." Grieved, the disciples one by one ask Jesus if it is one
of them. So impressed are they with their master's predictive ability and wisdom,
they do not consider that Jesus could be mistaken. Each wonders (all but one
innocently) if in light of what Jesus has just said he might not himself betray him.
Jesus confirms their worst fears; the betrayer is "one of the Twelve, one who dips
into the bowl with" his Master. Nevertheless, Jesus recognizes that this fate is foretold in Scripture; but its inevitability does not excuse the action of the betrayer.

Woe to him, for it would be "better for him if that man had not been born." Jesus' pronouncement of woe underscores the seriousness of the betrayal.

Jesus' mastery of the situation is seen in the fact that he is able to foretell his fate. He has announced his forthcoming suffering and death, even the manner of it (10:32–34); now he foretells the betrayal. Later he will foretell the disciples' desertion and Peter's three denials. At every point Jesus is in command of the unfolding events; nothing takes him by surprise, nothing causes him to stumble and shrink back from fulfilling his mission. Indeed, his impending death occasions the opportunity to speak to the significance of his death as will be seen in the next pericope.

E. The Institution of the Lord's Supper   (14:22–25)

Bibliography

Aalen, S. "Das Abendmahl als Opfermahl im Neuen Testament." *NovT* 6 (1963) 128–52. **Allen, W. C.** "The Last Supper Was a Passover Meal." *ExpTim* 20 (1908–9) 377. **Ambrozic, A. M.** *Hidden Kingdom.* 183–202. **Audet, J.-P.** "Esquisse historique du genre littéraire de la 'bénédiction' juive et de l'"eucharistie' chrétienne." *RB* 65 (1958) 371–99. **Badia, L. F.** *The Dead Sea People's Sacred Meal and Jesus' Last Supper.* Washington, DC: University Press of America, 1979. **Bahr, G. J.** "The Seder of the Passover and the Eucharistic Words." *NovT* 12 (1970) 181–202. **Bammel, E.** "$\mathfrak{P}^{64(67)}$ and the Last Supper." *JTS* n.s. 24 (1973) 189–90. **Barclay, W.** *The Lord's Supper.* London: SCM Press, 1967. **Barth, M.** *Das Abendmahl: Pasamahl, Bundesmahl und Messiasmahl.* Theologische Studien 18. Zollikon; Zürich: Evangelischer, 1945. **Bayer, H. F.** *Jesus' Predictions of Vindication and Resurrection: The Provenance, Meaning and Correlation of the Synoptic Predictions.* WUNT 2.20. Tübingen: Mohr-Siebeck, 1986. 29–53. **Beasley-Murray, G. R.** *Jesus and the Kingdom of God.* 258–73. **Beck, N. A.** "The Last Supper as an Efficacious Symbolic Act." *JBL* 89 (1970) 192–98. **Becker, J.** "Die neutestamentliche Rede vom Sühnetod Jesu." *ZTK* Beiheft 8 (1990) 29–49. **Benoit, P.** "The Accounts of the Institution and What They Imply." In *The Eucharist in the New Testament.* Ed. J. Delorme et al. Dublin; Baltimore: Helicon, 1964. 71–101. ———. "The Holy Eucharist." In *Jesus and the Gospel.* 2 vols. London: Darton, Longman and Todd; New York: Herder and Herder, 1973. 1:95–122. ———. "Jésus et le Serviteur de Dieu." In *Jésus aux origines de la christologie.* Ed. J. Dupont. BETL 40. Gembloux: Duculot; Leuven: Leuven UP, 1975. 141–86. **Berger, K.** *Die Amen-Worte Jesu: Eine Untersuchung zum Problem der Legitimation in apokalyptischer Rede.* BZNW 39. Berlin: de Gruyter, 1970. 54–59. **Best, E.** *Temptation and the Passion.* 144–47. **Betz, J.** "Die Eucharistie als sakramentale Gegenwart des Heilsereignisses 'Jesus' nach dem ältesten Abendmahlsberichte." *Geist und Leben* 33 (1960) 166–75. **Black, M.** "The Arrest and Trial of Jesus and the Date of the Last Supper." In *New Testament Essays.* FS T. W. Manson, ed. A. J. B. Higgins. Manchester: Manchester UP, 1959. 19–33. ———. "The 'Fulfilment' in the Kingdom of God." *ExpTim* 57 (1945–46) 25–26. **Blank, J.** "Der 'eschatologische Ausblick' Mk 14,25 und seine Bedeutung." In *Kontinuität und Einheit.* FS F. Mussner, ed. P. G. Müller and W. Stenger. Freiburg; Basel: Herder, 1981. 508–18. **Bokser, B. M.** "Was the Last Supper a Passover Seder?" *BRev* 3.2 (1987) 24–33. **Bonsirven, J.** "Hoc est corpum meum: Recherches sur l'original araméen." *Bib* 29 (1948) 205–19. **Bornkamm, G.** "Herrenmahl und Kirche bei Paulus." *ZTK* 53 (1956) 312–49. **Bosch, D.** *Die Heidenmission* *in der Zukunftsschau Jesu: Eine Untersuchung zur Eschatologie der synoptischen Evangelien.* ATANT 36. Zürich: Zwingli, 1959. 175–83. **Boughton, L. C.** "'Being Shed for You/Many': Time-Sense and Consequences in the Synoptic Cup Citations." *TynBul* 48 (1997) 249–70. **Box, G. H.** "The Jewish Antecedents of the Eucharist." *JTS* o.s. 3 (1901–2) 357–69. **Brown, R. E.** "The Date of the Last Supper." *TBT* 11 (1964) 727–33. **Burchard, C.** "The Importance of Joseph and Asenath for the Study of the New Testament: A General Survey and a Fresh Look at the Lord's Supper." *NTS* 33 (1987) 102–34. **Burkill, T. A.** *Mysterious Revelation.* 161–77. **Burkitt, F. C.** "The Last Supper and the Paschal Meal." *JTS* o.s. 17 (1915–16) 291–97. **Carl, W. J., III.** "Mark 14:22–25." *Int* 39 (1985) 296–301. **Carmichael, D. B.** "David Daube on the Eucharist and the Passover Seder." *JSNT* 42 (1991) 45–67. **Casey, M.** *Aramaic Sources.* 219–52. ———. "The Original Aramaic Form of Jesus' Interpretation of the Cup." *JTS* n.s. 41 (1990) 1–12. **Chilton, B. D.** "'Amen': An Approach through Syriac Gospels." *ZNW* 69 (1978) 203–11. ———. *A Feast of Meanings: Eucharistic Theologies from Jesus through Johannine Circles.* NovTSup 72. Leiden: Brill, 1994. 46–74. ———. *Galilean Rabbi.* 202. ———. *Pure Kingdom: Jesus' Vision of God.* Studying the Historical Jesus. London: S. P. C. K.; Grand Rapids, MI: Eerdmans, 1996. 123–26. ———. *The Temple of Jesus: His Sacrificial Program within a Cultural History of Sacrifice.* University Park, PA: Pennsylvania State UP, 1992. 137–54. **Chordat, J. L.** *Jésus devant sa mort dans l'évangile de Marc.* Lire la Bible 21. Paris: Cerf, 1970. 73–80. **Christie, W. M.** "Did Christ Eat the Passover with His Disciples? or, The Synoptics versus John's Gospel." *ExpTim* 43 (1931–32) 515–19. **Cohn-Sherbok, D.** "A Jewish Note on ΤΟ ΠΟΤΗΡΙΟΝ ΤΗΣ ΕΥΛΟΓΙΑΣ." *NTS* 27 (1980–81) 704–9. **Cooke, B.** "Synoptic Presentation of the Eucharist as Covenant Sacrifice." *TS* 21 (1960) 1–44. **Coppens, J.** "Les soi-disant analogies juives de l'Eucharistie." *ETL* 8 (1931) 238–48. **Crawford, B. S.** "Near Expectation in the Sayings of Jesus." *JBL* 101 (1982) 225–44. **Cullmann, O.** "La significa-tion de la Sainte-Cène dans le christianisme primitif." *RHPR* 16 (1936) 1–22. ———. "Neutestamentliche Wortforschung: ΥΠΕΡ (ΑΝΤΙ) ΠΟΛΛΩΝ." *TZ* 4 (1948) 93–104. ——— and **Leenhardt, F. J.** *Essays on the Last Supper.* Ecumenical Studies in Worship 1. London: Lutterworth, 1958. **Dalman, G.** *Jesus–Jeshua: Studies in the Gospels.* London: S. P. C. K., 1929. 86–184. **Daly, R.** "The Eucharist and Redemption: The Last Supper and Jesus' Un-derstanding of His Death." *BTB* 11 (1981) 21–27. **Daube, D.** *He That Cometh.* St. Paul's Cathedral Lecture. London: Diocesan Council, 1966. ———. "The Significance of the Afikoman." *Pointer* (Spring 1968) 4–5. **David, J. E.** "τὸ αἷμά μου τῆς διαθήκης Mt 16,28: Un faux problème." *Bib* 48 (1967) 291–92. **Davies, P. E.** "Did Jesus Die as a Martyr-Prophet?" *BR* 2 (1957) 19–30. **Deissmann, A.** *Light from the Ancient East.* London: Hodder & Stoughton; New York: Harper & Row, 1927. **Delekat, F.** "Methodenkritische und dogmatische Probleme angesichts der gegenwärtigen Exegese der neutestamentlichen Abendmahlstexte." *EvT* 12 (1953) 389–415. **Delorme, J.** "The Last Supper and the Pasch in the New Testament." In *The Eucharist in the New Testament.* Ed. J. Delorme et al. Dublin; Baltimore: Helicon, 1964. 21–67. **Derrett, J. D. M.** "The Upper Room and the Dish." *HeyJ* 26 (1985) 373–82 (repr. in J. D. M. Derrett. *Studies in the New Testament.* 5 vols. Leiden: Brill, 1989. 5:119–28). **Descamps, A.** "Les origines de l'Eucharistie." In *Jésus et l'Église: Études d'exégèse et de théologie.* BETL 77. Leuven: Peeters and Leuven UP, 1987. 455–96. **Dockx, S.** "Le récit du repas pascal: Marc 14,17–26." *Bib* 46 (1965) 445–53. **Dormeyer, D.** *Die Passion Jesu.* 100–110, 117–24. **Dupont, J.** "'This is my Body'—'This is my Blood.'" In *The Eucharist Today: Essays on the Theology and Worship of the Real Presence.* Ed. R. A. Tartre. New York: Kennedy and Sons, 1967. 13–28. **Du Toit, A. B.** *Der Aspekt der Freude im urchristlichen Abendmahl.* Winterthur: Keller, 1965. 76–102. **Eisler, R.** "Das letzte Abendmahl [I]." *ZNW* 24 (1925) 161–92. ———. "Das letzte Abendmahl [II]." *ZNW* 25 (1926) 5–37. **Emerton, J. A.** "The Aramaic Underly-ing τὸ αἷμά μου τῆς διαθήκης in Mk XIV.24." *JTS* n.s. 6 (1955) 238–40. ———. "Mark xiv. 24 and the Targum to the Psalter." *JTS* n.s. 15 (1964) 58–59. ———. "ΤΟ ΑΙΜΑ ΜΟΥ ΤΗΣ ΔΙΑΘΗΚΗΣ: The Evidence of the Syriac Versions." *JTS* n.s. 13 (1962) 111–17. **Emminghaus, J. H.** "Stammen die Einsetzungsworte der Eucharistie von Jesus selber?" *BibLeb*

53 (1980) 36–38. **Feld, H.** *Das Verständnis des Abendmahls.* EdF 50. Darmstadt: Wissenschaftliche Buchgesellschaft, 1976. Esp. 23–25. **Feneberg, R.** *Christliche Passafeier und Abendmahl: Eine biblisch-hermeneutische Untersuchung der neutestamentlichen Einsetzungsberichte.* SANT 27. Munich: Kösel, 1971. **Flusser, D.** "Die Essener und das Abendmahl." In *Jesus—Qumran—Urchristentum.* Vol. 2 of *Entdeckungen im Neuen Testament.* Neukirchen-Vluyn: Neukirchener Verlag, 1999. 89–93. ———. "The Last Supper and the Essenes." *Immanuel* 2 (1973) 23–27. Repr. in D. Flusser. *Judaism and the Origins of Christianity.* Jerusalem: Magnes, 1988. 202–6. **France, R. T.** *Jesus and the Old Testament.* 121–23. **Friedrich, G.** *Die Verkündigung des Todes Jesu im Neuen Testament.* Biblisch-theologische Studien 6. Neukirchen-Vluyn: Neukirchener, 1982. **Fuller, R. H.** "The Double Origin of the Eucharist." *BR* 8 (1963) 60–72. **Gaugler, E.** *Das Abendmahl im Neuen Testament.* ATANT 11. Basel: Zwingli, 1943. **George, A.** "Le bonheur promis par Jésus d'après le Nouveau Testament." *LumVie* 52 (1961) 37–58. **Gese, H.** "Psalm 22 und das Neue Testament: Der älteste Bericht vom Tode Jesu und die Entstehung des Herrenmahles." *ZTK* 65 (1968) 1–22 (repr. in H. Gese. *Vom Sinai zum Zion: Alttestamentliche Beiträge zur biblischen Theologie.* BEvT 64. Munich: Kaiser, 1974. 180–201). **Gilmore, A.** "The Date and Significance of the Last Supper." *SJT* 14 (1961) 256–69. **Gnilka, J.** "Wie urteilte Jesus über seinen Tod?" In *Der Tod Jesu.* Ed. K. Kertelge. QD 74. Freiburg: Herder, 1976. 13–50. **Goetz, K. G.** "Zur Lösung der Abendmahlsfrage." *TSK* 108 (1937–38) 81–107. **Gottlieb, H.** "ΤΟ ΑΙΜΑ ΜΟΥ ΤΗΣ ΔΙΑΘΗΚΗΣ." *ST* 14 (1960) 115–18. **Grässer, E.** *Der Alte Bund im Neuen: Exegetische Studien zur Israelfrage im Neuen Testament.* WUNT 35. Tübingen: Mohr-Siebeck, 1985. 117–23. ———. *Die Naherwartung Jesu.* SBS 61. Stuttgart: Katholisches Bibelwerk, 1973. 113–18. **Grassi, J. A.** "The Eucharist in the Gospel of Mark." *AER* 168 (1974) 595–608. **Gregg, D. W. A.** "Hebraic Antecedents to the Eucharistic *Anamnesis* Formula." *TynBul* 30 (1979) 165–68. **Grelot, P.** *Les poèmes du serviteur.* LD 103. Paris: Cerf, 1981. 158–64. **Grimm, W.** *Weil ich dich liebe.* 294–300. **Gubler, M.-L.** *Die frühesten Deutungen des Todes Jesu: Eine motivgeschichtliche Darstellung aufgrund der neueren exegetischen Forschung.* OBO 15. Göttingen: Vandenhoeck & Ruprecht, 1977. 230–42. **Gundry, R. H.** *The Use of the Old Testament in St. Matthew's Gospel with Special Reference to the Messianic Hope.* NovTSup 18. Leiden: Brill, 1967. 57–60. **Hahn, F.** "Das Abendmahl und Jesu Todesverständnis." *TRev* 76 (1980) 265–72. ———. "Die alttestamentlichen Motive in der urchristlichen Abendmahlsüberlieferung." *EvT* 27 (1967) 337–74. ———. "Zum Stand der Erforschung des urchristlichen Herrenmahls." *EvT* 35 (1975) 553–63. **Hasler, V.** *Amen: Redaktionsgeschichtliche Untersuchung zur Einführungsformel der Herrenworte "Wahrlich ich sage euch."* Zürich; Stuttgart: Gotthelf, 1969. 49–54. **Heawood, P. J.** "The Time of the Last Supper." *JQR* 42 (1951–52) 37–44. **Hein, K.** "Judas Iscariot: Key to the Last-Supper Narratives?" *NTS* 17 (1970–71) 227–32. **Hengel, M.** *The Atonement: The Origins of the Doctrine in the New Testament.* Philadelphia: Fortress, 1981. 33–75. ———. "Der stellvertretende Sühnetod Jesu: Ein Beitrag zur Entstehung des urchristlichen Kerygmas." *IKZ* 9 (1980) 1–25, 135–47. **Hiers, R. H.** *The Historical Jesus and the Kingdom of God: Present and Future in the Message and Ministry of Jesus.* UFHM 38. Gainesville: University of Florida, 1973. 98–101. **Higgins, A. J. B.** *The Lord's Supper in the New Testament.* SBT 6. London: SCM Press, 1952. 24–37. ———. "The Origins of the Eucharist." *NTS* 1 (1954–55) 200–209. **Hook, N.** "The Dominical Cup Saying." *Theology* 77 (1974) 625–30. ———. *The Eucharist in the New Testament.* London: Epworth, 1964. **Hooker, M. D.** *Jesus and the Servant: The Influence of the Servant Concept of Deutero-Isaiah in the New Testament.* London: S. P. C. K., 1959. 80–83. ———. *The Signs of a Prophet: The Prophetic Actions of Jesus.* Harrisburg, PA: Trinity Press International, 1997. 48–54. **Hupfeld, R.** *Die Abendmahlfeier.* Gütersloh: Bertelsmann, 1935. **Jaubert, A.** "La date de la dernière Cène." *RHR* 146 (1954) 140–73. ———. *The Date of the Last Supper.* Staten Island, NY: Alba House, 1965. **Jeremias, J.** "Das Brotbrechen beim Passamahl und Mc 14,22par." *ZNW* 23 (1924) 203–4. ———. *The Eucharistic Words of Jesus.* Philadelphia: Fortress, 1977. ———. *New Testament Theology.* 288–92. ———. "This is My Body . . ." *ExpTim* 83 (1971–72) 196–203. ———. "Zur Exegese der Abendmahlsworte Jesu." *EvT* 7 (1947–48) 60–63. **Johnson,**

P. F. "A Suggested Understanding of the Eucharistic Words." *SE* 7 [= TU 126] (1982) 265–70. **Johnston, L.** "The Date of the Last Supper." *Scr* 9 (1957) 108–15. **Jonge, M. de.** "Jesus' Death for Others and the Death of the Maccabean Martyrs." In *Text and Testimony*. FS A. J. Klijn, ed. T. Baarda et al. Kampen: Kok, 1988. 174–84, 208–11. ———. "Mark 14:25 among Jesus' Words about the Kingdom of God." In *Sayings of Jesus: Canonical and Non-Canonical*. FS T. Baarda, ed. W. L. Petersen et al. NovTSup 89. Leiden: Brill, 1997. 123–35. **Kahlefeld, H.** *Das Abschiedsmahl Jesu und die Eucharistie der Kirche*. Frankfurt am Main: Knecht, 1980. **Kertelge, K.** "Das Abendmahl Jesu im Markusevangelium." In *Begegnung mit dem Wort*. FS H. Zimmermann, ed. J. Zmijewski and E. Nellessen. BBB 53. Bonn: Hanstein, 1980. 67–80. ———. "Die soteriologischen Aussagen in der urchristlichen Abendmahlsüberlieferung und ihre Beziehung zum geschichtlichen Jesus." *TTZ* 81 (1972) 193–202. **Kessler, H.** *Die theologische Bedeutung des Todes Jesu: Eine traditionsgeschichtliche Untersuchung*. Themen und Thesen der Theologie. Düsseldorf: Patmos, 1970. 275–81. **Kilmartin, E. J.** "The Last Supper and the Earliest Eucharists of the Church." *Concilium* 40 (1969) 35–47. **Kilpatrick, G. D.** "Eucharist as Sacrifice and Sacrament in the New Testament." In *Neues Testament und Kirche*. FS R. Schnackenburg, ed. J. Gnilka. Freiburg: Herder, 1974. 429–33. ———. "Living Issues in Biblical Scholarship: The Last Supper." *ExpTim* 64 (1952–53) 4–8. **Klauck, H.-J.** *Herrenmahl und hellenistischer Kult: Eine religionsgeschichtliche Untersuchung zum ersten Korintherbrief*. NTAbh 15. Münster: Aschendorff, 1982. 306–14. **Knoch, O.** "Ursprüngliche Gestalt und wesentlicher Gehalt der neutestamentlichen Abendmahlsberichte." *BK* 15 (1960) 37–40. **Kodell, J.** *The Eucharist in the New Testament*. Zacchaeus Studies: New Testament. Wilmington, DE: Glazier, 1988. **Kollmann, B.** *Ursprung und Gestalten der frühchristlichen Mahlfeier*. GTA 43. Göttingen: Vandenhoeck & Ruprecht, 1990. **Kosmala, H.** "Das tut zu meinem Gedächtnis." *NovT* 4 (1960–61) 81–94. **Kremer, J.** *Das Ärgernis des Kreuzes: Eine Hinführung zum Verstehen der Leidensgeschichte*. Stuttgart: Katholisches Bibelwerk, 1969. 22–30. **Kuhn, K. G.** "Die Abendmahlsworte." *TLZ* 75 (1950) 399–408. ———. "The Lord's Supper and the Communal Meal at Qumran." In *The Scrolls and the New Testament*. Ed. K. Stendahl. New York: Harper & Row, 1957. Repr. New York: Crossroad, 1992. 65–93. ———. "Über den ursprünglichen Sinn des Abendmahles und sein Verhältnis zu den Gemeinschaftsmahlen der Sektenschrift." *EvT* 10 (1950–51) 508–27. **Lambert, J. C.** "The Passover and the Lord's Supper." *JTS* o.s. 4 (1902–3) 184–93. **Lang, F.** "Abendmahl und Bundesgedanke im Neuen Testament." *EvT* 35 (1975) 524–38. **Lebeau, P.** *Le vin nouveau du royaume: Étude exégétique et patristique sur la parole eschatologique de Jésus à la Cène*. Paris: Desclée de Brouwer, 1966. **Leenhardt, F. J.** *Le Sacrement de la sainte Cène*. Neuchâtel; Paris: Delachaux et Niestlé, 1948. **Léon-Dufour, X.** "Jésus devant sa mort à la lumière des textes de l'institution eucharistique et des discours d'adieu." In *Jésus aux origines de la christologie*. Ed. J. Dupont. BETL 40. Gembloux: Duculot; Leuven: Leuven UP, 1975. 141–68. ———. "'Prenez! Ceci est mon corps pour vous.'" *NRT* 104 (1982) 223–40. **Lietzmann, H.** "Jüdisches Passahsitten und der ἀφικόμενος: Kritische Randnotizen zu R. Eislers Aufsatz über 'Das letzte Abendmahl.'" *ZNW* 25 (1926) 1–5. **Lindars, B.** "Joseph and Asenath and the Eucharist." In *Scripture: Meaning and Method*. FS A. T. Hanson, ed. B. P. Thompson. Hull: Hull UP, 1987. 181–99. **Loeschcke, G.** "Zur Frage nach der Einsetzung und Herkunft der Eucharistie." *ZWT* 54 (1912) 193–205. **Loewe, H.** "Die doppelte Wurzel des Abendmahles in Jesu Tischgemeinschaft." In *Abendmahl in der Tischgemeinschaft*. Ed. H. Loewe. Kassel: Stauda, 1971. 9–22. **Lohmeyer, E.** "Das Abendmahl in der Urgemeinde." *JBL* 56 (1937) 217–52. ———. "Vom urchristlichen Abendmahl." *TRu* 9 (1937) 168–227, 273–312; 10 (1938) 81–99. **Lys, D.** "Mon corps, s'est ceci (Notule sur Mt 26,26–28 et par.)." *ETR* 45 (1970) 389–90. **Mack, B. L.** *Myth*. 298–304. **MacRae, G. W.** "A New Date for the Last Supper." *AER* 138 (1958) 294–302. **Magne, J. M.** "Les paroles sur la coupe." In *Logia: Les paroles de Jésus—The Sayings of Jesus*. Ed. J. Delobel. BETL 59. Leuven: Peeters and Leuven UP, 1982. 485–90. **Mahoney, J.** "The Last Supper and the Qumran Calendar." *Clergy Review* 48 (1963) 216–32. **Manson, W.** *Jesus the Messiah: The Synoptic Tradition of the Revelation of God in*

Christ. London: Hodder & Stoughton, 1943. 134–46. **Marcus, J.** *Way of the Lord.* 156–57. **Marmorstein, A.** "Das letzte Abendmahl und der Sederabend." *ZNW* 25 (1926) 1–5. **Marshall, I. H.** *Last Supper and Lord's Supper.* Exeter: Paternoster; Grand Rapids, MI: Eerdmans, 1981. **Martin, R. P.** *Mark: Evangelist and Theologian.* 197–200. **Marxsen, W.** *The Beginnings of Christology, Together with The Lord's Supper as a Christological Problem.* Philadelphia: Fortress, 1979. 87–122. **McCormick, S.** *The Lord's Supper: A Biblical Interpretation.* Philadelphia: Westminster, 1966. **McKnight, S.** *A New Vision for Israel: The Teachings of Jesus in National Context.* Studying the Historical Jesus. Grand Rapids, MI; Cambridge: Eerdmans, 1999. 5–14. **Meier, J. P.** *Marginal Jew.* 2:302–9. **Merklein, H.** "Erwägungen zur Überlieferungsgeschichte der neutestamentlichen Abendmahlstraditionen." *BZ* 21 (1977) 88–101, 235–44 (repr. in H. Merklein. *Studien zu Jesus und Paulus.* WUNT 43. Tübingen: Vandenhoeck & Ruprecht, 1987. 157–80, esp. 171–80). **Meyer, B. F.** "The Expiation Motif in the Eucharistic Words: A Key to the History of Jesus?" *Greg* 69 (1988) 461–87. **Milligan, G.** "The Last Supper Not a Paschal Meal." *ExpTim* 20 (1908–9) 334. **Minette de Tillesse, G.** *Le secret messianique.* 390–94. **Mohr, T. A.** *Markus- und Johannespassion.* 185–212. **Moo, D. J.** *Old Testament in the Gospel Passion Narratives.* 127–32, 301–11. **Morrice, W. G.** "Covenant." *ExpTim* 86 (1974–75) 132–36. **Navone, J.** "The Last Day and the Last Supper in Mark's Gospel." *Theology* 91 (1988) 38–43. **Oberlinner, L.** *Todeserwartung und Todesgewissheit Jesu: Zum Problem einer historischen Begründung.* SBB 10. Stuttgart: Katholisches Bibelwerk, 1980. 130–34. **Oesterley, W. O. E.** *The Jewish Background of the Christian Liturgy.* Oxford: Clarendon, 1925. **O'Flynn, J. A.** "The Date of the Last Supper." *ITQ* 25 (1958) 58–63. **Ogg, G.** "The Chronology of the Last Supper." In *Historicity and Chronology in the New Testament.* Ed. D. E. Nineham et al. London: SCM Press, 1965. 92–96. ———. Review of *La Date de la Cène*, by A. Jaubert. *NovT* 3 (1959) 149–60. **Otto, R.** *The Kingdom of God and the Son of Man: A Study in the History of Religion.* New and rev. ed. Lutterworth Library 9. London: Lutterworth, 1943. Repr. Boston: Starr King Press, 1951. 263–330. **Palmer, D. W.** "Defining a Vow of Abstinence." *Colloquium* 6 (1973) 38–41. **Patsch, H.** *Abendmahl und historischer Jesus.* Calwer theologische Monographien 1. Stuttgart: Calwer, 1972. Esp. 180–82. ———. "Abendmahlsterminologie ausserhalb der Einsetzungsberichte: Erwägungen zur Traditionsgeschichte der Abendmahlsworte." *ZNW* 62 (1971) 210–31, esp. 219–28. **Perrin, N.** *The Kingdom of God in the Teaching of Jesus.* NTL. London: SCM Press; Philadelphia: Westminster, 1963. 67–73. **Pesch, R.** *Das Abendmahl und Jesu Todesverständnis.* QD 80. Freiburg: Herder, 1978. ———. *Das Evangelium der Urgemeinde.* 169–73. ———. "The Gospel in Jerusalem: Mark 14:12–26 as the Oldest Tradition of the Early Church." In *The Gospel and the Gospels.* Ed. P. Stuhlmacher. Grand Rapids, MI: Eerdmans, 1991. 106–48. ———. *Wie Jesus das Abendmahl hielt: Der Grund der Eucharistie.* Freiburg: Herder, 1977. **Pigulla, W.** "Das für viele vergossene Blut." *MTZ* 23 (1972) 72–82. **Preisker, H.** "Der Verrat des Judas und das Abendmahl." *ZNW* 41 (1942) 151–55. **Preiss, T.** "Was the Last Supper a Paschal Meal?" In *Life in Christ.* SBT 13. London: SCM Press, 1954. 81–96. **Reumann, J. H.** "The Problem of the Lord's Supper as Matrix for Albert Schweitzer's 'Quest of the Historical Jesus.'" *NTS* 27 (1980–81) 475–87. **Ringgren, H.** "The Use of the Psalms in the Gospels." In *The Living Text.* FS E. W. Saunders, ed. D. Groh and R. Jewett. Lanham, MD: University Press of America, 1985. 39–43. **Robbins, V. K.** "Last Meal: Preparation, Betrayal, and Absence." In *The Passion in Mark: Studies on Mark 14–16.* Ed. W. Kelber. Philadelphia: Fortress, 1976. 21–40. **Robinson, D. W. B.** "The Date and Significance of the Last Supper." *EvQ* 23 (1951) 126–33. **Ruckstuhl, E.** "Neue und alte Überlegungen zu den Abendmahlsworten Jesu." SNTSU 5 (1980) 79–106 (repr. in E. Ruckstuhl. *Jesus im Horizont der Evangelien.* Stuttgarter biblische Aufsatzbände 3. Stuttgart: Katholisches Bibelwerk, 1988. 69–100). **Saldarini, A. J.** *Jesus and Passover.* New York: Paulist, 1984. **Sandvik, B.** *Das Kommen des Herrn beim Abendmahl im Neuen Testament.* ATANT 58. Zürich: Zwingli, 1970. **Schelkle, K. H.** "Das Herrenmahl." In *Rechtfertigung.* FS E. Käsemann, ed. J. Friedrich et al. Tübingen: Mohr-Siebeck; Göttingen: Vandenhoeck & Ruprecht, 1976. 385–402. **Schenk, W.** *Der Passionsbericht nach Markus.* 189–93. **Schenke, L.**

Studien zur Passionsgeschichte des Markus. 286–341. **Schenker, A.** *Das Abendmahl Jesu als Brennpunkt des Alten Testaments: Begegnung zwischen den beiden Testamenten: Ein bibeltheologische Skizze.* BibB 13. Fribourg: Schweizerisches Katholisches Bibelwerk, 1977. **Schermann, T.** "Das 'Brotbrechen' im Urchristentum." *BZ* 8 (1910) 33–52, 162–83. **Schlosser, J.** *Le règne de Dieu.* 373–417. **Schürmann, H.** "Jesu ureigenes Todesverständnis: Bemerkungen zur 'impliziten Soteriologie' Jesu." In *Begegnung mit dem Wort.* FS H. Zimmermann, ed. J. Zmijewski and E. Nellessen. BBB 53. Bonn: Hanstein, 1980. 273–309. ———. "Die Semitismen im Einsetzungsbericht bei Markus und bei Lukas (Mk 14,22–24/Lk 22,19–20)." *ZKT* 73 (1951) 72–77. ———. "Das Weiterleben der Sache Jesu im nachösterlichen Herrenmahl." *BZ* 16 (1972) 1–23, esp. 11–14. **Schwager, R.** "Geht die Eucharistie auf Jesus zurück?" *Orientierung* 39 (1975) 220–23. **Schweitzer, A.** *The Problem of the Lord's Supper according to the Scholarly Research of the Nineteenth Century and the Historical Accounts.* Vol. 1: *The Lord's Supper in Relationship to the Life of Jesus and the History of the Early Church.* Ed. J. Reumann. Macon, GA: Mercer UP, 1982. **Schweizer, E.** "Das Abendmahl eine Vergegenwärtigung des Todes Jesu oder ein eschatologisches Freudenmahl?" *TZ* 2 (1946) 81–100. ———. *The Lord's Supper according to the New Testament.* FBBS. Philadelphia: Fortress, 1967. **Senior, D. P.** "The Eucharist in Mark: Mission, Reconciliation, Hope." *BTB* 12 (1982) 67–72. ———. *Passion of Jesus in the Gospel of Mark.* 76–88. **Simonis, W.** *Jesus von Nazareth: Seine Botschaft vom Reich Gottes und der Glaube der Urgemeinde.* Düsseldorf: Patmos, 1985. 84–91. **Skehan, P. W.** "The Date of the Last Supper." *CBQ* 20 (1958) 192–99. **Smith, B. D.** "The Chronology of the Last Supper." *WTJ* 53 (1991) 29–45. ———. *Jesus' Last Passover Meal.* Lewiston; Queenston: Mellen, 1993. ———. "The More Original Form of the Words of Institution." *ZNW* 83 (1992) 166–86. **Smith, M. A.** "The Influence of the Liturgies on the New Testament Text of the Last Supper Narratives." *SE* 5 [= TU 103] (1968) 207–18. **Söding, T.** *Glaube bei Markus.* 178–86. **Stacey, W. D.** "Appendix: The Lord's Supper as Prophetic Drama." In M. D. Hooker, *The Signs of a Prophet: The Prophetic Actions of Jesus.* Harrisburg, PA: Trinity Press International, 1997. 80–95. **Steinbeck, J.** "Das Abendmahl Jesu unter Berücksichtigung moderner Forschung." *NovT* 3 (1959) 70–79. **Strobel, A.** "Die Deutung des Todes Jesu im ältesten Evangelium." In *Das Kreuz Jesu.* Ed. P. Rieger. Forum 12. Göttingen: Vandenhoeck & Ruprecht, 1969. 32–64. **Stuhlmacher, P.** "The New Testament Witness concerning the Lord's Supper." In *Jesus of Nazareth—Christ of Faith.* Peabody, MA: Hendrickson, 1993. 58–102. **Suffrin, A. E.** "The Last Supper and the Passover." *ExpTim* 29 (1917–18) 475–77. **Suggit, J. N.** "The Perils of Bible Translation: An Examination of the Latin Versions of the Words of Institution of the Eucharist." In *A South African Perspective on the New Testament.* FS B. M. Metzger, ed. J. H. Petzer and P. J. Hartin. Leiden: Brill, 1986. 54–61. **Suhl, A.** *Zitate.* 110–20. **Sykes, M. H.** "The Eucharist as 'Anamnesis.'" *ExpTim* 71 (1959–60) 115–18. **Tabor, J. D.** "Martyr, Martyrdom." *ABD* 4:574–79. **Taylor, V.** *Jesus and His Sacrifice.* 114–42. **Temple, S.** "The Two Traditions of the Last Supper." *NTS* 7 (1960–61) 77–85. **Thyen, H.** *Studien zur Sündenvergebung im Neuen Testament und seinen alttestamentlichen und jüdischen Voraussetzungen.* FRLANT 96. Göttingen: Vandenhoeck & Ruprecht, 1970. 154–63. **Torrey, C. C.** "In the Fourth Gospel the Last Supper Was the Paschal Meal." *JQR* 42 (1951–52) 237–50. **Trilling, W.** *Fragen zur Geschichtlichkeit Jesu.* Düsseldorf: Patmos, 1966. 124–30. **Turner, N.** "The Style of St Mark's Eucharistic Words." *JTS* n.s. 8 (1957) 108–11. **Vogels, H.** "Mk 14,25 und Parallelen." In *Vom Wort des Lebens.* FS M. Meinertz, ed. N. Adler. NTAbh 1. Münster: Aschendorff, 1951. 93–104. **Vögtle, A.** "Todesankündigungen und Todesverständnis Jesu." In *Der Tod Jesu.* Ed. K. Kertelge. QD 74. Freiburg: Herder, 1976. 51–113. **Wagner, V.** "Der Bedeutungswandel von *bĕrit hadaša* bei der Ausgestaltung der Abendmahlsworte." *EvT* 35 (1975) 538–44. **Wellhausen, J.** "ἄρτον ἔκλασεν, Mc 14,22." *ZNW* 7 (1906) 182. **White, J. L.** "Beware of Leavened Bread: Markan Imagery in the Last Supper." *Forum* 3.4 (1987) 49–63. **Wilkens, H.** "Die Anfänge des Herrenmahls." *Jahrbuch für Liturgie und Hymnologie* 28 (1984) 55–65. **Williams, S. K.** *Jesus' Death as Saving Event.* HDR 2. Missoula, MT: Scholars Press, 1975. **Winnett, A. R.** "The

Breaking of the Bread: Does It Symbolize the Passion?" *ExpTim* 88 (1977) 181–82. **Wojciechowski, M.** "Le naziréat et la passion (Mc 14,25a; 15,23)." *Bib* 65 (1984) 94–96. **Wrede, W.** "Miscellen: 2. Tὸ αἷμά μου τῆς διαθήκης.'" *ZNW* 1 (1900) 69–74. **Wrege, H.-T.** *Die Gestalt des Evangeliums: Aufbau und Struktur der Synoptiker sowie der Apostelgeschichte.* BBET 11. Bern; Frankfurt am Main: Lang, 1978. 74–78. **Zeller, D.** "Prophetisches Wissen um die Zukunft in synoptischen Jesusworten." *TP* 52 (1977) 258–71. **Ziesler, J. A.** "The Vow of Abstinence: A Note on Mark 15:25 and Parallels." *Colloquium* 5 (1972) 12–14. ———. "The Vow of Abstinence Again." *Colloquium* 6 (1973) 49–50.

Translation

²²*And while they were eating, he,*[a] *taking bread [and] blessing [it],*[b] *broke [it], and gave [it] to them*[c] *and said,*[d] *"Take,*[e] *this is my body."* ²³*And after taking the cup, giving thanks, he gave [it] to them,*[f] *and all were drinking from it.* ²⁴*And he said to them, "This is my blood of the covenant,*[g] *which is poured out in behalf of*[h] *many.*[i] ²⁵*Truly, I say to you that I shall not again drink from the fruit of the vine until that day when I may drink it new in the kingdom of God."*

Notes

[a] אA C L Σ Φ and other later MSS read ὁ Ἰησοῦς, "Jesus."

[b] The "it" is implied. A few later MSS add καὶ εὐχαριστήσας, "and giving thanks" (as in v 23).

[c] A few later MSS and versions read τοῖς μαθηταῖς, "to his disciples" (cf. Matt 26:26).

[d] A few later MSS and versions add αὐτοῖς, "to them."

[e] Σ and several later MSS read λάβετε φάγετε, "take, eat" (cf. Matt 26:26).

[f] W reads τοῖς μαθηταῖς, "to his disciples."

[g] A Σ Φ and many later MSS and versions read τὸ αἷμά μου τὸ τῆς καινῆς διαθήκης, "my blood of the new covenant." The adj. καινῆς, "new," is an addition, inspired by the language found in Luke 22:20; 1 Cor 11:25; 2 Cor 3:6; Heb 8:8 (cf. Jer 31:31); 9:15. The same corruption is found in many MSS in Matt 26:28. See *TCGNT*[1], 113.

[h] Gk. ὑπέρ. On ὑπέρ used in this context, see Luke 22:19; 1 Cor 11:24. It means either "in behalf of" sinners (cf. Rom 5:6, 7, 8: "Christ died in behalf of us") or "for" sins (1 Cor 15:3: "Christ died for our sins"). A Σ Φ and many later MSS read περί, "for" or "concerning," in Mark 14:24. This variant may be due to the influence of LXX Isa 53:4: "he bears our sins and is pained for us"; 53:10: "if you should give for sin."

[i] W and many later MSS and versions add εἰς ἄφεσιν ἁμαρτιῶν, "for the forgiveness of sins." This addition is drawn from Matt 26:28, though the prep. phrase is also found in Mark (cf. 1:4) and in Acts (cf. 2:38).

Form/Structure/Setting

In 14:22–25 we have the institution of the Lord's Supper or Eucharist (from εὐχαριστεῖν [v 23], meaning "to give thanks"). These verses may originally have constituted an isolated unit of tradition, independent of 14:12–16. If so, then the supper may not necessarily have been a Passover meal, as the context provided by 14:12–16 implies (see discussion in *Form/Structure/Setting* on 14:12–21). Bultmann (*History*, 276) regards the parallel Luke 22:14–18 as derived from a distinct line of tradition (cf. Dibelius, *Tradition*, 206; Johnson, 231), part of which (i.e., vv 15–16) stands in tension with the Passover identification of the supper. Taylor (543) wonders if Mark 14:23 ("and all of them were drinking from it") originally concluded the supper, viewing vv 24–25 as appended sayings. This may be the case, but Ernst (413), Gnilka (2:239), and Pesch (2:345, 354, 364–77; id., "Mark 14:12–26," 118–22) believe vv 22–25 form a unity. As the passage stands, each verse contributes a distinct element: (1) the blessing and distribution of the bread (v 22), (2) the giving of thanks and the passing of the cup (v 23), (3) the saying about the "blood of the covenant" (v 24), and (4) the vow not to drink wine until the opportunity to do so in the kingdom of God (v 25). Pesch ("Mark 14:12–26"; id., *Wie Jesu das Abendmahl hielt,* 69–90; cf. the favorable review by T. Holtz, *TLZ* 106 [1981] cols. 812–13) believes that this material is part of the oldest passion tradition, predating Mark and Paul (i.e., 1 Cor 11:23–26). See also Ruckstuhl, SNTSU 5 (1980) 79–106; and Meyer, *Greg* 69 (1988) 461–87.

The major interpretive issue concerns the meaning of Jesus' words in v 24: "This is my blood of the covenant, which is poured out in behalf of many." Pesch (2:362) believes that Jesus understood his death as having an expiatory value. It is because of the numerous Semitic features that Pesch believes the tradition of the Lord's Supper and words of institution to be essentially historical and quite primitive, as mentioned above. Recently Chilton (*Temple of Jesus,* 152–54; id., *Feast of Meanings,* 66–74; id., *Pure Kingdom,* 125–26), who also accepts the authenticity of the tradition, has argued that τὸ σῶμά μου, "my body" (v 22), and τὸ αἷμά μου, "my blood" (v 24), refer not to the body and blood of Jesus himself but to the sacrificial animal, that is, to *its* body and *its* blood. Because of the dubious manner in which sacrificial animals were being purchased and slaughtered, Chilton reasons, Jesus had withdrawn from the temple and had recommended bread and wine as a substitution. For Jesus, the bread and wine constituted his body (i.e., sacrificial animal) and his blood (i.e., the blood of the sacrificial animal). Chilton's intriguing interpretation may very well clarify significant halakic points of difference between Jesus and the ruling priests (particularly with reference to Hillel's teaching regarding the proper manner of possessing and presenting sacrificial animals; cf. *t. Ḥag.* 2.11; *y. Ḥag.* 2.3; *y. Beṣah* 2.4; *b. Beṣah* 20a–b; see *Comment* section on 11:15–19), but another interpretation of the words of institution should be sought. (One should also review the article by Derrett, *HeyJ* 26 [1985] 373–82, who sees Jesus' action of dipping the bread into the bowl as having priestly connotations. This line of interpretation, however, is freighted with too much symbolism.)

Is the traditional interpretation that Jesus attached atoning value to his death plausible? Could a first-century Jew have thought and spoken in terms of giving his life "in behalf of many" and, by doing so, have saved his people and/or effected a renewed covenant? And if he did, would it have made sense to his contemporaries? Dying in behalf of family, friends, or one's city or country is well known in Greek stories (see Hengel, *Atonement,* 9–14; e.g., Euripides, *Alc.* 968–69: Creon wishes "to die as an atoning Sacrifice for the city"; and many other examples), but is similar tradition found in Judaism of late antiquity? It is, and it is sufficient to answer our questions in the affirmative. Three passages in 4 Maccabees speak of the salvific value of the suffering or death of the righteous: "By their endurance they conquered the tyrant, and thus their native land was purified through them" (4 Macc 1:11b). In reference to "those who gave their bodies in suffering for the sake of religion," the author asserts: "Because of them the nation gained peace, and by reviving observance of the law in the homeland they ravaged the enemy" (4 Macc 18:3–4). Even more explicitly, and in language reflecting the cultus itself, the author declares that these martyrs became, "as it were, a ransom for the sin of our nation. And through the blood of these devout ones and their death as an expiation, divine Providence preserved Israel that previously had been afflicted" (4 Macc 17:21b–22).

These passages are discounted by some, either because they reflect Hellenistic influence and not necessarily ideas current among Palestinian Jews, or because 4 Maccabees may have been composed after the destruction of the temple, and the ideas in 17:21–22 (especially) therefore reflect compensation for this loss (cf. Chilton, *Feast of Meanings*, 124–25). However, there is no indication in 4 Maccabees that the temple has been destroyed. Moreover, some scholars think the book was composed sometime between 20 and 54 C.E. (cf. *OTP* 2:533–34). In any event, the idea of martyrdom for the benefit of Israel is expressed in the earlier books of the Maccabees and in other Palestinian traditions. According to 1 Macc 6:44, Eleazar, brother of Judas Maccabeus, "gave himself [ἔδωκεν ἑαυτόν] to save his people and to win for himself an everlasting name" (cf. Gal 1:4: "who gave himself [δόντος ἑαυτόν] for our sins"; Titus 2:14: "who gave himself [ἔδωκεν ἑαυτόν] for us"). In the gruesome account of the martyrdom of the mother and her seven sons, the youngest of the sons says to the king:

> If our living Lord is angry for a little while, to rebuke and discipline us, he will again be reconciled with his own servants. . . . I, like my brothers, give up body and life for the laws of our fathers, appealing to God to show mercy soon to our nation . . . and *through me and my brothers* to bring to an end the wrath of the Almighty which has justly fallen on our whole nation. (2 Macc 7:33, 37–38; emphasis added)

The shedding of the blood of the righteous will prompt God to act and to make expiation for his people (cf. Deut 32:43; see further discussion in de Jonge, "Jesus' Death for Others"). According to *L.A.B.* 18:5, Isaac's willingness to give his life resulted in God's election of the descendants of Abraham: "And because he did not refuse, his sacrifice was well pleasing to me, and on account of his blood I chose them." Charlesworth asserts that *Liber antiquitatum biblicarum* reflects "the milieu of the Palestinian synagogues at the turn of the common era" (*OTP* 2:300). Another Palestinian tradition, *Testament of Moses*, promotes the idea of righteous, beneficial death: Taxo urges his seven sons to "die rather than transgress the commandments of the Lord of Lords" so that by doing this their "blood will be avenged before the Lord. Then his [God's] kingdom will appear throughout his whole creation. Then the devil will have an end" (*T. Mos.* 9:6b–10:1). The apparent linkage between the death of the righteous and the appearance of the kingdom of God is of special interest with respect to Jesus, who also was a proclaimer and martyr of the kingdom of God. Similar ideas are found in later Palestinian rabbinic traditions. Commenting on 1 Kgs 20:42 and 22:34, Simeon ben Yohai (second century C.E.) is remembered to have said: "That single drop of blood which flowed from that righteous man [the prophet of 1 Kgs 20:37] effected atonement in behalf of [על *ʿal*] all Israel" (*y. Sanh.* 11.5). Two more Tannaitic traditions should be mentioned: "When Israelites are slain by the nations of the world, it serves them as expiation in the world to come" (*Sipre Deut.* §333 [on Deut 32:43]); "you find everywhere that the patriarchs and the prophets gave their lives in behalf of [על *ʿal*] Israel" (*Mek.* on Exod 12:1 [*Pisḥa* §1]). One should also consider the com-

ment in the *Community Rule* scroll from Qumran: "they shall atone for sin by doing justice and by suffering the sorrows of affliction" (1QS 8:3–4; cf. 5:6; 9:4).

From these texts and traditions it seems reasonable to conclude that Jesus in
all probability did attach atoning and salvific significance to his impending death
(see Wright, *Jesus and the Victory of God*, 579–84). Indeed, Jeremias's remark (*Eucharistic Words*, 231) is not excessive: "The sources compel the conclusion that *it is
inconceivable that Jesus should not have thought of the atoning power of his death*" (his
emphasis). Jesus had proclaimed the kingdom of God, whereby Israel's covenant
would be renewed, probably in reference to Jer 31:31–34 (see Hengel, *Atonement*,
71–75; Meyer, *Greg* 69 [1988] 461–87; and *Comment* on 14:24). As "son of man"
Jesus was authorized to forgive sins and commence the process of restoring Israel. Now facing the probability of death, it would only have been natural for him
to conclude that his death would advance God's purposes, just as surely as the
deaths of the Maccabean martyrs atoned for Israel's sin and paved the way for
national deliverance. Jesus' death would in fact establish the renewed covenant
and guarantee the consummation of the kingdom of God. So assured was Jesus
that he vowed not to drink wine again until he would drink it in the kingdom of
God (again, see Hengel, *Atonement*, 72).

The emergence of the tradition of the Eucharist in itself also attests the atoning significance that Jesus placed on his death. The solemnity of the occasion,
the words of institution with their reference to the "blood of the covenant," and
the deep impression made on the disciples gave rise to early Christianity's doctrine of atonement. Apart from Jesus' words at the Last Supper and their
connotations of atonement, the doctrine of atonement (as opposed to ideas of
simple martyrdom) that emerged cannot be easily explained. Moreover, the mere
fact of the institution of the Lord's Supper as something to be commemorated by
the church also corroborates the atonement orientation of Jesus' words. Recognizing Jesus' death as atonement and not simply as martyrdom, in combination
with the conviction that he was God's Son, would have greatly encouraged the
institution of the Eucharist.

Here the Jewish commemoration of Passover, celebrated with a special meal
(including the Jewish practice of sacrifice), and Greco-Roman traditions in honor
of the gods, also celebrated with sacramental meals and/or drinking, could converge in early Christian fellowship and worship. Several Greco-Roman examples
can be cited: "When unmixed wine is served during a meal, it is the custom to
greet it with the words, 'To the Good Deity!' but when the cup is passed around
after the meal diluted with water, to cry out, 'To Zeus Savior!'" (Diodorus Siculus,
Library of History 4.3.4). It is reported that Attis initiates used to say "I ate from
the drum; I drank from the cymbal; I carried the sacred dish" (*apud* Clement of
Alexandria, *Exhortation to the Greeks* 15.3). According to Apuleius, speaking of the
Isis cult: "Then they began to solemnize the feast, the nativity of my holy order,
with sumptuous banquets and pleasant meats; the third day was likewise celebrated
with like ceremonies, with a religious dinner" (*Metam.* 11). An inscription from
the cult of Zeus Panamaros reads "The deity invites all people to a meal, and he
prepares a common and honorable table for all, whatever their origin" (SEG 4.247;
cf. P.Oxy. 110). Justin complains of a sacramental meal observed by devotees of
the mysteries of Mithra, who take bread and wine (*1 Apol.* 66.3). In Judaism not
only was the Passover meal eaten, but various types of fellowship offerings and

sacrifices were eaten, as though in the presence of God. We also know of various sacramental meals observed by Essenes (1QS 6:4–6; 1QSa 2:17–21; Josephus, *J.W.* 2.8.5 §129–33) and by the closely related Therapeutae, whose banquets included the reading of Scripture, interpretation, homily, and the singing of hymns (Philo, *Contempl. Life* 37, 69–87). Jesus' words and the symbolism of the bread and wine are at home in the pre-Easter setting of first-century Jewish Palestine. Mark's version, though edited, represents important fragments of early tradition that in all probability reaches back authentically to the Last Supper.

Comment

22 καὶ ἐσθιόντων αὐτῶν λαβὼν ἄρτον εὐλογήσας ἔκλασεν καὶ ἔδωκεν αὐτοῖς, "And while they were eating, he, taking bread [and] blessing [it], broke [it], and gave [it] to them." The genitive absolute, ἐσθιόντων αὐτῶν, "while they were eating," is somewhat ambiguous, allowing either that Jesus and the disciples were well into their meal or that the meal had just begun. However, the context (cf. v 18) demands the first option. Jesus and his disciples have been eating, and he has already startled them with the prediction of betrayal; now he will utter the words of institution.

The words of institution are prefaced by a blessing. It is speculated that this blessing may have approximated the blessing found in *m. Ber.* 6:1: "Blessed are You, O Lord our God, King of the universe, who brings forth bread from the earth" (Taylor, 544; Johnson, 231; Gundry, 830). The words of institution are then uttered but are accompanied by important symbols: the bread and the cup, which are imbued with new meaning. Jesus takes ἄρτος, which can refer to either leavened or unleavened "bread" (ἄζυμος, "unleavened"; cf. Josephus, *Ant.* 3.6.6 §§142–43). Accordingly, Jeremias (*Eucharistic Words*, 62–66; cf. Gundry, 841) rightly argues that the use of ἄρτος does not rule out a Passover interpretation of the Last Supper (but it does nothing to support it either). According to Luke, Jesus takes the bread "when he had given thanks" (Luke 22:19), which agrees with Paul (1 Cor 11:24) and probably points to a primitive pre-Markan tradition (Gundry, 829). The bread is broken and given to the disciples. In acting this out, Jesus follows the example of OT prophets, who variously walked barefoot (Isa 20:2), broke a potter's jug (Jer 19:10), or wore a yoke (Jer 28:10). In Acts 21:11 the prophet Agabus binds Paul's feet and hands with his girdle to foretell the fate that awaits the apostle in Jerusalem. Jesus' action is a prophetic sign (אות *'ôt*) that is meant to signify something (Otto, *Kingdom of God,* 300–301; Taylor, *Jesus and His Sacrifice*, 118; Beck, *JBL* 89 [1970] 102–98; Stacey, "Prophetic Drama," 86–90).

The act of breaking the bread may adumbrate the violent fate that awaits Jesus: just as surely as the bread is broken, so too will his body be broken (Otto, *Kingdom of God,* 302). Taking Jesus' words in this way, an early Christian scribe adds κλώμενον, "broken," to 1 Cor 11:24, so that the Pauline tradition of the words reads: "This is my body, which is broken for you" (cf. ℵᶜ C³ Dᵇ·ᶜ G K P Ψ and many other authorities; cf. *TCGNT¹*, 562). However, the association of broken bread with Jesus' broken body may be a theological rereading of the story through later Christian interpretation and eucharistic tradition. Besides, breaking the bread is what has to be done if it is to be distributed (Gundry, 840). Therefore, the significance of Jesus' action is not the violence to his body (to which the reference to τὸ αἷμά μου, "my blood," will allude) but the act of sharing the bread (cf. Hooker, *Signs of a Prophet*, 48–49). In contrast to the reference to τὸ αἷμά μου τῆς διαθήκης, "my blood of the covenant" (v 24), the breaking of the bread probably has nothing to do with the atoning value of Jesus' sacrifice (*pace* Otto, *Kingdom of God*, 275; and others).

λάβετε, τοῦτό ἐστιν τὸ σῶμά μου, "Take, this is my body." Behind Jesus' reference to σῶμα, "body," probably lies the Aramaic גֵּשֶׁם gĕšēm (as in Dan 3:27–28, where the LXX [3:94–95] translates with σῶμα) instead of בִּשְׂרָא biśrā', "flesh," or נוּפָא gûpā', "body" or "corpse" (see Casey, *Aramaic Sources*, 239). Gundry (831) favors נוּפָא gûpā' and thinks Jesus' words could be translated "this is my corpse." He supports this interpretation by noting that σῶμα is used in reference to Jesus' burial (14:8; 15:43). After all, Jesus "was not buried alive." True, but he was *crucified* alive, and it is his suffering and death to which Jesus alludes here. His body, *while alive*, will undergo intense suffering; his blood will be poured out (in the beatings and crucifixion, not in the later burial; see further discussion of this issue in the next paragraph). Furthermore, Jesus' *corpse* is not broken; it is buried (even if hastily and incompletely). The *life* will be beaten and bled out of Jesus.

In addition to τοῦτό ἐστιν τὸ σῶμά μου, "this is my body," Luke also reads τὸ ὑπὲρ ὑμῶν διδόμενον, "which is given for you," and τοῦτο ποιεῖτε εἰς τὴν ἐμὴν ἀνάμνησιν, "Do this in remembrance of me" (Luke 22:19b), which closely parallels Paul's form of the tradition: τοῦτό μού ἐστιν τὸ σῶμα τὸ ὑπὲρ ὑμῶν· τοῦτο ποιεῖτε εἰς τὴν ἐμὴν ἀνάμνησιν, "This is my body which is for you. Do this in remembrance of me" (1 Cor 11:24). This material should be viewed not as secondary embellishments but as original components of the words of institution that the evangelist Mark has omitted (see Gundry, 831–33, who reasonably suggests that Markan interest in Jesus' predictive powers leads to the omission of some of the traditional material). Jesus' linking himself, and his anticipated suffering, to the bread may have been suggested in part by the "bread of affliction" (Deut 16:3; cf. Lachs, 407), but its principal association may concern something else.

The copula ἐστίν, "is," should be taken to mean "signifies" or "represents" (Taylor, *Jesus and His Sacrifice*, 122). Jesus does not mean to say that the bread is literally his body. The sense in Aramaic may have been "this (bread) represents me" (cf. Carmichael, *JSNT* 42 [1991] 55; cf. E. Schweizer, *TDNT* 7:1059: "originally σῶμα ["body"], like αἷμα ["blood"], denoted the whole person of Jesus"). But what do the breaking and distribution of the bread signify? Daube (*He That Cometh*, 6–14; id., *Pointer* [Spring 1968] 4–5) wonders if Jesus' action constitutes an implicit messianic claim whereby a portion of the unleavened bread (and Daube understands the Last Supper as a Passover Seder) is broken off at the beginning of the meal and then at the conclusion is consumed by all who are sharing in the meal. What is broken off is called the *afikoman* (אֲפִיקוֹמָן 'ăpîqômān, from Greek ἀφικόμενος, meaning "he who comes"; on the confusion of the derivation of this word, cf. *EncJud* 2:329; the Greek derivation proposed in Jastrow 1:104 [ἐπὶ κῶμον = *comissatum ire*, "to go revelling," i.e., "to the aftermeal entertainment"] is among several false derivations and etymologies), and it represents the portion of the meal that the Messiah will eat when he returns to celebrate with Israel. Jesus has broken off a piece of bread, signifying the *afikoman*, and then distributes it to his disciples. As he does so, he declares, "this is my body," or as recommended above, "this represents me." Jesus has identified himself as the *afikoman*, that is, as "he who comes," the Messiah. In accepting and eating the *afikoman,* thus identified, the disciples demonstrate their faith in Jesus as the Messiah.

Daube (*He That Cometh,* 2) believes that the *afikoman* tradition lies behind a saying credited to Hillel: "There shall be no Messiah for Israel, because they have already enjoyed him in the days of Hezekiah" (*b. Sanh.* 99a; cf. 98b). The word translated "enjoyed" literally is "eaten" or "consumed" (אכלו *ʾāklû*). Hillel reasons that Israel has already eaten the messianic *afikoman* in the person of King Hezekiah (who has lived up to the expectations of Isa 9:1–6), so further messianic expectation is unwarranted. Although some think this is the Hillel of ca. 300 C.E., others (E. Bammel, "Das Wort vom Apfelbäumchen," *NovT* 5 [1962] 219–28, esp. 225; Daube, *He That Cometh,* 2, 15 n. 9) think it is the older, famous contemporary of Jesus (ca. 15 B.C.E.). The association of the *afikoman* with the awaited Messiah is still attested in some Jewish circles (cf. *EncJud* 2:330). But there is perhaps more direct and more important evidence for this interpretation. Carmichael (*JSNT* 42 [1991] 59–60) has observed that in Melito's paschal homily (second century C.E., following the text edited by O. Perler, *Meliton de Sardes, sur la Paque* [Paris: Cerf, 1966]) Jesus is twice specifically called the ἀφικόμενος: "This one is he who comes [ἀφικόμενος] from heaven to the earth on account of the one who suffers" (*Peri Pascha* 467–68); "This is he who comes to you [ὁ πρός σε ἀφικόμενος]" (*Peri Pascha* 642). Carmichael suspects that this is why the risen Jesus is recognized when he breaks bread (Luke 24:30–31), for this action recalled Jesus' earlier breaking off and distribution of the *afikoman,* at which time he declared that it was he. It could also explain why early Christian communal meals are simply described as "breaking bread" (Acts 2:42, 46; 20:7) and why Paul speaks of *remembering* the Lord (i.e., what he did and what he claimed) and eating the bread and drinking the cup "until he comes" (1 Cor 11:24, 26).

The advantage of this interpretation is that it follows familiar Jewish convention and it does not require us to suppose that Jesus invited his disciples to eat his body or "flesh," as the Fourth Gospel puts it (cf. John 6:48–58; John does this because of the identification of Jesus as the Passover lamb, which is eaten, and as the "bread from heaven," the manna, which is also eaten). Nor has Jesus invited his disciples to drink his blood (see *Comment* on vv 23–24). Such cannibalistic symbolism as this would have been wholly unacceptable in a Jewish context (cf. John 6:41, 52, 60, 66). Jesus' claim to be the one who comes and then in v 24 his reference to his "blood of the covenant" parallel his earlier comment about John the Baptist: "But I tell you that Elijah [i.e., John] has come, and they did to him whatever they wished [i.e., they treated him with contempt and killed him]" (Mark 9:13). Like Elijah, so too the Messiah has come; like Elijah, so too the Messiah will die.

23 καὶ λαβὼν ποτήριον εὐχαριστήσας ἔδωκεν αὐτοῖς, "And after taking the cup, giving thanks, he gave [it] to them." The blessing pronounced over the cup again may have approximated the blessing found in *m. Ber.* 6:1: "Blessed are You, O Lord our God, King of the universe, who creates the fruit of the vine." Just as Jesus took bread and gave it to his disciples, so now he takes the cup and gives it to his disciples. But the actions are only loosely parallel. While breaking the bread, Jesus claimed that it (the bread) was he; that is, he was the portion of bread broken off and set aside in anticipation of the coming Messiah. Jesus claimed to be "he who comes," the Messiah. Now he takes the cup, but the significance that he will attach to it is strikingly different, even if it is theologically and eschatologically complementary.

καὶ ἔπιον ἐξ αὐτοῦ πάντες, "and all were drinking from it." We should recall that Jesus had told James and John that they would drink the cup that Jesus himself would have to drink (10:38–39). The attentive reader/auditor of Mark will have perceived in this comment a fulfillment of Jesus' promise, on the one hand, and a foreboding adumbration of future fulfillment, on the other. "All were drinking from" the cup again emphasizes the communal dimension, which is part of Jesus' emphasis on the restoration of Israel. He appointed the Twelve (3:14–15; 6:7–13), whose highly symbolic number pointed to eschatological renewal; now he asks the Twelve to share in the cup. The disciples had eaten the broken and distributed bread, and by doing so they implicitly endorsed Jesus' messianic identity and role. Now they all drink from the common cup; but Jesus has not yet explained what the cup signifies.

Juxtaposition of bread and cup (or wine) is found in Jewish texts that derive from late antiquity. One thinks of *Jos. Asen.* 8:5: a man "will eat blessed bread of life and drink a blessed cup of immortality"; 8:11: "let her eat your bread of life and drink your cup of blessing"; and 16:16: "Behold, you have eaten bread of life, and drunk a cup of immortality." In another tradition, as Jacob lay dying, we are told "Joseph and his brothers ate bread before their father; and they drank wine. And Jacob rejoiced greatly because he saw Joseph eating and drinking with his brothers before him" (*Jub.* 45:5). The last passage connotes little more than restored fellowship and so provides no meaningful background to the Last Supper, but the symbolism of the passages in *Joseph and Aseneth* is suggestive and loosely relates to the Jewish covenant (in this case to Aseneth's admission into the covenant). However, the point of the bread at the Last Supper only indirectly has anything to do with "bread of life" (though compare John 6:35), while the cup of the Last Supper probably alludes to suffering, not to immortality (though one could argue that the suffering is what provides for immortality).

24 τοῦτό ἐστιν τὸ αἷμά μου τῆς διαθήκης τὸ ἐκχυννόμενον ὑπὲρ πολλῶν, "This is my blood of the covenant, which is poured out in behalf of many." The true significance of the cup (v 23) is now clarified. The broken bread was Jesus, the longed-for "coming one," but the cup is Jesus' "blood of the covenant." The expression τὸ αἷμα τῆς διαθήκης, "blood of the covenant," recalls Exod 24:8: "And Moses took the blood and threw it upon the people, and said, 'Behold the blood of the covenant [דם־הברית *dam-habbĕrît;* LXX: τὸ αἷμα τῆς διαθήκης], which the LORD has made with you in accordance with all these words'" (cf. Taylor, 545; id., *Jesus and His Sacrifice,* 131; Pesch, 2:358; Casey, *Aramaic Sources,* 242). Jesus' words probably also allude to Jer 31(LXX 38):31 (see Meyer, *Greg* 69 [1988] 461–87): "Behold, the days are coming, says the LORD, when I will make a new covenant [ברית חדשה *bĕrît ḥădāšâ* LXX: διαθήκην καινήν] with the house of Israel and the house of Judah"; as well as Zech 9:11 (Taylor, 545): "by your blood of the covenant [בדם־בריתך *bĕdam-bĕrîtēk;* LXX: ἐν αἵματι διαθήκης], I will set your captives free from the waterless pit" (RSV, adapted). The last part of the saying, τὸ ἐκχυννόμενον ὑπὲρ πολλῶν, "which is poured out in behalf of many," may also allude to the Suffering Servant of Isa 52:13–53:12 (again see Meyer, *Greg* 69 [1988] 461–87; id., *Aims,* 64; cf. Higgins, *Lord's Supper,* 32; Gundry, *Use of the Old Testa-*

ment, 59: "Πολλῶν ['of many'] agrees with both the LXX and the MT, the conjunction with ἐκχυννόμενον ['poured out'] certifying an allusion to Is 53").

These various Scriptures may account, in part, for the variety of forms of the words of institution:

τοῦτό ἐστιν τὸ αἷμά μου τῆς διαθήκης τὸ ἐκχυννόμενον ὑπὲρ πολλῶν, "This is my blood of the covenant, which is poured out in behalf of many." (Mark 14:24)

τοῦτο γάρ ἐστιν τὸ αἷμά μου τῆς διαθήκης τὸ περὶ πολλῶν ἐκχυννόμενον εἰς ἄφεσιν ἁμαρτιῶν, "For this is my blood of the covenant, which is poured out for many for the forgiveness of sins." (Matt 26:28)

τοῦτο τὸ ποτήριον ἡ καινὴ διαθήκη ἐν τῷ αἵματι μου τὸ ὑπὲρ ὑμῶν ἐκχυννόμενον, "This cup which is poured out for you is the new covenant in my blood." (Luke 22:20)

τοῦτο τὸ ποτήριον ἡ καινὴ διαθήκη ἐστὶν ἐν τῷ ἐμῷ αἵματι, "This cup is the new covenant in my blood." (1 Cor 11:25)

τοῦτό ἐστι τὸ αἷμά μου, "This is my blood." (Justin, *1 Apol.* 66.3)

τοῦτό ἐστι τὸ αἷμά μου τὸ περὶ πολλῶν ἐκχυννόμενον εἰς ἄφεσιν ἁμαρτιῶν, "This is my blood which is poured out for many for the forgiveness of sins." (*Apos. Con.* 8.12.37)

Jesus' saying about the significance of the cup and his blood presupposes a collocation of related covenant texts (Exod 24:8; Jer 31:31; Zech 9:11) as well as the Suffering Servant Song (Isa 53:12). The foundational passage is Exod 24:1–8, in which the story is told of God's establishment of his covenant with Israel through Moses. The blood was thrown against the altar next to the twelve pillars that represented the twelve tribes; then it was thrown upon the people, who shouted that they would obey (Exod 24:4–8). While throwing the blood on the people, Moses cried out: "Behold the blood of the covenant" (cf. *Tg. Onq.*: "This is the blood of the covenant"). It is to this passage that Zechariah alludes: "by your blood of the covenant, I will set your captives free from the waterless pit" (Zech 9:11 [RSV, adapted]). It is unnecessary to paraphrase the passage to read "the blood of my covenant with you" (cf. RSV, NRSV), for the reciprocity of the covenant is clear enough (cf. C. L. Meyers and E. M. Meyers, *Zechariah 9–14*, AB 25C [New York: Doubleday, 1993] 138–40). The covenant is both God's (or "my," as some versions paraphrase) and Israel's ("your," which is how the Hebrew actually reads; the second-person pronoun occurs in some Greek MSS). Jesus has alluded to these passages when he says "my blood of the covenant." But the adjective καινή, "new," which modifies διαθήκη, "covenant" (Luke 22:20; 1 Cor 11:25), is derived from Jer 31(LXX 38):31, part of an oracle that anticipates the restoration of fallen Israel (Moule, 115). The last clause, τὸ ἐκχυννόμενον ὑπὲρ πολλῶν, "which is poured out in behalf of many," alludes to Isa 53:12, "he poured out [הֶעֱרָה *heʿĕrâ*] his soul to death, and was numbered with the transgressors; yet he bore the sin of many [רַבִּים *rabbîm*; LXX: πολλῶν]," a passage drawn to the exodus context in all probability by the similar language in Exod 29:12, "and the rest of the blood you shall pour out [תִּשְׁפֹּךְ *tišpōk*; LXX: ἐκχεεῖς] at the base of the altar." The Aramaic paraphrase of Zech 9:11, "You also, *for whom* a covenant *was made* by blood, *I have delivered from bondage to the Egyptians; I have supplied your needs in the wilderness desolate as an empty pit in which* there is no water" (emphasis indicating departures from the Hebrew), which alludes to the exodus event, may explain why this collocation of Scriptures was invoked at the Passover season (see also Exod 24:11, "And they beheld God, and ate and drank," which also lends itself to a Passover setting; Taylor, 545).

διαθήκη customarily translates בְּרִית *běrît* and means "covenant" (so Taylor, 546, and others) and not (*pace* A. Deissmann, *Light*, 337–38) "testament." The covenant of which Jesus speaks concerns the promise of the coming kingdom of God, the new covenant promised by Jeremiah. Jesus will give his own blood to effect the new covenant, the restoration of Israel, and the kingdom of God "having come in power" (cf. Mark 9:1).

τὸ ἐκχυννόμενον, "which is poured out," recalls the language of sacrificial atonement (cf. Lev 4:7, 18, 25, 30, 34; e.g., v 18: καὶ τὸ πᾶν αἷμα ἐκχεεῖ, "and all the blood he will pour out"; all of these passages employ τὸ αἷμα ἐκχεεῖ, "he will pour out the blood"). The language probably reflects Isa 53:12, but in Hebrew or Aramaic, not the Greek. Isaiah is further echoed in the prepositional phrase ὑπὲρ πολλῶν, "in behalf of many," which reminds Mark's readers of 10:45: "For the 'son of man' did not come to be served but to serve, and to give his life as a ransom for many [ἀντὶ πολλῶν]." This utterance, taken with the words of institution, provides compelling evidence that Jesus viewed his death as a "national sacrifice, offered to God on Israel's behalf, the death of one for the many" (McKnight, *New Vision*, 9). Jeremias (*ExpTim* 83 [1971–72] 203) remarks: "Without Is 53 the eucharistic words would remain incomprehensible." See also Lev 17:11: "For the life of the flesh is in the blood; and I have given it for you upon the altar to make atonement for your souls; for it is the blood that makes atonement, by reason of the life." For more on the OT background of the eucharistic words, see Hahn, *EvT* 27 [1967] 337–74.

Jesus' "cup word" is no more cannibalistic than his "bread word." He has not invited the disciples to drink his blood (*pace* Taylor, *Jesus and His Sacrifice*, 133–36), not even metaphorically (as in the discourse in John 6); he has asked his disciples to see in the cup a symbol of his impending death. Jesus finds in the cup and the pouring of the wine into it, as well as the draining of the cup, a parallel to his death. The pouring out of his blood takes on sacrificial and atoning connotations, which Jesus has linked to the covenant of the kingdom. Jesus has deliberately taken over the words "blood of the covenant" (Exod 24:8; Zech 9:11) and has applied them to his death with the eschatological perspective of Jer 31:31 and the vicarious aspect of Isa 53:12. Jesus' death will actually facilitate the coming of the kingdom and the redemption of Israel. It is probably in this sense that we should understand Jesus' statement that his death is "in behalf of many." By taking the blow that should fall heavily on Israel, Jesus will mitigate the severity of divine judgment and hasten the consummation of the kingdom.

25 ἀμὴν λέγω ὑμῖν, "Truly, I say to you." Many of Jesus' important utterances are prefaced with these words (e.g., 3:28; 8:12; 9:1, 41; 10:15, 29; 11:23; 12:43; 13:30; 14:9, 18, 25, 30). The asseverative use of ἀμήν, "truly," is distinctive to Jesus (see Guelich, 177–78; Chilton, *Galilean Rabbi*, 202; id., *ZNW* 69 [1978] 203–11; and *Comment* on 9:1).

οὐκέτι οὐ μὴ πίω ἐκ τοῦ γενήματος τῆς ἀμπέλου ἕως τῆς ἡμέρας ἐκείνης ὅταν αὐτὸ πίνω καινὸν ἐν τῇ βασιλείᾳ τοῦ θεοῦ, "I shall not again drink from the fruit of the vine until that day when I may drink it new in the kingdom of God." A fuller form of the tradition is found in Luke 22:15–16: "I have earnestly desired to eat this passover with you before I suffer; for I tell you I shall not eat it until it is fulfilled in the kingdom of God." The Lukan version of the tradition may suggest that Jesus expected to celebrate the next Passover "in the kingdom of God." He had desired to eat the Passover meal with his disciples (the next day), but because of his impending arrest he would not be able to. In Mark's form of the tradition, reference is made only to the "fruit of the vine": Jesus will not drink wine until he drinks it in the kingdom. Jesus' vow of abstinence may have been a Nazirite vow, but nothing is said of not cutting his hair (cf. Num 6:1–21; Judg 13:5–7; Acts 18:18). If we follow the Lukan parallel, Jesus' vow has only to do with abstaining from Passover food until the kingdom's appearance (so Gundry, 843). In essence, Jesus has declared that the fateful Passover that he has shared with his disciples will be the last one in the old order that he will observe; the next time he observes it, it will be in the kingdom.

De Jonge ("Mark 14:25") believes that v 25 may very well derive from Jesus, though the Markan evangelist has probably edited it. De Jonge thinks it probable that the saying reflects Jesus' restorative expectations. Zechariah's influence may be felt yet again. Not only do Jesus' words in v 24 allude to this prophetic book, but reference to drinking wine "in the kingdom of God" may also allude to Zech 14:9, which looks forward to the day when "the LORD will become king over all the earth," that is, when the kingdom of God (cf. *Tg.* Zech 14:9, "the kingdom of the LORD shall be revealed") will have come in its fullness (see Marcus, *Way of the Lord,* 156–57).

τοῦ γενήματος τῆς ἀμπέλου, "the fruit of the vine," reflects OT language; cf. Isa 32:12; Hab 3:17. The latter passage is part of an oracle that looks forward to the salvation of God.

It has been suggested that the somewhat odd usage of the word καινόν, "new" (Aram. חדת *ḥădat*), in the clause "until that day when I may drink it new in the kingdom of God," may somewhat inaccurately render the underlying Aramaic. The original Aramaic may have read "until I drink it having been renewed [אתחדתית *'ithadētît*] in the kingdom of God" (cf. Taylor, 547, following Black, *Aramaic Approach* [1946 edition], 171–72; contrast Casey, *Aramaic Sources,* 220–21, 242–43, who thinks Jesus spoke of "new" wine [cf. Mark 2:22]; and Gundry, 834, who takes καινόν adverbally, "anew"). Though speculative, the suggestion is plausible and gives significant meaning to the second part of Jesus' vow. When he drinks the fruit of the vine in the kingdom of God, he will do so renewed. This makes good sense, especially if Jesus anticipates his death and subsequent vindication (Taylor, 547: "The saying shows that at the Supper Jesus looked forward, beyond death, to the perfect fellowship of the consummated Kingdom"). It will not be the old Jesus who drinks wine at the next Passover; it will be the "new" Jesus who will drink it in the kingdom. In the Pauline tradition, it is the coming of Jesus himself that is linked to the Lord's Supper (cf. 1 Cor 11:26: "For as often as you eat this bread and drink the cup, you proclaim the Lord's death until he comes").

The Passover that Jesus anticipates celebrating in the kingdom may relate in some ways to expectations of a messianic banquet, a theme based on Scripture (Isa 25:6; 4 Ezra 6:52), alluded to elsewhere in Jesus' teachings (Luke 13:28–29;

14:15–24; 22:30) and adumbrated in his lifestyle (Matt 11:19 = Luke 7:34; Mark 2:16), regulated at Qumran (1QSa), and elaborated upon in later Jewish and Christian traditions (*1 Enoch* 60:7; 62:14; *2 Bar.* 29:5–8; Rev 19:9; *m. ʾAbot* 3:16; *b. B. Bat.* 74b; *Tg. Ps.-J.* Num 11:16). Jesus envisions a time of complete restoration of Israel, when the promises of God and his prophets come to fulfillment.

Explanation

Jesus' words of institution have to do with his anticipated suffering and the value he attached to it. He asks his disciples to share in this covenant in (his) blood, just as earlier he had told his followers that to be his disciples they must be willing to take up their cross and to lose their lives in the service of the kingdom (8:31–38; 10:38–39). In Mark, reference to the cup in the words of institution takes the readers and auditors back to 10:38–39, where Jesus warned James and John that they indeed would drink from the very cup from which Jesus himself would drink. But the cup of the Last Supper also anticipates Jesus' fearful prayer in Gethsemane (14:36), where he will ask God, if at all possible, to remove the cup of suffering from him. These metaphorical references to the cup, all of them having to do with suffering, should guide us in our interpretation of Jesus' reference to the cup in 14:23. Jesus has not asked his disciples to eat his body and drink his blood (in a metaphorically Johannine sense); he has asked them to recognize his messianic mission in the shared bread and the atoning, covenantal value of his death in the shared cup.

Jesus' vow not to drink wine again until he may do so in the kingdom of God extends the thought of covenant renewal and underscores how seriously he takes his mission. The kingdom of God will indeed come, and thereafter nothing will be the same. The vow of abstinence in the Passover setting is significant, for the Passover holiday celebrated God's act of delivering Israel from slavery in Egypt. Jesus has announced the kingdom of God, whose inbreaking and advancing power is attested by the exorcisms, which in turn document the retreat of the kingdom of Satan. Jesus will not drink of the fruit of the vine; that is, he will not celebrate Passover until he may do so in the kingdom of God, when God has completed his liberation and restoration of Israel. When he does celebrate the Passover (and/or the messianic banquet), he will do so renewed, or, in Christian language, glorified.

F. Peter's Denial Foretold   (14:26–31)

Bibliography

Anderson, H. "The Old Testament in Mark's Gospel." In *The Use of the Old Testament in the New and Other Essays.* FS W. F. Stinespring, ed. J. M. Efird. Durham, NC: Duke UP, 1972. 280–306, esp. 290–93. **Bayer, H. F.** *Jesus' Predictions of Vindication and Resurrection: The Provenance, Meaning and Correlation of the Synoptic Predictions.* WUNT 2.20. Tübingen:

Mohr-Siebeck, 1986. 174–76. **Berger, K.** *Die Amen-Worte Jesu: Eine Untersuchung zum Problem der Legitimation in apokalyptischer Rede.* BZNW 39. Berlin: de Gruyter, 1970. 49–50. **Best, E.** *Following Jesus.* 199–203, 210–12. ———. *Temptation and the Passion.* 173–76. **Brady, D.** "The Alarm to Peter in Mark's Gospel." *JSNT* 4 (1979) 42–57. **Bruce, F. F.** "The Book of Zechariah and the Passion Narrative." *BJRL* 43 (1960–61) 342–45. **Cangh, J.-M. van.** "La Galilée dans l'évangile de Marc: Un lieu theologique?" *RB* 79 (1972) 59–75. **Casey, M.** *Aramaic Sources.* 219–52. **Crossan, J. D.** "Redaction and Citation in Mark 11:9–10, 17 and 14:27." In *Society of Biblical Literature 1972 Seminar Papers.* Ed. L. C. McGaughey. 2 vols. SBLSP 11. Missoula, MT: SBL, 1972. 1:17–61, esp. 39–47. **Curtis, J. B.** "An Investigation of the Mount of Olives in the Judaeo-Christian Tradition." *HUCA* 28 (1957) 137–80. **Derrett, J. D. M.** "The Reason for the Cock-Crowings." *NTS* 29 (1983) 142–44 (repr. in J. D. M. Derrett. *Studies in the New Testament.* 4 vols. Leiden: Brill, 1986. 4:129–31). **Dormeyer, D.** *Die Passion Jesu.* 110–17. **Ellington, J.** "The Translation of ὑμνέω." *BT* 30 (1979) 445–46. **Ernst, J.** "Noch einmal: Die Verleugnung Jesu durch Petrus (Mk 14,54.66–72)." In *Beiträge und Notizen.* Vol. 1 of *Petrus und Papst: Evangelium, Einheit der Kirche, Papstdienst.* Ed. A. Brandenburg and H. J. Urban. Münster: Aschendorff, 1977. 43–62, esp. 50–55. **Evans, C. F.** "I will go before you into Galilee." *JTS* n.s. 5 (1954) 3–18. **France, R. T.** *Jesus and the Old Testament.* 107–9. **Geddert, T. J.** *Watchwords.* 163–66. **Glasson, T. F.** "Davidic Links with the Betrayal of Jesus." *ExpTim* 85 (1973–74) 118–19. **Grass, K.** "Zu Mc 14,28." *ZNW* 13 (1912) 175–76. **Gundry, R. H.** *The Use of the Old Testament in St. Matthew's Gospel with Special Reference to the Messianic Hope.* NovTSup 18. Leiden: Brill, 1967. 25–28. **Guyot, G. H.** "Peter Denies His Lord." *CBQ* 4 (1942) 111–18, esp. 111–12. **Hasler, V.** *Amen: Redaktionsgeschichtliche Untersuchung zur Einführungsformel der Herrenworte "Wahrlich ich sage euch."* Zürich; Stuttgart: Gotthelf, 1969. 49–54. **Hoskyns, E. C.** "Adversaria Exegetica." *Theology* 7 (1923) 147–55. **Iersel, B. M. F. van.** "'To Galilee' or 'in Galilee' in Mark 14,28 and 16,7?" *ETL* 58 (1982) 365–70. **Joüon, P.** "Marc 14,31: ὁ δὲ ἐκπερισσῶς ἐλάλει." *RSR* 29 (1939) 240–41. **Karnetzki, M.** "Die galiläische Redaktion im Markusevangelium." *ZNW* 52 (1961) 238–72. **Klein, G.** "Die Verleugnung des Petrus: Eine traditionsgeschichtliche Untersuchung." *ZTK* 58 (1961) 285–328 (repr. in G. Klein. *Rekonstruktion und Interpretation: Gesammelte Aufsätze zum Neuen Testament.* BEvT 50. Munich: Kaiser, 1969. 49–98). **Kosmala, H.** "The Time of the Cock-Crow." *ASTI* 2 (1963) 118–20; 6 (1968) 132–34 (repr. in H. Kosmala. *Studies, Essays, and Reviews.* 2 vols. Leiden: Brill, 1978. 2:76–78, 79–81). **Kremer, J.** *Das Ärgernis des Kreuzes: Eine Hinführung zum Verstehen der Leidensgeschichte nach Markus.* Stuttgart: Katholisches Bibelwerk, 1969. 31–35. **Lattey, C.** "A Note on the Cockcrow." *Scr* 6 (1953) 53–55. **Lightfoot, R. H.** "A Consideration of Three Passages in St. Mark's Gospel." In *In Memoriam Ernst Lohmeyer.* Ed. W. Schmauch. Stuttgart: Evangelischer Verlag, 1951. 110–15. ———. *The Gospel Message of St. Mark.* Oxford: Clarendon, 1950. 106–8. **Linnemann, E.** "Die Verleugnung des Petrus." *ZTK* 63 (1966) 1–32 (repr. in E. Linnemann, *Studien zur Passionsgeschichte.* 70–108). **Marcus, J.** *Way of the Lord.* 154–64. **Meye, R. P.** *Jesus and the Twelve.* 80–85. **Mohr, T. A.** *Markus- und Johannespassion.* 213–25. **Moo, D. J.** *Old Testament in the Gospel Passion Narratives.* 182–87, 215–17. **Odenkirchen, P. C.** "'Praecedam vos in Galilaeam' (Mt 26,32 cf. 28,7.10; Mc 14,28; 16,7 cf. Lc 24,6)." *VD* 46 (1968) 193–223. **Orge, M.** "'Percutiam pastorem et dispergentur oves' (Mc. 14,27; Mt 26,31)." *Claretianum* 7 (1967) 271–92. **Perrin, N.** "Towards an Interpretation of the Gospel of Mark." In *Christology and a Modern Pilgrimage: A Discussion with Norman Perrin.* Ed. H. D. Betz. Claremont, CA: New Testament Colloquium, 1971. 1–78, esp. 37–44. **Pesch, R.** *Das Evangelium der Urgemeinde.* 174–76. ———. "Die Verleugnung des Petrus: Eine Studie zu Mk 14,54.66–72 (und Mk 14,26–31)." In *Neues Testament und Kirche.* FS R. Schnackenburg, ed. J. Gnilka. Freiburg: Herder, 1974. 42–62, esp. 52–58. **Pieper, K.** "Einige Bemerkungen zu Mt. 26.31 und Mk. 14.27." *BZ* 21 (1933) 320–23. **Rusche, H.** "Das letzte gemeinsame Gebet Jesu mit seinen Jüngern: Der Psalm 136." *Wissenschaft und Weisheit* 51 (1988) 210–12. **Schenk, W.** *Der Passionsbericht nach Markus.* 223–29. **Schenke, L.** *Studien zur Passionsgeschichte des Markus.* 348–460. **Schmauch, W.** "Der Ölberg: Exegese zu einer Ortsangabe besonders bei Matthäus und Markus." *TLZ* 77 (1952) 391–96. **Schneider, G.**

Die Passion Jesu. 75–76. **Schoeps, H.-J.** "Ebionitische Apokalyptik im Neuen Testament." *ZNW* 51 (1960) 101–11, esp. 108–11. **Schroeder, R. P.** "The 'Worthless' Shepherd: A Study of Mk 14:27." *CurTM* 2 (1975) 342–44. **Smith, T. V.** *Petrine Controversies in Early Christianity: Attitudes towards Peter in Christian Writings of the First Two Centuries.* WUNT 2.15. Tübingen: Mohr-Siebeck, 1985. 178–85. **Stanley, D. M.** *Jesus in Gethsemane.* New York: Paulist, 1980. 119–54. **Stein, R. H.** "A Short Note on Mark. XIV. 28 and XVI. 7." *NTS* 20 (1973–74) 445–52. **Steinseifer, B.** "Der Ort der Erscheinungen des Auferstandenen: Zur Frage alter galiläischen Ostertraditionen." *ZNW* 62 (1971) 232–65. **Suhl, A.** *Zitate.* 62–65. **Tooley, W.** "The Shepherd and Sheep Image in the Teaching of Jesus." *NovT* 7 (1964–65) 15–25, esp. 16–19. **Trudinger, L. P.** "Davidic Links with the Betrayal of Jesus: Some Further Observations." *ExpTim* 86 (1974–75) 278–79. **Turner, C. H.** "Marcan Usage: Notes, Critical and Exegetical, on the Second Gospel." *JTS* o.s. 26 (1925) 12–20. **Vanhoye, A.** "L'angoisse du Christ." *Christus* 18 (1971) 382–89. **Walter, N.** "Die Verleugnung des Petrus." *TVers* 8 (1977) 45–61. **Wenham, J. W.** "How Many Cock-Crowings? The Problem of Harmonistic Text-Variants." *NTS* 25 (1978–79) 523–25. **Wilcox, M.** "The Denial-Sequence in Mark xiv. 26–31, 66–72." *NTS* 17 (1970–71) 426–36, esp. 427–33. **Zeller, D.** "Prophetisches Wissen um die Zukunft in synoptischen Jesusworten." *TP* 52 (1977) 258–71.

See also *Bibliography* for 14:66–72.

Translation

²⁶*And after singing a hymn, they went out to the Mount of Olives.* ²⁷*And Jesus says to them, "All of you will fall away,*[a] *because it is written: 'I will strike the shepherd, and the sheep*[b] *will be scattered.'* ²⁸*But after I am raised up, I shall go before you in Galilee."* ²⁹*But Peter*[c] *said to him, "Even if all will fall away,*[d] *I will not!"* ³⁰*And Jesus says to him, "Truly,*[e] *I say to you, today—this very night, before the cock crows twice—you will deny me three times."* ³¹*But he*[f] *was saying vehemently, "Even if I have to die with you, I will not deny you!" And all were likewise saying this.*

Notes

[a]Gk. σκανδαλισθήσεσθε, lit. "you will be offended" or "you will be made to stumble." A C² W Σ Φ and several later MSS add ἐν ἐμοὶ ἐν τῇ νυκτὶ ταύτῃ, "by me in this night" (cf. Matt 26:31).

[b]Several later MSS and authorities add τῆς ποίμνης, "of the shepherd" (cf. Matt 26:31).

[c]Syr. MSS read *kêpā'*, "Cephas."

[d]Gk. σκανδαλισθήσονται, lit. "they will be offended" or "they will be made to stumble." Several later MSS add ἐν σοί, "by you" (cf. Matt 26:33).

[e]Gk. ἀμήν. A few late MSS and authorities read ἀμὴν ἀμήν, "truly, truly." The duplication of ἀμήν reflects Johannine influence.

[f]A C N W Σ Φ and several later MSS add Πέτρος, "Peter" (cf. Matt 26:35), while some Syr. MSS add *šim'ôn*, "Simon."

Form/Structure/Setting

During the Last Supper Jesus foretold his betrayal (14:17–21). After retiring to the Mount of Olives Jesus now tells his disciples that they will all fall away. Peter, however, stoutly declares that he will not abandon Jesus, even if all the rest do. Jesus responds by specifying the nature of Peter's apostasy: he will deny Jesus three times before the morning rooster crows twice. The formal structure of this scene is reminiscent of the first prediction of the passion, in which Jesus foretells his passion, Peter contradicts him, and Jesus rebukes Peter (8:31–33). However, there are differences, for in 14:31 Peter continues to assure Jesus of his fidelity and in 14:66–72 Jesus' prediction is fulfilled literally.

Bultmann (*History*, 306) includes Mark 14:27–31 among the "faith legends" that reflect "apologetic motives." The passage may very well serve an apologetic interest in the Gospel of Mark: the apostasy of the disciples did not take Jesus by surprise; indeed, he foretold it, even the precise circumstances of the denials that issued from his principal disciple, Peter. But according to Dibelius (*Tradition*, 115–16), the prediction of Peter's denials "is not really told in legendary style." Taylor (*Formation*, 57–58) thinks Bultmann's skepticism is unjustified. In his commentary, Taylor (548) asserts that most of the tradition depends "ultimately on Petrine testimony." Cranfield (428–29) also evaluates the tradition as "Petrine." The passage may serve apologetic interests, but not well enough to explain wholesale fabrication. Why would early Christians have wanted to emphasize the embarrassing failure of the disciples, who having been forewarned, still lapsed so completely?

The passage is made up of six parts: (1) the setting (v 26, which could just as easily be described as the conclusion to the previous pericope), (2) Jesus' startling prediction of the apostasy of his disciples, supported by prophecy (v 27, citing Zech 13:7), (3) a second prediction, one involving resurrection and implied reunion with the disciples (v 28), (4) Peter's protest (v 29), (5) Jesus' even more specific prediction of Peter's denial (v 30), and (6) Peter's and the disciples' continuing protest against Jesus' prediction (v 31).

Comment

26 καὶ ὑμνήσαντες, "And after singing a hymn." According to Rusche (*Wissenschaft und Weisheit* 51 [1988] 210–12), Jesus and his disciples sang the *Hallēl Haggādôl* (the "Great Hallel [Praise]," i.e., Ps 136), which recounts God's mighty acts, connecting Israel's past with Jesus' passion. However, the hymn may have been drawn from the *Hallēl* (Pss 113–18), especially if the supper had been a Passover meal (cf. *m. Pesaḥ.* 10:7). Paul and Silas sing in Acts 16:25, though it has nothing to do with a meal or celebration of a holy day. There are allusions to singing, music, or melody elsewhere in the NT (cf. 1 Cor 14:26; Eph 5:19; Col 3:16; Heb 2:12[?]; Jas 5:13).

ἐξῆλθον εἰς τὸ ὄρος τῶν ἐλαιῶν, "they went out to the Mount of Olives." Jesus and his disciples have left the city of Jerusalem (i.e., the city proper within the walls) and have gone (outside the walls across the Kidron Valley) to the Mount of Olives. τὸ ὄρος τῶν ἐλαιῶν, "the Mount of Olives," overlooks the city of Jerusalem and the eastern side of the Temple Mount itself. It was first mentioned in Mark 11:1, when Jesus entered the city. It was mentioned again in 13:3, when Jesus gathered with Peter, James, and John and answered their questions about his prediction of the destruction of the temple (13:2). See *Comment* on 11:1 and *ABD* 5:13–15.

The retreat to the Mount of Olives, wherein was located the Garden of Gethsemane (14:32–42) and where Jesus taught his disciples about the end times, suggests that this was a favorite spot outside the city. Jesus' interest in this location may have been partly due to his interest in the prophecies of Zechariah (cf. Marcus, *Way of the Lord*, 156; and *Comment* on v 27 and on v 28).

27 πάντες σκανδαλισθήσεσθε, "All of you will fall away." Literally, Jesus says, "You all will be scandalized." σκανδαλίζειν, "to scandalize," is the common word used in the Greek NT for reference to stumbling. The word occurs eight times in Mark (4:17; 6:3; 9:42, 43, 45, 47; 14:27, 29), twenty-six times in the Gospels, and three times in Paul (1 Cor 8:13 [2x]; 2 Cor 11:29). In Mark 4:17 Jesus describes the shallow-rooted as those who fall away or are scandalized at the first sign of tribulation or persecution. In 6:3 the people of Nazareth are scandalized at Jesus. In 9:42–45 σκανδαλίζειν seems to mean "to sin," that is, "whoever causes one of these little ones to sin" (lit. "whoever scandalizes one of these little ones"; see *Comment* on 9:43–47). The word occurs rarely in the LXX (Sir 9:5; 23:8; 35:15; *Pss. Sol.* 16:7; and Dan 11:41 in some MSS), but its Hebrew equivalent כשל *kāšal* occurs frequently and coheres with NT usage. One may wonder if what Jesus said about the shallow-rooted person in his parable of the Sower applies to his disciples. Because they lack depth, they too will fall away the first time they encounter serious opposition. Not until the resurrection, when Jesus rejoins them in Galilee (v 28; cf. 16:7), will the disciples put down roots deeply enough to take on their apostolic duties.

ὅτι γέγραπται, πατάξω τὸν ποιμένα, καὶ τὰ πρόβατα διασκορπισθήσονται, "because it is written: 'I will strike the shepherd, and the sheep will be scattered.'" Jesus makes his disturbing prediction because of what is written in Scripture. What Scripture foretells cannot be avoided: Jesus will be struck down, and when he is, his disciples (the "sheep") will scatter from him. Suhl (*Zitate,* 62–64) and Wilcox (*NTS* 17 [1970–71] 429–30) think that the quotation of Zech 13:7 comes from the evangelist Mark, not from Jesus. On the contrary, because the prophecy speaks of divine judgment directed against the shepherd, it is unlikely that early Christians, including the Markan evangelist, would have appealed to Zech 13:7 as a prophetic reference to Jesus: "'Awake, O sword, against my shepherd, against the man who stands next to me,' says the LORD of hosts. 'Strike the shepherd, that the sheep may be scattered; I will turn my hand against the littles ones.'" Jesus' application of the Zech 13:7 to himself is similar to an interpretation found at Qumran, where this passage is cited in the *Damascus Document* with the understanding that the "sheep" are the "poor of the flock," that is, the members of the Qumran community, while the stricken "shepherd" is perhaps the Teacher of the Righteousness (CD 19:7–13; cf. C. Rabin, *The Zadokite Documents,* rev. ed. [Oxford: Clarendon, 1958] 31).

πατάξω τὸν ποιμένα, "I will strike the shepherd." Both the LXX and the MT are imperatival: "Strike [הַךְ *hak;* LXX: πάταξον (אc A Q)] the shepherd!" Jesus' first-person form of the quotation probably reflects the final clause of Zech 13:7: "And I will turn [or 'bring down'; וַהֲשִׁבֹתִי *wahăšibōtî;* LXX: ἐπάξω] my hand against the little ones" (cf. Gundry, *Use of the Old Testament,* 27).

Here again we find Jesus' interest in acting out an agenda informed by themes and images in the prophecy of Zechariah. That Jesus alluded to Zechariah while standing on the Mount of Olives is suggestive when one remembers Zech 14:4: "On that day his feet shall stand on the Mount of Olives which lies before Jerusalem on the east." Jesus departed from the Mount of Olives when he entered the city of Jerusalem mounted on a colt, in what probably was a deliberate acting out of Zech 9:9 (see discussion in *Form/Structure/Setting* on 11:1–11 above); he delivered his eschatological discourse from the Mount of Olives; and now having once again retired to the Mount of Olives, Jesus speaks of the judgment that will befall him and will scandalize his disciples (for discussion of the influence of Zechariah in Mark, see Marcus, *Way of the Lord,* 154–64).

καὶ τὰ πρόβατα διασκορπισθήσονται, "and the sheep will be scattered." Mark reverses the order of verb and noun (cf. LXX: καὶ διασκορπισθήσονται τὰ πρόβατα [Q]) to draw attention to the sheep, who will be scattered and lost without their shepherd (on differences between the Markan form of the quotation and the Greek OT, see Gundry, *Use of the Old Testament,* 25–28). The scattering of the sheep, of course, is a temporary undoing of the messianic task of gathering the sheep, the lost, and the exiles of Israel (cf. Num 27:17; 1 Kgs 22:17; 2 Chr 18:16; Ezek 34:8, 12, 15; Zech 10:2; Bar 4:26; *Pss. Sol.* 17:4, 21, 26–28; *Tg.* Isa 6:13; 8:18; 35:6; 53:8: "From chastisements and punishments he [the Messiah] will bring our exiles near"; *Tg.* Hos 14:8: "They shall be gathered from among their exiles, they shall dwell in the shade of their Messiah"; *Tg.* Mic 5:1–3).

28 ἀλλὰ μετὰ τὸ ἐγερθῆναί με προάξω ὑμᾶς εἰς τὴν Γαλιλαίαν, "But after I am raised up, I shall go before you in Galilee." The saying in Mark 14:28, which employs ἐγείρειν, "to raise up," may be either a Markan composition (so Marcus, *Way of the Lord,* 155) or an insertion of pre-Markan tradition (to prepare for 16:7; cf. Taylor, 549). In support of insertion is the smooth transition from v 27 to v 29: "'All of you will fall away, because it is written. . . .' But Peter said to him, 'Even if all will fall away. . . .'" Moreover, it is odd that there is no reaction to Jesus' reference to his resurrection. The saying, even if edited and inserted into its present context, may very well be a bit of authentic dominical tradition, part of the tradition of Jesus' prediction of his resurrection (on the authenticity of this tradition, see discussion in *Form/Structure/Setting* on 8:31–33 and *Comment* on 8:31).

Marcus (*Way of the Lord,* 155–57) has suggested that insertion of the reference to the resurrection here in v 28 may be further evidence of the influence of eschatological tradition associated with Zechariah. According to Zech 14:4, the Lord will come, and when his feet stand on the Mount of Olives, it will be split in two from east to west. In targumic tradition this verse is understood to refer to the resurrection of the dead. According to *Tg.* Song 8:5, "when the dead rise, the Mount of Olives will be split, and all Israel's dead will come up out of it." According to *Eccl. Rab.* 1:11 §1 and *Song Rab.* 4:11 §1, the "holy ones" whom God will bring when he comes (quoting Zech 14:5) are the prophets who (we are to infer) have been resurrected. Marcus raises the possibility that "the resurrectional reading of Zech. 14:1–5 was known and used by Mark 14:28." Moreover, implicit in the promise to "go before you" is anticipation of regathering the sheep that had been scattered when the shepherd was struck down (in v 27, quoting Zech 13:7). This feature may also reflect the imagery of Zechariah, for Zech 13:8–9 promises restoration of the scattered sheep.

According to van Iersel (*ETL* 58 [1982] 365–70), the phrase εἰς τὴν Γαλιλαίαν in 14:28 and 16:7 should be understood as "in Galilee." He reasons that the translation "into Galilee" or "to Galilee" is especially problematic for the interpretation of 16:7–8, while "in Galilee" is not. Van Iersel could be correct, for in Mark εἰς, "to, into," often does encroach upon ἐν, "in." A few obvious examples include 1:9, "he was baptized in [εἰς] the Jordan"; 1:21, "he was teaching in [εἰς] the synagogue"; 1:39, "and he was preaching in [εἰς] their synagogues in [εἰς] all Galilee"; 2:1, "it was reported that he was at [εἰς] home"; and many others (cf.

Turner, *JTS* o.s. 26 [1925] 14–20). In all of these examples we should have expected the preposition ἐν. If we read Mark's εἰς τὴν Γαλιλαίαν as "in Galilee," then apparently Jesus has promised his disciples that after being raised up, προάξω, "I shall go before," or lead them in Galilee, the original theater of ministry. Instead of simply promising to go to Galilee before the disciples themselves arrive (as Gundry, 845, takes it: Jesus "will arrive before they do"), Jesus promises to give them leadership "in Galilee," just as he used to do (cf. 10:32, where Jesus "goes before" his disciples as leader) before the fateful Passover visit to Jerusalem. The military usage of προάγειν, "to go before" (e.g., Thucydides 7.6; 2 Macc 10:1), supports this interpretation (cf. C. F. Evans, *JTS* n.s. 5 [1954] 9). As their commander, Jesus will continue to lead his disciples in Galilee.

29 ὁ δὲ Πέτρος ἔφη αὐτῷ, εἰ καὶ πάντες σκανδαλισθήσονται, ἀλλ᾽ οὐκ ἐγώ, "But Peter said to him, 'Even if all will fall away, I will not!'" Peter makes a prediction different from the one that Jesus has just made in v 27: others may fall away, but he will not. Jesus, however, is not persuaded, for Scripture says otherwise, and (we may infer) he knows Peter better than Peter does. Moreover, this is not the first time that Peter gets it wrong. Peter contradicts and is contradicted by Jesus in 8:31–33 and, more mildly and indirectly, by God himself in 9:5–7. Peter also has his expostulation answered by Jesus in 10:28–31. From these episodes we must not overdraw inferences. The Markan evangelist is not trying to make a fool out of Peter (as he is often portrayed in popular Christian sermons). Nor is Peter's incomprehension part of a Markan secrecy theme (cf. Wrede, *Messianic Secret*, 105). The point is that Jesus is vastly superior in power, insight, and faith in comparison to his own disciples, who have been privileged with private teaching and an ongoing relationship with Jesus. What ordinary people fail to comprehend and fear, Jesus comprehends and faces with dignity and composure. He is prepared to face death, even if his closest friends betray and abandon him.

30 ἀμὴν λέγω σοι ὅτι σὺ σήμερον ταύτῃ τῇ νυκτὶ πρὶν ἢ δὶς ἀλέκτορα φωνῆσαι τρίς με ἀπαρνήσῃ, "Truly, I say to you, today—this very night, before the cock crows twice—you will deny me three times." Jesus counters Peter's protest with an even more specific prediction: before the rooster crows twice, Peter will have denied Jesus three times (v 30). Roosters crow early in the morning (cf. *m. Yoma* 1:8; *m. Tamid* 1:2), even before first light, so Jesus' prophecy, if accurate, must be fulfilled soon. Before this terrible day is anywhere near over, Peter will have fulfilled Jesus' prediction. Mark's redundant language, "today—this very night, before the cock crows twice," lends certainty and urgency to Jesus' prediction (Cranfield, 429: "ascending accuracy"). Mark's δίς, "twice," should be retained; its omission in some MSS is owing to assimilation to the Matthean and Lukan parallels (*TCGNT* [1], 114). Often cited is Aristophanes, *Eccl.* 390–91: "when the rooster calls the second time."

ἀπαρνεῖσθαι, "to deny," is an important word in biblical vocabulary; it is the opposite of ὁμολογεῖν, "to confess" (cf. Matt 10:32–33//Luke 12:8–9), and often refers to the refusal to worship God. The wicked "recognized as the true God him whom they had before denied to know" (Wis 12:27); "the ungodly, refusing [lit. 'denying'] to know you, were scourged by the strength of your arm" (Wis 16:16). In loyalty to the faith, and in contrast to the wicked, the righteous man says, "I will not deny our noble brotherhood" (4 Macc 10:15). Striking an eschatological note, Isaiah prophesies, "For in that day people shall deny the works of their hands" (LXX Isa 31:7), that is, people will deny their idols. Similarly, Jesus asks his followers to deny themselves and take up their cross and follow him (8:34). Of course, true to Jesus' prediction, Peter will deny Jesus three times (esp. 14:68, 72). The threeness of the denial may signify completion (cf. Derrett, *NTS* 29 [1983] 142–44).

31 ὁ δὲ ἐκπερισσῶς ἐλάλει, ἐὰν δέῃ με συναποθανεῖν σοι, οὐ μή σε ἀπαρνήσομαι, "But he was saying vehemently, 'Even if I have to die with you, I will not deny you!'" Peter protests further: even if he must die with Jesus, he will not deny him. On previous occasions Peter has been befuddled, even frightened, but in this hour of crisis he determines to remain loyal to Jesus, even if no one else does. Peter offers συναποθανεῖν, "to die with," Jesus ἐὰν δέῃ, "if it may be necessary." His protestation is reminiscent of Job's assurance to the angel, who has warned the biblical worthy of his impending temptation: "Till death I will endure; I will not step back at all!" (*T. Job* 5:1). The examples of the famous Maccabean martyrs immediately come to mind, those who chose death rather than compromise their faith (e.g., 2 Macc 6–7). No doubt Peter has spoken sincerely, but little does he know how severe the testing will be.

ὡσαύτως δὲ καὶ πάντες ἔλεγον, "And all were likewise saying this." All of the disciples join in saying what Peter has said (cf. John 11:16: "Let us also go, that we may die with him"). In a group and unthreatened, they are brave. As it turns out, however, it is the predictions of Jesus that come true, not the assurances of his disciples. Mark's reader will discover that at every point Jesus gets it right. The predicted betrayal (14:20) will be fulfilled (14:42–46); indeed, already it has been fulfilled to a degree in 14:10–11. When arrested, "abandoning him, they all fled" (14:50). When questioned by the maid servant, Peter denies Jesus (14:66–72). The accuracy of Jesus' predictions only lends further credibility to his predictions of resurrection and of coming with the clouds as the "son of man."

Explanation

Jesus has already saddened his disciples by announcing at the supper that one of them, indeed, one of the Twelve, will betray him. Now, after retiring to the Mount of Olives, he stuns his disciples further by declaring that all of them will fall away in fulfillment of Scripture. Like the shepherd of Zechariah, Jesus will be struck down, and the sheep will be scattered. But Peter and his fellow disciples refuse to believe it. Others may fail, but they will not. Indeed, Peter, then the rest following his lead, avers that he would rather die with Jesus than deny him. Jesus, however, knows better. Before the rooster crows twice Peter will have denied his friend and master three times.

The citation of part of the oracle from Zechariah is important, for as a whole (see Zech 13:7–9) the oracle coheres with the context in which Jesus now finds himself (i.e., passion week, Mark 11–15). Jerusalem's rejection of Jesus has aroused God's wrath. The shepherd will be struck down, the sheep will be scattered, and the entire land will be judged. Only a remnant will be spared. When a repentant people call on the name of the Lord, they will be answered. The oracle of Zechariah summarizes the principal points of the eschatological discourse in Mark 13.

Jesus assures his disciples that after he is raised up, he will go before them in Galilee. With the Passover and week-long Feast of Unleavened Bread over, the disciples could be expected to return home. But when they have returned to Galilee, they will no longer be "like sheep without a shepherd" (Mark 6:34). The risen Jesus will be waiting for them and will give them leadership, as he had before the passion.

G. The Prayer in Gethsemane   (14:32–42)

Bibliography

Andrews, M. "Peirasmos—A Study in Form-Criticism." *ATR* 24 (1942) 229–44. **Armbruster, C. J.** "The Messianic Significance of the Agony in the Garden." *Scr* 16 (1964) 111–19. **Barbour, R. S.** "Gethsemane in the Tradition of the Passion." *NTS* 16 (1969–70) 231–51. **Barr, J.** "'Abba, Father' and the Familiarity of Jesus' Speech." *Theology* 91 (1988) 173–79. ———. "Abba Isn't Daddy." *JTS* n.s. 39 (1988) 28–47. **Barrett, C. K.** "Important Hypotheses Reconsidered, Pt 5: Spirit and the Gospel Tradition." *ExpTim* 67 (1956–57) 142–45. **Beck, B.** "Gethsemane in the Four Gospels." *Epworth Review* 15 (1988) 57–65. **Benoit, P.** *Passion and Resurrection.* 1–23. **Bernard, J. H.** "St. Mark xiv. 41,42." *ExpTim* 3 (1891–92) 451–53. **Best, E.** *Following Jesus.* 147–52. ———. *Temptation and the Passion.* 92–94. **Bishop, E. F. F.** "A Stone's Throw." *ExpTim* 53 (1941–42) 270–71. **Black, M.** *Aramaic Approach.* 225–26. ———. "The Cup Metaphor in Mark xiv. 36." *ExpTim* 59 (1947–48) 195. **Boman, T.** "Der Gebetskampf Jesu." *NTS* 10 (1963–64) 261–73. **Boobyer, G. H.** "ἀπέχει in Mark xiv. 41." *NTS* 2 (1955–56) 44–48. **Bratcher, R. G.** "Unusual Sinners." *BT* 39 (1988) 335–37. **Brongers, H. A.** "Der Zornesbecher." *OtSt* 15 (1969) 177–92. **Carle, P. L.** "L'Agonie de Gethsémani." *Divinitas* 21 (1977) 429–32. **Cavallin, A.** "(τὸ) λοιπόν: Eine bedeutungsgeschichtliche Untersuchung." *Eranos* 39 (1941) 121–44. **Charlesworth, J. H.** "A Caveat on Textual Transmission and the Meaning of *Abba.*" In J. H. Charlesworth, M. Harding, and M. Kiley. *The Lord's Prayer and Other Prayer Texts from the Greco-Roman Era.* Valley Forge, PA: Trinity Press International, 1994. 1–14. **Chase, T.** "τὸ λοιπόν, Matt. xxvi.45." *JBL* 6.2 (1886) 131–35. **Couchoud, P.-L.** "Notes de critique verbal sur St Marc et St Matthieu." *JTS* o.s. 34 (1933) 113–38, esp. 129–31. **Cranfield, C. E. B.** "The Cup Metaphor in Mark xiv. 36 and Parallels." *ExpTim* 59 (1947–48) 137–38. **Daube, D.** "Death as a Release in the Bible." *NovT* 5 (1962) 82–104. ———. "A Prayer Pattern in Judaism." *SE* 1 [= TU 73] (1959) 539–45. ———. "Two Incidents after the Last Supper." In *The New Testament and Rabbinic Judaism.* Jordan Lectures 2. London: Athlone, 1956. 330–35, esp. 332–35. **Dautzenberg, G.** *Sein Leben bewahren: ψυχή in den Herrenworten der Evangelien.* SANT 14. Munich: Kösel, 1966. 124–33. **Davies, W. D.,** and **Allison, D. C.** *The Gospel according to Saint Matthew.* 3:590–602. **Dibelius, M.** "Gethsemane." *Crozer Quarterly* 12 (1935) 254–65. **Dormeyer, D.** *Die Passion Jesu.* 124–37. **Dowd, S. E.** *Prayer, Power, and the Problem of Suffering: Mark 11:22–25 in the Context of Markan Theology.* SBLDS 105. Atlanta: Scholars Press, 1988. 151–58. **Dunn, J. D. G.** *Jesus and the Spirit: A Study of the Religious and Charismatic Experience of Jesus and the First Christians as Reflected in the New Testament.* London: SCM Press; Philadelphia: Westminster, 1975. 17–20. **Evans, C. A.** *Jesus and His Contemporaries.* 276–97, esp. 288–89. **Feldmeier, R.** *Die Krisis des Gottessohnes: Die Gethsemaneerzählung als Schlüssel des Markuspassion.* WUNT 2.21. Tübingen: Mohr-Siebeck, 1987. **Feuillet, A.** *L'Agonie de Gethsémani: Enquête exégétique et théologique suivie d'une étude du 'Mystère de Jésus' de Pascal.* Paris: Gabalda, 1977. 77–142. **Fiebig, P.** "Jesu Gebet in Gethsemane." *Der Geisteskampf der Gegenwart.* 66 (1930) 121–25. **Field, F.** *Notes.* 39. **Fitzmyer, J. A.** "Abba and Jesus' Relation to God." In *À cause de l'Évangile.* FS J.

Dupont. 2 vols. LD 123. Paris: Cerf, 1985. 1:15–38. **Geddert, T. J.** *Watchwords.* 90–111. **Giblet, J.** "La prière de Jésus." In *L'Expérience de la prière dans les prandes religions.* Ed. H. Limet and J. Ries. Homo Religiosus 5. Louvain-la-Neuve: Centre d'Histoire des Religions, 1980. 261–73. **Gnilka, J.** *Jesus of Nazareth: Message and History.* Peabody: Hendrickson, 1997. 262–63. **Gourgues, M.** *Le défi de la fidélité: L'expérience de Jésus.* Lire la Bible 70. Paris: Cerf, 1985. 77–109. **Grassi, J. A.** "Abba, Father." *TBT* 21 (1983) 320–24. ———. "*Abba*, Father (Mark 14:36): Another Approach." *JAAR* 50 (1982) 449–58. **Green, J. B.** "Jesus on the Mount of Olives (Lk. 22.39–46)." *JSNT* 26 (1986) 29–48. **Greig, J. C. G.** "Abba and Amen: Their Relevance to Christology." *SE* 5 [= TU 103] (1968) 3–13, esp. 5–10. **Grelot, P.** "L'arrière-plan araméen du 'Pater.'" *RB* 91 (1984) 531–56, esp. 538–42. ———. "Une mention inaperçue de 'Abba' dans le *Testament araméen de Lévi.*" *Sem* 33 (1983) 101–8. **Grimm, W.** *Weil ich dich liebe.* 209–22. **Hanson, A. T.** *The Wrath of the Lamb.* London: S. P. C. K., 1957. 27–39. **Héring, J.** "Simples remarques sur la prière à Gethsémané: Matthieu 26.36–46; Marc 14.32–42; Luc 22.40–46." *RHPR* 39 (1959) 97–102. ———. "Zwei exegetische Probleme in der Perikope von Jesus in Gethsemane (Markus XIV 32–42; Matthäus XXVI 36–46; Lukas XXII 40–46)." In *Neotestamentica et Patristica.* FS O. Cullmann, ed. W. C. van Unnik. NovTSup 6. Leiden: Brill, 1962. 64–69. **Holleran, J. W.** *The Synoptic Gethsemane: A Critical Study.* Analecta Gregoriana 191. Rome: Gregorian UP, 1973. **Hooker, M. D.** *Son of Man.* 161–63. **Howard, V. P.** *Das Ego Jesu in den synoptischen Evangelien: Untersuchungen zum Sprachgebrauch Jesu.* MTS 14. Marburg: Elwert, 1975. 123–32. **Hudson, J. T.** "Irony in Gethsemane? (Mark xiv. 41)." *ExpTim* 46 (1934–35) 382. **Huppenbauer, H.** "*Basar* 'Fleisch' in den Texten von Qumran (Höhle I)." *TZ* 13 (1957) 298–300. **Jannaris, A. N.** "Misreadings and Misrenderings in the New Testament." *Expositor* 5.8 (1898) 422–32, esp. 428–31. **Jeremias, J.** *The Central Message of the New Testament.* New York: Scribner's, 1965. 19–20. ———. *The Prayers of Jesus.* SBT 6. London: SCM Press, 1967. 11–65, 95–98, 108–15. **Kazmierski, C. R.** *Jesus, the Son of God.* 151–63. **Kelber, W.** "The Hour of the Son of Man and the Temptation of the Disciples (Mark 14:32–42)." In *The Passion in Mark: Studies on Mark 14–16.* Ed. W. Kelber. Philadelphia: Fortress, 1976. 41–60. ———. "Mark 14,32–42: Gethsemane: Passion Christology and Discipleship Failure." *ZNW* 63 (1972) 166–87. ———, **Kolenkow, A. B.,** and **Scroggs, R.** "Reflections on the Question: Was There a Pre-Markan Passion Narrative?" In *Society of Biblical Literature 1971 Seminar Papers.* Ed. J. L. White et al. 2 vols. SBLSP 10. Missoula: SBL, 1971. 2:503–85, esp. 537–43. **Kenny, A.** "The Transfiguration and the Agony in the Garden." *CBQ* 19 (1957) 444–52. **Kiley, M.** "Lord, Save My Life (Ps 116:4) as Generative Text for Jesus' Gethsemane Prayer (Mark 14:36a)." *CBQ* 48 (1986) 655–59. **Klausner, J.** *Jesus of Nazareth: His Life, Times, and Teaching.* London: George Allen, 1925. 330–32. **Knox, W. L.** *The Sources of the Synoptic Gospels.* 2 vols. Cambridge: Cambridge UP, 1953, 1957. 1:125–30. **Kremer, J.** *Das Ärgernis des Kreuzes: Eine Hinführung zum Verstehen der Leidensgeschichte nach Markus.* Stuttgart: Katholisches Bibelwerk, 1969. 36–40. **Kruse, H.** "'Pater Noster' et Passio Christi." *VD* 46 (1968) 3–29. **Kuhn, K. G.** "Jesus in Gethsemane." *EvT* 12 (1952–53) 260–85. ———. "New Light on Temptation, Sin, and Flesh in the New Testament." In *The Scrolls and the New Testament.* Ed. K. Stendahl. New York: Harper & Row, 1957. Repr. New York: Crossroad, 1992. 94–113, 265–70. **Le Déaut, R.** "Goûter le calice de la mort." *Bib* 43 (1962) 82–86. **Léon-Dufour, X.** "Jésus à Gethsémani: Essai de lecture synchronique." *ScEs* 31 (1979) 251–68. **Lescow, T.** "Jesus in Gethsemane." *EvT* 26 (1966) 141–59. **Linnemann, E.** *Studien zur Passionsgeschichte.* 11–40. **Lods, M.** "Climat de bataille à Gethsémane." *ETR* 60 (1985) 425–29. **Lohse, E.** *History of the Suffering and Death of Jesus Christ.* Philadelphia: Fortress, 1967. 55–68. **Lövestam, E.** *Spiritual Wakefulness in the New Testament.* Lund: Gleerup, 1963. 65–67, 90–91. **Mack, B. L.** *Myth.* 306–8. **Marchel, W.** "'Abba, Pater!' Oratio Christi et christianorum." *VD* 39 (1961) 240–47. ———. *Abba, Père! La prière du Christ et des chrétiens: Étude exégétique sur les origines et la signification de l'invocation à la divinité comme père, avant et dans le Nouveau Testament.* AnBib 19. Rome: Biblical Institute, 1963. 101–27. ———. *Abba, Vater! Die Vaterbotschaft des Neuen Testaments.* Die Welt der Bibel. Düsseldorf: Patmos, 1963.

33–46. **Martin, F.** "Literary Theory, Philosophy of History and Exegesis." *Thomist* 52 (1988) 575–604. **Martin, R. P.** *Mark: Evangelist and Theologian.* 203–5. **McCasland, S. V.** "'Abba, Father.'" *JBL* 72 (1953) 79–91. **Minear, P. S.** *Commands of Christ.* Nashville; New York: Abingdon; Edinburgh: St. Andrews, 1972. 157–64. **Mitton, C. L.** "The Will of God: 1. In the Synoptic Tradition of the Words of Jesus." *ExpTim* 72 (1960–61) 68–71. **Mohn, W.** "Gethsemane (Mk 14,32–42)." *ZNW* 64 (1973) 194–208. **Mohr, T. A.** *Markus- und Johannespassion.* 226–48. **Moo, D. J.** *Old Testament in the Gospel Passion Narratives.* 240–42. **Müller, K. W.** "ἀπέχει (Mk 14:41)—absurda lectio?" *ZNW* 77 (1986) 83–100. **Myllykoski, M.** *Die letzten Tage Jesu.* 144–58. **Pelcé, F.** "Jésus à Gethsémani: Remarques comparatives sur les trois récits évangéliques." *FoiVie* 65 (1966) 89–99. **Pesch, R.** *Das Evangelium der Urgemeinde.* 176–79. **Popkes, W.** *Christus Traditus: Eine Untersuchung zum Begriff der Dahingabe im Neuen Testament.* ATANT 49. Zürich: Zwingli, 1967. 152–69, 180–81. ———. "Die letzte Bitte des Vater-Unser: Formgeschichtliche Beobachtungen zum Gebet Jesu." *ZNW* 81 (1990) 1–20, esp. 11–17. **Robinson, B. P.** "Gethsemane: The Synoptic and the Johannine Viewpoints." *CQR* 167 (1966) 4–11. **Robson, J.** "The Meaning of Christ's Prayer in Gethsemane." *ExpTim* 6 (1894–95) 522–23. **Sanders, E. P.** *The Historical Figure of Jesus.* London; New York: Penguin, 1993. 263–64. **Saunderson, B.** "Gethsemane: The Missing Witness." *Bib* 70 (1989) 224–33. **Schelbert, G.** "Sprachgeschichtliches zu 'Abba.'" In *Mélanges Dominique Barthélemy: Études bibliques.* Ed. P. Casetti et al. OBO 38. Göttingen: Vandenhoeck & Ruprecht, 1981. 395–447, esp. 410. **Schenk, W.** *Der Passionsbericht nach Markus.* 193–206. **Schenke, L.** *Studien zur Passionsgeschichte des Markus.* 461–560. **Schlosser, J.** *Le Dieu de Jésus: Étude exégétique.* LD 129. Paris: Cerf, 1987. 130–39. **Schmahl, G.** *Die Zwölf im Markusevangelium.* 134–37. **Schwarz, G.** *Jesus und Judas.* 59–65, 183–88. **Simpson, M. A.** "The Kingdom of God Has Come." *ExpTim* 64 (1952–53) 188. **Smisson, E. A.** "Mark xiv. 41: ἀπέχει." *ExpTim* 40 (1928–29) 528. **Smith, T. V.** *Petrine Controversies in Early Christianity: Attitudes towards Peter in Christian Writings of the First Two Centuries.* WUNT 2.15. Tübingen: Mohr-Siebeck, 1985. 173–78. **Söding, T.** "Gebet und Gebetsmahnung Jesu in Getsemani: Eine redaktionskritische Auslegung von Mk 14,32–42." *BZ* 31 (1987) 76–100. ———. *Glaube bei Markus.* 344–55. **Speier, S.** "'Das Kosten des Todeskelches' im Targum." *VT* 13 (1963) 344–45. **Standaert, B. H. M. G. M.** "Crying 'Abba' and Saying 'Our Father': An Intertextual Approach to the Dominical Prayer." In *Intertextuality in Biblical Writing.* FS B. van Iersel, ed. S. Draisma. Kampen: Kok, 1989. 141–58. **Stanley, D. M.** *Jesus in Gethsemane: The Early Church Reflects on the Sufferings of Jesus.* New York: Paulist, 1980. 119–54. **Staples, P.** "The Kingdom of God Has Come." *ExpTim* 71 (1959–60) 87–88. **Suhl, A.** *Zitate.* 49–50. **Szarek, G.** "A Critique of Kelber's 'The House of the Son of Man and the Temptation of the Disciples.'" In *Society of Biblical Literature 1976 Seminar Papers.* Ed. G. W. MacRae. SBLSP 15. Missoula, MT: Scholars Press, 1976. 111–18. **Taylor, T. M.** "'Abba, Father' and Baptism." *SJT* 11 (1958) 62–71. **Taylor, V.** *The Passion Narrative of St Luke.* Cambridge: Cambridge UP, 1973. 69–72. **Thomas, J.** "La scène du jardin: Selon Marc 14,32–42." *Christus* 28 (1981) 350–60. **Tilborg, S. van.** "A Form-Criticism of the Lord's Prayer." *NovT* 14 (1972) 94–105, esp. 95–99. **Torrey, C. C.** *Four Gospels.* 103. ———. *Our Translated Gospels.* 12–16, 56–59. **Torris, J.** "L'agonie de Jésus (Marc 14,32–42): Intention, sources, historicité." *La Pensé et les hommes* 17 (1973) 75–77. **Trémel, Y.-B.** "L'agonie du Christ." *LumVie* 68 (1964) 79–104. **Unnik, W. C. van.** "Alles ist dir möglich (Mk 14,36)." In *Verborum Veritas.* FS G. Stählin. Ed. O. Böcher and K. Haacker. Wuppertal: Brockhaus, 1970. 27–36. **Vanhoye, A.** "L'agnoisse du Christ." *Christus* 18 (1971) 382–89. **Vermes, G.** *Jesus the Jew.* London: Collins, 1973. 210–13. **Vischer, W.** "Abba." *ETR* 54 (1979) 683–86. **Weinacht, H.** *Die Menschwerdung des Sohnes Gottes.* 154–57. **Westcott, B. F., and Hort, F. J. A.** *Introduction.* 2:26–27. **Wilcox, M.** "Semitisms in the New Testament." *ANRW* 2.25.2 (1984) 978–1029, esp. 995–98. **Wilson, W. E.** "Our Lord's Agony in the Garden." *ExpTim* 32 (1920–21) 549–51. **Wrege, H.-T.** *Die Gestalt des Evangeliums: Aufbau und Struktur des Synoptiker sowie der Apostelgeschichte.* BBET 11. Bern; Frankfurt am Main: Lang, 1978. 78–80. **Wulf, F.** "Der Geist ist willig, das Fleisch schwach." *Geist und Leben* 37 (1964)

241–43. **Zeller, D.** "God as Father in the Proclamation and in the Prayer of Jesus." In *Standing before God: Studies in Prayer in Scriptures and in Tradition*. FS J. M. Oesterreicher, ed. A. Finkel and L. Frizzel. New York: Ktav, 1981. 117–29, esp. 122–24. **Zwaan, J. de.** "The Text and Exegesis of Mark xiv. 41 and the Papyri." *Expositor* 6.12 (1905) 459–72.

Translation

³²*And they go to a place whose name is Gethsemane;* ᵃ *and he says to his disciples, "Sit here while* ᵇ *I pray."* ³³*And he takes along Peter* ᶜ *and James and John with him, and he began to be distressed and troubled.* ³⁴*And he says to them, "My soul is grieved to the point of death; remain here, and watch!"* ³⁵*And going on a little further, he fell* ᵈ *on the ground and was praying that, if it is possible, the hour might pass from him.* ³⁶*And he was saying, "Abba, Father, all things are possible for you. Remove this cup from me; yet not what I will, but what you will."* ᵉ ³⁷*And he comes* ᶠ *and finds them sleeping, and he says to Peter,* ᵍ *"Simon, are you sleeping? Were you not able to watch* ʰ *for an hour?* ³⁸*Watch and pray that you do not come into temptation. The spirit is willing, but the flesh is weak."* ³⁹*And again, going away, he prayed, saying the same thing.* ⁱ ⁴⁰*And again, coming, he found them* ʲ *sleeping, for their eyes were heavy, and they did not know how they should answer him.* ⁴¹*And he comes the third time, and says to them, "Are you still sleeping and resting? Is it far off?* ᵏ *The hour has come! Behold, the 'son of man' is delivered into the hands of sinners!* ⁴²*Arise;* ˡ *let us be going. Behold, the one who is betraying me has arrived."*

Notes

ᵃGk. γεθσημανί. The spelling of this name varies considerably in the Gk. MSS. ℵ reads γεθσημανεί; B reads γετσημανεί. D reads γησημανεί. Other spellings include γεθσεμανεί, γηθσεμανεί, γεθσιμανή, γεσσημανεί, γεδσημανί. The versions display a similar range of variation. The name comes from the Aram. שְׁמָנֵא גַּת *gat šĕmānê*, which means "oil-press." Cranfield (430) says that the word is derived from the Heb. שְׁמָנִים גַּת *gat šĕmānîm*, "press of oils," but the Gk. transliteration found in the Markan text more closely matches the Aram.

ᵇSeveral later MSS add ἀπελθών, "having departed" (in the sense of putting some distance between himself and his disciples; cf. Matt 26:36).

ᶜSyr. MSS read *kêpāʾ*, "Cephas."

ᵈD Σ and several later MSS add ἐπὶ πρόσωπον, "on his face" (cf. Matt 26:39).

ᵉIn the oldest and best authorities θέλεις, "you will," is not present, though it is clearly implied. D and several later MSS add the word.

ᶠA few later MSS make explicit what is understood by adding πρὸς τοὺς μαθητὰς αὐτοῦ, "to his disciples" (cf. Matt 26:40; Luke 22:45).

ᵍSyr. MSS read *kêpāʾ*, "Cephas."

ʰA few later MSS add μετ᾽ ἐμοῦ, "with me" (cf. Matt 26:40).

ⁱD omits τὸν αὐτὸν λόγον εἰπών, "saying the same thing."

ʲA C N W and several later MSS and authorities read καὶ ὑποστρέψας εὗρεν αὐτοὺς πάλιν, "and, returning, he found them again."

ᵏThe meaning of ἀπέχει is problematic. ἀπέχειν usually means "to abstain from, to hold off, to receive full payment, *or* to be far off." In the present context it is usually understood to mean that the disciples have slept "enough," or that Jesus has admonished them "enough." This meaning underlies the Latin *sufficit*, "it is enough." Some think ἀπέχει means "time is up." D W Φ and a few later MSS add τὸ τέλος, "the end," apparently meaning "the end has come," or "time has expired," which may in fact correctly interpret the rare impersonal use of ἀπέχει; cf. Westcott-Hort, *Introduction* 2:26–27. This reading underlies other Latin authorities, which read *consummatus est finis*, "the end has come." Metzger (*TCGNT*¹, 114–15) cites an old Latin reading (fourth to fifth century) that in effect offers a paraphrase of the passage: "and he came the third time and when he had prayed he says to them,

'Sleep on now; behold, he who betrays me has come near.' And after a little he aroused them and said, 'Now is the hour; behold, the son of man is betrayed.'" See further discussion in *Comment* on v 41.

[1]A few MSS read add ἐντεῦθεν, "from here" (cf. John 14:31).

Form/Structure/Setting

Jesus' prayer in the garden of Gethsemane is one of the most famous scenes in the Gospel story. As on several other solemn occasions, Jesus takes along Peter, James, and John. He confides in them that his soul is grieved to the point of death. He asks his closest disciples to remain with him and keep watch. He then goes off by himself, falls on the ground, and prays that, if it is possible, God may remove the cup of suffering from him. When he rejoins his disciples, he finds them sleeping. He exhorts them to keep watch and then retires again to pray. He returns two more times and finds them sleeping. He then announces the approach of his betrayer and rouses his disciples.

According to Bultmann (*History,* 267–68), Mark 14:32–42 is "an individual story of a thorough-going legendary character, which has not survived intact in Mark." It belongs to a "later stage of the tradition" (*History,* 284). Dibelius (*Tradition,* 182) finds "artificial links" in the story of Gethsemane, though he is not as skeptical as Bultmann. Taylor (551; cf. id., *Formation,* 58) is less skeptical still, saying that the story of Jesus' prayer in Gethsemane has strong claim to Petrine origin. Contemporary scholars remain divided, though many view the story as rooted in reliable tradition. Cranfield (430), who regards its origin as "probably Petrine," thinks "the historical value of the section is beyond serious doubt." He reasons rightly that it is inconceivable that the early church would create a scene in which Jesus appears panicked and begs God to cancel his impending martyrdom, and in which the disciples appear so feckless. Sanders (*Historical Figure,* 264) comments that the prayer "is perfectly reasonable" and that it shows that Jesus "hoped that he would not die, but he resigned himself to the will of God."

Kuhn (*EvT* 12 [1952–53] 260–85) has proposed that Mark 14:32–42 constitutes a combination of two pre-Markan traditions. Taylor (*St Luke,* 69–72) suspects that Luke 22:40–46 is independent of Mark, while Green (*JSNT* 26 [1986] 29–48) thinks Luke made use of Mark and another non-Markan source. Others think Heb 5:7–8 reflects independent tradition (cf. Brown, 227–33). Moreover, there may be independent material in the Fourth Gospel as well. It is impossible to reach certainty in such a complicated issue, but independent, pre-Markan tradition(s) would only lend additional support to the historicity of the story.

Some critics have claimed that the story of the prayer in Gethsemane cannot rest on historical tradition because the disciples slept. Saunderson (*Bib* 70 [1989] 224–33) asserts that the mysterious young man of 14:51–52 cannot be ruled out as a witness. Perhaps this is true, but this hardly puts the tradition on firmer ground. All that the tradition preserves of Jesus' prayer are three brief sentences (v 36). If the scene is a Christian creation, why not a larger inventory of dominical tradition as in John 17, for example? Dozing disciples may very well explain such meager preservation of dominical tradition. The contrast between Jesus, who prays earnestly, and the disciples, who are unable to concentrate on prayer, may very well serve parenetic purposes in the Markan community (cf. Söding, *BZ* 31 [1987]

76–100), but the parenetic function does not necessarily stand in tension with historicity.

Comment

32 The Mount of Olives was traditionally a place of prayer (Ezek 11:23; 2 Sam 15:32), and it was the place where God would appear in judgment (Zech 14:4). Jesus leads his disciples εἰς χωρίον οὗ τὸ ὄνομα Γεθσημανί, "to a place whose name is Gethsemane." The name comes from Aramaic, meaning "oil-press" (see *Note* a above). It is called a κῆπος, "garden," in John 18:1, where, we are told, Jesus often gathered with his disciples (John 18:2).

καὶ λέγει τοῖς μαθηταῖς αὐτοῦ· καθίσατε ὧδε ἕως προσεύξωμαι, "and he says to his disciples, 'Sit here while I pray.'" Several times in the Gospel of Mark Jesus prays or gives teaching on prayer: in 1:35 he arises before daybreak to pray in private; in 6:46 he sends his disciples on ahead, then retires to a mountain to pray; in 9:29 he tells his disciples that certain types of unclean spirits cannot be driven out except by prayer; in 11:17 Jesus criticizes the authorities for failing to make the temple a "house of prayer for all the nations" (alluding to Isa 56:7); in 11:24–25 he teaches his disciples about faith and prayer; in 12:40 he warns of avaricious scribes who offer up phony prayers; and in 13:18 he exhorts his disciples to pray that the coming day of tribulation not take place in winter. Asking the disciples to sit down while he prays nearby (v 35: "a little further") has its closest parallels in 1:35 and 6:46.

33 καὶ παραλαμβάνει τὸν Πέτρον καὶ [τὸν] Ἰάκωβον καὶ [τὸν] Ἰωάννην μετ' αὐτοῦ, "And he takes along Peter and James and John with him." On three prior occasions Jesus has taken along Peter, James, and John: in 5:37–43, where the three disciples witness the raising of the daughter of Jairus; in 9:2–8, where the three witness the transfiguration of Jesus and hear the voice of God; and in 13:37, where the three receive instruction concerning the end times. Jesus takes along these three disciples because he needs and wants their company and because he wishes to instruct them to the very end. It may also be that Jesus is concerned to have witnesses, "two or three" (cf. Deut 17:6; 19:15), in view of matters that lie ahead.

καὶ ἤρξατο ἐκθαμβεῖσθαι καὶ ἀδημονεῖν, "and he began to be distressed and troubled." This is the only time ἐκθαμβεῖσθαι, "to be distressed, amazed," is used of Jesus in the NT. The word describes great emotion. In 9:15 "all the crowd, seeing him, were greatly amazed [ἐξεθαμβήθησαν], and running up to him they greeted him." In this instance, the crowd is not distressed, but excited (see *Comment* on 9:15). In 16:5 the women will enter the tomb, see "a young man seated on the right, dressed in a white robe," and then be "amazed" (or "distressed"; cf. 16:5 below). In 16:6 the young man will say to them, "Do not be amazed. You seek Jesus the Nazarene, who was crucified. He has been raised; he is not here." Again, the meaning of ἐκθαμβεῖσθαι in these contexts has to do with excitement or agitation, not necessarily distress. Yet in 14:33 the appearance of ἐκθαμβεῖσθαι alongside ἀδημονεῖν, "to be troubled," suggests more than excitement or amazement. In context with this word, ἐκθαμβεῖσθαι conveys the idea of distress or anguish (BAG, 239; cf. Cranfield, 431). ἀδημονεῖν elsewhere in the NT is found only in the Matthean parallel (Matt 26:37, where it is coupled with λυπεῖσθαι, "to be pained"; the word choice was probably inspired by the next verse) and in Phil 2:26 (Epaphroditus "has been distressed because you heard that he was ill"). Jesus' comment (in v 34) only adds to the element of distress and sorrow.

34 περίλυπός ἐστιν ἡ ψυχή μου ἕως θανάτου, "My soul is grieved to the point of death." The word translated περίλυπος, "grieved," appears only one other time in Mark, in 6:26, where the tetrarch Herod Antipas "was grieved" (RSV: "was exceedingly sorry") that his boastful offer to his stepdaughter would result in the beheading of John the Baptist. For Jesus to say that his soul is grieved ἕως θανάτου, "to the point of death," is remarkable and appears to be a deliberate echo of biblical language: Ps 42:4–5, 11 (= LXX Ps 41:5, 6 [τί περίλυπος εἶ ψυχή], 12; MT Ps 42:5–6, 12); 43:5 (= LXX Ps 42:5: τί περίλυπος εἶ ψυχή); Jonah 4:9 (LXX: σφόδρα λελύπημαι ἐγὼ ἕως θανάτου); Sir 37:2. The latter text is especially interesting, given Jesus' knowledge of Judas's imminent betrayal: οὐχὶ λύπη ἔνι ἕως θανάτου / ἑταῖρος καὶ φίλος τρεπόμενος εἰς ἔχθραν, "Is it not a grief to the death / when a companion and friend turns to enmity?" Jesus' words could be understood more literally, "grieved to death" (as the RSV similarly translates Sir 37:2, "a grief to the death"), but "to the point of death," a sense ἕως will allow, seems truer to the intended meaning.

μείνατε ὧδε καὶ γρηγορεῖτε, "Remain here, and watch!" Both verbs are imperative; the present-tense γρηγορεῖτε, lit. "be watching!" lends emphasis to the command. Elsewhere in Mark, Jesus enjoins his disciples using γρηγορεῖν, "to watch." Three times in the eschatological discourse he uses γρηγορεῖν: in 13:34 it appears in the parable of the Doorkeeper, who is told to watch for the return of his master; in 13:35 Jesus uses the word when he applies the lesson to his disciples, saying, "Watch therefore"; and in 13:37 Jesus says to "all" (the Markan community?) "Watch!" The evangelist's use of βλέπειν, "to see," is approximately synonymous, appearing several times in the eschatological discourse (13:5, 9, 23, 33) and elsewhere in the sense of "beware" (e.g., 4:24; 8:15; 12:38). Because γρηγορεῖν appears in the eschatological discourse, Barrett (*ExpTim* 67 [1956–57] 144) thinks that here in 14:34 Jesus has asked his disciples to watch for the Parousia of the "son of man." However, this is doubtful (Cranfield, 432). If the command to "watch" adverts to the Parousia, to what does the command to "remain here" advert? The most likely meaning is that Jesus has asked his disciples to act as sentries, protecting Jesus' privacy and providing him with advanced warning should malefactors approach (Gundry, 854, rightly: "it has to do with watching for Judas' coming").

35 καὶ προελθὼν μικρὸν ἔπιπτεν ἐπὶ τῆς γῆς, "And going on a little further, he fell on the ground." Luke 22:41 says Jesus went "about a stone's throw." Falling to the ground attests to the distress that has overtaken Jesus. Matthew 26:39 says that Jesus ἔπεσεν ἐπὶ πρόσωπον αὐτοῦ, "fell on his face," which is probably how Mark should be understood. Normally Jews pray standing and looking up to heaven (cf. Mark 6:41: Jesus "looked up to heaven, and blessed"; Luke 18:11: "the Pharisee stood and prayed"; recall also the name of the famous Jewish prayer, the ʿAmîdâ, which means "standing"). Falling to the ground (or on one's face), though exceptional, nevertheless does reflect Middle Eastern custom in antiquity and has biblical precedent. In Gen 17:1–3 God appeared to Abram, and the great patriarch "fell on his face" (LXX: ἔπεσεν Ἀβρὰμ ἐπὶ πρόσωπον αὐτοῦ). In LXX Lev 9:24, when fire fell from heaven, the Israelites ἔπεσαν ἐπὶ πρόσωπον, "fell on their face." Several times in Numbers, Moses, Aaron, and the people fall on their faces, either in great religious distress or in the presence of God (Num 14:5; 16:4, 22, 45; 20:6). Other examples can be found outside the Bible, where praying/worshiping and falling on one's face are juxtaposed. Job's wife falls to the ground worshiping (*T. Job* 40:4), while Aseneth "fell on her face" while praying (*Jos. Asen.* 14:3).

προσηύχετο ἵνα εἰ δυνατόν ἐστιν παρέλθῃ ἀπ᾽ αὐτοῦ ἡ ὥρα, "praying that, if it is possible, the hour might pass from him." Mark's summary of the prayer anticipates Jesus' actual words, which will be reported in the next verse. Jesus prays that, "if it is possible," he may yet escape the violent fate that awaits him. εἰ δυνατόν ἐστιν, "if it is possible," will remind Mark's readers of Jesus' earlier teaching, when he told the distraught father, "All things are possible [πάντα δυνατά] for the one who has faith" (9:23); or when he warned his disciples that false messiahs and false prophets would offer signs and wonders to mislead, "if possible [εἰ δυνατόν], the elect" (13:22). More pertinent yet is the advice that Jesus gave his disciples when they wondered if anyone could be saved. They are told "With humans it is impossible, but not with God; for all things are possible with God [πάντα γὰρ δυνατὰ παρὰ τῷ θεῷ]" (10:27). In a moment, Jesus will say this very thing to God: "All things are possible for you." In effect, Jesus faces a severe testing of his own faith, not so much in himself as in God, whose kingdom he has been proclaiming and whose power he has been demonstrating since the inception of his ministry.

Jesus' prayer is that the hour παρέλθῃ ἀπ᾽ αὐτοῦ, "might pass from him." The hour will be defined shortly as being the time for the "son of man" to be "delivered into the hands of sinners" (v 41), who will then abuse and execute him, just as Jesus has predicted on several occasions (cf. 8:31; 9:31; 10:33–34). But because Jesus has also spoken of his death in terms of atonement (14:24: "This is my blood of the covenant," alluding to Exod 24:8 and other texts), thus implying that his death is in some sense a sin offering, he may very well have also feared divine wrath (Cranfield, 433–34). After all, in 14:27 he applied Zech 13:7 ("Strike the shepherd") to himself, thus implying that God's wrath would fall upon him. Moreover, at the very moment of his death Jesus will cry out, "My God, my God, why have you abandoned me?" (15:34). It is this abandonment that Jesus fears most. Perhaps this accounts for the intensity of Jesus' fear, in contrast to the equanimity seen in the Maccabean martyrs. Jesus hopes this severe experience "might pass from him," that is, "might pass him by" and miss him altogether. Mark's usage of παρέρχεσθαι, "to pass by," supports this interpretation (cf. 6:48, where Jesus walking on the water intends to "pass by" the disciples in the boat; 13:30, where the generation of the last days "will not pass away" until all is fulfilled; and 13:31, where hyperbolically Jesus says, "Heaven and earth will pass away, but my words will not pass away").

ἡ ὥρα, "the hour," is at most only loosely related to the Johannine hour motif (e.g., John 17:1); it offers no evidence of contact between the synoptic and Johannine traditions (*pace* H. Koester, *Ancient Christian Gospels* [London: SCM Press; Philadelphia: Trinity Press International, 1990] 211). The hour theme derives from Jesus himself, who probably drew upon vocabulary and themes from Daniel (4:17, 26; 5:5; 8:17, 19; 11:35, 40, 45), where the idea of "hour" figures prominently, often with eschatological overtones. The Johannine hour motif represents an independent and greatly developed expression of this theme.

36 καὶ ἔλεγεν, "And he was saying." It is gratuitous to claim that the disciples could not have heard Jesus pray because they were too far away and were sleeping. Jesus had only gone on ahead "a little further" (v 35), thus implying that the disciples were still within earshot. Moreover, prayer in antiquity was normally spoken aloud; silent prayer was exceptional (cf. 1 Sam 1:12–16, where Eli the priest mistakes Hannah's silent prayer for drunkenness). We should also assume that the disciples did not drop off to sleep so quickly that they heard nothing of what Jesus said. The imperfect ἔλεγεν, "he was saying," accommodates the repetition of the prayer in vv 36, 39, and 41 (implied).

ἀββὰ ὁ πατήρ, "Abba, Father," juxtaposes transliteration of the Aramaic אַבָּא 'abbā' and Greek translation. Both forms are probably to be understood as vocative. Jesus' manner of speaking of God as Father and his direct address to God as Father in prayer (cf. Luke 11:2: "Father, may your name be sanctified" [author's tr.]; and the expanded, liturgical form in Matt 6:9: "Our Father, who are in heaven, may your name be sanctified" [author's tr.]) have occasioned much scholarly discussion, often with reference to the work of J. Jeremias. In a series of studies Jeremias has claimed that Jesus' use of Father is original, even unique. Jeremias avers that "here there is something quite new, absolutely new—the word *abba*" (*Prayers of Jesus*, 96). He further claims, and has made famous in doing so, that Jesus' use of אַבָּא 'abbā' parallels the way children addressed their fathers or father-figures (e.g., the little children who run to Honi the Circle-Drawer, crying out "Abba, Abba!"; cf. *b. Ta'an.* 23b) and so could be legitimately translated "Daddy" (*Central Message*, 19–20). But this interpretation has been challenged more recently by Fitzmyer ("Abba and Jesus' Relation to God"), Barr (*JTS* n.s. 39 [1988] 28–47; id., *Theology* 91 [1988] 173–79), and others (see the synthesis provided by Charlesworth, "Meaning of *Abba*"; Davies and Allison, *Matthew* 1:601–2). Jesus' use of אַבָּא 'abbā' was not unique, nor did it necessarily imply a unique sense of divine sonship, but it was distinctive, perhaps even somewhat unconventional. This distinctiveness is one reason that scholars regard it as authentic (e.g., recently, Gnilka, *Jesus of Nazareth*, 262: "Jesus' manner of referring to God as Father, especially in the address of prayers, must be taken as authentic").

Jeremias and others made use of rabbinic and targumic materials, which have the disadvantage of postdating the NT by several generations and so may not reflect exactly the language or the conventions of first-century Palestine (for a succinct review of the most pertinent rabbinic material, see Vermes, *Jesus the Jew*, 210–12; for a review of the linguistic data, including targumic sources, see Fitzmyer, "Abba and Jesus' Relation to God"). But there are earlier sources that should be given priority. Precedent for addressing God as Father is found in Scripture itself: "Is not [the LORD] your father [אָבִיךָ 'ābîkâ], who created you, who made you and established you?" (Deut 32:6); "For you are our father [אָבִינוּ 'ābînû], though Abraham does not know us and Israel does not acknowledge us; you, O LORD, are our father [אָבִינוּ 'ābînû], our Redeemer from of old is your name" (Isa 63:16 NRSV); and others (Isa 64:7; Jer 31:9; Mal 1:6; Ps 68:6). In Ps 89:26 (MT 89:27) the Davidic heir is to cry out, "You are my Father [אָבִי 'ābî], my God, and the Rock of my salvation." Righteous Tobit in his prayer exhorts his fellow Israelites: "Make his greatness known there, and exalt him in the presence of all the living; because he is our Lord and God, he is our Father [πατὴρ ἡμῶν] for ever" (Tob 13:4). Yeshua ben Sira the sage prays: "O Lord, Father [πάτερ] and Ruler of my life, do not abandon me!" (Sir 23:1); "O Lord, Father [πάτερ] and God of my life, do not give me haughty eyes" (Sir 23:4). Neither of these verses in Sirach is preserved in Hebrew, either in the Cairo text or in the Dead Sea Scrolls. However, Sir 51:10, which reads confusedly in Greek: "I appealed to the Lord, the Father [πάτερα] of my lord, not to forsake me in the days of affliction," is preserved somewhat differently and more briefly in the Cairo text, which appears to echo Ps 89:27: "Yea, I exalted the LORD, 'You are my Father [אבי אתה *ʾābî ʾāttâ*], for you are the Mighty One of my salvation'" (the Hebrew version is superior; cf. P. W. Skehan and A. A. Di Lella, *The Wisdom of Ben Sira,* AB 39 [Garden City: Doubleday, 1987] 566–67). There are at least two relevant parallels from the Dead Sea Scrolls: Joseph prays, "My Father [אבי *ʾābî*], my God, do not abandon me to the Gentiles" (4Q372 [= 4QapocrJoseph^b] 1 16); "My Father [אבי *ʾābî*] and my Lord" (4Q460 [= 4QPseudepigraphic Works] 5 6). It should be noted that the address to God as Father is often found in the context of distress.

Jesus' distinctive style has left its mark outside of the Gospels themselves. Paul says in Rom 8:15–16: "When we cry, 'Abba! Father! [ἀββὰ ὁ πατήρ],' it is the Spirit himself bearing witness with our spirit that we are children of God"; and in Gal 4:6: "Because you are sons, God has sent the Spirit of his Son into our hearts, crying, 'Abba! Father! [ἀββὰ ὁ πατήρ].'" This Aramaic/Greek juxtaposition, identical to what we have in Mark 14:36, suggests that Jesus' style of addressing God as Father left a deep impression on early Christians. Paul's employment of this form of address in contexts emphasizing Christians' kinship and obedience to God may aid us in interpreting the significance of Jesus' prayer in Gethsemane, as Grassi (*JAAR* 50 [1982] 449–58; *TBT* 21 [1983] 320–24) has suggested. The cry "Abba! Father!" in imitation of Jesus is a mark of filial obedience. Faced with a severe testing, Jesus cried out "Abba! Father!" and then proclaimed his willingness to seek God's will, not his own. Grassi further speculates that Jesus' cry of "Father!" and his willingness to obey, even if it meant his death, may be modeled after Isaac's similar willingness to obey his father Abraham (Gen 22:1–19; cf. 22:7, where Isaac cries out, "My father!").

πάντα δυνατά σοι, "all things are possible for you." This statement is as much a request as it is a confession. It is as if to say, "I believe that you can do anything, including making it possible for me not to go through the horror of the passion." On what is δυνατός, "possible," see *Comment* on v 35.

παρένεγκε τὸ ποτήριον τοῦτο ἀπ᾽ ἐμοῦ, "Remove this cup from me." On παρένεγκε, "remove" or "take away," see Field, *Notes,* 39. On the cup of wrath, see Isa 51:17, where the prophet enjoins Jerusalem: "stand up, O Jerusalem, you who have drunk at the hand of the LORD the cup of his wrath [LXX: τὸ ποτήριον τοῦ θυμοῦ]." On removing or taking away the cup, see Isa 51:22, where a compassionate and forgiving God says, "Behold, I have taken from your hand the cup of staggering [LXX: τὸ ποτήριον τῆς πτώσεως]; the bowl of my wrath [LXX: τὸ κόνδυ τοῦ θυμοῦ] you shall drink no more." See also Ezek 23:32–34; Lam 4:21; Ps 11:6; *Mart. Ascen. Isa.* 5:13 (cf. Mark 10:38–39). Scriptural parallels such as these add color and backdrop to the words of Jesus' pleading prayer.

ἀλλ᾽ οὐ τί ἐγὼ θέλω ἀλλὰ τί σύ, "Yet not what I will, but what you will." Klausner (*Jesus of Nazareth,* 332) thinks this line is a Markan addition, stating, "who could not think that a prayer of the Messiah could be refused, or that the Messiah need plead to God like a child appealing to its parents." On the contrary, the mere

hint of tension between the will of Jesus and the will of his heavenly Father, something no Christian tradent would suggest, strongly points in the direction of
dominical origin. We must remember, too, the Lord's Prayer, which surely expresses the essence of Jesus' theology: "Our Father, who are in heaven, may your
name be sanctified; may your kingdom come; may your will [τὸ θέλημά σου] be
done on earth as it is in heaven" (Matt 6:9–10 // Luke 11:2–3 [author's tr.]; cf.
Swete, 344–45; Lukan redaction in 22:42, μὴ τὸ θέλημά μου ἀλλὰ τὸ σὸν γινέσθω,
"not my will but yours be done" [NRSV], which draws a closer parallel to the language of the Lord's Prayer, shows that this evangelist was familiar with the form
attested in Matt 6:10 but attested in only some MSS of Luke 11:3).

Kiley (*CBQ* 48 [1986] 655–59) argues that Jesus' cry in v 36a reflects the cry of
the psalmist in Ps 116:4: "O Lord . . . , save my life!" He believes that the context
of Mark 14 could have been perceived by the early church to reflect the experience of the "pray-er" of Ps 116. Kiley cites three principal points of contact (Kiley's
tr.): (*a*) Ps 116:11: "Every man is false/a liar" (cf. Mark 14:10–11, 17–21, 43–52,
which recounts the betrayal of Judas, the denial of Peter, and the word of a false
witness); (*b*) Ps 116:13: "I will take the cup of salvation" (cf. Mark 14:24, where the
covenant will be renewed through Jesus' blood "poured out for many"); (*c*) Ps
116:15: "Precious in the Lord's eyes is the death of his faithful ones" (cf. Mark
14:3–9, where the anointing by the woman at Bethany underscores the surpass-
ing value of Jesus' death). Kiley's parallels are interesting but vague. They are
insufficient in number and detail to hypothesize significant influence of Ps 116
on Mark 14.

Surrender to the will of God is known in Greco-Roman sources as well. Epictetus
the Stoic is remembered to have prayed, "Lead me on, O Zeus and Destiny. . . . If
it please the gods, so be it" (Arrian, *Epict. diss.* 3.22.95).

37 καὶ ἔρχεται καὶ εὑρίσκει αὐτοὺς καθεύδοντας, "And he comes and finds
them sleeping." Evidently Jesus had been apart from the disciples praying for
about one hour (or less). When he returns, he finds them asleep, thus failing to
watch, as Jesus had requested in v 34. Accordingly, he rouses Peter, and says to
him, Σίμων, καθεύδεις; οὐκ ἴσχυσας μίαν ὥραν γρηγορῆσαι, "Simon, are you sleeping? Were you not able to watch for an hour?" Luke 22:45 charitably reduces the
lapses from three to one and explains that the disciples were sleeping ἀπὸ τῆς
λύπης, "from sorrow," though when gripped in sorrow, one usually finds it difficult to sleep (cf. A. Plummer, *A Critical and Exegetical Commentary on the Gospel
according to S. Luke,* ICC [Edinburgh: T. & T. Clark, 1896] 511: "Prolonged sorrow
produces wakefulness"; similar ideas are found in Scripture: Isa 38:15: "All my
sleep has fled because of the bitterness of my soul"; Dan 2:1: "Nebuchadnezzar
had dreams; and his spirit was troubled, and his sleep left him"; 6:18; Prov 3:24).
The emotional abandonment of Jesus by his disciples during his time of prayer
in Gethsemane portends the literal abandonment that will take place soon. The
questions of Jesus directly to Simon Peter prepare the reader for the fulfillment
of Jesus' prediction that his chief disciple will indeed deny him three times. The
lonely scene in the garden depicts Jesus as increasingly isolated—from his people,
from his followers, and even from his closest disciples.

38 γρηγορεῖτε καὶ προσεύχεσθε, ἵνα μὴ ἔλθητε εἰς πειρασμόν, "Watch and
pray that you do not come into temptation." Jesus gives an exhortation to his
disciples (the verb is plural, so evidently Jesus is now addressing James and John

also). Earlier he had requested that they watch (v 34). Now he exhorts them to watch *and pray,* just as he himself has been doing. The content of the disciples' prayers will not be the same, of course. The conjunction ἵνα, "that," is not final (i.e., "so that") but introduces the content of the disciples' prayers (Cranfield, 434). They are to pray that they not enter into temptation. Into temptation of what? In the NT temptation, either the noun πειρασμός, "temptation," or the verb πειράζειν, "to tempt," often refers to temptation to sin, to yield to fleshly impulses (Acts 20:19; Gal 4:14; Jas 1:2; 1 Pet 1:6). This is not the meaning here. Jesus' warning has to do with the temptation to abandon the cause to which Jesus had called his disciples, in effect, to fall away from the faith (Keener, *Matthew,* 634), to go the way of Judas Iscariot, to betray Jesus and the kingdom of God. Jesus, who has been successfully waging war on the kingdom of Satan (cf. Mark 1:7–8; 3:27, where by inference Jesus is to be understood as the one stronger than the strong man, Satan), now anticipates a fearful counteroffensive. Jesus is himself frightened and worries that his closest friends do not sufficiently appreciate the dangers they face. Because they are insufficiently troubled to keep alert and to pray, they are vulnerable.

According to Torrey (*Our Translated Gospels,* 12, 14–16; cf. id., *Four Gospels,* 103), the Aramaic underlying Mark 14:38, "Watch [עוּרוּ *'ûrû*] and pray, lest you enter into temptation [תַּעֲלוּן בְּנִסְיוֹנָא *ta'ălûn běnisyônā'*]," has been misunderstood; the reading should be "Awake, and pray not to fail the test!" This is possible, but Mark's Greek makes sense as it stands.

τὸ μὲν πνεῦμα πρόθυμον ἡ δὲ σὰρξ ἀσθενής, "The spirit is willing, but the flesh is weak." Watchfulness and prayer are necessary to shore up the weak flesh (cf. the extended discussion of the antithesis between flesh and spirit in Rom 7–8, but this hardly justifies regarding v 38b as "Pauline"; Wellhausen, 120; Lohmeyer, 317). τὸ πνεῦμα, "the spirit," of which Jesus speaks here is not the Holy Spirit (*pace* Schweizer, 313–14, despite a possible parallel with "willing spirit" in Ps 51:12), which is powerful (cf. Mark 1:7–8), but the human spirit, which is fickle and all too often faithless (cf. 4:40). Humans may be eager to follow Jesus and participate in the advancement of the kingdom, but like the seed cast upon the shallow soil that sprouts up quickly and then withers under the hot sun (4:16–17), so they fall away at the first encounter with persecution. In the Gospels, πρόθυμος, "willing" (which can also mean "eager" or "ready"), occurs only here and in the Matthean parallel (Matt 26:41). The only other occurrence in the NT is Rom 1:15, where Paul tells the Christians of Rome "I am eager [πρόθυμον] to preach the gospel to you also who are in Rome." For examples in the LXX, see Hab 1:8; 1 Chr 28:21; 2 Chr 29:31; 2 Macc 4:14; 15:9: "Encouraging them from the law and the prophets, and reminding them also of the struggles they had won, he made them the more eager [προθυμοτέρους]"; 3 Macc 5:26. For examples of the nominal προθυμία, "willingness," see Sir 45:23; Acts 17:11; 2 Cor 8:11–12, 19; 9:2. In Scripture בָּשָׂר *bāśār*/σάρξ, "flesh," often represents the mortal, frail human being in contrast to the Almighty (e.g., Isa 31:3: "The Egyptians are human, and not God; their horses are flesh, and not spirit" [NRSV]; 40:5–6; Jer 17:5: "Cursed are those who trust in mere mortals and make mere flesh their strength, whose hearts turn away from the LORD" [NRSV]; 25:31; Zech 2:13[17]).

39 καὶ πάλιν ἀπελθὼν προσηύξατο τὸν αὐτὸν λόγον εἰπών, "And again, going away, he prayed, saying the same thing." After exhorting the disciples, particularly Peter, Jesus once again retires to his place of prayer (presumably the same place, not far from the disciples). Jesus' command to the disciples to pray is "confirmed by example" (Swete, 347). We are told that Jesus prayed τὸν αὐτὸν λόγον, "the same thing" (lit. "the same word"). However, these words, omitted by D and other authorities (principally Latin MSS), may be a gloss (Taylor, 535: "every appearance of being a gloss"; Anderson, 320). The Matthean evangelist takes the opportunity to supply the reader with Jesus' words, revealing that Jesus has resolved to do his Father's will (Matt 26:42: "My Father, if this cannot pass unless I drink it, your will be done" [NRSV]). In the Johannine account Jesus is even determined to drink the cup: "Shall I not drink the cup which the Father has given me?" (John 18:11).

40 καὶ πάλιν ἐλθὼν εὗρεν αὐτοὺς καθεύδοντας, ἦσαν γὰρ αὐτῶν οἱ ὀφθαλμοὶ καταβαρυνόμενοι καὶ οὐκ ᾔδεισαν τί ἀποκριθῶσιν αὐτῷ, "And again, coming, he found them sleeping, for their eyes were heavy, and they did not know how they should answer him." Jesus' exhortation in vv 37–38 has had little effect; the disciples have dozed off again. The description of the heaviness of the disciples' eyes refers to their sleepiness, not to their sheepishness in the presence of a disappointed Jesus (*pace* Gundry, 856). "From sorrow" is Luke's better excuse for Mark's "their eyes were heavy" (cf. *Comment* on v 37). But Mark's οὐκ ᾔδεισαν τί ἀποκριθῶσιν αὐτῷ, "they did not know how they should answer him," does refer to the disciples' embarrassment. The disciples simply cannot excuse themselves. Twice now they have slumbered, thus letting down their master.

41 καὶ ἔρχεται τὸ τρίτον καὶ λέγει αὐτοῖς, καθεύδετε τὸ λοιπὸν καὶ ἀναπαύεσθε, "And he comes the third time, and says to them, 'Are you still sleeping and resting?'" The triad of the disciples' failures adumbrates the triad of Peter's forthcoming denials. Their inability shows that the disciples are not up to the challenge that they soon will face in sharp contrast to the intense, prepared, praying Jesus. Gundry (857) takes the Greek verbs καθεύδετε and ἀναπαύεσθε as imperatival, not as interrogatory or accusatory. He thinks that Jesus speaks with exasperation: "Sleep for the remainder [of the time till the betrayer has drawn near] and rest." But that is unlikely, for in the same breath Jesus says, "The hour has come!" Would Jesus, even in exasperation, have told his disciples to go on sleeping when he knew the enemy's approach was near? This seems improbable. Moreover, the interrogative parallels the question in v 37, "Simon, are you sleeping?" The interrogative therefore is to be preferred.

ἀπέχει ἦλθεν ἡ ὥρα, "Is it far off? The hour has come!" The meaning of ἀπέχει is difficult (see *Note* k above). It is often translated "it is enough" (e.g., KJV, ASV, RSV, NASB, NRSV), meaning either that the disciples have slept enough or that Jesus has scolded them enough. Admittedly, ἀπέχειν has a wide semantic range, but "to be far off" or "to be far away" is the most common meaning (cf. LXX Isa 29:13 [quoted in Mark 7:6, the only other place in Mark where ἀπέχειν occurs]; 54:14; 55:9; Ezek 8:6; 11:15; 22:5; Joel 4:8[3:8]; intransitive use cited in LSJ: "to be away" or "to be far from"). The usage in the LXX should take precedence over the less germane evidence found in some papyri (cf. Field, *Notes,* 39; even the papyri [MM, 57–58] attest the meaning "to be far away" when intransitive).

Aramaic specialists have suggested that ἀπέχει reflects either misunderstanding or misreading of the underlying Aramaic. According to Torrey (*Our Translated Gospels,* 56, 58–59; cf. id., *Four Gospels,* 103), the Greek translator misunderstood the Aramaic כַּדּוּ *kaddû,* because in Syriac it means "enough" (equivalent of the Latin *satis,* "enough" or "sufficient"). But the true meaning is "already." Accordingly, Mark's original text would have read "Would you sleep now, and take your rest? Already the time has come" (*Our Translated Gospels,* 56). Black (*Aramaic Approach,* 225–26) disagrees with Torrey, pointing out that כַּדּוּ *kaddû* in both Aramaic and Syriac means "now" (equivalent to the Latin *iam,* "now" or "already"), something the translator would surely have known. Moreover, why would the translator choose ἀπέχει to express *satis est,* "it is enough," when the adjective ἱκανός, "sufficient," which occurs many times in the LXX and the NT (cf. Mark 15:15), or the verb ἀρκεῖν, "to suffice, satisfy, be enough," which occurs several times in the LXX and NT, would be more expected? Black accepts the reading in D (cf. W Θ and other authorities): ἀπέχει τὸ τέλος καὶ ἡ ὥρα, "far-off is the end and the hour." Because this meaning flies in the face of the context, Black suspects that the original Aramaic דְחֵיק *dĕḥêq,* "press, urge," was misread as רחיק *rĕḥîq,* "be distant, far off," a meaning illustrated in *b. Ber.* 64a: "He who tries to press the hour, him the hour presses." Accordingly, he thinks Jesus' saying originally was "The end and the hour are pressing." Taylor (556–57) also accepts D's reading of τὸ τέλος, "the end," and has sympathy for Black's suggestion. However, in the end he favors the older view set forth by Hudson (*ExpTim* 46 [1934–35] 382), who accepted D's reading and understood ἀπέχει as meaning "far away." Accordingly, Taylor (557) thinks Jesus' words originally were "Still asleep? Still resting? The End is far away? The hour has struck. Behold, the Son of Man is being delivered into the hands of sinners." The views of Hudson and Taylor are to be preferred, but it may not be necessary to accept the reading τὸ τέλος, which may be a scribal gloss that correctly captures the sense of ἀπέχει, "far off." Even without τὸ τέλος, the meaning seems clear enough: "Is it [i.e., the end] far off? [On the contrary,] the hour has come!" Taking ἀπέχει in this sense is favored because (1) "it is far off" is its most common meaning, and (2) it makes better sense in context; that is, the second question meaningfully follows up on the first question: Are the disciples still sleeping? Do they think they have plenty of time since the danger, the temptation of which Jesus has spoken, is far removed?

More recently, Müller (*ZNW* 77 [1986] 83–100) has suggested that ἀπέχει should be understood as the imperfect, third-person singular (ἀπεχεῖ), from the verb ἀποχεῖν, "to pour out." The meaning would then be that God has poured out his judgment into the cup that Jesus sees before him: "It was poured out." But this meaning seems strained; if Jesus fears drinking the cup of divine wrath (with which he the shepherd will be struck down), why would he say "It was poured out"? Why not something like "I shall drink it" or "I have drunk it"? Other options are listed in Cranfield, 435–36.

ἰδοὺ παραδίδοται ὁ υἱὸς τοῦ ἀνθρώπου εἰς τὰς χεῖρας τῶν ἁμαρτωλῶν, "Behold, the 'son of man' is delivered into the hands of sinners!" Jesus' declaration harks back to his passion predictions (8:31; 9:31; 10:33–34), e.g., "The 'son of man' is delivered into human hands" (9:31). What Jesus had several times predicted is now beginning to be fulfilled. The three disciples with Jesus would also have thought back to the Last Supper, concluded only a few hours earlier (14:18–21). The reference here to ἁμαρτωλῶν, "sinners," is ironic, given the criticism that Jesus' opponents had leveled against him earlier in his ministry: "Why does he eat with tax collectors and sinners [ἁμαρτωλῶν]?" (2:16). Those who had criticized Jesus for associating with sinners are now themselves acting as sinners in the worst way. Sinful opposition to the person and ministry of the "son of man" is thematic in the Markan Gospel: "For whoever should be ashamed of me and my words in this adulterous and sinful generation, indeed the 'son of man' will be ashamed of him" (8:38). Jesus' words, "delivered into the hands of sinners," may echo Ps 140:8 (LXX 139:9): μὴ παραδῷς με κύριε ἀπὸ τῆς ἐπιθυμίας μου ἁμαρτωλῷ, "Deliver me not, O Lord, to the sinner because of my lust."

42 ἐγείρεσθε, ἄγωμεν, "Arise; let us be going." Though the disciples have failed as sentries and fellow prayer warriors, Jesus nevertheless urges them to prepare to meet the approaching enemy. In military contexts ἄγωμεν is used as a command, "Forward," "March," or "Advance!" Similarly, Jesus has ordered his disciples to ready themselves (Anderson, 321).

ἰδοὺ ὁ παραδιδούς με ἤγγικεν, "Behold, the one who is betraying me has arrived." Jesus' prescience is here demonstrated. Before the actual arrival of the party sent out by the ruling priests, scribes, and elders (14:43), Jesus already knows who they are. Even more impressive, he knows that Judas Iscariot himself is with them, for Judas is the "one who is betraying"; the other men are no more than servants of their masters.

Explanation

Following the Last Supper, Jesus retires to the Mount of Olives to a place called Gethsemane with the disciples Peter, James, and John. He asks them to remain nearby and watch while he himself goes further and falls on the ground and prays that, if possible, the hour of trial might pass (vv 34b–35). The prayer itself, "Abba, Father. . . . Remove this cup from me" (v 35), reveals the human Jesus who recoils from the coming suffering. But it also paints an impressive picture. Jesus is fully aware of the severity of the trial that lies ahead. No aspect of it—the arrest, the abuse, the interrogations, the beatings, or the crucifixion itself—will take him by surprise. Mark's portrait is of one who is the master of the situation, not of a fanatic who in bewilderment sees his plans go awry.

The metaphor of the cup reminds us of the question that Jesus had earlier put to James and John: "Are you able to drink the cup that I drink? . . . The cup that I drink you will drink" (10:38–39). Before entering Jerusalem, Jesus had anticipated that he would have to drink the cup of suffering and death. The implication is that his disciples (indeed, all Christians) will face the same trials. Jesus' repeated prayers contrasted with the disciples' repeated failures to keep awake puts Jesus in a complimentary light. Indeed, Peter's falling asleep three times (vv 37, 40, 41) may be intended by the evangelist to parallel his later three denials. While Jesus gains strength through prayer, his disciples lose spiritual fortitude, thus becoming vulnerable to fear and faithlessness. There is in this dramatic scene a lesson for every Christian.

Jesus' prayer that God can do all things, even take away the cup of suffering, underscores the idea that Jesus' suffering is God's will. It is not Jesus' wish, but it is God's; and Jesus accepts it (v 36). His abrupt announcement, "The hour has come! Behold, the 'son of man' is delivered into the hands of sinners!" (v 41), again shows Jesus to be very much in control of the situation. Nothing has taken him by surprise. Ironically, it is Jesus who announces the arrival of the betrayer (v 42), not his feckless disciples who were supposed to be keeping watch.

H. The Betrayal and Arrest of Jesus (14:43–52)

Bibliography

Argyle, A. W. "The Meaning of καθ᾽ ἡμέραν in Mark xiv.49." *ExpTim* 63 (1951–52) 354. **Belcher, F. W.** "A Comment on Mark xiv.45." *ExpTim* 64 (1952–53) 240. **Benoit, P.** *The Passion and Resurrection of Jesus.* 25–48. **Black, M.** "The Arrest and Trial of Jesus and the Date of the Last Supper." In *New Testament Essays.* FS T. W. Manson, ed. A. J. B. Higgins. Manchester: Manchester UP, 1959. 19–33. **Blinzler, J.** *The Trial of Jesus: The Jewish and Roman Proceedings against Jesus Christ Described and Assessed from the Oldest Accounts.* Westminster: Newman, 1959. 174–216. **Broer, I.** *Die Urgemeinde und das Grab Jesu: Eine Analyse der Grablegungsgeschichte im Neuen Testament.* SANT 31. Munich: Kösel, 1972. 79–200. **Bruce, F. F.** *The 'Secret' Gospel of Mark.* Ethel M. Wood Lecture. London: Athlone, 1974 (repr. in F. F. Bruce. *The Canon of Scripture.* Downers Grove, IL: InterVarsity Press, 1988. 298–315). **Cantinat, J.** "Jésus devant le Sanhédrin." *NRT* 75 (1953) 300–308. **Cosby, M. R.** "Mark 14:51–52 and the Problem of the Gospel Narrative." *PRSt* 11 (1984) 219–31. **Crossan, J. D.** *Four Other Gospels: Shadows on the Contours of Canon.* Sonoma: Polebridge, 1992. 59–83. ———. "Thoughts on Two Extracanonical Gospels." *Semeia* 49 (1990) 155–68. **Derrett, J. D. M.** "The Iscariot, Meṣira, and the Redemption." *JSNT* 8 (1980) 2–23. ———. "Peter's Sword and Biblical Methodology." *BeO* 32 (1990) 180–92. **Dibelius, M.** "Judas und der Judaskuss." In *Botschaft und Geschichte: Gesammelte Aufsätze.* Ed. G. Bornkamm and H. Kraft. 2 vols. Tübingen: Mohr-Siebeck, 1953. 1:272–77. **Doeve, J. W.** "Die Gefangennahme Jesu in Gethsemane: Eine traditionsgeschichtliche Untersuchung." *SE* 1 [= TU 73] (1959) 458–80. **Dormeyer, D.** *Die Passion Jesu.* 138–50. **Dreisbach, A. R., Jr.** "Mark 14:51–52: Historical 'Fact' or Sindonological 'Spy-Clue.'" In *Symposium Proceedings: History, Science, Theology and the Shroud.* Ed. A. Berard. Amarillo, TX: Privately published, 1991. 113–23. **Emmet, P. B.** "St. Mark xiv.45." *ExpTim* 50 (1938–39) 93. **Field, F.** *Notes.* 40. **Fleddermann, H.** "The Flight of a Naked Young Man (Mark 14:51–52)." *CBQ* 41 (1979) 412–18. **Fortna, R. T.** "Sayings of the Suffering and Risen Christ: The Quadruple Tradition." *Forum* 3.3 (1987) 63–69. **Gourgues, M.** "À propos du symbolisme christologique et baptismal de Marc 16.5." *NTS* 27 (1981) 672–78. **Grappe, C.** "Jésus: Messie prétendu ou Messie prétendant? Entre les catégories de messianité revendiquée et de messianité prétendue." In *Jésus de Nazareth: Nouvelles approches d'une énigme.* Ed. D. Marguerat et al. Le monde de la Bible 38. Paris: Labor et Fides, 1998. 269–91. **Hall, S. G.** "Swords of Offence." *SE* 1 [= TU 73] (1959) 499–502. **Haren, M. J.** "The Naked Young Man: A Historian's Hypothesis on Mark 14,51–52." *Bib* 79 (1998) 525–31. **Horsley, R. A.** "Les groupes juifs palestiniens et leurs messies à la fin de l'époque du second Temple." *Concilium* 245 (1993) 29–46. ———. "Popular Messianic Movements around the Time of Jesus." *CBQ* 46 (1981) 409–32. ———. "Popular Prophetic Movements at the Time of Jesus: Their Principal Features and Social Origins." *JSNT* 26 (1986) 3–27. **Jackson, H. M.** "Why the Youth Shed His Cloak and Fled Naked: The Meaning and Purpose of Mark 14:51–52." *JBL* 116 (1997) 273–89. **Kermode, F.** *The Genesis of Secrecy: On the Interpretation of Narrative.* Cambridge, MA; London: Harvard UP, 1979. 55–64. **Klauck, H.-J.** *Judas, ein Jünger des Herrn.* QD 111. Freiburg: Herder, 1987. 64–70. **Knox, J.** "A Note on Mark 14:51–52." In *The Joy of Study.* FS F. C. Grant, ed. S. E. Johnson. New York: Macmillan, 1951. 27–30. **Koester, H.** *Ancient Christian Gospels: Their History and Development.* London: SCM Press; Philadelphia: Trinity Press International, 1990. 293–303. ———. "History and Development of Mark's Gospel (From Mark to Secret Mark and 'Canonical Mark')." In *Colloquy on New Testament Studies.* Ed. B. Corley. Macon, GA: Mercer UP, 1983. 35–57. **Kremer, J.** *Das Ärgernis des Kreuzes: Eine Hinführung zum Verstehen der Leidensgeschichte nach Markus.* Stuttgart: Katholisches Bibelwerk, 1969. 41–45. **Krieger, N.**

"Der Knecht des Hohenpriesters." *NovT* 2 (1957) 73–74. **Linnemann, E.** *Studien zur Passionsgeschichte.* 41–69. **McIndoe, J. H.** "The Young Man at the Tomb." *ExpTim* 80 (1968–69) 125. **McVann, M. E.** "Conjectures about a Guilty Bystander: The Sword Slashing in Mark 14:47." *Listening* 21 (1986) 124–37. **Merkel, H.** "Auf den Spuren des Urmarkus? Ein neuer Fund und seine Beurteilung." *ZTK* 71 (1974) 123–44. ———. "'Secret Gospel' of Mark." In *Gospels and Related Writings.* Vol. 1 of *New Testament Apocrypha.* Ed. W. Schneemelcher. Rev. ed. Cambridge: James Clarke; Louisville: Westminster John Knox Press, 1991. 106–9. **Meyer, M. W.** "The Youth in the *Secret Gospel of Mark.*" *Semeia* 49 (1990) 129–53. **Mohr, T. A.** *Markus- und Johannespassion.* 249–51. **Morrice, W. G.** "The Imperatival ἵνα." *BT* 23 (1972) 326–30. **Myllykoski, M.** *Die letzten Tage Jesu.* 158–67. **Neirynck, F.** "La fuite du jeune homme en Mc 14,51–52." *ETL* 55 (1979) 43–66 (repr. in F. Neirynck. *Evangelica: Gospel Studies—Études d'Évangile.* Ed. F. Van Segbroeck. BETL 60. Leuven: Peeters and Leuven UP, 1982. 215–38). **Nestle, E.** "Zum Judaskuss." *ZNW* 15 (1914) 92–93. **Nolle, L.** "The Young Man in Mk. xiv.51." *Scr* 2 (1947) 113–14. **Pesch, R.** *Das Evangelium der Urgemeinde.* 179–83. **Quesnel, Q.** "The Mar Saba Clementine: A Question of Evidence." *CBQ* 37 (1975) 48–67. **Ross, J. M.** "The Young Man Who Fled Naked." *IBS* 13 (1991) 170–74. **Rostovtzeff, M. I.** "οὖς δεξιὸν ἀποτέμνειν." *ZNW* 33 (1934) 196–99. **Saunderson, B.** "Gethsemane: The Missing Witness." *Bib* 70 (1989) 224–33. **Schenk, W.** *Der Passionsbericht nach Markus.* 206–15. **Schenke, H.-M.** "The Mystery of the Gospel of Mark." *SecCent* 4 (1984) 65–82. **Schenke, L.** *Der gekreuzigte Christus.* 111–24. **Schneider, G.** "Die Verhaftung Jesu: Traditionsgeschichte von Mk 14,43–52." *ZNW* 63 (1972) 188–209. ———. *Die Passion Jesu.* 43–50. **Schnellbächer, E. L.** "Das Rätsel des νεανίσκος bei Markus." *ZNW* 73 (1982) 127–35. **Schwarz, G.** *Jesus und Judas.* 184–96. **Scroggs, R.,** and **Groff, K. I.** "Baptism in Mark: Dying and Rising with Christ." *JBL* 92 (1973) 531–48, esp. 536–40. **Sellew, P.** "*Secret Mark* and the History of Canonical Mark." In *The Future of Early Christianity.* FS H. Koester, ed. B. A. Pearson. Minneapolis: Fortress, 1991. 242–57. **Smith, M.** *Clement of Alexandria and a Secret Gospel of Mark.* Cambridge: Harvard UP, 1973. **Standaert, B. H. M. G. M.** *L'évangile selon Marc.* 153–68. **Stock, A.** *Call to Discipleship.* 188–90. **Stock, K.** *Boten aus dem Mit-Ihm-Sein.* 150–54. **Suhl, A.** "Die Funktion des Schwertsreichs in den synoptischen Erzählungen von der Gefangennahme Jesu: Beobachtungen zur Komposition und Theologie der synoptischen Evangelien: Mk 14,43–52; Mt 26,47–56; Lk 22,47–53." In *The Gospels 1992.* FS F. Neirynck, ed. F. Van Segbroeck et al. 3 vols. BETL 100. Leuven: Peeters and Leuven UP, 1992. 1:295–323. **Trudinger, L. P.** "Davidic Links with the Betrayal of Jesus: Some Further Observations." *ExpTim* 86 (1974–75) 278–79. **Vanhoye, A.** "La fuite du jeune homme nu (Mc 14,51–52)." *Bib* 52 (1971) 401–6. **Viviano, B. T.** "The High Priest's Servant's Ear: Mark 14:47." *RB* 96 (1989) 71–80. **Vogler, W.** *Judas Iskarioth: Untersuchungen zu Tradition und Redaktion von Texten des Neuen Testaments und ausserkanonischer Schriften.* Theologische Arbeiten 42. Berlin: Evangelische Verlagsanstalt, 1983. 47–51. **Waetjen, H.** "The Ending of Mark and the Gospel's Shift in Eschatology." *ASTI* 4 (1965) 114–31, esp. 114–21. **Westcott, B. F.,** and **Hort, F. J. A.** *Introduction.* 2:27.

Translation

[43]*And immediately, while he was still speaking, Judas,*[a] *one of the Twelve, appears, and with him a* [b]*crowd with swords and clubs, [sent] from the ruling priests and the scribes and the elders.* [44]*But the one betraying him had given them a sign, saying, "Whomever I should kiss is he. Seize him, and lead him away under guard."* [45]*And when he had come, immediately approaching him,*[c] *he says,*[d] *"Rabbi!"*[e] *And he kissed him.* [46]*But they laid hands on him and seized him.* [47]*But [a certain] one of those standing by, having drawn a sword, struck* [f] *the servant of the high priest and cut off his ear.*[g] [48]*And responding, Jesus said to them, "As against an insurrectionist have you come out with swords*

and clubs to take me? [49]*Daily I was with you in the temple teaching, and you did not seize me. But in order that the Scriptures* [h] *should be fulfilled!"* [50]*And abandoning him, they* [i] *all fled.* [51]*And a certain young man was following him, with a linen sheet wrapped around his naked [body].* [j] *And they* [k] *seize him.* [52]*But leaving his linen sheet, the naked man fled.* [l]

Notes

[a]A Φ and several later MSS read ὁ Ἰσκαριώτης, "Iscariot"; D reads Σκαριώτης, "Scariot." On the variety of spellings and forms of this name, see *Note* a on Mark 14:10.

[b]A C D N W Σ Φ and a few later MSS and versions read ὄχλος πολύς, "great crowd" (cf. Matt 26:47).

[c]A few late MSS read προσελθὼν προσεκύνει αὐτῷ, "and approaching, he bowed to him." This appears to be a Matthean import (cf. Matt 8:2; 9:18; 15:25; 20:20; 28:9).

[d]N Σ and a few later MSS read τῷ Ἰησοῦ, "to Jesus."

[e]C² W Φ and several later MSS read χαῖρε, ῥαββί, "Greetings, Rabbi" (cf. Matt 26:49).

[f]Gk. ἔπαισεν. ℵ C D L W and several later MSS read ἔπεσεν, "he attacked."

[g]A few late authorities read τὸ ὠτάριον τὸ δεξιόν, "right ear." The addition of the adj. reflects Luke 22:50; John 18:10.

[h]N W Φ and several later MSS and versions add τῶν προφητῶν, "of the prophets," an addition inspired by Matt 26:56.

[i]N Σ and several later MSS add οἱ μαθηταί, "the disciples"; W adds οἱ μαθηταὶ αὐτοῦ, "his disciples" (cf. Matt 26:56).

[j]Gk. ἐπὶ γυμνοῦ, lit. "on naked." The word *body* has been added. A few OL MSS read *supra nudum corpus,* "over [his] naked body."

[k]W and a few later MSS read οἱ δὲ νεανίσκοι, "and the young men," which has been added to supply the verb with a subject; cf. Westcott-Hort, *Introduction* 2:27. The noun itself was suggested by its appearance at the beginning of the verse.

[l]A D N W Σ Φ and several later MSS and authorities add ἀπ' αὐτῶν, "from them." Metzger (*TCGNT* [1], 115) explains that this addition "is a natural expansion that refers to the unexpressed subject of κρατοῦσιν ['they seize']."

Form/Structure/Setting

With his arrest Jesus' passion predictions (8:31; 9:31; 10:33–34) now begin their fulfillment. In his usual vivid and direct manner, the evangelist narrates Jesus' arrest, the brief scuffle that ensues, the flight of the disciples, and the strange mention of the young man who flees naked. The pericope is made up of four parts, though it could be further subdivided: (1) The identification and arrest of Jesus (vv 43–46), (2) the wounding of the high priest's servant (v 47), (3) Jesus' rebuke of those arresting him (vv 48–49), and (4) the flight of the disciples and the curious notice of the young man (vv 50–52).

Bultmann (*History,* 268–69) believes that the story of the arrest of Jesus originally followed 14:27–31 (the walk to the Mount of Olives) and that it is "coloured by legend in the motif of the betrayal by a kiss and by what Jesus says in vv. 48f., which sounds very much like Church apologetics and dogmatics." Bultmann may be right with regard to his first point. Taylor (558) suspects 14:1–2, 10–11, 12–16, 17–21, 26–31, and 43–52 made up the original "narrative framework on which the Passion Narrative is built." But the story contains little that the early church would have cared to invent. The treachery of Judas, kiss and all, is not easily explained as apologetic. The injury of the high priest's servant, the flight of the disciples, and the odd notice of the young man who flees naked put the disciples,

who were to become the major apostles of the early church, in such an unflatter-
ing light that one may well wonder how such details can be explained as the
products of pious imagination, dogmatics, or apologetics. Jesus' retort in vv 48–
49 is very much what we should have expected him to say under the circumstances.
Jesus has shown no violent tendencies, heads up no army, and has threatened no
one, yet he is attacked. His indignation is perfectly understandable. The only
element that could pass as dogmatics or apologetics is his cry "But in order that
the Scriptures should be fulfilled!" (v 49b). But given the evangelist's very limited interest in scriptural fulfillment (Suhl, *Zitate*), this utterance is better explained
as dominical rather than redactional. The historical Jesus *did* believe that Scripture was being fulfilled in his ministry. How else would he have interpreted such
an incident? Was it a sign of the failure of his ministry? Was it an invalidation of
his calling? Certainly not. It too, like other events, was part of the divine plan,
foretold in the Scriptures.

Bultmann is right, of course, to note that legendary elements do find their
way into the story. We are told elsewhere that it was the right ear that was injured
(Luke 22:50; John 18:10), that the injured servant was named Malchus (John
18:10), that Jesus healed the injured servant (Luke 22:51), and that the disciple
who struck the servant was none other than Simon Peter (John 18:10). Items of
conversation attributed to Jesus (Matt 26:50, 52–53; Luke 22:48, 51, 53; John 18:4,
5, 7, 8, 11), the disciples (Luke 22:49), and even those arresting Jesus (John 18:5,
7) have also been added (while Matthew and Luke omit mention of the flight of
the young man). But we should not assume that all these details that appear in
Gospels written after Mark necessarily have no basis in fact. Mark may very well
have abridged his tradition since he has done so elsewhere (e.g., in the description of the Lord's Supper, 14:22–25).

Comment

43   καὶ εὐθὺς ἔτι αὐτοῦ λαλοῦντος παραγίνεται Ἰούδας εἷς τῶν δώδεκα, "And
immediately, while he was still speaking, Judas, one of the Twelve, appears." True
to Jesus' prediction in 14:17–21, his betrayer proved to be "one of the Twelve"
(14:20). The horror of this act from the perspective of Jesus' movement lay in
the fact that the Twelve represented a repentant and restored Israel, the foundation for a new beginning. Jesus himself had appointed the Twelve, entrusted his
message of the kingdom to them, empowered them to do his work of healing
and exorcism (3:13–19; 6:7–13), and promised them positions of authority in the
coming kingdom (by inference in 10:40–45; explicitly in Matt 19:28 = Luke 22:28–
30). Judas's betrayal constituted much more than simply the perfidy of one who
had previously professed loyalty and commitment to the cause. Judas betrayed
Jesus, "the son of man," to whom divine authority and kingdom had been entrusted and upon whom the very fate of Israel rested. Judas betrayed Israel as
much as he betrayed his master and friend.

As Jesus finished speaking, Judas Iscariot appeared καὶ μετ᾽ αὐτοῦ ὄχλος μετὰ
μαχαιρῶν καὶ ξύλων παρὰ τῶν ἀρχιερέων καὶ τῶν γραμματέων καὶ τῶν πρεσβυτέρων,
"and with him a crowd with swords and clubs, [sent] from the ruling priests and
the scribes and the elders." The existence of thugs armed with clubs working for
the ruling priests is attested in the turmoil of Jerusalem in the late 50s and early

60s. According to Josephus, "Such was the shamelessness and effrontery which possessed the ruling priests that they actually were so brazen as to send slaves to the threshing floors to receive the tithes that were due to the priests, with the result that the poorer priests starved to death" (*Ant.* 20.8.8 §181). Later, Josephus narrates: "But Ananias had servants who were utter rascals and who, combining operations with the most reckless men, would go to the threshing floors and take by force the tithes of the priests; nor did they refrain from beating those who refused to give. The ruling priests were guilty of the same practices as his slaves, and no one could stop them" (*Ant.* 20.9.2 §§206–7). Later rabbinic traditions recalled with chagrin the violence and oppression of the ruling priests in the first century C.E. (e.g., *t. Menaḥ.* 13.19–21; *t. Zebaḥ.* 11.16–17; *b. Pesaḥ.* 57a; *b. Yebam.* 86a–b; *b. Ketub.* 26a). First-century priestly corruption is attested in the *Testament of Moses,* which describes the ruling priests as avaricious, corrupt, thieving, and proud (5:3–6:1; 7:1–10, the latter passage being especially pertinent). Similar criticisms are lodged in the Dead Sea Scrolls (e.g., 1QpHab 8:12; 9:5; 10:1; 12:10; 4QpNah 1:11). The arrest of Jesus attests a similar strong-armed enforcement operative some thirty years earlier. The rough treatment of Jesus ben Ananias during the 60s (*J.W.* 6.5.3 §§300–309), who like Jesus of Nazareth appealed to Jer 7 and spoke of the temple's doom, fits this pattern of violence and intimidation.

44 δεδώκει δὲ ὁ παραδιδοὺς αὐτὸν σύσσημον αὐτοῖς λέγων, ὃν ἂν φιλήσω αὐτός ἐστιν, κρατήσατε αὐτὸν καὶ ἀπάγετε ἀσφαλῶς, "But the one betraying him had given them a sign, saying, 'Whomever I should kiss is he. Seize him, and lead him away under guard.'" In the darkness it was necessary for Jesus to be identified quite specifically, lest he bolt and elude capture. This is why Judas approaches Jesus, his "rabbi" (master or teacher), and, as a rabbi's *ḥābēr* (associate or disciple), kisses him (v 45). Not only would the quick and certain identification of Jesus be difficult in the dark, but most, if not all, of the men sent to arrest Jesus may not have seen him before and so would not have been able to identify him, even in broad daylight. ἀσφαλῶς, "under guard," is literally "safely" or "securely." However, in contexts such as the present one, where securing a fugitive or prisoner is in view, the adverb means "under guard." Judas has urged the men from the ruling priests to take care to secure Jesus. After all, if he should get away, Judas would not receive the promised payment.

45 καὶ ἐλθὼν εὐθὺς προσελθὼν αὐτῷ λέγει, ῥαββί, καὶ κατεφίλησεν αὐτόν, "And when he had come, immediately approaching him, he says, 'Rabbi!' And he kissed him." When Judas and company arrive, he immediately goes up to Jesus and greets him. Judas has wasted no time; he has moved quickly and has given Jesus no opportunity to attempt an escape. Judas has served the ruling priests well, not only by taking their servants to a lonely place at night, where Jesus would have few allies and no sympathetic crowds that could be counted on to fly to his assistance, but also by identifying Jesus with the prearranged sign, the kiss, a sign of affection and respect that a disciple has for his rabbi. Using this respectful greeting only heightens Judas's villainy and gives his actions a touch of hypocrisy. Lachs (416) points out that it was considered presumptuous for a disciple to address his rabbi first. On rabbis kissing colleagues or disciples, see 1 Esdr 4:47; *t. Ḥag.* 2.1; *b. Ḥag.* 14b; *b. Soṭah* 13a; *Pesiq. Rab Kah.* 1.3; *Qoh. Rab.* 6:2 §1; 9:5 §1. One also thinks of 2 Sam 20:9–10, where Joab (a soldier) kisses Amasa and then kills him.

46 οἱ δὲ ἐπέβαλον τὰς χεῖρας αὐτῷ καὶ ἐκράτησαν αὐτόν, "But they laid hands on him and seized him." Now that Jesus has been identified, the priests' deputies seize him, no doubt wishing to make him secure as Judas had urged. Seizure at night was intended to render Jesus' following leaderless and so discourage a coordinated counterattack (which those doing the priests' bidding may have feared). In biblical parlance, to "lay hands on" someone is to arrest or attack someone (e.g., Gen 22:12; 2 Sam 18:12; 2 Kgs 11:16; 2 Chr 23:15; Neh 13:21; Esth 2:21; 3:6; 6:2; 8:7; 9:12; Job 41:8; Acts 4:3; 5:18; 12:1; 21:27), though the same or similar words are also used to describe benevolent contact, either to bless or heal (as in Mark 6:5; 8:23, 25; 10:16).

47 εἷς δέ [τις] τῶν παρεστηκότων σπασάμενος τὴν μάχαιραν ἔπαισεν τὸν δοῦλον τοῦ ἀρχιερέως καὶ ἀφεῖλεν αὐτοῦ τὸ ὠτάριον, "But [a certain] one of those standing by, having drawn a sword, struck the servant of the high priest and cut off his ear." Reacting to this seizure, someone draws his sword and strikes the servant of the high priest, cutting off his ear (perhaps "ear lobe," for οὖς is the normal word for "ear," while ὠτάριον is found in the papyri in reference to the handle of a vessel; cf. MM, 704). The singular τοῦ ἀρχιερέως, "the high priest" (cf. 14:53, 60–61, 63, 66), in contrast to the plural τῶν ἀρχιερέων, "the ruling priests," in v 43 (cf. 8:31; 10:33; 11:18, 27; 14:1, 10), refers specifically to the high priest (and not simply to one of the ruling priests; Gundry, 879). Mark's ἔπαισεν, "struck," is not the best word to use in reference to a sword (παίειν usually means "to strike with the fist" or in colloquial speech "to slug" someone; cf. Matt 26:68 = Luke 22:64, where a blindfolded Jesus is buffeted about the head; LXX Num 22:28; Job 16:10; Lam 3:30). Both Matthew (26:51) and Luke (22:50) substitute the more appropriate πατάσσειν, "to strike" (πατάξας, "having struck," and ἐπάταξεν, "struck," respectively; for examples of strike [πατάσσειν] with the sword [μάχαιρα], cf. LXX Num 21:24; Deut 20:13; Josh 19:48; 2 Sam 15:14; 23:10; 2 Kgs 19:37; Isa 37:38; Jer 2:30; 33:23 [Eng. 26:23]). The Matthean/Lukan agreement over against Mark hardly constitutes real evidence against the two-source theory (see "Synoptic Problem" in the *Introduction*).

Brown (1:266–67; cf. van Iersel, 438–39) thinks that the person who struck the servant was neither Peter nor one of the disciples but someone who "belonged to a third group." This is possible, for animosities toward the ruling priests were not limited to Jesus' following. Bystanders who saw a group from the priests attempting to seize Jesus might have reacted violently against them. If one of Jesus' disciples did not commit the assault, however, one wonders why the Gospel tradition subsequently and with increasing specificity credits the violent act to one of the disciples. Jesus' rebuke and saying about living and dying by the sword (Matt 26:52–53) and the disciples' question "Shall we strike with the sword?" (Luke 22:49; cf. 22:35–38) are clear indications that Matthew and Luke thought that the high priest's servant was struck by one of Jesus' disciples. The Fourth Evangelist (John 18:10) specifically names Simon Peter. Although it must be admitted that Mark's "one of those standing by" is ambiguous and could refer to someone other than one of the disciples, the traditional interpretation is still to be preferred.

The disciple who struck the servant of the high priest is identified in John 18:10 as Simon Peter. In popular preaching, as well as in scholarly writing, this incident is regarded as one more impetuous and thoughtless act on the part of Peter. But given what Josephus says about violent men working for the ruling priests, who beat and stole from lower-ranking priests (see *Comment* on v 43), we should perhaps see the disciple's action as a brave attempt to protect Jesus by intercepting a man who was advancing on Jesus to deliver a blow. Peter does not miss his mark, as some preachers say ("All he got was an ear!"; this incident is not intended to be humorous; *pace* van Iersel, 441); rather, Peter lands a serious blow to the side of the servant's head, which among other things takes off a piece of his ear. It may have been that Peter, still smarting from Jesus' prediction that he would not only fall away with the others but would deny Jesus three times before the early morning crowing of the rooster, was eager to prove his loyalty, even if he "must die with" Jesus (cf. 14:31).

Viviano (*RB* 96 [1989] 71–80) argues that the servant of the high priest was not a lowly domestic but rather the prefect of the priests, the chief assistant or deputy of the high priest. The cutting of his ear lobe (ὠτάριον) constituted mutilation and disqualified him from the priestly office (see Lev 21:18; Josephus, *Ant.* 14.13.10 §§365–66; *J.W.* 1.13.9 §§269–70; *t. Parah* 3.8). When compared with literature from antiquity, this incident should not be understood as accidental; it is a symbolic wound intended to shame, not to kill. Viviano concludes, therefore, that this curious detail should be seen within the larger theme of the temple in Mark. Stock (372; id., *Call to Discipleship,* 188–90) finds irony in the incident, commenting that "the high priest's servant is reduced to the status of a robber" because the "loss of an ear was the punishment given a robber since Persian times." The irony is that Jesus was arrested as a robber (λῃστής).

48 ὡς ἐπὶ λῃστὴν ἐξήλθατε μετὰ μαχαιρῶν καὶ ξύλων συλλαβεῖν με, "As against an insurrectionist have you come out with swords and clubs to take me?" Jesus indignantly challenges those who arrest him: "As against an insurrectionist [λῃστήν] . . . ?" λῃστής can be translated as "robber," "brigand," "rebel," or "insurrectionist." The latter meaning is probably what is intended here, for Jesus is never accused of robbery or of any form of violent crime. He will be presented to the Roman governor in 15:1–5 as "king of the Jews." Josephus's use of λῃστής probably offers the best contemporary parallel and should be translated as either "rebel" or better as "insurrectionist." His choice of the word is no doubt pejorative, but it may also reflect popular usage of the term in the first century. There are several individuals who tried to become Israel's king (and perhaps even Messiah): some in the aftermath of the death of Herod the Great in 4 B.C.E. (e.g., Judas son of Hezekiah the "chief brigand" [*Ant.* 17.10.5 §§271–72; *J.W.* 2.4.1 §56]; Simon of Perea [*Ant.* 17.10.6 §§273–76; *J.W.* 2.4.2 §§57–59]; Athronges the shepherd of Judea [*Ant.* 17.10.7 §§278–84; *J.W.* 2.4.3 §§60–65]); at least one in the aftermath of the deposing of Archelaus in 6 C.E. (Judas of Gamala [Acts 5:37; *J.W.* 2.8.1 §118; *Ant.* 18.1.1 §§4–10; 18.1.6 §§23–25; 20.5.2 §102]); several at the outbreak of the war in 66 C.E. and subsequently (e.g., Menahem son of Judas of Galilee [*J.W.* 2.17.8–9 §§433–48]; John of Gischala [*J.W.* 2.20.6 §575; 2.21.1 §§585–89; 4.1.1–5 §§121–46; 4.7.1 §§389–94; 4.9.11 §566; 5.3.1 §§104–5; 5.6.1 §§250–51; 6.9.4 §433]; Simon bar-Giora [*J.W.* 4.9.3–8 §§503–44; 4.9.10 §§556–65; 4.9.11–12 §§573–84; 5.1.3–4 §§11–26; 5.6.1 §§248–54; 5.6.3 §§266–67; 5.7.3 §309; 5.13.1–2 §§527–40; 7.2.2 §§26–36; 7.5.6 §154]); one that we know of during the North African uprising of 115–16 C.E. (Lukuas of Cyrene [Eusebius, *Hist. eccl.* 4.2.1–4; Dio Cassius, *Roman History* 68.32; 69.12–13]; Dio calls this man "Andreas"); and, of course, the famous Simon ben Kosiba (Gk. Χωσιβά), who waged war with the Romans in 132–35 C.E. and whose sobriquet while winning was *bar kôkbā'*, "son of the star," but after his defeat was *bar kôzĕbāʾ*, "son of the lie" (cf. *y. Taʿan.* 4.5; *b. Sanh.* 93b; *b. Giṭ.* 57a–b; *Lam. Rab.* 2:2 §4; Dio Cassius, *Roman History* 59.13.3; Jerome, *Ruf.* 3.31).

In what ways, if any, Jesus compares with the various rebels and insurrectionists of his time is an important question; see Horsley (*CBQ* 46 [1981] 409–32) and Grappe ("Jésus"). The verb συλλαμβάνειν, "to take," often in the sense of "to arrest," is also used by Josephus to describe the arrest of Jesus son of Ananias, the prophet who had offended the ruling priests with his prophecy of the doom of the city and the temple (*J.W.* 6.5.3 §302). This is but one of several interesting parallels between Jesus of Nazareth and Jesus ben Ananias (see *Excursus:* "The Arrest of Jesus Son of Ananias").

49 καθ' ἡμέραν ἤμην πρὸς ὑμᾶς ἐν τῷ ἱερῷ διδάσκων καὶ οὐκ ἐκρατήσατέ με, "Daily I was with you in the temple teaching, and you did not seize me." καθ' ἡμέραν . . . ἐν τῷ ἱερῷ, "daily . . . in the temple," may suggest that Jesus spent more time in Jerusalem than Mark's narrative indicates, possibly supporting the Fourth Gospel's tradition of more time in the holy city (Cranfield, 437). Jesus' activity in the temple precincts is described as διδάσκων, "teaching," which is how Jesus is depicted throughout the Markan narrative (the word appears some seventeen times, mostly in the present and imperfect tenses, emphasizing habitual activity). In the Markan narrative, of course, Jesus is referring primarily to chaps. 11–12 (e.g., 12:14: διδάσκαλε, οἴδαμεν ὅτι ἀληθὴς εἶ . . . ἐπ' ἀληθείας τὴν ὁδὸν τοῦ θεοῦ διδάσκεις, "teacher, we know that you are true . . . you truly teach the way of God"; 12:35: ὁ Ἰησοῦς ἔλεγεν διδάσκων ἐν τῷ ἱερῷ, "Jesus was speaking, while teaching in the temple"). Jesus makes the point that had temple authorities wanted him, they could have taken him openly and in public. Instead, they have interrupted him during a time of private prayer. The implication is that the temple authorities have resorted to this tactic because they know that their actions would not win the approval of the public. Jesus' πρὸς ὑμᾶς, "with you," implies that some of those arresting him were present in the temple precincts, probably as security.

ἀλλ' ἵνα πληρωθῶσιν αἱ γραφαί, "But in order that the Scriptures should be fulfilled!" Jesus is unfazed; his time in prayer has prepared him for this moment. Therefore, he is able to believe that his arrest is happening "in order that the Scriptures should be fulfilled." Mark's reader immediately thinks of 9:12: "how is it written about the 'son of man'? That he should suffer many things"; or the more recent prediction of betrayal in 14:21: "For the 'son of man' goes, just as it is written concerning him" (for OT passages that may have been in mind, see *Comment* on 14:21). A verb is implied following the conjunction ἀλλά, "but." Cranfield (437) plausibly suggests γέγονεν, referring to Jesus' arrest. Thus, the whole thought would be: "It has happened, in order that the Scriptures should be fulfilled!" Matthew (26:56) fills out Mark's ellipsis further: "But all this has happened [τοῦτο δὲ ὅλον γέγονεν], in order that the Scriptures of the prophets should be fulfilled" (author's tr.). The formula ἵνα πληρωθῶσιν, "in order that . . . should be fulfilled," is found many times in the NT: six times in Matthew, thirteen times in the Johannine writings, seven times in the Paulines and deutero-Paulines, and once in Revelation. On the necessity of scriptural fulfillment, see *T. Naph.* 7:1: "These things must be fulfilled [δεῖ ταῦτα πληρωθῆναι] at their appropriate time."

Not only is Scripture fulfilled, but Jesus' own predictions begin to be fulfilled. He has been betrayed by one of his disciples, as he had said. And now all of his disciples take flight (v 50), as predicted earlier that night (14:27: "All of you will fall away"). Shortly Mark's readers will learn of Peter's denials. The complete collapse of Jesus' following is seen in the flight of the naked young man. Lane (527) suggests that what we may have here is an allusion to the picture portrayed in Amos 2:16, where in an oracle against Israel the prophet foresees that even the "stout of heart among the mighty shall flee away naked" in the day of judgment. Lane is probably correct, for this idea coheres with the earlier appeal to Zech 13:7, where the shepherd is struck down and the sheep are scattered (see *Comment* on 14:27). In rejecting her Messiah, Israel has brought upon itself judgments described in the prophets; the Scriptures are being fulfilled.

50 καὶ ἀφέντες αὐτὸν ἔφυγον πάντες, "And abandoning him, they all fled." In 14:27 Jesus had predictively told his disciples, "All [πάντες] of you will fall away." πάντες, "all," of his disciples disagreed (vv 29, 31). Now, however, true to Jesus' prediction, πάντες of the disciples flee (the three who had been with him in prayer and however many of the eight who had lingered nearby). In contrast to the placement of πάντες at the front of the sentence in the prediction in v 27, here the evangelist draws attention to πάντες by placing it in last position: "and abandoning him, they fled—all (of them)." By doing this, the evangelist underscores the literal fulfillment of Jesus' prediction.

51 καὶ νεανίσκος τις συνηκολούθει αὐτῷ περιβεβλημένος σινδόνα ἐπὶ γυμνοῦ, καὶ κρατοῦσιν αὐτόν, "And a certain young man was following him, with a linen sheet wrapped around his naked [body]. And they seize him." This is the first appearance of the νεανίσκος τις, "certain young man," in Mark's Gospel. However, in so-called *Secret Mark*, two passages of which are preserved in a letter written by Clement of Alexandria (ca. 180 C.E.), Jesus first meets the young man in Mark 10. If Clement's testimony is accepted, this youth, raised up by Jesus in a manner that reminds us of John 11, came to Jesus by night to be taught the secret of the kingdom of God (cf. Mark 4:11). That it is the same young man seems clear enough: ἔρχεται ὁ νεανίσκος πρὸς αὐτόν· περιβεβλημένος σινδόνα ἐπὶ γυμνοῦ, "the young man comes to him, with a linen sheet wrapped around [his] naked [body]" (Clement, *Letter to Theodore*, folio 2, recto, lines 7–8; for Greek text, see M. Smith, *Clement of Alexandria*, 450, 452). According to Clement, this passage is found in *Secret Mark* after Mark 10:34. Although *Secret Mark* has its defenders, who claim that this Gospel dates to the first century and perhaps predates the Synoptics themselves (e.g., Crossan, *Four Other Gospels*, 59–83; id., "Two Extracanonical Gospels," 161–67; Koester, *Ancient Christian Gospels*, 293–303; id., "History and Development of Mark's Gospel"; M. W. Meyer, *Semeia* 49 [1990] 129–53; Sellew, "*Secret Mark*"), it is probably nothing more than a second-century (Carpocratian?) recension of "public" Mark (as Clement himself maintains), and not the reverse. Moreover, the passage about the young man is judged by critics to be "too Markan" to be from Mark; that is, it is made up almost entirely of vocabulary and phrases drawn from Mark (see Quesnel, *CBQ* 37 [1975] 48–67; as well as the excursus on *Secret Mark* in Gundry, 603–23). It is hard to avoid the conclusion that *Secret Mark*, if such a recension did in fact exist, is little more than a pastiche of Markan materials (cf. E. Best, review of *Redactional Style in the Marcan Gospel*, by E. J. Pryke, *JSNT* 4 [1979] 75–76 [repr. as "Uncanonical Mark" in Best,

Disciples and Discipleship, 197–205]; Bruce, *'Secret' Gospel of Mark*, 12; Merkel, *ZTK* 71 [1974] 123–44, esp. 125–26; id., "'Secret Gospel,'" esp. 107; Neirynck, *ETL* 55 [1979] esp. 50–51; as well as several reviewers of M. Smith's books, e.g., R. M. Grant, *ATR* 56 [1974] 58–64, esp. 61; P. Parker, *ATR* 56 [1974] 53–57, esp. 56; C. C. Richardson, *TS* 35 [1974] 571–77, esp. 575; see "Are the Synoptics the Oldest Gospels?" in *Introduction*).

The evangelist provides us with no clue to the identity of the young man. He has been identified as John son of Zebedee, as John Mark (who in turn has been identified as the author of the Gospel of Mark), as James the brother of Jesus, and so on. He is perhaps related in some way to the young man whom the women encounter at the tomb (16:5–7), but that is far from certain. M. W. Meyer (*Semeia* 49 [1990] 129–53) thinks the young man of 14:51–52 is to be identified with the young man of 16:5 as well as with the man who had observed the Law from his "youth" (10:17–22 [v 20: ἐκ νεότητος]) and the youth in frags. 1 and 2 of *Secret Mark*. There is, however, no good reason to link the young man with the rich man of 10:17–22. Despite the tradition of referring to this man as the "rich young ruler" (his wealth is mentioned in v 22; his status as "ruler" is introduced in Luke 18:18), there is nothing that indicates that he was a νεανίσκος, "young man." Saying that he had observed the Law from his "youth" (v 20) does not necessarily imply that he was still a youth at the time of his conversation with Jesus. Appealing to *Secret Mark*, which has been judged as late and secondary, cannot shed any light on the question of the identity of the young man. Tradition has held that this curious story, which both Matthew and Luke understandably chose to omit, may be autobiographical. Cranfield (439) speculates further by suggesting that this figure, hearing of Judas's treachery, had dressed hurriedly and had dashed outside to warn Jesus of the approach of the party sent to arrest him. This may be the case, but we should translate περιβεβλημένος σινδόνα as "a linen sheet wrapped around" the young man's body, not "thrown over" as though in haste (cf. Acts 12:8; Diogenes Laertius 6.90; Field, *Notes*, 40). Cranfield's suggestion is plausible, but it is no more than speculation, as he himself admits (curiously, J. F. Williams, *Other Followers of Jesus*, 194–203, discusses the young man of 16:5–7 but says nothing of the young man of 14:51–52).

52 ὁ δὲ καταλιπὼν τὴν σινδόνα γυμνὸς ἔφυγεν, "But leaving his linen sheet, the naked man fled." The language used to describe the flight of the naked youth is reminiscent of Joseph's story about his escape from Potiphar's wife: κρατεῖ τὰ ἱμάτιά μου, γυμνὸς ἔφυγον, "she seized my clothes, and I fled naked" (*T. Jos.* 8:3; cf. καταλιπὼν τὰ ἱμάτια αὐτοῦ . . . ἔφυγε, "leaving his clothes . . ., he fled," in LXX Gen 39:12–13). But a Joseph typology seems doubtful. Amos 2:16 has also been suggested as a possible scriptural backdrop: "He who is stout of heart among the mighty shall flee away naked in that day." Ross (*IBS* 13 [1991] 170–74) thinks the incident was historical and so was handed down in the early church because it shows that the crucifixion was an element of the "day of the Lord" as foretold by Amos. The identity of the naked man is irrelevant to the meaning of the passage. However, the LXX Amos 2:16 reads, διώξεται, "will be pursued," not φεύξεται, "will flee." Besides, there is no indication that the young man of Mark would have been regarded "among the mighty." In what sense does he correspond to defeated and frightened troops? Fleeing naked is suggestive, but there is nothing else that points to Amos. Textual variants (such as the omission of ἐπὶ γυμνοῦ, "around his naked [body]" [v 51]) and the omission of vv 51–52 by Matthew and Luke suggest that the young man did indeed flee naked and not, as has been suggested, in his underclothes (as may be the meaning in John 21:7).

Puzzling over this passage has led to a variety of symbolic interpretations. Jackson (*JBL* 116 [1997] 273–89) has drawn attention to blind Bartimaeus, who threw aside his coat (10:50) and followed Jesus. Jackson thinks the two episodes should be studied together, for both men display contrasting yet complementary typologies. Schnellbächer (*ZNW* 73 [1982] 127–35) links the νεανίσκος, "young man," of 14:51–52 with the νεανίσκος of 16:5–7, suggesting that the young man who was stripped of everything at the time of Jesus' arrest is the one who will be restored in appearance after the resurrection, radiantly dressed and seated at the right hand (similarly Gourgues, *NTS* 27 [1981] 675). If so, what would this signify? Schnellbächer thinks that the young man symbolizes Jesus' death and rising, perhaps as a fulfillment of Isa 40:30–31: "Even youths shall faint and be weary, and young men shall fall exhausted; but they who wait for the LORD shall renew their strength, they shall mount up with wings like eagles, they shall run and not be weary, they shall walk and not faint." The parallel seems farfetched. Many other scholars have followed a similar line of interpretation, probing the significance of the twofold mention of a νεανίσκος in 14:51–52 and 16:5–7, each time with reference to a man's clothing (cf. Scroggs and Groff, *JBL* 92 [1973] 531–48; McIndoe, *ExpTim* 80 [1968–69] 125; Vanhoye, *Bib* 52 [1971] 401–6; Waetjen, *ASTI* 4 [1965] 114–31). According to Fleddermann (*CBQ* 41 [1979] 412–18) and Kermode (*Genesis of Secrecy*, 55–64), the young man functions as a type for all Christians who desert the faith because of persecution but may be restored upon returning in faith. According to Cosby (*PRS* 11 [1984] 219–31), this incident teaches that whereas Jesus faces his appointed destiny of suffering in accord with God's will (cf. 14:36), the disciples (who did not keep watch and did not pray) flee into the night, stripped of all their confident expectations of positions of power in the messianic kingdom. However, it is not clear that the naked young man was one of the disciples. More recently, M. W. Meyer (*Semeia* 49 [1990] 145) says of the young man: "Once dressed in the ritual garment of initiation, he has abandoned his baptismal robes and fled." Meyer is following up M. Smith's original idea (*Clement of Alexandria*, 186–87) that *Secret Mark* frag. 1 had originally functioned as part of an early Christian baptismal catechism. But where in *Secret Mark*, or in canonical Mark for that matter, do we find mention of baptism, water, or disrobing and rerobing? (For criticism, see Cosby, *PRS* 11 [1984] 219–31; Gundry, 619–20.)

The point the evangelist is trying to make is probably much simpler than the various theories that have been briefly surveyed. A major point made in Mark 14 is that whereas *Jesus* is prepared for the temptations and dangers that lie ahead, his *disciples* are not. When the arresting party approaches, the disciples fall into panic and disorder. One strikes at the high priest's servant, all flee, and then a young man, perhaps a would-be follower, narrowly escapes, fleeing in utter disgrace. All of this underscores the stunning accuracy of Jesus' prediction that they all would fall away. In stark contrast to his disciples' failure of nerve, Jesus stands his ground, ready to drink the cup that his Father has given him. In the next two passages, Jesus' prophecies will continue to be fulfilled as Peter denies Jesus three times.

Explanation

Preachers have often ridiculed Peter (for it is assumed that Peter was indeed the disciple who lashed out with his sword), speculating that in his rashness he did not take careful aim but only slightly wounded the servant of the high priest. Quite apart from whether the high priest's servant thought his wound was slight, such a line of interpretation is probably off target. Because the deputies were facing Jesus as they attempted to subdue him, the wound in the side of the head suggests that the aggressive disciple had attempted to intercept him. Far from missing, the disciple got his man. But before the altercation could get out of control, Jesus rebuked those who had come to seize him: "As against an insurrectionist have you come out with swords and clubs to take me?" (v 48). Jesus mocked the cowardice and villainy of his captors. He reminded them that daily he had taught in the temple precincts in the very backyard of the ruling priests. If they had wanted to take him, why not on those occasions? No, they could not seize him in public, out in the open, lest an angry public rise up against them. They had to use stealth, bribery, and treachery to take him, thus revealing the sort of men they were.

Mark's first-century readers and auditors would find in this passage a Jesus who stands in sharp contrast with those around him. Jesus' resolve to follow the will of God stands in contrast to the villainy of the arresting party, on the one hand, and to the cowardice and panic of his disciples, on the other. This contrast will continue in the hearing before the Jewish council, where false accusations are hurled at Jesus and where Peter falsely denies knowing Jesus. The evangelist has presented Jesus as a noble figure, one worthy of the Roman world's admiration and respect, one worthy of the Christian community's continuing devotion and allegiance.

I. The Trial of Jesus (and Peter)   (14:53–65)

Bibliography on the Sanhedrin Hearing

Abrahams, I. *Studies in Pharisaism.* 2:212. **Anderson, C. P.** "The Trial of Jesus as Jewish-Christian Polarization: Blasphemy and Polemic in Mark's Gospel." In *Paul and the Gospels.* Vol. 1 of *Anti-Judaism in Early Christianity.* Ed. P. Richardson. Waterloo, Ontario: Wilfrid Laurier UP, 1986. 107–25. **Bartsch, H.-W.** "Wer verurteilte Jesus zum Tode? Zu der Rezension des Buches von Paul Winter *On the Trial of Jesus,* durch Ethelbert Stauffer" *NovT* 7 (1964–65) 210–16. **Ben-Chorin, S.** "Wer hat Jesus zum Tode verurteilte?" *ZRGG* 37 (1985) 63–67. **Benoit, P.** *Jesus and the Gospel.* 2 vols. London: Darton, Longman & Todd; New York: Herder and Herder, 1973. 1:123–88. ———. *Passion and Resurrection.* 73–114. **Betz, O.** "Probleme des Prozesses Jesu." *ANRW* 2.25.1 (1982) 565–647. ———. "The Temple Scroll and the Trial of Jesus." *SWJT* 30 (1988) 5–8. **Blinzler, J.** "Geschichtlichkeit und Legalität des jüdischen Prozesses gegen Jesus." *Stimmen der Zeit* 147 (1950–51) 345–57. ———. "Das Synedrium von Jerusalem und die Strafprozessordnung der Mischna." *ZNW* 52 (1961) 54–65. ———. *The Trial of Jesus: The Jewish and Roman Proceedings against Jesus Christ Described* *and Assessed from the Oldest Accounts.* Westminster: Newman, 1959. **Bowker, J. W.** "The Offence and Trial of Jesus." In *Jesus and the Pharisees.* New York: Cambridge UP, 1973. 42–52. **Brandon, S. G. F.** "The Trial of Jesus." *Judaism* 20 (1971) 43–48. ———. *The Trial of Jesus of Nazareth.* London: Batsford; New York: Stein and Day, 1968. **Braumann, G.** "Noch einmal: Zur Blutgerichtsbarkeit des Synedrions." *ZNW* 33 (1934) 84–87. **Burkill, T. A.** "The Competence of the Sanhedrin." *VC* 10 (1956) 80–96. ———. "The Trial of Jesus." *VC* 12 (1958) 1–18. **Buss, S.** *The Trial of Jesus Illustrated from Talmud and Roman Law.* London: S. P. C. K., 1906. **Catchpole, D. R.** "The Problem of the Historicity of the Sanhedrin Trial." In *The Trial of Jesus: Cambridge Studies.* FS C. F. D. Moule, ed. E. Bammel. SBT 13. London: SCM; Naperville, IL: Allenson, 1970. 47–65. ———. *The Trial of Jesus.* StPB 18. Leiden: Brill, 1971. **Cohen, D.,** and **Paulus, C.** "Einige Bemerkungen zum Prozess Jesu bei den Synoptikern." *ZSSR* 102 (1985) 437–45. **Cohn, H.** "Reflections on the Trial of Jesus." *Judaism* 20 (1971) 10–23. ———. *The Trial and Death of Jesus.* New York: Harper & Row, 1967. **Cooke, H. P.** "Christ Crucified—And by Whom?" *HibJ* 29 (1930–31) 61–74. **Crossan, J. D.** *The Cross That Spoke: The Origins of the Passion Narrative.* San Francisco: Harper & Row, 1988. **Dabrowski, E.** "The Trial of Jesus in Recent Research." *SE* 4 [= TU 102] (1968) 21–27. **Danby, H.** "The Bearing of the Rabbinical Criminal Code on the Jewish Trial Narratives in the Gospels." *JTS* o.s. 21 (1919–20) 51–76. **Daube, D.** "Limitations on Self-Sacrifice in Jewish Law and Tradition." *Theology* 72 (1969) 291–304. **Derrett, J. D. M.** *An Oriental Lawyer Looks at the Trial of Jesus and the Doctrine of Redemption.* London: School of Oriental and African Studies, 1966 (repr. in J. D. M. Derrett. *Law in the New Testament.* London: Darton, Longman & Todd, 1970. 389–460). **Dodd, C. H.** "The Historical Problem of the Death of Jesus." In *More New Testament Studies.* Manchester: Manchester UP; Grand Rapids, MI: Eerdmans, 1968. 84–101. **Dormeyer, D.** "Die Passion Jesu als Ergebnis seines Konflikts mit führenden Kreisen des Judentums." In *Gottesverächter und Menschenfeinde? Juden zwischen Jesus und frühchristlicher Kirche.* Ed. H. Goldstein. Düsseldorf: Patmos, 1979. 211–38. **Ebeling, H. J.** "Zur Frage nach der Kompetenz des Synedrions." *ZNW* 35 (1936) 290–95. **Enslin, M. S.** "The Temple and the Cross." *Judaism* 20 (1971) 24–31. ———. "The Trial of Jesus." *JQR* 60 (1970) 353–55. **Feuter, K., Schweizer, E.,** and **Winter, P.** "Diskussion um den Prozess Jesu." In *Wer war Jesus vom Nazareth? Die Erforschung einer historischen Gestalt.* Ed. G. Strube. Munich: Kindler, 1972. 221–40. **Fiebig, P.** "Der Prozess Jesu." *TSK* 104 (1932) 213–28. **Flusser, D.** "Der Hohepriester Hannas und sein Geschlect." In *Jesus—Qumran—Urchristentum.* Vol. 2 of *Entdeckungen im Neuen Testament.* Neukirchen-Vluyn: Neukirchener Verlag, 1999. 185–92. ———. *Jesus.* 195–206. ———. "A Literary Approach to the Trial of Jesus." *Judaism* 20 (1971) 32–36. **Garnsey, P.** "The Criminal Jurisdiction of Governors." *JRS* 58 (1968) 51–59. **Goguel, M.** "À propos du procès de Jésus." *ZNW* 31 (1932) 289–301. **Goodenough, E. R.** *The Jurisprudence of Jewish Courts in Egypt: Legal Administration by the Jews under the Early Roman Empire as Described by Philo Judaeus.* New Haven, CT: Yale UP, 1929. **Grant, F. C.** "On the Trial of Jesus: A Review Article." *JR* 44 (1964) 230–37. **Grant, R. M.** "The Trial of Jesus in the Light of History." *Judaism* 20 (1971) 37–42. **Greenhut, Z.** "Burial Cave of the Caiaphas Family." *BAR* 18.5 (1992) 28–36, 76. **Haufe, G.** "Der Prozess Jesu im Lichte der gegenwärtigen Forschung." *ZZ* 22 (1968) 93–101. **Holzmeister, U.** "Zur Frage der Blutgerichtsbarkeit des Synedriums." *Bib* 19 (1938) 43–59. **Horbury, W.** "The 'Caiaphas' Ossuaries and Joseph Caiaphas." *PEQ* 126 (1994) 32–48. ———. "The Trial of Jesus in Jewish Tradition." In *The Trial of Jesus: Cambridge Studies.* FS C. F. D. Moule, ed. E. Bammel. SBT 13. London: SCM Press; Naperville, IL: Allenson, 1970. 103–21. **Imbert, J.** *Le procès de Jésus.* Paris: Presses universitaires de France, 1980. **Jaubert, A.** "Les séances du Sanhédrin et les récits de la passion." *RHR* 166 (1964) 143–69. **Jonge, M. de.** "The Use of Ο ΧΡΙΣΤΟΣ in the Passion Narrative." In *Jésus aux origines de la christologie.* Ed. J. Dupont et al. BETL 40. Gembloux: Duculot, 1975. 169–92. **Kennard, J. S., Jr.** "The Jewish Provincial Assembly." *ZNW* 53 (1962) 25–51. **Kertelge, K.,** ed. *Der Prozess gegen Jesus: Historische Rückfrage und theologische Deutung.* QD 112. Freiburg; Basel: Herder, 1988. **Kilpatrick, G. D.** *The Trial of Jesus.* London: Oxford UP, 1953. **Kim, S.** *The Son of Man as the Son of God.* WUNT 30.

Tübingen: Mohr-Siebeck, 1983; Grand Rapids, MI: Eerdmans, 1985. 79–81. **Klausner, J.** *Jesus of Nazareth: His Life, Times, and Teaching.* London: George Allen & Unwin, 1925. 339–48. **Klijn, A. F. J.** "Scribes, Pharisees, Highpriests and Elders in the New Testament." *NovT* 3 (1959) 259–67. **Klövekorn, P. B.** "Jesus vor der jüdischen Behörde." *BZ* 9 (1911) 266–76. **Koch, W.** *Der Prozess Jesu: Versuch eines Tatsachenberichts.* Cologne: Kiepenheuer & Witsch, 1966. **Kolping, A.** "'Standrechtlich gekreuzigt': Neuere überlegungen zum Prozess Jesu." *TRev* 83 (1987) 265–76. **Kremer, J.** "Verurteilt als 'König der Juden'—verkündigt als 'Herr und Christus.'" *BL* 45 (1972) 23–32. **Lapide, P. E.** "Jesu Tod durch Römerhand." In *Gottesverächter und Menschenfeinde? Juden zwischen Jesus und frühchristlicher Kirche.* Ed. H. Goldstein. Düsseldorf: Patmos, 1979. 239–55. ———. *Wer war schuld an Jesu Tod?* Gütersloh: Mohn, 1987. **Lietzmann, H.** "Bemerkungen zum Prozess Jesu." *ZNW* 30 (1931) 211–15; 31 (1932) 78–84. ———. "Der Prozess Jesu." In *Kleine Schriften II: Studien zum Neuen Testament.* Ed. K. Aland. TU 68. Berlin: Akademie, 1958. 251–63. **Lindeskog, G.** "Der Prozess Jesu im jüdisch-christlichen Religionsgespräch." In *Abraham unser Vater: Juden und Christen in Gespräch über die Bibel.* FS O. Michel, ed. O. Betz et al. AGSU 5. Leiden: Brill, 1963. 325–36. **Lohse, E.** "Der Prozess Jesu Christi." In *Ecclesia et Res Publica.* FS K. D. Schmidt, ed. G. Kretschmar and B. Lohse. Göttingen: Vandenhoeck & Ruprecht, 1961. 24–39. **Mantel, H.** *Studies in the History of the Sanhedrin.* Cambridge: Harvard UP, 1961. 254–90. **Matera, F. J.** "The Trial of Jesus: Problems and Proposals." *Int* 45 (1991) 5–16. **McLaren, J. S.** *Power and Politics in Palestine: The Jews and the Governing of their Land 100 B.C.–A.D. 70.* JSNTSup 63. Sheffield: JSOT Press, 1991. 88–101. **Meyer, F. E.** "Einige Bemerkungen zur Bedeutungen des Terminus 'Synhedrion' in den Schriften des Neuen Testaments." *NTS* 14 (1967–68) 545–51. **Millar, F.** "Reflections on the Trials of Jesus." In *A Tribute to Geza Vermes: Essays on Jewish and Christian Literature and History.* Ed. P. R. Davies and R. T. White. JSOTSup 100. Sheffield: JSOT Press, 1990. 355–81. **Müller, K.** "Jesus und die Sadduzäer." In *Biblische Randbemerkungen.* FS R. Schnackenburg, ed. H. Merklein and J. Lange. Würzburg: Echter, 1974. 3–24. ———. "Möglichkeit und Vollzu, jüdischer Kapitalgerichtsbarkeit im Prozess gegen Jesus von Nazaret." In *Der Prozess gegen Jesus: Historische Rückfrage und theologische Deutung.* Ed. K. Kertelge. QD 112. Freiburg; Basel: Herder, 1988. 41–83. **Ostrow, J.** "Tannaitic and Roman Procedure in Homicide." *JQR* 48 (1957–58) 352–70; 52 (1961–62) 160–67, 245–63. **Pesch, R.** *Der Prozess Jesu geht weiter.* Freiburg; Basel: Herder, 1988. ———. "Die Überlieferung der Passion Jesu." In *Rückfrage nach Jesus: Zur Methodik und Bedeutung der Frage nach dem historischen Jesus.* Ed. K. Kertelge. QD 63. Freiburg: Herder, 1974. 148–73. **Puech, E.** "A-t-on redécouvert le tombeau du grand-prête Caïphe?" *Le monde de la Bible* 80 (1993) 42–47. **Reich, R.** "Caiaphas' Name Inscribed on Bone Boxes." *BAR* 18.5 (1992) 38–44, 76. **Reichrath, H.** "Der Prozess Jesu." *Judaica* 20 (1964) 129–55. **Ritt, H.** "Wer war schuld am Jesu Tod? Zeitgeschichte, Recht und theologische Deutung." *BZ* 31 (1987) 165–75. **Rosenblatt, S.** "The Crucifixion of Jesus from the Standpoint of the Pharisaic Law." *JBL* 75 (1956) 315–21. **Roth, L.** "Caiaphas, Joseph." *EncJud* 5:19–20. **Rudberg, G.** "Die Verhöhnung Jesu vor dem Hohenpriester." *ZNW* 24 (1925) 307–9. **Sanders, E. P.** *Jesus and Judaism.* 294–318. **Sandmel, S.** "The Trial of Jesus: Reservations." *Judaism* 20 (1971) 69–74. **Schneider, G.** "Gab es eine vorsynoptische Szene 'Jesus vor dem Synedrium'?" *NovT* 12 (1970) 22–39. ———. "Jesus vor dem Sanhedrin." *BibLeb* 11 (1970) 1–15. **Schubert, K.** "Die Juden order die Römer? Der Prozess Jesu und sein geschichtlicher Hintergrund." *Wort und Wahrheit* 17 (1962) 701–10. ———. "Das Verhör Jesu vor dem Hohen Rat." In *Bibel und zeitgemässer Glaube II.* Ed. J. Sint. Klosterneuburg: Buch- und Kunstverlag, 1967. 97–130. **Schumann, H.** "Bemerkungen zum Prozess Jesu vor dem Synhedrium." *ZSSR* 82 (1965) 315–20. **Sherwin-White, A. N.** *Roman Law and Roman Society in the New Testament.* The Sarum Lectures, 1960–61. London: Oxford UP, 1963. 24–47. ———. "The Trial of Christ." In *Historicity and Chronology in the New Testament.* Ed. D. E. Nineham et al. Theological Collections 6. London: S. P. C. K., 1965. 97–116. **Sloyan, G. S.** "Recent Literature on the Trial Narrative of the Four Gospels." In *Critical History and Biblical Faith: New Testament Perspectives.* Ed. T. R. Ryan. Villanova, PA: Villanova UP, 1979. 136–76. **Smallwood, E. M.** "High Priests and

Politics in Roman Palestine." *JTS* n.s. 13 (1962) 14–34. ————. *The Jews under Roman Rule: From Pompey to Diocletian.* SJLA 20. Leiden: Brill, 1976. 145–80. **Sobosan, J. G.** "The Trial of Jesus." *JES* 10 (1973) 72–91. **Stewart, R. A.** "Judicial Procedure in New Testament Times." *EvQ* 47 (1975) 94–109. **Trilling, W.** "Der 'Prozess Jesu.'" In *Fragen zur Geschichtlichkeit Jesu.* Düsseldorf: Patmos, 1966. 130–41. **Watson, F.** "Why Was Jesus Crucified?" *Theology* 88 (1985) 105–12. **Winter, P.** "Marginal Notes on the Trial of Jesus." *ZNW* 50 (1959) 14–33, 221–51. ————. *On the Trial of Jesus.* Studia Judaica 1. 2nd ed. Rev. by T. A. Burkill and G. Vermes. Berlin; New York: de Gruyter, 1974. ————. "The Trial of Jesus and the Competence of the Sanhedrin." *NTS* 10 (1963–64) 494–99. **Zeitlin, S.** "The Political Synedrion and the Religious Synedrion." *JQR* 36 (1945) 109–40. ————. "Synedrion in Greek Literature, the Gospels and the Institution of the Sanhedrin." *JQR* 37 (1946) 189–98. ————. "Synedrion in the Judeo-Hellenistic Literature and Sanhedrin in the Tannaitic Literature." *JQR* 37 (1946) 307–15. ————. *Who Crucified Jesus?* New York: Harper & Row, 1942.

Bibliography on Mark 14:53–65

Bartsch, H.-W. "Historische Erwägungen zur Leidensgeschichte." *EvT* 22 (1962) 449–59. **Beavis, M. A.** *Mark's Audience: The Literary and Social Setting of Mark 4.11–12.* JSNTSup 33. Sheffield: JSOT Press, 1989. 115–23. ————. "The Trial before the Sanhedrin (Mark 14:53–65): Reader Response and Greco-Roman Readers." *CBQ* 49 (1987) 581–96. **Betz, O.** "Probleme des Prozesses Jesu." *ANRW* 2.25.1 (1982) 565–647, esp. 613–39. ————. *What Do We Know about Jesus?* London: SCM Press; Philadelphia: Westminster, 1968. 83–98. **Beyer, H. W.** "βλασφημέω, κ. τ. λ." *TDNT* 1:621–25. **Blinzler, J.** "The Trial of Jesus in the Light of History." *Judaism* 20 (1971) 49–55. ————. "Zum Prozess Jesu." In *Aus der Welt und Umwelt des Neuen Testaments: Gesammelte Aufsätze I.* SBB. Stuttgart: Katholisches Bibelwerk, 1969. 124–46. **Bock, D. L.** *Blasphemy and Exaltation in Judaism and the Final Examination of Jesus.* WUNT 2.106. Tübingen: Mohr-Siebeck, 1998. **Borrell, A.** *The Good News of Peter's Denial: A Narrative and Rhetorical Reading of Mark 14:54.66–72.* University of South Florida International Studies in Formative Christianity and Judaism 7. Atlanta: Scholars Press, 1998. **Brandon, S. G. F.** "The Trial of Jesus." *Horizon* 9 (1967) 4–13. ————. *The Trial of Jesus of Nazareth.* London: Batsford; New York: Stein and Day, 1968. 81–106. **Braumann, G.** "Markus 5, 2–5 und Markus 14, 55–64." *ZNW* 52 (1961) 273–78. **Büchsel, F.** "Die Blutgerichtsbarkeit des Synedrions." *ZNW* 30 (1931) 202–10. **Cantinat, J.** "Jésus devant le Sanhédrin." *NRT* 75 (1953) 300–308. **Catchpole, D. R.** "The Answer of Jesus to Caiaphas (Matt. XXVI.64)." *NTS* 17 (1970–71) 213–26. ————. *The Trial of Jesus.* StPB 18. Leiden: Brill, 1971. 174–203. **Donahue, J. R.** *Are You the Christ?* 53–102, 104–13. ————. "Introduction: From Passion Traditions to Passion Narrative." In *The Passion in Mark: Studies on Mark 14–16.* Ed. W. Kelber. Philadelphia: Fortress, 1976. 1–20. ————. "Temple, Trial, and Royal Christology (Mark 14:53–65)." In *The Passion in Mark: Studies on Mark 14–16.* Ed. W. Kelber. Philadelphia: Fortress, 1976. 61–79. **Dormeyer, D.** *Die Passion Jesu.* 149–50, 157–75, 288–90. ————. *Der Sinn des Leidens Jesu: Historisch-kritische und textpragmatische Analysen zur Markuspassion.* SBS 96. Stuttgart: Katholisches Bibelwerk, 1979. 49–61. **Edwards, J. R.** "Markan Sandwiches: The Significance of Interpolations in Markan Narratives." *NovT* 31 (1989) 193–216. **Evans, C. A.** "'Peter Warming Himself': The Problem of an Editorial 'Seam.'" *JBL* 101 (1982) 245–49. **Flusser, D.** "'Who Is It That Struck You?'" *Immanuel* 20 (1986) 27–32 (repr. in D. Flusser. *Judaism and the Origins of Christianity.* Jerusalem: Magnes, 1988. 604–9). **Fortna, R. T.** "Jesus and Peter at the High Priest's House: A Test Case for the Question of the Relation between Mark's and John's Gospels." *NTS* 24 (1978) 371–83. **France, R. T.** "Jésus devant Caïphe." *Hokhma* 15 (1980) 20–35. **Fredriksen, P.** "Jesus and the Temple, Mark and the War." In *Society of Biblical Literature 1990 Seminar Papers.* Ed. D. J. Lull. SBLSP 29. Atlanta: Scholars Press, 1990. 293–310. **Genest, O.** *Le Christ de la passion: Perspective structurale: Analyse de Marc 14,53–15,47, des parallèles et extra-bibliques.* Recherches 21: Théologie. Tournai: Desclée; Montreal: Bellarmin, 1978. 29–55. **Gnilka, J.**

"Die Verhandlungen vor dem Synhedrion und vor Pilatus nach Markus 14.53–15,5." In *Evangelisch-Katholischer Kommentar zum Neuen Testament: Vorarbeiten*. 4 vols. Neukirchen-Vluyn: Neukirchener Verlag, 1969–72. 2:5–21. **Gourgues, M.** *À la droite de Dieu: Résurrection de Jésus et actualisation du Psaume 110:1 dans le Nouveau Testament*. EBib. Paris: Gabalda, 1978. 189–208. **Gundry, R. H.** למטלם: 1Q ISAIAH a 50,6 and Mark 14,65." *RevQ* 2 (1960) 559–67. **Hengel, M.** *Studies in the Gospel of Mark*. 31–58, 138–61. **Hill, D.** "Jesus before the Sanhedrin—On What Charge?" *IBS* 7 (1985) 174–86. **Hooker, M. D.** *The Message of Mark*. London: Epworth, 1983. 88–104. **Jeremias, J.** "Zur Geschichtlichkeit des Verhörs Jesu vor dem hohen Rat." *ZNW* 43 (1950–51) 145–50. **Juel, D.** "The Function of the Trial of Jesus in Mark's Gospel." In *Society of Biblical Literature 1975 Seminar Papers*. Ed. G. W. MacRae. 2 vols. SBLSP 14. Missoula, MT: Scholars Press, 1975. 2:83–104. ———. *Messiah and Temple*. 59–79. **Kazmierski, C. R.** *Jesus, the Son of God*. 165–90. **Kempthorne, R.** "Anti-Christian Tendency in Pre-Marcan Traditions of the Sanhedrin Trial." *SE* 7 [= TU 126] (1982) 283–86. **Lamarche, P.** "Le 'blasphème' de Jésus devant le Sanhédrin." *RSR* 50 (1962) 74–85 (repr. in P. Lamarche. *Révélation de Dieu chez Marc*. Le point théologique 20. Paris: Beauchesne, 1976. 105–18). **Lee, M. Y.-H.** *Jesus und die jüdische Autorität: Eine exegetische Untersuchung zu Mk 11,27–12,12*. FB 56. Würzburg: Echter, 1986. 218–32. **Légasse, S.** "Jésus devant le Sanhédrin: Recherche sur les traditions évangéliques." *RTL* 5 (1974) 170–97. **Lentzen-Deis, F.** "Passionsbericht als Handlungsmodell." In *Der Prozess gegen Jesus: Historische Rückfrage und theologische Deutung*. Ed. K. Kertelge. QD 112. Freiburg; Basel: Herder, 1988. 221–32. **Linnemann, E.** *Studien zur Passionsgeschichte*. 109–35. **Lührmann, D.** "Markus 14.55–64: Christologie und Zerstörung des Tempels im Markusevangelium." *NTS* 27 (1980–81) 457–74. **Mack, B. L.** *Myth*. 293–95. **Martin, R. P.** *Mark: Evangelist and Theologian*. 177–81. **Minette de Tillesse, G.** *Le secret messianique*. 358–94. **Mohr, T. A.** *Markus- und Johannespassion*. 252–81. **Moo, D. J.** *Old Testament in the Gospel Passion Narratives*. 139–44, 346–47. **Myllykoski, M.** *Die letzten Tage Jesu*. 48–92. **Neirynck, F.** *Duality in Mark*. 133. ———. "ΤΙΣ ΕΣΤΙΝ Ο ΠΑΙΣΑΣ ΣΕ: Mt 26,68/Lk 22,64 (diff. Mk 14,65)." *ETL* 63 (1987) 5–47, esp. 6–14 (repr. in F. Neirynck. *Evangelica II*. Ed. F. Van Segbroeck. BETL 99. Leuven: Peeters and Leuven UP, 1991. 95–137, esp. 96–104). **Pesch, R.** *Das Evangelium der Urgemeinde*. 184–91. **Rudberg, G.** "Die Verhöhnung Jesu vor dem Hohenpriester." *ZNW* 24 (1925) 307–9. **Schenk, W.** *Der Passionsbericht nach Markus*. 215–23, 229–43. **Schenke, L.** *Der gekreuzigte Christus*. 23–46. **Schneider, G.** "Gab es eine vorsynoptische Szene 'Jesus vor dem Synedrium'?" *NovT* 12 (1970) 22–39, esp. 29–32. ———. *Die Passion Jesu*. 55–64. **Schreiber, J.** *Die Markuspassion: Wege zur Erforschung der Leidensgeschichte Jesu*. Hamburg: Furche, 1969. 54–58. **Schubert, K.** "Biblical Criticism Criticised: With Reference to the Markan Report of Jesus' Examination before the Sanhedrin." In *Jesus and the Politics of His Day*. Ed. E. Bammel and C. F. D. Moule. Cambridge: Cambridge UP, 1984. 385–402. **Standaert, B. H. M. G. M.** *L'évangile selon Marc*. 254–59. **Streeter, B. H.** *The Four Gospels: A Study of Origins*. Rev. ed. London: Macmillan, 1930. 325–29. **Strobel, A.** *Die Stunde der Wahrheit: Untersuchungen zum Strafverfahren gegen Jesus*. WUNT 21. Tübingen: Mohr-Siebeck, 1980. 7–14. **Suhl, A.** *Zitate*. 54–66. **Unnik, W. C. van.** "Jesu Verhöhnung vor dem Synedrium (Mc 14,65 par.)." *ZNW* 29 (1930) 310–11. **Winter, P.** "Marginal Notes on the Trial of Jesus." *ZNW* 50 (1959) 14–33, 221–51, esp. 221–34. ———. "Mk 14,53b.55–64 ein Gebilde des Evangelisten." *ZNW* 53 (1962) 260–63. ———. "The Markan Account of Jesus' Trial by the Sanhedrin." *JTS* n.s. 14 (1963) 94–102.

See also *Bibliography* for 14:66–72 for citations related to 14:53–54.

Bibliography on Mark 14:58

Ådna, J. "Jesu Kritik am Tempel: Eine Untersuchung zum Verlauf und Sinn der sogenannten Tempelreinigung Jesu, Markus 11,15–17 und Parallelen." Diss., University of Oslo, 1993. 202–51, 498–520. **Best, E.** *Following Jesus*. 213–16. **Crossan, J. D.** *In Fragments*. 306–10. **Donahue, J. R.** *Are You the Christ?* 104–13. **Ellis, E. E.** "Deity-Christology in Mark 14:58." In

Jesus of Nazareth: Lord and Christ: Essays on the Historical Jesus and New Testament Christology. FS I. H. Marshall, ed. J. B. Green and M. Turner. Grand Rapids, MI: Eerdmans, 1994. 192–203. **Evans, C. A.** "Predictions of the Destruction of the Herodian Temple in the Pseudepigrapha, Qumran Scrolls, and Related Texts." *JSP* 10 (1992) 89–147. **France, R. T.** *Jesus and the Old Testament.* 99–100. **Gärtner, B.** *The Temple and the Community in Qumran and the New Testament.* SNTSMS 1. Cambridge: Cambridge UP, 1965. 105–22. **Gaston, L.** *No Stone on Another: Studies in the Significance of the Fall of Jerusalem in the Synoptic Gospels.* NovTSup 23. Leiden: Brill, 1970. 66–243, esp. 102–5. **Geddert, T. J.** *Watchwords.* 130–33. **Hoffmann, R. A.** "Das Wort Jesu von der Zerstörung und dem Wiederaufbau des Tempels." In *Neutestamentliche Studien.* FS G. Heinrici. Leipzig: Hinrichs, 1914. 130–39. **Hooker, M. D.** "Traditions about the Temple in the Sayings of Jesus." *BJRL* 70 (1988) 7–19. **Howard, V. P.** *Das Ego Jesu in den synoptischen Evangelien: Untersuchungen zum Sprachgebrauch Jesu.* MTS 14. Marburg: Elwert, 1975. 135–42. **Jeremias, J.** "Die Drei-Tage-Worte der Evangelien." In *Tradition und Glaube: Das frühe Christentum in seiner Umwelt.* FS K. G. Kuhn, ed. G. Jeremias et al. Göttingen: Vandenhoeck & Ruprecht, 1971. 221–29. **Juel, D.** *Messiah and Temple.* 117–39, 143–57, 197–209. **Kleist, J. A.** "The Two False Witnesses (Mk 14:55ff)." *CBQ* 9 (1947) 321–23. **Linnemann, E.** *Studien zur Passionsgeschichte.* 116–27. **McElvey, R. J.** *The New Temple.* Oxford: Oxford UP, 1969. 67–79. **Moo, D. J.** *Old Testament in the Gospel Passion Narratives.* 247–49, 339–41. **Plooij, D.** "Jesus and the Temple." *ExpTim* 42 (1930–31) 36–39. **Sabbe, M.** "The Cleansing of the Temple and the Temple Logion." In *Studia Neotestamentica: Collected Essays.* BETL 98. Leuven: Peeters and Leuven UP, 1991. 331–54. **Sanders, E. P.** *Jesus and Judaism.* 71–76. **Sariola, H.** *Markus und das Gesetz.* 222–29. **Schiffman, L. H.** "Messianic Figures and Ideas in the Qumran Scrolls." In *The Messiah.* Ed. J. H. Charlesworth. Minneapolis: Fortress, 1992. 116–29. **Schlosser, J.** "La parole de Jésus sur la fin du Temple." *NTS* 36 (1990) 398–414. **Schnider, F.** *Jesus der Prophet.* OBO 2. Göttingen: Vandenhoeck & Ruprecht, 1973. 156–58. **Simon, M.** "Retour du Christ et reconstruction du Temple dans la pensée chrétienne primitiv." In *Aux sources de la tradition chrétienne.* FS M. Goguel. Neuchâtel: Delachaux & Niestlé, 1950. 247–57. **Sweet, J. P. M.** "A House Not Made with Hands." In *Templum Amicitiae.* FS E. Bammel, ed. W. Horbury. JSNTSup 48. Sheffield: JSOT Press, 1991. 368–90. **Theissen, G.** "Die Tempelweissagung Jesu: Prophetie im Spannungsfeld von Stadt und Land." *TZ* 32 (1976) 144–58 (repr. in G. Theissen. *Studien zur Soziologie des Urchristentums.* WUNT 19. 2nd ed. Tübingen: Mohr-Siebeck, 1983. 142–59; ET: "Jesus' Temple Prophecy: Prophecy in the Tension between Town and Country." In G. Theissen. *Social Reality and the Early Christians: Theology, Ethics, and the World of the New Testament.* Minneapolis: Fortress, 1992. 94–114). **Vögtle, A.** "Das markinische Verständnis der Tempelworte." In *Die Mitte des Neuen Testaments: Einheit und Vielfalt neutestamentlicher Theologie.* FS E. Schweizer, ed. U. Luz and H. Weder. Göttingen: Vandenhoeck & Ruprecht, 1983. 362–83 (repr. in A. Vögtle. *Offenbarungsgeschehen und Wirkungsgeschichte: Neutestamentliche Beiträge.* Freiburg: Herder, 1985. 168–88). **Wenschkewitz, H.** *Die Spiritualisierung der Kultusbegriffe Tempel, Priester und Opfer im Neuen Testament.* Angelos-Beiheft 4. Leipzig: Pfeiffer, 1932. 96–101. **Wise, M. O.** "*4QFlorilegium* and the Temple of Adam." *RevQ* 15 (1991) 103–32 (rev. and repr. in M. O. Wise. *Thunder in Gemini and Other Essays on the History, Language and Literature of Second Temple Palestine.* JSPSup 15. Sheffield: JSOT Press, 1994. 152–85). **Young, F. M.** "Temple Cult and Law in Early Christianity." *NTS* 19 (1972–73) 325–38.

Bibliography on Mark 14:61–62

Baarlink, H. *Anfängliches Evangelium.* 214–21. **Bammel, E.** "Erwägungen zur Eschatologie Jesu." *SE* 3 [= TU 88] (1964) 3–32. **Beasley-Murray, G. R.** "Jesus and Apocalyptic: With Special Reference to Mark 14,62." In *L'Apocalypse johannique et l'apocalyptique dans le Nouveau Testament.* Ed. J. Lambrecht. BETL 53. Gembloux; Leuven: Leuven UP, 1980. 415–29. ———. *Jesus and the Kingdom of God.* 296–304. **Berger, K.** "Die königlichen Messiastraditionen des

Neuen Testaments." *NTS* 20 (1973–74) 1–44, esp. 19–28. **Black, M.** "The Theological Appropriation of the Old Testament by the New Testament." *SJT* 39 (1986) 1–17, esp. 12–16. **Bock, D. L.** *Blasphemy and Exaltation in Judaism and the Final Examination of Jesus: A Philological-Historical Study of the Key Jewish Themes Impacting Mark 14:61–64.* WUNT 2.106. Tübingen: Mohr-Siebeck, 1998. **Borsch, F. H.** "Mark xiv.62 and 1 Enoch lxii.5." *NTS* 14 (1967–68) 565–67. ———. *The Son of Man in Myth and History.* London: SCM Press, 1967. 391–94. **Burkill, T. A.** "Blasphemy: St. Mark's Gospel as Damnation History." In *Christianity, Judaism and Other Greco-Roman Cults.* FS M. Smith, ed. J. Neusner. SJLA 12. Leiden: Brill, 1975. 51–74. **Burkitt, F. C.** "On Romans ix 5 and Mark xiv 61." *JTS* o.s. 5 (1903–4) 451–55, esp. 453–54. **Casey, P. M.** *Son of Man: The Interpretation and Influence of Daniel 7.* London: S. P. C. K., 1979. 178–84. **Catchpole, D. R.** "The Answer of Jesus to Caiaphas (Matt. xxvi.64)." *NTS* 17 (1970–71) 213–26. ———. "You have Heard His Blasphemy." *TynBul* 16 (1965) 10–18. **Conzelmann, H.** "Das Selbstbewusstsein Jesu." In *Theologie als Schriftauslegung: Aufsätze zum Neuen Testament.* BEvT 65. Munich: Kaiser, 1974. 30–41. **Dautzenberg, G.** "Psalm 110 im Neuen Testament." In *Liturgie und Dichtung: Ein interdisziplinäres Kompendium.* Ed. H. Becker and R. Kaczynski. St. Ottilien: EOS, 1983. 141–71, esp. 152–54. ———. "Zwei unterschiedliche 'Kompenden' markinischer Christologie? Überlegungen zum Verhältnis von Mk 15,39 zu Mk 14,61f." In *Evangelium Jesu Christi heute verkündigen.* FS C. Mayer, ed. B. Jendorff and G. Schmalenberg. Giessen: Selbstverlag des Fachbereichs, 1989. 17–32. **Donahue, J. R.** *Are You the Christ?* 88–95, 138–42, 172–77. **Dupont, J.** "'Assis à la droite de Dieu': L'interpretation du Ps. 110,1 dans le Nouveau Testament." In *Resurrexit: Actes du Symposium international sur la résurrection de Jésus (Rome 1970).* Ed. E. Dhanis. Rome: Libreria Editrice Vaticana, 1974. 340–422, esp. 347–72. **Evans, C. A.** "In What Sense 'Blasphemy'? Jesus before Caiaphas in Mark 14:61–64." In *Society of Biblical Literature 1991 Seminar Papers.* Ed. E. H. Lovering, Jr. SBLSP 30. Atlanta: Scholars Press, 1991. 215–34. ———. *Jesus and His Contemporaries.* 407–34. **Feuillet, A.** "Le triomphe du fils de l'homme d'après la déclaration du Christ aux Sanhédrites (Mc., xiv,62; Mt., xxvi,64; Lc., xxii,69)." In *La venue du Messie.* Ed. E. Massaux. RechBib 6. Bruges: Desclée de Brouwer, 1962. 149–71. **Flusser, D.** "'At the Right Hand of Power.'" *Immanuel* 14 (1982) 42–46 (repr. in D. Flusser. "Sitzend zur Rechten der Kraft." In *Jesus—Qumran—Urchristentum.* Vol. 2 of *Entdeckungen im Neuen Testament.* Neukirchen-Vluyn: Neukirchener Verlag, 1999. 105–9). **France, R. T.** *Jesus and the Old Testament.* 140–42. **Gaston, L.** *No Stone on Another: Studies in the Significance of the Fall of Jerusalem in the Synoptic Gospels.* NovTSup 23. Leiden: Brill, 1970. 388–90. **Glasson, T. F.** "The Reply to Caiaphas (Mark xiv.62)." *NTS* 7 (1960–61) 88–93. ———. *The Second Advent: The Origin of the New Testament Doctrine.* Rev. ed. London: Epworth, 1963. 54–62. **Goldberg, A.** "Sitzend zur Rechten der Kraft." *BZ* 8 (1964) 284–93. **Gourgues, M.** *À la droite de Dieu: Résurrection de Jésus et actualisation du Psaume 110:1 dans le Nouveau Testament.* EBib. Paris: Gabalda, 1978. 127–62, 189–208. **Haag, H.** "Sohn Gottes im Alten Testament." *TQ* 154 (1974) 223–31. **Hampel, V.** *Menschensohn und historischer Jesus: Ein Rätselwort als Schlüssel zum messianischen Selbstverständnis Jesu.* Neukirchen-Vluyn: Neukirchener, 1990. 174–85. **Hay, D. M.** *Glory at the Right Hand: Psalm 110 in Early Christianity.* SBLMS 18. Nashville; New York: Abingdon, 1973. 64–70. **Hengel, M.** "'Setze dich zu meiner Rechten!' Die Inthronisation Christi zur Rechten Gottes und Psalm 110,1." In *Le Trône de Dieu.* Ed. M. Philonenko. WUNT 69. Tübingen: Mohr-Siebeck, 1994. 108–94 (ET: "'Sit at My Right Hand!' The Enthronement of Christ at the Right Hand of God and Psalm 110:1." In M. Hengel. *Studies in Early Christology.* Edinburgh: T. & T. Clark, 1995. 119–225). **Héring, J.** *Le Royaume de Dieu et sa venue.* Paris: Alcan, 1937. 111–20. **Higgins, A. J. B.** *Jesus and the Son of Man.* London: Lutterworth, 1964; Philadelphia: Fortress, 1965. 66–74. **Hoffrichter, P.** "Das dreifache Verfahren über Jesus als Gottessohn, König und Mensch: Zur Redaktionsgeschichte der Prozesstradition." *Kairos* 30–31 (1988–89) 69–81. **Hooker, M. D.** *Son of Man in Mark.* 163–73. **Howard, V. P.** *Das Ego Jesu in den synoptischen Evangelien: Untersuchungen zum Sprachgebrauch Jesu.* MTS 14. Marburg: Elwert, 1975. 142–48. **Huntress, E.** "'Son of God' in Jewish Writings prior to the Christian Era." *JBL* 54 (1935) 117–23.

Jonge, M. de. "The Use of Ο ΧΡΙΣΤΟΣ in the Passion Narrative." In *Jésus aux origines de la christologie*. Ed. J. Dupont et al. BETL 40. Gembloux: Duculot, 1975. 169–92, esp. 173–82. ———. "The Use of the Word 'Anointed' in the Time of Jesus." *NovT* 8 (1966) 132–48. **Juel, D.** *Messiah and Temple*. 77–107. ———. *Messianic Exegesis: Christological Interpretation of the Old Testament in Early Christianity.* Philadelphia: Fortress, 1988. 141–46. **Kazmierski, C. R.** *Jesus, the Son of God.* 165–89. **Kempthorne, R.** "The Marcan Text of Jesus' Answer to the High Priest (Mark xiv 62)." *NovT* 19 (1977) 197–208. **Kingdon, H. P.** "Messiahship and the Crucifixion." *SE* 3 [= TU 88] (1964) 67–86. **Kremer, J.** "'Sohn Gottes': Zur Klärung des biblischen Hoheitstitels Jesu." *BL* 46 (1973) 3–21. **Lamarche, P.** "Le 'blasphème' de Jésus devant le sanhédrin." *RSR* 50 (1962) 64–85 (repr. as "La déclaration de Jésus devant le Sanhédrin." In P. Lamarche. *Christ vivant: Essai sur la christologie du Nouveau Testament.* LD 43. Paris: Cerf, 1966. 147–63). **Linton, O.** "The Trial of Jesus and the Interpretation of Psalm cx." *NTS* 7 (1960–61) 258–62. **Lövestam, E.** "Die Frage des Hohenpriesters (Mark.14,61, par. Matth. 26,63)." *SEÅ* 26 (1961) 93–107. **Maartens, P. J.** "The Son of Man as a Composite Metaphor in Mark 14:62." In *A South African Perspective on the New Testament.* FS B. M. Metzger, ed. J. H. Petzer and P. J. Hartin. Leiden: Brill, 1986. **Marcus, J.** "Mark 14:61: 'Are You the Messiah-Son-of-God?'" *NovT* 31 (1989) 125–41. **McArthur, H. K.** "Mark XIV.62." *NTS* 4 (1957–58) 156–58. **Minette de Tillesse, G.** *Le secret messianique.* 333–37, 358–63, 368–73. **Moo, D. J.** *Old Testament in the Gospel Passion Narratives.* 148–51. **Moule, C. F. D.** "The Gravamen against Jesus." In *Jesus, the Gospels, and the Church.* FS W. R. Farmer, ed. E. P. Sanders. Macon, GA: Mercer UP, 1987. 177–95. **Müller, M.** *Der Ausdruck "Menschensohn" in den Evangelien: Voraussetzungen und Bedeutung.* ATD 17. Leiden: Brill, 1984. 97–101. **Mussner, F.** "Die Wiederkunft des Menschensohnes nach Markus 13,24–27 und 14,61–62." *BK* 16 (1961) 105–7. **Neufeld, V. H.** *The Earliest Christian Confessions.* NTTS 5. Leiden: Brill, 1963. 108–11. **O'Neill, J. C.** "The Charge of Blasphemy at Jesus' Trial before the Sanhedrin." In *The Trial of Jesus: Cambridge Studies.* FS C. F. D. Moule, ed. E. Bammel. SBT 13. London: SCM Press, 1970. 72–77. ———. "The Silence of Jesus." *NTS* 15 (1969) 153–67. **Pace, S.** "The Stratigraphy of the Text of Daniel and the Question of Theological *Tendenz* in the Old Greek." *BIOSCS* 17 (1984) 15–35. **Perrin, N.** "The Christology of Mark: A Study in Methodology." *JR* 51 (1971) 173–87. ———. "The High Priest's Question and Jesus' Answer." In *The Passion in Mark: Studies on Mark 14–16.* Ed. W. Kelber. Philadelphia: Fortress, 1976. 80–95. ———. "Mark xiv.62: The End Product of a Christian Pesher Tradition?" *NTS* 12 (1965–66) 150–55. **Pesch, R.** "Die Passion des Menschensohns: Eine Studie zu den Menschensohnsworten der vormarkinischen Passionsgeschichte." In *Jesus und der Menschensohn.* FS A. Vögtle, ed. R. Pesch and R. Schnackenburg. Freiburg; Basel: Herder, 1975. 166–95, esp. 184–92. **Robinson, J. A. T.** "The Second Coming: Mark xiv.62." *ExpTim* 67 (1955–56) 336–40. **Rowe, R. D.** "Is Daniel's 'Son of Man' Messianic?" In *Christ the Lord: Studies in Christology.* FS D. Guthrie, ed. H. H. Rowdon. Leicester; Downers Grove, IL: InterVarsity Press, 1982. 71–96. **Schaberg, J.** *The Father, the Son and the Holy Spirit: Triadic Phrase in Matthew 28:19b.* SBLDS 61. Chico, CA: Scholars Press, 1982. 270–77. ———. "Mark 14.62: Early Christian Merkabah Imagery?" In *Apocalyptic and the New Testament.* FS. J. L. Martyn, ed. J. Marcus and M. L. Soards. JSNTSup 24. Sheffield: JSOT Press, 1989. 69–94. **Schenker, A.** "Gott als Vater—Söhne Gottes: Ein vernachlässigter Aspekt einer biblischen Metapher." *FZPhTh* 25 (1978) 3–55. **Scott, R. B. Y.** "Behold, He Cometh with Clouds." *NTS* 5 (1958–59) 127–32. **Seitz, O. J. F.** "The Future Coming of the Son of Man: Three Midrashic Formulations in the Gospel of Mark." *SE* 6 [= TU 112] (1973) 478–94. **Stauffer, E.** *Jesus and His Story.* London: SCM Press; New York: Knopf, 1960. 142–59. ———. "Messias oder Menschensohn?" *NovT* 1 (1956) 81–102. **Suhl, A.** *Zitate.* 54–56. **Taylor, V.** "The 'Son of Man' Sayings Relating to the Parousia." *ExpTim* 58 (1946) 12–15 (repr. in V. Taylor. *New Testament Essays.* London: Epworth, 1970; Grand Rapids, MI: Eerdmans, 1972. 119–26). **Thayer, H.** "σὺ εἶπας, σὺ λέγεις, in the Answers of Christ." *JBL* 13 (1894) 40–46. **Tinsley, E. J.** "The Sign of the Son of Man (Mk 14,62)." *SJT* 8 (1955) 297–306. **Unnik, W. C. van.** "Jesus the Christ." *NTS* 8 (1961–62) 101–16. **Vögtle, A.** "Todesankündigung und

Todesverständnis Jesu." In *Der Tod Jesu: Deutungen im Neuen Testament*. Ed. K. Kertelge. QD
74. Freiburg: Herder, 1976. 51–113, esp. 62–64. **Yadin, Y.** "A Midrash on 2 Sam. vii and Ps.
i–ii (4Q Florilegium)." *IEJ* 9 (1959) 95–98. **Zehrer, F.** "Jesus, der Sohn Gottes." *BL* 48 (1975)
70–81. **Zmijewski, J.** "Die Sohn-Gottes-Prädikation im Markusevangelium: Zur Frage einer
eigenständigen markinischen Titelchristologie." SNTSU 12 (1987) 5–34, esp. 9–32.

Translation

⁵³*And they led Jesus to the high priest,*ᵃ *and all the ruling priests and the elders and
the scribes come together.* ⁵⁴*And Peter* ᵇ *followed him from a distance, right into the courtyard of the high priest, and he was sitting with the officers and was being warmed by the
fire.* ⁵⁵*But the ruling priests and the entire council were seeking testimony* ᶜ *against Jesus,
in order to put him to death, but they were not finding any.* ⁵⁶*For many were giving false
testimony against him,*ᵈ *and the testimonies were not in agreement.* ⁵⁷*And some, standing up, testified against him falsely, saying,* ⁵⁸*"We heard him saying, 'I shall destroy this
temple made with hands, and after three days I shall build another not made with hands.'"*
⁵⁹*And not even their testimony was in agreement.* ⁶⁰*And standing up in the midst, the
high priest asked Jesus, saying, "Are you not going to reply? What are these men testifying against you?"* ⁶¹*But he* ᵉ *was silent, and answered back nothing. Again the high
priest interrogated him* ᶠ *and says to him, "Are you the Messiah, the son of the Blessed?"* ᵍ
⁶²*But Jesus said, "I am;* ʰ *and you will see 'the son of man' seated 'at the right hand' of
the Power* ⁱ *and 'coming with the clouds of heaven.'"* ʲ ⁶³*And* ᵏ *tearing his robes, the high
priest says, "Why do we still have need of witnesses?* ⁶⁴*You* ˡ *heard the blasphemy!*ᵐ *What
seems right* ⁿ *to you?" And they all condemned him to be deserving of death.* ⁶⁵*And some
began to spit on him,*ᵒ *and to cover his face, and to strike him, and to say to him,
"Prophesy!"* ᵖ *And the officers received* ۹ *him with slaps.*

Notes

ᵃA W and several later MSS read πρὸς τὸν ἀρχιερέα Καϊάφαν, "the high priest Caiaphas." The
name of the high priest does not occur in Mark. Its presence here is due to the influence of Matt
26:57. On the attestation of this name in Josephus and in a recent archaeological find, see commentary below.

ᵇSome Syr. MSS read *kêpā'*, "Cephas"; the Peshitta reads *šim'ôn*, "Simon."

ᶜGk. μαρτυρίαν, "testimony" or "witness." Reflecting the context, A and a few later MSS read
ψευδομαρτυρίαν, "false testimony" (cf. Matt 26:59).

ᵈA few later MSS read κατ᾽ Ἰησοῦ, "against Jesus."

ᵉℵ A and several later MSS and versions read Ἰησοῦς, "Jesus."

ᶠW Φ and a few later MSS and versions add ἐκ δευτέρου, "for the second time."

ᵍℵ* A and a few later MSS read ὁ υἱὸς τοῦ θεοῦ, "son of God" (cf. Matt 26:63). At least one MS
reads ὁ υἱὸς τοῦ ζῶντος, "son of the living One." This reading is prompted by the parallel in Matt
26:63, ἐξορκίζω σε κατὰ τοῦ θεοῦ τοῦ ζῶντος, "I adjure you by the living God," and by Peter's confession in Matt 16:16, σὺ εἶ ὁ χριστὸς ὁ υἱὸς τοῦ θεοῦ τοῦ ζῶντος, "you are the Christ, the Son of the
living God."

ʰSeveral later MSS read σὺ εἶπας ὅτι ἐγώ εἰμι, "You have said that I am." This reading may be derived from Matt 26:64. However, Matthew may reflect the original reading of Mark 14:62, which a later
scribe may have shortened in order to remove the ambiguity of Jesus' answer (see *Comment* on v 62).

ⁱA few late authorities read τῆς δυνάμεως τοῦ θεοῦ, "of the power of God" (cf. Luke 22:69).

ʲGk.: μετὰ τῶν νεφελῶν τοῦ οὐρανοῦ. D omits μετά, "with." G 33 and other MSS read ἐπί, "upon."
Some old Italian and Lat. MSS, including the Vg., read *cum*, "with," while others read *super*, "upon."
Similar variants are attested in other versions (Arm Eth Geo Syr). These variants reflect the discrep-
ancy in the Gk. OT itself, where we find ἐπὶ τῶν νεφελῶν τοῦ οὐρανοῦ, "upon the clouds of heaven"

(LXX Dan 7:13), and μετὰ τῶν νεφελῶν τοῦ οὐρανοῦ, "with the clouds of heaven" (Theodotion Dan 7:13). The latter reading, which the evangelist evidently has followed, reflects the underlying Aram. עם־ענני שמיא ʿim-ʿănānê šĕmayyāʾ, "with the clouds of heaven" (MT Dan 7:13), which in turn reflects the words of the Aramaic-speaking Jesus.

ᵏW and a few later authorities add εὐθέως, "immediately."

ˡN W Σ and several later authorities add πάντες, "all."

ᵐW and a few later authorities add τοῦ στόματος αὐτοῦ, "from his mouth" (cf. Luke 22:71).

ⁿGk. φαίνεται, lit. "it appears." A few MSS read δοκεῖ, "it seems" (cf. Matt 26:66).

ᵒGk. ἐμπτύειν αὐτῷ. A few late MSS read ἐμπαίζειν αὐτῷ, "to beat on him." D and a few other MSS read ἐμπτύειν αὐτοῦ τῷ προσώπῳ, "to spit in his face."

ᵖOne encounters a variety of readings among many late MSS. Some read προφήτευσον ἡμῖν, "prophesy to us"; προφήτευσον ἡμῖν, χριστέ, "prophesy to us, Messiah"; and προφήτευσον ἡμῖν, χριστέ, τίς ἐστιν ὁ παίσας σε, "prophesy to us, Messiah; who hit you?" (The latter is read by N W Σ 33 and several later MSS, and is taken from Matt 26:68.)

ᵠSome authorities read ἔβαλλον, "were throwing," or ἔβαλον, "threw," while one MS reads κατέβαλον, "threw down." See *Comment* on v 65.

Form/Structure/Setting

The Markan account of Jesus' interrogation by the high priest and his colleagues unfolds in six basic parts: (1) the leading of Jesus inside, where "all the ruling priests and the elders and the scribes" have gathered together, and Peter's trailing behind and entrance into the courtyard of the high priest (vv 53–54); (2) the attempts to find incriminating witnesses against Jesus (vv 55–61a); (3) the high priest's question concerning Jesus' identity (v 61b); (4) Jesus' affirmation of his messianic identity (v 62); (5) the high priest's charge of blasphemy and call for capital judgment (vv 63–64); and (6) Jesus' rough treatment at the hands of his accusers and the officers (v 65). The notation of Peter's following into the courtyard sets the stage for his denials in vv 66–72.

Bultmann (*History*, 269–70) asserts that 14:55–64 is a "secondary explanation of the brief statement in 15:1." V 65 originally belonged elsewhere (*History*, 271). Dibelius (*Tradition*, 213) points out that "an eyewitness' [*sic*] description of the proceedings when Jesus was interrogated before the high priest and before Pilate is impossible." He believes that the narrative grew out of the temple accusation in v 58 (*Tradition*, 182–83, 192–93). Taylor (*Formation*, 58) sees the story of Jesus before the priests as a later addition to the core of the Passion Narrative. In his commentary, Taylor (563) sees the story as pre-Markan, "an account based on tradition." Because it cannot be based on the testimony of Christian eyewitnesses, it is not necessarily discredited, "since knowledge of what happened . . . must have been available." Taylor is correct so far as he goes. However, the tradition may very well be Petrine, since Peter himself was present in the courtyard of the high priest's home (Cranfield, 439, doubts this because the "narrative seems too precise"). It is in fact hard to believe that this disciple, willing to risk being in the vicinity of those who had arrested Jesus, would not have been able to learn anything of the proceedings that took place inside. All that is reported—the several "false" witnesses, the question about Jesus' threat against the temple, the question and reply regarding Jesus' messianic claim, and the high priest's charge of blasphemy—does not constitute more than the bare bones of the proceedings. Jesus' reply, moreover, in which he conflates elements from Dan 7:13 and Ps 110:1, has links to his previous teaching, all of which has good claim to authenticity.

Attested throughout the dominical tradition is the self-reference "son of man," which reflects Dan 7:13, while Jesus' interpretation of Ps 110:1 (Mark 12:35–37) can hardly be the creation of the early church (see *Comment* on 12:35–37). One must also agree with Cranfield (439), who correctly opines that the story "is not as doctrinally coloured as it surely would have been, were it the free construction of the early community."

More recent source and form critics have proposed a bewildering number of complex theories that try to explain the origins and composition of the Jewish hearing. Linnemann (*Studien zur Passionsgeschichte,* 109–35) attempts to distinguish between two independent narratives, an "A" source (vv 53b, 57, 58, 61b, 60a, 61a) and a "B" source (55a, 56, 60a, 61c, 62, 63, 64). Schneider (*BibLeb* 11 [1970] 1–15; id., *NovT* 12 [1970] 22–39; id., *Die Passion Jesu,* 55–64) believes that the evangelist has created a "diptych" contrasting the confessing Jesus inside and the denying Peter outside, both of whom are accused in a series of three. Schenke (*Der gekreuzigte Christus,* 26–46) identifies vv 53a, 55–56, 60–61, and 63–65 as the original core, with vv 53b, 57–59, and 62 added later. Dormeyer (*Die Passion Jesu,* 149–50, 157–75, 288–90) believes that he has identified three overlapping sources in the trial story: a portion of a primitive Acts of a Martyr (in v 55), a secondary christological redaction of this source (as seen in vv 56, 61b, 62a, 63, 64, 65b), and a final Markan redaction, whereby Jesus as the suffering Son of God is portrayed as the exemplary figure (as seen in vv 53b, 57–61a, 62ab–65ac). The disparity seen in this sampling of scholarly work reveals the subjectivity in attempts to differentiate among source, pre-Markan redaction, and Markan redaction. That the material has been edited and that it took shape in stages seem to be unavoidable conclusions. Nevertheless, for reasons already given, the bulk of this material in all probability represents fragments of historical reminiscence, much of it Petrine, of the essential components of Jesus' hearing before Jewish authorities.

The story of Jesus before the priests raises a number of historical and interpretive questions: (1) What kind of judicial hearing was it? (2) What was false about the temple threat in v 58? If Jesus did say something to this effect, what did it mean? (3) Did Jesus affirm his messianic identity, and if he did, what did he mean by it? (4) In what sense did Jesus commit blasphemy, and how did that justify calls for his death? All of these questions will be addressed in the *Comment* below.

There is also a structural and source-critical question that needs to be addressed at the outset. Is the intercalation of Jesus' trial (vv 53, 55–65) into Peter's denials (vv 54, 66–72) yet one more Markan "sandwich," or is it traditional? Critics and commentators often assume that it is the former. Just as the Markan evangelist intercalated the demonstration in the temple (11:11, 15–19) into the story of the fig tree (11:12–14, 20–25), just as he intercalated the story of the anointing (14:3–9) into the story of the plot to betray Jesus (14:1–2, 10–11), and so forth (see the list in Neirynck, *Duality in Mark,* 133), so he has intercalated the trial into the denials (on this feature of the evangelist's style with reference to the trial and the denials, see Donahue, *Are You the Christ?,* 58–63; Edwards, *NovT* 31 [1989] 193–216). Peter is left outside in the courtyard "being warmed by the fire." After narrating the trial scene, the evangelist returns to Peter in the courtyard, "warming himself" (vv 66–67).

The problem in this case, however, is that the same intercalation is found in John 18. In John 18:15–18, Peter and the "other disciple" enter the courtyard of the priest (in this case it is Annas; cf. vv 13, 24), where Peter is left "warming himself" by the fire (v 18). John 18:19–24 relates the story of Jesus before the Jewish council; then in v 25 we return to Peter outside "warming himself," where he will deny Jesus. The presence of this intercalation in John 18 is an embarrassment to theories that assume intercalation in Mark 14:53–65. Accordingly, some scholars suggest that John 18 is evidence of dependence upon the Gospel of Mark (e.g., Donahue, "From Passion Traditions," 9; K. E. Dewey, "Peter's Curse and Cursed Peter (Mark 14:53–54, 66–72)," in *The Passion in Mark*, ed. W. Kelber, 98, 104). The problem with this proposal is that evidence of Johannine dependence on Mark or one of the other Synoptics is quite meager, with the result that many, perhaps even a majority, of Johannine scholars think John is literarily independent of the Synoptic tradition. More to the point, one wonders why John 18, intercalation and all, offers no other evidence of knowledge of Mark 14 (cf. Fortna, *NTS* 24 [1978] 375: the evidence that John used Mark is "virtually none"). John 18 has the Jewish hearing at the home of Annas, rather than at the home of Caiaphas; the questions put to Jesus and Jesus' replies are completely different from those of Mark 14; and the details of the questions put to Peter and Peter's replies are almost completely different. In essence, we are asked to believe that in depending on Mark 14 the author of John 18 only extracted the literary seam created as the story shifts from Peter, to Jesus, and then back to Peter again. This is not very plausible.

Another problem of the intercalation theory in 14:53–65 is that one wonders if a story of Peter's denials could have circulated independently (cf. Gundry, 891). The story of the anointing in 14:3–9 could have circulated independently; so also the story of the priest's offering money for information and Judas's decision to accept it (14:1–2, 10–11). The stories of the fig tree (11:12–14, 20–25) and the temple action (11:11, 15–19) could have circulated independently. But could a story of Peter's denials have circulated with no reference to the interrogation of Jesus taking place inside at the same time? Herein lies the principal difference between this intercalation and the others. The others involve sequence, one detail following another, separated by hours, even by days; the trial of Jesus and the denials of Peter, however, are events that take place *simultaneously*. Finally, the literary technique of digression and resumption is in evidence in late antiquity in texts where we have no reason to suspect the splicing together of sources (cf. C. A. Evans, *JBL* 101 [1982] 248–49; accepted by Gundry, 891). It is probable, then, that this story, intermingled as it is, was traditional and that the Markan evangelist, who may have edited it in places, especially at the beginning and at the end, is not responsible for the blending of the two plots. (The combined stories in 5:21–43 of Jairus's daughter and the woman with the hemorrhage may very well be another example of pre-Markan tradition, not Markan redaction; cf. Guelich, 292–93.)

Comment

53 καὶ ἀπήγαγον τὸν Ἰησοῦν πρὸς τὸν ἀρχιερέα, "And they led Jesus to the high priest." Mark does not say so, but the high priest he mentions is Joseph (called) Caiaphas. Caiaphas is mentioned by name nine times in Matthew, Luke, John, and Acts. He is not mentioned by name in Mark. In John 18:13 he is identified as the son-in-law of Annas (also called Ananus, or Ḥanan), while in Luke 3:2 the evangelist tells us that the word of God came to John the Baptist "in the high-priesthood of Annas and Caiaphas." This linkage of Caiaphas, the ruling high priest, with his father-in-law attests to the enduring influence of the former high priest, who served 6–15 C.E.

A recent archaeological discovery has renewed scholarly and popular interest in this figure. In an ornate first-century C.E. crypt found in 1990 in Jerusalem's Peace Forest, which is 1.5 kilometers south of the Old City, two ossuaries (now in the Israel National Museum) were found on which was inscribed the name Caiaphas, according to some scholars (Greenhut, *BAR* 18.5 [1992] 35; Reich, *BAR* 18.5 [1992] 40–44; Flusser, *Jesus*, 195–206). On one of the boxes two inscriptions read (on one end) יהוסף בר קיפא *Yĕhôsēp bar Qayyāpāʾ* and (on one side) בר קפא יהוסף *Yĕhôsēp bar Qāpāʾ*. This ossuary contained the bones of a sixty-year-old man (and those of two infants, a toddler, a young boy, and a woman) and could be the ossuary of Caiaphas, the high priest to whom Josephus refers as Joseph Caiaphas (cf. *Ant.* 18.2.2 §35 ['Ιώσηπος ὁ Καϊάφας, "Joseph, the one [called] Caiaphas"] and 18.4.3 §95 [τὸν ἀρχιερέα 'Ιώσηπον τὸν Καϊάφαν ἐπικαλούμενον, "the high priest Joseph, the one called Caiaphas"]; for mention of Annas, whose five sons became high priests in turn, see *Ant.* 20.9.1 §§197–98). The sloppy scrawl on the side of the ossuary may be the writing of the relative who placed his bones in the box (to keep a record of whose bones were in which box). A second ossuary in the tomb bears the name קפא *Qāpāʾ*. According to the Tosefta (ca. 300 C.E.), Rabbi Joshua said, "I hereby give testimony concerning the family of the house of ʿAlubaʾi of Bet Šebaʾim and concerning the family of the house of Qaipha [קיפא *Qaypāʾ*] of Bet Meqošeš, that they are children of co-wives, and from them have been chosen High Priests, and they did offer up sacrifices on the Temple altar" (*t. Yebam.* 1.10; cf. Roth, *EncJud* 5:19–20). Reich and Flusser are of the opinion that the name inscribed on the ossuary is none other than that of the high priest so well known to Christians. This identification is accepted by the Israel National Museum in Jerusalem, and the bones of the elderly man have been interred on the Mount of Olives as those belonging to the high priest Joseph called Caiaphas.

However, Horbury (*PEQ* 126 [1994] 32–48) and Puech (*Le monde de la Bible* 80 [1993] 42–47) have called the identification with Caiaphas into question. Their objections are several: (1) The letter identified as *yôd* in קיפא *Qyp* (on the end of the ossuary) may very well be a *wāw* (i.e., קופא *Qwp*). As a *wāw* it is probably a vowel, not a consonant (as *Qayyāpāʾ*, or Caiaphas, requires), and so should probably be vocalized as *Qôpāʾ* or *Qûpāʾ*. (2) The omission of the *yôd/wāw* in the inscription on the side of the ossuary (קפא *Qp*) supports the view that the *yôd/wāw* in the longer spelling of the name is a vowel, not a consonant. (3) The crypt in which the ossuary was found is not as ornate as one might expect in the case of a high-priestly family (as seen, for example, in the ornate and grand mauselea found in Akeldama). The crypt of Peace Forest may have been that of a fairly well-to-do Jerusalem family, but not one of a family that was among Jerusalem's very wealthy and politically powerful. Although the possible identification of the name on the ossuary and the skeletal remains of elderly man in it with the high priest of the Gospels has not been decisively ruled out, serious doubts have been raised.

Another box in this crypt contains the bones of a woman, bearing the name מרים ברת שמעון *Miryām bĕrat Šimʿôn,* "Miriam, daughter of Simon." In it a coin minted during the reign of Herod Agrippa I (42/43 C.E.) was found in the mouth of the skull, probably reflecting the pagan custom of payment to the Greek god Charon for safe passage across the River Styx (see Greenhut, *BAR* 18.5 [1992] 28–36, 76; Reich, *BAR* 81.5 [1992] 38–44, 76). Although we should not read too much significance into this curious feature, it does testify to the extent of penetration of pagan culture into Jewish life, even within upper, possibly priestly circles of the highest rank.

Bringing Jesus to the home of the high priest (as is made clear in v 54) late at night indicates that the hearing that will shortly take place is unofficial and ad hoc, notwithstanding mention in v 55 of ὅλον τὸ συνέδριον, "the entire council"; see *Comment* on v 55. The nocturnal assembling of such high-ranking figures attests to their great alarm and sense of urgency. Their hope is to dispatch Jesus quickly before the celebration of the Passover meal the following evening.

καὶ συνέρχονται πάντες οἱ ἀρχιερεῖς καὶ οἱ πρεσβύτεροι καὶ οἱ γραμματεῖς, "and all the ruling priests and the elders and the scribes come together." These are the men who have been Jesus' chief antagonists since his arrival in Jerusalem. Jesus has encountered some of them in his teaching and activities in the temple precincts (11:18, 27; 12:12, 28, 38; 14:1). The gathering of "the ruling priests and the elders and the scribes" harks back to Jesus' passion predictions, where these individuals were mentioned as those who would seek his death (8:31; 10:33).

54 ὁ Πέτρος ἀπὸ μακρόθεν ἠκολούθησεν αὐτῷ ἕως ἔσω εἰς τὴν αὐλὴν τοῦ ἀρχιερέως καὶ ἦν συγκαθήμενος μετὰ τῶν ὑπηρετῶν καὶ θερμαινόμενος πρὸς τὸ φῶς, "Peter followed him from a distance, right into the courtyard of the high priest, and he was sitting with the officers and was being warmed by the fire." In being brought before the high priest, all the ruling priests, the elders, and the scribes (v 53), Jesus now faces the most powerful men among the Jewish people. Peter, following at a safe, inconspicuous distance, enters the courtyard of the high priest, where he joins the attendants who are warming themselves by the fire. What happens to Peter will be narrated later. By gaining access to τὴν αὐλὴν τοῦ ἀρχιερέως, "the courtyard of the high priest," Peter is now in a position to learn what he can of the fate of his teacher and friend. He hopes to remain inconspicuous among the throng of officers and servants, some of whom were involved in the arrest. If Peter was indeed the person who struck the servant of the high priest in Gethsemane (14:47), then his wish for anonymity becomes all the more understandable. Even if he was not the one who assaulted the servant (and the evangelist does not say he was), the simple fact that he is a disciple of Jesus places him in jeopardy, and Mark's readers know it. The evangelist leaves the worried disciple θερμαινόμενος πρὸς τὸ φῶς, "being warmed by the fire," a detail that will be repeated in v 67 to draw readers back to this setting.

55 οἱ δὲ ἀρχιερεῖς καὶ ὅλον τὸ συνέδριον ἐζήτουν κατὰ τοῦ Ἰησοῦ μαρτυρίαν εἰς τὸ θανατῶσαι αὐτόν, καὶ οὐχ ηὕρισκον, "But the ruling priests and the entire council were seeking testimony against Jesus, in order to put him to death, but they were not finding any." οἱ ἀρχιερεῖς, "the ruling priests," are mentioned first and without "the elders and the scribes," who so often are in their company because they form the real power in Jewish politics, even if subordinate to their Roman overlords (cf. Josephus, *Ant.* 20.10.5 §251: "the ruling priests [οἱ ἀρχιερεῖς] were entrusted with the leadership of the nation"; Smallwood, *JTS* n.s. 13 [1962] 14–34; id., *The Jews under Roman Rule*, 148–50).

ὅλον τὸ συνέδριον, "the entire council," does not mean a formal sitting of the Sanhedrin, as has sometimes been claimed. What is probably meant is that several members of the Sanhedrin have convened at the home of Caiaphas and that most, perhaps all, of them were interested in seeking testimony against Jesus. The use of ὅλον, "entire," which is hyperbolic, may have been intended to underscore how fully Jesus' passion predictions had been fulfilled (Gundry, 883). If this gathering of priests and elders is recognized for what it is—an informal hearing designed to gain a consensus among Jewish authorities that Jesus should be handed over to the Romans with a capital recommendation—then objections that have been raised against its historicity on the grounds that the rules of capital trials have been violated (as laid down two centuries later in *m. Sanh.* 4–7) are quite beside the point (cf. Cranfield, 440).

The ruling priests ἐζήτουν κατὰ τοῦ Ἰησοῦ μαρτυρίαν εἰς τὸ θανατῶσαι αὐτόν, "were seeking testimony against Jesus, in order to put him to death." This μαρτυρίαν, "testimony," had to be eyewitness (and not simply circumstantial), and it had to be verified in accordance with Jewish law (see *Comment* on v 59). Although the hearing before the Jewish rulers was not a formal trial, certain rules of evidence nevertheless still applied. However, try as they might, οὐχ ηὕρισκον, "they were not finding any." Mark's imperfect ηὕρισκον, "were [not] finding," signifies the ongoing effort, while εἰς τὸ θανατῶσαι αὐτόν, "in order to put him to death," makes it clear that the priests were seeking evidence of capital crimes. As the Markan narrative will make clear, the ruling priests have no plan to put Jesus to death themselves; they expect Pilate to do this. Because the Roman governor would have little interest and little jurisdiction in a purely religious dispute (e.g., matters of temple polity), the ruling priests must secure testimony that will give rise to a charge that will be taken seriously by Rome.

56 πολλοὶ γὰρ ἐψευδομαρτύρουν κατ' αὐτοῦ, "For many were giving false testimony against him." γάρ, "for," elaborates on ἐζήτουν . . . μαρτυρίαν, "were seeking testimony," and οὐχ ηὕρισκον, "were not finding any," of v 55. Despite the *seeking*, the priests were *not finding* serious testimony, "for" or "because" the witnesses kept failing the test of agreement. From the evangelist's point of view, of course, those giving testimony against Jesus were false witnesses, who ἐψευδομαρτύρουν, "were giving false testimony" or "were falsely testifying." Their "pseudo" appellation reminds readers of Mark of Jesus' warning in 13:22: "False messiahs [ψευδόχριστοι] and false prophets [ψευδοπροφῆται] will be raised up and will offer signs and wonders in order to deceive, if possible, the elect." Already Jesus has encountered false witnesses, whose false testimony in all probability continues to be uttered in the time of the Markan community.

καὶ ἴσαι αἱ μαρτυρίαι οὐκ ἦσαν, "And the testimonies were not in agreement." Here lies the explanation of why the ruling priests were not finding any incriminating evidence against Jesus: αἱ μαρτυρίαι, "the testimonies," i.e., sworn statements, ἴσαι . . . οὐκ ἦσαν, "were not in agreement" (lit. "and equal [ἴσαι] the testimonies were not"). For the sense in which they were not equal, see *Comment* on v 59.

57 καί τινες ἀναστάντες ἐψευδομαρτύρουν κατ' αὐτοῦ, "And some, standing up, testified against him falsely." Some stood up before the seated priests and ἐψευδομαρτύρουν, "testified . . . falsely," as had been anticipated in v 56. In what sense their testimony was false, however, is not easy to determine.

58 ἡμεῖς ἠκούσαμεν αὐτοῦ λέγοντος ὅτι ἐγὼ καταλύσω τὸν ναὸν τοῦτον τὸν χειροποίητον καὶ διὰ τριῶν ἡμερῶν ἄλλον ἀχειροποίητον οἰκοδομήσω, "We heard him saying, 'I shall destroy this temple made with hands, and after three days I shall build another not made with hands.'" The evangelist scarcely prepares his readers for this accusation. In fact, the readers of Mark who are dependent on Mark alone are in no position to evaluate it. Mark's readers know, of course, that Jesus has engaged in controversy with the temple establishment (chaps. 11–12) and has predicted the temple's complete and utter destruction (13:2), and they know that Jesus *did not* say anywhere in Mark, "I shall destroy this temple . . . ." Because Jesus predicted the temple's destruction (cf. C. A. Evans, *JSP* 10 [1992] 89–147) and because the Johannine Jesus says something similar (cf. John 2:19: "Destroy this temple, and in three days I will raise it up"), most scholars today believe Mark 14:58 represents something that Jesus actually said or at least something close to something that he said (cf. Sanders, *Jesus and Judaism*, 71–76; Ådna, "Jesu Kritik am Tempel," 506–7).

There are other reasons for thinking Jesus did say something like this, for the saying appears to allude to the image of the stone cut from a mountain "by no human hand," which then destroys the image that represents the successive kingdoms of the earth (Dan 2:44–45; Ådna, "Jesu Kritik am Tempel," 507). There is much in dominical tradition that harks back to Danielic language and imagery, the "son of man" self-designation being the most obvious (cf. Dan 7:13; see *Comment* on Mark 8:31). Jesus may also have seen himself as the anointed one who would be cut off (Dan 9:26; see *Comment* on Mark 14:21), and he foretold the coming "abomination of desolation" that would signal the nearness of the appearance of the "son of man" (Dan 11:31; 12:5–13; see *Comment* on Mark 13:14). It could very well be that after his rejection in Jerusalem, Jesus began to speak of his death and of the temple's destruction (as in Mark 13:2), possibly even threatening to replace the temple built by Herod with one of heavenly origin. Incorporation of Daniel's stone that represents the kingdom of God is consistent with Jesus' use of Daniel and coheres with his proclamation of the kingdom of God. It should also be noted that elements from Dan 7:13 and 2:44–45 are combined in the messianic vision of 4 Ezra 13; cf. esp. vv 3, 6, 36: "that man flew with the clouds of heaven . . . he carved out for himself a great mountain, and flew upon it . . . the mountain carved out without hands."

There are some Jewish traditions in which the eschatological Messiah is expected to rebuild the temple of Jerusalem. This expectation may be rooted in the prophecy of Zech 6:12: "The man whose name is Branch . . . he shall build the temple of the LORD" (cf. *Tg.* Zech 6:12: "Behold, the man whose name is Messiah will be revealed, and he shall be raised up, and shall build the Temple of the Lord"). We may again have more evidence of the influence on Jesus of this prophetic book. The men of Qumran apparently looked for a new, eschatological temple. 4QFlor 1:6–7 may have some relevance for understanding the meaning of the saying attributed to Jesus: "And he told them to build for him a sanctuary of man [מקדש אדם *miqdaš 'ādām*]." Some have thought of this sanctuary (or temple) in spiritual or communal terms: i.e., because the Essenes do not have access to the temple in Jerusalem, or at least are unable to influence the *pragmata* (activities) of the cult, they have formed a human temple whereby they might worship God. Wise (*RevQ* 15 [1991] 103–32) has argued that the passage is speaking about a literal temple, one that will be built in the time of judgment and restoration. God has commanded the righteous to build the "Temple of Adam," at which time the bliss of paradise will be restored. Wise could be correct, for this seems to be the meaning in the Temple Scroll as well. According to this writing, God promises: "I shall dwell with them for all eternity. I shall sanctify my [Te]mple with my glory, for I will cause my glory to dwell upon it until the day of creation, when I myself will create my temple; I will establish it for myself for everlasting in fulfillment of the covenant that I made with Jacob at Bethel" (11QTemple 29:7–10). A new temple for the eschatological, restored Jerusalem is envisioned in *2 Bar.* 4:3: "This is the city of which I said, 'On the palms of my hands I have carved for you.' It is not this building that is in your midst now; it is that which will be revealed, with me, that was already prepared from the moment that I decided to create Paradise." Later rabbinic interpretation entertains the idea that it is God himself who builds the temple: "But when He built the [Solomonic] Temple . . . but when He came to build the Temple He did it, as it were, with both of His hands, as it is said, 'The sanctuary [מקדש *miqdāš*], O Lord, which Your hands have established'" (*Mek.* on Exod 15:17–21 [*Širātā'* §10]; cf. J. Z. Lauterbach, ed., *Mekilta de Rabbi Ishmael,* 3 vols. [Philadelphia: Jewish Publication Society of America, 1933–35] 2:79; Ådna, "Jesu Kritik am Tempel," 250). Although probably deriving from the period between the two great wars (70–132 C.E.), the Aramaic paraphrase of Isa 53:5, "and he [i.e., the Servant who in the Targum is identified as the Messiah] will build the sanctuary, which was profaned for our sins," probably reflects messianic ideas that were in circulation in earlier times.

Referring to the temple as χειροποίητον, "made with hands," in itself would have been offensive to the ruling priests, for in addition to denying the divine status of the temple such a statement would even hint at its idolatrous status. In the LXX, χειροποίητος, "made with hands," appears several times in reference to idols (translating פֶּסֶל *pesel* [cf. Lev 26:1]; or אֱלִילִים *'ĕlîlîm* [cf. Isa 2:18; 10:11; 19:1]; or various forms of "gods of gold, silver" [cf. Dan 5:4, 23; 6:28]). Such a connotation would only intensify the prophetic indictment of Jesus' saying: The temple establishment is likened to something human, perhaps even idolatrous, that will be destroyed when "the son of man" comes (cf. 14:62) and a temple ἀχειροποίητον, "not made with hands," is erected.

If the accusation that Jesus *himself* threatened to destroy the temple (and this is doubtful; cf. Sanders, *Jesus and Judaism,* 74: "he must have either predicted or threatened the destruction of the temple *by God*") could be confirmed, then Jesus would have been subject to serious punishment, perhaps execution. The possibility of execution for uttering threats against the temple is seen in the story of Jesus ben Ananias, who in 62 C.E. began prophesying the destruction of the temple. Outraged, ruling priests wanted him executed (Josephus, *J.W.* 6.5.3 §§300–309; see *Excursus:* "The Arrest of Jesus Son of Ananias"). Josephus also tells the story of Jeremiah, who was accused of having used divination against the king (and by implication the city of Jerusalem). The elite of Jerusalem demanded that the prophet be punished; therefore when he was brought to trial, many rulers cast votes against him (Josephus, *Ant.* 10.6.2 §§89–92). One also thinks of how Paul was mobbed in the temple precincts when rumors started to the effect that the apostle had brought a Gentile into the court of Israel (Acts 21:27–36; v 36: "Away with him!").

59 καὶ οὐδὲ οὕτως ἴση ἦν ἡ μαρτυρία αὐτῶν, "And not even their testimony was in agreement." According to Jewish law, two or three witnesses were required to establish the facts of a criminal case (cf. Num 35:30; Deut 17:6; 19:15). According to v 57, "some, standing up, testified against him." Mark's τινές, "some," at the very least implies two men; indeed, the evangelist may have wished to leave us with the impression that *several* men stood up and accused Jesus. The actual words of the testimony—"We heard him saying, 'I shall destroy this temple . . .'"— do not seem to be the issue. What Jesus is alleged to have said seems to have been agreed upon, unless the reader is to imagine that some of the witnesses testified that Jesus in fact said something else and so contradicted what the others said. But that does not seem to be the case here. In what sense then did their testimony lack being ἴση, "in agreement"? The example in Susanna, an apocryphal addition to the book of Daniel, is instructive and may answer our question. In this entertaining story, we are told of two lustful elders (πρεσβύτεροι) who attempt to seduce the beautiful Susanna. Catching her in a private garden while she bathes, they proposition her, threatening: "Look, the garden doors are shut, no one sees us, and we are in love with you; so give your consent, and lie with us. If you refuse, we will testify against [καταμαρτυρήσομεν] you that a young man was with you, and this was why you sent your maids away" (Sus 20–21 [Theodotion]). Susanna refuses and cries for help, whereupon the elders "shouted against her" (v 24). The next day the people gather at the house of Joakim, the husband of Susanna. The elders testify against her:

> As we were walking in the garden alone, this woman came in with two maids, shut the garden doors, and dismissed the maids. Then a young man, who had been hidden, came to her and lay with her. We were in a corner of the garden, and when we saw this wickedness we ran to them. We saw them embracing, but we could not hold the man, for he was too strong for us, and he opened the doors and dashed out. So we seized this woman and asked her who the young man was, but she would not tell us. These things we testify [μαρτυροῦμεν]. (vv 36–41 [Theodotion])

The informal Jewish court initially believes the testimony of the two elders. Accordingly, "they condemned her to die [κατέκριναν αὐτὴν ἀποθανεῖν]" (v 41 [Theodotion]). As Susanna is being led away to be put to death, the youthful Daniel intervenes. He questions separately each of her accusers. Where was Susanna when she was in the embrace of the young man? The separated elders give conflicting accounts (vv 52–59), Susanna is acquitted, and the wicked elders are executed (vv 60–62). In all probability, the lack of agreement to which the evangelist refers in Mark 14:56 and 59 was of this nature. Under separate cross-examination, the testimonies of these individuals did not agree and so were not admissible against Jesus.

60 καὶ ἀναστὰς ὁ ἀρχιερεὺς εἰς μέσον ἐπηρώτησεν τὸν Ἰησοῦν, "And standing up in the midst, the high priest asked Jesus." ἀναστάς, "standing up," in the midst of the council, as the false witnesses had just moments before, the high priest (i.e., Joseph called Caiaphas, son-in-law of Annas, a former high priest and still very much a major influence upon temple politics; see *Comment* on v 53) puts a question directly to Jesus. The witnesses that had been brought forward had proven ineffective. Caiaphas decides to take a more direct approach, shifting the burden onto the accused.

οὐκ ἀποκρίνῃ οὐδέν; τί οὗτοί σου καταμαρτυροῦσιν; "Are you not going to reply? What are these men testifying against you?" Mark's structure is awkward. Most translations see two questions: "Are you not going to reply?" and "What are these [men] testifying against you?" (cf. Taylor, 567; Cranfield, 442; and others). The high priest asks Jesus if he is not going to reply to the (unconfirmed) charges that have been brought against him. The first question is a challenge, even a dare. The second question is a demand. The high priest's strategy is plain enough: if the testimony that has been given thus far fails to incriminate Jesus, perhaps his replies to it will.

61 ὁ δὲ ἐσιώπα καὶ οὐκ ἀπεκρίνατο οὐδέν, "But he was silent, and answered back nothing." Jesus refuses to answer. Why he refuses here and then answers a moment later is not obvious. Jesus may have refused to answer the "false" testimony, as if not wishing to dignify it with an answer. But when asked correctly about his identity, he chooses to answer.

πάλιν ὁ ἀρχιερεὺς ἐπηρώτα αὐτόν, "Again the high priest interrogated him." Mark's πάλιν, "again," alludes to v 60. ἐπερωτᾶν occurs in Mark some twenty-five times. It is often translated "to ask," but that sometimes fails to convey the full sense of the word, for in some contexts the idea is "to interrogate." For example, in 5:9 Jesus interrogates the demonized man, demanding to know his name. In 8:27–29 Jesus interrogates his disciples, with reference to his identity in the opinion of the public and his disciples. Frequently Jesus is interrogated by his critics. In 7:5 Pharisees and scribes demand to know why Jesus' disciples do not follow the tradition of the elders. Pharisees question Jesus on the issue of divorce (10:2), Sadducees interrogate him on the question of resurrection (12:18), and a scribe wishes to know which commandment Jesus thinks is greatest of all (12:28). But Jesus himself interrogates his critics (11:29) and answers them so effectively that they no longer dare to interrogate him further (12:34). In vv 60–61, however, Jesus is faced with a much more dangerous interrogation. The high priest is no petty rival, irritated scribe, or indignant Pharisee; he is the highest Jewish authority, and he is not to be trifled with.

σὺ εἶ ὁ χριστὸς ὁ υἱὸς τοῦ εὐλογητου; "Are you the Messiah, the son of the Blessed?" The high priest's σύ, "you," is "emphatic and contemptuous" (Taylor 567), for εἶ by itself means "you are," or in this interrogative context "are you?" Thus the sense is: "Are *you* [!] the Messiah?" The high priest's question here is not a double one, as in v 61. In other words, he has not asked Jesus, "Are you the Messiah? [Are you] the son of the Blessed [i.e., God]?" (an option rightly rejected by Lövestam, *SEÅ* 26 [1961] 94–95). When the high priest qualifies χριστός, "anointed [one]" or "Messiah," as ὁ υἱὸς τοῦ εὐλογητοῦ, "the son of the Blessed," it is clear that he is talking about the anointed king, as opposed to an anointed prophet (1 Kgs 19:15–16; 1 Chr 16:22 = Ps 105:15) or anointed priest (Lev 16:32; 1 Chr 29:22). Only the Davidic, royal descendant was talked about as in some sense the "son of God," as seen, for example, in 2 Sam 7:12, 14: "I will raise up your [i.e., David's] offspring after you, . . . I will establish his kingdom. . . . I will be his father, and he shall be my son" (cf. 1 Chr 17:13); Ps 2:2, 7: "The kings of the earth set themselves . . . against the Lord and his anointed. . . . I will tell of the decree of the LORD: He said to me, 'You are my son, today I have begotten you.'" At Qumran, Nathan's oracle (2 Sam 7) was interpreted explicitly as referring to the eschatological Messiah: "'I will be a father to him, and he will be my son.'

This refers to the Shoot of David, who is to arise with the Interpreter of the Law, and who will arise in Zion in the last days" (4Q174 [= 4QFlorilegium] 3:11–12). Ps 2:2, 7, moreover, is probably alluded to in the poorly preserved and controversial 1QSa 2:11–12: "when God begets the Messiah with them." The texts at Qumran tell against the skepticism of some scholars (e.g., Haenchen, 512; Schweizer, 324), who have argued that in Jewish circles the Messiah was never called "son of God."

It has been claimed that Caiaphas's reference to God as τοῦ εὐλογητοῦ, "the Blessed," is a "pseudo-Jewish expression" that derives from Mark or Christian tradition before him (Juel, *Messiah and Temple*, 79; cf. Klausner, *Jesus of Nazareth*, 342: "This is not a Hebrew expression and must be a later addition"). But its appearance in Jewish liturgy suggests otherwise: "Rabbi Ishmael says: 'Bless the Lord who is blessed [*or* who is the Blessed: המבורך *hambôrāk*]" (*m. Ber.* 7:3; see the discussion where the opinion of Rabbi Ishmael prevails; see G. H. Dalman, *The Words of Jesus*, tr. D. M. Kay [Edinburgh: T. & T. Clark, 1902] 200; Abrahams, *Studies in Pharisaism* 2:212; Gundry, 910: it is "possible that τοῦ εὐλογητοῦ goes back to the passive participle המברך [*hambōrāk*]"). Juel (*Messiah and Temple*, 78–79) contends that the examples of המבורך *hambôrāk* in the mishnaic and talmudic (Jerusalem and Babylonian) tractates *Berakot* are adjectival ("who is blessed"), not substantival ("the Blessed [One]"). But this assumes more exactitude in translation and transmission from Hebrew/Aramaic to Greek than we should require. And in any case, Mark's τοῦ εὐλογητοῦ may in fact be adjectival and so could be rendered "the son of [him] who is blessed" (cf. the call to prayer in the synagogue: בָּרְכוּ אֶת יהוה הַמְבֹרָךְ *bārăkû 'et YHWH hambôrāk*, "Bless the Lord the Blessed [One]," or "Bless the Lord who is blessed"). Mark's "the Blessed" is not an *abbreviation* of the ubiquitous rabbinic circumlocution הקדוש ברוך הוא *haqqādôš bārûk hû'*, "the Holy One blessed be He," as Klausner (*Jesus of Nazareth*, 342) rightly denies; it is a *forerunner* of the later, expanded rabbinic expression (so Gundry, 909–10). One should also take into account *1 Enoch* 77:2, which speaks of "the Most High" and "the Eternally Blessed" (a partially preserved Enochic text at Qumran only loosely parallels the Ethiopic, reading "the Great One" [רבא *rabbā'*] instead of "the Most High" or "the Eternally Blessed"; cf. 4Q209 [= 4QEnastr^b ar] 23:3). The authenticity of the high priest's question is supported by the appearance of the circumlocution "the Blessed," for the Markan evangelist has no hesitation in saying "kingdom of God" (contrast Matthew's preference for "kingdom of heaven") or having characters identify Jesus as "son of God" (e.g., 3:11; 15:39; cf. 1:1) or "holy one of God" (e.g., 1:24).

Marcus (*NovT* 31 [1989] 125–41) sees in the high priest's qualification, "the son of the Blessed," a distinction between "son of God" and "son of David." It is possible that Jesus himself made such a distinction, and Marcus (*NovT* 31 [1989] 135–37) is correct to draw our attention to Mark 12:35–37, but it is doubtful that the high priest made this distinction. To be the Messiah, son of David, was to be in some sense the "son of God" (as in 2 Sam 7:12–14; Ps 2:2, 7). Whether Jesus was of a more political, restorative type (hoping to restore the Davidic, royal line) or of a more utopian type (thinking the world was about to end and a new one about to take its place; on this distinction, see L. H. Schiffman, "Messianic Figures," 128–29), or some middle combination, would scarcely have mattered to the high priest or to the Roman authorities. But the distinction in all probability was important to Jesus, who earlier had objected to the scribal epithet "son of

David," because it inadequately defined the Messiah (see *Comment* on 12:35–37). Jesus will qualify his messianic self-definition in his reply.

62 ἐγώ εἰμι, καὶ ὄψεσθε τὸν υἱὸν τοῦ ἀνθρώπου ἐκ δεξιῶν καθήμενον τῆς δυνάμεως καὶ ἐρχόμενον μετὰ τῶν νεφελῶν τοῦ οὐρανοῦ, "I am; and you will see 'the son of man' seated 'at the right hand' of the Power and 'coming with the clouds of heaven.'" According to Mark, Jesus answers with a simple ἐγώ εἰμι, "I am." But Matt 26:64 reads σὺ εἶπας, "You have said [it]," and Luke 22:70 reads ὑμεῖς λέγετε ὅτι ἐγώ εἰμι, "You say that I am." Taylor (568) believes there "is good reason to think that . . . Mark wrote σὺ εἶπας ὅτι ἐγώ εἰμι ['You have said that I am']," for this reading is attested in Θ fam. 13 472 543 565 700 1071 geo arm Origen, and it would explain the readings found in Matthew and Luke. Cranfield (443–44) and others agree. This view has much to commend it. One can understand that a scribe might wish to omit σὺ εἶπας ὅτι, "you have said that," so that Jesus' affirmation of his messiahship would be explicit. Moreover, the "you have said" is consistent with the indirectness of Jesus' messianic identity, as seen elsewhere in Mark. Indeed, if the reading stands, then we have Jesus properly confessed by both the highest Jewish authority in 14:61–62 ("Are you the Messiah, the son of the Blessed? . . . You have said that I am") and a high Roman authority, the centurion, in 15:39 ("Truly this man was the son of God"). But having Jesus directly affirm his messiahship may also be problematic, for it would strike Jewish readers as presumptuous. Simon ben Kosiba is discredited in *b. Sanh.* 93b by having him claim "I am the Messiah." Others may have confessed Jesus as the Messiah or as the son of God, but for Jesus to have done so in such a direct way may have caused some discomfort for early Jewish Christians. Matthew's "You have said [it]" and Luke's "You say that I am" may represent attempts to mitigate the presumptiveness of Jesus' bald statement, "I am." Inspired by the qualifications and feeling the same pressure, a later scribe copying Mark may have expanded and qualified Jesus' reply: "You have said that I am." The question is not easily settled. Because the external evidence for the longer reading is weak and internal considerations can cut in either direction, the shorter reading is preferred.

Jesus' reply, ἐγώ εἰμι, "I am," is a simple affirmation ("yes"); it is not an allusion to the divine name (rightly Betz, *ANRW* 2.25.1 [1982] 634; E. P. Sanders, *Jewish Law from Jesus to the Mishnah: Five Studies* [London: SCM Press; Philadelphia: Trinity Press International, 1990] 65). Compare *T. Job* 29:3–4: "'Are you [σὺ εἶ] Jobab, our fellow king?' . . . 'I am [ἐγώ εἰμι].'"

ὄψεσθε, "you will see," means that members of the Sanhedrin who have condemned Jesus will *see* him as the "son of man" who will come in judgment (cf. Dan 7:9–14). When Mark's Gospel was circulated ca. 69 C.E., this was no longer possible. With the delay of the Parousia such a saying would have become increasingly problematic. For this reason it is better to view it as a genuine fragment of Jesus' reply to the high priest rather than as a later Christian pesher (*pace* N. Perrin, *NTS* 12 [1965–66] 150–55; id., "Jesus' Answer," 85, based on Zech 12:10) or prophecy (*pace* N. Perrin, "Jesus' Answer," 91–95). Hengel ("'Sit at My Right Hand!'" 187) believes it is pre-Markan and probably authentic, though he is uncertain how close it is to the original form of the utterance. Hengel ("'Sit at My Right Hand!'" 188) also calls our attention to the association of the plural ὄψεσθε, "you will see," with Enochic traditions about the "son of man," or "elect one":

"you will see my elect one sitting on the throne of glory" (*1 Enoch* 55:4); "and they shall see and recognize him sitting on the throne of his glory" (62:3). Jesus' solemn statement "you will see" followed by a "son of man" self-reference would have in all probability brought to mind traditions such as these in which kings and rulers are depicted as groveling before the "son of man" seated on his glorious throne and presiding as judge.

Caiaphas and company will see τὸν υἱὸν τοῦ ἀνθρώπου . . . ἐρχόμενον μετὰ τῶν νεφελῶν τοῦ οὐρανοῦ, "'the son of man' . . . 'coming with the clouds of heaven.'" This is an unmistakable allusion to Dan 7:13. Some of Jesus' previous self-references as "the son of man" clearly alluded to the Danielic figure. The claim in 2:10 that "the son of man" has "authority on earth" to forgive sins implies that Jesus, as "the son of man" who in Dan 7:13–14 has been given authority in heaven, may now forgive sins "on earth." The claim in 2:28 that "the son of man" is "lord even of the sabbath" probably reflects the same concept. The forecasts in 8:38 and 13:26 of the coming of "the son of man . . . with the holy angels" and "in clouds with great power and glory" clearly allude to Dan 7:13–14. Even the passion sayings and related sayings in which reference to "the son of man" routinely appears (e.g., 8:31; 9:9, 12, 31; 10:33 [esp. 45, which qualifies Dan 7:14]; 14:21, 41) probably allude to the struggle depicted in Dan 7:15–27. The high priest and his priestly colleagues at the moment sit in judgment on Jesus, but the day will come when they will see him coming with the clouds as "the son of man."

Jesus enriches his bold self-identification and prophecy by drawing an element from Ps 110:1: "Sit at my right hand, till I make your enemies your footstool." By alluding to this verse, ἐκ δεξιῶν . . . τῆς δυνάμεως, "'at the right hand' of the Power," Jesus not only claims that he will sit next to God but implies that when he returns as "the son of man," he will come as judge of his (and God's) enemies, that is, the ruling priests who now sit in judgment on him. This image coheres with the Enochic texts quoted above, where "the son of man" sits on his throne of glory and judges the rulers of the earth, who bow before him. (For further discussion, see *Comment* on 11:28.)

Presupposing the Jewish exegetical principle of *gĕzêrâ šāwâ*, "an equivalent category," Jesus has drawn together Dan 7 and Ps 110. Both passages envision the enthronement of God: "thrones were placed and one that was ancient of days took his seat; . . . the court sat in judgment, and the books were opened" (Dan 7:9–10); "The LORD says to my lord: 'Sit at my right hand, till I make your enemies your footstool'" (Ps 110:1). The plural "thrones" of Dan 7:9 and God's invitation to the psalmist's "lord" to sit next to him create the picture that Jesus envisions: as "the son of man" Jesus will take his seat next to God himself (Ps 110:1); he will "come with the clouds" (Dan 7:13); the court will sit "in judgment" (Dan 7:9); and his "enemies" will become his "footstool" (Ps 110:1).

To be καθήμενον, "seated," in the presence of God is roughly paralleled in 4Q504 [= 4QDibHam[a]] 1–2 iv 5–8: "And you chose the tribe of Judah, and established your covenant with David, so that he would be like a shepherd, a prince over your people, and would sit in front of you on the throne of Israel for ever." But this text appears to be a review of Israel's history, not a messianic prophecy. The David referred to here is the historical David, not the Messiah. He sits "on the throne of [historical] Israel" and does so "in front of" God in a symbolic sense, not in the metaphysical, eschatological sense that Jesus has implied in his combination of Dan 7:13 and Ps 110:1. Potentially of more relevance is the "David-Apoca-lypse" from *Hekhalot Rabbati* §§125–26, attributed to Rabbi Ishmael, which describes David's crown as radiating a splendor that reaches from one end of the world to another "as David came and sat upon his throne, which was prepared in the pres-ence of the throne of his Creator" (P. Schäfer, *Übersetzung der Hekhalot-Literatur II §§ 81–334*, 2 vols., TSAJ 17 [Tübingen: Mohr-Siebeck, 1987] 2:56–59; cf. Hengel, "'Sit at My Right Hand!'" 195–96). This vision is eschatological, and David may possess messianic characteristics. It is not clear, however, if this tradition reaches back to the early part of the first century C.E. (For more examples and critical discussion of enthroned OT worthies, see D. L. Bock, *Blasphemy and Exaltation*, 115–62; Hengel, "'Sit at My Right Hand!'" 185–212.)

When Jesus returns as "the son of man," he will be seated at the right hand τῆς δυνάμεως, "of the Power." The expression τῆς δυνάμεως as a circumlocution for God is better attested than the τοῦ εὐλογητοῦ, "the Blessed," the circumlocu-tion used by the high priest. An exact parallel is found in a saying attributed to Rabbi Ishmael: "It was said by the mouth of the Power [הגבורה *haggĕbûrâ*]" (*Sipre Num.* §112 [on Num 15:31]; cf. *b. ʿErub.* 54b; *b. B. Meṣiʿa* 58b; *b. Šabb.* 88b; *b. Yebam.* 105b; *Tg.* Job 5:8: "from the Power [תקיפא *taqqîpāʾ*]"; 14:18 [var.]; 18:4 [var.]). There are references to "the Power that is above [כח של מעלה *kōaḥ šel maʿălâ*]" (*Sipre Deut.* §319 [on Deut 32:18]) and "in the eyes of the Power [הגבורה *haggĕbûrâ*]" (*ʾAbot R. Nat.* [A] 37.12). Note also *1 Enoch* 62:7: "For the Son of Man was con-cealed from the beginning, and the Most High One preserved him in the presence of his power." It is also possible that the word δυνάμεως, "Power," was suggested by LXX Ps 109:2 (cf. MT 110:2): "the Lord will send forth from Zion the rod of your power [ῥάβδον δυνάμεώς σου]." There is no good reason (*pace* Kazmierski, *Jesus*, 167–69) to regard the epithet "the Power" as an inauthentic Jewish Chris-tian circumlocution.

Juel (*Messiah and Temple*, 95), finding incongruous the juxtaposition of being "seated," which implies being stationary, and "coming," which implies movement, concludes that "two separate scenes" have been combined. However, this suppo-sition is unnecessary, for we find Ps 110:1 and Dan 7:13 combined in Jewish exegesis (cf. *Midr. Ps.* 2.9 [on Ps 2:7]), which suggests that ancient exegetes found nothing incongruous in linking these texts. But the incongruity itself vanishes when we recognize that the throne of which Dan 7:9 speaks is God's chariot throne, whose "wheels were burning fire" (cf. Ezek 1; 10). One can be *seated* and *moving* because one is in a chariot. It would seem that Jesus has claimed that he will return as the figure depicted in Daniel's vision, seated at the right hand of God in the divine chariot throne, and that he will return in judgment on his enemies. This dominical pronouncement is probably what lies behind the later revelatory tradition in Rev 3:21: "He who conquers, I will grant him to sit with me on my throne, as I myself conquered and sat down with my Father on his throne."

63 ὁ δὲ ἀρχιερεὺς διαρρήξας τοὺς χιτῶνας αὐτοῦ λέγει, τί ἔτι χρείαν ἔχομεν μαρτύρων, "And tearing his robes, the high priest says, 'Why do we still have need of witnesses?'" According to *m. Sanh.* 7:5, when the judges hear blasphemy, they are to "stand up on their feet and tear their garments, and they may not mend them again." The custom of tearing one's clothing reaches back to the earliest times of biblical history. The action conveyed great anguish and/or penitence: "When Reuben returned to the pit and saw that Joseph was not in the pit, he tore his clothes" (Gen 37:29 NRSV); "Tamar put ashes on her head, and tore the long robe that she was wearing; she put her hand on her head, and went away, crying aloud as she went" (2 Sam 13:19 NRSV); Eliakim, Shebna, and Joah "came to Hezekiah with their clothes torn and told him the words of the Rabshakeh" (2 Kgs 18:37 NRSV); "Then Job arose, tore his robe, shaved his head, and fell on the ground and worshiped" (Job 1:20 NRSV); "in their temples the priests sit with their clothes torn, their heads and beards shaved, and their heads uncovered" (Ep Jer 31 NRSV); "When the leaders of the Assyrian army heard this, they tore their tunics and were greatly dismayed, and their loud cries and shouts arose in the midst of the camp" (Jdt 14:19).

The high priest's action of tearing his robes anticipates his charge of blasphemy (in v 64). The charge is of sufficient gravity that witnesses are no longer necessary. They are not necessary because the judges themselves are now the witnesses, having heard with their own ears a stunning and, from their point of view, incriminating statement.

64 ἠκούσατε τῆς βλασφημίας· τί ὑμῖν φαίνεται, "You heard the blasphemy! What seems right to you?" Some critics have claimed that Jesus did not commit capital blasphemy (as later defined in the Mishnah). However, the usage of βλασφημεῖν, "to blaspheme," and βλασφημία, "blasphemy," in Scripture itself and in first-century writers like Josephus and Philo suggests a broader and more inclusive understanding (see the following *Excursus*).

Excursus: Blasphemy

Bibliography

Anderson, C. P. "The Trial of Jesus as Jewish-Christian Polarization: Blasphemy and Polemic in Mark's Gospel." In *Paul and the Gospels*. Vol. 1 of *Anti-Judaism in Early Christianity*. Ed. P. Richardson. Waterloo, Ontario: Wilfrid Laurier UP, 1986. 107–25. **Beyer, H. W.** "Βλασφημέω, κ. τ. λ." *TDNT* 1:621–25. **Bock, D. L.** *Blasphemy and Exaltation in Judaism and the Final Examination of Jesus*. WUNT 2.106. Tübingen: Mohr-Siebeck, 1998. **Evans, C. A.** "In What Sense 'Blasphemy'? Jesus before Caiaphas in Mark 14:61–64." In *Society of Biblical Literature 1991 Seminar Papers*. Ed. E. H. Lovering, Jr. SBLSP 30. Atlanta: Scholars Press, 1991. 215–34. **O'Neill, J. C.** "The Charge of Blasphemy at Jesus' Trial before the Sanhedrin." In *The Trial of Jesus: Cambridge Studies*. FS C. F. D. Moule, ed. E. Bammel. SBT 13. London: SCM Press, 1970. 72–77.

We may summarize the data concerning the concept of blasphemy in Jewish circles in the first century as follows, drawing on and supplementing the recent work of Bock (*Blasphemy and Exaltation*).

The principal Hebrew words referring to blasphemy are גדף *gādap*, "to revile *or* slander," קלל *qillēl*, "to revile *or* belittle," חרף *ḥērēp*, "to reproach," and נאץ *nāʾaṣ*, "to despise." A few examples will suffice. At Sinai, Israel is commanded not to "revile" (תְּקַלֵּל *těqallēl*) God (Exod 22:27 [Eng. v 28]). Lev 24 is especially important, for the subject of blasphemy is treated at length. Of great importance are vv 15–16: "And say to the people of Israel, Whoever curses [יְקַלֵּל *yěqallēl*] his God shall bear his sin. He who blasphemes [נֹקֵב *nōqēb*] the name of the LORD shall be put to death; all the congregation shall stone him; the sojourner as well as the native, when he blasphemes [בְּנׇקְבוֹ *běnoqbô*] the Name, shall be put to death." Literally, נקב *nāqab* is "to name" (LXX Lev 24:16: ὀνομάζων, "he who names," and ἐν τῷ ὀνομάσαι αὐτόν, "when he names"), but here in Lev 24:16 it means to make use of the name of God in an act of cursing. In 1 Kgs 21:13 Naboth is (falsely) accused of speaking against God and is executed. In Job 2:9–10, the suffering righteous man is advised by his wife to "curse God and die." According to Num 14:11–23, the people who disbelieved God, despite all the signs he performed in Egypt and in the wilderness, are said to have "despised" (יְנַאֲצֻנִי *yĕnaʾăṣunî*) God (v 11). Therefore they will not see the promised land. In Num 16:30 the earth swallows up the men who "despised" the Lord.

Most of this terminology appears in the Dead Sea Scrolls. According to 1QpHab 10:12–13, the wicked "will undergo fiery punishments because they blasphemed [גדפו *giddĕpû*] and reviled [יחרפו *yĕḥārĕpû*] God's chosen ones." In 1QS 4:11 we find mention of a "blaspheming tongue," while in 1QS 7:11 we read of a community rule whereby the one who utters a curse, because he is startled while reading Scripture or pronouncing a blessing, shall be permanently removed from the council of the community. CD 5:12 describes those who "have reviled the statutes of God's covenant, saying, 'They are not well-founded.'" Members of the community are to take care how they behave, especially with reference to wealth, lest outsiders "blaspheme" (ינדפו *yĕgaddĕpû*), or speak ill of, the community (CD 12:8). Qumran also speaks of a גדפן *gaddĕpān*, a "blasphemer." According to 4Q385 (= 4QJerC[b]) 44 i 6 = 4Q387 (= 4QpsEz[c]) 3 ii 8, "[the king]dom of [Israe]l will pe[rish in those days. . . . And then he shall arise, the Blasp]hemer [גדפן *gaddĕpān*]. He shall co[mmit abomination." The גדפן *gaddĕpān* is probably Antiochus IV (cf. Dan 7:8, 11, 20).

In the LXX βλασφημία, "blasphemy," βλασφημεῖν, "to blaspheme," and βλάσφημος, "blasphemous," occur some twenty-two times, often translating the Hebrew terminology already surveyed. About half of the occurrences of the Greek terminology are found in the deuterocanonical writings. In 1 Macc 2:6, the priest Mattathias "saw the blasphemies [βλασφημίας] which were happening in Judah and in Jerusalem." In 2 Macc 8:4, a repentant and mournful people implore God to look upon their pitiful condition and to remember the "blasphemies committed against his name." General usage of terms for blasphemy in Greek or in Latin is found in the pseudepigrapha. One example is especially interesting. In *1 Enoch* 27:2 Uriel the angel describes those who "speak hard things concerning [God's] glory." In the context of *1 Enoch* this is understood as the equivalent of blasphemy (cf. 1:9; 5:4; 101:3). Elsewhere the Greek tradition does employ βλασφημεῖν (and cognates βλασφημία and βλάσφημος) in translating גדף *gādap* (2 Kgs 19:6, 22; cf. Isa 37:6, 23; Ezek 20:27; Ps 44:16), נאץ *nāʾaṣ* / נאצה *nĕʾāṣâ* (Isa 52:5 [cited in Rom 2:24]; Ezek 35:12; cf. 2 Sam 12:14; 2 Kgs 19:3; Isa 37:3; Ps 74:10, 18), יכח *yācaḥ* (2 Kgs 19:4), שלו *šālû* (Dan [θ] 3:29 [96]), and the euphemism ברך *bērak* (Isa 66:3; cf. 1 Kgs 21:10, 13; Job 1:5; 2:9). βλασφημεῖν and cognates occur in those books of the Greek tradition where there either was no Hebrew original or the Hebrew original is no longer extant (Tob [א] 1:18; Wis 1:6; Sir 3:16; Bel [θ] 8 [9]; 2 Macc 8:4; 9:28; 10:4, 34, 35, 36; 12:14; 15:24).

Usage of the Greek terminology for blasphemy occurs frequently in Philo and Josephus. On βλασφημία in Philo, see *Migration* 20 §117 (where prayers and blessings, blasphemies and curses are contrasted); *Joseph* 14 §74 (blasphemy or hubris); *Moses* 2.38 §205 (the disciples of Moses must refrain from blasphemy, even in regard to idols, lest bad habits develop and they blaspheme God); *Decalogue* 19 §93 (let one refrain from blasphemies since he uses his mouth to pronounce the holiest of all names); *Flaccus* 5 §33, §35 (slanders and blasphemies against the king); 17 §142 (blasphemies against Flaccus); *Embassy* 46 §368 (Gentiles utter blasphemies against the Deity).

There are two important examples of the verb βλασφημεῖν in Philo. In *Moses* 2.38 §206, the philosopher-exegete states: "But if anyone, I will not say blasphemes [βλασφημήσειεν] the Lord of gods and men, but even ventures to utter His Name unseasonably, let him suffer the penalty of death." In *Flight* 16 §§83–84, Philo explains the biblical text:

> After directing, then, that the man who is profane and reviles things sacred be led away from the most holy spots and given up to punishment, he goes on to say, 'He

that smites father or mother, let him die,' and likewise, 'he that reviles father or mother, let him die' [Exod 21:15–16]. He [Moses] as good as proclaims in a loud voice that no pardon must be granted to those who blaspheme [τῶν . . . βλασφημούντων] the Deity. For if those who have reviled mortal parents are led away to execution, what penalty must be considered that those have merited who take upon themselves to blaspheme [βλασφημεῖν] the Father and Maker of the universe?

For Philo, the person who blasphemes God is deserving of death.

The usage of the terminology is similar in Josephus. On βλασφημία, see *Ant.* 3.7.7 §180 (Gentiles utter blasphemies against the Jewish people); 3.14.3 §307 (angry Israelites heap blasphemies upon Moses and Aaron); 6.11.10 §238 (Saul ran out of blasphemies for Jonathan); 6.13.7 §300 (Nabal insults David with blasphemies); 13.10.6 §§293–95 (Eleazar heaps blasphemies upon Hyrcanus; i.e., his mother had been a captive during the reign of Antiochus IV, but in §294 the Pharisees ask for leniency in behalf of Eleazar, for it did not seem right to condemn a man to death for calumny [λοιδορίας]); 16.3.1 §68 (youths direct blasphemies at Salome and Pheroras); 19.9.1 §357 (people hurl blasphemies against the deceased Agrippa I); 20.5.3 §109 (Cumanus is irked by the blasphemies directed against himself); 20.9.4 §213 (ruling priests abuse each other with blasphemies); *Ag. Ap.* 2.3 §32 (Apion's blasphemy against the Jews); *J.W.* 3.9.6 §439 (people of Jotapata heap blasphemies upon Josephus). In all of these cases, blasphemy basically is synonymous with insult. In one case death is threatened for having insulted the high priest Hyrcanus by saying that his mother had been a captive (thus implying that her offspring was suspect).

For the verb βλασφημεῖν in Josephus, see *Ant.* 4.8.6 §202 ("Let him who blasphemes God be stoned, then hung for a day, and buried ignominiously and in obscurity"); 6.9.3 §183 (as David approaches Goliath, he says: "Let this enemy then be reckoned even as one of those wild beasts, so long as he has insulted our army and blasphemed our God, who will deliver him into our hands"); 10.11.2–3 §233, §242 (Belshazzar blasphemes God by drinking, along with his concubines, from the vessels taken from the Jewish temple); 18.8.1 §257 (Apion blasphemed the Jews in Alexandria); 20.5.3 §108 (outraged at the soldier who mooned them, and so insulted God, the Jews blaspheme Cumanus); 20.8.7 §175 (Jews blaspheme the Syrians); *Life* 45 §232 (the inhabitants of Sepphoris refrain from blaspheming Josephus); *J.W.* 2.17.1 §406 (angry Jews blaspheme King Herod Agrippa II); 2.18.7 §492 (Jewish rioters in Alexandria blaspheme Tiberius); 2.21.3 §602 (Josephus himself is blasphemed by an angry mob); 5.9.4 §375 (Josephus is blasphemed by the besieged in Jerusalem); 5.11.2 §458 (the besieged blaspheme Caesar); 6.6.1 §320 (outwitted, Roman soldiers blaspheme the faithlessness of the clever boy who escapes them). Again, most of these examples describe insults against human beings. Three texts speak of the death penalty. The first example alludes to Lev 24:16, part of Josephus's summary of the Jewish law. The second example pertains to Goliath, who (it is implied) will die because of his taunting (or blaspheming) of the armies of the living God. The third example concerns a heathen king (Belshazzar) who blasphemes God, not by pronouncing his name but by making profane use of sacred vessels. We are not told that he dies, but God's wrath is seen in the overthrow of his kingdom.

Only material that predates Jesus or is approximately contemporary has been surveyed here. (Usage of the terminology of blasphemy in rabbinic and targumic literature is similar, excepting the legal discussion in *m. Sanh.* 6–7.) We find a broad range of meaning from insults with no religious connotation, to insults with religious connotation but no mention of the Deity, to insults of the Deity himself. In a few instances the death penalty is mentioned or implied. The legal technicalities and requirements found in the Mishnah are not attested in these early texts.

There is nothing in the Markan account of the high priest charging Jesus with blasphemy and calling for his execution that is inconsistent with sources that are contemporary with or predate the time of Jesus. It is anachronistic to read back the rules of the mishnaic tractate *Sanhedrin* into the early first century and then accuse the Markan evangelist of creating an impossible scene because so many mishnaic rules are violated. Some of the details of the Markan hearing may be explained by the later codified laws of *Sanhedrin,* and some of the rules of *Sanhedrin* may have been observed in Jesus' day, but lack of agreement between Mark's first-century narrative and Mishnah's late second-century, early third-century code cannot be taken as evidence against the historicity and veracity of the Markan account.

In the eyes of the high priest and those who agreed with him, Jesus committed blasphemy when he claimed a heavenly identity. He claimed to be the "son of God" in the highest sense, whereby he might even sit upon God's throne itself. Jesus did not claim a mere honorific title "son of God," which might be applied to a Davidic Messiah. He claimed to be God's "son" in heavenly terms, as "the son of man" who in heaven would approach the very throne of God and receive kingdom and authority. The unease that Jewish religious authorities may have had with such a notion is attested in a rabbinic tradition that claims to derive from the time of Aqiba (early second century C.E.). Its potentially embarrassing content, in that the great Aqiba is rebuked, argues for the authenticity of the tradition:

> "Till thrones were placed" [Dan 7:9]—what is there to say? One (throne) for Him and one for David, even as has been taught: "One was for Him and one was for David"—the words of Rabbi Aqiba. Rabbi Yose said to him, "Aqiba, how long will you profane the Shekinah? Rather, one (throne) is for justice and one for mercy." Did he accept (this answer) from him or not accept it from him? Come (and) hear what has been taught: "One (throne) is for justice and the other for mercy"—the words (now) of Rabbi Aqiba. Rabbi Eleazar ben Azariah said to him, "Aqiba, what do you have to do with Aggada? Occupy yourself with Nega'im and Ohaloth—but one as a throne and one as a footstool: a throne for a seat and a footstool for support of His feet." (*b. Sanh.* 38b; cf. *b. Ḥag.* 14a)

Aqiba understands the plural "thrones" of Dan 7:9 as teaching that one throne is God's and another is David's. Aqiba's suggestion that David (i.e., the Messiah) would take his seat next to God himself implies some sort of sharing of divine authority and status. Not only did Aqiba's contemporary, Yose the Galilean, object, but it is quite evident that the later editors of the Babylonian Gemara saw this as dangerously similar to the various heresies (such as Christianity and Gnosticism) which taught that there were two or more "Powers" in heaven. Therefore this passage was placed in a context dealing with "two Powers" heresies. (Aqiba is portrayed as changing his mind, and so abandoning his potentially heretical interpretation.)

Jesus also committed blasphemy by implicitly threatening the high priest at the time he came for judgment. Jesus could have been viewed as committing blasphemy against God's high priest and therefore in a certain sense against God himself. We must remember what befell Jesus son of Ananias for daring to pronounce doom on the temple. Ruling priests seized him, treated him roughly, and handed him over to the Roman governor with demands that he be put to death

(Josephus, *J.W.* 6.5.3 §§300–309). Josephus does not tell us that this later Jesus was accused of blasphemy (and he may have been); all we know is that the ruling priests were outraged that he dared to speak against the temple, and for that they wanted him put to death (see *Excursus:* "The Arrest of Jesus Son of Ananias"). Bock (*Blasphemy and Exaltation,* 236) rightly concludes that Jesus' blasphemy consisted of (1) his claim to possess comprehensive divine authority (cf. Gundry, 917), and (2) his threat to judge the ruling priests. Bock further concludes that Mark's brief story of the Jewish hearing has a strong claim to authenticity. The high priest's charge that these claims and threats were blasphemy and warranted a recommendation of execution is consistent with contemporary ideas of the sanctity of the temple and usage of the terminology for blasphemy.

According to Gundry (915–16), when the charge was made public, Jesus' words would have been paraphrased, using a circumlocution, i.e., "You will see 'the son of man' seated 'at the right hand' of the Power." But in keeping with the rules found in *m. Sanh.* 7:5 Jesus may not have employed a euphemism, saying instead, "at the right hand of YHWH." Upon hearing this, the high priest stood up and tore his robe. When the statement was later repeated before the public (which is how Peter and other followers of Jesus would have heard it), the circumlocution was employed. The legislation found in the mishnaic tractate *Sanhedrin* may very well be relevant, and it does seem to cohere with the details of the Jewish hearing that the Markan evangelist provides us (cf. Gundry, 917). However, whether or not Jesus actually pronounced the tetragrammaton, what he said could nevertheless have been viewed as blasphemy in that it presumed divine prerogatives and threatened the high priest and his priestly colleagues. Although the accusation that Jesus threatened to destroy the temple (v 58) had not received the required confirmation (v 59), the image of this allegation would have lingered in the minds of the priests and would have colored their interpretation of Jesus' allusion to Ps 110:1 and Dan 7:13. Whether pronunciation of the tetragrammaton was necessary for a capital charge in cases of blasphemy in the early first century is not known. The sources from this period suggest that charges of blasphemy and calls for execution did not require pronunciation of the tetragrammaton.

οἱ δὲ πάντες κατέκριναν αὐτὸν ἔνοχον εἶναι θανάτου, "And they all condemned him to be deserving of death." Mark's πάντες, "all," is probably hyperbolic and should be understood as "many" or "most." The quorum that assembled at the high priest's home was in all likelihood somewhat hand-picked to begin with and was probably sympathetic to Caiaphas's disposition. If there were any among the elders and priests who defended Jesus, we are not told. The Markan evangelist will later tell us of one Joseph of Arimathea, a respected member of the Sanhedrin, who was himself also looking for the kingdom of God (15:43). He requests the body of Jesus and gives it a decent burial, more decent than would have been expected for the body of an executed criminal. Was he in attendance at the hearing gathered at the home of Caiaphas? We are not told. Moreover, someone looking for the kingdom of God was not necessarily a supporter of Jesus. Matthew, however, identifies Joseph as "a disciple of Jesus" (27:57), as does John, adding that Joseph was a disciple "secretly" (19:38). Luke implies that Joseph was indeed present and that he "had not consented" to the Sanhedrin's judgment (23:50–51). More fancifully, the *Gospel of Peter* tells us that Joseph was "a friend of Pilate and of the Lord" (*Gos. Pet.* 2.3). Joseph desires to bury Jesus "since he had seen all the good he had done" (*Gos. Pet.* 6.23). Furthermore, in John 7:50–52 Nicodemus, who in 3:1 is identified as "a ruler of the Jews," defends Jesus before the Sanhedrin, and in 19:39–40 he assists in Jesus' burial. It is clear that in the passage of time there was an interest among Christians in finding some support for Jesus, however meager, from among the membership of the Jewish Sanhedrin. How much of this tradition, if any, has roots in the actual events is difficult to determine.

The Sanhedrin κατέκριναν, "condemned," Jesus ἔνοχον εἶναι θανάτου, "to be deserving of death," just as Jesus in 10:33 had predicted they would: "the 'son of man' will be handed over to the ruling priests and to the scribes, and they will condemn him to death [κατακρινοῦσιν αὐτὸν θανάτῳ] and will hand him over to the Gentiles."

On ἔνοχος, "deserving" or "guilty," elsewhere in Mark, see 3:29, "but whoever blasphemes against the Holy Spirit never has forgiveness, but is guilty [ἔνοχος] of an eternal sin." Compare LXX Gen 26:11: "And Abimelech commanded all his people, saying, 'All who touch this man or his wife shall be deserving of death [θανάτου ἔνοχος ἔσται].'"

65 καὶ ἤρξαντό τινες ἐμπτύειν αὐτῷ καὶ περικαλύπτειν αὐτοῦ τὸ πρόσωπον καὶ κολαφίζειν αὐτὸν καὶ λέγειν αὐτῷ, προφήτευσον, "And some began to spit on him, and to cover his face, and to strike him, and to say to him, 'Prophesy!'" This tradition seems to have been colored by Isa 50:6 (so Bultmann, *History,* 281), though not as much as Nineham (408) claims. Under the influence of Matt 26:68, a variety of variants have cropped up (see *Notes* n and o). Again the reader of Mark would recognize the literal and detailed fulfillment of Jesus' passion prediction: "And they will mock him, and spit upon him [ἐμπτύσουσιν αὐτῷ]" (10:34). The mockery is seen in the act of covering Jesus' face, striking him, and saying to him, "Prophesy!" Apparently, Jesus is supposed to possess prophetic clairvoyance and so be able to identify his assailant, even if he cannot see him. The way Mark's text stands, it is the priests and elders themselves who have spat on Jesus and have begun to strike him. Moments later the officers will take their turn.

ἐμπτύειν, "to spit upon," is a matter of great shame; e.g., Num. 12:14: "But the LORD said to Moses, 'If her father had but spit [LXX: ἐνέπτυσεν] in her face, should she not be shamed seven days? Let her be shut up outside the camp seven days, and after that she may be brought in again'"; Deut 25:9: "then his brother's wife shall go up to him in the presence of the elders, and pull his sandal off his foot, and spit [LXX: ἐμπτύσεται] in his face." Because in these verses it is in the transgressor's face that one spits, it is not surprising that some manuscripts of Mark 14:65 read "And some began to spit in his face" (see *Note* n).

καὶ οἱ ὑπηρέται ῥαπίσμασιν αὐτὸν ἔλαβον, "And the officers received him with slaps." The KJV reads "and the servants did strike him with the palms of their hands," accepting the reading ἔβαλον, "threw" or "struck," instead of the earlier and better attested ἔλαβον, "received" (see *Note* p; for discussion of the variant, see Field, *Notes,* 40). οἱ ὑπηρέται, "the officers," are the men outside with Peter, warming themselves by the fire (v 54). Mark's narrative will shortly return to them.

Explanation

In some ways 14:53–65 forms an important thematic climax to the Gospel of Mark. As predicted several times, Jesus has been taken into custody and has been brought before the ruling priests, elders, and scribes to face charges. Many accusations are brought before the assembly, including one claiming that Jesus has threatened to destroy and then rebuild the temple. But none of the accusations can be properly verified. Finally, the high priest himself directly asks Jesus if he is the Messiah, the son of the Blessed (i.e., God). The reader of Mark has been told in the first verse of the Gospel that Jesus is the Messiah, the son of God (1:1). From time to time Jesus' divine identity has been acknowledged by frightened spirits (1:24; 3:11; 5:7), by the disciples (8:29), or by God himself (1:11; 9:7). But now Jesus faces his mortal enemy, the high priest, who has been offended and threatened by Jesus' activities in Jerusalem the past week.

Jesus had expressed disappointment with respect to the function of the temple establishment. He had taken action in the precincts, overturning tables, and had prophetically reminded those present that the temple was to be "a house of prayer for all the Gentiles"; instead, it had become "a cave of robbers" (11:17, quoting Isa 56:7; Jer 7:11). Deep offense was taken, but Jesus continued teaching in the precincts. With a parable he predicted that the ruling priests would lose their stewardship and that he himself, the rejected son, would be vindicated (12:1–12); with irony he warned of avaricious scribes who oppress rather than assist the poor (12:38–40, 41–44); and with skill he answered all questions put to him (11:27–33; 12:13–17, 18–27, 28–34, 35–37).

Even without the passion predictions, Mark's reader would not fail to anticipate an inevitable clash between Jesus and the priestly establishment. Rome thus far had played no role, but anyone living in the Roman Empire would know that talk of the kingdom of God and presenting oneself as the divine anointed agent of this kingdom would ultimately lead to a collision with Roman power. Most of Mark's readers would already know that Jesus was crucified under the authority of Pontius Pilate, but many would not know the whole story. The hearing before the priestly authorities would fill in an important gap in the readers' knowledge. In this passage we have the transition from what had up to now been a Jewish affair. Now the reader would know how the story of Jesus moved from an intensely Jewish debate to a Roman crucifixion.

The high priest's demand that Jesus answer his question, "Are you the Messiah, the son of the Blessed?" sets the stage for Jesus' unequivocal affirmation: "I am; and you will see 'the son of man' seated 'at the right hand' of the Power and 'coming with the clouds of heaven.'" The meaning of the mysterious epithet "son of man," which Jesus had employed in reference to himself many times before, now becomes much clearer. The epithet is messianic after all and points to a messianism that is much more than being a mere "son of David." The anointed "son of man," who has received from God kingdom and authority is more than David's son; he is David's "lord" (12:35–37). He is also lord of the temple and its caretakers, as they will find out, when they see the "son of man" coming with the clouds, seated at the right hand of God. Implicit in Jesus' collocation of phrases from Dan 7:13 and Ps 110:1 is his divine status and the threat of judgment on those who judge him. Outraged, the priests condemn Jesus to death and send him out to be handed over to the Roman authorities.

J. Peter's Denial of Jesus   (14:66–72)

Bibliography

Auerbach, E. *Mimesis: The Representation of Reality in Western Literature.* Princeton, NJ: Princeton UP, 1968. 40–49. **Benoit, P.** *Passion and Resurrection.* 49–72. **Birdsall, J. N.** "τὸ ῥῆμα ὡς εἶπεν αὐτῷ ὁ Ἰησοῦς (Mk 14,72)." *NovT* 2 (1958) 272–75. **Boomershine, T. E.** "Peter's Denial as Polemic or Confession: The Implications of Media Criticism for Biblical Hermeneutics." *Semeia* 39 (1987) 47–68. **Borrell, A.** *The Good News of Peter's Denial: A Narrative and Rhetorical Reading of Mark 14:54.66–72.* University of South Florida International Studies in Formative Christianity and Judaism 7. Atlanta: Scholars Press, 1998. **Boyd, W. J. P.** "Peter's Denial—Mark xiv.68; Luke xxii.57." *ExpTim* 67 (1955–56) 341. **Brady, D.** "The Alarm to Peter in Mark's Gospel." *JSNT* 4 (1979) 42–57. **Buchanan, G. W.** "Mark xiv.54." *ExpTim* 68 (1956–57) 27. **Bussby, F.** "St. Mark 14,72: An Aramaic Mistranslation?" *BJRL* 21 (1937) 273–74. **Cantinat, J.** "Jésus devant le Sanhédrin." *NRT* 75 (1953) 300–308. **Catchpole, D. R.** *The Trial of Jesus.* StPB 18. Leiden: Brill, 1971. 160–74. **Danson, J. M.** "The Fall of St. Peter." *ExpTim* 19 (1907–8) 307–8. **Dassmann, E.** "Die Szene Christus-Petrus mit dem Hahn: Zum Verhältnis vom Komposition und Interpretation auf frühchristlichen Sarkophagen." In *Pietas.* FS B. Kötting, ed. E. Dassmann and K. S. Frank. Münster: Aschendorff, 1980. 509–27. **Derrett, J. D. M.** "I do not know nor understand (Mark 14,68)." *BO* 41 (1999) 41–45. ———. "The Reason for the Cock-Crowings." *NTS* 29 (1983) 142–44. **Dewey, K. E.** "Peter's Curse and Cursed Peter (Mark 14:53–54, 66–72)." In *The Passion in Mark.* Ed. W. Kelber. 96–114. ———. "Peter's Denial Reexamined: John's Knowledge of Mark's Gospel." In *Society of Biblical Literature 1979 Seminar Papers.* Ed. P. J. Achtemeier. 2 vols. SBLSP 18. Missoula, MT: Scholars Press, 1979. 1:109–12. **Dormeyer, D.** *Die Passion Jesu.* 150–55. **Ernst, J.** "Noch einmal: Die Verleugnung Jesu durch Petrus (Mk 14,54.66–72)." *Catholica* 30 (1976) 207–26 (repr. in *Beiträge und Notizen.* Vol. 1 of *Petrus und Papst: Evangelium, Einheit der Kirche, Papstdienst.* Ed. A. Brandenburg and H. J. Urban. Münster: Aschendorff, 1977. 43–62). ———. "Die Petrustradition im Markusevangelium—Ein altes Problem neu angegangen." In *Begegnung mit dem Wort.* FS H. Zimmermann, ed. J. Zmijewski and E. Nellessen. BBB 53. Bonn: Hanstein, 1980. 35–65, esp. 56–57. **Evans, C. A.** "'Peter Warming Himself': The Problem of an Editorial 'Seam.'" *JBL* 101 (1982) 245–49. **Fortna, R. T.** "Jesus and Peter at the High Priest's House: A Test Case for the Question of the Relation between Mark's and John's Gospels." *NTS* 24 (1977–78) 371–83. **Fox, R.** "Peter's Denial in Mark's Gospel." *TBT* 25 (1987) 298–303. **Frieling, R.** *Christologische Aufsätze.* Gesammelte Schriften zum Alten und Neuen Testament 3. Stuttgart: Urachhaus, 1982. 116–24. **Gardiner, W. D.** "The Denial of St. Peter." *ExpTim* 26 (1914–15) 424–26. **Gewalt, D.** "Die Verleugnung des Petrus." *LB* 43 (1978) 113–44. **Goguel, M.** "Did Peter Deny His Lord? A Conjecture." *HTR* 25 (1932) 1–27. **Guyot, G. H.** "Peter Denies His Lord." *CBQ* 4 (1942) 111–18. **Herron, R. W., Jr.** *Mark's Account of Peter's Denial of Jesus: A History of Its Interpretation.* Lanham, MD; New York: University Press of America, 1991. **Hunter, J.** "Three Versions of Peter's Denial." *Hudson Review* 33 (1980) 39–57. **Juel, D.** *Messiah and Temple.* 59–75. **Klein, G.** "Die Verleugnung des Petrus: Eine traditionsgeschichtliche Untersuchung." *ZTK* 58 (1961) 285–328 (repr. in G. Klein. *Rekonstruktion und Interpretation: Gesammelte Aufsätze zum Neuen Testament.* BEvT 50. Munich: Kaiser, 1969. 49–90 with "Nachtrag," 90–98). **Kosmala, H.** "The Time of the Cock-Crow." *ASTI* 2 (1963) 118–20; 6 (1967–68) 132–34. **Kosnetter, J.** "Zur Geschichtlichkeit der Verleugnung Petri." In *Dienst an der Lehre.* FS F. König, ed. Catholic Theological Faculty, University of Vienna. Wiener Beiträge zur Theologie 10. Vienna: Herder, 1965. 127–43. **Krauss, S.** "La défense d'élever du menu bétail en Palestine et questions connexes." *REJ* 53 (1907) 14–55, esp. 28–37. **Lampe, G. W.**

H. "St. Peter's Denial." *BJRL* 55 (1972–73) 346–68. ———. "St. Peter's Denial and the Treatment of the Lapsi." In *The Heritage of the Early Church*. FS G. V. Florovsky, ed. D. Neiman and M. Schatkin. OrChrAn 195. Rome: Pontifical Oriental Institute, 1973. 113–33. **Lattey, C.** "A Note on Cockcrow." *Scr* 6 (1953–54) 53–55. **LaVerdiere, E.** "Peter Broke Down and Began to Cry." *Emmanuel* 92 (1986) 70–73. **Lee, G. M.** "Mark 14,72: ἐπιβαλὼν ἔκλαιεν." *Bib* 53 (1972) 411–12. ———. "St. Mark xiv.72: ἐπιβαλὼν ἔκλαιεν." *ExpTim* 61 (1949–50) 160. **Lindars, B.** "Christ and Salvation." *BJRL* 64 (1981–82) 481–500. **Linnemann, E.** *Studien zur Passionsgeschichte*. 24–31, 70–108. **Masson, C.** "Le reniement de Pierre: Quelques aspects de la formation d'une tradition." *RHPR* 37 (1957) 24–35 (repr. in C. Masson. *Vers les sources d'eau vive: Études d'exégèse et de théologie du Nouveau Testament*. Publications de la Faculté de Théologie: Université de Lausanne 2. Lausanne: Payot, 1961. 87–101). **Mayo, C. H.** "St Peter's Token of the Cock Crow." *JTS* o.s. 22 (1921) 367–70. **McEleney, N. J.** "Peter's Denials—How Many? To Whom?" *CBQ* 52 (1990) 467–72. **Merkel, H.** "Peter's Curse." In *The Trial of Jesus: Cambridge Studies*. FS C. F. D. Moule, ed. E. Bammel. SBT 13. London: SCM Press, 1970. 66–71. **Meyer, F. E.** "Einige Bemerkungen zur Bedeutungen des Terminus 'Synhedrion' in den Schriften des Neuen Testaments." *NTS* 14 (1967–68) 545–51. **Mohr, T. A.** *Markus- und Johannespassion*. 276–81. **Murray, G.** "Saint Peter's Denials." *DRev* 103 (1985) 296–98. **Myllykoski, M.** *Die letzten Tage Jesu*. 99–105. **Pesch, R.** *Das Evangelium der Urgemeinde*. 191–93. ———. "Die Verleugnung des Petrus: Eine Studie zu Mk 14,54.66–72 (und Mk 14,26–31)." In *Neues Testament und Kirche*. FS R. Schnackenburg, ed. J. Gnilka. Freiburg: Herder, 1974. 42–62. **Ramsay, W. M.** "The Denials of Peter." *ExpTim* 27 (1915–16) 296–301, 360–63, 410–13, 471–72, 540–42; 28 (1916–17) 276–81. **Riesenfeld, H.** "The verb ἀρνεῖσθαι." *In honorem Antonii Fridrichsen*, ed. New Testament Seminar, University of Uppsala. ConNT 11. Lund: Gleerup, 1947. 207–19. **Rothenaicher, F.** "Zu Mk 14,70 und Mt 26,73." *BZ* 23 (1935–36) 192–93. **Ruhland, M.** *Die Markuspassion aus der Sicht der Verleugnung*. Eilsbrunn: Ko'amar, 1987. 29–36. **Schenk, W.** *Der Passionsbericht nach Markus*. 215–23. **Schenke, L.** *Der gekreuzigten Christus*. 15–22. **Schneider, G.** *Die Passion Jesu*. 73–79. **Seitz, O. J. F.** "Peter's 'Profanity': Mark 14,71 in the Light of Matthew 16,22." *SE* 1 [= TU 73] (1959) 516–19. **Smith, P. V.** "St. Peter's Threefold Denial of our Lord." *Theology* 17 (1928) 341–48. **Smith, T. V.** *Petrine Controversies in Early Christianity: Attitudes towards Peter in Christian Writings of the First Two Centuries*. WUNT 2.15. Tübingen: Mohr-Siebeck, 1985. 178–81. **Thomson, J. R.** "Saint Peter's Denials." *ExpTim* 47 (1935–36) 381–82. **Torrey, C. C.** *Our Translated Gospels*. 16–18. **Valentin, P.** "Les comparutions de Jésus devant le Sanhédrin." *RSR* 59 (1971) 230–36. **Walter, N.** "Die Verleugnung des Petrus." *TVers* 8 (1977) 45–61. **Wenham, J. W.** "How Many Cock-Crowings? The Problem of Harmonistic Text-Variants." *NTS* 25 (1978–79) 523–25. **Westcott, B. F.,** and **Hort, F. J. A.** *Introduction*. 2:27. **Wilcox, M.** "The Denial Sequence in Mark xiv. 26–31, 66–72." *NTS* 17 (1970–71) 426–36, esp. 433–36. **Wuellner, W. H.,** and **Leslie, R. C.** *The Surprising Gospel: Intriguing Psychological Insights from the New Testament*. Nashville: Abingdon, 1984. 55–62.

See also *Bibliography* for 14:26–31 and 14:53–65.

Translation

⁶⁶*And while Peter*ᵃ *was below in the courtyard, one of the maid servants of the high priest comes,*ᵇ ⁶⁷*and seeing Peter*ᶜ *warming himself, looking at him, she says,*ᵇ *"You also were with the Nazarene,*ᵈ *Jesus."* ⁶⁸*But he denied [it],*ᵉ *saying, "I neither know*ᶠ *nor understand what you are saying." And he went outside into the forecourt. [And a cock crowed.]*ᵍ ⁶⁹*And the maid servant, seeing him, began again to speak to those who were standing around, "This is one of them."* ⁷⁰*But again he denied it. And after a little while again those standing around were saying to Peter,*ʰ *"Truly you are one of them, for*

you also are a Galilean."ⁱ ⁷¹*But he began to curse and swear,*ʲ *"I do not know this man of whom you are speaking."* ⁷²*And immediately the cock crowed a second time.*ᵏ *And Peter*ˡ *remembered the word that Jesus had said to him, "Before the cock crows twice*ᵐ *you will deny me three times." And he began to weep.*ⁿ

Notes

ᵃA few Syr. MSS read *kêpāʾ,* "Cephas"; the Peshitta reads *šimʿôn,* "Simeon."

ᵇD and a few later authorities add πρὸς αὐτόν, "to him."

ᶜSyr. MSS read "him."

ᵈGk. Ναζαρηνοῦ. The Gk. MSS attest a great deal of variety: D reads Ναζορηνοῦ; other MSS read Ναζωρινοῦ, Ναζωρηνοῦ, Ναζωραίου, Ναζοραίου, Ναζαραίου. The versions attest a similar range of variants.

ᵉThe text actually reads ἠρνήσατο, "he denied." The "it" is implied. A few late MSS add αὐτόν, "him."

ᶠAt least one MS adds αὐτόν, "him" (cf. Luke 22:57). This addition smooths out the statement. Peter has declared that he neither knows Jesus nor understands what the maid servant is talking about.

ᵍThe words καὶ ἀλέκτωρ ἐφώνησεν, "and a cock crowed," are placed in square brackets in Nestle-Aland²⁷ and UBSGNT³ᶜ. They are read by A C D Θ Ψᶜ 067 and a great many later MSS, but they are not found in ℵ B L W Ψ* 579 892 2427 and several other authorities. Metzger (*TCGNT*¹, 115–16) admits to great uncertainty. He suspects that the words may have been added to the text "to emphasize the literal fulfillment of Jesus' prophecy" earlier in v 30. See also Westcott-Hort, *Introduction* 2:27. Lagrange (407), Taylor (574), and Cranfield (447) accept the reading. Swete (363), Lohmeyer (331), Nineham (409), Grundmann (418), and A. Stock (384) reject it. See *Note* k.

ʰSyr. MSS read *kêpāʾ,* "Cephas."

ⁱA Σ 33 and several later MSS add καὶ ἡ λαλιά σου ὁμοιάζει, "and your speech is like it." This addition is drawn from Matt 26:73. Cranfield (447), however, accepts the reading. See the reservations expressed by Gundry (921).

ʲD and a few later authorities have καὶ λέγειν, "and to say."

ᵏἐκ δευτέρου is omitted by ℵ C*ᵛⁱᵈ L and other authorities, under the influence of Matt 26:74; Luke 22:60. See *Note* g.

ˡSome Syr. MSS read *kêpāʾ,* "Cephas"; the Peshitta reads *šimʿôn,* "Simeon."

ᵐℵ C*ᵛⁱᵈ W Σ and a few later authorities omit δίς, "twice," to align the text with Matt 26:27 and Luke 22:61; other authorities rearrange the order: (*a*) δὶς φωνῆσαι τρίς με ἀπαρνήσῃ, "twice crows three times me you will deny" (B 2427); (*b*) φωνῆσαι δὶς ἀπαρνήσῃ με τρίς, "crows twice you will deny me three times" (A *f*¹·¹³ 33 1006 1506 Majority text syʰ samˢˢ bo).

ⁿA few late MSS read καὶ ἐξελθὼν ἔξω ἔκλαυσεν πικρῶς, "and having gone outside, he wept bitterly." The reading derives from Matt 26:75 and avoids the difficult ἐπιβαλών, "having begun" (see *Comment* on v 72).

Form/Structure/Setting

According to Bultmann (*History,* 269), the "story of Peter is itself legendary and literary." He believes (*History,* 278) that the story "could not originally have belonged organically to the Passion Narrative," because it does not link well with what follows and simply takes up too much space for an old, primitive narrative (cf. Dibelius, *Tradition,* 214: "much more ample than the main scene"). Bultmann (*History,* 269) also thinks that the story of Peter's denial of Jesus originally followed vv 43–52. He concludes (*History,* 279) that a primitive Passion Narrative emerged that told the story of Jesus' arrest, his condemnation by the Sanhedrin and Pilate, his journey to the place of crucifixion, and then the execution itself. Later, the story was supplemented with the story of the denials, the prophecy of the disciples' flight and of Peter's denials (14:27–31), which Bultmann thinks was probably composed when combined to the story of the denials, and various other items, such as the anointing in 14:3–9. Dibelius (*Tradition*, 214) is less skeptical than is Bultmann; he believes "an old tradition appears to be present in the narrative of Peter's denial." Taylor (*Formation*, 58) also sees the prophecy of the denials and the story of the denials as later additions to the Passion Narrative. However, Taylor believes that when the basic outline of the narrative was composed and began to circulate, it "awakened latent memories of other incidents which by degrees found their place within the communal Story" (*Formation*, 59). In general principle, Taylor's view is to be preferred.

Bultmann's critical analysis is problematic at several points, not least of which is the "ominiscience" (Taylor, *Formation*, 58) that is required to know the detail that is claimed. That the story of the denials and the account of Jesus' hearing before the priests had separate origins and then were later joined (by the evangelist Mark, as yet one more "sandwich") is doubtful, for the intertwining of the story of Peter outside and Jesus inside is probably traditional and not the work of the Markan evangelist (which is also *pace* Taylor, *Formation*, 58). The intercalation of these two stories reaches back to the very beginnings of the telling of the passion. For arguments in support of this position, see *Form/Structure/Setting* on 14:53–65. More important, it is very improbable that the early church would invent a story so disparaging of Peter, who by the 60s and later had gained great stature in the church. He not only denies Jesus three times, as had been foretold, but he curses (perhaps Jesus himself) in his craven panic to distance himself from his condemned master. Regardless of what value the dramatic fulfillment of Jesus' prophecy might have had for putting Jesus himself in an impressive light, the damage to Peter's credibility would surely have been seen as too high a price to pay for pious invention and christologically motivated apologetic. Peter's denials of Jesus were known and perhaps later readily admitted by the apostle himself. What could be salvaged from the sad episode was the memory that Jesus had anticipated it and that Peter had been restored.

The story itself is marked by dramatic escalation in the intensity of Peter's denials. He does not simply deny Jesus; he finally curses him. The pericope breaks down into three components, each centered on a denial: (1) first denial, where Peter is approached by one of the maid servants of the high priest (vv 66–68); (2) second denial, where the same maid servant points out Peter to others (vv 69–70a); and (3) third denial, where those standing around address Peter, Peter denies Jesus with curses, the cock crows twice, Peter remembers Jesus' words, and then Peter breaks down and weeps (vv 70b–72).

Comment

66 καὶ ὄντος τοῦ Πέτρου κάτω ἐν τῇ αὐλῇ ἔρχεται μία τῶν παιδισκῶν τοῦ ἀρχιερέως, "And while Peter was below in the courtyard, one of the maid servants of the high priest comes." In v 54 Peter had followed Jesus and the arresting crowd right εἰς τὴν αὐλήν, "into the courtyard." The evangelist now returns to him ἐν τῇ αὐλῇ, "in the courtyard." In the OT the courtyard of the temple is frequently mentioned. Royal palaces, ordinary homes, and especially the homes of the wealthy also had courtyards. The home of Caiaphas was probably large and impressive, if the ruins of the mansion in the Jewish quarter of Jerusalem (not too far from the southwest corner of the Temple Mount), unearthed in 1970, are indicative. The stone weight bearing the inscription קתרס בר[ד] *[dĕ]bar Qātrŏs*, "[of] the son of Qatros," found in the ruins of the "Burnt House" (70 C.E.), suggests that the nearby mansion may have belonged to the high priestly family of Qatros, one of the principal high priestly families that held sway in the last century or so of the Second Temple period. Later rabbis would remember these families in a critical light: "Woe is me because of the house of Qadros [קדרוס *Qādrôs*]. Woe is me because of their pen" (*t. Menaḥ.* 13.21; the woes go on to speak of the "house of Hanin," which probably refers to Annas, the father-in-law of Caiaphas). This Qatros/Qadros may be the Cantheras (Κανθήρας) mentioned by Josephus (*Ant.* 20.1.3 §16). If the mansion near the Burnt House did indeed belong to a high priestly family, then we have a pretty good idea of what the house of Caiaphas probably looked like: a large, imposing structure, two stories, with two or more cellars and various cisterns and a large courtyard surrounding much of the house. Part of this courtyard communicated with the street; it is here that Peter, the servants, and various officers spent the remainder of the evening trying to stay warm by the fire and making what conversation they could. Such large homes would be well staffed with servants. The nearby Burnt House was in all probability a dwelling in which a servant family had lived and possibly manufactured incense. For photographs and discussion of the "Burnt House," see N. Avigad, *Discovering Jerusalem* (Nashville: Abingdon, 1983) 120–36. For ancient traditions and recent archaeological data pertaining to Caiaphas, see *Comment* on 14:53.

67 καὶ ἰδοῦσα τὸν Πέτρον θερμαινόμενον ἐμβλέψασα αὐτῷ λέγει, καὶ σὺ μετὰ τοῦ Ναζαρηνοῦ ἦσθα τοῦ Ἰησοῦ, "seeing Peter warming himself, looking at him, she says, 'You also were with the Nazarene, Jesus.'" It must be admitted that this verse, which takes the reader back to 14:54 ("Peter . . . warming himself at the fire"), has every appearance of an editorial seam, of which the evangelist is fond (e.g., 14:18, 22). But in this case the structure of the story—leaving Peter at the fire, viewing Jesus before the high priest, and then returning to Peter at the fire—is probably pre-Markan, for the same seam appears in John 18. To argue that this is evidence of Johannine dependence on Mark creates more problems that it solves (cf. *Form/Structure/Setting* on 14:53–65).

There is nothing accusatory or threatening about the maid servant's observation, "You also were with the Nazarene, Jesus," especially when we remember that in Mark's narrative Peter was not identified as the one who struck the servant of the high priest. Peter's fear, however, is understandable; he has no idea what turn the hearing inside may take. After all, the ruling priests may decide to round up Jesus' closest followers, perhaps as witnesses for the prosecution or as fellow defendants. Initially, the maid servant glances at Peter (ἰδοῦσα, "seeing"); then studying him more closely (ἐμβλέψασα, "looking"), she correctly identifies him as one of those who had been with Jesus. We do not know how she made this identification, for she (presumably) had not been with those who arrested Jesus. She may have heard Peter speak and assumed that he was one of Jesus' Galilean followers (as v 70 seems to imply).

68 ὁ δὲ ἠρνήσατο λέγων, οὔτε οἶδα οὔτε ἐπίσταμαι σὺ τί λέγεις, "But he denied [it], saying, 'I neither know nor understand what you are saying.'" Peter categorically denies knowing Jesus. It is possible that the last clause is interrogatory, in which case Peter's denial would read "I neither know nor understand (you). What you are saying?" But it is not likely that Peter would pose a counterquestion, only encouraging the maid servant to pursue the conversation. He has no idea what she is talking about, so she should drop the matter. Of course, Peter already sounds like the lady in Shakespeare's *Hamlet* that "doth protest too much." Why is he present, warming himself by the fire at such an early hour? How can he be among the very persons who earlier had arrested Jesus and yet not know anything about Jesus or the matters at hand? His denial is not persuasive and only arouses more curiosity. Grundmann (418) calls our attention to *m. Šebu.* 8:3, 6: "'Where is my ox?' and he answered, 'I do not know what you are saying.'" Torrey (*Our Translated Gospels,* 16–18) thinks that the Aramaic has been misunderstood and that Peter's denial originally was "I am neither a companion of, nor do I know at all, him of whom you speak."

Mark's ἠρνήσατο, "he denied," calls to mind significant dominical utterances, such as Matt 10:33 (RSV, adapted): "Whoever denies me before humans, I also will deny before my Father who is in heaven" (cf. Luke 12:9); and the approximate parallel in Mark 8:38: "whoever should be ashamed of me, . . . indeed the 'son of man' will be ashamed of him." The tradition of Peter's denials stands sharply in tension with NT teaching regarding denying Jesus and denying the faith. Principal examples include Acts 3:14: "But you denied the Holy and Righteous One, and asked for a murderer to be granted to you"; 2 Tim 2:12: "if we endure, we shall also reign with him; if we deny him, he also will deny us"; 2 Pet 2:1: "But false prophets . . . false teachers . . . even denying the Master who bought them, bringing upon themselves swift destruction"; 1 John 2:23: "No one who denies the Son has the Father"; Jude 4: the ungodly "deny our only Master and Lord, Jesus Christ"; Rev 3:8: "you have kept my word and have not denied my name." The strength and uncompromising nature of this tradition works against the speculation that the story of Peter's threefold denial of Jesus was the result of pious, homiletical invention (cf. Schniewind, 193).

καὶ ἐξῆλθεν ἔξω εἰς τὸ προαύλιον [καὶ ἀλέκτωρ ἐφώνησεν], "And he went outside into the forecourt. [And a cock crowed.]" Despite losing the warmth of the fire, Peter finds it necessary to escape the observant woman. Peter exits the main αὐλή, "courtyard," and now enters the προαύλιον, "forecourt." καὶ ἀλέκτωρ ἐφώνησεν, "and a cock crowed," is probably a gloss designed to harmonize with ἐκ δευτέρου ἀλέκτωρ ἐφώνησεν, "the cock crowed a second time," and with Jesus' prediction that Peter would deny him three times πρὶν ἀλέκτορα φωνῆσαι δὶς, "before the cock crows twice" (v 72). The textual issues are in this case complicated, and the arguments could go the other way.

69 καὶ ἡ παιδίσκη ἰδοῦσα αὐτὸν ἤρξατο πάλιν λέγειν τοῖς παρεστῶσιν ὅτι οὗτος ἐξ αὐτῶν ἐστιν, "And the maid servant, seeing him, began again to speak to those who were standing around, 'This is one of them.'" Again catching a glimpse of Peter, who probably has stolen closer to the fire, the maid servant begins to speak of him. She is convinced; "This is one of them," she avers. Her certainty in the Markan version stands in contrast to the more deferential tone used in the Fourth Gospel: "You are not also of this man's disciples, are you? (John 18:17); and then later, the crowd asks: "You are not also of his disciples, are you?" (18:25, author's tr.).

70 ὁ δὲ πάλιν ἠρνεῖτο, "But again he denied it." We are not told what he said in the second denial. Matthew (26:72) says that Peter "denied it with an oath, 'I do not know the man.'" Luke (22:58) has Peter questioned by a man, to whom he responds: "Man, I am not!"

καὶ μετὰ μικρὸν πάλιν οἱ παρεστῶτες ἔλεγον τῷ Πέτρῳ, ἀληθῶς ἐξ αὐτῶν εἶ, καὶ γὰρ Γαλιλαῖος εἶ, "And after a little while again those standing around were saying to Peter, 'Truly you are one of them, for you also are a Galilean.'" The situation for Peter has now grown more grave, for it is no longer a single maid servant who has made the identification; it is the crowd itself. Although Mark does not say so, Peter's previous denials and other conversation have probably led to his being identified as a Galilean. Matthew (26:73) makes this explicit: "Certainly you are also one of them, for your accent betrays you." According to the Talmud (cf. *b. Ber.* 32a; *b. Meg.* 24b), Galileans are said to pronounce *'aleph* as *'ayin* and *'ayin* as *'aleph* (i.e., too much guttural for the *'aleph*, too little for the *'ayin*). One text pokes fun at Galilean pronunciation: "A certain Galilean went around saying to people, 'Who has *amar?* Who has *amar?*' They said to him, 'You Galilean fool, do you mean an ass (*ḥămār*) for riding, or wine (*ḥămar*) for drinking, wool (*'ămar*) for clothing, or a lamb (*'immar*) for slaughtering?'" (*b. 'Erub.* 53b; cf. G. H. Dalman, *The Words of Jesus,* tr. D. M. Kay [Edinburgh: T. & T. Clark, 1902] 80–81). An instance of being betrayed by one's speech is cited in G. H. R. Horsley, *NewDocs* 5:31: "His non-Greek (lit. barbaric) bearing and his speech [γλῶσσα] show him to be a foreigner" (from a fragment of the *Acts of the Pagan Martyrs*). According to Acts 2:7, the disciples are recognized by their speech as Galileans (cf. Acts 4:13).

71 ὁ δὲ ἤρξατο ἀναθεματίζειν καὶ ὀμνύναι ὅτι οὐκ οἶδα τὸν ἄνθρωπον τοῦτον ὃν λέγετε, "But he began to curse and swear, 'I do not know this man of whom you are speaking.'" Feeling the pressure of the crowd and fearing confirmation that he indeed is one of Jesus' disciples, Peter denies his master in the most emphatic manner possible. He begins ἀναθεματίζειν καὶ ὀμνύναι, "to curse and swear," that he does not know τὸν ἄνθρωπον τοῦτον, "this man," of whom they speak. In order to keep himself as distant as possible, Peter does not even mention Jesus' name. His cursing, or anathematizing, is perhaps directed against Jesus. At the very least he has called curses down upon himself (and those who have asked him?), should he be lying (Cranfield, 447–48). See the use of ἀναθεματίζειν in Acts 23:12, 14, 21, where certain zealous Jews "anathematize themselves" by vowing not to eat or drink until they should kill Paul. The usage in Acts may very well capture the idea here in Mark. In the LXX the word often translates חרם *ḥāram,* "to destroy."

72 καὶ εὐθὺς ἐκ δευτέρου ἀλέκτωρ ἐφώνησεν. καὶ ἀνεμνήσθη ὁ Πέτρος τὸ ῥῆμα ὡς εἶπεν αὐτῷ ὁ Ἰησοῦς, "And immediately the cock crowed a second time. And Peter remembered the word that Jesus had said to him." Mark says εὐθύς, "immediately," the cock crowed. No sooner were the words of the third, final, climactic denial out of his mouth when the cock crowed a second time. The ugly words of the third denial were still ringing in the ears of all. The fulfillment of Jesus' prophecy, brought to mind so suddenly and jarringly, heightens the drama and poignancy of the scene and the remarkable accuracy of Jesus' prophecy.

πρὶν ἀλέκτορα φωνῆσαι δὶς τρίς με ἀπαρνήσῃ, "'Before the cock crows twice you will deny me three times.'" Peter remembers what Jesus had said (14:30) and fully recognizes the exact correspondence between the prophecy and its complete fulfillment.

καὶ ἐπιβαλὼν ἔκλαιεν, "And he began to weep." ἐπιβαλών, "began," lit. "having begun," is a difficult reading whose meaning is uncertain. Cranfield (448) item-izes several suggestions: "when he thought thereon," "covering his head," "drawing his cloak about his face," "dashing out," "throwing himself on the ground," and "set to and." Cranfield settles on the last option, noting that it is also accepted by the great grammarian J. H. Moulton (and also by F. Debrunner). Field (*Notes*, 41–43) argues for "covering the head," citing several texts that use ἐπιβάλλειν in this sense. The difficulty is attested by the Matthean (26:75) and Lukan (22:62) evangelists, both of whom choose another word (ἐξελθών, "having gone out"; see *Note* n). The options proposed by Cranfield and Field are probably the two best. Of these two, the meaning "covering the head" is more problematic, for usually it has an object. The meaning "having begun" (or the quaint "set to") is attested in the papyri (cf. P.Teb. 50.12) and is accepted by Klostermann (157–58), Schniewind (192, 195), and MM (235), among others (cf. BAG, 289–90).

Explanation

In stark contrast to Jesus, who is inside before the high priest, the most powerful Jew in Israel, Peter stands outside quailing before a female servant, a person of no power. Peter is recognized as having been with the Nazarene, Jesus (v 67). But he denies it without qualification. He neither knows nor understands what she is talking about. The maid again sees Peter (and the Greek suggests that it is the same maid, though see Matt 26:71, which says "another maid") and says to the bystanders: "This is one of them" (v 69). But Peter again denies it (v 70a). A little while later, the bystanders say to Peter that he surely must be one of the followers of Jesus, for he is a Galilean (v 70b). The maid servant's persistence has now led to several suspecting that Peter is a disciple. Perceiving the growing danger, the panicked disciple invokes a curse on himself (i.e., "May I be damned if I am not telling the truth"), perhaps even on the man (i.e., Jesus) about whom they ask, and says that he does not know the one they are talking about (v 71). The words are hardly out of his mouth when the rooster begins to crow. Jesus' prediction is fulfilled instantly and impressively. Remembering the prediction and recognizing what he has done, Peter weeps (v 72).

Mark's portrait contrasting Jesus and Peter is masterful and has often been the subject of Christian preaching. Even while Jesus is inside before the ruling priests who mock him and ask him to prophesy (14:65), Peter is outside fulfilling the very prophecy of Jesus that foretold Peter's threefold denial. Peter's failing only makes Jesus look more impressive and at the same time provides a lesson for all Christians, many of whom have denied or will deny their Lord.

K. Jesus before Pilate   (15:1–15)

Bibliography on the Roman Trial

Allen, J. E. "Why Pilate?" In *The Trial of Jesus: Cambridge Studies.* FS C. F. D. Moule, ed. E. Bammel. SBT 13. London: SCM Press; Naperville. IL: Allenson, 1970. 78–83. **Bammel, E.** "Pilatus' und Kaiphas' Absetzung." In *Judaica: Kleine Schriften I.* WUNT 37. Tübingen: Mohr-Siebeck, 1986. 51–58. ———. "The Trial before Pilate." In *Jesus and the Politics of His Day.* Ed. E. Bammel and C. F. D. Moule. Cambridge: Cambridge UP, 1984. 415–51. **Becq, J.** "Ponce Pilate et la mort de Jésus." *BTS* 57 (1963) 2–7. **Benoit, P.** *Passion and Resurrection.* 115–51. **Betz, O.** "The Temple Scroll and the Trial of Jesus." *SWJT* 30 (1988) 5–8. **Blinzler, J.** "Der Entschied des Pilatus—Exekutionsbefehl oder Todesurteil?" *MTZ* 5 (1954) 171–84. ———. *The Trial of Jesus: The Jewish and Roman Proceedings against Jesus Christ Described and Assessed from the Oldest Accounts.* Westminster: Newman, 1959. 164–93. **Brandon, S. G. F.** *Jesus and the Zealots.* Manchester: Manchester UP; New York: Scribner's, 1967. 1–25. ———. "The Trial of Jesus." *Horizon* 9 (1967) 4–13. **Burkill, T. A.** "The Condemnation of Jesus: A Critque of Sherwin-White's Thesis." *NovT* 12 (1970) 321–42. ———. "The Trial of Jesus." *VC* 12 (1958) 1–18. **Catchpole, D. R.** *The Trial of Jesus.* StPB 18. Leiden: Brill, 1971. 183–202. **Chaval, C. B.** "The Releasing of a Prisoner on the Eve of Passover in Ancient Jerusalem." *JBL* 60 (1941) 273–78. **Chilton, B. D.** *The Temple of Jesus.* University Park, PA: Pennsylvania State UP, 1992. **Chilton, C. W.** "The Roman Law of Treason und the Early Principate." *JRS* 45 (1955) 73–81. **Cohn, H.** *Reflections on the Trial and Death of Jesus.* Jerusalem: Israel Law Review Association, 1967. **Colin, J.** "Sur le procès de Jésus devant Pilate et le peuple." *REA* 67 (1965) 159–64. **Crespy, G.** "Recherche sur la signification politique de la mort du Christ." *LumVie* 20 (1971) 89–109. **Crossan, J. D.** *Who Killed Jesus? Exposing the Roots of Anti-Semitism in the Gospel Story of the Death of Jesus.* San Francisco: HarperCollins, 1995. **Davies, S. L.** "Who Is Called Bar Abbas?" *NTS* 27 (1980–81) 260–62. **Doyle, A. D.** "Pilate's Career and the Date of the Crucifixion." *JTS* o.s. 42 (1941) 190–93. **Dunkerley, R.** "Was Barabbas Also Called Jesus?" *ExpTim* 74 (1962–63) 126–27. **Erhardt, A.** "Pontius Pilatus in der frühchristlichen Mythologie." *EvT* 9 (1949–50) 433–47. **Fitzmyer, J. A.** "Crucifixion in Ancient Palestine, Qumran Literature, and the New Testament." *CBQ* 40 (1978) 493–513. **Flusser, D.** *Jesus.* 146–73. **Garnsey, P.** "The Criminal Jurisdiction of Governors." *JRS* 58 (1968) 51–59. **Haacker, K.** "Wer war Schuld am Tode Jesu?" *TBei* 25 (1994) 23–36. **Harrison, E. F.** "Jesus and Pilate." *BSac* 105 (1948) 307–19. **Haufe, G.** "Der Prozess Jesu im Lichte der gegenwärtige Forschung." *ZZ* 22 (1968) 93–101. **Hengel, M.** *Crucifixion.* London: SCM Press; Philadelphia: Fortress, 1977. **Hill, D.** "Jesus and Josephus' 'messianic prophets.'" In *Text and Interpretation.* FS M. Black, ed. E. Best and R. McL. Wilson. Cambridge: Cambridge UP, 1979. 143–54. **Horbury, W.** "Christ as a Brigand in Ancient Anti-Christian Polemic." In *Jesus and the Politics of His Day.* Ed. E. Bammel and C. F. D. Moule. Cambridge: Cambridge UP, 1984. 197–209. **Horsley, R. A.** "Popular Messianic Movements around the Time of Jesus." *CBQ* 46 (1984) 471–96. **Horvath, T.** "Why Was Jesus Brought to Pilate?" *NovT* 11 (1969) 174–84. **Husband, R. W.** "The Pardoning of Prisoners by Pilate." *AJT* 21 (1917) 110–16. **Jensen, E. E.** "The First Century Controversy over Jesus as a Revolutionary Figure." *JBL* 60 (1941) 261–72. **Juster, J.** *Les juifs dans l'empire romain: Leur condition juridique, économique et sociale.* 2 vols. Paris: Geunther, 1914. 2:127–49. **Kingdon, H. P.** "Had the Crucifixion a Political Significance?" *HibJ* 35 (1936–37) 556–67. **Kinman, B. R.** "Pilate's Assize and the Timing of Jesus' Trial." *TynBul* 42 (1991) 282–95. **Koch, W.** *Der Prozess Jesu.* Berlin: Kiepenheuer & Witsch, 1966. **Langdon, S.** "The Release of a Prisoner at the Passover." *ExpTim* 29 (1917–18) 328–30. **Lattey, C.** "The Praetorium of Pilate." *JTS* o.s. 31 (1930) 180–82. **Légasse, S.** *Le procès de Jésus: L'histoire.* LD 156. Paris: Cerf, 1994. **Liberty, S.** "The

Importance of Pontius Pilate in Creed and Gospel." *JTS* o.s. 45 (1944) 38–56. **Lietzmann, H.** "Der Prozess Jesu." *Sitzungsberichte der Preussischen Akademie der Wissenschaften in Berlin* 14 (1931) 313–22. **Lohse, E.** "Die römischen Statthalter in Jerusalem." *ZDPV* 74 (1958) 69–78. **Maier, P. L.** "The Episode of the Golden Roman Shields at Jerusalem." *HTR* 62 (1969) 109–21. ———. "Sejanus, Pilate, and the Date of the Crucifixion." *CH* 37 (1968) 3–13. **Matera, F. J.** "The Trial of Jesus: Problems and Proposals." *Int* 45 (1991) 5–16. **McGing, B. C.** "The Governorship of Pontius Pilate: Messiahs and Sources." PIBA 10 (1986) 55–71. ———. "Pontius Pilate and the Sources." *CBQ* 53 (1991) 416–38. **Millar, F.** "Reflections on the Trials of Jesus." In *A Tribute to Geza Vermes: Essays on Jewish and Christian Literature and History*. Ed. P. R. Davies and R. T. White. JSOTSup 100. Sheffield: JSOT Press, 1990. 355–81. **Overstreet, R. L.** "Roman Law and the Trial of Christ." *BSac* 135 (1978) 323–32. **Pesch, R.** *Das Evangelium der Urgemeinde.* 194–201. **Pixner, B.** "Noch einmal das Prätorium: Versuch einer neuen Lösung." *ZDPV* 95 (1979) 56–86. **Riesner, R.** "Das Prätorium des Pilatus." *BK* 41 (1986) 34–37. **Ritt, H.** "'Wer war Schuld am Tod Jesu?' Zeitgeschichte, Recht und theologische Deutung." *BZ* 31 (1987) 165–75. **Rivkin, E.** *What Crucified Jesus? The Political Execution of a Charismatic.* Nashville: Abingdon, 1984. **Robbins, V. K.** "The Crucifixion and the Speech of Jesus." *Forum* 4.1 (1988) 33–46. **Rogers, R. S.** "Treason in the Early Empire." *JRS* 49 (1959) 90–94. **Schmidt, K. L.** "Der Todesprozess des Messias Jesus." *Judaica* 1 (1945) 1–40. **Schwartz, D. R.** "Josephus and Philo on Pontius Pilate." *The Jerusalem Cathedra* 3 (1983) 26–45. **Sherwin-White, A. N.** *Roman Law and Roman Society in the New Testament.* The Sarum Lectures, 1960–61. London: Oxford UP, 1963. 24–47. ———. "The Trial of Christ." In *Historicity and Chronology in the New Testament.* Ed. D. E. Nineham et al. Theological Collections 6. London: S. P. C. K., 1965. 97–116. **Sloyan, G. S.** *Jesus on Trial: The Development of the Passion Narratives and Their Historical and Ecumenical Implications.* Ed. J. Reumann. Philadelphia: Fortress, 1973. **Sobosan, J. G.** "The Trial of Jesus." *JES* 10 (1973) 72–91. **Soltero, C.** "Pilatus, Jesus et Barabbas." *VD* 45 (1967) 326–30. **Staats, R.** "Pontius Pilatus im Bekenntnis der frühen Kirche." *ZTK* 84 (1987) 493–513. **Strobel, A.** *Die Stunde der Wahrheit: Untersuchungen zum Strafverfahren gegen Jesus.* WUNT 21. Tübingen: Mohr-Siebeck, 1980. 61–99. **Sweet, J. P. M.** "The Zealots and Jesus." In *Jesus and the Politics of His Day.* Ed. E. Bammel and C. F. D. Moule. Cambridge: Cambridge UP, 1984. 1–9. **Twomey, J. J.** "Barabbas Was a Robber." *Scr* 8 (1956) 115–19. **Vardaman, J.** "A New Inscription Which Mentions Pilate as 'Prefect.'" *JBL* 81 (1962) 70–71. **Vincent, L.-H.** "Le lithostrotos évangélique." *RB* 59 (1952) 513–30. **Volkmann, H.** "Die Pilatusinschrift von Caesarea Maritima." *Gymnasium* 75 (1968) 124–35, plates 13–15. **Wansbrough, H.** "Suffered under Pontius Pilate." *Scr* 18 (1966) 84–93. **Winter, P.** *On the Trial of Jesus.* Studia Judaica 1. 2nd ed. Rev. by T. A. Burkill and G. Vermes. Berlin; New York: de Gruyter, 1974. ———. "The Trial of Jesus as a Rebel against Rome." *The Jewish Quarterly* 16 (1968) 31–37. **Yadin, Y.** "Pesher Nahum (4Q pNahum) Reconsidered." *IEJ* 21 (1971) 1–12.

See also *Bibliography* for 14:53–65

Bibliography on Pontius Pilate, Roman Prefect

Bajsic, A. "Pilatus, Jesus und Barabbas." *Bib* 48 (1967) 7–28. **Bammel, E.** "Pilate and Syrian Coinage." *JJS* 2 (1950–51) 108–10 (repr. in E. Bammel. *Judaica: Kleine Schriften I.* WUNT 37. Tübingen: Mohr-Siebeck, 1986. 47–50). **Benoit, P.** "Prétoire, lithostroton et Gabbatha." *RB* 59 (1952) 531–50. **Blinzler, J.** "Die Niedermetzelung von Galiläern durch Pilatus." *NovT* (1957) 24–49. **Bond, H. K.** "The Coins of Pontius Pilate: Part of an Attempt to Provoke the People or to Integrate them into the Empire?" *JSJ* 27 (1996) 241–62. ———. *Pontius Pilate in History and Interpretation.* SNTSMS 100. Cambridge: Cambridge UP, 1998. **Collins, M. F.** "Hidden Vessels in Samaritan Tradition." *JSJ* 3 (1972) 97–116. **Davies, P. S.** "The Meaning of Philo's Text about the Gilded Shields." *JTS* n.s. 37 (1986) 109–14. **Dibelius, M.** "Herodes und Pilatus." *ZNW* 19 (1915) 113–26. **Doyle, A. D.** "Pilate's Career and the Date of the Crucifixion." *JTS* o.s. 42 (1941) 190–93. **Flusser, D.** "A Literary Approach to the Trial of Jesus." *Judaism* 20 (1971) 32–36 (repr. in D. Flusser. *Judaism and the Origins of Christianity.* Jerusalem: Magnes, 1988. 588–92). **Fuks, G.** "Again on the Episode of the Gilded Shields at Jerusalem." *HTR* 75 (1982) 503–7. **Hedley, P. L.** "Pilate's Arrival in Judaea." *JTS* o.s. 35 (1934) 56–57. **Hofer, H.** "Aus den Papieren des Pilatus." *Reformatio* 15 (1966) 181–87. **Husband, R. W.** "The Pardoning of Prisoners by Pilate." *AJT* 21 (1917) 110–16. **Jones, A. H. M.** "Procurators and Prefects in the Early Principate." In *Studies in Roman Government and Law.* Oxford: Blackwell, 1960. 115–25. **Kindler, A.** "More Dates on the Coins of the Procurators." *IEJ* 6 (1956) 54–57. **Kinman, B. R.** "Jesus' 'Triumphal Entry' in the Light of Pilate's." *NTS* 40 (1994) 442–48. ———. "Pilate's Assize and the Timing of Jesus' Trial." *TynBul* 42 (1991) 282–95. **Kraeling, C. H.** "The Episode of the Roman Standards at Jerusalem." *HTR* 35 (1942) 263–89. **Krieger, K.-S.** "Pontius Pilatus—Ein Judenfeind? Zur Problematik einer Pilatusbiographie." *BN* 78 (1995) 63–83. ———. "Die Problematik chronologischer Rekonstruktionen zur Amtszeit des Pilatus." *BN* 61 (1992) 27–32. **Langdon, S.** "The Release of a Prisoner at the Passover." *ExpTim* 29 (1917–18) 328–30. **Lémonon, J. P.** *Pilate et le gouvernement de la Judée: Textes et monuments.* EBib. Paris: Gabalda, 1981. ———. "Ponce Pilate: Documents profanes, Nouveau Testament et traditions ecclésiales." *ANRW* 2.26.1 (1992) 741–78. **Maier, P. L.** "The Episode of the Golden Shields at Jerusalem." *HTR* 62 (1969) 109–21. ———. "Sejanus, Pilate, and the Date of the Crucifixion." *CH* 37 (1968) 3–13. **McGing, B. C.** "Pontius Pilate and the Sources." *CBQ* 53 (1991) 416–38. **McLaren, J. S.** *Power and Politics in Palestine: The Jews and the Governing of Their Land 100 B.C.–A.D. 70.* JSNTSup 63. Sheffield: JSOT Press, 1991. 81–87. **Merritt, R. L.** "Jesus Barabbas and the Paschal Parson." *JBL* 104 (1985) 57–68. **Oestreicher, B.** "A New Interpretation of Dates on the Coins of the Procurators." *IEJ* 9 (1959) 193–95. **Ollivier, J.** "Ponce Pilate et les Pontii." *RB* 5 (1896) 247–54, 594–600. **Overstreet, R. L.** "Roman Law and the Trial of Christ." *BSac* 135 (1978) 323–32. **Rigg, H. A.** "Barabbas." *JBL* 64 (1945) 417–56. **Roth, L.** "Pontius Pilate." *EncJud* 13:848. **Sandmel, S.** "Pilate, Pontius." *IDB* 3:811–13. **Schwartz, D. R.** "Josephus and Philo on Pontius Pilate." *The Jerusalem Cathedra* 3 (1983) 26–45. ———. "Pontius Pilate." *ABD* 5:395–401. **Sherwin-White, A. N.** "The Trial of Christ." In *Historicity and Chronology in the New Testament.* Ed. D. E. Nineham et al. London: S. P. C. K., 1965. 97–116. **Smallwood, E. M.** "The Date of the Dismissal of Pontius Pilate from Judaea." *JJS* 5 (1954) 12–21. ———. "High Priests and Politics in Roman Palestine." *JTS* n.s. 13 (1962) 14–34. ———. *The Jews under Roman Rule: From Pompey to Diocletian: A Study in Political Relations.* SJLA 20. 1976. Repr. Leiden: Brill, 1981. 160–74. **Staats, R.** "Pontius Pilatus im Bekenntnis der frühen Kirche." *ZTK* 84 (1987) 493–513. **Stauffer, E.** "Zur Münzprägung und Judenpolitik des Pontius Pilatus." *La nouvelle clio* 1–2 (1949–50) 495–511, plates 1–3. **Thatcher, T.** "Philo on Pilate: Rhetoric or Reality?" *ResQ* 37 (1995) 215–18. **Vincent, L.-H.** "L'Antonia et le Prétoire." *RB* 42 (1933) 83–113. ———. "Le lithostrotos évangélique." *RB* 59 (1952) 513–30. **Watson, F.** "Why Was Jesus Crucified?" *Theology* 88 (1985) 105–12.

Bibliography on the Pilate Inscription

Alföldy, G. "Pontius Pilatus und das Tiberieum von Caesarea Maritima." *Scripta classica Israelica* 18 (1999) 85–108. **Bartina, S.** "Poncio Pilato en una inscripción monumentaria palestinense." *CB* 19 (1962) 170–75. **Betz, A.** "Zur Pontius Pilatus-Inschrift von Caesarea-Maritima." In *Pro Arte Antiqua.* FS H. Kenner, ed. W. Alzinger et al. Österreichisches archäologisches Institut in Wien: Sonderschriften 18. Vienna; Berlin: Koska, 1982. 33–36, plate 14. **Boffo, L.** *Iscrizioni greche e latine per lo studio della Bibbia.* Brescia: Paideia Editrice, 1994. 217–33. **Brusa Gerra, C.** "Le Iscrizióni." In *Scavi di Caesarea Maritima.* Ed. A. Frova. Rome: Bretschneider, 1966. 217–20. **Burr, V.** "Epigraphischer Beitrag zur neueren Pontius-Pilatus-Forschung." In *Vergangenheit, Gegenwart, Zukunft.* Ed. W. Burr. Würzburg; Stuttgart:

Echter, 1972. 37–41. **Calderini, A.** "L'inscription de Ponce Pilateà Césarée." *BTS* 57 (1963) 8–14. **Degrassi, A.** "Sull' iscrizione di Ponzio Pilato." *Rendiconti della Reale Accademia nazionale dei Lincei: Classe di Scienze morali, storiche e filologiche.* Series 8. Vol. 19. (1964) 59–65. **Di Stefano Manzella, I.** "Pontius Pilatus nell' iscrizione di Cesarea di Palestina." In *Le iscrizioni dei cristiani in Vaticano: Materiali e contributi scientifici per un mostra epigrafica.* Ed. I. Di Stefano Manzella. Vatican City: Edizioni Quasar, 1997. 209–15, fig. 3.1.2. **Frova, A.** "L'iscrizione di Ponzio Pilato a Cesarea." *Rendiconti dell' Istituto Lombardo* 95 (1961) 419–34. ———. "Ponzio Pilato e il Tiberieum di Cesarea." *La Veneranda Anticaglia* 16–17 (1969–70) 216–17. **Gatti, C.** "A proposito di una rilettura dell'epigrafe di Ponzio Pilato." *Aevum* 55 (1981) 13–21. **Gauze, J. H.** *Ecclesia* 174 (1963) 137. **Guey, J.** "La dédicace de Ponce Pilate découverte à Césarée de Palestine." *Bulletin de la Société Nationale des Antiquaires de France* (3 February 1965) 38–39. **Labbé, G.** "Ponce Pilate et la munificence de Tibère: L'inscription de Césarée." *REA* 93 (1991) 277–97. **Lémonon, J.-P.** *Pilate et le gouvernement de la Judée: Textes et monuments.* EBib. Paris: Gabalda, 1981. 23–32. ———. "Ponce Pilate: Documents profanes, Nouveau Testament et traditions ecclésiales." *ANRW* 2.26.1 (1992) 748–52. **Lifshitz, B.** "Inscriptions latines de Césarée (Caesarea Palaestinae)." *Latomus* 22 (1963) 783–84, plates 63–64. **Merlin, A.,** ed. *L'année épigraphique* (1963) no. 104. ———. *L'année épigraphique* (1964) no. 39. **Prandi, L.** "Una nuova ipotesi sull'iscrizione di Ponzio Pilato." *CClCr* 2 (1981) 25–35. **Rinaldi, G.** "Cesarea di Palestina." *BeO* 4 (1962) 100–103. **Ringel, J.** *Césarée de Palestine: Étude historique et archéologique.* Paris: Ophrys, 1975. 97–103. **Solin, H.** "Analecta Epigraphica." *Arctos* 6 (1970) 101–12, esp. 108–10. **Stauffer, E.** *Die Pilatusinschrift von Caesarea Maritima.* Erlangen: Erlanger Universitätsreden, 1966. **Vardaman, J.** "A New Inscription Which Mentions Pilate as 'Prefect.'" *JBL* 81 (1962) 70–71. **Volkmann, H.** "Die Pilatusinschrift von Caesarea Maritima." *Gymnasium* 75 (1968) 124–35, plates 13–15. **Weber, E.** "Zur Inschrift des Pontius Pilatus." *BJ* 171 (1971) 194–200. **Yelnitsky, L. A.** "The Inscription of Pontius Pilate at Caesarea and Its Historical Significance." *Vestnik drevnei istorii* 93 (1965) 142–46 [Russian].

Bibliography on Mark 15:1–15

Aus, R. D. "The Release of Barabbas (Mark 15:6–15 par.; John 18:39–40), and Judaic Traditions on the Book of Esther." In *Barabbas and Esther and Other Studies in the Judaic Illumination of Earliest Christianity.* SFSHJ 54. Atlanta: Scholars Press, 1992. 1–27. **Bajsic, A.** "Pilatus, Jesus und Barabbas." *Bib* 48 (1967) 7–28. **Bammel, E.** "The Trial before Pilate." In *Jesus and the Politics of His Day.* Ed. E. Bammel and C. F. D. Moule. Cambridge: Cambridge UP, 1984. 353–64. ———. *The Trial of Jesus.* London: SCM Press, 1970. **Berger, K.** "Die königlichen Messiastraditionen des Neuen Testaments." *NTS* 20 (1973–74) 1–44, esp. 22–28. ———. "Zum Problem der Messianität Jesu." *ZTK* 71 (1974) 1–30, esp. 1–15. **Betz, O.** "Probleme des Prozesses Jesu." *ANRW* 2.25.1 (1982) 565–647, esp. 639–44. **Bond, H. K.** *Pontius Pilate in History and Interpretation.* SNTSMS 100. Cambridge: Cambridge UP, 1998. 94–119. **Brandon, S. G. F.** *Jesus and the Zealots.* Manchester: Manchester UP; New York: Scribner's, 1967. 252–64. **Braumann, G.** "Markus 15,2–5 und Markus 14,55–64." *ZNW* 52 (1961) 273–78. **Chaval, C. B.** "The Releasing of a Prisoner on the Eve of Passover in Ancient Jerusalem." *JBL* 60 (1941) 273–78. **Couchoud, L.,** and **Stahl, R.** "Jesus Barabbas." *HibJ* 25 (1927) 26–42. **Davies, S. L.** "Who Is Called Bar Abbas?" *NTS* 27 (1981) 260–62. **Deissmann, A.** *Light from the Ancient East.* London: Hodder & Stoughton; New York: Harper & Row, 1927. **Dormeyer, D.** *Die Passion Jesu.* 174–85. ———. *Der Sinn des Leidens Jesu: Historisch-kritische und textpragmatische Analysen zur Markuspassion.* SBS 96. Stuttgart: Katholisches Bibelwerk, 1979. 62–75. **Ford, J. M.** "'Crucify Him, Crucify Him' and the Temple Scroll." *ExpTim* 87 (1975–76) 275–78. **Foulon-Piganiol, C. L.** "Le rôle du peuple dans le procès de Jésus: Une hypothèse juridique et théologique." *NRT* 98 (1976) 627–37. **Genest, O.** *Le Christ de la passion: Perspective structurale. Analyse de Marc 14,53–15,47, des parallèles et extra-bibliques.* Recherches 21: Théologie. Tournai: Desclée;

Montreal: Bellarmin, 1978. 57–95. **Haacker, K.** "Einige Fälle von 'erlebter Rede' im Neuen Testament." *NovT* 12 (1970) 70–77. **Hagedorn, A. C.,** and **Neyrey, J. H.** "'It Was Out of Envy That They Handed Jesus Over' (Mark 15.10): The Anatomy of Envy and the Gospel of Mark." *JSNT* 69 (1998) 15–56. **Hedinger, U.** "Jesus und die Volksmenge: Kritik der Qualifizierung der óchloi in der Evangelienauslegung." *TZ* 32 (1976) 201–6. **Horvath, T.** "Why Was Jesus Brought to Pilate?" *NovT* 11 (1969) 174–84. **Irmscher, J.** "Σὺ λέγεις (Mk 15,2; Mt 27,1; Lc 23,3)." *Studii Clasice* 2 (1960) 151–58. **Jonge, M. de.** "The Earliest Christian Use of *Christos:* Some Suggestions." *NTS* 32 (1986) 321–43. **Kremer, J.** *Das Ärgernis des Kreuzes: Eine Hinführung zum Verstehen der Leidensgeschichte nach Markus.* Stuttgart: Katholisches Bibelwerk, 1969. 54–59. **Lee, G. M.** "Mark xv 8." *NovT* 20 (1978) 74. **Maccoby, H. Z.** "Jesus and Barabbas." *NTS* 16 (1969–70) 55–60. **Mack, B. L.** *A Myth of Innocence.* 295–96. **Matera, F. J.** *The Kingship of Jesus: Composition and Theology in Mark 15.* SBLDS 66. Chico, CA: Scholars Press, 1982. 7–20. **McLaren, J. S.** *Power and Politics in Palestine: The Jews and the Governing of Their Land 100 B.C.– A.D. 70.* JSNTSup 63. Sheffield: JSOT Press, 1991. 88–101. **Merritt, R. L.** "Jesus Barabbas and the Paschal Pardon." *JBL* 104 (1985) 57–68. **Mohr, T. A.** *Markus- und Johannespassion.* 282–301. **Moo, D. J.** *Old Testament in the Gospel Passion Narratives.* 148–51. **Myllykoski, M.** *Die letzten Tage Jesu.* 94–99. **Nicklin, T.** "'Thou Sayest.'" *ExpTim* 51 (1939–40) 155. **Rigg, H. A., Jr.** "Barabbas." *JBL* 64 (1945) 417–56. **Schenk, W.** *Der Passionsbericht nach Markus.* 223–49. **Schenke, L.** *Der gekreuzigte Christus.* 47–60. **Schneider, G.** *Die Passion Jesu.* 83–87, 94–98. ———. "The Political Charge against Jesus (Luke 23:2)." In *Jesus and the Politics of His Day.* Ed. E. Bammel and C. F. D. Moule. Cambridge: Cambridge UP, 1984. 403–14, esp. 403–4. **Schreiber, J.** "Das Schweigen Jesu." In *Theologie und Unterricht: Über die Repräsentanz des Christlichen in der Schule.* FS H. Stock, ed. K. Wegenast. Gütersloh: Mohn, 1969. 79–87. **Senior, D. P.** *Passion of Jesus in the Gospel of Mark.* 105–14. **Strobel, A.** *Die Stunde der Wahrheit: Untersuchungen zum Strafverfahren gegen Jesus.* WUNT 21. Tübingen: Mohr-Siebeck, 1980. 95–99. **Twomey, J. J.** "Barabbas Was a Robber." *Scr* 8 (1956) 115–19. **Winter, P.** *On the Trial of Jesus.* Rev. T. A. Burkill and G. Vermes. 2nd ed. Studia Judaica 1. Berlin; New York: de Gruyter, 1974. 131–43.

Translation

¹*And as soon as it was morning, having held a consultation,*[a] *the ruling priests with the elders and scribes and the whole council, [and]*[b] *having bound Jesus, carried [him]*[c] *away and handed [him]*[c] *over to Pilate.*[d] ²*And Pilate questioned him, "Are you the king of the Jews?" And replying, he*[e] *says to him, "You say it."*³*And the ruling priests were accusing him much.*[f] ⁴*But Pilate again questioned him, saying, "Do you answer nothing? Look how much they accuse you!"*⁵*But Jesus no longer gave any reply, so that Pilate was amazed.*

⁶*Now at the feast he*[g] *would release to them one prisoner whom they chose.*⁷*But there was one called Barabbas,*[h] *imprisoned with the rebels,*[i] *who had in the rebellion committed murder.*⁸*And going up,*[j] *the crowd began to request,*[k] *just as he used to do for them.*[l] ⁹*But Pilate answered them, saying, "Do you wish that I might release to you the king of the Jews?"*¹⁰*For he knew that because of envy the ruling priests had handed him over.*¹¹*But the ruling priests stirred up the crowd, so that he should rather release Barabbas*[m] *to them.*¹²*But Pilate, again answering, was saying to them, "What then [do you wish that] I should do with him [whom you call]*[n] *'the king of the Jews'?"*¹³*But again they shouted,*[o] *"Crucify*[p] *him!"*¹⁴*But Pilate was saying to them, "Why, what evil has he done?" But they shouted all the more, "Crucify*[p] *him!"*¹⁵*So Pilate, wishing to satisfy the crowd, released to them Barabbas,*[q] *and he handed Jesus over, having scourged [him],*[c] *that he might be crucified.*

Notes

[a]Gk. συμβούλιον ποιήσαντες. ℵ C L and a few later MSS read συμβούλιον ἑτοιμάσαντες. Metzger (*TCGNT*[1], 117) says that this reading represents an attempt to remove the ambiguity of the text so that it would clearly mean "having made a plan," or "having held a consultation," as opposed to "having convened the council."

[b]The bracketed conjunction καί, "and," is needed (and D and a few other MSS supply it), but it is probably not original.

[c]The bracketed word has been added to the text (though W and a few later MSS do add αὐτόν, "him").

[d]A few late MSS read Πόντιος Πιλᾶτος, "Pontius Pilate." The earliest Gk. spelling of Pilate is Πειλᾶτος (as in ℵ A B D), but in many of the later MSS the name is spelled Πιλᾶτος. (This applies to the other occurrences of the name in Mark 15.) Latin MSS spell the name *Pilatus,* which evidently reflects the way the governor himself spelled his name, as seen in the Pilate inscription found at Caesarea Maritima (see *Comment* on v 1).

[e]Ν Σ and a few later MSS add Ἰησοῦς, "Jesus."

[f]Ν W Σ 33 and several later MSS add αὐτὸς δὲ οὐδὲν ἀπεκρίνατο, "but he himself answered nothing" (cf. Luke 23:9).

[g]W and a few later MSS and authorities add ὁ ἡγεμών, "the governor" (cf. Matt 27:15).

[h]Gk. Βαραββᾶς. This name appears in a variety of forms and spellings: Βαραβᾶς, Βαρραββᾶς, Βαβαρραββᾶς, and most curious of all (read by W) Βαρναβᾶς, "Barnabas," the name of Paul's missionary companion. Βαραββᾶς transliterates the Aramaic name אבא בר *bar ʾAbbāʾ,* which means "son of the father."

[i]Α Σ 33 and several later MSS read συστασιαστῶν, "fellow rebels."

[j]Gk. ἀναβάς. ℵ[c] A C N W Σ and a few later authorities read ἀναβοήσας, lit. "calling out," a word that occurs nowhere else in Mark. In contrast, forms of ἀναβαίνειν occur in Mark several times.

[k]D and a few later MSS read ὅλος ὁ ὄχλος ἤρξατο αἰτεῖσθαι αὐτόν, "the whole crowd began to petition him" (an OL MS adds *Pilatum,* "Pilate").

[l]A few later MSS read κάθως ἔθος ἦν ἵνα τὸν Βαραββᾶν ἀπολύσῃ αὐτοῖς, "as was his custom, that he might release to them Barabbas."

[m]Again, variations in the forms and spellings of this name are attested. See *Note* h above.

[n]The words ὃν λέγετε are read in B 2427 but omitted by A D W Θ *f*[1.13] 205 565 700 2542 *pc* lat sy[s] sa. The words are placed in square brackets in Nestle-Aland[27] and UBSGNT[3c] to indicate that they are doubtful (see Metzger, *TCGNT*[1], 118). If they are omitted, the verse reads "What then shall I do with the 'king of the Jews'?"

[o]Several late MSS add ἀνασειόμενοι ὑπὸ τῶν ἀρχιερέων καὶ ἔλεγον, "having been agitated by the ruling priests, and they were saying."

[p]A few late MSS read σταύρου σταύρου, "crucify, crucify." The geminatum form probably derives from Luke 23:21.

[q]A few of the variations mentioned in *Note* h are attested in two or three late MSS.

Form/Structure/Setting

Mark 15:1–15 constitutes one of the most dramatic and memorable scenes in the Passion Narrative. The passage falls into two principal parts: (1) Jesus is handed over to the Roman governor to face the charge of claiming to be "king of the Jews" (vv 1–5), and (2) Pilate allows the crowd to decide between Jesus and Barabbas (vv 6–15). In the first part, Pilate interrogates Jesus, who remains silent (v 5), while in the second part, Pilate interrogates the crowd, who shout for Jesus' crucifixion (vv 13–14).

Bultmann (*History,* 272, 279) believes that a primitive narrative that briefly related Jesus' condemnation by Pilate underlies 15:1–15. Taylor (577) describes vv 1–15 as "loosely constructed" and as "more than a mere compilation of separate items of tradition." However, Bultmann senses tension between vv 1–2 (where

Jesus answers) and vv 3–5 (where Jesus does not answer). Moreover, he (*History,* 272, 284) thinks that v 2 is a secondary addition. However, Dibelius (*Tradition,* 213) thinks that v 2 may be quite primitive, reflecting the early church's knowledge of the Roman governor's verdict against Jesus. Dibelius is probably correct. Furthermore, Jesus' "You say it" (v 2, which is what probably underlies Matt 26:64) in contrast to his "I am" in 14:62 (see *Comment* on 14:62) implies a reticence to accept the Roman epithet "king of the Jews" (see *Comment* on v 2), whereas before the ruling priests Jesus was willing to accept the epithet "Messiah, son of the Blessed" (14:61). However, it is probable that v 1 is a Markan introduction that anticipates the priestly accusations in v 3. The core of the story is thus found in vv 2–15. Of this, the most problematic feature is the Barabbas tradition.

Bultmann (*History,* 272; cf. 284, 306) believes that the episode of Barabbas (vv 6–15) is "obviously a legendary expansion." His comment that v 12 resembles v 2 is valid, but his skeptical view of the material as a whole is unwarranted. Taylor (577) plausibly opines that the Barabbas episode in all probability never circulated as a separate, independent piece of tradition. Likewise Cranfield (448) comments that the "narrative is realistic and notably restrained, and clearly rests on primitive tradition." Johnson (247–48) adds that "it is so simple and straightforward, almost objective, using no emotional words and no theological interpretation." But Bultmann is not alone in his skepticism. C. G. Montefiore (2:373) remarks that the Barabbas episode is "very doubtful" historically, though he concedes that "some historical reminiscence is at the bottom of the tale." Taylor replies (577) that "while not the narrative of an eyewitness, it rests probably on primitive testimony." Nineham (411) regards the "chaffering" between Pilate and the crowd as unhistorical, though he gives no real reason why this must be so. Bultmann (*History,* 272 n. 2) avers that there "is no evidence in either Jewish or Roman law for the custom" of the so-called Passover Pardon. Nineham (413–14) suspects that Pilate did not regularly release a prisoner but "in a particular case" may have done so. It must be admitted that there is no evidence "in either Jewish or Roman law" for the custom to which the Markan evangelist alludes. But the impression is that Pilate's deed was an act of clemency on the part of the governor, and therefore provision for it in the law need not be expected. Although there is no direct evidence apart from the Gospels themselves that Pilate customarily released a prisoner at Passover, there are good reasons for accepting the historicity of this element of the Passion Narrative (see *Comment* on v 6).

A great deal of debate, sometimes heated polemic, centers on the question of the responsibility for Jesus' execution. Years ago Lietzmann (*Sitzungsberichte der Preussischen Akademie* 14 [1931] 313–22) argued that Mark—our "only" source (*sic*) for the story of Jesus' condemnation and execution—is unreliable. Since Jesus was crucified, which Lietzmann believes was a non-Jewish form of execution, his trial and death must have been entirely at the discretion of the Roman authorities. Winter (*On the Trial,* 131–43) agrees, claiming that it was the Roman governor, not the Jewish council, that condemned Jesus to death. Cohn (*Reflections,* 32) dogmatically asserts that the trial and execution of Jesus "were exclusively Roman." However, most scholars today agree that Jewish authorities acted together with Roman authorities in having Jesus put to death (e.g., Blinzler, *Trial of Jesus;* Burkill, *VC* 12 [1958] 1–18; Catchpole, *Trial of Jesus;* B. Chilton, *Temple of Jesus;* Haacker, *TBei* 25 [1994] 23–36; W. Koch, *Der Prozess;* Matera, *Int* 45 [1991] 5–16;

Ritt, *BZ* 31 [1987] 165–75; Rivkin, *What Crucified Jesus?;* Sloyan, *Jesus on Trial;* Strobel, *Die Stunde der Wahrheit*), with the principal responsibility lying with the Romans (e.g., Crossan, *Who Killed Jesus?;* Haufe, *ZZ* 22 [1968] 93–101). Although the older assumption that only Romans practiced crucifixion has now been called into question (e.g., Betz, *SWJT* 30 [1988] 5–8; Fitzmyer, *CBQ* 40 [1978] 493–513; Hengel, *Crucifixion,* 84–90; Yadin, *IEJ* 21 [1971] 1–12), there is no reason to doubt that Jesus' execution was carried out by Roman authority (*pace* Bammel, "Trial before Pilate," 437–51).

The Gospels' portrait of Pilate as wavering, wishing to release Jesus, but finally acquiescing to the demands of Jerusalem's influential elite has often been questioned. Many assume that this portrait grew out of apologetic interests that hoped to put Jesus and early Christianity on the side of Rome. It was the Jewish leaders, after all, not the Roman governor, who desired Jesus' death—so goes the argument. That the evangelists exploited the story of the wavering, uncertain Pilate is quite probable, but its wholesale invention is doubtful (see Brown, 2:695–705; McGing, *CBQ* 53 [1991] 416–38). When we remember the political and social setting of Jewish Palestine in the time of Pilate, we should not be surprised that Pilate was reluctant to execute in such a public and provocative manner a popular prophet from Galilee, whose many followers were present in Jerusalem. Stringing up Jesus could very well have instigated a riot, the very thing Pilate hoped to avoid. If Jesus had no military intentions, then he was little more than a pest. A beating and some jail time would suffice. But no, the ruling priests wanted him dead. Pilate obliged, but only when it had been made clear that the decision to have Jesus executed was not really his.

Comment

1 καὶ εὐθὺς πρωὶ συμβούλιον ποιήσαντες, "And as soon as it was morning, having held a consultation." Mark's συμβούλιον ποιήσαντες, "having held a consultation," does not mean that a second priestly hearing has taken place. The evangelist wishes only to remind his readers, after the interruption of the story of Peter's denials (14:66–72), that the priests had reached a decision during the night, and now that it was morning they were ready to act on this decision. Indeed, the ruling priests did not delay but acted εὐθὺς πρωὶ, "as soon as it was morning." The εὐθὺς πρωὶ modifies not the participial phrase συμβούλιον ποιήσαντες but the latter part of the verse: δήσαντες τὸν Ἰησοῦν ἀπήνεγκαν καὶ παρέδωκαν Πιλάτῳ, "having bound Jesus, carried [him] away and handed [him] over to Pilate." συμβούλιον ποιήσαντες refers to what happened the night before. (Mark's clumsy employment of modifiers is seen elsewhere, e.g., 6:16–18; 11:13; 16:3–4.)

οἱ ἀρχιερεῖς μετὰ τῶν πρεσβυτέρων καὶ γραμματέων καὶ ὅλον τὸ συνέδριον, "the ruling priests with the elders and scribes and the whole council." The evangelist reminds his readers of the principal players in the proceedings against Jesus. The triad of ruling priests, elders, and scribes has appeared earlier in Mark 11:27; 14:43, 53 (cf. the passion predictions in 8:31 and 10:33, minus the elders).

δήσαντες τὸν Ἰησοῦν ἀπήνεγκαν, "having bound Jesus, carried [him] away," could imply that Jesus' feet, as well as his hands, were bound so that he could not walk but had to be carried. However, this might be pressing the language too literally.

καὶ παρέδωκαν Πιλάτῳ, "and handed [him] over to Pilate." The priests' act of handing over (παρέδωκαν) Jesus to the Roman governor fulfills his earlier predictions: "The 'son of man' is delivered [παραδίδοται] into human hands" (9:31); and more closely, "the 'son of man' will be handed over [παραδοθήσεται] to the ruling priests and to the scribes, and they will condemn him to death and hand [παραδώσουσιν] him over to the Gentiles" (10:33). The priestly decision the preceding evening was that Jesus was worthy of death, so they hand him over to the governor. The language also recalls Judas's treachery, in handing Jesus over to his enemies (14:10, 11, 18, 21, 42, 44). One should also recall LXX Isa 53:6: "the Lord handed [παρέδωκεν] him over for our sins." On the act of the ruling priests handing over someone to the Roman governor, see *Excursus:* "The Arrest of Jesus Son of Ananias" and *Comment* on 11:27.

This is the first reference to Pontius Pilate (Π[ε]ιλᾶτος; his surname Πόντιος appears in Luke 3:1; Acts 4:27; 1 Tim 6:13; cf. Josephus, *Ant.* 18.2.2 §35), the Roman governor of Judea (26–37 C.E.; Ollivier, *RB* 5 [1896] 247–54, 594–600; but Schwartz, *ABD* 5:396–97, argues for the dates 19–37 C.E.). Pilate normally resided in Caesarea Maritima (on the Mediterranean), but during Passover and other holidays he took up residence in Jerusalem either in the Antonia (which is doubtful), which overlooked the temple precincts, or in Herod's palace (cf. Josephus, *J.W.* 2.14.8 §301, which says Gesius Florus, the last governor before the outbreak of the Jewish war against Rome, resided in Herod's palace). The Roman historian Tacitus (ca. 56–ca. 118 C.E.) states that "Christus . . . had suffered the death penalty during the reign of Tiberius, by sentence of the procurator Pontius Pilate [*per procuratorem Pontium Pilatum*]" (*Ann.* 15.44).

Calling Pilate a "procurator" is anachronistic, for prior to the brief reign of Agrippa I (41–44 C.E.), the Roman governors of Judea were prefects. This historical point was argued by A. H. M. Jones ("Procurators and Prefects") in 1960 and confirmed in 1961 by an inscription found at Caesarea Maritima (cf. Frova, *Rendiconti dell' Istituto Lombardo* 95 [1961] 424–25), which is frequently cited, though its reconstruction is much debated:

[CAESARIEN]STIBERIÉVM	[Caesarean]s' Tiberieum
[PON]TIVSPILATVS	[Pon]tius Pilate,
[PRAEF]ECTVSIVDA[EA]E	[Pref]ect of Juda[ea]
[D]É[DIT]	[d]e[dicates]

According to this reconstruction, Pontius Pilate has dedicated a "Tiberieum" to the people of Caesarea (i.e., *Caesarien[ibus]*). But in another, more recent reconstruction (cf. Alföldy, *Studia classica Israelica* 18 [1999] 106–7), the governor has restored a Tiberieum for the seamen:

[NAUTI]STIBERIÉVM	[Seamen']s Tiberieum
[PON]TIVSPILATVS	[Pon]tius Pilate,
[PRAEF]ECTVSIVDA[EA]E	[Pref]ect of Jude[a]
[REF]É[CIT]	[restor]e[s . . .]

Others reconstruct the inscription somewhat differently: Weber, *BJ* 171 (1971) 194–200: *[Kal(endis) Iulii]s Tiberiéum [M(arcus) ? Po]ntius Pilatus [praef]ectus Iuda[ea]e [dedicavit],* "The Tiberieum of July First Marcus (?) Pontius Pilate prefect of Judea has dedicated"; Degrassi, "Sull'iscrizione di Ponzio Pilato": *[Dis Augusti]s Tiberieum [Pon]tius Pilatus [praef]ectus Iuda[ae]e [fecit, d]e[dicavit]*, "The Tiberieum of the Divine Augusti [i.e., Caesar Augustus and Livia his wife, the mother of Tiberius] . . ."; Bartina, *CB* 19 (1962) 170–75: *[opu]s Tiberieum*, "The Tiberieum building"; Gatti, *Aevum* 55 (1981) 13–21: *[Iudaei]s Tiberieum*, "The Tiberieum of the Jews"; Burr, "Epigraphischer Beitrag": *[nemu]s Tiberieum*, "The Tiberieum of the [sacred] grove"; Labbé, *REA* 93 (1991) 277–97: *[munu]s Tiberieum*, "The Tiberieum [erected for the people]." For text, proposed reconstructions, and scholarly discussion, see *Bibliography on the Pilate Inscription* above (especially Alföldy, *Studia classica Israelica* 18 [1999] 85–108; Di Stefano Manzella, "Pontius Pilatus"; and Labbé, *REA* 93 [1991] 277–97). Alföldy (*Studia classica Israelica* 18 [1999] 85–108) has plausibly suggested that the inscription commemorates a rebuilding of the harbor of Caesarea Maritima, an achievement in which Pontius Pilate would have taken some pride. The Tiberieum itself may have been a lighthouse.

In the Gospels, Pilate, who in the inscription is called a *praefectus,* "prefect," is called a ἡγεμών (cf. Matt 27:2; Luke 3:1), which is a general term that means "leader" or "governor" and can serve as the Greek equivalent for either prefect or procurator. Although there are variations and inconsistencies in the terminology used by Greek writers, *praefectus* is usually rendered by ἔπαρχος, "commander," *procurator* by ἐπίτροπος, "steward, guardian." Mark does not mention Pilate's rank (though the plural ἡγεμόνων, "governors," appears in the eschatological discourse in conjunction with kings [13:9]). The prefect was more of a military office (i.e., a military governor), while the procurator had broader civil authority and was concerned to protect the emperor's financial interests.

The portrait of Pilate is quite negative in the writings of two Jewish contemporaries (Brown, 694–95, enjoins caution on this score). Philo of Alexandria describes the governor of Judea as a "man of an inflexible, stubborn, and cruel disposition," adding that "briberies, insults, robberies, outrages, wanton injuries, executions without trial, and endless and supremely grievous cruelty" marked his administration (*Embassy* 38 §§301–2). Philo's remarks here are primarily in reference to the incident of the golden shields that Pilate had placed in Herod's palace in Jerusalem. These criticisms are politically motivated and probably exaggerate the governor's faults.

Josephus, who also has no praise for the man, relates an incident in which one night Pilate transferred military standards bearing the image of the Roman emperor from Caesarea Maritima to Jerusalem (possibly another version of the same event described by Philo). A large group of Jews went to Caesarea imploring the governor to remove the standards. Only their willingness to die, unresisting, compelled Pilate to have the offensive standards returned to Caesarea (*J.W.* 2.9.2–3 §§171–74; *Ant.* 18.3.1 §§55–59). Josephus relates another incident in which Pilate dipped into the temple treasury to secure additional funding for a municipal project. The account from which the money was taken was the "sacred treasure known as *Corbonas* [κορβωνᾶς]" (*J.W.* 2.9.4 §175; *Ant.* 18.3.2 §§60–62). Josephus is here referring to the dedicated offering known as קָרְבָּן *qorbān,* that is, a gift given to God (cf. Mark 7:11: "'Qorban [κορβᾶν],' that is, 'gift'" [author's tr.]; cf. Guelich, 368–69; Matt 27:6: "It is not lawful to put them [i.e., Judas's pieces of silver] into the *Corbanas* [κορβανᾶν]" [RSV, adapted]). To take such consecrated items and put them to a secular use would have been highly offensive to the Jewish people.

Once again, the Jewish people protested and offered no resistance. Pilate sent soldiers, dressed as civilians, among the people. At a prearranged signal, these disguised soldiers began beating the people with clubs, killing some, injuring many others, and finally dispersing the crowd. In both of the incidents related by Josephus, the ruling priests are conspicuous by their silence. This is especially startling in the case of taking money from the *Corbonas,* for Pilate could not have done this, nor would he have dared to do this, without permission and assistance from the ruling priests themselves. Evidently, Caiaphas the high priest and Pilate the governor worked well together. It is not surprising that shortly after Pilate was removed from office in early 37 C.E. after his brutal assault on the Samaritans, Caiaphas was also removed from office (*Ant.* 18.4.2 §§88–89; 18.4.3 §95).

The Lukan evangelist alludes to a grisly event when Jesus is told "of the Galileans whose blood Pilate had mingled with their sacrifices" (Luke 13:1). This may be yet one more instance of the governor's violence against his subjects (see Brown, 698–705, for a convenient summary of six incidents involving Pilate; see also McLaren, *Power and Politics,* 81–87; Bond, *Pontius Pilate,* 24–93; Brown concludes that the Gospels' portrait of Pilate is not inconsistent with what we know of the governor of Judea, especially in reference to the incident of the standards; see also Bond's conclusion, pp. 119, 205).

2 σὺ εἶ ὁ βασιλεὺς τῶν Ἰουδαίων; "Are you the king of the Jews?" This is the first reference to Jesus as βασιλεὺς τῶν Ἰουδαίων, "king of the Jews." He will be called this again in vv 9, 12, 18, 26. "King of the Jews" is a Roman designation (cf. Josephus, *J.W.* 1.14.4 §282, where Mark Antony makes Herod "king of the Jews [βασιλέα . . . Ἰουδαίων]"; *Ant.* 14.3.1 §36; 15.10.5 §373; 15.11.4 §409; 16.9.3 §291; 16.10.2 §311). χριστός, "Messiah" (8:29; 12:35; 14:61; 15:32), υἱὸς Δαυίδ, "son of David" (10:47, 48; 12:35), βασιλεὺς Ἰσραήλ, "king of Israel" (15:32), and perhaps even υἱὸς τοῦ εὐλογητοῦ, "son of the Blessed" (14:61; cf. 3:11), were Jewish designations for Israel's king. Cranfield (449) wonders if Pilate had the charge, in which Jesus claimed to be the "king of the Jews?" before him in writing. Pilate asks Jesus, "Are *you* the king of the Jews?" utilizing the emphatic personal pronoun σύ as had Caiaphas in 14:61: "Are *you* the Messiah . . . ?" The emphatic pronoun carries with it a touch of mockery, perhaps suggesting that Pilate had anticipated meeting someone more impressive (i.e., "You? You must be kidding!"). The epithet will appear on the *titulus* near or upon the cross in 15:26, where mockery is surely intended (Taylor, 579).

Jesus replies in kind: σὺ λέγεις, "*You* say it." Jesus' use of the pronoun σύ, "you," conveys no sarcasm but calls attention to the inadequacy of the epithet. It is Pilate's choice of words, not the choice of Jesus. Jesus does not deny the identification, for he is indeed the "king of the Jews," but it is not his preferred self-designation (Taylor, 579), nor is it the evangelist's preferred designation for Jesus.

3 καὶ κατηγόρουν αὐτοῦ οἱ ἀρχιερεῖς πολλά, "And the ruling priests were accusing him much." Jesus' indirect answer, "You say it," and, we may surmise, Pilate's response (a questioning, even mocking glance at Jesus' accusers?) prompt the ruling priests to accuse Jesus vigorously. Earlier in Mark (3:2), Jesus was watched closely so that his opponents (Pharisees? cf. 2:24) might accuse him. But there the accusations concerned matters of the oral law regarding what was permissible on the Sabbath. Here the accusations are much more serious. Mark says the ruling priests were accusing Jesus πολλά, "much." πολλά could be the direct object, "(of) many things," or it could serve as an adverb, "much." The latter option is probably to be preferred (so Gundry, 924; cf. 1:45: "he began to preach much"). Moreover, the ruling priests do not really have a great number of charges to bring against Jesus; they have one serious charge, which they press upon the Roman governor with great emphasis. Not only did the priests repeat Jesus' own confession that he was the Messiah and "son of God," thereby implying that he indeed claimed to be Israel's king; they probably mentioned his threats against the temple and his disruptive behavior in the temple precincts.

4–5 οὐκ ἀποκρίνῃ οὐδέν; ἴδε πόσα σου κατηγοροῦσιν. ὁ δὲ Ἰησοῦς οὐκέτι οὐδὲν ἀπεκρίθη, ὥστε θαυμάζειν τὸν Πιλᾶτον, "'Do you answer nothing? Look how much they accuse you!' But Jesus no longer gave any reply, so that Pilate was amazed." Jesus refuses to discuss the matter with Pilate, and he refuses to reply to the charge that has been laid against him (vv 3–5). Pilate is amazed (v 5a), which casts Jesus once again in a favorable light. With calm and dignity Jesus stands before his accusers, who with vehemence accuse him and with befuddlement question him. Some commentators have wondered if Jesus' silence echoes Isa 53:7: "he opened not his mouth." By itself, the parallel is not impressive. But παρέδωκαν, "handed . . . over," of v 1, which may allude to LXX Isa 53:6 (see *Comment* on v 1), and the statement that Pilate θαυμάζειν, "was amazed," which may allude to LXX Isa 52:15, "thus nations will be amazed [θαυμάσονται] much at him," suggest that elements of the Suffering Servant hymn have colored the narrative. Pilate may well have been amazed at Jesus' silence because Roman law apparently presumed the guilt of those who refused to defend themselves (cf. Sherwin-White, *Roman Law*, 25–26).

Mark's readers will have been impressed by Jesus' silence and courage in the face of damning charges and threats. Jesus will have been seen as a just man able to face death nobly and with a stoic calm. Appreciation for these qualities are attested in the best of the Greco-Roman ethical tradition. Plutarch remarks that "many are silent under mutilation and endure scourging and being tortured by the wedge at the hands of master or tyrants without uttering a cry" (*Mor.* 498D–E = *An vit.* §2). Centuries earlier, Plato commented that "the just man will have to endure the lash, the rack, chains, the branding-iron in his eyes, and finally, after every extremity of suffering, he will be crucified" (*Republic* 2.5 §361e).

6 κατὰ δὲ ἑορτὴν ἀπέλυεν αὐτοῖς ἕνα δέσμιον ὂν παρῃτοῦντο, "Now at the feast he would release to them one prisoner whom they chose." Vv 6–15 narrate Pilate's offer to release one of the prisoners (the so-called *privilegium paschale* [special Passover law]). The imperfect ἀπέλυεν, "he would release," implies that this was the governor's custom (cf. also v 8: καθὼς ἐποίει αὐτοῖς, "just as he used to do for them"). Because there is no corroboration of Pilate's Passover pardon outside the NT Gospels, some critics think it is nothing more than a literary and theological invention. But the tradition is attested in at least two independent streams, Mark (followed by Matthew and Luke) and John (which is independent of the Synoptics). Is it probable that an inauthentic custom would spring up among Christians early enough and convincingly enough to find its way into the emerging streams of tradition, eventually making its appearance in two independent Gospel accounts?

Nevertheless, many doubt the historicity of Mark's report of Pilate's custom of Passover release (e.g, Winter, *On the Trial*, 134). But there is a measure of corroborating evidence that lends credibility to the evangelist's narrative. The

Mishnah says that "they may slaughter (the Passover lamb) for one . . . whom they have promised to bring out of prison" on the Passover (*m. Pesaḥ.* 8:6; cf. Chaval, *JBL* 60 [1941] 273–78; Strobel, *Die Stunde die Wahrheit,* 120–24). Who the "they" are is not made clear (Jewish authorities? Roman authorities?), but it is interesting that the promised release from prison is for the express purpose of taking part in the Passover observance. According to Deissmann, a papyrus (P.Flor. 61, lines 59–60, 64, ca. 85 C.E.), "containing a report of judicial proceedings, quotes these words of the governor of Egypt, G. Septimius Vegetus, before whom the case was tried, to a certain Phibion": "You were worthy of scourging . . . but I give you to the crowds" (Deissmann, *Light from the Ancient East,* 269–70, plate; Deissmann's tr. of the Gk. text is slightly adapted). Lagrange (414) and Lohmeyer (337) cite Pliny the Younger (ca. 61–112 C.E.), who says: "It was asserted, however, that these people were released upon their petition to the proconsuls, or their lieutenants; which seems likely enough, as it is improbable any person should have dared to set them at liberty without authority" (*Ep.* 10.31). An inscription from Ephesus (ca. 441 C.E.) relates the decision of the proconsul of Asia to release (ἀπολύειν, as also in Mark) prisoners because of the outcries of the people of the city (Deissmann, *Light from the Ancient East,* 269–70 n. 7; cf. W. M. Calder, "Christians and Pagans in the Greco-Roman Levant,"*Classical Review* 38 [1924] 29–30). Livy (5.13.8) speaks of special dispensations whereby chains were removed from the limbs of prisoners. When the procurator Albinus (62–64 C.E.) prepared to leave office in Judea, he released all prisoners incarcerated for offenses other than murder (Josephus, *Ant.* 20.9.5 §215). He did this hoping to gain a favorable review from the inhabitants of Jerusalem. And finally, years earlier Archelaus (4 B.C.E.–6 C.E.) hoped to appease his countrymen, and so gain his late father Herod's kingdom, by acquiescing to their demands that those imprisoned be released (Josephus, *Ant.* 17.8.4 §204: "Some demanded the release [ἀπόλυσιν] of the prisoners who had been put in chains by Herod").

The evidence as a whole suggests that Roman rulers, as well as at least one Herodian prince, on occasion released prisoners (as apparently did other rulers in the eastern Mediterranean; cf. Merritt, *JBL* 104 [1985] 57–68). This was done for purely political reasons to satisfy the demands of the crowds and to curry their favor. Another factor that supports the historicity of the Markan narrative is the improbability of asserting such a custom if there had been none. If Pilate had not released prisoners on the Passover or on other holidays, or at least on one occasion (so Gnilka, 301; Lührmann, 256), the evangelist's claim that he did so could have quickly and easily been shown to be false and would therefore have occasioned embarrassment for the early church. That all three of the later evangelists take over the story (and the Fourth Evangelist probably did so independently of the Synoptics) argues that no such embarrassment clung to the story. Bond (*Pontius Pilate,* 199) opines that "Pilate, and possibly other governors, may have occasionally released lesser criminals as a gesture of Roman goodwill, especially during such a potentially volatile festival as the Passover." For concise summaries of the scholarly positions on the pardon, see Bond, *Pontius Pilate,* 199–200, and McLaren, *Power and Politics,* 93 n. 2.

7 ὁ λεγόμενος Βαραββᾶς, "one called Barabbas." V 7 is not well placed; it would fit better after v 8 or v 10 (Taylor, 581). Nothing is known of the figure Barabbas. In Matt 27:16–17 he is twice called Jesus Barabbas or Jesus son of Abba (i.e., Jesus son of the father). Mark's text may have originally read this way (so Cranfield, 450; Nineham, 416; Taylor, 581; and others), i.e., "there was Jesus, called Barabbas," but an early Christian scribe, uncomfortable that a murderer was called by the same name, may have deleted the name Jesus. Barabbas is actually the Aramaic name אבא בר *bar 'Abbā'* (see *Note* h). Several rabbis are "bar Abba": Samuel bar Abba, Nathan bar Abba (cf. Swete, 370; St-B 1:1031). What may have drawn the detail of Barabbas into the Passion Narrative and into association with the trial of Jesus of Nazareth was this common name and the contrasting fates of the two men. Jesus Barabbas, who was (perhaps) a murderer ἐν τῇ στάσει, "in the rebellion," was released, but Jesus of Nazareth, who harmed no one—indeed, saved many—was condemned to death.

Mark says that Barabbas had been μετὰ τῶν στασιαστῶν δεδεμένος, "imprisoned with the rebels." It is impossible to determine which group of rebels this was. (In *J.W.* 6.2.8 §157, in reference to the later Jewish rebellion, Josephus describes an attack by Jewish "rebels" [τῶν στασιαστῶν] on Roman sentries on the Mount of Olives.)

οἵτινες ἐν τῇ στάσει φόνον πεποιήκεισαν, "who had in the rebellion committed murder." The οἵτινες, "who," is plural, referring to the rebels. The text does not state explicitly that Barabbas was himself a murderer, though his being lumped with those who had committed murder may imply it (Gundry, 926). However, Pilate's willingness to release this man argues against it, for surely the Roman governor would not have released a murderer (cf. Josephus, *Ant.* 20.9.5 §215), especially if in the rebellion Roman soldiers had been killed. What στάσει, "rebellion," the evangelist has in mind is impossible to determine. It is possible that Barabbas and comrades were participants in the violence that followed the protest over the appropriation of temple funds, but that is little more than a guess.

8 καὶ ἀναβὰς ὁ ὄχλος ἤρξατο αἰτεῖσθαι, "And going up, the crowd began to request." This ὄχλος, "crowd," is not the crowd of 14:43 who had arrested Jesus, for they would hardly have needed to be encouraged to call for Jesus' death. Rather, the crowd that has gone up to call for release of a prisoner probably consists primarily of supporters of Barabbas as well as others, perhaps, who hope to secure the release of someone else. They approach the governor's judgment seat the morning of Passover in anticipation of the annual Passover pardon, καθὼς ἐποίει αὐτοῖς, "just as he used to do for them."

9 θέλετε ἀπολύσω ὑμῖν τὸν βασιλέα τῶν Ἰουδαίων, "Do you wish that I might release to you the king of the Jews?" Pilate's offer may have been ironic—the crowd wants Barabbas, an insurrectionist; Pilate offers them the "king of the Jews"! How could the governor be more generous? Taylor (582) thinks Pilate's question is contemptuous. Cranfield (451) wonders if Pilate's question is innocent, reflecting a misunderstanding in which the governor heard people calling for the release of "Jesus" and so wondered which one—the one from Nazareth or the son of Abba? It is more likely that the governor's question is proactive, wishing to make it clear that he is more than willing to release the popular teacher.

10 ἐγίνωσκεν γὰρ ὅτι διὰ φθόνον παραδεδώκεισαν αὐτὸν οἱ ἀρχιερεῖς, "For he knew that because of envy the ruling priests had handed him over." This statement enhances Jesus' status. That is, Jesus is not surrendered to Pilate because he is a danger or because he is undesirable; he is given up because his enemies envy his person and qualities (Hagedorn and Neyrey, *JSNT* 69 [1998] 15–56).

Knowing that Jesus had been handed over to him on account of envy, Pilate treads
carefully. Before condemning Jesus to death, he seeks in essence a plebiscite. Did
the people really want Jesus executed, or was it only the few ruling priests who
brought the charges and demanded his death? There is no interest in justice here;
only politics are at work. Pilate probably knew that Jesus was popular. He was not
about to risk offending the populace, especially at Passover season, and so instigate a riot, the very thing he wished to avoid. Some might challenge this
interpretation by pointing to the incidents mentioned above where Pilate seemed
more than willing to use violence against his subjects. But in the cases described
by Josephus, Pilate was defending his own actions (the standards in Jerusalem
and the appropriation of temple funds). In the case of Jesus, Pilate has nothing
at stake other than maintaining the peace.

11 οἱ δὲ ἀρχιερεῖς ἀνέσεισαν τὸν ὄχλον, ἵνα μᾶλλον τὸν Βαραββᾶν ἀπολύσῃ
αὐτοῖς, "But the ruling priests stirred up the crowd, so that he should rather release Barabbas to them." The ruling priests urge the crowd to call for the release
of Jesus bar Abba, not Jesus of Nazareth. They have vigorously lobbied the governor. Now they vigorously lobby the crowd. From their point of view, the danger
that Jesus of Nazareth would be released is a very real one. After all, Jesus was
known as a popular teacher and healer, and led no army. He was therefore not
an obvious threat to Rome. At most, he was guilty of speaking of a coming kingdom of God and of having a key role in it—things not too different from visions
and dreams of others. Perhaps it was politically more expedient to release him
than make a martyr of him. Hence, the ruling priests encourage the crowd to call
for the release of bar Abba (Barabbas). On noisy crowds clamoring before a Roman authority, see Acts 24:1; Josephus, *Ant.* 18.8.2–4 §§264–73.

12 τί οὖν [θέλετε] ποιήσω [ὃν λέγετε] τὸν βασιλέα τῶν Ἰουδαίων, "What then
[do you wish that] I should do with him [whom you call] 'the king of the Jews'?"
If Jesus of Nazareth is not to be released, then what shall the governor do with
him? The alternatives are fairly obvious—either execution or imprisonment. But
Pilate forces the crowd to make the decision. This way he can wash his hands
(literally in Matt 27:24) of the matter. Politically, Pilate acts shrewdly and entirely
in keeping with his character as we know it from unsympathetic sources (i.e.,
Philo and Josephus; see *Comment* on v 1). On τὸν βασιλέα τῶν Ἰουδαίων, "the
king of the Jews," see *Comment* on v 2. ὃν λέγετε, "whom you call" (if it is to be
read; see *Note* n), again alludes to the original charge brought against Jesus.

13 οἱ δὲ πάλιν ἔκραξαν, σταύρωσον αὐτόν, "But again they shouted, 'Crucify
him!'" Once again οἱ, "they," that is, the crowd (cf. v 11) as well as the ruling priests
themselves, shout their demands to Pilate. They shouted for the release of Barabbas,
but in reference to Jesus, they shout "Crucify him!" They do not want prison for
Jesus; they want the ultimate penalty for Jesus—crucifixion. The death of Jesus will
hopefully end his movement and fatally discourage his closest followers. σταυροῦν,
"to crucify," originally meant "to fence with stakes" (cf. *TDNT* 7:581; BAG, 772–73,
MM, 586–87) and means "to crucify" in Polybius 1.86.4 and others (see Hengel,
Crucifixion, 22–32). See Esth 7:9 (Eng. 7:10), where תלה *tālâ*, "to hang," is translated
with σταυροῦν in the LXX. Romans referred to crucifixion as *servile supplicium*, "slaves'
punishment" (cf. Valerius Maximus 2.7.12; Tacitus, *Hist.* 2.72; 4.11). This probably
explains the association in the Philippian hymn of Jesus' death on the cross with
the status of slave (cf. Phil 2:7–8; Hengel, *Crucifixion*, 62–63).

14 τί γὰρ ἐποίησεν κακόν, "Why, what evil has he done?" Pilate has committed no "tactical blunder" (*pace* Lane, 556), nor is his answer "feeble" (Taylor, 583); he is happy to accommodate the ruling priests' recommendation that Jesus be put to death—as long as in doing so he incurs no political risks. His only concern is that his condemnation of Jesus not provoke the Jewish people or be seen as yet another example of Roman brutality. Pilate is not about to create a problem for himself; he wishes only to extricate himself from responsibility (as also does Gallio in Corinth, who judges the controversy set before him as a Jewish dispute and not one that falls under his jurisdiction; cf. Acts 18:12–17; K. L. Schmidt, *Judaica* 1 [1945] 1–40, esp. 35–36). If the crowd insists that Jesus be crucified, he would like to know why.

οἱ δὲ περισσῶς ἔκραξαν, σταύρωσον αὐτόν, "But they shouted all the more, 'Crucify him!'" The crowd provides no answer to Pilate's question. They simply "shouted all the more." The evangelist makes it clear that the ruling priests, along with a supportive crowd of laity (many of whom favored Barabbas), have demanded Jesus' death. The impulse to execute Jesus, therefore, does not come from the Roman governor. There can be no doubt that Mark and early Christians wished to underscore this point in their attempt to defend themselves against state persecution and the accusation that their master was a criminal and enemy of the empire. But apologetically motivated exploitation of the tradition does not mean that the tradition itself lacks reasonable claim to historicity. Jesus was crucified as "king of the Jews" (15:26), a well-established datum and a Roman datum at that. But the original accusers were the ruling priests. The narrative we have in Mark, substantially followed by Matthew and Luke, independently attested in John, and partially corroborated by Josephus (cf. *Ant.* 18.3.3 §§63–64, esp. "When Pilate, upon hearing him accused by the first men [= ruling priests; cf. *Ant.* 11.5.3 §§140–41; 18.5.3 §121] among us, had condemned him to be crucified"), fits the facts as we know them. Mark's portrait of Pilate—often caricatured in popular Christian preaching and writing—does not lack verisimilitude. Pilate is not weak; he is not vacillating. Shrewd, political, cruel, and corrupt may very well describe him—and he was finally recalled by Rome—but none of these attributes stands in tension with Mark's presentation if both Mark and the historical situation are critically appraised.

15 ὁ δὲ Πιλᾶτος βουλόμενος τῷ ὄχλῳ τὸ ἱκανὸν ποιῆσαι ἀπέλυσεν αὐτοῖς τὸν Βαραββᾶν, "So Pilate, wishing to satisfy the crowd, released to them Barabbas." Not wishing to provoke the crowd, Pilate releases Barabbas (on the "Paschal Pardon," see *Comment* on v 6 above). Again, this shows no more weakness than when Pilate relents in the episode of the shields. Indeed, in this case Pilate wishes not to offend his allies, the ruling priests. In his other controversies, the Roman governor came into conflict with the rabble, not the ruling priests. What he has done here is to accede to the wishes of the ruling priests, but not until he is satisfied that to do so is not a mistake.

παρέδωκεν τὸν Ἰησοῦν φραγελλώσας ἵνα σταυρωθῇ, "he handed Jesus over, having scourged [him], that he might be crucified." Having released Barabbas to the people, Pilate hands Jesus over to the Roman troops, who will carry out the crucifixion. But before Jesus is given over to their custody, the governor has him scourged (φραγελλώσας), which apparently was standard pre-crucifixion procedure (cf. *Dig.* 48.19.8.3; Josephus, *J.W.* 2.14.9 §306). Scourging (also μαστιγοῦν and cognates) was done with a whip made up of several leather straps to which were attached sharp, abrasive items, such as nails, glass, or rocks. Scourging resulted in the severe laceration of the skin and damage to the flesh beneath (e.g., Josephus, *J.W.* 6.5.3 §304: "flayed to the bone with scourges [μάστιξι μέχρι ὀστέων ξαινόμενος]"). As the Jewish revolt drew to an end, the Romans crucified many who ventured beyond the walls of Jerusalem in search of food: "They were accordingly scourged [μαστιγούμενοι] and subjected to torture of every description, before being killed, and then crucified [ἀνεσταυροῦντο] opposite the walls" (Josephus, *J.W.* 5.11.1 §449).

According to Cicero (*Verr.* 2.5.168) and Josephus (*J.W.* 7.6.4 §203), crucifixion was the worst form of death. Juvenal has this grim thought in mind when he writes, "The vulture hurries from dead cattle and dogs and crosses to bring some of the carrion to her offspring" (*Sat.* 14.77–78; Suetonius, *Aug.* 13.1–2: "the carrion-birds will soon take care of" one's "burial"!; Horace, *Ep.* 1.16.48: "hanging on a cross to feed crows"). A text from a later period expresses well how crucifixion compared to other forms of execution: "But hanging is a lesser penalty than the cross. For the gallows kills the victim immediately, whereas the cross tortures for a long time those who are fixed to it" (Isidore of Seville, *Etymologia* 5.27.34; cf. Seneca, *Dial.* 3.2.2: "long-drawn-out agony"). Another writer from late antiquity explains: "Whenever we crucify the condemned, the most crowded roads are chosen, where the most people can see and be moved by this terror. For penalties relate not so much to retribution as to their exemplary effect" (Pseudo-Quintilian, *Decl.* 274; cf. Josephus, *J.W.* 5.11.1 §§450–51). On a second-century epitaph, the deceased declares that his murderer, a slave, was "crucified alive [ζωὸν ἀνεκρέμασαν] for the wild beasts and birds" (*NewDocs* 8:1). For further examples, see also Hengel, *Crucifixion,* 22–32, and *Comment* on 15:20b–21.

Explanation

At first light the ruling priests, elders, and scribes hold a council and decide to bind Jesus and send him to Pilate, the Roman governor. Pilate's question, "Are you the king of the Jews?" (v 2a), makes clear what charge the ruling priests have brought against Jesus. Jesus' affirmation of messiahship and divine sonship, understood in the Jewish context, amounts to an unambiguous claim to kingship. The Roman Senate made kings (such as Herod the Great and later Herod's grandson Agrippa I). Self-proclaimed kings were viewed as treasonous rebels (and at that time Judea had been plagued with several would-be kings).

In replying, "You say it" (v 2b), Jesus does not refuse the title "king of the Jews," but neither does he say, "I am," as he had when Caiaphas asked him if he was the Messiah, the son of God (see *Comment* on 14:61). That Jesus' answer was not understood as rejection of the title is seen in his subsequent crucifixion and the mockery of him as "king of the Jews" (15:18, 26). Jesus is indeed the king of Jews, but not in the sense understood by Rome, her Jewish collaborators, or various Jewish would-be kings. Jesus' kingship derives entirely from God, from whom he, as the "son of man" of Dan 7, has received kingdom and authority.

Pilate's offer to release Jesus as a gesture of goodwill at the Passover season only heightens the hypocrisy and villainy of those who wish to destroy Jesus. Are they really concerned about law and order? Do they really have Rome's interests in mind? Evidently not, for they call for the release of one Barabbas, a rebel and associate of murderers, a man truly deserving of the death sentence (vv 6–11).

Excursus: The Arrest of Jesus Son of Ananias

There is an important historical parallel that may clarify the chain of events that begin with Jesus' action in the temple and end with his condemnation to death by Pontius Pilate, the Roman prefect. According to Josephus (*J. W.* 6.5.3 §§300–309):

> Four years before the war . . . there came to the feast, at which is the custom of all Jews to erect tabernacles to God, one Jesus son of Ananias, an untrained peasant, who, standing in the Temple, suddenly began to cry out, "A voice from the east, a voice from the west, a voice from the four winds, a voice against Jerusalem and the sanctuary, a voice against the bridegroom and the bride, a voice against all the people."
> . . . Some of the leading citizens, angered at this evil speech, arrested the man and whipped him with many blows. But he, not speaking anything in his own behalf or in private to those who struck him, continued his cries as before. There-upon, the rulers . . . brought him to the Roman governor. There, though flayed to the bone with scourges, he neither begged for mercy or wept. . . . When Albinus the governor asked him who and whence he was and why he uttered these cries, he gave no answer to these things. . . . Albinus pronounced him a maniac and released him. . . . He cried out especially at the feasts. . . . While shouting from the wall, "Woe once more to the city and to the people and to the sanctuary . . . ," a stone . . . struck and killed him.

There are several important parallels between the temple-related experiences of Jesus of Nazareth and those of Jesus son of Ananias. Both entered the precincts of the temple (τὸ ἱερόν: Mark 11:11, 15, 27; 12:35; 13:1; 14:49; *J. W.* 6.5.3 §301) at the time of a religious festival (ἑορτή: Mark 14:2; 15:6; John 2:23; *J. W.* 6.5.3 §300). Both spoke of the doom of Jerusalem (Luke 19:41–44; 21:20–24; *J. W.* 6.5.3 §301), the sanctuary (ναός: Mark 13:2; 14:58; *J. W.* 6.5.3 §301), and the people (λαός: Mark 13:17; Luke 19:44; 23:28–31; *J. W.* 6.5.3 §301). Both apparently alluded to Jer 7, where the prophet condemned the temple establishment of his day ("cave of robbers": Jer 7:11 in Mark 11:17; "the voice against the bridegroom and the bride": Jer 7:34 in *J. W.* 6.5.3 §301). Both were arrested by the authority of Jewish—not Roman—leaders (συλλαμβάνειν: Mark 14:48; John 18:12; *J. W.* 6.5.3 §302). Both were beaten by the Jewish authorities (παίειν: Matt 26:68; Mark 14:65; *J. W.* 6.5.3 §302). Both were handed over to the Roman governor (ἤγαγον αὐτὸν ἐπὶ τὸν Πιλᾶτον, "they brought him to Pilate": Luke 23:1; ἀνάγουσιν αὐτὸν . . . ἐπὶ τὸν . . . ἔπαρχον, "they brought him . . . to the . . . governor": *J. W.* 6.5.3 §303). Both were interrogated by the Roman governor (ἐρωτᾶν: Mark 15:4; *J. W.* 6.5.3 §305). Both refused to answer the governor (οὐδὲν ἀποκρίνεσθαι: Mark 15:5; *J. W.* 6.5.3 §305). Both were scourged by the governor (μαστιγοῦν/μάστιξ: John 19:1; *J. W.* 6.5.3 §304). Pilate may have offered to release Jesus of Nazareth, but did not; Albinus did release Jesus son of Ananias (ἀπολύειν: Mark 15:9; *J. W.* 6.5.3 §305).

Josephus says that τῶν . . . ἐπισήμων τινὲς δημοτῶν, "some of the leading citizens," arrested Jesus ben Ananias and "severely chastised him" (*J. W.* 6.5.3. §302). These "leading citizens" probably overlap with and perhaps are identical with the ruling priests, to whom Josephus sometimes refers as "first men" (cf. *Ant.* 11.5.3 §§140–41; 18.5.3 §121), the very ones who are said to have arrested Jesus of Nazareth and to have handed him over to Pontius Pilate (*Ant.* 18.3.3 §64; see *Comment* on v 14 above).

Given the numerous verbal parallels, is there some sort of literary relationship between *J. W.* 6.5.3 §§300–309 and the passion tradition? Probably not. First, the parallels comprise no more than nouns of place and context and verbs that mark the various steps in the judicial and penal process. In other words, the parallels are precisely what one would expect in cases where routine actions are being described. Second, aside from the single parallel cluster where we have a common verbal root, preposition, and Roman governor as object, there are no instances of parallel sentences or phrases. Literary relationships are suspected when there is a high concentration of common vocabulary, especially phrases and whole sentences. In short, the common vocabulary adduced above indicates a common judicial and penal process, but not a literary relationship. There is no indication that the story of one Jesus influenced the telling of the story of the other Jesus.

For our purposes, the value of the experience of Jesus son of Ananias lies in the independent illustration of the penal process in pre-70 Judea, particularly with respect to the interface between Jewish and Roman authorities. The Gospels' portrait of the ruling priests seizing Jesus, interrogating him, and then handing him over to the Roman governor with calls for his execution is found to be in essential agreement with the experience of Jesus son of Ananias. The story of this later Jesus, moreover, also illustrates the sensitivity of the ruling priests with respect to prophecies and criticisms directed against them and the temple. Both Jesus of Nazareth and Jesus son of Ananias, appealing to parts of Jer 7, spoke of the temple's doom. As a result, both encountered deadly opposition from the ruling priests (see *Comment* on 11:17).

L. Roman Soldiers Mock Jesus   (15:16–20a)

Bibliography

Bailey, K. E. "The Fall of Jerusalem and Mark's Account of the Cross." *ExpTim* 102 (1991) 102–5. **Benoit, P.** *Passion and Resurrection.* 115–51. ———. "Prétoire, Lithostroton und Gabbatha." *RB* 59 (1952) 531–50. **Berger, K.** "Zum Problem der Messianität Jesu." *ZTK* 71 (1974) 1–30, esp. 1–15. **Blinzler, J.** *Trial of Jesus: The Jewish and Roman Proceedings against Jesus Christ Described and Assessed from the Oldest Accounts.* Westminster: Newman, 1959. 173–76. **Bonner, C.** "The Crown of Thorns." *HTR* 46 (1953) 47–48. **Delbrueck, R.** "Antiquarisches zu den Verspottungen Jesu." *ZNW* 41 (1942) 124–45. **Dormeyer, D.** *Die Passion Jesu.* 187–91. **Genest, O.** *Le Christ de la passion: Perspective structurale: Analyse de Marc 14,53–15,47, des parallèles et extra-bibliques.* Recherches 21: Théologie. Tournai: Desclée; Montreal: Bellarmin, 1978. 57–95, 123–43. **Goodenough, E. R.,** and **Welles, C. B.** "The Crown of Acanthus (?)." *HTR* 46 (1953) 241–42. **Jonge, M. de.** "The Earliest Christian Use of *Christos:* Some Suggestions." *NTS* 32 (1986) 321–43. **Kremer, J.** *Das Ärgernis des Kreuzes: Eine Hinführung zum Verstehen der Leidensgeschichte nach Markus.* Stuttgart: Katholisches Bibelwerk, 1969. 54–59. **Kreyenbuehl, J.** "Der Ort der Verurteilung Jesu." *ZNW* 3 (1902) 15–22. **Maier, P. L.** *Pontius Pilate.* Garden City, NY: Doubleday, 1968. 215–40. **Matera, F. J.** *The Kingship of Jesus: Composition and Theology in Mark 15.* SBLDS 66. Chico, CA: Scholars Press, 1982. 21–24. **Mohr, T. A.** *Markus- und Johannespassion.* 302–12. **Moo, D. J.** *Old Testament in the Gospel Passion Narratives.* 139–44. **Pesch, R.** *Das Evangelium der Urgemeinde.* 201–2. **Pixner, B.** "Noch einmal das Prätorium: Versuch einer neuen Lösung." *ZDPV* 95 (1979) 56–86. **Riesner, R.** "Das Prätorium des Pilatus." *BK* 41 (1986) 34–37. **Schenk, W.** *Der Passionsbericht nach Markus.* 250–52. **Schenke, L.** *Der gekreuzigte Christus.* 54–55. **Schmidt, T. E.** "Mark 15.16–32: The Crucifixion Narrative and the Roman Triumphal Procession." *NTS* 41 (1995) 1–18. **Schneider, G.** *Die Passion Jesu.* 104–8. **Senior, D. P.** *Passion of Jesus in the*

Gospel of Mark. 105–14. **Winter, P.** *On the Trial of Jesus.* Rev. by T. A. Burkill and G. Vermes. 2nd ed. Studia Judaica 1. Berlin; New York: de Gruyter, 1974. 100–106.

Translation

[16] *And the soldiers led him*[a] *away into* [b] *the palace,*[c] *which is the praetorium, and they summon the whole battalion.* [17] *And they clothe him in* [d] *purple, and they place on him a crown, weaving together thorns.* [18] *And they began to salute him, "Hail, king*[e] *of the Jews!"* [19] *And they were striking his head with a reed and were spitting on him,*[f] *and bowing their knees, they were doing homage to him.* [20a] *And when they had mocked him, they stripped him of thec purple and put his own clothes on him.*

Notes

[a]C³ and a few later MSS add τὸν Ἰησοῦν, "Jesus."

[b]D P 1359 and other MSS read ἔσω εἰς τὴν αὐλήν, "inside, into the palace," apparently to smooth out the awkward expression ἔσω τῆς αὐλῆς, lit. "inside of the palace." Matthew omits the phrase and simply reads εἰς τὸ πραιτώριον, "into the praetorium" (Matt 27:27).

[c]αὐλή can mean "courtyard" (as in 14:54, 66), but here it means "palace" (cf. BAG, 121). A few late MSS (M Θ) add τοῦ Καϊάφα, "of Caiaphas," which Pesch (2:469 n. a) thinks is anti-Jewish.

[d]Several late MSS add χλαμύδα κοκκίνην καί, "scarlet mantle and" (cf. Matt 27:28).

[e]Gk. βασιλεῦ. The vocative, which is read by ℵ B D and several later MSS, implies that the Roman soldiers are addressing Jesus. A C² N Σ and several late MSS read ὁ βασιλεύς (nom.), i.e., "Hail, it is the king of the Jews!" (cf. John 19:3). This reading is probably secondary, anticipating the indic. form of the reading of the *titulus* in Mark 15:26. The voc. form is truer to the idea of the Roman triumph, in which soldiers address the emperor "Hail, Caesar!" See *Comment* below.

[f]Syr. and Copt. MSS read "in his face."

Form/Structure/Setting

Bultmann (*History*, 284, 304–6) thinks that the story of the Roman soldiers mocking Jesus is a legendary, novelistic embellishment, possibly from "pagan Hellenism." Taylor (584), however, believes that the story is "historical testimony." Cranfield (452) calls it "primitive tradition," while more recently Gnilka (2:306) and others judge it to be pre-Markan. There is some Markan redaction, as seen in v 16 ("which is the praetorium") and perhaps in v 19a ("And they were striking his head with a reed and were spitting on him"), which may may have been inspired by 14:65 (Gnilka, 2:306). Use of the reed, however, which coheres with other elements of the mockery, may be an original detail. Overall, there is nothing remarkable about the story that points either to the evangelist's special interest (though see *Comment* below) or to tension with history. Crucifixion victims were routinely scourged, abused, and mocked. The story constitutes a unified whole (Pesch, 2:469) but may be divided into three principal movements: (1) the gathering of the whole battalion (v 16), (2) the mockery of Jesus (vv 17–19), and (3) the ending of the mockery (v 20a).

The parallel found in the *Gospel of Peter* says that Jesus was clothed with purple, was seated on a "chair of judgment," and was told, "Judge justly, king of Israel!" (*Gos. Pet.* 3.7). The rest of the scene blends together other synoptic elements (Brown, 863; Gundry, 941). There is nothing about this version of the story that points to early, independent tradition.

Nineham (418) hears allusions to Isa 50:6–7, "I gave my back to smiters, and my cheeks to those who pulled out the beard; I hid not my face from shame and spitting," and 53:3, 5, but these are remote at best, though there are possible echoes of the Suffering Servant song elsewhere in Mark 15 (e.g., LXX Isa 53:6 in v 1; Isa 53:7 and LXX Isa 52:15 in v 5). In any event, the correspondence is not close enough to conclude that the Markan narrative has been shaped in any significant way by the Servant poems of Isaiah.

The mockery of Jesus as a Jewish king finds an approximate parallel in Philo, *Flaccus* 6 §§36–39. On the occasion of King Agrippa's visit to Alexandria, the people seized a lunatic named Carabas, a street person who was often made sport of. They

> drove the poor fellow into the gymnasium and set him up high to be seen by all and put on his head a sheet of byblus [papyrus] spread out wide for a diadem, clothed the rest of his body with a rug for a royal robe, while someone who had noticed a piece of the native papyrus thrown away in the road gave it to him for his sceptre. And when as in some theatrical farce he had received the insignia of kingship and had been tricked out as a king, young men carrying rods on their shoulders as spearmen stood on either side of him in imitation of a bodyguard. Then others approached him, some pretending to salute him, others to sue for justice, others to consult him on state affairs. Then from the multitudes there rang out a tremendous shout hailing him as *Mari* [Aramaic: "My lord"], which is said to be the name for 'lord' with the Syrians.

The mockery directed at Agrippa I is quite significant, well illustrating the mockery to which Jesus was subjected. It does not, however, require us to conclude that Mark is dependent in some way on this incident or on Philo's work itself.

Other incidents approximate the mockery of Jesus. One thinks of the harsh and humiliating treatment of deposed Vitellius (69 C.E.) at the hands of Roman soldiers, who mockingly made the former emperor revisit various stations where at one time he was held in honor (cf. Dio Cassius 64.20–21). We think too of the savage and humiliating treatment of Eleazar, who was stripped, scourged (μάστιξ), tortured, and then in his dying breath prayed for the salvation of Israel (4 Macc 6:1–30). One is also reminded of the deposition recording the words of the new emperor Hadrian and a Jewish embassy with reference to the Jewish revolt that occurred toward the end of Trajan's reign (115–17 C.E.). In this fragmentary document mention is made of the mockery of a would-be monarch: "Paulus (spoke) about the king, how they brought him forth and (mocked him?); and Theon read the edict of Lupus ordering them to lead him forth for Lupus to make fun of the king" (P.Louvre 68 1.1–7; for text, translation, and notes, see V. A. Tcherikover and A. Fuks, eds., *Corpus Papyrorum Judaicarum,* 2 vols. [Cambridge: Harvard UP, 1957–60] 2:87–99). Plutarch (*Pomp.* 24.7–8) relates a story in which pirates mocked a prisoner who had claimed the rights of Roman citizenship. They dressed him up ("threw a toga on him"), extended to him various honors (including falling to their knees), and then finally made him walk the plank (for a survey of examples of mockery in late antiquity, see Brown, 873–77).

The mockery mimics aspects of the Roman triumph (see T. E. Schmidt, *NTS* 41 [1995] 1–18), in which Caesar was hailed as emperor and received homage. The purple cloak, the crown of thorns (resembling the crown of ivy), the reed with which Jesus is struck on the head, and the bowing in mock homage are all components of the apparel worn and homage received by the Roman emperor, who at the triumph wore a purple robe and laurel wreath and held a scepter (e.g., Dio Cassius 6.23; 44.11 [Julius Caesar]; Appian, *Civil Wars* 5.130 [Augustus]; Dio Cassius 59.25.3 [Gaius Caligula]); for extended discussion and many more citations, see H. S. Versnel, *Triumphus* [Leiden: Brill, 1970] 56–57, 235–300; Schmidt, *NTS* 41 [1995] 2–4 nn. 6–12; Pesch, 2:470–71). Being dressed in purple would also recall the attire of Hellenistic kings of an earlier period (cf. 1 Macc 10:20: "purple robe and golden crown"; 10:62: "clothe him in purple"; 11:58: "to dress in purple"; 14:43–44: "clothed in purple"; Luke 16:19: "dressed in purple").

It is possible, given the evangelist's interest in portraying Jesus to some extent as Caesar's rival (see 1:1 and "Theology of Mark" in the *Introduction*), that the evangelist himself edited the tradition, especially the mockery, to correspond more closely with Roman imperial traditions, perhaps with the mockery of Agrippa I in mind. But it is hard to believe that the evangelist, or a Christian tradent before him, would invent a story in which Jesus is so shamefully abused and mocked. It is more probable that this story approximates what actually happened to Jesus, though in its transmission certain details may have been added. In the context of Mark's Gospel, the mockery will be reversed in the centurion's later confession that Jesus was indeed "son of God" (15:39).

Comment

16 οἱ δὲ στρατιῶται ἀπήγαγον αὐτὸν ἔσω τῆς αὐλῆς, ὅ ἐστιν πραιτώριον, "And the soldiers led him away into the palace, which is the praetorium." The στρατιῶται, "soldiers," are probably the auxiliaries, recruited from Palestine and other parts of the Roman Empire, who were under Pilate's command (M. P. Spiedel, *Roman Army Studies,* 2 vols. [Stuttgart: F. Steiner, 1992] 2:224–32; G. Webster, *The Roman Imperial Army,* 3rd ed. [London: A. & C. Black, 1981] 142–55). These soldiers lead Jesus into the αὐλῆς, "palace" (cf. 1 Macc 11:46; see *Note* c), that is, the praetorium. Mark's language ἔσω τῆς αὐλῆς, lit. "inside of the palace," is awkward, leading to the reading ἔσω εἰς τὴν αὐλήν, "inside, into the palace" (see *Note* b), which is not much of an improvement, and to the Matthean simplification εἰς τὸ πραιτώριον, "into the praetorium" (Matt 27:27). πραιτώριον is a Latin loanword (*praetorium*), which referred to the official residence of the governor (Cranfield, 452). The Roman praetorium of Jerusalem may have been located in the fortress Antonia (at the northwest corner of the Temple Mount), or in Herod's Upper Palace (near the Jaffa Gate), or somewhere on the western slope of the Tyropoeon Valley, opposite the southwest corner of the Temple Mount. Modern scholars have abandoned the first option (which seems to have its origins in Crusader ideas). The second option is recommended by Benoit (*RB* 59 [1952] 531–50), Blinzler (*Trial of Jesus,* 173–76), Maier (*Pontius Pilate,* 215–40), and others, while the third, which enjoys an ancient tradition of identification, is recommended by Pixner (*ZDPV* 95 [1979] 56–86) and others. It may be noted that Paul was detained in the praetorium of Caesarea Maritima (Acts 23:25; cf. Phil 1:13).

καὶ συγκαλοῦσιν ὅλην τὴν σπεῖραν, "and they summon the whole battalion." σπεῖρα, "batallion" (which originally meant a "coil"), translates the Latin *cohors,* a military term referring to a tenth of a Roman legion (cf. BAG, 768). *Cohors* came to mean a platoon and could number anywhere from two hundred to six hundred men. The opportunity to make sport of a "king of the Jews" was not to be missed; therefore the whole batallion was summoned to take part in the mockery that would ensue.

17 καὶ ἐνδιδύσκουσιν αὐτὸν πορφύραν καὶ περιτιθέασιν αὐτῷ πλέξαντες ἀκάνθινον στέφανον, "And they clothe him in purple, and they place on him a crown, weaving together thorns." The soldiers' mocking costume for Jesus gives him the appearance of a Hellenistic vassal king (Lane, 559; cf. 1 Macc 10:20; 11:58) or perhaps of the Roman emperor himself (Swete, 376; cf. Suetonius, *Tib.* 17.2: "clad in the purple-bordered toga and crowned with laurel"). (This topic is discussed in more detail above in *Form/Structure/Setting*.) The color may actually have been red, and therefore, as some have suggested, it was a soldier's cloak (e.g., Plutarch, *Phil.* 11.2: "They wore their soldiers' cloaks with scarlet tunics"). Apparently Matthew (27:28) has understood it this way, for he says that the soldiers wrapped Jesus in a χλαμύδα κοκκίνην, "scarlet cloak." Matthew (27:29) also mentions a reed, which may have been in Mark's text; the reed will appear in Mark's narrative in v 19. The reed, representing a king's scepter, would add to Jesus' mock royal garb and paraphernalia.

18 καὶ ἤρξαντο ἀσπάζεσθαι αὐτόν, χαῖρε, βασιλεῦ τῶν Ἰουδαίων, "And they began to salute him, 'Hail, king of the Jews!'" The soldiers' salute imitates the Latin imperial greeting, *Ave, Caesar, victor, imperator,* "Hail, Caesar, victor, emperor" (see, e.g., Suetonius, *Claud.* 21.6: "Hail, Emperor [*Ave, imperator*], we who are about to die salute you").

19 καὶ ἔτυπτον αὐτοῦ τὴν κεφαλὴν καλάμῳ καὶ ἐνέπτυον αὐτῷ, "And they were striking his head with a reed and were spitting on him." The reed is part of the trappings of the mockery (i.e., it represents a scepter); its use is not to inflict pain but to deride (Gundry, 942). The spitting perhaps mocks kissing and other signs of affection. In any case, it expresses disrespect and contempt in the extreme (see *Comment* on 14:65). The detail of spitting may owe its origin to 14:65 (Gnilka, 2:306), but its appearance in the present context is neither awkward nor unnatural.

καὶ τιθέντες τὰ γόνατα προσεκύνουν αὐτῷ, "and bowing their knees they were doing homage to him." Genuflecting completes the parody. The attentive reader/auditor of Mark will recall that earlier the Gerasene demoniac had run up to Jesus and done homage (προσεκύνησεν) to him, addressing Jesus as "Son of the Most High God" (5:6–7). Roman soldiers now bow before Jesus, much as they would to Caesar, who for them was the "son of God."

20a καὶ ὅτε ἐνέπαιξαν αὐτῷ, "and when they had mocked him," may summarize and bring to a conclusion the mockery scene. But it may actually introduce an escalation in the abuse of Jesus, for the word ἐμπαίζειν, "to mock," sometimes means to treat someone cruelly (see J. W. van Henten, *The Maccabean Martyrs as Saviours of the Jewish People: A Study of 2 and 4 Maccabees,* JSJSup 57 [Leiden: Brill, 1997] 112 and nn. 105–8, in reference to Antiochus IV's cruel torture of the seven sons and their mother in 2 Macc 7, esp. vv 7, 10). Sometimes ἐμπαίζειν functions as a euphemism for torture (cf. *TDNT* 5:631–33).

ἐξέδυσαν αὐτὸν τὴν πορφύραν καὶ ἐνέδυσαν αὐτὸν τὰ ἱμάτια αὐτοῦ, "they stripped him of the purple and put his own clothes on him." The time of mockery comes to an end. The soldiers remove the purple garment and return to Jesus his own clothes, for which later they will gamble (15:24).

Explanation

The soldiers mock Jesus by placing on him a purple cloth or robe and a woven crown of thorns. They salute him, "Hail, king of the Jews!" strike him on the head with a reed, and bow before him as if doing homage to a king. The Roman soldiers have acted out a mock salute of the Roman emperor, perhaps as was done during the celebration of a triumph. At such a time the emperor would wear an ivy crown and a robe with a purple mantle. His soldiers would shout "Hail, Caesar!" But the mockery of Jesus will later be turned on its head by the Roman centurion, who will supervise the crucifixion and subsequently confess his belief that Jesus is the "son of God." Right now Jesus' claim to kingship and divine sonship appears ludicrous; some hours later, when he dies and preternatural portents occur, these claims will take on new credibility.

The mockery of Jesus, as a prelude to a painful and shameful death on a cross, represents the nadir of the incarnation to which the primitive hymn in Phil 2:6–8 alludes: "who, though he was in the form of God, did not count equality with God a thing to be grasped, but emptied himself, taking the form of a servant, being born in the likeness of men. And being found in human form he humbled himself and became obedient unto death, even death on a cross."

M. The Crucifixion of Jesus   (15:20b–41)

Bibliography

Ayton, R. A. "'Himself He Cannot Save' (Ps xxii, 29 and Mark xv, 31)." *JTS* o.s. 21 (1919–20) 245–48. **Baarlink, H.** *Anfängliches Evangelium.* 264–65. **Bailey, K. E.** "The Fall of Jerusalem and Mark's Account of the Cross." *ExpTim* 102 (1990–91) 102–5. **Baker, N. B.** "The Cry of Dereliction." *ExpTim* 70 (1958–59) 54–55. **Bauckham, R. J.** *Jude and the Relatives of Jesus in the Early Church.* Edinburgh: T. & T. Clark, 1990. 9–15, 19–24. ———. "Salome the Sister of Jesus, Salome the Disciple of Jesus, and the Secret Gospel of Mark." *NovT* 33 (1991) 245–75. **Benoit, P.** *Passion and Resurrection.* 153–204. **Berger, K.** "Zum Problem der Messianität Jesu." *ZTK* 71 (1974) 1–30, esp. 1–15. **Best, E.** *Following Jesus.* 213–16. ———. *Temptation and the Passion.* 97–102. **Bligh, P. H.** "Christ's Death Cry." *HeyJ* 1 (1960) 142–46. ———. "A Note on *Huios Theou* in Mark 15:39." *ExpTim* 80 (1968) 51–53. **Blight, W.** "The Cry of Dereliction." *ExpTim* 68 (1956–57) 285. **Blinzler, J.** *Die Brüder und Schwestern Jesu.* SBS 21. Stuttgart: Katholisches Bibelwerk, 1967. 73–86. **Boman, T.** "Das letzte Wort Jesu." *ST* 17 (1963) 103–19. **Bratcher, R. G.** "Mark xv.39: the Son of God." *ExpTim* 80 (1968–69) 286. ———. "A Note on υἱὸς θεοῦ (Mark xv.39)." *ExpTim* 68 (1956–57) 27–28. **Braumann, G.** "Wozu? (Mk 15,34)." In *Theokratia: Jahrbuch des Institutum Judaicum Delitzschianum II. 1970–72.* FS K. H. Rengstorf, ed. W. Dietrich et al. Leiden: Brill, 1973. 155–65. **Brower, K. E.** "Elijah in the Markan Passion Narrative." *JSNT* 18 (1983) 85–101. **Buckler, F. W.** "Eli, Eli, Lama Sabachthani?" *AJSL* 55 (1938) 378–91. **Burchard, C.** "Markus 15,34." *ZNW* 74 (1983) 1–11. **Burgos Nuñez, M. de.** "Le comunión de Dios con el crucificado: Cristología de Marcos 15,22–39." *EstBib* 37 (1978) 243–66. **Caza, L.** *"Mon Dieu, mon Dieu, pourquoi m'as-tu abandonné?" Comme bonne nouvelle de Jésus Christ, Fils de Dieu, comme bonne nouvelle de Dieu,*

pour le multitude. Recherches 24. Paris: Cerf; Montreal: Bellarmin, 1989. Esp. 173–336.
———. "Le relief que Marc a donné au cri de la croix." *ScEs* 39 (1987) 171–91. **Chronis, H. L.** "The Thorn Veil: Cultus and Christology in Mark 15:37–39." *JBL* 101 (1982) 97–114. **Cohn-Sherbok, D.** "Jesus' Cry on the Cross: An Alternative View." *ExpTim* 93 (1981–82) 215–17. **Colwell, E. C.** "A Definite Rule for the Use of the Article in the Greek New Testament." *JBL* 52 (1933) 12–21. **Cowling, C. C.** "Mark's Use of ὥρα." *ABR* 5 (1956) 154–60. **Crossan, J. D.** *In Fragments.* 306–12. ———. "Mark and the Relatives of Jesus." *NovT* 15 (1973) 81–113, esp. 105–10. **Danker, F. W.** "The Demonic Secret in Mark: A Reexamination of the Cry of Dereliction (15:34)." *ZNW* 61 (1970) 48–69. **Daube, D.** "The Veil of the Temple." In *The New Testament and Rabbinic Judaism.* London: Athlone, 1956. 23–26. **Dautzenberg, G.** "Zwei unterschiedliche 'Kompenden' markinischer Christologie? Überlegungen zum Verhältnis von Mk 15,39 zu Mk 14,61f." In *Evangelium Jesu Christi heute verkündigen.* FS C. Mayer, ed. B. Jendorff and G. Schmalenberg. Giessen: Selbstverlag des Fachbereichs, 1989. 17–32. **Davies, J. G.** "The Cup of Wrath and the Cup of Blessing." *Theology* 51 (1948) 178–80. **Davis, P. G.** "Mark's Christological Paradox." *JSNT* 35 (1989) 3–18. **Donahue, J. R.** *Are You the Christ?* 190–209. **Dormeyer, D.** *Die Passion Jesu.* 191–208. ———. *Der Sinn des Leidens Jesu: Historisch-kritische und textpragmatische Analysen zur Markuspassion.* SBS 96. Stuttgart: Katholisches Bibelwerk, 1979. 76–89. **Elgvin, T.** "The Messiah Who Was Cursed on the Tree." *Them* 22.3 (1997) 14–21. **Fowler, R. M.** *Let the Reader Understand.* 202–9. **Geddert, T. J.** *Watchwords.* 140–45. **Genest, O.** *Le Christ de la passion: Perspective structurale: Analyse de Marc 14,53–15,47, des parallèles et extra-bibliques.* Recherches 21: Théologie. Tournai: Desclée; Montreal: Bellarmin, 1978. 97–143. **Gese, H.** "Psalm 22 und das Neue Testament." *ZTK* 65 (1968) 1–22. ———. *Der Sinn des Leidens Jesu: Historisch-kritische und textpragmatische Analysen zur Markuspassion.* SBS 96. Stuttgart: Katholisches Bibelwerk, 1979. 76–89. **Glasson, T. F.** "Mark xv. 39: The Son of God." *ExpTim* 80 (1969) 286. **Gnilka, J.** "Mein Gott, mein Gott, warum hast du mich verlassen? (Mk 15,34 Par.)." *BZ* 3 (1959) 294–97. **Grayston, K.** "The Darkness of the Cosmic Sea: A Study of the Symbolism in St Mark's Narrative of the Crucifixion." *Theology* 55 (1952) 122–27. **Greenlee, J. H.** "The Greek Definite Article." *BT* 1 (1949–50) 162–65. **Guichard, D.** "La reprise du psaume 22 dans le récit de la mort de Jésus (Marc 15,21–41)." *FoiVie* 87.5 (1988) 59–64. **Gunther, J. J.** "The Family of Jesus." *EvQ* 64 (1974) 25–41. **Guy, H. A.** "Son of God in Mk 15:39." *ExpTim* 81 (1969–70) 151. **Hahn, F.** "Das Verständnis des Glaubens im Markusevangelium." In *Glaube im Neuen Testament.* FS H. Binder, ed. F. Hahn et al. Biblisch-theologische Studien 7. Neukirchen-Vluyn: Neukirchener, 1982. 43–67, esp. 61–62. **Hanson, K. C.,** and **Oakman, D. E.** *Palestine in the Time of Jesus: Social Structures and Social Conflicts.* Minneapolis: Fortress, 1998. 90–95. **Harner, P. B.** "Qualitative Anarthrous Predicate Nouns: Mark 15:39 and John 1:1." *JBL* 92 (1973) 75–87. **Hengel, M.** *Crucifixion: In the Ancient World and the Folly of the Message of the Cross.* London: SCM Press; Philadelphia: Fortress, 1977. ———. "Maria Magdalena und die Frauen als Zeugen." In *Abraham unser Vater: Juden und Christen im Gespräch über die Bibel.* Ed. O. Betz et al. AGSU 5. Leiden: Brill, 1963. 243–56. ———. *The Son of God.* London: SCM Press; Philadelphia: Fortress, 1976. **Holzmeister, U.** "Crux Domini eiusque crucifixio ex archaeologia Romana illustrantur." *VD* 14 (1934) 149–55, 216–20, 241–49, 257–63. ———. "Die Finsternis beim Tode Jesu." *Bib* 22 (1941) 404–11. **Jackson, H. M.** "The Death of Jesus in Mark and the Miracle from the Cross." *NTS* 33 (1987) 16–37. **Jeremias, J.** *Golgotha.* Angelos 1. Leipzig: Pfeiffer, 1926. **Johnson, E. S.** "Is Mark 15:39 the Key to Mark's Christology?" *JSNT* 31 (1987) 3–22 (repr. in *The Synoptic Gospels: A Sheffield Reader.* Ed. C. A. Evans and S. E. Porter. Biblical Seminar 31. Sheffield: Sheffield Academic Press, 1995. 143–62). ———. "Mark 15,39 and the So-called Confession of the Roman Centurion." *Bib* 81 (2000) 406–13. **Jonge, M. de.** "The Earliest Christian Use of *Christos:* Some Suggestions." *NTS* 32 (1986) 321–43. ———. "Two Interesting Interpretations of the Rending of the Temple-Veil in the Testaments of the Twelve Patriarchs." *Bijdragen* 46 (1985) 350–62. **Juel, D.** *Messiah and Temple.* 117–39. ———. *Messianic Exegesis:*

Christological Interpretation of the Old Testament in Early Christianity. Philadelphia: Fortress, 1988. 114–16. **Kato, Z.** *Völkermission im Markusevangelium.* 162–87. **Kazmierski, C. R.** *Jesus, the Son of God.* 191–211. **Kiddle, M.** "The Death of Jesus and the Admission of the Gentiles in St. Mark." *JTS* o.s. 35 (1934) 45–50. **Killermann, S.** "Die Finsternis beim Tode Jesus." *TGl* 23 (1941) 165–66. **Kilpatrick, G. D.** "Mark xv.28." In *The Principles and Practice of New Testament Textual Criticism: Collected Essays.* Ed. J. K. Elliott. BETL 96. Leuven: Peeters and Leuven UP, 1990. 307–11. **Kim, T. H.** "The Anarthrous υἱὸς θεοῦ in Mark 15,39 and the Roman Imperial Cult." *Bib* 79 (1998) 221–41. **Kingdon, H. P.** "Messiahship and the Crucifixion." *SE* 3 [= TU 88] (1964) 67–86. **Kremer, J.** *Das Ärgernis des Kreuzes: Eine Hinführung zum Verstehen der Leidensgeschichte nach Markus.* Stuttgart: Katholisches Bibelwerk, 1969. 60–79. **Lamarche, P.** "La mort du Christ et le voile du temple." *NRTh* 106 (1974) 583–99. **Lapide, P. E.** *Er wandelte nicht auf dem Meer: Ein jüdischer Theologe liest die Evangelien.* Gütersloh: Mohn, 1984. 87–106. **Lee, G. M.** "Mark xv 21, 'The Father of Alexander and Rufus.'" *NovT* 17 (1975) 303. ———. "Two Notes on St. Mark." *NovT* 18 (1976) 36. **Légasse, S.** "Les voiles du temple de Jérusalem: Essai de parcous historique." *RB* 87 (1980) 560–89. **Léon-Dufour, X.** "Le dernier cri de Jésus." *Études* 348 (1978) 666–82. **Lindeskog, G.** "The Veil of the Temple." In *In honorem Antonii Fridrichsen sexagenarii.* Ed. B. Reicke. ConNT 11. Lund: Gleerup, 1947. 132–37. **Linnemann, E.** *Studien zur Passionsgeschichte.* 136–70. **Lofthouse, W. F.** "The Cry of Dereliction." *ExpTim* 36 (1924–25) 188–92. **Mahoney, A.** "A New Look at 'The Third Hour' of Mark 15,25." *CBQ* 28 (1966) 292–99. **Mann, C.** "The Centurion at the Cross." *ExpTim* 20 (1908–9) 563–64. **Manus, C. U.** "The Centurion's Confession of Faith (Mk 15:39)." *Bulletin of African Theology* 7 (1985) 261–78. **Martin, R. P.** *Mark: Evangelist and Theologian.* 181–84. **Matera, F. J.** *The Kingship of Jesus: Composition and Theology in Mark 15.* SBLDS 66. Chico, CA: Scholars Press, 1982. 29–48, 125–45. **McCasland, S. V.** "Portents in Josephus and the Gospels." *JBL* 51 (1932) 323–35. **McHugh, J. J.** *The Mother of Jesus in the New Testament.* London: Darton, Longman & Todd; Garden City, NY: Doubleday, 1975. 241–47. **Meye, R. P.** *Jesus and the Twelve.* 169–71. **Michaels, J. R.** "The Centurion's Confession and the Spear Thrust." *CBQ* 29 (1967) 102–9. **Miller, J. V.** "The Time of the Crucifixion." *JETS* 26 (1983) 157–66. **Mohr, T. A.** *Markus- und Johannespassion.* 313–50. **Montefiore, H. W.** "Josephus and the New Testament." *NovT* 4 (1960) 139–60, esp. 148–54. **Moo, D. J.** *Old Testament in the Gospel Passion Narratives.* 264–83. **Motyer, S.** "The Rending of the Veil: A Markan Pentecost?" *NTS* 33 (1987) 155–57. **Myllykoski, M.** *Die letzten Tage Jesu.* 124–30. **Nestle, E.** "Die Sonnenfinsternis bei Jesu Tod." *ZNW* 3 (1902) 246–47. **Oberlinner, L.** *Historische Überlieferung und christologische Aussage: Zur Frage der "Brüder Jesu" in der Synopse.* FB 19. Stuttgart: Katholisches Bibelwerk, 1975. 86–148, 357–60. **Osborn, G. R.** "Redactional Trajectories in the Crucifixion Narrative." *EvQ* 51 (1979) 80–96, esp. 81–86. **Paton, W. R.** "Die Kreuzigung Jesu." *ZNW* 2 (1901) 339–41. **Pelletier, A.** "Le 'Voile' du temple de Jérusalem est-il devenu la 'Portière' du temple d'Olympie?" *Syria* 32 (1955) 289–307. **Pesch, R.** *Das Evangelium der Urgemeinde.* 203–13. **Pobee, J.** "The Cry of the Centurion—A Cry of Defeat." In *The Trial of Jesus.* FS C. F. D. Moule, ed. E. Bammel. SBT 13. London: SCM Press, 1970. 91–102. **Powell, J. E.** "'Father, into Thy Hands . . .'" *JTS* n.s. 40 (1989) 95–96. **Read, D. H. C.** "The Cry of Dereliction." *ExpTim* 68 (1956–57) 260–62. **Rehm, M.** "Eli, Eli, lamma sabacthani." *BZ* 2 (1958) 275–78. **Reumann, J. H.** "Psalm 22 at the Cross: Lament and Thanksgiving for Jesus Christ." *Int* 28 (1974) 39–58, esp. 49–55. **Riesner, R.** "Golgota und die Archäologie." *BK* 40 (1985) 21–26. **Robbins, V. K.** "The Crucifixion and the Speech of Jesus." *Forum* 4.1 (1988) 33–46. ———. "The Reversed Contextualization of Psalm 22 in the Markan Crucifixion: A Socio-Rhetorical Analysis." In *The Four Gospels 1992.* FS F. Neirynck, ed. F. Van Segbroeck et al. 3 vols. BETL 100. Leuven: Peeters and Leuven UP, 1992. 2:1161–83. **Rodgers, P.** "Mark 15:28." *EvQ* 61 (1989) 81–84. **Rosenblatt, S.** "The Crucifixion of Jesus from the Standpoint of the Pharisaic Law." *JBL* 75 (1956) 315–21. **Rossé, G.** *The Cry of Jesus on the Cross.* New York: Paulist, 1987. **Sagne, J.-C.** "The Cry of Jesus on the Cross." *Concilium* 169 (1983) 52–58. **Sahlin, H.** "Zum Verständnis von drei Stellen des Markus-Evangeliums." *Bib* 33 (1952) 53–66, esp. 62–66. **Sanders, E. P.** *Jesus and Judaism.* 71–76. **Sariola, H.** *Markus und das Gesetz.* 222–29. **Scheifler, J. R.** "El Salmo 22 y la Crucifixión del Señor." *EstBib* 24 (1965) 5–83. **Schenk, W.** *Der Passionsbericht nach Markus.* 13–139. **Schenke, L.** *Der gekreuzigte Christus.* 77–110. **Schlier, H.** *Die Markuspassion.* Kriterien 32. Einsiedeln: Johannes, 1974. 72–85. **Schlosser, J.** "La parole de Jésus sur la fin du Temple." *NTS* 36 (1990) 398–414. **Schlüngel, P. H.** "Die Erzählung des Markus über den Tod Jesu: Verstehenshilfen in Mk 15." *Orientierung* 38 (1974) 62–65. ———. "Von Markus erzählt: Jesu Leiden bis zur Passion." *Orientierung* 39 (1975) 50–51. **Schmidt, T. E.** "Cry of Dereliction or Cry of Judgment? Mark 15:34 in Context." *BBR* 4 (1994) 145–53. ———. "Mark 15.16–32: The Crucifixion Narrative and the Roman Triumphal Procession." *NTS* 41 (1995) 1–18. **Schneider, C.** "Der Hauptmann am Kreuz: Zur Nationalisierung neutestamentlicher Nebenfiguren." *ZNW* 33 (1934) 1–17. **Schneider, G.** *Die Passion Jesu.* 109–28, 133–35. ———. "Die theologische Sicht des Todes Jesu in den Kreuzigungsberichten der Evangelien." *TPQ* 126 (1978) 14–22. **Schottroff, L.** "Frauen in der Nachfolge Jesu in neutestamentlicher Zeit." In *Frauen in der Bibel.* Vol. 2 of *Traditionen der Befreiung: Sozialgeschichtliche Bibelauslegungen.* Ed. W. Schottroff and W. Stegemann. Munich: Kaiser, 1980. 91–133. ———. "Maria Magdalena und die Frauen am Grabe Jesu." *EvT* 42 (1982) 3–25. **Schreiber, J.** *Der Kreuzigungsbericht des Markusevangeliums: Mk 15,20b–41: Eine traditionsgeschichtliche und methodenkritische Untersuchung nach William Wrede (1859–1906).* BZNW 48. Berlin; New York: de Gruyter, 1986. ———. *Theologie des Vertrauens.* 22–82, 91–109. **Schulz, A.** *Nachfolgen und Nachahmen: Studien über das Verhältnis der neutestamentlichen Jüngerschaft zur urchristlichen Vorbildethik.* SANT 6. Munich: Kösel, 1962. 49–54. **Schüngel, P. H.** "Die Erzählung des Markus über den Tod Jesu." *Orientierung* 38 (1974) 62–65. **Schützeichel, H.** "Der Todesschrei Jesu—Bemerkungen zu einer Theologie des Kreuzes." *TTZ* 83 (1974) 1–16. **Schweizer, E.** "Scheidungsrecht der jüdischen Frau? Weibliche Jünger Jesu?" *EvT* 42 (1982) 294–300. **Senior, D. P.** *Passion of Jesus in the Gospel of Mark.* 114–32. **Shiner, W. T.** "The Ambiguous Pronouncement of the Centurion and the Shrouding of Meaning in Mark." *JSNT* 78 (2000) 3–22. **Söding, T.** *Glaube bei Markus.* 251–80. **Steichele, H.-J.** *Der leidende Sohn Gottes.* 193–312. **Stenger, W.** "Bemerkungen zum Begriff "Räuber" im Neuen Testament und bei Flavius Josephus." *BK* 37 (1982) 89–97. **Stock, A.** "Hinge Transitions in Mark's Gospel." *BTB* 15 (1985) 27–31. **Stock, K.** "Das Bekenntnis des Centurio: Mk 15,39 im Rahmen des Markusevangeliums." *ZKT* 100 (1978) 289–301. **Stockklausner, S. K.,** and **Hale, C. A.** "Mark 15:39 and 16:6–7: A Second Look." *McMaster Journal of Theology* 1 (1990) 34–44. **Strobel, A.** *Kerygma und Apokalyptic.* Göttingen: Vandenhoeck & Ruprecht, 1967. 139–45. **Suhl, A.** *Zitate.* 47–52, 61–62. **Taylor, V.** "The Narrative of the Crucifixion." *NTS* 8 (1961–62) 333–34. **Torrey, C. C.** *Our Translated Gospels.* 129–32. **Trilling, W.** *Christusverkündigung in den synoptischen Evangelien.* Biblische Handbibliothek 4. Munich: Kösel, 1969. 191–211. **Trudinger, L. P.** "'Eli, Eli, Lama Sabachthani?' A Cry of Dereliction? or Victory?" *JETS* 17 (1974) 235–38. **Ulansey, D.** "The Heavenly Veil Torn: Mark's Cosmic Inclusio." *JBL* 110 (1991) 123–25. **Vanhoye, A.** "L'angoisse du Christ." *Christus* 18 (1971) 382–89. **Veale, H. C.** "'The Merciful Bystander.'" *ExpTim* 28 (1916–17) 324–25. **Vögtle, A.** "Das markinische Verständnis der Tempelworte." In *Die Mitte des Neuen Testaments: Einheit und Vielfalt neutestamentlicher Theologie.* FS E. Schweizer, ed. U. Luz and H. Weder. Göttingen: Vandenhoeck & Ruprecht, 1983. 362–83 (repr. in A. Vögtle. *Offenbarungsgeschehen und Wirkungsgeschichte: Neutestamentliche Beiträge.* Freiburg: Herder, 1985. 168–88). **Unnik, W. C. van.** "L'usage de σῴζειν 'sauver' et des dérivés dans les évangiles synoptiques." In *Sparsa Collecta.* Part One: *Evangelia, Paulina, Acta.* NovTSup 29. Leiden: Brill, 1973. 16–34. **Waal, A. de.** "Das Mora-Spiel auf den Darstellungen der Verlosung des Kleides Christi." *RQ* 8 (1894) 145–46. **Weeden, T. J.** "The Cross as Power in Weakness (Mark 15:20b–41)." In *The Passion in Mark: Studies on Mark 14–16.* Ed. W. Kelber. Philadelphia: Fortress, 1976. 115–34, esp. 129–34. **Weinacht, H.** *Die Menschwerdung des Sohnes Gottes.* 61–68. **Westcott, B. F.,** and **Hort, F. J. A.** *Introduction.* 2:27–

28. **Wilkinson, J.** "The Physical Cause of the Death of Christ." *ExpTim* 4 (1972) 105–7. ———. "The Seven Words from the Cross." *SJT* 17 (1964) 69–82. **Williams, J. F.** *Other Followers of Jesus.* 182–88. **Winter, P.** *On the Trial of Jesus.* Rev. by T. A. Burkill and G. Vermes. 2nd ed. Studia Judaica 1. Berlin; New York: de Gruyter, 1974. 153–57. **Wojciechowski, M.** "Le naziréat et la passion (Mc 14,25a; 15,23)." *Bib* 65 (1984) 94–96. **Worden, T.** "'My God, my God, why hast Thou forsaken me?'" *Scr* 6 (1953) 9–16. **Yates, J. E.** "The *Velum Scissum:* Mark 15.38." In *The Spirit and the Kingdom.* London: S. P. C. K., 1963. 232–37. **Zahn, T.** "Der zerrissene Tempelvorhang." *NKZ* 13 (1902) 729–56. **Zehrer, F.** "Jesus, der Sohn Gottes." *BL* 48 (1975) 70–81. **Zimmermann, F.** "The Last Words of Jesus." *JBL* 66 (1947) 465–66. **Zmijewski, J.** "Die Sohn-Gottes-Prädikation im Markusevangelium: Zur Frage einer eigenständigen markinischen Titelchristologie." SNTSU 12 (1987) 5–34, esp. 9–32.

Bibliography on the Crucifixion

Arnold, M. "La crucifixion dans le droit romain." *BTS* 133 (1971) 4. **Bammel, E.** "Crucifixion as a Punishment in Palestine." In *The Trial of Jesus: Cambridge Studies.* FS C. F. D. Moule, ed. E. Bammel. SBT 13. London: SCM Press, 1970. 162–65. **Baumgarten, J. M.** "Does *tlh* in the Temple Scroll Refer to Crucifixion?" In *Studies in Qumran Law.* SJLA 24. Leiden: Brill, 1977. 172–82. **Betz, O.** "The Temple Scroll and the Trial of Jesus." *SWJT* 30 (1987–88) 5–8. **Charlesworth, J. H.** "Jesus and Jehoḥanan: An Archaeological Note on Crucifixion." *ExpTim* 84 (1973) 147–50. ——— and **Zias, J.** "Crucifixion: Archaeology, Jesus, and the Dead Sea Scrolls." In *Jesus and the Dead Sea Scrolls.* Ed. J. H. Charlesworth. ABRL. New York: Doubleday, 1992. 273–89. **Cohn, H. H.** "Crucifixion." *EncJud* 5:1133–35. **Díez Merino, L.** "La crucifixión en la antigua literatura judía (Período intertestamental)." *EstEcl* 51 (1976) 5–27. **Fitzmyer, J. A.** "Crucifixion in Ancient Palestine, Qumran, and the New Testament." *CBQ* 40 (1978) 493–513 (repr. in J. A. Fitzmyer. *To Advance the Gospel: New Testament Studies.* New York: Crossroad, 1981. 125–46). **Flusser, D.** "The Crucified One and the Jews." *Imm* 7 (1977) 25–37. **Ford, J. M.** "'Crucify him, crucify him' and the Temple Scroll." *ExpTim* 87 (1976) 275–78. **Fransen, I.** "L'historien Flavius-Josephe et le supplice de la croix." *BTS* 133 (1971) 5. **García Martínez, F.** "4QpNah y la Crucifixión: Nueva hipótesis de reconstrucción de 4Q 169 3–4 i, 4–8." *EstBib* 38 (1979–80) 221–35. **Haas, N.** "Anthropological Observations on the Skeletal Remains from Givʿat ha-Mivtar." *IEJ* 20 (1970) 38–59. **Halperin, D. J.** "Crucifixion, the Nahum Pesher, and the Rabbinic Penalty of Strangulation." *JJS* 32 (1981) 32–46. **Hengel, M.** *Crucifixion in the Ancient World and the Folly of the Message of the Cross.* London: SCM Press; Philadelphia: Fortress, 1977. **Hewitt, J.** "The Use of Nails in the Crucifixion." *HTR* 25 (1932) 29–45. **Kuhn, H.-W.** "Die Gekreuzigte von Givʿat ha-Mivtar: Bilanz einer Entdeckung." In *Theologia Crucis—Signum Crucis.* FS E. Dinkler, ed. C. Andresen and G. Klein. Tübingen: Mohr-Siebeck, 1979. 303–34. ———. "Die Kreuzesstrafe während der frühen Kaiserzeit: Ihre Wirklichkeit und Wertung in der Umwelt des Urchristentums." *ANRW* 2.25.1 (1982) 648–793. ———. "Zum Gekreuzigten von Givʿat ha-Mivtar: Korrektur eigenes Versehens in der Erstveröffentlichung." *ZNW* 69 (1978) 118–22. **Maier, J.** *The Temple Scroll: An Introduction, Translation and Commentary.* JSOTSup 34. Sheffield: JSOT Press, 1985. 132–34. **Møller-Christensen, V.** "Skeletal Remains from Givʿat ha-Mivtar." *IEJ* 26 (1976) 35–38. **Naveh, J.** "The Ossuary Inscriptions from Givʿat ha-Mivtar, Jerusalem." *IEJ* 20 (1970) 33–37. **Tzaferis, V.** "Crucifixion: The Archaeological Evidence." *BAR* 11 (1985) 44–53. ———. "Jewish Tombs at and near Givʿat ha-Mivtar." *IEJ* 20 (1970) 18–32. **Vogt, J.** "Crucifixion etiam pro nobis: Historische Anmerkungen zum Kreuzestod." *IKZ* 2 (1973) 186–91. **Weber, H.-R.** *Kreuz: Überlieferung und Deutung der Kreuzigung Jesu im neutestamentlichen Kulturraum.* Stuttgart; Berlin: Kreuz, 1975. 153–74 (ET: *The Cross: Tradition and Interpretation.* Tr. E. Jessett. London: S. P. C. K.; Grand Rapids, MI: Eerdmans, 1979). **Wilcox, M.** "'Upon the Tree'—Deut 21:22–23 in the New Testament." *JBL* 96 (1977) 85–99. **Yadin, Y.** "Epigraphy and Crucifixion." *IEJ* 23 (1973) 19–22. ———. "Pesher Nahum (4QpNahum)

Reconsidered." *IEJ* 21 (1971) 1–12. **Zias, J.,** and **Sekeles, E.** "The Crucified Man from Giv'at ha-Mivtar: A Reappraisal." *IEJ* 35 (1985) 22–27. **Zugibe, F.** "Two Questions about Crucifixion: Does the Victim Die of Asphyxiation? Would Nails in the Hands Hold the Weight of the Body?" *BRev* 5 (1989) 35–43.

Bibliography on Mark 15:26

Baarlink, H. *Anfängliches Evangelium.* 210–11. **Bammel, E.** "The *titulus.*" In *Jesus and the Politics of His Day.* Ed. E. Bammel and C. F. D. Moule. Cambridge: Cambridge UP, 1984. 353–64. **Baumbach, G.** "Die Stellung Jesu im Judentum seiner Zeit." *FZPhTh* 20 (1973) 285–305. **Berger, K.** "Zum Problem der Messianität Jesu." *ZTK* 71 (1974) 1–30, esp. 1–15. **Catchpole, D. R.** "The 'Triumphal' Entry." In *Jesus and the Politics of His Day.* Ed. E. Bammel and C. F. D. Moule. Cambridge: Cambridge UP, 1984. 319–34. **Dahl, N. A.** "The Crucified Messiah." In *The Crucified Messiah and Other Essays.* Minneapolis: Augsburg, 1974. 1–36. **Evans, C. A.** *Jesus and His Contemporaries.* 314–15. **Haacker, K.** "Einige Fälle von 'erlebter Rede' im Neuen Testament." *NovT* 12 (1970) 70–77. **Lee, G. M.** "The Inscription on the Cross." *PEQ* 100 (1968) 144. **Marshall, C. D.** *Faith as a Theme.* 200–208. **Matera, F. J.** *The Kingship of Jesus: Composition and Theology in Mark 15.* SBLDS 66. Chico, CA: Scholars Press, 1982. 24–29. **Meyer, B. F.** *The Aims of Jesus.* London: SCM Press, 1979. 176–80. **O'Rahilly, A.** "The Title of the Cross." *IER* 65 (1945) 289–97. **Regard, P.-F.** "Le titre de la croix d'après les évangiles." *RAr* 28 (1928) 95–105. **Schneider, G.** "The Political Charge against Jesus (Luke 23:2)." In *Jesus and the Politics of His Day.* Ed. E. Bammel and C. F. D. Moule. Cambridge: Cambridge UP, 1984. 403–14.

Translation

[20b] And they lead him out, so that they might crucify him. [21] And they compel a certain passerby, Simon of Cyrene, coming from the country, the father of Alexander and Rufus, so that he might carry his cross. [22] And they bring him to the place Golgotha, which means "Place of the Skull." [23] And they were offering him [a] wine mixed with myrrh, which he did not take.[b] [24] And they crucify him and "divide his clothes, casting lots for them," [to determine] who should take what. [25] But it was the third [c] hour, and they crucified him. [26] And the inscription of the charge written against him was: [d] "The King of the Jews." [27] And with him they crucify two rebels, one on the right,[c] and one on his left.[ef] [29] And those passing by were ridiculing him, wagging their heads, and saying, "Ha! You who would destroy the temple [g] and build [another] in three days, [30] save yourself, having come down from the cross!" [31] Likewise also the ruling priests, mocking among themselves with the scribes, were saying, "Others he saved; himself he can't save! [32] Let the Messiah, the king of Israel, come down from the cross now,[h] so that we may see and believe!" [i] And those crucified with him were reviling him.

[33] And when the sixth hour had come, darkness fell over the whole land until the ninth hour. [34] And at the ninth hour Jesus cried with a loud voice, "Eloi, Eloi, lema sabachthani?" [j] which means, "My God, my God, why have you abandoned [k] me?" [35] And some bystanders, listening, were saying, "Behold, he calls Elijah." [l] [36] But someone, running up, having filled a sponge with vinegar, having placed it on a reed, gave it to him to drink, saying, "Permit [me]; let us see if Elijah [l] comes to take him down." [m] [37] But Jesus, after letting out a loud cry, expired. [38] And the veil of the temple was torn in two, from top to bottom. [39] But the centurion who stood opposite him, seeing that he had died [n] in this way, said, "Truly this man was the son of God!" [40] But there were also women

there watching from a distance, among whom were Mary ° *Magdalene, and Mary the mother of James the younger and of Joses,*ᵖ *and Salome,* ⁴¹*who, when he was in Galilee, were following him and were serving him; and many other women who had come up with him to Jerusalem.*

Notes

ᵃA C² D Σ and a few later authorities add πιεῖν, "to drink."

ᵇA few late MSS read ἠθέλησεν, "want" (cf. Matt 27:34).

ᶜA few late MSS read ἕκτη, "sixth." The variant results from an attempt to harmonize Mark's account with John 19:14; cf. Metzger, *TCGNT*¹, 118; Westcott-Hort, *Introduction* 2:27. One will find similar scribal efforts in John 19:14, where τρίτη, "third," replaces John's ἕκτη, "sixth."

ᵈ33 and a few late MSS add οὗτός ἐστιν, "this is" (cf. Matt 27:37).

ᵉIn some of the Latin MSS, names are given to these rebels. We are told that the name of the man on the right was Zoathan, while the name of the man on the left was Chammatha.

ᶠΛ Θ Σ 083 *f*¹·¹³ 33 892 1006 1506 Majority text lat syᵖ·ʰ add v 28: καὶ ἐπληρώθη ἡ γραφὴ ἡ λέγουσα· καὶ μετὰ ἀνόμων ἐλογίσθη, "And the Scripture was fulfilled, which says, 'And he was reckoned with lawless persons.'" This addition derives from Luke 22:37 (cf. Isa 53:12). The verse is not found in ℵ A B C D Ψ 2427 *pc* syˢ sa boᵖᵗ. See Westcott-Hort, *Introduction* 2:27–28. See *Comment* on v 28 below.

ᵍA few late MSS add τοῦ θεοῦ, "of God."

ʰA few later MSS read εἰ ὁ χριστὸς ἐστι ὁ βασιλεὺς Ἰσραήλ, καταβάτω νῦν ἀπὸ τοῦ σταυροῦ, "If this is the Messiah, the king of Israel, let him come down from the cross now."

ⁱC³ D Σ and several later MSS add αὐτῷ, "in him."

ʲMark's ἐλωί, ἐλωί, λεμὰ σαβαχθανί, "Eloi, Eloi, lema sabachthani," transliterates the Aram. אֱלָהִי אֱלָהִי לְמָא שְׁבַקְתָּנִי *'ĕlāhî 'ĕlāhî lĕmā' šĕbaqtanî* (cf. *Tg.* Ps 22:1, which offers only a partial parallel). Most of the authorities read ἐλωί, but D and a few other MSS read ἠλεί, which transliterates the Heb. אֵלִי *'ēlî*, "my God." The spelling λεμά is read by ℵ C L and several other MSS, but λιμά is read by A P 33 and other MSS. This is probably no more than a spelling variant. But λαμά, which is read by B D N and other MSS, represents the Heb. לְמָה *lāmâ*, "why?" There is a great deal of variety in the transliteration of שְׁבַקְתָּנִי *šĕbaqtanî*. Most MSS read σαβαχθανί (L 33 and others) or σαβαχθανεί (ℵᶜ C N Σ and others). But A reads σιβακθανεί, and B reads ζαβαφθανεί. D's ζαφθανί (which is followed in many Latin MSS with *zapthani*) is an attempt to transliterate עֲזַבְתָּנִי *'ăzabtānî*, "have you abandoned me," of Ps 22:1. The Heb. elements were suggested by the better-known and more accessible Heb. version of the OT and by the parallel in Matt 27:46, which itself represents a reading that has partially assimilated to the Heb.

ᵏD and a few late Latin MSS read ὠνείδισας, "reproached," possibly to avoid the idea of God abandoning Jesus; cf. Metzger, *TCGNT*¹, 120.

ˡGk. Ἠλίαν, which is read by B² C D L N Σ 33 and a few other MSS. Ἠλείαν is read by ℵ A B* and a few other MSS. Elijah in Heb. is אֵלִיָּה *'ēliyyâ*. The variation in the Gk. spelling is common.

ᵐA few late MSS and authorities read σῶσαι καὶ καθελεῖν αὐτόν, "to save him and take him down."

ⁿA C N Σ and a few later MSS and authorities read ὅτι οὕτως κράξας ἐξέπνευσεν, "how, crying out, he died" (and similarly in D W and a few other MSS and authorities). Metzger (*TCGNT*¹, 121) thinks that the addition of κράξας, "crying out," derives from Matt 27:50.

ᵒGk. Μαρία. B C W and several later MSS read Μαριάμ.

ᵖGk. Ἰωσῆτος. ℵ* A C N W Σ 33 read Ἰωσή. One OL MS reads *Ioseph*.

Form/Structure/Setting

Bultmann (*History*, 272–74) believes that the crucifixion narrative is laced throughout with legend and scriptural apologetic. Accordingly, v 24 is a prophecy (cf. Ps 21:19); v 25 is Markan redaction; v 26 is editorial, harking back to the hearing before Pilate; v 27 has been inspired by Isa 53:12; v 28 is later scriptural proof text; vv 29–32 "is a legendary formulation on the basis of a prophetic proof" (Ps 21:8; Lam 2:15); vv 29 and 31 are doublets; vv 33–39 is an account "strongly disfigured by legend"; v 34 is a "secondary interpretation of the cry of Jesus in v

37," based on Ps 21:2; vv 35 and 36b are secondary; v 36a may also be later and is probably legendary, based on Ps 68:22; vv 33 and 38 cannot be "ancient report, but only . . . Christian legend"; v 39 is also part of the legendary development; v 37 may be authentic, but even here there is doubt; vv 40–41, the women as witnesses, is as unhistorical as the tradition that they discovered the empty tomb. All that survives is an "ancient historical nàrrative" preserved in vv 20b–24a, with perhaps v 37. Taylor (*Formation,* 58) remarks that "the confidence with which Bultmann tells how the Markan Story came into being could be justified only by the gift of omniscience." He acknowledges that in the telling of the story certain details seen in the light of scriptural prophecy suggested themselves, and the narrative was edited to accommodate these points of contact. But the wholesale accretion that Bultmann finds is not the best explanation. Rather, Taylor (*Formation,* 59) thinks that a "historical nucleus attracted to itself traditional elements in free circulation and brought them together within the range of its own orbit."

The extent of the influence that OT Scripture had upon the Passion Narrative has been a topic of ongoing study (e.g., D. J. Moo, *Old Testament in the Gospel Passion Narratives,* 264–83). Marcus (*Way of the Lord,* 175) tabulates the allusions to and echoes of several lament psalms in the crucifixion and death scene as follows:

Mark	Topic	Psalms
15:24	division of garments	22:18
15:29	mockery, wagging head	22:7
15:30–31	Save yourself!	22:8
15:32	reviling	22:6
15:34	cry of dereliction	22:1
15:36	gave him vinegar to drink	69:21
15:40	looking on at a distance	38:11

That the narrative has been shaped and that materials have been selected, while perhaps others have been omitted, seem probable. But overarching midrashic and chiastic theories are less persuasive. As a case in point, Bailey's imaginative proposal (*ExpTim* 102 [1990–91] 102–5) suggests that Mark 15:20–39 constitutes a chiasmus, inspired by and alluding to Lam 2:15–16. The proposed chiasmus looks like this:

1. Simon of Cyrene, a Jew, passes by and carries the cross (v 21)
 2. Wine offered, garments divided, crucifixion (v 23)
  3. The third hour, "The King of the Jews" (vv 25–26)
   4. Two robbers (v 27)
    5. Those passing by wagged their heads and mocked him (vv 29–30)
     6. The chief priests mocked him (vv 31–32a)
   7. Two robbers (v 32b)
  8. Sixth hour, ninth hour, "My God, my God . . ." (vv 33–34)
 9. Vinegar offered, veil of temple torn, crucifixion (vv 36–38)
10. The centurion, a Gentile, sees and believes (v 39)

Bailey thinks that Mark has borrowed from Lam 2:15–16: "All who pass along the way clap their hands at you; they hiss and wag their heads at the daughter of

Jerusalem; 'Is this the city which was called the perfection of beauty, the joy of all the earth?' All your enemies rail against you; they hiss, they gnash their teeth, they cry: 'We have destroyed her! Ah, this is the day we longed for; now we have it; we see it!'" What had originally referred to the city of Jerusalem and the temple now refers to Jesus and his cross. Bailey's suggestion is ingenious, but it is not persuasive. The chiasmus looks contrived, with details unaccounted for (e.g., vv 22, 24, 35), and with material very unequally divided. Details such as hissing, wagging the head, and insulting remarks may have contributed to the telling of the Passion Narrative, or they may only reflect a common cultural milieu. It is improbable that Mark's readers would have perceived such a lengthy and complicated chiasmus and then associated Jesus with the city of Jerusalem.

Mark 15:20b–41 falls into two principal parts with the following subsections:

1. The crucifixion of Jesus (vv 20b–32)
   a. The leading of Jesus (and Simon of Cyrene) to the place of crucifixion (vv 20b–22)
   b. The crucifixion and division of clothing (vv 23–24)
   c. The temporal notation that it was "the third hour" that Jesus was crucified (v 25)
   d. The notation of the inscription (v 26)
   e. The mockery from criminals and priests alike (vv 27, 29–32)
2. The death of Jesus (vv 33–41)
   a. The second temporal notation that it was the "sixth hour" that darkness fell (v 33)
   b. The third temporal notation that Jesus cried out, with bystanders reacting to it (vv 34–36)
   c. The death of Jesus (v 37)
   d. The tearing of temple veil (v 38)
   e. The confession of the centurion (v 39)
   f. The notation that three Galilean women watched from a distance (vv 40–41).

Comment

20b καὶ ἐξάγουσιν αὐτὸν ἵνα σταυρώσωσιν αὐτόν, "And they lead him out, so that they might crucify him." The mockery over, the soldiers lead Jesus out of the praetorium (or out of the city itself; Swete, 377) to the place where they will crucify him. The next verse presupposes that Jesus is carrying his own cross (or at least one piece of it). It is curious that in light of the passion prediction in 8:34, "If someone wishes to follow after me, let him deny himself and take up his cross and follow me," the evangelist fails to mention this fact (see *Comment* on v 21). According to Plautus, the condemned man carried his cross (the *patibulum*) through the city to the place of crucifixion (*Carbonaria* frg. 2; *Mil. glor.* 2.4.6–7 §§359–60); so also Plutarch: "Every wrongdoer who goes to execution carries out his own cross [ἐκφέρει τὸν αὑτοῦ σταυρόν]" (*Mor.* 554A–B = *Sera* §9; for graphic descriptions of first-century crucifixions, see Seneca, *Dial.* 3.2.2; 6.20.3; Josephus, *J.W.* 5.11.1 §§449–51).

21 καὶ ἀγγαρεύουσιν παράγοντά τινα Σίμωνα Κυρηναῖον ἐρχόμενον ἀπ᾽ ἀγροῦ . . .

ἵνα ἄρῃ τὸν σταυρὸν αὐτοῦ, "And they compel a certain passerby, Simon of Cyrene, coming from the country . . . so that he might carry his cross." ἀγγαρεύειν, "to compel," an old Persian loanword, is not found in the LXX, but it is attested in the papyri (MM, 2), Josephus (BAG, 6), and rabbinic literature (i.e., the noun אנגריא 'angaryā'; cf. Jastrow, 81). According to Torrey, "Simon of Cyrene [קִרְנָי Qirrēnāy], coming from the field," constitutes a "slight corruption of the Aramaic," which originally read "Simon, a farmer [קִרְוָי qirwāy] coming from the field" (Our Translated Gospels, 129, 131–32). But this emendation is hardly necessary, for the text makes good sense as it stands. ἐρχόμενον ἀπ' ἀγροῦ, "coming in from the country," need not suggest tension with labor laws and holiday observance. Indeed, because he is Simon "of Cyrene," we should suppose that Simon was not a local resident with fields to work in the vicinity of Jerusalem. It probably only means that Simon had just entered or was just about to enter the city as the execution party approached (Cranfield, 454). It is also probable that Simon was compelled to carry the cross because Jesus himself was too weak to complete the journey. Against the claim that this is a fictional story (to exemplify Jesus' requirement that his disciples take up and carry their own crosses) is the fact that Jesus was unable himself to carry it (Brown, 2:913–14). Surely it would have been more impressive to make a point of Jesus' carrying the cross as an example for his followers than to have him unable to do the very thing he required of his followers.

τὸν πατέρα Ἀλεξάνδρου καὶ Ῥούφου, "the father of Alexander and Rufus." Simon, perhaps a Jew from Cyrene, is said to be the father of "Alexander and Rufus." Because the name Rufus appears in Rom 16:13 (and nowhere else in the NT), some have wondered if this is the same person, which then may explain why the evangelist mentions the names of Simon's sons. That is, these men, or at least Rufus, may have been known to Christians in Rome, where Mark's Gospel may have been composed and first circulated. This can be no more than speculation.

22 καὶ φέρουσιν αὐτὸν ἐπὶ τὸν Γολγοθᾶν τόπον, ὅ ἐστιν μεθερμηνευόμενον Κρανίου Τόπος, "And they bring him to the place Golgotha, which means 'Place of the Skull.'" Mark's Κρανίου Τόπος, "Place of the Skull," translates Γολγοθᾶν (= גלגלתא galgaltā', "round stone"). T. E. Schmidt (NTS 41 [1995] 10–11) has argued that Κρανίου Τόπος should be translated "Place of the Head" rather than "Place of the Skull." He speculates further that the Vulgate's Calvaria, "Skull" (quod est interpretatum Calvariae locus, "which is interpreted, 'Place of the Skull'"), and the "popular image associated with Gordon's Calvary" have influenced modern versions, which translate "Skull." If Mark's Κρανίου Τόπος be understood as "Place of the Head" (Latin Capitis locus), we may have yet another allusion to Roman tradition. As Schmidt observes, every Roman triumph reached its conclusion at the temple of Jupiter Capitolinus, the place of the "head" (see Livy 50.55.5–6, cited and discussed by Schmidt). Schmidt may be correct, but κρανίον does mean "skull" (in LSJ, not just in BAG), and the fact that the Aramaic גלגלתא galgaltā' means "round stone" supports "skull" as much as it does "head." Some think that the hill got its name from the legend that Adam's skull was buried at the site (see L. Ginzberg, The Legends of the Jews, 7 vols. [Philadelphia: The Jewish Publication Society of America, 1909–38] 5:125–27 n. 137).

23 καὶ ἐδίδουν αὐτῷ ἐσμυρνισμένον οἶνον· ὃς δὲ οὐκ ἔλαβεν, "And they were offering him wine mixed with myrrh, which he did not take." The offer of drink to the sufferer may have its roots in Scripture itself, as especially in Prov 31:6: "Give strong drink to him who is perishing, and wine to those in bitter distress." Part of this verse is appealed to as justification for showing mercy to one who is being executed. According to a late third-century rabbinic saying, "They give him who goes out to be executed a grain of frankincense in a cup of wine so that his mind becomes confused, as it is said, 'Give strong drink to him who is perishing, and wine to those in bitter distress' (Prov 31:6)" (*b. Sanh.* 43a). A similar teaching is found in one of the Talmud's minor tractates: the condemned are "given to drink wine containing frankincense so that they should not feel grieved" (*Sem.* 2:9).

But has wine mixed with myrrh (and not frankincense) been given to Jesus to numb the pain? There is no evidence that myrrh had analgesic properties. Moreover, the ones who offer the wine to Jesus are the soldiers who are crucifying him. It is difficult, therefore, to interpret this offer as an act of mercy. A Jewish custom would scarcely serve as a guide. Wine mixed with myrrh or other perfumes was thought of as a delicacy (cf. Pliny, *Nat.* 14.15 §92: "The finest wine in early days was that spiced with the scent of myrrh"; 14.19 §107). It is probable, then, that the offer of fine wine to Jesus was in fact part of the ongoing mockery (cf. vv 29–32). In effect, the soldiers were offering the finest wine to the "king of the Jews." In later tradition, the scented wine becomes "gall" (Matt 27:34) or "vinegar" (Luke 23:36). Indeed, the drink may have been referred to as fine wine mixed with myrrh as part of the mockery when in fact the soldiers offered Jesus gall or vinegar (though the potions mentioned in the later Gospels may have been inspired by Ps 69:21 or Lam 3:15). The evangelist Luke has correctly understood the intended mockery: "The soldiers also mocked him, coming up and offering him vinegar, and saying, 'If you are the king of the Jews . . .'" (23:36–37).

Jesus refuses the offered drink, but not because of his vow to abstain from wine until he may drink it in the kingdom of God (14:25), nor because of a Nazirite vow (*pace* Wojciechowski, *Bib* 65 [1984] 94–96), nor because he wishes not to dull his senses (which presupposes the problematical view that wine mixed with myrrh would have served as an analgesic) so that he might drink the cup the Father has given him to drink (10:38–39; 14:36). After all, Jesus could have drunk a bitter cup to symbolize his willingness to drink the cup of suffering that his heavenly Father had willed him to drink. Nor does Jesus refuse to drink the cup because drinking on the Day of Atonement was forbidden (cf. *m. Yoma* 8:1). Day of Atonement traditions (*pace* Davies, *Theology* 51 [1948] 178–80) have nothing to do with the Passover or with Mark's presentation of Jesus' death. No, Jesus refuses to drink because he refuses to participate in the mockery. This refusal is consistent with his earlier lack of participation in the jeering and mockery to which he had been subjected (14:65; 15:16–20) and with his silence before the priests (14:60–61) and before Pilate (15:4–5).

24 καὶ σταυροῦσιν αὐτὸν καὶ διαμερίζονται τὰ ἱμάτια αὐτοῦ βάλλοντες κλῆρον ἐπ᾽ αὐτὰ τίς τί ἄρῃ, "And they crucify him and 'divide his clothes, casting lots for them,' [to determine] who should take what." The discovery in 1968 of an ossuary (ossuary no. 4, at Givʿat ha-Mivtar) of one יהוחנן *Yĕhôḥānān*, who had been crucified, provides archaeological evidence and illumination on how Jesus himself may have been crucified. The ossuary and its contents date to the late 20s C.E. The remains of an iron spike (11.5 centimeters in length) are plainly seen, piercing the right ankle bone. Those who took down the body of Yehoḥanan apparently were unable to remove the spike, with the result that a piece of wood (from an olive tree) remained affixed to the ankle. Later, the skeletal remains of the body—spike, fragment of wood, and all—were placed in the ossuary. Forensic examination of the rest of the skeletal remains supports the view that Yehoḥanan was crucified with arms apart, hung from a horizontal beam or tree branch. However, there is no evidence that his arms or wrists were nailed to this cross beam (as claimed in early reports). Hengel (*Crucifixion*, 9) cites the following passage from a third-century C.E. author: "Punished with limbs outstretched . . . they are fastened (and) nailed to the stake in the most bitter torment, evil food for birds of prey and grim picking for dogs" (*Apotelesmatica* 4.198–200). The inscription on Yehoḥanan's ossuary may also have a bearing on how the man was crucified. The following can be found on the broad side of the ossuary (Naveh, *IEJ* 20 [1970] 35, plate 13):

יהוחנן	Yĕhôḥānān
יהוחנן	Yĕhôḥānān
בן חגקול	ben Ḥgqwl

The *gîmel*, which is the second letter of the second word in the third line is unclear. If it is a *zāyin* instead of a *gîmel*, then as חזקול *Ḥzqwl* (or חזקיל *Ḥzqyl*) it could be a corrupt form of "Ezekiel" (which normally is יחזקאל *Yĕhezqēʾl*). Yadin (*IEJ* 23 [1973] 19) suggests reading הגקול *haggāqûl*, that is, "the bowlegged one" (i.e., one with "knees apart"). Yadin then suggests that the second and third lines should read: "Yehoḥanan the son of the one (hanged) with his knees apart," that is, the one who was crucified. Yadin's suggestion is ingenious but suffers from the fact that "bowlegged" is actually spelled עקול *ʿāqûl* or עיקל *ʿiqqēl* (cf. *m. Bek.* 7:6). Yadin (*IEJ* 23 [1973] 19–20) thinks this discrepancy may be due to a spelling variation or to different pronunciation. In any case, he suggests that both father and son were buried in ossuary no. 4. Yehoḥanan, the man who was crucified, and his son, Yehoḥanan "son of the one (hanged) with his knees apart." For further discussion, see Charlesworth, *ExpTim* 84 (1973) 147–50; H.-W. Kuhn, "Die Gekreuzigte von Givʿat ha-Mivtar"; Zias and Sekeles, *IEJ* 35 (1985) 22–27; Charlesworth and Zias, "Crucifixion"; and the older work by J. Hewitt, *HTR* 25 (1932) 29–45, which now must be updated by the data gleaned from the Yehoḥanan ossuary.

The soldiers who have crucified Jesus διαμερίζονται τὰ ἱμάτια αὐτοῦ βάλλοντες κλῆρον ἐπ' αὐτά, "divide his clothes, casting lots for them." The phrase comes from Ps 22:18: "they divide my garments among them, and for my raiment they cast lots." The division of the crucifixion victim's property, including his clothing, was apparently customary (*Digest of Justinian* 48.20.1; Tacitus, *Ann.* 6.29: "people sentenced to death forfeited their property"), though there were exceptions (*Digest of Justinian* 48.20.6; cf. Tacitus, *Hist.* 4.3). The allusion to Ps 22:18 (which in John 19:24 becomes explicit) obviously derives from Christians who passed on the story, phrasing it to take on scriptural overtones. The casting of lots probably did not involve throwing dice (unless we are to imagine that someone thought to bring along his box of dice). Another game is probably in view, such as guessing how many fingers one is hiding behind one's back (cf. de Waal, *RQ* 8 [1894] 145–46; Brown, 2:955).

τίς τί ἄρῃ, "[to determine] who should take what." Taylor (590) remarks that "the blending of the two interrogatives is classical." For examples, see Field, *Notes*, 43–44.

25 ἦν δὲ ὥρα τρίτη καὶ ἐσταύρωσαν αὐτόν, "But it was the third hour, and they crucified him." The third hour was 9:00 A.M. According to John 19:14, "it was about the sixth hour," that is, noon. John may have delayed the time in order to have Jesus crucified at approximately the same time that the people began to slaughter the Passover lambs, which Cranfield (455–56) regards as the most probable explanation. However, he also notes the possibility of confusion between the *gamma* (Γ = 3) and the *digamma* (F = 6) in early MSS. Gundry (957) is not impressed with this solution. He rightly notes that Mark's use of τρίτη, "third," instead of a Γ, tells against the theory (though it does not necessarily rule it out). Gundry thinks that the Fourth Evangelist deliberately pushed Jesus' crucifixion deeper into the day, so that Jesus' death would take place at the same time the Paschal lambs were being killed. He is probably correct, which makes harmonizing theories unnecessary (*pace* J. V. Miller, *JETS* 26 [1983] 157–66). Mark's time accords better with the notice that Jesus had been presented to Pilate πρωΐ, "early in the morning" (v 1).

26 καὶ ἦν ἡ ἐπιγραφὴ τῆς αἰτίας αὐτοῦ ἐπιγεγραμμένη, ὁ βασιλεὺς τῶν Ἰουδαίων, "And the inscription of the charge written against him was: 'The King of the Jews.'" ἡ ἐπιγραφὴ τῆς αἰτίας, "the inscription of the charge," refers to the *titulus* (cf. John 19:19, where the Greek equivalent τίτλος appears), which stated the reason for punishment (*causa poenae*). In Latin the inscription probably read something like *[IESUS NAZARENUS] REX IUDAEORUM*, while the Hebrew may have read ישוע הנצרי] מלך היהודים [*yēšûaʿ hannoṣrî] melek hayyĕhûdîm*. (On the trilingual text of the *titulus*, see John 19:20.) Mark's Greek inscription parallels closely the forms found in the other Gospels (cf. Matt 27:37; Luke 23:38; John 19:19). W. Bousset (*Kyrios Christos* [Göttingen: Vandenhoeck & Ruprecht, 1913] 56) doubts the historicity of the *titulus*, seeing it as an "edifying meditation of the believing Jesus community" that constituted "mockery of the Jews." Haenchen (536) denies the historicity of the *titulus*, but for the opposite reason: it reflects the confession of the Jewish church. Following the skepticism of Bultmann (*History*, 272, 284; see discussion above), Catchpole ("'Triumphal' Entry," 328) also doubts the historicity of the *titulus*, suspecting that it has been drawn from the earlier material in Mark 15. Many other scholars, such as Wellhausen (130–31), Winter (*On the Trial of Jesus*, 108), E. Dinkler (*Signum Crucis* [Tübingen: Mohr-Siebeck, 1967] 306), Bammel ("The *titulus*," 363), and G. Schneider ("Political Charge," 404: the *titulus* is "historically unimpeachable"), among others (including many commentators; cf. Pesch 2:484: "no reasonable doubt is possible"), have accepted the historicity of the *titulus*.

It is improbable that ὁ βασιλεὺς τῶν Ἰουδαίων, "The King of the Jews," derives from Christian confession (or even more improbably from Christian mockery of the Jewish people). It certainly does not derive from the Markan evangelist, who wishes to portray Jesus as the "Christ" and the "son of God," not as the "king of the Jews." The epithet "king of the Jews" is of Roman coinage. The Roman Senate, and later emperor Augustus, recognized Herod the Great as "king of the Jews" (Josephus, *Ant.* 15.11.4 §409: ὁ τῶν Ἰουδαίων βασιλεὺς Ἡρώδης, "the king of the Jews, Herod"; cf. *J.W.* 1.14.4 §§282–85; *Ant.* 14.11.4 §280). Only Romans use this title of Jesus in Mark (a nuance missed by the author of the *Gospel of Peter*; cf. *Gos. Pet.* 4.11, where the *titulus* reads "This is the King of Israel"). The mocking priests call Jesus "king of Israel" (Mark 15:31–32), the Jewish flavoring of which is consistent with the high priest's question earlier put to Jesus: "Are you the Messiah, the son of the Blessed?" (14:61). But Christians regarded Jesus as the Messiah, the son of God, and not as king of Israel or king of the Jews.

The practice of producing a *titulus* that accompanied the victim is variously attested in antiquity (cf. Suetonius, *Cal.* 32.2: a thieving slave was ordered to "be led about among the guests, preceded by a *titulus* giving the reason for his punishment [*causam poenae*]"; *Dom.* 10.1: a man who insulted the emperor is thrown to the dogs, with a *titulus* that described his offense; Dio Cassius 54.3.6–7: before his crucifixion, a slave was required to carry around the Forum a notice giving the reason for his execution; 73.16.5; Eusebius, *Hist. eccl.* 5.1.44: Attalus the Christian "was led around the amphitheatre and a placard was carried before him on which was written in Latin, 'This is Attalus, the Christian'").

The Markan evangelist does not tell us where the *titulus* describing Jesus as "king of the Jews" was placed. The Matthean evangelist tells us that it was placed above Jesus' head (Matt 27:37). This notation has encouraged the traditional image of the † configuration of the cross (Brown, 2:948). This view may be found in Irenaeus (*Haer.* 2.24.4) and Tertullian (*Nat.* 1.12.7). The words σταυρός, "cross," and σταυροῦν, "to crucify," allow for other configurations, such as an X or T (supported by *Barn.* 9:8 and Justin, *Dial.* 91.2) or simply a vertical pole. The *patibulum* that Jesus, then Simon, carried (v 21) is assumed to have been a cross beam, thus ruling out the X and pole configurations. It is also generally assumed that Jesus was crucified in an upright posture (as again Matt 27:37 presupposes). Of course, if the mass crucifixions near the end of the Jewish revolt are anything to go on (cf. Josephus, *J.W.* 5.11.1 §451: "the soldiers out of rage and hatred amused themselves by nailing their prisoners in different postures"), people could have been crucified upside down and in any number of different positions.

27 καὶ σὺν αὐτῷ σταυροῦσιν δύο λῃστάς, ἕνα ἐκ δεξιῶν καὶ ἕνα ἐξ εὐωνύμων αὐτοῦ, "And with him they crucify two rebels, one on the right, and one on his left." The crucifixion of two λῃστάς, "rebels," along with Jesus raises intriguing questions. Who were these men? Were they in any way related to Jesus and his following? And if they are called λῃστάς, with what had they been involved, and did it have anything to do with Jesus' movement? It is impossible to answer these questions (unless we accept the political-military thesis of S. G. F. Brandon, *The Trial of Jesus of Nazareth* [New York: Stein and Day, 1968]). Perhaps the most plausible speculation is that these men were associates of Barabbas, who was himself involved in an insurrection in which murder was committed (cf. 15:7). These two violent men, who had probably been involved in the same insurrection, were only naturally associated with Jesus, who had himself been condemned for apparently claiming to be Israel's anointed king. In Pilate's view it was only fitting for the three of them to be executed together.

28 καὶ ἐπληρώθη ἡ γραφὴ ἡ λέγουσα· καὶ μετὰ ἀνόμων ἐλογίσθη, "And the Scripture was fulfilled, which says, 'And he was reckoned with lawless persons.'" This verse, which quotes part of Isa 53:12, is a scribal gloss drawn from Luke 22:37 (see *Note* f). However, Rodgers (*EvQ* 61 [1989] 81–84) has argued that the verse was an original part of Mark but was deleted by a harmonizing scribe. This is doubtful.

29 καὶ οἱ παραπορευόμενοι ἐβλασφήμουν αὐτὸν κινοῦντες τὰς κεφαλὰς αὐτῶν, "And those passing by were ridiculing him, wagging their heads." οἱ παραπορευόμενοι, "those passing by," is consistent with the convention of crucifying criminals in public places or along major thoroughfares (cf. *Digest of Justinian* 48.19.28). We again have an allusion to Ps 22, this time to v 7: "All who see me mock at me, they make mouths at me, they wag the head" (RSV, adapted; see also Lam 2:15). Mark's plural κινοῦντες τὰς κεφαλὰς αὐτῶν, "wagging their heads," does not agree with either the LXX (21:8: ἐκίνησαν κεφαλήν, "they wagged [the] head") or the MT (22:8: יָנִיעוּ רֹאשׁ *yānîʿû rōʾš*, "they wag [the] head"), which both use the singular "head." However, Mark's language is Septuagintal. Once again the language of the story has been colored by the language and imagery of Scripture (Taylor, 591). The agreement, however, is not sufficient to conclude that the whole scene is the creation of pious imagination (cf. Cranfield, 456).

Literally, Mark says the passersby ἐβλασφήμουν, "were blaspheming," Jesus (in contrast, LXX Ps 21:8 reads ἐξεμυκτήρισαν, "were mocking"), which is probably intended to be ironic. That is, Jesus, falsely accused of blasphemy in 14:64 for truthfully identifying himself as God's anointed Son (an opinion shared by God himself in 1:11 and 9:7), is now being blasphemed by his tormentors who falsely accuse him of something that had been dismissed in court.

οὐὰ ὁ καταλύων τὸν ναὸν καὶ οἰκοδομῶν ἐν τρισὶν ἡμέραις, "Ha! You who would destroy the temple and build [another] in three days." The second person ("you") is taken from the second-person imperative and reflexive pronoun in v 30 (σῶσον σεαυτόν, "save yourself"). The mockery alludes to the allegation that Jesus had threatened to destroy the temple, a threat that at least some witnesses had mentioned to the ruling priests at the time of Jesus' hearing (cf. 14:58). No doubt Jesus' threatening words had gained some currency in and about Jerusalem. Jesus' talk of building another temple "in three days" seems quite ludicrous now that he hangs from the cross.

30 σῶσον σεαυτὸν καταβὰς ἀπὸ τοῦ σταυροῦ, "save yourself, having come down from the cross!" If Jesus can't save himself, how can he build another temple? How can he restore Israel? The mere fact of the crucifixion appears flatly to contradict Jesus' previous preaching and prophesying. Mark's readers know, of course, that Jesus had foretold his death and that by dying he would accomplish his Father's will. They also know that Jesus did indeed have the power to save himself and to come down from the cross. But to do so now would be to fail in his mission (Cranfield, 457).

31 ὁμοίως καὶ οἱ ἀρχιερεῖς ἐμπαίζοντες πρὸς ἀλλήλους μετὰ τῶν γραμματέων, "Likewise also the ruling priests, mocking among themselves with the scribes." The mocking is realistic, for it goes to the heart of the controversy between Jesus and the ruling priests. The major dispute concerned Jesus' criticisms of the temple establishment and his very public demonstration (cf. 11:15–18) as well as his not so thinly veiled threat that the ruling priests would be replaced and judged (12:1–12; 14:62). With Jesus nailed to the cross, helpless and dying, his threatening, judgmental words seem ludicrous. The danger he posed is past; the ruling priests can now have their fun. In like manner in an apocryphal work, false prophets mock Isaiah as he is sawn in two (cf. *Mart. Ascen. Isa.* 5:2–3).

ἄλλους ἔσωσεν, ἑαυτὸν οὐ δύναται σῶσαι, "Others he saved; himself he can't save!" This taunt casts doubt on the reality and efficacy of Jesus' prior acts of saving others. Because he cannot now save himself, the implication is that he probably has saved no one else, no matter what is rumored of him. His inability to save himself thus invalidates the legitimacy of his mission, which was to save Israel.

32 ὁ Χριστὸς ὁ βασιλεὺς Ἰσραὴλ καταβάτω νῦν ἀπὸ τοῦ σταυροῦ, "Let the Messiah, the king of Israel, come down from the cross now." The invitation hearkens back to Jesus' affirmation of the high priest's question, "Are you the Messiah, the son of the Blessed?" (14:61), and to Jesus' bold affirmation, "I am; and you will see 'the son of man' seated 'at the right hand' of the Power and 'coming with the clouds of heaven'" (14:62). Of course, the ruling priests invite Jesus to come down from the cross *now* (νῦν), knowing that he will indeed be taken down *later,* when dead. Let him come down now, without further delay. Let him demonstrate to all that he is indeed who he has claimed to be.

ἵνα ἴδωμεν καὶ πιστεύσωμεν, "so that we may see and believe!" If Jesus proves himself by coming down from the cross, even the ruling priests, his archenemies, will believe in him. But they must see first before they can have faith. In essence, the ruling priests, like the Pharisees before them (8:11–12), are demanding a sign. The logic of seeing and believing finds expression in Wis 2:17–18: "Let us see [ἴδωμεν] if his words are true, and let us test what will happen at the end of his life; for if the righteous man is God's son [υἱὸς θεοῦ], he will help him, and will deliver him from the hand of his adversaries." Though the thought here is parallel, it is doubtful that this text underlies the saying in Mark (so Taylor, 592).

οἱ συνεσταυρωμένοι σὺν αὐτῷ ὠνείδιζον αὐτόν, "those crucified with him were reviling him." Jesus is completely alone; he has no allies, not even among those who share his fate. These men are συνεσταυρωμένοι σὺν αὐτῷ, "crucified with him," but clearly not in the Pauline sense (Rom 6:6; Gal 2:20). The prefix σύν, "with," indicates that they are crucified at the same time and place. In Paul it means to join with Jesus and to identify with his experience (as foretold to James and John in Mark 10:38–39). The rebels (v 27) revile Jesus out of their fear and anguish. Their own hopes and aspirations have been foiled, so they reproach Jesus for having made even grander plans that seemingly have also gone unfulfilled. If these men had been part of Jesus' following (and there is no evidence that they had been), then their rage at Jesus would be all the more understandable. The mockery of Jesus is now complete.

33 καὶ γενομένης ὥρας ἕκτης σκότος ἐγένετο ἐφ᾽ ὅλην τὴν γῆν ἕως ὥρας ἐνάτης, "And when the sixth hour had come, darkness fell over the whole land until the ninth hour." It is now noon; Jesus has hung on the cross for three hours (cf. v 25). At the brightest time of the day, "darkness fell over the whole land until the ninth hour," that is, until 3:00 P.M. This is the first of two preternatural events (the second is the tearing of the temple veil in v 38). In late antiquity in Jewish (*b. Mo'ed Qaṭ.* 25b) as well as in Roman traditions (Diogenes Laertius, 4.64: at the death of Carneades "the moon is said to have been eclipsed"; Plutarch, *Caes.* 69.3–5; Virgil, *Georg.* 1.463–68, where the sun hid its face in response to the death of Caesar), strange events and omens were thought often to attend the death of great figures. The darkness may also allude ominously to such biblical stories as Exod 10:22, implying that divine judgment is being visited upon the earth (cf. Jer 15:9; Joel 2:10; Amos 8:9). Gundry (947) thinks the darkness implies that God has hidden his son from the leering of his tormentors. In view of the cry of abandonment in v 34, perhaps it is better to think that God has hidden his face from his son.

34 καὶ τῇ ἐνάτῃ ὥρᾳ ἐβόησεν ὁ Ἰησοῦς φωνῇ μεγάλῃ, "And at the ninth hour Jesus cried with a loud voice." Jesus, having hung on the cross for six hours (from

9:00 A.M. to 3:00 P.M.), suddenly ἐβόησεν . . . φωνῇ μεγάλῃ, "cried with a loud voice." The loudness of the cry lends further drama to the scene. Jesus does not expire with a gasp or a whimper; he cries out loudly and unexpectedly.

ἐλωί ἐλωί λεμὰ σαβαχθανί; ὅ ἐστιν μεθερμηνευόμενον· ὁ θεός μου ὁ θεός μου, εἰς τί ἐγκατέλιπές με, "'Eloi, Eloi, lema sabachthani?' which means, 'My God, my God, why have you abandoned me?'" The darkness of the land signifies judgment; that Jesus cries out the way he does suggests that divine judgment has in part fallen on him. This is consistent with his earlier allusion to Zech 13:7 in Mark 14:27. In rejecting God's son (see the parable of the Vineyard Tenants in 12:1–12) God strikes his own people, beginning with Israel's shepherd. Darkness covers the land as God looks away from the obscenity that has taken place. (The variant in *Gos. Pet.* 5.19, ἡ δύναμίς μου, ἡ δύναμίς [μου], "My Power, [my] Power," is clearly a secondary, probably docetic, gloss.) Burchard (*ZNW* 74 [1983] 1–11) rightly comments that there is nothing in Mark's account that has prepared its readers for this shocking cry.

Jesus has quoted Ps 22:1, a psalm whose details have been echoed in various places in the Passion Narrative. Here we have an explicit quotation and one that is on the lips of Jesus (as was Zech 13:7 in Mark 14:27). Some wonder if Jesus has the whole psalm in mind, especially the concluding part that relates vindication and restoration:

> I will tell of thy name to my brethren;
>> in the midst of the congregation I will praise thee. . . .
> For he has not despised or abhorred the affliction of the afflicted;
>> and he has not hid his face from him,
>> but has heard, when he cried to him. . . .
> Posterity shall serve him;
>> men shall tell of the Lord to the coming generation,
> and proclaim his deliverance to a people yet unborn,
>> that he has wrought it. (vv 22, 24, 30–31)

Perhaps Jesus did have the whole of the psalm in mind, including the optimistic conclusion (see the excellent treatment in Marcus, *Way of the Lord,* 180–86), but the reality of his sense of abandonment must not be minimized. Jesus has not lost his faith in God, as the twofold address, "My God, my God," implies, but he feels utterly abandoned. It is not surprising that the later evangelists choose different concluding utterances: "Father, into thy hands I commit my spirit!" (Luke 23:46); "It is finished" (John 19:30).

Very problematic and unconvincing is Cohn-Sherbok's (*ExpTim* 93 [1981–82] 215–17) speculative suggestion that Jesus' Aramaic words have been misunderstood and misrendered into Greek and that he really said "My God, my God, why have you praised me?"

35 τινὲς τῶν παρεστηκότων ἀκούσαντες ἔλεγον, ἴδε Ἠλίαν φωνεῖ, "some bystanders, listening, were saying, 'Behold, he calls Elijah.'" Bystanders think Jesus has called for Elijah (ἐλωί = Aramaic אֱלָהּ *'ĕlāhî,* "my God" [see *Note* j], approximating the sound of אֵלִיָּה *'ēliyyâ,* "Elijah"; cf. Matt 27:46, whose Hebraizing ἠλί = אֵלִי *'ēlî,* "my God," more closely resembles the name of Elijah), an eschatological figure who would come (cf. 9:12: "Elijah, coming first, does restore all things"; Sir 48:10) and rescue the righteous (cf. *b. ʿAbod. Zar.* 17b; *b. Taʿan.* 21a; *Pesiq. Rab.*

Kah. 18.5; *Gen. Rab.* 33.3 [on Gen 8:1]; and Caza, *ScEs* 39 [1987] 171–91, who calls attention to traditions of Elijah coming to aid the afflicted). These bystanders are probably Jewish, for Gentiles were not likely to hear an Aramaic or Hebrew allusion to the name of Elijah (Cranfield, 459). Jesus again cries out and dies. The loud shout, instead of a dying moan, tells of Jesus' power even in death (Gundry, 947). Reference to Elijah is not an ironical allusion to John the Baptist, who has already come (*pace* Brower, *JSNT* 18 [1983] 85–101).

36 δραμὼν δέ τις [καὶ] γεμίσας σπόγγον ὄξους περιθεὶς καλάμῳ ἐπότιζεν αὐτόν, "But someone, running up, having filled a sponge with vinegar, having placed it on a reed, gave it to him to drink." Cranfield (459) thinks this τὶς, "someone," was a soldier. This would have to assume, given what he said, that he recognized the possible allusion to Elijah. Of course, he may have learned this from the Jewish bystanders. It may be that the "someone" who ran up to Jesus with the vinegar-filled sponge was one of the Jewish bystanders. If his act was one of mockery and not sympathy, the soldiers probably would not have hindered him. In any event, "wine mixed with myrrh" (v 23) had already been offered to Jesus. The tradition has been shaped somewhat by Ps 69:21 (= LXX 68:22), whose words ἐπότισάν με ὄξος, "they gave me vinegar to drink," are echoed in ὄξους . . . ἐπότιζεν αὐτόν, "with vinegar . . . gave it to him to drink."

ἄφετε ἴδωμεν εἰ ἔρχεται Ἡλίας καθελεῖν αὐτόν, "Permit [me]; let us see if Elijah comes to take him down." ἴδωμεν εἰ ἔρχεται Ἡλίας, "let us see if Elijah comes," may be part of the mockery and, if so, parallels what the ruling priests said in v 32: "Let the Messiah, the king of Israel, come down from the cross now, so that we may see [ἴδωμεν] and believe" (Marcus, *Way of the Lord*, 184). It is possible that a sympathetic bystander races up to Jesus to give him a stimulant to help keep him conscious long enough to see if Elijah would indeed appear either in his eschatological role (as Jesus, it would have been assumed, hoped) or in his occasional role as assistant of the troubled and stricken (see *Comment* on v 35). It is more probable, however, that the gesture is part of the mockery that has been going on periodically since the conclusion of the hearing before the ruling priests (14:65). While on the cross, Jesus has been mocked as the one who threatened to destroy and rebuild the temple in three days (v 29) and he has been invited to come down from the cross to convince skeptics that he really is Israel's King Messiah (v 32). Now the mockers wish to see if Elijah comes in answer to Jesus' anguished cry.

37 ὁ δὲ Ἰησοῦς ἀφεὶς φωνὴν μεγάλην ἐξέπνευσεν, "But Jesus, after letting out a loud cry, expired." Once again Jesus is said to have uttered, or more literally to have "let out" or to have "released" (ἀφείς), a φωνὴν μεγάλην, "loud cry," just as he had in v 34 (ἐβόησεν . . . φωνῇ μεγάλῃ, "cried with a loud voice"). The use of ἀφιέναι meaning "to let out" a voice is attested in Demosthenes 18.218 and Euripides, *Hipp.* 418; *El.* 59. Gundry (948) is correct in understanding that the act of shouting is itself the death. That is, Jesus does not shout out and then a moment later die. His death manifests itself *as a shout*. By telling it this way, the evangelist, if not the tradition before him, shows that Jesus' very death displays his power; the release of his spirit (as implied in the verb ἐξέπνευσεν, "expired") is awesome.

38 τὸ καταπέτασμα τοῦ ναοῦ ἐσχίσθη εἰς δύο ἀπ' ἄνωθεν ἕως κάτω, "And the veil of the temple was torn in two, from top to bottom." The power of Jesus is displayed in his death audibly in the loud shout of v 37, but it is displayed even more impressively and more tangibly in the tearing of the καταπέτασμα τοῦ ναοῦ, "veil of the temple." That the tearing of the veil is the result of Jesus' sudden expiration, and not merely a coincidental omen, is probable (Gundry, 948–50). This death shout and the tearing of the temple veil constitute a single action that counters all of the previous mocking. Jesus, mocked as a pseudo-prophet (14:65) and pseudo-messiah (15:32), who in his despair actually thinks Elijah might come to his aid (15:36), surprises the onlookers with an unexpectedly and inexplicably powerful shout, the force of which actually tears the temple veil. He who had spoken of the temple's destruction (cf. 13:2; 14:58) has now on the cross struck it with his dying breath, tearing the veil ἀπ' ἄνωθεν ἕως κάτω, "from top to bottom," that is, tearing it completely. Just as the descent of the Holy Spirit upon Jesus at his baptism tore the heavens (1:10, σχιζομένους), so now the loud exhalation of Jesus' spirit has torn (ἐσχίσθη) the veil of the temple. This interpretation gains support from a study by Ulansey (*JBL* 110 [1991] 123–25), who draws our attention to Josephus's description of the outer veil as "a panorama of the entire heavens" (*J.W.* 5.5.4 §214). Ulansey rightly wonders if in the tearing of this veil we have a parallel to the tearing of the heavens at the time of Jesus' baptism. The tearing of the veil is not a Markan Pentecost (*pace* Motyer, *NTS* 33 [1987] 155–57). Chronis (*JBL* 101 [1982] 97–114) is correct to say that in Jesus' death his true identity is revealed, as the centurion will himself immediately acknowledge (in v 39), but Chronis goes too far in saying that the torn veil is equivalent to God showing his "face."

The torn veil is but a token of the complete destruction that will someday befall the temple (cf. Jackson, *NTS* 33 [1987] 16–37), when "not one stone will be left here upon another that will not be thrown down" (13:2). It is also the first step in the promised judgment that will overtake Jesus' priestly judges (14:62). It is the second supernatural sign that has taken place during the crucixifion, the first being the odd darkness that fell upon the land (v 33). The parallel in the *Testaments of the Twelve Patriarchs* has occasioned discussion: "And you shall act lawlessly in Israel, with the result that Jerusalem cannot bear the presence of your wickedness, but the veil of the Temple will be torn [σχίσαι τὸ ἔνδυμα τοῦ ναοῦ], so that it will no longer conceal your shame" (*T. Levi* 10:3). H. C. Kee ("Testaments of the Twelve Patriarchs," in *OTP* 1:792 n. b) thinks that the text may have been tampered with by a Christian (some MSS of *T. Levi* in fact read καταπέτασμα, "veil"); it may originally have read "the garment of the Temple will be torn." The veil of the temple cannot be said to have concealed shame; Kee's proposed emendation is probably correct. But the prediction found in the *Lives of the Prophets* offers a more exact parallel: "And concerning the end of the Temple he [i.e., Habakkuk] predicted, 'By a western nation it will happen.' 'At that time,' he said, 'the curtain [ἅπλωμα] of the Dabeir [i.e., the holy of holies] will be torn into small pieces'" (*Liv. Pro.* 12:11–12). D. R. A. Hare ("Lives of the Prophets," in *OTP* 2:393 n. i) believes this is a genuine pre-70 prediction that reflects growing unease over the increasing presence of Gentiles in and around Jerusalem. According to Josephus (*J.W.* 6.5.3–4 §§288–315) and later rabbinic traditions (*y. Soṭah* 6.3; *b. Giṭ.* 56a; *b. Yoma* 39b), there were many odd occurrences in the temple that were interpreted as fearful omens that foretold the temple's destruction. Mark's story of the tearing of the temple veil will have impressed Mark's Jewish readers, who were perhaps familiar with some of these traditions (cf. also Tacitus, *Hist.* 5.13; Jerome, *Epist.* 120.8.1). The Talmud records a tradition (very probably apocryphal) that the Roman general Titus slashed the temple veil with his sword (*b. Giṭ.* 56b).

The veil (τὸ καταπέτασμα) should probably be understood as the veil that enshrouded the holy of holies. It is the word used in the LXX (e.g., Exod 26:31–37). However, the outer veil, which covered the entrance to the holy place (Exod 27:16) and was easier to see, may be what is in mind in the Markan story. Against identification with the outer veil is the fact that it is usually called τὸ κάλυμμα (as in LXX Exod 27:16 and elsewhere), though there are some exceptions. Commentators are divided on the question of which veil is meant, with some favoring the inner (Gould, 295; Swete, 388; Turner, 79; Rawlinson, 238) and others the outer (Klostermann, 186; Lohmeyer, 347; Jackson, *NTS* 33 [1987] 16–37; Ulansey, *JBL* 110 [1991] 123–25). Pesch (2:498) asserts that the evidence does not allow for determining which veil is meant. Taylor (*Formation,* 58) makes the intriguing suggestion that v 38 may have been "originally a Pauline comment."

39 ἰδὼν δὲ ὁ κεντυρίων ὁ παρεστηκὼς ἐξ ἐναντίας αὐτοῦ ὅτι οὕτως ἐξέπνευσεν, "But the centurion who stood opposite him, seeing that he had died in this way." That is, the centurion has observed the power of Jesus' expiration, his breathing out (ἐξέπνευσεν) that tore the temple veil. ὁ παρεστηκὼς ἐξ ἐναντίας αὐτοῦ, "who stood opposite him," should be taken to mean that the centurion is standing before Jesus, as opposed to behind him or off to the side. Thus, he witnesses fully the powerful shout and consequent tearing of the temple veil (Jackson, *NTS* 33 [1987] 28; Gundry, 950–51).

ἀληθῶς οὗτος ὁ ἄνθρωπος υἱὸς θεοῦ ἦν, "Truly this man was the son of God!" When the heavens were torn at Jesus' baptism, God declared, "You are my beloved Son!" (1:11 RSV, adapted). With the tearing of the temple veil, a human declares in agreement with God himself, "Truly this man was the son of God!" Impressed by the manner of Jesus' death and the signs that attend it, the Roman centurion confesses of Jesus what he should only confess of the Roman emperor. Caesar is not the "son of God"; Jesus, the crucified Messiah, is. The mockery is now over. In calling Jesus the "son of God," the centurion has switched his allegiance from Caesar, the official "son of God," to Jesus, the real Son of God (on the range of meanings of this epithet, see Hengel, *Son of God*). However, it is probably to read too much into the centurion's declaration to understand it as an "orthodox" Christian confession (*pace* Taylor, 597; cf. Davis, *JSNT* 35 [1989] 3–18; Johnson, *JSNT* 31 [1987] 3–22; id., *Bib* 81 [2000] 406–13) or as the signal that the veil of the messianic secret has finally been lifted (as is rightly criticized by Shiner, *JSNT* 78 [2000] 3–22). The centurion now ascribes to Jesus what he had earlier ascribed to Caesar: Caesar is not *divi filius,* "son of God" (alluding to the title of the great emperor Augustus), but Jesus ís (see Kim, *Bib* 79 [1998] 221–41; and "Theology of Mark" in the *Introduction*).

40 ἦσαν δὲ καὶ γυναῖκες ἀπὸ μακρόθεν θεωροῦσαι, "But there were also women there watching from a distance." The surprising confession of the centurion, brought on by the stunning and awesome shout of Jesus, brings the death scene to a close. But the evangelist must prepare for the discovery of the empty tomb in 16:1–8, so he appends the notice of the women who observe all that happened. They are witnesses to the amazing events that take place when Jesus is crucified, and they will be witnesses to the empty tomb, yet one more dramatic omen that attends the death of Jesus. (Noting that the women saw where Jesus was buried in 15:47 serves the same purpose.)

Μαρία ἡ Μαγδαληνή, "Mary Magdalene." There are several women in the NT named Mary. Μαρία is a Greek or Latin (*Maria*) form of the Semitic name מִרְיָם *Miryām*, "Miriam." Mary Magdalene is so named because she is from the town of Magdala (possibly meaning the "the fish tower"). She figures prominently in the Gospel tradition, particularly at the crucifixion and resurrection (Matt 27:56, 61; 28:1; Mark 15:47; 16:1, [9]; Luke 24:10; John 19:25; 20:1, 11, 16, 18). According to Luke 8:2, "seven demons had gone out" of Mary Magdalene.

Μαρία ἡ Ἰακώβου τοῦ μικροῦ καὶ Ἰωσῆτος μήτηρ, "Mary the mother of James the younger and of Joses." According to John 19:25, one "Mary the wife of Clopas" was near the cross with Mary Magdalene. Perhaps this should be understood as the same Mary who was the mother of James and Joses (or "Joseph" [Matt 27:56]).

Σαλώμη, "Salome." If we follow the Matthean parallel, then this Salome might be the otherwise unnamed "mother of the sons of Zebedee" (Matt 27:56). For further discussion, see Bauckham, *NovT* 33 (1991) 245–75.

41 αἳ ὅτε ἦν ἐν τῇ Γαλιλαίᾳ ἠκολούθουν αὐτῷ καὶ διηκόνουν αὐτῷ, "who, when he was in Galilee, were following him and were serving him." One of the interesting and unusual features of Jesus' ministry was the presence of several women who numbered among his disciples. Although they διηκόνουν, "were serving," Jesus and the other disciples, they also sat at his feet and were taught, even as were the men (Luke 10:38–42). This is why Mark says they ἠκολούθουν αὐτῷ, "were following him," which implies discipleship. For Jesus had called his male disciples to follow him (e.g., 1:16–20). Luke 8:3 also mentions the names of other women, such as "Joanna, the wife of Chuza, Herod's steward, and Susanna, and many others," who provided for Jesus and his disciples "out of their means." Given the high value that Jesus placed on serving (cf. esp. Mark 10:45) as well as generosity (cf. esp. Mark 10:21–22), the service of these women in the Jesus movement should not be viewed in a servile sense.

καὶ ἄλλαι πολλαὶ αἱ συναναβᾶσαι αὐτῷ εἰς Ἱεροσόλυμα, "and many other women who had come up with him to Jerusalem." The one who anointed Jesus' head (14:3–9) may very well have been one of these women. The evangelist says συναναβᾶσαι, "had come up," because the hills of Judea, especially those of Jerusalem itself, are higher in elevation than the lower lands of Galilee and especially the Jordan Valley.

Explanation

At Golgotha what Jesus foretold finally takes place. Several times he had predicted his passion (8:31; 9:31; 10:33–34) to frightened, uncomprehending disciples. Now he is taken out to be crucified, the most fearful, painful, shameful form of execution practiced in late antiquity. Although we are not told so explicitly, Jesus evidently is so weakened from the physical abuse that he had experienced during the night that he is unable to carry the cross beam of his cross to the place of execution. One Simon of Cyrene is compelled to carry the cross. Jesus is brought to Golgotha, that grim place whose name means "Place of the Skull." There Jesus is crucified and his clothing is divided among the soldiers. Following this indignity, Jesus is subjected to one form of mockery after another. The *titulus* that reads "The King of the Jews" on one level refers to the criminal charge, but on another level it is surely understood in an ironical sense. Jesus is ridiculed (or "blasphemed") and taunted with a variety of sarcastic remarks: "save yourself," "others he saved; himself he can't save," "let the Messiah, the king of Israel, come down from the cross," "behold, he calls Elijah; . . . let us see if Elijah comes to take him down." Jesus is all alone; his disciples abandoned him when he was arrested the night before, an arrest made possible by the treachery of Judas Iscariot. Even Peter, who had dared to follow the arresting party into the courtyard of the high priest's home, lost his nerve and denied knowing Jesus. Now hanging on the cross and being jeered at by his executioners and curious bystanders, the rebels crucified with him revile him. Even Jesus himself feels abandoned by his Father and so cries out, "My God, my God, why have you abandoned me?"

But important details appear in this sorrowful narrative that hint at divine vindication. A strange darkness suddenly falls over the land. Evidently, the execution of Jesus has not gone unnoticed by the heavens, which recoil from viewing the spectacle. When Jesus cries out in death, the force of his expiration tears the veil of the temple from top to bottom, prompting the centurion, who (we may rightly assume) only moments earlier had taken part in the cruel jesting, to confess of Jesus, "Truly this man was the son of God!" The abruptness and profoundness of the centurion's reassessment of Jesus would have stunned the Roman readership of Mark. The centurion acknowledges that this crucified Jesus of Nazareth is the true son of God, not "divine" Caesar as the imperial cult would have it. The omens witnessed thus far, the darkness and the torn temple veil, lend credibility to the centurion's confession and so do the many astounding feats performed by Jesus in his public ministry, but the most amazing omen of all is yet to take place.

The scene concludes with the notation of the women who witness the crucifixion. They stand in stark contrast to the disciples who had fled, and so in some ways model discipleship better than do the Twelve themselves. These women will also be the first to discover the empty tomb and to learn of the resurrection of Jesus. Their firsthand witness of the resurrection constitutes yet one more mark of distinction.

Thus far the reader of Mark's Gospel has seen that Jesus predicted his passion with uncanny accuracy. He was indeed condemned by the ruling priests, elders, and scribes and was handed over to Gentiles to be mocked, spit upon, scourged, and crucified. But Jesus also predicted that "after three days" he would be raised up. It is one thing to predict one's death and then die, but the fulfillment of one's predicted resurrection is another matter. In a short time the truth of this prediction will be known.

N. The Burial of Jesus   (15:42–47)

Bibliography

Ambrozic, A. M. *Hidden Kingdom.* 240–43. **Barrick, W. B.** "The Rich Man from Arimathea (Matt 27:57–60) and 1QIsaᵃ." *JBL* 96 (1977) 235–39. **Bauckham, R. J.** *Jude and the Relatives of*

Jesus in the Early Church. Edinburgh: T. & T. Clark, 1990. 9–15. **Benoit, P.** *Passion and Resurrection.* 205–30. **Blinzler, J.** *Die Brüder und Schwestern Jesu.* SBS 21. Stuttgart: Katholisches Bibelwerk, 1967. 73–86. ———. "Die Grablegung Jesu in historischer Sicht." In *Resurrexit: Actes du symposium international sur la résurrection de Jésus (Rome 31 Mars–6 Avril 1970).* Ed. E. Dhanis. Rome: Editrice Vaticana, 1974. 56–107. ———. "'Sindon' in Evangeliis: Rectificatio." *VD* 34 (1956) 112–13. ———. "Zur Auslegung der Evangelienberichte über Jesu Begräbnis." *MTZ* 3 (1952) 403–14. **Bornhäuser, K.** "Die Kreuzesabnahme und das Begräbnis Jesu." *NKZ* 42 (1931) 38–56. **Brändle, M.** "Die synoptischen Grabeserzählungen." *Orientierung* 31 (1967) 179–84. **Braun, F.-M.** "La sépulture de Jésus." *RB* 45 (1936) 34–52, 184–200, 346–63. **Briend, J.** "La sépulture d'un crucifié." *BTS* 133 (1971) 6–10. **Broer, I.** *Die Urgemeinde und das Grab Jesu: Eine Analyse der Grablegungsgeschichte im Neuen Testament.* SANT 31. Munich: Kösel, 1972. 79–82, 87–200. **Brown, R. E.** "The Burial of Jesus (Mark 15:42–47)." *CBQ* 50 (1988) 233–45. **Bulst, W.** "Untersuchungen zum Begräbnis Christi." *MTZ* 3 (1952) 244–55. **Cox Evans, L. E.** "The Holy Sepulchre." *PEQ* 100 (1968) 112–36. **Crossan, J. D.** "Empty Tomb and Absent Lord (Mark 16:1–8)." In *The Passion in Mark.* Ed. W. H. Kelber. 135–152. ———. *Historical Jesus.* 354–94. ———. "Mark and the Relatives of Jesus." *NovT* 15 (1973) 81–113, esp. 105–10. ———. *Who Killed Jesus?* San Franciso: HarperCollins, 1995. 160–88. **Dhanis, E.** "L'ensevelissement de Jésus et la visite au tombeau dans l'évangile de saint Marc (xv,40–xvi,8)." *Greg* 39 (1958) 367–410. **Dobschütz, E. von.** "Joseph von Arimathia." *ZKG* 23 (1902) 1–17. **Donfried, K. P.** "Mary in the Gospel of Mark." In *Mary in the New Testament: A Collaborative Assessment by Protestant and Roman Catholic Scholars.* Ed. R. E. Brown et al. Philadelphia: Fortress; New York: Paulist, 1978. 51–72, esp. 68–72. **Dormeyer, D.** *Die Passion Jesu.* 216–21, 235–37. **Fuller, R. H.** *The Formation of the Resurrection Narratives.* 2nd ed. Philadelphia: Fortress, 1980. 52–57. **Gaechter, P.** "Zum Begräbnis Jesu." *ZKT* 75 (1953) 220–25. **Grass, H.** *Ostergeschehen und Osterberichte.* 2nd ed. Göttingen: Vandenhoeck & Ruprecht, 1962. 173–83. **Hengel, M.** *Crucifixion in the Ancient World and the Folly of the Message of the Cross.* London: SCM Press; Philadelphia: Fortress, 1977. **Holtzmann, O.** "Das Begräbnis Jesu." *ZNW* 30 (1931) 311–13. **Jackson, C.** "Joseph of Arimathea." *JR* 16 (1936) 332–40. **Kennard, J. S., Jr.** "The Burial of Jesus." *JBL* 74 (1955) 227–38. **Kratz, R.** *Rettungswunder: Motiv-, traditions- und formkritische Aufarbeitung einer biblischen Gattung.* Frankfurt am Main; Bern: Lang, 1979. 500–510. **Kremer, J.** *Das Ärgernis des Kreuzes: Eine Hinführung zum Verstehen der Leidensgeschichte nach Markus.* Stuttgart: Katholisches Bibelwerk, 1969. 80–84. **Masson, C.** "L'ensevelissement de Jésus (Marc xv,42–47)." *RTP* 31 (1943) 192–203. **Matera, F. J.** *The Kingship of Jesus: Composition and Theology in Mark 15.* SBLDS 66. Chico, CA: Scholars Press, 1982. 48–56. **McCane, B. R.** "'Where No One Had Yet Been Laid': The Shame of Jesus' Burial." In *Society of Biblical Literature 1993 Seminar Papers.* Ed. E. H. Lovering, Jr. SBLSP 32. Atlanta: Scholars Press, 1993. 473–84 (revised and expanded in *Authenticating the Activities of Jesus.* Ed. B. D. Chilton and C. A. Evans. NTTS 28.2. Leiden: Brill, 1998. 431–52). **Mercurio, R.** "A Baptismal Motif in the Gospel Narratives of the Burial." *CBQ* 21 (1959) 39–54. **Meye, R. P.** *Jesus and the Twelve.* 167–71. **Mohr, T. A.** *Markus- und Johannespassion.* 351–64. **Oberlinner, L.** *Historische Überlieferung und christologische Aussage: Zur Frage der "Brüder Jesu" in der Synopse.* FB 19. Stuttgart: Katholisches Bibelwerk, 1975. 86–148. **O'Rahilly, A.** "The Burial of Christ." *IER* 58 (1941) 302–16, 493–503; 59 (1942) 150–71. **Perrin, N.** *The Resurrection according to Matthew, Mark, and Luke.* Philadelphia: Fortress, 1977. 14–38. **Pesch, R.** *Das Evangelium der Urgemeinde.* 213–15. ———. "Der Schluss der vormarkinischen Passionsgeschichte und des Markus-evangeliums: Mk 15,42–16,8." In *L'Évangile selon Marc.* Ed. M. Sabbe. 365–409. **Price, R. M.** "Jesus' Burial in a Garden: The Strange Growth of the Tradition." *Religious Traditions* 12 (1989) 17–30. **Riesner, R.** "Golgota und die Archaeologie." *BK* 40 (1985) 21–26. **Sariola, H.** *Markus und das Gesetz.* 115–17. **Schenk, W.** *Der Passionsbericht nach Markus.* 254–58. **Schenke, L.** *Auferstehungsverkündigung und leeres Grab.* SBS 33. Stuttgart: Katholisches Bibelwerk, 1968. 15–20. ———. *Der gekreuzigte Christus.* 78–83. **Schneider, G.** *Die Passion Jesu.* 136–40. **Scholz, G.** "'Joseph von Arimathäa' und 'Barabbas.'" *LB* 57 (1985) 81–94. **Schottroff, L.** "Frauen in der Nachfolge Jesu in neutestamentlicher Zeit." In *Frauen in der Bibel.* Vol. 2 of *Traditionen der*

Befreiung: Sozialgeschichtliche Bibelauslegungen. Ed. W. Schottroff and W. Stegemann. Munich: Kaiser, 1980. 91–133 (ET: "Women as Disciples of Jesus in New Testament Times." In L. Schottroff. *Let the Oppressed Go Free: Feminist Perspectives on the New Testament.* Louisville: Westminster John Knox, 1993). **Schreiber, J.** "Die Bestattung Jesu: Redaktionsgeschichtliche Beobachtungen zu Mk 15,42–47 par." *ZNW* 72 (1981) 141–77. **Schweizer, E.** "Scheidungsrecht der jüdischen Frau? Weibliche Jünger Jesu?" *EvT* 42 (1982) 294–300. **Senior, D.** *Passion of Jesus in the Gospel of Mark.* 132–35. **Smith, R. H.** "The Tomb of Jesus." *BA* 30 (1967) 74–90. **Standaert, B. H. M. G. M.** *L'évangile selon Marc.* 168–72. **Westcott, B. F.,** and **Hort, F. J. A.** *Introduction.* 2:28. **Williams, J. F.** *Other Followers of Jesus.* 188–91.

Bibliography on Jewish Burial Practices

Bloch-Smith, E. *Judahite Burial Practices and Beliefs about the Dead.* JSOTSup 123. Sheffield: JSOT Press, 1992. **Buchler, A.** "L'enterrement des criminels d'après le Talmud et le Midrasch." *REJ* 46 (1903) 74–88. **Cousin, H.** "Sépulture criminelle et sépulture prophétique." *RB* 81 (1974) 375–93. **Daube, D.** "The Anointing at Bethany and Jesus' Burial." *ATR* 32 (1950) 186–99 (repr. in D. Daube. *The New Testament and Rabbinic Judaism.* Jordan Lectures 2. London: Athlone, 1956. 312–24). **Figueras, P.** *Decorated Jewish Ossuaries.* DMOA 20. Leiden: Brill, 1985. ———. "Jewish Ossuaries and Secondary Burial: Their Significance for Early Christianity." *Imm* 19 (1984–85) 41–57. **Gafni, Y.** "Reinterment in the Land of Israel: Notes on the Origin and Development of the Custom." *The Jerusalem Cathedra* 1 (1981) 96–104. **Greenhut, Z.** "Burial Cave of the Caiaphas Family." *BAR* 18.5 (1992) 29–36, 76. ———. "The Caiaphas Tomb in North Talpiyot, Jerusalem." *ʿAtiqot* 21 (1992) 63–71. **Haas, N.** "Anthropological Observations on the Skeletal Remains from Givʿat ha-Mivtar." *IEJ* 20 (1970) 38–59. **Hachlili, R.** "Burials: Ancient Jewish." *ABD* 1:789–94. ———. "The Goliath Family in Jericho: Funerary Inscriptions from a First Century A.D. Jewish Monumental Tomb." *BASOR* 235 (1979) 31–65. ———. "A Second Temple Period Necropolis in Jericho." *BA* 43 (1980) 235–40. ———. "Wall Painting in the Jewish Monumental Tomb at Jericho." *PEQ* 117 (1985) 112–27. ——— and **Jeremias, J.** *Heiligengräber in Jesu Umwelt.* Göttingen: Vandenhoeck & Ruprecht, 1958. **Kahane, P.** "Pottery Types from the Jewish Ossuary Tombs around Jerusalem." *IEJ* 2 (1952) 125–39, 176–82; 3 (1953) 48–54. **Killebrew, A.** "Jewish Funerary Customs during the Second Temple Period in Light of the Excavations at the Jericho Necropolis." *PEQ* 115 (1983) 109–39. **Klein, S.** *Tod und Begräbnis in Palästina zur Zeit der Tannaiten.* Berlin: Itzowski, 1908. **Lieberman, S.** "Some Aspects of Afterlife in Early Rabbinic Literature." In *Texts and Studies.* New York: Ktav, 1974. 235–73. **Liebowitz, H.** "Jewish Burial Practices in the Roman World." *ManQ* 22 (1981–82) 107–17. **Meyers, E. M.** *Jewish Ossuaries: Reburial and Rebirth.* Rome: Pontifical Biblical Institute, 1971. ———. "Secondary Burials in Palestine." *BA* 33 (1970) 2–29. **Michel, O.** "Jüdische Bestattung und urchristliche Östergeschichte." *Judaica* 16 (1960) 1–5. **O'Rahilly, A.** "Jewish Burial." *IER* 58 (1941) 123–35. **Oren, E. D.,** and **Rappaport, U.** "The Necropolis of Maresha—Beth Guvrin." *IEJ* 34 (1984) 114–53. **Puech, É.** "Les nécropoles juives palestiniennes au tournant de notre ère." In *Dieu l'a resuscité d'entre les morts.* Les quatres fleuves 15–16. Paris: Beauchesne, 1982. 35–55. **Rahmani, L. Y.** "Ancient Jerusalem's Funerary Customs and Tombs." *BA* 44 (1981) 171–77, 229–35; 45 (1982) 43–53, 109–19. ———. "Jewish Rock-Cut Tombs in Jerusalem." *ʿAtiqot* 3 (1961) 91–120. ———. "A Jewish Tomb on Shahin Hill, Jerusalem." *IEJ* 8 (1958) 101–5. **Reich, R.** "Caiaphas Name Inscribed on Bone Boxes." *BAR* 18.5 (1992) 38–44, 76. **Strange, J. F.** "Late Hellenistic and Herodian Ossuary Tombs at French Hill, Jerusalem." *BASOR* 219 (1975) 39–67. **Toynbee, J. M. C.** *Death and Burial in the Roman World.* Ithaca, NY: Cornell UP, 1971. **Tzaferis, V.** "Jewish Tombs at and near Givʿat ha-Mivtar, Jerusalem." *IEJ* 20 (1970) 18–32. **Zias, J.,** and **Sekeles, E.** "The Crucified Man from Givʿat ha-Mivtar: A Reappraisal." *IEJ* 35 (1985) 22–27.

Translation

[42] *And when evening had already come, since it was [the day of] Preparation, that is, [the day] before the Sabbath,* [43] *Joseph from Arimathea,[a] a respected member of the council, who also himself was expecting the kingdom of God, having come, being bold, went to Pilate and requested the body[b] of Jesus.* [44] *But Pilate[c] was surprised that he had already died, and summoning the centurion, he asked him if he had by now[d] died.* [45] *And learning from the centurion [that he was dead],[e] he gave the corpse[f] to Joseph.[g]* [46] *And buying a linen shroud, [and] taking him down, he[h] wrapped [him] in the linen shroud, and laid him in a tomb, which had been hewn out of rock; and he rolled a stone[i] against the door of the tomb.[j]* [47] *Now Mary Magdalene and Mary the [mother][k] of Joses[l] were observing where[m] he had been laid.*

Notes

[a]Gk. Ἀριμαθαίας. ℵ^c D and a few late MSS read Ἀριμαθίας. ℵ* B* read Ἀρειμαθαίας. Other attested spellings include Ἀρημαθίας, Ἀριμαθέας, Ἀριματθαίας, and in Syr. MSS "Ramtha" and "Ramthis." A few late MSS add πόλεως, "city," an addition inspired by Luke 23:51. It is thought that Arimathea might be the city Ῥαμαθαίν, "Ramathain," mentioned by Josephus (*Ant.* 13.4.9 §127), which may be the city רָמָתַיִם *rāmātayim*, "Ramathaim," mentioned in 1 Sam 1:1 (see *Comment* on v 43).

[b]Gk. σῶμα. D reads πτῶμα, "corpse." An OL MS reads *cadaver*, "corpse." This variant is probably the result of agreement with v 45.

[c]On the spelling of Pilate's name, see *Note* d on Mark 15:1.

[d]Gk. πάλαι, lit. "long ago," which is read by ℵ A C L 33 and several later MSS and authorities. B D W and a few later MSS read ἤδη, "already." Metzger (*TCGNT*[1], 121) suspects that the appearance of the second ἤδη represents an effort to replace the odd-sounding πάλαι.

[e]The words "that he was dead" are the implied direct obj.

[f]Gk. πτῶμα, lit. "what has fallen," usually translated "corpse." A C W Σ and a few later MSS read σῶμα, "body," which is probably a deliberate agreement with v 43.

[g]B W read Ἰωσῆ, "Joses."

[h]D Σ and a few later MSS add ὁ Ἰωσήφ, "Joseph."

[i]ℵ and the Georgian MSS read λίθον μέγαν, "great stone" (cf. Matt 27:60).

[j]D and a few later authorities add καὶ ἀπῆλθεν, "and departed."

[k]The bracketed word is not present but is implied. W and a few later MSS add μήτηρ, "mother."

[l]Gk. Ἰωσῆτος. C N and several later MSS read Ἰωσῆ. D reads Ἰακώβου, "Jacob" or "James." Σ and a few later authorities read Ἰωσήφ, "Joseph"; cf. Westcott-Hort, *Introduction* 2:28. See *Note* p on Mark 15:40.

[m]D reads more stylistically τὸν τόπον ὅπου, "the place where."

Form/Structure/Setting

Bultmann (*History,* 274) surprisingly affirms that the story of the burial of Jesus "is an historical account which creates no impression of being a legend apart from the women who appear again as witnesses in v. 47, and vv. 44, 45 which Matthew and Luke in all probability did not have in their Mark. It can hardly be shown that the section was devised with the Easter story in mind." Bultmann is probably correct in every point. There is no hint of vv 44–45 in Matthew and Luke, who otherwise follow the Markan narrative fairly closely. Hagner (*Matthew* 2:857) believes that Matthew had these verses before him but chose to omit them. Likewise, Fitzmyer (*Luke* 2:1523) believes that Luke also omitted these verses. But it is hard to account for their complete omission in both of these Gospels. Such an agreement with each other while differing from Mark (with Markan priority assumed) is not easily explained. Bultmann is probably correct that the draft of Mark used by Matthew and Luke did not contain this material, which may have been added later to explain how it was that permission would have been given to take down a crucifixion victim the very day that he had been crucified— indeed, after hanging on the cross only a few hours. After all, those crucified normally suffered for days. The need for this explanation probably arose outside of Israel and without knowing that in Israel (in peacetime) crucifixion victims were normally taken down before the end of the day. The original edition of Mark probably did not have vv 44–45 because Palestinian Jewish Christians were familiar with this custom (as also was Pilate). Moreover, Bultmann is probably correct with regard to v 47, which seems to be an appendage (cf. Taylor, 599). Cranfield (461), however, thinks it is needless to bracket off vv 44–45 and 47.

Recently, Crossan (*Who Killed Jesus?* 160–88; cf. id., *Historical Jesus*, 354–94) has questioned the historicity of the burial scene, maintaining that it grew up out of legend and "prophecy" found in the Scriptures. It is "hope," not "history," Crossan avers, explaining that it was far more likely that the body of Jesus was unceremonially thrown into a ditch or shallow grave to be eaten by dogs. He admits that the bodies of crucifixion victims were sometimes taken down and buried, even on the day in which execution took place. He also acknowledges that the discovery of the ossuary of Yehoḥanan, who had been crucified and in whose right ankle bone the iron spike was still present (see *Comment* on 15:24), offers dramatic evidence of the complete and proper burial of a crucifixion victim. But the discovery thus far of only *one* crucifixion victim to have been buried decently demonstrates, reasons Crossan, the rarity of such burial. The majority of those crucified were never buried, their bodies being left to hang on the cross for animals and birds of carrion to feast upon. Crossan reasons, therefore, that it is probable that Jesus suffered the same fate. (See Crossan's comment in *Who Killed Jesus?* 188: "I keep thinking of all those other thousands of Jews crucified around Jerusalem in that terrible first century from among whom we have found only one skeleton and one nail.")

But Crossan's interpretation of the evidence is not convincing, and his dependence on the *Gospel of Peter* is problematic in its own right. Those Jewish persons in Israel left unburied almost always were victims during a time of war, when Rome had no regard for Jewish customs or sensibilities. This happened following the death of Herod the Great in 4 B.C.E., when it was necessary for Varus, the Roman legate of Syria, to move against uprisings in Judea, where he crucified two thousand (Josephus, *Ant.* 17.10.10 §295). It happened again, during the first great revolt of 66–70 C.E. Thousands of Jews were crucified outside the walls of Jerusalem (Josephus, *J.W.* 5.11.1 §450). Under such circumstances it is not at all surprising that the crucifixion victims were left hanging on their crosses to rot in the sun and to be picked apart by animals.

Even outside of Israel, Jewish sensibilities were normally respected. This is why Philo bitterly complains of Flaccus, Roman governor of Egypt. His conduct was exceptional in not allowing the bodies of crucifixion victims to be taken down and buried on the eve of a holiday: "I have known cases when on the eve of a holiday of this kind, people who have been crucified have been taken down and their bodies delivered to their kinsfolk, because it was thought well to give them burial and allow them the ordinary rites. . . . But Flaccus gave no orders to take down those who had died on the cross" (*Flaccus* 10 §83). Years later and returning to Israel, Josephus expresses outrage that the rebels who murdered two former high priests did not have the decency to bury them: "They actually went so far in their impiety as to cast out the corpses without burial, although the Jews are careful about funeral rites that even malefactors who have been sentenced to crucifixion are taken down and buried before sunset" (*J.W.* 4.5.2 §317). The desire to take down the dead before sunset stems from Deut 21:22–23, "you shall bury him the same day, for a hanged man is accursed by God; you shall not defile your land which the LORD your God gives you for an inheritance," and is attested in other Jewish texts (e.g., Tob 1:17–18; 2:3–8; Josephus, *J.W.* 3.8.5 §§377–78; 4.6.1 §§360–61).

Crossan's inference regarding the singularity of the discovery of the crucified Jew—crucified in the late 20s C.E., and therefore quite possibly under the authority of the prefect Pontius Pilate—is inappropriate. The discovery of this crucifixion victim with an iron spike still imbedded in his ankle is indeed exceptional, not because almost no crucifixion victims in peacetime were buried, but because the spikes were always removed. The only reason that the spike remained in the ankle of Yehoḥanan was that its tip had been bent back, thus making extraction impossible. The bones of Yehoḥanan actually provide evidence for the opposite of what Crossan wants to argue: in peacetime Jewish crucifixion victims were normally buried (though almost never with the iron spikes), just as Josephus himself says.

Jesus was crucified by Romans with the consent of (indeed, at the insistence of) the ruling priests. Rome was not at war with Israel. On the contrary, Roman and Jewish authorities were working together. Under such circumstances we should expect that crucifixion victims would normally, if not always, be taken down and buried. To leave the body of Jesus hanging on the cross or to have thrown it into a ditch where it might have been mauled by dogs would have been highly offensive to Jews, whether they were sympathizers of Jesus or not, especially so during the Passover season. Indeed, to leave the bodies of Jesus and the other two men hanging on the cross for several days at that time of year would have been dangerously provocative. (For an expert discussion of this issue, which supports the position taken here, see B. R. McCane, "'Where No One Had Yet Been Laid.'")

Finally, for some twenty years Crossan has maintained that "those who knew the site [where Jesus was buried] did not care and those who cared did not know the site" (Crossan, "Empty Tomb and Absent Lord," 152; id., *Historical Jesus*, 394). This dogmatic syllogism presumes too much and denies typical human behavior. Given the great importance the Jewish people placed on burial as well as the devotion Jesus' followers had for their friend and teacher, it is difficult to believe that "those who cared" about Jesus were unable to find out where he had been buried. Moreover, the tradition that women observed the burial firsthand and subsequently visited the tomb smacks of authenticity. Dismissal of this tradition is hard to understand and to justify. Inauthentic legend surely would enhance the eyewitness testimony by including male disciples, probably Peter himself. But, contrary to expectation, this is just what we do not find in the Gospels. The Gospels' restraint at this crucial point creates a strong presumption in favor of the authenticity of the tradition and shifts a heavy burden upon those who insist that a story that features women as the sole friendly witnesses of the place of burial and as the discoverers of the empty tomb the following Sunday morning is inauthentic and somehow serves a positive, theological purpose in the early Christian community.

The passage of the burial of Jesus breaks down into four principal units: (1) the request to bury the body of Jesus (vv 42–43), (2) the governor's surprise that Jesus was already dead and his ascertaining that this was so (vv 44–45), (3) the burial of Jesus (v 46), and (4) the notation that the two women observed the place where the body of Jesus was laid (v 47).

Comment

42 καὶ ἤδη ὀψίας γενομένης, ἐπεὶ ἦν παρασκευὴ ὅ ἐστιν προσάββατον, "And when evening had already come, since it was [the day of] Preparation, that is, [the day] before the Sabbath." Mark's syntax is once again convoluted. What he means to say is that the day's end is fast approaching. Jesus had died at about the ninth hour (15:34), that is, at 3:00 P.M. Evening is about to arrive, so the time is somewhere between 4:00 and 5:00 P.M. (4:00 P.M., according to Taylor, 599). The Passover meal will be observed soon (or, by Mark's reckoning, the evening meal of the day after Passover). Mark explains that παρασκευή, "[the day of] Preparation," is προσάββατον, "[the day] before the Sabbath," or perhaps more literally, the "pre-Sabbath" day. If the Sabbath began at about 6:00 P.M., then there was little time to prepare Jesus for burial.

43 Ἰωσὴφ [ὁ] ἀπὸ Ἀριμαθαίας εὐσχήμων βουλευτής, "Joseph from Arimathea, a respected member of the council." All four NT Gospels refer to Joseph from Arimathea (Matt 27:57; Mark 15:43; Luke 23:51; John 19:38). The town of Arimathea has been identified with Ramathaim-zophim (1 Sam 1:1), Rathamin (1 Macc 11:34), and Ramathain (Josephus, *Ant.* 13.4.9 §127), all of which are considered variant names for the same place (Fitzmyer, *Luke* 2:1526). If this city has been rightly recognized, it is about twenty miles northwest of Jerusalem. Crossan (*Who Killed Jesus?* 172–73) believes that the story of Joseph from Arimathea is a Markan invention that helps explain the circumstances that resulted in Jesus' burial (which Crossan thinks did not take place). But Joseph from Arimathea, as just mentioned, also appears in the Fourth Gospel (cf. John 19:38), which literarily is probably independent of the Synoptic Gospels (though not all scholars agree on this point). It is obvious that the later evangelists wish to enhance Joseph's status—in Matthew and John he is a "disciple of Jesus" (Matt 27:57; John 19:38, which adds, "but secretly, for fear of the Jews"), while in Luke he "is a good and righteous man, who had not consented to their [i.e., the council's] purpose and deed" (Luke 23:50–51)—but there is no compelling reason to conclude that the man did not exist and that he had nothing to do with the burial of Jesus. It is probable that there was such a person named Joseph, who was from Arimathea, but nothing else was known of him.

ὃς καὶ αὐτὸς ἦν προσδεχόμενος τὴν βασιλείαν τοῦ θεοῦ, "who also himself was expecting the kingdom of God." The first evangelist to give an explanation for Joseph's kindness and daring is Mark, who says that he ἦν προσδεχόμενος τὴν βασιλείαν τοῦ θεοῦ, "was expecting the kingdom of God"; that is, Joseph was in principle sympathetic to Jesus' goals, even if not necessarily committed to the Jesus movement itself. Mark's choice of words is intriguingly ambiguous and smacks of authenticity. If Joseph from Arimathea were no more than a Markan fiction (forgetting for a moment how this person then makes an appearance in the Fourth Gospel), then we must wonder why Mark is so noncommittal with regard to the man's attitude toward Jesus. Mark and the tradition before him know that one Joseph, a man from Arimathea, saw to the burial of Jesus' body in a rock-cut tomb. But who was he and why did he do this? Early Christians were not sure. Mark hazards that the man must have entertained hopes for the coming of the kingdom (and perhaps the man really did, and early Christians knew this) and then adds that he was εὐσχήμων, "respected" or "noble." For Matthew, Luke, and John, this is not reason enough: Joseph was either a righteous man who did not agree with the council's decision (so Luke) or, even better, he was indeed one of Jesus' disciples (so Matthew and John), though perhaps secretly (so John).

ἐλθὼν . . . τολμήσας εἰσῆλθεν πρὸς τὸν Πιλᾶτον καὶ ἠτήσατο τὸ σῶμα τοῦ Ἰησοῦ, "having come, being bold, went to Pilate and requested the body of Jesus." The attribution of boldness to Joseph is due to the potential danger for him to show concern for Jesus, a man condemned by the Roman governor (cf. Brown, *CBQ* 50 [1988] 233–45). By showing concern, Joseph might be suspected by Pilate of being one of Jesus' followers or at least one whose views coincided with those of Jesus and his movement. Moreover, as a member of the council he could not be seen showing concern for Jesus. Being labeled as a friend of Jesus could have seriously negative consequences for future advancement in social, religious, and political matters.

Why did Joseph take the trouble to bury Jesus? Joseph's request to take down the body (perhaps all three of the bodies?) would in the first place have been motivated out of a desire that the land not be defiled on the Passover (esp. in light of Deut 21:22–23; see *Form/Structure/Setting* above). Second, his request is in keeping with Jewish piety, in this case, concern that the dead receive a proper burial (cf. Brown, *CBQ* 50 [1988] 23–45). Third, if Mark's explanatory addition, "who also himself was expecting the kingdom of God," is based in fact, then Joseph may have believed in what Jesus stood for, even regarded Jesus as a prophet, and therefore believed that Jesus was very much deserving of a proper burial. Of course, many interpreters suspect that this explanatory addition is an apologetic gloss. This could be true, but the evangelist is not claiming that Joseph was an actual follower or disciple of Jesus (as do Matthew and John); he only claims that Joseph expected the kingdom. This implies that Joseph would have been in agreement, at least in broad terms, with Jesus' message. Joseph's compassion for Jesus, of course, does lend itself to Mark's apologetic interests. That a "respected" [εὐσχήμων] member of the council" was in essential agreement with Jesus' message and undertook to provide him a decent Jewish burial removes some of the shame of Jesus' execution and perhaps even lends a measure of honor to his burial.

Joseph knows that given the charges brought against Jesus, the Roman governor might very well refuse permission (see *Digesta* 48.24.1–2; 48.16.15, 3; Tacitus, *Ann.* 6.29). But Jewish custom was opposed to leaving bodies hanging on gibbets or crosses overnight (see Deut 21:23; *m. Sanh.* 6:6; *b. Sanh.* 46b), regarding burial of the dead as an act of piety (see 2 Sam 21:12–14; Tob 1:17–19; 2:3–7). Pilate, moreover, was probably only too happy to have the corpse of Jesus removed from public view.

44 ὁ δὲ Πιλᾶτος ἐθαύμασεν εἰ ἤδη τέθνηκεν καὶ προσκαλεσάμενος τὸν κεντυρίωνα ἐπηρώτησεν αὐτὸν εἰ πάλαι ἀπέθανεν, "But Pilate was surprised that he had already died, and summoning the centurion, he asked him if he had by now died." Pilate was surprised that Jesus had died so quickly because most crucifixion victims survived and suffered for two or three days, sometimes even longer, before succumbing (cf. Seneca, *Dial.* 3.2.2: "long-drawn-out agony"; Juvenal, *Sat.* 14.77–78; Isidore of Seville, *Etymologia* 5.27.34; Hengel, *Crucifixion,* 29–31; and *Comment* on 15:15). Accordingly, Pilate summons the centurion to ask if Jesus had in fact died. It was necessary for the governor to ascertain that Jesus had indeed died before he would grant the request for the body. In one satire a story is told of a family who takes down from the cross a relative while the Roman sentry is away from his post (cf. Petronius, *Satyricon* 111). Although a satire, it probably does reflect the possibility of thwarting justice by escaping the cross. Josephus tells us of three friends taken down from crosses while still alive, one of whom survived the ordeal (*Life* 75 §421).

45 καὶ γνοὺς ἀπὸ τοῦ κεντυρίωνος ἐδωρήσατο τὸ πτῶμα τῷ Ἰωσήφ, "And learning from the centurion [that he was dead], he gave the corpse to Joseph." When Pilate learns from the centurion, very probably the same centurion who had witnessed Jesus' dramatic death (in 15:37–39), that Jesus is indeed dead, he releases the corpse (τὸ πτῶμα) into Joseph's charge.

46 καὶ ἀγοράσας σινδόνα καθελὼν αὐτὸν ἐνείλησεν τῇ σινδόνι καὶ ἔθηκεν αὐτὸν ἐν μνημείῳ ὃ ἦν λελατομημένον ἐκ πέτρας, "And buying a linen shroud, [and] taking him down, he wrapped [him] in the linen shroud, and laid him in a tomb which had been hewn out of rock." This was standard burial procedure in this period of time. The Markan evangelist does not identify whose tomb this was. He and his readers perhaps assumed that it belonged to Joseph. However, it is highly improbable that Joseph's family tomb would have been in the vicinity of a place of execution (cf. Brown, *CBQ* 50 [1988] 233–45). Matthew says that Joseph laid the body of Jesus "in his own new tomb" (Matt 27:60), while Luke says the body was placed "in a rock-hewn tomb, where no one had ever yet been laid" (Luke 23:53). McCane ("'Where No One Had Yet Been Laid'") plausibly suggests that these redactional touches are attempts to mitigate the shame of Jesus' burial. Burial of the body of an executed criminal in the family tomb was not permitted until one year had elapsed and the bones had been gathered into an ossuary. Then the remains could be placed in the family crypt. In other words, the shame of a criminal's execution extended into the postmortem period. The tomb of Jesus was therefore regarded as a place of shame (which probably explains why no tomb was venerated in Christian circles until well into the fourth century; *pace* Jeremias, *Heiligengräber,* 145) and was probably a well-used crypt reserved for the burial of criminals (McCane, "'Where No One Had Yet Been Laid'"). Matthew and Luke know that the tomb into which Jesus was placed was not his family's (which presumably would have been in Galilee near Nazareth), but by saying that it was "new" (Matthew) or that "no one had ever been laid" in it (Luke), some of the shame is mitigated. The late and legendary *Gospel of Peter* adds more details, transforming Jesus' shameful burial into one of honor (cf. 6.22; 12.52–54).

Crossan (*Who Killed Jesus?* 173) asserts that Joseph did not bury the other two crucifixion victims. As a "pious Sanhedrist" he would have done this, but because he did not, Crossan maintains, we have another strong indication that the story is fiction. Crossan's argument, however, is based on silence. We do not know that Joseph did not bury the other two men. For that matter, we do not know that the other two men were not buried by their families or friends. The evangelists are not concerned with these two men, certainly including the Markan evangelist, who earlier had said that these men had reviled Jesus (15:32). Presumably all three were buried (as Jewish sensibilities would require and as our limited sources indicate was the custom). All the Markan evangelist knows is that a man named Joseph, who was from Arimathea, secured the body of Jesus, wrapped it in a linen shroud, and then placed it in a tomb hewn out of rock. The evangelist speculates that he was motivated by similar hope of the coming kingdom, but he shrinks from claiming that the man was a disciple (as Matthew and John claim) or a good and righteous man who had not consented to the council's decision (as Luke conjectures). It is possible that Jesus received somewhat better consideration than the other two crucified men, but that is only surmise. Crossan claims that Mark did not want to say that all three were buried because then the bodies, which probably would have ended up in the same crypt, could have become confused (*Who Killed Jesus?* 174). This highly speculative notion rests on a condescending misunderstanding of Jewish burial practices and Jewish competence (again, see McCane, "'Where No One Had Yet Been Laid'").

A σινδόνα, "linen shroud," is not mentioned in the Fourth Gospel, but we are told of τὰ ὀθόνια, "linen cloths." These are found lying on the floor of the tomb, separate from the face napkin, which is by itself, rolled up (John 20:4–7). A face napkin is not mentioned in Mark, and the linen shroud is not mentioned again. In Matt 27:59 we are told that it was a καθαρᾷ, "clean," linen shroud, which is probably yet another effort to mitigate the shamefulness of Jesus' burial. Matthew's "clean" perhaps implies that less care was taken with the burial of other criminals.

καὶ προσεκύλισεν λίθον ἐπὶ τὴν θύραν τοῦ μνημείου, "and he rolled a stone against the door of the tomb." A stone is rolled against the opening, thus sealing the tomb. Examples of this type of tomb with round stones by the opening can be seen in the vicinity of Jerusalem today. The famous Garden Tomb, a favorite with tourists, is probably not the tomb of Jesus. The evangelist mentions the stone because it will feature significantly in the discovery of the empty tomb.

47 ἡ δὲ Μαρία ἡ Μαγδαληνὴ καὶ Μαρία ἡ Ἰωσῆτος ἐθεώρουν ποῦ τέθειται, "Now Mary Magdalene and Mary the [mother] of Joses were observing where he had been laid." The evangelist again notes that women from among Jesus' following observed where he had been buried. Earlier we had been told that these women had looked on during the crucifixion (15:40–41). Women, including Mary Magdalene, will be the first to discover the empty tomb (16:1).

Explanation

The principal point of the story of the burial of Jesus is simply that he was buried in a tomb (with a modicum of dignity) and that two women knew where it was. The point of the story may be simple, but it is profoundly important, for the women must know where the tomb is if they are to visit it early Sunday morning and find it empty (16:1–8). There is present a touch of apologetic as well. Given the flight of the disciples and the denials of Peter, there was the distinct possibility that none of Jesus' following had any idea what had become of the body of their beloved master. Had Jesus' body not received proper burial, had the location of his tomb remained unknown, indeed, had Jesus' body not been buried at all (which was unlikely), then the disgrace of his shameful execution would only have been compounded. Mark's story reassures his readers that Jesus was indeed buried properly, even if without the usual mourning and other marks of honor, and that his place of burial was known. The report of Pilate's ascertaining that Jesus was indeed dead after having hung on the cross only six hours may have countered suspicions that Jesus had been taken down from the cross alive and that he had not truly been resurrected. That there were arguments such as these raised against early Christianity's Easter proclamation is attested by Matthew, who finds it necessary to counter claims that the body of Jesus had been removed from the tomb by his disciples (cf. Matt 27:62–66; 28:11–15).

O. The Resurrection of Jesus and the Discovery of the Empty Tomb   (16:1–8)

Bibliography

Aland, K. "Der Schluss des Markusevangeliums." In *L'Évangile selon Marc.* Ed. M. Sabbe. 435–70. **Allen, W. C.** "St. Mark xvi.8. 'They were afraid.' Why?" *JTS* o.s. 47 (1946) 46–49. **Alsup, J. E.** "John Dominic Crossan, 'Empty Tomb and Absent Lord': A Response." In *Society of Biblical Literature 1976 Seminar Papers.* Ed. G. W. MacRae. SBLSP 15. Missoula, MT: Scholars Press, 1976. 263–67. ———. *The Post-Resurrection Appearance Stories of the Gospel Tradition.* Calwer theologische Monographien 5. Stuttgart: Calwer; London: S. P. C. K., 1975. 85–107. **Anderson, H.** "The Easter Witness of the Evangelists." In *The New Testament in Historical and Contemporary Perspective.* FS G. H. C. MacGregor, ed. H. Anderson and W. Barclay. Oxford: Blackwell, 1965. 35–55, esp. 42–45. ———. *Jesus and Christian Origins: A Commentary on Modern Viewpoints.* New York: Oxford UP, 1964. 218–22. **Backhaus, K.** "'Dort werdet ihr Ihn sehen' (Mk 16:7): Die redaktionelle Schlussnotiz des zweiten Evangeliums als dessen christologische Summe." *TGl* 76 (1986) 277–94. **Bartsch, H.-W.** "Der Schluss des Markus-Evangeliums." *TZ* 27 (1971) 241–54. **Bater, R. R.** "Towards a More Biblical View of the Resurrection." *Int* 23 (1969) 47–65. **Benoit, P.** *Passion and Resurrection.* 231–61. **Berger, K.** *Die Auferstehung des Propheten und die Erhöhung des Menschensohns: Traditionsgeschichtliche Untersuchungen zur Deutung des Geschickes Jesu in frühchristlichen Texte.* SUNT 13. Göttingen: Vandenhoeck & Ruprecht, 1976. 177–79. **Best, E.** *Following Jesus.* 199–203. ———. *Mark.* 28–31, 72–78. **Bickermann, E.** "Das leere Grab." *ZNW* 23 (1924) 281–92. **Bindemann, W.** "Geht nach Galiläa! Vom Kult zum Gottesdienst im Alltag der Welt." *Texte und Kontexte* 11 (1981) 23–39. **Bode, E. L.** *The First Easter Morning: The Gospel Accounts of the Women's Visit to the Tomb of Jesus.* AnBib 45. Rome: Pontifical Biblical Institute, 1970. 29–45, 127–32. ———. "A Liturgical *Sitz im Leben* for the Gospel Tradition of the Women's Easter Visit to the Tomb of Jesus?" *CBQ* 32 (1970) 237–42. **Boffo, L.** *Iscrizioni greche e latine per lo studio della Bibbia.* Brescia: Paideia Editrice, 1994. 319–33. **Bolt, P. G.** "Mark 16:1–8: The Empty Tomb of a Hero?" *TynBul* 47 (1996) 27–37. **Boomershine, T. E.** "Mark 16:8 and the Apostolic Commission." *JBL* 100 (1981) 225–39. ——— and **Bartholomew, G. L.** "The Narrative Technique of Mark 16:8." *JBL* 100 (1981) 213–23. **Botha, P. J. J.** "οὐκ ἔστιν ὧδε

. . . : Mark's Stories of Jesus' Tomb and History." *Neot* 23 (1989) 195–218. **Bowman, D. J.** "The Resurrection in Mark." *TBT* 11 (1964) 709–13 (repr. in *Contemporary New Testament Studies.* Ed. M. R. Ryan. Collegeville, MN: Liturgical Press, 1965. 161–65). **Brändle, M.** "Narratives of the Synoptics about the Tomb." *TD* 16 (1968) 22–26. **Broer, I.** "Das leere Grab: Ein Versuch." *Liturgie und Mönchtum* 42 (1968) 42–51. ———. *Die Urgemeinde und das Grab Jesu: Eine Analyse der Grablegungsgeschichte im Neuen Testament.* SANT 31. Munich: Kösel, 1972. 87–137. ———. "Zur heutigen Diskussion der Grabesgeschichte (Mk 16, 1–18)." *BibLeb* 10 (1969) 40–52. **Brun, L.** "Der Auferstehungsbericht des Markusevangeliums." *TSK* 87 (1914) 346–88. **Bultmann, R.** *History.* 284–87. **Bush, R. A.** "Mark's Call to Action: A Rhetorical Analysis of Mark 16:8." In *Church Divinity.* Ed. J. Morgan. Bristol: Wyndham Hall, 1986. 22–30. **Cadbury, H. J.** "Mark 16:8." *JBL* 46 (1927) 344–50. **Cantinat, J.** *Réflexions sur la résurrection de Jésus (d'après Saint Paul et Saint Marc).* Paris: Gabalda, 1978. 79–89. **Catchpole, D. R.** "The Fearful Silence of the Women at the Tomb." *JTSA* 18 (1977) 3–10. **Cheek, J. L.** "The Historicity of the Markan Resurrection Narrative." *JBR* 27 (1959) 191–200. **Cranfield, C. E. B.** "St. Mark 16.1–8." *SJT* 5 (1952) 282–98, 398–414. **Creed, J. M.** "The Conclusion of the Gospel according to Saint Mark." *JTS* o.s. 31 (1930) 175–80. **Crossan, J. D.** "Empty Tomb and Absent Lord (Mark 16:1–8)." In *The Passion in Mark.* Ed. W. H. Kelber. 135–52. ———. "A Form for Absence: The Markan Creation of Gospel." *Semeia* 12 (1978) 41–55, esp. 48–51. **Cumont, F.** "Un rescrit impérial sur la violation de sépulture." *Revue historique* 163 (1930) 241–66. **Delorme, J.** "Les femmes au tombeau: Mc 16,1–8."*AsSeign* 2.21 (1969) 58–67. ———. "The Resurrection and Jesus' Tomb: Mark 16,1–8 in the Gospel Tradition." In *The Resurrection and Modern Biblical Thought.* Ed. P. de Surgy. New York: Corpus Books, 1970. 74–106. **Derrett, J. D. M.** *The Anastasis: The Resurrection of Jesus as an Historical Event.* Shipston-on-Stour: Drinkwater, 1982. Esp. 135–39. **Dhanis, E.** "L'ensevelissement de Jésus et la visite au tombeau dans l'évangile de saint Marc (xv,40–xvi,8)." *Greg* 39 (1958) 367–410. **Dibelius, M.** *Tradition.* 189–96. **Dietzfelbinger, D.** "Markus 16,1–8." In *Kranzbacher Gespräch der Lutherischen Bischofskonferenz zur Auseinandersetzung um die Bibel.* Ed. H. Schnell. Berlin; Hamburg: Lutherisches Verlaghaus, 1967. 9–22. **Dormeyer, D.** *Die Passion Jesu.* 221–35. **Evans, C. A.** "Mark's Use of the Empty Tomb Tradition." *SBT* 8.2 (1978) 50–55. **Evans, C. F.** "I Will Go before You into Galilee." *JTS* n.s. 5 (1954) 3–18. ———. *Resurrection and the New Testament.* SBT 12. London: SCM Press; Naperville, IL: Allenson, 1970. 67–81. **Farrer, A. M.** *A Study in St. Mark.* New York: Oxford UP, 1952. 172–81. **Fuller, R. H.** *The Formation of the Resurrection Narratives.* New York: Macmillan, 1971; London: S. P. C. K., 1972. 50–70. **Geddert, T. J.** *Watchwords.* 161–73. **Giesen, H.** "Der Auferstandene und seine Gemeinde: Zum Inhalt und zur Funktion des ursprünglichen Markusschlusses (16:1–8)." SNTSU 12 (1987) 99–139. **Goulder, M. D.** "The Empty Tomb." *Theology* 79 (1976) 206–14. ———. "Mark xvi. 1–8 and Parallels." *NTS* 24 (1977–78) 235–40. **Gourgues, M.** "À propos du symbolisme christologique et baptismal de Marc 16.5." *NTS* 27 (1980–81) 672–78. **Grass, H.** *Ostergeschehen und Osterberichte.* 4th ed. Göttingen: Vandenhoeck & Ruprecht, 1970. 15–23. **Grassi, J. A.** "The Secret Heroine in Mark's Drama." *BTB* 18 (1988) 10–15. **Grayston, K.** *Dying, We Live: A New Inquiry into the Death of Christ in the New Testament.* Oxford; New York: Oxford UP, 1990. 164–237. **Grimme, H.** "Harmonie zwischen Anfang und Schluss des Markusevangeliums." *TQ* 126 (1946) 276–89. **Güttgemanns, E.** "Linguistische Analyse von Mk 16,1–8." *LB* 11–12 (1972) 13–53. **Hamilton, N. Q.** "Resurrection Tradition and the Composition of Mark." *JBL* 84 (1965) 415–21. **Hanhart, K.** *The Open Tomb: A New Approach, Mark's Passover Haggadah (± 72 C.E.).* Collegeville, MN: Liturgical Press, 1995. **Harris, M. J.** *Raised Immortal: Resurrection and Immortality in the New Testament.* London: Marshall, Morgan & Scott, 1983; Grand Rapids, MI: Eerdmans, 1985. 14–18, 38–44. **Hebert, G.** "The Resurrection-Narrative in St. Mark's Gospel." *SJT* 15 (1962) 66–73. **Henaut, B. W.** "Empty Tomb or Empty Argument: A Failure of Nerve in Recent Studies of Mark 16?" *SR* 15 (1986) 177–90. **Hengel, M.** "Maria Magdalena und die Frauen als Zeugen." In *Abraham unser Vater: Juden und Christen im Gespräch über die Bibel.* FS

O. Michel, ed. O. Betz et al. AGSU 5. Leiden: Brill, 1963. 243–56. **Hester, J. D.** "Dramatic Inconclusion: Irony and the Narrative Rhetoric of the Ending of Mark." *JSNT* 57 (1995) 61–86. **Horst, P. W. van der.** *Ancient Jewish Epitaphs.* CBET 2. Kampen: Kok, 1991. 159–60. ———. "Can a Book End with γάρ? A Note on Mark xvi.8." *JTS* n.s. 23 (1972) 121–24. **Horstmann, M.** *Studien zur markinischen Christologie.* 128–34. **Horvath, T.** "The Early Markan Tradition on the Resurrection (Mk. 16,1–8)." *RUO* 43 (1973) 445–48. **Hug, J.** *La finale de l'Évangile de Marc (Mc 16, 9–20).* EBib. Paris: Gabalda, 1978. 187–215. **Iersel, B. M. F. van.** "'To Galilee' or 'in Galilee' in Mark 14,28 and 16,7?" *ETL* 58 (1982) 365–70. **Jenkins, A. K.** "Young Man or Angel?" *ExpTim* 94 (1983) 237–40. **Kahmann, J.** "'Il est ressuscité, le Crucifié': Marc 16,6a et sa place dans l'évangile de Marc." In *La Pâque du Christ: Mystère de salut.* FS F.-X. Durrwell, ed. M. Benzerath. LD 112. Paris: Cerf, 1982. 121–30. **Kloner, A.** "Did a Rolling Stone Close Jesus' Tomb?" *BAR* 25.5 (1999) 22–29, 76. **Knox, W. L.** *The Sources of the Synoptic Gospels.* Cambridge: Cambridge UP, 1953. 148–49. **Koch, G.** *Die Auferstehung Jesu Christi.* BHT 27. Tübingen: Mohr-Siebeck, 1965. 157–71. **Kraeling, C. H.** "A Philological Note on Mark 16:8." *JBL* 44 (1925) 357–64. **Kratz, R.** *Rettungswunder: Motiv-, traditions- und formkritische Aufarbeitung einer biblischen Gattung.* Frankfurt am Main; Bern: Lang, 1979. 500–510. **Kremer, J.** *Die Osterbotschaft der vier Evangelien: Versuch einer Auslegung der Berichte über das leere Grab und die Erscheinungen des Auferstandenen.* Stuttgart: Katholisches Bibelwerk, 1968. 13–31. ———. *Die Osterevangelien—Geschichten um Geschichte.* Stuttgart: Katholisches Bibelwerk, 1977. 30–54. **Kuhn, H.-W.** "Predigt über Markus 16,1–8." *EvT* 38 (1978) 155–59. **Lapide, P. E.** *The Resurrection of Jesus: A Jewish Perspective.* Minneapolis: Augsburg, 1977. **LaVerdiere, E.** "The End, a Beginning." *Emmanuel* 90 (1984) 484–91. ———. "It Was a Huge Stone." *Emmanuel* 92 (1986) 125–29. ———. "Robed in Radiant White." *Emmanuel* 90 (1984) 138–42. **Léon-Dufour, X.** *Resurrection and the Message of Easter.* London: Chapman, 1974; New York: Holt, Rinehart & Winston, 1975. 128–38. **Lightfoot, R. H.** *The Gospel Message of St. Mark.* Oxford: Clarendon, 1950. 80–97. **Lillie, W.** "The Empty Tomb and the Resurrection." In *Historicity and Chronology in the New Testament.* Ed. D. E. Nineham et al. Theological Collections 6. London: S. P. C. K., 1965. 117–34. **Lincoln, A. T.** "The Promise and the Failure: Mark 16:7, 8." *JBL* 108 (1989) 283–300. **Lindemann, A.** "Die Osterbotschaft des Markus: Zur theologischen Interpretation von Mark 16,1–8." *NTS* 26 (1979–80) 298–317. **Linnemann, E.** "Der (wiedergefundene) Markusschluss." *ZTK* 66 (1969) 255–87. **Magness, J. L.** *Sense and Absence: Structure and Suspension in the Ending of Mark's Gospel.* SBLSS. Atlanta: Scholars Press, 1986. **Manson, T. W.** *The Servant-Messiah: A Study of the Public Ministry of Jesus.* Cambridge: Cambridge UP, 1953. 50–56, 93–97. **Marin, L.** "Les femmes au tombeau." *Languages* 22 (1971) 39–50. **Marxsen, W.** *Mark the Evangelist.* 111–16. **Masson, C.** "Le tombeau vide." *RTP* 32 (1944) 161–74. **McIndoe, J. H.** "The Young Man at the Tomb." *ExpTim* 80 (1969) 125. **Merklein, H.** "Mk 16,1–8 als Epilog des Markusevangelium." In *The Synoptic Gospels.* Ed. C. Focant. BETL 110. Leuven: Peeters and Leuven UP, 1993. 209–38. **Metzger, B. M.** "The Ending of the Gospel according to Mark in the Ethiopic Manuscripts." In *Understanding the Sacred Text.* FS M. S. Enslin, ed. J. Reumann. Valley Forge, PA: Judson, 1972. 165–80 (repr. in B. M. Metzger. *New Testament Studies: Philological, Versional, and Patristic.* NTTS 10. Leiden: Brill, 1980. 127–47). ———. "The Nazareth Inscription Once Again." In *New Testament Studies: Philological, Versional, and Patristic.* NTTS 10. Leiden: Brill, 1980. 75–92. **Meye, R. P.** "Mark 16:8—The Ending of Mark's Gospel." *BR* 14 (1969) 33–43. **Mohr, T. A.** *Markus- und Johannespassion.* 365–403. **Moule, C. F. D.** "St. Mark xvi.8 Once More." *NTS* 2 (1955–56) 58–59. **Mussner, F.** *Die Auferstehung Jesu.* Biblische Handbibliothek 7. Munich: Kösel, 1969. 128–35. **Neirynck, F.** "ΑΝΑΤΕΙΛΑΝΤΟΣ ΤΟΥ ΗΛΙΟΥ (Mc 16,2)." *ETL* 54 (1978) 70–103 (repr. in F. Neirynck. *Evangelica: Gospel Studies—Études d'Évangile.* Ed. F. Van Segbroeck. BETL 60. Leuven: Peeters and Leuven UP, 1982. 181–214). ———. "John and the Synoptics: The Empty Tomb Stories." *NTS* 30 (1984) 161–87 (repr. in F. Neirynck. *Evangelica II.* Ed. F. Van Segbroeck. BETL 99. Leuven: Peeters and Leuven UP, 1991. 571–99). ———. "Marc 16,1–8: Tradition et rédaction: Tombeau vide et angélophanie." *ETL* 56 (1980) 56–88 (repr. in F. Neirynck. *Evangelica: Gospel Studies—Études d'Évangile*. Ed. F. Van Segbroeck. BETL 60. Leuven: Peeters and Leuven UP, 1982. 239–72). **Nicklin, T.** "St. Mark xvi.8." *ExpTim* 38 (1936–27) 429. **Niemann, F.** "Die Erzählung vom leerer Grab bei Markus." *ZKT* 101 (1979) 188–99. **Oberlinner, L.** "Die Verkündigung der Auferweckung Jesu im geöffneten und leeren Grab." *ZNW* 73 (1982) 159–82. **O'Collins, G.** "The Fearful Silence of Three Women (Mark 16:8c)." *Greg* 69 (1988) 489–503. **Odenkirchen, P. C.** "Praecedam vos in Galileam." *VD* 46 (1968) 193–223. **Oppermann, R.** "Eine Beobachtung in Bezug auf das Problem des Markusschlusses." *BN* 40 (1987) 24–29. **Osborne, G. R.** *The Resurrection Narratives: A Redational Study*. Grand Rapids, MI: Baker, 1984. 43–72, 193–219. **Ottley, R. R.** "ἐφοβοῦντο γάρ, Mark xvi 8." *JTS* o.s. 27 (1926) 407–9. **Palmer, D. W.** "The Origin, Form, and Purpose of Mark XVI.4 in Codex Bobbiensis." *JTS* n.s. 27 (1976) 113–22. **Paulsen, H.** "Mk xvi 1–8." *NovT* 22 (1980) 138–75 (repr. in *Zur neutestamentlichen Überlieferung von der Auferstehung Jesu*. Ed. P. Hoffmann. Wege der Forschung 522. Darmstadt: Wissenschaftliche Buchgesellschaft, 1988. 376–415). **Perkins, P.** "The Resurrection of Jesus of Nazareth." In *Studying the Historical Jesus: Evaluations of the State of Current Research*. Ed. B. D. Chilton and C. A. Evans. NTTS 19. Leiden: Brill, 1994. 423–42. **Pesch, R.** *Das Evangelium der Urgemeinde*. 215–22. ———. "Das 'leere Grab' und der Glaube an Jesu Auferstehung." *IKaZ* 11 (1982) 6–20. ———. "Der Schluss der vormarkinischen Passionsgeschichte und des Markusevangeliums: Mk 15,42–16,8." In *L'Évangile selon Marc*. Ed. M. Sabbe. 365–409. **Petersen, N. R.** "When Is the End Not the End? Literary Reflections on the Ending of Mark's Narrative." *Int* 34 (1980) 151–66. **Pokorný, P.** "'Anfang des Evangelium': Zum Problem des Anfangs und des Schlusses des Markusevangeliums." In *Die Kirche des Anfangs*. FS H. Schürmann, ed. R. Schnackenburg. ETS 38. Leipzig: St. Benno, 1977. 115–31. **Räisänen, H.** *'Messianic Secret' in Mark's Gospel*. 207–11. **Reedy, C. J.** "Mk 8:31–11:10 and the Gospel Ending: A Redactional Study." *CBQ* 34 (1972) 188–97. **Richardson, L. J. D.** "St. Mark xvi. 8." *JTS* o.s. 49 (1948) 144–46. **Rigaux, B.** *Dieu l'a ressuscité: Exégèse et théologie biblique*. Studii Biblici Franciscani Analecta 4. Gembloux: Duculot, 1973. 184–200. **Ritt, H.** "Die Frauen und die Osterbotschaft: Synopse der Grabesgeschichten (Mk 16,1–8; Mt 27,62–28,15; Lk 24,1–12; Joh 20,1–18)." In *Die Frauen im Urchristentum*. Ed. G. Dautzenberg et al. QD 95. Freiburg: Herder, 1983. 117–33. **Sandmel, S.** "Prolegomena to a Commentary on Mark." *JBR* 31 (1963) 294–300 (repr. in *New Testament Issues*. Ed. R. Batey. Harper Forum Books. New York: Harper & Row; London: SCM Press, 1970. 45–56; in S. Sandmel. *Two Living Traditions: Essays on Religion and the Bible*. Detroit: Wayne State UP, 1972. 147–57). **Schenk, W.** *Der Passionsbericht nach Markus*. 259–71. **Schlier, H.** "Die Osterbotschaft aus dem Grab (Markus 16,1–8)." *Katholische Gedanke* 27 (1971) 1–6. **Schmithals, W.** "Der Markusschluss, die Verklärungsgeschichte und die Aussendung der Zwölf." *ZTK* 69 (1972) 379–411. **Schneider, G.** "'Er ist auferweckt worden!' Eine Auslegung von Mk 16,1–8." *Der Katholische Erzieher* 17 (1964) 113–17. ———. *Die Passion Jesu*. 143–49. **Schnell, C. W.** "Tendencies in the Synoptic Tradition: Rudolf Bultmann's Legacy and an Important Christian Tradition." *Neot* 23 (1989) 177–94. **Schnellbächer, E. L.** "Das Rätsel des νεανίσκος bei Markus." *ZNW* 73 (1982) 127–35. **Schottroff, L.** "Frauen in der Nachfolge Jesu in neutestamentlicher Zeit." In *Frauen in der Bibel*. Vol. 2 of *Traditionen der Befreiung: Sozialgeschichtliche Bibelauslegungen*. Ed. W. Schottroff and W. Stegemann. Munich: Kaiser, 1980. 91–133 (ET: "Women as Disciples of Jesus in New Testament Times." In L. Schottroff. *Let the Oppressed Go Free: Feminist Perspectives on the New Testament*. Louisville: Westminster John Knox, 1993). ———. "Maria Magdalena und die Frauen am Grabe Jesu." *EvT* 42 (1982) 3–25 (ET: "Mary Magdalene and the Women at Jesus' Tomb." In L. Schottroff. *Let the Oppressed Go Free: Feminist Perspectives on the New Testament*. Louisville: Westminster John Knox, 1993). **Schweizer, E.** *Neues Testament und heutigen Verkündigung*. BibS(N) 56. Neukirchen-Vluyn: Neukirchener, 1969. 55–60. **Scroggs, R., and Groff, K. I.** "Baptism in Mark: Dying and Rising with Christ." *JBL* 92 (1973) 531–48, esp. 540–48. **Sheehan, T.** *The First Coming: How the Kingdom of God Became Christianity*. New York: Vantage

Books, 1986. 127–73. ———. "Two Easter Legends." *Philosophy and Theology* 1 (1986) 32–48. **Sint, J. A.** "Die Auferstehung Jesu in der Verkündigung der Urgemeinde." *ZKT* 84 (1962) 129–51. **Smith, R. H.** "New and Old in Mark 16:1–8." *CTM* 43 (1972) 518–27. **Stählin, G.** "'On the Third Day': The Easter Traditions of the Primitive Church." *Int* 10 (1956) 282–99. **Standaert, B. H. M. G. M.** *L'évangile selon Marc.* 579–85. **Stein, R. H.** "A Short Note on Mark. XIV. 28 and XVI. 7." *NTS* 20 (1973–74) 445–52. **Stenger, W.** *Die Ostergeschichten der Evangelien.* Schriften zur Katechetik 13. Munich: Kösel, 1970. 17–30. **Streeter, B. H.** *The Four Gospels: A Study of Origins.* Rev. ed. London: Macmillan, 1930. 333–60. **Synge, F. C.** "Mark 16.1–8." *JTSA* 11 (1975) 71–73. **Thomas, J. C.** "A Reconsideration of the Ending of Mark." *JETS* 26 (1983) 407–19. **Thurston, B. B.** "Faith and Fear in Mark's Gospel." *TBT* 23 (1985) 305–10. **Torrey, C. C.** *Our Translated Gospels.* 71–73. **Trompf, G. W.** "The First Resurrection Appearance and the Ending of Mark's Gospel." *NTS* 18 (1971–72) 308–30. ———. "The Markusschluss in Recent Research." *ABR* 21 (1973) 15–26. **Turner, C. H.** "Marcan Usage: Notes, Critical and Exegetical, on the Second Gospel." *JTS* o.s. 26 (1925) 12–20. **Vignolo, R.** "Una finale reticente: interpretazione narrativa di Mc 16,8." *RivB* 3 (1990) 129–89. **Vögtle, A.** "'Er is auferstanden, er is nicht hier!'" *BibLeb* 7 (1966) 69–73. **Waetjen, H.** "The Ending of Mark and the Gospels' Shift in Eschatology." *ASTI* 4 (1965) 114–31. **Weeden, T. J.** *Mark.* 101–17. **Westcott, B. F.,** and **Hort, F. J. A.** *Introduction.* 2:28. **White, P. O. G.** "The Resurrection and the Second Coming in the Gospel of Mark." *SE* 6 [= TU 112] (1973) 615–18. **Wichelhaus, M.** "Am ersten Tage der Woche." *NovT* 11 (1969) 45–66. **Wilckens, U.** "Die Perikope vom leeren Grab Jesu in der nachmarkinischen Traditionsgeschichte." In *Festschrift für Friedrich Smend zum 70. Geburtstag.* Berlin: Merseburger, 1963. 30–41. **Williams, J. F.** *Other Followers of Jesus.* 191–203. **Wilson, W. G.** "St. Mark xvi.8: A Modern Greek Parallel." *JTS* o.s. 50 (1949) 57–59.

Bibliography on the Resurrection of Jesus

Albertz, M. "Zur Formgeschichte der Auferstehungsberichte." *ZNW* 21 (1922) 259–69. **Alsup, J. E.** *The Post-Resurrection Appearance Stories of the Gospel Tradition.* London: S. P. C. K., 1975. ———. "Resurrection and Historicity." *ASB* 103 (1988) 5–18. **Anderson, H.** "The Easter Witness of the Evangelists." In *The New Testament in Historical and Contemporary Perspective.* FS G. H. C. MacGregor, ed. H. Anderson and W. Barclay. Oxford: Blackwell, 1965. 35–55. **Bartsch, H.-W.** "Der Ursprung des Osterglaubens." *TZ* 31 (1975) 16–31. **Benoit, P.** *Passion and Resurrection.* 231–61. **Bode, E. L.** *The First Easter Morning: The Gospel Accounts of the Women's Visit to the Tomb of Jesus.* AnBib 45. Rome: Pontifical Biblical Institute, 1970. **Brändle, M.** "Did Jesus' Tomb Have to Be Empty?" *TD* 16 (1968) 18–21. ———. "Early Christian Understanding of the Resurrection." *TD* 16 (1968) 14–17. ———. *Die Urgemeinde und das Grab Jesu: Eine Analyse der Grablegungsgeschichte im Neuen Testament.* SANT 31. Munich: Kösel, 1972. **Brown, R. E.** *A Risen Christ in Eastertide: Essays on the Gospel Narratives of the Resurrection.* Collegeville, MN: Liturgical Press, 1991. ———. *The Virginal Conception and Bodily Resurrection of Jesus.* New York: Paulist, 1973. 96–124. **Brun, L.** *Die Auferstehung Christi in der urchristlichen Überlieferung.* Giessen: Töpelmann, 1925. **Campenhausen, H. von.** "The Events of Easter and the Empty Tomb." In *Tradition and Life in the Early Church: Essays and Lectures in Church History.* Tr. A. V. Littledale. London: Collins; Philadelphia: Fortress, 1968. 42–89. **Cantinat, J.** *Réflexions sur la résurrection de Jésus (d'après Saint Paul et Saint Marc).* Paris: Gabalda, 1978. **Carmignac, J.** "Les apparitions de Jésus ressuscité et le calendrier biblico-qumrânien." *RevQ* 7 (1971) 483–504. **Carnley, P.** *The Structure of Resurrection Belief.* Oxford: Clarendon, 1987. **Cavallin, C. C.** *Life after Death: Paul's Argument for the Resurrection of the Dead in 1 Cor 15.* Part I: *An Enquiry into the Jewish Background.* Lund: Gleerup, 1974. **Craig, W. L.** "The Bodily Resurrection of Jesus." In *Studies of History and Tradition in the Four Gospels.* Ed. R. T. France and D. Wenham. Gospel Perspectives 1. Sheffield: JSOT Press, 1980.

47–74. ———. "The Empty Tomb of Jesus." In *Studies of History and Tradition in the Four Gospels.* Ed. R. T. France and D. Wenham. Gospel Perspectives 2. Sheffield: JSOT, 1981. 173–200. ———. "The Historicity of the Empty Tomb of Jesus." *NTS* 31 (1985) 39–67. ———. "On Doubts about the Resurrection." *Modern Theology* 6 (1989) 53–75. ———. "Pannenbergs Beweis für die 'Auferstehung Jesu.'" *KD* 34 (1988) 78–104. **Cranfield, C. E. B.** "The Resurrection of Jesus Christ." *ExpTim* 101 (1990) 169. **Crossan, J. D.** *The Cross That Spoke: The Origins of the Passion Narrative.* San Francisco: Harper & Row, 1988. **Davies, J. G.** "Factors Leading to the Emergence of Belief in the Resurrection of the Flesh." *JTS* n.s. 23 (1972) 448–55. **Davis, S. T., Kendall, D.,** and **O'Collins, G.,** eds. *The Resurrection.* Oxford: Oxford UP, 1997. **Descamps, A.** "La structure des récits évangéliques de la résurrection." *Bib* 40 (1959) 726–41. **Dhanis, E.,** ed. *Resurrexit: Actes du symposium international sur la résurrection de Jésus (Rome 31 Mars–6 Avril 1970).* Rome: Editrice Vaticana, 1974. **Dodd, C. H.** "The Appearances of the Risen Christ: An Essay in Form-Criticism of the Gospels." In *Studies in the Gospels.* FS R. H. Lightfoot, ed. D. E. Nineham. Oxford: Blackwell, 1955. 9–35. **Drane, J. W.** "Some Ideas of Resurrection in the New Testament Period." *TynBul* 24 (1973) 99–110. **Eddy, G. T.** "The Resurrection of Jesus Christ: A Consideration of Professor Cranfield's Argument." *ExpTim* 101 (1989–90) 327–29. **Evans, C. F.** *Resurrection and the New Testament.* SBT 12. London: SCM Press; Naperville, IL: Allenson, 1970. **Freudenberg, W.** *Ist er wirklich auferstanden? Eine Untersuchung der biblischen Auferstehungsberichte.* Wuppertal: Brockhaus, 1977. **Fuller, R. H.** *The Formation of the Resurrection Narratives.* New York: Macmillan, 1971; London: S. P. C. K., 1972. ———. "The Resurrection of Jesus and the Historical Method." *JBR* 34 (1966) 18–24. **Gaechter, P.** "Die Engelserscheinungen in den Auferstehungsberichten." *ZKT* 89 (1967) 191–202. **Galvin, J. P.** "The Origin of Faith in the Resurrection of Jesus: Two Recent Perspectives." *TS* 49 (1988) 25–44. ———. "A Recent Jewish View of the Resurrection." *ExpTim* 91 (1978–79) 277–79. ———. "Resurrection as *Theologia Crucis Jesu:* The Foundational Christology of Rudolf Pesch." *TS* 38 (1977) 513–25. **Gardner-Smith, P.** *The Narrative of the Resurrection: A Critical Study.* London: Methuen, 1926. **Gils, F.** "Pierre et la foi au Christ ressuscité." *ETL* 38 (1962) 5–43. **Goergen, D. J.** *The Death and Resurrection of Jesus.* Wilmington, DE: Glazier, 1988. **Goppelt, L.** "Die Auferstehung Jesu in der Kritik, ihr Sinn und ihre Glaubwerdigkeit." In *Grundlagen des Glaubens.* Ed. P. Rieger and J. Strauss. Munich: Kösel, 1970. 55–74. **Grass, H.** "Zur Begründung des Osterglaubens." *TLZ* 89 (1964) 405–14. **Grayston, K.** "The Empty Tomb." *ExpTim* 92 (1980–81) 263–67. **Gutbrod, K.** *Die Auferstehung Jesu im Neuen Testament.* Stuttgart: Calwer, 1969. **Gutwenger, E.** "The Narration of Jesus' Resurrection." *TD* 16 (1968) 8–13. ———. "Zur Geschichtlichkeit der Auferstehung Jesu." *ZKT* 88 (1966) 257–82. **Hayes, J. H.** "Resurrection as Enthronement and the Earliest Church Christology." *Int* 22 (1968) 333–45. **Hempelmann, H.** *Die Auferstehung Jesu Christi—Eine historische Tatsache? Eine engagierte Analyse.* Wuppertal: Brockhaus, 1982. **Hendrickx, H.** *The Resurrection Narratives of the Synoptic Gospels.* Rev. ed. London: Chapman, 1984. **Hengel, M.** "Ist der Osterglaube noch zu retten?" *TQ* 153 (1973) 252–69. **Hoffmann, P.** "Auferstehung: Neues Testament." *TRE* 4 (1979) 450–67. **Hübner, H.** "Kreuz und Auferstehung im Neuen Testament." *TRu* 54 (1989) 262–306. **Iersel, B. M. F. van.** "The Resurrection of Jesus: Information or Interpretation?" *Concilium* 60 (1970) 54–67. **Ittel, W.** *Ostern und das leere Grab.* Gütersloh: Mohn, 1967. **Jeremias, J.** *New Testament Theology.* 300–311. **Kasper, W.** "Der Glaube an die Auferstehung Jesu vor dem Forum historischer Kritik." *TQ* 153 (1973) 229–41. **Kegel, G.** *Auferstehung Jesu—Auferstehung der Toten: Eine traditionsgeschichtliche Untersuchung zum Neuen Testament.* Gütersloh: Mohn, 1970. **Kendall, D.,** and **O'Collins, G.** "The Uniqueness of the Resurrection Appearances." *CBQ* 54 (1992) 287–307. **Klumbies, P.-G.** "'Oster' als Gottesbekenntnis und der Wandel zur Christusverkündigung." *ZNW* 83 (1992) 163–64. **Koch, G.** *Die Auferstehung Jesu Christi.* BHT 27. Tübingen: Mohr-Siebeck, 1965. **Kremer, J.** *Das älteste Zeugnis von der Auferstehung Christi.* 3rd ed. SBS 17. Stuttgart: Katholisches Bibelwerk, 1970. ———. *Die Osterbotschaft der vier Evangelien: Versuch einer Auslegung der Berichte über das leere Grab und die Erscheinungen des Auferstandenen.* Stuttgart: Katholisches Bibelwerk, 1968.

———. "Zur Diskussion über 'das leere Grab.'" In *Resurrexit: Actes du symposium international sur la résurrection de Jésus (Rome 31 Mars–6 Avril 1970)*. Ed. E. Dhanis. Rome: Editrice Vaticana, 1974. 137–68. **Ladd, G. E.** *I Believe in the Resurrection of Jesus*. London: Hodder & Stoughton; Grand Rapids, MI: Eerdmans, 1975. **Lake, K.** *The Historical Evidence for the Resurrection of Jesus Christ*. London: Williams & Norgate; New York: Putnam's Sons, 1907. **Lapide, P.** *The Resurrection of Jesus: A Jewish Perspective*. Minneapolis: Augsburg, 1983. **Legault, A.** "Christophanies et angélophanies dans les récits évangéliques de la résurrection." *ScEs* 21 (1969) 443–57. **Leipoldt, J.** "Zu den Auferstehungs-Geschichten." *TLZ* 73 (1948) 737–42. **Léon-Dufour, X.** *Resurrection and the Message of Easter*. London: Chapman, 1974; New York: Holt, Rinehart & Winston, 1975. **Lohfink, G.** "Der Ablauf der Osterereignisse und die Anfänge der Urgemeinde." *TQ* 160 (1980) 162–76 (repr. in G. Lohfink. *Studien zum Neuen Testament*. SBA 5. Stuttgart: Katholisches Bibelwerk, 1989. 149–67). ———. "Die Auferstehung Jesu und die historische Kritik." *BibLeb* 9 (1968) 37–53. ———. "The Resurrection of Jesus and Historical Criticism." *TD* 17 (1969) 110–14. **Lorenzen, T.** "Ist der Auferstandene in Galiläa erschienen? Bemerkungen zu einem Aufsatz von B. Steinseifer." *ZNW* 64 (1973) 209–21. **Mánek, J.** "The Apostle Paul and the Empty Tomb." *NovT* 2 (1958) 276–80. **Marböck, J.** "Henoch—Adam—der Thronwagen." *BZ* 25 (1981) 103–11. **Marxsen, W.** *Jesus and Easter: Did God Raise the Historical Jesus from the Dead?* Nashville: Abingdon, 1990. ———. *The Resurrection of Jesus of Nazareth*. London: SCM Press; Philadelphia: Fortress, 1970. **Mildenberger, F.** "Auferstanden am dritten Tage nach den Schriften." *EvT* 23 (1963) 265–80. **Moule, C. F. D.** "The Post-Resurrection Appearances in the Light of Festival Pilgrimages." *NTS* 4 (1957–58) 58–61. ———, ed. *The Significance of the Message of the Resurrection for Faith in Jesus Christ*. SBT 8. Naperville, IL: Allenson, 1968. **Mussner, F.** *Die Auferstehung Jesu*. Biblische Handbibliothek 7. Munich: Kösel, 1969. **Nauck, W.** "Die Bedeutung des leeren Grabes für den Glauben an den Auferstandenen." *ZNW* 47 (1956) 243–67. **Neyrey, J. H.** *The Resurrection Stories*. Collegeville, MN: Liturgical Press, 1990. **Nickelsburg, G. W. E.** *Resurrection, Immortality and Eternal Life in Intertestamental Judaism*. HTS 26. Cambridge: Harvard UP, 1972. **O'Collins, G.** *Interpreting the Resurrection: Examining the Major Problems in the Stories of Jesus' Resurrection*. New York: Paulist, 1988. ———. "Is the Resurrection an 'Historical' Event?" *HeyJ* 8 (1967) 381–87. ——— and **Kendall, D.** "Mary Magdalene as Major Witness to Jesus' Resurrection." *TS* 48 (1987) 631–46. **Pannenberg, W.** "Did Jesus Really Rise from the Dead?" *Dialog* 4 (1965) 18–35. **Perkins, P.** *Resurrection: New Testament Witness and Contemporary Reflection*. Garden City, NY: Doubleday, 1984. **Perrin, N.** *The Resurrection according to Matthew, Mark and Luke* (British title: *The Resurrection Narratives: A New Approach*). London: SCM Press; Philadelphia: Fortress, 1977. **Pesch, R.** "Zur Entstehung des Glaubens an die Auferstehung Jesu." *TQ* 153 (1973) 201–28. **Ponthot, J.** "Gospel Traditions about Christ's Resurrection: Theological Perspectives and Problems of Historicity." *Lumen Vitae* 21 (1966) 66–90, 205–24. **Rengstorf, K. H.** *Die Auferstehung Jesu: Form, Art und Sinn der urchristlichen Osterbotschaft*. Witten-Ruhr: Lutherverlag, 1952. **Ruckstuhl, E.** "Auferstehung, Erhöhung und Himmelfahrt Jesu." In *Jesus im Horizont der Evangelien*. SBA 3. Stuttgart: Katholisches Bibelwerk, 1988. ———. "Die evangelischen Ostererzählungen." In *Die Auferstehung Jesu Christi: Heilsgeschichtliche Tatsache und Brennpunkt des Glaubens*. Ed. E. Ruckstuhl and J. Pfammatter. Lucerne; Munich: Rex, 1968. 31–59. **Schenke, L.** *Auferstehungsverkündigung und leeres Grab*. SBS 33. Stuttgart: Katholisches Bibelwerk, 1968. **Segal, A. F.** "The Risen Christ and the Angelic Mediator Figures in the Light of Qumran." In *Jesus and the Dead Sea Scrolls*. Ed. J. H. Charlesworth. ABRL. Garden City, NY: Doubleday, 1992. 302–28. **Seidensticker, P.** *Die Auferstehung Jesu in der Botschaft der Evangelisten*. SBS 26. Stuttgart: Katholisches Bibelwerk, 1967. **Smit, D. J.** "The Resurrection of Jesus—What Was It? Plurality and Ambiguity in the Christian Resurrection Hope." *Neot* 23 (1989) 159–75. **Smith, J. J.** "Resurrection Faith Today." *TS* 30 (1969) 393–419. **Smith, R. H.** *Easter Gospels: The Resurrection of Jesus according to the Four Gospels*. Minneapolis: Augsburg, 1983. **Staudinger, H.** "The Resurrection of Jesus Christ as Saving

Event and as 'Object' of Historical Research." *SJT* 36 (1983) 309–26. **Steinseifer, B.** "Der Ort der Erscheinungen des Auferstandenen: Zur Frage alter galiläischer Ostertraditionen." *ZNW* 62 (1971) 232–66. **Stuhlmacher, P.** "Kritischer müssen mir die Historisch-Kritischen sein!" *TQ* 153 (1973) 244–51. **Tabor, J. D.** "'Returning to the Divinity': Josephus' Portrayal of the Disappearance of Enoch, Elijah and Moses." *JBL* 108 (1989) 225–38. **Talbert, C. H.** "The Concept of Immortals in Mediterranean Antiquity." *JBL* 94 (1975) 419–36. **Teeple, H. M.** "The Historical Beginnings of the Resurrection Faith." In *Studies in New Testament and Early Christian Literature.* FS A. P. Wikgren, ed. D. E. Aune. NovTSup 33. Leiden: Brill, 1972. 107–20. **Turner, H. E. W.** "The Resurection." *ExpTim* 68 (1956–57) 369–71. **Vögtle, A.** "Wie kam es zum Osterglauben?" In *Wie Kam es zum Osterglauben?* Ed. A. Vögtle and R. Pesch. Düsseldorf: Patmos, 1975. 11–131. **Vorster, W. S.** "The Religio-Historical Context of the Resurrection of Jesus and Resurrection Faith in the New Testament." *Neot* 23 (1989) 159–75. **Walker, D. A.** "Resurrection, Empty Tomb and Easter Faith." *ExpTim* 101 (1989–90) 172–75. **Ware, R. C.** "The Resurrection of Jesus." *HeyJ* 16 (1975) 22–35, 174–94. **Watson, F.** "'Historical Evidence' and the Resurrection of Jesus." *Theology* 90 (1987) 365–72. **Wengst, K.** *Ostern—Ein wirkliches Gleichnis, eine wahre Geschichte: Zum neutestamentlichen Zeugnis von der Auferweckung Jesu.* Kaiser Taschenbücher 97. Munich: Kaiser, 1991. **Whitaker, D.** "What Happened to the Body of Jesus?" *ExpTim* 81 (1969–70) 307–11. **Wilckens, U.** *Resurrection: Biblical Testimony to the Resurrection: An Historical Examination and Explanation.* Atlanta: Knox, 1978. **Worschitz, K. M.** "Ostererscheinungen—Grundlagen des Glaubens." *Diakonia* 22 (1991) 6–17. **Zehrer, F.** *Die Auferstehung Jesu nach den vier Evangelisten: Die Osterevangelien und ihre hauptsäche Probleme.* Vienna: Mayer, 1980.

Translation

¹*And when the Sabbath was past, Mary Magdalene, and Mary the mother of James, and Salome bought spices*[a] *so that, going, they might anoint him.*[b] ²*And very early in the morning of the first day of the week they come to the tomb, before the sun had risen.* ³*And they were saying to themselves, "Who will for us roll the stone away from the door of the tomb?"*[c] ⁴*And looking up, they see that the stone was rolled away; for it was very large.* ⁵*And going into the tomb, they saw a young man seated on the right, dressed in a white robe, and they were distressed.* ⁶*But he says to them, "Do not be distressed.*[d] *You seek Jesus the Nazarene, who was crucifed. He has been raised; he is not here. Behold the place where they laid him.* ⁷*But go, tell his disciples and Peter, 'He is going*[e] *before you in Galilee. There you will see him, just as he told you.'"* ⁸*And going outside, they fled from the tomb, for trembling*[f] *and amazement had taken hold of them. And they said nothing to anyone, for they were afraid.*

Notes

[a]A few late MSS read πορευθεῖσαι ἡτοίμασαν ἀρώματα, "having gone, they prepared spices."
[b]Several late MSS read τὸν Ἰησοῦν, "Jesus."
[c]The OL codex Bobiensis (it[k]) inserts the following between vv 3 and 4: *Subito autem ad horam tertiam tenebrae diei factae sunt per totum orbem terrae, et descenderunt de caelis angeli et surgent in claritate vivi Dei simul ascenderunt cum eo, et continuo lux facta est. Tunc illae accesserunt ad monimentum,* "But suddenly at the third hour of the day there was darkness over the whole circle of the earth, and angels descended from the heavens, and as he was rising [reading *surgente eo*] in the glory of the living God, at the same time they ascended with him; and immediately it was light. Then the women went to the tomb" (based on the translation in Metzger, *TCGNT* ¹, 121–22). Westcott and Hort (*Introduction* 2:28) speculate that this insertion is based on an apocryphal source. They could be correct, for the resurrection scene of Bobiensis is reminiscent of the more fanciful account found in the *Gospel of Peter*: "A

loud voice rang out in heaven, and they saw the heavens opened and two men descending from there in great brightness and drawing near to the tomb. . . . [A]gain they see three men coming out of the tomb—two of them supporting the one, and a cross following them—and the heads of the two reached to heaven, but (the head) of the one being led by the hand extended above the heavens" (*Gos. Pet.* 9.35–10.40).

[d]D W and several later MSS and authorities read μὴ φοβεῖσθε, "Fear not" (cf. Matt 28:5). These words echo those of Jesus in Mark 6:50.

[e]Several late MSS read ὅτι ἠγέρθη ἀπὸ νεκρῶν καὶ ἰδοὺ προάγει, "that he was raised from the dead, and behold, he is going before" (cf. Matt 28:7). This variant probably echoes the language of the passion predictions, e.g., Mark 9:9.

[f]Gk. τρόμος. D W and a few later authorities read φόβος, "fear."

Form/Structure/Setting

Bultmann (*History,* 287) believes that the "purpose of the story is without doubt to prove the reality of the resurrection of Jesus by the empty tomb." There is some truth to this, to be sure, but one wonders how well it applies to Mark, whose text in our oldest MSS contains no account of the resurrection itself, only a report of it (in vv 6–7). Bultmann's point has validity only if Mark originally did contain a resurrection narrative. After all, failure to narrate what one hopes to prove is an odd way of proceeding. (Of course, Bultmann, *History,* 285, does believe that Mark's Gospel originally ended with a resurrection appearance in Galilee.) Furthermore, Bultmann (*History,* 284–87) believes that Mark 16:1–8 is a secondary formulation that fits awkwardly with the preceding pericopes (as seen in repeating the names of the women [15:40, 47; 16:1] and in the impression that Jesus' preparation for burial has been left incomplete [15:46; 16:1]). Awkward transitions, however, are not unusual in Mark, often indicating the presence of sources and at the same time testifying to the evangelist's limited editorial skills. Taylor (602) rightly suggests that the awkward fit of 16:1–8 (esp. v 1) suggests that this pericope has been drawn from a cycle of tradition distinct from much of what underlies chaps. 14–15. The evangelist has constructed the narrative "on the basis of tradition." Taylor's view is in agreement with that of Dibelius (*Tradition,* 190, 192), who asserts that "Mark did not create the story of the empty grave" and that "the grave-legend is no invention of Mark's."

One of the most famous, rationalizing interpretations of the story of the empty tomb is the so-called Wrong Tomb Theory. According to Lake (*Historical Evidence,* 251–53), early Sunday morning the women went to the tomb they thought contained the body of Jesus and met a young man, who guessed the purpose of their errand and told them: "He is not here; see the place where they laid him." The young man then "probably pointed to the next tomb." Frightened, the women fled, misunderstanding the words of the young man. Later learning of the resurrection, they concluded that the tomb they had visited was "empty." Lake (*Historical Evidence,* 263) concludes: "The empty tomb is . . . doctrinally indefensible and is historically insufficiently accredited."

How sufficiently accredited the narrative must be before Lake will accept it is unclear. There are probably two independent accounts of the empty tomb: Mark's and John's (though scholars dispute the independence of John). But perhaps the most important aspect of this question centers on the simple fact that from the earliest moment on, Jesus' followers spoke of "resurrection" (ἀνάστασις) or of being "raised" (ἐγείρειν, ἀνιστάναι), which in a Jewish Palestinian setting would strongly imply the abandonment of the grave (cf. Dan 12:2: "And many of those who sleep in the dust of the earth shall awake, some to everlasting life, and some to shame and everlasting contempt"). Apart from the discovery of the empty tomb, the Easter appearances of Jesus would in all probability have been interpreted as ghost stories, in effect turning Easter into Halloween. The unanimous, unopposed, and unrivaled interpretation among early Christians that Jesus died, was buried, and was raised (cf. 1 Cor 15:3–4: "raised on the third day") is best explained not as the result of visions of the living Christ only but as the result of the discovery of the empty tomb, which then gave meaning to the visions, leading Christians to speak of them in terms of *resurrection* and not merely ghostly, phantasmal apparitions.

The major factor that supports the historicity of the empty tomb tradition is the potentially awkward admission that the tomb was first visited by women, not Jesus' leading male disciples. Here the criterion of embarrassment is invoked. In Paul's proclamation of the resurrection, men figure prominently; indeed, there is no mention of women at all (cf. 1 Cor 15:3–8). The most plausible explanation for the story recounted in Mark 16:1–8 is that it reflects what the early church knew actually happened: some women went to Jesus' tomb, not expecting resurrection but to mourn and perhaps augment the abridged burial procedures. To their great astonishment, the tomb was vacant. The subsequent appearances of the risen Christ made it clear that these women were not mistaken. The empty tomb, in turn, made it clear that the appearances of Christ should be understood in terms of resurrection.

The strong presupposition in favor of the historicity of the discovery of the empty tomb by women tells against Crossan's contention that the *Gospel of Peter* contains the earliest account of Easter that underlies the accounts in the four canonical Gospels (cf. *Cross That Spoke*). According to the *Gospel of Peter*, a whole host of credible (and hostile) witnesses were on hand to witness Jesus' resurrection. Because of the obvious lack of historical verisimilitude in this account (such as Jewish elders and ruling priests spending the night in a cemetery!), Crossan believes a later editor made changes in the story. But why were *women* introduced as the first to discover the empty tomb and bear witness to the resurrection? Would not the later evangelists in revising the *Gospel of Peter* have depicted Peter and other male disciples finding the tomb? The Markan narrative, which is followed by Matthew and Luke, strongly resists this sequence. It is highly improbable that the *Gospel of Peter* predates the Synoptics and served as their principal passion and resurrection source. It is therefore very probable that the discovery of the tomb by women is bedrock historical tradition and that later details (such as the women reporting the discovery to the disciples and the disciples confirming their story, as in the other canonical Gospels; or a guard posted at the tomb, as in Matthew; or myriads of hostile witnesses, as in the *Gospel of Peter*) represent embellishments meant to clarify or defend the remarkable claim of the resurrection. (E.g., was Jesus really resurrected or was his appearance only a ghost? The former, says Luke, because the Jesus who appeared ate food [Luke 24:36–43]. But how did the disciples know the apparition was really Jesus? Maybe it was someone else. There was no mistake in identity, says John, because Jesus showed the disciples the marks of the nails in his hands [John 20:19–29].)

More recently, arguments have been made that the empty-tomb story was Mark's deliberate, redactional conclusion to his Gospel (e.g., Crossan, "Empty Tomb and Absent Lord"; cf. Weeden, *Mark*, 45–51, 101–17). If this claim can be sustained, then it lends strong support to the view that Mark's Gospel originally did conclude at v 8. However, Crossan's conclusion that Mark ended his narrative with the empty tomb and without a resurrection appearance so as to reinforce his emphasis on suffering and service in opposition to an obsession with miracles and apparitions on the part of his alleged opponents is not convincing. And in any case, would not the young man's statements that "he has been raised" (v 6) and that "he is going before you in Galilee. There you will see him" (v 7) have negated Mark's thrust as Crossan understands it? Would not these hypothetical advocates of miracles and apparitions have been perfectly satisfied with Mark's narrative? After all, the evangelist had given them nine chapters of miracles and extraordinary events, including the transfiguration, in Mark 1–9, and then at the conclusion of the Gospel provided an eerie narrative in which a mysterious young man announced that Jesus had indeed been raised, just as originally promised, and had gone on ahead of disciples to Galilee where he would meet them. If Jesus' teaching on the need for endurance in the face of suffering was peppered with confident predictions of resurrection "after three days," how did the evangelist guard his flank against his hypothetical opponents?

The empty-tomb story has inspired many symbolic interpretations, but none is compelling. Botha (*Neot* 23 [1989] 195–218) believes that the empty-tomb narrative, whereby Jesus is resurrected despite crucifixion and being sealed in a tomb with a large stone, is the evangelist's way of illustrating how God is able to save people in mysterious ways. Vignolo (*RivB* 3 (1990) 129–89) thinks the puzzlement produced by Mark's abrupt ending stimulates the reader to imagine what the conclusion of the narrative should be. Intrigued by the women who mysteriously appear (15:40–41) and disappear (16:8), the reader is drawn into the search for Jesus. Lincoln (*JBL* 108 [1989] 283–300) finds in the Markan ending encouragement for the readers of the Gospel to persevere despite failure and disobedience as exemplified by the disciples. Giesen (SNTSU 12 [1987] 99–139) finds in the empty-tomb story encouragement not to focus on the absence of the Lord or on the women's fear, but to focus on the living, resurrected Christ as experienced in the community and in daily life.

Individual details in the narrative are also subject to highly symbolic interpretation. According to LaVerdiere (*Emmanuel* 92 [1986] 125–29), notice that the stone "was very large" (v 4) underscores the gravity of death, but its being rolled away from the opening of the tomb symbolizes the proclamation of the gospel. LaVerdiere (*Emmanuel* 90 [1984] 138–42) also believes that the clothing of the young man encountered at the tomb symbolizes the baptized Christian whose person reflects the brilliance of the risen, transfigured Lord. Jenkins (*ExpTim* 94 [1983] 237–40), however, thinks that the white robe indicates the heavenly state of a martyr, whose presence at the tomb is a challenge to Jesus' followers to face death, if necessary, for the sake of the gospel. The subjectivity and unverifiability of these interpretations and many others should be obvious.

The empty tomb would have impressed readers in the Roman Empire, both Jewish and Gentile. At least two omens took place during Jesus' execution: the darkness that befell the land (15:33) and the tearing of the temple veil when

Jesus expired with a loud cry (15:37–38). The mysterious absence of Jesus' body and the announcement of the young man would have created a sense of awe and wonderment in the readers of Mark's Gospel. But the telling of the story in a manner calculated to impress Roman readers does not mean that the story itself grew out of Roman traditions. Contrary to Hamilton (*JBL* 84 [1965] 415–21) and Bickermann (*ZNW* 23 [1924] 281–92), Bolt (*TynBul* 47 [1996] 27–37) rightly doubts that the empty-tomb tradition owes its origin to Greco-Roman ideas of the hero who mysteriously abandons his grave. The empty tomb of Jesus has nothing to do with the empty tomb of a hero or with traditions of translation.

Because he has become convinced that Jewish-Christian dialogue is inhibited by Christians' belief in a literal resurrection of Jesus, Hanhart (*Open Tomb*, ix) seeks a new understanding of Mark 16:1–8. He contends that the "ending of Mark should be read as midrashic aggadah expressing his indomitable faith and hope in God in a time of great crisis," not as literal history. Perhaps Hanhart should converse with Lapide (*Resurrection*), a Jewish scholar who thinks that Jesus was indeed resurrected and who is more than happy to discuss it with Jews and Christians. In any event, perceived theological needs or personal preferences are hardly legitimate criteria for concluding what happened historically or what was intended exegetically. Lapide argues first from history and exegesis and then reflects theologically on what it all means. He concludes on historical and exegetical grounds that Jesus was resurrected, although he asserts that this does not necessarily make Jesus Israel's Messiah.

An inscription from Nazareth of uncertain date, though probably pre-70, may have some bearing on our understanding of the sanctity of the grave in late antiquity. The Nazareth inscription reads (see Boffo, *Iscrizioni*, 319–33; Cumont, *Revue historique* 163 [1930] 241–66; Metzger, "Nazareth Inscription"; van der Horst, *Ancient Jewish Epitaphs*, 159–60):

> Ordinance of Caesar: It is my pleasure that graves and tombs—whoever has made them as a pious service for ancestors or children or members of their house—that these remain unmolested in perpetuity. But if any person lay information that another either has destroyed them, or has in any other way cast out the bodies which have been buried there, or with malicious deception has transferred them to other places, to the dishonor of those buried there, or has removed the headstones or other stones, in such a case I command that a trial be instituted, just as if they were concerned with the gods for the pious services of mortals. For beyond all else it shall be obligatory to honor those who have been buried. Let no one remove them for any reason. If not, however [i.e., if anyone does so], capital punishment on the charge of tomb robbery I will to take place.

Metzger ("Nazareth Inscription," 91) comments: "If in fact the ordinance was published in Palestine some time prior to the death of Jesus, then . . . at the time of the resurrection there was in force a severe law against tampering with buried bodies, the consequences of infringing which the panic-stricken disciples are very unlikely to have braved" (cf. Boffo, *Iscrizioni*, 333; Brown, 1293–94).

Mark's narrative of the empty tomb is made up of four principal components: (1) the approach of the women to anoint Jesus' body (vv 1–3), (2) the discovery of the open tomb (v 4), (3) the message of the young man (vv 5–7), and (4) the flight and fear of the women (v 8).

Comment

1 καὶ διαγενομένου τοῦ σαββάτου, "And when the Sabbath was past," that is, after 6:00 P.M. Saturday, the women would then have been permitted to purchase items and to engage in work, such as preparing perfumes and ointments for Jesus' body. This they planned to do the following day, very early in the morning (v 2).

Μαρία ἡ Μαγδαληνὴ καὶ Μαρία ἡ [τοῦ] Ἰακώβου καὶ Σαλώμη, "Mary Magdalene, and Mary the mother of James, and Salome." These women have been named in 15:40 (see *Comment* there), and two of them have been named in 15:47.

ἠγόρασαν ἀρώματα ἵνα ἐλθοῦσαι ἀλείψωσιν αὐτόν, "bought spices so that, going, they might anoint him." Because of the short interval between Jesus' death, his removal from the cross, and his interment, the preparation of his body according to Jewish burial conventions in all probability had been abridged. This scenario of haste lends additional support to Mark's tradition of Joseph from Arimathea. This Joseph is no devoted disciple; he regards the burial of Jesus as a religious duty. It is done with dispatch (as no doubt it was for the other two crucifixion victims), but not with devotion. The women, who were devoted to Jesus (cf. 14:3–9), now hope to complete the process. Due care for the corpse was very important to Judaism of late antiquity and is reflected in an apocryphal tradition that tells of angels who tend to the burial of righteous Abraham: "and they bore his precious soul in their hands in divinely woven linen. And they tended the body of the righteous Abraham with divine ointments and perfumes until the third day after his death. And they buried him in the promised land" (*T. Abr.* 20:10b–11).

2 καὶ λίαν πρωῒ τῇ μιᾷ τῶν σαββάτων . . . ἀνατείλαντος τοῦ ἡλίου, "And very early in the morning of the first day of the week . . . before the sun had risen." Mark's language is confusing—contradictory in its present form and possibly redundant. It is contradictory if we allow it to stand as found in the Greek text: λίαν πρωῒ . . . ἀνατείλαντος τοῦ ἡλίου, "very early in the morning . . . the sun having risen." But it is possible that an οὔπω, "not yet," has dropped out of the text. If so, the text is simply redundant: "very early in the morning . . . the sun not yet having risen." Torrey (*Our Translated Gospels,* 71–73) suspects a problem in the Aramaic. If corrected, the concluding genitive absolute of v 2 (ἀνατείλαντος τοῦ ἡλίου, "the sun having risen") would then be taken with the beginning of v 3, which would then read: "When the sun had risen, they were saying to themselves. . . ." Perhaps this is the source of the misunderstanding, but the problem is in the Greek. It may be assumed that the text is in some way corrupt, so the translation "before the sun had risen" has been adopted here. If this is correct, then the women have set out for the tomb around 5:00 A.M. Since it is so early in the morning, the women must have bought their spices Saturday evening "when the sabbath was past" (v 1). Mark's narrative knows nothing of the earthquake and the angel who descends from heaven to roll away the stone (cf. Matt 28:2–4).

ἔρχονται ἐπὶ τὸ μνημεῖον, "they come to the tomb." The women are able to find their way to the tomb, having seen where Jesus' body had been laid (cf. 15:47). Mark says nothing about a guard at the tomb (a tradition found in Matt 27:62–66 and greatly embellished in the *Gospel of Peter*), so the women's only concern is gaining access, not permission, to Jesus' body.

3 τίς ἀποκυλίσει ἡμῖν τὸν λίθον ἐκ τῆς θύρας τοῦ μνημείου, "Who will for us roll the stone away from the door of the tomb?" The stones used to seal the openings to tombs were anywhere from five to six feet in diameter with varying thickness. An average stone weighed hundreds of pounds. Although some of these stones rolled along a flat channel, they usually leaned against the outer wall of the tomb itself, thus creating a great deal of friction. The three women assume that they do not possess the size and strength to roll the stone aside. They wonder who might do it for them. Because of the early hour, the women likely assume that no one will be available to assist them. It is here that Mark should explain that the stone is very large, but he withholds this information until the end of v 4.

4 καὶ ἀναβλέψασαι θεωροῦσιν ὅτι ἀποκεκύλισται ὁ λίθος, "And looking up, they see that the stone was rolled away." Quite unexpectedly the women find the stone already rolled away. The problem that they had discussed on the way has been resolved, though they have no idea how.

ἦν γὰρ μέγας σφόδρα, "for it was very large." The Markan evangelist now belatedly explains why the women were concerned about rolling the stone aside to gain access to the body of Jesus (v 3): the stone was μέγας σφόδρα, "very large." (On Mark's clumsy placement of the qualifying modifier, see *Comment* on 11:13.) By stating this, the evangelist may also be suggesting that the stone's movement in itself points to supernatural power at work, for such a large stone could not be easily moved.

Kloner (*BAR* 25.5 [1999] 22–29, 76) calculates that approximately 98 percent of stones used to close the entrances to tombs in Jesus' day were square block stones. Larger, wheel-shaped stones were used only by the wealthy. He concludes therefore that the stone that closed Jesus' tomb was probably the smaller block stone and that the verb ἀποκεκύλισται, "was rolled away," could still be used in reference to the square stones. However, since the Gospel tradition remembers that the tomb belonged to a wealthy man, the stone that closed Jesus' tomb may very well have been of the larger, wheel-shaped variety.

5 καὶ εἰσελθοῦσαι εἰς τὸ μνημεῖον, "And going into the tomb." The Fourth Evangelist says it was necessary to stoop (παρακύπτειν) to see into the tomb (John 20:5). This is because the opening of a rock-cut tomb was normally about one meter square; one could not enter such a tomb without stooping. Hence a stone of about four feet in diameter was sufficient to cover the opening. Only when the women actually enter the tomb through its small opening will they be able to see what or who is inside.

εἶδον νεανίσκον καθήμενον ἐν τοῖς δεξιοῖς περιβεβλημένον στολὴν λευκήν, "they saw a young man seated on the right, dressed in a white robe." The women expected to see the body of Jesus; instead, they see a νεανίσκον, "young man." The identity of this person has been endlessly debated. The only other occurrence of νεανίσκος, "young man," in Mark is found in 14:51–52, the story of the young man who leaves behind the linen sheet, the only thing he is wearing, and flees naked into the night. Several theories have been proposed that try to find a meaningful linkage between the disrobed and robed young men. Most of these theories suffer from an excess of subjective symbolism (see *Comment* on 14:51–52).

It is often remarked that contrary to Matt 28:3, 5, which describes the young man as an ἄγγελος, "angel," and as having an appearance ὡς ἀστραπή, "like light-

ning," and clothing λευκὸν ὡς χιών, "white as snow," Mark describes the messenger at the empty tomb only as a νεανίσκον, "young man." But angels are sometimes
described in this manner: "Two young men also appeared to him [δύο
προσεφάνησαν αὐτῷ νεανίαι], remarkably strong, gloriously beautiful and splen-
didly dressed" (2 Macc 3:26); "While the High Priest was making the offering of
atonement, the same young men [νεανίαι] appeared again to Heliodorus dressed
in the same clothing" (3:33). As is made clear in context, these young men are
angels. And according to Josephus: "Now once when his [Manoah's] wife was
alone, an angel [ἄγγελος] appeared to her from God, in the likeness of a comely
and tall youth [νεανία]" (*Ant.* 5.8.2 §277). The story of Tobit is instructive (cf.
Tob [א] 5:5, 7, 10), in that the angel first appears in the narrative as a man and
only later is revealed as a protective angel.

Mark also says the young man was περιβεβλημένον στολὴν λευκήν, "dressed in a
white robe." This apparel also suggests an angelic figure. In 2 Macc 5:2, angels
are seen wearing διαχρύσους στολάς, "golden robes." Comments about the apparel of an angel or mysterious person are typical (cf. *L.A.B.* 9:10: "Behold a man
in a linen garment stood and said to me"; Rev 7:9: περιβεβλημένους στολὰς λευκάς,
"dressed in white robes"; 7:13: οὗτοι οἱ περιβεβλημένοι τὰς στολὰς τὰς λευκάς,
"these who are dressed in white robes"; 10:1: ἄλλον ἄγγελον . . . περιβεβλημένον
νεφέλην, "another angel . . . dressed in a cloud"). The transfigured Jesus, whose
clothing took on a heavenly look, was said to have become "exceedingly white
[λευκά] as a launderer on earth cannot whiten [λευκᾶναι]" (Mark 9:3).

Matthew clearly and correctly understands Mark's young man as an angel. To
be sure, the Matthean evangelist has embellished Mark's version of the story, but
he has not significantly altered it by transforming a mortal into an angel (Taylor,
606–7). All things considered, it is probable that Mark intends the young man in
16:5 to be understood as an angel (so most commentators; see also Brown, 1:300).

The evangelist says that the young man is καθήμενον ἐν τοῖς δεξιοῖς, "seated
on the right," perhaps suggesting authority or honor, perhaps even as a parallel
to the risen Christ who shortly will be ἐκ δεξιῶν καθήμενον, "seated 'at the right
hand,'" of God (as prophesied in 14:62; cf. Ps 110:1). Being at the right, presumably right of the place where the body of Jesus had been laid, may suggest that
authority to speak for the risen Christ has been delegated to this young man,
though it is doubtful that this "makes the young man represent Jesus" (as Gundry,
990, understands).

καὶ ἐξεθαμβήθησαν, "and they were distressed." The women were distressed
(or "amazed") at the discovery of the opened tomb and the presence of the young
man. The word ἐκθαμβεῖν, "to amaze, distress," usually expresses great emotion.
In 9:15 "all the crowd, seeing him, were greatly amazed [ἐξεθαμβήθησαν], and
running up to him, they greeted him." Apparently they were amazed at Jesus'
appearance following his descent from the Mount of Transfiguration (see *Comment* on 9:15). In 14:33 Jesus ἤρξατο ἐκθαμβεῖσθαι, "began to be distressed," which
is probably what ἐκθαμβεῖν means here in parallel with ἀδημονεῖν, "to be troubled"
(see *Comment* on 14:33). Here in 16:5, however, the women are not only amazed,
but they are probably also distressed at the discovery of the open tomb and the
mysterious stranger. Has Jesus' body been removed? Will they be able to complete the planned anointing?

The Matthean and Lukan evangelists seize on the ambiguity and mysteriousness of the Markan scene and rewrite it—independently of one another—in such a way that the supernatural elements are greatly enhanced. In Matthew (28:5) the young man becomes an angel of the Lord (which carries with it important OT images), while in Luke (24:4) he is expanded into two figures (cf. John 20:12) whose unearthly dress clearly implies their angelic identities (cf. Luke 24:23) and attests to Luke's penchant for dual witness (cf. Luke 10:1).

6 μὴ ἐκθαμβεῖσθε, "Do not be distressed." The young man enjoins the women that there is nothing to be worried about; all is as it should be.

Ἰησοῦν ζητεῖτε τὸν Ναζαρηνὸν τὸν ἐσταυρωμένον, "You seek Jesus the Nazarene, who was crucified." The young man quickly reassures the women by stating matter-of-factly the purpose of their visit. He knows they are followers of Jesus and that they have come to minister to him.

ἠγέρθη, οὐκ ἔστιν ὧδε· ἴδε ὁ τόπος ὅπου ἔθηκαν αὐτόν, "He has been raised; he is not here. Behold the place where they laid him." The young man now explains the absence of Jesus' body: ἠγέρθη, οὐκ ἔστιν ὧδε, "He has been raised; he is not here." As if to respond to looks of disbelief and incomprehension on the faces of the women, the young man bids them to examine ὁ τόπος ὅπου ἔθηκαν αὐτόν, "the place where they laid him." Mark's readers are reminded of 15:47: "Mary Magdalene and Mary the [mother] of Joses were observing where he had been laid [ποῦ τέθειται]." The women knew where Jesus' body had been laid; they are therefore invited to search the tomb and ascertain that Jesus' body is in fact οὐκ . . . ὧδε, "not here." Mention should be made of the interesting parallel in *T. Job* 39:11–12: "And they left to dig (up Job's deceased children), but I (Job) forbade it, saying, 'Do not trouble yourselves in vain. For you will not find my children, since they were taken up into heaven.'"

7 ἀλλὰ ὑπάγετε εἴπατε τοῖς μαθηταῖς αὐτοῦ καὶ τῷ Πέτρῳ, "But go, tell his disciples and Peter." Having satisfied the women's fears and doubts, the young man now commands them to report back to Jesus' disciples and (especially) to Peter. Why is Peter singled out? Taylor (607) is correct to say that "there can be little doubt that the Denial is in mind." Again, the fact that women are the conveyors of the good news of Easter strongly urges the historicity of the tradition. Pious fiction would resist assigning such an important role to minor followers of Jesus (as the women would have been viewed).

προάγει ὑμᾶς εἰς τὴν Γαλιλαίαν· ἐκεῖ αὐτὸν ὄψεσθε, καθὼς εἶπεν ὑμῖν, "He is going before you in Galilee. There you will see him, just as he told you." The young man gives the women the message they are to repeat to Peter. The plural ὑμᾶς, "you," indicates that the message is for all of the disciples, not just for Peter. προάγει, "he is going before," implies leadership, not simply prior arrival in Galilee. Accordingly, εἰς τὴν Γαλιλαίαν should be rendered "in Galilee," rather than "to" or "into Galilee," for frequently in Mark εἰς, "into," is used in place of ἐν, "in" (e.g., 1:9: "he was baptized in [εἰς] the Jordan"; 1:21: "he was teaching in [εἰς] the synagogue"; 1:39: "he was preaching in [εἰς] their synagogues in [εἰς] all Galilee"; cf. Turner, *JTS* o.s. 26 [1925] 14–20; van Iersel, *ETL* 58 [1982] 365–70; and *Comment* on 14:28). This means that the risen Christ will be going before his disciples or leading the way for them in Galilee. The implication is that the ministry of proclaiming and advancing the kingdom, broken off for a short time in order to make the fateful journey to Jerusalem, will now resume. ἐκεῖ αὐτὸν ὄψεσθε, "there you will see him," makes it clear that the apostolic faith in the resurrection will rest on eyewitness, firsthand experience, not hearsay (i.e., the report of the women). The young man's message should hardly occasion surprise, for Jesus himself had foretold this very thing: "But after I am raised up, I shall go before you in Galilee" (14:28).

8 καὶ ἐξελθοῦσαι ἔφυγον ἀπὸ τοῦ μνημείου, εἶχεν γὰρ αὐτὰς τρόμος καὶ ἔκστασις, "And going outside, they fled from the tomb, for trembling and amazement had taken hold of them." After having this startling message revealed to them, the women bolt from the tomb, gripped with τρόμος καὶ ἔκστασις, "trembling and amazement." They are so excited by what they have seen and heard that their bodies begin to shake.

καὶ οὐδενὶ οὐδὲν εἶπαν, "And they said nothing to anyone." The women act contrary to what the young man had commanded them only a moment before. Mark's double negative, οὐδενὶ οὐδέν, literally "nothing to no one," adds emphasis. Even if the women have failed to recover and carry out their orders, the reader knows that the risen Christ will indeed appear to his disciples in Galilee. The reader of Mark by now knows that Jesus' predictions invariably come to pass (such as his repeated predictions of his passion and resurrection "after three days").

ἐφοβοῦντο γάρ, "for they were afraid." The women are frozen into inactivity and silence by their fear. Perhaps readers are to assume that once they recover they will fulfill their commission to report to the disciples and to Peter the message of the young man (cf. Creed, *JTS* o.s. 31 [1930] 175–80; Moule, *NTS* 2 [1955–56] 58–59; Cranfield, 469). Of course, the original Markan narrative may very well have continued for a few more paragraphs, perhaps concluding with the predicted appearance to the disciples in Galilee. But the oldest MSS of Mark's Gospel end here at v 8 (see discussion of 16:9–20). The question of whether Mark ends at 16:8 has been hotly debated, with many scholars arguing that v 8 is the original ending (e.g., Wellhausen, 137; Lohmeyer, 356–60; Lightfoot, *Gospel Message*, 80–97, 106–16; Crossan, "Empty Tomb and Absent Lord"; Lane, 591–92; Bush, "Mark's Call to Action") and many others contending that the original ending has been lost, whether accidentally or intentionally, or that perhaps the author was prevented from writing it (e.g., Swete, 399; Turner, 82–83; Cranfield, 471; Taylor, 609; Gundry, 1009–12).

Aland ("Der Schluss," 461–64) has shown that γάρ, "for," can conclude a whole document, not just a sentence. Sandmel (*JBR* 31 [1963] 54–55) thinks Mark's abrupt ending is deliberate:

> it brilliantly passes a scornful judgment on the scorned disciples. That Mark closes without a Resurrection appearance would no longer be a surprise, for how could an artful author depict Jesus as appearing to the disloyal and the deniers? The words 'Tell his disciples and Peter that he is going before to Galilee' (16:7) now take on a new sense, for they are not so much the promise they are usually thought to be, but are instead a prime rebuke, meant to be understood as conveying contempt.

Sandmel may in part be correct, but it is doubtful that the evangelist intends his conclusion or the words of the young man to be a "scornful judgment" or a "rebuke" meant to convey "contempt." The focus of the passage is christological, not parenetic. Jesus has been vindicated, and his frightened disciples, who failed him in his hour of need, are to be told that this prophecy that they had not understood has been fulfilled: "He has been raised; he is not here. . . . He is going before you in Galilee. There you will see him, just as he told you" (vv 6–7; cf. 14:28).

Gundry (1009–12) marshals significant evidence in support of his view that the final sentence of v 8, "And they said nothing to anyone, for they were afraid," was in fact the beginning of a new paragraph, the rest of which is now lost. Some of his points include: (1) Mark has consistently narrated the fulfillment of Jesus' various predictions, such as seeing God's power having come at the transfiguration, securing a colt, finding the upper room, and the passion predictions themselves. (2) If the final sentence was to be understood as disobedience of the young man's command to report to the disciples, we should expect an adversative δέ or ἀλλά, "but," not καί, "and," which Mark usually uses to introduce new pericopes. (3) Both Matthew and Luke continue their Easter narratives with the women, implying that Mark's lost account also continued with the women. (4) There is material in the Easter stories of Matthew and Luke that points to a common source, and that source is probably Mark. (5) The Markan evangelist usually begins rather than ends pericopes on a note of fear (5:33, 36; 6:20, 50; 9:6; 10:32; 11:32). (6) Only 10 percent (i.e., six out of sixty-six) of Mark's γάρ, "for," clauses conclude pericopes. This statistic favors the view that the last part of v 8 begins a new pericope rather than ends the one that precedes. Similarly, the rarity of books ending with γάρ should caution against accepting v 8 as the conclusion of Mark. (7) The centrality of the Easter appearances in early Christian preaching supports the presumption that Mark's Gospel, like the other three canonical Gospels, also concluded with an appearance of the risen Christ (cf. Cranfield, 471; Taylor, 609; Osborne, *Resurrection Narratives*, 64–65).

The cumulative effect of this evidence, taken with Gundry's arguments, tips probability in favor of the view that v 8 was not the intended ending of the Gospel and that either a narrative resurrection appearance was composed, but then later was lost, or was planned, but then was not penned. Although the earliest extant MSS end here, later MSS of Mark go on to narrate resurrection appearances. These later MSS of Mark provide two endings, which will be briefly considered in the next section of the commentary.

Explanation

Because Jesus had been buried in haste and probably because his criminal status had placed restrictions on the burial rites, three brave women risk going to the tomb early Sunday morning to complete the burial process and to weep quietly at the tomb. They wonder who will roll back the heavy stone. It is ironic that not one of Jesus' male disciples is available to offer this assistance. But the question quickly becomes moot; when they arrive at the tomb, they find that the stone has already been rolled back. Entering the tomb they see a young man. The evangelist Mark does not call him an angel, but the description probably would have made most of Mark's readers (including the Matthean evangelist) think that he was an angel.

The young man tells the astounded women that Jesus of Nazareth is risen and is not to be found in the tomb. He bids them to look upon the very place where his body had lain. Jesus is indeed gone. They are to go and tell the disciples, especially Peter, that he will go before them in Galilee; there they will see him. There is an element of irony here. The disciples have fled and have presumably begun their journey for home, leaving behind their dead master. But not so; Jesus will arrive in Galilee before they do and will "go before" them "in Galilee," implying that the resurrected Jesus will continue to lead his disciples in the ongoing ministry of the kingdom of God.

Mark's Gospel ends abruptly with the notation that the women were so astonished that they were left frightened and speechless. In all probability the narrative continued with the women fulfilling their assignment and with Jesus making an appearance to the disciples just as had been promised. Mark's Gospel ends with a dramatic finish, emphasizing once again the awesome power of Jesus, who not only astounded people during his ministry but also astounded people in his death and in his resurrection. At the beginning of the Gospel Jesus is identified as the "son of God" (1:1), an identity later confirmed by the heavenly voice (1:11). At the end of the Gospel the Roman centurion, the very man who supervised the execution of Jesus and who probably had taken part in the mockery of Jesus, confesses that the crucified one is indeed the "son of God" (15:39), a confession confirmed by the resurrection, the discovery of the empty tomb, and the young man whom the women encountered. Jesus had drunk the cup that his Father had given him, which required that he "give his life as a ransom for many" (10:45). However, as confidently predicted, he has been raised from the dead and will go before his disciples and continue to give leadership. Therefore, the mission of his disciples, chosen and commissioned earlier in the ministry, may now continue with renewed vigor and vision.

P. Two Endings (16:9–20)

Bibliography

Aland, K. "Bemerkungen zum Schluss des Markusevangeliums." In *Neotestamentica et Semitica.* FS M. Black, ed. E. E. Ellis and M. Wilcox. Edinburgh: T. & T. Clark, 1969. 157–80. ———. "Der Schluss des Markusevangeliums." In *L'Évangile selon Marc.* Ed. M. Sabbe. 435–70. ———. "Die wiedergefundene Markusschluss? Eine methodologische Bemerkung zur textkritischen Arbeit." *ZTK* 67 (1970) 3–13. **Alsup, J. E.** *The Post-Resurrection Appearance Stories of the Gospel Tradition.* Calwer theologische Monographien 5. Stuttgart: Calwer; London: S. P. C. K., 1975. 117–25. **Amphoux, C. B.** "La 'finale longue de Marc': Un épilogue des quatre évangiles." In *The Synoptic Gospels.* Ed. C. Focant. BETL 110. Leuven: Peeters and Leuven UP, 1993. 548–55. **Baarda, T. J.** "An Unexpected Reading in the West-Saxon Gospel Text of Mark 16.11." *NTS* 41 (1995) 458–65. **Bacon, B. W.** "Again the Authorship of the Last Verses of Mark." *Exp* 6.12 (1905) 401–13. **Bartsch, H.-W.** "Der Schluss des Markus-Evangeliums: Ein überlieferungsgeschichtliches Problem." *TZ* 27 (1971) 241–54. ———. "Der ursprüngliche Schluss der Leidensgeschichte: Überlieferungs-geschichtliche Studien zum Markus-Schluss." In *L'Évangile selon Marc.* Ed. M. Sabbe. 411–33. **Becquet, G.** "La mission universelle de l'Église par la foi et ses signes (Mc 16,15–20)." *Esprit & Vie* 80 (1970)

297–300. **Benoit, P.** *Passion and Resurrection.* 263–87, 313–42. **Berger, K.** *Die Auferstehung des Propheten und die Erhöhung des Menschensohns: Traditionsgeschichtliche Untersuchungen zur Deutung des Geschickes Jesu in frühchristlichen Texte.* SUNT 13. Göttingen: Vandenhoeck & Ruprecht, 1976. 163–67. **Birdsall, J. N.** Review of *The Last Twelve Verses of Mark,* by W. R. Farmer. *JTS* n.s. 26 (1975) 151–60. **Bode, E. L.** *The First Easter Morning: The Gospel Accounts of the Women's Visit to the Tomb of Jesus.* AnBib 45. Rome: Pontifical Biblical Institute, 1970. 44–45. **Boomershine, T. E.,** and **Bartholomew, G. L.** "The Narrative Technique of Mark 16:8." *JBL* 100 (1981) 213–23. **Bruce, F. F.** "The End of the Second Gospel." *EvQ* 17 (1945) 169–81. **Brun, L.** "Bemerkungen zum Markusschluss." *TSK* 84 (1916) 157–80. **Bruns, J. E.** "A Note on Mk 16,9–20." *CBQ* 9 (1947) 358–59. **Burgon, J. W.** *The Last Twelve Verses of the Gospel according to S. Mark.* Oxford: James Parker, 1871. **Cadbury, H. J.** "Mark 16:8." *JBL* 46 (1927) 344–50. **Cantinat, J.** *Réflexions sur la résurrection de Jésus (d'après Saint Paul et Saint Marc).* Paris: Gabalda, 1978. 89–94. **Colwell, E. C.** "Mark 16:9–20 in the Armenian Version." *JBL* 56 (1937) 369–86. **Comfort, P. W.** *The Quest for the Original Text of the New Testament.* Grand Rapids, MI: Baker, 1992. 137–38. **Conybeare, F. C.** "Aristion, the Author of the Last Twelve Verses of Mark." *Exp* 4.8 (1893) 241–53. ————. "On the Last Twelve Verses of St. Mark's Gospel." *Exp* 5.2 (1895) 401–21. **Cowper, B. H.,** ed. *Codex Alexandrinus.* London; Edinburgh: Williams & Norgate, 1860. 106 (contains the long ending of Mark). **Cox, S. L.** *A History and Critique of Scholarship concerning the Markan Endings.* Lewiston, NY; Queenston, Ontario: Mellen, 1993. **Creed, J. M.** "The Conclusion of the Gospel according to Saint Mark." *JTS* o.s. 31 (1929–30) 175–80. **Descamps, A.** "La structure des récits évangéliques de la résurrection." *Bib* 40 (1959) 726–41. **Dodd, C. H.** "The Appearances of the Risen Christ: An Essay in Form-Criticism of the Gospels." In *Studies in the Gospels.* FS R. H. Lightfoot, ed. D. E. Nineham. Oxford: Blackwell, 1955. 9–35 (repr. in C. H. Dodd. *More New Testament Studies.* Manchester: Manchester UP; Grand Rapids, MI: Eerdmans, 1968. 102–33). **Dunn, J. W. E.** "The Text of Mark 16 in the English Bible." *ExpTim* 83 (1971–72) 311–12. **Elliott, J. K.** "The Text and Language of the Endings to Mark's Gospel." *TZ* 27 (1971) 255–62. **Evans, H. H.** *St. Paul the Author of the Last Twelve Verses of the Second Gospel.* London: Nisbet, 1886. **Farmer, W. R.** *The Last Twelve Verses of Mark.* SNTSMS 25. Cambridge: Cambridge UP, 1974. **Fegley, H. N.** "An Exegetical Study on Mark 16,17–20." *Lutheran Church Review* 11 (1891) 241–50. **Fuller, R. H.** "Longer Mark: Forgery, Interpolation, or Old Tradition?" In *Protocol of the Eighteenth Colloquy, 7 December 1975, The Center for Hermeneutical Studies in Hellenistic and Modern Culture.* Ed. W. Wuellner. Berkeley: The Center for Hermeneutical Studies in Hellenistic and Modern Culture, 1976. 1–11. **Goodspeed, E. J.** "The Original Conclusion of the Gospel of Mark." *AJT* 9 (1905) 484–90. ————. "The Original Conclusion of Mark." *Exp* 45 (1919) 155–60. **Gourgues, M.** *À la droite de Dieu: Résurrection de Jésus et actualisation du Psaume 110:1 dans le Nouveau Testament.* EBib. Paris: Gabalda, 1978. 199–208. **Gregory, C. R.** "Das Freer-Logion." *Theologisches Literatur Blatt* 29 (1908) 74–75. **Grimme, H.** "Harmonie zwischen Anfang und Schluss des Markusevangeliums." *TQ* 126 (1946) 276–89. **Guy, H. A.** *The Origin of the Gospel of Mark.* London: Hodder & Stoughton, 1954. 157–63. **Haacker, K.** "Bemerkungen zum Freer-Logion." *ZNW* 63 (1972) 125–29. **Harnack, A.** "Neues zum unechten Marcusschluss." *TLZ* 33 (1908) 168–70. **Harris, J. R.** "On the Alternative Ending of St. Mark's Gospel." *JBL* 12 (1893) 96–103. **Hartmann, G.** *Der Aufbau des Markusevangeliums mit einem Anhang: Untersuchungen zur Echtheit des Markusschlusses.* NTAbh 17. Münster: Aschendorff, 1936. **Hay, D. M.** *Glory at the Right Hand: Psalm 110 in Early Christianity.* SBLMS 18. Nashville; New York: Abingdon, 1973. 42–45, 104–15. **Helzle, E.** "Der Schluss des Markusevangeliums (Mk 16,9–20) und das Freer-Logion (Mk 16,24 W), ihre Tendenzen und ihr gegenseitiges Verhältnis." *TLZ* 85 (1960) 470–72. **Herklotz, F.** "Zu Mk 16,9–20." *BZ* 15 (1918–19) 149–50. **Horst, P. W. van der.** "Can a Book End with γάρ? A Note on Mark xvi.8." *JTS* n.s. 23 (1972) 121–24. **Hubbard, B. J.** *The Matthean Redaction of a Primitive Apostolic Commissioning: An Exegesis of Matthew 28:16–20.* SBLDS 19. Missoula, MT: SBL, 1974. 137–49. **Hug, J.** *La finale de l'Évangile de Marc (Mc 16, 9–20).* EBib. Paris: Gabalda, 1978. **Jeremias, J.** "The Freer Logion." In *Gospels* *and Related Writings*. Vol. 1 of *New Testament Apocrypha*. Ed. W. Schneemelcher. Rev. ed. Cambridge: James Clarke; Louisville: Westminster John Knox, 1991. 248–49. **Katz, P.** "The Early Christians' Use of Codices instead of Rolls." *JTS* n.s. 44 (1945) 63–69. **Kenyon, F. G.** "Papyrus Rolls and the Ending of St. Mark." *JTS* n.s. 40 (1939) 56–57. **Kevin, R. O.** "The Lost Ending of the Gospel according to Mark: A Criticism and a Reconstruction." *JBL* 45 (1926) 81–103. **Kilpatrick, G. D.** "Some Thoughts on Modern Textual Criticism and the Synoptic Gospels." *NovT* 19 (1977) 275–92 (repr. in G. D. Kilpatrick. *The Principles and Practice of New Testament Textual Criticism: Collected Essays*. Ed. J. K. Elliott. BETL 96. Leuven: Peeters and Leuven UP, 1990. 80–97). **Knox, W. L.** "The Ending of St. Mark's Gospel." *HTR* 35 (1942) 13–23. **Koch, H.** "Der erweite Markusschluss und die kleinasiatischen Presbyter." *BZ* 6 (1908) 266–78. **Koester, H.** "Response to Reginald Fuller's Paper." In *Protocol of the Eighteenth Colloquy, 7 December 1975, The Center for Hermeneutical Studies in Hellenistic and Modern Culture*. Ed. W. Wuellner. Berkeley: The Center for Hermeneutical Studies in Hellenistic and Modern Culture, 1976. 29–32. **Kolenkow, A. B.** "Response to Reginald Fuller's Paper." In *Protocol of the Eighteenth Colloquy, 7 December 1975, The Center for Hermeneutical Studies in Hellenistic and Modern Culture*. Ed. W. Wuellner. Berkeley: The Center for Hermeneutical Studies in Hellenistic and Modern Culture, 1976. 33–34. **Legault, A.** "Christophanies et angélophanies dans les récits évangéliques de la résurrection." *ScEs* 21 (1969) 443–57. **Liese, H.** "In Ascensione Domini (Mc 16,14–20)." *VD* 12 (1932) 129–34. **Lightfoot, R. H.** *The Gospel Message of St. Mark*. Oxford: Clarendon, 1950. 80–97. **Linnemann, E.** "Der (wiedergefundene) Markusschluss." *ZTK* 66 (1969) 255–87. **Linton, O.** "Der vermisste Markusschluss." *TBl* 8 (1929) 229–34. **Lubsczyk, H.** "Kyrios Jesus: Beobachtungen und Gedanken zum Schluss des Markusevangeliums." In *Die Kirche des Anfangs*. FS H. Schürmann, ed. R. Schnackenburg et al. ETS 38. Leipzig: St. Benno, 1977. 133–74, esp. 146–73. **Mader, J.** "Der Markusschluss." *BZ* 3 (1905) 269–72. **Maly, K.** "Mk 16,14–20." *Dienst am Wort* 3 (1966) 85–90. **Martin, J. P. P.** *Partie pratique*. Vol. 2 of *Introduction à la critique textuelle du Nouveau Testament*. Paris: Maisonneuve freres et C. Leclerc, 1884. 1–554. **Metzger, B. M.** "The Ending of the Gospel according to Mark in the Ethiopic Manuscripts." In *Understanding the Sacred Text*. FS M. S. Enslin, ed. J. Reumann. Valley Forge, PA: Judson, 1972. 165–80 (repr. in B. M. Metzger. *New Testament Studies: Philological, Versional, and Patristic*. NTTS 10. Leiden: Brill, 1980. 127–47). ———. *The Text of the New Testament: Its Transmission, Corruption, and Restoration*. 3rd ed. Oxford; New York: Oxford UP, 1992. 226–29. **Mirecki, P. A.** "The Antithetic Saying in Mark 16:16." In *The Future of Early Christianity*. FS H. Koester, ed. B. A. Pearson. Minneapolis: Fortress, 1991. 229–41. **Mitton, C. L.** "Some Further Studies in St. Mark's Gospel." *ExpTim* 87 (1975–76) 297–301. **Nauck, W.** "Die Bedeutung des leeren Grabes für den Glauben an den Auferstandenen," *ZNW* 47 (1956) 243–67. **Osborne, G. R.** *The Resurrection Narratives: A Redactional Study*. Grand Rapids, MI: Baker, 1984. **Ottley, R. R.** "ἐφοβοῦντο γάρ, Mark xvi 8." *JTS* o.s. 27 (1926) 407–9. **Petersen, N. R.** "When Is the End Not the End? Literary Reflections on the Ending of Mark's Narrative." *Int* 34 (1980) 151–66. **Pokorný, P.** "'Anfang des Evangelium': Zum Problem des Anfangs und des Schlusses des Markusevangeliums." In *Die Kirche des Anfangs*. FS H. Schürmann, ed. R. Schnackenburg. ETS 38. Leipzig: St. Benno, 1977. 115–31, esp. 117–20. **Powell, E.** *The Unfinished Gospel: Notes on the Quest for the Historical Jesus*. Westlake Village, CA: Symposium Books, 1994. **Reedy, C. J.** "Mk 8:31–11:10 and the Gospel Ending: A Redactional Study." *CBQ* 34 (1972) 188–97. **Rigaux, B.** *Dieu l'a ressuscité: Exégèse et théologie biblique*. Studii Biblici Franciscani Analecta 4. Gembloux: Duculot, 1973. **Roberts, C. H.** "The Ancient Book and the Ending of St. Mark." *JTS* o.s. 40 (1939) 253–57. **Rohrbach, P.** *Der Schluss des Markusevangeliums, der Vier-Evangelien-Kanon und die kleinasiatischen Presbyter*. Berlin: Georg Nauck, 1894. **Roloff, J.** *Kerygma und der irdische Jesus*. 184. **Rördam, T. S.** "What Was the Lost Ending of Mark's Gospel?" *HibJ* 3 (1905) 769–90. **Schearer, W. C.** "The Last Twelve Verses of St. Mark's Gospel." *ExpTim* 5 (1893) 227–28. **Schmidt, H.** "Zur Frage des urprünglichen Markusschlusses." *TSK* 80 (1907) 487–513. **Schmithals, W.** "Der

Markusschluss, die Verklärungsgeschichte und die Aussendung der Zwölf." *ZTK* 69 (1972) 379–411. **Schneider, G.** "Die Missionsauftrag Jesu in der Darstellung der Evangelien." In *Mission im Neuen Testament.* Ed. K. Kertelge. QD 93. Freiburg: Herder, 1982. 71–92, esp. 72–81. **Schwarz, G.** "Zum Freer Logion—Ein Nachtrag." *ZNW* 70 (1979) 119. **Scott Moncrieff, C. E.** "The Lost Ending of Mark." *Theology* 12 (1926) 218–20. **Scrivener, F. H.,** ed. *Bezae Codex Cantabrigiensis.* Cambridge: Deighton, Bell, 1864. 325 (contains the first part of the long ending, i.e., vv 9–15). **Stagg, F.** "Explain the Ending of the Gospel of Mark, Mark 16:17–18." In *What Did the Bible Mean?* Ed. C. Frazier. Nashville: Broadman, 1971. 122–25. **Streeter, B. H.** *The Four Gospels: A Study of Origins.* Rev. ed. London: Macmillan, 1930. 333–60. **Taylor, C.** "Some Early Evidence for the Twelve Verses St. Mark 16,9–20." *Exp* 4.8 (1893) 71–80. **Ternant, P.** "La prédication universelle de l'évangile du Seigneur: Mc 16,15–20." *AsSeign* 2.28 (1969) 38–48. **Thomas, J. C.** "A Reconsideration of the Ending of Mark." *JETS* 26 (1983) 407–19. **Torris, J.** "Les fins de l'évangile selon Marc." *Cahiers Renan* 12 (1966) 67–74. **Trompf, G. W.** "The First Resurrection Appearance and the Ending of Mark's Gospel." *NTS* 18 (1971–72) 308–30. ———. "The Markusschluss in Recent Research." *ABR* 21 (1973) 15–26. **Turner, C. H.** "Did Codex Vercellensis (a) Contain the Last Twelve Verses of St Mark?" *JTS* o.s. 29 (1927–28) 16–18. **Wagenaars, F.** "Structura litteraria et momentum theologicum pericopae Mc 16,9–20." *VD* 45 (1967) 19–22. **Westcott, B. F.,** and **Hort, F. J. A.** *Introduction.* 2:28–51. **Williams, C. R.** "The Appendices to the Gospel according to Mark: A Study of Textual Transmission." *Transactions of the Connecticut Academy of Arts and Sciences* 18 (1915) 353–447. **Williams, C. S. C.** *Alterations to the Text of the Synoptic Gospels and Acts.* Oxford: Blackwell, 1951. **Zahn, T.,** and **Resch, A.** "The Authorship of the Last Verses of Mark." *Exp* 4.10 (1894) 219–32. **Zwemer, S. M.** "The Last Twelve Verses of the Gospel of Mark." *EvQ* 17 (1945) 13–23.

Translation

In the ancient MSS that contain the whole of Mark, we find four endings: (1) at 16:8, "for they were afraid"; (2) at 16:20, the so-called Long Ending; (3) at 16:8, plus the so-called Short Ending; and (4) at 16:20, plus the Short Ending. Many of the older MSS have asterisks and obeli marking off the Long or Short Endings as spurious or at least doubtful.

Long Ending[a]

[9]*But when he rose early on the first day of the week, he appeared first to Mary Magdalene, from whom he had cast out seven demons.* [10]*That woman, going, announced to those who had been with him,*[b] *as they were mourning and weeping.* [11]*And they, having heard that he was alive and had been seen by her, did not believe.*

[12]*But after these things he appeared in another form to two of them as they were walking, going in the country.* [13]*And when they returned, they reported to the rest; but they did not believe them.*

[14]*Later, he appeared to the eleven themselves as they reclined; and he reproached their unbelief and hardness of heart, because they had not believed those who had seen him risen.*[c] [15]*And he*[d] *said to them, "Having gone into all the world, preach the gospel*[e] *to every creature.* [16]*The one who believes and is baptized will be saved; but the one who does not believe will be condemned.*[f] [17]*But these signs will accompany those who believe: in my name they will cast out demons; they will speak in new*[g] *tongues;* [18]*[and with their hands]*[h] *they will pick up snakes, and if they drink any deadly poison, it will not hurt them; they will lay hands on the sick, and they will recover."*

[19]*Then the Lord Jesus,*[i] *after he had spoken to them, was taken up into heaven, and sat down at the right hand of God.*[j] [20]*But going out, they preached everywhere, while the Lord worked alongside and confirmed the message through the accompanying signs.*[k]

SHORT ENDING

[1]*But all that they had been told they reported briefly to those with Peter. But after these things, even Jesus himself*[m] *sent out by means of them, from east to west, the sacred and imperishable proclamation of eternal salvation. Amen.*[n]

SUBSCRIPTIONS

B: κατὰ Μᾶρκον, "according to Mark."

ℵ A C L W 33: εὐαγγέλιον κατὰ Μᾶρκον, "Gospel according to Mark."

D: εὐαγγέλιον κατὰ Μᾶρκαν ἐτελέσθη· ἄρχεται πράξεις ἀποστόλων, "Gospel according to Mark is finished; the Acts of the Apostles begins."

71 251 470: τέλος τοῦ κατὰ Μᾶρκαν εὐαγγελίου, "The end of the Gospel according to Mark."

G S 28 128: τὸ κατὰ Μᾶρκαν εὐαγγέλιον ἐξεδόθη μετὰ χρόνους ι´ [or: ιβ̄] τῆς τοῦ Χριστοῦ [G: κυρίου] ἀναλήψεως, "The Gospel according to Mark was given ten [*or* twelve] seasons after the ascension of Christ [G: the Lord]."

483 484: τὸ κατὰ Μᾶρκαν εὐαγγέλιον ἐξεδόθη μετὰ χρόνους ι´ τῆς τοῦ ἀναλήψεως. καὶ ἐκηρύχθη ἐκ Ῥώμης ὑπὸ Πέτρου, "The Gospel according to Mark was given ten seasons after the ascension of Christ. And it was declared from Rome by Peter."

13 124 346: εὐαγγέλιον κατὰ Μᾶρκαν ἐγράφη ρωμαιστὶ ἐν Ῥώμῃ μετὰ ιβ̄ ἔτη τῆς ἀναλήψεως τοῦ κυρίου, "The Gospel according to Mark was written in Latin in Rome twelve years after the ascension of the Lord."

293: ἐγράφη ἰδεωχειρῶς αὐτοῦ τοῦ ἁγίου Μάρκου ἐν τῇ πρεσβυτέρᾳ Ῥώμῃ μετὰ χρόνους δέκα τῆς τοῦ Χριστοῦ καὶ τοῦ θεοῦ ἡμῶν ἀναλήψεως καὶ ἐξεδόθη παρὰ Πέτρου τοῦ πρωτοκορυφαίου τῶν ἀποστόλων τοῖς ἐν Ῥώμῃ οὖσι πιστοῖς ἀδελφοῖς, "It was written by Saint Mark's very own hand, in the Roman presbytery, ten seasons after the ascension of our Christ and God; and it was given out from Peter, the leader of the apostles, to the faithful brothers in Rome."

M Χ Θ Π 69 476 481: no subscription.

INSCRIPTIONS

ℵ B: κατὰ Μᾶρκον, "according to Mark."

A C D L W F 33: εὐαγγέλιον κατὰ Μᾶρκον, "Gospel according to Mark."

G: τὸ κατὰ Μᾶρκον, "The [Gospel] according to Mark."

80 89 128 241: τὸ κατὰ Μᾶρκον ἅγιον εὐαγγέλιον, "The holy Gospel according to Mark."

vg and a few OL MSS: *incipit secundum Marcum,* "[Here] begins [the Gospel] according to Mark."

Notes

[a]The question of the originality of these endings is addressed in the *Form/Structure/Setting* below. For descriptions of the MS evidence, see Westcott-Hort, *Introduction* 2:28–51; Metzger, *TCGNT*[1], 122–28.

[b]A few late MSS read τοῖς μαθηταῖς αὐτοῦ, "to his disciples."

[c]A C* 33 and several later MSS add ἐκ νεκρῶν, "from the dead." W adds:

κἀκεῖνοι ἀπελογοῦντο λέγοντες ὅτι ὁ αἰὼν οὗτος τῆς ἀνομίας καὶ τῆς ἀπιστίας ὑπὸ τὸν σατανᾶν ἐστιν, ὁ μὴ ἐῶν τὰ ὑπὸ τῶν πνευμάτων ἀκάθαρτα τὴν ἀλήθειαν τοῦ θεοῦ καταλαβέσθαι δύναμιν· διὰ τοῦτο ἀποκάλυψόν σου τὴν δικαιοσύνην ἤδη, ἐκεῖνοι ἔλεγον τῷ χριστῷ. καὶ ὁ χριστὸς ἐκείνοις προσέλεγεν ὅτι πεπλήρωται ὁ ὅρος τῶν ἐτῶν τῆς ἐξουσίας τοῦ σατανᾶ, ἀλλὰ ἐγγίζει ἄλλα δεινά· καὶ ὑπὲρ ὧν ἐγὼ ἁμαρτησάντων παρεδόθην εἰς θανατὸν ἵνα ὑποστρέψωσιν εἰς τὴν ἀλήθειαν καὶ μηκέτι ἁμαρτήσωσιν ἵνα τὴν ἐν τῷ οὐρανῷ πνευματικὴν καὶ ἄφθαρτον τῆς δικαιοσύνης δόξαν κληρονομήσωσιν.

And those ones excused themselves, saying, "This age of lawlessness and unbelief is under Satan, who does not permit the truth and [reading καί] power of God to overcome the unclean things of the spirits. Therefore reveal your righteousness now." [Thus] they were speaking to Christ. And Christ was replying to them, "The term of the years of the authority of Satan has been fulfilled, but other terrible things draw near. And in behalf of those who sinned I was delivered over to death, that they might return to the truth and no longer sin, in order that they might inherit the spiritual and incorruptible glory of righteousness which is in heaven." (tr. adapted from Taylor, 614–15)

This agraphon, called the Freer Logion, is discussed by J. Jeremias, "The Freer Logion," in *New Testament Apocrypha*, ed. W. Schneemelcher, rev. ed., 2 vols. (Cambridge: James Clarke; Louisville: Westminster John Knox, 1991) 1:248–49. Jeremias rightly views this logion as apocryphal, but primitive. He observes that it is replete with echoes of various NT (and OT) themes and passages.

[d]A few OL MSS read *Iesus*, "Jesus."

[e]The Peshitta reads "my gospel."

[f]W reads κατακριθεὶς οὐ σωθήσεται, "being condemned, will not be saved."

[g]C* L and a few later authorities omit καιναῖς, "new."

[h]Nestle-Aland[27] and UBSGNT[3c] place these words in square brackets. They are not found in A D W and several later MSS.

[i]W adds χριστός, "Christ." An OL MS reads *dominus Iesus Christus*, "Lord Jesus Christ."

[j]A few late authorities read τοῦ πατρός, "the Father."

[k]A few late MSS read τέλος, "[The] end," or ἀμήν, "Amen."

[l]L reads φέρεταί που καὶ ταῦτα, "Somewhere these things also are in circulation." Other late MSS read ἐν ἄλλοις ἀντιγράφοις οὐκ ἐγράφη ταῦτα, "In other copies these things are not written"; or ἐν τισὶν ἀντιγράφων ταῦτα φέρεται, "In some of the copies these things are in circulation."

[m]A few late MSS read ἐφάνη, "appeared," or ἐφάνη αὐτοῖς, "appeared to them." The text would then read: "Jesus himself appeared to them. By means of them he sent out, from east to west, the sacred and imperishable. . . ."

[n]L and a few later authorities omit ἀμήν, "Amen."

Form/Structure/Setting

Although scholars are almost evenly divided over the question of whether v 8 was the original conclusion of the Gospel of Mark (see *Comment* on 16:8), almost all regard both the so-called Long Ending (i.e., vv 9–20) and the Short Ending as textually spurious (Taylor, 610: "almost universally held conclusion"). Most think the longer passage is a late secondary conflation of traditions found in Matthew, Luke, John, and Acts, enriched with a few legendary details.

Perhaps the most interesting suggestion of authorship comes from H. H. Evans (*St. Paul the Author*), who has proposed that the Apostle Paul wrote Mark 16:9–20. This far-fetched proposal, however, has gained no following. (In another work, Evans also advanced the theory that Paul wrote Luke-Acts!) Conybeare (*Exp* 4.8 [1893] 241–53) suggested that Mark 16:9–20 was composed by the second-century apologist Aristion. Nineteenth-century contemporaries Burgon (*Last Twelve Verses*) and J. P. P. Martin (*Partie pratique*) argued that Mark 16:9–20 is authentic, while very recently Powell (*The Unfinished Gospel*) has suggested that Mark's lost ending is preserved in John 21.

Farmer (*Last Twelve Verses*) finds the evidence for and against the originality of Mark 16:9–20 evenly divided. He is himself inclined to view it as original. According to his understanding of the synoptic relationships this means that the last twelve verses of Mark are a conflation of details found in Matthew and Luke. If the ending is genuine, then Farmer would have his best evidence for the posteriority of Mark. However, it is much more probable that the ending is not original, even if it does preserve some details that may have been part of the original ending.

Parts of Mark's long ending appear to be based on various elements found in the other Gospels and Acts. Some of the most obvious elements are as follows:

V 11: Lack of belief (cf. Luke 24:11)
V 12: Two on the road (cf. Luke 24:13–35)
V 14: Reproach for unbelief (cf. John 20:19, 26)
V 15: Great Commission (cf. Matt 28:19)
V 16: Salvation/Judgment (cf. John 3:18, 36)
V 17: Speaking in tongues (cf. Acts 2:4; 10:46)
V 18: Serpents and poison (cf. Acts 28:3–5)
V 18: Laying hands on the sick (cf. Acts 9:17; 28:8)
V 19: Ascension (cf. Luke 24:51; Acts 1:2, 9)
V 20: General summary of Acts

The material appears to be abbreviated and/or summarized from these sources (cf. Pesch, 2:545–46: Mark 16:9–20 is "ein kompilatorisches Exzerpt von den Evangelien vorausliegenden Traditionen" ["a compiled excerpt from previously existing traditions in the Gospels"]; see also Metzger, *TCGNT* [1], 122–28; Thomas, *JETS* 26 [1983] 407–19). This point can be illustrated by comparing a portion of the spurious ending to Mark's Gospel (Mark 16:12–13) to the much longer description of the two disciples on the road to Emmaus (Luke 24:13–35). The whole Markan passage is provided, but only parallel fragments from Luke are provided:

Mark 16:12–13	*Luke 24*
μετὰ δὲ ταῦτα	καὶ ἰδού [v 13]
"but after these things"	"and behold"
δυσὶν ἐξ αὐτῶν	δύο ἐξ αὐτῶν [v 13]
"to two of them"	"two of them"
περιπατοῦσιν	περιπατοῦντες [v 17]
"as they were walking"	"while walking"
ἐφανερώθη ἐν ἑτέρᾳ μορφῇ	μὴ ἐπιγνῶναι αὐτόν [v 16]
"he appeared in another form"	"not to recognize him"
πορευομένοις εἰς ἀγρόν	ἦσαν πορευόμενοι εἰς κώμην [v 13]
"going in the country"	"they were going to a village"
κἀκεῖνοι ἀπελθόντες	ὑπέστρεψαν εἰς Ἰερουσαλήμ [v 33]
"and when they returned"	"they returned to Jerusalem"
ἀπήγγειλαν τοῖς λοιποῖς	καὶ εὗρον . . . τοὺς ἕνδεκα καὶ τοὺς σὺν αὐτοῖς [v 33]
"they reported to the rest"	"and they found . . . the eleven and those who were with them"
	καὶ αὐτοὶ ἐξηγοῦντο τὰ ἐν τῇ ὁδῷ [v 35]
	"and they told what had happened on the road"
	ἀπήγγειλαν ταῦτα πάντα τοῖς ἕνδεκα [v 9; cf. Matt 28:8]
	"they told all these things to the eleven"
οὐδὲ ἐκείνοις ἐπίστευσαν.	βραδεῖς τῇ καρδίᾳ τοῦ πιστεύειν [v 25; cf. Matt 28:17]
"but they did not believe them"	"slow of heart to believe"

All the elements in Mark 16:12–13 have their counterpart in the longer story in Luke 24. Most of the vocabulary in Mark 16:12–13 is found in Luke 24. Is the Markan passage a secondary summarizing pastiche, or is it a primitive, pre-synoptic tradition? Given the spurious status that most textual critics assign to the Longer Ending of Mark's Gospel, not too many scholars would be seriously inclined to view Mark 16:12–13 as the original form of the story and to view Luke 24:13–35 as an expanded and embellished version.

Mark's version of the Great Commission leaves one with the same impression. Verbal and conceptual parallels are as follows:

Mark 16:15–17	*Matt 28:18–20*
καὶ εἶπεν αὐτοῖς "and he said to them"	καὶ . . . ἐλάλησεν αὐτοῖς λέγων "and . . . he spoke to them, saying"
πορευθέντες "having gone"	πορευθέντες "having gone"
εἰς τὸν κόσμον ἅπαντα "into all the world"	πάντα τὰ ἔθνη "all nations"
πάσῃ τῇ κτίσει "to every creature"	πᾶσα ἐξουσία ἐν οὐρανῷ καὶ ἐπὶ γῆς "all authority in heaven and on earth"
βαπτισθείς "[the one who] is baptized"	βαπτίζοντες "baptizing"
ἐν τῷ ὀνόματί μου "in my name"	εἰς τὸ ὄνομα . . . τοῦ υἱοῦ "in the name . . . of the Son"

The parallels with Acts and the other Gospels, the high concentration of vocabulary found nowhere else in Mark, the absence of these verses in our oldest copies of Mark (e.g., א B) and in the earliest fathers (e.g., Clement of Alexandria and Origen), and the awkward connection between vv 8 and 9 have led most scholars to conclude that the Long Ending of Mark was not part of the original Gospel.

Comment on Long Ending

9 ἀναστὰς δὲ πρωῒ πρώτῃ σαββάτου ἐφάνη πρῶτον Μαρίᾳ τῇ Μαγδαληνῇ, παρ' ἧς ἐκβεβλήκει ἑπτὰ δαιμόνια, "But when he rose early on the first day of the week, he appeared first to Mary Magdalene, from whom he had cast out seven demons." πρωῒ, "early," is a favorite word in Mark; its usage here is inspired by 16:2: "And very early [λίαν πρωῒ] in the morning of the first day of the week they come to the tomb." On ἐφάνη, "he appeared," cf. Matt 2:13: "an angel of the Lord appeared [φαίνεται] to Joseph in a dream." On Mary Magdalene, παρ' ἧς ἐκβεβλήκει ἑπτὰ δαιμόνια, "from whom he had cast out seven demons," cf. Luke 8:2: ἀφ' ἧς δαιμόνια ἑπτὰ ἐξεληλύθει, "from whom seven demons had gone out" (and *Comment* on Mark 15:40).

10 ἐκείνη πορευθεῖσα ἀπήγγειλεν τοῖς μετ' αὐτοῦ γενομένοις πενθοῦσι καὶ κλαίουσιν, "That woman, going, announced to those who had been with him, as they were mourning and weeping." ἐκείνη, "that woman" (i.e., Mary Magdalene), goes τοῖς μετ' αὐτοῦ γενομένοις, "to those who had been with him" (i.e., the disciples), so that she may fulfill the command of the young man encountered at the empty tomb (cf. 16:7). The language recalls John 20:18: ἔρχεται . . . ἀγγέλλουσα τοῖς μαθηταῖς, "she goes . . . , announcing to the disciples." The disciples are said to be πενθοῦσι καὶ κλαίουσιν, "mourning and weeping." Following his denials, Peter ἔκλαιεν, "began to weep" (Mark 14:72). On πενθεῖν, "to mourn," cf. Matt 9:15: "Can the wedding guests mourn [πενθεῖν] as long as the bridegroom is with them? The days will come, when the bridegroom is taken away from them, and then they will fast."

11 κἀκεῖνοι ἀκούσαντες ὅτι ζῇ καὶ ἐθεάθη ὑπ᾽ αὐτῆς ἠπίστησαν, "And they, having heard that he was alive and had been seen by her, did not believe." ζῆν, "to be alive," is found in Mark 5:23; 12:27, but the wording here may be indebted to Luke's resurrection narrative (24:5: "Why do you seek the living [τὸν ζῶντα] among the dead?"; 24:23: "[they] did not find his body; and they came back saying that they had even seen a vision of angels, who said that he was alive [ζῆν]"). θεάεσθαι, "to see," which is found frequently in John, does not appear elsewhere in Mark (Taylor, 611). The response of unbelief, "they did not believe [ἠπίστησαν]," is probably inspired by Luke 24:11: "but these words seemed to them an idle tale, and they did not believe [ἠπίστουν] them" (cf. Luke 24:41; Matt 28:17; John 20:25).

12 Μετὰ δὲ ταῦτα δυσὶν ἐξ αὐτῶν περιπατοῦσιν ἐφανερώθη ἐν ἑτέρᾳ μορφῇ πορευομένοις εἰς ἀγρόν, "But after these things he appeared in another form to two of them as they were walking, going in the country." We have here a clear allusion to the story of the two disciples walking on the road to Emmaus (Luke 24:13–35). In Luke's story, Jesus appears to two men who are πορευόμενοι, "going" (24:13), to a village that is about seven miles from Jerusalem. When Jesus encounters them, they are out of the city in the country. Mark 16:12 says Jesus was ἐν ἑτέρᾳ μορφῇ, "in another form," which explains Luke 24:16: "But their eyes were kept from recognizing him."

13 κἀκεῖνοι ἀπελθόντες ἀπήγγειλαν τοῖς λοιποῖς· οὐδὲ ἐκείνοις ἐπίστευσαν, "And when they returned, they reported to the rest; but they did not believe them." This is precisely what the two men on the road to Emmaus do (cf. Luke 24:33–35). The second unbelieving response is probably inspired by the second unbelieving response in Luke 24:41 (cf. the first unbelieving response in Luke 24:11).

14 ὕστερον [δὲ] ἀνακειμένοις αὐτοῖς τοῖς ἕνδεκα ἐφανερώθη καὶ ὠνείδισεν τὴν ἀπιστίαν αὐτῶν καὶ σκληροκαρδίαν, "Later, he appeared to the eleven themselves as they reclined; and he reproached their unbelief and hardness of heart." Jesus appears to the eleven while they reclined, which again is inspired by the setting in Luke 24 (cf. 24:41, where Jesus requests something to eat). The risen Jesus rebukes the disciples, asking them, "Why are you troubled, and why do questionings rise in your hearts?" (Luke 24:38). On σκληροκαρδία, "hardness of heart," cf. Mark 10:5. On ἀπιστία, "unbelief," cf. Mark 6:6.

ὅτι τοῖς θεασαμένοις αὐτὸν ἐγηγερμένον οὐκ ἐπίστευσαν, "because they had not believed those who had seen him risen," represents a later perspective. No doubt many in the early church marveled at the apostles' reluctance to believe the first reports of the resurrection (cf. John 20:19, 24–29).

Codex W adds a lengthy insertion to v 14 (the so-called Freer Logion; see *Note* c above).

15 πορευθέντες εἰς τὸν κόσμον ἅπαντα κηρύξατε τὸ εὐαγγέλιον πάσῃ τῇ κτίσει,

"Having gone into all the world, preach the gospel to every creature." The Matthean Great Commission (Matt 28:18–20) has inspired this command. πάσῃ τῇ κτίσει, "to every creature," is to be preferred to "to all creation" (so Cranfield, 473). Cf. the commission in ʾAbot 1:12: "Be of the disciples of Aaron, loving peace and pursuing peace, loving mankind and bringing them nigh to the Law."

16 ὁ πιστεύσας καὶ βαπτισθεὶς σωθήσεται, "The one who believes and is baptized will be saved." For an example of the combination of πιστεύειν, "to believe," and σώζειν, "to save," see Luke 8:50.

ὁ δὲ ἀπιστήσας κατακριθήσεται, "but the one who does not believe will be condemned." Cf. John 3:18: "He who believes [ὁ πιστεύων] in him is not condemned [κρίνεται]; he who does not believe is condemned already, because he has not believed in the name of the only Son of God"; 3:36: "He who believes [ὁ πιστεύων] in the Son has eternal life; he who does not obey the Son shall not see life, but the wrath of God rests upon him"; 20:23: "If you forgive the sins of any, they are forgiven; if you retain the sins of any, they are retained."

17 σημεῖα δὲ τοῖς πιστεύσασιν ταῦτα παρακολουθήσει, "But these signs will accompany those who believe." The promise of accompanying (lit. "following") signs is probably inspired by John 14:12: "Truly, truly, I say to you, he who believes [ὁ πιστεύων] in me will also do the works that I do; and greater works than these will he do, because I go to the Father"; and perhaps Acts 5:12: "Now many signs [σημεῖα] and wonders were done among the people by the hands of the apostles."

ἐν τῷ ὀνόματί μου δαιμόνια ἐκβαλοῦσιν, γλώσσαις λαλήσουσιν καιναῖς, "in my name they will cast out demons; they will speak in new tongues." In the book of Acts the disciples cast out demons (16:18) and speak in tongues (2:3–4; 10:46; 19:6; cf. 1 Cor 12:28).

18 [καὶ ἐν ταῖς χερσὶν] ὄφεις ἀροῦσιν κἂν θανάσιμόν τι πίωσιν οὐ μὴ αὐτοὺς βλάψῃ, "[and with their hands] they will pick up snakes, and if they drink any deadly poison, it will not hurt them." We may have here an allusion to Paul's experience with the poisonous viper that the apostle shook off with no ill effect (Acts 28:3–6). In Luke 10:19 Jesus tells his disciples that they tread upon serpents (ὄφεων; i.e., unclean spirits). See *T. Joseph* 6:2, 7; *T. Benj.* 3:5; 5:2. Stories of suffering no ill effects from poison or deadly snakes begin to emerge in the second century.

ἐπὶ ἀρρώστους χεῖρας ἐπιθήσουσιν καὶ καλῶς ἕξουσιν, "they will lay hands on the sick, and they will recover." Through the laying on of hands, Paul regains his sight (Acts 9:12, 17) and the Spirit is received (Acts 8:17; 19:6).

19 ὁ μὲν οὖν κύριος Ἰησοῦς μετὰ τὸ λαλῆσαι αὐτοῖς ἀνελήμφθη εἰς τὸν οὐρανὸν καὶ ἐκάθισεν ἐκ δεξιῶν τοῦ θεοῦ, "Then the Lord Jesus, after he had spoken to them, was taken up into heaven, and sat down at the right hand of God." κύριος Ἰησοῦς, "Lord Jesus," is found in Acts (1:21; 4:33; 7:59; etc.) and in Paul (Rom 14:14; 1 Cor 5:4, 5; 11:23), but never in the Gospels. ἀνελήμφθη εἰς τὸν οὐρανόν, "was taken up into heaven," is probably inspired by Luke's version of the Ascension (cf. Luke 24:51; Acts 1:2, 11, 22; compare also 1 Tim 3:16). Cf. *2 Bar.* 46:7: "I shall be taken up."

20 ἐκεῖνοι δὲ ἐξελθόντες ἐκήρυξαν πανταχοῦ, "But going out, they preached everywhere." ἐξελθόντες, "going out," probably refers to departure from Galilee (*pace* Taylor, 613, who suggests departure from Jerusalem). The Long Ending surely presupposes the fulfillment of Mark 16:7: "He is going before you to Galilee." Having seen the resurrected Jesus in Galilee, where he upbraided them for their lack of faith and then commissioned them, the disciples now obey the risen Jesus and ἐξελθόντες, "going out," from Galilee, ἐκήρυξαν πανταχοῦ, "preached everywhere." This language recalls Luke 9:6: "And they departed [ἐξερχόμενοι] and went through the villages, preaching the gospel and healing everywhere [πανταχοῦ]." Paul says in 1 Cor 4:17 that he teaches πανταχοῦ, "everywhere."

τοῦ κυρίου συνεργοῦντος καὶ τὸν λόγον βεβαιοῦντος διὰ τῶν ἐπακολουθούντων σημείων, "while the Lord worked alongside and confirmed the message through the accompanying signs." We have here a general summary of the activity of the disciples, assisted by the Lord, in the book of Acts. Parts of the language may find a parallel in Heb 2:3–4: "how shall we escape if we neglect such a great salvation? It was declared at first by the Lord, and it was attested [ἐβεβαιώθη] to us by those who heard him, while God also bore witness by signs [σημείοις] and wonders and various miracles and by gifts of the Holy Spirit distributed according to his own will."

Comment on Short Ending

Some MSS preserve the so-called Short Ending to Mark (L Ψ 099 0112). Almost all of those that do also contain the Long Ending. The Short Ending too has no compelling claim to authenticity, for it contains a high precentage of non-Markan vocabulary and exhibits a rhetorical tone found nowhere else in Mark.

Πάντα δὲ τὰ παρηγγελμένα τοῖς περὶ τὸν Πέτρον συντόμως ἐξήγγειλαν, "But all that they had been told they reported briefly to those with Peter." This sentence fulfills the expectation of Mark 16:7. The women have gone to the disciples and to Peter and have told them what the young man at the tomb had explained to them and had commanded.

Μετὰ δὲ ταῦτα καὶ αὐτὸς ὁ Ἰησοῦς ἀπὸ ἀνατολῆς καὶ ἄχρι δύσεως ἐξαπέστειλεν δι᾽ αὐτῶν τὸ ἱερὸν καὶ ἄφθαρτον κήρυγμα τῆς αἰωνίου σωτηρίας, "But after these things, even Jesus himself sent out by means of them, from east to west, the sacred and imperishable proclamation of eternal salvation." The Matthean Great Commission (Matt 28:18–20) and the general thrust of the book of Acts are here presupposed. The lateness of the Short Ending is indicated by the devotional language employed (i.e., "the sacred and imperishable proclamation of eternal salvation").

ἀμήν, "Amen." The Short Ending is brought to a conclusion with a prayerful, liturgical touch.

Taylor (614) rightly notes that the Short Ending, which represents a distinct tradition that perceived the need for a conclusion to the Gospel of Mark, came to be pushed aside in favor of the superior Long Ending.

Explanation

The two endings of Mark, which must be regarded as later, secondary endings, testify to the widespread belief that Mark's narrative did not abruptly conclude with frightened, silent women at the tomb, ostensibly unwilling or unable to obey the mysterious young man who commanded them to tell the disciples and Peter that the risen Jesus would go before them in Galilee. These endings wish to confirm the resurrection of Jesus and at the same time to underscore the missionary directive.

Apart from a stunning manuscript discovery, we shall never be certain how Mark's Gospel concluded. But the message of the book as a whole is plain enough: Jesus of Nazareth was God's Son, who through extraordinary power, witnessed in miracle and in teaching, proclaimed the kingdom of God and willingly went to the cross to fulfill his mission. Because of the resurrection and the subsequent promise that the risen Christ will continue to lead his disciples, that mission may yet be fulfilled, and the Christian community may continue to proclaim with its Lord, "Repent, the kingdom of God is at hand!"

Index of Modern Authors

Index of Principal Topics

Index of Biblical and Other Ancient Sources

The Old Testament

The New Testament

Old Testament Apocrypha

Old Testament Pseudepigrapha and Early Jewish Literature

Dead Sea Scrolls

Josephus

Early Christian Literature

Nag Hammadi Tractates

Greek and Latin Literature

Papyri

Inscriptions and Ostraca